THE TECHNIQUE OF PSYCHOTHERAPY

FOURTH EDITION

LEWIS R. WOLBERG, M.D.

Clinical Professor of Psychiatry
New York University Medical School
and Emeritus Dean
Postgraduate Center for Mental Health
New York, New York

PART TWO

GRUNE & STRATTON
Harcourt Brace Jovanovich, Publishers
Orlando · New York · London · Philadelphia
San Diego · San Francisco
Sydney · Tokyo · Toronto

Library of Congress Cataloging in Publication Data
Wolberg, Lewis R. (Lewis Robert), 1905–
The technology of psychotherapy.

Bibliography: p.
Includes indexes.
1. Psychotherapy.   I. Title.   [DNLM: 1.
Psychotherapy.   WM 420 W848t]
RC480.W6   1988   616.89'14   87-34863
ISBN 0-8089-1877-X

Grune & Stratton, Inc.
Philadelphia, PA 19105

Library of Congress Catalog Number 87-34863
International Standard Book Number 0-8089-1877-X
Printed in the United States of America

Contents

Contents

IV. The Terminal Phase of Treatment

V. Special Aspects

men and women, 1050; books on family problems and crises, 1050; books on family living and adjustment, 1051; books on general child care and guidance, 1051; books on infants and young children, 1052; books on adoption and foster care, 1052; books on the child's middle years, 1052; books on how to understand and relate to the adolescent, 1052; books on how to explain sexuality to children, 1053; books about sexuality to read to or be read by children, 1053; books for adolescents, 1053; books about exceptional, handicapped, and emotionally ill children, 1054; books on self-understanding and self-help books, 1054; books for families with a mentally ill relative, 1055; books on problems of retirement and old age, 1055; books for the advanced reader, 1055; pamphlet sources, 1055). Educational Films and Videotapes, 1056 (general child care and guidance, 1056 [infants and young children; child's middle years; how to understand and relate to the adolescent]); marriage and alternate life styles, 1057 [issues facing single parents; human sexuality; pregnancy and childbirth]; family problems and crises, 1057 [alcoholism; bulimia; substance abuse; dying]; families with a mentally ill relative, 1058 [Alzheimer's disease]; family living and adjustment, 1058 [bereavement, aging]; exceptional, handicapped, and emotionally ill children, 1059; self-understanding, 1059; drug therapy and ECT, 1059; problems of vocational change, retirement and old age, 1059; mental health film sources, 1059–1060).

Preface to the Fourth Edition

What inspired a fourth edition of this book were a number of important developments in mental health that are having an impact on contemporary psychotherapeutic practice. Among these are (1) the availability of new psychopharmacological agents that are singularly effective for symptoms of anxiety, panic, obsessive reactions, depression, mania and schizophrenia; (2) a greater use of short-term approaches not only because third party payers have placed limitations on the number of reimbursable sessions, but also because brief therapy has established its validity beyond traditional limited goals; (3) a shift toward the sicker end of the spectrum of patients seeking help in outpatient clinics and private practice due to the reduction of inpatient facilities, and emphasis on short-term hospitalization, deinstitutionalization, and many other factors; (4) the continuing development of creative symptom-oriented and problem-solving, supportive, behavioral, milieu and outreach approaches as well as family, marital, and group treatments; (5) greater efforts toward more scientific treatment planning with emphasis on differential therapeutics; (6) expanding experimentation in reconstructive therapy through methods oriented around object relations theory and self-psychology, which have led to changes in the way the more severe personality problems are being conceptualized.

While the field of psychotherapy is virtually bursting with luxuriant techniques and expanding dimensions of application, little attempt has been made to integrate the information that we have available today. This poses a problem for students learning ways of managing emotional illness. Added to their befuddlement is the persistent fervor of some established groups to maintain ideological purity. Sugary pieties about the need for unity have not succeeded in halting adversarial verbal dueling.

What we have come to realize more and more is that psychotherapy is not a homogeneous operation, being burdened by many contradictory variables. It is not only the actual interventions that determine the outcome, but also the degree to which the patient accepts and utilizes them, the skill of the therapist, and the climate of the therapeutic alliance. Countless snags and resistances arise in treatment that can sabotage the efforts of the most dedicated therapists and best motivated patients. And many non-specific factors influence therapeutic results for the good and bad. Yet there is a possibility that all good therapists operate in somewhat similar ways if they are to achieve worthwhile results, and this is irrespective of the theories they espouse and the explanations they offer of what they do.

When the original edition of this book was published in 1954, partial solutions for some of the quandaries in psychotherapy were offered. I had acquired a bulk of data of how therapists with different orientations conducted psychotherapy that registered a positive effect on their patients. The locus of this information was a community health center in New York City, the Postgraduate Center for Mental Health, which my wife, a psychiatric social worker and clinical psychologist, and I founded in 1945 under the name The New York Consultation Center. The Center provided a laboratory for study, and the relatively large numbers of patients being treated served as a rich resource for empirical observations. Our case load in the early days consisted of a sizeable number of civilian patients as well as veterans of World War II who had come back from the European and Asian theaters and who were sent to us for treatment as a contract clinic of the Veterans Administration. In a short while we were deluged with veterans being discharged from the service, and to treat this mass of emotionally disturbed patients as well as our habitual caseload of civilians in need of help, we had to enlarge our staff greatly.

World War II having ended, the army medical officers with psychiatric training were going back into private practice. Drawing on this group, we developed a large staff of psychiatrists and a few clinical psychologists, all of whom had been trained in diverse methods of psychotherapy and belonged to practically every school of psychological thought existing at the time. Although their theoretical belief systems varied widely, and their focus on pathology differed, we soon discovered that there were those who obtained good results and those who did not. We tried to substantiate what it was that successful therapists did.

Our initial hypothesis was that good therapists, irrespective of discipline, established rapid rapport with their patients, displaying empathy in dealing with expressed emotion. They developed a theory about the patient's illness and around this formulated a treatment plan involving the patient in at least some of the decision making. They took the time to resolve unreasonable expectations and to enhance motivation for therapy. They adapted their techniques to the needs of each patient, e.g. utilization of structured approaches with confused and helpless patients and less structured ones with more highly organized individuals. They did not hesitate to employ confrontation with patients with whom they had a good relationship in order to create a better learning medium through affect arousal. They worked within the framework of the patient's belief systems where possible, but when these interfered with treatment they tactfully attempted to alter distorted cognitions. Analytically oriented therapists did not hesitate to work toward symptom alleviation where symptoms were self-defeating, diverting the patient from self-observation. Aware of transferential projections, they controlled their own untoward countertransferential feelings. The more intuitive therapists employed their personal feelings to divine what was on the patient's mind, conscious and unconscious. They aggressively dealt with evasions and resistances, recognizing the carry-over of defenses and value distortions from the past. They provided reinforcements for constructive behavior. Finally, where the goal was not personality reconstruction, which was most often the case, they terminated therapy at a point where the patient could reasonably manage on his or her own in order to avoid a therapeutic stalemate in dependency. All of these maneuvers were done irrespective of cherished theories.

As the Center expanded, it developed an organized interdisciplinary training program in psychotherapy and psychoanalysis, obtaining a charter for this from the Board of Regents of the State of New York. It became one of the largest outpatient continuous treatment centers in the country, servicing a steady caseload of over 1600 patients in its Adult Clinic, Clinic for Children and Adolescents, Social Rehabilitation Clinic, Group Therapy Clinic, Family Therapy Clinic and Clinic for Alcoholism. Its clinics were licensed by the New York State Department of Mental Hygiene and approved by the Joint Commission on Accreditation of Psychiatric Facilities of the AMA. Apart from the Fellowship program in psychotherapy and psychoanalysis, training programs for qualified personnel were developed within each of the clinics in child psychiatry, analytic group therapy, family therapy, supervision of the therapeutic process, and alcoholism. The Department of Community Services and Education developed a counseling service and a training program in counseling for social workers, clergymen, teachers, rehabilitation workers, and other personnel dealing with problems encountered in their work. A two-year part-time mental health consultation course for certified psychotherapists enabled the servicing of over 600 agencies, institutions, and industrial groups in the community. As part of public education an ongoing lecture series was developed for the general public. Continuing education programs for mental health professionals rounded out the activities of the Center.

All of the foregoing activities enabled detailed observation of aspects related to the practice of psychotherapy and, coupled with studies of cases in my own private practice, inspired later editions of this book.

Because of the wide range of its coverage and step-by-step delineation of techniques, the book became known as the "cookbook of psychotherapy," and was also referred to as a treatment manual. However, it was never intended as either a "cookbook" or treatment manual with standard recipes of operation. Too many variables exist in the continuum of patient-therapist-environment to allow for universal formulas applicable for all patients and therapists under differing environmental circumstances. Although the methods described in the book have been tested, they are best utilized as guidelines to be altered to the needs of individual patients and the styles and personalities of practicing therapists.

Throughout the book allusions have been made to a dynamic way of thinking about what goes on in psychotherapy. The reason for this is that even though the methods employed by the therapist may be non-analytic, one sometimes cannot escape intrapsychic interferences such as those that issue out of the pool of early developmental conditionings. The form of these interferences are embodied in transferential corruptions and manifold resistances, identification of which would seem to fall within the premises of psychoanalysis. Although in the past few decades we have witnessed the erosion of psychoanalysis as a preferred method of treatment, this has not lessened its value in understanding operative forces in psychotherapy. "Psychoanalytically oriented psychotherapy" accordingly has become the most common form of psychotherapy in use today.

The psychotherapist who has not been trained as an analyst may still be able to identify transference and resistance, and one may recognize some countertransferential responses within oneself. In utilizing psychoanalytic concepts in treatment, as in the identification and resolution of resistance, the therapist may still be effective even though not practicing formal psychoanalysis. Since over 90 percent of patients cannot afford, or tolerate, or constructively utilize intensive psychoanalysis, psychotherapy will constitute the best approach for most patients. Blending dynamics with a skilled use of techniques, the therapist may enable the patient, not only to achieve symptomatic relief, but also to gain sufficient self-understanding to effectuate some important reconstructive personality changes. The present volumes detail methods through which such changes may be accomplished.

It is impossible to include all of the sources I have drawn on for help in the research and writing of this new edition. I am particularly grateful to my colleagues at the Postgraduate Center for Mental Health who perused parts of the manuscript and offered valuable suggestions: Dr. Ava Siegler on Child and Adolescent Psychiatry; Dr. David Phillips on Social Workers and Casework Approaches; Dr. Marvin Aronson on Group Psychotherapy; Dr. Harold Kase on Rehabilitative Approaches; Dr. Gary Ahlskog on Pastoral Counseling and Religious Approaches, Dr. Maria Fleischl on Eastern Philosophies, Dr. Zane Liff and Dr. Henry Kellerman on Psychologists in Psychotherapy. Thanks are due to Dr. Cyril Franks for his help on Behavior Therapy, to Dr. Norman Sussman on Pharmacotherapy and to Dr. Susanne Lego on The Nurse in Psychotherapy. I am especially grateful to Lee Mackler for her meticulous work on the sections on Bibliotherapy, Selected Texts, and Films, Audiotapes, and Videotapes. Thanks are also due to my publishers for allowing me to utilize material from my books: to Brunner/Mazel "The Practice of Psychotherapy," to Thieme-Stratton "The Handbook of Short-Term Psychotherapy, to Grune & Stratton "Short-Term Psychotherapy" and "The Dynamics of Personality." Finally thanks are due my secretary, Jeannine Matthews, for her help with the physical preparation of the manuscript.

The Middle Phase of Treatment (continued)

46
The Handling of Resistances to Cure

Despite our best intentions and the most heroic efforts, even where patients express hope and determination to conquer their problems, they may sometimes be unwilling to relinquish them. Personality change is painful as progress takes hold. Anachronistic patterns regressively pull the individual back to the dreams and demands of the past. Temporary secondary gains and the desire to avoid anxiety at all costs hold patients in a grip from which they may be unable to release themselves.

Interpretations of these defensive operations help patients gradually to an understanding of their unhealthy patterns and to a discovery of what, if any, vicarious satisfactions they gain from them. In this way the patients learn to master some of the anxiety that made the defenses necessary. However, because certain drives serve a protective function and yield intense gratifications, the individual is apt to fight treatment desperately. Under these circumstances, therapy is interpreted as an assault on secret wishes and expectations.

FORMS OF RESISTANCE

In his book, *Inhibitions, Symptoms and Anxiety,* Freud (1966) emphasizes five types of resistance: (1) "repression resis-tance," which is motivated to protect the ego from anxiety; (2) "transference resis-tance," inspired by a refusal to give up hopes for regressive gratifications from the analyst, along with a desire to frustrate him or her; (3) "episonic gain resistance," which follows upon a need to indulge secondary gains and the advantages of symptoms; (4) "repetition compulsion resis-tance," motivated by a drive to repeat neurotic impulses under the lash of a self-destructive principle; and (5) the need for punishment to appease guilt. Psychoanalysis is a "never ending duel between the analyst and the patient's resistance" (Menninger, KA, 1961).

Resistance operates not only in psychoanalysis but in all forms of psychotherapy. This is not remarkable because therapy threatens to upset the delicate balance between various elements of the personality. To give up defenses, however, maladaptive as they may be, expose patients to dangers or deprivations that they consider more upsetting than the inconveniences already suffered as a result of the symptoms.

Resistance may take myriad forms, limited only by the repertory of the individual's defenses. Patients may spend time on evasive and aggressive tactics: fighting the therapist; or proving the therapist is wrong; or winning the therapist over with gestures of helplessness, praise, or devotion; or seeking vicarious means of escaping; or evading treatment. Fatigue, listlessness, inhibitions in thinking, lapses in memory, prolonged silences, intensification of complaints, pervasive self-devaluation, resentment, suspiciousness, aggression, forced flight into health, spurious insight, indulgence in superficial talk, engagement in irrational acts and behavior (acting-out), and expressed contempt for normality may occupy patients to the detriment of their progress.

Resistances may consume the total energy of the patient, leaving little zeal for positive therapeutic work. Sometimes a skilled therapist may bypass resistance by prodding reality into the face of the patient. Sometimes it may be handled by interpretations. Often it operates in spite of attempts to dissipate it, bringing the best efforts of the therapist to a halt. Because resistance is so often concealed and rationalized, it may be difficult to expose. Even an experienced therapist may be deceived by its subtleties.

In supportive therapy resistance may be manifested in a refusal to acknowledge environmental disturbance or in a defensiveness about one's life situation. There may be a greater desire to cope with present known vexations than to chance unknown and perhaps grievous perils. There may be a reluctance to yield inimical conditions that gratify needs for self-punishment and justify one's recriminations against the world. In reeducative therapy, resistance to the changing of modes of relating to people cannot be avoided. New interpersonal relations are, in the mind of patients, fraught with danger. They can be approached only tentatively and with great hesitation. The patients may accordingly remain oblivious to their interpersonal distortions, no matter how frequently they are brought to their attention and how thoroughly they are interpreted. They will repeat the same patterns, with continuous bouts of suffering, and seemingly little insight into what is going on. In cognitive therapy, attempts to alter values or modify belief systems are often met with a confounding reluctance to yield anachronistic and debilitating self-statements. In reconstructive therapy impediments are even more manifest. A most complex array of resistances may materialize. This is especially the case where a weak ego creates an inability to face and to master anxiety related to unconscious conflicts.

Suppression and Repression

Any material that is emotionally disturbing will be suppressed or repressed by the patient until enough strength is gained to handle the anxieties evoked by its verbalization. This material may seem, and actually may be, insignificant or innocuous. It is essential to remember, however, that it is not so much the events or ideas that are disturbing, but rather the meanings given to them and the feelings they inspire.

Thus, a female patient suffering from feelings of hopelessness and depression, relieved through excessive alcoholic indulgence, could talk freely about her bouts of antisocial behavior that bordered on the criminal, with little disturbance; yet she required one year of therapy before she could relate an experience of removing the clothing of her younger brother and observing and handling his penis. The excitement of this experience and the guilt engendered by it were so intense that she had isolated the memory in her mind.

Only when I had proved myself to be a noncondemning person, who would not punish or reject her for the desires that produced this incident, was she able to bring it up and to reevaluate it in the light of her present-day understanding.

Intensification of Symptoms

One of the earliest symptoms of resistance to cure is a reenforcement of those neurotic devices that had previously kept the individual free from anxiety. Something to anticipate, consequently, during therapy is an acute exacerbation of neurotic symptoms. An explanation that the patient may possibly get worse before getting better is often a safeguard against interruption of therapy.

Self-devaluation

An insidious type of resistance is that of self-devaluation. Here patients refuse to concede that there is anything about them of an estimable nature or that they have any chance whatsoever of achieving worthwhile status. To every interpretation, they respond with the allegation that they are lost, that there is no need for them to continue, that they are hopeless, that it is too late in life to expect a change for the better. The inner image of themselves is often that of a hideous, contemptible person, and any attempt to explain to them that this is a distorted picture usually falls on deaf ears; their self-contempt is used as a bulwark to progress in therapy. There may be, in addition, a deep wish to be cared for like a child by rendering themselves helpless (parental invocation). The desire to depreciate themselves may be in the nature of escaping criticism by anticipatory self-punishment. A masochistic indulgence is also a cover for a fear that if one acknowledges oneself to be an able person, active and independent efforts will be expected of one. Patients with this misconception will hang on to their self-contempt with a determination that is astonishing, and only painstaking analysis of this resistance can lead them out of their morass. Sometimes self-devaluation is masked by surface narcissism and grandiosity.

Forced Flight into Health

Another form of resistance is "forced flight into health." Here individuals try to convince themselves and the therapist that they are well and that they no longer need treatment. Any implication that they are not making a good adjustment is resisted with vigor. Actually, patients may conduct their affairs with a semblance of normality in that they appear to be confident, self-reliant, and normally assertive. Yet the trained observer may detect a false note and often can perceive the tremendous effort that is needed to maintain the illusion of health. This form of resistance is usually associated with the need to maintain a rigid watch over everything one says for fear one will lose control. From a pragmatic point of view, it makes little difference if a patient flies, swims, walks, or crawls to health, as long as one gets there. However, assumed health, fashioned by resistance, is generally short-lived.

Intellectual Inhibitions

The urge to ward off the therapist may result in a reluctance to think, to talk, or to feel. The patient, yielding to this urge, will insist that there is nothing pressing to talk about. Thus a singular sterility in the associations develops with an inability to think constructively about pressing problems.

The patient may break appointments, come late, forget to mention significant aspects of the day, block off memory of the dreams and fantasies, manifest inattention, show an inability to concentrate or to remember what has gone on before, relapse into silence during the interview, or display a mental fogging that persists both inside and outside of therapy.

The following excerpt from a session illustrates this phenomenon.

The patient, a divorcee of 32 years of age, with an hysterical, infantile personality, involved sexually with 2 men who were supporting her, came to therapy after making a suicidal attempt. After one year of treatment, her recognition of her dependency caused her to decide to get rid of her lovers and to get a productive job. The patient came a half hour late for the session that follows:

Pt. (apologetically) I've been forgetting

things lately. Absent-mindedness for about 6 months. Last week I forgot to go to an important meeting. I will make appointments and completely forget them. I forget things to do.

Th. Let's explore that and see if we can learn something about it.

Pt. I keep forgetting names and telephone numbers. I don't know why. Maybe I'm so preoccupied with what's to become of me.

Th. Are you preoccupied?

Pt. I am. I can't remember anything.

Th. What *is* on your mind?

Pt. I have the constant worry that I better hurry and do what I have to do. I am concerned with dying. I keep thinking I may not be here long. I noticed yesterday that my shoes on the floor were empty. I then said, "What will people do with my shoes when I die? I wonder who'll go over my papers."

Th. What's this all about? Do you feel the life you are now living is not worth living?

Pt. I feel threatened by giving up these people who are supporting me. I wonder if I can live and get along. What will become of me?

Th. Maybe you resent giving up these dependent patterns?

Pt. I must resent it; yet even though I do, I can't tolerate them any longer. I've gotten to the point where I can be casual with my supporters and tell them exactly what I feel. I told Max that I can't go to bed with him; he's too old for me. This is terribly threatening for me because the instant I do that my income is cut off.

Th. Mm hmm.

Pt. And Max told me he would give me money without strings tied to it.

Th. This must be a great temptation.

Pt. It is, and I see myself not wanting to give it up. I've accepted it in my mind to try it out.

Th. You may be in a great conflict between being dependent and being active and independent.

Pt. Yes, I don't know which to do.

Th. That's something that you yourself will have to work through.

Pt. I suppose my mind is in a fog because I don't know what to do, but somehow I feel I'm getting stronger. [*The mental fog and her coming late for the session are apparently signs of resistance.*]

Very frequently, negativistic resistant states develop several weeks or several months after the patient appears to have entered into the spirit of treatment, spontaneously analyzing difficulties and making what appears to be good progress. Sud-denly, without warning, a blocked, inhibited pattern develops.

Acting-out

Along with unwillingness to verbalize ideas and impulses, the patient may indulge in irrational acts and behavior in everyday life. This "acting out" appears to be a way of supporting the inability to talk during treatment. The acts serve to drain off anxiety and leave little energy available for work during the treatment hour.

Superficial Talk

Another form of resistance is a veering around one's problems in superficial talk. Here verbal comments are used as a defense to ward off basic issues. The patient may spend the entire time of treatment in talk that embraces topics of the day, current events, or past experiences portraying personal tragedy and martyrdom. There is little of deep significance in the conversation, and, if allowed to do, the patient may continue for years to discuss material that is interesting enough but that actually has little to do with significant problems. Often the patient will want to monopolize the interview and will resent the therapist getting a comment or an interpretation in edgewise. Rarely will the patient talk about attitudes toward the therapist, who may begin to feel merely like a sounding board for the patient's boasts and diatribes. It is almost as if in superfluous conversation the patient defies the world to make him or her talk about innermost problems. Associated with this, there may be an attempt to intellectualize, to figure out convoluted connections, and to present a rigid and logical system of what must have happened to one.

Insight as Resistance

A device that is apt to be confusing to the therapist is the use of insight as a form of resistance. Here patients routinely will go through a detailed accounting of how well they understand themselves, using the best accepted terminology, presenting the dynamics and mechanisms of their disorders in approved textbook style. To all appearances they have gained complete insight into the origin of their problems, into their compulsive trends and distorted relationships, and into the consequences and destructive influences of their neuroses. Yet in their daily experiences they go right on with their usual neurotic modes of adjustment, manifesting the same symptoms that originally brought them to treatment. It is probable in such cases that the patient's insight is a highly intellectualized affair that is employed to confuse himself or herself and the therapist.

There are many reasons why a person utilizes insight as a smoke screen behind which to indulge customary neurotic trends. One of the most common reasons is the desire to escape criticism and detection. Here, a dissociation exists between how the patient thinks and feels. It is often easy for the therapist to minimize the seriousness of the patient's disorder when confronted during treatment with a beautiful recitation of psychopathology. Behind the camouflage of insight it is apparent that the patient uses knowledge of mechanisms as an instrument to allay guilt and to forestall criticism in regard to daily actions.

This mechanism is often found in extremely dependent patients who have magical expectations of what therapy will do for them. The chief motivation for entering treatment is the feeling that the therapist will bring about those neurotic objectives that they, themselves, have failed to obtain through their own efforts. Compliance here is the keynote, and the patients, by reciting their spurious insights, will feel that the therapist must reward their aptitudes in learning with anticipated bounties. The facade is at least partially unconscious, and the patients may really believe that they understand themselves thoroughly. The clue to what is going on is usually furnished by the outbursts of hostility and criticism that eventually are pointed toward the therapist when, after months of precise and punctilious performance, the patients do not magically get from therapy what they originally set out to achieve.

Dissociating the Treatment Hour from Life

Sometimes resistance takes the form of the patient's utilizing the treatment hour as a special event dissociated from life. Regarding it as such, the patient will go into the mechanisms of interpersonal relationships with complete freedom, displaying insight that seems to end after he or she exits from the therapist's office. It is obvious that with the therapist, the patient is operating under a set of standards entirely different from those used with other people in general. There seems to be something recondite about the treatment hour, for it is set apart from all other experiences. The special resistance here is that of not seeing how the material that is uncovered in the treatment hour relates to everyday situations. This isolation of treatment from life is often rationalized by the patient on the basis that the therapist is a scientist, who does not condemn one for acts for which one would be punished by others. In this way the patient will lead a dual existence and seemingly be unable to fill the chasm between what happens in treatment and experiences outside of treatment.

Contempt for Normality

An insidious kind of resistance expresses itself in a fear of, or a contempt for, normality. Associated is a refusal to assume responsibility or to make an effort on one's own. By substituting new patterns for old, patients believe that they are yielding up something valuable, something they may never be able to replace, that they will become a prosaic bore, or that they may be exposing themselves to dangers with which they will be unable to cope. This type of resistance appears most intensely in reconstructive therapy after the patients have gained insight and are ready to execute it into action.

A patient with a phobic reaction extended to subway travel made a trip to my office by subway for the first time since treatment had started. She entered the room sullenly and remarked fretfully that she was furious with me. Her anger had started when she discovered that she had no great anxiety riding on the train. A fragment of the session follows:

Pt. I am so angry and resentful toward you. (*pause*)

Th. I wonder why.

Pt. I feel you are gloating over my taking a subway. I feel mother is gloating too. [*Originally accompanied to my office by her mother with whom she had been living since her divorce, the patient with therapy gradually overcame her agoraphobia except for riding on the subway.*] I resent her too. I felt she was pushing me, trying to force me to break away from her. She gloats if I do something that makes me independent. I feel that when I go ahead you gloat too. [*The patient had become so pathologically dependent on her mother that she was scarcely able to let mother out of her sight. Mastering some dependency and walking alone was achieved previously in therapy, although the patient was very reluctant to give up this aspect of her dependent relationship.*]

Th. It sounds as if you are angry about being able to travel on the subway.

Pt. Mother seems to be anxious to give up her responsibility for me. I resent that. But I also don't like the idea of my being so close to mother too.

Th. I see, as if you want to continue being dependent and yet resenting it.

Pt. When I get sick at night, I ask her to make me some tea; and then I resent her patrician attitude when she does this.

Th. But what about your feeling about me?

Pt. It's like giving in to you. But yesterday I felt liberated by the idea that I'm in the middle of a conflict and that coming here offers me hope. I realize that my neurosis is threatened by my getting well. (*laughs*)

Th. What part of your neurosis do you want to hold onto?

Pt. (*laughs*) None. But I have a feeling that I don't want to be normal, that in giving in to you I'll be like anybody else. Also that you'll expect more things of me. And (*laughs*) that if I get too well you'll kick me out. [*Here the patient verbalizes a variety of resistances: namely, a desire for uniqueness, a contempt for normality, a fear she will be expected to face more anxiety-provoking situations, a reluctance to give up her dependence on me, a punishing of her mother and of me by refusing to acknowledge improvement, and an unwillingness to yield her masochism and the various secondary gain elements accruing to her neurosis.*]

Occasionally a psychosomatic complaint may be a manifestation of resistance, as illustrated in the following fragment from a session with a male patient:

Pt. Everything was going well until this morning when I got stomach cramps. They have been with me all day.

Th. Mm hmm.

Pt. I find it hard to concentrate because my stomach bothers me so much. Mondays I always have a hard time for some reason. It's happened the last few Mondays.

Th. Seems like an unlucky day for you. (*pause*)

Pt. I was thinking about how long it takes to get well, and I was wondering if others did any better than I do. Of course, things are a lot better now, and I was thinking of taking a course in journalism up at the New School. The only thing is that it comes on Mondays, and that's hard. I . . . uh . . . uh . . . (*Patient brings hand to his abdomen.*) I had something I wanted to say . . . but I can't think of anything but these cramps. (*He takes a cigarette from a pack, reaches into his pocket for matches but cannot find them.*) Do you have a match?

Th. I believe so. Here's one. (*pause*)

Pt. Well . . . (*coughs*)

Th. You were saying that Mondays are pretty tough on you? Perhaps something happens to you on Mondays that upsets you.

Pt. I . . . I . . . I don't know.

Th. You do come *here* on Mondays.

Pt. Why . . . yes . . . yes . . . I mean I do.

Th. Maybe something is upsetting you in coming here?

Pt. I don't know what it might be. (*pause*) Maybe I'm upset that you feel I'm not doing well. [*We discuss his feelings that he is not living up to expectations. This is what has been giving him anxiety. His cramps are manifestations of internalized resentment and act in the service of resistance.* [*The symptoms soon vanished completely when he could see their connection with his faulty assumptions.*]

Reluctance to Yield the Pleasure Values of the Treatment Hour

A form of resistance that is frequently overlooked is one that involves reluctance to yield the positive pleasures that the patient gets out of the treatment itself. The patient may derive such comfort from the therapeutic hour that other gratifications seem dubious, and may refuse to give up the neurosis because of a desire to continue therapy indefinitely. This is frequently the case in a very dependent patient, who looks forward to the hour to get a "fix," who perhaps pays lip homage to all the dynamic principles uncovered during treatment, but whose chief motive for therapy is to get suggestions and courage to carry on with daily routines. Unless one watches oneself carefully, the therapist will fall into a trap laid out by the patient and may, by the patient's helplessness and apparent inability to do things voluntarily, feel forced to feed the patient with doses of advice and admonishments, which the patient absorbs as if these were pronouncements from the Deity.

Transference Resistances

Perhaps the most common and disturbing of resistances are those that are produced in response to the relationship with the therapist or that take the form of transference. Contact with the therapist is understandably disturbing when it mobilizes attitudes, impulses, and feelings that threaten the repressive forces. Patients will, in the attempt to escape from the associated anxiety, exhibit their usual characterologic defenses to detach themselves, make themselves helpless, control and overwhelm the therapist, or render themselves invincible by pseudo-aggressiveness. In supportive and some types of reeducative psychotherapy the patients will manage to restore their equilibrium through the medium of such defenses, and they will, more or less successfully, repress disturbing irrational, unconscious drives. In reconstructive therapy, on the other hand, the therapist constantly interprets the nature and purpose of the various defenses as they arise. This constitutes an assault on the integrity of the repressive system and will precipitate much tension. Eventually the patient cannot help coming to grips with the emotions and drives that hitherto have been successfully avoided. The patient will then mobilize further protective devices to reinforce the crumbling repressions.

One of the earliest manifestations of this struggle is an intensification of symptoms, which seems to serve the desperate function of restoring psychic equilibrium. Soon the struggle becomes more personalized as the patient realizes that relationship with the therapist is the womb of the distress. Resistance once exerted against awareness of the original unconscious material is now shown toward projected and animated representations in the transference.

The patient may exhibit a disarming dependent attitude toward the therapist, who is regarded as the embodiment of all that is good and strong and noble in the universe. This kind of resistance is often found in individuals who are characterologically submissive, subordinate, and ingratiating and who strive to adjust to life by clinging parasitically to a more powerful person. It is as if the individual had an amputated self that could be restored only by symbiosis with a stronger individual. There is even an associated tendency to overvalue the characteristics and qualities of the therapist. This type of relationship is extremely shaky because the patient regards therapy as a magical means to security and power. Consequently, the therapist must always live up to inordinate expectations that are sheerly in the realm of fantasy, beyond possibility of fulfillment. The patient will make unreasonable demands on the therapist, and, failing to get what he or she secretly wants, be filled with outrage.

Another form of relationship resistance is based on an intense fear of the therapist as one who is potentially capable of injuring or enslaving the patient. This attitude stems from a hostile image of the parent that usually is applied to selected authoritative individuals. Treatment in such cases proceeds only when the patient realizes that the therapist does not desire to punish or condemn for the impulses or fantasies, but instead is benevolently neutral toward them. Little progress is possible until the patient accepts the therapist as a friend, not foe.

Sometimes patients display a disturbing need to be victimized and unfairly treated. They will maneuver themselves into a situation with the therapist in which they feel they are being taken advantage of. They may even exhibit various symptoms that they attribute to the harmful effects of therapy. In order to reinforce their waning repressive system, they thus seek to transform the therapist into a stern authority who commands and punishes them. Where this happens, they will experience severe anxiety if the therapist is tolerant and condones their inner impulses.

When resistance is displayed in the form of hostility, the resulting reaction patterns will depend on the extent to which the patients are able to express aggression. Where the character structure makes it mandatory to inhibit rage, the patients may respond with depression and discouragement. They may then want to terminate therapy on the grounds that they have no chance of getting well. They may mask their aggression with slavish conformity and perhaps evince an interest in the therapist's personal life, assuming an attitude of comradery and good fellowship. There is in such efforts a desire to ally themselves with the enemy in order to lessen the danger to themselves.

On the other hand, where the patients are able to express hostility, they may exhibit it in many ways especially where the transference becomes intense. They may become critical, then defiant, challenging the therapist to make them well. Irritability is often transmuted into contempt, and the patients may accuse the therapist of having exploitative or evil designs on them. Feeling misunderstood and humiliated, they will manufacture, out of insignificant happenings in their contact with the therapist, sufficient grounds to justify their notion of being mistreated. They will become suspicious about the therapist's training, experience, political convictions, and social and marital adjustment. They may enter actively into competition with the therapist by reading books on psychoanalysis to enable them to point out the therapist's shortcomings. They may become uncooperative and negativistic.

Sometimes hostility is handled by attempts at detachment. The need to keep the therapist from getting too close may burn up a great deal of the patients' energy. They may refuse to listen to what the therapist says. They may ridicule in their minds proffered interpretations. They may forget their appointments or seek to discontinue therapy, inventing many rationalizations for this. They may strive to ward the therapist off by discussing irrelevant subjects or by presenting a detailed inventory of their symptoms. In their effort to keep aloof they may attempt to take over therapy, interpreting in advance their unconscious conflicts, the existence of which they suspect or fabricate. An insidious type of defense is a preoccupation with childhood experiences. Here the patients will overwhelm the therapist with the most minute details of what must have happend to them during childhood, presenting a fairly consistent and logical survey of how previous inimical experiences must have produced all of their present difficulties.

Occasionally the impulse toward detachment is bolstered by contempt for the therapist's values; the patients will feel that their own standards are what really count. Because of this they will be convinced that the therapist cannot like them and will "let them down." They will rationalize these feelings and say to themselves that the therapist is no good, or incompetent, or of no importance, or that psychotherapy is nothing but nonsense.

The desire to control the situation may reflect itself in many ways. Some patients may seek to shower the therapist with gifts and favors, or they may develop a sentimental attachment that assumes a sexual form. Therapy may be regarded as a seduction, the patient experiencing in it intense erotic feelings. One of the motives involved in falling in love with the therapist is to put the latter in a position where there will not be too close probing into the patient's deepest secrets. The incentive may be to devaluate, test, influence, get the whip hand, or fuse with the therapist; in this way taking a shortcut to cure.

Many patients come to treatment not because they desire to function more adequately in their interpersonal relationships, but rather because they seek to obtain from treatment the fulfillment of neurotic demands that they have been unable to gratify through their own efforts. In such cases resentment and resistance develop when the patient does not receive from the therapist the specific type of help that was expected.

Upon analyzing what the patient wants from the therapist, it turns out that what is sought is not a cure for the neurosis, but an infallible method of making it work. Many patients desire to achieve neurotic expectations without having to pay the penalty of suffering. The individual with a power drive may thus insist on a formula whereby one can function invincibly in all activities. The perfectionist will want to find a way to do things flawlessly, with as little effort as possible. The dependent individual will expect to amalgamate with the therapist and to have all whims gratified without reciprocating. The detached soul will seek the fruits of social intercourse, while maintaining distance from people. When these drives are not gratified in therapy, when patients sense that these are instead being challenged, they will become tremendously resistive.

In sicker patients, resistance is sometimes exerted against accepting the idea that it is possible to function adequately without repairing a fantasied injury to the genital organs. In the female this may be expressed in the expressed refusal of continuing life without the possibility of ever procuring for herself a penis, which she regards as the bridge to activity and self-fulfillment. In males, the assumption of a passive role is often interpreted as equivalent to being castrated, and resistance may be directed against assuming any role that does not involve aggressive "masculine" fighting or "machoism." Even accepting help from the therapist may symbolize passivity.

Psychotherapy may produce other unfavorable resistance reactions in patients with immature ego structures. The transference can become so dramatic and disturbing to these patients that they respond to it in an essentially psychotic manner. They will accuse the therapist of being hostile, destructive, and rejecting, and they will refuse to acknowledge that their attitudes may be the product of their own feelings. The reasonable ego here is very diminutive and cannot tolerate the implications of some surfacing of unconscious drives and conflicts. The patient acts out inner problems and constantly avoids subjecting them to reason. The acting-out tendency permits the neurosis to remain intact. Where the therapist is seen as a cruel or lecherous or destructive being who threatens the patient with injury or abandonment, any action or interpretation is twisted in the light of this delusional system. Fear and anxiety issuing from the patient's irrational strivings lie like boulders in the path, barring the way to a more congenial therapeutic relationship. In such cases therapy will be prolonged, and the relationship must be worked on actively so as to constitute for the patient a gratifying rather than threatening human experience. (See also Chapter 42)

METHODS OF HANDLING RESISTANCE

Little has been written on how definitely to solve the paradox of the patients who seek help yet resist any external control or guidance toward change. What would seem to be indicated is a participant model for therapy in which the patients take responsibility in treatment, monitoring their own behavior and determining the nature of their interactions, environment, and their future plans.

In psychoanalysis, early in treatment the patients gather from the passivity of the analyst that they have to make their own decisions and work through their blocks toward utilizing insight in the direction of change. Interpretation of resistances is the prime modality used and the analyst hopes that the patients will in the resolution of these obstructions generalize their learnings in therapy toward making new constructive adaptations.

In psychoanalytically oriented therapy, the therapist is more active and employs techniques in addition to interpretation to help the patients effectuate change. These techniques often draw from many schools and are more or less eclectic in nature.

In behavior therapy, the therapist is highly active, utilizing when necessary a rich assortment of devises, including systematic desensitization, operant conditioning, modeling of preferred behaviors, role playing, work assignments, and cognitive therapy. These treatments are sometimes blended with counseling.

At the outset it often becomes apparent that what some patients want from therapy is to overcome suffering without giving up attitudes and behaviors that are responsible for their suffering. What is required before any progress can be made is to work toward motivating the patient to change and to formulate worthwhile objectives in treatment. In behavior therapy these are deliniated and presistently pursued.

In his chapter on self-management methods, Kanfer (1980) describes a behavioral model drawn from Skinnerian methods and research findings in social and cognitive psychology as well as current clinical practices. Through various techniques, the patient acquires skills for use in problem-solving. The patient is also trained in altering noxious elements of the environment. Development of constructive repertoires is conducted through negotiations with the patient. Past experiences are reviewed only to provide information during behavioral analysis on the circumstances surrounding the original conditions when the maladaptive behavior was developed, and to point out the present inappropriateness of this behavior.

In controlled environments like a hospital or in military organizations, reinforcement contingencies may be relatively easily applied. But in one's ordinary living environment these are not so readily arranged, and it is for this reason that manipulation of cognitive variables through cognitive behavior therapy can be valuable in order to help evolve constructive self-reinforcing attitudes. A good deal of support will be required from the therapist at the start of treatment, but this will diminish as the patient becomes more skilled in self-management. A contract is usually negotiated, details of which spell out the required behavior, the time goal, the reinforcements for fulfillment of obligations, some aversive consequences of nonfulfillment of the contract, and the way reviews and evaluations will be conducted. Where required behaviors occur outside the range of observation of the therapist, self-monitoring is mandatory and here the patient will benefit from keeping a careful record of his or her behaviors. Assignment of tasks expedites self-observation and hastens the development of new behavioral repertoires. Techniques are employed to set up environmental conditions unfavorable to the undesired behavior, and to establish contingencies for self-reinforcement. Discussions cover the patient's experiences in self-management with the object of helping to transfer learnings and skills to situations that may develop in the future. There are other models one may follow if one is pursuing a behavioral program, but the one I have outlined seems to cover the essential points.

As soon as the therapist realizes that resistance is interfering with therapy, it is necessary to concentrate on the resistance to the exclusion of all other tasks. This may be done in a number of ways. In supportive and reeducative approaches, this is done by reassurance, persuasion, and various manipulative and strategic maneuvers. In reconstructive approaches a cognitive attach or the resistance itself is instituted.

Identifying the Resistance and Exploring Its Manifestations

Calling the patient's attention to the resistance itself and exploring its manifestations are essential procedures.

For example, a patient has for the past few sessions arrived 5 to 10 minutes late. The sessions are spent in a discursive account of family events, including the impending marriage of his son, the forthcoming graduation of his daughter, and the attacks of "gall-bladder trouble" suffered by his wife for which she may need an operation. The responsibilities imposed on him by his business and social position also occupy his attention. He mentions having suggested a 2-week vacation in Florida, but his wife promptly vetoed the idea. He pauses in his conversation and then remarks that there is nothing on his mind.

Sensing resistance, I direct the interview along the following lines:

Th. I wonder if there is something on your mind that bothers you that you are not talking about.

Pt. Why, no, not that I'm aware of.

Th. The reason I bring this up is that you have been coming late to your sessions, and during your sessions you have kind of rambled along, not talking about things that bothered you too much. At least I have that impression. [*pointing out possible resistances*]

Pt. Why no, I mean you want me to talk about anything on my mind. I'm supposed to do that, am I not?

Th. Yes.

Pt. Well, I haven't had anything else bothering me.

Th. Perhaps not, but have you had any symptoms that upset you?

Pt. No. I've noticed though that my jaws tighten up sometimes. And my wife tells me I'm grinding my teeth in my sleep.

Th. Mm hmm. That sounds like tension of some kind.

Pt. I know I feel a little tense.

Th. A little tense?

Pt. I've been upset that I have to do, do, do for other people, give, give, give, and get little in return.

Th. As if people expect things from you and do not want to give anything?

Pt. Yes, I'm getting fed up with my life, the way it's been going.

Th. I see. This could be upsetting.

Pt. I suppose you'd say I feel frustrated.

Th. Well, what do *you* say?

Pt. (*laughs*) It's hard to admit it, but I am. Sometimes I'd like to chuck up the whole thing, and be single again, without responsibilities, to do what I want to do.

Th. I should think you would feel frustrated that you can't. If this is what you really feel this is what you want.

Pt. Lately I've been getting this way. [*The patient discusses his secret ambition of wanting to be a writer and admits that he was embarrassed to talk about this. He also was, he remarks, afraid to admit that he resents being tied down to a routine family life and has fantasized divorce. His resistance to talk about these things along with his internalized rage at his life situation seem responsible for his muscular symptoms.*]

Pointing Out Possible Reasons for the Resistance

Where patients are cognizant of their resistance but do not recognize its purpose, the therapist should point out various possibilities for the resistance. The defensive object of the resistance may be interpreted along with the facades; the patients may be shown that their resistance protects them against the threat of change. Thus, a patient hesitates repeatedly during a session; the periods of silence are not broken by the usual interview techniques.

Th. I wonder what the long silences mean.

Pt. Nothing comes to my mind, that's all. I kind of wish the time was up.

Th. Perhaps you are afraid to bring up certain things today. [*suggesting that her silence is a resistance to prevent her from bringing up painful material.*

Pt. Like what?

Th. Well, is there any event that happened since I saw you that you have not mentioned to me?

Pt. (*silence*) Yes, there was. I met a man last Wednesday who sent me. I made a big play for him and am going to see him Sunday. [*The patient's infidelity to her husband is one of her symptoms, of which she is ashamed.*]

Th. I see.

Pt. I have wondered why I did this. I realized you wouldn't tell me not to, but I feel guilty about it.

Th. Was that the reason why you were silent?

Pt. (*laughing*) Honestly, I thought there wasn't much to talk about. I minimized the importance of this thing. But I realize now that I didn't want to tell you about it.

Th. What did you think my reaction would be?

Pt. (*laughs*) I guess I thought you'd think I was hopeless or that you'd scold me.

Reassuring Tactics

Reassuring the patient in a tangential way about that which is being resisted necessitates an understanding by the therapist of the warded-off aspects.

For instance, a woman with an obsessional neurosis comes into a session with symptoms of exacerbated anxiety. She has no desire to talk about anything but her suffering. This seems to me a sign of resistance. When I inquired about dreams that she may have had, the patient reveals one that, in a disguised way, indicates murderous attitudes toward her offspring. The idea occurs to me that she is attempting to suppress and repress thoughts about her children.

A significant portion of the session follows:

Th. I wonder if you haven't been overly concerned about thoughts of your children.

Pt. I'm frightened about them, the thoughts.

Th. You know, every mother kind of resents being forced into playing the role of housewife. This is a cramped life to many persons. Most women may resent their children and from time to time wish they weren't around. It's natural for them to feel that. [*reassuring the patient about possible hostility*]

Pt. (*rapidly*) That's how I feel.

Th. They may even get a feeling sometime that if the children pass away, that will liberate them. Not that they really want that, but they look at it as an escape. [*more reassurance*]

Pt. That's what I didn't want to say. I've felt that it was horrible to be like that.

Focusing on Material Being Resisted

Bringing the patient's attention to the material against which the resistance is being directed must be done in a very diplomatic way, preferably by helping the patients to make their own interpretation or by a tentative interpretation.

A patient with a problem of dependency complained of an intense headache and a general feeling of disinterest in life.

The interview was rather barren, but enough material was available to bring the patient to an understanding of what he was trying to repudiate.

Pt. My wife has been telling me that I just am not like the other husbands. I come home and read the newspaper and don't go grubbing around in the garden.

Th. What does that make you feel like?

Pt. I guess she's right. But as hard as I try, I know I'm being a hypocrite. I just gave that up.

Th. But your wife keeps pounding away at you.

Pt. Well, what are you going to do. I don't help her around the place. She resents my being as I am.

Th. But what do you feel your reaction is to her pounding away at you?

Pt. (*fists clench*) It drives me nuts. I'd like to tell her to stop, but I know she's right.

Th. Is it possible that you resent her attitude, nevertheless, and would prefer her laying off you when you don't do the chores? [*a tentative interpretation of the material against which there is resistance*]

Pt. God damn it. I think she is being unreasonable when she sails into me. [*The patient takes courage from my interpretation and expresses resentment.*]

Th. Mm hmm.

Pt. After all, I come home tired and I find no interest in planting cucumbers. Besides, it's crazy. My neighbors plant dollar tomatoes. Each tomato costs them a dollar. It's no economy. The whole thing is silly. [*The patient continues in a diatribe, venting his resentment about his wife's attitude. At the end of the session his headache has disappeared.*]

Handling Acting-out

Acting-out is a common manifestation that has been given various interpretations (Abt, 1965). Fenichel (1945) defines acting-out as "an acting which unconsciously relieves inner tension and brings a partial discharge to warded-off impulses (no matter whether these impulses express directly instinctual demands, or are reactions to original instinctual demands, i.e., guilt feelings); (the present situation, somehow associatively connected with the repressed content, is used as the occasion for the discharge of repressed energies, the cathexis is displaced from the repressed memories to the present, 'derivative,' and this displacement makes the discharge possible.") Aronson (1964a) considers the essential features of any acting-out sequence to be a reenactment of a childish ("pregenital") memory or fantasy, of which there is no conscious recollection, precipitated by transference or resistance during psychotherapy, displacing itself to some organized "ego-syntonic" action, thus permitting a partial discharge of inner tension. At the same time there is no awareness of any relationship of the old memory or fantasy with the current action.

Prior to coming to therapy the patient, having indulged in acting-out tendencies as a way of expressing unconscious impulses and feelings, may have gotten into certain scrapes. During psychotherapy acting-out may occur even in patients who have, before treatment, shown no evidence of it in their behavior.

There are some psychotherapists who take the view that acting-out can serve a useful purpose in some patients, that it may be growth inducing and, particularly where basic problems originated in the preverbal state, they constitute a means toward assertiveness and a preliminary step toward gaining insight. Consequently, they tend to encourage and even to stimulate acting-out. Other therapists, however, regard acting-out as always detrimental to therapeutic progress since it drains off the tension that should be employed for a requisite understanding and working through of conflicts. Between these two extremes an intermediate viewpoint may be taken, acting-out being managed in accordance with whether it serves as an obstruction to or as an intermediate stage toward learning.

Some patients who were overindulged and poorly disciplined as children will engage in untoward acting-out behavior to goad the therapist into a setting of limits such as they had never experienced with their own parents. On the other hand, where parents have been too authoritarian and have cowed the patient to a point where the slightest emergence of defiant or antisocial conduct inspires fear of a counterattack, acting-out may constitute a breaking out of restraints. The handling of acting-out in these two instances will be different.

Where acting-out occurs as a resistance to therapy, it is usually inspired by the transference situation. Because patients refuse to verbalize prior to acting-out and because they may conceal and rationalize their behavior, it may be difficult to deal with it therapeutically. For instance, a prudish female patient, shortly after starting therapy, confessed having involved herself in extramarital love affairs with several men. It was only through a dream that I was able to get a glimpse of her guilt feelings at sexual actions that were totally foreign to her personality. Confronting her with the existence of sexual guilt brought forth divulgence of the information that she had, during the past month, become so sexually aroused that she felt forced to seek satisfaction in outside affairs. Focusing on her feelings about me, the patient was soon brought to an awareness of how closely she had identified me with her father, and of how her incestuous impulses were being displaced. The establishment of the connections of her current behavior with its infantile roots enabled her to control her acting-out and to work through her fantasies within the therapeutic situation.

The therapist should consequently be alert to extraordinary behavior patterns that occur in the patient. Thus, a man who is ordinarily restrained may engage in random, multiple sexual affairs to the point of satyriasis, or involve himself in dangerous but exciting aggression-releasing situations that are potentially disastrous to him. One patient, for instance, whenever provoked by hostility toward her therapist, would get into her car and drive speedily and recklessly. Only when she narrowly escaped an accident would she slow down.

When acting-out is recognized, it is necessary to bring this to the attention of the patient. The therapist may suggest that there are reasons why the patient feels forced to engage in certain behaviors. Talking about feelings *prior* to putting them into action will help the therapeutic process. Acting compulsively the way that the patient does tends to interfere with therapy. Should the patient accept these statements and verbalize, enough energy may be drained off in the interview to forestall acting-out. Interpretation may also help to dissipate the need for unrestrained behavior. Interpretive activities will require a repeated pointing out to the patient of manifestations of acting-out conduct. At the same time attempts are made to link actions to fantasies or impulses that are preconsciously perceived. Material from free associations and dreams may be valuable here. What helps in most instances is bringing the patient to an awareness of evidences of transference. Should any of the acting-out manifestations contain healthy elements, the therapist should attempt to reinforce these. The strategic timing of interpretations is important. Where acting-out occurs during a session as a manifestation of transference and resistance, interpretations will be particularly effective; nevertheless, a prolonged period of working through may still be required.

Should acting-out persist and should this be potentially dangerous to the patient, the therapist may direct the patient to desist from the acts on the basis of their destructive nature, while encouraging talking about impulses. Of course, in some instances, it may be impossible for the patient voluntarily to stop acting-out. Exhibitionism, voyeurism, transvestism, and masochistic sexual activities are examples. However, with persistence it may be possible to get patients to talk freely about their temptations and to help them, to an extent at least, to gain some voluntary control. Increasing the frequency of sessions and giving patients the privilege of telephoning the therapist whenever the impulse to act-out occurs are often helpful. As a last resort, if patients continue dangerous acting-out, the therapist may threaten to withdraw from the therapeutic situation unless control over impulses is exercised. Behavioral aversive conditioning techniques are sometimes employed as a means toward checking acting-out that cannot be controlled in any other way. Cooperation of the patient will, of course, be necessary. The patient may also be told, "If you want to continue in this self-destructive behavior, you can do it by yourself; you don't need me. If you want to change, I can help you."

It goes without saying that acting-out within the therapeutic session, like physical attacks on the therapist and lovemaking gestures, are to be discouraged or prohibited. Patients may be told that they can talk about anything they please, but that unrestrained actions are not permitted by rules of therapy. Experience has shown that these interfere with the therapeutic process.

Handling Transference Resistances

Where transference has developed to the point where it constitutes resistance to treatment, it will have to be resolved. If it is not dissipated, it will seriously interfere with the working relationship. Treatment may become interminable, the patient utilizing the therapeutic relationship solely as a means of gratifying neurotic impulses at the expense of getting well. Frustrated by the absence of what the patient considers to be the proper response to reasonable demands, the patient may terminate treatment with feelings of contempt for or antagonism toward the therapist.

Superficial manifestations of transference may often be adequately handled by maintaining a steadfast attitude and manner, constantly bringing the patient back to reality. Sometimes a studied avoidance of the role that the patient wants the therapist to play, or acting in an opposite role, minimizes transference. For instance, if the patient expects the therapist to be directive and controlling, on the basis of a conviction that all authority is this way, the therapist deliberately acts permissive, tolerant, and encouraging of those activities toward assertiveness and freedom that the patient

cherishes but which he or she believes the parents had prohibited. Such role playing rarely is successful because the patient will usually see it as a ruse. It is better to interpret to the patient what the therapist believes is behind the patient's reactions.

A female patient, conditioned to expect punishment for infractions by a punitive parent, appears for a session depressed and guilt-ridden. She seems to demand that the therapist scold and punish her for having drunk to excess the evening before and for having acted sexually promiscuous. Not being able to stimulate this reaction in the therapist, the patient launches into an attack, upbraiding the therapist for passivity. The therapist continues to react in a tolerant and nonjudgmental manner, but interprets the responses of the patient in terms of her desires for punishment and forgiveness to propitiate aroused guilt feelings.

Severe manifestations of transference being rooted in infantile conditionings will usually require prolonged "working through." Strategically timed interpretations of the sources of transference in childhood experiences and fantasies, and of its present functions, will be required.

Among the most disturbing of transference resistances is that of the sexual transference, which takes the form of insistence that one can be cured only in a sexual relationship. While therapy may set off a temporary sexual attraction toward the therapist, this fascination usually disappears as therapy progresses or upon the simple structuring of the therapeutic situation. However, in some patients the sexual preoccupation becomes intense and persistent. A male patient, for example, will pick out from the behavior of a female therapist minor evidences that he will enlarge to justify his belief that the therapist must be in love with him. The protestations of the patient may greatly flatter the therapist, and the urgency of the expressed demands may tempt her to respond partially by touching or holding the patient. These advances are most provoking to the patient and incite greater sexual feeling. Should the therapist engage in any kind of sex play with the patient, this can have only the most destructive effect on both participants. Once the patient has even partially seduced the therapist, he may develop contempt for her weakness and for her abandonment of ethical principles. The therapeutic situation will obviously terminate with any expressed intimacy.

It is important in handling sexual transference not to make the patient feel guilty about sexual feeling. Rather, the feeling should be accepted and an attempt made to find out what it means in terms of the patient's past sexual attitudes and behavior. For instance, sex may indicate being accepted or preferred by someone. It may perhaps have the connotation of vanquishing or humiliating others. Sometimes reassuring comments are helpful in abating the patient's reactions. Thus the patient may be told, "It is usual for persons to develop such feelings for their therapist," or "It is good that you have these feelings because they will enable you to work out important attitudes and relationships," or "The *feeling* you have toward me is a step in your ability to feel and to relate to other people," or "This will serve as a means toward better relations with others." Where the patient brings in dreams and fantasies, it may be possible to interpret, with all the precautions already mentioned, the sources of the patient's transference reactions.

Another disturbing resistance is that of the hostile transference. Here the patient will react to the therapist as if convinced of the reality of the therapist's unfriendliness, destructiveness, ineptness, seductiveness, and maliciousness. The patient will be importunate, irrascible, and insistent that it is the therapist who misinterprets and not he or she. The patient may become retaliatory or destructive in response to the therapist's fancied hostility, or may experience panic, depression, or psychosomatic symptoms.

A resolution of hostility by the introduction of reality and by interpretation is indicated, following some of the suggestions given for the management of the sexual transference.

Where transference cannot be handled in any other way, active steps will have to be taken to minimize it. Such measures include a focusing in the interview on the current life situation rather than on early childhood experiences, avoidance of dreams and fantasies, discouraging discussion of the patient's relationship to the therapist, abandonment of the couch position and free association if these have been employed, decreasing the frequency of the interviews, presenting interpretations in terms of the character structure and current life situation rather than in terms of genetic determinants, and greater activity in the interview.

THE NEED FOR WORKING THROUGH RESISTANCE

Resistance may burn up the entire energy of the patient, who may self-defensively concentrate on fighting the therapist, or proving the therapist to be wrong, or winning the therapist over with gestures of helplessness, praise, or love, or seeking various means to escape or to evade treatment. The struggle is an intense one and usually goes on below the level of awareness.

When one appreciates the purpose of resistance, one realizes that patience is a great virtue. The therapist must bear with the neurotic individual as he or she progresses and takes refuge over and over again in customary defenses. Resistance is yielded only after a great struggle, for change is a painful affair.

Since resistance has a dynamic function, an effort is made to help the patient to relinquish it slowly. Too sudden removal may produce severe anxiety and may provoke a reinforcement of the neurotic defenses intended to protect the individual.

Relinquishment of resistance will thus be blocked by a threat of repetition of the anxiety experience.

Resistance is best managed by demonstrating its presence, its purpose, its ramifications, its historical origin, and the manner of its operation in the patient's present relationships with the therapist and with people in general. As resistances are gradually analyzed and resolved, repressed material appears in consciousness in a less and less disguised form. Resistances require a constant working through. A single interpretation of a resistance is hardly effective.

The therapist should allow resistance to evolve fully before taking it back to its origins. If a second resistance develops, the therapist must handle it by returning to the first one and demonstrating to the patient the interrelationship of the two. Tackling the patient's defensive reactions inevitably causes the patient to feel threatened and to dispute interpretations of his or her resistance. This reaction is opposed by a contrary motive, that of retaining the good will of the therapist. Often the patient will attempt to satisfy both of these motivations at the same time by abandoning his or her defense in the forms recognized by the therapist and changing it to a less obvious type. The understanding of these elaborations and their continued exposure forces the patient to take a real stand against them and, finally, to abandon them entirely.

It is always essential to remember that resistance has a strong protective value. Patients will usually reject any insight that is too traumatic, perhaps toying with it for a while, then forgetting it. However, through careful handling, insight into how and why the resistance is operating may be gained. First, the patient must be made aware of the resistance. Merely calling attention to it alerts attention to a specific task. It prevents burning up energy in pursuit of maintaining the resistance, constructively diverting it toward tracing down its meaning. Once a resistance develops, it is essen-

tial to abandon other tasks until it is resolved, because the patient will not be productive while battling the therapist. It is best at first not to probe too deeply for unconscious material, but rather to work intensively upon the immediate interpersonal relationship. To aid in the process, the patient must be impressed with the fact that there is nothing morally bad about showing certain defensive attitudes in the form of resistance.

The dealing with transference resistances may be a prolonged affair in the personality disorders. Here the ego seems blocked in absorbing the full meaning of the oppositional behavior as it becomes apparent. The patient may acknowledge the presence of certain drives. The patient may even understand their irrational nature and historical origin. but this pseudoinsight provokes little change in the customary life adjustment. The entire therapeutic process is intellectualized, the patient perhaps using insight to fortify himself or herself against anxiety. The patient's relationship with the therapist never proceeds to a level of good feeling that is shorn of hostility and inordinate expectations.

In infantile, narcissistic character structures particularly, intellectuality serves as a defense against unconscious impulses. Habitually there is a repression of the feeling aspects of the patient's personality, and mastery is sought through intellectual control. Any experience of feeling is regarded as catastrophic. By a curious transformation the defense itself may become a vicarious means of gratifying nonpermissible drives as represented in hostile and sexual impulses.

Patients, who have a tendency to isolate emotional components from emerging unconscious material, may make the latter acceptable to themselves by repressing the affective content. Frequently they strive to neutralize their panic by means of attempted foresight and reason. During therapy they give the impression of being very active and at first seem to work extraordinarily well. Even though they make a brilliant feat of minutely analyzing their inner mental processes, little change occurs. Such patients may involve the therapist in long dialectic arguments that take on the nature of debates. Words replace action and constitute a defense against feelings.

Interpretation of this type of defense is bound to create great turmoil in the patient. The patient is prone to feel attacked and criticized by the therapist. "Negative therapeutic reactions" are common, the patient responding to important interpretations not with insight or relief, but with depression and discouragement. Hostility may be directed at the therapist in an effort to annihilate the therapeutic work.

It is essential to remind every patient not to get too distressed if cure is not immediate. Some patients are confounded and depressed when they find, in spite of therapy, that they go on reacting in their usual ways. It may be necessary to explain that reaction patterns that have become established over a long period cannot be removed in a few sessions. They are habits that call for extended working through and reeducation.

In the event the patients insist they cannot get well because they are hopeless, the therapist may say, "You can express your hopelessness, but I will not go along with it. You can spend your energies feeling hopeless, and you don't need me for this; or you can spend your energies doing something about getting well in which case I can help you."

ILLUSTRATIVE CASE MATERIAL

Example 1

In this session, a female homosexual patient with a problem of dysphoria introduces a number of different resistances that block her progress.

Pt. I keep losing my keys constantly. My mind can't seem to concentrate lately. I notice that the only time I want to think about my problem is when I come here. The minute I get out I feel relieved. When I leave here I notice my hands as very cold. [*This sounds like resistance in the form of intellectual inhibition.*]

Th. I see. Can you tell me more about this?

Pt. When I get out of the office, in waiting for the elevator, I push myself up against the wall pretending the wall to be Helen (*the patient's homosexual love object*). I actually kiss that wall and I say, "Who does he think *he* is, trying to pull me away from my darling Helen. I won't have it, I just won't have it." [*This device seems to be a magical way of neutralizing therapy, which she interprets as a threat to her homosexuality.*]

Th. What does it remind you of when you do that?

Pt. Like being united with my mother. Everything seems to be O.K. again, and I can go on living. [*Having lost her mother in childhood, the patient's homosexuality, in part, is a neurotic attempt to reunite herself with her mother.*]

Th. Mm hmm.

Pt. You see. I do that.

Th. But why do you think I want to take you away from your mother?

Pt. I see that. You see, the information I get here, I feel, is going to get rid of the old regime and bring on a new regime.

Th. And the old regime is what?

Pt. Homosexuality. That's strong. It's easier to live in than the new regime.

Th. And the new regime?

Pt. Is getting rid of the mother fantasy and working it out.

Th. So that you would consider any insights that you get here in a certain way.

Pt. As dangerous to my ability to function (*pause*) for the moment.

Th. So when you come here, I upset the balance and you may want to go to the opposite extreme.

Pt. I shift to the opposite extreme so I can function.

Th. You must perhaps think of me as a terrible person to do this to you. [*probing our relationship*]

Pt. You are a horror. (*said facetiously*) I adore you, you know.

Th. You do? Why?

Pt. You know I do. [*Our relationship, though ambivalent, seems good.*]

Th. In spite of what I do?

Pt. In spite of it. (*coughs*)

Th. Maybe I better stop doing this to you. [*challenging her desire for health*]

Pt. Hell, no. I don't go wild. There is a certain amount of control.

Th. The fact that you know all the reasons that exist for your problem . . .

Pt. (*interrupting defiantly*) Doesn't do me any good.

Th. You are still the arbiter of whether you'll do anything about the situation or not. But at least you have the right to know all the facts. There is no magic about this. The whole thing is your choice. Nobody is going to take anything away from you, you don't want to let go of.

Pt. But I don't have the ability to make a choice rationally. (*yawns*)

Th. Right now your choice would be irrational?

Pt. Yes, I'd choose homosexuality. But, not really. You know, my mind is wandering. I'm trying not to listen to you. You know what I'm doing now? I'm trying to figure out my school homework. [*Patient is aware of her resistance.*]

Th. Not paying attention to what I'm saying.

Pt. Isn't that awful. First I yawn and then my mind wanders. And I wasn't even aware of what I was doing. [*Again she recognizes her resistance.*]

Th. But now you've caught yourself.

Pt. I caught myself.

Th. There must be a reason why it's dangerous for you to integrate what we talk about. [*pointing out possible reasons for her resistance*]

Pt. I just won't listen to you. (*coughs*) I'll bet this throat business has something to do with it. Obviously.

Th. You sense your own resistance. Do you want me to leave you alone?

Pt. No, no. But I do want to get well.

Th. It may take time for you to overcome this problem. It started far back in your childhood. And you have been reacting automatically since.

Pt. You know, I didn't hear a word you said. My mind keeps wandering. [*more resistance*]

Th. Do you remember anything we talked about the last session?

Pt. Nothing. My mind's a complete blank. I can't pull myself together at all. (*coughs*) And you know why I can't do this?

Th. Why?

Pt. Because you are sitting back and judging me on my little speeches.

Th. I'm judging you?

Pt. It's not true, but that's how I feel. I sort of feel I'm on trial and that I'm likely to do things wrong. The same thing happens when I get up and speak in class. It's funny that I don't remember a damn word of what you said today.

Th. How about what I said to you last time?

Pt. Oh, I remember that, but I can't put it together.

Th. Suppose you try.

Pt. It's like the only thing that can give me pleasure is my homosexuality and my torture fantasies with masturbation. I feel that you will take these from me. I say to myself that if I let you take these things away, the time will come when I'll need them and I'll be without them. Take life's last spark away.

Th. No wonder you can't concentrate here, if you think this is what really is going to happen. As if there can't be a good substitute for your present pleasures.

Pt. But it's not entirely what I feel because I do want to get well. But I can't seem to do it today. When I leave here, I suppose I'll kiss that wall to get my equilibrium back. Or I will get a hopeless desire and sexual attraction for you. I don't want to listen to what you have to say. I just want to be close to you. [*transference resistance*]

Th. In a way that's the same thing as clinging to and kissing the wall? (I am not trying to discourage her transference, but merely to control its intensity.)

Pt. It is exactly the same thing. It's the same thing I have about Helen. Intellectually I'm not interested. I want to get into bed with her. So stop talking and let's have sex. That's how I feel about you. Same kind of feeling.

Th. Sex appeases your tension? Is that what you really want exclusively?

Pt. Obviously not, but I can see how this operates. And another crazy thing I do. When I leave here and get onto the street, I imagine you are watching me from the window. I get into my car and roar off.

Th. What does that mean to you?

Pt. It's like I get my masculinity back again.

Th. Which means you feel you lose it when you come here?

Pt. (*laughs*) Yes, I really do. I know that's

silly. I say, "I'll show him. I'll roar off. I'll show him he can't make me into a woman." I try to get my feeling of power. (*laughs*) How silly can you get?

Example 2

A patient comes in with a hoarseness so severe that she can hardly talk. This symptom came on her several hours prior to her session and was not accompanied by any other signs of a head cold. Exploration reveals the symptom to be a manifestation of various resistances.

Th. I wonder if you have been at all emotionally upset prior to this hoarseness. [*focusing on possible emotional sources of the symptom*]

Pt. I don't know what you mean.

Th. Are you aware of anything emotional that is happening right now? (*long pause*) What about your feeling about therapy?

Pt. The only thing I can say now, which is nuts, is that I'm scared to death of you. (*pause*)

Th. The way you look at me is suggestive that you are afraid of me. (*The patient has a frightened expression on her face.*)

Pt. I was always aware that I had a tenseness before, but it never was like this. (*The patient is so hoarse it is difficult to make out what she is saying.*)

Th. What do you think this is all about?

Pt. I don't know. (*pause*)

Th. Have you had any dreams?

Pt. Yes, I had one dream I can hardly remember. It's scrambled. (*pause*) I dreamed I was in some sort of clinic. It was your clinic. (*pause*) And there was a young chap there who was very attracted to me. He was there for treatment too. I liked him, and he liked me. But I was a patient at the clinic and I was working there, both. I talked to a group of people on the stairs. You were there as an onlooker in a benevolent way. And I was kidding. I said I want to go to Paris and live a couple of years. But this guy I liked and I decided we would have to take you with us. We have to take Dr. Wolberg with us because we have to finish this treatment. I looked at you and said, "That's involved for you, isn't it?" You laughed. It was all said in fun. Then this young chap and I decided to go home, and we walked and walked. And all of a sudden it occurred to me that I was walking without any trouble at all. (*Among the patient's problems are muscular pains and arthritis com-*

plaints in both legs which make it hard for her to walk.)

Th. Mm hmm.

Pt. (*pause*) And then I was back in the clinic, and this young chap said he wanted me to do his analysis. I said that's impossible. And he sort of grinned at me and disappeared out of the door. That's all I can remember. [*The thoughts that come to my mind are that the patient may represent herself in the dream as her feminine component and the young man as her masculine component. She wants to return to narcissism (loving the man) and feels she can function this way (being able to walk). However, she is unwilling to give up her dependency on me (returns to the clinic) and she relinquishes her masculine component (the man disappears out of the door). Another possibility is that the young man is a disguised symbol for me toward whom the patient feels she can express an erotic feeling. In this way she can dissociate her sexual feeling for me from her therapy. Working further on the dream may disclose its meaning.*]

Th. When did this dream occur?

Pt. Last night.

Th. What are your associations to it?

Pt. (*pause*) I'm blocked off on associations, (*pause*) I'm blocked off on thinking. I'm in a complete state of suspension. [*intellectual resistance*]

Th. What in the dream might give you clues about your fear of me? What might you be planning or thinking of that would make you afraid of me?

Pt. Well, when I said I want to go to Paris, I might want to run away.

Th. What does Paris mean?

Pt. If I could do what I want to do, I'd go to Paris for a couple of years. I love it, just adore it. I love the French people, their relaxation and acceptance. It was wonderful.

Th. What does Paris symbolize to you?

Pt. Fun and sex. It's a sexy place.

Th. And here you wanted to go with this young man.

Pt. Yes, he was cute. (*laughs*)

Th. Was there a sexual feeling about that dream?

Pt. Oh, yes, sure. I was all for this guy. I'll tell you who he was. I never thought of it until now. He was a guy I met at Bob's party last Wednesday night. He turned out to be a young psychiatrist, and he knew you. Which is connected with you. So there you are.

Th. So you really felt attracted to him.

Pt. Yes, but had to take you along.

Th. Why do you think you had to?

Pt. Obviously you two are the same.

Th. So that you may have sexual feelings for me and project them onto another person, or you have a fear of sex and also fear disappointment. [*tentative interpretation*]

Pt. (*sighs*) Couldn't that be the same thing?

Th. It might. There may also be a desire to leave your therapy and run off and have fun, and wonder about my disapproval of that. There may be many things. What do you think? [*tentative interpretations*]

Pt. Consciously I'm not aware of wanting to run away from therapy. It's very painful to me as you can see. I wouldn't be happy getting out of it; I'd only be happy getting through with it. But the sexual thing troubles me.

Th. What about any sexual feelings toward me?

Pt. I think I've always had that. I block off though and can't talk about it. It's almost impossible. [*She recognizes her resistance.*]

Th. What does talking about the feelings do?

Pt. Make me scared of you. I don't want to talk about it. I'm sure that's what's happening to me now, (*pause*) I'm just preventing talking, that's all. (*pause*) And I feel silly. [*This indicates an awareness that her hoarseness may be a form of resistance against verbalizing sexual feelings toward me.*]

Th. Silly about your feelings?

Pt. Mm hmm. *I* think it does. All my life I've covered up important things, so to let it out is an almost impossible thing. I talk about sex often in a pseudosophisticated way. I can make smart cracks faster than anybody I know, but it has nothing to do with me. To talk about my sexual feelings—no, no. The minute it touches me, I clam up.

Th. Yet you haven't been too inhibited in your sex life.

Pt. I think I was a great deal, even though I didn't act it. (*pause*) I just thought of a dream I had in which you kissed me. I told you about it two months ago. From that time on I haven't been able to talk about my sexual feelings for you.

Th. Mm hmm.

Pt. When I'm lonesome I say you are very attractive to me sexually. (*pause*) I feel sexual contact with you is forbidden, like it would be with a father. (*The patient's voice is much clearer now, as if her hoarseness is vanishing.*)

Th. If it's true that you feel extremely guilty about having sexual thoughts about me, that would cause you not to want to tell me your thoughts. [*interpreting her resistance*]

Pt. That comes close to it, I think. It's silly. (*laughs*) I'm beginning to see through you. (*The patient's voice is very clear at this point, her hoarseness having subsided considerably.*)

Th. What do you mean?

Pt. You're trying to make me talk about you. All right. (*laughs*) I have varying emotions about you. First, I say, "To hell with that bastard, I won't go back to see him." Then I say, "That's what he expects me to do, so I shall go back to see him." And then I say you are trying to be my friend, trying to do something decent. Then I get contrite about having had bad thoughts. All of which is a bunch of crap. I know it as well as you know it.

Th. So you must feel resentful toward me sometime.

Pt. I feel, (*long pause*) I feel now, and I have for the last few times I've seen you, that all of the threads that have bothered me have all come together in one knot, which knot has become *you*. If I can get that knot untied, then I'll be free. All the other things that bothered me are minor. I'm pulling out everything I have to resist you.

Th. Resist me in what reference?

Pt. Horribly enough I'm afraid it's a resistance to getting cured. [*recognition of resistance of normality*]

Th. You sound disgusted with yourself.

Pt. I am.

Th. What might cure do to you?

Pt. Well, it could put me back to work. It could eliminate all my excuses for not doing things. It could make me take an aggressive and active role. It could make me stop drinking and take that fun away from me. It could make me take a decisive action about George (*her husband*). I've come through the labyrinth and I'm up to the door, and I'm just resisting like hell. [*The patient elaborates her many resistances against normality.*]

Th. You must be frightened. Because that door is the door people want to reach.

Pt. That's what I've been coming here to reach.

Th. And now that you're approaching it, you are a little afraid of it.

Pt. I'm scared as hell, but I'm beginning a little to understand it.

The following is an excerpt of the very next session that brings out some interesting points:

Pt. I had a very peculiar reaction. Of course, it is almost impossible for me to say it, a very peculiar reaction last time. And I don't know what it was that was said, whether it was something I said or something you said, I don't know. But it was something in connection with our conversation, our relationship. Then all of a sudden I got a "cat-and-canary" deal, which you knew perfectly well, because you couldn't help but see it on my face. I don't see how you couldn't, and then just as I left, I said, "I feel like you're laughing at me." I knew that you weren't laughing at me in the sense of being nasty, but you knew damned well I wouldn't tell you what was on my mind. And, of course, that's the hell of the "cat-and-mouse" thing, because I'm perfectly aware that you know what's on my mind. Or at least you know very well whether I'm holding something back and won't say it or not. And I know that you know; so, therefore, I get into one of these, as I say, "cat-and-mouse" deals.

Th. What makes you feel that I can read your mind, that I know what you're holding back?

Pt. I'll bet 99 times out of 100 you do. It's very difficult, and I feel very silly. Whatever it was, whether that was a part of it or something else, I got a reaction of being very silly and ingenue, and very ridiculous, and I couldn't get over that feeling. Now what tossed me into that?

Th. When did you get this feeling?

Pt. Sometime during the last part of our conversation last time. I don't remember very much what we said, only that I think you asked me how I feel about you.

Th. How *do* you feel?

Pt. Giddy.

Th. Giddy?

Pt. Yeah. I think when I use the word "silly" I probably mean that. (*pause*)

Th. How did you feel *I* must have viewed you? Was it that you thought *I* thought you were silly?

Pt. Yeah. I imagine that's it.

Th. Well, why?

Pt. (*pause*) My reaction when I left was that I wanted to put my arms around you and kiss you. Now whether that is a little-girl reaction or not, I don't know. But that was the feeling I had.

Th. You felt affectionate?

Pt. Yeah. And then I think that's probably why I felt embarrassed. I felt I (*laughs*) wanted to go over and sit on your lap, like a little girl, and I'm probably older than you are.

Th. You think I think you're silly if you want to do that?

Pt. Probably because I had the idea that you've been trying to make me grow up. And goddamn it, I don't want to grow up.

Th. If this is what you feel, this is what you feel. Let's try to understand it. Suppose you do feel like putting your arms around me or sitting on my lap. Do you think there is something wrong with that?

Pt. Apparently I do. I don't think so, but I *feel* there is. I must or I wouldn't react that way. And when I get the "cat-and-canary," as they say, the "cat-that's-robbed-the-canary-look" on my face, I usually have something in my head, which I entertain, which I think is not in order. (*pause*)

Th. You know it is rather interesting that you find it so hard to mention to me what had happened. [*focusing on resistance*]

Pt. Sometimes I'll go for months and won't mention some things to you. And it isn't because I want to hide something. That's the goddamned mechanism of this thing. I blurted out and told you the last time, but, of course, by the time I get to talking about things, it's just when I'm putting on my coat. Like last time I kicked myself around the block when I got outside. I thought, why that's perfectly silly, why shouldn't I have said that; I've said every other goddamned thing. It's a wonder I came back today and said it. Because sometimes I might go for months and I might talk about every subject in the world. But some little thing like that which apparently has significance for me, I can't talk about.

Th. Perhaps it had such deep significance to you for a special reason?

Pt. Well, I find you attractive. (*laughs*) It's silly, but I have a thought it would be nice . . . last time what I failed to say was that I thought it would be nice to go to bed with you. But it kills me to tell you that. [*sexual transference*]

Th. Perhaps you wonder what my reaction would be.

Pt. I can remember one instance now. I don't suppose it was the type of person. It was probably the way I was feeling at the time. But usually men have approached me and I pretty much took what I wanted and left what I didn't want alone. That's always the case. A few times I thought someone was awfully cute, and I have deliberately gone after it, trying to look undeliberate. The exception was this once, and I can't remember who this man was. I think I'd read it in a novel, and I decided to try to ask a man to sleep with me, and did. And the result was disastrous. He ran like he was hit by a poisoned arrow.

Th. I see.

Pt. This guy ran. I don't think I ever did see him again. I remember now. Yeah. To show you that I'm embarrassed about it, I can't remember his name. Anyway, he was a guy that I went to Vriginia with. I was going on my business. He was going on his business. He was trying to make a business deal with me. He was very good looking, and he was my type. He was dark and not too damned tall and big, and I thought he was very attractive. I had lunch with him several times. And so I was going to Richmond. And I said at lunch one day that I was going to go to Richmond on such and such a day. And he said, "What are you taking?" And I told him the train number. And I got on the train, and he had the compartment right next to me. That I've never figured out. Maybe it was just luck. So anyway, he started making love to me. He came in to my compartment, and we were having a couple of drinks, and we were talking. And he started making love to me and all in a round-about way, an inch at a time, an inch at a time. He put his arms around me first, and all the pow-wow they go through. So I thought this is going to be silly. I'd been thinking about it for weeks. That looks good. I'd like to have that when I can get a hold of it. So I just turned and looked at him. I said, "You don't have to go through all this, because I *want* to sleep with you." And it scared the hell out of him.

Th. Do you feel that maybe you're afraid of being outspoken with me too?

Pt. Goddamn it, yes. (*laughs*) I see it now. I must be afraid. You will run off and leave me if I'm too outspoken. My parents never let me speak my mind. Everything I learned I got out of being on the go with the other kids on the street. [*We continue to explore her sexual feelings toward me.*]

47

The Management of Untoward Attitudes in the Therapist, Including Countertransference

Two people locked up in the same room are, sooner or later, bound to find their difficulties rubbing off on each other, each personality influencing the other. The patient will regard the therapist in many ways, such as (1) an idealized parental figure, (2) a symbol of the parents and of authority, and (3) a model after whom one seeks to pattern oneself. A therapist too responds to a patient in various ways. There is a tendency to project onto the patient one's own prejudices and values as well as to identify the patient with individuals from one's own past. The therapist's reactions are bound to influence those of the patient. In recognition of the fact that a therapist cannot truly act as a blank screen, no matter how thoroughly adjusted one is, many therapists have devoted themselves to a delineation of the clinical effects of what they have called *countertransference* (Balint & Balint, 1939; Berman, L, 1949; Bonime, 1957; Cohen, M, 1952; Gitelson, 1952; Heiman, P, 1950; Little, M, 1951; Orr, 1954; Rioch, 1943; Salzman, 1962; Tauber, 1964; Winnicott, 1949; Wolstein, 1959). The importance of countertransference is that it influences all forms of psychotherapy—supportive, reeducative, or reconstructive—sometimes to their detriment, sometimes to their benefit.

The idea that countertransference is always bad has in recent years been revised (see Chapter 5, 57). Countertransference may be used in a therapeutic way. Therapists, recognizing that their own neurotic feelings are being activated, may look not only into themselves, but also into what neurotic needs and drives in their patients are activating in their personal reactions. They may then bring up these provocations as foci for exploration. They may ask, "Is the patient aware of aberrant impulses and behaviors? What does the patient want to accomplish by them?" Confronting the patient with the behavior may have a therapeutic impact.

Accepting the benefits of some countertransference reactions, we shall in the remainder of this chapter concern ourselves with its negative effects that account for a great many failures in psychotherapy.

Conceptions about countertransference are multifaceted. These range from the traditional idea that it is exclusively confined to feelings derived from repressed unresolved parental atachments (Winnicott, 1949) to strivings provoked by anxiety (Cohen, M, 1952) to the total range of attitudes of the therapist toward the patient (Alexander F, 1948). The tendency to dilute countertransference with reactions emerging from the habitual character structure has created some confusion. Befuddlement also comes from the tendency to identify all positive or negative feelings toward the patient as forms of countertransference. The therapist as a functioning human being will have a warmth toward, a liking for, and empathy with patients—more with some than with others for realistic reasons. The therapist will also be candidly angry with certain actions of patients, the display of which toward the patient may not at all be destructive. Indeed, the patient may be traumatized by the therapist's failure to respond to provocations with justified indignation or rage. However, the reactions we are concerned with most in psychotherapy are responses of the therapist not justified by reality but which issue either out of the therapist's own transference or that emerge as expressions of the neurotic character structure. Therapeutic manipulations fostered by the therapist's needs, rather than by those of the patient, are bound to create rather than to solve problems (Lorand, 1963a).

Where disciplined in self-observation, the therapist may become cognizant of troublesome attitudes and feelings toward patients before expressing them in behavior. The more insight one has into one's interpersonal operations, the more capable one is of exercising any necessary control. Where there is little understanding of one's unconscious dynamisms, the therapist is most apt to respond with unmanageable negative countertransference.

An illustration of how countertransference may act to the detriment of therapeutic competence may be cited by the case of a male therapist who, well trained and endowed with more than the usual warmth toward people, was able to achieve good results in psychotherapy with most patients. Notably defective, however, were his results with male patients who had serious difficulties with women. The therapist himself was involved in conflict with his wife, the details of which he was not at all loath to verbalize. This was undoubtedly a manifestation of his unresolved problems with women. Whenever his male patients divulged their difficulties with their wives, the therapist would immediately respond with rancor and vehemently denounce the chicanery of scheming females. This attitude, while temporarily comforting to some patients, ultimately resulted in their distrust of the therapist, engendered by a realization that they could never work through with him some of their basic life problems.

It is rare indeed that a therapist, irrespective of how free one is from personality blemish, can respond with completely therapeutic attitudes toward all patients. With some patients one may display an adequate degree of sensitivity, flexibility, objectivity, and empathy, so helpful to good psychotherapy. With other patients one may manifest a lack of these qualities and an inability to perceive what is happening in the treatment process. There will be a failure to recognize neurotic projections in the relationship, and to remain tolerant in the face of the patient's irrational and provocative behavior. Thus, infantile requests by the patient for exclusive preference, or sexual responsiveness, or expressions of resentment and hostility, or unfounded complaints of being exploited, may bring out in the therapist attitudes that interfere with a working relationship.

If the analyst cannot identify with the patient, he will encounter difficulties, but identification in turn leads to other difficulties . . . the analyst then experiences the patients' intense anxieties fears, rages, lusts and conflicts as his own, and unless he faces these problems and deals with them directly, he may resort to controlling devices to allay the patient's anxiety and his own—such as excessive tenderness or other devices similar to those employed by the patient's parents, or he may resort to primitive defenses similar to those used by the patient, especially paranoid defenses. (Savage, 1961).

Character distortions in the therapist

will inevitably have an effect on the patient. Thus, a need in the therapist to be directive and authoritarian, while advantageous in supportive approaches, tends, in insight therapy, to interfere with the individual's growing sense of self, expanding assertiveness, and independence. Authoritarian attitudes also pander to dependency strivings in the patient and coordinately nurture rebellious tendencies. Some therapists are driven by pompousness to make too early and too deep interpretations, which they hope will impress the patient with their erudition and perceptiveness. They may also attempt to force the patient into actions before the latter is ready for them. However, this playing of a directive role with the patient to satisfy certain emotional needs in the therapist must not be confused with a deliberate extension to the patient of emotional support when this is therapeutically indicated. The former is usually based on the motivation to parade one's power and omniscience; the latter is a studied, measured giving of help that is inspired by the needs of the patient.

Tendencies toward passivity and submissiveness in the therapist may also have a detrimental effect on treatment since it is sometimes necessary to be firm with the patients, as in helping them to avoid retreat, to execute insight into action, and in offering them essential guidance and reassurance. Submissive traits in the therapist, furthermore, operate to bring out sadistic, hostile attitudes in the patients.

Impulses toward detachment may develop in the therapist as a defense against entering into close contact with some patients. This trait is particularly destructive to the therapeutic relationship. The patient may be able to establish some sort of relatedness with a domineering or a passive therapist, but is totally unable to relate to one who is detached.

A therapist who, because of personal anxiety or a depriving life situation, is thwarted in the expression of certain basic drives may attempt to live through them vicariously in the experiences of the patient. The therapist may, therefore, tend to overemphasize certain aspects of the patient's behavior. Thus, if the patient is in a position of fame, or is financially successful, or is expressing sexual or hostile impulses, the therapist, if there is the unconscious need to satisfy such strivings, will focus unduly on these perhaps to the exclusion of other vital psychic aspects. This loss of perspective is particularly pronounced where there is any overidentification with the patient.

Neurotic ambitiousness may cause the therapist to glory in the patient's accomplishments and to push the patient inexorably into areas that are calculated to lead to success and renown. Overambitiousness may also be extended toward seeking rapid results in treatment. Here the therapist will be unable to wait for the gradual resolution of resistance. Accordingly, the exploratory process will be promoted too hurriedly at the beginning of therapy. Perturbed by the slowness with which the patient acquires insight, the therapist may interpret prematurely, and then respond with resentment at the oppositional tendencies of the patient. The therapist may also propel the patient too vigorously toward normal objectives and then become frustrated at the patient's refusal to utilize insight in the direction of change.

Due to anxiety or guilt, it may be difficult for the therapist to countenance certain needs within himself or herself. When such needs appear in the patient, the therapist may exercise attempts to inhibit their expression. Difficulties here especially relate to impules toward sexuality, hostility, and assertiveness. Should the patient introduce these topics, the therapist may act disinterested or may focus deliberately on another area. The therapist may be unaware of these personal psychic blind spots that prevent exploring anxiety-inspiring conflicts in the patient. Thus, a therapist who has problems in dealing with hostility, may, upon encountering hostile expressions, reassure the patient compulsively or channelize verbalizations toward a less threatening topic. Fear of hostility may also cause the therapist to tarry, to lose initiative, and to evidence confusion on occasions when the patient attempts to act in an aggressive or assertive way. Fear of special aspects of the patient's unconscious may cause the therapist to circumvent the discussion of pertinent material to the detriment of reconstructive therapeutic goals.

Other limiting personality manifestations may reflect themselves in neurotic attitudes toward money with an overemphasis of fees and payments, in an inability to tolerate acting-out tendencies in the patient, and in a tremendous desire for admiration and homage. Perfectionistic impulses may cause the therapist to drive the patient compulsively toward goals in treatment that are beyond the patient's capacities. At times some therapists, under pressure of their own neurotic drives, may set up a situation in treatment that parallels closely the traumatizing environment of the patient's childhood. When this happens, the patient's transference may become extreme and perhaps insoluble. Certain patients may mobilize in the therapist strong feelings of rejection and intolerance, which will destroy the emotional climate that is so important for personality development. Other therapists, burdened with narcissism, and needing to impress the patient constantly with their brilliance, may utilize interpretation too freely and water down the therapeutic process with intellectualizations.

It must not be assumed that all neurotic displays on the part of the therapist will have a bad effect. If they play into the patient's immediate needs, they may bring the patient to a rapid homeostasis. Thus, a sadistic therapist may be eagerly responded to by a masochistic patient. An authoritarian, domineering therapist may satisfy the dependent impulses of a depressed person. Restoration of equilibrium will not, of course, alter the basic personality structure. Important to consider also is that growth in a psychotherapeutic relationship with a neurotic therapist may occur in patients with essentially good resources. Such patients will select out of positive aspects of the therapeutic situation elements that they can utilize constructively. They may rationalize the therapist's neurotic weaknesses, or not pay attention to them, or simply blot them out of their cognitive field. It is to be expected that perceptive patients will eventually discover some neurotic patterns or traits in their therapists. This may at first result in disillusionment, anxiety, resentment, or insecurity. If the relationship is a good one, however, there need be no interference with the therapeutic process, the patients ultimately adjusting themselves to the reality of a less-than-ideal therapist image. It may actually be helpful to discard the mantle of perfection with which the therapist has been draped in the early part of therapy. The degree and kind of neurotic disturbance in the therapist is what is important.

At certain phases in treatment therapist improprieties may become more pronounced than at others. For instance, during periods of resistance the therapist may respond with aggressive or rejecting behavior. Some actions of the patient may also stimulate countertransference. A patient who is frankly seductive may stimulate sexual feelings in the therapist; one who is openly antagonistic may precipitate counterhostile attitudes. The patient may be sensitive to the moods of the therapist and work on these for specific gains, the most insidious effect of which is a sabotaging of the treatment effort.

Because countertransference may result in therapeutic failure, it must be handled as soon as possible. Where recognized, the therapist may be able to exercise some control over it. There are therapists, who, though unanalyzed themselves, have an excellent capacity for self-analysis and an ability to restrain annoying expressions of countertransference. This permits the therapeutic process to advance unimpeded. A therapist who has undergone successful personal psychotherapy or psychoanalysis will still be subject to countertransference from time to time. Nevertheless, one should, by virtue of one's training, be capable of detecting and of managing troublesome reactions as soon as they develop.

Instead of denying a neurotic response to the patient, which is so common, some therapists, detecting their own untoward responses, admit them openly and even analyze them with the help of the patient. Alger (1964) suggests that the therapist should "deal with these feelings in no way different than he deals with any other of his reactions. By this is meant that he be willing to include all the reactions he has while he is with his patient as part of the analytic data of that particular situation. . . . In this view, the analysis then becomes a joint activity in which two participants attempt by mutual effort to assemble and openly share with each other their perceptions, their concepts, and most importantly their own feelings." Such therapeutic license will call for great skill on the part of therapist, to say nothing of personal courage.

One way of acquiring this skill is to examine oneself honestly rather than defensively when attacked or criticized by a patient. To be sure, it is impossible for a therapist to maintain a consistent attitude toward or interest in patients at all times. Names and events may be forgotten, indicating to the patient lack of rapport; appointments may be broken or confused, connoting unconcern; irrelevant comments may be made, pointing to "noncaringness"; tension and anxiety may be expressed, suggesting instability. Irrespective of the reasons for the therapist's reactions, awareness of what one is doing and willingness to admit one's failings when they are discerned by the patient is of paramount importance. There is nothing so undermining to a patient as to have an observation, predicated on fact, dismissed as fanciful, or to have an obvious error on the part of the therapist converted into a gesture for which the patient is held responsible. Where the therapist is capable of admitting a blunder and of conveying to the patient that this does not vitiate respect and interest, the liability may actually be converted into an asset.

Certain therapists have taken this as license to articulate every aberrant thought and impulse to the patient, and even to act out with the patient. While this may be accepted by some patients as indications of the therapist's genuineness, it is destructive for most patients who expect the therapist to function as a rational authority. Therapists who are basically detached, and who are obsessively preoccupied with neurotic impulses, may, nevertheless, come through to the patient more sincerely as people when they engage in such random and undisciplined behavior than when they assume the straitjacket of a "therapeutic" attitude. From this experience of unrestraint, however, they may devise a theory and formulate methodologies, predicated on being free and abandoned in the therapeutic relationship, a stance that for most professionals will prove to be antitherapeutic.

Detection of countertransference and character distortions may not be possible where deep unconscious needs are pressing. It is this unawareness of their inner drives that so frequently causes therapists to rationalize them. Indeed, the very selection of certain methodologies and kinds of therapeutic practice are often determined by unconscious motivations. Thus, a therapist, basically passive, who fears human contacts and has evolved a detached manner as a defense, may be attuned to schools in which extreme passivity and nondirectiveness are the accepted modes. Or, if by personality domineering and aggressive, a therapist may be inclined toward endorsing the doctrines of those schools that advocate directive or coercive techniques.

MANAGEMENT OF COUNTERTRANSFERENCE

Those aspects of countertransference that reflect the projection of a patient's unconscious process may enable a sensitive therapist to detect unverbalized needs and conflicts. How to deal with countertransferential feelings constructively will depend on how skillful the therapist is in making interpretations and the readiness of the patient to accept such interpretations. It is essential that confirmation of the therapist's intuitive hunches be obtained from other sources of information such as the patient's nonverbal behavior, dreams, slips of speech, free associations, and acting out episodes. The therapist may have to delay interpretations until a strategic time presents itself. The manner in which interpretations are made will also determine how they will be accepted (see Chapter 45, p. 754).

Some of the patient's actions may stir up realistic angry feelings in the patient that have nothing to do with countertransference. Here it is necessary to judge how propitious a disclosure of such feelings may be. It is sometimes important to verbalize one's angry feelings toward a patient who is behaving in a self-defeating and provocative manner, especially when there is no need to build up a transference neurosis. Such verbalization is not done in a punitive way, but rather as a means of bringing the patient to an awareness of how the patient comes through with people and why reactions toward him or her are less than congenial. Where the patient is in a negative transference toward the therapist or the transference is acting as resistance to therapy, the therapist must control angry feelings and

work on the interpretation of the transference to get therapy "back on the tracks."

Since some negative countertransferential reactions are unavoidable, most likely breaking through when the therapist's emotional reserve is taxed or when the therapist is distraught and upset, the question arises as to what one can do to neutralize their antitherapeutic effect. Signs of countertransference include impatience with the length of a session or resentment at having to terminate it, doing special out-of-the-ordinary things for select patients, dreaming about a patient, making opportunities to socialize with the patient, sexual fantasies about the patient, unexplained anger at the patient, boredom with the patient, impulses to act out with the patient, and refusal to terminate when planned goals have been achieved.

In order to become sensitized to one's own neurotic manifestations when they appear, all therapists should subject themselves to self-examination throughout the course of therapy. Such questions as the following are appropriate:

1. How do I feel about the patient?
2. Do I anticipate seeing the patient?
3. Do I overidentify with, or feel sorry for the patient?
4. Do I feel any resentment or jealousy toward the patient?
5. Do I get extreme pleasure out of seeing the patient?
6. Do I feel bored with the patient?
7. Am I fearful of the patient?
8. Do I want to protect, reject, or punish the patient?
9. Am I impressed by the patient?

Should answers to any of the above point to problems, the therapist may ask why such attitudes and feelings exist. Is the patient doing anything to stir up such feelings? Does the patient resemble anybody the therapist knows or has known, and, if so, are any attitudes being transferred to the patient that are related to another person? What other impulses are being mobilized in the therapist that account for these feelings? What role does the therapist want to play with the patient? Mere verbalization to oneself of answers to these queries, permits of a better control of unreasonable feelings. Cognizance of the fact that one feels angry, displeased, disgusted, irritated, provoked, uninterested, unduly attentive, upset, or overly attracted may suffice to bring these emotions under control. In the event untoward attitudes continue, more self-searching is indicated. Of course, it may be difficult to act accepting, noncritical, and nonjudgmental toward a patient who is provocatively hostile and destructive in attitudes toward people, and who possesses disagreeable traits that the therapist in everyday life would criticize.

The ability to maintain an objective attitude toward the patient does not mean that the therapist will not, on occasion, temporarily dislike many of the things the patient does or says. Indeed, one may become somewhat irritated with any patient on certain occasions, especially when being subjected to a barrage of unjust accusations, criticisms, and demands. The stubborn resistances of the patient to acquiring insight and to translating insight into action, and the clinging of the patient to attitudes and action patterns that are maladaptive and destructive, will tax the endurance of any therapist, no matter how well integrated one's personality may be. But the capacity to understand one's own feelings will help the therapist better to tolerate the neurotic strivings of the patient and to maintain a working relationship.

To illustrate how a therapist may control countertransference, we may consider the case of a patient who is having an affair with the wife of his best friend and feels exultant about this situation. The therapist, repulsed by the enthusiasm and sexual abandon displayed by the patient, may, therefore, have a temptation to interpret the situation as a disgraceful one, with the

object of putting pressure on the patient to give up his paramour. With this in mind, the therapist may enjoin, order, or suggest that the patient stop seeing the woman in question or desist from having sexual relations with her. Should the therapist step in boldly in this way, the interference will probably be resented by the patient. Indeed, transference may be mobilized, the patient regarding the therapist as a cruel, depriving, dangerous mother or father who prohibits sex or freedom. An artificial note will thus be injected into the relationship, the patient utilizing his affair as a means of defying the therapist. Not only will the patient continue in his infatuation, but the therapeutic situation may deteriorate. Or the patient may yield to the therapist's suggestion and give up the relationship with the woman and then become depressed and detached, as if he has been forced to relinquish something precious. He will feel that his independence has been violated.

In attempting to control one's responses, the therapist may indulge in self-searching. Realizing moralistic attitudes, the therapist is better capable of keeping in the forefront the general principle that, right or wrong, the patient is the one who must make the decision about continuing in the affair or giving it up. Accordingly, instead of suggesting to the patient that he stop the illicit relationship, the therapist may say:

"Now here is a situation that seems to have a good deal of value for you. You get fun out of seeing your friend's wife, but you also see that there are difficulties in the situation. Now suppose we discuss the good and bad sides of your predicament." The patient then will verbalize his feelings about the virtues as opposed to the liabilities of his intrigue. Thereupon, the therapist may remark: "Here, you see, there are values as well as liabilities in the situation. It is important for you to consider all the facts and then decide the course of action you want to take." In this way the therapist strives to keep personal feelings from influencing the patient. The patient is then better equipped to evaluate what is happening and to plan his own course of action.

It is unnecessary for therapists to feel that they must strap themselves into an emotional straitjacket to avoid upsetting the patient. Nor is it essential that they be paragons of personality virtues to do good psychotherapy. As long as one is reasonably flexible, objective, and empathic, and provided that a working relationship exists, one may indulge a variety of spontaneous emotional responses, even some that are neurotically nurtured, without hurting the patient or the therapeutic situation. Actually, the patient will adjust to the therapist's specific personality, if it is sensed that the therapist is a capable, honest, nonhostile person who is interested in helping the patient get well.

For example, a therapist may be inclined to be active and somewhat domineering. The patient may then exhibit toward the therapist the usual attitudes toward domineering and authoritative people: the patient may become fearful, or hostile, or submissive, or detached. As the therapist interprets these reactons without rancor, the patient may challenge the therapist's overbearing manner. The therapist, if not threatened by this stand, will acknowledge the operation of some domineering tendencies. The very fact that the therapist admits responsibility, may give the patient a feeling that he or she is not dealing with the image of imperious authority. The patient may then question the facades and defenses that automatically are employed with authority, and may countenance a new kind of relationship. In working out this aspect of the problem, the patient will undoubtedly see connections with other personality facets and begin working on these also.

If, on the other hand, the therapist acts in a passive, retiring way, basic attitudes toward passive people may emerge. Thus, the same patient may become disappointed, sadistic, or depressed. The therapist, observing such reactions, will be able to bring the patient to an awareness of why these tendencies are being manifested. The patient will learn by this that the therapist is really not an inconsequential person, in spite of a quiet manner. Indeed, the patient may discover personal qualities of need for a godlike authority as well as contempt for any lesser kind of human being. An important aspect of the problem will then be resolved. With this resolution other aspects will come up for consideration, such as the patient's attitudes toward domineering people. Thus, even though the patient deals with two entirely different reactions on the part of the therapist, basic difficulties will have been managed and hopefully worked out.

What is important, therefore, is not whether the therapist has an impeccable personality that admits no negative countertransference, but rather that prevailing distortions can be sufficiently reduced, controlled, or explicated to provide the patient with a suitable medium in which to work through neurotic patterns.

48
Translating Insight into Action

A basic assumption in insight approaches is one made originally by Freud that was to the effect that once the individual becomes aware of unconscious motivations, one can then alter one's behavior and get well. That this fortunate consequence does not always follow (a circumstance also recognized by Freud) is the disillusioning experience of many young therapists, who have predicated their futures on the premise that analysis of resistances will inevitably bring forth insight and cure like a sunbeam breaking through a cloud.

The fact that a patient acquires a basic understanding of the problems and delves into their origins as far back as childhood, does not in the least guarantee being able to do anything about them. Even if an incentive to change is present, there are some patterns that cling to a person obstinately as if they derive from a world beyond the reach of reason and common sense. The patient is somewhat in the position of the inveterate smoker who has been warned by the physician to give up tobacco at the risk of an early demise, or of the obese hypertensive who pursues gluttony with avidity while reviling his or her weakness and lamenting an inevitable doom. Chided by the physician to reduce weight to avert the threat of a cornonary attack, the patient is unable to avoid overstuffing with the foods marked taboo on the reducing chart, irrespective of how thoroughly the patient appreciates the folly of intemperance. In the same way, repetitive compulsive patterns lead an existence of their own seemingly impervious to entreaty or logic.

Complicating this enigma further is the fact that the acquisition of even inaccurate insights may register themselves with beneficial effect, particularly if the therapist interprets with conviction and the patient accepts those pronouncements on faith. Marmor (1962) has implied that "insight" usually means the confirmation by the patient of the hypotheses of the therapist that have been communicated by various verbal and nonverbal cues. Having arrived at a presumably crucial understanding as indicated by approving responses from the therapist, the patient experiences what is essentially a placebo effect. The restoration of the sense of mastery reinforces further belief in the validity of the supposition, and encourages the patient to search for further validations, which most certainly is bound to be found by the patient in the suggestive pronouncements of the therapist.

One of my patients reported to me what he considered a significant flashback that almost immediately resolved his anxiety: "This," he avowed, "was a cock-sucking experience I reconstructed from what must have happened to me in childhood. It involved an affair with a Chinaman. My father gave me shirts to take to the Chinaman who had a laundry nearby. I got the slip, but when I brought my father along to collect the laundry, I took him by mistake to another Chinese laundry. My father had a fight with the Chinaman over the slip. Then I remembered and brought my father to the right laundry. We lived in Cleveland at the time. That's why I know it happened before I was 6. Seems young to be running errands, but I had a dream that convinced me that the Chinaman sucked my cock. I remember he gave me leechie nuts.''

This memory served to convince the patient that he now had the key to his fear of wandering away from home and his sexual problems. It required no extensive work to reveal this bit of insight as false, although it had a most astonishing effect on the patient.

This does not mean that some of the insights patients arrive at may not be correct. But not too much wisdom is needed to recognize that, with all of the doctrines of psychodynamics current among contemporary schools of psychotherapy, each one of which finds its theories confirmed in work with patients, factors other than their precepts, reflected as insights, must be responsible for at least some of the cure. The nonspecific windfalls of insight do not invalidate the specific profits that can accrue from a true understanding of the forces that are undermining security, vitiating self-esteem, and provoking actions inimical to the interests of the individual.

In opening up areas for exploration, a therapist should, in the effort to minimize false insight, confine oneself as closely as possible to observable facts, avoiding speculations as to theory so as to reduce the suggestive component. The more experienced one is, the more capable one will be of collating pertinent material from the patient's verbal content and associations, gestures, facial expressions, hesitations, silences, emotional outbursts, dreams, and interpersonal reactions toward assumptions that, interpreted to the patient, permit the

latter to acknowledge, deny, or resist these offerings. Dealing with the patient's resistances, the therapist studies the patient's behavior and continues to reexamine original assumptions and to revise them in terms of any new data that come forth.

The collaborative effort between patient and therapist made in quest of insight is in itself a learning experience that has an emotional impact on the patient that is at least as strong as any sudden cognitive illumination (Bonime, 1961). Malvina Kramer (1959) has pointed out that ''what appears from the patient-analyst viewpoint to be a matter of insight and intrapsychic rearrangement turns out to be a far more complex process which depends on fields of multiple interaction on many levels.''

Improvement or cure in psychotherapy may be posited on the following propositions:

1. The patient successfully acquires an understanding of the nature of the problem by developing the capacity to conceive of it in terms that are meaningful.
2. On the basis of this understanding, the patient begins to organize a campaign of positive action, acquiring symbolic controls, replacing destructive with adaptive goals, and pursuing these in a productive way.

True insight is helpful in this process. It acts as a liberating and an enabling force; it upsets the balance between the repressed and repressing psychic elements; it creates motivations to test the reality of one's attitudes and values; it gives the person an opportunity to challenge the very philosophies with which one's life is governed. But insight is not equivalent to cure; by itself it is insufficient to arrest the neurotic process and to promote new and constructive patterns.

Indeed, the development of insight may surprisingly produce not relief from distress, but an accentuation of anxiety.

The ensuing challenge to change one's modus operandi, and the sloughing off of neurotic protective devices make the possibility of exposure to hurt all the more real. No longer is one capable of hiding behind one's defense mechanisms. One must tear down one's facades and proceed to tackle life on assertive terms. Prior to acquiring insight, one may have envisaged "normality" in fantasy as a desirable quality, but the approaching new way of life fills the individual with a sense of foreboding.

Thus a man with an impotency problem may learn in therapy that his impotence is a defense against a fear of being mutilated by destructive, castrating women. Realizing that his defense is realistically unfounded, he must still expose himself to intercourse. This will continue to be extremely frightening to him until he convinces himself, through action, that the imagined dangers will not come to pass. A woman, working in an advertising agency, may discover that a fear of competition with men is associated with her repudiation, on the basis of anxiety, of a desire for masculinity. Her knowledge then opens up the possibility of her being able to stand up to men. Specifically, she may practice her new insight on a man in her office who has advanced himself professionally over her, because she had assumed a retiring and passive attitude. The understanding that she is playing a role with men akin to the subordinate role she had assumed as a child with her brother does not ameliorate the anxiety that she feels at having to compete with her office associate.

To protect themselves from facing the threatened perils of action, patients may throw up a smokescreen of resistance. They may reinforce old and employ new defensive mechanisms. They may devaluate strivings for health even though these had constituted strong incentives for starting therapy. The original motivations may be submerged under the anxiety of impending fulfillment and the patients may then interrupt treatment.

It is an unfortunate fact that only too often does therapy grind to a halt at a point where insight must be converted into action. The impediment encountered by the patient is complicated by resistance against releasing intolerable unconscious fantasies associated with action. In psychoanalysis action inhibition may symbolically be repeated in transference, and analysis of the resistance may liberate the patient. The therapist, while permitting the verbal expression of the unconscious fantasy in the relationship, does not participate in it; nor does the therapist encourage its sexual or hostile acting-out. Any interventions are predicated on the patient's need, not the countertransferential demands of the therapist. But even under those circumstances translation of insight into action may fail.

MODERN LEARNING THEORY AND PSYCHOTHERAPY

The difficulties that invest the resolution of old patterns and the elaboration of new ones make it necessary for therapists to use every stratagem at their disposal. Since psychotherapy involves a learning process in which the patient acquires abilities to abandon neurotic adjustment in favor of an adaptation consonant with reality, it may be interesting to consider the therapeutic situation in the light of a theory of learning. A number of attempts have been made to coordinate psychotherapy with the principles of modern learning theory. None of these has proven successful since the various propounded theories—including the stimulus–response and cognitive theories—are unable to account for the complexities of ego functioning, both normal and pathological. The ego seems to operate under laws of its own that have scarcely been embraced by any of the learning theories. Furthermore, there are various kinds of learning to which different postulates may be applied. The unsolved problems of learning would seem too diffuse to permit of any real application of learning theory to the phenomena of psychotherapy.

It may be helpful, nevertheless, to consider a number of well-known learning principles and to attempt to apply them to psychotherapeutic situations.

Learning is most effective where the individual participates directly in the learning experience. For this reason, the greatest impact on a patient is registered by patterns that come out during the encounter with the therapist—patterns that are a product of the collaborative relationship. Such a learning experience gives the patient a basis on which to reconstitute ideas of reality. It permits the patient to experiment with the therapist as a new kind of authority in association with whom the patient can evolve a more wholesome image of the self.

This eventuality, however, does not always develop in therapy, and when it happens, it does not guarantee an integration of understanding toward productive behavioral change. First, the patient may have an investment in the maladaptive patterns that subserve spurious security needs. To give them up exposes the individual to fantasied dangers or to deprivations. For example, a homosexual man may learn that he seeks in the homosexual relationship a virile image to repair his own damaged genitalia. He learns also that avoidance of women is both a safety measure to withdraw him from competition with other men and a way of preventing his being overwhelmed and infantilized by a mother figure. These insights do not subdue his intense sexual interest in males nor stop him from seeking men as a source of gratification. They do not lessen his disgust toward women, with whom he continues to maintain a casual, detached, demanding, or hostile relationship.

A second factor that may hinder the occurrence of a meaningful learning experience in therapy is the fact that a patient's reactions may have become so automatic and conditioned that knowledge of their unreasonableness does not suffice to inhibit them; they continue in an almost reflex way. One patient as a boy was constantly being taken to physicians by a hypochondriacal mother. Threats of operations were used as measures to exact the cooperation of the boy for various injections and diagnostic procedures. In later life, the patient developed a profound fear of doctors to a point where he refused to expose himself to essential medical contacts. An understanding of the sources of these fears, and an attempt to control them, did not inhibit explosive physiological reactions at the sight of a physician.

A third instance in which the learning experience in therapy may not be effective occurs when the attitudes and behavior of the therapist do not provide the conditions most conducive to change; because patterns, perhaps inspired by countertransference, may reinforce the patient's neurotic expectations. A woman patient, burdened in her work by damaging competitiveness with other women and constantly involved in winning the attentions of her male associates through her seductive manner, realizes during therapy the origin of these drives in her competitiveness with her mother for her father's favors. Yet she may cleverly maneuver the therapist into acting overprotective and reassuring toward her by playing on the therapist's personal interest in attractive women.

Repeated attempts to execute healthy responses may lead to their reinforcement. Nevertheless, repeated practice of rational reactions does not necessarily inhibit neurotic responses. The power of the repetition compulsion often neutralizes effective learning. Thus, a man who compulsively fails as soon as success becomes imminent may, on the basis of insight into this distortion, force himself diligently to take advantage of any emoluments his life situation yields. Yet the impulse to fail will become so overbearing that he may yield to failure even while trying to succeed. Learning, nevertheless, goes on in the medium of neurotic relapse, provided that the individual is aware of what is happening and has ideas of why he needs to foster his failure. This working through is helped by the therapist who is in a position to be objective. It may be achieved by the person alone if he has the motivation to examine and to correct his behavior.

Learning is facilitated through satisfaction of important needs, such as gaining of rewards and an avoidance of punishment. However, in the light of our experiences in psychotherapy, we have to recast our ideas about rewards and punishments due to the disordered values of the patient. Rewards to a neurotic person may most keenly be the expressed residues of surviving infantile needs, such as dependency or defiance, which are more or less unconscious. They may be organized around maintenance of various neurotic mechanisms of defense that reduce anxiety. In the latter case the individual will develop not health-oriented behavior but more sophisticated methods of supporting defenses. Thus, a married man, pursuing at the sacrifice of his safety and economic security, a disturbed young woman, who constitutes for him a maternal symbol, is suffused with pleasure whenever the woman favors him with her attention. Due to her narcissism, immaturity, and fears of men, she rejects his advances, yet she demands that he protect and support her. Fearful that he will lose her affection, the man yields to the unsatisfactory arrangement of financing the irresponsible expenditures of the young woman in the hope that she will eventually bestow her favors on him. His hostility and anxiety mount as he becomes more and more trapped by his dependence. In therapy what the man seeks is freedom from his symptoms and, covertly, expert stratagems of breaking down the young woman's resistance to loving him unstintingly. After a period in treatment, he learns the meaning of his involvement. The rewards that he obtains in integrating this learning is the immediate approval of the therapist and the promised reward that his symptoms will be relieved if he extricates himself from his untenable situation. These satisfactions threaten the rewards he really seeks in terms of overcoming the young woman's rejection of him and of establishing himself as her favorite "son" and lover. What he does then is to utilize his psychological insights to understand the reactions of his desired mistress in order to outmaneuver her. Momentary sexual yieldings are followed by her executing violent scenes and threats of separation, which, precipitating anxiety in the man, binds him more firmly in his enslavement. The punishment that he receives is really no deterrent to his continued acting-out of this drama. Indeed, it fulfills an insidious need to appease his guilt feeling. Thus, as in many psychological problems, punishment becomes a masochistic reward.

We cannot, therefore, apply the same criteria of rewards and punishments to the complex problems of learning in psychotherapy as we do to some other forms of learning. This is why conditioning techniques that are utilized in behavior therapy fail to influence certain kinds of neurotic disturbance. As the working-through process continues in treatment, the patient may, however, eventually rearrange his value systems. He may then approximate healthy goals as rewards and conventional pain and suffering as punishments. Conditioning under these circumstances may then prove successful.

Rational understanding is a *sine qua non* of learning. Rational understanding in itself, as has repeatedly been emphasized, does not seem to help many emotional problems. This is because behavioral change is predicated on complex rearrangements of thinking, feeling, and acting that are bound together in tangled disorder. We attempt a disentwining of this complex yarn by plucking away at the surface strands. There may be no other way of getting at the disorganized psychosociophysiological structure. Hopefully, our efforts will be rewarded. Even from superficial intellectual unravelings behavioral, and even physiological, readjustments may ensue. As S. Freud (1928) once said, "The voice of the intellect is a soft one, but it does not rest until it has gained a hearing." Ultimately our therapeutic operations may overcome the tumultuous emotions of the psychologically ill individual. Unfortunately, patterns and values acquired early in life may obstruct meaningful adult learning. The most obstructive interferences are systems that have been repressed and yet obtrude themselves in devious ways. For example, sexual education as it is now being taught in high schools and colleges may have little impact on a young woman who has developed, as a result of childhood anxieties, the practice of shunting sexual material out of her mind. Defiance of authority, developed to preserve autonomy and to neutralize overprotective and interfering parental figures, may subtly block the incorporation of factual data. Perfectionistic tendencies and fear of failure, residues of a damaged self-image, may interfere with effective recall in situations where performance is a measure of self-worth. The powerful imprint of early impressions and experiences on the total behavior of the individual cannot be overemphasized, and learning may be blocked until some resolution of inner conflict has been instituted.

Is it completely hopeless, then, to try to take advantage of any basic learning propositions in order to expedite psychotherapy? Let us attempt to answer this question by considering some of the positive learning factors that Hilgard (1956) has described so well.

Motivation is important in learning. Individuals who are motivated to learn will apply themselves to the learning task and more readily overcome their resistances. Rewards are much more effective learning stimulants than are punishments. In psychotherapy, rewards may be offered to patients in the form of encouragement and approval when they have come to important understandings or have engaged in constructive actions. The benefits of their activities may be pointed out in terms of what progress will do for them.

When learning failures occur, the person may be helped to tolerate them by pointing out previous successes. In psychotherapy failures are inevitable, partly due to resistance and partly to the repetitive nature of neurotic drives. Reassurance of the patients when they become discouraged by failure and helping them to see why the failure occurred may encourage them to try again. The therapist may accent the patient's constructive activities that were initiated in the past.

Setting realistic goals during learning is an important step. Individuals may be unable to achieve success where their objectives are beyond their capacities or opportunities. Where their goals are too modest, also, they will not make the effort that would be most rewarding. In psychotherapy, where the therapist senses that the patient is overly ambitious and that his or her plans are unrealistic, it is essential that the therapist bring the patient back to earth. There are some memories the patient may be unable to recover, some patterns so imbedded in the past that they cannot be overcome. Pointing some of these facts out may prevent the individual from engaging in frustrating efforts that discourage productive learning. On the other hand, when the individual's targets are too limited, for instance, where one insists that one is so seriously and irretrievably ill that one cannot achieve certain gains or execute essential actions, the therapist has a responsibility in stimulating the patient toward more ambitious aims.

Learning is most effective where there is a good relationship with the teaching authority and where mutual respect prevails. This is, of course, the essence of good psychotherapy. Where habitual contacts with authority are predicated on fear, hostility, or excessive dependence, the patient will probably display these patterns, which will then inhibit learning. The patient may be diverted from the task of learning toward fulfillment of regressive needs in the association with the therapist. The therapist must be alert to these maneuvers and must constantly keep the working relationship at the proper pitch, devoting efforts to this above all other tasks.

Active participation by individuals in the learning process is more effective than a passive feeding of materials to them. If the learner is able to figure out facts and to apply these to a variety of situations, he or she will learn most readily. In therapy problem-solving tasks are given to the patients; questions are directed at them; a thinking through of solutions is encouraged. The motto is "Let's figure this thing out together" rather than "Here are the answers." The patients are constantly encouraged to enter into new situations and to observe their reactions to these challenges.

Where learning materials and tasks are understood by individuals, they will integrate knowledge better than where these are meaningless. Knowledge of how to perform well in the learning task, recognition of errors in operation, and the understanding of what constitutes effective performance are most helpful. In therapy the treatment situation is structured for the patient; the purpose of different techniques is presented to the patient in terms that can be understood. There are a number of routines that may seem mysterious to the patient,

for instance, the refraining from advice given and the employment of dreams. A careful explanation of their rationale is conducive to greater cooperation.

Repetition makes for the greatest success in learning. Where recall can be spaced over an expanded span, material will be better retained. In psychotherapy the patient is continuously engaged in examining neurotic behavior; the patient acquires an increasing understanding of why one acts in certain ways. Repetition of successful behavioral responses is encouraged. The working-through process constitutes a continuous learning experience.

BUILDING MOTIVATION FOR ACTIVITY

If empirically we are to pay credence to these concepts of learning, we have to abide by the rule that the first step in helping patients to translate insight into action is to build adequate incentives toward the abandoning of old patterns of living. A constant analysis of the significance of the individual's habitual drives—their purpose, origins, contradictions, and resultant conflicts—casts doubt on the value of such drives. Gradually patients realize that their strivings do them more harm than they do them good, that they are responsible for much of their maladjustment, and that they promote many of their own symptoms. Eventually they understand that the pleasures that they derive from the fulfillment of their patterns are minute, indeed, compared to the devastation that are created in their lives. They then become willing to challenge the validity of their customary modes of adjustment. Whether they will change their behavior is a choice they themselves have to make.

For example, a woman with a strong dependency drive discovers that her need for dependence dominates every aspect of her thinking and feeling. Finding an omnipotent person on whom to lean fills her with a sense of goodness and security. Life than becomes a bountiful place; she is suffused with vitality, imagination, and creativeness. But not long after this metamorphosis a curious change takes place in the way that she feels. Fear and panic begin to overwhelm her; she becomes sleepless and she feels depressed; headaches, dyspepsia, and muscle tension develop. To her consternation she seems to invite suffering, masochistically assuming the manner of a martyr, and then undermining the person who acts as her host. She appears also to want to capitalize on her plight, by holding forth physical weakness and infirmity as reasons for her avoidance of responsibility.

These patterns become apparent to her during psychotherapy in relation to her husband who she variantly adores, fears, and despises, making for a tumultuous marriage. She learns that while she is driven to submit herself to him as a powerful parental agency, this crushes her assertiveness and fosters feelings of helplessness. Exploration of the genesis of her patterns may show her how her dependency resulted from subjugation by an overprotecting mother, who stifled her independent emotional growth. This knowledge gives impetus to her desires for freedom. She sees how continued pursuit of dependency since childhood causes reflex helplessness and crushing of independence. Such insights are fostered in a nonjudgmental and tolerant treatment atmosphere, the therapist never is represented as an authority who orders the patient to change her way of life.

On the basis of her new understanding much dissatisfaction may be created in the patient with her present life situation. She will also be motivated to experiment with different modes of adjustment. The desire to give up dependency as a primary adaptive technique may, however, be blocked by a fear of, and a contempt for, normal life goals. Anxiety here may mask itself as anhedonia—an indifference to or boredom with pleasures and impulses accepted as valuable by the average person—for, compared with the ecstatic, albeit spurious, joys of neurotic fulfillment, customary routines seem uninspiring indeed. The therapist accordingly engages in a constant analysis of misconceptions about normality in terms of their anxiety–avoidance components.

When our patient, for instance, manifests disinterest in certain people, it may be possible to show her that she harbors contempt for any individual who does not possess glamorous strength and omniscience. She may actually classify people into two categories: those who are superior and who potentially can serve as parental substitutes and those who are inferior and, therefore, are utter bores. The immense narcissism and grandiosity inherent in her attitudes about herself may become apparent to the patient as she realizes how she strives to gain omnipotence through passive identification with a godlike figure. At this point the patient may become aware of why she refuses to have children. She realizes that she does not want to be replaced as the favorite child of her husband. She does not want to "give" and be a parent to a child, since she herself wants to be that child. She conceives it her right to take from others.

This analysis of anxieties and expectations, and the continued verbalization by the patient of fears and anticipated pleasures, provides increased motivation to attempt a different life expression. But no new patterns can be learned unless the motivation to acquire them is greater than the motivation that promotes the survival of the existing neurotic habits. Therapist activities, therefore, must embrace encouragement of any desires that the patient voices for mental health, emotional growth, and freedom from suffering. The therapist must attempt to undermine the pleasure and security values that the patient seeks from the prosecution of her neurosis. Thus, the therapist may show the patient that the rationale of her dependency need is inescapable if one accepts the premise that she is incorrigibly helpless. While it is true that conditions in her childhood made dependency and related patterns necessary, she now continues to operate under assumptions that are no longer true. Her expectations of injury approximate those of a child. If she analyzes her situation today, she will see that conditions no longer necessitate anachronistic reactions that are so destructive to her adjustment. She is challenged to revise her assumption of life as a repetitive phenomenon that is blackened by shadows of her need for parenting.

PROVIDING A FAVORABLE ENVIRONMENT FOR ACTION

With expanding insights the patient tends to affiliate neurotic strivings with suffering and maladjustment. Their operation and even their appearance begin to evoke discomfort. This provides motivation for their inhibition. Involved in the inhibitory response are incidental stimuli or cues that are associated with the neurotic patterns and that once could initiate them. More and more the patient becomes capable of controlling reactions and of engaging in productive responses.

It may be necessary for the therapist to prepare the patient in advance for any foreseen disappointments that may occur in the course of executing a new response. Thus, if our dependent patient decides that she must assert herself with her husband, she may resolve to do this by asking him for a regular allowance weekly, from which she can budget her household expenses, purchase her clothing, and provide for certain luxuries. Hitherto her husband has doled out funds whenever she needed to make a purchase, requesting an itemized accounting in order to check on her spending. He has considered his wife irresponsible—an attitude the patient has sponsored, partly

out of need to avoid responsibility and partly out of hotsility—because she has made many unnecessary purchases. He has for this reason restricted her spending. We may, therefore, anticipate that he will react negatively to her suggestion that he provide her with a weekly sum and that she be entrusted with the family purchasing. Because she has chosen this area as a test for her assertiveness, a negative or violent reception of her assertive gesture will probably mobilize anxiety and result in defeat. She may then suffer a decisive setback in her therapy and perhaps never again dare to approach her husband assertively.

To forestall this contingency, the therapist may ask her to anticipate her husband's reaction when the patient presents her plan. The patient may be fully expectant that her husband's response will be negative. She may then be asked to anticipate her own reaction should he refuse to cooperate. The therapist may even predict for the patient a violent response on the part of her husband and get her to verbalize how she would feel if he became recalcitrant and punitive. Once the patient accepts the possibility that her request may bring forth hostility and once she recognizes that her husband may, on the basis of her past performance, perhaps be justified in his refusal to trust her management, the therapist may encourage her to approach her husband on a different basis. Discussing with him the need for practice in making herself more independent, she may suggest that he allow her to assume greater responsibility in the handling of finances. However, since even this prudent method of presentation may be rejected, the patient should be prepared for a disappointment. What is accomplished by this tactic is that the patient is desensitized to failure and musters the strength to cope with an absence of rewards for her new responses.

In many patients insight is translated into action without too great activity on the part of the therapist. In some patients, however, considerable activity may be required before therapeutic movement becomes perceptible. Although the therapist may have been more or less passive during the first two phases of therapy, this phase necessitates more energetic measures, and greater pressure and confrontation because of the patient's reluctance to face anxiety.

PSYCHODRAMATIC TECHNIQUES

In occasional instances role playing may be efficacious, the therapist taking the role of the individual with whom the patient seeks to relate on different terms. Or the therapist may suggest that the patient assume the role of that individual, while the therapist takes the part of the patient. The patient, in addition to building up immunity to rebuffs, enjoys in this technique an opportunity for emotional catharsis. The therapist is, in turn, possessed of a means of making the patient aware of one's undercurrent feelings and responses. If the therapist does group psychodrama, the patient may be introduced into the group while continuing to be seen on an individual basis too.

Conferences with Family Members

An element often overlooked in the resistance to getting well is the impact of the reactions on the patient of significant other persons. The patient's interpersonal relationships are bound to change as the shackles of the neurosis are broken by the patient. The threat to the existing family balance will mobilize defensive attack and withdrawal maneuvers on the part of those with whom the patient is in close bond and who are threatened by change. Often this creates such turmoil that the patient will block off progress and perhaps retreat to former patterns of interaction, only to be rewarded by a return of symptoms. The therapist may imagine that it is the therapy that is ineffective, an unhappy thought that the patient may well instigate and sustain. By being constantly on the lookout for possibilities of retrenchment into former behavioral patterns, the therapist will best be able to explain failure of progress as a form of resistance. This phenomenon is most clearly apparent in children, adolescents, and young people who live closely with their families, particularly those who are withdrawn and schizoid. Therapy in releasing independent or rebellious activities in the identified patient may create a crisis in the family homeostasis.

Family therapy with the significant others present may be very successful where the related persons are not too emotionally disturbed. Where an adult patient lives in a close relationship with another person, like a spouse, the person is bound to react with anxiety when the patient threatens to upset present routines. Thus, the mate of our female patient with the dependency problem will probably regard any change in the patient in her striving for freedom as an assault on his own rights. He may then attempt to undermine the patient's treatment.

Surmising such a contingency, we might find it expedient to arrange for a talk with the spouse. The consultation will have to be secured with the knowledge and even cooperation of the patient. One or several conferences with the spouse can often make the difference between success or failure in the patient's initial effort at a new response. Once the spouse sees the rationale of the new plan of action (and senses that he is not being blamed by the therapist), and he realizes that his own problems and needs are being taken into account, he may voluntarily cooperate. Even hostile reactions of the patient may be tolerated by him, if he is alerted to the possibilities of such reactions. In our dependent patient, for example, an interview may be geared around the discussion with the husband of what he has noticed about his wife. Any troublesome attitudes and behavior mentioned may then be pointed out as manifestations of her problem of lack of assertiveness. In order for her to overcome this problem, which is so crippling to her adjustment, including her marital adjustment, it will be necessary to give her an opportunity to grow. Even though she may make mistakes, the husband is enjoined to exercise tolerance, since this is how people learn and grow. It would be better for her to make a few mistakes, for instance, in the way that she budgets her allowance, and to help her to learn through her mistakes, than to let her continue in her present state of turmoil.

Obviously, in order for the husband to adjust to the patient's assertiveness, it will be necessary for him to master some of his own needs that are being satisfied by the patient's passivity and dependence. A fear for his own masculinity, and/or a compulsive striving for superiority and power may demand that his wife relate to him as a subordinate. Consequently, the husband may have to experience a therapeutic change himself in order to allow his wife to exercise assertiveness in the relationship. He may go through an emotional crisis before this happens, even though he appreciates the purpose behind the plan as explained to him by the therapist. Naturally the husband's dynamics would not be thrown at him during an interview because he would most certainly reject the interpretations. Rather he may be told: "I know this is asking a good deal from you to let your wife experiment. You may not be able to do it, many people can't." This challenge may be enough to get his cooperation.

The following excerpt from a session with a woman whose dependency problem resembled that of the hypothetic patient we are considering as an example illustrates this point:

Pt. And Sunday morning I was in church and I got a little nervous. Then when I came home, my husband started acting funny, wanting to go here, wanting to go there. I told him I thought he didn't really want to go anywhere. He brought up a lot of things. All of a sudden I looked at him and saw hatred on his face, and my mind stopped working. He said, "You care more about the doctor than you do me." He acted very jealous, and I got upset.

Th. I see.

Pt. And in the last few months we had been getting along so well. You know I just am never going to go back again to what I was. I got upset at his attitude and wanted to throw something at him, but instead I turned it on me. I cried and tore my hair. He got me so angry, I lost control. I don't want to live with a man I have to appease. I told him he is a mean man and that I would leave him.

Th. And then what happened?

Pt. He got upset and cried. He told me it was his fault. He said he always was this way and that he could see he was wrong. Then I started feeling sorry for him. Then I got mad at him. I don't think I can stand him. He's brutal and mean. He isn't happy until he sees me groveling on my knees. Then he's happy. Maybe I'm not the woman for him. (*pause*)

Th. But you *could* assert your rights. You *could* define what you feel your rights to be.

Pt. But I have. I don't see what I did to aggravate him. I know he has a problem in wanting to treat me like a slave. Maybe someone else could stand it, but I can't. And I told him and threatened to walk out. (*pause*)

Th. So what happened then?

Pt. Surprising. He broke down and cried. Then he said it was all his fault. He said he could see how he treated me, that it was all his fault. He said he didn't know how I could stand it so long. He said he would try to treat me more like an equal.

There are many instances in which improvement in therapy of one marital partner results in increasing emotional disturbance of the mate. Indeed, a disturbed adaptation of the patient may be a condition necessary for the equilibrium of the mate. Thus, a husband, domineered by a power-driven wife, may satisfy masochistic needs under a domain of tyranny. He may be unwilling to give up his masochistic indulgences and adjust to an atmosphere of cooperative equality brought about by the wife's improvement through psychotherapy. Or a frigid woman, receiving treatment, may make sexual demands on her impotent husband who will then develop strong anxiety. Where the mate of the patient has good ego strength, he or she may possibly be able to adapt spontaneously adjusting to the new demands presented by the patient toward a healthier adjustment. The outcome of psychotherapy in one partner then will be emotional improvement in both members. However, it may be necessary for the mate of the patient to receive psychotherapy also where spontaneous improvement does not occur. Conjoint marital therapy and even family therapy, including as many involved members of the family as possible, may be in order.

Adjusting the Patient's Environment

Where the patient's environment is disturbed, it may have to be altered before insight can adequately be translated into action. Thus, if there is undernourishment, shabby physical attire, bad housing, and other consequences of a subminimal budget standard, which are outside of the patient's control, a community or private agency may have to render assistance. An individual who is living with a brutal or neurotic parent or marital partner may be unable to achieve adequate mental health until an actual separation from the home is brought about. Domineering parents who resent their offspring's self-sufficiency may cause a patient to feel hopeless since compliance seems to be a condition for security.

The majority of patients are capable of modifying their environment through their own actions, once the disturbance is clearly identified and the proper resources are made available to them. Occasionally the adjunctive series of a trained social worker

may be required, especially with children and patients with weak ego structures. The therapist, with the help of a social worker, may materially alleviate certain problems by simple environmental manipulation. This is particularly the case where the people with whom the patient lives are capable of gaining insight into existing defects in the family relationship. Such factors as favoritism displayed toward another sibling, lack of appropriate disciplines and proper habit routines, the competitive pitting of a child against older siblings, overprotective and domineering influences of the patient's parents or mate may sometimes be eliminated by proper psychoeducation. Correction of sources of discord and tension frequently is rewarded by alleviation or disappearance of symptoms.

Such situational treatment, while admittedly superficial, can have defnite therapeutic value and may permit an individual to proceed to more favorable development. Often family members become so subjectively involved with the problems of the patient, so defensive and indignant about them that they are unable to see many destructive influences that exist in the household. An honest and frank presentation of the facts may permit intelligent people to alter the situation sufficiently to take the strain off the patient.

It must not be assumed, however, that all situational therapy will be successful, even when gross disturbances exist in the household. Frequently the family is unable or unwilling to alter inimical conditions because of severe neurotic problems in members other than the patient or because of physical factors in the home over which they have no control. Here the social worker, through repeated home visits, may start interpersonal therapy that may bring the family around toward accepting the recommendations of the therapist. The worker may, in specific instances, render material aid to the family, or may assist in the planning of a budget or a home routine. Direct contact of the social worker with the family may reveal that others need attention or therapy.

Another function that the social worker can fulfill is to make available to the individual the various church, school, and neighborhood recreational facilities. Persons with emotional problems frequently become so rooted to their homes, out of a sense of insecurity, that they fear outside contacts. Establishing a relationship with and introducing the patient to groups outside the home may start a social experience that becomes increasingly meaningful for helping to release forces that make for self-development. A day hospital, day-care center, or rehabilitation unit are often of great value.

In cases where the destructive elements within the family are irremediable or where the individual is rejected with little chance of eventual acceptance, it may be necessary to encourage the individual to take up residence elsewhere. Temporary or permanent placement in a foster family or rest home may be essential. Although there is evidence that such change of environment rarely has an effect on deeper problems, residence in a home with kindly and sympathetic adults may serve to stabilize and to give the individual an opportunity to execute in action the insight learned. The most significant factor in changes of residence is the meaning that it has to the patient. If the patient regards it as another evidence of rejection, it can have an undermining rather than a constructive influence. Instead of getting better, the patient may regress to more immature patterns of behavior. Above all, the patient must be adequately prepared for residence change or placement and should look forward to it as a therapeutic experience rather than as a form of punishment.

Caution must, however, be exercised in effecting drastic and permanent changes in the work or home situation, and thorough study of the patient is essential before one is justified in advising anything that may recast the patient's entire life. This applies particularly to problems of divorce and separation.

Many married patients seek therapeutic help while on the crest of a wave of resentment that compels them to desire separation or divorce. Mere encouragement on the part of the therapist serves to translate these desires into action. The therapist should, therefore, always be chary of giving advice that will break up a marriage unless completely convinced that there is nothing in the marital situation that is worthy of saving or until certain that the relationship is dangerously destructive to the patient and that there is no hope of abatement. This precaution is essential because the patient may completely bury, under the tide of anger, positive qualities of the mate to win sympathy from the therapist or to justify the resentment felt toward the mate.

When the therapist is swept away by the patient's emotion and encourages a breakup of the home, many patients will be plunged into despair and anxiety. They will blame the therapist for having taken them so seriously as to destroy their hopes for a reconciliation. It is advisable in all cases, even when the marital situation appears hopeless, to enjoin the patient to attempt the working through of problems in the present setting, pointing out that the spouse may also suffer from emotional difficulties for which treatment will be required. The patient will, in this way, not only be helped, but also the spouse, and constructive features of the relationship will be preserved. It is wise to get the patient to talk about positive qualities possessed by the spouse instead of completely being absorbed by the latter's negative characteristics.

On the other hand, it is undesirable, indeed manifestly impossible, to restrict every patient from making fundamental changes during therapy. Conversion of understanding into action presupposes that the life situation must be altered. The rule that no changes be made during the period of therapy is more honored in its breach than its observance. The important thing is that the patient discuss with the therapist plans to effectuate change *before* making them in order to lessen the possibilities of a neurotic decision, for instance one that may be in service of masochistic self-defeating impulses.

Learning New Patterns within the Therapeutic Relationship

The reexperiencing by the patient, within the therapeutic situation, of early unresolved fears, attitudes, and needs and the proper management by the therapist of these strivings are important means of learning. The patient has an opportunity to work out, in a more favorable setting, problems that could not be resolved in relationships with early authorities. The new patterns resulting are gradually absorbed and become a part of the patient's personality.

For this to happen, the therapeutic situation must serve as a corrective experience and must not repeat early disappointments and mishandlings. The patient while motivated to grow and to develop within the relationship, is hampered by anxiety, residual in expectations of hurt from domineering, rejecting, overprotecting, and punitive authority. This is why the therapist must not be tempted by the patient's unprovoked attitudes and behavior to repeat the prohibitions, penalties, and retribution of authoritative figures in the patient's past. Should the therapist respond in this way, the patient's convictions that authority is not to be trusted will be reinforced. No modifications of attitudes can occur under these circumstances.

Realizing that the patient must verbalize or act out unreasonable strivings in order to get well, the therapist will have an opportunity to react to these in an entirely

different way from that anticipated by the patient. The therapist acts in a warm, accepting, and nonjudgmental manner. These attitudes inspire the patient to retest the original traumatic situation. The patient does this anticipating hurt. If the therapist, by virtue of understanding and the ability to remain objective, can avoid repeating the punitive and rejecting threats, the patient may be helped to live through in a new setting crucial experiences that should have been resolved as a child. The therapist will constantly have to interpret to the patient the latter's expectation of hurt, and to help the patient to realize that the circumstances under which one failed to develop security and self-esteem were peculiar to a disturbed childhood.

This will call for a high degree of mental health on the part of the therapist, whose own value system is bound to incorporate many of the judgments and arbitrary attitudes residual in the culture, which, incorporated in the parent's attitudes, have crushed the patient's growth.

Within the therapeutic relationship itself, therefore, the patient is helped to find a new and healthier means of adjustment. A virtue of the working alliance is that it acts as a prototype of better interpersonal relationships. It fosters the patient's faith in other people and ultimately in the self.

One way that the working relationship is utilized is to battle resistances to action. It is sometimes necessary to encourage patients to face certain situations that have paralyzed them with fear. Utilizing the relationship as a fulcrum, the patients may be urged to experiment with new patterns while observing their responses. A program sometimes may be planned cooperatively with the patients, the therapist occasionally making positive suggestions. While advice giving is best eschewed, the advantages and disadvantages of alternative courses of action may be presented, the patients being encouraged to make a final choice for themselves. Thus, if a patient wants the therapist to make the decision on an issue, the therapist may ask, "What do *you* feel about this?" Possibilities of failure, as well as anticipated reactions to entering into new situations may be explored. The patient may be cautioned by such statements as, "It isn't easy to do this" or "This may be hard for you." A method of stimulating action is to confront the patient with the question, "What are you doing about this situation?" whenever dissatisfaction is expressed by the patient on his or her progress.

Even with these promptings the patient may shy away from executing actions that threaten to promote old anxieties. If the initiative is put in the patient's hands, a stalemate may result. Although an analysis of resistances may encourage a cautious step into dangerous territory, the patient may need a gently firm push by the therapist before boldly approaching a new activity. In phobias, for instance, the patient may have to be strongly urged to face the phobic situation, on the basis that it is necessary to learn to master a certain amount of anxiety before one can get well. Where the relationship with the therapist is good, the patient will be motivated to approach the situation that seems dangerous with greater courage.

Success and pleasure in constructive action constitute the greatest possible rewards for the patient. Occasionally the therapist may indicate approval in nonverbal or in cautiously phrased verbal terms. Conversely, whenever the patient fails in an attempted action, sympathy, reassurance, encouragement, and active analysis of the reasons for the failure are indicated. The patient may be reminded that the difficulty has been present a long time and that one need not be discouraged if one does not conquer one's trouble abruptly. The patient may be given an explanation such as the following: "You know, an emotional problem is often like a hard rock. You can pound on it with a hammer one hundred times without making any visible impression. The hundred-and-first time, however,

it may crumble to pieces. The same thing happens in therapy. For months no visible change is present, but the neurotic structure is constantly being altered under the surface. Eventually in therapy, and even after therapy, signs of crumbling of the neurosis occur."

Eventually the rewards of positive achievement and enjoyment issue out of the new and healthy patterns themselves. Surcease from suffering, reinforced by joys of productive interpersonal relationships, enable the patient to consolidate gains.

Adjunctive devices are often helpful during the action phase of therapy. These include the prescription of tranquilizing drugs, to help master anxiety associated with attempting new tasks, as well as hypnosis, self-hypnosis, and behavior therapy. (See Chapters 56 and 51.)

ILLUSTRATIVE CASE MATERIAL

The following is a portion of a session in which a man with a personality problem of dependency, submissiveness, passivity, and detachment indicates how he has put his insight into action and asserted himself.

Pt. There has been a great change in me. I haven't felt this way in my whole life. And it has been going on for weeks.

Th. Is that so?

Pt. Yes. Of course, I used to have spurts of good feeling for different reasons. Once I felt as happy as a lark when I was about 13. I had had eczema for years and x-ray treatments took it away. I felt grand for a short time. And then I felt wonderful when I met my wife, but it lasted only a short while. But all these things came from external causes. The way I feel now seems to be coming from inside of me. All my life I seem to have been a zombie, really dead, because I carried inside of me all sorts of standards of other people. I was like an automaton. If you would press a button, I would react in a certain way. I never had a sense of myself.

Th. Mm hmm.

Pt. Things have happened these weeks, which I think I handled well, and my reactions were good too. I have never had a prolonged period like this. Several times I'd say to myself, "I wonder if I can keep this up?" People mean different things to me now, you know. They are not powerful and threatening. My daughter was operated on at the hospital, for example. I regarded it in a sensible way. I said, "It's a minor operation. I'm concerned about her, but it's a simple thing and nothing to be upset about." I used to have a whole string of emotional responses that go along with illness. Now my wife has this worrying but that was instilled in her by her mother. So I had to go along handling various things with her feelings which used to suck me into a trap before and arouse guilt feelings in me.

Th. I see.

Pt. So she started to hammer at me a few days before the operation to see to it that the room in the hospital was a good one, that there was a television set there, and so on. Now this is a good hospital, I know, but their policy is annoying. I know they have a program, and you could stand on your ear and get nowhere by ordering them around. So I said to my wife, "I'm not going to follow out your directions and do this and do that because I don't think it's right. Everything will go smoothly." So I did it my way, and everything went smoothly.

Th. Previously how would you have done it?

Pt. To tell you this is a revolution is an understatement. I'd always appease my wife like I did my mother. I'd do what she said without questioning it. This time I did what *I* wanted, and I felt no guilt. I had a sense of power. Everything went smoothly. When I got to the hospital, my wife was frantic because they gave my daughter a rectal sedative and she expelled it. The nurse was all confused and didn't know what to do. Then they called for her to go to the operation. I said, "I won't let her out of the room until she is properly sedated. I don't care if they get the whole hospital on my head; I'm just not going to do it." And I did this with ease. There was nothing to it. Before this I would say, "Look, I'm making these people wait, and so forth, and so forth." So the intern came up and gave her a sedative. They called the surgeon who agreed that the child shouldn't come down until she was sedated. *(laughs)* Everyone was chewing their nails, but I stuck to my guns. Not that I was unreasonable, but I did stick to what I felt was right.

Th. And things came out well?

Pt. Better than well. It's like a miracle. To think how fearful I was, before therapy, to take a stand with anybody. Especially, I wasn't able

to be firm with my wife. When I got home, though, my wife started on me and said that I should have acted more cooperative. That burned me up because that questioned my stand. I told her calmly *(laughs)* that I had sized up the situation and felt this is what had to be done, and the proof was that things turned out well. Even if they didn't, I was sure I was doing the right thing.

Th. I see.

Pt. I then realized that my wife was under a strain, and I told her I was sorry if I talked rough to her. And then she said, "Yes, you're sorry," sarcastically. I said to her, "Look, I said I was sorry. I'm not going to crawl; I'm not going to stand on my head or any goddamn thing." And I didn't feel any anxiety or any guilt or anything. This morning my wife was as happy as a lark, as if nothing had happened.

Th. That made you feel you could take a stand and nothing bad would happen.

Pt. I just brought that up to show that I wasn't drawn in; I felt I was right and I wasn't going to try to dope out my wife's neurotic reactions to things and turn myself inside out trying to please her. I felt wonderful about this. So that was that.

Th. Yes.

Pt. I get a lot of resentment now at certain women mostly, and say, "Why did I have to knock myself out for years? What's so great about them? They are just people, and there are plenty of them around. Why were women so important to me?" I know what it springs from, and it seems so crazy to me now. *(laughs)*

Th. What *did* it spring from actually? [*testing his insight*]

Pt. Well, I would say that there were many factors involved and the picture becomes clearer; my whole life becomes clearer all the time. I would say it all started out, leaving psychologic terms out, with getting a terrible deal with my mother—she killed me. She must have acted in such a way that I was terribly uncertain of her love, and I must have gotten the feeling that if I didn't do exactly as she wanted me to do, she wouldn't love me anymore. And there was no approbation given to me as a person. I became a thing. I became something that was used as a ground for other people's neurotic problems. My mother, on the one hand, being defeated in her life, used me to a point of smothering me with affection, which, I have a feeling now, covered a lot of repressed hostility and a lot of rebellion against being a mother. My father, on the other hand, showered on me his own lack of confidence as a man. He impressed me with what a man should be, that when he was with people, he wouldn't let them get away with anything. If a cab driver said anything to him, he'd beat him up. He had a tremendous temper. He'd say, "You got to fight; don't take anything from anybody." He never gave me any affection. He couldn't. I think he has a lot more qualities than my mother, but he is very compulsive in the matter, as shown by the fact that he couldn't be warm. He was compulsive about his own work and emphasized to me not to procrastinate or put off tomorrow what could be done today. The approbation came from getting good marks in school. That was the big thing.

Th. Yes.

Pt. So, I grew up with two big areas that were involved—the love area with my mother and the work area with my father. And then, in addition to that, my mother presenting the picture of what a bastard an aggressive man is. My father was a bastard, she said. "I love you," she said, "so don't be a bastard to me. If you do certain things that I don't like, then you are a bastard to me." So I grew up that way with no confidence in myself, no feeling about myself as having worth. The only worth I had was getting good marks to please my father and giving in to please my mother. So with one thing and another I started to crack up.

Th. What happened with your wife?

Pt. She became a mother, and the same thing would have happened with every woman. No matter what the woman was, she was irreplaceable because I had no confidence I could get another woman.

Th. How would you say your attitudes are now in that respect?

Pt. Well, I would say, number one, I know they are not irreplaceable. I think I use sex in an abnormal way. First, it was to prove being a man and to get this feeling of being approved and accepted by a woman like my wife, which after a while stopped working because it proved nothing. So I feel now they are not irreplaceable. I know they have problems, and I don't have to get involved in their problems. I don't have to be sucked in again into being an automaton who is prey to their whims. Pleasing a woman, no matter what her problems, is good as long as it is a reciprocal thing; but doing it just to please her becomes detrimental to the relationship. I suppose in our culture women are more insecure than men and have problems; but I don't have to get involved in their problems. I also have learned that making a woman insecure by making her feel uncertain about you is not the answer. Because, while it works temporarily to incite her interest, it breaks up the relationship after a while.

Th. So that you feel your attitudes are altogether more wholesome.

Pt. My, yes. I realized that my feelings and my needs are just as important as the woman's. All this time I've been making an intellectual exercise about resolving conflict. Instead, the drives I feel now are healthy and good. After all, if it's a fifty-fifty proposition; you can't be too submissive and you can't be too aggressive. I feel a lot more strength within myself. I feel more alive and more vital. The reactions of other people don't matter as much as my own, or I'd say better that my reactions are equally important as the opinions of other people.

49
The "Working-through" Process

Mental health is won only after a long and painful fight. Even in supportive therapy, where goals are minimal, the person clings to symptoms with a surprising tenacity. In reeducative therapy the patient returns repetitively to old modes of living while making tentative thrusts in a new and more adaptive direction. In reconstructive therapy the struggle is even more intense, the patient shuttling back and forth, for what seems to be an interminable period, between sick and healthy strivings.

The initial chink in the patient's neurotic armor is made by penetrations of insight. The patient tries stubbornly to resist these onslaughts. The implementation of any acquired insight in the direction of change is resisted even more vigorously. Only gradually, as anxieties are mastered, does the patient begin to divest neurotic encumbrances.

Change is never in a consistently forward direction. Progress takes hold, and the patient improves. This improvement is momentary, and the patient goes backward with an intensified resistance, retrenching with all previous defenses as the problem is investigated more deeply. Anxiety forces a reverse swing toward familiar modes of coping with fear and danger. This is not a setback in the true sense because the individual integrates what has happened into the framework of rational understanding. With the gain achieved from this experience another step forward takes place. Again, anxiety forces a return to old methods of dealing with stress or resorting to disguised adaptations of one's defenses. In association with this there may be discouragement and a feeling of helplessness. But this time, the reintrenchment is more easily overcome. With the development of greater mastery there is further progress; and there may again be a regression to old defenses. The curve of improvement is jerky, but with each relapse the patient learns an important lesson. The neurotic way of adaptation is used less and less, and as patients gain strength through what is happening to them, they are rewarded with greater and greater progress.

It is discouraging to some therapists to encounter such curious reluctances in their patients toward moving ahead in treatment. The therapist is bound to respond with discouragement or resentment when, after having made an estimable gain, the patient experiences a recrudescence of the symptoms. Should the therapist communicate dismay to the patient, the latter is apt to regard this as a sign of hopelessness or of having failed the therapist. Actually, there is no need for despondency or pessimism should the patient fumble along, repeat the same mistakes, or backslide when logic dictates that one forge ahead.

One way the therapist may maintain control of personal feelings is to anticipate setbacks in all patients. No patient will be able to acquire new patterns overnight. Each patient has a personal rate of learning, which may not be accelerated by any technical tricks.

Before structural psychic change can take place, it is necessary for patients to amalgamate changes that they have achieved in one area with other areas of their personalities. Analogically, it is as if in a business institution that is failing specific enlightenment comes to one department of the organization. After a new policy is accepted and incorporated by this department, it is presented to the other organizational divisions for consideration. Resistance against changing the status quo will inevitably be encountered, with eventual painful yielding by department heads, executives, and other administrative personnel. Many months may go by before the recommended reforms are generally accepted and put into practice. Not until then will the influence on the business be felt. In emotional illness, too, enlightenment produced by understanding of one facet of the individual's behavior will have little effect on the total behavior until it is reconciled with the various aspects of the patient's personality.

This process of *working through* is usually extremely slow, particularly where basic character patterns are being challenged. One may painstakingly work at a problem with little surface change. Then, after a number of months something seems to "give," and the patients begin responding in a different way to their environment. Gaining satisfaction from the new response, they integrate it within their personalities. The old patterns continue to appear from time to time, but these become increasingly susceptible to influence and replacement with new more adaptive reac-

tions. Having achieved a partial goal, one is motivated to tackle more ambitious aims. The investigative operation is extended toward these new objectives, and the working-through exercise then goes on with retreats and advances until constructive and established action eventuates.

Thus, a patient with a disturbing personality problem came to therapy because of the symptom of impotence. Understanding of his sexual misconception, with a working through of his fear of performance, opened up the possibility of more advanced objectives. A portion of an important session with this patient follows:

Pt. I saw Jane after I spoke to you. Sexually we got along better than we ever had. She had a good orgasm, and it was really the first time. We've been seeing each other for about 5 months, so it was sort of a milestone as far as I was concerned. And yet, I wasn't, I didn't feel as though I'd done a great thing, as though I'd "arrived" or anything like that.

Th. Previously you had felt—I can even recapture your own words—that if an occasion ever occurred with a person like Jane where you could really function to your own satisfaction and to hers, it would really mean you had achieved your goal. Now that it's come about, it hasn't proved to be anything like you anticipated.

Pt. I said to myself that something seems to be stopping me almost from thinking about it. I said, "Now, let's think about this thing because this is supposedly very important." And I just didn't grasp it, as though there's something you want so much, and you get it, and it doesn't mean anything. I said this ought to give you a wonderful feeling; this should be good for you, that this happened. It was good, but it didn't solve all my problems like I imagined it would. And I don't know whether it's because it's become less important to me. It continually demonstrates this business of I could do such-and-such, if only this were the case. How foolish that is because I thought to myself, "Well, really it's just once. Maybe it should be another time. Maybe I should prove myself again. Once really isn't enough." But I feel I could do it three or four times, or a hundred, and it still wouldn't be enough. [*The patient is apparently aware of the fact that sexual success will not solve all of his problems.*]

Th. As a matter of fact, it is possible that the

reason you weren't functioning well sexually with her is that you weren't permitting yourself to enjoy sex for the pleasure value but rather for its value in building you up. [*interpreting his neurotic use of sex*]

Pt. I would guess that I have certainly dhanged in that respect. It bothered me though that it didn't mean more to me than it did. I thought, "Well maybe that's why it happened," because it didn't mean so much to me. So that we're still really on the same basis, as far as this business is concerned.

Th. Mm hmm.

Pt. I say to myself, "Well, there's three women, Barbara, Martha, and Jane, that I'm sleeping with. I have now reached a point where I, they've all been able to have orgasms. It made me feel comfortable, but not . . . maybe I could be better off if I could think, 'Jesus, I'm terrific, or what a great man I am now'." But I don't feel that way.

Th. It would be a very neurotic thing to build up your self-esteem solely and completely, or largely, on the basis of how you function sexually. That's a facade that will cross you up.

Pt. It would be like evaluating a man on the basis of his appetite. If I would be with a woman and I could only have one orgasm, I would think to myself, "Well, you're not as much of a man as if you had two or three orgasms." And yet, it would be like saying, "If a man eats a plate of oysters, if he eats only one plate, he's not as much a man as if he'd eaten two or three plates." I realize my attitude is ridiculous.

Th. But still you seem to think one way and feel the other way.

Pt. It really is a tough situation. This sort of thing seems to be pretty much the kernel of my difficulty. It radiates in all actions and all spheres. I mean the sexual element now seems to, right now, this week anyhow, seems to be receding somewhat into the background and other aspects becoming important. I see where it's necessary to do more, to alter your personality and your attitudes. A whole new set of values have to be evolved, what's good and what's bad, what's right and what's wrong, the sort of life you want to live and what you want to do about it, which, I presume most people never really figure out. I have toyed with the idea before, but now I want to get into myself more.

Another patient with sexual fears and problems in his marital life was, with continued working through, able to make good progress. His relationship with his wife improved. Sexuality became less compulsive

a function; he began to achieve greater assertiveness and a feeling of increased self-esteem. These changes are illustrated in the following fragment of the session that follows:

Pt. Tuesday night I decided to bring some flowers home. It was like a miracle, a tremendous response. In fact my wife's face was so overjoyed that I really felt a little sorry that—well, she'd been so miserable—it just required little things like that, not much to make her happy. I talked to her last night about my work, and she interpreted my actions as rejection. But it wasn't so, I told her. I said the things you really want are the important ones. She said that it's true. I explained to her about my work and eventually I thought I'd be able to spend more time with the children, and I was working toward that end. I feel much more comfortable in the situation. I was afraid that I'd have a compulsion to want to do as many things as possible along these lines, so that she'd know I was thinking of her. And the result would be that I'd have a conflict between wanting to do those things and other things like my work. But I find it's not so. I feel very comfortable, much more comfortable in the situation. I feel that I can do those things if I want to. If I think of something to make her know that I'm thinking of her, it's not an effort really on my part. I don't feel a compulsion to want to do them. In fact, when I got the flowers, I really enjoyed getting them. I would say right now that my situation, therefore, on the whole is a little better. These other things aren't important to me. My wife is enjoyable. I'm more in control of the situation.

Th. You'll be able to make even further progress if you can think objectively about your situation and not act impulsively as you once did.

Pt. Yes, I guess so. I guess being tied up in a situation makes you lose your perspective, but I was so interested in the things that she was actually finding fault with me for, I felt that I concentrated on those, taking them as a personal affront, instead of realizing what they were. I suppose that the situation will change again in some way, but right now I guess things are fairly peaceful, considering everything. I have a great deal of work to do, but I think I'm less neurotic about it; for the first time, I would say, since I've been in business, I am willing and eager to strip myself of as much detail work as possible. Before I was just holding on to it. I made up my mind that this work has to be done and that until I do it, I won't be able to take it easy. The work has to be done before I can take it easy. So I said to myself, "Well, it's really awful because if I had three days like Saturday, where no one bothered me, in a row, I could do it all." So I told my wife that I'm going to have to work a few nights and she said O.K. In fact, last night, I did one of the things that she complained about, I came home late again. But it was wonderful; she didn't complain about it. She greeted me with a smile and said nothing about it. So I could see that that wasn't the important thing. I would say that I feel on the whole that I sort of climbed a little and reached a little plateau, if such a thing is possible.

Th. Well, let us examine that plateau, and see what incentives there are to move ahead. Because virtually, in terms of your goals that you came to see me for originally, you've pretty much achieved those, haven't you?

Pt. I suppose so. The physical symptoms that I had, I don't have them any more. I assume they'll just fade away, because I never think of them. Sexually, I'm functioning much better than I ever did before. So I guess on those two counts I've come a long way. That's true.

Th. In your assertiveness, in your capacity to stand up for your own rights, what about that?

Pt. Well, I'd say there is probably less progress made on that score. We haven't been working on it as much as the other thing.

Th. Well, do you feel that it's been a problem? Do you feel that that constitutes a problem for you?

Pt. Yes, definitely, but now I feel more like a person with rights and things like that, more of an individual than I felt before. But I think I still have a long way to go to feel really an assertive person, I would say. And this may be just a temporary peace that I've achieved. All the elements that caused me anxiety for the past few months have reached the point of equilibrium.

Therapeutic progress is gauged by the ability of the patient to apply what has been learned toward a more constructive life adaptation. The recognition of disturbing drives and the realization that they are operating compulsively do not guarantee that any modification will occur. Nor do they mean that the patient has the capacity for change. The ability to progress depends upon many factors. Foremost is the desire for change. Among the motivating influences here are a sense of frustration induced by an inability to fulfill normal needs and growing awareness that neurotic strivings are associated with suffering far in excess of compensatory gratifications.

The detection of contradictions in the personality structure also acts as a powerful incentive to change. It is, however, merely the first step in the reintegrative process. Thus, if a patient exhibits a pattern of compulsive dependency, the mere recognition of dependency and its consequences will not alter the need to cling tenaciously to others. While it may point the way to the more basic problem of inner helplessness and devaluated self-esteem, there is still a need to examine the meaning of the patient's impaired self-esteem as well as to determine its source. Furthermore, there is required an appreciation of the motivating factors in the individual's present life that perpetuate feelings of helplessness. Understanding the origins of one's dependency trend and tracing it to determining experiences with early authorities are important steps, but these too are usually insufficient for cure. As long as basic helplessness continues, dependency has subjective values the individual cannot and will not relinquish. While the irrationality of one's drives may be recognized as well as the unfortunate consequences, one will desperately cling to them, at the same time rationalizing prevaling motives. Partial insight regarding deep dependency promptings will not eradicate them nor dim their acceptance the remainder of one's life.

Working through, as has been previously indicated, is especially difficult in reconstructive therapy and a description of the process may at this point be helpful. The releasing of the self from the restraint and tyranny of an archaic conscience, freeing it from paralyzing threats of inner fears and conflicts, is an extremely slow process. Ego growth gradually emerges, with the development of self-respect, assertiveness, self-esteem, and self-confidence. It is associated with liberation of the individual from a sense of helplessness and from fears of imminent rejection and hurt from a hostile world.

The process of ego growth is complex and merits a more elaborate description. Fundamentally to encourage such growth it is necessary to cajole the ego into yielding some of its defenses. Within the self the individual feels to weak to do this and too terrified to face inner conflicts. Unconscious material is invested with such anxiety that its very acknowledgment is more than the patient can bear. Rooted in past conditionings, this anxiety possesses a fantastic quality, since it is usually unmodified by later experiences. It is as if the anxiety had been split off and were functioning outside the domain of the ego. In therapy it is essential to reunite the conscious ego with the repressed material and its attendant anxiety, but resistance constantly hampers this process. Promoting resistance is the hypertrophied set of standards and prohibitions that developed out of the individual's relationships with early authorities. These standards oppose not only the uncovering of unconscious material, but also the expression of the most legitimate personal needs.

Working through in reconstructive therapy must be accompanied by a strengthening of the ego to a point where it can recognize the disparity between what is felt and what is actually true, where it can divest the present of unconscious fears and injuries related to the past, where it can dissociate present relationships with people from attitudes rooted in early interpersonal experiences and conditionings. Ego growth is nurtured chiefly through a gratifying relationship with the therapist. The exact mechanism that produces change is not entirely clear. However, the therapist–patient relationship acts to upset the balance of power between the patient's ego, conscience, and repressed inner drives. The ultimate result is a liberation of the self and a replacement of the tyrannical conscience

by a more tolerant conscience patterned around an identification with the therapist.

The relationship with the therapist may, however, light up the individual's fears of injury, as well as inordinate expectations, drives, and forbidden erotic and hostile desires. Despite the lenity of the therapist, the patient will keep subjecting the therapist to tests in order to justify a returning to the old way of life. If the therapist is too expressive in tolerance of the patient's deepest impulses, the patient will look upon treatment as a seduction for which one will pay grievous penalties later on. On the other hand, a repressive attitude expressed by the therapist will play in with the patient's residual concept of authority as restrictive and, therefore, deserving of customary evasions and chicaneries. At all times the patient will exploit usual characterologic defenses to prevent relating the self too intimately to the therapist. The patient has been hurt so frequently in previous interpersonal relationships that there is the conviction that danger lurks in the present one. Under the latter circumstance the working-through experiences may take place within the transference relationship itself particularly when the patient is in long-term therapy and the therapist encourages the development of a transference neurosis. Obsiously the therapist must have had psychoanalytic training to lead the patient through the rigors of the neurotic transference experience.

Many months may be spent in dealing with resistances that ward off the threat of a close relationship with, and the acknowledgment of certain irrational feelings toward, the therapist. The therapist acts to dissolve these facades by direct attack. Perhaps for the first time patients permit themselves to feel, to talk, and to act without restraint. This freedom is encouraged by the therapist's attitude, which neither condones nor condemns destructive impulses. The patients sense that the therapist is benevolently neutral toward their impulses and will not retaliate with counterhostility in response to aggression. Gradually the patients develop reactions to the therapist that are of a unique quality, drawing upon emotions and strivings that have hitherto been repressed. The release of these submerged drives may be extremely distressing to the patients. Because they conflict so outrageous with standards, bound to reject them as wholly fantastic or to justify them with rationalizations. There is an almost psychotic quality in projected inner feelings and attitudes, and the patients may fight desperately to vindicate themselves by presenting imagined or actual happenings that put the therapist in a bad light.

As the patients experience hostility toward the therapist and as they find that the dreaded counterhostility does not arise, they feel more and more capable of tolerating the anxiety inevitable to the release of their unconscious drives. They find that they can bear frustration and discomfort and that such tolerance is rewarded by many positive gains. Finally, they become sufficiently strong to unleash their deepest unconscious drives and feelings, which previously they had never dared to express. Projecting these onto the person of the therapist, the patients may live through infantile traumatic emotional events with the therapist that duplicate the experiences initially responsible for their disorders. The latter phase occurs when the patients have developed sufficient trust and confidence in the therapist to feel that they are protected against the consequences of their inner destructive impulses.

Sexual wishes, hostile strivings, and other drives may also suddenly overwhelm the patients and cause them to react compulsively, against their better judgment. The patients almost always will exhibit behavior patterns, both inside and outside the therapeutic situation, that serve either to drain off their aroused emotions or to inhibit them. They may, for instance, in response to feelings of rage, have a desire to

frustrate and hurt the therapist. Accordingly, they will probably have but tend to suppress imprecations and derisive feelings about the therapist, minimizing the latter's intelligence, or emphasizing any shortcomings. They may become sullen, or mute, or negativistic.

These reactions do not always appear openly and may be manifested only in dreams and fantasies. Sometimes hostility is expressed more surreptitiously in the form of a sexual impulse toward the therapist, which may have its basis in the desire to undermine or to depreciate. At the same time the patients realize that they need the love and help of the therapist, and they may feel that expression of hostility will eventuate in rejection. They may then try to solve their conflict by maintaining a detached attitude toward the therapist, by refusing to verbalize freely, by forgetting appointments, or by terminating treatment.

A danger during this working-through process is that the patients may act out inner impulses and feelings and fail to verbalize them. This is particularly the case where the patients are given no chance to express everything that comes to mind. Such acting-out has a temporary cathartic effect, but it is not conducive to change. If the patients do not know what they are reliving, they will think that their reactions are completely justified by reality. If acting-out goes on unchecked, it may halt the therapeutic process. The most important task of the therapist here is to demonstrate to the patients what in the therapeutic relationship is being avoided by acting-out.

As the patients realize that their emotions and impulses are directly a product of their relationship with the therapist, they will attempt to justify themselves by searching for factors in the therapist's manner or approach that may explain the reactions. Inwardly they are in terror lest the therapist call a halt to therapy and thus bring to an end the possibility of ever establishing an unambivalent relationship with another human being. Yet they continue to respond with contradictory attitudes. On the one hand, they seek praise and love from the therapist, and, on the other, they try to repudiate and minimize the therapist. They resent the tender emotions that keep cropping up within themselves. The battle with the therapist rages back and forth, to the dismay of both participants.

One of the effects of this phase of the therapy is to mobilize ideas and fantasies related to past experiences and conditionings. The transference relationship is the most potent catalyst the therapist can employ to liberate repressed memories and experiences. As the patients express irrational impulses toward the therapist, they become tremendously productive, verbalizing fantasies and ideas of which they were only partially aware.

Sooner or later the patients discover that their attitudes and feelings toward the therapist are rooted in experiences and conditionings that date to the past; they realize that these have little to do with the therapist as a real person. This has a twofold effect: first, it shows them why exaggerated expectations and resentments develop automatically in their relationships with others; second, it permits them to see that they are able to approach people from a different point of view.

The transference is a dynamic, living experience that can be intensely meaningful to the patient. Recovery of repressed material is in itself insufficient. The material has to be understood, integrated, and accepted. During reconstructive therapy much material of an unconscious nature may come to the surface, but the patients will, at first, be unable to assimilate this material because it lies outside the scope of their understanding. In the transference relationship the patients are able to feel their unconscious impulses in actual operation. They realize them not as cold intellectual facts but as real experiences. The learning process is accelerated under such circumstances.

The transference not only mobilizes the deepest trends and impulses, but also it teaches the patients that they can express these without incurring hurt. This is unlike the ordinary authority–subject relationship, in which the person feels obligated to hold back irrational feelings. Because of the therapist's tolerance, the patients become capable of countenancing certain attitudes consciously for the first time. They appreciate that when they express destructive attitudes toward the therapist, these do not call forth retaliatory rejection, condemnation, or punishment. They gradually develop a more tolerant attitude toward their inner drives, and they learn to reevaluate them in the light of existing reality rather than in terms of unconscious fantasies and traumatic events in the past. As they undergo the unique experience of expressing their deepest strivings without retaliation, they also begin to permit healthy attitudes to filter through their defenses. The therapist becomes an individual who fits into a special category, as less authority and more the friend.

The tolerant and understanding attitude of the therapist provides a peculiar attribute of protectiveness; for the patients alone are unable to accept inner conflicts and impulses and use the therapist as a refuge from danger. The conviction that they have a protector enables them to divulge their most repulsive dreams, impulses, emotions, memories, and fantasies, with an associated release of affect. Along with growing awareness of their unconscious drives with placement in the time frame of earliest childhood, the patients sooner or later discover that there is a difference between what they feel and what it actually going on in reality; they find that their guilt feeling and anxiety actually have no basis in fact.

The patients may bring up more and more painful material. Encouraged to express themselves, they begin to regard the therapist as one who bears only good will toward their repressed drives. They will continue to exhibit all of their customary interpersonal attitudes and defenses in their relationship with the therapist, but they can clarify these to themselves under a unique set of conditions—conditions in which they feel accepted and in which there is no condemnation or retaliatory resentment.

The reorientation in their feelings toward the therapist makes it possible for them to regard the therapist as a person toward whom they need nurture no ambivalent attitudes. Their acceptance of the therapist as a real friend has an important effect on their resistances. These are genetically related to the hurt that they experienced in their relationships with early authorities. The lowering of resistances is dynamically associated with an alteration in their internalized system of restraints, for, if they are to yield their defenses, they must be assured that the old punishments and retributions will not overtake them. It is here that their experiences with the therapist play so vital a role because in it they have gained an entirely new attitude toward authority. Their own conscience is modified by adoption of a more lenient set of credos.

One of the chief aims of reconstructive therapy is to render the conscience less tyrannical and to modify it so as to permit the expression of impulses essential for mental health. Perhaps the most important means toward this alteration is through acccceptance of the therapist as a new authority whose standards subdue and ultimately replace the old and intolerable ones. In the course of the therapeutic relationship the patients tend to identify themselves with the therapist and to incorporate the therapist's more temperate values. The ultimate result is a rearrangement of the dynamic forces of the personality and a reduction in the harshness of the superego.

Identification with the therapist also has a remarkable effect on a patient's ego. Progress in reconstructive therapy is registered by the increasing capacity of the reasonable ego to discern the irrationality of its actions, feelings, and defenses. The rebuilding of ego strength promotes a review of old repressions, some of which are lifted, while others are accepted but reconstructed with more solid material, so that they will not give way so easily to unconscious fears. Growth in the rational power and judgment of the ego makes it possible to identify these destructive strivings, which, rooted in past experiences, are automatically operative in the present.

Ego strength, consequently, results both from liberation of the self from the repressive and intolerant standards of the tyrannical conscience, and also identification with the accepting, nonhostile figure of the therapist. Ultimately, ego growth involves an identification with a healthy group. This is, of course, the final aim in therapy, and a good relation with the group eventually must supplement and partly replace the personal identification.

The undermining of the superego and the strengthening of the ego give the patients courage to face their fearsome impulses, such as hate. They become increasingly more capable of expressing rage openly. The possibility of their being physically or verbally attacked by the therapist becomes less and less real to them. As they resolve their hate and fear, they are likely to experience an onrush of loving emotions. Particularly where a transference neurosis has been allowed to develop, these may burst forth in a violent form, as in a compulsive desire for sexual contact. In this guise feelings may be loathsome and terrifying and may become promptly repressed. Sexuality, to the mind of the patients, may mean unconditional love or surrender or a desire to attack or to merge with another person. Inextricably bound up with such destructive feelings are healthful ones, but because the patients have been hurt so frequently in expressing tender impulses, they have customarily been forced to keep feelings under control. In their relationships with the therapist they learn that normal demands for understanding and affection will not be frustrated and that these have nothing to do with hateful and sexual attitudes.

As the therapist comes to be accepted as an understanding person, the unconscious impulses come out in greater force, and the patients discover that they are better able to tolerate the anxiety that is created by such expression. In contrast to what occurs in real life, resistance to one's divulgence is not reinforced by actual or implied threats of retaliation or loss of love. The patients then become conscious of the fact that their terror has its source within themselves rather than in an implied threat of hurt from the therapist. This insight does not help much at first, but gradually it permits the patients to experiment in tolerating increased doses of anxiety.

The development of the capacity to withstand pain makes it possible for the patients to work out more mature solutions for their problems, instead of taking refuge in repression, a defense hitherto necessitated by an inability to tolerate anxiety. The discovery that they have not been destroyed by their impulses and the realization that they have not destroyed the therapist, whom they both love and hate, are tremendous revelations, lessening the inclination to feel guilty and to need punishment, and contributing to their security and self-respect.

At this stage in therapy the patients become more critical of the therapist and more capable of injecting reality into the relationship. They attempt to test out their new insights in real life. They do this with considerable trepidation, always anticipating the same kind of hurt that initially fostered their repression. As they discover that they can express themselves and take a stand with the therapist, a new era of trust in the therapist is ushered in with a definite growth of self-confidence. Over and over they work through with the therapist their own characterologic strivings, reexperiencing their unconscious impulses and the accompanying reactions of defense against them. Gradually they become aware of the meaning of their emotional turmoil, as well as of the futility of their various defenses. The continuous analysis of the transference enables them to understand how their neurotic drives have isolated them from people and have prevented expression of their healthy needs.

A new phase in their relationships with the therapist ensues. Realizing that the therapist means more to them than does anyone else, they seek to claim this new ally for themselves. They may wish to continue the relationship indefinitely, and they may look upon the completion of therapy as a threat. Clinging to their illness may then have positive values. However, they soon begin to understand that there are reality limitations in their present relationship, and they begin to realize that they do not get out of it the things that they are beginning to demand of life, that the outside world is the only milieu in which they can gratify their needs. They find the relationship with the therapist gratifying, but not gratifying enough; their reality sense becomes stronger, and their ability to cope with frustration is enhanced. Finally, they set out in the world to gain those satisfactions that they have never before felt were available to them.

The working-through process is not always accompanied by the intensive transference manifestations such as have been described. Indeed, the relationship with the therapist may be maintained on a more or less equable level, the working through of attitudes, feelings, and conflicts being accomplished exclusively in relation to persons and situations outside of therapy. This is particularly the case in supportive, reeducative, and psychoanalytically oriented psychotherapies in which a transference neurosis is more or less discouraged. But even in the latter therapies it may not be possible to keep direct transference from erupting; if this occurs, some of the working through will have to be focused on the patient–therapist relationship.

Again it must be emphasized that circumvention and avoidance of a transference neurosis do not necessarily limit the extent of reconstructive change that may be achieved by skilled therapists with less intensive therapies than classical analysis. Nevertheless there are some patients in whom repression is so extreme that only a transference neurosis will serve in its resolution. (See also Chapter 42)

EXPEDITING WORKING THROUGH

It is salutary to avoid reinforcing the patient's concept that one is a laboratory of pathological traits. Our focus on symptoms, conflicts, defenses, and personality distortions may divert us from accenting the sound, constructive, and healthy elements that coexist. Patients are sufficiently alarmed by their difficulties not to need constant reminders of the various ways that these obtrude themselves in their lives. In a subtle way they perceive that the therapist is more interested in their pathological traits than in other aspects, and they may respond to this reinforcement by concentrating on them at the same time that they build a shell of hopelessness around themselves. As they repetitively indulge their neuroses, and the therapist keeps pointing this out to them, they may begin to feel out of control. Ultimately, they may give up and assume the attitude that if they are unavoidably neurotic, they might as well act like heroes in a Greek legend, marching with head up to their inevitable doom.

Neurotic trends are tenacious things and do not yield by constant exposure of their existence or source. They must gradually be neutralized through replacement with more effective and adaptive substi-tutes. This process will require that the therapist mobilize all positive resources at the disposal of the patients. While one should not avoid acquainting the patients with what they are doing to sabotage their adjustment, and perhaps the reason why, one should at the same time point out what constructive elements are present simultaneously. For example, a saleswoman in therapy who is burdened by a need to fail, destroys again the opportunity of advancement by insulting the vice president of the company, who is in charge of her operations and who is considering her and a colleague for a post that is more interesting, better paying, and more prestigious. The patient eager to have this new job, to her own consternation finds herself engaging angrily in complaints and recriminations about the company's policies and operations charging that the vice president must in some way be involved. The patient reports to her therapist.

Pt. I did it again. I was so furious with myself. I even realized what I was doing while I was letting off steam. I'm just a mess.

Improper Response

Th. You aren't, but what you're doing to your life is. You shouldn't have allowed yourself to criticize your superior directly.

Proper Response

Th. It's obvious to me that you care enough about yourself to be disturbed by what happened. When a similar situation presents itself that invites you to fail, you will most likely be able to anticipate your response in advance and alert yourself to any sabotage talk.

The patient should be apprised of her active need for cooperation. She must be told that one cannot change without experimenting with certain new actions. Like any experiments she must take some risks, and she must be prepared to face some failure and disappointments, even a few hurts. Successes cannot occur without some failures. The therapist should extend as much help and encouragement as is necessary—

but no more. It is important that the patient assume as much responsibility as possible. Role playing here can be helpful.

To summarize, the following principles may be found helpful:

1. Patients must proceed at a pace unique for themselves and contingent on their readiness for change and on their learning abilities.
2. Reinforcement for progress is needed in the form of therapist verbal approval whenever the patient takes a reasonable step forward.
3. If resistances to movement develop, the focus on therapy must be concentrated on understanding and interpreting the patient's resistances.
4. Adjuncts, like assigning homework practice sessions, for the gradual mastery of certain problems may help deal with obdurate resistances.
5. Encouraging the patient to generalize from the immediate situation one aspect of experience, or the control of a symptom, to other experiences may be important. This eventually enables a view of the immediate disturbance in the light of the total personality structure.
6. Adjuncts like role playing may be indispensable.

ILLUSTRATIVE CASE MATERIAL

Illustrative of the working through of transference is the case of a young divorcée with a personality problem of detachment, whose marriage had broken up largely because of her general apathy. Sexually frigid and with little affectionate feeling for people, she had never been able to establish a relationship in which she could feel deep emotion. After a prolonged period of working on her resistances, she began to evince positive transference feelings toward me, as manifested in the following fragment of a session:

Pt. I had a dream yesterday. We were dancing together, and then you make love to me. Then the scene changes, and there is a fellow sitting on a bench, and you kiss me and in jest ask him to leave. And then you sit down, and I lie down with my head against you. You put your arms around me. And then the scene shifts again, and you and I are in the kitchen. And my daughter, Georgia, is climbing over the sink toward the window, and I pull her in. Then I'm standing there with my son, John, in the hallway and you very professionally ask if there is anyone else I am waiting for. You came to find out about John. You forget the fact that you asked me for dinner, and I'm very let down and wake up with that let-down feeling.

Th. What are your associations to this dream?

Pt. I awoke with the feeling that I'm very much in love with you. I want you to love me very much. It's a desperate feeling that I can't control.

Th. How long has this feeling been with you?

Pt. It's been accumulating over a time, but it suddenly hit me last night, and when I awoke this morning, I knew. (*pause*) This is a funny thing to ask you, but I feel sexually attracted to you. Is it ever permissible to . . . to . . . I mean (*blushes*)

Th. You mean to have an affair?

Pt. Yes.

Th. Well, I appreciate your feeling very much. It often happens that in therapy the patient falls in love with the therapist. This is understandable because the patient takes the therapist into her confidence and tells him things she wouldn't dare tell herself. But in therapy for the therapist to respond to the patient by making love would destroy therapy completely.

Pt. I can understand perfectly. But I felt that you responded to me, (*laughs*) that *you* were in love with me. I think you are the most wonderful man in the world.

Th. You may possibly feel I reject you. It is important though to explore your feelings for me, no matter what these may be.

Pt. I agree, agree with you, of course. I can't see how this happened to me though. It never happened before. It's a hell of a note, but as you say, it must inevitably happen.

There ensued a prolonged period of strife in which the patient veered from sexual to hostile and destructive feelings toward me. The following session, for example, reflects negative impulses.

Pt. I'm furious at you. I don't, didn't want to come today.

Th. Can you tell me why?

Pt. Because you've gotten, gotten me to feel like a human being again instead of a piece of wood, and there's nothing to do about it. You know very well there's nothing to do about it.

Th. You mean, now you're able to feel about people and there's nothing you can do about expressing yourself?

Pt. (*angrily*) Oh, please be quiet will you. (*pause*) Here you went and got me all stirred up for absolutely nothing. It's like you want to torture and hurt me.

Th. What makes you think that I want to torture you and hurt you?

Pt. I didn't say you wanted to. I don't believe I've reproached you at all. I never reproach anybody for anything, I never have.

Th. But . . .

Pt. Have I ever implied or said one word of reproach to you? I don't believe I have.

Th. No.

Pt. No. I don't think so. I don't reproach anybody for anything. I don't want you to do anything at all, except just let me walk out of that door.

Th. Do you really want to walk out of that door?

Pt. I'm going to walk out of that door. You see, what you don't know about me yet is that I've a very, very strong will. (*pause*) You sit there in that chair, and I sit here opposite you, and you've got that lovely warm darn way of speaking, and before I reach that door, you'll freeze like an icicle. And I can do exactly the same thing, exactly the same thing.

Th. You mean just to get even with me?

Pt. Have you ever seen me try to get even with anybody? I don't think you have. I'm not a very vindictive person.

Th. Do you think I really act icy to you?

Pt. But you do.

Th. When?

Pt. I went out of here the last time ashamed of myself. I went down that street crying. I was crying. I felt you rejected me, cold to me.

Th. You felt that I rejected you? You felt that I acted cold toward you? When did I act cold toward you?

Pt. Let's drop that rejection business, shall we? It isn't a question of being rejected. It has nothing to do with it at all. And if we get right down to it, what difference does it make whether you do or you don't?

Th. It makes this difference, that I am very much interested in helping you.

Pt. If I walked out of this room, you'd never think of me again.

Th. You feel that if you walk out of this room, I'll never even think of you again.

Pt. That's exactly how I feel! Exactly what I feel. Yes. Suppose you had to do the same thing for every patient. You couldn't last, any more than any other doctor could last, any more than any trained nurse could last. They can't. (*pause*) Well, I'm feeling a lot better getting that off my chest.

Th. I'm glad you're feeling better.

Pt. Yes. I'm sure. I think you owe me quite a little time. I don't believe I've ever stayed here 45 minutes, have I? I don't think so. I've always looked at that clock and I've gone. I've gone to the second at 40 minutes after I got here. [*This is not exactly correct, but I decide not to challenge it.*]

Th. Why?

Pt. Because I don't want anything from anybody. Because I don't want one minute of anybody's time.

Th. You just want to be completely independent?

Pt. Yes, I do.

Th. I wonder if you trust me?

Pt. I've always trusted you. What do you think I'm coming here for? There isn't anybody that is forcing me to come. Who is it that drags me any place on a chain? If I didn't want to come, there isn't anybody that could make me come.

Th. Indeed. You know, too, that it's good that there's nobody that forces you to be here. It has to be completely a free thing with you, a voluntary thing with you, a thing that you really believe in.

Pt. I don't know what I'm going to do when I have to leave you, when I'm through with this.

Th. Why?

Pt. I can't depend on anybody, see?

Th. You're afraid to get dependent on me?

Pt. I'm afraid to get dependent on any human being, because there isn't a living human being that I can trust. Not even you. I can't trust anybody on earth. And that's the truth.

Th. I can't force you to trust me, but I hope you will. I'll do everything in my power to be worthy of that trust. But I can appreciate the suffering and torment that you must go through as you begin to feel feelings for me.

Pt. But you do torment me.

Th. How do I torment you?

Pt. I think you resent me, even despise me.

Th. Did I ever do anything to give you that impression?

Pt. No, but . . . I guess I must *think* you reject me. But you really don't.

The brief samples of the interviews contained here do not permit the detailed and painful elucidations of the genetic origins of the patient's problem. This was rooted in relationship to her early parenting figures. Her mother was a vain, rejecting, narcissistic woman and her father a cold, detached individual to whom she could never get close. She was made to feel that human beings should at all times control their emotions. Her dreams in therapy left no doubt in my mind that she was transferring her repressed feelings related to her father toward me. The working through of her feelings toward a more constructive solution is shown in this portion of an interview that occurred several months after the initial onset of transference:

Pt. When I came to you, you were exactly what I needed at that moment, and you comforted me when I came, and for the first few weeks—it was no more than that—then I began to like you. I liked you more and more, and it was interesting to me that I could feel that way about a person because I had not up to that point. You were the first person that I felt anything for since many, many years ago. So I reasoned it out, and I felt that you were probably . . . I didn't know what you were like as a man. I knew you only from a professional standpoint, what you were like. Maybe I would not feel that way if I did know you, I don't know. I was trying to tell myself I didn't know enough about you to feel that way. It wasn't anything sound. And another thing I felt was that you were probably a symbol of what I would like to have or feel for someone, that you just were a symbol. Actually, I didn't know enough about you to feel that way, and I kept telling myself that, and, during your vacation when I left I thought I didn't know how I was going to get along without seeing you. It was really the high point of my week when I came to see you. I looked forward to it, and I really enjoyed that more than anything else that I did. So, during the summer, I thought, "Well, I am going to miss him. How will I get along?" I sort of leaned on you, and I had gotten so much comfort. Then, something began to happen to me, and I felt that even if I felt that way, maybe you did like me very much, maybe you didn't. I don't know whethe[r] you say is all professional. I felt that as [far as] you were concerned, even if you did like [me,] and I liked you as you said, which was wh[at I] had figured out for myself, that any sort of v[ery] close friendship was not possible and isn't pra[c]tical. I felt that I needed you much more as [a] doctor than a man at that point and that I should forget about it. So it was something that I was putting on. I probably needed something, maybe it wasn't necessarily you. So I sort of started to look around at men. I was aware more of the attention they paid me. I responded more, which I had never done. I found that I was giving them a little more encouragement because I never radiated any encouragement. I felt that if I were to find someone, I was very happy that I could feel that way about someone. I really was because I didn't think I could any more, I just didn't. I missed seeing you, which was very unusual for me, because I hadn't felt that way about anyone in many years. So I started to look around; as I say I have responded, but I haven't found anyone that I do feel that way about. Of course, I haven't had the opportunity.

Th. At least you are not running away and are not guilt-ridden. You may feel that if the right sort of person came along, there may be a possibility for a relationship. But what about me right now?

Pt. Well, I'll tell you how I feel about that. When I first came here, not the first few weeks, but a little later, I felt that you did like me personally. I don't know how justified I was, but I did feel that.

Th. You mean that I was in love with you?

Pt. Not that you were in love with me, but that you were attracted to me, that you did like me. But, of course, again I said that maybe I was so keyed up; I thought maybe I had sort of colored it, which was unusual for me, because I have never in all my life responded to any man or made the first steps without his feeling a great interest in me. I have never, so that if it was so, it was different than it had ever been because that was never so before. I have never made the first move or picked someone and said I liked him and want to know him, and I'd like to be in love with him. I never felt that way.

Th. It was always as a result of somebody's else's actions first.

Pt. Of somebody radiating more than the usual amount of interest. So that I felt that it was different and I was rarely wrong, I mean, I was always right, but, of course, as I say, I was in a different state of mind than I am today. I am much calmer, probably see things a little clearer.

.t love me, and I
way I wanted it, and
d you didn't because I
elt it was wrong because
erson, because you are my
omebody else," I said to my-
a matter of fact a very funny
d. I ran into my uncle who re-
you shortly after first starting with
beginning to feel that way about you,
as curious about you. I met him in a
ant. We talked for a few minutes. He
d me how I was getting along. I said I was
king progress. He asked me how I liked you,
and I said very much indeed, you were grand.
He said he thought so too. You were practical,
and he recommended you because he thought
you would be what I needed. So I said, "Is he
married?" And I was blushing. So he said, "He
has an awfully nice wife and some lovely children." I realized then that probably I had radiated something that I hadn't intended to. I must
have radiated some interest.

Th. Your reaction to me was one that occurs commonly in psychotherapy.

Pt. I realize this.

Th. Sometimes it's necessary to have such a
reaction to get well.

Pt. That's the thing, that's the reason I
bring it up.

Th. You might never get well if you didn't
have a positive attitude toward me. That attitude
we can use as a bridge to better relationships
with men. There is a possibility that you may not
find a man right away. There is a possibility of
that, but at least you will know that it's not because of any block in you; it's not because you
have no capacity to love.

Pt. Well, it's been, and I'll tell you it's been
an amazing thing. I used to wonder at it myself
because I certainly am not cold. I used to wonder at myself because it didn't seem to concern
me. I mean sex. That's the truth of it. But I'm
getting myself interested now.

50
Supportive and Reeducative Techniques during Middle Treatment Phase

With the accent on cost-effectiveness demanded by third party payers, short-term therapy has been coming into prominence, and this has tilted the scales toward goals of symptom control and problem-solving. These necessitate supportive and reeducative interventions. There are still a substantial number of therapists who believe methods aimed at symptom control, while rapidly palliating suffering and perhaps even reinstating the previous psychological equilibrium, operate like a two-edged sword. Justifiable as symptom control may seem, these skeptics insist that it fails to resolve the *underlying* problems and difficulties that nurture the current crisis. Irreconcilable unconscious needs and conflicts continue to press for fulfillment, and, therefore, they insist, we may anticipate a recrudescence or substitution of symptoms. These assumptions are based on an erroneous closed-symptom theory of personality dynamics. Symptoms once removed may actually result in productive feedback that may remove barriers to constructive shifts within the personality system itself. Even though these facts have been known for years (Alexander, F, 1944; Alexander et al, 1946; Avnet, 1962; Wolberg, LR, 1965; Marmor, 1971) and have been corroborated

in the therapeutic results brought about by active psychotherapeutic methods, the time-honored credo branding symptom removal as worthless persists and feeds lack of enthusiasm for symptom-oriented techniques. The supportive process, however, may become more than palliative where, as a result of the relationship with the helping agency, the person gains strength and freedom from tension, and substitutes for maladaptive attitudes and patterns those that enable one to deal productively with environmental pressures and internal conflicts. This change, brought about most effectively through the instrumentality of a relationship either with a trained professional in individual therapy or with group members and the leader in group therapy, may come about also as a result of spontaneous relearning in any helping situation. Some dependency is, of course, inevitable in this kind of a therapeutic interaction, the adequate handling of which constitutes the difference between the success or failure of the therapeutic relationship in scoring a

Excerpts of this chapter are reprinted with permission from Wolberg LR: The Handbook of Short-term Psychotherapy. New York, Thieme-Stratton, Inc., 1980 true psychotherapeutic effect. Dependency of this kind, however, can be managed therapeutically and constitutes a problem only in patients who feel within themselves a pathological sense of helplessness. The sicker and more immature the patient, the stronger the dependency is apt to be. It is essential that the helping agency be able to accept the patient's dependency without resentment, grading the degree of support that is extended and the responsibilities imposed on the patient in accordance with the strength of the patient's defenses.

The evidence is thus overwhelming that symptom-oriented therapy does not necessarily circumscribe the goal. The active therapist still has a responsibility to resolve as much of the patient's residual personality difficulties as is possible within the confines of the available time, the existing motivations of the patient, and the basic ego strengths that may be relied on to sustain new and better defenses. It is true that most patients who apply for help only when a crisis cripples their adaptation are motivated merely to return to the dubiously happy days of their neurotic homeostasis. Motivation, however, can be changed if the therapist clearly demonstrates to the patient what really went on behind the scenes of the crisis that were responsible for the upset.

Supportive approaches are employed during the middle phases of treatment under the following conditions:

As a Principal Form of Therapy

1. Where the patient possesses a fairly well-integrated personality but has temporarily collapsed under severe stress, a short period of palliative psychotherapy may suffice to restore the habitual stability. Supportive techniques may also be efficacious where the problem has not yet been structuralized, as in behavior disorders in chil-dren. Actually, supportive therapy under these circumstances may be the treatment of choice in a sizable number of patients who consult a psychotherapist.

2. Patients who require more intensive psychotherapy, but are temporarily too ill to utilize reconstructive therapy, may benefit from supportive approaches as an interim measure.

3. Supportive therapy is often mandatory in patients whose symptoms interfere drastically with proper functioning or constitute sources of danger to themselves and to others. Among such symptoms are severe depression, suicidal impulses, homicidal or destructive tendencies, panic reactions, compulsive acting-out of perverse sexual strivings, severe alcoholism, drug addiction, and disabling physical symptoms of psychologic origin.

4. Where motivation for extensive therapeutic goals is lacking in patients who seek no more than symptom relief or problem-solving, supportive treatment may prove sufficient. After such partial goals have been achieved, it may be possible to motivate the patient to work toward reconstructive goals.

5. Where the personality has been severely damaged during the formative years so that there is little on which to build, the objective may be to stabilize the individual through supportive measures. Some patients with severe infantile, dependent personality disorders, and with borderline and psychotic reactions, may be unable to tolerate the anxieties of exploration and challenge.

6. Supportive treatment may be indicated where the available time and finances are limited, or where there is extreme character rigidity, or where the personality is so constituted that the patient can respond only to commanding authoritative injunctions. Even though manifest neurotic difficulties continue

in force following therapy, life may become more tolerable and the individual may adopt a more constructive attitude toward reality.

As an Adjunctive Form of Treatment during Reeducative and Reconstructive Therapy

1. Where the coping resources of the ego are failing, as evidenced in feelings of extreme helplessness, severe depression, intense anxiety, and disabling psychosomatic symptoms, extension of support is usually necessary.
2. In cases where the environment is grossly disturbed so as to impede progress, supportive techniques like environmental manipulation may be required.

MODE OF ACTION OF SUPPORTIVE THERAPY

Supportive therapy owes its efficacy to a number of factors:

1. A correction or modification of a disturbed environment or other stress source may serve to strengthen coping resources.
2. The improvement that results may permit the individual to exact gratifications essential to one's well-being.
3. The patient may fulfill, in the supportive relationship with the therapist, important interpersonal needs, the deprivation of which has created tension. The supplying of emotional needs in the relationship constitutes what is sometimes known as *transference cure*. For instance, the patient, feeling helpless, may desire the protection and security of a stronger individual on whom one may become dependent. Finding this with the therapist, the pa-tient feels the comfort akin to a child who is being cared for by a loving and powerful parental agency. The patient is thus relieved of responsibility and filled with a sense of comfort and security. Reinforcing these effects are the influences of the placebo element and of suggestion.
4. In the medium of the therapeutic relationship, the patient may verbalize freely and gain a cathartic release for fears, guilt feelings, damaging memories, and misconceptions that have been suppressed or repressed, having no opportunity for such discharge in the customary life setting. The draining off of tension, which has been converted into symptoms, brings about relief and usually a temporary abatement of symptomatic complaints.
5. The patient may rebuild shattered old defenses or erect new ones that serve to repress more effectively offending conflicts. Supportive therapy is suppressive in nature, helping to keep conflicts from awareness or modifying attitudes toward the elements of conflict.
6. Under the protective aegis of the therapist, the patient is enabled to face and to master life problems that were hitherto baffling. Greater capacity to deal with these problems not only helps to rectify current sources of stress, but also gives the patient confidence in the ability to adjust to other difficult aspects of the environment. The resultant expansion of security may eliminate the patient's need to exploit inadequate defense mechanisms.
7. There may be alleviation of guilt and fear through reassurance or through prohibitions and restrictions, which, imposed by the therapist, are interpreted as necessary disciplines by the patient.
8. Certain measures, like drugs and relaxing exercises, may remove tension or moderate its effects.

9. An outlet for excessive energy and ten-
    sion may be supplied through pre-
    scribed physical exercises, hobbies,
    recreations, and occupational therapy.

THE THERAPIST–PATIENT RELATIONSHIP IN SUPPORTIVE THERAPY

The different techniques employed in
supportive therapy presuppose a relationship of therapist to patient that varies from
strong directiveness to a more passive permissiveness. In most cases the therapist is
essentially authoritarian.

Success in treatment usually is contingent on acceptance of the therapist as a
wise or benevolent authority. A consistent
effort is made to establish and maintain a
congenial atmosphere. Because hostile attitudes oppose the incorporation of therapeutic suggestions, it is essential to try to avoid
a negative transference. An attempt is
made to win the patient over to a conviction
that the therapist is a helpful friend. Whenever the patient manifests attitudes that interfere with the relationship, therapy is focused on discussion and clarification in the
attempt to restore the original rapport.
Much skill may be required to halt negative
feelings as soon as they start developing;
but unless this is done, the therapist may
encounter resistance that cannot be controlled.

Forcefulness of personality, and an
ability to inspire confidence are important
qualities in the therapist for this type of
therapy. The ideal attitude toward the patient is sympathetic, kindly, but firm. The
most successful therapists never derive sadistic pleasure from the patient's submission nor resent the latter's display of aggression or hostility. They do not succumb
to blandishments of praise or admiration. A
noncondemning, accepting attitude, shorn
of blame or contempt, secures best results.

The neurotic patient may, of course, display provocative impulses and attitudes;
but if the therapist is incapable of controlling his or her resentment, this practitioner
will probably be unable to do productive
work with the patient. The irritation cannot
usually be concealed by a judicious choice
of words.

The attitudes of the therapist are important because some of the patient's responses have been conditioned by antagonistic reactions of other people. At the start
of therapy the patient will expect similar
displays from the therapist, especially rejection or condemnation. When such responses do not appear even under badger-
ing, the patient's attitude toward the
therapist hopefully will change. Different
from how he or she acts in other relationships, the patient may begin to feel accepted as is, and genuine warmth toward
the therapist may begin to trickle through.
The patient may then recognize the therapist as an ally with whom one can identify
and whose values one may respect.

There are therapists who attempt, in a
supportive framework, to deal boldly with
pathogenic conflicts by manipulating the
therapeutic relationship. Here they deliberately play a role with their patients in order
to reinforce or subdue the parental image or
to introduce themselves as idealized parental substitutes. Transference responses are
deliberately cultivated by employing permissiveness or by enforcing prohibitions
graded to a desire effect. Acting a "good"
parental figure is considered helpful with
patients who need an accepting "giving"
situation. Deprived in childhood of an understanding maternal relationship, certain
patients are presumed to require a "living
through" with another human being of an
experience in which they are protected and
loved without stint. Another role assumed
by the therapist is that of a commanding,
stern authoritarian figure. This is believed
to be helpful in patients whose superegos

are relatively undeveloped, who still demand control and discipline from the outside.

Sometimes role playing is arranged so that it simulates early patterns of parents, on the theory that it is essential for the patient to live through with the therapist emotional incidents identical in type with the traumatizing experiences of childhood. Only by dramatizing one's problems, it is alleged, can the patient be prodded out of the rigid and circumscribed patterns through which one avoids coming to grips with life. In order to mobilize activity and to release inner drives, the therapist attempts to create a relationship that is charged with tension. The ensuing struggle between patient and therapist is said to catalyze the breaking down of the neurosis.

One may rightfully criticize this technique on the grounds that the patient may actually experience too much frustration as a direct result of the therapeutic situation. The tension and hostility that are mobilized may eventually become sufficiently strong to break through repression, with an acting-out of impulses that are destructive to the patient and to the therapeutic relationship.

A misdirected positive use of role playing is also to be impugned. Even though open demonstrations of affection may seem logical in making the patient feel loved and lovable, such gestures are usually ineffective because of the patient's ambivalence. Love is so fused with hate that the patient may completely misinterpret affectionate tokens. This does not mean that the therapist must be cold and withdrawn, for a refrigerated attitude will even more drastically reinforce the patient's feelings of rejection.

Manipulations of the relationship call for a great deal of skill and stamina on the part of the therapist. They are responded to best by relatively healthy persons. Borderline patients, schizophrenics, paranoiacs, and profoundly dependent individuals may react badly to such active gestures, and perceptive patients easily see through the play acting as not genuine.

GUIDANCE

In the supportive technique of guidance the therapist acts as a mentor, helping the patient to evolve better ways of adjusting to the reality situation. Therapeutic interviews are focused around immediate situational problems. While the therapist may formulate an hypothesis of the operative dynamics, this is not interpreted to the patient unless the dynamics are clearly manifest and the interpretation stands a chance of being accepted by the patient without too great resistance. The employment of guidance requires that the therapist encourage the patient toward a better understanding and evaluation of the reality situation, toward a recognition of measures that will correct the patient's difficulty, and toward the taking of active steps in effectuating a proposed plan. The patient is usually required to make the choices, although the therapist may clarify issues, outline the problem more succinctly, present operational possibilities, suggest available resources, and prompt the patient to action. Reassurance is utilized in proportion to the existing need, while as much responsibility is put on the patient as one can take.

Guidance suggestions must always be made in such a manner that the patients accept them as the most expedient and logical course of action. It may be essential to spend some time explaining the rationale of a tendered plan until the patients develop a conviction that they really wish to execute it. In this choice the patients should always be led to feel that their wishes and resistances will be respected by the therapist.

There are, however, a few patients whose personalities are so constituted that they resent a kindly and understanding authority. Rather they are inclined to demand a scolding and commanding attitude without which they seem lost. Such patients appear to need punitive reinforcement of their conscience out of fear of yielding to inner impulses over which they have little control. At the start of therapy it may sometimes be tempting to respect the needs and demand of such personalities, but an effort must always be made later on to transfer the disciplinary restraints to the individual. Unless such an incorporation of prohibitions is achieved and becomes an integral part of the individual's conscience, one will demand greater and greater displays of punitive efforts on the part of the therapist. To complicate this, when one has responded to dictatorial demands, one will burn inwardly with resentment toward the therapist, and will feel self-contempt for being so weak as to need authoritative pressure.

One way of conducting the guidance interview is to try to avoid, as much as possible, the giving of direct advice. Rather, the therapist may couch ideas and suggestions in a way that patients participate in the making of decisions. Furthermore, advice should be proffered in a nondictatorial manner so that patients feel they may accept or reject it in accordance with their own judgment.

The sicker the individuals, the more likely they will make erratic choices, and the more they will need active guidance and direction. How long the supportive relationship will have to be maintained will depend on the strength of the patient's ego. Usually, as patients gain security and freedom from symptoms, they will want to take more and more responsibility for their own destiny. Even those persons who offer resistance to assertiveness and independence may be aided in developing incentive toward greater independence. This may require considerable time and patience, but in many instances such constructive motivation can be achieved.

ENVIRONMENTAL MANIPULATION

The special environment in which the individual lives may sponsor conditions inimical to mental health. This does not mean that mental health will be guaranteed by a genial atmosphere because personal conflicts will continue to upset the individual even under the most propitious circumstances. One may be burdened with blocks that obstruct taking advantage of available opportunities. One may initiate and foster a disturbance of the environment where none has existed in order to satisfy inner needs. Be this as it may, the therapist has a responsibility to help rectify discordant living conditions so as to give the patient the best opportunities for growth. Though the effort may be palliative, the relief the patient experiences, even temporarily, will provide the most optimal conditions for psychotherapy. It is obviously best for patients to execute necessary changes in the environment for themselves. The therapist, however, may have to interfere directly or through an assistant by doing for the patients what they cannot do for themselves.

Conditions for which environmental manipulation may be required are the following:

1. *Economic situation.*
    a. Location of resources for financial aid.
    b. Budgeting and managing of income.
    c. Home planning and home economics.
2. *Work situation.*
    a. Testing for vocational interests and aptitudes. (Referral to a clinical psychologist may be required.)
    b. Vocational guidance and vocational rehabilitation. (Referral to a clinical psychologist or rehabil-

itation resource may be required.)

3. *Housing situation.*
   a. Locating new quarters.
   b. Adjusting to the present housing situation.
4. *Neighborhood situation.*
   a. Moving to a new neighborhood.
   b. Locating and utilizing neighborhood social, recreational, or educational resources.
   c. Adjusting to the present neighborhood.
5. *Cultural standards.*
   a. Interpreting meaning of current cultural patterns.
   b. Clarifying personal standards that do not conform with community standards.
   c. Clarifying legality of actions.
6. *Family and other interpersonal relations.*
   a. Consulting with parents, siblings, relatives, mate, child, or friend of patient.
   b. Promoting education in such matters as sexual relations, child rearing, and parenthood.
   c. Helping in the selection of a nursery school, grade school, camp, or recreational facilities for the patient's children.
   d. Referring patient to legal resources in critical family or interpersonal situations.
7. *Daily habits, recreations, and routines.*
   a. Referring patient to resources for correction of defects in dress, personal hygiene, and grooming.
   b. Referring patient to appropriate recreational, social, and hobby resources.
8. *Health.*
   a. Clarifying health problems to patient or relative.
   b. Referring patient to hospital or institution.
   c. Referring patient to resources for correction of remediable physical disabilities.

The therapist may have to interfere actively where the environmental situation is grossly inimical to the best interests of the patient. This usually implies work with the patient's family, since it is rare that a patient's difficulties are limited to himself or herself. Various family members may require psychotherapy before the patient shows a maximal response to treatment. Indeed, the cooperation of the family is not only desirable, but in many instances unavoidable. A good social worker can render invaluable service to the therapist here. In some cases family therapy may be required.

Where the immediate environment does not offer good opportunities for rehabilitation, the patient may be referred to resources that will reinforce the therapist's efforts, such as day-and-night hospitals, halfway houses, sheltered workshops, rehabilitation centers, and social therapy clubs. For instance, day-and-night hospitals manage even moderately disturbed patients in the community and help support their work capacities. Halfway houses serve as a sheltered social environment in which the patient's deviant behavior is better tolerated than elsewhere. The patient is capable of experimenting there with new roles while being subject to the modifying pressures of group norms. Discarding of disapproved patterns and adoption of new attitudes may become generalized to the social environment (Wechsler, H, 1960b, 1961). Sheltered work programs have been shown to help patients make a slow adjustment to conditions and conflicts at work (Olshansky, 1960). Tolerating an individual's reactions allows the individual to restructure defenses at his or her own pace without countenancing violent or rejecting responses on the part of supervisors and employers. A reconditioning process that prepares the patient for a regular occupation in the community may in this way be initiated. Rehabilitation centers, such as Altro Health and Rehabilitation Services, provide a variety of benefits that are made available to patients and that permit them to achieve the best adjustment within the limitations of their handicaps. At such centers the following may be accomplished:

1. Handling the patient's lack of motivation and resistance to work.
2. Helping patients in their efforts at reality testing.
3. Educating patients in methods of coping with daily problems as well as in developing working skills.
4. Aiding patients in recognizing early signs of emotional upset and suggesting means of removing themselves from sources that upset them before they go to extremes.
5. Working with the patient's family to secure their cooperation and manage problems within the family structure.
6. Providing aftercare services to prevent relapses (Benney et al, 1962; Fisher & Beard, 1962).

Social therapy clubs provide an extraordinary medium for a variety of experiences, either in themselves or as part of a therapeutic community (Bierer, 1948, 1958; Ropschitz, 1959; Lerner, 1960; Fleischl, 1962, 1964; Waxenberg & Fleischl, 1965).

EXTERNALIZATION OF INTERESTS

The turning of the patient's interests away from the self may be considered important in planning a supportive program. Hobbies, occupational therapy, and recreational activities may be considered here.

A most effective hobby is one that provides an acceptable outlet for impulses that the person cannot express directly. The need to experience companionship, to give and to receive affection, to be part of a group, to gain recognition, to live up to certain creative abilities, and to develop latent talents may be satisfied by an absorbing hobby interest.

External activities can provide compensations that help the individual to allay some inferiority feelings. Instead of concentrating on failings, patients are encouraged to develop whatever talents and abilities they possess. For instance, if they are proficient as tennis players or have good singing voices, these aptitudes are encouraged so that the patients feel that they excel in one particular field. Whatever assets the individual has may thus be promoted. Calisthenics and gymnastics, even setting-up exercises, act as excellent outlets for tensions that have no other way of being drained off.

Some patients harbor within themselves strong hostilities with needs to vanquish, defeat, and overwhelm others. These drives may have to be repressed as a result of fear of retaliatory rejection or punishment. Sometimes even ordinary forms of self-assertiveness may be regarded as aggression. The device of detachment may be used in order to avoid giving expression to what are considered forbidden impulses. For such patients hobbies that do not involve competition will be most acceptable, at first. The ultimate object is to evoke interest in a hobby that has some competitive element. The patients may come around to this themselves. For example, one patient chose photography as an outlet principally because it involved no contact with other people. Gradually, as she became more expert, she exhibited her work to friends, and, finally, she entered pictures in various photographic contests. Later on, with encouragement she learned to play bridge, which acted as a spur to an interest in active competitive games and sports.

The ability to relieve tension through activities that involve the larger muscle groups permits of an effective way of helping disquieting aggression. Boxing, wrestling, hunting, archery, marksmanship, fencing, and such work as carpentry and stone building can burn up a tremendous amount of energy. In some individuals the mere attendance at games and competitive sports, such as baseball, football, and boxing, has an aggression-releasing effect. It must be remembered, however, that this release is merely palliative; it does not touch upon difficulties in the life adjustment of the person that are responsible for the generation of hostility.

Many other impulses may be satisfied through occupational or diversional activities. Hobbies may foster a sense of achievement and can help the individual to satisfy a need for approval. Energy resulting from inhibited sexual strivings may gain expression sometimes in an interest in pets or naturalistic studies. Frustrated parental yearnings may be appeased by work with children at children's clubs or camps.

One must expect that patients will try to employ hobbies as a means of reinforcing the neurotic patterns that rule their lives. If they have a character structure oriented around perfectionism, they will pursue their hobbies with the goal of mastering intricate details. If they are compulsively ambitious, they will strive to use their interest as a way to fame or fortune. The same driving need holds true for any other prevailing character traits.

Most patients gain some temporary surcease from neurotic difficulties during the period when they are working at a new interest; however, their troubles escalate when the hobby fails to come up to their expectations. In spite of this, diversions may open up avenues for contact with others that neutralize this reversal.

Neurotic difficulties often cause individuals to isolate themselves from the group. Pleasures derived from social activities do not lessen the tensions and anxieties incurred in mingling with people. Occupa-tional therapy, hobbies, and recreations give the person an opportunity to regulate the degree of participation with others in a project of mutual enjoyment. Pleasure feelings to some extent help lessen defenses against people. They may even lead to the discovery of new values in relating to a group. Once the patient has established a group contact, sufficient pleasures may sustain interest. It is to be expected, nevertheless, that customary withdrawal defenses may create tension. But the benefits derived from the group may more than make up for the discomfiture.

In some instances it may be possible to convince the patient to engage in activities or work that contribute to the general welfare of the community. This can stimulate a feeling of active participation with others and a conviction of social usefulness.

REASSURANCE

Reassurance may be necessary at certain phases of psychotherapy. This is sometimes given in verbal form; more commonly it is indicated through nonverbal behavior, as by maintenance of a calm and objective attitude toward the patient's feelings of crisis whenever they burst out.

Verbal reassurance, when used, should not be started too early, since the patient at first may not have sufficient faith in the therapist to be convinced of the latter's sincerity. The patient may imagine that the therapist is secretly ridiculing him or her, or does not know how serious the situation really is, or is merely delivering therapeutic doses of solace without deep conviction.

In practicing reassurance, the therapist must listen to the patient with sincerity and respect, pointing out that the difficulties may perhaps seem overwhelming at present, but that there are undoubtedly more solutions than appear on the surface. Under no circumstances should the patient be disparaged for illogical fears. The patient often appreciates that worries are senseless, but is unable to control them.

One of the most common fears expressed by the neurotic person is that of going insane. Panicky feelings, bizarre impulses, and a sense of unreality lead to this assumption. There is great fear of losing control and perhaps inflicting injury on oneself or others. Fear of insanity may be justified by revelations of a mentally ill relative from whom a taint was believed inherited. It is essential to accent the facts that fear of insanity is a common neurotic symptom and that there is scarcely a family in which one cannot find cases of mental illness. A presentation may be made of the facts of heredity, with an explanation that insanity is not inevitable even in families that have a history of mental illness. Further reassurance may be given that the patient's examination fails to reveal evidence of insanity.

Another ubiquitous fear relates to the possession of a grave physical disease or abnormality. Patients may believe that through physical excesses, or masturbation, or faulty hygiene they have procured some irremediable illness. A physical examination with x-ray and laboratory tests should be prescribed if necessary, even though negative findings may not convince the patients that their fears are founded on emotional factors. Assurance may be given to the patients that anxiety and worry can produce physical symptoms of a reversible nature. Where fears are not too integral a part of the patient's neurosis, these explanations may suffice. Even where fears are deep, as in obsessional patients, and where patients do not accept the results of the physical examination, their more rational self will toy with the idea that they may be wrong. At any rate, the absence of manifest physical illness will give the therapist the opportunity to demonstrate to the patients that their problems are not really just a physical one and that feelings of being ill or damaged may serve an important psychologic function.

Masturbatory fears are often deepseated and operate outside the awareness of the person. Patients may, through reading and discussions with enlightened people, rationalize their fears, or they may conceal them under an intellectual coating. Either because of actual threats on the part of early authorities, or through their own faulty deductions, they may believe that their past indulgences have injured them irreparably. They may shy away from masturbatory practices in the present or else engage in them with conscious or unconscious foreboding. Assurance that they have misinterpreted the supposedly evil effects of masturbation, coupled with assigned reading of books that present scientific facts on the subject, have remarkably little effect on their qualms. They are unable to rid themselves of childish misapprehensions that seem invulnerable to reason. Nevertheless, the therapist's point of view should be presented in a sincere and forthright manner, with the statement that the patients, for emotional reasons, may not now be able to accept the explanation. Eventually, as they realize the depth of their fears, they may be able to understand how victimized they have been all their lives by faulty ideas about masturbation absorbed during their childhood.

Reassurance may also be needed in regard to other aspects of the individual's sexual life. Frigidity, for instance, is the concern of many women who often expect that it will disappear automatically with marriage. Projecting their disappointment, some women tend to blame their mates for sexual incompetence. In therapy misconceptions will have to be clarified carefully with a focusing on possible causes of guilt and other provocative conflicts.

In men, reassurance may be required in conditions of temporary impotence. Many males are excessively concerned with their sexual prowess and have exorbitant expectations of themselves in sexual performance. Discussions may be organized around the theme that episodes of impotence are quite natural in the lives of most men. Temporary feelings of resentment toward a marital partner or attempts at intercourse during a state of exhaustion, or without any real desire, will normally inhibit the erective ability. On the basis of several such failures, the individual may become panicky, and his tension may then interfere with proper sexual function thereafter. The patient may be shown the necessity for a different attitude toward sex, treating it less as a means of performance and more as a pleasure pursuit. Reassurance that his impotence is temporary and will rectify itself with the proper attitude may suffice to restore adequate functioning.

Another concern shown by patients is that of homosexuality. Fears of homosexuality may be disturbing. It is helpful sometimes to reassure the patient regarding homosexual fears or impulses which are equated with a devalued self-image. Elucidation that a liking for people of the same sex may occasionally be associated with sexual stimulation, that this impulse is not a sign that one is evil or depraved, and that it need not be yielded to, may be reassuring. An effort may be made to explain how, in the development of a child, sexual curiosities and sex play are universal and may lead to homosexual explorations. Usually this interest is later transferred to members of the opposite sex, but in some persons, for certain reasons, an arrest in development occurs. The patient may be informed that when homosexuality represents a basic attitude toward people as part of a neurotic problem, it need not be considered any more significant than any other problem that requires psychological treatment.

Reassurance is often necessary in the event of infidelity of one's marital partner.

Where a man or woman is extremely upset because a spouse has been unfaithful, one may feel not only a threat to security, but, more importantly, a shattering of self-esteem. The therapist may affirm that infidelity on the part of one's marital partner is indeed hard to bear, but that it is far from a unique experience in our culture. The patient must be urged not to be stampeded into a rash divorce simply because of feelings of outrage. It is natural that knowledge of a spouse's infidelity does justify indignation, but in one's own interest, one must not act precipitously, even though encouraged by friends, family, and public opinion to hate and cut off from the erring spouse. There is good logic in resisting a dramatic act and not precipitating a divorce over an affair that is in all probability quite insignificant. Such reassurance may convince the patient to try to work out a better relationship with the spouse and perhaps discover why a drift from each other had occurred.

One use of reassurance practiced by some therapists is toward helping the process of ego building. Patients become so preoccupied with their defects that they are apt to lose sight of constructive aspects of their personality. The therapist here selects for emphasis positive aspects of the individual's life adjustment and personality that the patient has underestimated. Qualities of the patient may be highlighted with emphasis on how these have been sabotaged by the patient's preoccupation with troubles. Reassurance in response to inferiority feelings, however, is generally futile. One of the most common symptoms of neurosis is devaluated self-esteem, which fosters inhibitions in action, perfectionistic strivings, and feelings of worthlessness, inadequacy, and self-condemnation. Any attempt here to inflate the patient's ego by reassurance accomplishes little.

Self-devaluation may be a symptom that serves a useful purpose for the patients, protecting them from having to live up to the expectations of other people or of their own ego ideal. Rebuilding their self-esteem by reassurance, therefore, threatens to remove an important coping mechanism. Many persons who devalue themselves insidiously do penance for forbidden strivings and desires. Reassurance here may actually plunge the person into anxiety. If patients have sufficient ego resources, reassurance even though necessary should be tempered, the patients being apprised that responsibility for investigating their patterns has to be borne by themselves. If this precaution is not taken, the patients will lose initiative in getting at the source of their difficulties, and they will tend to seek more and more reassurance from the therapist.

PERSUASION

Persuasive techniques are sometimes helpful as supportive measures, particularly in obsessive-compulsive personalities. The object is to try to master conflict by forces of will power, self-control, and powers of reasoning. Positive results are contingent on accepting the therapist as a wise benevolent authority whose mandates must be followed. (see also Chapter 9, p. 123).

Persuasive suggestions have arbitrarily been subdivided into several categories. They represent a point of view and a slant on life that may not always be accurate but that, *if accepted by the patient,* may help alleviate distress. In general, suggestions tend toward a redirection of goals, an overcoming of physical suffering and disease, a dissipation of the "worry habit," "thought control" and "emotion control," a correcting of tension and fear, and a facing of adversity. These suggestions consist of homespun bromides, slogans, and cliches. But their pursuit is considered justified by some therapists as a means of helping the patient control symptoms. The following sugges-

tions are a summary of a number of different "systems" of persuasion. Superficial as they sound they are sometimes eagerly accepted by patients, who are not amenable to other approaches and seem to need a wise authority to structure their lives.

Redirection of Goals

If the patient's goals in life are obviously distorted, the patient is instructed that the most important aim in living is inner peace rather than fame, fortune, or any other expedient that might be confused with real happiness. In order to gain serenity, one may have to abandon hopes of becoming rich, famous, or successful. One may be causing oneself much harm by being overambitious. If one is content to give up certain ambitions, and to make an objective in life that of mental serenity and enjoyment, one should try living on a more simple scale. It is important to give up struggling for success. Health and freedom from suffering are well worth this sacrifice.

One can attain happiness and health by learning to live life as it should be lived, by taking the good with the bad, the moments of joy with the episodes of pain. One must expect hard knocks from life and learn to steel oneself against them. It is always best to avoid fearsome anticipations of what might happen in the future. Rather one should strive for a freer, more spontaneous existence in the present. One should take advantage of the experiences of the moment and live for every bit of pleasure that one can get out of each day. The place to enjoy life is here. The time is now. By being happy oneself, one can also make others happy.

It is profitable to concern oneself with the problems of other people. Many persons who have suffered pain, disappointment, and frustration have helped themselves by throwing their personal interests aside and living to make others happy. We are social creatures and need to give to others, even if we must force ourselves to do so. Thus, we can take a little time out each day to talk to our neighbors, to do little things for them. We can seek out a person who is in misery and encourage one to face life. In giving we will feel a unity with people.

A person may be enjoined to avoid the acting-out of a sense of despair. A pitfall into which most "nervous" people fall is a hopeless feeling that paralyzes any constructive efforts. One must not permit oneself to yield to feelings of hopelessness, for life is always forward moving. Hopelessness and despair are a negation of life. If we stop holding ourselves back, we will automatically go forward, since development and growth are essential parts of the life process.

Overcoming Physical Suffering and Disease

The patient, who may be suffering from ailments of a physical nature, may be told that physical symptoms are very frequently caused by emotional distress. Studies have shown that painful thoughts can affect the entire body through the autonomic nervous system. For instance, if we observe an individual's intestines by means of a fluoroscope, we can see that when the person thinks fearful or painful thoughts, the stomach and intestines contract, interfering with digestion. On the other hand, peaceful, happy thoughts produce a relaxation of the intestines and a restoration of peristaltic movements, thus facilitating digestion. The same holds true for other organs.

Understanding the powerful effect that the mind has over the body lucidly demonstrates that physical suffering can be mastered by a change in attitudes. By directing one's thoughts along constructive lines, by keeping before the mind's eye visions of peace and health, a great many persons who have been handicapped by physical ail-

ments, and by even incurable diseases, have conquered their suffering and even have outlived healthy people. This is because a healthy mind fosters a healthy body and can neutralize many effects of a disabling malady.

Physical aches and pains, and even physical disease, may be produced by misguided thoughts and emotions. The body organs and the mind are a unity; they mutually interact. Physical illness can influence the mind, producing depression, confusion, and disturbed thought process. On the other hand, the psyche can also influence the body, causing an assortment of ailments. In the latter instance the institution of proper thought habits can dispel physical distress.

It is natural for persons who are suffering from physical symptoms to imagine that there is something organically wrong with them. They cannot be blamed if they seek the traditional kinds of relief. But palliation is not found in medicines or operations. Relief is found in determining the cause of their troubles and correcting the cause. Worry, tension, and dissatisfaction are causes for many physical complaints; the treatment here lies in abolishing destructive thoughts.

The first step in getting relief from physical suffering is to convince oneself that one's troubles are not necessarily organic. The difficulties may lie in one's environment, but usually they are due to improper thinking habits. If there is a remediable environmental factor, this must, of course, be remedied. Where it cannot be altered, the person must learn to change oneself so that one can live comfortably in one's difficult environment. In the latter case one has to reorganize one's patterns of thinking.

Where patients actually have an organic ailment that is not amenable to medical or surgical correction, an attempt may be made to get the patients not only to accept the illness, but also to change their attitudes toward it. It is essential to help the patients reorganize their philosophy so that they can find satisfactions in life consistent with their limited capacities.

In physical conditions of a progressive nature, such as coronary disease, cancer, or malignant hypertension, the patients may be in a constant state of anxiety, anticipating death at any moment. Here it is wise to emphasize the fact that death is as much a part of living as is life and that the horrors attached to it are those that come from a misinterpretation of nature. Life must go on. Babies are born, and people pass on to a peaceful sleep that is death. The chances are that the one still has a long useful life ahead that can be prolonged by adopting a proper attitude toward one's condition. If suffering and pain do not exist, this should be pointed out as a fortunate occurrence. The person should think about the present and avoid dwelling too much on the future. No one can anticipate what the future may bring. Accidents can happen to anyone, and even a young person in the best of health does not know when an illness or accident will strike. The only rational philosophy is to glean whatever pleasure one can from the moment and to leave the future to take care of itself. Hypnosis and self-hypnosis may be employed as aids for the alleviation of tension, pain, and physical distress.

The patients are encouraged to develop hobbies and to engage in activities that will divert their thinking from themselves. A list of diversions that the patients can pursue may be prepared and the patients guided into adopting new interests.

Dissipating the "Worry Habit"

Patients who are obsessed with worrying about themselves may be urged to remember that much energy is expended ruminating about one's problems and fears instead of doing something positive about a solution. Worry tends to magnify the importance of petty difficulties; it usually paralyzes initiative. The worrier is constantly preoccupied with ideas of fear, dread, and morbid unpleasantness. These thoughts have a disastrous effect on the motor system, the glands, and other organs.

In order to overcome the "worry habit," it is first necessary to formulate in one's mind the chief problem with which one is concerned. To do this it will be necessary to push apprehensions boldly aside. In a seemingly insurmountable problem, one should attempt to reformulate the situation to bring clearly to mind the existing difficulty. If one is honest with oneself, one will realize that most of one's energy has been spent in hopeless despair, in anxiety, or in resentful frustration rather than in logical and unemotional thinking that can bring about tranquility.

First, it is necessary to review all possible answers to the problem at hand. Next, the best solution is chosen, even though this may seem inadequate in coping with all aspects of the problem. A plan of action must then be decided on. It is necessary to proceed with this design immediately and to abandon all worry until the plan is carried out as completely as possible. Above all the person must stick to the project, even if it is distasteful.

If the person cannot formulate a scheme, the therapist may help to do so. The patient should be told that it is better to be concerned about a constructive partial plan than to get tangled up in the hopelessness of completely resolving an apparently insoluble problem. Until the patient can work out something better, it is best to adjust to the present situation, striving always to externalize energy in a constructive way.

The patient may be urged to stop thinking painful thoughts. He or she may be told that forgetting is a process that goes on of its own accord if one does not interfere with it. Worry is a process that has been learned. One can, therefore, help oneself by controlling one's thoughts and avoiding painful ideas. If action is impossible for the moment, one can try to crowd out apprehensions by simply resolving to stop worrying.

Discussing painful topics with other people should also be avoided. If the patient must ventilate disturbing feelings, this should be done with the therapist. "Blowing off steam" and relating troubles to friends often does more harm than good because the suggestions offered are usually unsound. It is better for the patient to understand one's difficulties than to become too emotional about them. It may be necessary to ask friends and relatives to stop talking about the patient's personal problems, if such discussions are aggravating. It is understandable that people close to one will be much concerned with the patient's illness, but they must be reminded that their solicitude may aggravate the patient's condition. Trouble may often be forestalled by insisting that one "feels fine" when questioned by others about one's health.

"Thought Control" and "Emotion Control"

Patients who seem to be at the mercy of painful thoughts and emotions may be enjoined never to permit their minds to wander like flotsam, yielding to every passing thought and emotion. It is necessary to try to choose deliberately the kinds of thoughts to think and the kinds of emotions to feel. It is essential to eschew ruminating about resentments, hatreds, and disappointments, about "aches and pains," and about misery in general.

One must think thoughts that nourish the ego and permit it to expand to a better growth. A woman with multiple complaints unresponsive to various types of psychotherapy was told by her therapist that if she wants to be without pain, she must fill her mind with painless ideas. If she wants to be happy, she must smile. If she wants to be well, she must act as if she *were* well. She must straighten her shoulders, walk more resolutely, talk with energy and verve. She must face the world with confidence. She must look life in the face and never falter. She must stand up to adversity and glory in the struggle. She must never permit herself to sink into the quagmire of helplessness or give herself up to random worries, thus feeling sorry for herself. She must replace thoughts of doubt and fear with those of courage and confidence. She must think firmly of how she can accomplish the most in life, with whatever resources she has. She must feel those emotions that lead to inner harmony.

She must picture herself as above petty recriminations, avoiding the centering of her interest around herself. Even if she suffers from pain and unhappiness, she must stop thinking about her daily discomforts. She must give to others and learn to find comfort in the joys of giving. She must become self-reliant and creative. Emancipation from tension and fear can come by training one's mind to think joyous and peaceful thoughts. But new thought habits do not come immediately. One must show persistence and be steadfast in one's application. One must never permit oneself to be discouraged. One must practice, more and more. Only through persistent practice can perfection be obtained so that the mind shuts out painful thoughts automatically.

It is not necessary to force oneself impetuously to stop worrying or feeling pain. Will power used this way will not crowd out the painful emotions. One must instead substitute different thoughts or more appropriate actions. If one starts feeling unhappy or depressed, one should determine to rise above this emotion. One should talk cheerfully to others, try to do someone a good turn; or one may lie down for a short while, relax the body and then practice thinking about something peaceful and pleasant. As soon as this occurs, unhappy thoughts will be eradicated. A good practice is to think of a period in one's life when one was happiest. This may have been in the immediate past or during childhood. One may think of people one knew, the pleasant times one had with them. This substitution of pleasant for unpleasant thoughts may take several weeks before new thinking habits eventuate.

These injunctions had an almost immediate effect on the patient. Instead of preoccupying herself with her symptoms she concentrated on putting into practice the suggestions of her therapist, with a resultant dramatic cessation of complaints.

Correcting Tension and Fear

Where undifferentiated tension and fear exist, the patient may be told that difficulties may come from without, but that one's reactions to these difficulties are purely personal and come from within. By changing these reactions, one can avoid many of the consequences of stress. If one is confronted with tension, anxiety, or feelings of inner restlessness, it is best to start analyzing the causes. Are these emotions due to disappointment or failure? Or are they the product of a sense of hopelessness? Once the cause is found, it is necessary to face the facts squarely and take corrective steps. It is urgent to plan a course to follow and to execute this immediately. If facts cannot be altered, one must change attitudes toward them. It is essential to stop thinking about the painful side of things and to find instead something constructive on which to concentrate.

One may be unable to prevent anxious thoughts from coming into one's mind, but they can be prevented from staying there. The person must stop saying, "I can't," and think in terms of "I can." As long as one says, "I can't," one is defeated. Being resolute and persistent in saying "I can" will eventually bring results.

The first step in overcoming tension is to stop indulging oneself in self-pity. Tension will drag one's life down if not interrupted. It is necessary to learn to love life for the living. One must learn not to exaggerate troubles. One must let other people live *their* lives, and one should live one's own.

Many people suffering from tension and fear have helped themselves by saying, "Go ahead and hurt all you want; you will not get me down." Fears are best faced by courageously admitting them. They can be conquered by stopping to fight them or by refraining from trying to master them by sheer will power. Acknowledging that one is afraid is the first step. Thereafter one must determine to rid oneself of fear by developing the conviction that one will overcome it. A sense of humor is of unparalleled help here. If one laughs at one's fears instead of cringing before them, one will not be helpless and at the mercy of forces one cannot control.

Practicing relaxation sometimes is useful. Each day one may lie on one's back, on the floor or on a hard surface, for 20 minutes, consciously loosening up every muscle from forehead to feet, even fingers and toes. The individual may then start breathing deeply, with slow, deep exhalations through pursed lips. At the same time the individual may think of a peaceful scene at the mountains or seashore. Mental and muscular relaxation are of tremendous aid in overcoming states of tension. (see also Chapter 56, pp. 965–969).

Facing Adversity

In the event patients have an irremediable environmental difficulty, they may be reminded that there are many dire conditions in one's environment that cannot be changed no matter how diligently one tries. Poor financial circumstances, an unstable mate, overactive youngsters who make noise and tax one's patience, a physical handicap, or an incurable physical illness can create a great deal of worry, tension, and anxiety. It is not so much these difficult conditions that are important as it is the reaction of the person to them. Life is usually full of struggle; but individuals need not permit themselves to get embroiled in the turmoil and misery of the world. There are many persons who are deformed, or deprived of sight, hearing, and of vital parts of their body, who live happily and courageously because they have learned to accept their limitations and to follow the rule to live life as it is right now. There are many persons who, forced to exist under the most miserable conditions of poverty, with no resources or education, are not distressed by worry or nervousness because they have not yielded themselves to their emotions.

It is a human tendency to exaggerate one's plight. If one compares oneself with many other people, however, one will discover that one is not so badly off. Individuals may not be able to achieve all of the ambitions that they have in life. They may not be as intellectual as they want to be, or as strong, or successful, or rich, or famous. They may have to earn a living at work they detest. As bad as they imagine their state to be, if they were to be faced with the possibility of changing places with some other persons, they would probably refuse to do so. They might be dissatisfied with their appearance, and may long for features that would make them look more handsome and distinguished or beautiful and sophisticated. If this were possible, they might instead find their health had become impaired or their intellect was not up to its present level.

It is necessary to make the most out of the little one has. Every person possesses weaknesses and must learn to live with them. Each of us must pattern our life so as to make our weaknesses as little manifest as possible. We must expand all of our good qualities to the limit. One's facial appearance may not be handsome, but one may have nicer hair and teeth than many other people. These may be emphasized in hair style or proper facial expression. One can appear well groomed with well-tailored clothing. If one's voice is good, one should cultivate it. In this way one may take advantage of every good feature one possesses.

Instead of resigning oneself to a sense of hopelessness, it is wise to turn one's mind toward creative activities and outlets. It will take much perseverance to conquer feelings of helplessness and frustration, but this can be done, particularly by living honestly and courageously. The wealthiest person is one who has not riches but strength of spirit. If individuals are dissatisfied with themselves, they may try to imagine themselves as the kind of person who they would like to be. They may then find that they can do those things that they have hitherto felt were impossible. They must never yield to despair or discouragement. Crippled persons have learned to walk by sheer perseverance of will. On the other hand, one should not set goals for oneself that are impossible of fulfillment. Thwarted ambition can give rise to bitterness and greed.

A sign of character is to change those conditions that can be remedied and to accept those that cannot be changed. To accomplish this one must face the problem squarely. What is to be done about a difficult situation? What can be done? How will one go about accomplishing the change? This calls for a plan of action that, once made, must be pursued diligently without discouragement.

There are always, of course, situations one must accept. Unalterable facts must be faced. If one cannot change things as they are, one can change one's own attitude so that one will not overreact to one's difficulties. As soon as a person has decided to make the best of things, his or her condition will improve immediately. If one is unable to possess the whole loaf, one must learn to content oneself with part of a loaf. One must disregard minor discomforts, and pay less and less attention to them. One's symptoms may be annoying, but they are not fatal. Keeping two written lists, outlining on one side the things that have troubled one, on the other side the things that have gone in one's favor, will often convince the person, after a while, that the balance is on the positive side.

It is particularly important to train oneself to overcome the effects of frustration and disappointment. These may be expressed in the form of quarreling, or holding grudges against others, or by depression or physical symptoms. There are many dangers associated with permitting onself to become too discouraged. It is best here to forestall despair before it develops, by adopting the attitude that one will not allow oneself to get too upset if things go wrong. One must force oneself to regard all adversity dispassionately, with the idea of modifying the cause if possible, or changing one's point of view, if the cause cannot be removed.

The above persuasive suggestions do not represent a scientific point of view. However, their use is believed, especially by nondynamically oriented therapists, to be consonant with a pragmatic approach to therapy in certain patients who do not respond well to insight of other more sophisticated approaches.

EMOTIONAL CATHARSIS AND DESENSITIZATION

Release of painful feelings and desensitization to their effects constitutes an important supportive technique (see also p. 31). Patients are encouraged to talk about those things in their past life or in their present-day relationships that bother them most. Their responsiveness will depend on the confidence and trust they have in the therapist.

The patient may be told that most people have bottled up within themselves memories and experiences that, though

seemingly under control, continue to have a disturbing effect on them. The attempt to obliterate emotional experiences by banishing them from the mind is not ordinarily successful. Disturbing ideas keep obtruding themselves into the stream of thought. Even when will power triumphs and suppression succeeds, casual everyday happenings may remind one of one's conflict. In addition to memories, there are also impulses and desires of which one is thoroughly ashamed and which one dares not permit oneself to think about. Among these are desires for extramarital sexual gratification, homosexual interests, hostile strivings, and impulses of a fantastic and infantile nature.

Emotional catharsis must never be foisted on patients. To force them to reveal inner fears of a traumatic nature prematurely may cause them such panic that their resistance to further revelations will be increased. Actually, the patients have built up so hard a crust of repression that it keeps them from admitting their deepest fears even to themselves. It is essential to let them feel their own way and choose their own pace with casual encouragement.

In continued discussions with the patients it may be emphasized that every individual has difficulties and problems to be ashamed of, that they also probably are no exception and may have had experiences that make them feel that they are wicked. Discussing the patient's problem in this roundabout way makes it possible to talk about worries more openly. For instance, where it is obvious that the patient has a suppressed homosexual wish, the therapist may weave into the discussions the fact that every person, at certain times in life, develops friendships with and crushes on people of the same sex. This is by no means abnormal; it is merely a developmental phase in the life of the individual. Some persons, for certain reasons, continue to have ideas that were normal at an earlier phase of growth. As a matter of fact, most people have fears of homosexuality. The patient may be told that it would be unusual not to have such ideas at one time. The patient may then casually be asked whether or not this is so. In opening up discussions about latent tendencies there are certain risks that must be countenanced. Sometimes patients prevent themselves from acting-out their desires by not thinking about or exposing them. Such persons may interpret the therapist's interest as condonation of their suppressed impulses, particularly where the therapist relieves them too freely of their guilt. Guilt, of course, is, not too trustworthy an opposing force, but it may be the only deterrent to rebellious tendencies that the patient has. An effort to supply the patient with rational deterrents should be made where cravings may involve the patient in unforeseen dangers.

The ability of the patient to discuss impulses, fears, and experiences openly, without encountering condemnation, enables the patient to tolerate the implications of the suppressed material.

In the event patients confess to a truly reprehensible incident in their lives, the ventilation of these facts may have to be followed by active reassurance. They may be reminded that the incidents they have revealed do not necessarily pollute them, that many persons are compelled, for neurotic reasons, to do things that they regret later, and that their subsequent actions can fully neutralize what they have done. Patients may be urged to spend their energy doing something positive in the present rather than to wear themselves out regretting the past. They may, if they desire, make some restitution to any person who has been injured by their acts, or to society in general.

In cases where individuals have irrational feelings that issue out of their relationships with people or where they have phobias, they repeatedly may be urged, for purposes of desensitization, to talk about if not to expose themselves to those situations that incite painful emotions. Their experiences are then subjected to discussion, and the patients are trained to face those situations gradually, without quaking. For instance, if patients have a fear of closed spaces, they may be instructed to lock the door of their rooms for a brief instance for the first day, to increase the interval to the count of 10 the next day, then to one-half minute, extending the time period daily, until they discover through actual experience that they can tolerate the phobic situation. Other phobias may be treated in a similar way with selected pertinent suggestions. The therapist must appreciate, of course, that the patient's fears may be rooted in established conditionings and may not yield to such desensitization techniques until a behavioral analysis is instituted and tactics sensibly organized. These tactics actually are reeducative and therefore will be discussed in the next chapter on Behavior Therapy.

MISCELLANEOUS SUPPORTIVE MEASURES*

Relaxation exercises and massage may be prescribed for muscle tension, spasms, contractures, and tremors, the patient being referred to a physiotherapist when this is necessary. Enforced rest is sometimes advised for fatigue and exhaustion in the form of a prolonged vacation or a sojourn in a spa or country place. Subcoma insulin therapy is sometimes prescribed for unyielding anxiety states, delirium tremens, and confusional syndromes. Electrical (convulsive) therapy is helpful in bipolar disorders, endogenous depression, and senile depression. Drug therapy is employed where indicated; for example, sedatives, hypnotics, and tranquilizers in excitement or insomnia, antidepressants in depression

---

* See also Chapter 56, "Adjunctive Aids in Psychotherapy."

or listlessness, Antabuse in alcoholism, and glandular products in endocrine disorders. These somatic therapies will be discussed later. Inspirational group therapy is a helpful procedure in certain problems, for instance, for dependent, characterologically immature, alcoholic, drug addictive, and mentally ill patients.

Supportive measures during reconstructive treatment must be employed cautiously because the patient may invest the therapist with directive, authoritarian qualities that interefere with a good working relationship. Moreover, alleviation of symptoms and suffering may remove a most important motivation for continued treatment in some patients.

There are, nevertheless, certain circumstances under which support is necessary. The challenging of one's defenses exposes basic conflicts and may revive the early anxieties that inspired them. A period of some instability and turmoil is to be expected with reconstructive procedures, and the therapist may, where the reactions are severe, temporarily have to assume the role of a helping authority.

The specific kinds of supportive measures implemented here vary according to the patient's needs. Where severe environmental disturbance exists, the therapist may suggest available resources that hold forth promise of mediation. The therapist may also aid the patient in resolving resistances toward utilizing the prescribed resources effectively. Active reassurance may be dispensed where the patient harbors gross misconceptions or where there is a threat of a dangerous shattering of the ego. There may be a cautious extension of advice when the patient is thoughtlessly embarking on a potentially destructive course of action. Encouragement certainly may be voiced when the patient does a significant job in thinking through a problem or in effectuating insight into action.

The degree of emotional support employed will depend upon the strength of the patient's ego. A withholding of support by the therapist, when the patient actually needs it, may be harmful. On the other hand, excessive support may interefere with assertiveness and activity. The person's reactions to support will depend on its symbolic meaning to the person. The most common response is an abatement of symptoms and a cessation of anxiety. Occasionally, however, anxiety breaks out due to fears of being overwhelmed and mutilated in a protective relationship. These reactions will have to be handled promptly, should they emerge.

REEDUCATIVE APPROACHES*

Reeducative measures are employed both as a complete goal-limited form of treatment and as interventions that are strategically incorporated into a reconstructive therapeutic program.

Current interest in cognitive therapy (Beck AT, 1971, 1976) accents the value of certain reeducational techniques during psychotherapy. The individual's cognitive set often determines what one feels and how one interprets reality. Utilizing this paradigm, patients are enjoined to examine how their *interpretation* of an event determines their feelings and whether the interpretation is based on facts or insubstantialities. Sometimes patients are asked to keep a diary and jot down the thoughts that immediately precede certain feelings. In this way they learn first to identify provocative thinking patterns that inspire upsetting feelings and then to challenge the validity of their ideas.

The value of examining the connection of events with succeeding disturbing emotions is shown by the pilot study of A. T. Beck and Kovacs (1977), in which de-

---

* See also Chapters 10 and 51, "Reeducative Therapy," "Techniques in Behavior (Conditioning) Therapy," and "Adjunctive Aids in Psychotherapy," respectively.

pressed patients who were treated with cognitive therapy did better than those who were given antidepressant drugs. Some forms of cognitive therapy focus on the various ego states of individuals during their daily operations. There is exploration of the interfaces of these states, elaboration of the dissimilar roles assumed during these states, explication of the multiform self-representations, and differentiations between self and object, and identification of the values and needs emerging with each ego state. In this way individuals become aware of habitual shifts in their orientations, some of the forces producing the shifts, and perhaps tactics through which control may be achieved before their emotions take over. During therapy, an integration of dissociated self- and object representations is attempted, with the aim of bringing the patient's self-concepts to a more mature level. Sicker patients, such as those who are borderline cases and those who have narcissistic character disorders, are apt to show splitting and confusion of self-object identities. Here the patients may utilize the therapist as an aspect of themselves during transference. This will call for therapeutic interventions, such as interpretations, that are more attuned to reconstructive than reeducative premises.

In some forms of reeducative therapy efforts are made to rehabilitate the individual as rapidly as possible by discovering and modifying factors that provoked the emotional illness and by surveying the available assets and liabilities in order to mobilize positive forces of the personality. In the medium of a warm relationship with the therapist, the patients are brought to an awareness of certain interpersonal conflicts that have contaminated their adjustment. Maladaptive attitudes are explored to point out to the patients the difficulties that these create for them. Individuals get viewpoints of how their reactions became conditioned and why they persist. Finally, they are helped to adjust with new, healthful, more

adaptive patterns. In behavior and conditioning approaches, there is a minimization of insight and a concentration on learning and reconditioning.

In reeducative therapy less weight is placed on exploring the origins of patterns, while more emphasis is put on reorganization of habits, regardless of their sources in constitution or in specific inimical experiences. During the process of retraining, early difficulties that originally produced disturbing character traits may spontaneously be remembered by the patient. As part of their schooling, the patients must be taught to face early childhood experiences and, if necessary, to change attitudes toward them.

The patients are encouraged to rectify remediable environmental difficulties, to adjust to irremediable handicaps while finding adequate compensations and sublimations, to enhance personality resources through education and activity, to abandon unrealistic goals, and to coordinate ambitions with capacities. The therapist concentrates on all of the healthy personality elements, actual and potential, that can neutralize, control, or rectify pathologic adjustment.

In dealing with abnormal traits and patterns, the therapist may strive to bring patients to where they can reason unemotionally, facing facts bravely, adjusting to painful memories and impulses without panic, meeting stresses of life with courage, and forsaking fantasy in thinking. Each trait that the patients exhibit may be taken up in detail, discussing its origin, purpose, value, and the ways it interferes with their happiness and adjustment. More adaptive substitive patterns may then be explored, and the patients may be urged to take positive courses of action.

A discussion of the patient's life history may reveal to the therapist that the patient has an awareness of the inordinate attachment to a domineering parent or parental surrogate who continues to infantalize him or her. Evidences of how dependency undermines the patient are brought to his or her attention, and the patient may be shown how some symptoms are produced by conflict over dependent need. If the patient evidences a desire to overcome dependency on the family, the wisdom of making decisions and of finding outlets for energy and interests may be indicated. It is to be expected, because neurotic reaction patterns are so deeply imbedded, that this advice will not be heeded at first; but as the patient constantly experiences untoward emotions associated with the giving up of independence, the patient may agree with the therapist's observations and gradually experiment with new modes of adjustment.

Where patients are too compliant and recognize their compliance, it may be pointed out that they have probably always felt the need to be overrespectful to authority. Their security is perhaps bound up with this reaction. However, they have a right, as a human being, to their own opinions, and they need not accept the wishes or orders of other people unless they want to do so. They can review in their mind the pros and cons of any advice given them, and they may then accept or reject it as they see fit. If they do not wish to abide by the orders or judgments of other people, they can try to explain to them why their own plans seem best. Should they decide to conform with the wishes of others, they must be sure that this is what they really want, and that it is not what they feel forced to want. Above all, they must be logical rather than emotional in their choices of action. Specific ideas on how to function independently may be advanced. The help of other people with whom the patient lives may be enlisted in this training process.

An individual who is aware of a power drive may be shown how this is a dominating force in life, preoccupying thoughts and actions. Individuals may be partly aware of how they strive for power and strength in all of their interpersonal relationships.

What they may not realize is how mercilessly their drive rules them and how it results in their forfeiting normal goals. The person may be advised how a power trend brings him or her into conflict with others and evokes retaliatory hostilities. It is necessary to get the patients to see the need of adopting a more mature attitude and of readjusting their standards in line with the reality situation. Other outlets than power may then be suggested to satisfy the patient's drive for self-assertiveness and self-esteem.

The same technique may be used in dealing with other compulsive neurotic patterns, such as detachment, aggression, and perfectionism. Their manifestations are repeatedly brought to the patient's attention, and the patient is shown why they stir up difficulties. The patient is challenged in his or her assumption that these are the only means adjusting to life, and substitutive responses are suggested.

Patients may be acquainted with the ways in which their character drives operate insidiously. They may be shown that, unknown to themselves, they lash out at others, or vanquish them in actual deeds or in fantasy, or render themselves invulnerable and strong, or retreat from competition, or engage in any number of facades that become for them basic goals in life, making average pursuits meaningless.

Such unhealthy attitudes perhaps might be understandable were we to insist on what is probably not true—that they really are an inferior persons who have to eliminate adult and realistic methods of dealing with their problems. The patients must be shown the need to stop taking refuge in childhood defenses, and they must be apprised of the wisdom of facing their difficulties with decision and courage. However, because they have utilized their defenses for so many years, they must understand that these will not vanish immediately. Indeed, defenses will keep cropping up from time to time. Above all, there is no need for discouragement. When they become sufficiently strong, their defenses will no longer be required. Yet, they must not abandon their patterns out of a sole conviction that orders must be followed, or to please the therapist. Rather, as they realize the implications of their neurotic drives, they will want to substitute creative goals and patterns for those that have resulted in their present unhappiness.

The therapist should, in this way, actively encourage a conscious analysis by the patients of their customary trends as well as stimulate them to substitute new ways of thinking and acting. If the old patterns reappear, it may be necessary for the patients to try to bring them to as complete a halt as possible by deliberate effort. The patients should be encouraged to feel that they have the capacity to change, that others sicker than themselves have done so successfully.

Usually the patients will be dismayed to find that their character patterns are regarded as problems because they have accepted them as natural and normal. As they realize that these constantly bring them into difficulties with people and are responsible for much of their turmoil, they are supplied with a valid motivation to alter their scheme of life. They are confronted with a choice for which they, themselves, will have to assume a full measure of responsibility.

Many persons faced with this choice are unwilling or unable to give up their destructive drives. The knowledge that frustration or pain will follow observance of their patterns is not enough to make them give up the gratifications that accrue from the propitiation of neurotic goals. Extreme examples of this are the alcoholic who appreciates the physical, social, and moral hardships that inevitably follow the bouts of drinking but seems unable to do anything about it, or the smoker who developing emphysema continues to live in an atmosphere of tobacco fumes, or the obese individual with hypertension who overstuffs with fattening foods. In cases where patients refuse to abandon their destructive habits or immature objectives, the knowledge that they are responsible for their own plight is healthier, from a therapeutic viewpoint, than the conviction that may have existed previously, to the effect that the sources of their misery lay outside of themselves.

Where one is convinced that one's adjustment is eminently unsatisfactory, where one realizes that one's gratifications do not compensate for the suffering that comes from indulgence of one's immature drives, where one is aware of how one's patterns interfere with mature goals, one may be motivated toward experimenting with new reactions toward people and toward oneself.

Once patterns that are inimical to adjustment are clearly defined and more adaptive substitutive reactions are suggested, a long period of experiment and training is necessary before unhealthy attitudes are replaced by those of a more mature nature.

Even where patients have the motivation to change, a struggle will be necessary to achieve reeducative effects. In spite of all good resolutions, the patients, at first, will find themselves responding automatically, in line with their customary habits. They will, however, become more and more conscious of their reactions, and, as they occur, they will better be able to subject them to analysis and control. Even though this may fail to stop them from following their usual patterns, they will become more and more aware of their irrational motives, and they may develop greater determination to substitute more constructive behavior tendencies.

For instance, perfectionistic persons may become conscious of the fact that the impulse to do everything meticulously extends itself into every aspect of their lives and poisons relationships with people. They will see, as the therapist brings it to their attention, that the slightest failure to perform flawlessly suffices to create tension and panic. They may learn that the reason for their disturbance lies in the fact that when they are not perfect, their image of themselves is shattered and they feel unloved and unlovable. Life then becomes a constant series of frustrations, since it is obviously impossible to do things perfectly every minute of the day and still be human. The patients will, as they become aware of their inordinate expectations, find themselves toying with a more self-tolerant philosophy, which they will not wish to accept at first, probably because being mediocre is equivalent to being no good at all, and be-

cause they are unconvinced that perfectionism is not really the keynote of life. As they test the truth of the therapist's exhortations and as they realize the extent to which their perfectionistic strivings dominate them, they may attempt to restrain themselves before yielding to perfectionistic impulses. They will review in their mind the reasons why they must be perfect on every occasion. They may eventually even try to substitute for this impulse the attitude that they can do things casually without needing to be perfect.

To expedite these reeducational aims, behavior therapy may be helpful, a description of which follows in the next chapter.

51
Techniques in Behavior (Conditioning) Therapy

The Freudian economic concept of the personality as a closed energy system sponsored the idea that libido removed from one area must be relocated and that energy released by symptom removal must inevitably wreak its mischief elsewhere. The removal of symptoms, therefore, was considered irrational and the rewards dubious since energy soon displaced itself in other and perhaps more serious symptoms. No myth has survived as tenaciously as has this concept, which continues to be promulgated as dogma despite the fact that in practice symptoms are constantly being lifted with beneficial rather than destructive results.

In its early days behavior therapy was viewed by some clinicians as a viable and powerful means of bringing about symptom relief and removal. The assumption was that, even when effective, the net outcome would be primarily of an adjunctive or patching-up nature that had to be supplemented by more depth-directed, nonbehavioral approaches geared toward the total personality. Contemporary behavior therapy, however, is multidimensional and aims, in systematic fashion, at the modification of every relevant facet of the personality. This will include both maladaptive behavioral excesses (e.g., tics) and/or deficits (e.g., lack of assertion). It will embrace affective and cognitive modes of functioning; it will stress control from within (self-control) rather than control from without. It will take the form of a collaborative project with the patient rather than a *laissez faire,* "leave it to the patient to decide or not to decide," direction, on the one hand, or authoritarian direction, on the other.

Behavior therapy as it developed was rooted in concepts derived from conditioning and learning theory (Hilgard, 1956; Kimble, 1961), particularly from formulations of Pavlov, Skinner, and Hull, as well as from experimental and social psychology (Brady, 1985; Paul & Lentz, 1977; Pomereau & Brady, 1979). It was based on the hypothesis that since neurosis is a product of learning, "its elimination will be a matter of unlearning" (Wolpe, 1958). It gradually embraced a wide and seemingly disparate array of procedures, all of which share certain common attributes: an unswerving allegiance to data and the methodology of the behavioral scientist, a rejection of metaphysical concepts and mentalistic processes, and predilection for what is now known as social learning theory (Wolpe & Lazarus, 1966; Bandura, 1969; Wolpe,

1971; Birk et al, 1973; O'Leary & Wilson, 1975). These techniques may be directly physiological or narrowly S-R (stimulus–response) in nature (e.g., aversive conditioning), highly imaginal (e.g., real-life—graded desensitization of an elevator phobia), stimulus specific (e.g., thought stoppage), stimulus situation complex (e.g., assertion training, behavioral rehearsal), of a contractual nature (e.g., contingency contracting), directly cognitive (e.g., cognitive behavior therapy, rational emotive therapy) conducted with the individual or in groups, or utilizing complex interpersonal interactions as in group behavior therapy (not to be confused with behavior therapy in groups), etc. etc. Affects, cognitions, and behavior will all come within the purview of the behavior therapist of the 80s and 90s (as contrasted with the behavior therapist of a decade ago) indicated by the outcome of carefully engineered behavior analysis of the total situation. As more therapists apply themselves to this area of treatment, they introduce their own original procedures and unique interpretations regarding operative learning mechanisms. The rapid growth of behavior therapy and the introduction into its orbit of a profusion of techniques had led to some confusion, although attempts are being made to establish a methodical way of looking at the different approaches (Brady, 1985) as follows: 1. The situations where problem behaviors occur, i.e., which situations exaggerate and which ameliorate the behaviors; 2. the special ways the problem behaviors manifest themselves and the intensity of their manifestations; 3. the effect of the behaviors on the patient and on others, as well as the consequences to the patient, to others, and to the environment; 4. the personal assets and resources available to support anticipated changes, and the areas in the environment on which we may draw for help; and 5. the possible impact on the patient and on others of anticipated improvement or cure. The past life and conditionings that have acted as a seed-

bed for problem behaviors, and the past and present reinforcements that have initiated and are now sustaining the behavior are also examined. A hierarchy of problem behaviors is composed on paper with the object of establishing a priority regarding which problems to select for immediate focus and which for a possible later focus. Goals in therapy are discussed in terms of what the patient wants from therapy and what changes in behavior are necessary to achieve this. Some behavior therapists recommend a *Behavioral Self Rating Check List* (Cautela & Upper, 1975), which contains 73 kinds of behavior it is possible to change. The therapist must agree that the patient's goals are acceptable and not unreasonable. Next, a definition of the problem includes the situations in which problem behaviors occur, their frequency, the patient's thoughts and feelings that accompany them, the environmental consequences, and their effect on the behaviors. A clinical assessment, including history-taking, follows. Certain forms may be used, such as a *Reinforcement Survey Schedule* (Cautela & Kastenbaum, 1967) and the *Fear Survey Schedule* (Wolpe & Lang, 1964).

The patient may be asked to write down the reactions during an episode where problem behaviors occur (e.g., a phobic inspiring situation). The patient is also asked to quantify the reactions, to write down the number of times a day the symptoms occur, and to note the circumstances that surround their appearance. What is searched for are the stimuli that set off problem behaviors and their reinforcements. In several interviews sufficient information should have been gained. After presenting the therapist's hypothesis of the patient's difficulty and gaining acceptance of this, a treatment plan is devised and a contract with the patient drawn up. Therapy focuses on set goals. Should the individual fail to respond well in relation to the limited selected target, a wider range of targets, perhaps calling for different behavioral techniques, may be required.

The practice of behavior modification is most expediently executed where the therapist and patient both agree on the behaviors to be altered or required, on immediate and ultimate goals, and on the methods to be employed to achieve these objectives. Where the patient is unable to make adequate decisions, these determinations are sometimes made with a relative or other representative, who is kept informed about progress and changes in goals or methods. An assessment of the problem initially (the "behavioral analysis") includes the history of the behavioral difficulty, the circumstances under which it now appears, its frequency, and the consequences following its occurrence. A careful record of the frequency of the distortion is generally kept during therapy by the patient or a member of the family. A search for overt or hidden reinforcements that maintain the noxious behavior is also pursued. The formulation of the treatment plan will depend on many factors, including the type of symptom, the forces that bring it about and maintain it, and the kind of environment in which the patient functions, including the influence of individuals with whom the patient is living.

The chief avenues to behavioral therapy are through desenitization modeling and cognitive approaches, and operant (instrumental) conditioning.

There are literally hundreds of techniques currently available to behavior therapists. Superficially, these might seem to share few common elements, ranging, as they do, from the naively simple to the complex, from the strictly physiological to the totally cognitive, etc. However, at least in principle if not always in fact, all possess certain common characteristics: acceptable only if adequately validated for the contemplated purpose; preceded by behavioral assessment, monitored throughout the ongoing intervention, and outcome evaluation carried out; stemming no matter how loosely from some form of clearly articulated learning theory framework.

SYSTEMATIC DESENSITIZATION

Techniques organized around classical conditioning are tailored for anxiety situations such as phobias, the product of unfortunate associations that continue to burden the individual without too much secondary gain or other subversive benefits. Therapy consists of a progressive desensitization to the anxiety situation, either by a slow exposure to gradually increasing increments of the anxiety stimulus, under as pleasurable or otherwise rewarding circumstances as possible, or by a mastery of fantasies of such stimuli in ever increasing intensity in the presence of an induced state of inner relaxation. Even where the anxiety situation is highly symbolized—for instance, phobic projection, which nonbehavioral therapists view as a product of deep inner conflict—it may be possible to overcome the symptom without the formality of insight. However, an understanding of the sources of the problem may be helpful in avoiding a relapse by dealing correctively with some of the core problems that initiate the anxiety. This, too, would be taken into account by modern behavior therapists in their treatment strategy without recourse to concepts such as the unconscious or the achievement of insight. On the other hand, insight alone, without reconditioning, may leave the symptom unrelieved. An understanding and use of behavioral approaches can be helpful even to the practitioner who aims at personality reconstruction. These techniques may be especially valuable during phases of treatment where the patient offers severe resistances to the execution of insight into action.

While increasingly deemphasized in the armamentarium of the beahvior therapist, perhaps the best known approach, and the easiest one to learn, is that of desensitization. In desensitization methods anxiety-provoking cues are presented in a positive or pleasurable climate. These cues must be graduated so that the responses that they evoke are always of lesser intensity than the positive feelings that coexist. In this way the aversive stimuli are gradually mastered in progressively stronger form. The method is most readily applicable to anxiety that is set loose by environmental cues. In the arrangement of stimulus hierarchies both environmental and response-produced cues are listed to encompass as many complex aversive social stimuli as possible. The most common positive anxiety-reversing stimulus, jointly presented with and calculated to neutralize and eventually extinguish the aversive stimuli, is muscular relaxation, often induced by hypnosis.

To his use of this technique Wolpe (1958) has given the name "reciprocal inhibition." Treatment is initiated by the construction of an "anxiety hierarchy." The patient is given the task to prepare a list of stimuli to which he or she reacts with unadaptive anxiety. The items are ranked in accordance with the intensity of anxiety that they induce. The least anxiety-provoking stimulus is placed at the bottom. The most disturbing stimulus is put at the top. The remainder are placed in accordance with their anxiety-arousing potential. The patient is then hypnotized and relaxed as deeply as is possible. In the trance it is suggested that the patient will imagine the weakest item in the anxiety hierarchy. If the patient is capable of doing this without disturbing the relaxation state, the next item on the list is presented at the following session. With each successive session the succeeding intense anxiety stimulus is employed during relaxation until "at last the phobic stimulus can be presented at maximum intensity without impairing the calm relaxed state." At this point the patient will presumably have ceased to react with the previous anxiety, and to be able to face in life "even the strongest of the once phobic stimuli."

Wolpe denies that his therapy is useful only in simple phobias. He believes that even difficult "character neurosis" can be treated, since they consist of intricate systems of phobias that have been organized in complex units. "This," he says, "is not remarkable, if as will be contended, most neuroses are basically unadaptive conditioned anxiety reactions." Wolpe insists that in contrast to measures of success by all methods of therapy, ranging from traditional counseling to psychoanalysis, of a recorded 50 percent, his special method brings about an "apparently cured" and "much improved" rate of over 90 percent. It is important, however, to stress, as do sophisticated behavior therapists, that the presenting complaint is not necessarily either the one that requires desensitization or, if it is, that it may not be the one that should be given sole, or even primary, attention. For example, to desensitize an attorney to a fear of public speaking (the presenting complaint) may be of far less significance than desensitization to the fear of losing face should the attorney not win the case. Which desensitization strategy to employ, or whether to employ desensitization at all, or what other necessary behavioral techniques to employ in the restructuring of this particular individual's life can only be determined by a detailed and comprehensive behavioral analysis of the total life style of that individual and the relevant contingencies operating in the individual's life and the lives of meaningful others.

Attempts to standardize Wolpe's procedure have been made by Lazovik and Lang (1960). The pretraining procedure of five sessions includes the construction of an anxiety hierarchy (a series including the phobic object, graded from most to least frightening). Training in deep muscle relaxation after the method of Jacobson (1938) is followed by training in hypnosis, efforts being made to get the patient to learn to visualize hypnotic scenes vividly. Eleven sessions of systematic desensitization follow the pretraining period. During these the patient is instructed to relax deeply, and items on the anxiety hierarchy are presented as scenes that are to be visualized clearly. The least frightening scene is presented first. When this is experienced for about 3 to 10 seconds without anxiety, the next item in the hierarchy is introduced. All scenes are presented at least twice. If any of the scenes make the patient anxious or apprehensive, the patient is instructed to raise the left hand a few inches. Should this happen, the scene is immediately discontinued and not repeated until the next session; rather, the last successfully completed item of the hierarchy is presented. From 2 to 4 scenes are attempted during each session of 45 minutes. The authors confirm Wolpe's method as remarkably effective for treating cases of phobia and insist that there is no substitution of other fears. This has also been my personal experience.

Edward Dengrove has prepared a leaflet for "fearful" patients that introduces them to the technique of systematic desensitization:*

The type of treatment that is being offered to you is known as systematic desensitization. It is based upon scientific studies of conditioned reflexes and is particularly helpful to persons who are fearful. It makes little difference what these fears are: whether of closed places, or being alone, walking alone, driving or flying; or whether one fears loss of self-control, criticism by others, and the like.

Kindly list *all* of the fears that disturb you. Make the list as complete as possible. We will go over the list together and reduce it to its basic units. Treatment will be directed to each individual fear.

The next step will be to teach you how to relax. There are several methods by which this may be accomplished. The particular method that suits your needs will be chosen. This is very important, for the more relaxed you are, the

more rapid your progress to health. You cannot be relaxed and remain anxious or fearful at the same time.

When you are completely relaxed—not partially, but completely—I shall present to your visual imagination a series of situations. These will be based upon your presenting fears. They will be organized in series, graded from the most mild to the most intense. Each forms a hierarchy.

As you visualize each scene in the relaxed state, you may find yourself unmoved by what you see. Or you may experience an uneasiness or restlessness (anxiety). This is a critical point in treatment, and must be signalled to me. No matter how slight, I must be made aware of it.

I may ask, "Do you feel relaxed? Do you feel at ease?" If you do, then move your head up and down ever so slightly. If you do not, move it from side to side.

This is a critical point, for we can only proceed as fast as you are able to accept these visualized situations with ease. I shall not push or prod you. It is only by the ability to maintain your relaxed state that you are able to overcome these fears.

The desensitization takes place gradually by getting you to cope with small doses of anxiety at first, then gradually increasing the dosage a small amount at a time.

With children, desensitization is done in a less subtle manner. Consider a child who is afraid of dogs. The child is held by a trusted person who allows him to suck on a lollipop and point to a dog on a leash in the distance. A little later, the child, still held, is encouraged to view a dog through a pet-shop window. Still later, he is brought closer to a dog; and later, closer still. With the pleasure of the food and security of being held by a trusted person, the child gradually overcomes his fear. At first there are pictures of dogs, then toy dogs, small, friendly dogs, medium-sized dogs, and so forth. At last, he will be able to reach out and touch a dog.

This gives you a clue to a second part of treatment. You are to do the very things that you fear. One cannot overcome a fear by avoiding it, as you have done in the past, nor by trying to drown it out with continued medication. Medicine is helpful, but only a crutch, to be reduced and gradually thrown away.

The same principles of gradual desensitization must be employed. You are not to attempt any activity that produces overwhelming anxiety. However, you can and should try those tasks that are only mildly upsetting, at the same time attempting to quiet yourself. If the anxiety

_____

* Reprinted with the permission of Dr. Dengrove.

persists, stop what you are doing, for this will only set you back. Instead, return to doing those things that you can do without getting upset.

With this approach you will find yourself gradually doing more of these tasks that you avoided in the past. One can get used to almost any new situation that is approached gradually.

Interestingly, as the milder fears are overcome, the more strong ones lose their intensity and lessen, much as the contents of a gum machine diminish with the discharge of each piece of gum. The more one attempts with relaxation, the more rapid the improvement. But one must keep in mind that these attempts deal only with those productive of mild anxiety.

A warning: everyone must proceed at his or her own pace. Some slowly, others more rapidly. There is no reason to feel guilt or shame if one's progress is slow. The process of desensitization cannot be hurried by rushing into highly anxious situations. You will not be thrown into the water and made to swim or sink on your own. At times, under the pressure of need or anger, a few of you will make large strides but this is the exception to the rule.

Consider the woman who is afraid to leave her home. Her first move is to step outside her front door and back again into the house. From there she gradually makes it to the street in front of her home, then around the house—by herself or with someone or while someone trusted is in the house. Each day this is extended until she is able to walk a house away, then two houses, then half-a-block; with someone, without someone, with someone at home, with no one there. Again, no new step is made until the previous step is mastered, and until it can be accomplished without any anxiety whatsoever. Each fear is attacked individually, daily or as frequently as this can be done.

Gradually you find yourself doing things without thinking about them. Sometimes it will be only after you have done something that you realize you have done it without forethought or anxiety. It may be that someone else will point out to you that you have done something you would not have attempted in the past.

A cooperative spouse is not only helpful and understanding but an essential part of this approach. He or she can be tremendously important to this undertaking. Marital problems tend to hold back progress and should be resolved.

It is by doing what we do in the office, and what you do for yourself away from the office, that will lead you to health. One or other of these techniques may be used alone, but when both are employed, progress is so much faster.

Systematic desensitization is sometimes expedited by the use of drugs, like Brevital, 1% solution, in small doses (Brady, 1966; Friedman & Silverstone, 1967). Slow intravenous injections to produce relaxation without drowsiness are particularly valuable for patients who are unable to relax or who are extraordinarily anxious. Pentothal (2% solution) is preferred by some therapists to Brevital.®

IMPLOSIVE THERAPY (FLOODING)

Implosive therapy is a modality utilized to help extinguish avoidance responses (e.g., phobias) as an alternative to relaxation–desensitization treatment (Kirchner & Hogan, 1966; Hogan & Kirchner, 1967; Stampfl, 1967). Exposure to a fear-provoking stimulus with no attempt to escape from it will tend to weaken the strength of the stimulus (Boulougouris & Marks, 1969). The patient here is instructed to approach the phobic situation and to tolerate it (by relaxing the muscles and by trying mentally to change the meaning of the danger imagined to invest the situation).

Eventually it is hoped that the fear will be extinguished. The therapist may model the proper approach behavior as an example of how controls can be established. Experience convinces that in vivo desensitization is superior to desensitization through imagery, as, for example, in systematic desensitization. However, desensitization through imagery may be used as a preliminary therapy in order to reduce the level of an intense anxiety reaction that can prevent the patient from even attempting to expose oneself to a real situation. A trusting relationship with the therapist is of the greatest help to the patient whose terrors have kept the patient from confronting the phobic situation.

A massive form of in vivo desensitization, *implosive therapy or flooding,* exposes the patient to fear-provoking stimuli, escape from which is not permitted. Induced exaggerated forms of fearful imagery related to the phobia may precede actual immersion in the phobic situation, the therapist purposefully magnifying the sinister nature of the fantasy stimulus. After the patient learns to tolerate the imagery, the real stimulus in force is employed. Remaining in a fearsome position until the anxiety disappears may result in substantial improvement or cure. In some cases where a phobic situation exists outside the office, the therapist accompanies the patient to the site (bus, subway, elevator, funeral parlor, crowded street, etc.) and stays with the patient through the latter's anxiety attack until it is dispelled. In other cases, particularly where the patient for physical reasons cannot endure too strong anxiety, withdrawal from the scene is permitted as soon as the patient feels moderately uncomfortable. In obsessive-compulsive reactions the exposure is to the stimuli that produce the rituals and the patient is discouraged or blocked from engaging in them. For example, in hand-washing compulsions produced by touching dirt, the therapist first models rubbing the hands on the shoes or the floor and then enjoins the patient to do the same. The therapist sits with the patient, encouraging the patient not to go to the bathroom to scrub the hands. The results with this kind of therapy have been encouraging; however, "The therapist must not back away from the elicitation of anxiety, no matter how uncomfortable the patient becomes, and must not terminate the session before the extinction of anxiety is complete" (Seligman, 1979). Agreement must be reached with the patient in advance of using this technique that the patient will be willing to tolerate a certain amount of discomfort in overcoming the handicap, the advantages in time-saving being pointed out. It cannot be emphasized enough that the therapeutic alliance must be a firm one in order for the patient to trust the massive exposure to flooding techniques. Time may have to be spent consolidating the relationship prior to suggesting the technique to the patient.

The exact way flooding works is not entirely known. There are so many variables in therapy that one cannot credit results exclusively to the methods employed, since the skill of the therapist, personality, case selection, etc. crucially influence results. Be this as it may, implosive therapy in the hands of a skilled operator may dramatically cure certain phobias.

Some patients reject implosive therapy out of panic, or they may not physically be able to tolerate the great anxiety release because of cardiac illness or a vulnerable ego structure that may shatter with resultant psychosis. Here systematic desensitization is best or *graded* exposure, where approach to the phobic object or situation in small steps is employed (Wilson, GT, 1980). In both flooding or graded exposure, the therapist or empathic assistant may accompany the phobic patient to the situation that requires mastery and this can have great reassurance value. It is important here that the therapist withdraws from the therapy gradually to avoid a dependency stalemate.

In extremely upset patients intravenous infusions of a short-acting barbiturate are sometimes helpful. The patient at the start of therapy may be given a slow intravenous injection of Pentothal® (thiopental sodium) in dilution of 2%, sufficient to produce relaxation without drowsiness. Pentothal® is available in 500 mg vials in combination packages with diluent of 20 mL vial of sterile water. Some therapists utilize a 1.25% concentration (Hussain, MZ, 1971), but the diluent here should be sterile sodium chloride to prevent hemolysis. Convenient sterile prefilled cartridge-needle units (Tubex, Wyeth Laboratories) are also available with 1½ grains of Pentothal.® A very slow injection of the drug is essential to avoid sleepiness. Once relaxation is obtained, the patient is shown pictures related to the phobic object or phobic situation and asked to picture himself or herself touching or holding the object or being involved in the situation. This continues throughout the session, the patient being asked to continue to imagine being immersed in the scene. Where artificial objects similar to the phobic object can be obtained (snakes, worms, mice, roaches, etc.), the patient is enjoined to handle these. The session is brought to an end with the patient in a drug-relaxed state. As mastery occurs, sessions are conducted with lesser and lesser amounts of the drug and finally without it. Some therapists prefer a 1% solution of Brevital® (methohexital sodium) to Pentothal.®

Home practice sessions may be valuable for some patients. These can cover a wide range of themes. A paradoxical technique that I have found valuable for some phobias is illustrated by the following directions given to patients:

> Running away from fearful situations or trying to crowd out of your mind a fearsome thought only reinforces your fear. If you practice producing the fearful situation deliberately in your mind as completely as possible, while studying your bodily reactions, you will begin extinguishing the fear. If when you are not practicing the fear comes upon you, do not push it aside; try to exaggerate it, experiencing the fear as fully as possible. Practice bringing on the fear at least three times daily. If you have a sympathetic friend whom you can talk to about your reactions while practicing, this can help.

OPERANT CONDITIONING

Techniques of operant (instrumental) conditioning, in which the subject is active in bringing about a situation toward achieving reward or avoiding punishment, supplement classical Pavlovian conditioning procedures (Krasner, L, 1971). Essentially, these techniques consist of reinforcements in the form of rewards or the withdrawal of an aversive (punishing) stimulus or event as soon as the subject executes a desired act. The subject is free to respond or not to respond instead of, as in classical conditioning, being passively subjected to events over which there was no control. The techniques are designed to strengthen existing constructive responses and to initiate new ones.

Operant approaches depend on the fact that human beings like other animals are influenced toward specific kinds of behavior by the reinforcers they receive for this behavior. Where a desired behavior is sought, the patient must first be able to accept the desirability of this behavior in terms of the rewards that will accrue from it. Many patients are confused regarding appropriate courses of action. The therapist's positive attention and approval following a remark that indicates a willingness to try a tactic, or the execution of the desired behavior itself, or approximations of this behavior, may be reinforced through nodding, utterances of approval, or paying rapt attention to these desirable responses, or by granting material rewards. However, when the patient repeats a pathological pattern or verbally indicates nonproductive choices, the therapist may act disinterested and fail to respond to this behavior.

Operant conditioning works best in an environment that can be controlled. It is indicated in nonmotivated patients in institutions whose behavior must be modified to enable them to adjust more appropriately. The "token economy" of Ayllon and Azrin (1968), established in a state institution, illustrates an imaginative use of substitutive reinforcers. Since the desired reinforcers (ground passes, TV, cigarettes, canteen purchases, trips to town, and ordering items from a mail order catalogue) would not in all cases be immediately produced, tokens to exchange for these when available were found to be effective. Tokens were earned for better self-care and for work on and off the ward. The results in terms of morale and behavioral improvement, which in some cases led to recovery, were astonishing.

Bachrach (1962) provides an example of anorexia nervosa treated by operant conditioning techniques. Since food obviously did not have its expected reinforcing characteristics, a study was made of the stimuli that could act as reinforcers. Because the subjects enjoyed visits from people, music, reading, and television, they were at first deprived of these by being put in a barren room. Being visited by people, listening to records, seeing television, or reading books were made contingent upon eating and weight gain. In a little over a year of such operant conditioning, the patients' weight increased twofold.

Ayllon and Michael (1959) describe an experiment in operant-conditioning therapy done on the ward of a mental hospital by the nursing staff working under the supervision of a clinical psychologist. The patient sample consisted of 14 schizophrenics and 5 mentally defective patients. The kind of disturbing behavior (psychotic talk, acts, etc.) in each patient was recorded along with the nature and frequency of the naturally occurring reinforcements (giving the patient attention, social approval, candy, ciagrettes). Then the nurses were instructed to observe the patients for about 1 to 3 minutes at regular intervals, to give them reinforcements only during desirable behavior, and to ignore undesirable behavior. Nonsocial behavior was to be reinforced temporarily if it replaced violent behavior. For instance, two patients who refused to eat unless spoon fed had a penchant for neat and meticulous appearance of their clothing. The nurses were instructed to spill food on their clothing during periods when they resisted feeding and to present social reinforcements when the patients fed themselves. The patients soon spontaneously began to reach for their spoons and eventually were feeding themselves. In a group of mentally defective patients who were collecting papers, rubbish, and magazines in their clothing next to their skin, the nurses were instructed not to pay attention (i.e., not to reinforce) this behavior, while flooding the ward with magazines to overcome the shortage. The hoarding tendency was overcome.

In the experimental control of behavior the specification of the response is usually simple to describe, but the identification of the stimulus that brings on the response may be obscure. Hence, one must work toward the desired response employing appropriate scheduled reinforcements in terms of what the subject considers to be significant rewards. At first, the most that can be expected are approximations of the final response. Reinforcement is restricted progressively to responses that are closer and closer to the end response. In this way behavior is shaped. Complex behavior patterns may be evolved by developing a series of coordinated responses, linking them together like a chain. Thus, employing food as the reinforcing stimulus, Ayllon and Michael (1959, 1964), as described above, brought chronic schizophrenics out of their disturbed behavior and psychotic isolation. Lindsley (1960) has also written about the operant conditioning of severely sick patients, and N. R. Ellis and his colleagues (1960) have had some interesting experience in retraining disturbed mental defectives.

Operant conditioning is suited for the removal of habits and patterns that serve a neurotic function from which people derive some immediate benefit (such as delinquent behavior, temper tantrums, etc.) at the expense of their total adjustment. It is also helpful in developing new constructive patterns that are not in the individual's current repertoire. In the main, the treatment procedure consists of an identification of the untoward patterns and a careful delineation of the stimuli that bring them about. Next, the nature of the reinforcements to be employed are determined (attention, food, bribes, etc.) as well as the nature of any aversive stimuli that may help to interrupt the pattern to be corrected. In general, reinforcements are withheld (or aversive stimuli applied) when the behavior to be corrected is manifested, but reinforcements are given (or aversive stimuli removed) when substitutive and more adaptive behavior is displayed. In this way the individual is helped to develop more frustration tolerance and to control untoward behavior in favor of acts for which rewards are forthcoming.

Ferster (1964), in an article that details the tactics of operant conditioning, describes the treatment of autistic children. As is known, tantrums and destructive behavior in autistic children are usually reinforced by the persons with whom the children are in contact by their yielding to the children and satisfying their whims. Thus, the children may have learned that they can get candy if they scream loud enough or bang their head on the floor. Much of the child's behavior is operant, being contingent on reactions from the social environment. Ferster found that food was the most effective reinforcing agent. The sound of the candy dispenser prior to the release of candy acted as a secondary reinforcer. With some training, coins became the conditioned reinforcer, the coins operating devices within the room that could deliver the candy reward. Later, the coins were to be held for a period prior to their use before the reward was allotted. Then five coins were to be accumulated. Delays were increased by introducing a towel or life jacket that later could be used in swimming or water play (another reinforcer) following the experimental session. While the repertory of the autistic child was limited, it was possible for the child to develop some frustration tolerance and controls.

Next, Ferster examined the circumstances in the early life of the child that originally had brought about, and still could bring about, behavioral disorders. The parental environment was also put under surveillance to see what factors weakened the child's performance, the resultant behavior, and the effect of this behavior on the people surrounding the child. This was done to determine what reinforcements were operating and the possible ways of discouraging such reinforcements. It is likely that the atavistic and uncontrollable behavior of the autistic child starts with the reinforcement of small magnitudes of behavior such as whining. A shaping into violent responses occurs by differential reinforcement. By refusing to provide reinforcements of the child's behavior, we may expect the child gradually to abandon the behavior (extinction). Changing the environment gradually may be helpful in this respect, since the habitual reinforcing agencies on whom and which the child depends on are no longer present. By withholding positive reinforcements and rewarding conduct that slowly approximates adaptive behavior, it may be possible to effectuate behavioral change not only in psychotic children but also in psychotic adults without using aversive stimuli.

The techniques of operant conditioning are particularly suited for patients who are not accessible for traditional interviewing techniques, e.g., delinquents, psychopaths, drug addicts, psychotics, and mental defectives. The results may be rewarding where the reinforcements stem from objective environmental sources, such as reasonable and relatively nonneurotic individuals with whom the patient is in contact. The results are not so good where the agencies, such as parents, participate in the family neurosis and support the patient's acting-out as a way of satisfying their own needs. It is indeed difficult to prevent reinforcement of the patient's untoward behavior in many families since the inspiring motives are usually unrecognized and subject to conscious denial. Thus parents may become frustrated when their child begins to get better. Subtly the child may be maneuvered back to the old way of behavior with restoration of the defensive protesting of the parent.

Where the reinforcements are of an inner, perhaps unconscious nature, such as sexual excitation and a masochistic desire for punishment, operant conditioning may be of little use. For example, where shoplifting in a well-to-do matron occurs against all reason, it is difficult to find external reinforcements to put this antisocial behavior to halt in case stealing serves to gratify unsatisfied urgent unconscious orality with needs for compulsive acquisition.

In intelligent patients, however, a recognition of some of their unconscious motivations may enable them to execute the principles of operant conditioning for themselves. An executive in a large business firm, presumably happily married and adjusted, periodically would involve himself with prostitutes, whom he enjoined to strap him down to a bed and beat him unmercifully. Struggling to escape from this humiliation, he responded with a strong orgasm. After this experience his shame and guilt feelings, as well as his fears of being discovered, overwhelmed him to the point of depression and suicidal impulses. Although he pursued every device at his command, including exercise, prayer, and involvement in charitable activities to counteract his desire, his intervals of abstinence from flagellant desires would, without reason, be interrupted and he would go forth again toward another beating orgy.

In studying this case it was determined that what particularly delighted this man was sailing in Long Island Sound, where he had a boat. This, it was felt, could be employed as a reinforcement for the ability to control his masochism. It was first necessary, however, to add to the leverage of his will power some understanding of the meaning of his peculiar deviation. This, it was determined from dreams and free associations, related particularly to spankings from his mother during his childhood when he masturbated or was otherwise "bad." A fusion of orgiastic feelings with punishment apparently was the conditioning underlying his symptom. The origins of this affiliation were blunted but memories were activated through analytic techniques. This provided him with a new motivation to decondition himself. A plan was organized so that sailing was to be indulged only in the intervals of control. If a relapse occurred and he acted out his masochism, sailing was to be avoided for a month thereafter. If the impulse appeared and he could control it, he was rewarded by taking a short sea voyage (which he enjoyed as much as sailing) to Bermuda. During the winter, if he had been able to vanquish his symptom, he was to take a sailing vacation in southern waters. Within a year of this regime the patient's symptom was arrested, and whenever the desire returned minimally, he was able to overcome it by reviewing the history of the original development of the symptom. Coordinate with symptom improvement was a better personal and sexual relationship with his wife.

The problem in utilizing operant conditioning as an adjunctive technique consists in finding external reinforcements that are sufficiently interesting and important for patients to induce them to challenge patterns that have open and subversive values. However, if the therapist reviews areas of interest with a patient who is willing to cooperate, a sufficiently provocative reward or diversion that will help incite the patient to change may be uncovered.

The schedules of reinforcement may preferably be arranged at varying intervals and at unpredictable times. This is to produce an anticipatory set and to help prevent the extinguishing of a response that may come about if the patient expected reinforcement uniformally as a consequence of a new behavior. It may so happen that circumstances make it impossible to reward new behaviors each time. If the patient does not envision fulfillment without fail, the patient will not be too disappointed and angry when reinforcements do not appear. Rather, the patient will anticipate their arrival at some point.

Other conditioning techniques have been employed. For instance, Efron (1964) helped a patient stop uncinate seizures by inhaling from a vial odors of various aromatic chemicals (these had been proven effective in controlling the seizures) that were conditioned to a nonspecific visual stimulus, namely an inexpensive silvered bracelet. This was done by presenting simultaneously every 15 minutes, for a period of 8 days, the concentrated odor of essence of jasmine and the bracelet. The instructions were to stare intently for 15 to 30 seconds at the bracelet while sniffing a vial of jasmine. Except for 7 hours of sleep at night, the conditioning continued during the rest of the 17-hour period. At the end of 8 days of conditioning, the bracelet alone presented to the patient produced the effects of jasmine, which receded in a few seconds when the bracelet was removed from the patient's sight. The patient was exposed to reinforcements twice a day for the next week. A spontaneous seizure developing during the second week was stopped by the patient's merely staring at the bracelet for a few seconds. Thereafter the bracelet continued without fail to arrest seizures.

An excellent account of conditioning techniques toward painless childbirth is given by Bonstein (1958). Contained in the article are general suggestions for pain control.

Conditioning techniques have been utilized as diagnostic aids. Gantt (1964), employing the methods of Krasnogorsky and of Ivanov-Smolensky, has described a method for the study of motor conditional reflexes that can be applied to psychiatric diagnosis. Through the use of his technique he claims to be able to distinguish psychogenic from organic psychoses. This is because in psychogenic problems patients inhibit the expression of the elaborated conditional reflex, while in organic psychoses they fail absolutely in the function of forming new adaptive responses. L. Alexander (1964), employing a conditional psychogalvanic reflex technique, has developed a test for the differentiation of physical from psychogenic pain. Ban and Levy (1964) describe a diagnostic test based on conditioned-reflex therapy that measures evidence of change in patients exposed to any treatment regime. Conditioned-reflex techniques have also been employed to investigate the effectiveness of drugs in psychiatry (Alexander, L, 1964). How conditioning may enter into the genesis of attacks of asthma is discussed by Dekker, Pelser, and Groen (1964).

PUNISHMENT AND DEPRIVATION

Behavior therapists now recognize that punishment rarely works as a means of halting undesirable behavior. It is usually temporary in its effect and likely to exaggerate rather than solve problems. Getting individuals to stop hurtful activities because they get adequate rewards in exchange is much more effective. The patients may not be able to anticipate the rewards that accrue from constructive behavior until they have yielded their destructive activities, and it will be necessary for the therapist to provide interim reinforcements.

A child who consistently misbehaves, who refuses to eat, sleep, or give up childish habits like thumb-sucking and bedwetting will frustrate the parents and provoke angry responses. The parent will be tempted to punish the child for refusing to cooperate. This may do little other than to mobilize the child's guilt feelings and lead to self-punitive activities (masochism) or to stimulate retaliating anger and defiance. Logic has little to do with these reactions. Or the parent may be tempted to remove certain privileges, such as taking away something that the child enjoys (e.g., allowance, desserts, or TV viewing). The consequences of such deprivation are usually the same as punishment. Yet punishment and deprivation may rarely be an expedient in temporarily stopping destructive behavior that the child refuses to halt. For instance, of their own accord, older children who are mercilessly beating a younger sibling may be forcefully required to retire to their rooms until they feel they can control themselves. But the expedient of punishment or deprivation must be used only in emergencies to put a stop to immediate destructive outbursts that do not yield to reason, verbal reprimand, or the ignoring of the behavior. In any event, the punishment or deprivation should be reasonable and never so drastic as to leave an enduring residue of anger and desire for revenge. It should always be used in conjunction with positive reinforcement for constructive behavior.

Far more effective are actions that tend to *extinguish* improper behavior. This may require little more than refusal to reinforce the behavior by paying too much attention to it or being ostensibly provoked by it. Thus, a parent may interrupt an undesirable activity by diverting a child's attention and substituting another activity for the disturbing one. Reinforcing the substitute activity by providing a proper reward for its indulgence will help extinguish the unwanted activity.

AVERSIVE CONTROL

There are times when all methods employed to halt disturbing behavior, particu-

larly those that are life threatening or destructive, may fail, and the therapist may, with the consent and cooperation of the patient, have to resort to measures of blocking the behavior by associating it with unpleasant stimuli (Cautela, 1967; Rachman & Teasdale, 1969; Lovibond, 1970; Meletsky, 1980).

Aversive conditioning is sometimes employed to overcome certain undesirable behavioral components. Emetic drugs (apomorphine or emetine hydrochloride) were used for years in the treatment of alcholism by conditioning methods. Miller, Dvorak, and Turner (1964) have described a technique of establishing aversion to alcohol through the employment of emetics in a group setting. A unique form of aversive stimulus-paralysis and suppression of respiration through intravenous injection of succinylcholine-chloride dihydrate has been reported by Sanderson et al. (1964). In addition to drugs, electric shock has been employed as an aversive stimulus for a variety of syndromes (McGuire & Vallance, 1964). Needless to say, unless one has an excellent working relationship with a patient, aversive conditioning poses some risk and may play into a patient's masochistic need. And, as noted in the preceding section, punitive conditioning is never employed in isolation by the modern behavior therapist; nowhere is this more evident than in the behavioral treatment of the alcoholic (Franks & Wilson, 1975). Hypnosis may be induced, if desired, and the aversive conditioning, if it is essential to use it, employed in the trance state.

In certain cases self-induced aversive conditioning may be helpful in controlling violently upsetting thoughts or impulses, such as occur in compulsive-obsessive reactions. The patient is supplied with a toy "shocking machine." This may be purchased in a store that sells tricks for the practical joker. It consists of a simulated book with a spicy title or a pack of cards, which, when opened, delivers a shock from a battery within. The shock (buzz) is harmless, yet annoying and even frightening. The patient, with the contraption in the hands, is requested to shut his or her eyes and then bring offensive thoughts to mind. As soon as they appear, the patient is to open the book or cards and keep it open until the thoughts completely disappear. After six to ten trials patients are usually surprised to find themselves unable to bring obsessive ideas to their minds, even when they try to force themselves to do so. The patient may be asked to practice this "exercise in thought control" two times daily, with as many trials as are necessary to eliminate the obsessions or impulses, even when the patient tries to bring them on.

Aversive conditioning may give patients confidence in their ability to occupy themselves with useful rather than self-destructive concerns. Carrying the device in their pocket may become a conditioned reassuring stimulus even though it is not used. Should the patients complain that the shock is too strong, they may reduce its intensity by interposing a piece of facial tissue between their fingers and the box. An alternative pain stimulus may be provided by a rubber band around the wrist that is snapped whenever an aversive measure is required.

A typewritten form such as the following may be given to the patient to be practiced at home:

HUMAN AVOIDANCE OR AVERSIVE CONDITIONING (HOMEWORK)*

You can help yourself to get rid of undesirable, torturesome thoughts and habits after you and the doctor or his associates have agreed that these thoughts or habits are damaging to you. Repeated practice is necessary for most people at least one or more times per day in the beginning and then at gradually decreasing intervals until the thought or habit is gone. The doctor or his associates may help prescribe the intervals and amount of time most helpful to you as well as other helpful ideas.

I. Repetitive, self-damaging thoughts (thought-stopping)**

    a. Close your eyes, hypnotize, or relax yourself and force the repetitive thought or the picture of the undesirable habit to be visualized in your mind for at least 2–3 seconds.

    b. Almost immediately, shout STOP or if this is not possible, think STOP or if this is not possible, think STOP emphatically and promptly give yourself an unpleasant buzz with the buzzer at the same moment. Holding your breath can be used with the buzzer, or something unobtrusive for you, e.g., a clenched fist can be used at the same time in place of "STOP." (It is important that during the pleasant and restful

time after you have stopped the shock, visualize a successful, positive, helpful image or valuable substitute activity.) As soon as these secondary things (breath holding, fist, etc.) work, use buzzer less and less frequently.

Repeat this entire procedure at the same sitting until you can no longer get the thought at that time or until at least 20 satisfactory repetitions have occurred. The entire procedure is to be repeated up to six times per day for 1 to 15 weeks. This will be prescribed in accordance with the severity of your problem and the length of time you have had it. Make a note each day on the back of an appointment card or some other record such as a homework sheet of how frequently and for what number of repetitions you have been using the buzzer, or the word STOP, breath holding, fist, etc. A list of possible pleasant thoughts, activities, assets should be available.

II. Modification

In addition, you can carry the buzzer, or special pen if you prefer, with you and use it whenever you find yourself thinking repetitively or continuing your undesirable habit. If circumstances are such that it is impossible for you to use the buzzer during the larger part of the day, think the word STOP, etc. and imagine the uncomfortable buzz when you find yourself going back to the thought or habit. This will gradually become more successful after actual practice when practice is possible. Unless good success is being maintained with the STOP, breath holding, or other simultaneous gesture, and the pleasant thought or activity substitution, report to doctor.

---

* Reprinted by permission of the author, Dr. Irwin Rothman.
** Modified by Rothman after J. Wolpe.
Note: The buzzer should be held firmly with two fingers and the buzz should not be pleasant. If it seems too much to endure, however, even though it contains only a single pen-light type of battery, a single thickness of Kleenex placed under the fingers will modify the buzz sufficiently.

Another form of aversive control is the withholding of positive reinforcements, such as the loss of certain privileges or the levying of fines, as a consequence of certain behaviors. Even though the effects of aversive control may be limited, it may have to be resorted to where self-injurious behavior cannot be stopped by any other method. For example, I have had referrals of patients with hair plucking that had failed to respond to years of insight therapy. They stopped their self-denuding habit after several sessions with a small shocking machine, which they carried with them thereafter. Obviously, desirable behavior that opposes the noxious habit should be rewarded. A variation of aversive control is "overcorrection," whereby individuals are obliged not only to restore the original situation disrupted by their behavior, but also to engage in other corrective tasks that can prove tedious (Foxx & Azrin, 1972; Webster & Azrin, 1973).

IMAGERY TECHNIQUES

In desensitization through imagery it has been shown that the pairing of fear and relaxation responses reduces the intensity of phobic reactions. Following Wolpe's method of systematic desensitization ("reciprocal inhibition") a hierarchy of fearful situations is constructed (see p. 000). The overcoming of lower level fear images encourages a progressive ascension in the hierarchial scale until the top level fearful situation is mastered in fantasy. A state of muscle relaxation is first produced, along with the image of a relaxing scene. The subject is then asked to visualize the lowest level fearful image. When this is tolerated with comfort, the next higher image is introduced. Should fear arise at any point, the scene is shifted away from the hierarchy to the relaxing image, and the relaxing muscle exercises are repeated. The scene prior to the one that produced fear is then reintroduced and progression up the scale continued. As fear reduction in imagery continues, patients are encouraged to actually expose themselves to graduations of the phobic situation that brought them to therapy. It is assumed, of course, that in the initial "behavioral assessment" a study has been made of the various reinforcement contingencies and that these are considered as part of the total treatment plan. Some patients are unable to learn relaxation procedures, or cannot use imagery successfully, or hesitate to report sensations of anxiety, or are unwilling to practice for weeks without immediate relief (which is sometimes what it takes for a proper response to develop), and hence will not be able to utilize this technique.

The patient may also practice self-imagery for purposes of ego building. The patient can be given instructions that may be easily followed at home. A mimeographed or typed sheet, such as the one that follows, will enable the patient to select that which is best. A small shocking machine or snapping a rubber band on the wrists is used to deliver an umpleasant stimulus in indicated sections of the sheet. A number of useful fantasies for self-imagery are detailed in the book by Kroger and Fezler (1976). See also Chapter 12 (Guided Imagery).

ASSERTIVE TRAINING

Among the most annoying deficits are not being able to stand up for one's rights, rejecting criticism even of a constructive nature, acceding to being coerced or manipulated by others, expressing one's desires and preferences only with guilt or embarrassment, and countenancing rejection as a sign of being worthless and debased. These deficits are usually associated with a devalued self-image and a hypertrophied and punitive conscience. Related as they are to such basic personality distortions, it is difficult to see how they can be altered without self-understanding.

A way of facilitating self-understanding, important to enduring change, is to bring patients to awareness of their anxieties, evasions, and other defenses through plunging them into situations where they must assert themselves. Whether thinking and acting in ways consonant with a positive self-concept can in themselves correct a devalued self-image is debatable, although some therapists assume "that if a patient behaves and thinks in a manner indicating a positive self concept, he has, in fact, acquired one" (Seligman, 1979). In my opinion, some cognitive alteration is essential.

A format that is often used for assertiveness training is a time-limited group of eight to ten patients led by a man/woman therapist team. A questionnaire rating reactions to certain situations may be found helpful (Gambrill & Richey, 1975). Patients are taught to differentiate acting assertive (expressing one's rights) from acting aggressive (putting others down). Discussions

IMPROVING HUMAN SELF-IMAGES RAPIDLY*
(some newer and some experimental methods)

INTRODUCTION: You and the doctor or his associates have agreed that a less self-critical self-image of yourself is desirable; or a self-concept in which you feel less inferior and more self-confident, or less childlike, more active at finding a new job—remedying a situation—doing more housework—getting more exercise—or more comfortable physical and social activity—or some other changes in your innermost self-concept are necessary or desirable.

Method I: Ego Building . Under self-hypnosis or relaxation leave yourself with the self-image of pleasant feelings and times in your life you, and possibly others, thought you were at least somewhat successful. Tell yourself, "I promise to act in accordance with this image."

Method II: A gradual stepladder of improved self-images can be used under self-hypnosis or relaxation, and you can move up this imaginary ladder of improved self-images until you feel a

tinge of anxiety. Step down to the last comfortable self-image you could get. As soon as possible, act in daily life according to this improved image—as if it is now you.

Method III: Visualize your "lazy" or passive self-image as perhaps you have looked after avoiding some important work—a picture that we have agreed should be changed. After imagining this picture for 2–3 seconds, give yourself a buzz, usually until the image stops. Repeat as prescribed, usually for about 20 pictures at a sitting, with at least daily repetition. Substitute an image of a time when you were slightly more pleased with yourself each time you relax from the buzz.

Method IV: This can be used if you have been taught self-hypnosis with body imagery changes. (a) Hypnotize yourself to picture how some of your character (expressed as face and body) looks to you. Usually the doctor or his associates will have agreed with you on a given signal or word for this unconscious image to appear clearly. If you find difficulty in separating "bad mother or bad father" (or other image previously discussed with the therapist) from your image, i.e., they stick, then try using the buzzer to break up the fusion and leave you with an independent self-image, or with "good" mother and father's love. (b) Then you may attempt to modify by fusing your image with someone who has, as you and your therapist have agreed, some desirable traits you'd gradually like to work toward in a realistic fashion. (c) If the old image is stubborn in leaving, or fusing with the image you and your therapist have agreed upon, use the buzzer as described in Method III and #1 under AVERSIVE CONDITIONING to modify the old image by buzzing it and thereby speeding up the desired fused image. Report changes to your therapist, and keep your goals practical and within easy steps forward.

NOTE: It is most important that you keep careful records of frequency of use, and just what happens with the images, and discuss this with the therapist. These methods are not the same as daydreaming. Homework time is limited to approved and improved images as prescribed and should be tried out in reality.

* Reprinted by permission of the author, Dr. Irwin Rothman.

involve self-assessment of assertiveness by the group members. Modest goals are then set for each at first. The actual training procedures include such techniques as behavior rehearsal, role-playing, imagery and cognitive behavior therapy (relabeling certain acts), etc. (Smith, MJ, 1975). Homework is assigned with the object of increasing assertive responses and lowering nonassertive ones. A diary is kept of experiences. Modeling by the therapist is often employed. Patients set up problem situations in which there is practice in asking for a favor, saying "no" to an unreasonable request, making a date with a person of the opposite sex, etc. The ability to accept rejection without anger, shame, or feelings of being inferior is developed by role-playing and discussion of feelings.

Coincident with such assertive performances, analytically trained therapists may explore individually or in a group format each individual's underlying conflicts that have been responsible for and that are sustaining the devalued self-image. This combination of behavioral and dynamic therapy is offered for the purpose of giving the patient the best opportunity for correcting problems in assertiveness on a permanent level. Dynamic therapy alone over a long-term period may get at the core of the responsible personality distortions, but the treatment may bog down when, after insight is gained, the patients resist putting their insights into action. Starting off with assertive training, on the other hand, almost immediately puts the patients in a position where they are confronted by their anxiety and the defenses that prevent them from resolving their problem. They have to deal with these as realities, not as theories.

It is interesting that in the face of this confrontation and in breaking through the resistance by practicing assertive exercises, many patients acquire insight into the dynamics of their problem. A dynamically oriented therapist will be able to expedite insight by examining and interpreting the patient's dreams, behavioral acting-out, and transference reactions. Past sources of trouble and early conflicts may surface; by working on these the therapist may connect them with the patient's current personality problems and more pointedly with the self-image pathology that expresses itself in symptoms. Even where the therapist is not dynamically oriented, some patients will put the pieces together by themselves.

Generally, in assertiveness training the patient is first taught to distinguish between assertiveness and aggressiveness. Too often they are considered identical. Assertiveness implies the need to stand up for one's rights and to refuse to relinquish one's rights. Aggression means a violation of another person's rights.

The ideal setting for assertive training is a group, although where a group is not available individual sessions can be productive. Patients keep a diary in which they record situations where they wanted or needed to act assertively, or to deny a request they felt was unreasonable, along with a notation of their feelings, their actual behavior, and their reactions to their behavior. A hierarchy of situations is constructed on paper, ranging from low level situations that are slightly difficult to handle to high level situations that the patient has found it impossible to manage. In role-playing one starts with low level situations, gradually working up to high level ones as mastery progresses. Some therapists advise the patient's utilizing a scale (*Subjective Units of Distress Scale*—SUDS) developed by Wolpe and Lazarus (1966) for record-keeping and role-playing. Other therapists employ biofeedback (EMG) to coordinate the items on the SUDS scale with subjective feelings of tension.

After role-playing promotes some confidence, the patients are encouraged to attempt low level assertive tasks in life itself, such as requesting things from people that are not too difficult for them to give. Should failure occur, the patients are told they are not yet ready for the assignment rather than that they failed at it. Discussions of the tasks and reactions are carried on in the group, who cheer successes but do not castigate the patient for failures. Videotape feedback can be helpful in providing the patients with data on visible defenses. Progressively more demanding requests are encouraged until the patients gain confidence in asserting themselves without hesitation. A variety of other programs to enhance assertiveness may be set up, such as those of Eisler et al. (1973b; 1974), Hersen et al. (1973a, b), Whiteley & Flowers, 1977), Flowers & Booraem (1980).

The following outline, modified after J. Wolpe and prepared by I. Rothman and M.L. Carroll, provides examples of practice exercises in assertiveness:

SELF-DESENSITIZATION OR ANXIETY REDUCTION TECHNIQUES IN MAN*

A.   Frequently you will be given a choice of self-relaxation or self-hypnotic techniques described in a booklet or in instructions given to you by the doctor. Practice the method you choose. Other types of training for self-help may also be shown you.

B.   Make a written stepladder of situations which disturb you or are problems to you. Arrange these in order from the most disturbing to the least, or from least to most if you prefer. Please provide a clear copy of your stepladder for the doctor.

C.   During your 70% successful relaxation periods, visualize dramatically (get a vivid mental picture of) yourself successfully handling the stiuations (going up your stepladder) from the least to slightly disturbing until you feel slightly tense, then stop. Relax until you are again at ease. This procedure should be done daily, usu-

ally for not more than 10 minutes at bedtime, or some other convenient time. This visualization should be about things you actually want and intend to do and not just daydreaming. Make it a practice to try the things you have successfully pictured yourself doing whenever possible. After a few days, longer or more frequent practice periods or several separate stepladders may be prescribed.

D.   Try to record where you are on the list daily. The faithfulness with which you practice daily visualization is an indication of how much your healthy self is willing to cooperate in the treatment against your self-destructive side. If your mind wanders from successful picturing, repeat the last successful picture. Remember that the mind can only concentrate on one thing at a time, although it may skip quickly. Bring back the thought you wish to work with for at least 2–3 seconds at a time. Your visualization will improve with practice. Stop when you feel anxiety at the same step on the stepladder more than three times, go back to a comfortable relaxation, and later add extra smaller steps between the worrisome ones.

E. The situations listed below are merely suggestions of areas which <u>may</u> be problems to you and how to handle them with this method. If any of the examples <u>do</u> apply to you, include them in your own stepladder (s), along with any other problem areas <u>not</u> listed here. Each area can be divided into <u>as many as 20 or more gradual steps</u> to visualize <u>and to conquer in actuality. If you</u> do not experience any anxiety while first visualizing situations which you find much too difficult to accomplish in real daily life, consult the doctor or his associates concerning this.

EXAMPLES:

(The first example is broken down to give you an idea of how to place situations on your own list.)

I.   ASSERTION EXAMPLES:

Asserting yourself with other people without guilt, listing different types of people in order of decreasing difficulty from the boss (possible #1) to the office boy (possible #9) to the janitor (possible #15). This is a most important category for people with depression, strong self-damaging tendencies, and anxieties in dealing with other people.

Picture yourself:

(a) expressing affection openly for (1) pets, (2) children, (3) immediate family, (4) more distant relatives, (5) friends, (6) acquaintances—possibly in that order of difficulty for you.

(b) being assertive with your family, clerks, waitresses, policemen, and authority figures in the degree and order of difficulty fitting you.

(c) Discussing topics which are of interest to you with your family, other relatives, and close friends.

(d) Making an effort and succeeding in discussing their interests.

(e) Stating your wishes without guilt to family, relatives, and close friends.

(f) Expressing disagreement without guilt to family, friends, other relatives.

(g) Following the same steps with casual friends and acquaintances.

(h) Requesting firmly that clerks, janitors, or any subordinates do their jobs promptly and properly.

(i) Expressing disagreement or your feeling of annoyance with those who do not fulfill their duties correctly.

(j) Talking about your job with fellow workers or firmly requesting that they do their share of any mutual job.

(k) Giving a report and expressing disagreement if necessary with your immediate superior in a tactful way.

(l) Giving a report and expressing disagreement if necessary to the highest superior with whom you must deal in a tactful way.

Other problem areas which can be broken down may include:

II.   FEAR OF CRITICISM, REJECTION, DISAPPROVAL, OR HEALTHY DISAGREEMENT:

(1) Successfully facing sarcasm from family, friends, or associates

(2) Successfully facing direct disapproval or criticism from family, friends, or associates

(3) Successfully arguing and being unafraid of arguments

(4) Successfully facing feelings of being excluded by others

(5) Successfully facing being ignored or reprimanded

(6) Successfully dealing with persons you feel dislike you, etc

III.   MEDICAL SYMPTOMS: Symptoms you have been told have no medical importance: getting busy with activities and ignoring symptoms such as rapid heartbeat, buzzing in ears, constant or intermittent pain from rheumatism, or similar symptoms if you know that they are not medically important. Arrange a stepladder of increasing time for enduring them and carrying on despite them.

IV.   STAGE FRIGHT: successfully speaking to a group. Perhaps start with an empty room and gradually increase the number of people present to 100.

V.   SOCIAL FRIGHT: enjoying entertaining and parties of increasing size from one friendly couple to any number of relative strangers.

VI.   CROWDS: At ease in crowds of increasing

size (elevators, trains, cramped quarters, open spaces, etc.).

VII. JOB SEEKING: Being at ease in applying for a job, starting with one you do not really want. Actually having several interviews before taking a job.

VIII. OPPOSITE SEX: Being at ease with members of the opposite sex, starting with someone unimportant to you and increasing periods of time and difficulty.

IX. DECISION MAKING: Being at ease in making your own decisions, without regrets and afterthought. Start with small decisions and increase importance.

* Reprinted by permission of the authors, Dr. I. Rothman and M. L. Carroll.

MODELING

Modeling can serve as a valuable means of social learning and personality development (Perry & Furukawa, 1980). The process involves both observational and performance aspects, theories of which have been adequately explicated in the literature (Bandura, 1977). By acting as a model, the therapist strives to provide cues for the patient that will help develop new behavioral skills, halt aberrant attitudes, and aid in problem-solving (Bandura, 1969). Both symbolic modeling (use of videotapes, films, audiotapes, written scripts) and live modeling (the therapist performing a certain exemplary behavior like facing a phobic situation) may be employed. Multiple models have an advantage over single models since the opportunities for identification are greater. For example, a child fearful of dogs, observing other children petting a puppy may be induced to experiment with approach behaviors.

To reduce anxiety that may be aroused in the patient, relaxation exercises can be used in advance of the modeling activity. Thus, if patients have a great fear of having their blood pressure taken, the therapist may initially utilize systematic desensitization with the patients to calm them down, demonstrating the use of the blood pressure apparatus on himself or herself. Priming the patient by explaining what the patient will see in the modeling activity is also useful. Once the patient executes the modeled behavior, active rehearsal of the behavior along with reinforcements (comments of approval, material rewards) will tend to establish it more firmly.

Graded participant modeling consists of the setting up of a hierarchy of activities related to a feared object or situation. For example in a phobia of airplanes, flying is at the top of the list, and calling the airline for information about a special flight at the bottom. In between are driving to the airport, going to the counter to talk to the attendant, sitting in the waiting room, walking to the gates, watching planes landing and taking off. The therapist may model the behavior for all of these gradients, then repeat the least anxiety provoking and ask the patient to execute this. As anxiety is completely resolved, the patient is enjoined to try progressively difficult tasks until actual flying occurs.

New behaviors must of course be transferred by the patients to the settings in which they live, work and function, and here the patients may not get the same reactions and reinforcements they receive in the training settings. Preparing the patients for the trials of performance generalization and reviewing with them their experiences in the transfer of learning to different settings are an integral part of the training process.

Recommended readings that give examples of the actual modeling process itself are: Bandura et al. (1969) in relation to overcoming phobias; Melamed and Siegel (1975) in anxiety reduction for children facing hospitalization and surgery; Csapo (1972) for correcting disturbed classroom behavior in withdrawn or disturbed children; Perry and Cerreto (1977) for training of living skills in mentally retarded persons; Hingtgen et al. (1967) for working with autistic children; Gutride et al. (1974) for helping psychotic patients reinstate adaptive behaviors; Sarason and Ganzer (1973) for rehabilitating juvenile delinquents; and Reeder and Kunce (1976) for preparing heroin addicts for adjustment following treatment. Modeling may also be used in professional training programs for counselors and therapists, e.g., to develop greater capacities for empathy (Perry, 1975).

COGNITIVE BEHAVIOR THERAPY

Recognizing that complex human behavior cannot be explained solely by conditioning paradigms, behaviorists since 1970 have turned to higher level processes, exploring what they have called "cognitive behavior therapy." As we might expect, different authorities have experimented with and developed innovative ways of implementing this new dimension. For example, some have focused on illogical thought patterns that in the past have forced the patient to draw false inferences from certain events, to overgeneralize from solitary incidents, and to fail to correct distortions even though life experience has pointed to the falsity of their assumptions (Beck, AT, 1976). Others have advocated more active training procedures, working with patients toward employing positive, constructive self-statements along with practicing relaxation techniques (Meichenbaum, 1977). Still others continue to use Ellis' (1962) technique of actively presenting rational solutions to replace the patient's maladaptive ones ("rational emotional imagery").

Instead of attempting to win patients over toward adopting a new philosophy toward life, or different attitudes toward themselves and others, as in persuasion (q.v.) the patients are given daily relearning exercises to change their thinking habits toward rational goals that they are trying to achieve. First, the patients are trained for several sessions in rational self-analysis to get at the basis of their problem. Next they are enjoined to practice rational emotive imagery for a minimum of 3 10-minute periods each day during which the patients see themselves acting in constructive ways in relation to the upsetting or challenging situations in their lives (Maultsby, 1970).

Social learning precepts are prominently employed in training procedures with the object of rational restructuring of thought processes; of altering mental sets in line with optimistic rather than pessimistic expectations; of liberating oneself from the tyranny of conventional beliefs; of abandoning the notion that one has always to be right, loved, perfect, important, and happy; and of relinquishing the idea that one's past indelibly stamps out one's destiny.

Patients are aided in acquiring coping skills by (1) putting themselves into challenging or upsetting situations in fantasy and verbalizing their feelings, and (2) role-playing constructive solutions. There is accumulating experimental evidence that these techniques help to reduce anxiety and to change attitudes that create pathologic feelings and behavior. Skill in problem-solving is encouraged by showing the patient that attitudes, positive or negative, will definitely influence the outcomes; that it is essential to define and formulate the problem at hand for which a solution is needed; that alternative approaches should be designed in the event a chosen solution proves to be inadvisable; that a definite decision of a course of action must be made; and that verification of the validity of this choice in terms of achievement of set goals must finalize the process (Goldfried & Davison, 1976).

An example of how cognitive therapy is executed is provided by the treatment of depressive disorders. The cognitive theory of depression assumes that a cognitive triad exists (Beck & Young, 1985). Depressed patients have a starkly negative view of themselves, conceiving of themselves as worthless, unlovable, and deficient. They see the environment as overwhelming and believe they cannot cope with the pressures around them. They regard the future as hopeless. Events are distorted and twisted through illogical thinking to confirm these apprehensions with unjustifiable arbitrary inferences, overgeneralization, selective obstruction, and magnification. Early negative schemas, evolved during early childhood and operative outside of awareness, act as predisposing factors and are activated by later life events. These cognitive distortions always contribute to depression with its physiological effects.

Cognitive therapy, which may be done on an individual or couples format, draws upon a number of techniques to change depressive thinking. The most difficult patients for either kind of format are severe endogenous depressions, bipolar depressions, organic brain syndromes, psychotic depression, schizoaffective disorders, and borderline personalities. Neurotic and mild endogenous depressions do best. But even in the severer depressions, cognitive therapy can be useful in combination with pharmacotherapy, milieu therapy, and supportive therapy. Apart from the usual empathic qualities essential in a therapist, considerable skill is needed along with the ability to communicate confidence and hopefulness. Goals, the specific problems to be focused on, and the agenda for each session are set collaboratively. Since patients may not understand a therapist's formulations yet avow that they do out of a need to please, the therapist should encourage feedback to make sure the meaning of the communications has been grasped. At the end of each session the therapist summarizes what has been done and asks the patient to write down the main points of the discussion. Homework assignments are important in-

cluding readings, self-relaxation, and diversionary activities.

Cognitive techniques involve a search for automatic thoughts and maladaptive assumptions through questioning, imagery, and role playing. Once an automatic thought is elicited in the form of interpretations of an event, an analysis of the thought is jointly embarked on to test its validity. Here the patient's use of words may come up for study. Rectification of the habit of self-accusation necessitates reattribution of blame. Alternative solutions are encouraged, maladaptive assumptions are challenged. Faulty beliefs are analyzed. Behavioral techniques are utilized especially when a patient is highly passive and withdrawn. These include activities to improve mastery and enhance pleasure, training in self-reliance and assertiveness, role playing, and diversion techniques.

Some cognitive therapists utilize psychological inventories as part of the assessment procedure. Among these are the Beck Depression Inventory (BDI) that scores the degree of depression, the Young Loneliness Inventory Score (Young, 1982) that reveals the degree of distress due to lack of intimate ties, and other tests. Interviewing is conducting mainly by a therapist focussing on the most distressing problem that concerns the patient and probing the "automatic thoughts" through questioning in order to understand the patient's perspective. A good area to explore at first is the inactivity and withdrawal that highlight and characterize depressive symptomology. Instead of criticizing, blaming, condemning, and reassuring the patient, the therapist continues to enjoin the patient to examine the immediate assumptions ("collaborative empiricist"). The therapist may ask the patient to select a small problem to work on together. Any suggested activity the patient brings up that can possibly bring the patient out of preoccupation with hopelessness is selected for "graded tasks" in the form of questions to break down resistance to following through with its execution. The patient may be asked to write out an activity schedule for the week. Some therapists routinely have their patients fill out the Beck Depressive Interview before each session so that progress can be monitored. Negative thoughts are chosen for questioning and probing of ways of coping with these and finding constructive alternatives. The therapist is alerted for dominant schema that control the patient's attitudes and relationships. Periodically, summaries are given to the patient of the themes that may be operating in the automatic thoughts. If the patient is planning a major decision, postponement may be recommended until a more realistic perspective is obtained.

Obviously, as one works with a patient character patterns will display themselves as reflected in the relationship to the therapist and to the therapeutic process itself. Distortions in the way the patient appraises things are clarified with the hope that through questioning and a "guided discovery" approach there will be a more realistic appraisal ("reattribution"). Continuing homework assignments may include keeping a daily record of dysfunctional thoughts by listing situations that lead to unpleasant thoughts and the stream of automatic daydreams or recollections that produce unpleasant emotions. A diary or *Weekly Activity Schedule* may also be kept to list and grade the degree of instances of mastery and pleasure. In therapy, maladaptive assumptions are continuously explored especially "in the context of a concrete event" with the object of replacing automatic thoughts with rational thoughts. A technique *Point Counterpoint* is sometimes utilized to help such a replacement. Here in role playing, the therapist plays the devil's advocate by expressing the patient's own negative thinking while the patient defends a more rational stance. Hopefully, underlying destructive assumptions will be undermined with practice in and out of therapy.

Other strategies may be devised to test the validity of one's assumptions that lead to depressive thinking and feeling. Patients are enjoined to test other hypotheses on which their assumptions, early schemas, and automatic thoughts are based. In vivo experiments within the patient's life situation are set up to test habitual beliefs and, during therapy, successes and failures are reviewed. Self-help homework assignments aid the patient in facing problems more realistically, and correcting thinking patterns that can lead to resolution of depression and to adaptive behavior.

CONTINGENCY CONTRACTING

Some behavior therapists try to direct the patient toward productive change through reinforcements in *contingency contracting*. It is agreed that the execution of desired behaviors (socialization, assertiveness, dietary abstinence, etc.) will result in certain positive rewards. The contract is drawn up between the patient and the therapist, or in couples therapy between the two partners. The selection of appropriate reinforcements may be aided by use of a *Reinforcement Survey Schedule* (Cautela & Kastenbaum, 1967). The contract is time-limited and specifies the behavior patients are to perform (e.g., smoking control, weight loss, assertive behaviors, etc.) and the rewards they are to receive for such behavior. The patients collect data in writing on the daily frequency of such behaviors and their reactions to their execution. The rewards must be reasonable, but must be sufficiently intense and meaningful for the patients to compensate them for whatever deprivations they undergo in performance of assigned tasks. The patients, for example, must feel that they are attaining a previously denied or absent prize and that they have earned it through their own efforts. If money is the reward, paid by a third party, this should not be accumulated but should be spent as soon as possible since saving may dilute the effort put into performance. Thus, a child who is rewarded with money for certain socializing behaviors should not be requested to save the money for college. Rewards to adults may consist of vacations, trips, and various kinds of entertainment. Sometimes when patients reward themselves with money, they deposit money with the therapist, who then distributes it in accordance with a patient's compliance with the contract. In contracts between couples (contingency or exchange contracts), the desired behaviors on the part of one member are rewarded with specified behaviors on the part of the other member.

Do sought-for behaviors continue after the contract ends? The claim made by behavior therapists is that in well-conducted therapies the patient begins to enjoy the behaviors for their own sake and for what they do to self-image and self-respect.

A GENERAL OUTLINE OF BEHAVIOR THERAPY PRACTICE

There are many designs for the practice of behavioral modification. One that I have found useful follows:

1. Ask patients which behaviors they wish to strengthen and which they wish to diminish or extinguish.
2. Find out the situations under which undesirable traits or symptoms lessen or increase. Do not be concerned with explaining why the problem developed except insofar as the positive and aversive reinforcements that maintain it can be detected.
3. Select jointly with the patient (on the basis of the patient's priorities) which behaviors or reactions are to be altered first, leaning toward those that, in your opinion, are most modifiable.
4. Explore the degree of motivation of the patient for therapy, the conse-

quences of present demeanor and the rewards anticipated from newly developed behavior. Challenge and work on the patient's motivation until it is certain that the patient unequivocally wishes to change for himself or herself and not to please others.

5. Examine in depth the behavioral constellation to be altered or strengthened, going into past history to determine the reinforcements that have maintained the problem. Can patients clearly define what it is that they desire to change? Do they accept your formulation of the problem? If not, you, the therapist, assume an educational role to teach the patient the full implications and complete description of the behaviors that are appropriate for the desired change. Do patients clearly understand what is expected of them?
6. Identify the rewards (reinforcers) if any that are to be employed making sure that they have value for the patient. These reinforcers are made contingent on the desired behavior. A contract—verbal or, better, written— is drawn stating what is expected of the patient and the rewards for maintenance of the contract. The contract time should be made short, say a few days, with the idea of renewing the contract at the end of the contract time.

Sometimes contingency contracting is utilized, the patient and therapist deciding mutually not only on the kind of reinforcements that the patient is to receive on controlling problem behaviors or substituting constructive alternatives, but also the penalties to be imposed, if any, for perpetuation of disturbed behaviors. We, the therapists, may also impose penalties on ourselves should we not live up to our contract (appearing late for appointments, missing appointments, etc.), for example, reducing or cancelling fees. Token reinforcement systems may be set up, the patients receiving tokens for constructive behavior that they can exchange for luxuries, privileges, etc. (Ayllon & Azrin, 1968; O'Leary & Drabman, 1971). Token economies have been found to work well in some institutions and classrooms (Paul & Lentz, 1977).

7. Work out a planned schedule with patients to begin to approach their new behaviors under the least traumatic circumstances possible. If interpersonal relations are involved in the plan, the least challenging individuals are selected so that the patient may be minimally uncomfortable. In the shaping of a difficult behavior, the start should strive for minimal gains and immediate reinforcements, with the object of approximating the desired change, more and more reinforcements being given step by step as changes progress.

8. Ask the patient to keep a diary that lists each day the frequencies of new behaviors practiced. Praise is proferred for each success, but no criticism is given for failure. If no progress occurs, explore with the patient the reasons for failure. Encourage the patient to try again and make suggestions as to new assignments that the patient is prepared to execute. Explore attitudes, beliefs, systems and other cognitions that may be acting as resistances to progress.

Behavior modeling by the therapist and role playing are introduced when necessary. If anxiety prevents the patient from following through on behavioral assignments, systematic desensitization may be tried and/or a mild tranquilizer suggested such as Xanax for a brief period of time only, recognizing its addictive potential. At each session the patient is given homework to expand on skills.

9. Where it is obvious that the patient is confused in acting in a constructive way, try behavior rehearsal (Casey, GA, 1973).

Here the therapist rehearses the patient in what to say and how to say it, covering a broad zone of interpersonal behavior, with both real and fantasied authorities and peer figures. The gestures to make, the words to say, the facial expressions to exhibit are all acted out. The rehearsal will bring out feelings in the patient that will need discussion. Sometimes it is helpful to make a recording (audio and video if available) to play responses back for the patient after each rehearsal. The therapist advantageously can play dual roles: first, that of the individual with whom the patient cannot seem to deal with in real life, and then, by changing chairs with the patient (role reversal), that of the patient with appropriate comments and gestures to indicate preferred reactions (modeling) while the patient is asked to put himself or herself in the position of the adversary. The patient may need constant or periodic coaching while this role playing goes on.

10. Individual sessions may later be complimented with family and group sessions where these are deemed helpful.

In family therapy sessions the attendant members are apprised of the circumstances that create and maintain behavioral difficulties. Appropriate ways of reacting with each other are suggested. Group sessions are usually conducted with the object of allowing each member about 10 minutes of time to describe what each has accomplished since the last session and the reactions. The members then make suggestions to each other as to how difficulties may be overcome or progress increased.

11. Should a relapse occur, the best way to manage it is not to reward it with too much attention. Ignoring the re-

lapse must be followed by adequate reinforcement when improvement resumes. Punishment should assiduously be avoided.

12. In the event resistance is obdurate and no progress occurs, explore frankly and openly the relationship with the patient. You as the therapist may very well look into your own feelings about the patient (countertransference) to see if you can perceive deleterious effects on the relationship.

There is, in my opinion, no reason why behavioral therapy cannot be practiced in a dynamic framework, although this may horrify some behavioral purists. Often dreams will reveal the nature of the resistance more readily than any other communication. Once the resistance is detected and explored, clarification or interpretation may turn the tide toward success in the behavioral effort.

A great deal of ingenuity is required to set up the design that will govern behavior therapy in a particular case. The treatment undergoes continued modifications in line with the observed behavioral change. Wide differences exist in the susceptibility of subjects to conditioning. However, the greater the quantum of anxiety, the more easily are conditioned responses established and the more difficult are these to extinguish. Generalized anxiety does not respond too well to behavior therapy unless it is possible to differentiate the conditioned stimuli that sponsor anxiety. It may be possible to break down anxiety or disturbed behavior into a number of phobic hierarchies and to deal with each hierarchy as a separate unit.

52
Techniques in Group, Family, and Marital Therapies

Group psychotherapy is a valuable and, in some cases, indispensible treatment method. Its historical development and uses in supportive (see page 140), reeducative (see page 190), and reconstructive (see page 318) approaches have been amply delineated and some of the important bibliography listed in the respective chapters. Group therapy may be employed both as an adjunctive aid to individual psychotherapy and as a treatment modality in its own right. There are some therapists who claim that not only are the results they obtain with groups equivalent to those of individual treatment, but in many cases even superior to it. Consequently, they dispense with individual therapy, except as an adjunct to a group approach. Other therapists, not so skilled in its use, tend to depreciate the effect and "depth" of group treatment. Among experienced therapists there is a feeling that combined or conjoint group and individual therapy is the treatment of choice. Problems show up in a group setting that never become apparent in a dyadic therapeutic relationship.

Evolving in a group are a number of processes that are intimately bound up with the outcome. Among the most important are the developing group cohesiveness and mutual assistance. What one finds evolving in the group are manifestations of empathy, support, challenge, confrontation, and interpretation; availability of identification models; opportunities for introducing projective identifications; investigative explorations; and a joint sharing of problems.

Needless to say, the specific way that the group is employed; its composition; the degree of activity or passivity of the therapist; the extent of the therapist's directiveness, maneuvers, and kinds of participation; the pursuits sanctioned within and outside the group; and the nature of interpretations will vary with the skill, experience, theoretical bias, and personality of the therapist. For example, some therapists assume an almost completely detached attitude on the assumption that this will dredge up the resentments of the group members, in the wake of which basic inner conflicts will be exposed. Other therapists cast anonymity to the winds and virtually become participating patients in the group, acting-out as enthusiastically as any other member. Both methods in the opinion of their sponsors are promoted as the "best" and even "only way" to do group therapy. Actually, there is no "best" group method; this will vary with the predilections of the therapist. After blundering through a number of sessions, each therapist will settle down to a procedure that works best for him or her.

Group therapy may be utilized (1) independently, during which both intrapsychic and interpersonal operations are considered; (2) in combination with individual therapy conducted by the same therapist ("combined therapy")—individual sessions deal with the patient's resistances, transferential responses to the therapist, and primary separation anxiety, while group sessions focus chiefly on interpersonal phenomena; (3) in conjunction with individual therapy conducted by another therapist ("conjoint therapy"); and (4) as leaderless groups particularly after formal group therapy has ended (Kline, 1975).

Meetings in independent, combined, conjoint therapy may take place one or two times weekly and, in institutional settings, even daily. They may be supplemented with regularly scheduled meetings that are not attended by the therapist ("coordinated meetings")—the members may congregate before a regular session ("premeetings"), after a regular session ("postmeetings"), or at other times at specially designated places ("alternate meetings"). Coordinated meetings enable patients to discuss their feelings about the therapist more freely. They are generally less formal and more spontaneous than regular meetings. Acting-out is more than a casual possibility here, which may or may not prove to be beneficial to the patient. ("Closed groups" maintain a constant membership although new members may be added for special reasons. "Open groups" operate continuously with new members being added as regular members complete therapy and leave the group.)

Treatment in group therapy may be "therapist-centered," in which therapists take a directive and more authoritarian role, moderating member-to-member communication, presenting interpretations, and limiting the patients' intragroup and extra-group activities ("triangular communication"). It may be "group-centered," in which the group operates as the primary authority, therapists functioning in a kind of consultative role. Here peer (sibling) and authority (parental) relationships are considered equally important; rotating leadership is encouraged; there is no interference with the relationships between patients ("circular communication"), which are constantly being broken, restored, and reorganized, the therapists controlling their anxiety about neurotic alliances; or "authority-denying" ("horizontal communication") may occur in which the therapists are on an equal plane with the patients, a structured relationship between therapists and patients being considered limiting to growth. In the latter case emotional interactions are considered most important; direct experience in the group is encouraged, therapists presenting their own problems to the group ("The group can grow if I grow with them.").

The group therapist, regardless of orientation, must be a good leader, requiring skills above and beyond those of a therapist.

How a therapist conducts a group will be determined

1. By the goals that the therapist sets—supportive, reeducative, or reconstructive.
2. By the constituent members—alcoholics, drug addicts, psychotics, stutterers, delinquents, psychoneurotics, character disorders, patients with heterogeneous problems.
3. By the therapist's training—group dynamics, rehabilitation, behavior therapy, cognitive therapy, existential therapy, psychodrama, psychoanalytically oriented psychotherapy, psychoanalysis.
4. By the therapist's personal ambitions

and needs—characterologic and countertransferential.

INFLUENCES OF THE GROUP ON THE INDIVIDUAL

When people gather together in a group, phenomena are mobilized that may have an influence on each individual. One of the effects is an immediate impression of strangeness and embarrassment. This soon gives way to a realization that others present are not too different from oneself in problems, weaknesses, and ways of relating. This encourages one to express oneself openly. The person soon discovers that the group fosters free expression of feelings or attitudes on any subject. There are no social taboos on content usually avoided in everyday interactions. The ability to open up varied forbidden topics, and the recognition that fellow members harbor the same fears and doubts, can be reassuring. Apart from the emotional catharsis experienced, the individual finds that problems can be shared with others without rejection or ridicule. Self-esteem and self-confidence are thereby enhanced. The individual begins to realize that he or she is not a reprehensible person deserving of blame or repudiation. The usual drives through which one achieves status and prestige may receive no sanction in the group. Indeed, they may be dealt with harshly or analyzed in terms of their neurotic components.

Humans are group creatures constantly looking to others for acceptance and validation of their own ideas. One of the most powerful molding influences in any group is the impact of group standards and values. These can have a markedly transforming influence on the personal persuasions by which individuals customarily govern themselves. A gradual incorporation of group convictions and judgments in a cohesive and developed group tends to neutralize self-oriented neurotic needs. The presence of the therapist acts as a safeguard against prevailing group values that are inappropriate. There is some validity in the belief that patients in a group may reinforce each other's rational reactions. This is because they collectively make up the norm from which they individually deviate. This is particularly true in a therapeutic group presided over by a therapist with healthy values; it is not so true in a group left to its own destiny, which so often will be diverted and taken over by a charismatic and power-driven member with qualities of leadership.

Group patterns evolve related to the roles members assume and the ways they perceive themselves; how and when they take over leadership; the specific motives assigned to them by other members; and the existing defensive maneuvers, such as competitiveness, struggles for control, dominance, submissiveness, ingratiation, masochistic devices, aggressiveness, and violence. The fluctuating group interaction is influenced by levels of tension that affect participation, the sharing of ideas, and decision making. Arguments, the taking over of a session by a monopolizer, coming late, absenteeism, and the formation of subgroup clusters manifesting special likings and dislikings raise tensions that stimulate corrective action; however, if tension is too high, it will paralyze action. Extremes of harmony and congeniality will also tend to subdue activity.

A successful solution to an interpersonal problem enables the individual better to extend his success to relationships with people outside the group. It is to be expected that reactions to different members will selectively indulge a full range of prejudices. Displays of awe, infatuation, disgust, anger, hate, and sexual interest may be manifested toward members identified as archaic or vulgar or idealized models. Whereas these feelings are controlled and verbalizations related to them suppressed or repressed in the usual group setting; they are encouraged and even rewarded in the therapeutic group by approval from the therapist. The reactions of the person with whom one is immediately entangled presents opportunities to examine the reasonableness or unreasonableness of one's responses. The individual gradually learns to accept criticism and aggression without falling apart. This is a most crucial lesson; indeed soon recognized is the fact that aggression and criticism can be either proper or unjustified and that one can differentiate the two and manage responses accordingly.

The effect of interpretations from other group members may be striking. The individual begins to distinguish prejudiced opinions from factual ones, and may then generalize tolerance to the world at large. The fear of becoming violent and in turn being subject to physical attack and humiliation lessen. The group judgment is a moving force that cannot be resisted. Where a number of members share an opinion about an individual or behavior, the effect may be more intense than an interpretation by the therapist. As one patient put it: "If a person in a group calls you a horse, you have a right to be indignant. If a second person in the group calls you a horse, you have a right to be insulted. If a third person in a group calls you a horse, you better look into yourself to see if you are acting like a horse." The group strengthens the individual's ability to express feelings toward the therapist, whether rational or irrational; one may be unable to do this during individual therapy.

One of the most important consequences of being in a group geared toward reconstructive goals is learning how emotional processes operate by observing how other members talk about and solve their problems. Dynamic thinking soon becomes a dominant mode in the group. Immediate symptoms are related to basic adaptational patterns. As these are traced to destructive past conditionings, resistance and transference may be mobilized and explored. In this way the patient begins to think more dynamically about himself or herself, the genetic origins of patterns, their manifestations in his or her present life, and the defensive maneuvers they inspire. Awareness of inner psychological operations is also sharpened through emotional involvements with other group members, through one's own spontaneous discoveries, and through interpretations from fellow members and the therapist. Instead of withdrawing, as in a usual life situation, the patient is encouraged to hold his or her ground and to express and analyze feelings and defenses. It is here that a psychotherapist trained in reconstructive therapy can make the greatest impact on the patient.

ADVANTAGES OF GROUP VERSUS INDIVIDUAL THERAPY

Group therapy has certain advantages over individual treatment. It is capable of registering deep impressions by virtue of the fact that the patient is exposed to the judgments of not one person, but a host of people. In individual therapy the patient soon learns how to cope with and to neutralize the influence of the therapist. It is much more difficult to do this in a group setting. Change is scored on different levels of the intrapsychic organization. This includes one's system of values, which is altered through percussion of disparate ideologies in the group. It is much easier for the individual to recast one's standards in a setting that is a reflection in miniature of the world than in the isolated confines of the dyadic therapeutic relationship.

Diversified intrapsychic defenses come out toward members of the group with whom the patient plays varying roles. Multiple transferences, both sequential and simultaneous, are readily established. The opportunity to relate in different ways to fellow members enables the individual to work through insights in the direction of change. Thus, if the patient finds it difficult to express him or herself aggressively or assertively, practice with the least threatening member may be in order. Thereafter there may be progressive challenge to others who are more threatening. In individual treatment the therapist may continue to be too powerful a figure to override. Moreover, even though the patient masters fear and guilt, he or she may find it difficult to transfer what has been learned during individual therapy to the environment outside the therapeutic setting.

Within the group the patient feels more protected, both by the therapist and by members with whom alliances have been formed, and he or she may be able to practice new attitudes more propitiously. For example, if Mary Smith has a problem in accepting any aggression and hostility that are directed toward her, the group will offer her the opportunity of exposure to these emotions in graduated doses. She will become more and more tolerant of the resentment extended toward her. She will learn to accept criticism—to reflect on it and to see whether it is justified or not—instead of reacting automatically with indignant or violent responses. Rigid character defenses often yield in group therapy as patients observe their ego-syntonic traits operating in others.

On the other hand, one advantage of individual therapy is that the focus is on the patient's personal problems, which often become diluted in a group setting. With so many other members of the group expressing themselves, it is not always possible for the patient to clarify significant feelings at the time he or she is experiencing them. Individual therapy enables the patient to look into the private world of fantasy and conflict and to explore intrapsychic mechanisms in greater depth. It permits a concentrated working through of past difficulties developed with parental authorities.

Outlining some of the benefits a patient may derive from group therapy, we may include (1) the opportunity to see that one is not alone in one's suffering and that problems felt to be unique are shared by others; (2) the opportunity to break down one's detachment and tendencies to isolate oneself; (3) the opportunity to correct misconceptions in ideas about human behavior by listening to others and by exposing oneself to the group judgment; (4) the opportunity to observe dynamic processes in other people and to study one's own defenses in clear perspective in relation to a variety of critical situations that develop in the group; (5) the opportunity to modify personal destructive values and deviancies by conforming with the group norm; (6) the opportunity to relieve oneself of tension by expressing feelings and ideas to others openly; (7) the opportunity to gain insight into intrapsychic mechanisms and interpersonal processes, (particularly as multiple and split transferences develop), the group acting as a unit that replicates the family setting and sponsors reenactment of parental and sibling relationships; (8) the opportunity to observe one's reactions to competition and rivalry that are mobilized in the group; (9) the opportunity to learn and to accept constructive criticism; (10) the opportunity to express hostility and to absorb the reactions of others to one's hostility; (11) the opportunity to consume hostility from others and to gauge the reasonableness of one's reactions; (12) the opportunity to translate understanding into direct action and to receive help in resolving resistances to action; (13) the opportunity to gain support and reassurance from the other members when one's adaptive resources are at a breaking point; (14) the opportunity to help others which can be a rewarding experience in itself; (15) the opportunity to work through problems as they precipitate in relationship with others; (16) the opportunity to share difficulties with fellow members; (17) the opportunity to break down social fears and barriers; (18) the opportunity to learn to respect the rights and feelings of others, as well as to stand up to others when necessary; (19) the opportunity to develop new interests and make new friends; (20) the opportunity to perceive one's self-image by seeing a reflection of oneself in other people; (21) the opportunity to develop an affinity with others, with the group supplying identification-models; (22) the opportunity to relate unambivalently and to give as well as to receive; (23) the opportunity to enter into productive social relationships, the group acting as a bridge to the world.

ORGANIZING A GROUP

In organizing a group the therapist will be limited by the patients available. Nevertheless, one should choose patients who are sufficiently advanced in their understanding of themselves to be able to perceive their patterns as they will appear in the group setting. While the clinical diagnosis is not too important, experience shows that the following conditions and patients do poorly in a group; except perhaps when implemented by an experienced group therapist in a homogeneous group within an inpatient setup through supportive or reeducative group methods.

1. Psychopathic personalities and those with poor impulse control
2. Acute depressions and suicidal risks
3. Stutterers
4. True alcoholics
5. Hallucinating patients and those out of contact with reality
6. Patients with marked paranoidal tendencies
7. Hypomanics
8. Patients with a low intelligence

The age difference should preferably not exceed 20 years. Homogeneity in educational background and intelligence is desirable but not imperative. A well-balanced group often contains an "oral-dependent," a "schizoid-withdrawn," a "rigid-compul-

sive," and perhaps a "provocative" patient, such as one who is in a chronic anxiety state. This variety permits the members to observe a wide assortment of defense mechanisms and to experience tensions they might otherwise evade.

The number of group members may range optimally from 6 to 10. If a therapist feels uncomfortable with a large group, then the size of the group should be reduced. Marital status is relatively unimportant. A balance of males and females in the group allows for an opportunity to project and to experience feelings in relation to both sexes, although acting-out is more likely in a mixed group.

A heterogeneous group in terms of age, sex, and syndrome is most effective for reconstructive goals. A homogeneous group, composed of patients with the same problem, is best for alcoholism, substance abuse, obesity, smoking, sexual problems, insomnia, phobias, depression, delinquency, stuttering, criminality, marital problems, divorce, and geriatric problems, although an occasional person with such problems may do well with and stimulate activity in a hetergeneous group. The goals are both supportive and reeducative. Severely handicapped persons, such as paraplegics, women who have had mastectomies, patients undergoing renal dialyses, and laryngectomized patients, feel unrelated to the norm and do better in homogeneous groups. Adolescents seem to be more responsive in same-sex, same-age groups.

In introducing the matter of group therapy to a prospective member the therapist may explain that a group is being organized for purposes of treatment. Talking over problems or ideas in a group tends to expedite getting well. The patient may then be invited to join with the statement that perhaps a group may facilitate his or her progress. This, if the patient is in individual treatment, may be presented as a "promotion."

One of the problems that plagues neurotic individuals is the loss of a sense of group belongingness. To an extent, it is because they devalue themselves and feel rejected by others; partly it is because they anticipate that their own hostility will be reciprocated. As a consequence of this isolation, they lose identity with people and thus are robbed of a vital source of security. When a suggestion is made that they enter a group, they may imagine that their worst fears will come to pass. They will then pose a number of questions that usually reflect their resistance, and the therapist will be obliged to answer them.

The following are common questions and suggested replies:

Q. How can other mixed-up people like myself help me?

A. People in a group actually do help each other. They become extremely sensitive and perceptive about problems, and they often may be of considerable service to other members. In the group the person has an opportunity to observe how he or she interacts and to witness the nature of reactions to one. The therapist is present during the sessions to see that it goes along well. It's normal to feel some anxiety the first few sessions which provide "grist for the mill."

Q. I would be ashamed to bring up my problems to a group of people I don't know.

A. This is understandable. It is not necessary for you to divulge anything you do not wish to talk about. [*Actually this reassurance does not retard the patient from divulging the most intimate problems readily as soon as he or she begins to articulate.*] Without your permission I shall not bring up anything about you or your problems. This is up to you. Most people fear not being able to talk in a group. In reality, being with a group with whom you can be yourself is consoling, not frightening.

Q. What am I supposed to do in the group?

A. There is no need for you to do anything special. You may talk or you may remain silent as you wish. Generally one is not as embarrassed as one would imagine.

Q. Won't these people reveal things about each other outside the group?

A. One of the rules is that no mutual confidences are to be revealed to outsiders. Should this happen (and it rarely does), the person is dropped from the group.

Q. Supposing I meet someone in the group I know?

A. When it happens, it may actually prove to be an advantage. Any problems between two people who know each other can often be worked out.

Q. Won't the problems of the other people rub off on me?

A. Without any reservation I can say, "no." On the contrary, you may gain a great deal from observing how other people face and resolve their troubles. It can be a great educational experience for you.

Q. Do I continue seeing you individually?

A. Generally yes, but we will decide how frequently. Sometimes I may want you to try the group alone, but if that comes up, we can talk about it.

Q. Can I raise any issues I want in the group, even about you?

A. Unless you do, you will not get as much benefit out of the group as you might. It is important to talk about your feelings and ideas in relation to yourself, to outside people, to the group members, and to me. That is, if you wish to do so.

Q. Supposing my feelings are unreasonable?

A. This is why the group is of such value. In life there is very little opportunity to examine the reasonableness or unreasonabless of one's attitudes and responses. The group offers you an opportunity to test your assumptions. In the protected setting of the group a person can express one's ideas and emotions.

The length of a group therapy session is approximately 1½ to 2 hours. The frequency of meetings is one to two sessions weekly, with alternate sessions once weekly if desired. The best seating arrangement is in a circle.

There are many advantages in employing cotherapists in a group, provided that problems between them do not prevent their working together. The literature on the subject of cotherapy and the difficulties that can occur between cotherapists that can sabotage their usefulness and destroy the group process are pointed out by J. B. Strauss (1975). Her own study deals with the results of a questionnaire that explores the ways therapists conceptualize their problems and how they try to cope with them. A most interesting finding was the difference of role perceptions of male and female therapists. Many problems can be overcome if the cotherapists meet periodically together with a supervisor whom both respect.

THE OPENING SESSIONS

At the first session the members are introduced by their first names, and the purpose of group discussions is clarified. This will vary with different therapists and different groups. Advanced patients will already have worked through some of their individual resistances in their sessions alone with the therapist. Newer patients may need more explanations in the group setting. The more passive-dependent the patient, the more leadership will be demanded of the therapist. The technique employed during the opening session will be determined by the therapist's orientation and level of anxiety. Many therapists who use the group as an adjunct may assume a very passive role so as to elicit spontaneous reactions from different members for use in later individuals sessions.

Some therapists begin by simply stating that the group offers members an opportunity to talk about their feelings and eventually to understand their individual patterns. It is not necessary for the members to feel compelled to reveal something that they want to keep to themselves. However, communicating freely will help them to get a better grip on their problems. For instance, each member must have had certain definite feelings about entering the group; he or she may have been embarrassed, upset, or fearful. The therapist may then attempt to elicit these emotions, and, as one member expresses freely, others will join in, leading to a general airing of difficulties shared by all.

Before the close of the first session, some therapists find it advisable to stress the confidential nature of the meetings and to caution that each member is expected not to reveal to others the identity of the members and the subject matter discussed in the group. While no member will have to divulge secrets before he or she is ready, each will be encouraged to relate any incidents involving accidental or planned contacts with other members of the group outside of the sessions. Therapists who strongly believe that acting-out is deleterious will, in all probability, discourage any contact outside of the group. Sexual involvements may be forestalled by fostering verbalization of the patients' feelings and impulses toward each other. Usually the anxiety level drops markedly at the end of the first session, but rises temporarily at the outset of the second session.

During the early stages of treatment some therapists who are anxious to prevent acting-out at any cost will, at first, assume a despotic role that contrasts sharply with their role in individual sessions. Parenthetically, this may lead to more acting-out. They may try to keep patients from exposing painful revelations before the group is ready to support them. On the other hand, free verbal interaction may be encouraged in the group in order to bring out each member's customary facades and defenses.

Later in the course of therapy authority is shared by various members, who are, from time to time, "elevated" and "dethroned" by the group according to its needs. Often individual members in their temporary authority posts may initiate ways of eliciting meaningful material. This may take the form of giving each person an opportunity to express him or herself at each session, or there may be a much more informal arrangement with the members spontaneously expressing what is on their minds at the moment. Actually, by the time emotions are beginning to flow freely within the group, there is no further need for procedural structuring; indeed, this should not be rigidly controlled at any time. The content of discussions will vary greatly, covering current incidents of importance in the lives of each member, dreams, attitudes toward others in the group or toward the therapist, and general areas, such as family relations, sex, dependancy, and competition.

In previous chapters, principles of supportive and re-educative group therapy have been described. In this chapter, principles of group psychotherapy oriented around reconstructive goals are considered. In addition, behavior (p. 902), experiential (encounter and marathon, p. 905), transactional analytic (p. 909), psychodramatic and role playing (p. 911), family (p. 914), and marital (couple, p. 923) interventions are considered.

LATER SESSIONS

Ezriel (1973) believed that principles of classical individual psychoanalysis could be advantageously adapted to group therapy. Essentially mechanisms of the unconscious are uncovered and their meaning explicated through interpretation. The core of the neurotic process are unconscious need structures that constantly strive for satisfaction through transference reactions and that are dynamically related to resistances. "Here-and-now interpretations" of transference maneuvers with group members does not preclude examination of extra-transference projections toward persons outside of the group. However, the therapists must be constantly on the alert for covert transference manifestations that relate directly to them but are being diluted by references to others. Interpretation of transference with the therapist ("the required relationship") brings the patient closer to behavior patterns that the patient has been repudiating ("the avoided relationship") and permits reality testing that can demonstrate that anticipated calamities will not come to pass. Often such experiences enable the patient to make a connection between contemporary life and unre-

solved infantile conflicts. Unconscious common group tensions lead to the development of a group structure within which each member seeks to express transference needs. The therapist can advantageously analyze the structure of the group as it displays itself in a particular session and designate the roles played by the different members, thus delineating the defense mechanisms displayed by the individual members. Interpretation can thus be both individual-centered and group-centered; ideally the focus is on the two during each session. All activity in the group, as in classical individual analysis, other than interpretation must be assiduously avoided to prevent gratification of transference needs, which, while momentarily tension relieving, keeps basic conflicts alive.

Other authorities, especially in the United States, insist that the classical model is too limiting and introduce many modifications and active maneuvers such as the structural interventions of Minuchin (1974b). A dynamic viewpoint, nevertheless, is desirable even if nonanalytic methods are employed. It is essential, however, always to attune therapy to the presenting complaints. Where this is not done, one can expect poor results.

As the group becomes integrated and develops an "ego" of its own, members feel free to air intimate vexations. The patient gains more insight into personal difficulties recognizing that many troubles previously believed unique have a common base. The therapist should, therefore, direct energies toward stimulating thinking around universally shared problems, getting responses from other group members even though the subject under consideration is out of the ordinary. The patients may be asked to talk about personal impressions of the role the therapist is playing in the group. Thereafter the group is asked to discuss the verity of each patient's assumptions.

As Grotjahn (1973) has pointed out

transference is a most important element of the group experience. He describes three trends in transference: (1) transference to the therapist and central figure (e.g., paternal figure), (2) transference to peers (e.g., sibling), and (3) transference to the group itself (e.g., pregenital mother symbol). These different transference relationships are always present simultaneously, patients treating the group as if it were their own family. In working through transference and defenses dreams are advantageously utilized; but they are utilized in a somewhat different manner than in individual therapy, the group members and the therapist associating directly to the dream especially focusing on the thoughts and feelings it evokes in themselves, without waiting for the associations of the dreamer. In this way the dream becomes a part of group experience. Sometimes the therapist's reactions to a group member may be perceived correctly by a third member and interpreted.

Many therapists practicing individual psychoanalysis contend that group therapy waters down transference reactions, minimizes regressive reactions, and neutralizes emergence of a genuine transference neurosis. Character changes in depth are, therefore, circumvented. Durkin and Glatzer (1973) have elaborated on how a constant focus on process rather than content and how selective exploration of origins of defensive behavior during group therapy can effectively bring forth pre-oedipal as well as oedipal conflicts. Systematic analysis of intragroup transferences may act as a vehicle for successful transference interpretations and can lead to reconstructive personality changes of a deep and enduring nature.

Of vital importance is the opportunity for the development of multiple transferences during which varying members of the group function as vehicles for the projection of feelings, attitudes, and relationships with important persons in the individual's past existence. Of significance, too, is the fact that the group situation allows for "split transferences"—for example, projection of a "good" mother image on one member (or the therapist or the group as a whole) and of a "bad" image on another.

The basic rule in a group setting is for members individually to express themselves as freely and without restraint as possible. This encourages the disclosure of forbidden or fearsome ideas and impulses without threat of rejection or punishment. The patterns of some individual members usually irritate and upset others in the group, mobilizing tension and stimulating appropriate and inappropriate responses. The monopolizing of most of the session's time and competitiveness for the therapist's attention bring about rapid responses from the other members. Many patients will react to a trait in a member that they despise in themselves, even though they may not be immediately aware of possessing that trait.

Some therapists work even at the start on group resistance. For example, they may believe that mobilization and release of hostility is essential toward the development of positive and cooperative attitudes. The activity they engage in, therefore, is designed to stir up hostility and to facilitate hostile verbalizations. Other therapists try to facilitate the activity of the members as "adjunct therapists." The interactional processes virtually do put the various group members in the role of cotherapists. Under the guidance of the therapist this role can be enhanced. The specific effect of member "cotherapists" may be analytic or it may be more supportive, encouraging, accepting, and empathic, thus providing an important dimension to supplement the work of the therapist. One way to enhance cotherapeutic participation is, even at the start, to analyze motivations of one or more members to stimulate curiosity and communication. The members are invited to put themselves into the place of a member chosen for focus, e.g., to imagine dreaming the same dream as the member and to interpret the meaning.

A patient finds it easier to examine the inner feelings that have been repudiated when sensing that the group and the therapist are supportive. If expressed feelings seem to elicit a sympathetic response from other members, the ensuing discussion often leads to a lifting of tension and a sharpening awareness of the patient's neurotic patterns. In the kaleidoscopic illuminations of the group each person's vision is broadened by taking advantage of the opportunity to observe and study his or her own and other members' reactions within the group—e.g., manifestations of hostility, fear, suspicion, or sexual feeling—and to relate them to the basic character structure. In this context the difficulties and antagonisms among members may, through analysis of the operative projections, lead to a constructive solution.

Among the therapist's activities are clarifying, structuring, focusing, timing, interpreting individual and group resistances, encouraging group interaction, and clarifying group interrelations. The therapist's ability to accept hostility and criticism from one member paves the way for other members to engage in verbalizing and a working through of their own hostile emotions.

Reactions of the patient occur in complex clusters as a release of feeling within the group is accelerated. Lack of restraint in one group member often results in a similar lack of restraint in the others. A climate that tends to remove repression enables the patient to work toward a better understanding of inner conflicts.

The matter of alternate sessions calls for special attention. Although it is regarded by some as a sanctioned vehicle for acting-out, experience shows that it can provide opportunities for free interaction, testing, and exploring. It enables some patients to speak more freely about their feelings about the therapist and thereby to consolidate their separation from parental authority. It is essential, however, that activities at alternate sessions or elsewhere involving group members with each other be reported at the regular group sessions. Acting-out members should be seen also in individual therapy.

TECHNICAL OPERATIONS OF THE GROUP THERAPIST

The role of the group leader is to catalyze participation of the various members, to maintain an adequate level of tension, to promote decision making and problem solving, to encourage identifications, to foster an interest in the goals to be achieved, and to resolve competitiveness, resentments, and other defenses that block activity. Groups have a tendency to develop many resistances; for instance, the members form cliques, they come late, they socialize too much, they get frozen into interlocking roles. The therapist has a responsibility to deal with these overt obstructions, as well as with those that are more concealed and come through in acts like passivity, detachment, and ingratiation. The group interactions will permit the therapist to witness how individuals function with others, their enmities, and their alliances.

How the leader communicates to the group will vary with the orientation and personal idiosyncrasies of the leader. Some leaders are mercilessly authoritarian, and they take over firm control, directing the various activities with despotic regulation. Others are so passive that they scarcely make their presence known. There are therapists who conceive of their role as a benevolent authority who grace their subjects with kindly guidance. There are those who insist the the function of the leader is to liberate the affects of patients that cause their paralysis as people. This, they believe, is accomplished best not by interpretation, but by establishing meaningful, deep relationships. Accordingly, a therapist must avoid setting up as a paradigm of health or virtue, one who is falsely objective, which may be merely a cover for the therapist's omnipotence. Some therapists contend that there is no reason why the therapist cannot reveal weaknesses and grow with patients, relating to their strengths. Experience convinces, however, that most therapists will do best in group therapy if they function with some discipline and if they sensitize themselves for counter-transference manifestations, which are more easy to elicit and more difficult to control in a group than in an individual setting since they too may unconsciously experience the group as their personal family. This does not mean that one must keep oneself in a straitjacket and not react to provocations. Expression of anger toward the group when this is justified, without threatening recriminations, may be exactly what the group needs.

There is always a temptation in group therapy to allow the group to indulge in social chatter, in endless mutual analysis, and in the recounting of dreams and personal experiences at length. This interferes with proper interaction in the group. The therapist must constantly remind the members that they are not there to act as professional psychoanalysts, attempting to figure out dynamics and to expound on theory. The best use of their time is in exploring their own immediate reactions. The principle activity of the therapist will be to resolve resistances to talking about feelings regarding one another and to try to break up fixed role behavior patterns.

The specific communicative media will also vary with the training of the therapist and the goals in treatment. A recounting of dreams, and particularly recurrent dreams and nightmares, may be activated by most analytically oriented therapists, as may the reporting of fantasies and daydreams. Interpersonal interaction may be facilitated by encouraging the free association of each patient about the others in what Alexander Wolf (1950) has called "going around." Patients are enjoined to recite whatever comes to their minds about their fellow members, whether logical or not. Free association about the therapist is also invited. Interpretation is an instrumentality considered essential for the proper working-through of pathogenic conflicts.

Other therapist activities include

1. Focusing the conversational theme around pertinent subjects when topics become irrelevant.
2. Creating tension by asking questions and pointing out interactions when there is a slackening of activity in the group.
3. Posing pointed questions to facilitate participation.
4. Dealing with individual and group resistances.
5. Supporting upset members.
6. Encouraging withdrawn members to talk.
7. Interfering with hostile pairings who upset the group with their quarreling.
8. Reminding the group that communication about and understanding of mutual relationships is more important than interpreting dynamics.
9. Managing silence, which tends to mobilize tension in the group.

Role playing and psychodrama may be introduced periodically. They have advantages and liabilities, as may touching (Spotnitz, 1972).

An important aspect of the therapist's function in the group is that of gauging and regulating group tension and anxiety. It is well known that some degree of anxiety is one of the moving forces in therapy facilitating growth and change. But anxiety can also be disorganizing—if too much of it is aroused, the group cannot function; there is low cohesiveness, and dropouts occur. It is up to the therapist to step in and deal with excessive tension and maintain not a minimal level of tension, but an optimal one. If too little tension exists, a "dead" session may be resuscitated by requesting that the members "go around" associating freely about each other. A group that has settled into pallid social interchanges may also be revived by introducing a new active, disturbed member.

Perhaps the main task of the therapist is to detect resistances of the group as a whole as well as of the individual members. The dealing with resistance will depend on its manifestations and functions. The question is sometimes asked, "Should one share one's feelings with one's patients and act as a 'real' person rather than as a detached observer?" This depends on how it is done and the kind of relationship that the therapist has with the patients. To bring out one's *serious neurotic problems* may destroy the confidence of some group members in the therapist's capacity for objectivity, as well as the ability to help them, and the impair effectiveness of the therapeutic process. On the other hand, to share *feelings and reactions* will reveal the therapist as more human and less omniscient and give the patients confidence to talk more openly about their own anxieties.

As has been mentioned, a huge variety of resistances precipitate out in group therapy. Their dissolution has resulted in many innovative techniques. In a humanistic contribution Livingston (1975) describes two major forms of resistance that block progress in group therapy: contempt and masochism (sadomasochism). These defenses may, through the assumption of a special role on the part of the leader, be broken through in what the author calls the "vulnerable moment." During such intervals a patient allows himself or herself to be open and honest, and through a constructive sharing of an experience with the group and therapist, the patient may score substantial reconstructive gains. Describing how awareness of such readiness for change came about in his own group therapy as a patient, Livingston suggests techniques, some derived from Gestalt therapy, that may facilitate the working-through process.

A particularly insidious and masked form of resistance is acting-out. The initial reaction to a therapeutic group experience is generally a profoundly inspiring one. A good deal of the reaction is marshalled by hope, the patient projecting wishes to be accepted, understood, and loved without qualification. While defenses continue to operate, these are softened by the emotional catharsis that is experienced in verbalizing to strangers and by an idealization that projects onto them. Sooner or later he or she plummets back to the original defensive baseline as the patient discovers flaws in the idealized images of the group, as criticisms, challenges, and attacks justifiably and unjustifiably are leveled at him or her; and as multiple transference reactions come forth that, unfoundedly, make the group a facsimile of the patient's original family, with some members even sicker than those of the patient's own family. Frustration, disappointment, and even despair are apt to dominate responses, and acting-out may then occur verbally and behaviorally.

In groups conducted by unsophisticated therapists the acting-out dimension may be openly encouraged, the patients being helped or goaded into unrestrained speech and behavior without relating personal responses to underlying motivations. The temporary relief of tension and the pseudoassertive expostulations are confused with cure. Follow-up almost invariably demonstrates how futile are the results. Many of the members become welded into reciprocal sadomasochistic alliances, and therapy becomes interminable. Others find excuses to leave the group.

The ability of the therapist to establish and to maintain proper communication is the principal means of averting this therapeutic impasse. A. Wolf (1975) illustrates how a therapist may utilize his or her own personality characteristics, for example, solicitude, capacity for healthy engagement, self-discipline, and sheer human decency, to resolve resistances and to enhance interaction. He refers to methods employed by Asya Kadis, which tend to encourage working through rather than acting-out and help foster character restructuring.

The control of acting-out requires a differentiation of acting-out behavior from impulsive and compulsive acts (Spotnitz, 1973). It is generally agreed that there is a greater tendency toward acting-out in group therapy than in individual treatment. A primary function of acting-out, according to Spotnitz, is to avoid experiencing unpleasant emotions, often of preverbal origin, that cannot be tolerated. Action becomes tension alleviating. It often conveys information in a dramatic form to the effect that the individual is unable to verbalize freely. More constructively, it may serve as a means of attempting to master traumatic events, and it may actually help prevent the outbreak of psychosomatic illness or psychosis by discharging tension. However, the validity of acting-out is always justifiably challenged unless it results in reality testing or enables a patient to master a tendency toward resistive emotional action. Under these circumstances the patient's actions may be considered constructive and in some instances even maturational. If, on the other hand, investigation reveals that emotional action serves as a resistance to communication, it must be therapeutically handled as a form of resistance. Particularly damaging are actions that are destructive to the continuity of the group or to any of its members. Inadequate communication of understanding on the part of the therapist and failure to meet the patient's emotional needs may be responsible for acting-out, which may then take the form of the patient dropping out of the group. Awareness of this contingency may help the therapist deal with such behavior at its inception.

Another type of resistance is encoun-tered on the part of members who refuse to participate in the treatment process. Innovative therapeutic approaches here may cut through the defensive system through the use of videotape recording and playback. R. L. Beck et al. (1975) describe such a program in which dance movement therapy is employed to demonstrate how incongruence between verbal and behavioral communication as a form of resistance may be resolved. Success may sometimes be scored through this approach (whereas traditional therapeutic modes are ineffective) and can lead to a more constructive use of verbal psychotherapy.

Special patients and syndromes may also require innovative methods. The unique personality needs and defenses of adolescents (for example, their lability of affect, their struggle for identity) require an atypical format in the conduct of group psychotherapy. There are differences in respect to activity, depth and content of discussion, and roles taken within the group. Adolescents bring into the group (which influences its Gestalt) the rapidly shifting values of the contemporary social scene and their distinctive reactions to delights and horrors of our modern technological era. Their reactions differ from those of their parents, who were subjected to a different type of social conditioning. Moreover, the ease with which runaways may survive away from home in a commune and participation in the drug culture that surrounds them must be taken into account in any group psychotherapeutic plan. Kraft and Vick (1973) present an approach that acknowledges the pressing need in adolescents for expressions of their identity and creativeness by introducing into the group psychodramatic techniques and artistic activities, such as dance or movement, music, poetry, and various visual stimuli and by employing where indicated auxiliary therapists. Major conflicts of adolescents worked through in the group included individual excessive competitive behavior versus withdrawal tendencies, inadequate outlets for emotional expression versus emotional blocking, growing up toward individual responsibility versus dependency, and self-identification versus expected role assumption and various breakdowns in defensive operations. This type of group, according to the authors, provides a growth experience for the members, results being reflected in enhanced school performance, better peer relationships, and a general strengthening of ego functioning.

Riess (1973) describes in the conduct of a group of adolescents, or family of the adolescent, a structured "consensus technique" that he believes is ideally suited for diagnostic and therapeutic purposes. In this technique a problem situation in written or oral form is presented to each member who writes out what would be the appropriate outcome or way of action. The members then discuss the "solutions" and are given a limited time to come to a unanimous decision. In the course of the ensuing interactions, individual styles, reactions, and defenses become apparent and relationship problems emerge. The results may be utilized diagnostically. By mobilizing conflict and anxiety, defensive operations precipitate out rapidly, and where the therapist is trained dynamically to deal with defenses, therapy may become catalyzed.

One of the poignant problems of the group therapist is how to deal with "difficult" borderline patients, that is, those who do not respond to the usual tactics or maneuvers during the group session, who are extraordinarily self-involved, sensitive, dissatisfied, and angry. Their impact on the group may be intense and not always constructive, since they attempt to destroy, to monopolize, and to provoke counteraggression from other members. Moreover, they engage in struggles with the group leader that can be disturbing to the latter, to say the least. Pines (1975) has described the dy-

namics of the "difficult" patient, employing some of the ideas of Foulkes, Kohut, and Kernberg. He makes some useful suggestions on how to manage their reactions and resistances.

Efforts to expedite group therapy and catalyze movement have resulted in therapists' evolving their own unique techniques. Thus, Vassiliou and Vassiliou (1974) employ a transactional method "synallactic collective image technique," which actualizes psychodynamic concepts within the framework of general systems theory. Utilizing artistic creations made by group members (free paintings, doodlings, or scribblings), the participants choose, through majority vote, one creation around which discussion is organized. In this way the members "talk" to each other through a common stimulus. Gradually, as different projections evolve, communalities are compared and a "collective image" of the group emerges that revolves around a central theme with individual variations. Throughout, the therapist operates actively in a key "catalytic regulatory" role, participating continuously in the group transaction.

Encounter and marathon techniques are capable, through the intense emotional atmosphere that they create, of cutting through defenses and rapidly reaching repressed feelings and impulses rarely accessible through the use of conventional techniques. However, such active procedures are unfortunately utilized by therapists as a means of dealing with their own countertransference. Thus, the sessions may be employed as an outlet for the therapist's hostility, boredom, need for social and physical contact, desire for dramatic "instant insights," and solution of professional and personal identity conflicts. The avoidance by encounter therapists of traditional concepts and practices, such as the analysis of countertransference, is a great liability and accounts for the bulk of negative therapeutic reactions and treatment failures. A. W. Rachman (1975) points out the importance of countertransference analysis and suggests methods of examining countertransference.

Corsini (1973) describes a "behind-the-back" (BTB) technique that may serve a useful purpose for groups of people. The problem in ordinary group therapy is that people find it hard to be honest with one another to their faces. The BTB technique is a stylized and formalized procedure that requires a minimum amount of time on the part of the therapist and is one that a suitable group may utilize. Members of the group are prepared by informing them that the method is designed to help express oneself to others and to learn what others really think of one. They are then asked to volunteer their participation as both patients and therapists. Each member in the present and following sessions is given a half hour to tell his or her story without interruption. At the end of this time the involved patient is requested to sit with his back to the group while each member talks about the "absent" member. This requires 20 to 40 minutes. The absent member is asked to face the group again while the therapist briefly summarizes what has been said. The patient is given about 5 minutes to make a rebuttal, responses being studied by the therapist in terms of denials, agreements, evasions, and other defenses. Then the patient sits in the center of the group exposed to the interrogation of the group. The therapist may interrupt these questions and terminate the session by sending the patient out of the room should emotions become too violent. It is to be expected that the patient will be upset by his inquisition, but this very turmoil causes the patient to unfreeze, better to face up to problems, realizing how he or she impresses others. At the very next session the patient is asked to summarize the meaning of the past session. The BTB technique is planned to facilitate the release of emotions and to expedite change through altered behavior.

It is sometimes propitious, in the opinion of some therapists, once a dynamic understanding of a patient's emotional problems becomes clear, to expedite change through arranging an appropriate scenario that encourages the patient to act out conflicts in a controlled way. E. E. Mintz (1974) presents a number of such episodes from her experience with marathon groups. The procedures employed, some of which draw from psychodramatic and Gestalt therapeutic techniques, are bounded only by the imagination and dramatic proclivities of the group leader and participant members. Patients who are vulnerable or resistant to "interpretations" in individual sessions are often, with this technique, better capable of cutting into core problems and facing their difficulties. Moreover, the process stimulates the other group members to open up many personal painful areas for discussion.

Bach (1974) utilizes and describes a technique of aggressive therapeutic group leadership through participating actively in fights that occur between members of marathon groups. He considers neutrality and passive objectivity, the preferred stance of psychoanalysis, a form of alienation and not caring, which violates the intimate participative spirit of the marathon experience. The therapist "attacks" by frank verbal explosions and expressions of frustration, irritation, and indignation justified by what is happening in the group. Such actions may be leveled at a passive cotherapist who refuses to participate actively in the group work, at a whole group of "ground-rule" violators (e.g., people who avoid confronting each other with their feelings), at subgroups (e.g., those who hide in a cozy, pairing maneuver), and at individual members who manifest patterns that interfere with the group experience (e.g., monopolizing, controlling, etc.). Bach provides amusing examples of his "attack therapy," which, though seemingly countertransferentially inspired at times, appear, according to his accounts, to result in a more intimate, experience-sharing communion among the members. He expresses his philosophy of therapy in this way: "We must all relearn how to fight to regain our genuineness. Only after this are we ready to share love."

C. Goldberg (1975), on the other hand, stresses an existential stance and believes that patients can be actively taught skills in interpersonal relationships that can mediate their own and others' loneliness and despair, and which can probe ubiquitous alienation and existential exhaustion. Toward this end, the group leader actively participates in the group through openness, self-disclosures, display of congruence of feeling, and modeling of behavior. There is a minimization of verbal and nonactive interaction. Interpersonal skills are actively taught through such methods as a deciphering of nonverbal "body language," a listing and checking of one's irrational attitudes and an exposure of one's manipulations and defenses in order to influence situations outside the group and to revise strategies and core attitudes.

Many other group interventions have been described and are contained in the annual overview of group therapy by Wolberg & Schwartz (1973) and Wolberg & Aronson (1974–1983).

SPECIAL PROBLEMS

It can be seen from the previous discussion that some group therapists develop their unique techniques and ways of looking at group phenomena that, while valid for them, may not be sound, plausible, or found useful by every psychotherapist. Experimenting with these procedures and ideas, however, will reveal their value.

The mangement by the therapist of special problems among patients will be essential where they obstruct group interaction. The following are some of these.

The Silent Patient

Behind silence may lurk a variety of dynamisms. Sometimes detached, withdrawn persons may be drawn out by the therapist's asking them a pointed question in relation to what is currently going on in the group: "How do *you* feel about this?" Since the response will be hesitant and unsure, more aggressive patients may attempt to interrupt to take the floor over for themselves. The therapist may block this subterfuge and continue to encourage the reluctant patient to articulate. The patient may also be asked directly to report on any dreams. Sometimes it helps to allot a certain amount of time to each member, say, 5 minutes.

The Monopolizer

The person who attempts to monopolize the session may be manifesting a power struggle with the therapist or a masochistic maneuver to bring on the wrath of the therapist and other group members. The aggressive, narcissistic patient who insists on dominating the session will usually be interrupted by one or more members who resent this takeover. Where this does not occur, the therapist may halt the patient by asking another member what he or she is thinking about or by directing a question at the group as to whether they want the monopolizing patient to carry on all the discussion. The same tactics may apply to an interacting pair who interminably carry on a discussion between themselves.

The Quarreling Dyad

A manifestation of unresolved sibling or parental rivalry is two patients who constantly engage in verbal dogfights. This eventually becomes boring for the rest of the group and may sponsor a withdrawal into fantasy. The best way to deal with this phenomenon is by working toward each participant's tracing of the transferential roots of the enmity in order to recognize how both are projecting unconscious aspects of themselves on each other. This should not be too difficult from their dreams and associations. An interruption by the therapist of uncontrollable outbreaks of bickering is, of course, in order.

Acting-out Patients

Because groups are action oriented, because multiple transferences are set loose, because individuals other than the therapist are available for the discharge of erotic or hostile impulses, because not enough opportunity is given each patient to verbalize, and because upsetting revelations on the part of the group members may set off identical problems in a patient, acting-out can be a disturbing phenomenon in groups. The therapist may caution the members to talk out rather than to act out. The group members may be required to report at a regular session the activities engaged in between members outside the group. The therapist may try to reduce the anxiety level of the group. It is possible that the therapist's own countertransference is encouraging the acting-out. One should be constantly on guard for this. It may be necessary to reorganize the group when too many acting-out members are present. The therapist may insist on acting-out members being simultaneously in individual therapy.

The Private Session in the Group

Some patients will attempt to utilize the group time to get a private session with the therapist. They will look at and direct their conversation to the therapist, ignoring the presence of the group. This reaction is especially common in a patient who was an only child in the family of origin or who wants to be the preferred sibling. When this happens, the therapist may ask the patient to focus remarks on the group, may question the group as to how they feel about the patient's carrying on an intimate discussion with the therapist, may ask other members to associate to the patient's verbalizations, and finally, may suggest that the patient come in for a private session.

The Habitual Latecomer

Drifting into the session after it is under way will mobilize resentment among the members, particularly where it is repetitive. This resistance should be handled as a special problem, requesting the patient to try to understand what is behind this neglectful conduct. The latecomer ultimately may be threatened with removal from the group if he or she does not come on time. This may bring to the surface the resentment toward the group that is expressed in this symptom. The group members should be encouraged to deal with this problem, not just the therapist.

The Patient Who Insists that He or She Is Getting Worse not Better

There are patients who display a negative therapeutic reaction that they are only too eager to communicate to the group. Dependent patients who have been in the group for years, and who cling to it for emotional sustenance, usually join in to complain regarding the ineffectuality of therapy. This can influence the group morale and may be disturbing, especially to new members. The therapist may handle such a reaction by nondefensively citing examples from the progress made by various members of the group to disprove the thesis that therapy does not help and, where applicable, may point out the aim of the complainant to drive certain members (especially new members) out of the group.

The Accessory Therapist

A variety of mechanisms operate in the patient who is trying to replace the therapist. It may be a protest on the part of a dependent patient to the therapist's passivity. It may be an attempt to undermine the authority of the therapist. It may be a way of seeking favor with the therapist. It may be a gesture to compete with and replace the therapist. Irrespective of its basis, the patient may soon gather about him a group of followers as well as adversaries. The best way to handle this maneuver is to ask the other members what they think is happening, until the therapeutic pretender quiets down. The therapist may also ask the competing patient why he or she feels obliged to "play psychoanalyst."

Mobilizing Activity

Where progress has bogged down and members seem to be in a stalemate, one may stir up activity by (1) asking the group why this is so, (2) introducing psychodrama or role playing, (3) asking a member to talk about the role assumed in the group, then going around the group requesting the other members to comment, (4) asking each member to talk about feelings concerning the two people on either side of him or her, (5) utilizing one or more techniques of encounter or Gestalt therapy, (6) extending the length of a session up to the extent of a marathon session, (7) introducing several new members into the group, (8) determining the nature of the resistance and interpreting it, (9) shifting some old members to a new group, (10) introducing a borderline patient into the group whose anxiety level is high, (11) taking and playing back video tapes of the group in action, (12) pointing out which stimuli in the group release repetitive patterns in each patient and interpret-

ing their ramifications in outside relationships.

When a Therapist Becomes Bored with a Session

In this situation the therapist may ask, "Is anybody else besides me bored with this conversation?" Then the group could explore the basis for such a reaction.

MISCELLANEOUS GROUP APPROACHES

Preintake and Postintake Groups

Preintake groups, which act as a forum for discussion and orientation, are a valuable aspect of clinic functioning where a delay is unavoidable before formal intake. Up to 20 people may attend, and sessions may be given at weekly, bimonthly, and even monthly intervals. Parents of children awaiting intake may be organized into a group of this type, which may meet for 3 to 6 monthly sessions. Postintake groups may take place before permanent assignment, and meetings may be spaced weekly or up to 1 month apart. Here some therapeutic changes are possible as disturbing problems are introduced and elaborated. These preliminary groups serve as useful means of selecting patients for ongoing group therapy. They are worthy orientation and psychoeducation devices and help prepare and motivate patients for therapy.

Special Age Groups

Group therapy with children is usually of an activity nature. The size of children's groups must be kept below that of adult groups (Geller, 1962). For instance, in the age group up to 6 years, two or three children constitute the total. Both boys and girls can be included. Single-sex groups are

(1) from 6 to 8 years, which optimally consist of three to five members; (2) from 8 to 12 years, which may have four to six members; (3) from 12 to 14 years, which may contain six to eight youngsters; and (4) from 14 to 16 years, which have the same number. Mixed-sex groups at the oldest age level are sometimes possible.

Play therapy is the communicative medium up to 12 years of age, the focus being on feelings and conflicts. It is obvious that the ability to communicate is a prerequisite here. Beyond 12 years discussions rather than play constitute the best activity medium. Techniques include analysis of behavior in the group, confrontation, and dream and transference interpretation. Both activity (during which acting-out may be observed) and discussion take place at various intervals. Interventions of the therapist should be such so as not to hamper spontaneity. Discussion is stimulated by the therapist, and silences are always interrupted. Ideally, individual therapy is carried on conjointly with group therapy, particularly at the beginning of treatment.

Group psychotherapy with older people has met with considerable success in maintaining interest and alertness, managing depression, promoting social integration, and enhancing the concept of self in both affective and organic disorders (Goldfarb & Wolk, 1966). Where the goal is reconstructive, oldsters may be mixed with younger people.

Behavior Therapy in Groups

Behavioral techniques (Lazarus 1968; Meacham & Wiesen, 1974; Wolpe, 1969; Liberman, 1970; Fensterheim, 1971) lend themselves admirably to group usage, and results, as well as controlled studies, indicate that behavioral change may be achieved by the employment of methods such as behavioral rehearsal, modeling, discrimination learning, and social reinforcement. The group process itself tends to accelerate behavioral strategies. Homogeneous groups seem to do best, the selection of members being restricted to those who may benefit from the retraining of specific target behaviors. Thus, the control of obesity, shyness, speaking anxiety, insomnia, and phobias (flying insects, mice, closed spaces, etc.) can best be achieved in a group where the participants are focused on the abolition of similar undesirable behaviors. In institutional settings, particularly with psychotic patients, group decision-making strategies may be practiced, reinforcement being offered through token economies. Short-term hospitalization for severe obsessive-compulsives, and perhaps alcoholics and drug addicts, treated in special groups of populations with similar maladaptive behaviors can often be a rewarding enterprise (Rachman, S., et al, 1971).

Individually oriented behavioral interventions [see Chapter 51, Techniques in Behavior (Conditioning) Therapy] may be employed alone in a group setting, or in combination with psychodrama, role playing, Gestalt tactics, encounter maneuvers, or formal group therapy procedures (inspirational, educational, or analytic) depending on the training and flexibility of the therapist.

A routine practiced commonly is to see the patient initially in individual therapy to take a history, to explore the problem area in depth as to origin, circumstances under which it is exaggerated, reinforcements it receives as well as secondary gains, and goals to be approached, employing the traditional behavioral analysis. If group therapy is decided on, it is best to introduce the patient into a newly formed group with persons suffering from the same difficulties and who have approximately the same level of intelligence and knowledge of psychological processes. The size of the group varies from 5 to 10 individuals. A cotherapist is valuable and sometimes indispensable as in the treatment of sexual problems. The initial few sessions may be relatively unstructured to help facilitate the group process. The time of sessions varies from $1\frac{1}{2}$ to 3 or 4 hours. During the starting sessions members are encouraged to voice their problems and to define what they would like to achieve in the sessions, the therapist helping to clarify the goals.

A. P. Goldstein and Wolpe (1971) have outlined the following operations important in group behavioral treatment: feedback, modeling, behavior rehearsal, desensitization, motivational stimulation, and social reinforcement. *Feedback* is provided with confrontation of the reactions of the other members to the patient's own verbalizations and responses. This gives the patient an opportunity to alter these if it is desired. *Modeling* oneself after how others approach and master the desired behavior is an important learning modality. The therapists may engage in role playing or psychodrama to facilitate modeling. *Behavior rehearsal* similarly employs role playing involving the patient directly. Repetition of the process with different members helps solidify appropriate reactions, the patient engaging in role reversal when necessary. Here video playbacks may be important so that patients may see how they come across. Counterconditioning and extinction methods (systematic desensitization, role playing with the introduction of the anxiety-provoking stimulus, encouraging expression of forbidden emotions in the group like anger) eventually lead to *desensitization*. The therapist provides direction and guidelines for appropriate behavior, which with the pressure of the group, helps create *motivation* and *social reinforcement*. Support is provided the patient when necessary. Specific assignments outside the group may be given the patient.

Relaxation methods may be employed in a group for the relief of tension and such symptoms as insomnia. Any of the hypnotic or meditational methods outlined in this volume (q.v.) may be utilized; their impact is catalyzed by implementation in a group atmosphere.

Behavioral tactics are ideally suited for habit disorders related to eating, such as obesity, smoking, gambling, alcoholic overindulgence, and substance abuse. Members for each group must be chosen who suffer from the same problem and possess adequate motivation to cooperate with the interventions.

Where problems are centered around lack of assertiveness, assertiveness training can be highly effective. Fensterheim (1971) describes his method of dealing with this problem. Groups of 9 or 10 consisting of men and women in approximately the same number, roughly homogeneous as to age, marital status, achievement, education, and socioeconomic status (to enhance modeling) meet $2\frac{1}{4}$ hours once weekly. Seats are arranged in a horseshoe configuration, the opening serving as a stage for role playing and behavior rehearsal. Sessions are begun by each member reporting on the assignment proposed the previous week. Successes are rewarded with approval by therapist and members. Failures are discussed. On the basis of the report the assignment for the following week may be formulated. Special problems will evoke discussion by the group. Members are asked to keep their own records of assertive incidents that they indulged in during the past week. Special exercises are employed with role playing depending on problems of individual members, such as talking in a loud voice, behaving unpleasantly, telling an interesting story, expressing a warm feeling toward other group members, practicing progressive expressions of anger (reading a dialogue and portraying an angry role, improvising one's own dialogue, role playing angry scenes and incidents reported by other members, and role playing scenes from one's own life and experience). About

5 to 10 minutes of each session is spent doing these exercises over a 4-month period. Roughly 10 to 15 minutes may be used for systematic group desensitization from a common hierarchy prepared by the group. At the end of each session members formulate their own next assignment or if they are blocked, this is suggested.

Phobias respond remarkably well to group behavioral methods. Here the patient selection must also be homogeneous as in assertive training. Aronson (1974) describes a program that has been successful in 90 percent of his patients completing it. The program is designed for fear of flying (but the ideas can be adapted to other phobias, such as fear of cars, ships, elevators, tunnels, bridges, high places, etc.). Initial individual consultations are geared toward establishing a working relationship with the applicant, and essentially to do a behavioral analysis, although Aronson stresses a dynamic accent. A high degree of motivation is desirable. "How much do you want to get over this fear?" may be asked. At the first session the therapist structures the program (the first five sessions devoted to a discussion of fear of flying; one or two educational briefings with safety experts, pilots, and other air personnel to answer questions; seven to eight sessions on discussion and methods of overcoming the fears). The optional size of the goup is 8 to 12 persons. Meetings are for $1\frac{1}{2}$ hours once weekly. Presession and postsession meetings of ½ hour each without the therapist may be recommended. Pertinent reading materials on air travel and development should be available.

The following rules are delineated. (a) Each member will within the time limitations, be permitted to talk freely about existing fears. (b) At the second session each member is to bring in a drawing depicting the most pleasurable aspect that he or she can imagine about a commercial air flight and a second drawing depicting the most unpleasant consequences. The individual is also invited to talk about any personal dreams about travel (In recounting such dreams no associations are encouraged nor interpretations made regarding defenses.) (c) The following exercises aimed at anxiety control are introduced.

1. While lying down or seated comfortably on a chair, visualize all the sensations and anxieties you experience while on a plane. Simply visualizing yourself on a plane may make you anxious at first. You may find yourself wanting to avoid thinking about it. If so, let your mind dwell on pleasant thoughts for a while. As soon as you feel somewhat more relaxed, reenter the fantasy of being anxious on a plane. Focus initially on the least frightening aspects of flight. Gradually allow yourself to visualize more frightening fears. Each time you practice this exercise you will be able to get closer to the dangerous situation and stay with it longer. Do this exercise twice a day for a week (based on Wolpe, 1969).

2. Picture yourself in the *most pleasant* situation you can imagine. Let your mind dwell on this situation as long as possible. Then imagine yourself on a plane. Some of the positive feelings you experienced in your fantasy will come back with you and help allay your anxiety when you next imagine yourself on a plane on the ground or actually flying (based on Perls, 1969).

3. Visualize the most unpleasant situation you can possibly think of—a situation even *more unpleasant* to you than being on a plane. You will find that when you leave this fantasy and imagine yourself flying or actually on a flight, you will experience less anxiety (based on Perls, 1969).

Should any of these exercises stir up anxiety, the members must indicate this to prevent it from getting too deep. (d) Should members start feeling strongly hostile to each other, the therapist encourages verbalization and explains that strong, positive feelings among all group members will be necessary for success. (e) Talking about personal matters other than those related to fears of flying is to be discouraged. (f) After the fourth or fifth session one or two educational sessions are held with local airline representatives to answer technical questions about flying and safety measures. (g) After the eighth session the entire group visits an airport and, if possible, meets in a stationary airliner for about 1 hour. Members talk about their fears every step of the way. Around the tenth and twelfth session the group leader suggests a target date for a short flight. If too much anxiety prevails, this date can be temporarily postponed until the anxiety recedes. The leader must set the time with the airline representatives and accompany the group. After the flight the group reconvenes to discuss the reactions. (h) Members are encouraged to arrange their own flights and to continue in group therapy for a few sessions thereafter.

Other phobias may be treated in a group setting following this format, introducing whatever modifications are essential considering the nature of the target symptom. Videotaping and playback may be employed, should the therapist possess the apparatus, particularly for role-playing exercises.

Experiential (Encounter and Marathon) Therapy

The group therapy movement has mushroomed out to include a variety of forms. The traditional model, which focused on inspiration, education, and insight acquisition, has been supplemented by groups whose objective is experiential with a wide variety of techniques. Many names have been given to these new arrangements including Gestalt, human relations training, human awareness, leadership training, T-groups, sensitivity therapy, and encounter therapy. The time element (traditionally 90 minutes) has been stretched sometimes to several hours, 12 hours, 24 hours, or several days with time off for sleep (marathon groups). Encounter therapy may be an ongoing process like any other form of group therapy, or it may be brief, from one to a dozen sessions.

A constructive group experience with a small group of people who are educationally on a relatively equal level and who permit themselves to disclose their self-doubts and personal weaknesses can be most liberating to the participants. The fact that one can expose oneself to others and reveal fears and desires of which one is ashamed, without being rejected or ridiculed, can be reassuring and strengthening. The person feels accepted for oneself, with all of the flaws, rather than for the pose presented to the world. Whereas previously the individual may have regarded interpersonal relationships as threatening, they can now embrace a sustaining richness. As communication between the members broadens, they share more and more their hidden secrets and anxieties. They begin to trust and accept themselves as they learn to trust and accept the other participants. Interpersonal confrontations, while temporarily upsetting, may even ultimately bring the individual into contact with repudiated aspects of himself or herself.

By communicating without restraint the members are enabled to learn that other individuals have problems similar to and even more severe than their own. The realization enables them to relax their guards and to open up more with one another. The "encounters" in the group will probably sooner or later release underlying patterns of conflict, such as hostility toward certain members, excessive tendencies to defy and obstruct, inferiority feelings, unrealistic expectations, grandiose boastings, and other maneuvers that have little to do with the immediate group situation but rather are manifestations of fundamental characterologic flaws. Under the guidance of a skilled group leader the encounter group becomes a means through which the members become aware of how they are creating many of their own troubles. By talking things out they are able to correct some of their misperceptions.

Some observers would call this process psychotherapy. We are dealing here with semantics. The effects of the encounter group can be psychotherapeutic, particularly in persons who are ready for change and who already have, perhaps in previous psychotherapeutic experiences, worked through their resistances to change. But psychotherapy, in most cases, is not the achieved objective. What is accomplished is an educational realignment that challenges certain attitudes and teaches the person how to function better in certain situations. If one happens in the course of this education to change a neurotic pattern of behavior, so much the better, but it must be emphasized that psychotherapeutic groups are run differently from encounter groups. They are organized on a long-term basis and focused on neurotic symptoms and intrapsychic processes.

Even though there is some evidence that encounter group experiences may have a therapeutic effect on neurotic personality structure, our observations at the Postgraduate Center for Mental Health indicate that personality changes, when they do occur, are temporary, rapidly disappearing once the participant leaves the encounter group and returns to one's habitual life setting. We have worked with the staffs of various institutional units, including psychiatric clinics, correctional institutions, schools, and a host of professional and nonprofessional organizations. Our delight at "depth" changes brought about by encounter techniques has been generally short-

lived when we do follow-up studies after a reasonable time has elapsed. This fact does not depreciate what the encounter group can do for a participant, because in many instances it does alert the individuals to many neurotic shortcomings and motivates them to seek psychotherapy on a more intensive level. Many of our "cured" encounter clients have later asked for thorough psychotherapeutic help, once they have an inkling of their problems.

The usual marathon group exposes group members to constant association of approximately 30 hours, generally in the course of which a 5-hour break is taken. During the first 15 hours of interaction there is a gradual sloughing off of defenses, and, in the last hours, a "feedback" is encouraged in which the therapist enjoins the patients to utilize the understanding of themselves to verbalize or execute certain constructive attitudes or patterns. Highly emotional outbursts are encountered with this intensity of exposure, and corrective emotional experiences seem to occur. The therapist participates actively with the group, expressing his or her own reactions to the members but avoiding interjecting personal needs and problems. A variety of techniques may be employed. For example, at Esalen a combination of theories and methods were used, including Perls' Gestalt therapy, Freud's unconscious motivational ideas. Rolf's structural integration and body balance, Lowen's bioenergetic theory, Moreno's psychodrama. Shutz's encounter tactics, and other sensitivity training methods (Quaytman, 1969). Some of these techniques have more recently been taken over by Erhard Seminars Training (EST).

Experiential therapies are sometimes resorted to by psychotherapists when their patients have reached a stalemate in individual or group therapy. In many cases the specific working on the resistance resolves such blockage of progress without the need for dramatic interventions. However, in spite of this, there are some patients who seem unable to move ahead. Productions dry up, boredom develops, motivation to continue therapy dwindles away. Under these circumstances some therapists have found that referring their patients for encounter therapy or a weekend marathon suddenly opens them up, producing a flood of fresh material to work on, and sponsoring more enthusiasm for continued treatment.

Not too many therapists are qualified to do experiential therapy. Apart from that which may be gained by participation as a patient in encounter groups or in several marathons, it requires a special personality structure of great extraversiveness, spontaneous enthusiasm, and histrionic inventiveness. Sufficient flexibility must exist to permit a rapid switching of tactics and changing of formats to meet individual and group needs. The role of the leader will vary, of course, with the individual. Most therapists view themselves as participant observers who, while admitting and sharing some of their own problems, hold themselves up as models of expected behavior. Emotional stability of the therapist and control of countertransference are under these circumstances vital. The presence of a trained cotherapist is often of value in the service of objectivity. Both therapists who do marathon therapy and patients who receive it are usually enthusiastic. Follow-up studies have been more conservative as to the actual benefits. The immediate experience may be an intensely moving one, and participants usually believe that they have benefited and are reluctant to end their relationship. They feel that they have acquired a new understanding of themselves. Often they do. But we may anticipate that benefits will not persist unless the environment to which the member returns reinforces the new behaviors and attitudes that have been learned. This is usually not the case, however. One would anticipate that unless some intrapsychic change has occurred, the old defensive balances will usually be restored. It is for this reason that results will be best if the individual continues in individual or group therapy to work on the significance to him or her of the encounter or marathon experience.

It has been the practice, unfortunately, to offer encounters or marathons for unscreened applicants willing to pay the price of admission on the theory that even a bit of confrontation, challenge, and encounter can provide fruitful bounties. Undoubtedly, there are persons who may get a good deal out of an intensive interpersonal experience without formally entering into structured psychotherapy. This does not compensate for the unstable souls, balanced precariously on the razor edge of rationality, who can be damaged by exposure to such groups. There are some patients (usually borderline cases) who cannot tolerate the intense emotional relationships of the marathon experience (Stone, WN, & Tieger, 1971; Yalom & Lieberman, 1971). Such individuals may develop frank psychoses as a result of breakdown of their defenses. Unless the therapist is well trained and does diagnostic interviews on all applicants (which is not often the case), he or she is risking trouble, however infrequent this is reported.

Even where an initial diagnostic study qualifies a person for this type of therapy, difficulties can occur in those with fragile defenses. The task of the leader is to pick out of the group those members who in their speech and behavior are beginning to lose control. Removing such vulnerable persons from the group, temporarily by assigning to them isolated tasks and perhaps giving them supportive reassurance in a brief interview, may permit some of them to reenter the group when their reality sense is restored. The therapist will have to interrupt any challenges or attacks that are levied at such persons, refocusing attention elsewhere.

Generally, the individual entering an

experiential or marathon group is instructed in the responsibility that he or she has in the group, the need for physical restraint and abstinence from drugs and alcohol, and the fact that while one's behavior in the group is related to one's life style, that there may be new and better ways of relating that one can learn. Sometimes a contract is drawn up as to what changes a person desires to achieve. Accordingly, the individual may gauge for oneself how far ahead to move. Emphasis is on the "here-and-now" rather than on the past.

As to encounter techniques, these vary with the inventiveness of the leader. In a small group the members may be asked to "go around" and give their impressions of all the other members, positive and negative. The leader may then say, "Reach out and put your hands on the shoulders of the person next to you. He or she will do likewise. Look into each other's eyes and say whatever comes into your mind." Or, "Hold the hands of the person next to you, and describe what you feel these hands are saying."

Utilizing art materials (crayons, chalk, pastels, etc.), the members may be asked to draw anything that represents how they feel and also how they would like to feel. The group later associates to or discusses these productions. The same may be done with clay or plasticene materials.

Two members may be asked to approach each other in front of the group and to communicate in nonverbal terms, i.e., by touching, gestures, facial expressions, etc. The group then discusses the nature of the communication.

Schutz (1967a) has described a number of "warm-up" and other techniques that may be used. One technique in helping a person give up rigid controls and distrust of others is to encourage him or her to stand with back to the therapist and to shut the eyes and fall straight back with trust that the therapist will surely prevent falling. Patients show many defenses to this maneu-

ver, and the discussion of their fears and other feelings provides a stimulus for elaboration in the group. Later members may try this maneuver with each other when they develop confidence in permitting themselves to fall back.

Many touching maneuvers are employed for the same purpose. One is to invite patients to stretch out on a couch and to have them lifted by many hands and passed along, their bodies being stroked in the process. Associations to this are, as may be imagined, often interesting. In encounter groups, participants often play out their needs, impulses and conflicts not only through "verbal interchanges but also various nonverbal devices such as touching, massaging, holding, hugging, dancing, exercising, playing games, eyeball to eyeballing, acting out dreams and fantasies, etc." (Harper, 1975). Such groups which encourage an unrestrained expression of emotion may be helpful, at least temporarily, for inhibited, repressed individuals who require peer approval and modeling by a leader who also enjoins them to come forth with their feelings. But they may be harmful to vulnerable individuals who, having let the lid off their emotions, are left with residues of guilt and confusion after the group has disbanded. Dangers come from lack of provision for adequate postsession discussion, clarification, support, and interpretation; from inadequate selection procedures for members; and from inexperienced and untrained leaders who, though high in enthusiasm, are low in therapeutic understanding and sophistication.

Negative outcomes with experiential groups are to be expected in view of the superficial screening of the participants and the large number of untrained leaders who contact these groups with few or no limits on the selection of techniques. It would seem propitious to set up certification and licensure requirements for potential leaders of encounter groups to minimize hazards (Hartley, Roback, & Abramowitz, 1976).

It is to be expected that when people come together for an extended therapeutic experience that hopes are high and that there may be unreasonable expectations of benefit. Despite efforts to control postures and defenses and to substitute for them conventional modes of relating, the facades soon break down, particularly when the individual is criticized and challenged. The close contact, the extended time period of interaction, the developing fatigue, and actual and implied pressures for change all add to the uniqueness of the experience. Intimacies develop that the participant needs to control since subgroups and pairing are strongly discouraged. As the individual realizes the consequence of one's acts for the reactions of others, motivation for change may be increased. This is further augmented by reinforcements that one receives in the form of group approval for any changes that are exhibited. Where patients are not in ongoing groups or individual therapy, it is advisable to schedule a follow-up meeting 3 to 4 weeks later to discuss postmarathon impressions and experiences.

Because many participants have failed to achieve the hoped for relief from alienation, personal growth, and self-realization, the popularity of encounter groups has waned during the past decade.

The literature on encounter (experiential groups) has proliferated since the mid 1960s. The following are recommended: Back (1972), Burton (1969), M. Goodman (1972), Kuehn and Crinella (1969), E.E. Mintz (1967), Perls (1969), Rabin (1971), C.R. Rogers (1970), M. Rosenbaum (1969), Strean (1971–1972). The list continues to grow. Ample material has in the past been published on marathon therapy. A sampling follows: Bach (1966, 1967a–d), Casriel and Deitch (1968), Dies and Hess (1971), A. Ellis (1970), Gendzel (1970, 1972), J. Mann (1970), Rachman (1969, 1975), Sklar et al. (1970), Spotnitz (1968), Stoller (1967, 1968), Teicher et al. (1974), and Yalom and Lieberman (1971). In recent years interest in marathons has diminished.

Transactional Analytic Groups

Transactional analysis is a highly structured group of procedures, developed by Eric Berne in 1950 (see page 313), that is designed to help people achieve an expanded awareness of their interpersonal operations. It is predicated on the idea that human beings carry within themselves a threefold set of directives that influence their behavior in positive and negative ways. The first group of prescripts are residues of parental conditionings, the individual functioning as if driven by the values and attitudes of the parents. When this happens the "parent" (P) within is said to take over. The second group of regulations are the survival remnants of the "child" (C) and consist of immature promptings and habitudes, parcels of the past. The third group, the "adult" (A), is the logical, grown-up self that mediates a reasonable disposition. These divisions roughly correspond to Freud's superego, id, and ego; indeed, there is much in transactional analysis that parodies traditional dynamic formulations. What is unique and original about the method is the crisp, humorous, provocative language tabs assigned to different patterns that people display in their relationship with each other. This enables some persons, confused by the complex concepts and vernacular of psychoanalysis, to acquire insight into their drives and defenses rapidly, to accept more readily responsibility for them, and to work toward a primacy of the "adult" within themselves. It is little wonder that the volumes *Games People Play* by Berne (1964) and *I'm OK— You're OK* by T. Harris (1967) have stirred the popular imagination, plummeting the books to the top of the best-seller list.

Not all therapists, however, are able to do transactional analysis. What is required is a combination of special traits that include an extremely keen sense of humor, a facility for dramatics, a quick ability to perceive patterns as they come through in the patient's speech and behavior, and a unique capacity to label their use with relevant salty titles.

Treatment in transactional analysis begins with several individual interviews. Patients are instructed in the dynamics of the transactional approach and may be given assigned readings (Berne, 1964; Harris, 1967). A treatment "contract" is drawn up describing the goal of therapy in a specific and clear-cut way, and the patient is introduced to the group. Four overlapping phases of therapy are generally described (Karpman, SB, 1972).

The first phase is structural analysis concerned with understanding and recognizing "ego states," which objectively demonstrate themselves in body attitudes, tone of voice, vocabulary, and effect on others. Only one ego state manifests itself within the person at a time. Thus the individual's "parent" (P) may come through in vocabulary and behavior expressing what is right and wrong and what people should or should not do. The parent can be prejudiced, critical, pompous, and domineering, or nurturing, sympathetic, forgiving, reassuring, smothering, oversolicitous, infantilizing. The "adult" (A) is the "sensible, rational, logical, accurate, factual, objective, neutral, and straight-talking side of the personality." The "child" (C) can be "free," i.e., happy, intuitive, spontaneous, adventurous, and creative; or the child can be "adapted," i.e., showing reactions akin of those of parents like being sulky, frightened, guilty, sad, etc. The patient in the group during the first several weeks is encouraged to identify the ego states within oneself and as they come through in one's behavior toward the others in the group. The patient learns also of "skull transactions" (i.e., the internal dialogue that goes on between the ego states) as well as ways

of "getting the trash out of your head" (i.e., the adult decision to start new internal dialogues—"A 'go away' or 'That's my Parent talking' often quickly helps a patient 'divorce the parent' "). Catchy slogans are used to identify and describe attitudes of P, A, and C. Decision making, views of the world, modes of cataloging external information, and even examining resistance to therapy are referred to the separate outlooks of parent, adult, and child.

The second phase of therapy is transactional analysis (TA), which deals with the clarifying and diagraming of conversations with others, as by drawing arrows from one of the ego states of the person to one of the ego states of the other person. One's child may talk to another's child ("fun talk"), or adult to adult ("straight talk"), or parent to child ("helpful talk"). Various combinations can thus exist. In a group a patient's transactions can be drawn on a blackboard. In this way the patient learns the typical "games" that he or she plays with people. Transference is handled as a "typical transaction" and the precedents traced to early family transactions.

The third phase is "game analysis." "Games" are involved transactions of a number of people that lead to a "payoff" unless interrupted. They have social and psychological dimensions. Repetitive patterns and defenses are defined by provocative or humorous titles enabling the individual to accept them as part of the personality without too great anxiety. This is one of the virtues of transactional analysis. It is less apt than other dynamic therapies to set up resistance to the acknowledgment of destructive drives. The individual is more likely to accept the fact that he or she is driven by neurotic drives if these are presented humorously as universal foibles. The patient becomes less defensive and more willing to relinquish them.

One of the four basic positions is taken toward the world: (1) "I'm OK, you're OK," (2) "I'm OK, you're not OK," (3)

"I'm not OK, you're OK," (4) "I'm not OK, you're not OK." Games are played for figurative "trading stamps" for the purpose of collecting important prizes. "For instance, a man needing only two more books of 'mad' stamps comes home from work, starts a fight with his wife, collects the two books of 'mad' stamps, and cashes them in at the bar for a justifiable drink." Discussion focuses on developing rapidly an awareness of both social and psychological levels of behavior—not in abstract terms but by recognizing how one utilizes people to perpetuate one's own aims ("payoffs"). Sooner or later, the individual is able to interrupt the games (avoid being "hooked," achieve a "quit point") before they eventuate into his habitual acting-out patterns. Thus a cynical attitude toward the games provides motivation to stop them.

The fourth phase is "script analysis." A script is the individual's life plan evolved in early childhood. A "script matrix" charts the relationship with the parents and the crucial injunctions that have circumscribed the individual's life. The "script story" delineates the patient's life pattern and outlines the predicted end of the script. In the course of exploring the script early memories may be revived. The object of working with scripts is to give up old unwanted ones and "get a new show on the road." " 'Permission' in therapy is given to break the 'witch mother' injunctions. This is followed by a necessary period of up to 6 weeks of protection for the new ego, and this is dependent on the therapist having more potency than the witch parents. Patients gain a final autonomy in therapy and choose their own style of life or even live script free.' " Countertransference is recognized. "The therapist should be alert to detect witch messages in his own script and should not pass these on to his patients."

Transactional analysis for groups at one time attracted a sizable number of therapists, some of whom joined the International Transactional Analysis Association, which held seminars and study groups in many cities. Clinical membership was acquired after 2 years of supervised therapy and a written and oral examination. Publication on the subject has been ample, although interest somewhat has drifted away from transactional analysis during the past few years.

Psychodrama and Role Playing

Moreno (1934, 1946, 1966b) created a useful group therapy method, "psychodrama," which he first introduced in 1925 and that has evolved into a number of clinical methods, including sociodrama, the axiodrama, role playing, and the analytic psychodrama. Many of these have been incorporated into modern Gestalt, encounter, and marathon therapy.

In the hands of a skilled therapist psychodrama is a valuable adjunct in helping patients work through resistances toward translating their insights into action. The initial tactic in the group is the "warm-up" process to facilitate movement. This may take the form of the director (the therapist) insisting that the group remain silent ("cluster warm-up") for a period. As tension mounts, it will finally be broken by some member expostulating about a problem, the verbalizations drawing a "cluster" of persons around the member. Other members may similarly come forth with feelings and stimulate "clusters" interested in what they are saying. Soon the whole group is brought together around a common theme. The "star" chosen is the person whose personality reflects the problem area most clearly. Another warm-up method is the "chain of association." Here the group spontaneously brings up fears and associations until an engrossing theme evolves. The star chosen is the person who is most concerned with the theme. A third warm-up is initiated by the director ("directed warm-up") who, knowing the problems of the constituent members, announces the theme. A "patient-directed warm-up" is one in which a patient announces to the group the subject with which he or she would like to deal.

The star is groomed for the roles to play with representatives of important people in the patient's past and current life, selected from other group members ("auxiliaries") whose needs for insight preferably fit in with the parts they assume. The director facilitates the working together of the group on their problems, while focusing on one person (the "protagonist"). Among the techniques are (1) "role reversal," during which a protagonist and auxiliary reverse positions; (2) "the double," another member seconding for and supporting the protagonist; (3) "the soliloquy," characterized by a recitation by the protagonist of self-insights and projections; and (4) "the mirror," auxiliary egos portraying what the protagonist must feel.

By forcing themselves to verbalize and act parts, the members are helped to break through blocks in perceiving, feeling, and acting. Sometimes the therapist (the director) decides which life situations from the patient's history are to be reenacted in order to work at important conflictual foci. A technique often followed is that assumed by "auxiliary egos," who are trained workers or former patients "standing in" for the patient and spontaneously uttering ideas and thoughts that they believe the patient may not yet be able to verbalize, thus helping "to bring his personal and collective drama to life and to correct it" (Moreno, 1966a). As the patient reenacts situations, not only the self role, but also roles of other significant persons in his or her life, such as parents or siblings. The therapist, in the role as "director," may remain silent or inject questions and suggestions. Material elicited during psychodrama is immediately utilized in the presence of the "actor" patient and the group "audience." This technique usually has an emotionally cathartic value, and

it may also help the patient understand problems revealed by one's personal actions and thoughts as well as those reflected by other members of the group. By venting feelings and fantasies in the role of actor, the patient often desensitize to inner terrors, achieves hidden wishes, prepares for future contingencies, and otherwise helps to resolve many deeper problems and conflicts. Psychodrama may, instead of being protagonist-centered, i.e., focused on private problems of the patient, be group-centered, concerning itself with problems facing all members of the group.

A valuable function of the auxiliary egos is to represent absentee persons important in the life of the protagonist. Auxiliary egos, thus, are best recruited from those persons present in the group who come from a sociocultural environment similar to that of the patient. The auxiliary egos portray the patient's own internal figures, forcing the patient to face them in reality. In this way the symbolic representatives of the inner life are experienced as real objects with whom the patient has an opportunity to cope. The director enters into the drama that is being portrayed with various instructions and interpretations. Choice or rejection of the auxiliary egos is vested in the protagonist or the director. Since auxiliary egos are representations, they may play any role, any age, either sex, even the part of a dead person whose memory is still alive in the protagonist. If necessary, and where the protagonist can tolerate it, bodily contact is made between the patient and the auxiliary ego to supply reassurances and to restore aspects of closeness that the protagonist has lacked. Thus, a person who never experienced real "fathering" may get this from the actions of an auxiliary ego.

Props are sometimes used, such as an "auxiliary chair" which may represent an absentee personage. Living or dead family members may be portrayed by several empty chairs around a table, each chair in fantasy being occupied by a different relative. In the dramatic interactions the protagonist may play the role of the relative with whom there is momentary concern by sitting in the special chair and speaking for that person. Sometimes a tall chair is employed to give a protagonist sitting in it a means of assuming a position of superiority. A fantasy prop sometimes used is the "magic shop," in which the shopkeeper dispenses to all the members of the group imaginary items cherished by each in exchange for values and attitudes that are to be identified and surrendered by each member.

Role reversal is a useful technique in psychodrama, two related individuals, for example, taking the role of one another expostulating how they imagine the other feels or portraying the behavior of the other. Where a protagonist is involved emotionally with an absent person, the latter may be portrayed by an auxiliary ego.

Rehearsal of future behavior is an aspect of psychodrama. The protagonist here will play out a situation that necessitates the execution of skills or the conquest of anxiety that is presently felt to be unmastered. Verbalizing inner doubts and fears, and applying oneself to the task of overcoming these, may be helpful in easing one through actions in real life.

The controlled acting-out of fearsome strivings and attitudes helps to expose them to clarification. Thus, obsessive gentleness may be revealed as a defense against the desire to lash out at real or imagined adversaries. A protagonist so burdened may be encouraged to swing away at imagined persons who obstruct. A woman whose spontaneity is crushed may be enabled to dance around the room, liberating herself from inhibitions that block expressive movement. A suicidal person may portray going through the notions of destroying himself in fantasy, thus helping the therapist to discuss openly an impulse that otherwise may be translated into tragic action.

Moreno (1966a) explains the value of psychodrama in these words:

> Because we cannot reach into the mind and see what the individual perceives and feels, psychodrama tries, with the cooperation of the patient, to transfer the mind 'outside' the individual and objectify it within a tangible, controllable universe. . . . Its aim is to make total behavior directly visible, observable, and measurable.

In this way, patients are presented "with an opportunity for psychodynamic and sociocultural reintegration."

The psychodramatic technique has given rise to a number of *role-playing methods* that are being applied to education, industry, and other fields. Recognizing that the mere imparting of information does not guarantee its emotional acceptance or its execution into action, role playing is employed as a way of facilitating learning (Peters & Phelan, 1957a,b). As an example, a group of four participants and a group leader may be observed by four observers who sit apart from and in the rear of the participants. Initial interviews of 1 hour with each participant and observer are advantageous to determine motivations, expectations, and important psychopathological manifestations. Preliminary mapping of the procedure considers group combinations, problems to be considered, objectives and desired modes of interaction. A short warm-up period is employed at the beginning of each session to establish rapport. Then the participants are assigned roles in a selected conflict situation. A discussion by the group of the issues involved, with delineation of possible alternative courses of action, is followed by the leader's interpretation of why various participants reacted the way that they did. Repetition of the conflict situation with the same participants gives them an opportunity to try out new adaptive methods and tests their capacities for change. It also fosters reinforcement of a new mental set. At the end of the session the group leader renders ego support in the form of praise for individual contributions and reassurance to lower any mobilized tension or anxiety. Approximately six 1-hour group sessions are followed by individual consultation with each member to determine ongoing reactions. Another series of six group sessions, or more, may be indicated. These procedures, while effectively altering attitudes and promoting skills, may not effectuate significant changes in the basic personality structure. More extensive role-playing tactics have been described by Corsini (1966) that are designed to deal with extensive inner conflicts.

Quality of Change in Group Psychotherapy

One must not be deceived regarding the quality and depth of changes observed among members of a group as a consequence of continued interaction. Changes are dramatic: the attacking and aggressive person becomes quiet and considerate; the dominant individual shows abilities to be submissive; the withdrawn person comes out of a shell and relates flexibly to the other members; the dependent, clinging soul is encouraged to express assertiveness. These effects will become apparent, sooner or later, as products of both group dynamics and the interpretive activities of the therapist and group members. But whether there will be a transfer of learning to the outside world sufficient to influence a better life adaptation is another matter. Often what we find in group therapy (as we witness it also in individual therapy) is that the individual fits the group reactions into a special slot. The role played in the group is disparate from the roles in other situations. The group expects one to behave in certain ways, and one obliges. It offers a shelter from the harsh realities of the external world. One can "be oneself" in the group; but defenses may be checked at the therapist's door, and when leaving the thera-

pist's office or the group at postsessions and alternate sessions, one may reclaim them. Only in this haven of safety can one trust oneself to act differently.

This confounding resistance is testimony to the fact that interpersonal change is not the equivalent of intrapsychic change. The former change may merely reflect the acquisition of a new set of social roles that the individual fastens onto and that enhance the repertoire of patterns. It is like acquiring a new wardrobe to be worn on special occasions. The individual underneath remains the same. From this one must not assume that group therapy is of no real consequence. Intrapsychic changes are possible if the person has the courage appreciably to test the changed assumptions and to apply new learning in the group to the other roles played in life. The therapist has a responsibility here in seeing that the patient does not lock into a comfortable stalemate in the group. The patient may be asked whey there are differences in his or her feelings and behavior inside as compared with those outside the group, and if there has been no change, why not. Sometimes the patient's resistance is a persistence of the desire to recreate the patient's original family in the group, with all the ambivalences that this entails from which the patient refuses to break loose. Supplementary individual sessions may be specifically applied to these questions.

FAMILY THERAPY

Families are composed of units of individuals engaged in continuing interrelationships that significantly influence mutual behaviors (see p. 197). Pathology in one member can have a determining effect on the entire family system, which, in turn, will modulate the degree and form of individual dysfunctions. Therapeutic interventions therefore must concern themselves with the organizational distortions of the family as a system. It follows from this that correction of psychopathology in any one or more members presupposes a restructuring of the family organization, which is, to say the least, a difficult undertaking. At the start of treatment, the therapist is usually confronted with the fact that the family, dysfunctional as it may be, has reached a level of stability (homeostasis) that tends to resist modification. Attempts to alter faulty indigenous communication patterns, or efforts to move family boundaries outwardly toward remedial community resources are apt to be resisted. Family therapy is designed to deal with these rigidities (Gurman & Kniskern, 1981).

Contemporary techniques in family therapy are not uniform even though many of them are implemented under the rubric of presumably standard theories. They are essentially organized within the framework of three schools: structural family therapy, strategic family therapy, and intergenerational family therapy (Steinglass, 1984). Structural family therapy (Minuchin, 1974b; Minuchin & Fishman, 1981) focuses on the behavior of the family during the treatment session, and searches for patterns of alliance between two or more members as well as the firmness of their boundaries. Strategic family therapy emphasizes the symptomatic consequences of bad problem-solving. Homework is often assigned in the form of tasks for the different members, sometimes employing ambigious instructions. Patterns of communication may also be explored (Watzlawick, Weakland et al, 1974; Watzlawick et al, 1967), family problem-solving tactics investigated (Haley, 1976), and certain remedial or paradoxical tasks prescribed (Haley, 1976; Selvini-Palozzoli et al, 1978; Madanes, 1981). Intergenerational family therapy searches for patterns of "fusion" and "differentiation" that are passed along from one generation to another (Bowen, 1976). The theories and techniques of these three schools may seem worlds apart, but the effect on families of all of them can be significant when practiced by skilled and empathic family therapists.

Such practice can become quite involved, necessitating an understanding of individual and group therapy, systems theory, sociology, and group dynamics. During treatment the therapist must skillfully weave back and forth among the various members as resistance, transference, and defensive manifestations break loose. Countertransference is a fluid phenomenon in the process; identification with one or more the patients in the group commonly occurs. Since the actual difficulties are produced by the behavior of the individuals in the system, the resolution of such difficulties will necessitate changes in the behavior of the persons involved in the disorganizing interactions. This is sometimes referred to as the "interactional" approach in family therapy. Problems are not regarded as the tip of the iceberg, so to speak, emerging from buried inner manifestations, but as the iceberg itself. A good number of the therapeutic interventions are directed at the activities that are being used as "solutions" to control or eliminate undesired behavior. These activities usually sustain and reinforce the difficulty. Since such solutions often serve merely to aggravate the problem, therapy is concentrated on eliminating these futile solutions. New problem-solving methods are encouraged, focused on behavioral alterations rather than intellectual insights. A behavioral change in any member of a system can produce a change in the entire system. Accordingly, treatment may concentrate on the member who is most responsible for bringing about difficulties in the system, although the family as a whole is taken into consideration.

Many models for family therapy exist—and are still developing as psychotherapists of different professions, with varying theoretical viewpoints, evolve modes of working in relation to the needs of families and the structure and function of the agencies through which treatment is being implemented (Sager & Kaplan, 1972). Understandably, therapists have special ways of looking at family pathology and they organize their ideas, as has been pointed out, around favorite systems, such as behavioral family therapy, structural family therapy, psychodynamically oriented family therapy, and systems family therapy. Yet a therapist's clinical operations with families are influenced more by individual style of working with patients and the therapist's own unresolved family problems than by the theories espoused. This results in many different forms of practice that vary in such areas as selection of the unit of intervention (i.e., identified patient and parents, or total immediate family including siblings, extended family, distant relatives, etc.); time allotted to sessions (1 hour to several days [marathon family therapy]); duration of therapy (one session to many months); activity during sessions (listening, supporting, challenging, confronting, guiding, advising, censoring, praising, reassuring, etc.); relative emphasis on insight and behavioral alteration; and employment of adjunctive procedures (videotaping, use of one-way mirrors, role-playing, etc.).

How to manage resistance in family therapy is another area of discrepancy. Families struggle to maintain the homeostasis of a neurotic family system by preserving pathologic ways of relating. A great many of the current writings about family therapy specify contrasting ways of dealing with such resistance, and one is impressed with the lack of agreement for proper management of this disturbing phenomenon.

Sometimes family therapy is undertaken in clinics and family organizations, particularly those dealing with children for the purpose of reducing waiting lists. Under these circumstances therapy may be started even at the first interview as part of the intake and diagnostic process. Sometimes a group of workers visit the family in the home after an intake interview with the family and a diagnostic interview with the child (Hammer & Shapiro, 1965). Visiting the home has certain advantages since the members will demonstrate less defensiveness at home than at the clinic or office, displaying habitual reactions more easily.

Multiple therapists are often employed, circumventing to an extent the countertransference that develops in a one-to-one relationship. Individual therapy may be done concurrently by the different members of the team with selected members of the family (Hammer, 1967). Resistance is also more easily managed when more than one team member approaches a patient from a different perspective. The family facade is then more easily dissolved, and family members are more readily motivated to relate with their inner and latent feelings.

Sundry problems are experienced by therapists when dealing with another therapist who is treating a member within the family group. Disagreements will occur in observation, in emphasis of what is important, in diagnosis, and in the type of intervention best suited for specific situations. Competitiveness between therapists may interfere with their capacity to be objective. They may be offended by disagreements with or criticisms of their operations. There is finally the matter of expense and the finding of qualified professionals who can make their time coincide with that of the therapist. Opportunities are obviously better in a clinic than in a private setting, since fixed staff is available. There is an advantage in doing multiple therapy in a training center since a trainee may gain a great deal working with a more experienced therapist. Constructive collaboration between therapists tends to reinforce the impact of interpretations. It helps the resolution of resistance.

Working with a family group may serve purely as a diagnostic procedure, to spot psychopathology, and to aid in the assignment of therapists to individual family members who most need help. The focus may be on the relationships between parents, parents and children, and parents and grandparents. If a tangible problem exists, this may constitute the area around which explorations are organized. Short-term goals usually deal with a family crisis (Barten, 1971). Long-term goals are fluid and have to be adapted to the needs of the family. The objective, for example, may be to hold the members together in a fragmented family. It may be to help adolescents separate and find their own individuality. Sometimes asking each member of the family "What would you like to see changed in the family?" helps provide a focus. Each member may have a different idea about what should be changed. This will give the therapist valuable clues. At the end of the first session, a statement may be made to the family by the therapist as to what the problem seems to be.

It is vital in family therapy to understand and to respect the cultural background. The therapist must not deviate much from the accepted cultural system since this will offend some of the members and create resistance. Sometimes it is helpful to introduce an individual into the family group as a cotherapist who is part of the same subcultural setting, and who is capable of better translating the family code. This individual must, of course, have had some training at least as a paraprofessional.

Desirable goals of family therapy include resolution of conflicts, improved understanding and communication among family members, enhanced family solidarity, and greater tolerance for and appreciation of individuality (Zuk, 1974). All of these goals may not be achievable. In crisis resolution, for example, the total of one to six sessions, *which is the maximum number* acceptable to many lower-class families, may achieve little other than an overcoming of the immediate emergency. Somewhat more extensive are the objectives of short-term family therapy, which, though of longer duration, still may produce little

other than symptom reduction, largely because of the reluctance of the family members to involve themselves in extensive verbal interchange. Middle-class families are more willing to regard therapy as a learning experience and, accordingly, do not set strict time limits on treatment, usually accepting up to 25 to 30 sessions. They are often rewarded with more enduring changes. Sophisticated middle-class and upper middle-class families are generally better disposed to the more extensive goals of long-term therapy, e.g., alteration of values.

It is surprising how much can be done in from 3 to 15 family sessions, but follow-up individual or group therapy may be required. Parents soon begin to realize that problems that have exploded into crises have a long history, the roots of which extend into their own early upbringing. Guilt feelings, defensiveness, indignation, and attacking maneuvers may give way to more rational forms of reaction when even a partial picture of the dynamics unfolds itself.

Individual therapy may be done conjunctively with family therapy or at phases when work on a more intensive level is required. For instance, a husband whose authority is being challenged may require help in mastering his anxiety and in giving him some understanding of what is happening. Or a mother and father may need education regarding the processes that go on during adolescence, which can help them understand and deal with their own rebellious child. The family therapist, accordingly, will need the combined skills of the individual therapist, group therapist, sociologist, educator, and social worker.

A number of ethical issues are involved in doing family therapy (Morrison et al. 1982; Hines & Hare-Mustin, 1978; Sider & Clements, 1982). Among these is the question of whose interest is primary, the individual being seen by the therapist or the family? Maintaining the integrity of the family and its other members may mean sacrificing goals that the individual wants desperately to achieve. For example, where a married man seeks a divorce because of an involvement with another woman, should the therapist encourage this knowing that a family with small children and a handicapped wife, who by herself cannot manage the household, will have to be devastated by the family break-up? Another issue is the matter of confidentiality. Are therapists privileged to reveal information that seems vital for other family members to know? Further questions involve such points as to whether traditional ideas of an ideal family model should be held sacrosanct, whether the same therapist who does family therapy should also see individual members when they need it, how and when to arrange for conferences between outside therapists doing individual therapy with a group member and the family therapist, and whether members should be encouraged to reveal all, some, or no secrets they have concealed.

Doing family therapy is not without its risks, since the neurotic disturbance of one or more members may be the penalty the family is paying for holding itself together. Complementary symbiotic patterns may, when examined and resolved, tend to leave the members without defenses and worse off than before. A child's rebellion may be the only way that the child can preserve his or her integrity against a neurotic or psychotic parent. To interfere with this show of automomy may prevent the child from achieving any kind of self-actualization, resulting in crippling inhibitions. Disorganization of the family structure may be a consequence of insight into the neurotic basis for the existing relationships. Divorce, for example, may enable a woman with colitis to live her life without abdominal pain. But she may find herself, as a result, in empty waters, isolated and burdened with children she may not be able to rear by herself. Her need for her husband may then become painfully apparent. Mindful of these contin-

gencies, it is important to work against the too rapid precipitation of drastic changes in the family structure. It is here that life experience as well as professional experience will stand the therapist in good stead. Intensive individual psychotherapy may have to be employed at points where drastic changes in the life situation are imminent.

Some family therapists insist that the initial consultation include all family members. This is possible where family therapy is specifically requested. Usually one member of the family applies or is sent for help; this will necessitate one or more preliminary interviews prior to involving the entire family. Dealing with the resistance of a family to the securing of help, or of a patient to involving the family will call for skillful explanation and negotiation. All members of the immediate family and important members of the extended family as well as intimate friends are best included at least at the beginning. The therapist must be prepared to deal with explosive anger and accusations, channeling and defusing these to prevent the withdrawal of key members and breakup of treatment before it gets a start.

Great tact is needed in avoiding the show of favoritism since members usually attempt to woo the therapist to their side in the arguments that ensue. A delicate point is how to handle personal "secrets" revealed to the therapist during an individual session, the exposure of which may have an unforseen effect, good or bad, on the family. It is best that the therapist treat the secret as confidential information and that members themselves make the decision when, if ever, to reveal what they dread bringing to light. Another important point is the matter of establishing a verbal contract regarding the areas to be dealt with and the hoped for objectives in order to avoid later misunderstanding. Sessions are usually held once weekly for $1\frac{1}{2}$ to 2 hours. It goes without saying that the goals of selective problem solving will require fewer sessions than those of extensive reconstructive changes in the family members. Video recording with playback is a strikingly useful tool, and among the techniques is "cross-confrontation," during which a family unit is exposed to tape recorded excerpts demonstrating interactions.

Insofar as actual techniques are concerned (supportive, reeducative, and reconstructive), the existing styles are many even within the same practice models—structural, behavioral, psychodynamic, family systems, strategic, or experiential. An example of one stage of a structure, of diagnostic technique is described by Satir (1964a & b). The total interview consists of seven tasks.

The first task ("Main Problem") involves interviewing each family member separately, starting with the father, then the mother and the children in order of their age. Each is asked to discuss briefly: "What do you think is the main problem in your family?" They are each requested not to discuss their answers with other family members until later. Then the same question is asked of the group as a whole, gathered together in the interviewer's office. They are requested to arrive at some kind of consensus. This will expose the interactions and defenses of the members.

The second task ("Plan Something") is composed of a number of parts: (1) The family as a whole is requested to "plan something to do as a family." This enables the therapist to see how the family approaches joint decisions. (2) Next each parent is requested to plan something with all of the children and then the children to plan something that they can all do together. (3) The father and mother are asked to plan something that they can do as a couple. This reveals data of the operation of family subunits.

The third task ("The Meeting") includes the husband and wife only. The question asked them is, "How, out of all the people in the world, did you two get together?" The role each spouse plays in answering this is noted.

The fourth task ("The Proverb") consists of giving the husband and wife a copy of the proverb, "A rolling stone gathers no moss." Five minutes are devoted to getting the meaning from the couple and coming to a conclusion. They then are asked to call the children in and teach them the meaning of the proverb. This enables the therapist to perceive how the parents operate as peers and then as parents, how they teach things to their children, and how the children react.

The fifth task ("Main Fault and Main Asset") requires that the family sit around a table; then each person is given a blank card on which to write the main fault of the person to the left. The therapist, after stating that this will be done, writes two cards and adds them to the others. These contain the words "too good" and "too weak." The therapist then shuffles the cards and reads out the fault written on the top card. Each person is asked in turn to identify which family member has this fault. This exposes the negative value system of the family and prepares the family for the phase of treatment when the task is assigned to avoid open and direct criticism. Following this, each person is requested to identify his or her own main fault. This is succeeded by the assignment for each person to write on a card what he or she admires most about the person to the left. The therapist also fills out two cards: (1) "always speak clearly" and (2) "always lets you know where you stand." Experience shows that this part of the task, which is most difficult, exposes the positive value system of the family.

The sixth task ("Who is in charge") consists of asking the family, "Who do you think is in charge of the family?" This yields clues regarding how members perceive the leadership structure and their feelings about it.

The seventh task ("Recognition of Resemblance and Difference") requests the husband and wife to identify which of the children is like him or her and which like the other spouse. Then each child is asked which parent he or she believes to resemble most and the similar and the similar and different characteristics possessed in relation to both parents. The parents are also asked how each is like and unlike the other spouse. This points to the family identification processes.

These structured interviews last from 1 to 1½ hours and are employed as research diagnostic, and therapeutic tools. The network of communication patterns forms the basis for therapeutic intervention.

Further active procedures include (1) preparation of a list by each member of what they would like to see changed (this may act as a focus for negotiating a joint decision), (2) asking the family to discuss a recent argument, (3) asking each member to discuss what he likes and dislikes about other members, (4) changing the seating order periodically, (5) using puppets with members talking through them.

Zuk (1971a), Minuchin (1965, 1974b), and Minuchin and Montalvo (1967), have outlined a number of other strategies along structural lines that therapists have found useful. A search is instituted for alliances and splits in the family, the existing power hierarchies, family modes of conflict management with restoring authority lines, rearranging alliances, and reconstituting normal boundaries. Seating rearrangements and homework tasks are instituted to promote these objectives. Passivity on the part of the therapist will bring few rewards. The idea of allowing a family to engage in a free-for-all squabble often accomplishes nothing more than to encourage greater antagonism between the members. Providing some structure in the session, on the other hand, can be most helpful. This is done by asking specific questions, directing the different members to explore certain areas of feeling, and suggesting what behavior changes should be undertaken. Goals for the family

are set by the therapist, at the same time that the family members are encouraged to utilize their own resources in moving toward behavior change. For diagnostic purposes, if the therapist deems that it is appropriate to do so (and that the family will not be lost after the first session), it may be advisable to observe an undirected family in action in order to get a biopsy of the existing pathology and the distorted lines of communication. Once this is done, the therapist will be in a better position to structure, guide, direct, educate, and set goals.

In psychodynamic models insight and self-understanding are the goals of a family therapy with emphasis on the unconscious promotion of patterns of behavior, and the relationship of such patterns to past conditionings. The systems model, such as that of Bowen (1960), stresses the need for differentiation from one's family in order to achieve true identity. The understanding and resolution of relationship triangles that exist within the family is essential. A search for transgenerational transmission of problems is executed in quest of helping the patient achieve self-differentiation. In the strategic model resistance is not bypassed but joined, nondangerous symptoms may paradoxically be encouraged, and unusual home assignments given to the members. In assigning tasks in family therapy, the therapist attempts to alter the existing family system by asking members to engage in unusual activities that are foreign to their customary roles. This entails some risk because the assignments may spark resentment and sabotage. To avoid this, some therapists join the neurotic system by paradoxically emphasizing that for the time being the members must keep things as they are. Then, when the confidence of the family is gained, slow alterations in role are suggested followed by more extensive changes.

In the behavioral model, some therapists find a self-rating check list such as the one by Cautela and Upper (1975) useful as an assessment tool. An effort is made to identify the stimuli that activate symptoms and problem behaviors. Can these be controlled? How does the patient participate in bringing them on? Further information is occasionally obtained by the patient filling out certain standardization forms (Walsh, 1967, 1968). Observation of the patient in actual situations where problem behaviors occur (with family at home, in phobia mobilizing situations, etc.) may be helpful if this can be arranged. The use of visual imagery to identify cognitive elements associated with problem behaviors has been described by Meichenbaum (1971). The next step is quantification of the problem. The frequency and duration of problem behaviors are charted, recording how often and under what circumstances difficulties occur (Homme, 1965). A man with headaches, for example, is given homework to report the days and times when his headaches appear, the immediate circumstances preceding the onset of headaches, the consequences of his headaches to himself and others around him, and what if anything he does to relieve them. The third step is examining the reinforcing contingencies. Are there any gains the patient derives from symptoms or problem behaviors, like sympathy from those around him, freedom from responsibility, etc. If so, can these reinforcers be supplied by altered activities less destructive to the patient? Is the patient aware of such gains? A woman with periodic fainting spells was brought to the realization that these episodes focused attention on her by her family. Assured regarding their functional nature by the family physician who had been summoned to several such emergencies, the therapist suggested the family show studied neglect after a spell. On the other hand, the members were to lavish attention and praise on the patient when she engaged in constructive family activities. The fourth step is outlining the treatment plan. Once sufficient information is available, a hypothesis is presented to the patient, the treatment plan is formulated, agreement is reached on the focus and goals, and a contract is executed.

In actual family therapy practice several of these models may be combined depending on the kinds of problems that must be treated. The management of socially aggressive children especially constitutes a challenge to parents in our contemporary society. Belligerent and hostile children can stir up trouble for the entire family. A number of approaches have developed dealing with this specific problem; one of the best known being the methods developed by G. R. Patterson and his associates (Patterson & Gullion, 1968; Patterson, 1971; Patterson et al, 1975). A social learning approach teaches families to discover the ways in which they reinforce the disturbed child's behavior and how unwittingly they are taught to respond destructively to the child's provocations, thus adding fuel to the fire. Some techniques include immediate *isolation* of the child for 3 to 5 minutes (no more) when misbehaving, writing a contract with the child defining desirable and undesirable behaviors and prescribing good behavior that may be swapped for privileges.

Hostility that emerges in family therapy often derails the therapeutic process. How to deal with it is an important technical question. Usually the hostility is directed at a selected member who may be the identified patient or a parent who may be blamed for the events leading to the crisis. Unless hostile interchanges are interrupted, the status quo will tend to remain. One method is to divert the hostility by asking questions related to nonpersonal areas: the housing situation, arrangement of rooms, daily routines, employment, certain historical events, etc. Some therapists, who feel they have a good relationship with the family, sometimes try to focus the hostility on themselves to take it away from the scapegoated member. This may be done by asking: "I wonder if there is something I have done or not done that upsets you. I am suggesting that you are really angry at me." Opening up areas of transference can be highly productive at times, but the therapist must be able to control his or her own countertransference. The best way of dealing with hostility, of course, is to interpret it in terms of the personality needs, and defenses of the attacker. This is possible only after a therapeutic alliance has been established, the family pathology comprehended, and the dynamics of the individual family members understood.

The most difficult problem that the therapist will encounter in family therapy is the need and the determined effort (despite protests avowing a desire for change) to maintain the status quo. Yet there are healthy elements that exist in each family on which the therapist can draw. It is important to emphasize these in therapy rather than the prevailing psychopathology.

Reconstructive family therapy may require sessions for several months or several years, depending on the family pathology and goals. It is often articulated with individual or group reconstructive psychotherapy for family members who need special help. The focus here is on intrapsychic experience. The methodology will vary with the relationship designs and the communication systems. The focus is on transferential reverberations and resistances. During the group session it may become apparent that the "identified patient" is not the one who needs most intensive help. Since the patient may be responding to neurotic provocations from another family member, the latter may be the one who should be seen individually. The following case-history brings this out:

The primary patient is a 22-year-old man whose chief symptom is undiluted anxiety that interferes with his functioning. His relationships are highly competitive with males, the patient assuming a submissive self-castigating role. With females the patient detaches, fantasies of sexual engagement inspiring anxiety. At home the family is involved in constant quarreling, the patient engaging principally with his father, complaining that his father is excessively passive, manipulated by his mother, who is extraordinarily demanding of and ambitious for him. The two younger sisters display rebellious and withdrawal tendencies that have not yet become too pathological. In individual sessions the father presents himself as a misunderstood martyr. During the first few family sessions, however, it becomes obvious that he dominates and incessantly criticizes the family, especially the mother. The patient and sisters constantly take pot shots at him for acting too strong and dictatorial. The father responds with the expression that any weakness is inadmissible; it is important to deny illness or fear. This, it soon follows, is a pattern that prevailed in the father's own family. The father's father forced himself to work almost constantly as a duty. He died from a cardiac attack at an early age after refusing to see doctors for what seems to have been anginal pains. The father expresses admiration for his own father's "guts." During this recital the patient slumps in his chair interrupting with deprecatory comments. On questioning, he admits feeling defeated and under attack. Recognizing the father's role in stirring up the family, the father was referred for interviews with a therapist. This resulted in a rapid abatement of the patient's symptoms and a more congenial atmosphere at home.

A multiple family group of several families from the same background and socioeconomic level permits mutual exploration of common problems, the ability to observe difficulties in a more objective light, and the availability of a peer group to whom a family can relate who can help educate and be educated (Laqueur, 1968, 1972). The family code is more likely to become translated by a peer family than by a therapist who may come from a different background.

In reviewing 58 outcome studies of family therapy as compared to alternative treatments (i.e., individual therapy, group therapy, hospitalization, and drug therapy) Kniskern and Gurman (1980) found that 41 (i.e., 70 percent) of the family therapy outcomes were found to be superior, 15 (i.e., 25 percent) were found to be equal, and only two (i.e., 4 percent) were found to be inferior. Many of the primary patients in the studies complained of clinical problems (such as depressions) for which individual psychopathology traditionally is believed implicated. However, the authors, probably with good reason, state that interactional difficulties, such as marital problems, are the most likely conditions to respond best to family and conjoint marital therapy. Compared to such approaches, individual therapy, concurrent marital therapy (where one therapist sees each partner separately), and collaborative marital therapy (where each spouse is seen by different therapists) produce less impressive results. What is interesting, nevertheless, is that individual psychopathological difficulties, other than interactional problems, do respond well to good family therapy methods. Family therapy is highly desirable because the problems do not start or stop with the patient. The least that can be accomplished is the achievement of better lines of family communication and a softening of scapegoating. Family therapy may be one of the most effective ways of reducing rehospitalization, in addition to safeguarding maintenance medication. Many problem families exist, the members sometimes being entangled in complex interpersonal difficulties that seem impossible to unravel. The untrained therapist is apt to encounter insuperable difficulties with these families. On the other hand, an effective family therapist may accomplish good results impossible to achieve by another method.

MARITAL (COUPLE) THERAPY

Marital therapy is important for a variety of reasons. First, it presents an in vivo scan of the relationship operations of the patient who seeks treatment vis-a-vis the marital partner. From a diagnostic viewpoint this is advantageous because it reduces speculation about the patient's interpersonal psychopathology. Second, it enables enlisting the cooperation of the spouse toward helping the patient execute a therapeutic program for management of severe symptoms by serving in the role of cotherapist. Third, it permits observation of and dealing with emerging anxieties and defenses of the spouse that ordinarily might sabotage the progress being made by the patient. Fourth, it permits a more direct entering into and correction of the communication system of the patient as it displays itself in emotional interchanges. Marriage is a vehicle through which people constantly try to satisfy an assortment of needs and influences. It is often regarded by neurotic people as a way of overcoming defects in their own development and handicaps in their current life situation. The marital partner is therefore cajoled, seduced, or terrorized to perform and is held responsible for any deficiency in projected assignments. This imposes an enormous burden on the healthier of the two spouses since the demands made are usually impossible to fulfill.

On top of it all, the habitual hostilities, anxieties, defenses and coping devices that have plagued the individual since childhood become transferred over to the most conveniently available recipient—the spouse. The expression of such improprieties is complicated by reactive guilt feelings, remorse, and attempts at reparation, which in turn invite attack from the injured spouse, perpetuating the continuing chain of indignation, anger, and counterattack. Couples often get locked into this sadomasochistic circuit. It would seem that the battling partners need each other to act out mutual neurotic needs, which insidiously may keep the marriage together while serving as a platform for combat. A final neurotic gesture is the blaming of each other for personal shortcomings, mediocrities, failings, and even symptoms. Disillusionment is inevitable unless the spouses are willing to compromise. But where the needs of a marital partner are too insistent and the initial idealization and expectancies are too high, the explosive mixture gradually accumulates until detonated by some (perhaps minor) incident that will tend to blow the marriage apart. One severely neurotic member preying on a more healthy spouse is bad enough, but where both members are working on each other, the atomic stockpile builds up to frightening proportions.

Marriage calls for intricate adjustments. It involves not only dealing with one's personal difficulties but also the normal problems and the irrationalities of one's partner. Because marital adjustment is one of the most difficult and stressful human challenges, it is little wonder that so many people get disturbed under its impact. Problems in marriage and difficulties with a spouse account for almost 50 percent of the reasons why people seek professional help (Martin & Lief, 1973; Sager et al, 1968).

The task of marital therapy is twofold. First, it endeavors to help the patient overcome disturbing symptomatic complaints. Second, it strives to keep a shaky marriage together where there is even a small chance of its success, strengthening the couple's psychological defenses in the process, or, if the marriage cannot be saved, helping the partners separate with a minimum of conflict and bad feeling, particularly where children are involved.

Marital relationships are commonly sabotaged by the emotional defects of one or both partners. Where a marriage has deteriorated and the couple is motivated to work toward its betterment, there is a good chance that with proper treatment the relationship will improve. This does not mean that all marriages can be saved. In some cases the "chemical" combination of the union is irreconcilably explosive. Husband and wife are too much at loggerheads in their ideas, values, and goals to achieve even a reasonable meeting of the minds; or there is a barrenness of love and unabating cruelty toward each other; or sexual incompatibilities exist of too great severity; or there is uncontrollable and continued violence toward the children. Many couples are already virtually separated but still living together interlocked in a marital death grip from which they cannot loosen themselves before coming to therapy. Here the marriage may not be worthy of saving. The goal, as has been mentioned, may be to help the couple master their guilt and achieve the strength to separate. Generally, however, where couples are not too contentious and are willing to face their feelings and examine their behavior, marital therapy can help a marriage survive.

Marital therapy techniques draw from multiple fields, including psychoanalysis, behavior therapy, family therapy, group therapy, marriage counseling, child therapy, and family casework. Although the objects are the mastery of neurotic suffering and alteration of the relationship between the couple, a hoped-for, and usually serendipitous objective is intrapsychic change, which surprisingly may come about in those with a readiness for such change and relief from the distracting cross-fire between the two spouses. Conceptual schemes for the actual conduct of marital therapy are not unified, but the most successful approaches stress the importance of communication (Watzlawick et al, 1967; Minuchin, 1974) toward effecting changes in the transactional system. A system behavioral approach is particularly helpful, concentrating "on observable behavior and rules of current communication (Bolte, 1970; Hurvitz, 1970; Kotler, 1967; Mangus, 1957) without immediate recourse to a historical 'Why' " (Berman & Lief, 1975).

Greene (1972) has pointed out that the great variations in marital patterns require flexibility in therapeutic techniques. He proposes a "six-C" classification of therapeutic modalities:

I. Supportive Therapy
   A. Crisis counseling

II. Intensive Therapy
   A. Classic psychoanalytic psycho-
      therapy
   B. Collaborative therapy
   C. Concurrent therapy
   D. Conjoint marital therapy
   E. Combined therapies
      1. Simple therapy
      2. Conjoint family therapy
      3. Combined-collaborative
         therapy
      4. Marital group psychother-
         apy

"Crisis counseling" stresses sociocultural forces in the "here-and-now" situation. The "classic approach" is the usual
dyadic one-to-one relationship with both
partners seeing separate therapists who do
not communicate. The focus here is on the
individual's personal difficulties with the
marriage as the backdrop. It is used where
one partner has severe acting-out problems
of which the other partner is unaware (e.g.,
continuous infidelity or homosexuality),
where there is preference for this approach,
where one partner refuses to share the therapist, and where spouses have widely divergent goals in terms of the marriage problem. The "collaborative approach" is
similarly dyadic, but it sanctions communication between the two therapists by regularly scheduled meetings (Martin & Bird,
1963). The same therapist treats both partners individually in the "concurrent approach," which is aimed at bringing about
insight into behavior patterns as they affect
each member (Solomon & Greene, 1963).
This approach results in the lowest divorce
rates. Where strong sibling rivalry attitudes
exist, or where there are severe character
disorders, psychoses, or paranoid reactions, the concurrent approach cannot be
used.

These dyadic methods may be educationally oriented, focused on the marital relationship and on strategies of straightening

it out by utilizing a variety of counseling
and behavioral techniques. Should it become apparent that the patient has a severe
personality or emotional problem being
projected into the marital situation, individual psychotherapy may be indicated. In a
considerable number of cases the marital
equilibrium will be restored, and the spouse
will change with the stabilization and better
adaptation of the patient. However, where
the spouse is incapable of change and the
patient is unable to adapt to this impasse,
the marriage will continue as a traumatic
source for both.

The "conjoint marital approach,"
which is the most common form (Satir,
1965; Fitzgerald, 1969), is used both for
counseling and intensive therapy. Here the
partners meet jointly with the therapist at
the same session. This approach fosters
communication between the partners and
brings out more clearly the marital dynamics. With the "combined therapies" (1)
the "simple" form combines individual,
concurrent, and conjoint sessions in various arrangements; (2) "conjoint family
therapy" includes one or more of the children; (3) the "combined-collaborative"
form permits regular meetings of the partners together with the two therapists at the
same session; and (4) "marital group therapy" consists of group therapy with four
couples and one or two therapists (Blinder
& Kirschenbaum, 1967; Framo, 1973).

Thus, there are many ways of working
with couples but one of the most popular
short-term methods is based on a social
learning model and involves no more than
12 to 16 one hour to $1\frac{1}{2}$ hour sessions.
(Hahlweg & Jacobson, 1984; Jacobson &
Margolin, 1979; Lieberman et al. 1980; Stuart, 1980). Such behavioral marital therapy
focuses on securing better communication,
relationship, conflict reducing, and problem
solving skills through an active, directive
approach aided by consistent assigned
homework exercises. Usually the therapist

sets the agenda with input from the couple regarding progress or difficulties with the homework assignments.

We would make an assumption that if the couple appears for therapy or counseling they are interested in staying together. We would assume also that at one time they had a good relationship. Accordingly, it might be a strategic start in therapy to ask the couple how they originally happened to meet and how they got along at the beginning. From this the history of their difficulties would naturally follow. In recalling the circumstances of their early meeting and the congeniality that existed at one time, it may be possible to get the couple off the track of their bitterness and disillusionment with each other. Many couples forget that they have had a pleasing or happy background at one time, a foundation on which they can repair their present demoralization and wreck of a relationship. Talking about a happier past may give the two partners some hope that they can overcome their bitterness and develop better modes of communication and problem solving.

The actual techniques that are employed will vary with goals in treatment and whether we envisage therapy as solely a means of restoring harmony to the distressed couple or whether structural personality changes in one or both partners are possible. Where deep personality problems exist in one or both of the members, marital therapy, which is a short-term approach, will probably need reinforcement with individual dynamic therapy, since negotiation of differences may prove to be of no avail. Some therapists start with the short-term goal and only later move toward a more intensive process when it becomes obvious that severe personality problems interfere with progress.

In certain cases one member comes for treatment with the presenting complaint of a symptom, such as migraine, depression, agoraphobia or other neurotic disorders even though the true source of stress that provokes the symptom lies in the marital relationship. Indeed, a denial mechanism may exist of such severity that the therapist will have to approach the marital problem obliquely. In most cases however marital stress becomes an important complaint, but the patient may believe that nothing can be done about it since, in the opinion of the patient, the partner refuses to cooperate.

It is rare that marital difficulties are totally one-sided. It is rare, too, that the mate will not come in to see the therapist if the latter handles the situation correctly. The presenting patient may be asked if he or she can convince the mate to come in to see the therapist. The following is from a recording of an interview:

Pt. She's impossible. She won't listen. She says I'm nuts and it's all my doing—the mess we're in. I can't talk to her.

Th. Do you think she would come into see me if you asked her?

Pt. I already asked her to come here with me, and she refused. Frankly, I think it would be a waste of time.

Th. You must have had some hope that coming here would help the situation.

Pt. I suppose I'm looking for magic. I know she won't change.

Th. Would you mind if I telephoned her to come to see me about your problem? I would tell her it will be of help to me in helping you if she could give me an idea of what you're like. (*smiles*) Sometimes this defuses things. She won't feel I'm getting her here to accuse her.

Pt. By all means, maybe she'll come in if you convince her it's all my fault.

Th. I'm sure it isn't, but I'll do my best to ease her into talking things out.

The entire object of getting the mate into the therapist's office is to start a relationship with her or him. By listening with an empathic ear, emphasizing how difficult things must be, the therapist usually can gain confidence. In the case cited the following telephone conversation took place:

Th. Is this Mrs. B?

Mrs. B. Yes.

Th. This is Dr. Wolberg. I hope you will forgive me for calling you. I know it's an imposition. But your husband came in to see me, as you know.

Mrs. B. Yes, I do.

Th. I know it's been extremely difficult for you. But it would help me to help your husband if you could come in and tell me a little bit about him, and about what's happening.

Mrs. B. If I came in, I wouldn't stop talking. (*laughs*)

Th. So much the better, you could give me an idea of him and what has been going on. It must have been very rough.

Mrs. B. I'll be glad to come in.

The interview with Mrs. B went along smoothly, and little difficulty was experienced in starting therapy with the couple.

Unless one of the marital partners is paranoidal or completely unwilling to alter the marriage relationship, it should not be too difficult to convince both members to work with the therapist. The design of therapy will vary with the presenting problems and the preferred style of the therapist. Some therapists begin joint sessions immediately after the initial interview. Others prefer seeing the mate alone to assess the problem before starting joint sessions. It is helpful to ask each partner about the relationship their parents have had with one another. Sometimes just talking about this, patients discover that they are acting out roles patterned after parental models.

Where a marital problem is acknowledged by both partners and they seem willing to do something about it, the couple may be seen together right from the start of therapy. But where denial mechanisms are strong, it may be advantageous for the same therapist to begin individual therapy separately with both spouses, different appointments being given the two (*concurrent marital therapy*). They may not yet be ready for couple therapy, which can be instituted later. Where hostility between the partners is high, and appropriate communication is difficult, the therapist may be able to start a relationship individually with each partner, being wisely careful not to fall into the trap of being used by either against the other. It takes a good deal of ingenuity to do this. The therapist may anticipate competitiveness for attention, desires to be the preferred one, misinterpretations of what the therapist says to support an importunate demand on the part of one spouse, and resentment at the partner and therapist for presumed collaboration. Where the spouse of the patient seeking help refuses to see the therapist, one may try a referral to another professional or suggest that there be a personal selection of a therapist. In such a case the different therapists sometimes may have conferences to exchange information and discuss developments and plans (*collaborative marital therapy*). Where the spouse absolutely refuses any kind of therapy, treatment may be started with the presenting patient alone (*individual marital therapy*), trying to influence the reluctant partner indirectly.

Assuming that one is finally able to bring the partners together in therapy, the initial session may be initiated by asking each of the partners to discuss why they are coming for help as each sees it. The couple may then be queried as to how they originally met and how they happened to decide to get married or to live together. Whenever the two get into an argument or fire charges at each other, the therapist may interrupt the negative exchanges and get them back to talking about positive things that were or are happening. Some therapists find it helpful to spend at least one session alone with each of the spouses, reviewing the past histories, experiences, and problems of each particularly their relationship with each other, sexual and otherwise. At individual sessions, information may come up that will not readily be exposed in joint sessions. The matter of confidentiality should be stressed. Some therapists rely heavily on questionnaires to fill out such as the "Areas of Change Questionnaire," "Marital Status Inventory," the "Dyadic Adjustment Scale," the "Marital Precounseling Inventory," the "Marital Activities Inventory," and the "Sexual Interaction Inventory" (Wood & Jacobson, 1985), which will help in developing a treatment plan.

We usually find that central to many of the problems of marital couples are difficulties in communication. Behavioral approaches to communication training contain a number of procedures geared toward acquisition of communication skills with provision for feedback instructions and behavioral rehearsal. Dynamically oriented therapists may use these as part of their treatment with marital problems.

During joint sessions the therapist will have observed patterns of communication issuing out of the interaction of the couple, and will be able to offer the couple information about their verbal and nonverbal exchanges (criticisms of one by the other, attacks, praise, protectiveness, etc.) in descriptive terms without interpreting the deeper meaning or motivations for such exchanges (which, of course, can be made in a dynamic approach). Immediate feedback to both partners of provocative and disturbed communication patterns may help break the chain reaction of attack, counterattack or retreat that is characteristic of the couple's verbal interactions. With adequate preparation, video feedback may also be used with some advantage. In employing feedback the therapist should not lose any opportunity to comment on *positive* communication patterns in the hope of reinforcing these. Thus when a partner praises his or her mate the therapist may say, "I liked the way you complimented (or praised) him (her)."

Generally couples are not fully aware of their abrasive thrusts at each other or their corrosive answers to comments. Following an unjustified verbal blast, the therapist may ask a partner to reconsider what the spouse has said and then to give an alternative response. Sometimes the therapist may model a response, playing the roles of both the husband and the wife to avoid a sense of discrimination or favoritism. Cotherapists, if this is the format, may

each play the role of one of the spouses and model communication.

Behavior rehearsal is an important part of the relearning process, in that couples may practice in order to increase their skills of communication. Here the therapist provides instructions and modeling if necessary, giving continuing feedback. A valuable technique is *role reversal,* each spouse taking the role of the other in talking about a special situation. In this way, marital partners may teach each other problem-solving skills.

One of the most common difficulties is the insistent use of aversive control strategies by one or both partners ("If you do that again, I'm going to leave you"). Verbal threats and coercion increase until the only way left to deal with mutual intimidation is by detachment techniques, which cause estrangement from one another, further enhancing conflict. By arriving at some sort of agreement regarding areas of change through discussion, an avenue is opened for problem-solving which can be kept alive and expanded by proper reinforcements. Before changes in behavior can be proposed, however, there must be a clear definition of the problem (Jacobson & Margolin, 1979).

The sessions in a short-term format are generally highly structured and understandably call for a good deal of empathy, flexibility, and playing of many roles. "The therapist serves as a director, sympathizer, teacher, evaluator, instigator, and a juggler balancing these roles while providing perspective and insight as necessary." (Wood & Jacobson, 1985).

It is important to inform a couple that they should expect no immediate improvement in their relationship but after a few sessions devoted to studying the problems, they should *if they cooperate with the procedures that will be prescribed,* notice that matters between them are taking on a more optimistic turn. In this way, one can forestall the disappointment that follows when magical expectations of immediate change do not come to pass. Generally, some precipitating factor will have brought the marital conflict to a head and the couple will be anxious to talk about it. The discussion, arguments, angry displays, and frustrations that become manifest will be like a biopsy of the basic pathological issues. A therapist who steps into a marital melee will have more than was bargained for, particularly when each of the participants attempts to recruit the therapist as an ally against the other partner. It is here that the therapist may become emotionally involved, being tempted to fulfill the roles of arbiter, judge and high priest, rendering verdicts, making decisions, establishing criteria, and setting values. Personal standards and prejudices will unfailingly impose themselves and the therapist's own unresolved problems will vigorously come to the fore.

A great deal has been written about countertransference in psychotherapy, but in no other area than marital therapy is it apt to be so pronounced, particularly in cases where the therapist's own marriage is a mess. No wiser words have been said than for the marital therapist to look at his or her own marital values before the marriages of others can effectively be dealt with. Even though a therapist has some personal problems, an awareness of these and of how judgment may be warped by certain offensive behaviors or attitudes on the part of the therapist's patients should permit greater objectivity. The therapist therefore should carefully avoid being brought into assuming the role of a referee or judge who decides who is right or who is wrong; or ally with one or the other antagonists. This may be difficult for some therapists to do since it is natural to try to assess blame. A guiding principle in marital therapy is to try to search out and to enhance the strengths of a relationship not the weaknesses. Consequently, the therapist may emphasize positive factors that exist and to remind the couple that their relationship

has not always been a bad one. A good deal of time may also have to be spent in talking about existing environmental problems that have initiated or that are sustaining the difficulties between the two.

It is important from the outset not to express any condemnatory attitude toward either partner for behavior or characteristics that they are exhibiting either in the interview or outside. There will be ample opportunity later to interpret what is happening, and this is aimed toward insightful rather than punitive objectives. A woman may resent the role that she believes her husband expects of her as a dutiful wife, and she may respond by being defiant and neglectful. Her husband may counterattack by detaching himself from her and the family and by impotence. The chasm of misunderstanding grows deeper and deeper until each has accumulated an enormous bag of justifiable grievances. A therapist who takes sides will probably lose both patients. Once the dynamics become clear, the therapist may point out the inevitability of misunderstanding on the basis of the background, upbringing, value systems, and pressures that are being exerted by the partners on each other without laying down strict rules about male and female roles. If the therapist has the confidence of the couple, they will turn to him or her for some constructive guidance, which may be offered without being dictatorial about what should be done. It may be pointed out that difficulties exist in all relationships and that some compromise is always necessary, the ground rules to be negotiated through constructive communication.

Willy-nilly, the therapist will find a role assigned, by both members as an arbiter, guide, and potential ally to justify mutual opinions, disgruntlements, and claims. It takes a good deal of fancy footwork to avoid being maneuvered into a judgmental role. Countertransference is to be expected, and one's ability to detect one's own prejudices and predilections borne out of one's background and experience will help keep the therapeutic situation afloat. There are instances where one mate is manifestly unfair in behavior toward the other, or in liberties assumed, and the therapist may find it difficult to remain neutral. It will take ingenuity to get one mate to alter his or her behavior or to help the other member accept the situation with whatever compromises can be negotiated.

For example, one of my male patients who had married late in life, insisted on staying out late "with the boys" two nights weekly. His wife objected on the basis that she felt neglected and lonesome. At interview it was apparent that she suspected infidelity, which she tried to substantiate on the basis of decreasing frequency of intercourse. I was able to convince her, from my interview with her husband, that staying out late constituted a means by which some husbands maintain their independence which is being threatened by feelings of increasing devotion to their wives. This is what happened in this particular case. The husband, a detached person, had avoided close involvements with women until he met his wife. Thwarting his need for independence would, I hazarded, result in increasing detachment from her as a defense and perhaps a development of impotency. The patient's depression, related to hostility at being challenged and "browbeaten," lifted as his wife recognized the dynamics and accepted her husband's need for greater freedom. Joint sessions during which each partner unburdened themselves and traced their attitudes to past experiences resulted in a firming up of the relationship.

Taking an area in which a desire for change has been expressed, each member may be asked to discuss briefly how he or she believes the issue may be resolved with the object of negotiating an agreement on a suitable solution. Communication and problem-solving skills are studied here. Some therapists provide each of the coup-

les with a checklist and a rating scale to score daily happy and non-pleasing exchanges (Patterson, 1976; Weiss & Cerreto, 1980). These instruments have a therapeutic value in pointing out areas of possible improvement as well as providing the therapist with a means of comparing the appraisals of both members.

All of the foregoing measures are useful in devising a treatment plan that is discussed with the couple and to which the couple can add input. Agreement to abide by the terms of the plan is best obtained to enhance the collaborative effort. To repeat, the therapeutic process focuses on increasing positive and eliminating coercive and aversive exchanges. It is hoped that this will spontaneously be developed and carried through by both members. Any difficulty that emerges offers an opportunity for trouble-shooting to analyze the problem and to provide alternative solutions ("brain storming"). Communication skills are taught by suggestion and modeling and are practiced both during sessions and as part of homework. The ability to accept criticism and to have the courage to avoid responding in kind to a negative remark or act is encouraged.

Contracts may be negotiated to try to help firm up behavioral changes. Contingency contracting which operates on the basis of quid pro quo conciliations plays an important part in marital therapy, particularly in its behaviorally oriented forms. Here couples by negotiation come to a written agreement of what each member has to do in the relationship to produce changes with which both members are in harmony.

In contingency contracts each partner promises to alter some aspect of behavior the other partner finds disagreeable. Contingency contracting is for those in whom verbal resolutions alone are not sufficient to put a restraint on their impulsiveness. The presence of a legal-like document helps to promote compliance with prescribed behaviors. When carried out, positive actions produce reciprocal pleasing responses that act as reinforcers for mutually constructive behaviors. The contract should be specific, spelling out exactly the kind of activities to be executed; otherwise arguments may break out as to meanings of vague expressions. The behavioral changes of each should also be sufficiently equivalent so that both partners feel they are getting an equal share of benefits.

One must keep in mind that the very behaviors that a spouse grumbles about may subversively be reinforced by certain actions of the offended spouse because such behaviors satisfy unconscious needs or defenses in the latter. Thus, a woman complaining about infrequency of sexual relationships may during the sexual experience act in a disinterested, bored, or sarcastic manner. In this way, she punishes the very behavior she desires to increase. When we investigate why these ambivalent attitudes exist, we may find that, in spite of a surface interest, sexuality is laden with a great deal of fear, guilt, and shame. Or her anger at or disgust with her husband forbids carnal intimacy. Or perhaps there is a prohibitive incestuous barrier to sexual activity. Such dispositions, which have their origin in earlier conditionings, might cause us to anticipate that the wife would be unable to halt her punishing activities even though in the contingency contract she promised to do so. This may actually be the case in instances where underlying needs and defenses are intensely and urgently pressing. On the other hand, even where such tendencies act as negative reinforcers, experience teaches that people can exercise a considerable degree of willful control over inner impulses, and through self-discipline and continuing practice gradually master adverse predispositions. It is, of course, helpful to provide in the contract positive reinforcements of some kind for the control of repugnant reactions. In the case cited, the husband may reward his mate for refraining from her customary reactions with praise and some material or behavioral bounty that is significant to his wife. Where no improvement in the sexual situation occurs, however, it may be necessary to utilize a more psychoanalytically oriented approach aimed at expanding the couple's understanding of their motivations and behavior.

The matter of confidentiality is especially important. The patient is told that information given in private sessions will not be revealed to the other member of the couple. The members may be encouraged to talk freely and not hold anything back, but that is up to them. The therapist will not bring up topics that are taboo unless asked to. This encourages the disclosure of secrets so one can work with what comes out.

It is to be expected that where couples have been living in neurotic symbiosis that an alteration in the accustomed response of one member to the other's provocations will arouse anxieties in one or both members. Resistance will generally take the form of a desire to halt joint sessions. Interpretations of the resistance and the reasons behind it are necessary to keep the couple in therapy.

During sessions one may observe physical movements between husbands and wives that serve as forms of nonverbal communication to convey emotional meanings. These are in the form of approach and separation movements and, at different stages of treatment, seating rearrangements among couples, which may be explored with the object of analyzing the underlying dynamics. In the process one may observe one's own countertransference responses, which one should attempt to understand and to resolve.

While the therapist may make suggestions from time to time, it is vital that patients be made aware of the fact that they must work out their own solutions utilizing their own free will.

There are several impasses that may occur in marital therapy. One of the most difficult is the spouse who has a fixed position about divorce. This usually means that he or she does not want therapy except to try to convince the mate to accept the position. Often the lawyer of one mate may be responsible for this impasse. Another problem is when one member of the couple is in individual therapy with another therapist who differs in philosophy and goals from the marital therapist. Then a conference with the other therapist may be in order. Once contact has been established, coordinated therapy may be essential to break up an impasse. Where the marital breakdown has proceeded to a point of no return, both therapists may encourage utilizing divorce mediation procedures to minimize the trauma on the partners and children.

Important adjuncts to marital therapy are role playing and sexual therapy methods (Masters & Johnson, 1970; Kaplan, 1974). Alger (1967a) illustrates the use of the paradigmatic approach in marital therapy, the goal of which is to imitate a pattern one of the partners displays by acting out a part. Alger (1967b) also employs videotape recordings and playback in couple's sessions. His technique consists of a video recording of the first 15 minutes of a joint marital session, which is immediately played back over a television monitor. The participants may ask to stop the recording at any point to comment on the effect of their behavior on others. Viewing themselves as they talk and interact stimulates a great deal of feeling and expedites communication. Video viewing is now being employed with increasing frequency (Alger & Hogan, 1969; Berger, MM, 1969).

The presence of two therapists (cotherapists) lessens the possibility of exclusive alliances and of a dyadic impasse (Alger, 1967a; Markowitz, 1967). Each of the therapists may function as an alternate ego for one of the patients aerating ideas and sentiments the patient does not dare express. In this way the patient may gain the strength to face impulses and attitudes on the periphery of awareness. Substantiating the value of cotherapy are four truisms: (1) Two heads are better than one. (A second therapist may be able to illuminate areas missed by the first. Each may be able to correct bias and detect countertransference in the other.) (2) One therapist may support a patient under attack by mate when he or she needs a helping hand. (3) One therapist may engage in confrontation and challenging maneuvers while the other therapist interprets reactions of the patient or supports the latter if necessary. (4) Two therapists lessen the danger of the therapist being utilized as a judge or as a guru who knows and gives all the answers.

A mixed male-female team has advantages in providing opportunities for identification. The disadvantages of cotherapy are competitiveness and friction between the therapists and alliances of one therapist with one patient against the other therapist and the other patient. These may be modified by conferences together or in some cases with a trusted colleague acting in a supervisory capacity. There are advantages and disadvantages in conjoint marriage therapy with a husband-and-wife team (Bellville et al, 1969). The inevitable differences arising between the therapist couple are more volatile and unrepressed than in an unrelated couple and can threaten the therapeutic process. In their resolution, however, they offer the patient couple an opportunity to observe how a well-related couple negotiate differences, make compromises, and adapt themselves to each other's individual way of looking at things. It stands to reason that the therapist couple both must be reasonably adjusted, have an understanding about the therapeutic process, and preferably have been in personal therapy or coupled therapy themselves.

The behavioral approaches described may not be able to help marital difficulties that are too firmly anchored in intrapsychic disturbances. The prescription of tasks and exercises that are intended to influence couples to be less abrasive toward each other, to communicate more constructively, and to foster a balanced relationship will therefore not succeed in those couples whose behavior is intractably motivated by urgent unconscious needs and impelling inner conflicts. For example, if a wife transferentially relates to a husband as if he represents a hateful brother with whom she was in competition during early childhood, she may resent being nice to him and continuously fail in her therapeutic assignments. A husband who is struggling with a dependency need, idealizing his wife as a mother figure who must love, nurture and take care of him, may be unable to give up acting irresponsibly, resisting the independent role his wife insists he must assume as a condition for more fruitful living together.

We should not minimize the utility of the various persuasive, behavioral, and cognitive techniques practiced to expedite marital congeniality. They can be valuable, but they will miss their mark if one utilizes them while ignoring the enormously important developmentally inspired motivational forces that are constantly maneuvering marital partners to act against their best interests. These more insistently dictate the terms of conduct than any injunctions, maxims, precepts, recipes, prohibitions, and interpretations.

Whether or not the therapist deals with factors of transference or projective identification and utilizes dreams will depend on the training of the therapist, the goals desired, and the level of understanding of both patients. Dramatic results are sometimes obtained where marital partners associate to each other's dreams. This helps them become less defensive with each other. By the same token, transference phenomena brought out into the open as they relate to the therapist and to each other, aired without restraint, will bring forth emotions that with proper interpretation can prove helpful. Sager (1967) points out that it is important for anyone doing marital therapy "to be aware and work through reactions to, and general philosophy regarding, maleness and femaleness, maturity, marriage roles, career, money, relationship to children, and a host of other cathected concepts." Flexibility and tolerance for values other than their own are important assets for marital therapists.

The hope is that change occurring in the office and at home will be generalized to other relationships. Any relapses provide opportunities to anticipate future problems. The couple is requested to search for any cues that can trigger difficulties and to practice dealing with them before trouble precipitates.

In many cases progress is enhanced by couples working together in couple groups. As communication improves and relationship skills consolidate, intervals between sessions are increased. Couple groups may continue for a while without the presence of the therapist. Problems and relapses are anticipated and ways of managing them are discussed.

Follow-up sessions with the marital partners after therapy are wise to prevent a falling back into the old destructive patterns, the intervals between follow-up visits gradually being increased in the event improved adjustment continues.

53
Homework Assignments*

One of the most neglected aspects of psychotherapy is assigning homework through which patients can facilitate means of controlling or eliminating self-defeating patterns. It is often assumed that the lessons absorbed in the therapist's office will automatically carry over into everyday life. This cherished hope does not always come to pass. The average patient generally dissociates the learnings in the therapist's office from behavior at home, at school, at work, and in the community. After psychologically purging oneself during a session, outside the office the patient often slips back into familiar patterns. It can be helpful, therefore, in consolidating therapeutic gains to insist that therapy does not stop with the exit from the treatment room. The patient must put into practice what is learned during the sessions in order for any change to register itself permanently. And when treatment has ended, the patient will certainly need to reinforce new modes of coping by continuing homework; otherwise, in returning to the customary environment, relapse may be inevitable.

The assigned tasks are usually related to what is immediately going on in therapy, whether they involve exploring the nature of one's problems, charting the frequency of symptoms and recording the circumstances under which they appear, recognizing the constructive and destructive elements in the immediate environment, observing behavioral patterns and reinforcing those that are adaptive, picking out situations that enhance or lower self-esteem, studying one's relationships with people, examining dreams and fantasies, or seeing what resistances block the putting of understanding into productive action. Practice sessions devoted to assertive and other constructive forms of behavior are especially helpful. Some of the assigned exercises strive to inculcate new values and philosophies that contribute to a more productive adjustment. A relaxing and ego-building casette tape (see p. 1019) as well as assigned readings are additional useful accessories.

Instructions may be given the patient along the following lines:

1. *Look squarely at your immediate life situation.* What elements are to your liking? Are these elements good for you and constructive, and do they need reinforcement? Or should they be minimized or eliminated because they get you into problems? What elements are

* This chapter was incorporated from Wolberg LR: Handbook of Short-term Psychotherapy. New York, Thieme-Stratton, 1980 with permission.

destructive? What can you do to make them less destructive? Should they be eliminated completely? How can you go about doing this? Once you have decided on a plan of action, proceed with it a step at a time, doing something about it each day.

2. *What patterns of behavior would you like to change, patterns that should be changed?* How far back do they go? Do you see any connection between these patterns and things that happened to you as a child? Realize that you may not have been responsible for what happened to you as a child, but you are responsible for perpetuating these patterns now, for letting these patterns ruin your happiness at the present time. *You can do something about them.* When you observe yourself acting these patterns out, STOP. Ask yourself are you going to let them control you? Say to yourself, "I am able now to stop this nonsense," *and do it.* For example, every time you beat yourself and depreciate yourself, or act out a bad pattern and say you are helpless to control it, are you doing these things to prove that you are defenseless and that therefore somebody should come along and take care of you? Are you punishing yourself because you feel guilty about something? It is easy to say you are a crippled child and that some kind person must take care of you. But remember you pay an awful price for this dependency by getting depressed, feeling physically ill, and destroying your feelings of selfworth. Every time you control a bad pattern, reward yourself by doing something nice for yourself, something you enjoy and that is good for you.

3. *What patterns of behavior would you like to develop that are constructive?* Would you like to be more assertive for instance? If so, plan to do something that calls for assertiveness each day.

These assignments may be given verbally to the patient in the therapist's own words. If a relaxing and ego-building cassette tape (see p. 1019) has been made, remind the patient that results are contingent on utilizing the tape preferably at least twice daily. Keeping a diary and jotting down one's reactions and discoveries may prove to be a valuable adjunct.

In addition to the above, some patients may benefit from a printed or typewritten set of directions, such as suggested below. These may be adapted to specific problems. The list may be given to and discussed with the patient shortly before termination.

1. *Whenever you get upset or your symptoms return or get worse, ask yourself why this is so.* Try to establish a relationship between the symptoms and happenings in your environment. Did something occur that made you feel guilty or angered you or that you didn't like? Are you punishing yourself because you feel guilty? Is something going on in your relationship with a person who is close to you or with the people who are around you that is hard for you to take? Or is something bothering you that you find difficult to admit even to yourself? It is often helpful to keep a written record of the number of times daily that your symptoms return and approximately when they started and when they stopped. If you jot down the things that happened immediately before the symptoms started, and the circumstances, if any, that relieved them, you may be able to learn to control your symptoms or eliminate them.

2. *What are the circumstances that boost and the things that diminish the feelings about yourself?* When do you feel good about yourself and when do you feel bad? Are these feelings connected with your successes or your failures? What makes you feel inferior, and what makes you feel superior? Do you feel

better when you are alone and away from people, or do you feel better when you are with people? What kind of people?

3. *Observe the form of your relationship with people.* What tensions do you get with people? What kind of people do you like and dislike? Are these tensions with all people or certain kinds of people? What do people do to upset you? In what ways do you get upset? What do you do to upset them or get yourself upset when you are with them? What do you do and what do they do that tends to make you angry? What problems do you have with your parents, mate, children, boss, associates at work, authorities, people in general? Do you tend to treat anyone in a way similar to the patterns that you established with your father, mother, siblings? How is your reaction to people above you, below you, equal to you? What are your expectations when you meet a very attractive person of the opposite sex? Do you try to make yourself too dependent on certain people?

4. *Observing daydreams or night dreams.* A useful outline for observing the meaning of one's day or night dreams includes three questions: What is your feeling about yourself in the dream? What problem are you wrestling with in the dream? By what means do you reach, or fail to reach, a solution to the problem that presents itself in the dream?

    Recurring dreams are particularly significant because they represent a continuing core problem in one's life. Again, whenever possible, you should attempt, if you can, to relate the content of your dreams to what is happening in your life at that time. One man found that he had recurring dreams of bloodshed but that those dreams only occurred after he had made an attempt to assert himself by asking for a raise in pay or by going out with a girl that he liked. He was much surprised to discover that his frightening dreams were actually evidence that he still had some old childish fears about standing up for himself.

5. *Observing resistances to putting understanding into action.* Expect inevitable resistance when you try to stop neurotic patterns. And there can be tension and fear when one faces a challenge that formerly has been evaded. When delaying and avoidance continue to occur, it is well to question the reasons for the delay and ask why one is afraid—and then to take heart and deliberately challenge the fear to see if it can be overcome.

The disciplined practice of these principles of self-observation can lead to progressive growth. Patterns have to be recognized and revised if one is to achieve more satisfying goals in life. But as everyone knows, the habits of years give ground grudgingly and slowly. Ideally, however, the process of personality understanding and growth is marked by several discrete features: There is the awareness that one's problems do not occur fortuitously but are intimately connected with the events (especially the human interactions) of one's life. For a given individual there is a certain quality of human event that generates anxiety, conflict, and stress. These phenomena, once detected, may lead next to a searching for the origin and history of these patterns. It is not impossible to see how these patterns operated as far back as a person can remember—perhaps even the very earliest memory contains something of the same thing. Seeing the conditions under which fears originate, and under which they are not retriggered, one may next determine whether one can be more the master of one's life rather than a victim of it. Could we be different from the way we have always known ourselves to be? And ever so slowly, we may challenge one habitual childish fear at a time, pushing ourselves to break out of the prison of our neurotic self-defeating patterns. Success breeds success, and victory leads to victory. Defeats are reanalyzed in accord with their place in the psychic structure. Seeing ourselves defeated by the same old enemies, we are buoyed up in knowing that formulations about our personalities are correct, and we are then encouraged to fight on. Increasingly, we can express a claim to a new life; we find ourselves able to be more expressive. Self-recriminations diminish. Our capacities expand, and we gratify more of our needs. Feeling less frustrated in life, and therefore less angry, we can enter into relationships with people with more openness and a greater ability to share.

These are idealistic goals, but they represent a guide along the way toward greater self-observation and richer living. Fidelity to the practice of self-observation, together with the actual translation of understanding into action, can be a lifelong quest marked by high adventure and notable results.

The knowledge of oneself and how one reacts continues to constitute a health and mature behavior.

The above tasks given to the patient as an assignment in therapy can provide material to be discussed during the treatment hour. In addition to problem solving and symptom control, an attempt may be made to alter the individual's sense of values by developing a different way of conceptualizing himself or herself and of coping with the stresses and strains of everyday life.

Evolving a More Constructive Life Philosophy

One of the ways psychotherapy influences people is by helping them to develop new values and philosophies of living. However, the history of the majority of patients, prior to their seeking therapy, attests to futile gropings for some kind of philo-

sophical answer to their dilemmas. The search may proceed from Christian to Oriental philosophies, from prurience to moralism, from self-centeredness to community mindedness. What at first seems firmly established soon becomes dubious as new ideas and concepts are proffered by different authorities. It is far better to evolve philosophies that are anchored in some realistic conception of one's personal universe than to accept fleeting cosmic sentiments and suppositions no matter how sound their source may seem. Even a brief period of pschotherapy may till the soil for the growth of a healthier sense of values. We may be able during this span to inculcate in the person a philosophy predicted on science rather than on cultism.

The question that naturally follows in a therapy program is: Can we as therapists expedite matters by acting in an educational capacity, pointing out faulty values and indicating healthy ones that the patient may advantageously adopt? If so, what are the viewpoints to be stressed?

Actually, no matter how nondirective a therapist may imagine him or herself to be, the patient will soon pick up from explicit or implicit cues the tenor of the therapist's philosophies and values. The kinds of questions the therapist asks, the focus of interpretive activities, confrontations and acquiescences, silences and expressions of interest, all designate points of view contagious to the patient, which the patient tends to incorporate, consciously and unconsciously, ultimately espousing the very conceptual commodities that are prized by the therapist. Why not then openly present new precepts that can serve the patient better? Superficial as they sound, the few precepts that can be tendered may be instrumental in accelerating a better adjustment.

The precepts presented to the patient for practice at home may embody persuasive suggestions on how to isolate the past from the present, modes of managing anxiety, learning to endure a certain amount of tension and anxiety, tolerating a certain measure of anger and hostility, handling frustration and deprivation, correcting remediable elements in one's environment, adapting oneself to irremediable elements in one's life situation, using willpower to stop engaging in destructive activities, stopping unreasonable demands on oneself, challenging a devalued self-image, deriving the utmost enjoyment in life that is possible, and accepting one's social role. Not all patients need these directives, but they may be helpful especially in supportive and reeducative programs. But even in reconstructive therapy there are many patients who can benefit from them. The degree of authoritativeness in giving suggestions will vary ranging from highest in supportive therapy and lowest in reconstructive therapy.

Isolating the Past from the Present

All persons are victimized by their past, which may operate as mischief mongers in the present. A good adjustment presupposes modulating one's activities to present-day considerations rather than resigning to promptings inspired by childish needs and misinterpretations. In therapy the patient may become aware of the early patterns that repeat themselves in adult life. This may provide one with an incentive for change. On the other hand, it may give the patient an excuse to rationalize defects on the basis that unalterable damage has been done by the parents, who are responsible for all of his or her trouble. The therapist may remind the patient that the patient, like anyone else, has a tendency to project outmoded feelings, fears, and attitudes into the present. Early hurtful experiences undoubtedly contribute to the patient's insecurity and to devalued self-esteem. They continue to contaminate one's adjustment *now*, and, therefore, must try to overcome

them. Thus, the therapist would make a statement similar to the following:

Th. Ruminating on your unfortunate childhood and bitter past experiences are indulgences you cannot afford. These can poison your present life if you let them do this. It is a credit to you as a person to rise above your early misfortunes. Attempt to restrain yourself when you fall back into thinking about past events and you no longer can control or when you find yourself behaving childishly. Remember, you may not have been responsible for what happened to you when you were a child, but you *are* responsible for perpetuating these patterns in the present. Say to yourself, "I'm going to release myself from the bonds of the past." And work at it.

Handling Tension and Anxiety

The patient may be reminded that tension and anxiety may appear but that something positive can be done about them.

Th. Everytime you experience tension, or any other symptoms for that matter, ask yourself why? Is it the immediate situation you are in? Is it something which happened before that is stirring you up? Is it something you believe will happen in the future? Once you have identified the source of your tension or trouble, you will be in a better position to handle it. The least that will occur is that you will not feel so helpless since you know a little about its origins. You will then be in a better position to do things to correct your trouble.

The idea that one need not be a helpless victim of symptoms tends to restore feelings of mastery. A patient who was given this suggestion went to a new class. While listening to the lecturer, she began to experience tension and anxiety. Asking herself why, she realized she was reacting to the presence of a classmate who came from her own neighborhood and knew her family. She then recognized that she felt guilty about her interest in one of the men in the class. This happened to be the real reason why she registered for the course. She realized that she feared the neighbor's revealing her interest in the man to her parents if she sat near him or was friendly to him. She then thought about her mother who was a repressive, punitive person who had warned her about sexual activities. With this understanding, she suddenly became angry at her classmate. When she asked herself why she was so furious, it dawned on her that she was actually embittered at her own mother. Her tension and hostility disappeared when she resolved to follow her impulses on the basis that she was now old enough to do what she wished.

Tolerating a Certain Amount of Tension and Anxiety

Some tension and anxiety are inherent parts of living. There is no escape from them. The patient must be brought around to the fact that one will have to tolerate and handle a certain amount of anxiety.

Th. Even when you are finished with therapy, a certain amount of tension and anxiety are to be expected. All persons have to live with some anxiety and tension, and these may precipitate various symptoms from time to time. If you do get some anxiety now and then, ride it and try to figure out what is stirring it up. But, remember, you are no worse off than anyone else simply because you have some anxiety. If you are unable to resolve your tensions entirely through self-observation, try to involve yourself in any outside activities that will get your mind off your tensions.

Tolerating a Certain Amount of Hostility

If the patient can be made to understand that he or she will occasionally get resentful and that if the reason for this is explored, the patient may be able to avoid projecting anger or converting it into symptoms.

Th. If you feel tense and upset, ask yourself if you are angry at anything. See if you can figure out what is causing your resentment. Permit yourself to feel angry if the occasion justifies it, but express your anger in proportion to what the situation will tolerate. You do not have to do anything that will result in trouble for you; nevertheless, see if you can release some of your anger. If you can do nothing more, talk out loud about it when you are alone, or engage in muscular exercises to provide an outlet for aggression, like punching a pillow. In spite of these activities you may still feel angry to a certain degree. So long as you keep it in hand while recognizing that it exists, it need not hurt you. All people have to live with a certain amount of anger.

Tolerating a Certain Amount of Frustration and Deprivation

No person can ever obtain a full gratification of all of one's needs, and the patient must come to this realization.

Th. It is important to remember that you still can derive a great deal of joy out of eighty per cent rather than one hundred percent. Expect to be frustrated to some extent and learn to live with it.

Correcting Remediable Elements in One's Environment

The patient may be reminded of the responsibility to remedy any alterable factors in one's life situation.

Th. Once you have identified any area of trouble, try to figure out what can be done about it. Lay out a plan of action. You may not be able to implement this entirely, but do as much of it as you can immediately, and then routinely keep working at it. No matter how hopeless things seem, if you apply yourself, you can do much to rectify matters. Do not get discouraged. Just keep working away.

Adjusting to Irremediable Elements in One's Life Situation

No matter how much we may wish to correct certain conditions, practical considerations may prevent our doing much about them. For example, one may have to learn to live with a handicapped child or a sick husband or wife. One's financial situation may be irreparably marginal. There are certain things all people have to cope with, certain situations from which they cannot escape. If the patient lives in the hope of extrication from an unfortunate plight by magic, he or she will be in constant frustration.

Th. There are certain things every person has to learn to accept. Try your best to alter them as much as you can. And then if some troubles continue, just tell yourself you must live with some of them, and resolve not to let them tear you down. It takes a good deal of courage and character to live with your troubles, but you may have a responsiblity to carry them. If you start feeling sorry for yourself, you are bound to be upset. So just plug away at it and build up insulation to help you carry on. Say to yourself: "I am not going to respond to trouble like a weather vane. I will remedy the trouble if I can. If I cannot, I will adjust to it. I will concentrate on the good things in my life and minimize the bad."

Using Will Power to Stop Engaging in Destructive Activities

One of the unfortunate consequences of a dynamic approach is that the patient believes the idea that he or she is under the influence of unconscious monsters that cannot be controlled. The patient will, therefore, justify the acting-out on the basis of "automatic repetition-compulsions." Actually, once the patient has a glimmer of what is happening, there is no reason why the cooperation of will power cannot be enlisted to help inhibit himself or herself.

Th. If you know a situation will be bad for you, try to divert yourself from acting it out even if you have to use your will power. There is no reason why you can't work out substitute solutions that are less destructive to you even though they may not immediately be so gratifying. Remember, a certain amount of deprivation and frustration is normal, and it is a complement to you as a person to be able to give up gratifications that are ultimately hurtful to you. Remember, too, that some of the chief benefits you get out of your symptoms are masochistic, a kind of need to punish yourself. You can learn to over-come this too. When you observe yourself acting neurotically, stop in your tracks and figure out what you are doing.

A conventional housewife was involved sexually with two of her friend's husbands. She found herself unable to resist their advances, even though the sexual experiences were not particularly fulfilling. She felt ashamed and was guilt-ridden by her actions. There was obviously some deeper motive that prompted the patient to act out sexually, but the threat to her marriage and relationship with her husband required an immediate halting of her activity. I remarked to her: "Until you figure out some of your underlying feelings, it is best for you to stop your affairs right now. How would you feel about stopping right now? Let's give ourselves a couple of months to figure out this thing. Frankly, I don't see how we can make progress unless you do." The patient reluctantly acquiesced; but soon she was relieved that somebody was supporting her inner resolution to resist. The interval enabled us to explore her disappointment with her husband, her resentment toward him, and to find outlets for her desires for freedom and self-expression in more appropriate channels than sexual acting-out. If the patient has been given a chart detailing the interactions of dependency, low feelings of independence, hostility, devalued self-esteem and detachment, their manifestations as well as reaction formations to neutralize them, he or she may be enjoined to study the chart and see how one's own drives and needs, with their consequences, fit into the overall design.

Stopping Unreasonable Demands on Oneself

Pushing beyond the limits of one's capacities or setting too high personal standards require sober self-assessment. Are they to satisfy one's own ambitions or those of parents? Are they to do things perfectionistically? If so, does the patient feel greater independence or stature as a person when he or she succeeds?

Th. All people have their assets and liabilities. You may never be able to accomplish what some persons can do; and there are some things you can do that others will find impossible. Of course, if you try hard enough, you may probably do the impossible, but you'll be worn down so it won't mean much to you. You can still live up to your creative potentials without going to extremes. You can really wear yourself out if you push yourself too hard. So just try to relax and to enjoy what you have, making the most out of yourself without tearing yourself to pieces. Just do the best you can, avoiding using perfectionism as a standard for yourself.

Challenging a Devalued Self-image

Often an individual retires on the investment of conviction of self-devaluation. What need is there for one to make any effort if one is so constitutionally inferior that all of the best intensions and well-directed activities will lead to naught? It is expedient to show the patient that he or she is utilizing self-devaluation as a destructive implement to bolster helplessness and perhaps to sponsor dependency. In this way one makes capital out of a handicap. Pointing out realistic assets the patient possesses may not succeed in destroying the vitiated image of oneself; but it does help to reevaluate potentialities and to avoid the despair of considering oneself completely hopeless. One may point out to the patient instances of personal successes. In this respect, encouraging the patient to adopt the idea that he or she can succeed in an activity in which he or she is interested, and to expand a present asset, may prove to be a saving grace. A woman with a deep sense of inferiority and lack of self-confidence was exhorted to add to her knowledge of horticulture with which she was fascinated. At gatherings she was emboldened to talk about her specialty when an appropriate occasion presented itself. She found herself the center of attention among a group of suburbanites who were eager to acquire expert information. This provided her with a means of social contact and with a way of doing things for others that built up a more estimable feeling about herself.

Logic obviously cannot convince a person with devalued self-esteem that he or she has merit. Unless a proper assessment is made of existing virtues, however, the person will be retarded in correcting the distorted self-image.

Th. You do have a tendency to devalue yourself as a result of everything that has happened to you. From what I can observe, there is no real reason why you should. If you do, you may be using self-devaluation as a way of punishing yourself because of guilt, or of making people feel sorry for you, or of rendering yourself helpless and dependent. You know, all people are different; every person has a uniqueness, like every thumbprint is unique. The fact that you do not possess some qualities other people have does not make you inferior.

Deriving the Utmost Enjoyment from Life

Focusing on troubles and displeasures in one's existence can deprive a person of joys that are one's right as a human being. The need to develop a sense of humor and to get the grimness out of one's daily life may be stressed.

Th. Try to minimize the bad or hurtful elements and concentrate on the good and constructive things about yourself and your situation. It is important for every person to reap out of each 24 hours the maximum of pleasures possible. Try not to live in recriminations of the past and in forebodings about the future. Just concentrate on achieving happiness in the here and now.

Accepting One's Social Role

Every adult has a responsibility in assuming a variety of social roles: as male or female, as husband or wife, as a parent, as a person who must relate to authority and on occasions act as authority, as a community member with obligations to society. Though one may feel immature, dependent, hostile, and hypocritical, the individual still must try to fill these roles as completely as possible. If the patient is destructively involved with another person with whom one must carry on a relationship, like an employer, for example, he or she must attempt to understand the forces that serve to disturb the relationship. At the same time, however, one must try to keep the relationship going in a way that convention details so that personal security will not be jeopardized.

Th. One way of trying to get along with people is to attempt to put yourself in their position and to see things from their point of view. If your husband [wife, child, employer, etc.] is doing something that is upsetting, ask yourself: "What is he [she] feeling at this time: what is going on in his [her] mind? How would I feel if I were in his [her] position?" At any rate, if you can recognize what is going on, correcting matters that can be resolved, adjusting to those that cannot be changed; if you are able to relate to the good rather than to the bad in people, you should be able to get along with them without too much difficulty."

The form by which the above guidelines are verbally or graphically communicated to the patient will vary, and each therapist may decide whether they are useful in whole or in part for specific patients. Reading assignments may also be given and suggestions for continued self-education made after therapy has ended. A full list of reading materials will be found elsewhere (see Ch 56, "Bibliotherapy").

IV

The Terminal Phase of Treatment

54
Goals in Terminating Treatment

Theoretically, psychotherapy is never ending, since emotional growth can go on as long as one lives. Consequently, it is necessary to employ some sort of yardstick in order to determine when to discontinue treatment.

The problem of goals in psychotherapy is one about which there are differences of opinion. On the one hand, there are those who believe that a definition of goals is vital in any psychotherapeutic program. On the other hand, there are many professionals who consider goals to be an extremely arbitrary matter—a manifestation of the authoritarianism of the therapist who seeks to impose on the patient artificial values and standards. "Goallessness" has been mentioned as the procedural stance essential to technical analytic work (Wallerstein, 1965). Nevertheless, therapists of different orientations aim at outcome targets that reflect their special conceptions of dynamics.

Psychological processes may be conceived of in many ways including:

1. As energy exchanges within various divisions of the psychic apparatus (the Freudian hypothesis).
2. As interpersonal events mediated by characterologic distortions (the neo-Freudian hypothesis).
3. As forms of faulty learning and conditioning (the pavlovian hypothesis).

Goals in psychotherapy are fashioned by theoretical conceptions of personality. Thus, in Freudian theory the goal in therapy is genital maturity in which fixations of libido on pregenital levels that foster regression have been resolved. In neo-Freudian theory the objective is self-actualization that frees the individual in interpersonal relationships, enhances self-image, and expands creativity and productiveness. In conditioning theory it is the extinction of destructive old patterns and the learning-through-reinforcement of new and adaptive ones.

Irrespective of how one feels about the uses made of them, goals are understandably of concern to the psychotherapist, for success or failure in the treatment effort can be gauged only in the context of set objectives. Before describing goals, however, we must admit that judgments of "success" in psychotherapy are really a matter of definition and may be viewed differently from the standpoints of the patient, society, and the therapist.

SUCCESS JUDGMENTS

From the Standpoint of the Patient

There is a story about a man who confided to a friend that he had just successfully completed an extensive course of psychotherapy. "Why did you need psychotherapy?" asked the friend. "Because," revealed the man, "I thought I was a dog." "Was the treatment successful?" queried the friend. "Decidedly," replied the man, "feel my nose."

Estimates by the patient as to what has been accomplished in therapy are in themselves not a reliable index of therapeutic success. Most patients regard symptomatic relief as the best measurement of positive gain. This index, however, is not a completely valid one in assaying the effectiveness of treatment.

Symptomatic improvement may be achieved in several ways. First, it may be associated with the giving up of vital aspects of personality functioning. For example, where anxiety and guilt are aroused by sexual impulses, the abandonment of all forms of sexual expression may relieve symptoms. Or where close interpersonal relations are conceived of as dangerous, the patient may, in the course of therapy, detach from people. the bargain that the patient makes with anxiety here cannot be regarded as successful therapy, even though suffering is relieved. Second, the patient may, during treatment, propitiate certain neurotic drives, gaining thereby a spurious kind of security. Thus, one may make oneself dependent on the therapist, acquiring a regressive fulfillment of security needs. Symptoms will abate as long as one conceives of the therapist as a bountiful, loving, and protecting parent. This happy situation may, nevertheless, be placed in jeopardy whenever the therapist fails to live up to the patient's expectations. Under these circumstances we cannot consider

the surcease of symptoms a sign of cure. Third symptom relief may be produced by the repression of damaging conflicts. Many annoying but relatively innocuous symptoms may be blotted out of awareness in the course of supportive therapy, only to be replaced by substitutive symptoms of a more serious nature. Thus, the symptom of anxiety may be relieved during therapy by repressive techniques of one sort or another. Anxiety equivalents may, however, appear in the form of psychosomatic complaints. Damage to viscera may later eventuate, of which the patient is not conscious until an irreversible somatic ailment develops, perhaps years after the presumed "success" in therapy had occurred.

The patient's estimates of failure in therapy must also not be accepted at their face value, since concepts of failure are based on a false premise. Thus, one may consider treatment unsuccessful where hoped for ideal traits have not been achieved. For example, one patient may have secret notions of being a genius, that are now latent but that will be released through therapy. Another patient may regard therapy as unsuccessful unless one has developed complete equanimity and the ability to remain tranquil, to endure tension, and to vanquish discomfort, even in the face of the most devastating environmental conditions. The failure to develop these and other traits, which are, in the patient's mind, considered indices of health, security, and self-esteem, may cast a shadow on even estimable therapeutic results.

From the Standpoint of Society

Judgments as to success in therapy from the standpoint of social standards must also be held suspect. The patient's family, mate, or friends may have ideas about the kind of individual that they want the patient to become that may not correspond with standards of mental health. For instance, parents may expect and even demand that the therapist mold the patient into a creature who is cooperative and pleasant at all times and who never challenges parental authority. A mate may insist that the patient develop a personality that tolerates his or her own shortcomings and never gives vent to resentment. Friends may have stringent standards of character that might apply to themselves but not necessarily to the patient.

The culture or subculture may also impose arbitrary norms that differ from those of the patient or of the therapist. Political and economic forces in one group may make for a value system that is not accepted by, or acceptable to, another group. Thus, a "normal" individual in a totalitarian framework would be expected to submit willingly to the yoke of dictatorship and to subordinate personal freedom for the welfare of the state. In another cultural framework the individual's personal rights and the ability to make one's own choices would be paramount; one would not be expected to yield completely to authoritative demands. It is accordingly, important not to regard as goals of normality traits and drives that, though culturally condoned, may prove to be at variance with mental health.

From the Standpoint of the Therapist

The therapist may fashion therapeutic goals around certain set standards and values. These may relate to personal concepts of normality or to a general ideal of mental health.

One may, reflecting cultural concepts, pronounce certain traits as normal believing that the patient must acquire these before being considered emotionally balanced. Another therapist may personally operate under a cherished set of attitudes that constitute for one the highest goal.

Thus, if a value is put on ambitiousness, perfectionism, detachment, dependency, narcissism, or power devices, one is apt to consider these real assets toward which one must aim the therapeutic sights. A word of caution must especially be voiced in regard to that group of attitudes collectively embraced under the term of compliance. A reasonable compliance to authority is a necessary thing, but compliance is too often utilized by neurotic persons as a form of security. This is most often the case in those cultures in which the child is considered a relative nonentity who is expected to submit without question and to yield without complaint to the dictates and commands of the stronger, more authoritative individuals with whom the child lives. Where therapists themselves have been reared in an atmosphere that makes compliance tantamount with good breeding, they may expect the patient to adopt a submissive attitude. The patient may sense this trend in the therapist and try hard to please, even at the price of crushing self-strivings and needs for independent thought and action. Therapists may also, because of their own character structure, consider any aggression a sign of recalcitrance and ill will. They must be careful not to try to pattern their patients after their own image, for they, themselves, may be the victims of values that are basically faulty.

From the Standpoint of Mental Health Objectives

"Ideal" objectives of mental health are many. They require that the person be capable of deriving pleasure from creature comforts in life—from food, rest, relaxation, sex, work, and play. The individual is capable of satisfying these impulses in conformity with the mores of the group. Mobilizing whatever intellectual and experiential resources are required, one is able to plan creatively and realistically and to execute one's plans in accordance with existent opportunities. This involves an appraisal of one's aptitudes and limitations, and a scaling down of one's ambitions to the level of one's true potentialities. It includes the laying down of realistic life goals, an acceptance of one's abilities and a tolerance of one's shortcomings. Presupposed is a harmonious balance between personal and group standards, and those cultural and individual ideals that contribute both to the welfare of the self and of the group. The individual must be able to function effectively as part of the group, to give and to receive love, and otherwise to relate oneself congenially to other humans. One must be capable of engaging in human relations without indulging neurotic character strivings of detachment, needs to dominate or to be enslaved, or desires to render oneself invincible or perfect. One must be able to assume a subordinate relationship to authority without succumbing to fear or rage and yet, in certain situations, be capable of assuming leadership without designs of control or power. One must be able to withstand a certain amount of disappointment, deprivation, and frustration without undue tension or anxiety when these are considered to be reasonable, shared, or necessary to the group welfare or when the consequences of impulse indulgence entail more than their worth in compensatory pain. One's capacities for adjustment must be sufficiently plastic to adapt to the exigencies of life without taking refuge in childish forms of defense or in fantasy. To achieve a healthy self-regard an individual must have a good measure of self-respect, the capacity to be comfortable within oneself, a willingness to face the past and to isolate from the present anxieties relating to childhood experiences. The individual must possess self-confidence, assertiveness, a sense of freedom, spontaneity, and self-tolerance.

Unfortunately, limitations are imposed by a variety of factors on the achievement through therapy of such ideal goals. Chief among these are obstacles within the pa-

tient, such as lack of incentives for change, diminished ego strength, and practical considerations of insufficient time and money. Additionally, society itself imposes insuperable embargoes on certain aspects of functioning. It supports many neurotic values that necessitate the maintenance of sundry defenses for survival reasons. A personality structure that is ideally integrated might actually serve as a source of conflict where the individual has to operate in the framework of a severely neurotic culture.

TOWARD A PRACTICAL GOAL IN THERAPY

Modern philosophers contend that achievement of enduring happiness, while worthy of pursuit, is undoubtedly a dream. Total adaptation must be measured against the backdrop of humanity's continuing involvement with violence, exploitation, and devastation of the earth's resources. These and other inescapable calamities are bound to disturb our equilibrium. Achievement of the most ambitious goal in therapy—reconstruction of the personality structure—would theoretically be most helpful in adapting to society's ills while sponsoring constructive efforts to rectify them. However, goals in therapy are more or less patient regulated. No matter how well trained and skilled the therapist may be, nor how extensive the desire to reconstruct the patient's personality, the latter is always in a position to veto the therapist's intentions. The patient is in a position strategically to thwart the ideal goal of personality maturation—the most difficult of all objectives. Irrespective of how thoroughly conversant we, the therapists, may be with the technique of reconstructive psychotherapy, our efforts may prove unsuccessful.

Even where conditions are most favorable, reconstructive efforts may fail. The patient may be able to afford extensive psychotherapy and to make the necessary time arrangements; he or she may desire to achieve deep change, yet may gain little or no benefit from therapy. This fact has confounded many therapists as well as their patients who are wont, as a result, to regard reconstructive psychotherapy as ineffectual.

When we investigate failures in reconstructive therapy in patients who are adequately motivated, we find a number of operative factors. The patient may have sustained such personality damage during the formative years of life that the chances for complete growth are remote. The secondary gain factors may be so powerful as to make health a handicap rather than an asset. Environmental conditions may be irremediably destructive, and the patient may need some neurotic defenses in order to survive them. Disintegrative forces within the personality may be so strong as to threaten to break loose with the employment of uncovering procedures. Finally, neurotic symptoms or character distortions may constitute the only means of adjusting the patient to conflicts, even though one possesses insight into their nature.

There are some patients who can make an adaptation solely by employing such neurotic facades. While partially debilitating, they help prevent regression and the upsurge of disintegrative tendencies. Thus, a psychosomatic ailment may serve to drain off hostile and masochistic impulses which, deprived of a somatic expression, may shatter the ego and produce a psychosis.

While the ideal goal of absolute resolution of blocks in personality maturation, with achievement of complete functioning in all areas of living, is a cherished aim in every patient, in practice very few people if any can reach this objective. Lorand (1946) recognized this when he said that in doing psychoanalysis it is sometimes essential to satisfy oneself with "practical" though superficial results that permit the patient to get along more satisfactorily than before

therapy. Many other analysts years ago also recognized the impossibility of achieved ideal goals.

Clara Thompson (1950), in an excellent discussion of what constitutes a "cure" in therapy, describes the need for goal modification. She contends that the patient (1) must be relieved of neurotic suffering, (2) must also be able to relate to others with a minimum of unrealistically perpetuated attitudes that have their origins in early significant relationships, (3) must be capable of achieving as complete a development of personal powers as education and life circumstances will permit. If life situation and the culture in which functions are favorable, he or she will be most capable of relating to the group constructively; if not favorable, he or she may have to learn to endure relative isolation. As long as the person does not deceive oneself through neurotic escape mechanisms, one may remain reasonably healthy even under inimical conditions. However, since we live in a sick society, some neurotic compromises are necessary in order to function. An absolute cure is thus not possible. As long as the person is relieved of anxiety, inferiority feelings, and other destructive elements and is capable of coping effectively with life difficulties as they arise, this may constitute as much as can be done in treatment.

While classical analysts in theory contend that theirs is the only therapy that can regularly and deliberately bring about deep and permanent changes (Strachey, 1937; Menninger, KA, 1958; Wallerstein, 1965), they are not so confident that they can in practice always achieve these all-embracing results. Annie Reich (1950) considers that the bringing about through analysis of an absolute state of health "would appeal to the narcissistic omnipotence fantasies of the analyst." She adds that an analyst cannot hope to produce perfect human beings, that one should be content if one frees a patient from symptoms, enabling ability to work, to adjust to reality, to engage in "adult object relations," and to accept some limitations. Oberndorf (1942) speaks of a "practical success" of symptomatic relief, and admits that in many psychoanalytic cases "the structure of the disorder with recovery of infantile memories has not been worked out, to say nothing of being worked through." Wallerstein (1965) remarks, "Suffice it to say, that though the most ambitious of therapies in its overall outcome goals, in practice analysis often achieves no more than other less ambitious therapeutic approaches."

These formulations actually repeat what Freud himself conceded were limitations in man's capacities for change. In "Analysis terminable and interminable" (1937) he stated that what analysis accomplishes "for neurotics is only what normal people accomplish for themselves without its help," namely, a "taming" of their instincts to bring them into harmony with the ego. Where the ego for any reason becomes enfeebled, as in illness or exhaustion, the "tamed" instincts "may renew their demands and strive in abnormal ways after substitution satisfaction." Proof of this statement is inherent in what takes place in sleep when in reaction to the lessening of the ego's forces there is an awakening of instinctual demands. In altering the character structure, Freud was pessimistic of the outcome. It was not possible, he said, to predict a natural end to the process. "Our object will be not to rub off all the corners of the human character so as to produce 'normality' according to schedule, nor yet to demand that the person who has been 'thoroughly analyzed' shall never again feel the stirrings of passion in himself or become involved in any internal conflict. The business of analysis is to secure the best possible psychological conditions for the functioning of the ego; when this has been done, analysis has accomplished its task."

R. P. Knight (1941) has condensed the aims of psychoanalytic therapy as follows:

1. *Symptom disappearance.*
2. *Improvement in mental functioning* with (a) understanding of the childhood sources of conflict, the part played by precipitating reality factors, the modes of defense against anxiety, and the specific character of the morbid process, (b) tolerance of the instinctual drives, (c) realistic self-appraisal with the ability to accept oneself objectively, (d) relative freedom from enervating tensions and crippling inhibitions, (e) liberation of aggressive energies required for "self-preservation, achievement, competition and protection of one's rights."
3. *Improved adjustment to reality* with (a) better interpersonal relationships, (b) more productive work capacity, (c) ability to sublimate more freely in recreation and avocations, and full heterosexual functioning.

A realistic approach to all forms of psychotherapy, including psychoanalysis, recognizes principles of goal modification. It acknowledges that we may have to content ourselves with the modest objective of freedom from disturbing symptoms, the capacity to function reasonably well, and to experience a modicum of happiness in living. The patient may continue to be burdened by outbursts of neurosis, which escapes control from time to time. Realistically, some habitual activities will have to be circumscribed, and certain protective devices developed that are a bit restrictive in certain areas. Yet one will be as well adjusted as most persons, which means that average life objectives can be reached while living with some handicaps.

In the process of modifying goals, cognizance is paid to the fact that while each person is capable of change, there are various levels of change—from the altering of relatively superficial attitudes to the modification of the deepest strata of personality. The strength of the ego in itself may bear no relationship to the extensiveness of goals approached during therapy. Thus, in many patients with strong egos, who have successfully dealt with infantile conflicts through repression, compensation, and sublimation and whose present illness consists of a breakdown of these defenses, the goals may advantageously be oriented around mediating the stress situation that has provoked collapse, restoring to the person the habitual defenses.

In patients with a weak ego who have dealt with infantile conflicts unsuccessfully, with a serious thwarting of maturation, one may also have to be content with the goal of restoring repression and of strengthening defenses to bring the person back to customary equilibrium.

There are, in general, three types of patterns that exist in all persons that influence potentialities for personality modification even with depth therapy.

1. *Conditionings acquired during the preverbal period of life that have become so integral a part of the individual that they continued to operate in a reflex way.* Reorganization of these paradigms may be unsuccessful even after prolonged reconstructive or conditioning therapy, especially where they fulfill important needs, promote gratifications, or serve as defenses. Surviving in almost pristine form, they defy logic and resist corrective influences.

2. *Systems developed in early life that have been symbolized, then repressed and repudiated because they mobilize anxiety or foster such intense guilt that they cannot be acknowledged.* These patterns, often related to sexual, aggressive, and assertive needs, may break through periodically in direct or modified form rationalizations for them being elaborated. Alteration of these configurations may be possible once insight into their nature is gained, their pleasure or adaptive values harnessed, and motivation for their obliteration developed with substitution of more adaptive trends. Where pleasure gains are high and sacrifice of such gains is resented, or where substitution of more mature ways of behaving is resisted, insight will not remove or control their expression. Here selective reinforcements may be partially successful.

3. *Patterns developed in later childhood and in adult life of which the individual is aware.* One may be able to modify or to control these patterns through will power once one understands their nature and consequences. Yet one may also be motivated to retain these destructive modes because of their pleasure and anxiety-reducing values.

Amendment in all of these categories is possible. Some changes come about "spontaneously" in the medium of a rewarding, bountiful environment that does not repeat the frustrating upsetting experiences of the past. They may be the consequence of a constructive human relationship that acts as a corrective experience, rectifying distortions in past relationships. They occur most frequently, however, through a good psychotherapeutic experience with a skilled empathic therapist, the patient gaining some cognitive understanding of one's conflicts, drives, and defenses, and being helped to develop new ways of reacting and relating. In all persons some residues of the disturbed past will remain irrespective of how bountiful one's environment may be, how exhaustively one knows oneself, or how thoroughly one has relearned new patterns.

Were we, in summary, to attempt the definition of a practical goal in therapy, we might say that it is *the achievement by the patient of optimal functioning within the limitations of one's financial circumstances, existing motivations, ego resources, and the reality situation.* Such a goal would put upon the therapist the responsibility of resolving the patient's resistance in working toward the ideal objective of personality reconstruction. It would, however, admit of the expediency of adopting modified goals, such as dealing with only those aspects of the patient's problem that can be practically handled during the present therapeutic effort.

55
Technical Problems in Termination

The conditions under which termination of therapy is indicated are

1. Achievement by the patient of planned treatment goals.
2. Decision by the patient or therapist to terminate on the basis of incomplete goals.
3. The reaching of an impasse in therapy or the development of stubborn resistances that cannot be resolved.
4. Countertransference that the therapist is unable to control.
5. Occurrence of physical reasons, such as moving of the residence of patient or therapist.

TERMINATING THERAPY UPON REACHING SET GOALS

Therapy may be terminated after the patient has achieved planned goals, such as the disappearance of symptoms, the mediation of environmental stress sources, the acquisition of greater happiness, productivity and self-fulfillment, the resolution of difficulties in interpersonal relationships, or the establishment of creative and productive patterns in living, with the evolution of greater emotional maturity. It is to be hoped that some intrapsychic structural changes will have occurred in which, through a reworking of infantile conflicts, new defenses crystallize and adaptive solutions for old conflicts take place.

With the accomplishment of the purposes of therapy, termination is best effectuated by discussing the possibility of ending treatment with the patient, handling any resistance displayed, warning of the possibility of relapses, and inviting the patient to return after therapy has ended whenever necessary or desired.

Discussing Termination with the Patient

In advance of the termination date it is wise to discuss with the patient the matter of ending therapy. A tapering-off period may be suggested, and a termination date set, which ideally should be from 6 to 8 weeks. The frequency of sessions may be reduced, and the intervals between visits steadily increased. The following is an excerpt from a session with a patient with a phobic disorder who has achieved adequate improvement in therapy:

Th. It sounds as if you are reaching the end of treatment. How do you feel about stopping?
Pt. Oh, of course I am glad that I am feeling so well, and I am very thankful to you, doctor.

Th. Actually, you did the bulk of the work. Of course, we could go on with treatment indefinitely, reaching more extensive goals in your personality development, but frankly I don't see the need for that, unless you do.

Pt. Well, I suppose I can benefit, but as you say, I am comfortable and happy now with Jim [*the patient's husband*] being so much better now to live with, and all these fears and things are gone now.

Th. If you agree with me that we should begin to terminate, we can cut down our visits to a session every 2 weeks for the time being and then space them at intervals.

Pt. All right, doctor.

During the tapering-off period, any relapses or resistances are handled, sessions being again increased, but only if the patient's condition demands this. In occasional cases it may be decided to terminate therapy abruptly without tapering off, in order to expose the patient to a complete break with the therapist. Forced to function on one's own, the patient may marshall inner strength more rapidly.

Handling Resistances to Termination

If the therapist has conducted the treatment sessions with the full participation of the patient, and if the therapist has avoided playing too directive a role, termination will not pose too great a problem in the average patient. In supportive therapy, however, where the patient has accepted the therapist as a guiding authority with whom he or she has conformed, or in insight therapy where the patient has, on the basis of a residual dependency drive, made the therapist a necessary factor in adjustment, termination may present difficulties.

Termination of therapy is no problem in most patients who are adequately prepared for it, or who are characterologically not too dependent, or who are seen for only a few sessions and discharged before a strong relationship with the therapist develops, or who are so detached that they ward of a close therapeutic contact. It may,

however, become a difficult problem in other cases. Patients who in early childhood have suffered rejection or abandonment by or loss of a parent, or who have had difficulties in working through the separation individuation dimensions of their development are especially vulnerable and may react with fear, anger, despair, and grief. A return of their original symptoms when the termination date approaches will tend to confound the patient and inspire in the therapist frustration, disappointment, guilt feelings, and anger at the patient for having failed to respond to therapeutic ministrations.

In some patients in whom no manifest dependency operates in the relationship with the therapist, termination may still be troublesome. The patient may be fearful of giving up the protective situation in the therapeutic relationship. Memories of past suffering and anxiety may cause a patient to want to hold on to the security achieved, even at the cost of continuing in therapy indefinitely. M. Hollander (1965) has pointed out "that the role of being a patient in psychotherapy, like being a student in school or a patient on a medical service, may become a way of life instead of a means to an end."

The therapeutic tasks prior to termination with all patients involve analysis of the dependency elements in the relationship, a search for needs in the patient to perpetuate dependency, and a helping of the patient to achieve as much independence and assertiveness as possible. A shift in the character of the relationship may be necessary where the therapist has operated in a directive manner. Here the therapist behaves nondirectively with the patient, with the object of helping the patient establish new goals and values.

Resistances in the average dependent patient are multiform. Some patients bluntly refuse to yield dependency, adopting all kinds of dodges, even to relapse in their illness, in order to demonstrate their helplessness. Other patients exhibit a profound fear of assertiveness, perhaps promoted by a neurotic equation of assertiveness with aggression. Resolution of such resistances may consume a great deal of time.

In some patients, and especially in the third phase of treatment (see Chapter 48) it may be necessary to interpret continuously to the patient the reasons for this self-paralysis and to emphasize the need to make one's own choices no matter how revolutionary these may seem. The patient may be told that if a person has never developed full confidence in oneself as an individual, the right to experience oneself as an independent being may be startling. The insidious operation of this dependency may be illustrated, and the patient may be shown how dependency has crippled efforts toward self-growth. In the relationship with the therapist it is natural for the patient to expect the therapist to give the answers and to make the patient's decisions. Should the therapist do this, however, the patient will never develop inner strength. The therapist may keep emphasizing the patient's need to take complete responsibility for personal decisions. The patient may be apprised of the fact that some of decisions may be wrong; but even though one makes mistakes, the very fact that they are one's own mistakes will teach more than being told what to do at all times. The therapist does not want to withhold support from the patient, but it is necessary to do so now out of consideration for the patient's right to develop.

When the patient accuses the therapist of being cold and distant, the therapist may say:

The reason I'm not more demonstrative is that if I were to act like the traditional authority, it would eventually infantilize you; you would have to keep me around as a leaning post the rest of your life. You'd have to come to me for every decision with such queries as, "Am I doing something wrong?" or "Am I doing the right thing?" Rather, it's better for you to make mistakes, bad as they may be, and to feel that these are your own decisions than for me to tell you what to do.

A definition of the nondirective nature of therapy is given with the object of supplying the patient with an incentive to take responsibility. This will not serve to liberate the patient completely from dependency demands. Neurotic attitudes and behavior patterns will continue to press for expression. The patient may still exhibit toward the therapist the same insecurity, submissiveness, and aggression that he or she always has manifested toward authority. Habitual ineptitudes in dealing with life and people, destructive acting out and continuing detachment may go on, but with a slight difference: doubts that these aberrations are really necessary.

The following excerpt of a treatment session with a patient resisting termination illustrates some of these points:

Th. You want me to tell you exactly what to do, how to do it, and when. If you really feel that you just don't have strength to do things for yourself, I will do them for you, provided you understand it isn't going to be of help to you if I make your decisions. I'll leave it up to you to decide. If you really feel as bad as you say you do, and you haven't got the confidence to make your own decisions, I'll let you depend upon me, if you *really* want that. [*This statement is offered as a challenge to the patient. There are very few patients that take advantage of it. This patient actually has become quite assertive through therapy but is evincing a regressive dependency reaction to prevent termination.*]

Pt. I do feel just as badly as I told you, but at the same time I can hang on to various little things, one of which is that I long ago accepted the idea that you know what you're doing and I don't want to go against it. [*She seems to doubt the wisdom of her desire to have me function as a parental image.*]

Th. You don't want to go against what I have outlined as the best for you? What do you feel about making your own choices and your own decisions completely, with absolutely no help from me?

Pt. Oh, I think it's great, except that there doesn't seem to be much I can do about it.

Th. Well, what do you think would happen

if I told you what to do, if I took you over and acted like a parent?

Pt. I feel two ways about it. I feel, first of all, that it might be an excellent idea because I'm certainly amenable to letting you take me over. But the other way I feel about it is that all this time I've been trying to, more or less, cooperate with you. I trust your judgment and I can see very well that keeping throwing decisions at me is what will in the end make me self-sufficient. Yes, I can see it, but right now I just can't imagine it ever happening or my being able to stand on my own feet. I feel very much as if I have slipped constantly downward during the last few weeks. [*This is since termination was suggested.*] That's all. I mean it's not as if I don't have lucid moments every now and then, but they're very few and far between.

Th. All right, then would you want me to play the role of telling you what to do on the basis that you can't come to decisions for yourself?

Pt. If it was making decisions, I might be able to do it; but I just can't see any decisions to make. There's nothing clear-cut. I don't know where I am at all.

Th. So that you'd like to just let yourself be taken care of by somebody?

Pt. It sounds nice, but I know perfectly well that it wouldn't be so good for me.

Th. You mean my making the decisions for you wouldn't be so good?

Pt. Well, certainly not.

Th. But some people seem to want that.

Pt. Grown people?

Th. Yes, grown people. Their feeling about themselves is so diminutive, their capacity to function so low that they want a parent watching over them all the time. If you'd like to adjust on this level all your life, you'd need to have me around to make your decisions for you indefinitely.

Pt. And then if I wasn't living here, I'd try to find someone else to do it, if I let you go ahead with this plan. [*This is a healthy reluctance to accepting dependency.*]

Th. If you don't develop strengths within yourself so you can figure things out and plan your life and follow it through, right or wrong, then you're going to need somebody around all the time.

Pt. I'd rather not depend on you then.

Because the therapist operates in a more passive role, the patient will be encouraged to act with greater assertiveness, to initiate actions, and to follow them through. There is increasing incentive to take personal responsibility for one's actions, to make plans and express choices. Failure may occur, but there will be successes too. And inner strength will grow on the bedrock of successes. New feelings of integrity and a more complete sense of self will be developed.

Ego growth will thus be catalyzed during the terminal phase, eventuating in the patient's desire to manage one's own life. Such growth is contingent to a large extent on the continued permissiveness of the therapist and the persistent encouragement of the patient's activity and self-expressiveness. The fact that the patient successfully figures things out during the session eventually shows the patient that he or she is not at all at the mercy of forces on the outside. Ultimately the patient comes to the conclusion that one can live one's life, not because one is given permission, but because one has the right to do so. The patient feels equality with the therapist and a growing sense of self-respect. The self-confidence developed in therapy promotes an extension of assertive feeling toward the extratherapeutic environment.

The proper conduct of therapeutic sessions during the terminal phase of therapy requires that the therapist be so constituted that he or she can permit the patient to feel equality and to allow separation from treatment. The personalities of some therapists are essentially so authoritarian that they will not be able to function on equal terms with their patients. Automatically they will set themselves up as leaders, making judgments, giving directives, and setting goals for the patient that they insist must be followed. They may respond with hostility if challenged or abused by the patient. This is least apt to occur where the therapist has had personal psychotherapy and can analyze and control neurotic countertransference before it acts to interfere with the treatment situation.

Even the therapist who has undergone

personal therapy may manifest attitudes that support the resistances of the patient to termination. There may be a compulsion to overprotect or domineer the patient and thus an inability to assume a nondirective role. Economics may play a part when new referrals are scarce, and the therapist anticipates hard times ahead. This may lead to interminable therapy, until the patient forcefully asserts himself or herself by the marshalling of aggression, and in this way violently breaks ties with the therapist.

In some instances the therapist may have to be contented with only partial reduction of the patient's dependence. Here the dependency is reduced as to innocuous a level as possible, by encouraging contact with an outside group or, in sick patients who require prolonged treatment, by maintaining a casual therapeutic relationship at extended intervals over an indefinite period.

Warning of the Possibility of Relapses

No matter how thoroughly the patient's neurotic patterns seem to have been eradicated, particularly in reconstructive therapy, shadows of old reactions persist. One may be incapable of eliminating them completely, as one cannot obliterate entirely the recorded tracings in the brain of aspects of the patient's past. Under conditions of great insecurity, when the patient's sense of mastery is threatened, or during periods of disappointment, frustration, and deprivation, old defenses and strivings characteristic of past neurotic modes of adaptation are apt to be awakened.

Symptoms may return insidiously without the patient even being aware of having entered into the old conflictual situations that propagated them. Thus, migrainous attacks may recur in a man who, having learned to channel hostility constructively and to avoid competitive relationships that create damaging resentment,

changes his job to one where he is judged solely on the basis of comparison of his productivity to that of other employees. A woman with a propensity for dependent involvements may experience a return of her helplessness and her symptoms when she falls in love with, and acts submissive toward, a power-driven individual who constitutes for her an omnipotent father figure. Unconsciously she has yielded to a childish yearning for complete protection, and she is again paying the price in shattered self-esteem and its attendant symptomatic penalties.

It is essential for the patient to realize that getting well does not guarantee further nonexistence of symptoms. Indeed when confronted with truly crucial decisions some patients respond with a return of complaints. Also when stress becomes too powerful to manage, a temporary relapse is possible. However, if the causes of any relapse are investigated and analyzed, not only will the patient have the best opportunity of subduing suffering, but will also be in a better position to forestall the future return of symptoms. Some therapists find it profitable to tell patients at termination that they do not consider a person cured until a relapse or two has occurred and been overcome. Such a warning may prevent a patient from classifying therapy as a failure should recrudescence of symptoms ensue. It alerts one to the insidious operation of inner anxieties and promotes continuing self-analysis. The ability to utilize lessons learned in therapy strengthens newly acquired traits and expands personality growth. The therapist may tell the patient:

You are apt to get a flurry of anxiety and a return of symptoms from time to time. Don't be upset or intimidated by this. The best way to handle yourself is first to realize that your relapse is self-limited. It will eventually come to a halt. Nothing terrible will happen to you. Second, ask yourself what has been going on. Try to figure out what created your upset, what aroused your tension. Relate this to the general patterns that you have been pursuing that we talked about. Old habits hold on, but they will eventually get less and less provoking.

Inviting the Patient to Return for Further Sessions

The therapist may advantageously invite the patient to return for additional interviews in the event of a relapse the patient cannot work out alone. Should the patient take advantage of this invitation, it will be possible for the therapist rapidly to help the patient gain insight into the patterns that have been revived, to connect this understanding with what the patient already has learned in therapy, and to analyze why the patient was unable to deal with the relapse through his or her own efforts. This review will usually occasion much relief in the patient and provide a greater sense of mastery. Relatively few sessions will be required to effectuate this objective.

The patient may also desire to return to therapy in order to achieve more extensive objectives. Growth is a never ending process, and the patient may be so dissatisfied with the present status that a more exhaustive self-inquiry will be insisted on.

For example, a patient in an anxiety state, mobilized by involvement in a love affair that she has been unable to control with her habitual character defense of detachment, may utilize the therapeutic situation to break the relationship with the young man of whom she has become so hopelessly enamored. Restoring her detached defenses and again functioning satisfactorily without anxiety, she may decide that she has accomplished her treatment objective. However, because she has become aware of a conflict that makes close relationships dangerous for her, necessitating withdrawal, she may develop, after she has stopped treatment, an incentive to return to therapy for more extensive work. She will do this with a new goal in mind; namely to be able to relate closely to a person without needing to invoke her defense of detachment. With this expanded motivation, a reconstructive approach may be possible.

A suitable way of terminating therapy is to consider the increased spacing of sessions part of the treatment plan. As soon as the therapist decides on treatment termination, the patient is instructed that it is important to extend the intervals between sessions as part of the treatment plan. A 2-week interval is followed by increasing intervals between sessions. When it becomes apparent that the patient is coping well, a yearly session is planned.

Encouraging the Patient to Continue Therapeutic Self-Help

A consistent application of what has been learned in psychotherapy is essential. The patient may be encouraged to engage in self-observation and to challenge neurotic patterns directly should they return, both by trying to understand what brought them back and by actively resisting and reversing them. In some cases the patient may be taught the process of self-relaxation or self-hypnosis to help reduce tension when upset and also to enable the patient, through self-reflection, to arrive at an understanding of elusive precipitating factors that have revived conflicts.

Even where there has been only supportive or a more superficial type of reeducative therapy, the patient may be inspired, as much as possible, (1) to utilize will power for the purpose of facing reality situations, (2) to push one's mind away from ruminative obsessional thinking and preoccupations, (3) to cultivate, if possible, a sense of humor about oneself and situation, (4) to develop the philosophy of living in the present rather than regretting the past and dreading the future, (5) to practice expressing controlled resentment in justifiable situations, and (6) to examine any tensions, anxieties, or irrational impulses in terms of possible meanings, connecting them with what one knows of one's basic neurotic patterns. These precepts and others contained in Chapter 53 on Homework Assignments may be extremely helpful. Self-help relaxation methods (see p. 968), meditation (see p. 965) the playing of an audio tape that the therapist prepares for the patient (see p. 1019) for purposes of relaxation and ego building, may be prescribed for some patients. See also Chapter 57, pp. 1112–1114.

TERMINATING ON THE BASIS OF INCOMPLETE GOALS

Therapy may have to be terminated prior to the achievement of planned goals. There are a number of reasons for this, most important of which is insoluble resistance. Thus, a patient may, with psychotherapy, lose certain symptoms, but other symptoms may cling to one obstinately. One may relinquish many neurotic patterns but continue to exploit a few without which one may feel oneself incapable of functioning. One may develop a number of new potentialities, yet be unable to progress to as complete emotional maturity as either the patient or the therapist may desire. Working on resistance accomplishes little, and the therapist may then deem it advisable to interrupt treatment.

A countertransference obstacle that may require resolution is a too strong ambition in the therapist who expects too much from a patient. Therapeutic objectives may have to be scaled down considerably in certain individuals. Thus, we may be dealing with a sick borderline patient who is on the verge of a schizophrenic break and who is insistent that he be brought in therapy to a point where he can be more normal than normal. This wish, while admirable, is not realistic, for the patient does not possess the fortitude to endure the rigors of a reconstructive approach. Because he does not

have sufficient ego strength to work out a better adaptation, one may have to make a compromise with projected goals.

Sometimes therapy is started with a patient whose motivations are unalterably defective. For instance, a woman may have a tremendously arrogant notion of her capacities, and she may seek treatment solely because she has read somewhere that psychotherapy can bring out an individual's buried potentialities. The bloated self-image that the patient supports may be the only way she has of counteracting feelings of inner devastation or of rectifying a contemptuous self-image. Therapy with such a patient may be extremely difficult and may have to be terminated due to impenetrable resistance.

The therapist may be confronted with a patient whose life situation obstructs his or her progress. The environmental difficulty is so irremediable that possibilities of correction are remote, and hence the patient must be helped to live with it or be desensitized to its effect. Or the patient's symptoms may possess so strong a defensive value that their removal will produce a dangerous reaction. Therapy may have to be terminated on the basis of only partial symptomatic relief.

It may be impossible, due to other obstructions, to get some patients to progress beyond a certain point in therapy. To continue treatment may prove discouraging to the therapist and undermining to the patient. It is better here for the patient to retain some neurotic drives than to be exposed to interminable and frustrating therapy to which, in all probability, the patient will be unable to respond.

As soon as the therapist decides that maximum improvement has been obtained or that a stalemate has been reached, the therapy may be brought to a halt by utilizing the techniques described for termination after the achievement of planned goals. The therapist will, however, have to explain the reason for termination in such a way that the patient does not arrive at the conclusion that matters are hopeless and that no further progress is possible. Thus, the patient may be told that therapy has alleviated some symptoms, has brought about an awareness of basic problems, and has pointed the way to a more productive life. Because the patient's difficulties have existed a long period, resistances may persist for awhile. Putting lessons learned in therapy into practice, however, will provide the best opportunity to achieve a more complete development.

The mere mention of termination, and the discussion of resistances that seem to have blocked progress, may stimulate incentives to break through these hindrances. If a termination date has been set, the patient may work through resistances prior to the expiration date. On the other hand, the termination techniques may not resolve the many impediments to further change. Yet, after the patient has left treatment, spectacular progress may be experienced. The fact that no headway was made while in therapy may have been due to the operation of a subtle transference situation that acted as resistance. For example, hostility toward the therapist may have expressed itself in a refusal to go forward; or dependence on the therapist may have taken the initiative away from the patient. Once the patient is functioning away from therapy under one's own power, such resistances diminish and a spurt in development is possible.

Planned Interruption of Therapy

Instead of outright termination, a vacation from treatment may be suggested. During this period the learnings from therapy should be put into practice. The interruption can serve as an opportunity to observe the exact manner that one's personal problems interfere with proper functioning and to analyze what hindrances come up in try-

ing to cope with such problems on one's own. The proposed interruption may be presented to the patient as in the following excerpt:

Th. It seems to me that we have reached a plateau in your therapy and that a vacation from treatment may be indicated. How do you feel about that?

Pt. I just can't seem to get any further. I've been thinking of that. How long would you suggest?

Th. Suppose we plan on a month's vacation. After a month call me, and we'll arrange an appointment.

Pt. Do you believe that will be of help?

Th. I do. You might observe yourself during this period and see if you can determine what is happening, what stirs up your symptoms and what alleviates them. We might learn something important, and the interlude may help pull you out of the plateau.

Transferring the Patient

Sending the patient to another therapist may sometimes be preferable to outright termination. Where one seems unable to deal with the patient's resistances, or where one cannot control destructive countertransference, or, for any other reason, feels incapable of helping the patient any more, the decision may then be that the patient will do better with a different therapist. Sometimes a transfer is arranged when it is presumed the patient will benefit by a kind of therapeutic experience other than that provided by the present therapist. For instance, a therapist trained mainly in reconstructive approaches may feel that the patient needs supportive therapy and may consequently want to refer the patient to a professional person who is highly skilled in supportive techniques. Or a change to a therapist of the opposite sex may be considered advisable. Should a transfer be indicated, the therapist may discuss the matter with the patient as illustrated in this fragment of a session:

Th. For some time I have felt that we haven't been making very much progress.

Pt. Yes, I was worried about this. I wondered if you were getting impatient.

Th. Of course not, except that sometimes a snag like this does happen, and a person may be able to work it out better with another therapist.

Pt. You mean you want me to see somebody else?

Th. My desire is for you to get well. What would you feel about seeing someone I would recommend and who I believe can help you? I have a feeling you may do better with another type of technique, and Dr. _____ is very excellent at this.

Pt. Well, I don't know.

Th. Why don't you talk to Dr. _____ after I determine that he has the time for you? Then, after a couple of sessions you can see how you feel.

Pt. If you think this is best, I'll do it.

Th. I do, and I'll make all the arrangements and call you.

TERMINATION NOTE

At the time of termination a note should be entered in the patient's case record indicating the reasons for termination, the patient's condition of discharge, the areas of improvement, the patient's attitude toward the therapist, the recommendations made to the patient, and the final diagnosis. A form, such as in Appendix H may be found useful.

FOLLOW-UP

Prior to discharging the patient, then it is advisable to ask whether he or she would object to receiving an occasional letter from the therapist asking regarding one's progress. Most patients are delighted to cooperate and consider the therapist's gesture a mark of interest in their development. Follow-up letters, briefly inquiring into how things have been progressing, may be sent to the patient yearly, preferably for at least 5 years. This enables the therapist to maintain a good check on what has been happening over a considerable period of time. The patient's replies to the follow-up inquiry may be entered in the case record, and, if necessary, a brief notation may be made of the contents.

Follow-up is an essential practice where one wishes to determine the efficacy of one's clinical activities. It is an important aspect of outcome research. In doing follow-up we must remember that a single contact may not tell us too much. A person does not live in a vacuum after completing psychotherapy, and many intercurrent events can temporarily augment, detract from, or destroy the benefits of treatment. Thus an individual who has achieved a good result and has left therapy in a satisfactorily improved state may be subject to catastrophes that are beyond one's power to avoid or resolve. One may be in a state of depression at the time of follow-up but can later rally and pull oneself out of despair. This may not be evident unless provision is made for further contacts. Personal interviews are far more useful for follow-up than communication by mail, although practical considerations, such as changes in domicile to a remote area, may pose problems. Sometimes follow-ups done over the telephone may be much more satisfactory than by mail. However, patients tend to be more guarded here than in private interviews even where they have had a good relationship with their therapists.

Ideally, appraisals of the patient by other persons with whom the patient is living or working can be helpful, but this may be difficult to arrange. A simple statement of "feeling better" or "worse" means little unless areas of improvement or decline are delineated. Unless the case record has detailed categories of problems and deficits existing at the start of treatment estimates of change may be inaccurate. Researchers who have had no personal contact with a patient are especially handicapped, but even the primary therapist may without recorded backup be prejudiced by optimistic hunches.

PATIENTS' REACTIONS TO THE END OF THERAPY

What follows are some reactions voiced by patients when they finished therapy:

1. All people have problems, and I know now that mine are no worse than anybody else's.
2. I realize I considered my symptoms a sign of weakness. I realize they aren't. I don't pay attention to them and they pass. They aren't such a big deal now.
3. One of the big problems I had was considering myself the center of the universe. It now isn't so important for me to feel so important.
4. When I was so full of guilt, I felt I would burst. When I talked things out, I realized my standards were a lot more strict than those of other people. As a matter of fact, I would purposefully do things to prove I was bad; now I don't have to.
5. The price I would pay for my indulgences was just too high. So I don't burn the world up! So I don't get as much of a bang out of doing ridiculous things! The quietness I feel more than compensates for the high life I was leading.
6. Why knock yourself out climbing on top of the heap? You're nowhere when you get there. You kill yourself trying. I was so ambitious and perfectionistic that I had no time for living. Now I try

to find pleasure in little things, and it works.
7. I don't have to blame my parents anymore for my troubles; whatever happened, happened. Why should I let the past poison my present life? I feel I can live now for what life has to offer me right now.
8. I used to torture myself about the future. Worry about it so much I couldn't enjoy anything. I knew I was silly, but I couldn't stop it. Now I just don't care. I do the best I can now and I know the future will happen as it will happen no matter how much I worry about it. I take things as they come.

These ideas are not capricious whims. They are formulations developed after a working through of important conflicts. They indicate an attempt at solution of basic problems, which permit of a style of living more in keeping with reality.

Interestingly, the essence of such precepts may be found in proposals and rules of living laid down by poets and philosophers from the earliest times that humans recorded their hopes and fears and formulated ways of resolving them. Sometimes individuals arrive at such philosophies spontaneously without therapy, usually during emotional crises that force upon them adaptive ways of thinking and behaving. Sometimes the philosophies are evolved as a result of authoritative pressures or out of respect for leaders whom the individual elevates to a protective or powerful position. A good psychotherapeutic experience, however, will give the individual the best opportunity to remold values and to arrive at a more constructive way of being and living.

V

Special Aspects

56
Adjunctive Aids in Psychotherapy

The principle adjuncts in psychotherapy are relaxation exercises, biofeedback, somatic therapy, hypnosis, narcotherapy, videotape recording, and bibliotherapy.

RELAXATION EXERCISES AND MEDITATION

A certain amount of tension is a normal phenomenon, and every human being experiences it as a concomitant of daily living. It is probably helpful to problem solving and creative adaptation. In psychotherapy it acts as a stimulant to experimentation with new modes of defense and behavior. In excess, however, like too much anxiety, it paralyzes productive work and provokes a variety of physiological and psychological symptoms that divert the victim from concentrating on therapeutic tasks. Its control, consequently, becomes an expedient objective. While the therapeutic relationship serves to solace the patient, it may not be sufficient to subdue pathological tension. Minor tranquilizing drugs are effective, but they have side effects and may, in susceptible persons, lead to habituation. Fortunately, there are other available modes of tension control that can serve as an adjunct to psychotherapy.

As explained in a previous chapter, there are a number of ways that relaxation may be achieved, including meditation, Yoga practices, self-hypnosis, Zen, autogenic training, biofeedback, and simple breathing exercises. In all of the foregoing similar general principles prevail (Benson et al, 1974).

In meditation there is a *control of external stimuli*. This is achieved by a quiet environment devoid of distractions. An isolated room, a secluded seashore, or quiet woods can suffice. Other people may be present provided that they too participate in the relaxation experience, maintaining strict silence. Experienced meditators are able to "turn off" in almost any environment, withdrawing into themselves, but this will not apply to the great majority of people. Second, *attention is focused* on a simple sound, the repetition of a word or monotonous phrase, or gazing at an object. Some subjects utilize a metronome or listen to their own quiet deep breathing; some stare at a spot in the ceiling; still others recite to themselves a syllable or meaningless expression ("mantra"). Whenever the attention wanders and thoughts and ideas invade one's mind, the subject is enjoined to return to the fixation stimulus. Third, a free-floating, unpressured, languid, unresisting attitude must prevail: the *individual surrenders to passivity*. As images, reflections, ruminations, sentiments, and varied thoughts emerge from inner mental recesses, the subject lets them drift by without concentrating or being concerned with them. This is probably the most difficult task for the subject to learn, but with practice there is less and less focus on performance and greater ability to let things take their own course. Fourth, *a comfortable position* is essential, such as sitting in a chair or, if one is nimble, kneeling. Lying down is conducive to sleep and may defeat some of the aims of the experience.

The specific technique that one employs to achieve the relaxation experience is largely dependent on what is most meaningful for the individual. Some persons are so impressed with the mysteries of the esoteric Eastern philosophies that they are especially attracted to these.

In the practice of Zen Buddhism the meditation experience (Zazen) plays an important part. This, performed in a quiet atmosphere, with eyes open, the mind drifting while focused on breathing, produces a unique kind of physical-mental experience. Strived for are episodes of deep clarity (samadhi), of enlightened unity (satori), and a buildup of energy (joriki). To learn this type of meditation, one practices in a group (sangha), preferably under the guidance of a Zen master.

Transcendential meditation is perhaps the most widely employed form of relaxation utilized in the United States. Introduced by a guru, Maharishi Mahesh Yogi, it resulted in a movement that had gained mementum over the years with development of a large number of societies distributed throughout the land. The method continues to be used by some individuals. It is taught by a trained instructor who designs a word, sound, or phrase (mantra) presumably uniquely fitting to the subject, which is supposed to remain secret. This constitutes the fixation object.

Other forms of meditation include Yoga, Sufism, Taoism, Krishna Consciousness, and a wide variety of nonreligious practices focused on achieving a higher reality and greater knowledge than can be gathered through the senses. This is done by finding a "unity of being" in the quietness of inner tranquility. Each brand of relaxation has its devotees who attest to its singular usefulness. An excellent review of meditation is found in the book by Carrington (1977).

A description of the method designed by Dr. Maria Fleisch and Joan Suval, of basically two aspects of meditation therapy follows.

One involves effort and concentration, focusing attention upon a particular object or sensation, and the other, a simple watchfulness and observation, allowing a free flow of perceptions. The aims of this approach to meditation are twofold; to give a "total rest to the mind," relieving tension and anxiety, and to clear the mind, so that it is more aware and better able to cope with everyday problems.

The meditation therapist begins the group session by suggesting that the meditators close their eyes, take a deep breath, release it slowly, and allow their shoulders, chest, arms, legs, etc., to relax—to "let go completely." For a few moments focus will be on different parts of the body so that tension can be released in those areas. The therapist may then suggest that the meditators direct their attention for a while to the natural movement of their breathing, or to see if they can be aware of the various pulsations and sensations going on within the body. Other areas of focus could include listening to the sounds coming from the outdoors, or the footsteps in the halls, or the steady vibration of an air conditioner. The meditators are reminded throughout this part of the session that if certain thoughts distract their attention, they should simply observe that this is happening, refocusing their attention each time this occurs.

After 10 to 15 minutes of this aspect of the meditation involving effort and concentration, the therapist then suggests that the meditators now allow their attention to move wherever it is attracted—to a sound, a sensation, a thought—permitting a free flow of perceptions, an "effortless awareness." The therapist reminds the group, from time to time, that it is fine if thoughts are coming and going easily without causing any disturbance, but if the meditator finds that he or she is becoming anxious because of *thinking* about thoughts, one should then focus attention for a few moments on an area such as one's breathing, sensations within the body, sounds outside, etc., until the thoughts have subsided and one feels calmer. Then the meditator can return to watching a free flow of perceptions. Sometimes the therapist will ask the meditators to open their eyes "halfway" so that their gaze is directed downward for a few moments. This allows the meditator to discover that the watchfulness and effortless awareness can be going on even when the eyes are open. The therapist ends the meditation by once again suggesting that the meditators take a deep breath, exhale slowly, and gradually open their eyes.

Meditators are encouraged to schedule a 15- to 20-minute formal meditation period for themselves at home, either in the morning or the evening, or both, following the same procedure as outlined above. In addition, the therapist points out that this watchfulness and effortless awareness can go on while the person is involved in everyday activities—traveling on a bus, in a train, walking, listening to a conversation, observing the thoughts one has following an argument, etc. This allows one to be in closer "touch" with one's thoughts, feelings, what one actually IS at each particular moment of observation. Often when a meditator is simply watching a free flow of perceptions in this way, repressed thoughts can come to the surface. The meditation therapist stresses the importance of moving away from thought that creates tension and anxiety, calming the mind by focusing attention on an area that is not one of conflict, and then, when the mind is clear and quiet, allowing one to look once again at the thoughts or the situation that had caused the disturbance. When the mind is quiet and free from anxiety, it can see more easily which thoughts are negative and destructive and which are positive and constructive.

It should be pointed out that this approach to meditation is different from that of transcendental meditation, which limits itself to a formal meditation period, with the meditator concentrating attention on the silent or verbal repetition of an assigned "mantra" or Sanskrit word or phrase, so that one can enter into a state of relaxation. As indicated earlier, relaxation and concentration are important aspects of the meditation, but even more vital and beneficial is that this practical approach involves an effortless and choiceless awareness that the meditator can incorporate into daily life, enabling one to be in closer contact with oneself and to function more effectively in relationships.

In addition to the formal meditation period, the therapist answers questions that are asked and stimulates group discussion whenever possible. A strong supportive personality is an important requirement for the meditation therapist, who must also be watchful that there not be overdependency on the part of the meditators. The therapist can avoid this by encouraging individuals to meditate at home and throughout the day, modifying their approach according to their own needs and convenience.*

An outline such as that in Table 56-1 may also be given to the patient as an alternative method.

Meditation is employed not only as a means of tension control but also by some therapists as a way of facilitating imagery and free association. This is akin to the injunctions by early analysts to their patients to shut their eyes and allow themselves to relax completely, and then report the thoughts and phantasies that paraded themselves before their minds. As an adjunct in psychoanalytically oriented psychotherapy, meditation, like hypnosis, may release transference feelings that must be dealt with as part of the treatment process.

Biofeedback is another way of achieving relaxation through the use of instrumentation. This allows an individual to recognize and influence certain internal bodily states, like muscle tension, that interfere with relaxation. Among the most useful instruments are the electromyograph and temperature machines. Except where certain pathological physiological states exist, like very marked hypertension, dangerous tachycardia, and arrhythmias and severe migraine, there may be little advantage over the simple relaxation exercises outlined above for tension control.

Schultz's autogenic training (Schultz &

_____

* Reprinted with permission of Dr. Maria Fleishal and Joan Suval.

Table 56-1
Self-help Relaxation Methods

I. *Letting Go:* For most, it is a mistake to "try to relax." Just tense the muscle group and then visualize and verbalize to the muscle group "let go and keep on letting go."

II. *Breathing:* A Yogic style of deep slow breathing (6000 years old). Fill up with air from the lower belly (abdomen and diaphragm) toward the chest, like filling a glass of water, and *exhale slowly* thru the nostrils. You can first tense, or suck in the belly and feel tension in these muscles, and then say, "I will allow these muscles to let go," visualizing letting go on exhalation. Place hand below "belly button" and feel area move up on inhalation and down on exhalation. Relaxed breathing should continue throughout remaining exercises of tensing and relaxing.

III. *Forearm:* Many people can most quickly be aware of tensing the forearm and relaxing it on exhalation. Making a fist is one way of tensing and visualizing.

IV. *Face and Forehead:* Wrinkle forehead as tightly as possible, and then say to muscles, "Let go and keep on letting go." Practice this often. Furrow between the brows often and say, "Let go and continue to let go." Clench teeth, feel jaw muscles tighten, and let go with lips and teeth slightly parted. Show teeth and relax these muslces. *Push* tongue against upper palate (top of mouth) and let it relax between lower teeth (just almost touching bottom teeth). Close eyelids tightly and let go slowly. *IMPORTANT:* Look as far to left as possible with eyes closed, lids relaxed, and then let go and let eyes go and drift. Same to right and up and down. (Rolling eyeballs up with Yogic breathing and keeping them up is one way to be helpful for inducing self-hypnotism and later sleep in insomniacs.) Visualize and let the entire face smooth out as though you are smoothing it with both hands and let it stay smooth. (*Relaxation of eyes and tongue often controls unwanted thoughts and helps with insomnia.*)

V. If mind wanders, get it back to thinking of breathing and muscle group pictures as best you can. Tighten on inhalation and let go on exhalation.

VI. *Repetition:* Do not become discouraged since tension patterns have existed all of your life. Practice whenever possible. Soon shortcuts such as deep breathing and words "calm," or "let go," or "relax" or words or pictures of your choosing may help form relaxing a habit. You may find for yourself certain muscle groups, such as face, shoulders, or breathing muscles, that allow you to relax most adequately.

VII. *Neck Practice:* The same procedures of breathing and tensing muscle groups apply to all part of body. You can, especially in the beginning, bend head back, relax. Head to the left and right.

VIII. *Shoulders:* Hunch up as far as possible and let go. Backward and forward also.

IX. *Lower Extremities:* Pinch buttocks together; feel tension and let go. Tighten and let go toes.
General: Practice at every available moment to do things in a relaxed fashion: then let yourself consciously breath deeply and relax in situations ordinarily causing tension. If possible, condition or habituate the relaxation of the entire musculature or letting go to deep breathing and the same key words or words that seem to suit you.
Time: Persistence and review are worthwhile since everyone agrees on the desirability and harmlessness of relaxation.

Reprinted by permission of Dr. Irwin Rothman, modified from E. Jacobsen and J. Wolpe.

Luthe, 1959; Luthe, 1969) is another way of achieving tension control. An outline of modified autogenic training exercises is included at the end of the following section on biofeedback.

What all forms of relaxation correctly done achieve is a decrease in activity of the sympathetic nervous system with lowering of the heart rate, respiration, oxygen consumption, blood lactate level, blood pressure, muscle tension, and probably an increase in alpha brain waves. Where highly charged emotions and conflicts lay dormant, their upsurge into awareness may reverse these physiologic changes, but the proper technique will suppress such interferences. Hypnosis can be useful for the relaxation response, but where the object is to release repressed components through suggestion, cathartic liberation of emotions can occur. However, should strict tension control be the objective, there is no attempt made in hypnosis to probe for conflicts.

For many years this author has utilized hypnosis for simple tension control and has taught patients self-hypnosis (which can easily be learned), shying away from ego-building or exploratory suggestions so as to limit the extraneous suggestions and to focus the objective on relaxation. The technique is simple. The patient is enjoined to practice for 20 minutes, twice daily, sitting in a comfortable chair in a quiet room, shutting the eyes and breathing gently but deeply, concentrating on the sound of one's breathing. The patient is then asked to relax muscles progressively starting with the forehead and working down to the fingertips and then shoulders to toes. The reverse can also be done, that is, starting with the toes and slowly relaxing muscle groups to the forehead. Finally, the patient counts very slowly from 1 to 20 listening to his or her breathing. After the count the patient is enjoined to let the mind become passively languid, avoiding concentrating on thoughts and ideas. Should these obtrude themselves, the patient is to revert back to listening to breathing. In a short period these exercises may be learned achieving what the more complex meditation practices accomplish without unnecessary adornments. In some instances this author has made a cassette recording for the patient utilizing the format outlined in the section on hypnosis later in this chapter, but eliminating the ego-building suggestions and summation of suggestions. Such relaxation practices have been extremely helpful to patients under excessive tension, without interfering with the psychotherapeutic process.

A letter written by a physician who personally tried meditation to reduce pressures and tensions explains some of the benefits to be derived from it:

I'm getting back to meditating twice a day instead of just once (after four months of down to once a day). It really makes a big difference for me to have regular meditation. It certainly helps me see things in the larger perspective and less egotistically and egocentrically. Also it's a recharging of my mental battery, clearing the static of constant mental chatter out by tuning in to a clearer, more positive channel. You know, I actually feel much more ''free-floating'' after meditating—like the contrast between having all that subconscious mental chatter and no mental chatter brings the chatter back into acute focus. It seems like I then have greater access to my subconscious. I feel more creative, more in control, and less driven somehow.

BIOFEEDBACK

Through the use of electronic instruments it has been shown that an individual may become aware of changes in bodily functions of which one is usually ignorant, including skin temperature, blood pressure, muscle tension, and brain wave patterns. Changes in these functions activate the instruments designed to measure them and deliver signals (sounds or lights) to the subject permitting one to become aware of certain feelings or states of mind that influence alterations in the studied parameters. The subject gradually learns how to reproduce such feelings or states to secure desired physiological effects. Body and mind become affiliated through this feedback process so that eventually the individual can reproduce reactions without the use of instruments. The full value of biofeedback must still be evaluated. It has certain substantiated uses, but whether it is superior for this purpose to other techniques (yoga, autogenic training, meditation, self-hypnosis, progressive muscle relaxation, drug treatment, psychotherapy) has not yet been determined. There are some individuals who are extremely impressed with and hence responsive to gadgetry. A powerful placebo effect accompanies biofeedback instrumentation (Frank, 1982) but this does not entirely account for the benefits.

The conditions for which biofeedback may be helpful are generally those of any relaxation training program, i.e., conditions associated with tension and anxiety, either their raw manifestations or the somatic consequences. Biofeedback also serves to induce a state of relaxation during the application of behavioral techniques such as systematic and in vivo desensitization. Finally, it has some use in psychodynamic psychotherapy by helping the patient develop initial rapport with the therapist on the basis that something positive is being done for one. The patient is provided with a technique of controlling anxiety and thus may be more willing to participate in the painful task of exploring repressed needs and dealing with repudiated ideas and conflicts. Moreover, the patient will react to the instrumentation and to the routines expected of one with usual characterologic manipulations and defenses that can provide the therapist with ample dynamic material for scrutiny. During interviewing biofeedback encourages the release of imagery. Anxiogenic themes may be verbalized, particularly by thermal and electrodermal instrumentation, facilitating the exploration of significant fantasies, memories, and conflicts.

Biofeedback is particularly acceptable to those who are fearful of the labels of psychotherapy and mental health, such as executives suffering from tension and psychosomatic symptoms who do not wish to compromise their chances for advancement by having it appear on their record that they received "treatment for mental illness." Usually a patient is seen once or twice a week by the therapist, and is also encouraged to practice exercises at home each day and when symptoms occur. Twenty to forty formal sessions are usually required to learn tension reduction through instrumentation.

Biofeedback is being employed in Raynaud's disease, migraine, cardiac arrhythmias, hypertension, phobias, bruxism, torticollis, low back pain, cerebral palsy, peripheral nerve-muscle damage, upper motorneurone hemiplegia, some cases of tardive dyskinesia, Raynaud's syndrome, temperomandibular joint pain, insomnia, narcotic withdrawal, attention deficit disorder, tension headaches, asthma, irritable colon, fecal incontinence, chronic pain, seizure disorders, and neuromuscular ailments with reported promising results. But biofeedback cannot be recommended for everyone. It is valueless in serious psychiatric problems and it may create anxiety in some patients such as paranoid conditions. In combination with psychotherapy it proves most helpful, and therefore treatment should be executed or supervised by a trained psychotherapist. It requires time for learning, studied application, and practice, in which not all patients are willing to indulge. It requires also instruments that may be an expensive investment. In spite of these drawbacks, biofeedback is an area whose full possibilities and applications have opened up a fertile field of research (J. Segal, 1975). A number of volumes of collected research on feedback have already appeared as well as critical reviews of the literature (Basmajian, 1983; Gaarder & Montgomery, 1977; D. Shapiro & Schwartz, 1972; Blanchard & Young, 1974). A journal, *Biofeedback and Self-Regulation* has been published.

In the technique of biofeedback "a meditative state of deep relaxation is conducive to the establishment of voluntary control by allowing the individual to become aware of subliminal imagery, fantasies, and sensations" (Pelletier, 1975). This facilitates a link between physiological and psychological processes. The combination of relaxation exercises and biofeedback instrumentation facilitates identification of subjective imagery and physiological sensations that are quieting to the bodily organs.

Where a patient with a serious gastrointestinal, cardiovascular, migrainous, or psychosomatic illness is unable to achieve relief through psychotherapy with the adjunctive use of relaxation exercises, biofeedback training should be considered. Which instruments to employ will depend on the illness and the learning capacities of the patient. Many practitioners have found the galvanic skin reflex (GSR) electromyograph (EMG) and temperature machines most useful.

In muscle tension retraining through the use of an EMG information may be obtained regarding muscular activity below the threshold of sensory awareness. One may measure the average intensity of neuron firing in microvolts on a meter. An audible feedback delivers sounds registering increases in muscular activity, and by utilizing a threshold control one may provide conditions for optimal training. Where muscle relaxation is the goal, the threshold is set at a high level to produce sound; and as the patient learns to relax, the sound lessens then disappears. The electrodes are in a band that fits around the muscle to be utilized for training purposes. The most useful location is the forehead, the elec-

trodes being placed about 1 inch above the eyebrows.

Signals are picked up not only from the frontalis muscle, but also from other muscles in the head, face, and neck. Thinking activates anxiety thoughts, which can cause a rise in muscular activity. "Turning off thinking" causes a fall.

Relaxation of the frontalis muscle tends to generalize to the entire body. When the level reaches below 4 microvolts, the subject may report a feeling of weightlessness or floating and alterations in the body image. This may create temporary anxiety and increase muscle tension. Should this happen, the patient is reassured that these sensations are normal and to enjoy them. As tension decreases, those patients who are repressing anxiety strongly may experience a sudden burst of anxious thoughts and feelings. Should this happen, the patient is encouraged to verbalize them. In this way biofeedback may be useful in dynamic psychotherapy (Glucksman, 1981, Adler & Adler, 1972). Biofeedback can create a state of relaxation helpful in verbalization during psychotherapy and desensitization procedures in behavior therapy. The effect on the therapeutic alliance is generally a constructive one and the learning of self-regulation may have an influence on the establishing of inner controls.

When the subject has been able to maintain EMG activity below 4 microvolts for about 15 minutes, one should instruct the subject to examine internal sensations and feelings associated with deep relaxation in order to recreate the state without the feedback unit. In this way muscle relaxation may be obtained rapidly without the use of instruments.

GSR gives data as to emotional arousal, and its control may help lessen tension. The blood volume may also be assessed by special machines, especially through temperature measurements, in this way redirecting the blood flow from one

Table 56-2
Relaxation Training Procedure

Part I	
Sit quietly in a comfortable position.	Take another deep, slow breath.
Take a deep, slow breath. Hold the breath for several seconds. Slowly exhale.	Hold the breath while tightening your stomach and neck muscles. Feel the tension.
Take another deep, slow breath. Hold the breath and pull your toes toward your head, tightening your leg and calf muscles. Feel the tension.	Breathe out and let your muscles go limp. Take another deep, slow breath. Hold the breath and tighten every muscle in your body until you feel your whole body start to tremble with tension.
Breathe out and let go completely. Take another deep, slow breath. Hold the breath and make a fist with both hands, tightening your arm and shoulder muscles. Feel the tension.	Now breathe out and let go completely. Take another deep, slow breath. Hold the breath and tighten every muscle in your body. Hold on to the tension.
Breathe out and let go completely. Take another deep, slow breath. Hold the breath and bit down as hard as you can, tightening your jaw muscles. Feel the tension.	Now breathe out and let go completely. Take another deep, slow breath. Hold the breath and tighten every muscle in your body. Hold the tension.
Breathe out and let go completely.	Now breathe out and let go, relaxing completely.

Part II	
Concentrate on slow, deep breathing throughout this entire section.	My stomach and the whole center portion of my body feel heavy and relaxed.
Slowly repeat each of these phrases to yourself as you hear them.	My stomach and the whole center portion of my body feel heavy and relaxed. My hands feel heavy and relaxed.
I feel very calm and quiet. I feel very comfortable and quiet. I am beginning to feel quite relaxed. I am beginning to feel quite relaxed. My feet feel heavy and relaxed. My feet feel heavy and relaxed. My ankles feel heavy and relaxed. My ankles feel heavy and relaxed. My knees feel heavy and relaxed. My knees feel heavy and relaxed. My hips feel heavy and relaxed. My hips feel heavy and relaxed. My feet, my ankles, my knees and my hips all feel heavy and relaxed. My feet, my ankles, my knees and my hips all feel heavy and relaxed. My neck, my jaws and my forehead all feel heavy and relaxed. My whole body feels heavy and relaxed.	My hands feel heavy and relaxed. My arms feel heavy and relaxed. My arms feel heavy and relaxed. My shoulders feel heavy and relaxed. My shoulders feel heavy and relaxed. My hands, my arms and my shoulders all feel heavy and relaxed. My hands, my arms and my shoulders all feel heavy and relaxed. My neck feels heavy and relaxed. My neck feels heavy and relaxed. My jaws feel heavy and relaxed. My jaws feel heavy and relaxed. My forehead feels heavy and relaxed. My forehead feels heavy and relaxed. My neck, my jaws and my forehead all feel heavy and relaxed. My left elbow, my left shoulder feel warm and heavy.

My whole body feels heavy and relaxed.
My breathing is getting deeper and deeper.
My breathing is getting deeper and deeper.
I can feel the sun shining down on me warming the top of my head.
The top of my head feels warm and heavy.
The top of my head feels warm and heavy.
The relaxing warmth flows into my right shoulder.
My right shoulder feels warm and heavy.
My right shoulder feels warm and heavy.
My breathing is getting deeper and deeper.
The relaxing warmth flows down to my right hand.
My right hand feels warm and heavy.
My right hand feels warm and heavy.
The relaxing warmth flows back up to my right arm.
My right arm feels warm and heavy.
My right arm feels warm and heavy.
The relaxing warmth spreads up through my right elbow into my right shoulder.
My right elbow, my right shoulder feel warm and heavy.
My right elbow, my right shoulder feel warm and heavy.
The relaxing warmth flows slowly throughout my whole back.
I feel the warmth relaxing my back.
My back feels warm and heavy.
My back feels warm and heavy.
The relaxing warmth flows up my back and into my neck.
My neck feels warm and heavy.
My neck feels warm and heavy.
The relaxing warmth flows into my left shoulder.
My left shoulder feels warm and heavy.
My left shoulder feels warm and heavy.
My breathing is getting deeper and deeper.
The relaxing warmth flows down to my left hand.
My left hand feels warm and heavy.
My left hand feels warm and heavy.
The relaxing warmth flows back up to my left arm.
My left arm feels warm and heavy.
My left arm feels warm and heavy.
The relaxing warmth spreads up through my left elbow into my left shoulder.
My whole body is heavy, warm, relaxed.

My left elbow, my left shoulder feel warm and heavy.
The relaxing warmth flows to my heart.
My heart feels warm and easy.
My heart feels warm and easy.
My heartbeat is slow and regular.
My heartbeat is slow and regular.
The relaxing warmth flows down into my stomach.
My stomach feels warm and quiet.
My stomach feels warm and quiet.
My breathing is deeper and deeper.
My breathing is deeper and deeper.
The relaxing warmth flows down into my right thigh.
My right thigh feels warm and heavy.
My right thigh feels warm and heavy.
The relaxing warmth flows down into my right foot.
My right foot feels warm and heavy.
My right foot feels warm and heavy.
The relaxing warmth flows slowly up through my right calf, to my right knee, to my right thigh.
My right leg feels warm and heavy.
My right leg feels warm and heavy.
My breathing is deeper and deeper.
My breathing is deeper and deeper.
The relaxing warmth flows down into my left thigh.
My left thigh feels warm and heavy.
My left thigh feels warm and heavy.
The relaxing warmth flows down into my left foot.
My left foot feels warm and heavy.
My left foot feels warm and heavy.
The relaxing warmth flows slowly up through my left calf, to my left knee, to my left thigh.
My left leg feels warm and heavy.
My left leg feels warm and heavy.
My breathing is deeper and deeper.
My breathing is deeper and deeper.
The relaxing warmth flows up through my abdomen, through my stomach and into my heart.
My heart feels warm and easy.
My heart feels warm and easy.
My heart pumps relaxing warmth throughout my entire body.
My whole body is heavy, warm, relaxed.
My whole body is heavy, warm, relaxed.

(continued)

Table 56-2 (*continued*)

I am breathing deeper and deeper.	I feel serene, secure, still.
I am breathing deeper and deeper.	My thoughts are all turned inward.
My whole body feels very quiet and very serene.	I am at ease, completely at ease.
My whole body feels very comfortable and very relaxed.	Deep within my mind I can visualize and experience myself as relaxed.
My mind is still.	I am comfortable and still.
My mind is quiet.	My mind is calm and quiet.
My mind is easy.	I feel an inward peace.
I withdraw my thoughts from my surroundings.	I feel a new sense of well being.
Nothing exists around me.	I am breathing more and more deeply.

Part III

Now lift your arms slowly, high over your head.	You are breathing deeper and deeper.
Take a deep, deep breath.	Slowly say the following phrases to yourself.
Hold the breath and slowly lower your arms and hands.	My whole body feels quiet, comfortable and relaxed.
When your arms and hands touch your chair breathe out and go completely limp.	My hands and arms feel heavy, warm and relaxed.
Hold your hands in front of you as if you were praying.	My legs feel heavy, warm and relaxed.
Take a deep, deep breath.	My mind is quiet.
Press your hands together until you feel your arm muscles tremble.	I withdraw my thoughts from my surroundings.
Breathe out and go completely limp.	I feel serene and still.
Take a deep, deep breath.	My thoughts are turned inward.
Hold the breath and slowly draw your hands toward your face.	I am at ease.
When your hands touch your face, breathe out and let go.	Deep within my mind I can visualize and experience myself as comfortable and still. My mind is calm and quiet.
Go completely limp.	I feel an inward peace and quiet.
You are breathing deeper and deeper.	I am now relaxed and alert. [*If biofeedback training is to be utilized, simply say:* I am now ready to begin my training session.]

Reprinted by permission of the Cyborg Corporation, 342 Western Blvd. Boston Massachusetts 02135.

area of the body where blood engorgement causes symptoms (e.g., the brain in migraine attacks) to other areas (e.g., the hand). A blood pressure apparatus and an electrocardiographic (EKG) machine are also employed to control blood pressure and the heart rate. The electroencephalogram (EEG) is occasionally used in epileptic patients to teach them to increase the sensorimotor density rhythm in order to reduce the frequency of seizures. There is some evidence that penile tumescence, the operation of sphincters, repiratory activities, optic and stomach functions may be mediated through special instruments in this way, helping impotence, fecal incontinence, excess gastric acidity, asthma, and myopia. The work in these areas is still incomplete.

To control migraine, it is necessary to learn control of blood circulation in the brain to minimize engorgement of the blood vessels. Utilizing the thermal machine, one may learn to send the blood flow from the head to the hand. The machine has two probes that record the surface temperature (a measure of the blood flow). To monitor blood flow between the head and hand, one probe is placed on the forehead, the other probe on the middle finger of the right hand. The thermal unit (machine) detects minute changes in temperature differential. As a difference in temperature occurs between forehead and finger, a slowly pulsed audible tone will be heard in the earphones. The sound means the blood is flowing in the right direction. Training sessions after the relaxation exercises should last no longer than 5 to 10 minutes.

There is no reason why biofeedback cannot be utilized in combination with behavior therapy (e.g., systematic desensitization) and dynamic psychotherapy. In this way the patient monitors their own anxiety level by EMG feedback and becomes more insightful of his or her fantasy material in an atmosphere of objective detachment (Budzynski et al, 1970).

A useful means of achieving relaxation prior to biofeedback instrumentation is Schultz's autogenic training or a modification of this as in Table 56-2. Practically no scientifically controlled studies exist that truly establish the effectiveness of biofeedback, but the clinical reports are optimistic, perhaps overly optimistic. There is danger in this overoptimism of misuse of the method, and of arousing false hopes that biofeedback is a panacea. Should this happen, we may expect a backlash reaction leading to the denigration and premature elimination of biofeedback as a viable technique. What is needed are carefully designed studies with adequate controls.

A good text is the one by Gaarder and Montgomery (1977). Affordable monotoring modules are now available that measure physiological activities with considerable accuracy.

SOMATIC THERAPY

In a previous chapter the rationale and indications for the somatic therapies have been detailed (Chapter 9). In this section we shall consider some practical applications helpful for the psychotherapist in deciding which patients require medicaments adjunctively and which drugs to prescribe. If the therapist is a nonphysician, it will be necessary to work collaboratively with the prescribing medical person, supplying the proper data in order that the most suitable drug be selected.

Somatic therapy has proven itself to be a great boon to patients suffering from schizophrenia, endogenous depressions, manic phases of manic-depressive psychosis, acute puerperal psychosis, and severe toxic confusional states. Moreover, somatic treatments have had a positive effect on the morale of patients and their families and have helped to increase discharge rates om mental hospitals (Freyhan, 1961). The prevailing attitude of the public regarding the hopelessness and incurability of severe mental illness has given way to optimism that dread psychiatric diseases may now be interrupted and perhaps even cured. Employed in outpatient departments of hospitals and clinics, somatic therapy has brought early psychoses to a halt before they have progressed to a point where patients have had to be institutionalized. It has also helped in the rehabilitation of chronic psychotic patients.

Somatic therapy, particularly drug administration, has also exerted a beneficial effect in psychotherapy (Linn, 1964; Kalinowsky, 1965; Kalinowsky & Hippius, 1969; Hollister, 1973). While some therapists continue to shy away from the use of medications, situations do arise during psychotherapy when drugs may prove helpful, even in psychoanalysis (Ostow, 1962). An important factor is to prescribe drugs in sufficient dosage and over a sufficiently long period to test their efficacy.

Pharmacotherapy*

Psychotropic drugs during the past two decades have proven themselves to be of incalculable value in dealing with the biological correlates of certain mental and emotional disorders. They have not replaced psychosocial interventions, which concern themselves with the developmental, conditioning, extrapsychic, interpersonal, social, and philosophic-spiritual links in the behavioral chain. Nevertheless, in rectifying biochemical and neurophysiological dysregulations, they have by feedback influenced positively the various other bodily systems in the interests of better adaption. While they do not cure the disease, they alleviate many of the symptoms. Thus they have influenced, beyond the placebo effect, a variety of unwholesome behavioral symptoms, such as hyperactivity, agitation, excitement, violent rage, listlessness, social withdrawal, thinking disturbances including hallucinations and delusions, depression, tension, eating disorders, panic and anxiety. Initial improvements have been sustained, and many patients on a drug regimen even for over 10 years have not been deprived of any of their vital functions (Redlich & Freedman, 1966). Drug therapy helps to keep psychotic patients out of hospitals and enables them to assume some productive role in the community. During psychotherapy it permits of a modulation of anxiety, particularly where the individual is so immersed in dealing with its effects that one is unable to apply oneself to the tasks of psychological exploration and working through. It may make disturbed patients more accessible to psychotherapy. It also reverses some depressive reactions that drain energy and block initiative. All patients on psychoactive drugs should be under close medical supervision.

---

* Table 56-3 outlines some of the principal medications in use today. New substances are constantly being introduced.

The exact action of drugs is not entirely known; however, they appear to act both on the underlying disorder and on the secondary reactions (e.g., withdrawal, undermined self-esteem, etc.) of a patient to illness. They may dissociate symptoms from their attached emotional components; for example, the psycho-inhibiting medicaments, namely phenothiazines, can isolate delusional systems in schizophrenia. They may make available more psychic energy, thus enabling the patient to deal more readily with his or her conflicts. For instance, the energizing drugs vitalize the individual and increase general feelings of well-being. They may disrupt the psychic organization, giving symptoms a new meaning, as during psychedelic experiences with LSD. Tranquilizing and energizing drugs are sometimes employed singly or in combination (e.g., Trilafon and Elavil from two to four times daily), and with this alone (with no uncovering of dynamics and no insight) the patient may achieve a psychological balance. Lowinger et al. (1964), in a follow-up study on drug treatments as the exclusive therapeutic agency, found that the favorable outcome rates were comparable to other treatment approaches in similar patients. After a short period of time on medication some patients will reconstitute themselves; others may require prolonged drug administration. The dosage should be reduced in elderly patients and children. In selecting alternate drugs, it is important to inquire as to what has been effective in the past with the patient and with relatives who were or are on medications (since genetic factors influence drug responses).

Among the impediments in utilizing psychotropic drugs are:

1. Their side effects, such as allergic responses—hepatocanalicular jaundice with the phenothiazines and tricyclic antidepressants, and agranulocytosis with the phenothiazines and occasion-

ally imipramine (Tofranil) and amitriptyline (Elavil); pigmentary reactions in the skin, lens and cornea with phenothiazines; cardiac changes with certain phenothiazines and tricyclic compounds (especially Mellaril and Tofranil).

2. Their tendency to produce adverse physical and behavioral reactions—for example, hypotension with the phenothiazines and MAO inhibitors; adrenergic crisis in the sympathetic amines (amphetamine, dextroamphetamine); hypertensive crises with MAO inhibitors when tyramine foods are eaten; dyskinesia and Parkinsonism with the neuroleptics; problems in males of impotence and retarded ejaculation and anorgasmia in females. Antidepressant drugs may be contraindicated in some cardiac arrhythmias and in pheochromocytoma, and used with great caution in thyroid disease, angle-closure glaucoma, prostatic hypertrophy and renal failure.

3. Properties that lead to habituation—for instance, the sympathetic amines (Desoxyn, Dexedrine), the barbiturates (Nembutal), meprobamate (Miltown), chlordiazepoxide (Librium), and diazepam (Valium).

Side effects and allergic responses are not too common and mostly are annoying rather than dangerous. They do not justify discontinuing drug treatments. They usually occur during the early states of administration and may be controlled by antagonistic substances (like Cogentin or Artane in Parkinsonism). A disturbing and lasting effect of phenothiazines on chronic psychiatric patients in long-term therapy is tardive dyskinesia, which may not respond to any treatment. Habituating drugs, such as sedatives and hypnotics, may be regulated and should be at least temporarily discontinued after their effects have registered themselves to the benefit of the patient.

Some psychiatrists avoid personal prescription of tranquilizers in reconstructive therapy when they are needed on the basis that this introduces a guidance-supportive element in the relationship. If tranquilizers are indicated, they recommend that the patient consult the regular family physician. Actually, the giving of tranquilizers need not interfere with the management of reconstructive therapy, for the patient's reaction to the therapist as a guiding authority may be handled as part of the treatment process. Prescribing tranquilizers, giving interpretations, sending monthly bills, canceling appointments, and any other active transactions will be utilized by the patient as vehicles around which ideas about authority are organized, providing rich material for study. The nonmedical therapist will certainly need the cooperation of a physician, preferably a psychiatrist, in the event that prescription of a drug is necessary.

In review, drugs are no substitute for psychotherapy. But, as has been indicated, drugs can provide adjunctive help during certain phases of psychotherapeutic management. Caution is essential in prescribing drugs for minor emotional illness, not only because of their potential side effects, and the existence of allergies and sensitivities in the patient, but also because the temporary relief from symptoms that they inspire may induce the patient to utilize them as the first line of defense whenever conflict and tension arise, to the neglect of a reasoned resolution of a developing problem. In certain personality types tranquilizing and energizing drugs may come to fashion the individual's way of life, dependence on them producing a habituation whose effects are more serious than the complaints that they initially were intended to subdue. These disadvantages should not act as a deterrent to the proper employment of such medicaments, which, in their judicious use, will tend to help, not hinder, a psychotherapeutic program. Side effects and tendencies to habituation may be managed if therapists alert themselves to developing contingencies. A great deal of prudence must be exercised in evaluating the worth of any drug, since, as more and more medicaments are introduced into the market, their virtues are flaunted with spectacular and often unjustified claims.

In the main, tranquilizing drugs are employed in psychotherapy during extreme anxiety states when the patient's defenses crumble or when the patient is so completely involved in protecting him or herself from anxiety as to be unable to explore its sources. In neurotic patients the principal medicaments employed for anxiety are Xanas, Librium, Valium, and Serax. In borderline patients who are decompensating (depersonalization, extreme anxiety, psychotic-like ideation) low doses of neuroleptics, e.g., Stelazine and Haldol may be temporarily tried. In schizophrenia associated with apathetic and depressive symptoms, Stelazine and Trilafon may be employed. In schizophrenic excitement, Thorazine is an excellent drug, although, in office practice, Mellaril is effectively used. In psychotic reactions with apathy and withdrawal, Stelazine and Trilafon are helpful. Manic phases of manic-depressive psychosis may be approached with lithium and Haldol. For mood elevation in mild depressions, Ritalin may sometimes be employed, especially in older people. For moderate and neurotic depressions the monoamine oxidase (MAO) inhibitors, Nardil and Parnate, are sometimes utilized, recognizing the side effects and dangers that may accompany their use. Tofranil, Desipramine, and Norpramine apply themselves well to retarded depressions, while Elavil is often helpful in agitated depressions. For suicidal depressions electroconvulsive therapy is preferred. In drug addiction and alcoholism certain drugs may be valuable—for instance, methadone in the former and antabuse in the latter.

People react uniquely to drugs, not only because of their constitutional physiological makeup, but also because of their mental set, their attitudes toward the medication, and the specific lines of their expectation influencing both beneficial and side effects. Experimentation will be required in dosage and type of drug. The very young and the very old may exhibit a sensitivity to drugs that require either a reduction of dosage or contradict their use. Drug administration must be under the direction and control of a qualified psychiatrist who first examines the patient and then prescribes the best chemical adjunct. The psychiatrist should see the patient periodically thereafter to ascertain the results of drug treatment, to manage side effects, and to alter the dosage when necessary.

The monitoring by laboratory tests of blood levels of psychotropic medications may be important in patients who are not responding well to these medications. Patients show variations in their absorption of drugs from the gastro-intestinal tract as well as in the metabolism of the drugs. If drugs other than the principal one are being taken, these may influence the absorption process causing blood levels that are too low for clinical relapse or too high with precipitated toxicity. Many patients forget or refuse to follow proper drug intake regimens and monitoring of blood levels can detect whether too little or too much medication is being used in order to regulate side effects, and to ensure compliance. Standard therapeutic dosages do not influence all patients the same way, some under-responding and others experiencing toxic effects. Moreover, in patients with cardiovascular illness on antidepressants, for example, careful monitoring may enable maintaining the patient on a therapeutic level with the lowest drug concentrations to reduce the risks. The monitoring of neuroleptic blood concentrations in shcizophrenia helps identify the optimal plasma levels for good dopamine receptor binding at the lowest concentrations thus reducing extrapyramidal effects and the danger of tardive dyskinesia.

ANTIPSYCHOTIC DRUGS (NEUROLEPTICS)

Neuroleptics are used to reduce or eliminate the symptoms of psychosis in conditions such as schizophrenia, psychotic depression, mania, schizoaffective disorder, delirium, drug-induced psychosis and paranoid disorder. Such symptoms include disordered thinking, delusions, hallucinations, suspiciousness, extreme anger, markedly aggressive behavior, and agitated excitement. Given in periods of remission from psychosis, antipsychotic drugs may prevent a relapse and social and cognitive deterioration.

How these drugs work is not yet clearly known, but it is believed that they regulate at the receptor level the activity of the neurotransmitter dopamine (which operates excessively in schizophrenia). These medications also block other receptors producing quinidine-like activity and calcium-channel blockade, which may produce some undesirable side effects.

There are five distinctive classes of antipsychotic drugs for clinical use in the United States that are equally effective in antipsychotic activity, but vary in their pharmacologic profiles. This is all to the good since different individuals respond better to some of these classes than to others. The first and oldest class of drugs are the phenothiazines, which are of low potency, and hence require high dosage to be effective. Three common forms are available which vary slightly in chemical composition and produce somewhat different side effects. For example, the aliphatic phenothiazines (like chlorpromazine or Thorazine) produce marked sedation and are often used in overactive and aggressive psychotic patients. They do, however, lower the blood pressure (hypotension) and moderately promote extrapyramidal symptoms such as tremors, rigidity and masklike facial expression (Parkinsonism), which may necessitate neutralization by an anti-Parkinsonian drug. The second variant of phenothiazines is the piperidine phenothiazine group like thioridazine (Mellaril), which has the same effect as Thorazine but produces a lower incidence of extrapyramidal symptoms. The third variant is the piperazine phenothiazine group like trifluoperazine (Stelazine), perphenazine (Trilafon), and fluphenazine (Prolixin), which because of higher potency require lower dosage, hence produce less sedation and lowering of blood pressure (hypotension). Their disadvantage, however, is the higher incidence neurological (extrapyramidal) symptoms.

The second class of neuroleptics, the butyrophenones, have much the same effect as the piperazine phenothiziazines. The most widely used of these is halperidol (Haldol) which has a reduced tendency to cause undesired sedation, anticholinergic effects and hypotension, but a high incidence of extrapyrmidal symptoms. The third class are the thioxanthenes: Thiothixene (Navane) which has similar side effects as Stelazine, Trilifon, and Prolixin; and chlorprothixene (Taractan), which has some properties like Thorazine. The fourth class is represented by dihydroindolone Molindone (Moban) and produces moderate side effects. The fifth class consists of dibenzoxazapine or loxapine (Loxitane) which often produces sedation and extrapyramidal symptoms, but only moderate hypotension and anticholinergic effects. New drugs will undoubtedly come into the marketplace that exercise antipsychotic effects without the danger of tardive dyskinesia. For example, an investigative drug, Clozapine, has been found effective without the side effects of the neuroleptics. But even Clozapine has its destructive side effects in some cases affecting the blood through production of agranulocytosis.

The present available drugs vary in their choice and degree of receptor blockage, and hence the propensity for side effects. Excessive dopamine receptor blockage results in extrapyramidal movement disorders and tardive dyskinesia; blockage of muscarinic acetylcholine receptors are anticholinergic causing urinary retention, constipation, dry mouth and memory dysfunction; histamine receptor blockage produces sedation, weight gain and hypotension, tachycardia and lightheadedness. By selecting drugs that have a lessened capacity for side effects, disturbing symptoms can be minimized. Since patients respond differently to medications and only a clinical trial can determine which neuroleptic will best be tolerated. Some therapists start therapy with the older drugs like chlorpromazine (Thorazine), thioridazine (Mellaril), or fluphenazine (Prolixin), and only where uncomfortable side effects occur do they shift to drugs with a lower receptor affinity like molindone (Moban) and loxapine (Loxitane).

Given any of the commonly used antipsychotic drugs administered over an adequate period in proper dosage, they all exert approximately the same antipsychotic influence. Side effects may be different among the different groups and often the selection of a medication is determined by whether we want to eliminate a selected side effect. Thus he anticholinergic sedative reaction of drugs like Thorazine, Mellaril, and Taractan may be troublesome for some patients and here we would use the less sedating drugs like Haldol, Prolixin, or Stelazine. On the other hand extrapyramidal symptoms, like restlessness, (akithesia) muscle spasms (dystonia) and muscle rigidity (parkinsonism) are intolerable in susceptible patients and Mellaril, Navane, or Moban would be used, with less of an extrapyramidal effect. In elderly or cardiac patients, a selection of drugs should avoid those that lower blood pressure or depress heart action, e.g., Thorazine, Mellaril, and Taractin. If dangerous toxic reactions occur, the more innocuous drug Moban is best to use. It is important not to mix the different neuroleptics. In elderly patients who

display disturbing or unmanageable psychotic symptoms as part of an organic brain syndrome, severe depression, mania, paranoidal condition, or schizophrenia, antipsychotics may be indicated, but because of susceptibility to toxic reactions in the elderly, the dose should be reduced to one-third to one-half of the usual adult dose. High potency medications in small amounts like Prolixin and Haldol are preferred, administered in divided small doses to avoid the anticholinergic sedative and autonomic effects of the low potency drugs. However, extrapyramidal neurological side effects may occur with high potency medications. Sometimes medium potency drugs, like Trilafon work well with older patients, and in cardiac conditions Moban and Haldol may be prescribed.

Since there are some patients who seem to respond better to some classes of drugs than to others, after trying one medication for a sufficiently long period with gradually increasing dosage and achieving no success, one may then experiment with a new drug. In spite of some reports regarding the stimulating effect of the high potency antipsychotics like Prolixin, Permitil, and Haldol, there is little evidence for this and they should not be prescribed for this purpose. High potency neuroleptics like Prolixin, which have neurological (extrapyramidal) side effects and which may retard sexual functioning should be avoided where these effects are likely to upset a patient, for example, a paranoid individual. Too early use of long-term single dose injections (Prolixin Decanoate, Haldol Decanoate) may be responsible for noxious effects.

In adolescent schizophrenia, disturbed thinking and behavioral patterns may be helped by neuroleptics although the dosage must be monitored and adjusted in relation to the degree of impairment produced by side effects. The low potency sedating antipsychotics, like Thorazine and Mellaril are best avoided in favor of the high potency drugs like Stelazine, Navane, Prolixin, and Haldol, which are less sedating.

There is some evidence pointing to the positive effects of low doses of antipsychotics in certain borderline and schizotypal personality disorders. In patients with symptoms of "psychotism," illusions, ideas of reference, obsessive compulsive symptoms, and phobic anxiety, Goldberg, et al. (1986) found that Thiothixene (Navane) in an average daily dose of 8.7 mg produced favorable results. Soloff et al. (1986) discovered that an average dose of 7.24 mg of haloperidol (Haldol) relieved symptoms of depression, anxiety, hostility, "psychotism," and paranoid ideation in borderline patients.

Rapid intensive "neuroleptization" has not fulfilled promises of great effectiveness as compared to standard treatment. Time may be needed before results become apparent. Attempts to reduce this time by massive increases of dosage succeed in toxicity more often than in treatment success. After several weeks of studied treatment without results, trials with increased daily doses (like 1200 mg Thorazine or equivalent) may be in order.

Side effects are to be expected in all of the neuroleptics no matter which are chosen, and the patient should be told that they are usual and indicate the drug is having an effect. Should the patient continue to be drowsy, the bulk of the dose may be administered at night which will help sleep. Dryness of the mouth usually abates. Constipation may appear in older people. Rarely, some female patients develop a secretion from the breasts; they may manifest a weight gain and amenorrhea. Because skin sensitivity is increased, patients should be warned not to expose themselves deliberately to the sun during summer months. If skin sensitivity to sun lasts, Narvane is the best drug. Should dizziness occur due to postural hypotension, the patient may be instructed to stand up slowly from a lying or sitting position. Parkinsonism is considered by some authorities to be a welcome sign, a guidepost to maximum dosage. If it or dystonia or akithesia occurs, the patient should receive Artane (1–6 mg daily) or Cogentin (1–2 mg two or three times daily), or Kemadrin (2.5–5 mg three times daily). A rare side effect is agranulocytosis, and if the patient complains of a sore throat, a white blood cell and differential count should be obtained. In the event agranulocytosis is present, the drug should be immediately discontinued, and a medical consultation obtained to forestall complications. Jaundice is not too important, occurring mainly in 0.5 or 1 percent of older people. Reactions of skin, retinal, and corneal pigmentation are very rare.

Some side effects can be especially distressing and are usually responsible for patients discontinuing medication. Such side effects should therefore be anticipated, discussed with the patient, and managed by prolonged supervision. Without supervision one can expect a high incidence of drug disuse and relapse of illness. Anticholingeric effects may be neutralized by some medications, like bethanechol (Urecholine) or in emergencies by physostigmine (Antilirium). Among recipients of high potency drugs, extrapyramidal neurologic symptoms are reversible with the discontinuance of medication or can be neutralized by appropriate drugs like benztropine (Cogentin), trihexyphenidyl (Artane), diphenhydramin (Benadryl), and amantadine (Symmetral). The muscle spasms of the tongue and mouth (dystonias), the "restless legs" and fidgetiness (akithisias), tremors of the extremities and difficulties in walking (parkinsonism) can alarm the patient and relatives, but are not really too serious since they can be alleviated readily with appropriate medications mentioned above.

One complication is serious and develops in about 20 to 25 percent of patients, especially older persons on prolonged exposure to antipsychotic drugs, although in some cases it may develop in young patients after 3 to 6 months of therapy. This is tardive dyskinesia with peculiar movements of the tongue, jaws, face, and extremities. Withdrawal from drugs at first exaggerates the symptoms. No form of therapy has proven consistently successful. Another very serious but rare complication is the "neuroleptic malignant syndrome" that is not related to dose or drug interactions most likely to occur in young men, patients with brain disorders, and those subjected to heat stress, physical exhaustion, and dehydration. Long-term use (beyond 6 to 12 months) of neuroleptics is justified only when there are disturbing symptoms of schizophrenia, paranoia, and certain neurological diseases that do not respond to psychosocial treatments alone; short-term use (for up to 6 months) should be restricted to acute psychosis, severe mania, or agitated depression that are not relieved by alternate therapies. Where tardive dyskinesia appears, neuroleptic and anticholingeric medications should be discontinued. Low doses of benzodiazepines may be tried and psychosocial treatments intensified. Some patients, however, because of the severity of their illness, will still require neuroleptic therapy. In this case, a chemically dissimilar neuroleptic should be tried other than the one that precipitated the reaction. In view of possible malpractice suits, patients and relations should be appraised of risks and benefits in using and continuing neuroleptics, if they are required after a year, and record of notations of this filed in the case records. In all cases, psychosocial treatment should be utilized and neuroleptics lowered in dosage or stopped where the patient is capable of getting along without them.

Benefits from drug therapy do not usually occur immediately, but may require 3 or 4 weeks before results are seen. Side effects, however, may be experienced early in therapy and should not encourage premature termination of medication unless they are serious. A trial of 6 to 8 weeks with proper dosage is advisable and if some dysphoric side effects develop these should be treated with proper medications such as Cogentin.

Some caveats and routines are important to mention. Combinations of antipsychotic drugs are occasionally used to achieve a better balance between therapeutic and adverse effects, but this practice is generally avoided since psychotic drugs do not differ in their impact on target symptoms, and in combination may increase side effects. Neuroses, character disorders, anxiety reactions, and alcoholic upsets should never be treated even in low dosage with this powerful class of medications because of the risk of side effects. Before using drugs, a complete physical examination, blood count, liver profile and electrocardiogram should be done. In starting therapy the dosage is best at a low level (equivalent of 100 mg of Thorazine) and the dosage titrated upward watching the therapeutic response and side effects. Since absorption of medication is delayed by food and decreased by antacids, administration should be between meals and 2 hours after antacids. Following a few days of therapy, the total dosage may be given at bedtime provided the blood pressure does not decrease too drastically. Megadoses of drug should be avoided, but adequate dosage must be maintained (e.g., the equivalent of 400 to 600 mg of Thorazine for an acute schizophrenic episode). Inadequate doses yield side effects without therapeutic benefits. Finally chronic schizophrenia with symptoms of withdrawal and apathy usually will not respond to any of the neuroleptics. Because of the complications occurring in drug therapy it is important that a psychiatrist experienced in pharmacotherapy be put in charge of this dimension of the treatment process.

Maintenance drug therapy may be required and should be given in the lowest dosage (usually about 20–30 percent of the acute treatment doses) to keep the patient in some kind of functional equilibrium. More than 50 percent of schizophrenic patients rapidly relapse in a psychosis without drugs as compared with less than 20 percent of those on antipsychotic agents. How long to continue medications is difficult to assess. One rule of thumb is to extend treatment with drugs for 1 year after the first attack, for 2 years after the second; and indefinately after the third attack. "The safest guideline is to use the least medication for the shortest time necessary . . ." Baldessarini (1977). In all cases the rule should obtain to reduce the quantity of drug slowly once optimal symptom control has been obtained. This may be accompanied by total abstinence once, then twice weekly to allow the patient to try to make a drug-free adjustment. Psychotherapy and environmental adjustment to relieve the patient from undue stresses should be coordinately instituted. Should symptoms return, the dose levels can be adjusted upward. There are some patients who will need periodic drug therapy for the rest of their lives. Yet it is at least theoretically possible to secure adjustment in most cases without medication, provided adequate educational, rehabilitative, and psychotherapeutic facilities are available and utilized. Even hardcore institutional mental patients on long-term maintenance drug therapy have been withdrawn from medications with benefit where social-environmental treatment programs were organized (Paul et al, 1972). With the increasing incidence of malpractice lawsuits involving tardive dyskinesia, the prescription of neuroleptics has become more carefully controlled. The estimate that a large percentage of psychiatric and geriatric patients on psychotropic drugs for 2 to 3 years have some symptoms of this complication is inspiring a more conservative use of major tranquilizers and a more sensitive diagnosis of early signs of their devastating side effects. Many states are mandating the patient's right to informed consent as a prerequisite to the employment of psychotropic drugs. The fact that studies indicate a more benign course for schizophrenia than the hopeless outlook in past years, and an understanding of how improved community care, better work opportunities, and social integration can constitute the preferred treatment plan is sponsoring a more aggressive drug-free orientation (Warner, 1985).

Because some patients who require maintenance therapy are loath to use oral medications or forget to take them, parenteral long-acting phenothiazines (Prolixin Enanthate, Prolixin Decanoate, Haldol Decanoate) may be given. Such maintenance antipsychotic drugs have been found to play a crucial role in the prophylactic treatment of patients with schizophrenia who resist oral therapy. Nonmotivated patients may be brought in to the doctor's office by a relative. As a last resort, some reward, by arrangement with the relative, may be given the patient by the doctor (e.g., his allowance) each time he appears for an injection. In a sizable number of patients schizophrenia that has existed for years may "burn out," particularly where the environment poses few stresses and the adaptive level has improved. Should relapse follow on withdrawal, medications may be reinstated.

Mania. Lithium carbonate (300–600 mg taken three times daily) is an effective therapeutic and prophylactic agent (with no undue sedative effect) for bipolar disorders (manic-depressive psychosis) where manic attacks are part of the recurrent illness. It has also been used in acute nonorganic psychosis where an affective element exists. Some depressions, unresponsive to antidepressants have been helped by administration of lithium. Certain cases of schizophrenia (Hirschowitz et al, 1980) and alcoholism (Merry et al, 1976) are said to be responsive. Since lithium acts slowly, an excited, manic reaction may require initial antipsychotics, like Haldol or Thorazine orally or parenterally. This use is temporary since side effects may occur with the combination. The patient may be started on 300 mg of lithium three times daily, serum levels being tested twice during the first week. The usual dose is 600 mg three times daily, but this must be individualized and regulated by the blood level response. Regular determination of lithium serum levels by a good laboratory at least every month to maintain the proper concentration is essential. The range of lithium levels is kept between 0.8 to 1.5 milliequivalents (mE$_q$1) but during maintenance can be as low as 0.6 or 0.4 mE$_q$1 tested every 2 months. Side effects are tremor, dry mouth, stomach discomfort, muscular weakness, fatigue, and a metallic taste. Urinary, cardiac and blood problems may develop with sensitivity to lithium and overdose. Because of its effect on the kidneys and other organs, lithium should be prescribed and the patient closely observed by a psychiatrist skilled in its use. Where a manic patient fails to respond to lithium, alternative drugs like carbamazepine (Tegretal) and clonazepam (Clonopin) may be tried.

A thorough examination of kidney function is in order prior to lithium administration, since lithium is excreted through the kidneys and impairment of kidney function may lead to lithium toxicity. Lithium also affects the thyroid gland and an examination of this organ may avoid complications. Toxicity may occur at usual therapeutic serum concentrations of lithium, so monitoring of side effects is important especially in the elderly and brain damaged. Signs of toxicity include weakness, tremor, ataxia, drowsiness, tinnitus, nausea, vomiting, nystagmus, seizures, coma, urinary symptoms, gastric distress, hand tremor, and thyroid effects. Lithium should be avoided in severe renal or cardiovascular disease, and where there is dehydration and sodium depletion.

Antipsychotic drugs are considered nonhabituating, and withdrawal symptoms are rare. However long-term administration should be accompanied by periodic blood and liver studies (Bloom et al, 1965). Some therapists make it a rule to have their patients who are on substantial medication examined every three months neurologically, in order to forestall development of unfortunate complications.

ANTIDEPRESSANT DRUGS

On the whole, antidepressant drugs are inferior to electroconvulsive therapy in the treatment of severe and suicidal depressions. They do have an important utility, however, in nonsuicidal depressions provided that the selection of the drug is one that will fit in with the prevailing profile of symptoms. A caution to be exercised relates to the fact that antidepressants tend to intensify schizophrenic reactions and, especially in bipolar depression, to precipitate manic symptomatology.

Helpful in overcoming fatigue and oversedation is the sympathomimetic amine: dextroamphetamine (Dexedrine) and methamphetamine (Desoxyn), which are not used much today due to the potential for abuse. Methylphenidate (Ritalin) and Pemoline (Cylert) are similar in their effects to the sympathomimetic amines, but relatively weaker. Hyperkinetic children (ages 6 to 14) with both organic brain syndromes and functional disorders respond well to d-amphetamine, which has a calming rather than stimulating affect on them (Zrull et al, 1966). Amphetamine dependency may have serious consequences in the form of restlessness, irritability, insomnia, weight loss, aggressiveness, and general emotional instability (Lemere, 1966). Personality changes may progress to outright psychosis, the form of disorder being patterned by existing inner psychological needs and mechanisms (Commission on Alcoholism & Addiction, 1966). Prolonged addiction may result in permanent organic damage to the brain. It is essential, then, that administration of amphetamines be very carefully supervised.

Imipramine (Tofranil) is particularly valuable in inhibited endogenous depressions, approximately one-third being arrested and one-third improved. It is probably not as effective as ECT (minimum of eight treatments), but it may be a substitute where for any reason ECT cannot be easily administered. Imipramine has also been found useful in enuresis (Munster et al, 1961) panic reactions, and bulimia (Klein & Davis, 1969, Pope et al, 1983).

Since in some cases it may produce insomnia, Kuhn (1960) recommends that the first dose of imipramine be given at bedtime. If the drug helps the patient sleep, it may be taken throughout the day. If insomnia occurs, it should not be given after 3 pm. Starting with one 25-mg tablet three times daily, the dose is increased by one tablet each day until eight tablets daily are taken. When the symptoms remit, the dose is reduced by one tablet daily until a maintenance level is reached. Older people respond more intensely to imipramine and may do well on the smaller 10-mg tablets. Because agranulocytosis has been reported, occasional blood checks are recommended. Imipramine is contraindicated in glaucoma. Should side effects of a disturbing nature occur (skin itching, confusion, loss of appetite, etc.) the drug should be stopped and a phenothiazine substance administered. If an MAO inhibitor (Parnate, Nardil, Marplan) is being taken, this should be discontinued for at least 2 weeks prior to introducing imipramine, since the combination is dangerous. Kline, differing from the majority of opinion, claimed that small doses of one can be used in combination with the other (Kline, NS, 1966). This defection has now recently been sub-stantiated by others who claim that some patients resistive to all conventional therapies have been helped by a combination of a tricyclic and MAO inhibitor drug (Ayd, 1986). Agitated depressions may require a neuroleptic like Thorazine or Trilafon in addition to imipramine or a sedative antidepressant like Elavil. Following ECT, imipramine may be prescribed for a period to reinforce the antidepressive influence. Anticholinergic side effects include dryness of the mouth, tachycardia, arrhythma, sweating, dizziness, constipation, visual disorders, urinary retention, and, occasionally, agitation, which may be controlled by regulating the dosage. In many cases the total dose can be given at night. Imipramine can produce orthostatic hypotension and tachycardia, and prolong atrioventricular conduction time. It must be used with great caution in patients with bundlebranch disease of the heart. Side effects of arrthymia may be treated with physostigmine (2 mg intramuscularly or intravenously very slowly injected).

The newer imipramine and amitriptyline substances—desipramine (Norpramine, Pertofrane) and nortriptyline (Aventyl)—apppear to be no more effective than the parent compounds. They do have more stimulating properties and hence appear best suited for retarded depressions. Since they aggravate preexisting anxiety and tension, they should not be used where these symptoms are present, except perhaps in combinations with a sedative- tranquilizer.

Amitriptyline (Elavil) is a useful antidepressant with more sedative features than imipramine. Benefits are usually felt within a few weeks (Feldman, PE, 1961; Dorfman, 1961). Depression, tension, loss of appetite, disinterest in the environment and insomnia may be reduced or eliminated in somewhat more than half of the patients to whom the drug is given. It is administered in 25 mg dosages three times daily, increasing the dose by 25 mg daily until a 150-mg daily intake has been reached. In some cases a dose of 200, 250, and even 300 mg will be required. Older patients do well with a smaller dose, 10-mg tablets being substituted for the 25-mg tablets. The side effects, the contraindications, and the incompatability with the MAO inhibitors are similar to those of imipramine. Elavil potentiates alcohol, anaesthetics, and the barbiturates, and the quantities of the latter substances, if taken, should accordingly be reduced. Where a psychotic (delusional) depression exists, a combination of amitriptyline and a neuroleptic like perphenazine (Triavil for example) provides better results then either drug alone.

Monoamine oxidase (MAO) inhibitors, such as tranylcypromine (Parnate) and phenelzine (Nardil), while less successful than ECT, Tofranil, and Elavil, have some use, especially in the neurotic or hysterical depressions (Dysthmic Disorder) or where a tricyclic cannot be used as in glaucoma, cardiovascular disease, or prostatic enlargement with urinary retention. There is some evidence that they are especially useful in panic disorder, bulimia, and atypical depressions. If a patient has not responded to a tricyclic in 3 to 6 weeks, one can go from a tricyclic to a MAO inhibitor after a waiting period of 2 weeks. Beneficial effects may not occur for about 3 weeks. MAO inhibitors must not be given with other medicaments such as cold tablets, nasal decongestants, hay fever medications, "Pep pills," antiappetite medications, and asthma inhalants. Cheeses, pickled herring, chicken livers, beer, Chianti wine, coffee and tea in quantity, and over-the-counter cold remedies must also be eliminated from the diet. Side effects with the MAO inhibitors are potentiation of other drugs (such as barbiturates and amphetamine), hypotension, constipation, dysuria, reduced sexual activity, edema, and occasional liver toxicity (Ayd, 1961a & b). Such side effects may require an adjusting of the dose. N. S. Kline (1966), differing from other authorities in this country, contends that oral amphetamines and monoamine oxidase inhibitors are not incompatible and that the combination often eliminates the abrupt letdown that is a drawback in using MAO inhibitors alone.

Doxepin (Sinequan) is a useful antidepressant that has fewer side effects than Tofranil or Elavil. It may be given for neurotic depression, depression associated with alcoholism, depression or anxiety related to organic disease, and psychotic depressions with associated anxiety including involutional depression and manic-depressive disorders. It is relatively safe for and well tolerated by elderly patients. The dose for mild or moderate depression is 25 to 50 mg three times daily and for severe depression 50 to 100 mg three times daily. It may be used when the patient is taking guanethidine for hypertension in contradistinction to other tricyclics.

In the event the tricyclics (Tofranil, Elavil, Sinequan) produce too great sedation, Ritalin (10–20 mg) after breakfast may be prescribed. A nonbarbiturate hypnotic, like Doriden or Noludar, may be used for insomnia. Birth control pills should not be taken since they depress the plasma level of tricyclics. Patients over 60 should not be given the total dose at nighttime. Rather, one-half the dose after the evening meal and one-half at bedtime should be prescribed. After recovery the total dose should be continued for 3 months, then gradually lowered over several months, and finally discontinued. If the patient fails to respond to tricyclics, a MAO inhibitor (Nardil, Parnate), as mentioned, may be tried with the usual precautions. Some patients find the anticholinergic effects of the standard antidepressants intolerable. When this occurs the therapist may try one of the newer tetracyclic drugs such as trazodone (Desyrel). Because of its sedative effect it may be given at nightime which can be valuable for light sleepers. Maprotiline (Ludiomil) and trimipramine (Surmontil) are other antidepressants sometimes tolerated well despite their anticholinergic and other side effects. In the event a depressed patient has a cardiac illness, wellbutrin (Buprion) may be considered a good choice. This drug has few anticholinergic or sedative effects. Amoxapine (Asendin) is another medication that acts more rapidly than the other antidepressant and it has a wide range of actions useful in mild as well as psychotic depression.

Combinations of drugs have been developed for treatment of agitated and anxious depressions (Smith ME, 1963). For example, Triavil and Etrafon are mixtures of perphenazine (Trilafon) and amitriptyline (Elavil). This combination is supplied in several strengths, as outlined in Table 56-3. Other combinations are Parnate and Stelazine, Nardil and Trilafon, and Thorazine and Dexedrine, the doses being adjusted in accordance with which target symptom (depression, anxiety, agitation) is most in need of control. Such combinations are considered unnecessary by some authorities who advise giving single drugs in adequate dosage and adding accessory drugs only when it is necessary to control certain symptoms not influenced by the original drug.

It is advisable in prescribing antidepressants to instruct and reassure patients regarding possible side effects. The patient should be given a typewritten sheet, such as in Appendix T, including dosages and times to take pills. This is especially necessary for geriatric patients who have a tendency to forget. The patient should be instructed that no alcohol is to be taken for the first 2 weeks of using antidepressant medications. However, after this one can, if desired, drink moderately provided that the medication is not taken at the same time.

If a patient is coordinately using other medications for a physical condition, these medications may dictate the preferred antidepressant to use. For instance, in hypertension where guanethidine (Ismelin, Esimil) is being taken, doxepin (Sinequan) is a suitable antidepressant to use.

ANTIANXIETY DRUGS (ANXIOLYTICS)

It is unsound to assume that a high level of anxiety is needed to motivate a patient for therapy or to make greater efforts to explore one's problems. While tolerable anxiety and tension may require no medication, there is no reason to withhold psychotropic drugs where the patient is in real discomfort. A double-blind study by Whittington et al. (1969) with an unrelated outpatient population experiencing anxiety showed a greater perseverance in and acceptance of treatment of those receiving psychotropic drugs as compared with those receiving placebos. The fact that the patient gets relief from medicaments prescribed by the therapists seemed to help the relationship and to give the patient greater confidence in continuing therapy. The main anxiolytics are the benzodiazepines that are among the most frequently prescribed substances and owe their popularity to their effectiveness in subduing anxiety, calming stress, and quieting psychosomatic symptoms. They attach to highly specific receptor sites in the brain potentiating the inhibitory effects of the neurotransmitter GABA (y-aminobutyric acid). In higher dosage they possess a high level of safety, but in sensitive persons and the elderly they may produce ataxia, and when mixed with alcohol the combination can be dangerous. On the whole, however, their beneficial influence far outweighs their untoward consequences and they have an important place in the therapeutic armamentarium. Tolerance to benzodiazepines is very much less than to other anxiety agents like barbiturates, prolonged use of which necessitates increased doses of the drug to secure the same effects.

There is some difference in the profiles of the different benzodiazepines due mainly to the duration of their half-life which is determined by their rate of elimination. Diazepam (Valium) acts rapidly and main-

Table 56-3
Uses, Characteristics, and Doses of Psychotropic Drugs (see page 1000 for key)

Drug (How Dispensed)	Uses	Dosage	Miscellaneous (Action and Side Effects)
Psychostimulants			
1. Sympathetic amines	1. Very mild depression; appetite control; oversedation and fatigue; enuresis, attention deficit disorder with hyperactivity in children, narcolepsy.		1. Rapid action. Do not use in schizophrenia, agitation, and hypertension. Can cause irritability and insomnia. Habituation danger serious; use for no more than 3 months. Monitor blood pressure, especially in hypertension.
a. dextroamphetamine (Dexedrine; S 5, 10, 15 mg; T 5)		a. 5–15 mg at 9 am & 2 pm; (S) 10–15 mg at 9 am.	
b. methamphetamine (Desoxyn: T5 mg, Gradumet T 5, 10, 15 mg)		b. 5 mg at start, raise 5 mg weekly. Usual dose 20–25 mg d.	
2. Methylphenidate (Ritalin: T 5, 10, 20 mg; SR 20 mg)	2. As in (1), but effects are weaker.	2. 10-20-30 mg (T) at 9 am & 2 pm. In children start with 5 mg (bid) gradually raised	2. As in (1). Do not use in anxiety Tournette's syndrome, drug dependent patients.
3. Pemoline (Cylert: T 18.75, 37.5, 75 mg; chewable T 37.5 mg)	3. Attention deficit disorders	3. Single morning dose-start with 37.5 mg/day, increase by 18.75 mg at 1 wk intervals until desired effect.	3. Clinical improvement is gradual. May require 3–4 weeks for good effects. Do not use in psychotic children or in kidney disease.

Antidepressants

1. Tricyclics

a. imipramine (Tofranil: T 10, 25, 50 mg; P 25 mg in 2 cc; Tofranil PM, 75, 100, 125, 150 mg sustained action)	1. a. For retarded endogenous depression	a. 25 mg qid increased to 50 mg qid. Max. 250 mg d. Use the 10-mg size in older patients. P-IM-to 100 mg in divided doses.	a. Action in 7–21 days. Do not give with MAO inhibitors. Do not use in schizophrenia, epilepsy, glaucoma, urinary retention. Use cautiously in cardiovascular illness. Avoid cimetidine. Dryness of mouth and perspiration are side effects. Insomnia and hypotension seen occasionally. Desipramine not recommended for children.
desipramine (Norpramine, T 10, 25, 50, 75, 100, 150 mg. Pertofrane: caps 25, 50 mg)		100–200 mg daily. In elderly 25–100 mg.	
b. amitriptyline (Elavil: T 10, 25, 50, 75, 100, 150 mg; P 10 mg per cc)	b. A sedating, antianxiety antidepressant; for agitated depression.	b. 25 mg tid increased to 50 mg tid; max. 250 Use the 10 mg size in older patients. Maintenance 50–100 mg.	b. As in (a) but with more sedative features. Action in 10–30 days. Potentiates alcohol and barbiturates.
nortriptyline (Aventyl: T 10, 25 mg; liquid 10 mg per 5 cc); (Pamelor C 10, 25, 75 mg; liquid 10 mg per 5 cc)		10 mg bid increased to 10 mg qid; in 1 week 25 mg bid increased to 25 mg qid.	Avoid in cardiovascular disease. Not recommended for children.

(continued)

Table 56-3 (*continued*)

Drug (How Dispensed)	Uses	Dosage	Miscellaneous (Action and Side Effects)
c. doxepin (Sinequan: caps 10, 25, 50, 75, 100, 150 mg; oral concentrate 10 mg per cc) (Adapin: caps 10, 25, 50, 75, 100 mg)	c. For neurotic, alcoholic, and psychotic depression especially when accompanied by anxiety.	c. 25 mg tid increased to 50 mg tid (for mild or moderate depression) 50 mg tid increased to 100 mg tid (for severe depression.)	c. Side effects less than other tricyclics. A preferred drug for cardiac patients. Action in 10–21 days.
d. protriptyline (Vivactil: T 5, 10 mg)	d. Slight stimulant qualities.	d. 5 to 40 mg daily divided into 3 or 4 doses. Max. 60 mg. Lower dose in adolescence and elderly.	d. Potentiates response to alcohol and barbiturates.
e. amoxapine (Asendin: T 25, 50, 100, 150 mg)	e. Slight sedative qualities.	e. 50 mg bid or tid raised to 200 to 300 mg daily; max. 400 mg. In elderly 1/2 this dosage.	e. Somewhat more rapid action than imipramine or amitriptyline. Has neuroleptic advantages and dangers. Use cautiously in cardiac and convulsive disorders.
f. trimipramine (Surmontil: caps. 25, 50, 100 mg)	f. Antianxiety sedative antidepressant.	f. 25 mg. tid gradually increased to 150 mg. daily. Max. 300 mg d. Maintenance 50 to 150 mg daily.	f. Not recommended for children. Avoid in cardiovascular disease. Antichollnergic side effects.
2. MAO inhibitors	2. For neurotic and atypical depression.		2. Action in 1–4 weeks.

a. phenelzine (Nardil: T 15 mg)

a. 15 mg tid (max. d 90 mg) reduce slowly; maintenance d 15 mg.

a. Potentiates amphetamines, alcohol and barbiturates. May intensify schizophrenia. Produces hypotension, dry mouth, blurred vision, dizziness. Do not use in liver, kidney, or heart diseases. Sexual dysfunction may occur. Avoid tyramine foods and over-the-counter medicaments. Avoid in hypertension, cardiovascular disease.

b. tranylcypromine (Parnate: T 10 mg)

b. 10 mg at 9 am & 2 pm; in 2 weeks, 20 mg at 9 am & 10 mg at 2 pm.

b. Action in 2–21 days. As in (a).

3. Trazodone (Desyrel: T 50, 100, 150 mg)

3. Serotonin uptake inhibitor. Sedative qualities. No anticholinergic side effects, which is of advantage in glaucoma, urinary retention, constipation, or for elderly.

3. 50 mg tid increase by 50 mg/day every 3 days to max. of 400 mg d.

3. Side effects occasionally of priapism and cardiac arrhythmia may require cessation of drug. Generally less cardiotoxic than tricyclics.

4. Maprotiline (Ludiomil: T 25, 50, 75 mg)

4. A tetracyclic drug that helps depressions with anxiety, dysthmic disorders (neurotic depression), and major depressive disorders.

4. Start with 25 mg tid, after 2 weeks, gradually increase to 150 mg (max. 225). In elderly start with 25 mg increased to 75 mg if necessary.

4. Avoid in seizure disorders. Anticholinergic side effects. Caution in patients with cardiac disease, urinary retention, glaucoma. Long half-life. Avoid in patients on thyroid medication.

(continued)

Table 56-3 (*continued*)

Drug (How Dispensed)	Uses	Dosage	Miscellaneous (Action and Side Effects)
5. Wellbutrin (Buprion T 75 mg)	5. antidepressant with little cardiovascular effect.	5. 75 mg tid, increase by 75 mg every 3 days to 450 mg max. d.	5. Low incidence of daytime drowsiness, anticholingergic effects, or sedation. Little effect on weight, heart rate, and blood pressure. Avoid in seizure disorders, psychotic depression, history of psychosis.
6. Combination drugs perphenazine + amitriptyline (Triavil: *2-10, 2-25, 4-10, 4-25, 4-50* mg. Etrafon *2-10, 2-25, 4-10, 4-25* mg.	6. For anxious and agitated depression as well as depression in schizophrenia.	6. One T tid or qid., (max. d. 2 T tid); maintenance 1 T bid, tid or qid.	6. Contraindicated in glaucoma, urinary retention. Action in a few days or a few weeks. See amitriptyline and perphenazine. Some authorities feel combination drugs are unnecessary and even contraindicated.

Neuroleptics

1. Phenothiazines

a. chlorpromazine (Thorazine: T 10, 25, 50, 100, 200 mg; S 30, 75, 150, 200, 300 mg; P25 mg in 1 cc, 50 mg in 2 cc, 250 mg in 10 cc; syrup, 10 mg in cc; suppositories 25, 100 mg; concentrate 30 mg in 1 cc and 100 mg in 1 cc)	a. The sedative phenothiazine for paranoidal, agitated, confused, and hyperactive reactions in schizophrenia, manic-depressive reactions, agitated senile dementia. Safest for children and young adults.	a. 10–25 mg tid; after 1–2 days increase by 20–25 mg semiweekly to 1000 mg if necessary. P 25 mg for excitement IM, repeat in 1 hr. if necessary then oral 25–50 mg tid.	a. Action in a few days. Potentiates barbiturates. Drowsiness, dryness of mouth, stuffiness of nose, tachycardia, hypotension, photosensitivity, allergic skin reactions, jaundice may occur. Use cautiously in atherosclerosis, cardiovascular diseases. Rarely skin pigmentation, ocular changes, blood dys-

crasias. Parkinsonism requires Cogentin, Artane or Kemadrin (qv below).

b. thioridazine (Mellaril: T 10, 15, 25, 50, 100, 150, 200 mg; concentrate 30 mg per cc and 100 mg per cc)

b. Excellent sedative phenothiazine for ambulatory out-patient treatment of hyperkinetic and agitated psychoses. Helps some depressive reactions and hyperactive disturbed children.

b. Nonpsychotic patients: 10–25 mg tid or qid. Psychotics: 100 mg tid or qid (Max. 800 mg d).

b. Minimum of side extra pyramidal reactions. Action is rapid. High doses may cause pigmentary retinopathy. Use in neurological problems and in elderly. Avoid in severe cardiac illness.

c. trifluoperazine (Stelazine: T 1, 2.5 10 mg; P 2 mg per cc; concentrate 10 mg per cc)

c. For apathetic, depressed, withdrawn schizophrenics. Low dosage relieves tension and agitation. High dose for manic states, agitated depression, active schizophrenia.

c. Office patients: 1–2 mg bid or tid. Hospital patients; 5 mg tid or qid (max. 40–50 mg d) P 1–2 mg IM repeated 4–6 hours. In non-psychotic anxiety up to 5 mg d. max. 12 weeks.

c. Side effects in high dosage are common, namely extra-pyramidal reactions-dystonia and parkinsonism require Cogentin, Artane, or Kemadrin (qv below.) Lower anticholinergic effects.

d. perphenazine (Trilafon: T 2, 4, 8, 16 mg; repetabs 8 mg; concentrate 16 mg per 5 cc; P 5 mg in 1 cc)

d. For psychotic disorders with apathy, and control of severe nausea and vomiting in adults.

d. 2–4 mg tid; increased to 4 mg qid, max. 8 mg tid; 1–2 repetabs bid.

d. As above (c). Tolerated by elderly.

e. fluphenazine (Permitil: T 0.25, 2.5, 5, 10 mg; oral concentrate 5 mg per cc)

e. For psychotic agitation, hostility, aggression, behavior problems in children, and senile agitation.

e. Office patients: 0.5 mg d to 10 mg. Hospital patients 2–5 mg bid (max. 20 mg d). (Children and elderly: 0.25–0.5 mg d; (max. 1 mg).

e. As above (c).

(continued)

Table 56-3 (*continued*)

Drug (How Dispensed)	Uses	Dosage	Miscellaneous (Action and Side Effects)
(Prolixin: T 1, 2.5, 5, 10 mg; elixir: 0.5 mg per cc; P 2.5 mg per 5 cc IM only)	As above.	As above. Divided doses at 6–8 hour intervals. Maintenance 1–5 mg. d; P 1.25 mg increased 6–8 hr intervals to total of 10 mg.	As above. After IM injections for emergencies continue on 2–3 times P does with oral T.
f. fluphenazine enanthate (Prolixin Enanthate: P25 mg in 1 cc preassembled syringes; vials of 5 cc)	Potent long-acting injectable phenothiazine derivative for psychotic disorders.	25 mg (1cc.) IM or subcutaneous every 2 weeks. Adjust dose according to response from 12.5–100 mg every 2 weeks.	Action in 24–48 hours, lasting about 2 weeks. Useful where oral medication cannot be depended on. Extrapyramidal reactions frequent, which can be controlled with antiparkinsonian drugs. Contraindicated in subcortical brain damage.
g. fluphenazine decanoate (Prolixin Decanoate: P 25 mg in 1 cc preassembled syringes; vials of 5 cc)	Potent, long-lasting injectable phenothiazine derivative for schizophrenia.	12.5–25 mg IM or subcutaneous every 4 weeks. Adjust dose in small increments to 50 or 100 mg.	Action in 24–72 hours, lasting about 4 weeks. Useful where oral medication cannot be depended on. Extrapyramidal reactions frequent and will require antiparkinsonian drugs.
2. Dibenzoxazepines			
a. loxapine succinate (Loxitane: C 5, 10, 25, 50 mg; concentrate 25 mg per cc; P 50 mg per cc, IM)	a. Tranquilizes and suppresses aggressive activities in schizophrenia.	a. 10–25 mg bid, usual maintenance dose 60–100 mg d.	a. Action in $\frac{1}{2}$–2 hours for 12 hours. Contraindicated in drug-induced depressive states (alcohol, barbiturates). Lowers convulsive threshold. Fewer antichol inergic and hypotensive effects, but

Drug	Uses	Dosage	Remarks
			use cautiously in cardiovascular disease. Extra-pyramidal reactions frequent.
3. Butyrophenones			
a. Haloperidol (Haldol: T½, 1, 2, 5, 10 mg; concentrate 2 mg per cc; P 5 mg per cc)	a. For psychotic disorders and severe tics. Use where sedation is undesirable. Good for paranoidal patients, manic excitement, assaultive behavior, alcoholic delirium, neurological disorders, torticollis, intractable hiccups and vomiting, and confused and negativistic geriatric patients.	a. Moderate symptoms and older patients: ½–2 mg bid or tid. Severe symptoms: 3–5 mg bid or tid (max. 100 mg); P2-5 mg repeated if necessary.	a. May be tolerated in some patients better than phenothiazines. Extra-pyramidal reactions common. Low anticholinergic and cardiac complications.
(Haldol Decanoate P 50 mg per cc)	Sustained protection against schizophrenic relapses.	Start with 10–15 times previous oral dosage of Haldol (max. 100 mg) adjust dose required as needed. Give by deep intramuscular injection into glutial region. In exacerbation of symptoms supplement with oral Haldol.	Peak level in 6 days; half-life 3 weeks. Before starting convert to and stabilize pt. on oral Haldol from any other neuroleptic being taken.
4. Thioxanthenes			
a. thiothixene (Navane: C 1, 2, 5, 10, 20 mg; concentrate 5 mg per cc; P 2 mg per cc)	a. For psychotic disorders; esp. with depressive and anxiety symptoms.	a. Mild symptoms: 2 mg tid (max. d 15 mg). More severe symptoms: 5 mg bid to 30 mg (max. d 60 mg).	a. May be tolerated in some cases better than phenothiazines. Less sensitivity to sunlight. Lower extrapyramidal and myocardial effects.

(continued)

Table 56-3 (*continued*)

Drug (How Dispensed)	Uses	Dosage	Miscellaneous (Action and Side Effects)
b. chlorprothixene (Taractan: T 10, 25, 50, 100 mg; concentrate 100 mg per tsp; P 25 mg in 2 cc)	b. Agitated, anxious, depressed schizophrenics.	b. 25–50 mg tid or qid. Max. 600 mg d. P 25–50 mg up to tid or qid.	b. Avoid in cardiac and respiratory disease.
5. Dihydroindolones			
a. molindone (Moban: T 5, 10, 25, 50, 100 mg; concentrate 20 mg per cc)	a. For psychotic disorders.	a. 50–75 mg/d increased to 100 mg/d in 3–4 days. Mild symptoms: 5–15 mg tid or qid; moderate 10–25 mg tid or qid. Severe symptoms: up to 225 mg total.	a. Side reactions less than phenothiazines.
6. Antimanic drugs			
a. (Lithium carbonate (T 300 mg) (Also see Haldol, Thorazine, and Mellaril above.)	a–d. For control and prophylaxis of manic episodes in manic-depressive psychosis (Bipolar disorder (manic).	a. Usual dose, 300–600 mg tid. Adjust dosage to maintain serum levels between 1–1.5 mEq/1.	a. Action in 1–3 weeks. Contraindicated in colitis and severe renal and cardiovascular disease, or where diuretics are taken. Test serum levels twice weekly acute phase; in maintenance therapy at least every 2 months. Some skin eruptions and renal impairment possible in long-term therapy.
b. Lithane T 300 mg.		b. As above	
c. Lithobid: slow release T 300 mg.		c. 1800 mg/d; maintenance 900–1200 mg/d	
d. Cibalith-S: Syrup 300 mg per tsp.		d. 2 tsp tid; maintenance 1 tsp tid or qid.	
7. Anti-Parkinson Drugs (1) (Cogentin T 0.5,1,2 mg; P 1 mg in 1 cc)	7. For dystonia, akithisia, parkinsonism. Do not use prophylactically.	(1) Usual dose, 1–2 mg d. or P 1–2 mg.	After symptoms disappear for 1–2 weeks, withdraw to determine need for drug. For temporary use only; withdraw within 4–12 weeks.
(2) (Artane T 2.5 mg;		(2) 1 mg 1st day; 2 mg 2nd	

elixir 2 mg each tsp; sustained release C 5 mg)

(3) (Kemadrin T 5 mg)

(4) Symmetral: C 100 mg. Syrup 50 mg per tsp.

Anxiolytics

a. diazepam (Valium: T 2, 5, 10 mg; P 5 mg per cc)

b. chlordiazepoxide (Librium: caps 5, 10, 25 mg; P 100 mg in 5 cc)

c. alprazolam (Xanax: T 0.25, 0.5, 1 mg)

d. oxazepam (Serax: caps 10, 15, 30 mg; T 15 mg)

---

a. Anxiety, muscle spasms, drug and alcohol withdrawal, insomnia due to anxiety, status epilepticus.

b. Excellent tranquilizer with palliating qualities for anxiety, alcoholism, muscle spasms. IV in delirum tremens and as an anticonvulsive.

c. Anti-anxiety agent with antidepressant qualities.

d. Anxiety, alcoholic withdrawal, senile agitation.

---

day, increased if necessary to 5–15 mg d.

(3) 2.5 mg tid increased to 5 mg tid or/qid.

(4) 200 mg d.

a. 5 mg d to tid. Severe anxiety 10 mg tid or qid; P: IM or IV 2–20 mg repeated if necessary in 3–4 hours.

b. 10 mg tid or qid. Severe anxiety: 20–25 mg tid or qid; P 50–100 mg IM or IV, repeated if necessary in 2–6 hours.

c. 0.25 to 0.5 mg tid Max. d. 4 mg. In elderly start with 0.25 mg bid or tid. Increase or reduce as necessary. Larger doses needed to prevent panic attacks.

d. Mild anxiety: 15 mg qid. Severe anxiety; 30 mg tid or qid. Older patients; 10 mg tid.

---

a. Avoid in glaucoma and epilepsy. Drowsiness possible. Reduce dose in elderly patients. Avoid alcohol. Long half-life.

b. Ataxia, especially in older persons. Avoid alcohol.

c. Short half-life. Temporary drowsiness and lightheadedness may occur. Avoid alcohol.

d. Initial drowsiness usually passes.

(continued)

Table 56-3 (*continued*)

Drug (How Dispensed)	Uses	Dosage	Miscellaneous (Action and Side Effects)
e. lorazepam (Ativan: T 0.5, 1.0, 2.0 mg; P 2 & 4 mg per cc)	e. Short-term relief of anxiety and neurotic depression. IV & IM used prior to surgical procedures.	e. 2–6 mg daily in divided doses; no more than 2 mg in elderly in divided doses. IV 2 mg; IM 4 mg.	e. Sedation in 16 percent of patients; dizziness less frequently. Avoid alcohol. Short half-life.
f. hydroxyzine (Vistaril: caps 25, 50, 100 mg: P 25–50 mg in 1 cc; oral suspension 25 mg per tsp) (Atarax: T 10, 25, 50 mg; syrup 10 mg per tsp)	f. Mild anxiety, psychophysiological reactions. IM or IV for extreme anxiety and alcoholic withdrawal. Antihistamine antipruretic, antiemetic properties. For chronic urticaria and dermatitis.	f. 25–100 mg tid or qid. P & IM: 50–100 mg repeated as necessary, 4–6 hours.	f. Side effects mild. May be used with psychotherapy. Potentiates barbiturates and narcotics.
g. clorazepate dipotassium (Tranxene: (3.75, 7.5, 15 mg; Tranxene SD: 11.25, and 22.5 mg)	g. Anxiety	g. 15–60 mg d. Elderly or debilitated patients: 7.5–15 mg d.	g. Avoid in depression or psychosis.
h. meprobamate (Miltown, Equanil: T 200, 400, 600 mg)	h. Anxiety, tension headache, muscle spasms, insomnia. Use is diminishing in favor of benzodiazepines.	h. Adults: 400 mg d to tid (max. 2400 mg d). Children 100–200 mg bid.	h. Potentiates alcohol and sedatives. Hypotension possible, especially in older persons. Habituation with prolonged use. Avoid driving until drug dose is stabilized. Avoid rapid withdrawal of drug. Drowsiness, allergic reactions possible. Tolerated by older persons.
i. buspirone (BuSpar T5, 10 mg.)	i. a non-benzodiazepine anxiolytic useful in generalized anxiety reactions. Relatively	i. 5 mg tid. Increase by 5 mg. ov. 2–3 days up to 60 mg. max. Optional 20–30 mg d.	i. Does not potentiate alcohol sedation or impair psychomotor skills.

non-sedating and non-addictive with few side effects

Sedatives and Hypnotics
Barbiturates

1. Helpful in short-term allaying of tension, anxiety, and insomnia. P; IV or IM for convulsions.			1. Use with caution in liver disease. Habituation, tolerance, and addiction possibilities great; not for prolonged use.
a. phenobarbital sodium T 15, 30, 60, 100 mg. P 30, 60, 130 mg Elixir 20 mg in tsp.	a. Short-term sedative and hypnotic.	a. Sedation: 15–30 mg tid. Hypnotic: 100–200 mg.	a. Slow acting; long duration.
b. amobarbital sodium (Amytal: T 15, 30, 50, 100 mg. P250, 500 mg.	b. (as in a) IV amytal solution useful in narcosynthesis.	b. Sedation: 65–200 mg d. Hypnotic: 100–200 mg P (IV or IM) 60–500 mg (10% sol.) 0.5 to 1.0 cc per minute.	b. Moderately rapid acting; medium duration.
c. butabarital Sodium Butisol: T 15, 30, 50, 100 mg. Elixir 30 mg per tsp)		c. Sedation: 15–30 mg tid or qid. Hypnotic: 50–200 mg.	c. Rapid acting; short duration.
d. pentobarbital sodium Nembutal: caps 50–100 mg. P 50 mg per cc). Suppositories 30, 60, 120, 200 mg)		d. Hypnotic: 50–100 mg; P 150–200 mg IM, 100–500 mg IV. Suppositories: children 30–60 mg; Adults 120–200 mg.	d. Moderately rapid acting; short duration.
e. Secobarbital sodium (Seconal: pulvules 50–100 mg. P 50 mg in 1 cc)		e. Hypnotic: 100 mg; P (IV or IM) 50–100 mg.	e. Moderately rapid acting; short duration.
f. amobarbital and secobarbital sodium (Tuinal: caps 50, 100, 200 mg)		f. Sedation: 50 mg; Hypnotic: 50–200 mg.	f. Moderately rapid acting; medium duration.

(continued)

Table 56-3 (*continued*)

Drug (How Dispensed)	Uses	Dosage	Miscellaneous (Action and Side Effects)
Nonbarbiturates			
a. flurazepam hydrochloride (Dalmane: caps 15–30 mg)	a. Effective hypnotic for all types of insomnia.	a. 15–30 mg before retiring.	a. Low incidence of dependence, but avoid too prolonged administration. Avoid in pregnancy.
b. temazepam (Restoril C 15, 30 mg)	b. A short acting benzodiozepine. Anti-insomniac agent.	b. 15–30 mg; 15 mg in elderly.	b. Avoid in pregnancy.
c. triazolam (Halcion T 0.25, 0.5 mg)	c. A very short acting anti-insomniac agent.	c. 0.25 to 0.50 mg; 0.125 to 0.25 mg in elderly.	c. Avoid in pregnancy.
d. glutethimide (Doriden: T 250, 500 mg; caps 500 mg)	d. Useful in elderly and chronically ill patients. For 3–7 days only.	d. Sedation: 250 mg. Hypnotic: 500 mg.	d. Onset in 15–30 minutes; duration 6 hours. Occasional skin rash. Avoid in chronic insomnia.
e. methylprylon (Noludar: T 50, 200 mg; caps 300 mg)	e. Well tolerated and effective. For short-term use.	e. Sedation: 50–100 mg. Hypnotic: 300 mg.	e. Onset in 15–45 minutes; duration 5–8 hours. Avoid in chronic insomnia.
f. chloral hydrate (Noctec: caps 250–500 mg; syrup 500 mg per tsp)	f. Low toxity; well tolerated in chronic illness.	f. Sedation: 250 mg tid Hypnotic: 500–1000 mg.	f. Onset in 20 minutes. Avoid in cardiac, kidney, and liver disease.
g. ethchlorvynol (Placidyl: caps 200, 500, 750 mg)	g. Insomnia due to anxiety or excitement. For 3–7 days only.	g. Hypnotic: 500–1000 mg.	g. Do not give to patients with suicidal tendency. Avoid in chronic insomnia.
h. paraldehyde	h. A safe hypnotic and anticonvulsant in psychotic patients.	h. $\frac{1}{2}$–$1\frac{1}{2}$ tsp in iced fruit juice or milk; 2 tsp in agitation. P 1-2 cc IM (Sterile sol.)	h. Onset in 20 minutes. Avoid in gastrointestinal and liver disease.

d=daily; bid=2 times daily; tid=3 times daily; qid=4 times daily.
T=tablets; P=parenteral; S=spansules; caps=capsules; IM-intramuscularly; IV=intravenously; SR=sustained release.
max=maximum; av=average; gr=grain; mg=milligrams; cc=cubic centimeters.

tains its effect due to slow elimination. Chlordiazepoxide (Librium) acts more slowly and also has a long half-life. Chlorazepate (Tranxene), halazepam (Paxipam), and prazepam (Centrax) produce metabolites similar to Valium, and apart from their rate of absorption very much act in the same way. Alprazolam (Xanax) and lorazepam (Ativan) have the shortest half-life of the benzodiazepines.

Over the years some diazepines have been differently utilized, for example, chlordiazepoxide (Librium) for alcoholic withdrawal symptoms, lorazepam (Ativan) and alprazolam (Xanax) for anxiety with depression, hydroxyzine (Atarax, Vistaril) for allergic reactions and itching, alprazolam (Xanax) for some panic reactions and agorophobia, and flurazepam (Dalmane), triazolam (Halcion), and temazepam (Restoril) for insomnia.

All of these drugs should be employed with caution since tolerance and habituation is possible with prolonged use. To prevent withdrawal reactions the drugs should be discontinued gradually in those who have used them for more than 2 months, or in some cases even less, especially short-acting varieties like Ativan, Xanax, Halcion, and Restoril. For example, in the use of Xanax, dose reduction of no more than 1 mg every 3 days is advisable. Withdrawal symptoms generally consist of anxiety, depersonalization, and various physical symptoms that may frighten the patient greatly. Where large doses of medications have been taken and withdrawal is sudden, symptoms similar to barbiturate withdrawal, e.g., convulsions, may occur.

In prescribing anxiolytics, symptoms can sometimes be used as a guide for determining which tranquilizers to use. Thus, inhibited, motor-retarded, and anxious patients may do best on diazepam (Valium); the overactive, anxious patients on chlordiazepoxide (Librium); and the hostile, anxious patients on oxazepam (Serax). Where anxiolytics fail to control anxiety in borderline patients, close to a breakdown, one may try neuroleptic drugs like Stelazine. Other than this one should never use neuroleptics in nonpsychotic patients. Occasionally, barbiturates like phenobarbital work better in some anxiety-ridden patients than any other drugs. There are some anxieties that do not respond to any psychotropic drugs. These are often found in obsessive individuals who cannot stand the emotional straightjacket that tranquilization imposes on them. Anxiolytics are sometimes used along with antidepressants and major tranquilizers where anxiety is great.

Of all the minor tranquilizers, diazepam (Valium), chlordiazepoxide (Librium), and alprazolam (Xanax) are probably most used. With the introduction of buspirone (BuSpar ® Bristol-Myers Company, Evansville, Illinois), which holds promise of being an ideal anxiolytic drug, and whose influence is not through sedation, we may possess an important therapeutic and research tool. Most neurotic anxieties can be treated psychotherapeutically without drugs. It is only where the anxiety is so intense that the patient cannot function or because the anxiety interferes with psychotherapy that drugs should be used. In some cases where the patient as a result of psychotherapy is ready to face a fearful situation but avoids this, a drug can help to break through. There is, however, a tendency to overdose. One way of regulating the dosage of tranquilizers is suggested by Hollister (1974) with Valium. Two hours before bedtime the patient is enjoined to take 2.5 mg Valium and to make a note whether he or she falls asleep earlier than usual, sleeps longer, and has a slight hangover next morning. If these do not occur, 5 mg are taken the second night. Should the patient still not respond, 10 mg are taken the third night. The hangover effect may be sufficiently great to last the patient throughout the day. If not, one-fourth of the evening dose may be taken during day.

The indications for Valium and Librium besides anxiety are certain depressions that may respond to its mildly euphoriant effect. They are also valuable in treating the agitation of chronic alcoholics in alcoholic withdrawal, including delirium tremens. In *severe* anxiety relatively large doses of Valium may be necessary. The starting oral dose is 5 mg three or four times daily. The patient is asked to telephone in 3 days to report how he or she feels. If there is no effect, the dose is raised to 10 mg four times daily so that the patient takes a total of 40 mg. The patient should be seen 4 days later, and if the symptoms continue, the dosage may be raised to 20 mg three or four times daily. The evening dose may be the largest one in the case of insomnia. When the patient feels better (tranquilization, mild mood elevation, increased appetite), one dose may be removed; 2 weeks later, a second dose is removed; 4 weeks later, all but the evening dose is taken away. Such regulation of the dosage will tend to prevent addiction. With higher doses patients may become ataxic and drowsy. Should this happen, the dose is lowered (it requires about 4 days to eliminate the drug from the system; consequently side effects may last during this period). Rapid symptomatic relief in alcoholic agitation, acute delirium tremens, hallucinosis, acute anxiety, and acute phobic and panic reactions may sometimes be obtained with 50 to 100 mg of Librium injected intramuscularly or intravenously, repeating in 4 to 6 hours if necessary. Caution in the use of Librium is to be heeded in older people who may become ataxic with even moderate doses.

Meprobamate (Miltown, Equanil) is another drug that has anxiety-alleviating properties when given over a sufficiently extended period, but is now not used as frequently as before having been replaced by the more effective and less habituating benzodiazepines. Indications for meprobamate are similar to those of chlordiazepoxide, except that it should not be employed in depressed patients. It is particularly use-ful where skeletal muscle spasm is present. The symptom profile of anxiety and tension may be helped with 400 mg three or four times daily, which may slowly be increased to as much as 2400 mg daily, this high dose being maintained for only a short time. Allergic reactions (fever, urticaria, bronchial spasm, angioneurotic edema) should be treated by discontinuing the drug and administering antihistamines, epinephrine, and possibly cortisone. Dependence and habituation are possible, consequently meprobamates should not be used for more than 3 months. Withdrawal from high doses should be gradual over a 1- to 2-week period.

Other minor tranquilizers include oxazepam (Serax) and alprazolam (Xanax). Serax (15–30 mg three or four times daily) has been utilized to control anxiety, neurotic depression, alcoholic tremulousness and withdrawal. The agitated reactions of older people also may respond to Serax (10 mg three times daily). Xanax in recent years has proven itself to be an effective anxiolytic and has additionally antidepressant and antipanic effects.

These minor tranquilizers have a disadvantage of leading to addiction over a long-term period, although the addiction potential of the benzodiazepines has been exaggerated. In a study of the long-term use of Valium, Hollister et al. (1981) found that in 108 patients suffering from severe pain and muscle spasm due to musculoskeletal disorders of the spine, who had been treated with the drug over an average period of 5 years, with a median dose of 15 mg/day (ranging from 5 to 40 mg/day) 83 percent of patients claimed benefit and ". . . diazepam seemed to retain its efficacy and did not lead to any clear-cut abuse". Nevertheless, withdrawal symptoms do occur when stopping benzodiazepines even where therapeutic doses have been used no matter how gradual withdrawal takes place and the reactions can be distressing (Ayd, 1984). Where a person has an addictive personality (alcoholic, barbiturate user, etc.), it is best not to prescribe anxiolytics. Some new investigational antianxiety agents are in the process of being tested. One such non-benzodiazepine substance, buspirone (BuSpar), which has recently been released is helpful in patients with a generalized anxiety disorder. It has few side effects, is nonsedating, and has less potential for withdrawal symptoms, and less abuse potential.

In obsessional individuals who cannot tolerate losing control or not functioning with top efficiency, lowering performance may prove so upsetting as to obliterate any benefit from these drugs. Such persons may be taught to monitor their own minimal doses while being given reassurance to quiet them down.

Benzodiazepines are diminished in effectiveness when antacids and anticholinergic drugs (often sold over the counter) are concomitantly used.

Propranolol (Inderal) in doses of 10–40 mg three or four times daily may be of value in anxieties associated with beta adrenergic overstimulation, as in psychocardiac disorders. Inderal and other beta blockers require high doses, in which case careful monitoring of the heart is necessary to prevent excessive depression of cardiac function. Studies have shown that beta blockers are less effective in chronic anxiety and with agoraphobic or panic attacks than diazepam (Valium) although there is a possibility of addiction with the latter drug when utilized over a long-term period.

SEDATIVES, HYPNOTICS, AND PSYCHOSTIMULANTS

Since the advent of the benzodiazepines barbiturates have suffered a setback in popularity. Yet, in a few selected cases, they may still be the best drugs to use as daytime sedatives. Butabarbital (Butisol), phenobarbital sodium, and Tuinal in small dosage may be utilized here. However, in most cases the benzodiazepines are being employed for sedation as well as insomnia.

Insofar as insomnia is concerned, many substances have been used, abused, and then discarded in mankind's quest for a harmless substance that can hasten and sustain sleep. We still do not have such a substance, but currently the least harmful, though still not perfect are the benzodiazepines, which have now replaced alcohol, bromides, opiates, barbiturates, ethchlorvynol, glutethimide and methaqualone as the most frequently prescribed drug for insomnia. Chloral hydrate is still employed occasionally as a safe and effective hypnotic although some patients complain about its unpleasant taste and irritating effect on their stomachs.

Benzodiazepine hypnotics are useful aids if taken occasionally when stress distracts the normal sleep tendency. When taken regularly for sleep insurance, hypnotics eventually defeat their purpose by exercising a generally negative effect. Without a pharmacological "straight jacket" no sleep is anticipated with the feared consequence of not being able to function alertly or at all the next day. On the other hand, where benzodiazepines are not prescribed, a stressed individual may resort to alcohol or more dangerous drugs which cannot be monitored.

The most popular benzodiazepines are the long-acting flurazepam (Dalmane) with a half-life of 78 to 200 hours, the short-acting temazepam (Restoril) with a half-life of 9.5 to 12.5 hours, and the ultrashort-acting triazolam (Halcion) whose half-life lasts only 1.5 to 2.5 hours. Elderly persons who require daytime alertness and good psychomotor performance are best given triazolam (Halcion) in dosage of 0.125 mg, which may be increased to a limit of 0.5 mg. It is also given to persons who require a short boost in sleeping like those with jet lag with awakening in the middle of the night. Temazepam (Restoril) in dosage 15 mg to 30 mg is helpful to those who anticipate sleep difficulties. Flurazepam (Dalmane) with a dosage of 15 to 30 mg is highest in sedation and may impair performance. It has a utility for individuals who require at least some sedation.

Psychostimulants are now very rarely utilized for depression and diet control because of dangers of habituation. Amphetamines (Dexedrene, Desoxyn), methylphenidate (Ritalin), cocaine, and pemoline (Cylert) are easily acquired illicitly, and are used and abused by large groups of people for their stimulant effect, their control of overeating, and the relief of fatigue. Consistent use of agents such as amphetamines is likely to induce an organic brain syndrome with manic and paranoidal symptoms.

Some of the stimulants are medically indicated being for the treatment of certain syndromes (Baldessarini, 1972; Wobraich, 1977, Sprague & Sleator, 1973). Attention deficit disorders of children, hyperkinesis, poor impulse control, low frustration tolerance, and emotional lability may often be helped by dextroamphetamine (Dexedrine) or methylphenidate (Ritalin). Since the response to stimulants varies from child to child, adjustment of recommended dosage upward or downward will be necessary. These drugs have a calming effect on a hyperactive child and lessen the risk of later emotional problems that evolve from the acting-out and defensive patterns developed as a result of the hyperkinetic and attention deficit symptoms. In narcolepsy the heightened drowsiness, loss of muscle tone, and uncontrollable need to sleep may respond to high doses of amphetamine and methylphenidate, reinforced if necessary by imipramine.

PSYCHODYSLEPTIC (PSYCHOTOMIMETIC) DRUGS

Employed for the setting of model psychoses (see Chapter 9, page 136) LSD-25, mescaline, and psilocybin were once advocated to induce perceptual and cognitive crises in patients, release emotions, promote abreaction, revive memories, and open up channels to the unconscious. The effect on the individual was influenced by the environmental setting, the existing relationship with the therapist and activity of the therapist. Some patients, frozen in their affects, suddenly were transported into a psychedelic experience which enabled them to restructure their value systems somewhat after the manner of a mystical experience (see Chapter 10, page 207).

The extraordinary perceptual and hallucinatory irregularities induced by these drugs unfortunately appeal to adolescents in rebellion, thrill seekers, and psychopaths who subject themselves to a wondrous "widening of consciousness" in quest of new insights and powers. "It permits you to see, more clearly than our perishing mortal eye can see, vistas beyond the horizons of this life, to travel backwards and forwards in time, to enter other planes of existence, even—to know God" (Wasson, 1963). Psychiatric patients, disappointed in psychoanalysis, hypnosis, drug therapy, and electroconvulsive therapy (ECT), often express a demand for the drug on the basis of its vaunted effects on the psyche. Unfortunately, on the debit side of the ledger is the capacity of psychodysleptics, particularly in vulnerable borderline patients, of sweeping away defenses that keep the individual in some kind of functional relationship to reality. "Our accumulating day-to-day experience with patients suffering the consequences of the hallucinogens demonstrates beyond question that these drugs have the power to damage the individual psyche, indeed to cripple it for life" (*JAMA*, 1963).

Favorable reports on LSD therapy with almost every syndrome have been published by Abramson (1956a & b), Bender et al. (1962), Chandler and Hartman (1960), S. Cohen and Eisner (1959), Cutner (1959), Dahlberg (1963a & b), Eisner and S. Cohen (1958), Feld et al. (1958), Heyder (1964), D. J. Lewis and Sloane (1958), Martin (1957), Sandison and Whitelaw (1957), Savage et al. (1964), Schmiege (1963), Simmons et al. (1966), and Whitelaw (1959). The book, *Uses of LSD in Psychotherapy* (Abramson, 1960), published by the Josiah Macy, Jr., Foundation, has a wealth of experimental and clinical data. The paper by Spencer (1964) also contains material helpful in evolving a technique. A conference held at South Oaks, Long Island (NY), devoted to LSD therapy expounded its potentialities (Abramson, 1966). LSD has been particularly recommended in the treatment of alcoholism (Hoffer, 1965; Jensen, 1962; Kurland et al, 1966, 1971; McCabe et al, 1972; MacLean et al, 1961; Pahnke et al, 1970; Savage et al, 1969, 1973; Smith, CM, 1958).

Beneficial uses in group psychotherapy have been described by Bierer (1963) who claims good results for LSD (in combination with methedrine) in "acute neuroses and for some sex difficulties. In addition, our experience with LSD as one aspect of an individual and group psychotherapeutic program for psychotic patients has been sufficiently encouraging to merit its continued use on an experimental basis." Bierer insists that it is not dangerous to treat psychotic, psychopathic, and emotionally immature patients with LSD. Eisner (1964) has also described the facilitating use of LSD in group therapy.

More recent work has shown that beneficial effects with single large doses of psychodysleptic drugs, or multiple small dose usage are not sufficient to justify recommending this therapy as adjuncts to psychotherapy. On the contrary, it may exert an adverse effect on the psyche in the form of an immediate "bad trip" and more insidiously repetitive frightening flashbacks.

This should not deter from continuing careful research on how psychodysleptic drugs influence mental functioning. The problem of evaluating the effect of these substances in psychotherapy is as great as, if not greater than, that of assessing any other adjunct in psychotherapy. Of basic importance is how the therapist (who must be with the patient for 5 hours or more)

works with and relates to the patient who is under the influence of the drug. Where the patient becomes too upset, the psychosis may rapidly be abolished by intravenous administration of 50 mg of chlorpromazine. Motor activity is reduced by chlorpromazine, verbal objectivity lessened, anxiety resolved, feelings of unreality and depersonalization abolished, and though hallucinations or somatic delusions continue, the patient may not react to them adversely.

What is essential in utilizing hallucinogens experimentally is familiarity with the effects of the particular drugs employed. Sufficient time must be spent with a patient prior to the administration of the drug to establish a working relationship and a feeling of trust. The therapeutic surroundings must be congenial, and the therapist and preferably a psychiatric nurse should be with the patient during the period the drug is in effect (which may be as long as 10–12 hours) to render support if necessary.

Recently a new drug MDMA (3-4-methylene-dioxymethamphetamine) has been employed experimentally in the attempt to enhance psychotherapy (The Psychiatric Times, 1986). This drug is said to evoke a highly comfortable experience that invites intensification of feelings and self-exploration. The drug is taken in doses of 75–175 mg by mouth and its effects begin in 30–45 minutes. It is said to have few complications. Although the drug has been around for at least 15 years there have been few publications. It awaits further testing before its general use can be recommended.

ORTHOMOLECULAR PSYCHIATRY AND MEGAVITAMIN THERAPY

There is a theory that schizophrenia is the product of an endogenous hallucinogen that accumulates in susceptible individuals as a result of faulty metabolism. Implicated frequently, it is avowed, is adrenochrome, formed from oxidation of adrenalin and released in large quantities by the excessive methylation of noradrenalin. On the basis of this theory, Hoffer (1966, 1971) administered large quantities of nicotinic acid (3 g or more daily), which he and his associates believed could restore metabolic balances. The theory, as well as the cure, have been rejected by a number of scientific investigators who have been unable to confirm the chemical changes postulated. Nevertheless, a sizable group of psychiatrists (who call themselves "orthomolecular" psychiatrists, a term originated by Linus Pauling) have endorsed the value of large quantities of vitamins (nicotinic acid, nicotinamide, vitamin B6, vitamin C, vitamin B12, and pyridoxine) for schizophrenia in combination with other accepted therapies, such as phenothiazines, ECT, and psychotherapy.

A task force of the American Psychiatric Association was appointed to examine the claims and appraise the results of megavitamin therapy. The report rejected both the theory and practice of orthomolecular treatments (Lipton et al, 1973). The extravagent claims of the orthomolecular psychiatrists in the public media were considered unfortunate. According to the task force, it has been impossible to replicate the results of the advocates of this form of therapy. Other studies, such as a five year multihospital project sponsored by the Canadian Mental Health Association, have concluded that large doses of nicotinic acid (3000 mg per day or more), the cornerstone of megavitamin therapy, have no therapeutic value other than as a placebo.

Against these reports, the orthomolecular psychiatric group have claimed unfairness and bias. Members of the group cite their own research, including double-blind studies, that substantiate the value of megavitamin treatments in acute cases, often in conjunction with ECT and other therapies (Hawkins & Pauling, 1973). They repudiate the results of attempts to replicate their findings on the basis that the research designs have been faulty. Hoffer claims

that where the megavitamin program outlined by him has been followed exactly, all reports published have duplicated his original claims. Pauling (1974) insists that "There is evidence that an increased intake of some vitamins, including ascorbic acid, niacin, pyridoxine, and cyanocobalamin, is useful in treating schizophrenia and this treatment has a sound theoretical base."

The controversy illustrates the difficulty of validating outcome research findings where faith or lack of faith in the modality, along with nonspecific therapeutic elements, are unavoidable contaminants.

Electroconvulsive Therapy

Public and legislative distaste for electroconvulsive therapy (ECT), distortions promulgated by movie depictions of the method, malpractice insurance rates 400 percent higher than rates where practitioners do not use this modality, and professional misunderstanding about its operations and utility have tended to cast a shadow on a technique that in syndromes for which it is intended is better, quicker, and in some ways less dangerous than pharmacotherapy. While few people are frightened by the use of electricity in converting an arrhythmic heart to alpha rhythm, applying electricity to the skull to regulate mental rhythms bring out visions of medieval torture, inhumane manipulations of the mind, and irretrievable brain damage that have not vanished with the publication of countless studies detailing the established virtues and safety of this most misunderstood intervention. The facts speak for themselves. ECT is more effective and safer than psychotropic drugs for serious debilitating and suicidal depressions. In the hands of competant operators it is painless and without danger. A convulsive seizure that lasts 15 seconds in an anesthetized, relaxed patient results in no pain, no discomfort, and no recollection of the procedure. Only four serious complications occur in 100,000 treatments and this figure includes the treatment of 90 year olds. Compare this figure with any current medical and surgical procedure existing today. The argument that it should not be used because we do not know how it works is preposterous. We do not know how aspirin works or how electricity works, but we utilize both with benefit. Misused, both can be dangerous, and ECT in the past has been misused by applying it indiscriminately to minor emotional problems that it could not possibly influence.

ECT cures three-quarters of depressed patients in contrast to the best antidepressant drugs that relieve symptoms in from one-half to two-thirds cases. It has saved many lives that otherwise would have been extinguished by suicide. "Clearly ECT has demonstrated its efficacy beyond doubt. It should not be permitted to fall into disuse; if it is abandoned, patients will suffer." (JAMA, 1979). A panel organized by the National Institutes of Health, conceding that the risks of serious side effects are relatively low, gave ECT an endorsement to the effect that "not a single controlled study has shown another form of treatment to be superior to ECT in the short-term management of severe depressions." (Science, 1985). The most bothersome side effect is, in most cases, temporary memory loss for the period immediately surrounding the period of ECT and "some patients suffer no memory loss at all." The panel noted that the complication rate was 1 in 1700 treatments and the mortality risk no different from that associated with the use of short-acting barbiturate anesthetics. The question then is why there is such persistent and fierce opposition to ECT. For example, not long ago the citizens of Berkeley, California voted overwhelmingly to ban the use of ECT within the city limits (Science News, 1982). Even some psychiatrists maintain a continuing prejudice despite new technical developments in the concomitant use of muscle relaxants, anesthesia, unilateral electrode placements, hyperoxygenation,

and monitoring of seizures that reduce complications.

While ECT is effective in catatonia, its use in other forms of schizophrenia is controversial since antipsychotic drugs are usually adequate although blighted by the risk of tardive dyskinesia. In manic patients lithium has replaced ECT except in rare cases where violent excitement necessitates immediate intervention. In neurotic depression (dysthmic disorder), psychosocial and pharmacological approaches are the preferred treatment modalities rather than ECT. ECT has not been found useful for chronic schizophrenia, and adjustment disorders with depressant moods. Informed consent is required from the patient who is presented with the options available, the possible benefits and risks, and the sequelae of confusion and memory loss. Obviously the family must be involved in the decision-making process. Before treatment is started drugs such as monoamine oxidase inhibitors and lithium should be discontinued. A thorough physical and neurological examination is essential and any cardiac problems are closely monitored. Agitated and excited reactions and intense chronic anxiety will require concentrated ECT sessions until the symptoms are under control. ECT has been employed as a preventive measure in manic-depressive psychosis, being administered bimonthly or monthly following full recovery. More commonly following ECT, the prescription of antidepressant drugs or lithium (in bipolar disorders) is usually carried out as a preventive measure.

Adjunctive drugs have been employed with ECT, although caution prescribes that drugs like neuroleptics be employed only after the course of ECT is ended except in severely resistant patients (with the caution that the morning dose should not be given prior to ECT).

It is essential in using ECT to make sure that an adequate number of treatments are given. In general, depressions and manic excitements require approximately six or eight ECTs.

For the most part, the therapist will refer patients for ECT who are severely depressed. An adequate number of treatments (generally three) are needed during the first week where the patient is a suicidal risk. Following this, one treatment at weekly intervals may suffice. A total of 6 to 10 ECTs are usually required. Intervals should be so spaced that the patient is prevented from developing confusion and excessive memory loss. Excited and panicky schizophrenic or borderline patients may also require referral. Here treatments on the basis of three times weekly may be needed, reduced only to control confusion or regression. The last few treatments are given once weekly. In a few cases "maintenance ECT" has been used on a prolonged basis to keep the vulnerable patient from dissociating. Usually, however, borderline patients with a depressive or panicky overlay which interferes with psychotherapy may be made more accessible and kept from memory impairment by one, two, or three or more ECTs spaced sufficiently apart (Kalinowsky, 1965). Memory loss for recent events generally reverses itself within a few weeks.

Unilateral ECT reduces the post-treatment confusion and memory loss of conventional bilateral ECT by placing the treatment electrodes over one side of the head only: the nondominant hemisphere (usually the right side in a right-handed individual). Generalized seizures are obtained with this method, which is otherwise given with anesthesia and muscle relaxation exactly as bilateral ECT. The striking absence of memory loss with unilateral ECT permits treatment to be given on a daily basis (Abrams, 1967). The depression-relieving effects of unilateral ECT are less than for bilateral ECT (Abrams, 1972), however, and this observation has stimulated attempts to increase the therapeutic effects of unilateral ECT by giving more than one

treatment in a single session (Abrams & Fink, 1972). If there is no pressure of time and no clinical urgency (e.g., suicidal risk, progressive weight loss, reckless overactivity), unilateral ECT should be given initially, changing to bilateral ECT only if improvement has not occurred after four to six ECTs. Unilateral ECT is also useful for ambulatory patients or those whose work requires unaltered memory function during the treatment course. Unilateral ECT may also be used to avoid cumulative memory loss (retrograde amnesia) in patients who have improved after receiving their first few treatments with bilateral ECT.

Concentrated regressive ECT in the form of two ECTs daily to produce an organic brain syndrome is not recommended. Following ECT treatments, antidepressants for unipolar or lithium for bipolar depression may be given to forestall relapse.

The immediate consequences of ECT are confusion, headache, and transient memory loss. The confusion and headache disappear shortly, but memory loss may persist for weeks.

Basic Suggestions for Proper Drug Usage: Summary

There is a general agreement among clinicians regarding the selection and use of psychotropic drugs although the methods of employment may vary depending on the degree of expertise and the nature of the patient population. Standard medications and practices do exist which have been tested and validated in rigorous trials. A number of basic rules are in order: (1) One should never allow oneself to be influenced by anecdotal accounts of "novel" drug therapies. More often than not the drugs are worthless if not hazardous. (2) Nutrient supplements do not substitute for time-tested agents. (3) Nonmedical therapists must refer patients in need of drug therapy to psychiatrists qualified in pharmacotherapy. (4) The patient should be informed about the likelihood of using medications at the beginning of treatment in the event there is a drug-responsive disorder. (5) A negative transference should be suspected where there is noncompliance with prescribing instructions (Sussman, 1983). (6) Should a patient fail to respond to properly selected and administered medications, referral for specialized help with experimental drugs should be made only to a practitioner or clinic with experience in new pharmacological agents.

The proper use of psychotropic medication should result in maximal benefits for the patient at a minimal degree of risk. There is much more involved in pharmacotherapy than knowing the proper drug to select and writing a prescription. The following suggestions may be helpful.

1. Take a history of each patient regarding previous and present psychotropic drug usage, including which drugs were effective, the dosage, and any side effects. Ask about the use of psychotropic medications by other blood relatives. Due to genetic factors, the patient may have similar reactions to the same drugs. Inquire into existing physical illness since certain conditions may be dangerously aggravated by some drugs. For example, if the patient is taking certain medications for illness, these may be incompatible with some psychotropic drugs, for example, guanethidine for hypertension and tricyclics for depression do not mix.

2. A diagnosis is important in order to prescribe the proper drug; thus neuroleptics would be used for schizophrenia, lithium for mania, and antidepressants for psychotic depression.

3. Try to avoid some drug combinations, like hypnotics and antidepressants; they can lower the desired effect. Where combinations are necessary, one should be aware that the total

therapeutic effect may be reduced. Thus, benztropine (Cogentin) to eliminate parkinsonian symptoms may lower the plasma level of a neuroleptic drug so that psychotic symptomatology can reappear, necessitating greater dosage.

4. Side effects tend to be dose-related. However, some patients experience adverse drug reactions at the lowest doses, while other patients tolerate extremely high doses with no unwanted effects. Management of intolerable drug related symptoms involve lowering the dosage to the lowest possible therapeutically effective level, or switching to a drug with a lower side effect profile. For example, a patient who experiences severe extrapyramidal reactions to haloperidol (Haldol), and is unable to tolerate the anticholinergic effects of an antiparkinsonian drug (Artane, Cogentin, Kemedrin), may be given chlorpromazine or thioridazine that cause extrapyramidal reactions far less frequently.

5. Adequate dosage over a sufficiently long period is essential to test the efficacy of a drug. Build up dosage as rapidly as possible and sensible. If a patient fails to respond to one class of drugs during a sufficiently long time, switch to one of the other classes, as from aliphatic phenothiazines (Thorazine, Mellaril) to the butyrophenones (Haldol), to the thioxanthenes (Navane), to the dihydroindolones (Moban). If the patient still fails to respond after two months of antipsychotic or antidepressant drug therapy, the chances are the individual is not a good candidate for pharmacotherapy. Failure to respond to a benzodiazepine antianxiety or hypnotic drug within the first week should raise doubts about the eventual efficacy of the drug. Patients who benefit from benzodiazepines experience some re-

duction of anxiety or insomnia, even at low doses, at the outset of treatment.

6. Since most drugs are retained in the body for relatively long periods, a single total dose at nighttime, once a therapeutic effect has been obtained, is preferable to multiple doses during the day. Sleep is enhanced, and there is less tendency to forget to take the medications.

7. If a patient has had a good premorbid personality, has related well to people, and has broken down only under the impact of extremely severe stress, psychological treatments are likely to be most effective. The use of drugs may only be necessary for extremely severe or recalcitrant symptoms. An "acute psychotic break," particularly in a young person, may really be an identity crisis, a consequence of drug abuse, or a phase of a seizure disorder. It is better, therefore, not to prescribe psychotropic medications routinely. In many cases hospitalization suffices to stabilize the patient. One may wait a few days and then institute psychotherapy and reassurance to see if the patient's inner strengths will suffice to bring about a remission.

8. Where possible, concurrent psychotherapy should be employed in a psychotropic drug regimen to help reduce destructive interpersonal patterns, to lower self-imposed standards impossible of attainment, to teach social skills, and to facilitate environmental adjustment. Psychotherapy will enable the patient to make an adaptation more rapidly without the need, or with a reduced need, for medications.

9. Patients should be informed of the nature of side effects associated with psychotropic drug use. When antipsychotic drugs are prescribed, patients and their families should be told of the nature of extrapyramidal symptoms, particularly acute dystonic reactions. The therapist should not fear that an open discussion of side effects will deter the patient from agreeing to take medication, particularly if it is made clear that the benefits of treatment outweigh the risks. Patients receiving short-acting hypnotic drugs should be warned of possible rebound insomnia on the nights immediately after medication is discontinued.

10. Several drug preparations are marketed that contain fixed combinations of compounds with different clinical indications. The most widely used combination drugs are Triavil and Etrafon (both of which contain antipsychotic perphenazine and antidepressant amitriptyline) and Limbritol, a combination of chlordiazepoxide and amitriptyline. These three combination drugs may account for 20 percent of all prescriptions of antidepressant drugs. Nevertheless, except in a few special circumstances, there is little rational basis for the use of these combinations since the mixture of the drugs in fixed doses exposes the patient to unnecessary amounts of at least one of the compounds. This, in turn, causes a higher incidence of side effects. Whether drugs are used alone or in combination, dosage should be individualized according to clinical response.

11. Every class of psychotropic medication has been shown to increase the risk of birth defects. Though evidence that antipsychotic drugs produce congenital malformations is contradictory, the teratogenetic effects of lithium, anxiolytics, and tricyclic antidepressants is documented. Considering the consequences of birth defects for the parents and offspring, it is strongly suggested that women who

intend to become pregnant or who are pregnant be managed by nonpharmacological modalities. If the use of medication is being considered for psychotic women, hospitalization is advisable to see whether a structured secure environment obviates the need for drugs. In cases of depression during pregnancy, ECT is preferable to antidepressant medication. However, at times drug therapy is unavoidable, particularly when the patient's illness threatens the lives of both herself and the fetus.

12. The therapist should be mindful of the fact that according to the law patients have a qualified constitutional right to refuse psychotropic and antipsychotic medications, and this right has been recognized by a number of federal courts. In cases of incompetency, judgment about drug treatment decisions must be entrusted to a court.

13. Discussion with patients who require maintenance drug therapy can be reassuring to the patient, even to schizophrenics when informed about tardive dyskinesia. No increase in relapse or treatment noncompliance need be anticipated. (Munetz & Roth, 1985).

14. A patient who consents to take a drug should be told the name of the medication, whether it is intended to treat the disease or relieve symptoms, and how important it is to take it regularly, how to tell when it is working, what to do if it is not working, when and how to take it (before or after meals), how long to continue taking it, side effects and what to do about them, possible effects on driving and work with precautions on what to do, and interactions with other medications. (Drug and Therapeutic Bulletin, 1981).

15. Useful texts in pharmacotherapy are: Appleton and Davis (1980), Baldessarini (1984a & b), Hollister (1978), Klein et al. (1980), Mason and Granacher (1980), Simpson (1983).

CONFRONTATION

Psychodynamic theory and psychoanalytic methods are often accused of helping patients avoid responsibility for their behavior, blaming inner conflicts foisted on them by their parents or by past experience over which they had no control. In confrontation techniques it is assumed that the patient must accept responsibility for actions and take the consequences for behavior that is counterproductive. The patient is exposed to a surprise or shock stimulus from which there is no escape and to which he or she must respond. Retreats into unreality and evasive defense are cut off. The patient is invited to explore the reactions with the aid of the therapist. He or she must justify aspects of verbalizations and behavior that the therapist believes are significant. There are some people who learn best by being subjected to such psychological assault. This acts as an aversive stimulus to force a different mode of thinking and behavior, to doubt habitual coping devices, and to reach for new adaptations. The patient may then either be left to ingenuity to find alternative patterns, or possible solutions may be suggested in the hope the patient will grapple onto one of them. The effectiveness of this intervention will depend on the acceptance of the therapist as an authority whose injunctions must be incorporated at face value, as well as readiness for and ability to change. The timing of confrontation is important. We are all aware of how frequently the challenging of pathological character traits merely makes them more rigid. Careful empathic interpretation may have to precede forceful confrontation.

The selection of a proper area for confrontation will depend on the perceptiveness and diagnostic skill of the therapist. There are some therapists who, wedded to a special way of thinking about dynamics, impose this on the patient. Thus if therapists believe that masochism is a univeral liability and at the bottom of all pathology, they will interpret the symptoms of the patient in this light. Lewin (1970), for example, believes that every symptom serves both self-tormenting purposes as well as a means of provoking others. Even character patterns are interpreted as a masochistic need to suffer and punish people. The patient is helped "to see what he wants to do and what his conscience forces him to do" and how the disparity creates difficulties. The contrast between a healthy conscience that guides while inhibiting destructive actions and the patient's existing sadistic conscience that viciously torments and punishes is pointed out. It becomes essential for the patient to recognize that an intemperate and merciless conscience is the "*common enemy* against which the therapist is his ego's strong ally." No immediate interpretations are made of specific conflicts. "The initial confrontations are confined to the patient's need for self-punishment and his masochistic responses to anger."

The universality of this concept about masochism may be doubtful but sometimes masochism *is* at the basis of an individual's problems. Accident proneness, obsessional self-torment, suicidal tendencies, and hypochondriacal self-torment, suicidal tendencies, and hypochrondriacal preoccupations, for example, may be indications of a generalized masochism. Where this is apparent, an explanation such as the following may be offered: "You feel angry at what your parents did to you as a child. But you also feel guilty for your anger and thoughts. So you punish yourself for these thoughts and feelings. Your symptoms and your behavior seem to me to be the results of your punishing yourself. Now what are you going to do about what you are doing to

yourself?" Should these explanations and injunctions fail to produce results, some therapists resort to stronger challenges and confrontations.

While aggressive confrontation under these circumstances may prove profitable in some patients with good ego strength, it may not be applicable to sicker patients unless the confrontations are toned down to a point where they are executed in an empathic reassuring way. Even then it may be necessary to wait until a good working relationship has been established, and then only after it becomes apparent that masochistic maneuvers are obviously being employed by the patient in the interests of resistance—"You seem to be punishing yourself by refusing to get well."

Other explanations than masochism may be offered by therapists trained in specific schools of psychology or psychiatry. One universal basic cause is presented for all types of emotional illness, and this single etiological factor is tortured to fit in with *every* symptom and behavioral manifestation. Thus, the patient may be dazzled by brilliant explanations of the malfunctions of pregenital splitting, or of the Oedipus complex, or of the devalued self-image, or of subversive archetypes, or of conditioned anxiety, or of any of the countless theories around which current psychological ideologies are organized. While such single explanations may not be accurate, they may be temporarily effective, especially when dogmatically stated. In the long run, however, they will not hold up.

Most therapists who utilize confrontation employ it in the medium of a wide assortment of eclectic methods like role playing, Gestalt therapy, psychodrama, transactional therapy, encounter therapy, existential therapy, and psychoanalytically oriented psychotherapy.

Utilizing a transactional model, Garner (1970) has developed a confrontation technique that "focuses on the patient's conflict between the unconscious or conscious desire to approach a certain goal and the avoidance tendencies." The technique is characterized by interventions in the form of frequent directive statements made to the patient, with the question, "What do you think or feel about what I told you?" The patient's response is studied, whether it be complete compliance, compliance with critical appraisal, or critical appraisal. In this way an attempt is made to probe *reactions* to statements and to avoid the parroting of insight. The challenging question of the therapist requires that the patient explore the role of the therapist and the interactional dynamics of the relationship. It forces the patient also to examine the stereotyped nature of thoughts and behavior. The patient is invited to work out a mutually satisfactory solution to conflicts.

The focus may be limited or may involve the resolution of a core conflict that existed in the early life of the patient. For example, patients with dependency problems or separation anxiety may be confronted with, "Stop believing you are incapable of taking care of yourself," or "You are acting like the most helpless, inept person in the world." After each of these statements there is added, "What do you think or feel about what I have told you?" The latter question acts like a lever to explore compliance or noncompliance tendencies and to engage in problem-solving activities.

The confrontation formulations may be employed adjunctively in any form of insight therapy when a clearly defined conflict is exposed. They may be employed to reinforce a constructive defense or to challenge a neurotic defense, as in peer groups with addicts (Adler, G, & Buie, 1974). Among their uses is testing how thoroughly the patient has understood a point stressed by the therapist. In this way misinterpretations may be immediately corrected. Confrontation may also be used as an adjunct to behavioral and other educational methods as a wedge into cognitive areas. Obviously, sicker patients, such as borderline cases and schizophrenics, do not respond well to the technique.

GESTALT THERAPY

Establishing its position in the Human Potential Movement, Gestalt therapy (see Chapter 11 page 305) gets its inspiration from Gestalt psychology, existentialism, psychodrama, and psychoanalysis (particularly character analysis). It stresses the immediacy of experience in the here and now and nonverbal expressiveness (Fagan & Shepherd, 1970). It describes itself as a philosophy of living in the present rather than the past or future, of experiencing rather than imagining, of expressing rather than explaining or justifying, or avoiding the "shoulds" or "oughts," of taking full responsibility for one's actions, feelings, and thoughts, and of surrendering to "being as one is" (Naranjo, 1971).

By observing the patient's positive gestures and bodily movements, Gestalt therapists attempt to discern aspects that reflect unconscious feelings. The therapist points out these tendencies and asks the patient to exaggerate them, to express any feelings associated with them. The object is to expand the patient's awareness of the self, bodily sensations, and the world around one. Gestalt techniques are sometimes employed to catalyze other therapies. (Perls, 1973; Polster & Polster, 1973).

As to the actual techniques, Gestalt therapists have different ways of operating. Many follow the precepts of Fritz Perls (1969), particularly in working in the here and now, eschewing the "why" in favor of the "how." Since it is contended that review of the past cannot change what has happened, the past is avoided, the focus being on the immediate I-Thou therapeutic relationship. There is insistence on the patient taking full responsibility for the choices and decisions he or she makes. Only by self-acceptance, it is avowed, can meaningful contact be made with others. Closely observing ambiguous nonverbal behaviors and confronting the patient with these without analysis or interpretation may open up channels of repressed ideations and feelings. The patient may be asked to repeat or exaggerate unusual movements and amplify or adopt opposing modes of verbalization. "The whisperer experiments with yelling, the yeller experiments with whispering, the intellectual explainer who drowns everyone with words experiments with babbling sounds, enabling new awareness of sharing and holding back" (Kriesgfeld, 1979). An important objective is restoration to one's total being of split-off and dissociated aspects of the self. The person is consequently exposed to a group of "therapeutic experiments" in order to come to grips with repressed and repressing aspects of oneself. A patient may be requested to hold conversations with various parts of the body that feel tense or painful, or with people and objects in dreams. One may project these parts, people, or objects onto an empty chair and engage in a dialogue with these. A number of texts are available detailing gestalt techniques (Perls, 1969; Smith, 1976).

The patient may be asked to observe things about the therapist's waiting room and to comment on them, particularly to speculate on the kind of a person the therapist is believed to be from this data. If the patient becomes aware of certain bodily sensations like heart beating, deep breathing, neck stiffening, etc., he or she may be asked to talk to the heart, lungs, neck, etc. The projective elements of anything that one says are inquired into by asking the patient to relate comments about others to oneself. The patient is encouraged to do, and even to exaggerate doing things that he or she avoids or is ashamed of, at first in fantasy and then slowly in reality. All aspects of the patient's dreams are considered part of the self, and the patient is asked to play these parts, dramatizing them while verbalizing feelings freely. Many of the Gestalt techniques lend themselves to groups as well as individual therapy. The techniques used for the most usual situations encountered in therapy are summarized here:

1. *Dealing with conflict:* When elements of a conflict are perceived (e.g., dominant desires versus passive impulses; masculine versus feminine, etc.), the patient is asked to play both roles in turn, utilizing the empty chair in which an imagined significant person is seated or the counterpart aspect of the self is seated.

2. *Unresolved feelings:* When detected, the therapist may insist that these be expressed.

3. *Difficulties in self-expression:* A game is often played wherein the patient makes a statement and ends it by saying, "And I take responsibility for it."

4. *Fear of offending others:* In a group the patient goes around expressing attitudes and feelings frankly to each member.

5. *Testing projections:* A patient who believes another individual has a problem or characteristic is asked to play a role as if the problem or characteristic is one's own.

6. *Challenging reaction formations* (e.g., excessive prudishness): Here the therapist may ask the patient to play the opposite role deliberately (e.g., verbalizing sexual freedom).

7. *Managing anxiety:* The therapist says, "Why not let it build as far as it likes. Don't try to stop it. Emphasize your shaking. Try to bring it on."

8. *Tendencies to detachment and withdrawal:* The patient is asked to focus on the situations or inner feelings that cause withdrawal.

9. *Exploring the meaning of gestures or unusual verbal statements:* When these are noticeable, the patient is

asked to exaggerate them and detail associations.

10. *Difficulties in making assertive statements:* The patient is encouraged to say before each statement, "Of course" and "It is certain that."

11. *Use of dreams:* Each aspect of the dream is believed to represent a part of the individual. The patient is asked to identify with each aspect of the dream and act out a role talking to various aspects of oneself.

12. *Dealing with distorted values:* The therapist often tries to act as a model by verbalizing and sharing with the patient his or her personal values and feelings.

HYPNOSIS

Trance phenomena have been utilized as part of religious and healing rituals in all ages and cultures since the earliest of recorded history. The loss of control by the subject in the trance, the bizarre muscular movements, and the vivid imagery that is released have suggested "possession" by spirits and extramundane forces that have led observers to link hypnosis with mysticism and the paranormal. It is only relatively recently that attempts have been made at scientific investigation of hypnosis in the effort to understand how it influences behavior and particularly its therapeutic potentials. Modern uses of hypnosis embrace its employment within the matrix of a number of paradigms, such as social influence, dissonance reduction, indirect metacommunications, employment of paradox, imagery evocation, double binds and a variety of other interventions. Most recently the dramatic innovative techniques of Milton Erickson have been analyzed (Rossi, 1980; Zeig, 1985a and b) with the object of distilling from them strategies that can enhance the therapeutic process. Some new ideas have emerged from this contemporary work including "neuro-linguistic programming" (Bandler & Grinder, 1975) through which an attempt is made to manipulate unique individual thought processes in order to effectuate changes in behavior and feelings.

Such studies have shown that employed by reasonably trained professionals within the context of a structured therapeutic program, with awareness of limits of its application, hypnosis can make a contribution as an adjunct to any of the manifold branches of psychotherapy, whether these be supportive, reeducative, or psychoanalytic.

Most professionals who are fearful of hypnosis as a therapeutic tool, or exaggerate its virtues, either have never experimented with it for a time sufficient to test the method or else are victims of superstition, prejudices or naive magical expectancy. A number of spokesmen for hypnosis, some writing extensively, help to discredit it by overdramatizing the process, by exaggerating its powers, by participating in and publishing results of poorly conceived experiments, by engaging in naively organized therapeutic schemes, by offering therapeutic formulations that violate the most elementary precepts of dynamic psychology, or by promulgating its presumed dangers for which there is little basis in fact (Wolberg, LR, 1956).

How hypnosis aids in securing therapeutic effects is not entirely clear, but we may postulate two important influences. First, hypnosis rapidly produces a remarkable rapport with the therapist. Irrespective of the fact that this is probably linked to some anachonistic regressive dependency need, a strong impact is registered on the therapeutic working relationship. The placebo influence, a component of all therapies, is strongly enhanced. Suggestion, another universal component of all treatment processes, is so expanded in hypnosis that the patient responds sensitively and with dramatic readiness to both indirect, subtle persuasions by the therapist and to direct commands and injunctions that are not too anxiety provoking. The relationship with the therapist, in a surprisingly short time, becomes one in which the therapist becomes endowed with noble, protective, and even magical qualities. The ultimate result of these combined forces can be substantive relief from tension, a restoration of homeostasis, and a recapturing of a sense of mastery, which in themselves may restore adaptive defenses and produce a symptomatic cure.

The second influence of hypnosis is upon the intrapsychic processes. Hypnosis promotes an altered state of consciousness. As such, repression may temporarily be lifted with exposure of emotionally charged impulses that have been denied direct expression and that have hitherto partly drained themselves off through substitutive symptomatic channels. This can lead to a release of vivid imagery and emotionally cathartic verbalizations. Such spontaneous outbursts usually occur only in persons who are strongly repressed while nurturing explosive inner conflicts. On the other hand, a therapist utilizing exploratory techniques to probe unconscious ideation may, by direct suggestion or regression and revivification, expose less highly charged but significant fantasies, verbal associations, and memories, thus opening roads to greater self-understanding.

Hypnosis as a relaxing agency has been employed in physical and psychological disturbances that are characterized by stress and tension. Since stress may have a damaging effect on all bodily functions, its amelioration can be important for healing (Wolberg, LR, 1957). Tension relief may, on the basis of suggestion during the trance state, be supplemented perhaps by self-hypnosis (Wolberg, LR, 1965) or by such techniques as autogenic training (Luthe, 1963; Schultz & Luthe, 1959; Luthe et al, 1963).

Where the symptom does not bind too much anxiety or where its pleasure and masochistic values are not too intense, it may be possible to alleviate it by hypnotic suggestion without symptom substitution. Not only may the ensuing relief initiate a better adjustment, but also it may set off a chain reaction that, reverberating through the entire personality structure, influences its other dimensions. Suggestive hypnosis may also be of value in controlling the ruminations of chronic obsessive-compulsive patients whose preoccupations immerse them in interminable misery. By helping such victims to divert their thinking into more constructive channels, it may initiate relief of anxiety and a better adaptation. With caution hypnosis may be adopted as a suggestive instrument in controlling certain habits, such as overeating, excessive smoking, and insomnia. The phrasing of suggestions here is important.

Some therapists still use hypnosis like a magic wand to dissipate in thin air symptoms that hamper the adjustment of the patient. While symptom removal by hypnosis is justified where the symptom blocks therapy, as in emergencies or where more extensive therapy cannot be applied, one must realize its limitations. For so long as we depend solely upon the authoritarian powers with which the hypnotic situation automatically invests us, our therapeutic effectiveness will be no greater, and often will be less than miraculous healing. Christian Science, and other therapies dependent upon faith, magic, and prayer. Because of the evanescent effects of suggestive hypnosis, hypnotic therapy has historically enjoyed brief spurts of popularily followed by disappointment and abandonment of the method.

Hypnosis may prove itself to be singularly successful in overcoming resistance, exposing segments of the person's inner life that are deeply buried within and which have hitherto evaded detection. In rare instances this exposure of memories and experiences, as well as the related emotions, will result in the relief of a symptom. In my own work I have been able to remove isolated amnesias, motor paralysis, blindness, and anesthesias through the hypnotic revival of some early experience that resulted in these hysterical symptoms. This is what Freud did in his original work at the turn of the century, which resulted in his pioneer psychoanalytical discoveries. Hypnotic removal of symptoms should if possible be followed by further explorations for conflicts that have generated hysterical defenses.

The use of hypnosis in exploratory psychotherapy, such as in the insight approaches, is contingent upon the influence of hypnosis on unconscious resistance that in resolution helps the individual establish closer contact with repressed needs and conflicts. It may thus be possible to bring to the surface significant memories and repressed impulses that expedite the analytic process. (Wolberg, 1964a; 1986)

Hypnosis is particularly useful in freeing verbalizations, in liberating transference, and in helping the patient to recall dreams. Where anxiety blocks speech, the mere induction of a trance may serve to release a verbal discharge. Moreover, the provocation of transference feelings may bring to the surface painful emotions as well as fantasies that sometimes burst through with intense violence. Where free associations have been blocked for one reason or another, hypnosis may suffice to restore this form of communication. Hypnosis may serve also as a means of stimulating dreams in patients who are unable to remember them or who have "dried up" in their analytic productiveness.

In behavior therapy hypnosis is useful in various ways. First, it establishes in the mind of the patient the authority of the therapist, who will act as the reinforcing agency. Under these circumstances positive counterconditioning, aversive conditioning, extinction, and other tactics will be catalyzed. Second, by promoting relaxation through hypnosis a positive stimulus is supplied that becomes affiliated with the conditioned stimulus and helps to extinguish it. Third, on the basis of suggestion, the objectives of the therapist, once explicitly defined, may be more easily accepted. The patient is encouraged to behave in emotionally constructive ways, in quest of reversing established patterns or correcting behavioral deficits. Thus, in the method of desensitization through reciprocal inhibition anxiety-provoking cues are presented in a climate of relaxation in progressively stronger form.

There is no way of predicting in advance the exact influence hypnosis may have on the patient or problems since each individual will respond uniquely to the phenomenon of hypnosis in line with the special personal meanings. The mental set toward hypnosis, the motivations to be helped, the depth and quality of resistances, the preparation for induction, ideas about the therapist and particularly the image conjured up of the therapist, the skill of the therapist as a hypnotist, the quality of the suggestions administered, the management of the patient's doubts and oppositional tendencies, and the nature of the transference and countertransference will all enter into the responsive Gestalt.

Potentially, hypnosis may catalyze every aspect of the therapeutic process. Whether or not a therapist will want to employ it will depend largely on how much confidence one has in hypnosis and how well one works with hypnotic techniques.

Hypnosis is an intense emotional experience that may affect both patient and therapist. In the trance a dynamic configuration of many kinds of phenomena are constantly interacting in response to functional psychophysiological changes within the individual and the specific significance of the hypnotic interpersonal relationship. As attention is shifted from the external world toward the inner self, there is an expansion of self-awareness and a lifting of repressions, with exposure of certain repudiated aspects of the psyche. A regressive kind of relationship develops between the subject and operator, the latter being promoted into the post of a kind of magical authoritative figure.

Hypnosis may also release powerful feelings in the therapist, aspects of which, in the form of countertransference, may be inimical to the therapeutic objective. Particularly obstructive are omnipotent, sadistic, and sexual strivings. Only by experimenting with hypnosis can a therapist determine whether one is personally capable of employing it as a therapeutic adjunct. While one may be able to do good psychotherapy with the usual psychotherapeutic techniques, attempts at hypnosis may alter one's manner toward the patient in ways that will prove antitherapeutic. Thus, a therapist may act aggressively toward patients perceived to be in a helpless state. Coordinately, one may become suffused with feelings of grandiosity. Or one may, as a projected Svengali figure, find oneself sexually attracted to a patient whom one regards as passively seductive. Should these feelings arise in spite of measures to control them, it is best to pursue a pattern of caution and refrain from employing hypnosis in practice.

Hypnosis, then, is merely a device to facilitate the psychotherapeutic process rather than to substitute for it. No problems need be anticipated in the induction of hypnosis, and in the application of hypnotic and hypnoanalytic procedures, if the therapist masters at least one of the standard techniques, applies it confidently, while constantly observing the reactions of the patient and of oneself. Protracted dependency reactions are no more common than in psychotherapy without hypnosis. It goes without saying that hypnosis is no substitute for careful training, extensive experience, and technical competence. It will not make up for lacks in judgment or skill. However, a sophisticated psychotherapist

who has learned how to utilize hypnosis has available a most important adjunctive tool.

Induction of Hypnosis

Hypnosis is extremely easy to induce. The object is to bring the patient to a hypersuggestible state. Toward this end the operator executes a number of maneuvers, the most common one being a state of muscular relaxation and the fixation of attention. Important rules to follow are these:

1. Engage the attention of the patient by assigning a task, (muscle relaxation, hand clasp, hand levitation), descriptions of which will follow.
2. Approach the induction with a confident manner. Any faltering or unsureness in vocal expression will influence the patient negatively. Adopt a persuasive, calm, reassuring tone of voice, droning suggestions rhythmically and monotonously.
3. Employ repetition in suggestions to focus the patient's attention.
4. Excite the imagination of the patient by building word pictures so that the patient practically lives and feels what is suggested. (In children one can engage their attention by asking them to imagine watching a television screen and observing their favorite programs.)
5. Use positive rather than negative suggestions. For example, where pain is to be deadened, do not say, "You will have no pain." Say, "The sensation will change so that instead of feeling what you have been feeling, it will feel dull, numb, and tolerable." If a hypodermic injection is to be given, do not say, "This will not hurt," but rather, "This will be like a tiny mosquito bite."
6. Should the patient at any time open the eyes and insist he or she is not hypnotized, put your fingers on the eyelids to shut them and say, "That doesn't mat-

ter, I just want you to relax." Then continue with suggestions.

7. Almost universally, patients, after the first induction, even those who have been deeply hypnotized, will insist they were not in a trance. Reply with, "Of course you weren't asleep or anesthesized. You were in a state of relaxation and this is all that is necessary. You may go deeper next time, but it really doesn't matter." Give the patient a typewritten copy of material describing some phenomena of hypnosis (see Appendix U).

8. Some operators find it important to tell the patient that all that will be achieved in the first session is not hypnosis but a state of relaxation that will help the patient quiet the symptoms: "If you fall asleep, that is fine; if you feel completely awake, that too is fine. The effect will still be there." To some people the word "hypnosis" has many unfortunate connotations. It often embraces expectations of an immediate miracle cure. When the patient fails to go into the depth of trance imagined he or she should achieve with the "hypnotic" indication, one may become upset, feel hopeless, and lose confidence in the therapist.

A simple technique that I have found valuable, particularly for suggestive-persuasive-reeducative therapy, involves muscle relaxation. This method lends itself to teaching the patient self-hypnosis to carry on suggestions by oneself. It is helpful in this direction to supply the patient with a tape recording (the patient may bring a machine and a recording may be made directly on it; or if the therapist's recorder is compatible with that of the patient, he or she may be given the recorded tape at the end of the session). The patient may be requested to lean back in a chair and shut the eyes (if preferred one can be supine on a couch) and the material below may be dictated, *slowly*, in a persuasive tone (the therapist may have to practice reading the material so that it does not come through in a stereotyped mechanical way). As a preliminary, I tell the patient, "I would like to teach you a simple relaxing technique that should help you." If the patient agrees, I continue.

Making a Relaxing and Ego Building Audiotape

Having prepared the recorder and inserted a blank cassette, the therapist, prior to dictating into the microphone says:

All that will happen is that you will be pleasantly relaxed, no sleep, no deep trances, just comfortable. Now just settle back and shut your eyes. [*At this point the therapist may read the following material. If a recording is to be made, start the recording.*] Breathe in deeply but gently through your nostrils or mouth, right down into the pit of your stomach. D-e-e-p-l-y, d-e-e-p-l-y, d-e-e-p-l-y; but not so deeply that you are uncomfortable. Just deeply enough so that you feel the air soaking in. In . . . and out. D-e-e-p-l-y, d-e-e-p-l-y. In . . . and out. And as you feel the air soaking in, you begin to feel yourself getting sleepy and r-e-l-a-x-e-d. Very r-e-l-a-x-e-d. Even d-r-o-w-s-y, d-r-o-w-s-y and relaxed. Drowsy and relaxed.

Now I want you to concentrate on the muscle groups that I point out to you. Loosen them, relax them while visualizing them. You will notice that you may be tense in certain areas and the idea is to relax yourself completely. Concentrate on your forehead. Loosen the muscles around your eyes. Your eyelids relax. Now your face, your face relaxes. And your mouth . . . relax the muscles around your mouth, and even the inside of your mouth. Your chin; let it sag and feel heavy. And as you relax your muscles, your breathing continues r-e-g-u-l-a-r-l-y and d-e-e-p-l-y, deeply within yourself. Now your neck, your neck relaxes. Every muscle, every fiber in your neck relaxes. Your shoulders relax . . . your arms . . . your elbows . . . your forearms . . . your wrists . . . your hands . . . and your fingers relax. Your arms feel loose and limp; heavy and loose and limp. Your whole body begins to feel loose and limp. Your neck muscles relax; the front of your neck, the back muscles. If you wish, wiggle your head if necessary to get all the kinks out. Keep breathing deeply and relax. Now your chest. The front part of your chest relaxes . . . and the back part of your chest relaxes. Your abdomen . . . the pit of your stomach, that relaxes. The small of your back, loosen the muscles. Your hips . . . your thighs . . . your knees relax . . . even the muscles in your legs. Your ankles . . . your feet . . . and your toes. Your whole body feels loose and limp. [*Pause.*] And now, as you feel the muscles relaxing, you will notice that you begin to feel relaxed all over. Your body begins to feel v-e-r-y, v-e-r-y relaxed . . . and you are going to feel d-r-o-w-s-i-e-r, and d-r-o-w-s-i-e-r, from the top of your head right down to your toes. Every breath you take is going to soak in deeper and deeper and deeper, and you feel your body getting drowsier and drowsier.

And now, I want you to imagine, to visualize the most relaxed and quiet and pleasant scene imaginable. Visualize a relaxed and pleasant quiet scene. Any scene that is comfortable. ([*The following may be introduced at the first, and perhaps the second induction to give the patient an idea of the kind of imagery that is suitable. Once the patient selects a scene, these suggestions need not be repeated. If a recording is being made, the recorder should be turned off at this point to eliminate the remainder of this paragraph.*] It can be some scene in your past, or a scene you project in the future. It can be nothing more than being at the beach watching the water breaking on the shore. Or a lake with a sailboat floating lazily by. Or merely looking at the sky with one or two billowy clouds moving slowly. Any scene that is quiet and pleasant and makes you feel drowsy. Or a sound like Beethoven's sonata, or any other selection that is soothing.) Drowsier and drowsier and drowsier. You are v-e-r-y weary, and every breath will send you deeper and deeper and deeper. [*The recorder may now be turned on again.*]

As you visualize this quiet scene, I shall count from one to twenty, and when I reach the count of twenty, you will feel yourself in deep. [*The count should be made very slowly.*] One, deeper, deeper, Two, deeper and deeper and deeper. Three . . . drowsier and drowsier. Four, deeper and deeper. Five . . . drowsier and drowsier and drowsier. Six . . . seven, very very, very relaxed. Eight, deeper and deeper. Nine . . . ten, drowsier and drowsier. Eleven, twelve, thirteen; deeper and deeper. D-r-o-w-s-i-e-r and d-r-o-w-s-i-e-r. Fourteen, drowsier and drowsier and drowsier. Fifteen . . . sixteen . . seventeen, deeper and deeper. Eighteen . . . nineteen . . . and finally twenty.

The following "ego-building" suggestions of Hartland (1965)* may be employed in supportive and some reeducative approaches. They are introduced at this point.

As I talk to you, you will absorb what I say d-e-e-p-l-y into yourself. "Every day . . . you will become physically *STRONGER* and *FITTER*. You will become *MORE ALERT* . . . *MORE WIDE AWAKE* . . . *MORE ENERGETIC*. You will become *MUCH LESS EASILY TIRED* . . . *MUCH LESS EASILY FATIGUED* . . . *MUCH LESS EASILY DEPRESSED* . . . *MUCH LESS EASILY DISCOURAGED*. Every day . . . you will become *SO DEEPLY INTERESTED IN WHATEVER YOU ARE DOING* . . . *SO DEEPLY INTERESTED IN WHATEVER IS GOING ON* . . . *THAT YOUR MIND WILL BECOME MUCH LESS PREOCCUPIED WITH YOURSELF* . . . *AND YOU WILL BECOME MUCH LESS CONSCIOUS OF YOURSELF* . . . *AND YOUR OWN FEELINGS*.

"*Every day* . . . *YOUR NERVES WILL BECOME STRONGER AND STEADIER* . . . *YOUR MIND WILL BECOME CALMER AND CLEARER* . . . *MORE COMPOSED* . . . *MORE PLACID* . . . *MORE TRANQUIL*. You will become *MUCH LESS EASILY WORRIED* . . . *MUCH LESS EASILY AGITATED* . . . *MUCH LESS FEARFUL AND APPREHENSIVE* . . . *MUCH LESS EASILY UPSET*. You will be able to *THINK MORE CLEARLY* . . . you will be able to *CONCENTRATE MORE EASILY* . . . *YOUR MEMORY WILL IMPROVE* . . . and you will be able to *SEE THINGS IN THEIR TRUE PERSPECTIVE* . . . *WITHOUT MAGNIFYING THEM* . . . *WITHOUT ALLOWING THEM TO GET OUT OF PROPORTION*.

"*Every day* . . . you will become *EMOTIONALLY MUCH CALMER* . . . *MUCH MORE SETTLED* . . . *MUCH LESS EASILY DISTURBED*.

"*Every day* . . . you will feel a *GREATER FEELING OF PERSONAL WELL-BEING* . . . *A GREATER FEELING OF PERSONAL SAFETY* . . . *AND SECURITY* . . . than you have felt for a long, long time.

"*Every day* . . . *YOU will become* . . . and *YOU will remain* . . . *MORE AND MORE*

---

* Reprinted with permission of Dr. John Hartland and the editor of the *American Journal of Clinical Hypnosis*, 3:89–93, 1965.

COMPLETELY RELAXED . . . AND LESS TENSE EACH DAY . . . BOTH MENTALLY AND PHYSICALLY.

"And, AS you become . . . and, AS you remain . . . *MORE RELAXED . . . AND LESS TENSE EACH DAY . . . SO, you will develop MUCH MORE CONFIDENCE IN YOURSELF.*

"*MUCH more confidence in your ability to DO . . . NOT only what you HAVE to do each day, . . . but MUCH more confidence in your ability to do whatever you OUGHT to be able to do . . . WITHOUT FEAR OF CONSEQUENCES . . . WITHOUT UNNECESSARY ANXIETY . . . WITHOUT UNEASINESS. Because of this . . . every day . . . you will feel MORE AND MORE INDEPENDENT . . . MORE ABLE TO 'STICK UP FOR YOURSELF, . . . TO STAND UPON YOUR OWN FEET . . . TO 'HOLD YOUR OWN' . . . no matter how difficult or trying things may be. And, because all these things WILL begin to happen . . . EXACTLY as I tell you they will happen, you will begin to feel MUCH HAPPIER . . . MUCH MORE CONTENTED . . . MUCH MORE CHEERFUL . . . MUCH MORE OPTIMISTIC . . . MUCH LESS EASILY DISCOURAGED . . . MUCH LESS EASILY DEPRESSED.*"

These are broad suggestions that cover most problems. The therapist may interpolate specific suggestions in accord with the special needs of the patient.

Now relax and rest for a minute or so, going deeper, d-e-e-p-e-r, d-e-e-p-e-r, and in a minute or so I shall talk to you, and you will be more deeply relaxed. [*Pause for one minute.*]

In summary, there are four things we are going to accomplish as a result of these exercises, the 4S's: symptom relief, self-confidence, situational control and self-understanding. First, your various symptoms [*enumerate*] are going to be less and less upsetting to you. You will pay less and less attention to them, because they will bother you less and less. You will find that you have a desire to overcome them more and more. As we work at your problem, you will feel that your self-confidence grows and expands. You will feel more assertive and stronger. You will be able to handle yourself better in any situations that come along particularly those that tend to upset you [*enumerate*]. Finally, and most importantly, your understanding of yourself will improve. You will understand better

and better what is behind your trouble, how it started and why your symptoms developed. Whenever you feel your symptoms coming on you will be better able to understand what is bringing them about, and you will be able to do something constructive about this, more and more easily. You will continue working on what is behind your problem. [*Pause.*]

You should play the recording at least twice daily. The time is up to you. Remember it makes no difference if you are just pleasantly relaxed, or in a deep state, or asleep, the suggestions will still be effective. [*Pause.*]

Relax and rest and, if you wish, give yourself all the necessary suggestions to *yourself* to feel better. Using the word "you." Take as long as you want. Then you can go to sleep or arouse yourself. When you are ready, you will arouse *yourself* no matter when that is, by counting slowly to yourself from one to five. You will be completely out of it then—awake and alert. Remember, the more you practice, the more intense will be your response, the more easily will your resistances give way. Keep on practicing. And now go ahead—relax—and *when* you are ready—wake *yourself* up.

If a recording is being made, the machine may now be turned off. The patient may be able to arouse himself or herself as desired, or, if too long a period transpires, the patient may be aroused by saying:

Now, when I count to five, you will be awake. Your eyes will open, you will feel alert and well. One . . . [*pause*] . . . two [*pause*] . . . three . . . [*pause*] . . . four . . . [*pause*] . . . five . . . Lift your eyes.

The above induction may prove invaluable in short-term therapy and if it is recorded on an audiotape and given to the patient to talk about the posthypnotic feeling gains made during the active period of therapy. Understandably, as directive as it is, hypnosis will stimulate transference responses, positive and negative. Asking the patient to talk about the posthypnotic feelings may elicit material that can be useful to work productively with resistances and defenses. A dynamically oriented therapist may ask for dreams and associations and often the reactions of the patient to the hypnotic induction will open up interesting areas for exploration. Suggestions given a patient to dream will usually expedite dream reporting. This is especially helpful in patients who do not remember their dreams. Sometimes a suggestion to redream a forgotten dream during hypnosis may restore the memory; while dreams distorted by secondary elaborations may be corrected, or forgotten fragments reassembled. During hypnosis a patient may be directed to dream about selected subjects such as feelings about certain people, including the therapist.

Other Induction Methods

Other induction techniques may be employed although the foregoing induction method may be all that the therapist needs to use. Elsewhere, detailed accounts of trance induction have been elaborated (Wolberg, LR, 1948, pp. 98–185; 1964a, pp. 31–67). In brief, the required steps are these:

1. Promoting motivations that will lead to hypnosis by associating the desire to get well with cooperation in the hypnotic process.
2. Removing misconceptions and fears about hypnosis by explanation and clarification.
3. Introducing a suggestibility test, like the hand clasp test, to demonstrate that the patient can follow directions.
4. Giving the patient a short preparatory talk to the effect that the patient will not really go to sleep, even though sleep suggestions will help one relax, and that one will not be asked embarrassing questions or forced to do anything one does not want to do.
5. Inducing a trance by any chosen method.
6. Deepening the trance by suggest-

ing more and more complex hypnotic phenomena.
7. Making therapeutic suggestions.
8. Awakening the patient.
9. Discussing with the patient his or her trance experiences.

One of the easiest ways of inducing hypnosis is by means of the suggestibility test of the hand clasp. To do this, the patient is made comfortable in an armchair and asked to relax the body progressively, starting with the muscles in the forehead, then the face, neck, shoulders, arms, back, thighs, and legs. Following this, the patient is enjoined to clasp the hands, a foot or so away from the eyes. With eyes fixed on the hands, the hands are clasped together more and more firmly as the therapist counts from one to five stating that then, it will be difficult or impossible to separate the hands. After the patient has cooperated with this suggestion, the patient is to stare at the hands while the eyes begin to feel tired and the eyelids heavy. The eyelids progressively will get heavier and heavier until the eyelids feel like lead. The eyes will soon close and a pleasant sense of relaxation will sweep over the patient. These suggestions are repeated over and over in a monotonous cadence and in a firm, reassuring tone until the eyes close. The hands are then unclasped with or without the help of the therapist.

An effective way of inducing a deep trance is by means of hand levitation (Wolberg, 1948). This method is more difficult to master than the other techniques and calls for greater effort and persistence on the part of the therapist. With the patient's hands resting lightly on the thighs, the patient is asked to concentrate attention on everything the hands do. Sensations will be noticed, such as the warmth of the palms of the hands against the thighs, the texture of clothing, and perhaps the weight of the hands pressing on the thighs. Then the fingers will wiggle a little. As soon as this happens, the finger that moved first should be raised. Then the patient is commanded to raise the finger that moved first. Thereafter, gazing at the right hand it is anticipated that the fingers will fan out, the spaces between the fingers getting wider and wider. When this happens, suggestions are made that the fingers will slowly lift from the thigh; then the hand will rise as the arm becomes lighter and lighter; the eyes will become tired and the lids heavy. However, much as he or she wants to, the patient is not to fall asleep until the arm rises and the hand touches the face. As one gets more and more relaxed, and the lids get heavier and heavier, the arm and hand will get lighter and rise higher until it touches one's face. When it touches the face, the patient will be relaxed and drowsy and the eyes will be firmly shut. Suggestions are repeated constantly until they are acted on by the patient. Asking the patient to imagine a string tied around one or both wrists with a balloon at the free end which rises and pulls the hands up until they touch the face, at which point one will fall asleep, is sometimes also effective.

The traditional method of hypnosis through staring at a fixation object continues to be useful. Here a coin, pencil, or shiny object is held above the head, the patient being asked to stare at it while suggestions are made to the effect that one is getting sleepy, that one's eyes begin to water, and one's lids blink until one no longer can keep the eyes open.

As soon as the eyelids close by the use of any of the above methods, the trance may be deepened by suggesting, progressively, heaviness and stiffness of the left arm (limb catalepsy), heaviness of the lids until the patient cannot open them (lid catalepsy), inability to move the extremities or to get out of the chair (inhibition of voluntary movements), hyperesthesia of the hand, anesthesia of the hand, and, perhaps, auditory and visual hallucinations. Some

therapists do not go through the formality of deepening hypnosis (the first method of trance induction through muscle relaxation described above illustrates this). However, if probing techniques are to be employed, it is wise to induce as deep hypnosis as possible (see Wolberg 1948, 1964a). As to the actual syndromes helped by hypnosis, many therapists find that is valuable in the following ways:

1. As a means of removing certain conversion symptoms, like paralysis, aphonia, and some psychophysiologic reactions.
2. As a way of controlling the drinking urge in some alcoholic patients.
3. As a vehicle of establishing the authority of the therapist, which the patient does not dare to defy, thus inhibiting acting-out, especially in psychopathic personalities.
4. As a means of bolstering persuasive therapy in obsessive-compulsive reactions.
5. As treatment for certain habit disorders, like smoking, sexual difficulties, insomnia, overeating, and nail biting.
6. As a mode of reinforcing desensitization and counterconditioning in behavior therapy, as in phobias.

During insight therapy hypnosis may result in the following:

1. Removal of amnesia in post-traumatic stress reactions with release of repressed memories and emotions.
2. Lifting of repression in conversion and dissociative reactions.
3. Resolution of repression in the treatment of other conditions, like anxiety reactions and phobic reactions.
4. Dissipation of certain transference and content resistances.
5. Facilitation of dreams and free associations.

In supportive therapy, where an authoritarian relationship cannot be set up with facililty, hypnosis may put the therapist in a sufficiently omnipotent position to produce better results.

There is another use of hypnosis that has not received the attention it deserves, that is, as an experience in relationship. All therapy requires the establishing of a working relationship between therapist and patient. It is impossible, without good rapport, to help the patient to an understanding of the problem and to the resolution of the manifold resistances in utilizing insight in the direction of change. The mere induction of a trance produces a feeling of closeness and trust in a remarkably short time, resolving certain transference resistances and enabling the patient to proceed toward the exploration of anxiety-provoking inner conflicts. In some patients one may employ hypnosis at the start of therapy, and once a relationship has crystallized, one may go on to implement the traditional psychotherapies without hypnosis. This may cut down on the time required for the establishing of a working relationship.

Another technique utilized occasionally during the exploratory phase of therapy is the training of the patient in self-hypnosis, suggesting that one will investigate spontaneously, through dreams and fantasies in the self-induced trance state, puzzling aspects of the problem and also that one will work out various resistances that may arise. In this way the patient actively participates in the investigative process and time may be saved. The first induction method above may easily be adapted to self-hypnosis. More details may be found elsewhere (Wolberg LR, 1964a). Self-hypnosis may be employed on a maintenance basis where necessary. Qualms about its use need not be felt; addiction to and dependency on self-hypnosis has not occurred in my experience. Appendix V contains an outline for self-relaxation that may be given to the patient. Practice may result in the capacity for self-hypnosis.

Symptom removal through hypnosis should not pose undue risks. The consequences will depend on the way the removal took place and the attitude of the hypnotist. One does not rush into a complex psychiatric picture like a bull in a china shop. Unfortunate aftermaths are usually the product of a disturbed relationship rather than the result of hypnosis. Unsettling reactions to hypnosis do not seem to be greater than untoward responses to any other therapeutic relationship. A study by Litton (1966) of 19 cases of hysterical aphonias was undertaken to test the hypothesis that rapid removal of a symptom will eventuate in substitutive symptoms or in the precipitation of a breakdown in homeostasis. Removal of the symptom through hypnosis was successful in 14 cases and resisted in 5. Follow-up showed no unpleasant sequelae. In 2 cases there was a return of the symptom after 7 months, and in 1 case after 12 months. Readministration of hypnosis rapidly removed the symptom. As explained before, hypnosis provides a dynamic interpersonal situation that evokes processes in the patient that may be productively examined as a biopsy of how the patient responds to an intensive interpersonal relationship. The patient will project into the hypnotic situation his or her basic defenses and demands. Responses to hypnotic induction, and to the trance experience itself, may constitute the material around which the therapeutic work is organized. The specific meaning to the patient of being put into a trance can bring forth various irrational defenses and fears. For instance, a patient with frigidity was referred to me by her psychoanalyst for some hypnotic work. After the third induction, the patient revealed that she was aware of her need to keep her legs crossed during the entire trance state. So tightly did she squeeze her thighs together that they ached when she emerged from the trance. Prior to the next induction, I instructed her to keep her legs separated. As I proceeded with suggestions, she became flushed, opened her eyes, and exclaimed that she knew what upset her. I reminded her of her grandfather who, on several occasions, when she was a small child, tossed her into bed and held her close to his body. She had felt his erect penis against her body, which both excited her and frightened her. It became apparent that the hypnotic experience constituted for her an episode during which she hoped for and feared a repetition of this sexual seduction, and her leg crossing constituted a defense against these fantasies. Continued trance inductions desensitized her to her fears and were followed by an improved sexual functioning with her husband.

The hypnotic situation may also enable the patient to recall important past experiences. A man of 45 years with a claustrophobic condition of 10 year's duration was referred by an analyst who had treated the patient for several years. While his analysis (four times weekly for $2\frac{1}{2}$ years) had enabled the patient to mature considerably in his relationship with people, the phobic problem remained as an obstinate block to the financial success he potentially could achieve in his business. The phobia made it impossible for him to dine with people, and, whenever he was forced in a situation in which he had to eat with others, he excused himself several times during the meal so that he could go to the bathroom to disgorge his food.

The patient was inducted into a hypnotic state, and the suggestion was made that he would go back to the period in his life when he had first experienced a feeling similar to that in his phobia. After several minutes had gone by, it became apparent from his sweating, bodily movements, and moaning that the patient was undergoing a profound emotional reaction. Asked to talk, he murmured, in a voice scarcely audible:

I have a peculiar feeling; the chair is narrow and you are closer. I get a good feeling, a secure feeling [*breaks out into crying*]; my father, I hated him. He rejected me. He was very critical.

He never praised me for anything. There was something in him that wouldn't permit him to like me. I hate him. I hate him. [*The patient beats the side of the chair.*] I feel all choked up. I think of my mother. I am little. I see her [*compulsive crying*].

[*On being brought back to the waking state, the patient exclaimed*] This is one of the most remarkable experiences I ever had. This peculiar feeling. I felt the chair was much narrower than it is and that you were getting closer. I felt a good feeling, a secure feeling, like I sometimes felt when I went to see my analyst. But then something happened. I see myself in a restaurant with my parents, a child. I am that child. I am downstairs eating lobster. I felt as if I was going to throw up, and I didn't want to throw up at the table. I kept it in and went into a panic. I thought of my father. I hated him. He rejected me. He was extremely critical. He never praised me for anything. Something in him that wouldn't permit him to compliment me. When I was 3 or 4 years old, mother used to push food into me and I used to vomit it. When I was 10, I had polio and I was afraid to be alone. I was afraid to let Mother go out. I was afraid that something would happen to her. If an accident occurred, what would happen to me? I was afraid to stay alone. I had great anxiety until she came home. Before I was 13 I wasn't allowed to go myself. My mother was a terrific worry-wart about my physical condition and about where I was at nighttime.

The patient's recall of his early traumatic incident enabled us to get into other intimacies. An important one was his relationship with his analyst. It became apparent that he had become bogged down in transference resistance. Discussing this appeared to change his feeling toward his analyst, from one of resentment to that of gratitude that he had been helped significantly in many dimensions. Soon he desensitized himself to the phobic situation.

In working with resistances to giving up symptomatic complaints, the way suggestions are made may help avoid precipitating too much anxiety. If the therapist feels the patient is unable to tolerate recovery for the moment, one may say: (1) "Perhaps there is some information you do not wish to tell me at this time. It is all right to hold this back until the next time you see me or whenever you are ready." Or (2) "I wonder how long it will be before you will want to let yourself give up these uncomfortable symptoms. I do not want you to give them up all at once. Try hard to hold on to one bit of your symptom and not to let it disappear for at least a week or so after you feel comfortable.''

In reconstructive therapy hypnosis may be employed to expedite free association in patients who are blocked. It may also foster dream recall. A patient came to me for hypnosis to help her recover a dream that kept eluding her, but which she felt was significant. It had first appeared, she claimed, a long time ago during her psychoanalysis, but she had forgotten it. Try as hard as she could, she was not able to bring it back. Years had gone by after she had stopped her analysis, but periodically she had the impression that the dream returned, only to vanish with daylight. The situation intrigued her and she asked for referral for hypnosis, during which I told her that if she had a spontaneous dream, she would remember it. On awakening she revealed that a most interesting thing had happened to her while she was relaxing. The meaning of the forgotten dream had flashed through her mind.

"All of a sudden I realized that the dream was that I was all alone and I don't want to be alone. I don't want to be alone. I shed copious tears.'' This experience brought about a "heavy sadness'' which haunted the patient for several days. A spontaneous dream followed: "I go over the rooms that we lived in as a child. The rooms are empty. I'm all alone. Where is everybody? My mother, father, sister, brothers, where are they? There is nobody there. Ours was a busy house. Copious tears.'' Burdened by an even deeper depressive feeling to which she could not associate in the waking state, the patient was rehypnotized and requested to say what was on her mind. She replied: "Please everybody, please everybody, come back, come back. Don't leave me alone again.

What did I do, what did I do that this should happen.'' In bitter tears she revealed a memory of having as a tiny child been sent to a hospital after burning herself. Separation from her mother for a protracted period had initiated fear that she would be punished and sent away if she did "anything bad.'' The traumatic incident (which was validated) was followed by separation of her father from her mother when she was 3 years of age, for which the patient blamed herself unfairly. Therapy including teaching the patient self-hypnosis, during which she was enjoined to revive these images, to master the emotions related to them, and to revalue them in her mind. It was through this means that she desensitized herself. Ultimately her depression was resolved. Hypnotically induced dreams may, in this way, where insight is fragmented, serve to weave unrelated mental threads into a meaningful fabric.

A case illustration of how hypnosis may aid in the uncovering process, with a recording of hypnosis through the handclasp method, may be found in Chapter 44; page 744.

NARCOTHERAPY (NARCOSYNTHESIS, NARCOCARTHARSIS, NARCOANALYSIS)

The difficulty of inducing hypnosis in certain subjects, the relatively long time required to produce a trance even in susceptible persons, and the inability on the part of some therapists to acquire skill in trance induction, some time ago brought into prominence a simple technique of promoting hypnosis by the intravenous injection of a hypnotic drug, such as, Sodium Amytal (sometimes called the "Amytal interview'') or Sodium Penthothal (Horsley, 1936, 1943; Grinker & Spiegel, 1945; Sargant & Shorvon, 1945; Hoch & Polatin, 1952). It was most prominently used for the therapy of traumatic neurosis (Posttraumatic Stress Disorder) during and after World War II.

Injected narotic substances produce a cortical depression with relaxation and heightened susceptibility to suggestion, reassurance, and persuasion. The name given to this combined use of narcosis and supportive therapy is "narcosuggestion." The psychologic regression in narcosis, as in hypnosis, incites archaic dependency feelings toward the therapist and expedites authoritative supportive procedures. Acute anxiety reactions, some manic and catatonic reactions which constitute emergencies, or assaultive or self-destructive tendencies may sometimes be approached by narcosuggestion as may other conditions that call for supportive measures. In very resistent phobias the patient, in a light state of narcosis, may be exposed to counterconditioning techniques of behavioral therapy, for instance to Wolpe's "reciprocal inhibition" technique (see Chapter 51). As a diagnostic aid narcotherapy is sometimes employed to unmask a schizophrenic tendency that is concealed by defensive reactions in the waking state. This can help in treatment planning.

Releasing of cortical inhibition liberates charges of pent-up emotion that have been kept from awareness by repression. The result is an emotional catharsis. This effect may also be facilitated in narcosis by suggestion, by persistent questioning and probing, and by encouraging the patient to explore painful areas of his or her life. Recollection of repudiated traumatic memories and experiences may remove mental blocks, flurries of anxiety, depression, and psychosomatic symptoms associated with the repression of such harassing foci. These effects have been found helpful in the treatment of certain emotional problems, particularly acute stress reactions, (transportation and industrial accidents, catastrophes like floods and fire, and war neuroses), and some anxiety and hysterical reactions. In the war neuroses, particularly, beneficial results are possible especially in cases of recent origin treated before rigid defenses have organized themselves. The working through of the repressed or suppressed material in both narcotic and waking states helps to insure the permanency of the "cure." In chronic war and civilian neuroses, however, the patient does not seem to benefit so readily, since the illness has structuralized itself and stubborn resistances block progress. Another effect of drug interviews is to release pleasant positive feelings, which I. Stevenson et al. (1974) have found is conducive to symptomatic improvement. The effect of narcosis consequently can be both emotionally releasing as well as sedating depending on whether exposure is to challenging confrontations or calming suggestions.

While narcotherapy is principally employed for purposes of short-term therapy, it is sometimes introduced during the course of long-term insight psychotherapy where little material is forthcoming or obdurate resistance blocks the exploratory effort. Here one may occasionally save a treatment situation that has come to a stalemate by inducing narcosis and liberating repressive forces through concerted probing. Transference phenomena that have evaded both patient and therapist sometimes become dramatically operative as emotionally charged material is released. An emergency use of narcotherapy is in the sedating of acute uncontrollable anxiety and panic states that occur during the course of long-term therapy. These symptoms may be so severe that they threaten the therapeutic relationship. In obsessional neurosis, for instance, occasional sessions of light narcosis may prevent alarming reactions at phases when defensive forces subside too rapidly. The secret of narcosynthesis in chronic neurosis lies in the facilitated communication that it induces in severely repressed patients.

Where repressed incidents are of relatively recent origin, cathartic release may provide a dramatic improvement or cure. However, in most cases a structuralization of traumatic events has occurred, barricaded by many defenses, including protective character traits, so that the exposure during narcosis (no matter how dramatic the results) seems to do little for the patient. It is essential, therefore, as soon as the patient is capable of remembering seemingly important events to subject this material to repeated examination in the waking state, particularly probing for associated emotions. During this process periodic sessions with narcosis may be helpful. Should anxiety be strong or repression too interfering, the anxieties and defensive reactions may yield, and the need for narcosis will then be unnecessary.

Another use of narcosis is to expedite the induction of hypnosis in resistant subjects. During narcosis it may be possible to give patients suggestions to the effect that they will be susceptible to hypnosis. Suggestions must be detailed and specific, covering every aspect of the induction process. For example, the patient may be told when shown a fixation object, the eyes will water, lids will get heavy, the breathing will deepen, and sleep will get deeper and deeper. They will be as deeply asleep as at present. These suggestions should be repeated and the patient may be asked if he or she understands what to do. If confusion exists, the suggestions should be repeated when the drug effect is not so pronounced. As soon as the patient understands what is expected, he or she is asked to repeat what will happen at the next session. After the narcotic session, and before the patient is fully awake, he or she is shown the fixation object and given suggestions that the next time the object is presented drowsiness will occur faster and more deeply. Again, before leaving the room, this suggestion is repeated. The technique works best when positive transference phenomena are operative in the narcotic state. It may not succeed in the event the patient does not understand what to do, or if the patient is in a state of hostile resistance.

Induction of Narcosis

The actual technique of inducing narcosis is simple. Most therapists consider amobarbital sodium (Amytal) the drug of choice. There are various techniques of administration. Sodium Amytal is supplied in sterile powder form in ampules. Ampules of sterile water are also available. The 500-mg (7$\frac{1}{2}$ gr) size of Amytal size is generally utilized, sterile water being added while rotating (not shaking) the ampule to dissolve the drug. It is important to employ fresh solutions (no older than 30 minutes) and to see to it that they are clear (not cloudy). Rarely some patients require large amounts of the drug, and a second ampule of 7$\frac{1}{2}$ gr may be necessary. A small gauge intravenous needle attached to a large syringe is used for administration. The injection should be slow, about 1 cc per minute, to avoid depressing the respiration. While the injection takes place, the patient is asked to count backward from 100 to 1. When the patient becomes confused, mumbles, or stops counting, the injection should stop and treatment begun, such as questioning the patient about feelings, attitudes, and memories. Should too great anxiety intervene, more drug is slowly injected. However, in many cases reassurance that one will feel better after talking will alone suffice without the need for further sedation. The patient may be given interpretations and suggestions that one can if one wishes remember any of the material talked about after awakening or forget it until ready to talk about it. The patient may be requested to remember dreams. After the narcotic session he or she may be allowed to rest or sleep. An ampule of methamphetamine or similar stimulant is held in readiness in the event of respiratory embarrassment, and at the termination of the interview it may be introduced to facilitate awakening. Some therapists inject the 20 mg of methamphetamine intravenously at first. Slowly then, through the same needle, sodium Amytal (500 mg in 20 cc sterile water) is injected until drowsiness and dysarthia appear. Or, 500 mg of sodium Amytal in 9 cc sterilized distilled water are combined with a 20 mg ampule of amphetamine and introduced intravenously at the rate of 1 cc per minute.

Various drugs have been employed instead of amobarbital. Penothal sodium (supplied in sterile vials) and injected at the rate of 2 cc per minute is a common substitute, the dosage (approximately the same as Amytal) varying with individual patients. Methohexital sodium (Brevital), a short-acting barbiturate, is another substitute being supplied in sterile powder in ampules of 500 mg, 2.5 g, and 5 g. It may be utilized as a continuous drip, 500 mg of Brevital being added to 250 cc of sterile isotonic sodium chloride solution. This provides a 0.2 percent solution. For slow intermittent injection a 1 percent solution is used titrating the amount injected against the reaction of the patient. Sometimes methamphetamine is given intravenously following a intravenous drip of Brevital (Green, DO, & Reimer, 1974). Scarborough and Denson (1958) described a Pentothal-Desoxyn combination similar to that of Rothman and Sward (1956).

Because of the abuse potential, injectable Desoxyn is no longer available. If a substitute amphetamine can be found, this may be employed in proper dosage.

Methylphenidate hydrochloride (Ritalin) has been found helpful in breaking through blocks in the exploration of the problems of alcoholics (Hartert & Browne-Mayers, 1958). Exploratory interviews are carried out after intravenous injection of 20 to 40 mg of the drug. The patients respond by verbalizing freely with greater introspection and critical self-evaluation as well as more intensive involvement in the therapeutic situation. Since Ritalin in injectable form is not now available, oral administration prior to interviews may be considered with caution since Ritalin may be substituted by the alcoholic for alcohol.

In the course of narcotherapy, as has been mentioned previously, drug injections should be halted temporarily if the patient gets excessively incoherent. Should the patient become too alert, more drug is introduced. It goes without saying that adequate preparations must be made for the patient so that one can sleep off the effects of the medication.

In the event psychotic material is brought up during narcosis, giving evidence of a potential disintegrative tendency, therapeutic goals and methods should be reappraised. Where the patient becomes too upset through release of traumatic material, it is best not to let the excitement mount to the point of overtaxing the ego. More drug is injected to put the patient to sleep, which will enable one to overcome the cathartic effects of the narcosis.

The therapist questioning the patient during narcosis may have to utilize a firm authoritative tone. In posttraumatic stress disorders especially, one builds a dramatic word picture that approximates the original traumatic scene: military combat, rape, assault, fire, accident, flood, earthquake, etc. Kolb and Mutalipassi (1932) have introduced an audio tape with battle noises during narcosis which almost immediately may bring the veteran with combat stress back to the traumatic event. Abreaction takes many forms ranging from controlled talking about the fearsome incident to a violent acting out—muscularly, emotionally, verbally—the anxieties and fantasies that are being repressed. Sufficient time should be set aside to discuss with the patient feelings and memories after one comes out of narcosis. Generally, repeated sessions of narcosis tend to desensitize the patient allowing the repressed incident to be faced with diminished fear. Some therapists make audiotapes and videotapes of the narcotic sessions which they play back to their patients, and this stimulates animated discussions and provides material for interpretation. It goes without saying that individual and group psychotherapy are important following narcosynthesis in order to deal with the personality vulnerabilities that have predisposed the patient to the dissociative reactions displayed following the trauma.

Narcosis should be avoided in patients with manifest or latent porphyria, or who have liver, cardiac, respiratory or kidney disease. It should not be used in persons who are or were addicted to sedatives or hypnotics. Because of the danger of respiratory depression some therapists prefer to have the acutal narcosis done by a trained anesthesiologist who can stand by in case of emergencies.

VIDEOTAPE RECORDING

Videotape technology has been advancing at a rapid rate and it is being adapted to increasing areas of health and science. Among its many possibilities are self-observation and self-confrontation (Berger MM, 1971; Melnick & Tims, 1974, Roche Report, 1973, 1974a), which have been applied to the teaching and learning situation (Torkelson & Ramano, 1967). The evolvement of video psychiatry has followed in the wake of this. Videotapes are being produced to teach psychopathology, child development, and psychiatric treatment. A cassette entitled "Electronic Textbook of Psychiatry" has been prepared by the New York State Psychiatric Institute's Department of Educational Research. Written linear programmed texts are being arranged with interdigitating videotaped clinical illustrations to enliven the teaching of psychiatry. [See section on selected videotapes.]

The recording of psychotherapy sessions with opportunity for repeated playback offers patients an unparalleled learning experience that can catalyze the entire therapeutic process. As recorders and cameras have become less and less expensive, the video adjunct has been employed with increasing frequency in clinics and private practice, particularly in group, family, and marital therapy (Alger & Hogan, 1969; Czajkoski, 1968; Danet, 1969; Stoller, 1967, 1969). In behavior therapy (Bernal, 1969; Melnick & Tims, 1974), and in role playing and psychodrama, its employment is proving valuable. In selected cases persons in individual therapy may find self-observation of substantial value (Geertsma & Reivich, 1965; Paredes et al, 1969). An additional dividend is the fact that a therapist may observe one's own therapeutic performance and interpersonal conduct including countertransference, which can enhance one's own development and sharpen one's skills. The objective data issuing from even fragments of a single session can provide material for study and discussion over weeks and months. Progress or regress may also be scrutinized by comparing the productions of successful sessions. The videotape recording may also be utilized for the purpose of supervising a therapist's work, providing more authentic data than can be conveyed orally by the therapist.

The technique is simple. There is no need to conceal the equipment because after going through the preliminary brief anxiety and self-consciousness phases, patients readily make an adaptation to videotaping. For use of the tape in therapy, 10 minutes of the beginning of the session may be recorded and then played back through the monitor, or recording may be started when a significant period of the session is being approached. The patients are instructed to interrupt the playback if they wish to comment on discrepancies of behavior or if they desire to describe the feelings that they had at the time or have now.

Replay of small segments over and over may be rewarding either for the purposes of clarification and discussion or for desensitization where patients manifest a "shock" reaction at their images. Most patients are surprised at how often their appearance and behavior fails to reveal their shyness, anger, fear, distress, and other emotions. They become sensitive to the pervasive contradictory and paradoxical communications from verbal and nonverbal sources. For example, some patients are not aware of how angry, argumentative, and unpleasant they are in an interpersonal situation until they objectively see and listen to themselves. Opportunities for clarification, heightened awareness, and more constructive reactions are many. Where, as in group, family, or marital therapy, a patient's responses have been maladaptive and the patient realizes this, one may benefit from repeatedly playing back sessions to grasp incongruities of messages. Patients may be asked to try to repeat messages until they communicate clearly. Should resistance develop in therapy or a stalemate have been reached, videotaping may open up dimensions that succeed in breaking through the block. The availability of split-screen and special-effects generators through which one may obtain video multiimage distortions to elicit repressed material is an interesting new use for this adjunct (Roche Report, 1973). Original and unique ways of employing tapes are being elaborated by researchers and clinicians, and innovations will undoubtedly continue to emerge. These eventually will provide material for scientifically controlled studies to test their utility and validity.

Melnick and Tims (1974) make some excellent suggestions regarding the physical surroundings and equipment for videotaping. The room should be of ample size to accommodate comfortably the patients while providing enough space to operate the camera. It should be well ventilated. Generally a 15 feet by 18 feet size is good for a group of 8 to 10 people. If a group is the subject, the patients are seated in a semicircle with the open end accommodating the camera. Sound-absorbing materials and furniture in the room, such as accoustic tile on the ceiling, carpeting on the floor, draperies on the windows, and cloth covered chairs help the acoustics. As to selection of equipment, various machines are readily available. One-half inch decks and video cameras are available at moderate price and are usually ample for the average psychotherapist. A camera with a zoom lens will require an operator to focus on the entire group and on individuals. The operator can be the therapist, cotherapist, or a group member. Where taping is on the entire group and not on individuals, selecting a camera with a wide-angle lens (12.5 mm) is convenient since once set up it does not need an operator. The best microphone is an omnidirectional dynamic table microphone placed on a table or microphone stand. A monitor for the video and sound signals is the final piece of equipment, and for this purpose an ordinary television set is usually ample. Additional optional equipment is also available, such as the use of two cameras with a camera switcher, split-screen apparatus, a special-effects generator, and a second recorder with an electronic editor, where tapes are to be used for educational purposes. The original choice of equipment should allow for expansion with optional items should the latter be contemplated. If one cannot afford or utilize the most sophisticated apparatus, the simple portable one-half-inch deck and an inexpensive camera and microphone are sufficient, and they may well merit an investment.

THE TELEPHONE

Discrete use of the telephone as an adjunctive device is valuable in emergencies that arise in the course of psychotherapy. These fortunately are rare. Therapists may, for their patients' own good and for their own peace of mind, discourage patients calling for anything other than severe problems that cannot await solution until the next treatment session. Should it become apparent that the patient is taking advantage of the privilege of discrete telephoning, the therapist may focus during interviewing on the patient's need for telephone contact. The patient may be reminded that making one's own decisions during therapy is both strengthening and helpful even where such decisions do not turn out well since this provides material for exploration. If the patient is given sanction to telephone at will the flood of inconsequential calls that can result will very likely annoy the therapist and create severe resentments; this annoyance will adversely affect relations with the patient. In addition, if allowed at all, the therapist may be unable to stop the calls without hurting the working relationship.

There are several exceptions, however, to the rule. First, patients with a suicidal tendency do need the assurance of immediate contact when necessary. Here the therapist may have to insist that the patient telephone when too depressed. The lives of many patients have been saved by their ability to communicate with the therapist in crisis situations, and prior to the effective working of prescribed psychotropic drugs. Moreover, should the patient have taken an overdose of drugs, unintentially or with suicidal design, reporting this will enable the therapist to call an ambulance or the police to bring the patient to an emergency unit of a hospital for therapy. Second, patients for whom drug therapy has been prescribed should routinely be requested to telephone if they have peculiar or upsetting reactions to the medication. Hypotension, symptoms of blood dyscrasias, and severe dystonic reactions may need immediate medical intervention.

It goes without saying that the telephone is a vital therapeutic instrument for crisis intervention (Lester & Brockopp, 1973; Williams T, 1971). "Hotlines" exist in larger cities where young polydrug abusers, suicidally inclined persons, rape victims, and others seeking help for some misfortune or for general information can make contact with knowledgeable persons for guidance and counseling. There are for some clients advantages in retaining anonymity over the telephone and also in talking to an anonymous person onto whom the client can project fantasies of a helping person suited to one's needs (Lester D, 1974). It is vital where nonprofessional persons staff such services that they be adequately supervised by professionals. The telephone is an important resource, functioning to provide people with a reassurig human contact and a conduit for referral to available agencies in the community.

Telephone therapy also has a place where patients, for one reason or another, are unable for physical reasons to come to treatment in person (Miller WB, 1972; Robertiello, 1972). There are times where ill health, or absence of transportation, or travel away from home makes it impossible for a patient in psychotherapy to keep appointments, and yet a continuity of treatment is vital. Interestingly, a telephone may make it easier for a patient to reveal certain kinds of information than a face-to-face interview, particularly where a transference reaction exists. This may initiate a breakthrough when the patient returns for regular sessions.

PLAY THERAPY

Play therapy provides children with a means of giving vent to conflicts, ideas, and fantasies that they cannot ordinarily verbalize. One may look upon it as a special nonverbal language through which a child communicates. It is, in a certain sense, an acting-out, permitting through varied activities overt, nonverbal expressions to innermost feelings. "Play therapy does not belong to any specific school of therapy. Each therapist must first learn to understand and to master this particular language of the child, and then integrate the mastery of the therapeutic tool with the particular tenet of one's own therapeutic orientation. The child's play, in and by itself, is no more therapeutic than the patient's free associations and relating of dreams. It is the therapist's skill and sensitivity which helps the adult patient to understand the often meaningless stringing together of seemingly unrelated thoughts in free association. In a similar way the child therapist helps the child to understand the real meaning behind his spontaneous play activities '' (Woltman 1959).

Children, in line with their developmental growth, play act and think differently at different age levels. A 3-year-old may be playing with only a single toy, while an 8- or 10-year-old child may build a complicated structure. It must further be recognized that a child will select that kind of play activity which is best suited for the expression of a particular problem. Burning paper, throwing paper airplanes, or playing out elaborate automobile crashes can be properly used in therapy as long as one alerts oneself to the fact that all three activities may constitute an acting-out of aggressive impulses. The specific meanings that play materials and activities have for the child have been described by R. E. Hartley et al. (1952 a & b), who also has summarized play activities of children in terms of year levels (1957). A comprehensive study of children's play activities with miniature life toys has been presented by Lois Murphy (1956). The seminal contributions of schools of therapy to play therapy are found in the writings of Melanie Klein (1935, 1955), Anna Freud (1928), and Virginia Axline (1947), who is a follower of Carl Rogers. Specific play media and activities described many years ago may still be useful in the therapeutic treatment of children (Bender & Woltmann, 1936, 1937; Erickson EH, 1944, 1951; Gondor, 1954;

Lowenfeld, 1939; Lyle & Holly, 1941; Trail, 1945; Whiles, 1941; Woltmann, 1940, 1950, 1951, 1952, 1955, 1956). Play group therapy has been described by Ginott (1961). The free play technique of Gitelson (1939) is helpful in some cases. Where it is difficult to create in the child an attitude that is conducive to spontaneous play, or where specific problems or time limitations play a decisive role, the methods described by Conn (1938), D. Levy (1937, 1939), J. C. Solomon (1938, 1940, 1951), Muro (1968), Nelson (1967), and Nickerson (1973) may be applicable.

The methods of play therapy appear to be particularly suited to the expression of unconscious aggression and to the acting-out of jealousies in relation to a parent or sibling. They are also an excellent media for exploration of sexual and excretory fantasies. The beneficial effects of play therapy in part accrue from the insight patients gain into their drives and problems. More immediately, a child acts out in play, hostile, sexual, excretory, and other fantasies as well as anxiety-provoking life situations. The cathartic effect of play therapy temporarily alleviates tension. This is not as important as the gradual understanding that develops into the nature and effects of unbridled impulses. The noncondemning attitude of the therapist, who neither criticizes nor restricts the patient, but accords the child freedom in expressing overtly impulses and fantasies of a dreaded nature, alleviates guilt feelings, and eventually makes is possible for the child to acknowledge and to tolerate repressed drives. As these are repeatedly acted out in play, the child becomes desensitized to their influence. Understanding and control are developed by the therapist's carefully timed interpretations.

Controversy exists regarding the preferred approach in play therapy. A research study of play therapy some years ago in 298 outpatient child clinics in the United States indicated that 75 percent of the reporting clinics regard their theoretical orientation as psychoanalytic, 17 percent as nondirective, 5 percent as directive, and 3 percent as between directive and nondirective (Filmer & Hillson, 1959). At the same time, the majority of clinics considered Frederick Allen (1942) as the authority most representative of their orientation. Allen, whose concepts, reflecting those of Rank, stressed the relationship fostered through play therapy as the very core of the therapeutic process. This is in contrast with the approach of Melanie Klein (1955 a & b), which bypasses ego defenses and actively and immediately interprets the deep unconscious meanings of the child's play. The less radical approach of Anna Freud (1946) advocates interpretation of unconscious motivation only after a relationship has been established with the child. At the present time there is some shift toward behavioral theory and practice.

ART THERAPY

The use of artistic media, such as drawing, painting, and finger painting, as ways of exploring and working through unconscious conflict has been advocated by many therapists (Arlow & Kadis, 1946; Bender, 1937; Brick, 1944; Fink et al, 1967; Hartley RE, & Gondor, 1956; Levick, 1973; Mosse, 1940; Napoli, 1946, 1947; Naumburg, 1947, 1953, 1966; Schopbach, 1964; Stern, MM, 1952 a & b). These productions, whatever their nature, serve as means of emotional catharsis and as vehicles for revealing inner problems, wishes, and fears. Art therapy is particularly valuable in patients who find it difficult to talk freely. It is predicated on the principle that fundamental thoughts and feelings, derived from the unconscious, often find expression in images rather than in words (Naumburg, 1966). Through art a method of symbolic communication develops between patient and therapist. Though untrained in art, individuals can often project their conflicts into visual forms, to which they may then expeditiously associate freely. Dreams, fantasies, and childhood memories may also more readily be represented in a pictorial way rather than in speech. Patients who are blocked in verbalizing may find that drawing or painting their dreams and fantasies expedites translation of their thoughts and feelings into words. The function of the art therapist, according to many authorities in the past, is not to interpret, but to encourage the patient to discover for oneself the meaning of productions that provide symbolic ways of representing unconscious phenomena (Lewis NDC, 1928; Griffiths, 1935; Fairbairn, 1938a & b; Pickford, 1938; McIntosh & Pickford, 1943). The patient projects in the creations significant emotional meanings. This is very much similar to what happens in the Rorschach test (Vernonon, 1935). Furthermore, the symbolized content permits of an expression of inner impulses without too many guilt feelings. The art therapist accepts the patient's projections without punitive or judgmental responses. Interpretations are offered to the patient at strategic times. Interpretive approaches to art symbols have been described by Appel (1931), Jung (1934), Pfister (1934), Liss (1938), Baynes (1939), Harms (1939, 1941), Reitman (1939), Mira (1940), Naumburg (1944, 1950), and E. Kris (1952). Other informative articles are those of Levy (1934), F. J. Curran (1939), Despert (1937), Mosse (1940), and Bychowski (1947). Traditional concepts about art therapy are still currently accepted.

In the actual technique, the patient may draw or paint during the treatment hour, or may work at home and bring the productions to the therapist. Drawing and painting may be employed not only individually, but also in groups (Naumburg & Caldwell, 1959), being especially valuable in therapy with children (Kramer, 1972).

Simple, easily manipulable art materials must be made available to patients, particularly if they have never drawn or painted. Semihard pastels and casein or poster paints are to be preferred to oil paints. The therapist may have to instruct and encourage beginners by what is known as the "scribble technique." In this the patient is instructed to draw without a conscious plan by making a continuous line which may assume an irregular pattern as it meanders over the paper in various directions. The patient is then encouraged to search for a design, object, animal or person while holding the paper in different directions. Once the patient has done this, he or she is enjoined to work in art as spontaneously as possible using different materials.

Where a patient appears emotionally blocked or does not express appropriate feeling toward a special person or situation, instruction to construct an image or make a drawing representing the person or situation may release productive emotions and associations. The fact that the patient can control the drawings gives one a feeling of greater leverage over affective life. This is especially important in individuals with weak defenses who in being encouraged to draw have an option of how far they wish to go.

An attempt may be made to influence mood by asking the patient to draw something that depicts a special emotion. Thus, a depressed person may be asked to draw a happy scene, an anxiety-ridden soul to depict a relaxed and peaceful sketch. In a more cathartic vein, a patient may be requested to delineate on paper exactly how he or she feels or one would like to express if one could. The patient may also be encouraged, and perhaps helped, to depict the completion of an action essential for one's well-being on the theory that one may through this means symbolize a breakthrough of the stalemate and then respond behaviorally. Sometimes the psychothera-

pist may utilize as an adjunctive helper an art therapist. When such a person is used, regular conferences of the two must be held.

In group therapy some therapists find it useful to suggest that patients draw pictures on a common theme. Comparing the drawings and getting the group members' associations can provide much stimulation and enhance group activity. This technique has also been employed with smaller groups, as in family therapy (Kwiatowska, 1967).

The activity of the therapist in relation to the patient's drawings will vary. One may sit quietly and observe what is being drawn, waiting for the patient's explanations, or may comment on or ask questions about the images, or may interpret what one believes the patient is trying to say. The patient may be encouraged to draw certain items, (i.e., dreams, memories, fantasies, family members, etc.). The therapist may even sketch on the patient's picture or suggest additions or alterations. Questions about the symbols may be asked, and the patient may be encouraged to make associations.

Where a patient responds to images drawn with fear, anger, or detachment, it is likely that he or she has not been able cognitively to integrate what has been produced. This may provide valuable leads for the interview focus. Encouragement to repeat the same theme in drawing may result in therapeutic desensitization and conflict resolution.

There is a tendency among some art therapists to overvalue the medium of communication—the art production—and to confuse the latter with the therapeutic process itself. While therapy may thus be regarded as a constant uncovering phenomenon that brings up interesting material, there may be a denial or minimization of the true therapeutic vehicle—the relationship between patient and therapist. The use of art as an adjunct in therapy is, nevertheless, considered by some analysts as help-ful to patients who express themselves bet-ter in drawing and in other artistic ways than in free association or dreams. While the content of therapy may be focused on the art expression, the therapeutic process goes through the usual phases of transfer-ence and resistance as in any reconstruc-tive form of psychotherapy.

SEX THERAPY

People with sexual problems as their presenting complaint generally are not mo-tivated to seek intensive treatment. What they desire is to function sexually as rapidly and normally as possible. Catering to this wish is a group of new sex therapies (Ka-plan HS, 1974; Leiblum & Pervin, 1980), originated by the research team of Masters and Johnson (1966, 1970), which are short term, behaviorally oriented, and sympto-matically effective for most patients. What some of the authors advocated is a short intensive course of instruction and guid-ance in proper sexual attitudes and tech-niques administered to the patient and his or her sexual partner by a dual-sex team.

This format is undoubtedly an excel-lent one. Some therapists combine behav-ioral methods with exploratory techniques. They encourage their patients to verbalize their fears, guilt feelings, and misgivings and deal with resistances in traditional psy-chotherapeutic ways. Ideally, therapy fol-lowing the intensive initial course continues on a weekly basis for a period until the newly acquired patterns are solidly inte-grated and the patients are able to manage relapses by themselves.

There are obviously advantages to the couples working with the dual-sex thera-peutic team since cooperation of both pa-tient members is more easily obtained, re-sistances can be dealt with directly, misconceptions about sexuality can be ef-fectively brought out in the open, questions about technique are less likely to be dis-torted, and desensitization of embarrass-ment and alleviation of guilt feelings are en-hanced. In many cases the core problem is that of communication, particularly in rela-tion to mutual sexual feelings. Breaking into the facade that sex is dirty, not to be talked about, practiced in the dark, etc. can release both partners and lead to a more natural and spontaneous functioning.

Practical considerations, however, may make it impossible to utilize a dual-sex team, and the therapist may have to operate without a cotherapist. In some cases it will be impossible to get the patient's spouse or sexual partner to come for interviewing. Then the therapist will have to work with the patient alone, briefing him or her on how to instruct and work with the partner. If both partners are available, a 2-week va-cation period to initiate treatment is best since there will be less distractions. Here, too, modifications may be necessary; thus when the couple is ready for sexual exer-cises, a 3- or 4-day holiday may be all that is necessary.

A diagnostic assessment of any sexual problem is vital to the choice of treatment (Wasserman et al, 1980). It is important to determine which of four phases of sexual response is implicated. Is the disorder of one of inhibited desire, or inability to main-tain excitement and genital tumescence, or to control or achieve orgasm, or to achieve postorgasmic relaxation and well-being? (Kaplan and Moodie, 1984; Lief, 1981). Distinction of these phases of sexual re-sponse is important because varying mech-anisms and neural pathways are operative in each and different therapeutic interven-tions may be called for. For example, inhib-ited sexual desire may be the product of guilt about and repression of sexuality pro-duced by overmoralistic promptings in childhood, with consequent needs for self-punishment, indulgence in rape or bondage phantasies and masochistic practices as a condition for the release of sexual feeling. Conquest of these developmentally inspired sexual inhibitions may provoke the individual to imagine or to act out violent fantasies sadistically (sexual sadism), with antisocial behavior serving to subdue or symbolically destroy one's conscience or the projected representations. Guilt feelings and masochistic self-punishment usually follow these releases, but rarely eliminate them. Treatment when sought will require psychotherapy, preferably dynamically oriented, and only later behavioral approaches should sexual functioning continue to fail. Inhibited sexual desire may also be associated with failing release triggers that open the gates to sexual feeling, such as fetishism, transvestism, zoophilia, pedaphilia, exhibitionism and voyeurism, which must be approached psychotherapeutically although prognosis for recovery in these ailments is guarded. Sexual desire can be deadened by ailments like depression. Finally, the relationship with a marital partner may be pathological (e.g., incestuous) or so steeped in ongoing hostility as to deaden all thoughts of sex. Here marital therapy and dynamic psychotherapy may be essential.

Appropriate treatment for all of these foregoing conditions will therefore require accurate diagnosis. In the case of inhibited sexual excitement with frigidity and impotence, once organic factors (endocrinopathies, diabetes, arteriosclerosis, etc.) and medicinal agents (antihypertensives, beta-adrenergic drugs, alcohol, tranquilizers, etc) have been ruled out, behavioral sex therapy may be effective in itself, especially when the onset has been recent or the causes minor. But where personality difficulties exist, or anxieties and phobias are strong, coordinate psychotherapy and behavioral sex therapy may be necessary. The same may be said for inhibited female and male orgasm, premature ejaculation, dyspareunia and functional vaginismus. For the fourth phasic disturbance of inhibited postorgasmic relaxation and well-being, such treatments as cognitive therapy to alter meaning systems, and dynamic psychotherapy to explore conflicts may be useful.

Sexual problems do not occur in isolation. They appear as a manifestation of coordinate physical, marital, interpersonal, or interpsychic difficulties that are overshadowed by the patient's concern with the sexual symptom. The initial successes scored with the traditional behavior approaches consequently have not been as consistently sustained as was originally anticipated (DeAmicis et al, 1984). One difficulty that is now becoming apparent is the symptom of low sexual desire, which is often masked by defective motivation for therapy.

What appear as limited or absent sexual feelings (Kaplan, 1979) are now being recognized as a symptom of emotional disorder. In many cases such sexual inhibitions are the product of repressed fear, anxiety and anger. Application of a probing dynamic approach will usually bring such repressed feelings to the surface. Nonanalysts deal with this dimension by what they call "experiential sensory awareness exercises." The object is to recognize that inhibited sexual desires do not exist as a permanent passive state but are actively being promoted by emotions and attitudes that are in need of clarification and correction. Not only is psychoeducation required to rectify misconceptions about the right to experience pleasure and sexuality, but faulty belief systems and self-statements will require interpretation and restructuring. The action phase of the therapeutic process involves behavioral assignments and that concern the patient and a cooperative partner. Where marital problems exist these will have to be worked out, otherwise therapy will be sabotaged by one or both members. It goes without saying that physical causes of sexual disinterest such as diabetes, depression, use of cardiac medications, etc., will have to be considered in addition to working with psychological factors.

The presence of both members is an essential part of the treatment process. They are given an explanation of the number of sessions that will be involved (usually 15 to 25) and the fact that homework with sexual exercises will be employed. Brief mention may be made that all extramarital affairs, if any, must be halted for treatment to be successful. Readings may be suggested such as Heiman et al. (1976) and Zilbergeld (1973). In addition to meeting with the couple, individual sessions may be necessary. A usual form of therapy involves four phases: (1) experiential sensory awareness, (2) insight, (3) cognitive restructuring, and (4) behavioral assignments (Friedman & Hogan, 1985).

Several sessions of history taking and interviewing to gather relevant data and to clarify misconceptions are customary before starting behavioral conditioning. Important too is determination of what medications an individual is currently taking since heart and blood pressure drugs (e.g., beta-blockers, hydrochlorothiazides, antianginal pills, psychoactive drugs (e.g., tranquilizers, sedatives, antidepressants, neuroleptics), gastrointestinal drugs (e.g., Tagamet, Librax), hormonal drugs (e.g., estrogen, progesterone) and other drugs (e.g., fenfluramine, metronidazole, phenytoin) may cause loss of libido, impotence, ejaculatory dysfunction, and anorgasmia. Consultation with the patient's internist to see whether alternate medications can be prescribed will be important. There are a number of organic conditions, such as diabetes, hypopituitarism, hypothyroidism, vascular disorders, and neurogenic disturbances that may be implicated and that will require correction. Once these factors are eliminated, preliminary sessions may be started. These are best done individually with the partners

since many personal sensitive areas and confidential secrets may be exposed. Where a dual-sex team is used, the male therapist interviews the man and the female therapist interviews the woman. Patients will often ask the therapist not to reveal secrets to their mates. Such material ranges from masturbation to past and present sexual affairs. Some of these confidences are not as dreadful as the patient imagines, and their revelation could clear the air between the couple. However, the therapist must promise (and hold to the promise) not to expose the patient. If it turns out that therapy cannot continue without bringing up the secret, the therapist must ask the patient's permission. But in all likelihood the revelation may not be necessary.

The sexual history should cover the following.

1. The earliest memory of sexual feeling.
2. The kinds of sexual information expounded to the individual as a child.
3. Preparation for and reactions to menstruation in the female and the first ejaculation in the male.
4. The first sexual experience (masturbating or in relation to another person, animal, or object).
5. Sexual feelings toward parents or siblings.
6. Early homosexual or heterosexual activities. (The first sexual experiences are very important and the patient may never have gotten over them).
7. Present sexual behavior and accompanying feelings and fantasies.
8. Sexual dreams.
9. Attitudes toward masturbation.
10. Conditions under which orgasm occurs.
11. If married, the kind of relationship with mate.
12. Tendencies toward promiscuity.

Attitudes toward sexuality should be explored, for example, how the patient feels about kissing of the mouth, breast, body, and genitals, about manual manipulation of the genitals, about mouth-genital contact, and about different sexual positions. What does the patient feel (like, dislike) about the partner? What makes him or her angry? What makes him or her feel sexy? The therapist should look for what positive and pleasurable things are present in the relationship, since these can be reinforced. Often the *way* the patient responds to these questions, the hesitancies, embarrassment, etc., will yield as much information about attitudes as the content of the answers.

The bulk of patients who come for sexual therapy are well motivated. This is very much in their favor and permits the use of short-term approaches. The great majority of these patients can be helped without too great delving into dynamics. The empathic liberated attitude of the therapist coupled with correcting misinformation about sex may in itself suddenly liberate the patient.

Some of the more common questions plaguing patients are the following, suggested answers being indicated.

Q. What is the normal frequency of intercourse?

A. There is no such thing as "normal" frequency. Sexual needs vary with each person and the desire for pleasuring oneself can range from daily to bimonthly.

Q. Doesn't masturbation take away desire for intercourse?

A. If people learn better ways of pleasuring themselves, they engage in self-manipulation less frequently, although they can still derive pleasure from it.

Q. Isn't genital intercourse the most desirable form?

A. Sex has several forms and genital intercourse is certainly desirable, but at times other variations of pleasuring, like oral–genital contact, are indulged by many.

Q. I feel my penis is too small. Isn't this objectionable to women?

A. This is a common foolish concern of many men. The vagina is a flexible organ, accommodating itself and capable of being pleasured by all sizes. If you stop worrying about size and concentrate on pleasure in love-

making, your partner will undoubtedly be more than satisfied.

Perhaps the most important element in the treatment is the manner and attitude of the therapist (or therapeutic team). In working with patients who are seeking to liberate themselves from their sexual fears and inhibitions, the therapist presents as a model of a permissive authority. Therapists have tremendous leverage in working with sexual therapy because they fit into the role of idealized parental figures who can make new rules. An easygoing, noncondemning, matter-of-fact approach is quite therapeutic in its own right. The ideal therapeutic philosophy is that the patient has been temporarily diverted from attaining the true joys of sex and that if there is the desire to do so, it is possible to move toward reaching this goal of enjoyable pleasure without guilt and fear. This posture is difficult to simulate if the therapist has "hang-ups" about sex or harbors Victorian sentiments that harmonize with the patient's particular ideas or misconceptions. Many therapists falsely regard their own sexual attitudes and behavior as a norm. If these are too restrictive, they will prevent a full release of the patient's potentialities.

In brief sexual therapy, countertransference phenomena can fleetingly occur. One must expect that a patient of the opposite sex will sometimes openly or covertly express sexual transference. This is usually handled by a casual matter-of-fact attitude of nonresponse. Problems occur when the therapist is deliberately or unconsciously seductive with patients.

The following concepts will have to be integrated by the patient, hence they should be accepted by the therapist:

1. Sex is a normal and natural function.
2. The primary purpose of sex is pleasure not performance.
3. People have many different ways of pleasuring themselves. They can derive satisfaction through manual manipula-

tion, oral-genital contacts and genital-genital contacts. Unfortunately, the way we are brought up teaches many of us wrong attitudes about sexuality.

4. People have a right to liberate themselves from these crippling attitudes.
5. All people have the potential of enjoying sexuality.

If the therapist has scruples about these concepts, personal inhibitions may be passed on to the patient. Therefore, it may be preferable to refer patients with sexual difficulties to another therapist or team skilled in sexual therapy.

It is important to avoid the words "abnormal" or "pathological" since these may have frightening connotations. It is best to shy away from the word "masturbation" but rather refer to it as "deriving pleasure manually or through fondling the genitals oneself." The term "mutual masturbation" should also be avoided. Instead one may say "pleasuring each other manually." It is advisable to ask the patient, "Are there thoughts or fantasies or objects that turn you on?" People often have wild fantasies and even covet harmless fetishes, symbolic residues of past conditionings, which help them to release sexual feelings. To ridicule or condemn these when they are revealed will serve merely to discourage the patient. The proper therapeutic stance is casually to emphasize that people have different ways of pleasuring themselves. The therapist may say, "For every lock there is a key, and each person has his own key for the release of sexual feeling. If there is something harmless that turns you on, there is nothing to be afraid of or ashamed of." The reason why it is important not to interfere with sexually releasing fantasies is that removing them too soon, before other more satisfactory sexually releasing stimuli are developed, may result in paralyzing inhibitions or in resentments that will drive the patient away from therapy.

The patient should be asked to have a complete physical examination if one has not been recently obtained. There are some physical conditions as has been mentioned that result in impairment of functioning as well as medications that are inhibiting to libido. It may be necessary to reduce or to substitute drugs that are not so sexually incapacitating.

Where a depression exists, antidepressant medications may be necessary (buprion [Wellbutrin] is a good antidepressant here) and instead of inhibiting sexual feeling they may release it. Loss of libido is one of the first signs of a depression. In the case of excessive tension *mild* tranquilization may help. Buspirone (BuSpar) is an anxiolytic that has a minimal adverse effect on sexual feeling.

After taking a history, joint conference of partners and therapist (or dual-sex team) is held with the object of outlining the problem or problems and of discussing effective ways that the partners can participate in helping each other toward a better adjustment. An idea is given the couple about the roles of each, played in the past, that have produced the difficulty. The therapist also comments on the behavior of the couple to each other. Transferential data especially should be looked for: "The way you treat your wife [husband] it seems to me is how you described your mother [father] treated your father [mother]." Empathy must be displayed, and it is urgent to set up as good a working relationship as is possible. Reassurance is important. Sometimes women who have had hysterectomies believe that they will not be able to function sexually again. This mistaken notion should be clarified by the therapist, who may point out that the sexual response has nothing to do with the uterus. People with hysterectomies can function normally sexually. In males who have had suprapublic or transurethral prostatectomies any impotence that follows the operation usually disappears. This information can be reassuring to the prostectomized patient.

It may be advisable to use charts or illustrations to clarify the sex anatomy of male and female, even where no ostensible problems appear to exist. It is astonishing how ignorant some people are of their genital makeup. No matter how sophisticated they may imagine themselves to be, a great gap can exist in their education about how they are built.

Misconceptions will also have to be covered such as (1) that erections and orgasm can be brought on by will power, (2) that all sexual play must lead to intercourse, (3) that orgasms must be simultaneous, (4) that a clitoral orgasm is not an orgasm, (5) that orgasm is always essential during sexual contact, (6) that as one gets older desire for sex disappears.

The couple is then enjoined to start a new mode of sexual communication with each other. The therapist may interject these comments:

1. "Don't ask your spouse what he [she] wants in sex. Start every sentence with 'I want' or 'I would like.' "
2. "Express your feelings rather than act on them. If you are angry, say so. The minute you *act* angry with each other something has gone wrong."
3. "There is no reason not to reveal your performance fears to each other." The couple (or patient) should also be told at the start of therapy: "Until I [we] have given you the permission, to do otherwise, you are to limit your sexual activities to getting turned on with each other. There is to be no real intercourse in the meantime." Pressure removed from the male to penetrate with his penis and the female to have an orgasm may almost immediately lead to penile erections and vaginal lubrication. This can form the basis for fruitful reconditioning of responses.
4. "You will make mistakes, but that is the best way to learn."
5. "You are not to analyze your performance, just let things happen as they will. The goal is pleasure, not how well you are doing."
6. "You don't have to have intercourse to give your partner sexual satisfactions."

The basic first step to be practiced* by the couple is what Masters and Johnson have called "sensate focus." The couple is instructed to begin in privacy the following assignment:

Th. You are, in a comfortably warm room, to get into bed completely undressed. Turn on a soft light.

Some couples have actually never closely looked at each other nude. The partner with the problem, or with the most severe problem, is instructed:

Th. You are to do with him [or her] whatever you always wanted to do, like touching the face, body, thighs, etc. But *not* the breasts or genitals. There is absolutely to be no intercourse. If you do anything that causes discomfort, your partner must tell you. Your partner is to get what he [or she] can get out of it. But the important thing is for you to experience pleasure in what you are doing. Do this for 5 to 15 minutes, no more. Then your partner is to do the same thing with you.

Very often this exercise will mobilize strong sexual feelings. Impotent men will have erections; nonorgasmic women will lubricate: premature ejaculators will maintain an erection.

The couple may also be told that if they get aroused too much, they may pleasure themselves (masturbate) in the presence of each other, but not to the point of orgasm. Couples often lose their guilt and feel released by the therapist giving them "permission" for them to manipulate themselves in the presence of each other.

If the couple is seen only once weekly rather than the intensive 2-week course at the beginning, they may be told to practice "sensate focus" only twice during the week or at the most three times. They may also utilize a warm body lotion if they desire.

After such practice, the couple, seen together, is asked individually what has happened. The therapist may ask: "Describe how you felt when *you* did it; how did you feel when it was done to you." A good deal of benefit that comes from sexual therapy derives from the emotional catharsis that relieves patients of guilt, fear, and shame as they talk about their preoccupations and feelings. The fact that the therapist is empathic toward and noncondemning of past experiences and current fantasies and compulsions helps them to approach their problems from a less defiant and more objective perspective. They get the impression that there is nothing really "bad" or "evil" about what they are thinking, feeling, or doing; rather they feel that they can move ahead toward areas of greater sexual and emotional freedom and fulfillment. The therapist should search for factors that create anxiety and mutual hostilities. If not corrected, these may neutralize the effects of therapy. Where necessary, the therapist supplies data about physiology, prescribes books, and discusses techniques of symptom control. Useful suggestions may be found in the illustrated book by Helen Kaplan (1974). What went right and what went wrong? The accounts will usually vary. If things did not go well, this should be discussed and the couple sent out to repeat the exercises with the addendum: "Each person is to tell the other what he [or she] likes to have done." A common complaint is being ticklish. If this is the case, the ticklish partner should put his (or her) hands over that of the partner who does the stroking. They may be enjoined, "When you are more relaxed, the tickling will cease." Should the couple complain that there was no sexual feeling, they may be told: "This is not a sexual performance. It is a practice session." Successes should be praised but not analyzed.

As soon as this phase has gone well, the couple may be encouraged to practice genital pleasuring. "You may now gently stroke each others' genitals, directing each other as you go along. It is not necessary to have an orgasm unless you want to and are sufficiently stimulated. But spend not more than 15 minutes from the start." The man may be told: "It is enjoyable for a woman to be touched gently on the clitoris. You can put your forearm on her tummy and let your hand fall over the pubis." The woman is to direct the man's hand on her own pubis, the lips, and the clitoris, and tell him when to stop. If the woman does not lubricate, lubrication should be employed especially on the clitoris.

Where an intensive 2-week program is utilized, it may be arranged as follows, varying it according to the reported reactions:

First day: History taking.
Second day: Joint session. Educational explanations. Correcting misconceptions about sex. Directions about "sensate focus."
Third day: Round table (therapists and couple) to discuss reactions. Directions to examine each other avoiding genitals and breast.
Fourth day: More sensate focus. If no anxiety, genitals may be included.
Fifth day: Sensate focus with stimulation of genitals, but not to orgasm. Orgasm may be reached by pleasuring self if desired.
Sixth day: If no anxiety is reported, a mutually pleasurable thing is to be done.
Seventh day: No sexual practice.
Eighth day: As desired with or without practice.
Ninth day: Insertion of penis into vagina for pleasure, but no orgasm, is essential. The goal is pleasure, not orgasm, even if the penis goes inside. If there is no erection, the soft penis with KY jelly or other lubrication can still be introduced. It should contact the clitoris if not inserted. "Even the soft penis gives pleasure."
Tenth day: Repetition of ninth day.

If after four or five sensate focus sessions the couple is not responding and moving ahead, they should not be made to feel that they are failures. Some other form of treatment (like psychoanalytically oriented psychotherapy) may be necessary. The failure is not with the couple. It is due to the limitations of this particular kind of therapy. There is a group of patients such as those with inhibited sexual desire whose defenses prevent them from enjoying sex. Often obsessive ideas about performance interfere with the drive, excitement, and orgasm phases of the sexual act. In some cases the patient may be taught to disregard or bypass obsessive thoughts. In other cases the problem is too invested with unconscious conflict to disappear with simple sex therapy along behavioral lines. A combined dynamic and behavioral approach is best here.

Some special techniques may be necessary for different problems. In *premature ejaculation* the "squeeze" technique may be helpful. Here the man lies on his back. The woman with legs spread faces his pelvis. She strokes his body and then the penis until there is erection. She continues stroking the penis and randomly places thumbs on the raphe under the glans on the underside of the penis and the forefinger on the other side. She squeezes four times in 15 seconds, but not to the point of pain. Then he lies on his back, and she squats over him. She slowly inserts the lubricated penis and stops all movement for a moment. Then she moves slowly at a 45° angle, and he announces when he is getting too much pleasure. He then withdraws the penis, and the squeeze technique is utilized. Modifications of this technique may be used (Tanner BA, 1973). Where the female sexual partner becomes upset and *insists* on a "better performance," the problem of rapid ejaculation is augmented by guilt and conviction of failure. Tension builds up, which exaggerates the symptom. Here dynamic marital therapy along with sexual therapy along behavioral lines is the preferred approach.

A problem that disturbs many women is that of being *nonorgasmic*. Where the patient has sensuous feelings and can achieve orgasm with masturbation, the difficulty is generally not a serious one. Should a block to sensuous feelings exist, it is expedient to explore with the patient further the history of her sexual development from childhood and the store of misinformation that she has retained about sexuality.

The first step is helping the patient to develop greater sensuous feeling by exercises in relaxing, stroking her body, and self-pleasuring (masturbating). A book like *The Sensuous Woman,* by Lyle Huart, may be helpful. The sensate focus technique described above is then taught the couple with the object of pleasuring each other while avoiding intercourse. Pleasure in giving pleasure to the partner is the object while providing feedback of how they both feel during the exercises.

McCarthy (1973) describes a technique that may be found helpful.

First day: Stroking and kissing various parts of the partner's body with eyes shut and no genital touching.
Second day: Sensate focus, eyes shut and couple guiding each other with no genital touch.
Third day: Sensate focus, guiding each other and eyes open.
Fourth day: Abstinence.
Fifth day: Sensate focus with lotion, no genital touch.
Sixth day: Sensate focus and genital touch with eyes closed.
Seventh day: Guided sensate focus with genital touch, eyes open.

After this greater spontaneity and experiment are encouraged. Some couples may take several days to execute the directions assigned for one day. When the exercises have been completed, once-a-week visits are possible. Teaching the couple sexual positions may be part of the instructions starting with the "no-demand" position. Oral-genital stimulation techniques may also be introduced and feelings aired about this. Should anxiety develop during any of the stages, a return to sensate focus techniques is advocated. Finally, after orgasms are reached by manual and oral-genital techniques, actual intercourse is encouraged. As much as 2 or 3 months of preliminary stimulation may be required before full intercourse is "permitted." Naturally, if full intercourse occurs prior to this, the therapist acts pleased.

Some therapists skilled in hypnosis have been able to bring their female patients to orgasm by training them in fantasy formation while the patients are in a trance. They are told they will have feelings of gentle warmth in the vaginal area and will be able to accept these feelings and feel excited and passionate deeply inside the vagina. Thereafter scenes are suggested of the patient meeting her secret lover and making exciting love with him. Because repressive barriers are down and the imagination is so vivid in the trance, some patients are able to experience their first orgasm through such training. Posthypnotic suggestions are made to the effect that orgasms will come with intercourse without guilt or fear. The therapist must be a bit of a romantic poet to make such suggestions sound realistic. Should the therapist decide to utilize this technique, it is wise to have a female helper quietly present during and after trance induction for medico-legal reasons.

The use of vibrators should be avoided in nonorgasmic women, since they will probably respond to the intense stimulation and then find the actual sex experience nonstimulating. Moreover, if the vibrators are used too much, they may cause vaginal ulceration.

Where the complaint is *impotence,* we must differentiate between primary and secondary varieties. In *primary impotence,* the patient has never been able to sustain an erection with a partner sufficient for the sexual act. Some individuals here realize their failing, but they ascribe it to moral scruples, which they imagine will be resolved when they get married. Marriage fails to correct the condition and, recognizing that an annulment is imminent, husband and wife usually seek help from a minister or physician who, in turn, may refer the couple to a psychotherapist. Generally, primary impotence is an aspect of a severe personality problem characterized by strong feelings of inadequacy, inferiority, and doubts about one's masculinity. The principal approach here is dynamic psychotherapy with sex therapy as a supplementary, albeit useful, accessory that should involve the patient and his partner.

Secondary impotence is where, following a period of more or less successful intercourse, the male experiences a loss of erection. This may occur when he is fatigued, or physically ill, or excessively tense and anxious about some situational problem, or most frequently when he is feeling hostile toward his partner. Ever since women have come to regard sex as a right rather than a burden, the incidence of secondary impotence has risen. Especially affected are men who regard their partner's expectations as a challenge to their masculinity. Their reaction to "failure" is usually related to their self-image. If they have a low feeling about themselves, they will overrespond and look forward to the next attempt with a sense of dread. The need to perform becomes more important to them than the desire to achieve pleasure in the sex act. Hypnosis in some cases, may be emminantly successful as a reinforcing intervention in impotency and premature ejaculation (Wolberg, 1948) utilizing suggestions patterned after the directions discussed previously.

Let us assume that we have eliminated physical causes (for example, diabetes, which is sometimes the source of secondary impotence) for the impotence. Therapy will involve restoration of confidence in the ability to function. No more may be required than clarification that impotence can occur temporarily in all males and that it will rectify itself if the person has no stake in maintaining it. The therapist should emphasize and reemphasize, "The best advice to follow is to forget the need for performance and to attempt satisfying yourself to the limit of your capacity without or with an erection." Treatment with sensate focus is generally successful, but cooperation of the partner is mandatory.

We sometimes encounter a situation where a middle-aged man is secondarily impotent with his wife and has become involved in an erotic stimulating situation with a younger woman. He is sexually disinterested in his wife, who he complains is getting obese, is losing her body firmness, developing wrinkles, neglects her grooming, and exposes him to a boring, stereotyped sexual experience. Often the relationship with the wife has deteriorated into one where the man regards her as a maternal substitute. He may come to therapy spontaneously out of guilt and with the hope the therapist will work some miracle and produce an erection even though he may not be interested so much in pleasing himself as in pleasing his wife. Generally, if the man is emotionally involved with the other woman, sex therapy will not work too well and the restoration of adequate sexual functioning will be unsuccessful. At some point it will be necessary to break up the triad. The therapist may under some circumstances, at the start, where the man's motivation to correct the situation is strong, have to tell him that he will need to break up his relationship with the young woman before therapy can be successful. In other cases where the man is deeply entangled in the affair, immediate rupture can be traumatic and may be strongly resisted. Here, gradually the effort may be made to help the man see the inadequacy of the relationship with his mistress, an effort that may or may not prove successful. Marital therapy is sometimes useful where the relationship between husband and wife has not deteriorated too badly.

Brief periods of *frigidity* in women are normal, the product resulting from temporary physical disability or fleeting anxieties, tensions, and depressions. Frigidity can also occur when there is anger or irritation with a sexual partner. Short-term therapy with reassurance given that there is nothing seriously wrong, while permitting free verbalization of hostility toward the partner, may be all that is required.

Persistent frigidity may be divided into primary and secondary varieties. In *primary frigidity* the woman has never had an orgasm even during sleep or with masturbation, although she may have experienced some sexual arousal. Usually arousal reaches a pitch and then loss of feeling ensues without orgasm. Responsible for this may be fears of loss of control, of rejection, or of acting foolishly. In *secondary frigidity* the person was once orgasmic and then ceased to respond. Here untoward emotions and attitudes are often implicated, like hostility, distrust, disgust, and fear. Sometimes orgasm may be possible with certain fantasies, like being raped or punished, or with some practices, like being treated roughly, tied down, abused, etc. Sometimes masturbation succeeds while intercourse remains distasteful. Sex therapy may enable some women with secondary frigidity to respond satisfactorily. Should a patient require fantasies, the therapist should not disparage these. The patient may be encouraged to substitute thoughts about her present sexual partner at the start of orgasm in an effort to recondition a new way of thinking.

Long-standing primary frigidity, however, does not usually yield to sex therapy, particularly where it is a product of severe personality problems stemming from disturbed family relationships. There may be a fear of functioning like a woman, a repudiation of femininity, a disgust with and desire to renounce the female sexual organs, consciously or unconsciously conceived of as dirty or repulsive. There may be marked competitiveness and hostility toward men. Long-term psychoanalysis or dynamic psychotherapy offers chances for improvement or cure after reconstructive changes have been brought about.

In *dyspareunia* and *vaginismus* intercourse is so painful that it becomes aversive rather than pleasurably rewarding. Here the patient should be sent to a gynecologist to rule out organic causes. Trauma during the birth of a child, episiotomy, a painful past abortion, a hysterectomy, endometriosis, allergic reactions to birth control sprays and jellies, and other physical factors may be at the root of the problem. In most cases, however, the cause is psychogenic. During vaginismus the muscles go into spasm, a kind of defensive splinting. Penetration is difficult or impossible even for the little finger. Reaction to erotic approaches then sponsors a panicky withdrawal. Sometimes vaginismus is a secondary response to premature ejaculation or impotence in a husband or lover. The woman's reaction frightens and discourages the man and aggravates his problem, which, in turn, creates further symptoms in the woman. The triad of dyspareunia, vaginismus, and impotence are often at the basis of an unconsummated marriage. Couples sometimes shamefacedly seek help for this situation, and sex therapy may be tried.

A useful method of fealing with these reactions is to recondition the pain response through the use of graduated dilators. These may be obtained in a surgical supply house, one form being known as Young's Dilators. The smallest size, well lubricated, is slowly inserted by the woman, at first in the presence of her husband. She is encouraged to retain it for a while. Then gradually each day a larger size, well lubricated, is introduced. Next the husband slowly inserts the dilators in graduated size. The time dilators are retained in the vagina is increased from 15 minutes to 2 hours. The patient must be reassured that the dilators will not disappear in her body, a fearful misconception of some patients. Success rates are close to 100 percent, assuming no serious psychiatric problem coexists.

BIBLIOTHERAPY

Attempts are sometimes made by therapists to change faulty attitudes and to influence poor motivation in certain patients through the assigned reading of articles, pamphlets, and books. By these measures the patient is helped to understand how personality is evolved, why adaptation breaks down, the manifestations of collapse in adaptation, and how psychotherapy may help repair the damage. Advice on the handling of specific problems in adjustment, marriage, and child rearing may also be obtained from some reading materials. This therapeutic use of reading (psychoeducation) has been designated as "bibliotherapy."

Bibliotherapy is of value chiefly to persons who have had little contact with psychotherapy and who require more information about emotional illness before they can admit of its existence in themselves or can recognize that beneficial results may be obtained from treatment. It may correct misconceptions about mental health, psychiatry, and psychotherapy. It is sometimes effective in correcting misconceptions through acceptance of written authoritative statements and directives that help the person to suppress inner fears, to gain reassurance, and to adopt socially acceptable attitudes and values. The latter influence makes bibliotherapy a useful adjunctive device in certain patients receiving psychotherapy. Patients may gain from readings a number of methods by means of which they may regulate their life, inspirational formulas that help in the achievement of happiness and success, and devices that permit of a regulation of those conflicts and strivings that are more or less under volitional control.

Bibliotherapeutic approaches to mental health, while praiseworthy, have definite limitations. People often refuse to accept facts due to a complete or partial unawareness of ego-syntonic personality distortions. To tell parents they must accept and love their children in order for the children to grow into healthy adults, does not mean that they will appreciate the significance of these precepts. Indeed, even though children are being rejected, spouses despised, and family life desecrated, the culprits may not consider their behavior in any way unusual. They may even hold themselves up as parental ideals.

In other instances the person may acknowledge one's difficulties but be totally unable to do anything about them. Educational media that warn people of the disasters to children or to society of their reactions may mobilize counterreactions and actually exaggerate the existing problems.

The manner in which reading materials are prepared and presented is important. If they apprise of the fact that all parents commit errors, that children are resilient and can stand many mistakes if they feel loved and respected, and that youngsters with even severe difficulties can change, readings may create a corrective atmosphere.

On the whole, reading adjuncts will not prove to be remarkably corrective for the patient who is in reconstructive therapy. This is because no intellectual approach is of great service in modifying deeply repressed conflicts or in ameliorating symptoms that have strong defensive virtues for the individual. Indeed, the educational materials may be utilized by the patient as resistance, items being extracted out of context to justify neurotic patterns. The relative ineffectuality of reading materials in severe neurotic difficulties is attested to by the fact that scores of patients come to psychotherapy after having read more extensively from the psychiatric literature than has the therapist.

Nevertheless, bibliotherapy may help certain individuals to break through specific resistances and to gain limited insight, as, for instance, those patients who, uncon-vinced of the value of psychotherapy, require examples from the experiences of others of how therapy helps. Resistance to working with dreams may sometimes be handled by asking the patient to read books in which the rationale of dream interpretation is explained. A patient who has in therapy resolved crippling sexual inhibitions may be aided in achieving a more complete sexual life by reading appropriate materials dealing with marriage. Or a patient having problems with children may benefit greatly from books on child psychology. Personal involvement in short stories and case histories is also possible, and McKinney (1975) lists a bibliography that can be useful.

As a therapeutic medium, bibliotherapy is utilized in child therapy. Children readily get "caught up" in a story. A child identifies with one or more of the characters and releases emotional energy vicariously. This may result in greater awareness by the child of personal needs, feelings, and motivations (Ciancilo, 1965; Nickerson, 1975). Some of the ways that bibliotherapy is employed are described by Bell and Moore (1972), Chambers (1970), Dinkmeyer (1970), Gardner (1974), Heimlich (1972), Mulac (1971), Myrick and Moni (1972), and J. A. Wagner (1970).

The following is a list of recommended books and pampthlets, should the therapist decide that bibliotherapy is indicated. (The source abbreviations are spelled out at the end of these references (see pages 1059–1060).

BIBLIOTHERAPY SUBJECTS

General Psychology, Psychiatry, and Psychoanalysis.
Explaining How Personality Problems Operate.
Explaining How Psychiatry and Psychotherapy Help.
Marriage and Alternative Life Styles.
Human Sexuality.
Family Planning.

Pregnancy and Childbirth.

Men and Women.

Family Problems and Crises (Alcoholism, Child Abuse, Death, Divorce, Drug Abuse and Addiction, Family Violence, Incest, Mental Illness, Suicide, Teenage Pregnancy, Unemployment).

Family Living and Adjustment.

General Child Care and Guidance.

Infants and Young Children.

Adoption and Foster Care.

Child's Middle Years.

How to Understand and Relate to the Adolescent.

How to Explain Sexuality to Children.

About Sexuality to Read to or to be Read by Children.

For Adolescents.

About Exceptional, Handicapped, Developmentally Disabled, and Emotionally Ill Children.

On Self-understanding and Self-help books.

Families with a Mentally Ill Relative.

Problems of Vocational Change, Retirement, and Old Age.

For the Advanced Reader.

Books on General Psychology, Psychiatry, and Psychoanalysis

Berne E: A Layman's Guide to Psychiatry and Psychoanalysis, New York, Ballentine, 1982 (paperback)

Brill AA: Basic Principles of Psychoanalysis. Lanham, MD, University Press of America, 1985

Freud S: Introductory Lectures on Psychoanalysis: A General Introduction to Psychoanalysis. New York, Liveright, 1977. (paperback). Orig. Title: General Introduction to Psychoanalysis.

Grinker RR, Sr.: Psychiatry in Broad Perspective. New York, Behavioral Publications, 1975

Lichtenberg JD: The Talking Cure: A Descriptive Guide to Psychoanalysis. Hillsdale, NJ, Analytic Press, 1985

Wrightsman LS et al: Psychology; a scientific study of human behavior, 5th ed. Monterey, CA, Brooks/Cole, 1979

Books Explaining How Personality Problems Operate

English OS, Pearson GH: Emotional Problems of Living (3rd ed). New York, Norton, 1963

Fromm E: The Sane Society. New York, Fawcett World, 1977 (paperback)

Horney K: The Neurotic Personality of Our Time. New York, Norton, 1937 (paperback)

Menninger K: The Vital Balance: The Life Process in Mental Health and Illness. Mongolia, MA, Peter Smith, 1973.

Wolberg LR, Kildahl JP: The Dynamics of Personality. New York, Grune & Stratton, 1970

Books Explaining How Psychiatry and Psychotherapy Help

Herink R: The Psychotherapy Handbook. New York, New American Library, 1980

Horney K: Are You Considering Psychoanalysis? New York, Norton, 1963 (paperback)

Kovel J: A Complete Guide to Therapy: From Psychoanalysis to Behavior Modification. New York, Pantheon, 1977 (paperback)

Quinnett PG: The Troubled People Book: A Comprehensive Guide to Getting Help. New York, Continuum, 1982

Rubin TI & Rubin E: Not to Worry: The American Family Book of Mental Health. New York, Viking, 1984

Ruitenbeek H: Psychotherapy: What It's All About. New York, Avon, 1976

Pamphlets

Compulsive Gambling (Milt H). PAP (#598), 1981. $1.00

Depression: Causes and Treatment (Irwin R). PAP (#488), 1970 $1.00

Help for Emotional and Mental Problems (Ogg E). PAP (#567), 1987 $1.00

The Psychotherapies Today (Ogg E). PAP (#596), 1981. $1.00

Some Things You Should Know About Mental and Emotional Illness. (NMHA). (n.d.)

Troubled Children, Troubled Families–Techniques in Child and Family Therapy (Ogg E). PAP (#605), 1982. $1.00

What Everyone Should Know About Mental Health (n.d.) CLB

When Things Go Wrong, What Can You Do? (n.d.) NMHA. 30¢

Who's Who in Mental Health Care. 1981. CLB (Review copy: Free)

Books on Marriage & Alternate Life Styles

Belkin GS & Goodman N: Marriage, Family & Intimate Relationships. Boston, Houghton Mifflin, 1980

Bell RR: Marriage & Family Interaction, (6th ed). Chicago, Dorsey, 1983

Bernard J: The Future of Marriage. New Haven, Yale University Press, 1982

Lederer WJ: Creating a Good Relationship. New York, Norton, 1984

Rogers CR: Becoming Partners: Marriage and its Alternatives. New York, Delacorte, 1973 (also paperback, New York, Dell)

Stuart RB & Jacobson B: Second Marriage. New York, Norton, 1985

Pamphlets

Building a Marriage on Two Altars (Genne E&W). PAP (#466), 1971. $1.00

The Early Years of Marriage (Klemer RH, MG). PAP (#424), 1968. $1.00

Marriage and Love in the Middle Years (Peterson JA). PAP (#456), 1970. $1.00

New Ways to Better Marriages (Ogg E). PAP (#547), 1977. $1.00

One-Parent Families (Ogg E). PAP (#543), 1976. $1.00

Saving Your Marriage (Duvall E, S). PAP (#213), 1954 $1.00

Sexual Adjustment in Marriage (Klemer RH, MG). PAP (#397), 1966. $1.00

Stepfamilies–A Growing Reality (Berman C). PAP (#609), 1982. $1.00

Strengthen Your Marriage Through Better Communication (Bienvenu M Sr). PAP (#642), 1986. $1.00

What Makes a Marriage Happy (Mace DR). PAP (#290), 1959. $1.00

Yours, Mine & Ours: Tips for Stepparents. U.S. GPO (#S/N 017-024-00833-8), 1984. $3.50

Books on Human Sexuality

Barbach LG: For Yourself: The Fulfillment of Female Sexuality. Garden City, NY, Anchor/Doubleday, 1975 (paperback)

Bell AP et al: Sexual Preference: Its Development in Men & Women. Bloomington, Indiana University Press, 1981

Kitzinger S: Women's Experience of Sex. New York, C.P. Putnam's 1983

Marmor J: Homosexual Behavior: A Modern Reappraisal. New York, Basic Books, 1980

Masters W: The Pleasure Bond: A New Look at Sexuality and Commitment. Boston, Little, Brown, 1975

Money J, Tucker P: Sexual Signatures: On Being a Man or a Woman. Boston, Little, Brown, 1975

Pleck JH & Sawyer J (eds): Men and Masculinity. Englewood Cliffs, NJ, Prentice-Hall, 1974

Silverstein C: A Family Matter: A Parent's Guide to Homosexuality. New York, McGraw-Hill, 1978

Zilbergeld B & Ullman J: Male Sexuality. New York, Bantom Books, 1978

Pamphlets

Changing Views of Homosexuality (Ogg E). PAP (#563), 1978. $1.00

Sex Education for Disabled Persons (Dickman IR). PAP (#531), 1975 $1.00

Books on Family Planning

Publications dealing with the subjects of contraception, fertility, or menopausal hormone therapy may not reflect the results of current research. Readers are urged to consult their physicians.

Bromwich PD & Parsons AK: Contraception. York, Oxford University Press, 1984

Calderon MS: Manual of Family Planning & Contraceptive Practice, (2d ed). Melbourne, FL, Krieger, 1977

Goldstein M & Feldberg M: The Vasectomy Book: A Complete Guide to Decision Making. Boston, Houghton Mifflin, 1982

Guttmacher A: Pregnancy, Birth & Family Planning, revised by Irvin H. Kaiser. New York, NAL, 1986 (paperback)

Hatcher RA et al: It's Your Choice: A Personal Guide to Birth Control Methods for Women . . . & Men, Too! New York, Irvington Publisher, 1982

Ory HW et al: Making Choices: Evaluating the Health Risks & Benefits of Birth Control Methods. New York, Alan Guttmacher Institute, 1983

Pamphlets

Basics of Birth Control. Rev ed. PPFA, 1982. $.50

A Guide to Birth Control: Seven Accepted Methods of Contraception, PPFA, 1982. $.50

Abortion: Public Issue, Private Decision, (Pilpel, HF, Zuckerman, RJ & Ogg E). PAP (#527), 1975. $1.00

Preparing Tomorrow's Parents (rev ed) (Ogg E).
PAP (#520A), 1983. $1.00

Books on Pregnancy and Childbirth

Boston Children's Medical Center. Pregnancy, Birth and the Newborn Baby: A Publication for Parents. New York, Delacorte/Seymour Lawrence, 1972

Colman AD, Libby L: Pregnancy: The Psychological Experience. New York, Seabury, 1972

Cook WA: Natural Childbirth: Fact & Fallacy. Chicago, IL, Nelson-Hall, 1982

Guttmacher A: Pregnancy, Birth & Family Planning. New York, New American Library, 1984. (paperback)

Schaefer G, Zisowitz ML: The Expectant Father. New York, Simon & Schuster, 1964

Pamphlets

Childbirth Today: Where and How to Have Your Baby (Jacobson B). PAP (#628), 1984. $1.00

Pregnancy and You (Auerbach AB, Arnstein HS). PAP (#482), 1972 $1.00

A Pregnancy Primer: The Importance of Prenatal Care (Jacobson B). PAP (#636), 1985. $1.00

Prenatal Care. rev., 1983. Administration for Children, Youth, and Families. U.S.G.P.O., S/N 017-091-00237-1. $2.50.

The Very New Baby: The First Days of Life (Schwartz JV, Botts ER). PAP (#553), 1977. $1.00

Books on Men and Women

Bernard J: Women, Wives, Mothers: Values and Options. Chicago, Aldine, 1975

de Beauvoir S: The Second Sex. New York, Random House, 1974 (paperback)

Komarovsky M: Dilemmas of Masculinity: A Study of College Youth. New York, Norton, 1976.

Mead M: Male and Female. New York, Dell, 1984 (paperback)

Pamphlets

Male "Menopause": Crisis in the Middle Years (Irwin T). PAP (#526), 1975. $1.00

Men and Women–What We Know about Love (Lobsenz NM). PAP (#592), 1981. $1.00

Men's Jobs for Women: Toward Occupational Equality (Jaffe N). PAP (#606), 1982. $1.00

Books on Family Problems and Crises

Atkin E, Rubin E: Part-Time Father: A Guide for the Divorced Father. New York, Vanguard, 1976

Ausubel DP: What Every Well-Informed Person Should Know About Drug Addiction. Chicago: Nelson-Hall, 1980

Caine L: Widow. New York, Morrow, 1975

Heilman RO (ed): Early Recognition of Alcoholism & Other Drug Dependence. Center City, MN, Hazelden, 1973

Jones CL & Battjes R: Etiology of Drug Abuse, Implications for Prevention. (NIDA Research Monograph 56). Washington, D.C., Government Printing Office, 1985

Kubler-Ross E: Death: The Final Stage of Growth. New York, Simon & Schuster, 1986

Meryman R: Children of Alcoholism, a Survivor's Manual. Boston, Little, Brown, 1984

Milt H: Alcoholism—Its Causes and Cures. New York, Scribner, 1976

Nida PC & Heller WM: The Teenager's Survival Guide to Moving. New York, Macmillan, 1985

Sandmaier M: The Invisible Alcoholics: Women and Alcohol Abuse in America. New York, McGraw-Hill, 1981

Stuart IR, Abt LE (eds): Children of Separation and Divorce. New York, Grossman, 1981

Pincus L: Death and the Family: The Importance of Mourning. New York, Pantheon, 1976

Seixas J & Youcha G: Children of Alcoholism: A Survivor's Manual. New York, Harper-Row, 1986 (paperback)

Steinmetz SK & Straus MA (eds): Violence in the Family. New York, Harper-Row, 1974

Pamphlets

AIDS: Fears and Facts (Irwin, M). PAP (#639), 1986. $1.00

Assaults on Women: Rape and Wife Beating (Jaffe N). PAP (#579), 1980. $1.00

Caring About Kids: When Parents Divorce. U.S. GPO (#S/N 017-024-01102-9), 1984. $3.25

Children and Drugs (Saltman J). PAP (#584), 1980. $1.00

Dealing with the Crisis of Suicide (Frederick CJ, Lague L). PAP (#406A), 1967. $1.00

A Death in the Family (Ogg E). PAP (#542), 1976. $1.00

Drinking, Drugs and Driving. NCA, 1986. $.10

Drugs–Use, Misuse, Abuse: Guidance for Families (rev ed) (Hill M). PAP (#515A), 1985. $1.00

The Dying Person and the Family (Doyle N). PAP (#485), 1972 $1.00

Help for the Troubled Employee (Brenton M). PAP (#611), 1982. $1.00

Helping Children Face Crises (Barman A). PAP (#541), 1976. $1.00

How Teens Set the Stage for Alcoholism (O'Gorman, P & Stringfield S). NCA, 1978. $.40

How to Cope with Crises (Irwin T). PAP (#464), 1971. $1.00

If One of Your Parents Drinks Too Much What Are Your Problems Going to Be? (Block MA & Heing FV), 1965, AMA. $.20

Incest: Family Problem, Community Concern (Strouse E). PAP (#638), 1985. $1.00

The Many Faces of Family Violence (Saltman J). PAP (#640), 1986. $1.00

The Right to Die with Dignity (rev ed) (Ogg E). PAP (#587A), 1983. $1.00

Single Parent Families. U.S. GPO (#S/N 017-091-00229-1), 1984. $4.50

Teenage Pregnancy–What Can Be Done? (Dickman IR). PAP (#594), 1981. $1.00

To Combat and Prevent Child Abuse and Neglect (Irwin T). PAP (#588), 1980. $1.00

Understanding and Dealing with Alcoholism (Milt H). PAP (#580), 1980. $1.00

Unmarried Teenagers and Their Children (Ogg E). PAP (#537), 1976. $1.00

What to Do When You Lose Your Job (Weinstein GW). PAP (#617), 1983. $1.00

What You Should Know about Drug Abuse (rev ed) (Saltman J). PAP (#550A), 1984. $1.00

Women and Abuse of Prescription Drugs (Brenton M). PAP (#604), 1982. $1.00

When Parents Divorce. U.S. GPO (DHHS #(ADM) 81-1120) 1981. n.p.

When a Family Faces Cancer (Ogg E). PAP (#286), 1959. $1.00

When a Parent Is Mentally ILL: What to Say to Your Child (Armstein HS) JBFCS, 1974; paper) 1974, $1.50

Women and Alcohol–1980. AA, 1979. $.20

Books on Family Living and Adjustment

Arnstein HS: Between Mothers-in-Law & Daughters-in-Law: Achieving a Successful & Caring Relationship. New York, Dodd, 1985

Bradley B: Where Do I Belong? A Kids' Guide to Stepfamilies. Reading, Mass, Addison-Wesley, 1984

Denton W & Denton JH: Creative Couples: The Growth Factor in Marriage. Philadelphia, Westminster, 1983

Duvall EM & Miller B: Marriage & Family Development, (6th ed). New York, Harper-Row, 1984

Edwards M & Hoover E: The Challenge of Being Single. New York, New American Library, 1975

Kornhaber A: Between Parents & Grandparents. New York, StMartin's 1986

Rosenbaum V & Rosenbaum J: Stepparenting. Novato, CA, Chandler & Sharp, 1977

Satir V: Peoplemaking. Palo Alto, CA, Science & Behavior Books, 1972

Spock B: Raising Children in a Difficult Time. New York, Norton, 1985

Pamphlets

Handling Family Money Problems (Weinstein W). PAP (#626), 1984. $1.00

Making Ends Meet (Weinstein GW). PAP (#624). 1984. $1.00

One-Parent Families (Ogg E). PAP (#543), 1976. $1.00

Preparing to Remarry (Berman C). PAP (#647), 1986. $1.00

Stepfamilies–A Growing Reality (Berman C). PAP (#609), 1982. $1.00

You and Your In-laws: Help for Some Common Problems (Brenton M). PAP (#635), 1985. $1.00

Books on General Child Care and Guidance

Chess S et al: Your Child Is a Person: A Psychological Approach to Parenthood Without Guilt. New York, Penguin, 1977

Erikson EH: Childhood and Society (rev ed). New York, Norton, 1964 (also in paperback).

Ginott HG: Between Parent and Child: New Solutions for Old Problems. New York, Macmillan, 1969

Lamb ME: The Father's Role: Applied Persepctives. Somerset, NJ, John Wiley, 1986

Montessori M: From Childhood to Adolescence. New York, Schocken, 1973

Stone LJ, Church J: Childhood and Adolescence: A Psychology of the Growing Person (rev ed). New York, Random House, 1973

Pamphlets

Environmental Hazards to Children (DiPerna P). PAP (#600), 1981. $1.00

Helping Children Face Crises (Barman A). PAP (#541), 1976. $1.00

How to Discipline Your Children (Baruch D). PAP (#154), 1949. $1.00

Immunization–Protection against Childhood Diseases (rev ed) (Saltman J). PAP (#565A), 1983. $1.00

Motivation and Your Child (Barman A). PAP (#523), 1975. $1.00

Playmates: The Importance of Childhood Friendships (Brenton M). PAP (#525), 1975. $1.00

Pressures on Children (Barman A). PAP (#589), 1980. $1.00

Teaching Children about Money (Weinstein GW). PAP (#593), 1981. $1.00

What Should Parents Expect from Children (Archer J, Yahraes DL). PAP (#357), 1964. $1.00

When Your Child is Sick (rev ed) (Seaver J, Schwartz JV). PAP (#441A), 1978. $1.00

Your Child's Emotional Health (Wolf AWM). PAP (#264), 1958. $1.00

Your Child's Sense of Responsibility (Neisser EG). PAP (#254), 1957. $1.00

Books on Infants and Young Children

Arnstein HS: Billy & Our New Baby. New York, Human Sciences Press, 1973

Fraiberg S: The Magic Years: Understanding and Handling the Problems of Early Childhood. New York, Scribner, 1984

Snyder A: First Step. New American Library, 1976

Spock B: Baby and Child Care (4th ed). New York, Pocket Books, Simon & Schuster, 1983

Pamphlets

Breastfeeding (Riker AP). PAP (#353S), 1964. $1.00

Caring for the New Baby–The First 18 Months (Schwartz JV, Botts ER). PAP (#616), 1983. $1.00

Enjoy Your Child–Ages 1, 2, and 3 (Hymes JL Jr). PAP (#141), 1948. $1.00

The Pocket Guide to Babysitting. U.S. GPO, 1982. S/N 017-091-00236-3

Three to Six: Your Child Starts to School (Hymes JL Jr). PAP (#163), 1950. $1.00

Your Child From One to Six. U.S. GPO, 1984. S/N 017-091-00219-3. $2.00

Your First Months with Your First Baby (Barman A). PAP (#478), 1972. $1.00

Books on Adoption and Foster Care

Cautley RW: New Foster Parents: The First Experience. New York, Human Sciences Press, 1980

Churchill SR et al: No Child Is Unadoptable: A Reader on Adoption of Children with Special Needs. Beverly Hills, CA, Sage, 1979

Curto J: How to Become a Single Parent: A Guide for Single People Considering Adoption or Natural Parenthood Alone. Englewood Cliffs, NJ, Prentice-Hall, 1983

Day D: The Adoption of Black Children. Lexington, MA, Lexington Books, 1979

Festinger T: No One Ever Asked Us: A Postscript to Foster Care. New York, Columbia University Press, 1984

Pamphlets

Adopting a Child (Phillips M). PAP (#585), 1980. $1.00

Raising an Adopted Child' (Berman C). PAP (#620), 1983. $1.00

Books on the Child's Middle Years

Elkind D: A Sympathetic Understanding of the Child Six to Sixteen. Boston, Allyn & Bacon, 1978 (also paperback)

LeShan E: What Makes Me Feel This Way: Growing Up with Human Emotions. New York, Macmillan, 1974

Pamphlets

Early Adolescents: Understanding and Nurturing Their Development (Redl F). ACEI (ISBN 0-87173-087-1), 1978. $2.40

How to Help Your Children Achieve in School. U.S.G.P.O., 1983. S/N 065-000-00176-4. (Dept. of Education) $3.75.

Understand Your Child–From 6 to 12 (Lambert C). PAP (#144), 1948. $1.00

Your Child From 6 to 12. U.S.G.P.O., 1984. S/N 017-091-00070-1. $2.75.

Books on How to Understand and Relate to the Adolescent

Ginott H: Between Parent & Teenager. New York, Avon, 1971

Josselyn IM: The Adolescent and His World. New York, Family Service Association, 1952 (paperback)

Mead M: Culture and Commitment. Garden City, NY, Doubleday, 1970

Winship EC: Reaching Your Teenager. Boston, Houghton Mifflin, 1983

Pamphlets

An Adolescent in Your Home. Washington, D.C. U.S. GPO (#S/N 017-091-00202-9), 1984. $3.50

Adolescent Suicide: Mental Health Challenge (Freese AS). PAP (#569), 1979. $1.00

Anorexia Nervosa and Bulimia: Two Severe Eating Disorders (Jacobson B). PAP (#632), 1985. $1.00

Coming of Age: Problems of Teenagers (Landis PH). PAP (#234), 1956. $1.00

Helping the Handicapped Teenager Mature (Ayrault EW). PAP (#504), 1974. $1.00

Marijuana: Current Perspectives (Saltman J). PAP (#539), 1976. $1.00

Parent-Teenager Communication: Bridging the Generation Gap (Bienvenu MJ Sr). PAP (#438), 1969. $1.00

Parents and Teenagers (Hill M). PAP (#490), 1973. $1.00

The Problem with Puberty (Tepper SS). RAJ Publications, 1981. $1.50

Runaway Teenagers (Koestler FA). PAP (#552), 1977. $1.00

Teenagers and Alcohol: Patterns and Dangers (Saltman J). PAP (#612), 1983. $1.00

You and Your Alcoholic Parent (Hornik EL). PAP (#506), 1974. $1.00

Books on How to Explain Sexuality to Children

Bell R et al: Changing Bodies, Changing Lives: A Book for Teens on Sex & Relationships. New York, Random, 1981

Calderone MS & Ramey JW: Child Study Association of America. What to Tell Your Child about Sex. Northvale, NJ, Jason Aronson, 1983

Calderone MS & Johnson EW: The Family Book About Sexuality. New York, Harper-Row, 1981

Pierson JD: Planned Parenthood Federation of America Staff. How to Talk With Your Child about Sexuality: A Parent's Guide. New York, Doubleday, 1986

Pamphlets

How to Tell Your Child about Sex (Hymes JL Jr). PAP (#149), 1949. $1.00

Schools and Parents–Partners in Sex Education (Gordon S, Dickman IR). PAP (#581), 1980. $1.00

Sex Education: The Parents' Role (Gordon S, Dickman IR). PAP (#549), 1977. $1.00

Sexually Transmitted Diseases–Epidemic among Teenagers (rev ed) (Saltman J). PAP (#517A), 1982. $1.00

Talking to Preteenagers about sex (Hofstein S). PAP (#476), 1972. $1.00

Books about Sexuality to Read to or Be Read by Children

Andry AC & Schepp S: How Babies Are Made. Alexandria, VA, Time-Life Books, 1968

Gordon S & Gordon J: Did the Sun Shine Before You Were Born? A Sex Education Primer. Fayetteville, NY, Ed-U Press, 1982

Gordon S: Girls are Girls and Boys are Boys–So What's the Difference? Fayetteville, NY, Ed-U Press, 1979.

Johnson CB & Johnson E: Love and Sex and Growing Up. New York, Bantam Books, 1979

Johnson E: Love & Sex in Plain Language, (rev ed). New York, Harper-Row, 1985

Madaras L & Madaras A: What's Happening to My Body? A Growing up Guide for Mothers and Daughters. New York, New Market Press, 1983

Pomeroy WB: Boys & Sex, (rev ed). New York, Delacorte, 1981

Pomeroy WB: Girls & Sex, (rev ed). New York, Dell, 1986

Waxman S: Growing Up Feeling Good: A Child's Introduction to Sexuality. Los Angeles, CA, Panjandrum Books, 1979

Pamphlets

How was I Born? (Nilsson L). DEL, 1975. $10.95

It's My Body: A Book to Teach Young Children How to Resist Uncomfortable Touch (Freeman L), PPSC, 1982. $2.95

Books for Adolescents

Betancourt J: Am I Normal? An Illustrated Guide To Your Changing Body. New York, Avon Books, 1983

Betancourt J: Dear Diary: An Illustrated Guide to Your Changing Body. New York, Avon Books, 1983

Burns C: How to Survive Without Feeling Frustrated, Left Out or Wicked. New York, Harper & Row, 1986

Choice: Changes: You and Your Body. Philadelphia, CHOICE, 1978

Gordon S: The Teenage Survival Book: The Complete Revised, Updated Edition of YOU. New York, Times Books, 1981

Hanckel F & Cunningham J: A Way of Love, A Way of Life: A Young Person's Introduction to What it Means to be Gay. New York, William Morrow, 1979

Hunt M: The Young Person's Guide to Love. New York, Farrar Strauss Giroux, 1975

LeShan E: You and Your Feelings. New York, Macmillan, 1975

Lieberman EJ & Peck E: Sex and Birth Control: A Guide for the Young, rev ed. New York, Harper & Row, 1981

Nida RC & Heller WM: The Teenager's Survival Guide to Moving. New York, Macmillan, 1985

Satir V: Self Esteem: A Declaration. Berkeley, CA, Celestial Arts, 1975

Pamphlets

What Every Teenager Should Know About Alcohol. CLB, 1981

Books about Exceptional, Handicapped, and Emotionally Ill Children

Blodgett HE: Mentally Retarded Children: What Parents and Others Should Know. Minneapolis, University of Minnesota Press, 1972

Brown DL: Developmental Handicaps in Babies & Young Children: A Guide for Parents. Springfield, IL, Thomas, 1972

Heisler V: Handicapped Child in the Family: A Guide for Parents. Orlando, FL, Grune, 1972

Lowenfeld B: Our Blind Children: Growing and Learning with Them (3rd ed). Springfield, IL, Thomas, 1977

Meyer DJ et al: Living with a Brother or Sister with Special Needs: A Book for Sibs. Seattle, University of Washington Press, 1985

Myklebust HR: Your Deaf Child. Springfield, IL, Thomas, 1979 (paperback)

Pamphlets

Asthma—Episodes and Treatment (Saltman J). PAP (#608), 1982. $1.00

Getting Help for a Disabled Child—Advice from Parents (Dickman IR, Gordon S). PAP (#615), 1983. $1.00

Help for Your Troubled Child (Barman A, Cohen L). PAP (#454), 1970. $1.00

Learning Disabilities: Problems and Progress (Yahraes H). PAP (#578), 1979. $1.00

The Legal Rights of Retarded Persons (Ogg E). PAP (#583), 1980. $1.00

Mental Retardation—A Changing World (Lippman L). PAP (#577), 1979. $1.00

No Easy Answers: The Learning Disabled Child. U.S. GPO, 1984 (National Institute of Mental Health) S/N 017-024-00687-4 $6.50

The Retarded Child Gets Ready for School (rev ed) (Hill M). PAP (#349A), 1982. $1.00

You and Your Alcoholic Parent (Hornik EL). PAP (#506), 1974. $1.00

Books on Self-understanding and Self-help Books

Benson H: The Relaxation Response. New York, Morrow, 1976

Fromm E: The Art of Loving. New York, Harper & Row, 1974 (also paperback—New York, Bantom)

Gaylin W: Feelings: Our Vital Signs. New York, Harper-Row, 1979

Gould RL: Transformations: Growth and Change in Adult Life. New York, Simon & Schuster, 1978

Johnson TC: Doctor! What You Should Know About Health Care Before You Call a Physician. New York, McGraw-Hill, 1975

McCormick J: The Doctor: Father Figure or Plumber? Dover, NH, Longwood Publishing Group, 1979

Newman M, Berkowitz B: How to Be Your Own Best Friend. New York, Random House, 1981

Rubin TI: The Angry Book. New York, Macmillan, 1970 (paperback)

Rubin TI: Compassion & Self-Hate: An Alternative to Despair, (rev ed). New York, Macmillan, 1986 (paperback)

Sheehy G: Passages: Predictable Crises of Adult Life. New York, Dutton, 1977

Weiss RS (ed): Loneliness: The Experience of Emotional and Social Isolation. Cambridge, Mass, M.I.T. Press, 1974

Wheelis A: How People Change. New York, Harper & Row, 1974 (also paperback)

Pamphlets

Friendship Throughout Life (Barkas JL). PAP (#618), 1983. $1.00

How to Handle Stress: Techniques for Living Well (Bienvenu M). PAP (#622), 1984. $1.00

Listen to Your Body: Exercise and Physical Fitness (Dickman IR). PAP (#599), 1981. $1.00

Partners in Coping: Groups for Self and Mutual Help (Ogg E). PAP (#559), 1978. $1.00

Understanding Your Medical Examination (Block I). PAP (#630), 1984. $1.00

Books for Families with a Mentally Ill Relative

Benziger BF: The Prison of My Mind. New York, Walker, 1981

Greist JH & Jefferson JW: Depression and Its Treatment Help for the Nation's #1 Mental Problem. Washington, D.C., American Psychiatric Press, 1984

Korpell HS: How You Can Help: A Guide for Families of Psychiatric Hospital Patients. Washington, D.C., American Psychiatric Press, 1984

Milt H: Basic Handbook on Mental Illness, rev. ed. Maplewood, NJ: Scientific Aids Publications, 1978.

Park CC & Shapiro LN: You are Not Alone: Understanding & Dealing with Mental Illness. Boston, Little, Brown, 1976

Pamphlets

How to Help the Alcoholic (Cohen P). PAP (#452), 1970. $1.00

Phobias: The Ailments and the Treatments (Milt H). PAP (#590), 1980. $1.00

Understanding and Dealing with Alcoholism (Milt H). PAP (#580), 1980. $1.00

The Woman Alcoholic (Lindbeck V). PAP (#529), 1975. $1.00

When Mental Illness Strikes Your Family (Doyle KC). PAP (#172), 1951. $1.00

Books on Problems of Retirement and Old Age

Bradford L & Bradford M: Retirement: Coping with Emotional Upheavals. Chicago, Nelson-Hall, 1979

Butler RN: Why Survive? Being Old in America. New York, Harper-Row, 1985

Dickinson PA: The Complete Retirement Planning Book. New York, Dutton, 1984

Lieberman M & Tobin S: The Experience of Old Age: Stress, Coping, & Survival. New York, Basic Books, 1983

Mace E & Mace V: Letters to a Retired Couple. Valley Forge, PA, Judson Press, 1984

Maddox G et al: Nature & Extent of Alcohol Problems among the Elderly. New York, Springer Publishing, 1986

Pamphlets

After 65: Resources for Self-Reliance (rev ed) (Irwin T). PAP (#501A), 1982. $1.00

Ageism–Discrimination against Older People (Dickman IR). PAP (#575), 1979. $1.00

The Brain and Aging: The Myths, the Facts (Freese AS). PAP (#591), 1981. $1.00

Family Neglect and Abuse of the Aged: A Growing Concern (Milt H). PAP (#603), 1982. $1.00

Living the Retirement Years (Weinstein G). PAP (#643). $1.00

Planning Your Retirement Income (Weinstein GW). PAP (#634), 1985. $1.00

Social Security: Crises, Questions, Remedies (Kelman E). RAP (#621), 1983. $1.00

The Unseen Alcoholics–The Elderly (Buys D, Saltman J). PAP (#602), 1982. $1.00

Books for the Advanced Reader

Freud A: The Ego and the Mechanisms of Defense. New York, International Universities Press, 1967

Freud S: Collected Papers, 5 vols. New York, Basic Books, 1959

Jahoda M: Current Concepts of Positive Mental Health. New York, Basic Books, 1979 (Monograph No. 1, Joint Commission On Mental Illness and Health), Reprint of 1958

Joint Commission on Mental Illness and Health: Final Report. Action for Mental Health. New York, Basic Books, 1961

Leighton AH: My Name is Legion. New York, Basic Books, 1959

Lidz T: The Person: His and Her Development Throughout the Life Cycle (rev ed). New York, Basic Books, 1976

White R: Lives in Progress: A Study of the Natural Growth of Personality (3rd ed). New York, Holt, Rinehart, Winston, 1975

Pamphlet Sources

ACEI: Association for Childhood Education International, 1141 Georgia Ave., Suite 200, Weaton, MD 20902

AA: Al-Anon, 1 Park Ave., New York, NY 10016

AMA: American Medical Association, 535 North Dearborn St., Chicago, IL 60610

CLB: Channing L. Bete Company, South Deerfield, MA 01373

DEL: Delacorte Press, 1 Dag Hammarskjold Plaza, New York, NY 10017

JBFCS: Jewish Board of Family & Children's Services, Library, Inc. 120 West 57th Street, New York, NY 10019

NCA: National Council on Alcoholism, 733 Third Avenue, New York, NY 10017

NIMH: National Institute of Mental Health, 5600 Fishers Lane, Rockville, MD 20852

NMHA: National Mental Health Association, 1021 Prince St., Arlington, VA 22314

PPFA: Planned Parenthood Federation of America, 810 7th Avenue, New York, NY 10019

PAP: Public Affairs Pamphlets, 381 Park Avenue South, New York, NY 10016

PPSC: Planned Parenthood of Snohomish County, 2722 Colby, Suite 515, Everett WA 98201 or Parenting Press 7750 31st Ave., NE Seattle, WA 98115

RAJ: RAJ Publications, P.O. Box 18599, Denver, CO 80218

U.S. GPO: Superintendent of Documents U.S. Government Printing Office Washington, D.C., 20402

EDUCATIONAL FILMS AND VIDEOCASSETTES

The following is a list of audiovisual aids that the therapist may want to show to patients. The titles have been selected for their value in stimulating group discussions on various aspects of mental health. These present yet another medium as an adjunct to help change attitudes, provide insight, and increase self-understanding.

General Child Care & Guidance

And We Were Sad, Remember? 30 min, sd., color, 1979–80. Also video. Producer: US Dept of HEW. Order Source: NAVC. Purchase: $305. Rental: $30

Shows why children need to know about death, and how parents can help them deal with death when it happens.

It's My Decision As Long As It's What You Want. 13 min, videocassette, color, nd. Distributor: IV.

Parent-child relations.

Oh Brother, My Brother. 14 min, color, 1979.

Source: Pyramid. Distributor: UCEMC. Rental: $28

Sensitive look at the loving and affectionate relationship of two young brothers.

Spare The Rod (Discipline). 23 min, videocassette, color, nd. Distributor: IV.

Discipline as a potentially positive experience.

Pinks and the Blues, The. 57 min, color, 1982. Source: T.L. Distributor: UCEMC. Rental: $53

Shows how sex role stereotyping and traditional patterns of socialization continue today.

Infants and Young Children

Nurturing. 17 min, color 1973. Source: DAVF. Distributor: UCEMC. Rental: $38

Demonstrates the important role of the care-giver in infant development.

Child's Middle Years

From Sociable Six to Noisy Nine. 22 min, b & w, 1955. Source: WPIC. Produced by NFBC.

An illustration of the behavior that may normally be expected in children ages six to nine. Because the ages dealt with roughly correspond to those of first to third graders, this film will prove of particular interest to teachers in elementary grades and teachers in training as well as with parents and all who work with children.

How to Understand and Relate to the Adolescent

Alcohol, Drugs and You . . . a Losing Combination. 24 1/2 min, 16 mm color, 1982. Produced by SAIF. Order Source: BARR. Purchase: $490. Rental: $49.

Teenagers who have used drugs and alcohol discuss how they began and their feelings about themselves and their lives.

Childhood's End: A Look at Adolescent Suicide. 29 min, 16 mm, color, video, 1981. Order Source: CANFDS and FLMLIB. Purchase: $450 for 16 mm, $400 for video. Rental: $50 for 16 mm.

Probes the reasons for attempted sui-

cide by two adolescents through interviews with the adolescents themselves, their parents and close friends. Junior high school through adult level.

Personality: Adolescence. 21 min, color, 1978. Source: McG-H. Distributor: UCEMC. Rental: $30

Dramatized vignettes to illustrate some of the key traits in adolescent personality development.

Loving Parents. 24 min, 16 mm, color, video, 1978. Order Source: TEXFLM. Purchase: $330. Rental: $45

Each of the vignettes shows a variety of communication styles between parents and children while covering a specific sex-related topic.

Marriage and Alternative Life Styles

Make-Believe Marriage. 35 min. & 50 min. color, 1979. Director Robert Fuest. Distributor: LCA.

A high-school jock and the class feminist are paired off in their "trial marriage" class. As they face the realization and tests of "married life," they grow as individuals and fall in love. Dramatic film. An ABC after-school special. Blue Ribbon, American Festival. S-A.

Single Parent. 40 min, color, 1975. Distributor: UCEMC: Source: MEDIAG. Rental: $39

Cine-verité portrait of a divorced woman with children aged 11, 9, and 6.

Single Parents and Other Adults. 25 min, videocassette, color, nd. Distributor: IV.

Issues Facing Single Parents

Single Parents And Their Children. 18 min, videocassette, color, 1981. Distributor: IV.

Fourteen vignettes on difficult situations facing single parents.

Human Sexuality

A Family Talks About Sex. 29 min, videocassette, color, nd. Distributor: IV.

Discussion of questions about sex with young people.

Seasons of Sexuality. 14 min, 16 mm, color, video, 1980. Produced by Planned Parenthood of Syracuse. Order Source: PE. Purchase: $249 for 16 mm, $224 for video. Rental: $29

Dramatizes sexuality at various stages of human development from infancy through old age.

Sex Role Development. 22 min, 16 mm, color, 1974. Order Source: CRM and MCGH. Rental Source: IUAVC. Rental: $14.00

Examines some of the major sex-role stereotypes, tracing their transmission to children by way of the socialization process.

Update On The Homosexualities. 60 min, videocassette, color, nd. Distributor: HEM. Purchase: $295. Rental: $95

Dr. Alan Bell raises questions for discussion on sexuality, presents findings of researchers on "Homosexualities." Myths concerning homosexuals are debunked.

Pregnancy and Childbirth

Emotional Aspect of Pregnancy. 25 min, 16 mm, color, 1977. Order Source: PE.

Prepares expectant mothers and fathers for emotional changes experienced by both partners during pregnancy.

Miracle of Life. 57 mm, color, 1983. Source: T-L. Distributor: UCEMC. Rental: $53

Microphotography illustrates the process of human reproduction and presents footage of the actual conception of human life.

Family Problems and Crises (Alcoholism, Bulimia, Substance Abuse, Sexual Abuse, Dying

A Family Talks About Alcohol. 25 min, videocassette, color, nd. Distributor: IV.

Coping with an alcoholic in the family.

A Time To Die. 49 min, videocassette, color, 1982. Distributor: IV.

Facing death illustrated with FOCUS, a self-help group.

Angel Death. 33 min, 16 mm, color, 1979. Distributor: PSUPCR. Rental: $21

Paul Newman and Joanne Woodward narrate this documentary depicting the devastating mental and physical effects of the drug Angel Dust (PCP).

Bulimia. Videocassette. nd. Distributor: CMC. Purchase: VHS $150. BETA $150 3/4" $165. Shipping chg. $2. Rental: $50

Explains causes of bulimia, what bulimia is and interviews a recovering bulimic.

Wasting Away: Understanding Anorexia Nervosa and Bulimia. 45 min, color, videocassette, 1985. Produced by Barbara Castro Productions. Source: WPIC.

Preventive education for the at-risk age group on eating disorders. Physiological dangers are examined. Available treatment is discussed. Includes program guide for H.S. and college students and parents.

Changing Images of Women Drinkers. 24 min, videocassette, color, 1976. Distributor: ARF.

Videotape presents and examines current misconceptions about female alcohol abusers from a social-historical perspective.

Children of Denial. 28 min, color, 1983. Source: MAG. Distributor: UCEMC. Purchase: $450. Rental: $40

Explores the ways in which the children of alcoholics are affected by their parents' alcoholism.

Cocaine. 18 min, videocassette, color, 1979. Distributor: ARF.

Dramatizes the dilemma of a group of young adults concerning their potential use of cocaine.

Family Problems: Dealing with Crisis. Distributor: WDEMCO. 6 cassettes, 6 sound filmstrips (35 mm), 6–11 min. each, 1980.

Counsels children on moving, death, and divorce. Titles are "Looking at death," "Grieving," "When parents separate," "After the divorce," "When families move," and "The new neighborhood."

Hidden Alcoholics: Why Is Mommy Sick? 23 min, videocassette, color, nd. Distributor: IV.

Alcoholism in women.

I Want It All Now! 52 min, videocassette, color, nd. Distributor: IV.

Effects of divorce on adults and children.

Loved, Honoured and Bruised. 25 min, 16 mm, color, video, 1982. Produced by NFBC. Order Source: MEDIAG. Purchase: $445 for 16 mm, $310 for video. Rental: $50

Presents the story of an abused wife, what she endured, how she escaped and how she was assisted in starting a new life.

Marijuana—the facts. 25 min, videocassette, color, 1979. Distributor: ARF.

Film answers questions about marijuana.

The Last Taboo. 28 min, videocassette, color, nd. Distributor: IV.

Scenes from workshops on the effects and treatment of sexual abuse.

Families with a Mentally Ill Relative; Alzheimer's Disease

After the Tears: Teens Talk About Mental Illness in Their Families. Video tape, 1/2 VHS, 3/4 Umatic, 20 min, color. Producer/Distributor: UMHI. Order Source: WPIC.

Teens express their feelings about living with a mentally ill person in discussion with psychiatrist and psychologist.

Alzheimer's Disease. You Are Not Alone. 28 min, color, videocassette, 1985. Producer: WITF-TV. Source: WPIC.

Examines Alzheimer's Disease and its effects on its victims, their families and care givers.

Family Living and Adjustment (Bereavement, Aging)

Does Anybody Need Me Anymore? 29 min, 16 mm, color, 1977. Order Source: LCA.

A 46-year-old housewife painfully comes to terms with her empty nest; she has to decide what to do with the rest of her life.

Grieving: Suddenly Alone. 28 min, color, 1982. Source: CF. Distributor: UCEMC, Rental: $37

The typical emotional stages experienced by widows.

Trigger Films and Videotapes On Human Interaction Series 9. 16 mm, color, 9 video, 1981. Order Source: HUSED and MTITE. Purchase: $350 ea. for 16 mm. Rental: $60 ea. for 16 mm.

A series of short films promoting group discussions on topics including communication, assertiveness, women's issues, single and stepparents.

You and Your Aging Parents. 59 min, color, 3/4" video. Also Beta 2 and VHS. 1985. Producer/Sponsor: USNIH. Purchase: $155

Challenges of the "sandwich generation": middle-aged people caught between raising their own children and caring for aging parents are addressed. Guidelines for coping are offered along with recent scientific findings on aging.

Exceptional, Handicapped, Developmentally Disabled, Suicidal etc.

David And Lisa. 94 min, b & w, 1982. Source: Sterling. Distributor: UCEMC. Rental: $83

Sensitive drama of the tense but tender relationship between two deeply disturbed adolescents in a special therapeutic school.

Family Problems and Crises (Divorce, Illness, Unemployment, Death) Help Me! The Story of a Teenage Suicide. 25 min, 16 mm, color, video, 1981. Order Source: PHENIX and SLFP. Purchase: $395. Rental: $35

Dramatizes a teenage girl's suicide, based on case histories and professional knowledge. Outlines life crises, confusion and tension leading to teenage suicide.

Feeling Good About Yourself. 22 min, videocassette, color, nd. Distributor: IV.

Fostering self-esteem and socialization skills in the developmentally disabled.

First Steps. 25 min, videocassette, color, nd. Distributor: IV.

Training Educable Retarded Children

Parenting the Special Needs Child. 25 min, videocassette, color, nd.

Raising children with special needs.

Drug Therapy and ECT

Madness and Medicine. 49 min, color, 1977. Film, videocassette. Produced by ABC News. Source: WPIC. Commentator Howard K. Smith.

A mental institution is explored. Doctors and patients discuss use of drug therapy. Patients discuss re-orientation into society problems.

Shock Therapy: ABC News. "20/20" Documentary Film, 1/2 VHS, 3/4 Umatic, 16 min, color. Producer ABC News. Source: SI, Purchase: $95. nd. Speakers, Hugh Downs & Dr. Tim Johnson.

Patients discuss their ECT experience candidly. Medical authorities discuss pros and cons of ECT in a balanced presentation.

Problems of Vocational Change, Retirement, and Old Age

Bella. 55 min, 16 mm, video, 1982. Order Source: LTB. Purchase: $750 for 16 mm, $300 for video. Rental: $50

Many of the problems and concerns of the elderly are addressed in this dramatization of a vibrant older woman and her son's determination to have her lead a more sedate life.

Growing Old. 29 min, color, 1978. Source: McG-H. Distributor: UCEMC. Rental $26

Explores the problems of aging in America.

Chillysmith Farm. 55 min, 16 mm, color, 1981. Produced by Mark and Dan Jury. Source: FL. Purchase: $800. Videocassette: $650. Rental: $80

Raises issues on values, family life, birth, death, and individual responsibility for the aging.

Mental Health Film and Videotape Sources

ARF: Addiction Research Foundation, 33 Russell Street, Toronto, Ontario, Canada M552S1
BARR: Barr Films, 3490 E. Foothill Blvd., P.O. Box 5667, Pasadena, CA 91107
CANFDS: Canadian Filmakers Distribution

Centre, 144 Front St., W., Suite 430, Toronto, Ontario, Canada MSJ 2L7

CMC: Center for Medical Communication, School of Medicine, East Carolina University, Greenville, NC 27858-4384

CNEMAG: Cinema Guild, Division of Document Associates, 1697 Broadway, New York, NY 10019

FEIL: Edward Feil Productions, 4614 Prospect Avenue, Cleveland, OH 44103

FL (FLMLIB): Filmaker's Library, 133 East 5th St., New York, NY 10022

HEM: Health and Education Multimedia, Inc., 50 East 72 Street, New York, NY 10021 (212) 288-2297

HUSED: Human Services Development, 1616 Soldiers Field Rd., Boston, MA 02135

IUVAC: Indiana University, Audio-Visual Center, Bloomington, IN 47405

IV: Illinois Video. University of Illinois Film Center, 1325 South Oak Street, Champaign, IL 61820 1-800-252-1357

LCA: Learning Corporation of America, 1350 Ave of the Americas, New York, NY 10019

LTB: Little Theater Building, 240 West 44th St., New York, NY 10036

McG-H: CRM/McGraw-Hill Films, 110 15th St., Del Mar, CA 92014

MEDIAG: Media Guild, 11526 Sorrento Valley Rd. Suite J, San Diego, CA 92121

MTITE: MTI Teleprograms Inc., 3710 Commercial Ave., Northbrook, IL 60062

NAVC: National Audiovisual Center, Customer Services PJ, 8700 Edgeworth Dr., Capitol Heights, MD 20743-3701

NFBC: National Film Board of Canada, 1251 Avenue of the Americas, 16th Floor, New York, NY 10020

PE: Perennial Education, 477 Roger Williams, P.O. Box 855, Ravinia, Highland Park, IL 60035

PHENIX: Phoenix/BFA Film & Video, 468 Park Avenue, S., New York, NY 10016

PSUPCR: Psychological Cinema Register, Pennsylvania State University, University Park, PA 16802

SI: Somatics, Inc., 910 Sherwood Drive, Unit 18, Lake Bluff, IL 60044

SLFP: S-L Film Productions, Box 41108, Los Angeles, CA 90041

TEXFLM: Texture Films, Inc., 1600 Broadway, New York, NY 10019

T-L: Time-Life Multimedia, c/o Time-Life Video, 100 Eisenhower Drive, Paramus, NJ 07652

UCEMC: University of California, Extension Media Center, 2223 Fulton St., Berkeley, CA 94720

UMHI: United Mental Health, Inc., 401 Wood Street, Pittsburgh, PA 15222

USNIH: Department of Health, Education and Welfare, Public Health Service, National Institutes of Health

WDEMCO: Walt Disney Educational Media, Customer Service, 500 S. Buena Vista Dr., Burbank, CA 91521

WPIC: Western Psychiatric Institute and Clinic-Audiovisual Center, 3811 O'Hara Street, Pittsburgh, PA 15213, (Institutional Membership Available)

57
Short-Term Psychotherapy

Most of the psychotherapeutic treatments given in this country are short-term by the patients' choice. At the Postgraduate Center for Mental Health, one of the largest outpatient clinics in the United States, for example, patients are seen for psychoanalytically oriented psychotherapy with no limit set for the number of sessions to be given. Patients terminate treatment when they have decided they need no more help. Under these circumstances, the average number of sessions given comes to 17, and this is accompanied by an improvement rate of over 80 percent. Even though the Center is a psychoanalytic training unit, and patients are encouraged to remain in long-term therapy, only 15 percent are deemed suitable candidates for protracted treatment focused on reconstructive goals.

Follow-up studies on patients who have improved with short-term therapy have shown that the majority retain their gains and that some continue to progress by themselves once the start has been made during formal treatment. This does not mean that they would not have improved even more with long-term therapy. It merely indicates that short-term therapy is an important cost-effective approach for many psychiatric problems. It also has been shown by the nation's pioneer health maintenance organization to reduce utilization of medical resources. Yet there are still many therapists who are reluctant to accept the value of short-term approaches. Hoyt (1985) has listed the following reasons for this reluctance: (1) the belief that "more is better" and that long-term methods are more penetrative and thorough, (2) the idea that one should not contaminate the "pure gold" of analysis with baser metals of a supportive nature, (3) the therapist's predetermined notion that long-term therapy is indicated in spite of the patient's wishes, (4) the belief that short-term therapy involves an overwhelming investment of work and evergy, (5) the subtle economic factor of maintaining a steady rather than fluctuating source of income, (6) countertransference and undue therapist reactions to termination.

A number of studies have appeared that bear out that short-term therapy is a most efficient means of bringing about at least symptomatic improvement or cure. More than 25 years ago, this was proven by an experimental program of Group Health Insurance, Inc., in which 1200 participating psychiatrists treated a large sample of patients suffering from a wide spectrum of emotional problems (Avnet, 1962). At the end of the limited treatment period a 76 percent cure or improvement rate was scored. Follow-up investigation 2.5 years later recorded 81 percent of patients as having achieved recovery or improvement (Avnet, 1965). On the basis of these studies, it was grossly predicted that four of five patients receiving brief forms of treatment would report or feel some kind of improvement, even with current treatment methods executed by long-term oriented therapists.

That depth changes are also possible has been reported by psychoanalytically trained psychotherapists who present evidence that far-reaching and lasting changes may occur even with a limited number of dynamically oriented sessions (Sifneos, 1967, 1972; Davanloo, 1978; Malan, 1964a, 1976; Mann, 1973; Wolberg, 1980). This contention has understandably been subject to challenge. Personality distortions have a long history. They involve habit patterns and conditionings dating to childhood that have become so entrenched that they resist dislodging in a brief period. Repetitively they force the individual into difficulties with oneself and others, and they may persist even after years of therapy with an experienced psychoanalyst have revealed their source, traced their nefarious workings through developmental epochs, and painstakingly explored their present-day consequences. We can hardly expect that the relatively few sessions available for short-term therapy can effectuate the alchemy of extensive reorganization not possible with prolonged treatment. Reconditioning any established habit requires time; and time is of the essence in molding personality change if change is at all possible. *But experience persuades that this time need not be spent in all cases in continuous psychotherapy.* Removing some misconceptions about one's illness and one's background may dislodge the cornerstone, crumble the foundations, and eventually collapse some of the neurotic superstructure. This development may not be apparent until years have passed following a short-term treatment effort. Obviously, this bounty cannot always be realized. We may

hypothesize that the more experienced, highly trained, and flexible the therapist, the more likely it is to occur. Yet the environment in which the individual functions will undoubtedly also have a determining effect on any reconstructive changes that will evolve, since the milieu may sponsor and encourage or vitiate and crush healthy personality growth. But without having had the benefit of therapy, however brief it may have been, even the most propitious environment will have registered little improvement, save for exceptional cases.

There are patients who by themselves have already worked through a considerable bulk of their problems and who need the mere stimulation of a few sessions with a proficient therapist to enable them to proceed to astonishing development. Such an extensive dividend may not come about, nor should they be expected with many patients in short-term treatment, even where the therapist is sufficiently endowed by personality, training, and experience to do good psychotherapy.

Reasonable anticipations of what short-term treatment should accomplish in the average person are (1) relief of symptoms, (2) restoration to the optimal level of functioning that existed prior to the present illness, and (3) an understanding of some of the forces that initiated the immediate upset. When dynamic short-term therapy has been employed, we may, in addition, hope for (1) recognition of some pervasive personality problems that prevent a better life adjustment, (2) at least partial cognizance of their origin in past experiences and childhood conditionings, (3) recognition of the relationship between prevailing personality problems and the current illness, and (4) an identification of remediable measures that can be applied to environmental difficulties and perhaps to aspects of personality distortions as a whole. If treatment is managed well, patients will be given an opportunity to move beyond restoring their customary emotional balances. Should they possess sufficient motivation to propel them toward further development, should neurotic secondary gain elements be minimal, and should their environment be sufficiently accommodating to sponsor their continued movement, deeper alterations may occur. We may accept any reconstructive change as a welcome blessing if it comes, but, should it not, we must be satisfied that the patients have derived something worthwhile, even though goal limited, out of their sparse sessions. If therapy is interrupted at the peak of the improvement curve, before the idealized relationship projections dissolve in the acid substratum of transference and resistance, and before dependency has had an opportunity to establish a permanent beachhead in the relationship, the rate of improvement can be substantial.*

SELECTION OF CASES

While the best patients are undoubtedly those who are adequately motivated for therapy, intellectually capable of grasping immediate interpretations, proficient in working on an important focus in therapy, not too dependent, have had at least one good relationship in the past, and are immediately able to interact well with the therapist, they generally constitute only a small percentage of the population who apply to a clinic or private practitioner for treatment. The challenge is whether patients not so bountifully blessed with therapeutically positive qualities can be treated adequately on a short-term basis with some chance of improving their general modes of problem solving and perhaps of achieving at least a minor degree of personality reconstruction.

In practice one may distinguish at least

_____

* Some of the material in this chapter has been utilized and adapted, with the permission of the publishers from my books: Handbook of Short-Term Psychotherapy. New York, Thieme-Stratton, 1980; and Short-Term Psychotherapy, New York, Grune & Stratton, 1965.

five classes of patients who seek help. We have categorized them as class 1 through 5. In general, classes 1 to 3 require only short-term therapy. Classes 4 and 5 will need management for a longer period after an initial short-term regimen of therapy.

Class 1 Patients

Until the onset of the current difficulty class 1 patients have made a good or tolerable adjustment. The goal in therapy is to return them to their habitual level of functioning. Among such patients are those whose stability has been temporarily shattered by a catastrophic life event or crisis (death of a loved one, divorce, severe accident, serious physical illness, financial disaster, or other calamity). Some individuals may have been burdened with extensive conflicts as far back as childhood but up to the present illness have been able to marshall sufficient defenses to make a reasonable adaptation. The imposition of the crisis has destroyed their capacities for coping and has produced a temporary regression and eruption of neurotic mechanisms. The object in therapy for these patients is essentially supportive in the form of *crisis intervention* with the goal of reestablishing the previous equilibrium. Reconstructive effects while not expected are a welcome dividend. Generally, no more than six sessions are necessary.

An example of a class 1 patient is a satisfactorily adjusted woman of 50 years of age who drove a friend's automobile with an expired license and in the process had a severe accident, killing the driver of the car with which she collided and severely injuring two passengers in her own car, which was damaged beyond repair. She herself sustained a concussion and an injured arm and was moved by ambulance to a hospital, where she remained for a week. Charged with driving violations, sued by the owner of the car she borrowed and by the two injured passengers, she developed a dazed, depressed reaction and then periods of severe dizziness. Therapy here consisted of a good deal of support, reassurance, and help in finding a good lawyer, who counseled her successfully through her entangled legal complications.

Sometimes a crisis opens up closed traumatic chapters in one's life. In such cases it may be possible to link past incidents, feelings, and conflicts with the present upsetting circumstances enabling the patient to clarify anxieties and hopefully to influence deeper strata of personality. In the case above, for example, the patient recalled an incident in her childhood when while wheeling her young brother in a carriage, she accidentally upset it, causing a gash in her sibling that required suturing. Shamed, scolded, and spanked, the frightened child harbored the event that powered fear and guilt within herself. The intensity of her feelings surprised her, and their discharge during therapy fostered an assumption of a more objective attitude toward both the past and the immediate crisis event. It may not be possible in all cases, but an astute and empathic therapist may be able to help the patient make important connections between the past and present.

Class 2 Patients

The chief problem for class 2 patients is not a critical situation that has obtruded itself into their lives, but rather maladaptive patterns of behavior and/or disturbing symptoms. The object here is symptom cure or relief, modification of destructive habits, and evolvement of more adaptive behavioral configurations. Multiform techniques are employed for 8 to 20 sessions following eclectic *supportive-educational* models under the rubric of many terms, such as short-term behavioral therapy, short-term reeducative therapy, and so forth.

A phobia to air travel exemplifies the complaints of a class 2 patient. This was a great handicap for Miss J since job advancement necessitated visits to remote areas. The origin of the patient's anxiety lay in the last flight that she had taken 8 years previously. A disturbance in one of the engines reported to the passengers by the pilot necessitated a return to the point of origin. Since that time Miss J had not dared enter a plane. Therapy consisted of behavioral systematic desensitization, which in eight sessions resulted in a cure of the symptom.

In utilizing the various eclectic techniques, therapists alert themselves to past patterns that act as a paradigm for the present symptom complex, as well as to manifestations of resistance and transference. In a certain number of cases the patient may be helped to overcome resistances through resolution of provocative inner conflicts and in this way achieve results beyond the profits of symptom relief.

Class 3 Patients

Those in whom both symptoms and behavioral difficulties are connected with deep-seated intrapsychic problems that take the form of personality disturbances and inappropriate coping mechanisms make up the class 3 classification. Such patients have functioned at least marginally up to the time of their breakdown, which was perhaps initiated by an immediate precipitating factor. Most of these patients seek help to alleviate their distress or to solve a crisis. Some come specifically to achieve greater personality development. On evaluation either they are deemed unsuitable for long-term treatment, or extensive therapy is believed to be unnecessary, or for sundry other reasons cannot be done. They often possess the desire and capacity of work toward acquiring self-understanding.

The goal for class 3 patients is personality reconstruction along with symptomatic and behavioral improvement. Techniques are usually psychoanalytically oriented, involving interviewing, confrontation, dream and transference interpretations, and occasionally the use of adjunctive techniques like hypoanalysis. Some therapists confine the term *dynamic short-term therapy* to this class of patients and often employ a careful selection process to eliminate patients whom they feel would not work too well with their techniques (Buda, 1972; Davanloo, 1978, Malan, 1963; Sifneos, 1972; Ursano & Dressler, 1974).

An example of a class 3 patient is a young mother who brought her son in for consultation because he was getting such low marks in the final year of high school that the chances of his getting into college were minimal. Moreover, he firmly announced his unwillingness to go to college, insisting on finding a job after graduation so that he could buy an automobile and pursue his two hobbies: baseball and girls. During the interview with the boy it was obvious that he had motivation neither for further college education nor for any kind of therapeutic help. It was apparent too that his stubborn refusal to study and to go on to higher learning was a way of fighting off the domination of his mother and stepfather. Accordingly, the mother was advised to stop nagging the boy to continue his schooling. Instead she was urged to permit him to experiment with finding a job so that he could learn the value of a dollar and to discover for himself the kinds of positions he could get with so little education.

The next day the mother telephoned and reported that she had followed the doctor's instructions. However, she asked for an appointment for herself since she was overly tense and suffered from bad backaches that her orthopedist claimed were due to "nerves." What she wanted was to learn self-hypnosis, which her doctor claimed would help her relax. Abiding by her request, she was taught self-hypnosis—not only for relaxation purposes, but also to determine the sources of her tension. Through interviewing aided by induced imagery during hypnosis, she was able to recognize how angry she was at me for not satisfying her desire to force her son to go to college. Images of attacking her father, who frustrated and dominated her, soon brought out her violent rage. She realized then that her obsequious behavior toward her husband was a cover for her hostility. Acting on this insight, she was soon able to express her anger and to discuss her reactions with her husband and the reasons for her rages. This opened up channels of communication with a dramatic resolution of her symptoms and an improvement in her feelings about herself and her attitudes toward people, confirmed by a 5-year follow-up.

Patients are generally considered unsuited for dynamic short-term psychotherapy if they are not motivated to search for sources of their problems, are unable to withstand the frustration of receiving immediate symptomatic relief, cannot establish a close interpersonal relationship, do not have the ability or ego strength to tolerate anxiety consequent to the challenging and yielding of neurotic patterns of behavior, are not sufficiently "psychologically minded" to be able to reflect on reasons for their maladjustment, or resort habitually to the abuse of tranquilizers, alcohol, or drugs as a way of dealing with tension.

Class 4 Patients

Patients of the class 4 category are those whose problems even an effective therapist may be unable to mediate in a brief span and who will require more prolonged management after the initial short-term period of formal therapy has disclosed what interventions would best be indicated. The word "management" should be stressed because not all long-term modalities need be, and often are not, best aimed at intrapsychic alterations. Among individuals who appear to require help over an extended span are those whose problems are so severe and deep-rooted that all therapy can do for them is to keep them in reasonable reality functioning, which they could not achieve without a prolonged therapeutic resource.

Class 4 patients include the following:

1. Individuals with chronic psychotic reactions and psychoses in remission who require some supervisory individual or group with whom contact is regularly made over sufficiently spaced intervals to provide some kind of human relationship, however tenuous this may be, to oversee essential psychotropic drug intake, to regulate the milieu, and to subdue the perils of psychotic processes when these are periodically released. Such patients do not usually require formal prolonged psychotherapy or regular sessions with a psychotherapist; they could do as well, or better, with the supportive help of an empathic counselor. Milieu therapy, rehabilitation procedures, and social or group approaches may be useful.

2. Persons with serious character problems with tendencies toward alcoholism and drug addiction who require regular guidance, surveillance, group approaches, and rehabilitative services over an indefinite period.

3. Individuals with uncontrollable tendencies toward acting-out who need controls from without to restrain them from expressing impulses that will get them into difficulties. Examples are those who are occasionally dominated by dangerous perversions, desires for violence, lust for criminal activities, masochistic needs to hurt themselves, accident proneness, self-defeating gambling, and other corruptions. Many such persons recognize that they need curbs on their uncontrollable wayward desires.

4. Persons so traumatized and fixated in their development that they have never overcome infantile and childish needs and defenses that contravene a mature adaptation. For instance, there may be a constant entrapment in relationships with surrogate parental figures, which usually evolve for both subjects and hosts into a sado-masochistic purgatory. Yet such persons cannot function without a dependency prop, and the therapist offers to operate as a more objective and nonpunitive parental agency. Some of these patients may need a dependency support the remainder of their lives.

   Many of the patients in this category fall into devastating frustrating dependency relationships during therapy or alternatives to therapy from which they cannot or will not extricate themselves. Realizing the dangers of this contingency, we can, however, plan our strategy accordingly, for example, by providing supportive props outside of the treatment situation if support is needed. Nor need we abandon reconstructive objectives, once we make proper allowances for possible regressive interludes. In follow-up contacts, I was pleased to find, there had been change after 5,10, and in some cases 15 years in patients who I believed had little chance to achieve personality alterations.

5. Persons with persistent and uncontrollable anxiety reactions powered (a) by unconscious conflicts of long standing with existing defenses so fragile that the patient is unable to cope with ordinary demands of life or (b) by a noxious and irremediable environment from which the patient cannot escape.

6. Borderline patients balanced precariously on a razor edge of rationality.

7. Intractable obsessive - compulsive

persons whose reactions serve as defenses against psychosis.

8. Paranoidal personalities who require an incorruptible authority for reality testing.

9. Individuals with severe long-standing psychosomatic and hypochondrical conditions, such as ulcerative colitis, or chronic pain syndromes that have resisted ministrations from medical, psychological, and other helping resources. Often these symptoms are manifestations of defenses against psychotic disintegration.

10. People presenting with depressive disorders who are in danger of attempting suicide and require careful regulation of antidepressive medications or electroconvulsive therapy followed by psychotherapy until the risk of a relapse is over.

Class 5 Patients

In class 5 we place those individuals who seek and require extensive reconstructive personality changes and have the finances, time, forbearance, and ego strength to tolerate long-term psychoanalysis or psychoanalytically oriented psychotherapy. In addition, they have had the good fortune of finding a well-trained, experienced, and mature analyst who is capable of dealing with dependent transference and other resistances as well as with one's personal countertransferences. Patients who can benefit more from long-term reconstructive therapy than from dynamically oriented short-term therapy are often burdened by interfering external conditions that may be so strong, or by the press of inner neurotic needs so intense, that they cannot proceed on their own toward treatment objectives after the short-term therapeutic period has ended. Continued monitoring by a therapist is essential to prevent a relapse. In certain cases the characterologic detachment is so great that the patient is unable to establish close and trusting contact with a therapist in a brief period, and a considerable bulk of time during the short-term sessions may be occupied with establishing a working relationship.

In addition to adults a special group of patients requiring long-term therapy are highly disturbed children and adolescents who have been stunted in the process of personality development and who require a continuing relationship with a therapist who functions as a guiding, educational, benevolent parental figure.

Long-term patients in classes 4 and 5 usually constitute less than one-quarter of the patient load carried by the average psychotherapist. The bulk of one's practice will generally be composed of patients who may adequately be managed by short-term methods.

ESSENTIAL COMPROMISES IN SHORT-TERM THERAPY

Apart from the fact that acceptance of abbreviated goals may be necessary in short-term therapy, a number of other compromises may be essential. Prominent among these are (1) the employment of greater activity than in longer term treatment, (2) the flexible practice of differential therapeutics, (3) the overcoming of prejudices related to the "depth" of therapy, (4) avoiding denigration of short-term as compared with long-term approaches, and (5) utilization of interrupted rather than continuous treatments.

Encouragement of Therapist Activity

Anathema to short-term therapy is passivity in the therapist. Where time is of no object, the therapist can settle back comfortably and let the patient pick his or her way through the lush jungles of the psyche. To apply the same tactics in the few sessions that are available in short-term therapy will usually bring meager rewards. Treatment failures are often the product of lack of proper activity. It is for this reason that the conventional non-directive, detached attitude is unwise, as are free association and the use of the couch. Focused interviewing in the sitting up position is almost mandatory.

There are some therapists, of course, whose personalities support a passive role. Such practitioners may still be able to make an effort at involving themselves more actively, assuming as their objective a rapid assay of the central problem, dealing with its most obvious aspects. If one concentrates one's fire, one will be able to hit the target with greater certainty. At least the therapist will prevent the patient from steering the course of treatment into unproductive channels.

In short-term therapy, one cannot afford the luxury as in prolonged treatment of permitting the patient to wallow in resistance until he or she somehow muddles through. Resistance will, of course, occur, but it must be dealt with rapidly through an active frontal attack before it paralyzes progress.

One of the most difficult things to teach students aspiring to become short-term therapists is that activity in the relationship, with an involvement of oneself as a real person, and open expressions of interest, sympathy, and encouragement, are permissible. Somehow passivity has become synonymous with doing good psychotherapy with the result that at the end of the prescribed sessions the patient is no further advanced toward resolution of the problem than when therapy first started. Often therapists are not aware of how uninvolved they are until observed working behind a one-way mirror or through videotaping and their passivity is pointed out to them by a supervisor. Whether they can do anything about their impassiveness is another matter, but, in my experience, encouragement to express a more open interest, to engage oneself more vigorously in the interview, to give one's facial expressions a free release, to offer advice where needed, and to make

interpretations when necessary may vitalize the therapeutic situation sufficiently to convince that a stoic bearing, a blankness of countenance, and an unresourceful adherence to a phlegmatic role are not necessarily the "scientific" way of doing therapy. This does not mean that therapists will have to revolutionize their personalities in order to do short-term therapy. Individuals are constituted differently. Some therapists by nature are quiet and reserved; forcefulness is not within their behavioral range. But they will still be able to exercise the essential activity through a communicative and reassuring relationship. Activity means being interested in the patient and immediate life problems; it does not mean being controlling of the patient. Neither does it give the therapist license to cuddle the patient, make the patient's decisions and otherwise rob the patient of the responsibility of doing things for himself or herself.

Use of Differential Therapeutics

Insofar as the use of a differential therapeutics is concerned (see page 552) psychoanalytically trained therapists are particularly fearful of therapeutic contaminants. Mindful of the long struggle for acceptance of analytic covenants, they are reluctant to take what they consider to be a backward step by dignifying nonanalytic techniques. In this attitude they attempt to delay Freud's prediction that it eventually may be necessary to blend the "gold" of psychoanalysis with the "copper" of other therapies.

Short-term therapy requires a combination of procedures from psychiatric, psychoanalytic, psychological, and sociological fields. Sometimes utilized in the same patient are psychotherapeutic techniques, casework, drugs, hypnosis, group therapy, psychodrama, and desensitization and reconditioning procedures. This fusion of methods, in which there are extracted from the different approached tactics of proven merit, promise the most productive results. To implement such an eclectic regimen, a degree of flexibility is required that enables the therapist to step outside the bounds of training biases and to experiment with methods from fields other than habitual ones.

Here we run headlong into prejudices about what will happen to a personally cherished system of psychotherapy if one introduces into it foreign elements. It may reassure therapists to keep reminding themselves that there is nothing sacred about any of our present day modes of doing psychotherapy. They all work in some cases and fail in others. We actually owe it to our patients, as well as to ourselves to experiment with as many techniques as we can in order to learn which of these will be effective and which do not yield good results. Certain rigidities in the therapist will interfere with the proper experimentation. Eclecticism does not sanction wild therapy. It presupposes a scrupulous empirical attitude, assaying the values of the different methods for the great variety of conditions that challenge the therapist in daily practice.

Overcoming Prejudices About Depth

Important also is the overcoming of prejudices about "depth." Before a therapist is capable of doing effective short-term therapy he or she will need to abandon value judgments about "superficial" versus "deep" therapy. There is a tendency on the part of psychotherapists to put varying significances on levels of depth as they apply to the content of the therapeutic interviews. Material that relates to the past, from the dredgings of the unconscious, and from transferential interactions become emblazoned with special virtue. All else is labeled "superficial" from which little may be expected insofar as real personality change is concerned. Such notions are the product of a misuse of psychoanalytic wisdom that purports that the only true road to cure is through the alleys of the unconscious. This in spite of the fact that clinical experience

persuades that the divulgence of unconscious content carries no guarantee that a patient will get well.

Psychotherapy is no mining operation that depends for its yield exclusively on excavated psychic ore. It is human interaction that embraces a variety of dimensions, psychological and social, verbal and nonverbal. Some of these elements are so complex that we can scarcely express them in words. How can we, for example, describe such things as "faith," "hope," "trust," "acquisition of insight," "meaning," "restoration of mastery," "self-realization," and "development of capacity to love." These are aspects of therapy fluctuating within the matrix of change. In the architecture of personality building, no one tissue or girder stands alone. They are all interrelated. Revelation of the unconscious blends into the total therapeutic Gestalt. It does not constitute it.

Even though in short-term therapy we can only deal with the immediate and manifest, we may ultimately influence the total personality in depth, including the unconscious. Human warmth and feeling, experienced by a patient in one session with an empathic therapist, may achieve more profound alterations than years with a probing, detached therapist intent on wearing out resistance. This does not mean that one should be neglectful of the unconscious. Within a short span of therapy, repressed psychic aspects may still be elicited and handled.

Correcting Misconceptions About Time in Therapy

Rectification of prejudices about the superiority of long-term over short-term therapy is another must. It may be argued that if a few sessions can potentially induce corrective change, would not prolonged treatment do the job even more effectively, enabling the individual to apply to current life situation the kinds of discipline that sponsor a healthy perspective? There is no question that an extended time period permits the therapist to handle resistance that some patients mobilize toward the giving up of their neuroses. There is no question, too, that some patients, for instance, those that are masochistically inclined, gain a subversive gratification out of their neurotic misery and are loathe to yield it too readily. Here the therapist functions as a sentinel, alerting the patient to the presence and particular manifestations of resistance. Such patients would probably do better in prolonged treatment if we could avoid the trap of dependency and could successfully deal with transference elements that unleashed tend to enmesh the patient in the tangled folds of the past.

On the other hand, we may overemphasize the need for long-term treatment in many patients. We may assume that all persons possess healthy and resilient elements in their personality, which given half a chance, will burgeon forth. A brief period of treatment may be all that is required to set into motion a process of growth.

The question of the superiority of long-term over short-term therapy is therefore a rhetorical one. Experience persuades that some patients get nowhere with long-term therapy and do remarkably well with short-term approaches. There are others in whom short-term treatment does not succeed in denting the surface of their problem and who require a prolonged period of therapy before the slightest penetration is made. As has been pointed out the problem of selection of cases is as poignant a one as is the utilization of proper techniques. It is doubtful that we can always define syndromes that best will respond to either approach. Factors other than symptomatology and diagnosis determine how the patient will progress. Nor is it possible to delineate precisely special tactics that can expedite treatment in all cases. What works with one therapist and patient may not work with others. Each therapist will need to experiment with methods best suited to individual style and personality.

At the present stage of our knowledge, long-term treatment is not always an indulgence. If the patient is so constituted as to be able to take advantage of explorations into the psyche, and if the therapist is equipped to work on a depth level, extended therapy may be a rewarding adventure. Without question the "working-through" of psychological blocks, and the resolution of the manifold facades and obstructions the mind concocts to defeat itself, can in some persons best be accomplished in a prolonged professional relationship. Here the therapist concentratedly and continuously observes the patient, dealing with resistances as they develop, and bringing the patient to an awareness of the basic conflicts that power defensive operations. Given the proper patient with a personality problem of long-standing, who possesses an adequate motivation for change, with an ego structure sufficiently plastic, an environment that is malleable, a social milieu that will accept the patient's new found freedoms, who can afford luxuries of time and finances, and who relates constructively in a treatment experience with a well-trained psychotherapist, long-term therapy will offer the best opportunity for the most extensive personality change.

Moreover, there are certain chronic conditions that respond to no other instrumentality than continuous psychotherapy, no matter how assiduously the therapist is applied toward releasing forces of health within the patient. The situation is akin to diabetes in which the patient survives solely because he or she receives life-giving insulin. In certain problems, dependency is so deep-rooted that the patient can exist only in the medium of a protective relationship in which the patient can receive dosages of support. The patient appears to thrive in therapy and seemingly may be utilizing insights toward a better integration. But this improvement is illusory; the patient constantly needs to maintain a life-line to the helping authority to whom he or she clings with a desperation that defies all efforts at treatment termination. Such patients obviously will not do well with short-term methods, although long-term approaches may be inadequate also.

From the foregoing one may get the impression that long-term therapy is the preferred treatment where the patient has a severe personality disorder. This is not always the case. There are some risks in employing prolonged treatment in many patients. Dependent individuals who have been managing to get along on their own, albeit on a tenuous independency level, may become more and more helpless, and importune for increasing demonstrations of support with an exaggeration rather than a relief of their symptoms. Individuals with fragile ego structures will tend to develop frightening transference reactions in prolonged treatment, or they may go to pieces in the process of releasing repressions.

Patients who have been found to respond best to short-term therapy are those who possess a resilient repertoire of coping mechanisms, and who, prior to their immediate upset, were functioning with some degree of satisfaction. It is essential here to qualify the finding that acute problems are best suited for short-term approaches. Our frame of reference is the conventional body of techniques that we utilize today. There is no reason to assume that with the refinement of our methodology even severe personality difficulties may not be significantly improved on a short-term basis. This author has personally observed chronic cases treated with short-term methods, including obsessive-compulsive neurosis and borderline schizophrenia, and has noted many gratifying results. Indeed, had I believed that these patients should continue in extended therapy, I am certain that some would have marooned themselves in permanent treatment waters that would have swamped their tiny surviving islands of independence.

The best strategy, in this author's opinion, is to assume that every patient, irrespective of diagnosis, will respond to short-term treatment unless proven refractory to it. If the therapist approaches each patient with the idea of doing as much as reasonably possible within the span of up to 20 treatment sessions, the patient will be given an opportunity to take advantage of short-term treatment to the limit of potential. If this expediency fails, a resort to prolonged therapy may be taken.

Use of Interrupted Treatments

Realization that therapy is not a close-ended matter with permanent beginning, middle, and end phases has introduced a new model for the delivery of services. This is oriented around the principle that termination of psychotherapy with a successful outcome does not necessarily immunize the individual against future emotional illness. Conditions outside the individual related to career, status, economic stability, marital situation, and social milieu, as well as within the person, e.g., increased vulnerabilities associated with aging, value change, and physical well-being may impose stresses beyond habitual adaptive capacities. Returning for treatment on a short-term basis may be as important for many people as visiting their personal physicians throughout their life for unexpected ailments that periodically develop. The idea that one can discharge a patient and never see the patient again is an erroneous one and should not be encouraged. This means that all therapy is relevant to a time frame, and that patients are seen as "evolving, receptive to and needing different interventions at different times" (Bennett, 1983).

CATEGORIES OF SHORT-TERM THERAPY

A number of attempts have been made to subdivide short-term therapy into a number of distinctive categories. In general these fall into three groupings (1) crisis intervention, (2) supportive-educational short-term therapy, and (3) dynamic short-term therapy. The goals of crisis intervention usually differ from those in the other brief methods. Here, after from 1 to 6 sessions, an attempt is made to restore habitual balances in the existing life situation. Supportive educational approaches, such as behavior therapy, constitute forms of intervention that are undertaken, along with educational indoctrination, to relieve or remove symptoms, to alter faulty habit patterns, and to rectify behavioral deficits. To attain these objectives, a variety of eclectic techniques is implemented, depending on the idosyncratic needs of the patient and the skills and methodological preferences of the therapist. The number of sessions varies, ranging from 6 to 25. In some cases less than six sessions may be ample, and occasionally even one session has proven productive (Rockwell & Pinkerton, 1982; Bloom, 1981). In dynamic short-term therapy the thrust is toward achieving or at least starting a process of personality reconstruction. Sessions here may extend to 40 or more.

In crisis intervention, sessions may have to be prolonged, psychotropic medications may have to be employed, family members may have to be actively involved, and a multidisciplinary treatment team may have to be available at times. Less urgent forms of crisis intervention that are being practiced are indistinguishable from the kind of counseling commonly done in social agencies. The focus is on mobilizing positive forces in the individual to cope with the crisis stiuation, to resolve remediable environmental difficulties as rapidly as possible, utilizing if necessary appropriate resources in the community, and to take whatever steps are essential to forestall future crises of a similar or related nature. No attempt is made at diagnosis or psychodynamic formulation. Other kinds of crisis intervention attempt provisionally to detect underlying intrapsychic issues and past formative experiences and to relate these to current problems. More extensive goals than mere emotional stabilization are sought.

The "social-counseling" forms of crisis intervention are generally employed in walk-in clinics and crisis centers where large numbers of clients apply for help and where there is a need to avoid getting involved too intimately with clients who might get locked into a dependent relationship. Visits are as frequent as can be arranged and are necessary during the first 4 to 6 weeks. The family is often involved in some of the interviews, and home visits may have to be made. The interview focus is on the present situational difficulty and often is concerned with the most adaptive ways of coping with immediate pressing problems. Vigorous educational measures are sometimes exploited to activate the patient. The employment of supportive measures and the use of other helping individuals and agencies is encouraged.

More ambitious, goal-directed forms of crisis intervention are often seen operating in outpatient clinics and private practice. If the assigned number of sessions has been exhausted and the patient still requires more help, referral to a clinic or private therapist or continued treatment with the same therapist is considered.

Brief supportive-educational approaches have sponsored a variety of techniques, such as traditional interviewing, behavior therapy, relaxation, hypnosis, biofeedback, somatic therapy, Gestalt therapy, sex therapy, group therapy, etc., singly or in combination. The number of sessions will vary according to the individual therapist, who usually anchors the decision on how long it takes to control symptoms and enhance adaptation.

The philosophy that enjoins therapists to employ dynamic short-term treatment is the conviction that many of the derivatives of present behaviors are rooted in needs, conflicts, and defenses that reach into the past, often as far back as early childhood. Some of the most offensive of these components are unconscious, and while they obtrude themselves in officious and often destructive ways, they are usually rationalized and shielded with a tenacity that is frustrating both to the victim and to those around. The preferred way, according to prevailing theories, that one can bring these mischief makers under control is to propel them into consciousness so that the patient realizes what he or she is up against. By studying how the patient utilizes the relationship with the therapist, the latter has an opportunity to detect how these buried aberrations operate, projected as they are into the treatment situation. Dreams, fantasies, verbal associations, nonverbal behavior, and transference manifestations are considered appropriate media for exploration because they embody unconscious needs and conflicts in a symbolic form. By training, therapists believe themselves capable of decoding these symbols. Since important unconscious determinants shape one's everyday behavior, the therapist tries to establish a connection between the patient's present personality in operation, such as temperament, moods, morals, and manners, with early past experiences and conditionings in order to help the patient acquire some insight into how problems originated.

METHODOLOGY

A variety of short-term therapeutic methods have been proposed by different therapists (Barten, 1969, 1971; Bellak, 1968; Bellak & Small, 1965; Castelnuovo-Tedesco, 1971; Davanloo, 1978; Gottschalk et al, 1967; Harris, MR, et al, 1971; Levene et al, 1972; Malan, 1964, 1976; Mann, J, 1973; Patterson, V, et al, 1971; Sifneos, 1967; 1972; Wolberg, LR, 1980). There obviously are differences among therapists in the way that short-term therapy is implemented—for example, the focal areas cho-

sen for attention and exploration, the relative emphasis on current as compared to past issues, the attention paid to transference, the way resistance is handled, the depth of probing, the dealing with unconscious material that surfaces, the precise manner of interpretation, the degree of activity, the amount of advice giving, the kinds of interventions and adjunctive devices employed, and the prescribed number of sessions. Moreover, all therapists have to deal with their own personalities, prejudices, theoretical biases, and skills, all of which will influence the way they work. In spite of such differences, there are certain basic principles that have evolved from the experiences of a wide assortment of therapists working with diverse patient populations that have produced good results. The practitioner may find he or she can adapt at least some of these principles to his or her own style of operation even though continuing to employ methods that have proven themselves to be effective and are not exactly in accord with what other professionals do. While many of the suggestions as to technique discussed in previous chapters are applicable, in the pages that follow 20 techniques are suggested as a general guide for short-term therapy.

The important operations consist of (1) establishing a rapid positive working relationship (therapeutic alliance), (2) dealing with initial resistances, (3) gathering historical data, (4) selecting a focus for therapy, (5) defining precipitating events, (6) evolving a working hypothesis, (7) making a tentative diagnosis, (8) conveying the need for the patient's active participation in the therapeutic process, (9) making a verbal contract, (10) utilizing appropriate techniques in an active and flexible manner, (11) studying the reactions and defenses of the patient to the techniques being employed, (12) relating present-day patterns to patterns that have operated throughout the patient's life, (13) watching for transference reactions, (14) examining possible countertransference feelings, (15) alerting oneself to resistances, (16) assigning homework, (17) accenting the termination date, (18) terminating therapy, (19) assigning continuing self-help activities, and (20) arranging for further treatment if necessary.

These operations explained below, may be utilized in toto or in part by therapists who can adapt them to their styles of working.

Establish as Rapidly as Possible a Positive Working Relationship (Therapeutic Alliance)

An atmosphere of warmth, understanding, and acceptance is basic to achieving a positive working relationship with a patient. Empathy particularly is an indispensible personality quality that helps to solidify a good therapeutic alliance.

Generally, at the initial interview, the patient is greeted courteously by name, the therapist introducing oneself as in this excerpt:

Th. How do you do, Mr. Roberts. I am Dr. Wolberg. Won't you sit down over there (*pointing to a chair*), and we'll talk things over and I'll see what I can do to help you (*patient gets seated*).

Pt. Thank you, doctor. (*pause*)

A detached deadpan professional attitude is particularly fatal. It may, by eliciting powerful feelings of rejection, provoke protective defensive maneuvers that neutralize efforts toward establishing a working relationship.

It is difficult, of course, to delineate exact rules about how a therapeutic alliance may be established rapidly. Each therapist will utilize himself or herself to achieve this end in terms of own techniques and capacities in rapport. Some therapists possess an extraordinary ability even during the first session, as the patient describes the problem and associated feelings, of putting the patient at ease, of mobilizing faith in the effectiveness of methods that will be utilized, and of subduing the patient's doubts and concerns. A confident enthusiastic manner and a conviction of one's ability to help somehow communicates itself nonverbally to the patient. Therapist enthusiasm is an important ingredient in treatment.

The following suggestions may prove helpful.

Verbalize What The Patient May Be Feeling

Putting into words for the patient what he or she must be feeling but is unable to conceptualize is one of the most effective means of establishing contact. "Reading between the lines" of what the patient is talking about will yield interesting clues. Such simple statements as, "You must be very unhappy and upset about what has happened to you" or "I can understand how unhappy and upset you must be under the circumstances" present the therapist as an empathic person.

Encourage The Patient That The Situation Is Not Hopeless

It is sometimes apparent that, despite presenting oneself for help, the patient is convinced that he or she is hopeless and that little will actually be accomplished from therapy. The therapist who suspects this may say "You probably feel that your situation is hopeless because you have already tried various things that haven't been effective. But there *are* things that can be done, that *you can do* about your situation and I shall guide you toward making an effort." Empathizing with the patient may be important: "Putting myself in your position, I can see that you must be very unhappy and upset about what is happening to you."

Sometimes it is useful to define the patient's role in developing and sustaining the problem in a nonaccusing way: 'You probably felt you had no other alternative than to do what you did." "What you are doing now seems reasonable to you, but there may be other ways that could create fewer problems for you."

While no promise is made of a cure, the therapist must convey an attitude of conviction and faith in what is being done.

Pt. I feel hopeless about getting well. Do you think I can get over this trouble of mine?

Th. Do you really have a desire to get over this trouble? If you really do, this is nine-tenths of the battle. You will want to apply yourself to the job of getting well. I will point out some things you can do, and if you work at them yourself, I see no reason why you can't get better.

Where the patient becomes self-deprecatory and masochistic, the positive aspects of reactions may be stressed. For example, should the patient say that he or she is constantly furious, one might reply, "This indicates that you are capable of feeling strongly about things." If the patient claims detachment and does not feel anything, the answer may be, "This is a sign you are trying to protect yourself from hurting." Comments such as these are intended to be protective in order to preserve the relationship with the therapist. Later when it becomes apparent that the relationship is sufficiently solid, the therapist's comments may be more provocative and challenging. The patient's defenses being threatened, anxiety may be mobilized, but the patient will be sustained by the therapeutic alliance and will begin to utilize it rather than run away from it.

Deal With Initial Resistances

Among the resistances commonly encountered at the first session are lack of motivation and disappointment that the therapist does not fulfill a stereotype. The therapist's age, race, nationality, sex, appearance, professional discipline, and religion may, as emphasized in previous chapters, not correspond with the patient's ideas of someone in whom he or she wants to confide.

Th. I notice that it is difficult for you to tell me about your problem.

Pt. (*Obviously in discomfort*) I don't know what to say. I expected that I would see an older person. Have you had much experience with cases like me?

Th. What concerns you is a fear that I don't have as much experience as you believe is necessary and that an older person would do a better job. I can understand how you feel, and you *may* do better with an older person. However, supposing you tell me about your problem and then if you wish I will refer you to the best older therapist who can treat the kind of condition you have.

This tactic of accepting the resistance and inviting the patient to tell you more about himself or herself, as stated before, can be applied to other stereotypes besides age. In a well-conducted interview the therapist will reveal as an empathic understanding person, and the patient will want to continue with him or her in therapy.

Another common form of resistance occurs in the person with a psychosomatic problem who has been referred for psychotherapy and who is not at all convinced that a psychological problem exists. In such cases the therapist may proceed as in this excerpt.

Pt. Dr. Jones sent me here. I have a problem with stomachaches a long time and have been seeing doctors for it for a long time.

Th. As you know, I am a psychiatrist. What makes you feel your problem is psychological?

Pt. I don't think it is, but Dr. Jones says it might be, and he sent me here.

Th. Do you think it is?

Pt. No, I can't see how this pain comes from my head.

Th. Well, it might be organic, but with someone who has suffered as long as you have the pain will cause a good deal of tension and upset. [*To insist on the idea that the problem is psychological would be a poor tactic. First the therapist may be wrong, and the condition may be organic though undetectable by present day tests and examinations. Second, the patient may need to retain the notion of the symptom's organicity and even to be able to experience attenuated pain from time to time as a defense against overwhelming anxiety or, in certain serious conditions, psychosis.*]

Pt. It sure does.

Th. And the tension and depression prevent the stomach from healing. Tension interferes with healing of even true physical problems. Now when you reduce tension, it helps the healing. It might help you even if your problem is organic.

Pt. I hope so.

Th. So what we can do is try to figure out what problems you have that are causing tension, and also lift the tension. This should help your pain.

Pt. I would like that. I get tense in my job with the people I work. Some of them are crumbs. [*Patient goes on talking, opening up pockets of anxiety.*]

The object is to accept the physical condition as it is and not label it psychological for the time being. Actually, as has been indicated, it may be an essential adaptational symptom, the patient needing it to maintain an equilibrium. Dealing with areas of tension usually will help relieve the symptom, and as psychotherapy takes hold, it may make it unnecessary to use the symptom to preserve psychological homeostasis.

Motivational lack may obstruct therapy in other situations, as when a patient does not come to treatment on his or her own accord but is sent or brought by relatives or concerned parties. Additional examples are children or adolescents with behavior problems, people who are addicted (drug, alcohol, food, gambling), and people receiving pensions for physical disabilities. More on handling lack of motivation is detailed elsewhere (p 573).

Gather Historical Material and Other Data

Through "sympathetic listening" the patient is allowed to tell the story with as little interruption as possible, the therapist interpolating questions and comments that indicate a compassionate understanding of the patient's situation. It is hoped that the data gathered in the initial interview permits a tentative diagnosis and a notion of the etiology and possibly the psychodynamics. Should the patient fail to bring up important immediate concerns and problems, the therapist can ask direct questions. Why has the patient come to treatment at this time? What has been done about the problem to date? Has the patient arrived at any idea as to what is causing the difficulty? What does the patient expect or what would he or she like to get from therapy?

It is often advantageous to follow an outline (see Ch. 24) in order to do as complete a history or behavioral analysis as possible during the first session or two. This may necessitate interrupting the patient after the therapist is convinced that he or she has sufficient helpful data about any one topic.

Among the questions to be explored are the following:

1. Have there been previous upsets that resemble the present one?
2. Were the precipitating events of previous upsets in any way similar to the recent ones?
3. What measures aggravated the previous upsets and which alleviated the symptoms?
4. Apart from the most important problem for which help is sought, what other symptoms are being experienced (such as tension, anxiety, depression, physical symptoms, sexual problems, phobias, obsessions, insomnia, excessive drinking?
5. What tranquilizers, energizers, hypnotics, and other medications are being taken?

Statistical data are rapidly recorded (age, education, occupation, marital status, how long married, and children if any). What was (and is) the patient's mother like? The father? Any problems with brothers or sisters? Were there any problems experienced as a child (at home, at school, with health, in relationships with other children)? Any problems in sexual development, career choice, occupational adjustment? Can the patient remember any dreams, especially nightmarish and repetitive dreams? Were there previous psychological or psychiatric treatments?

To obtain further data, the patient may be exposed to the Rorschach cards, getting a few responses to these unstructured materials without scoring. This is optional, of course. The therapist does not have to be a clinical psychologist to do this, but he or she should have read some material on the Rorschach. The patient may also be given a sheet of paper and a pencil and be asked to draw a picture of a man and a woman. Some therapists prefer showing the patient rapidly the Thematic Apperception Cards. What distortions appear in the patient's responses and drawings? Can one correlate these with what is happening symptomatically? These tests are no substitutes for essential psychological tests where needed, which can best be done by an experienced clinical psychologist. But they can fulfill a useful purpose in picking up gross defects in the thinking process, borderline or schizophrenic potentialities, paranoidal tendencies, depressive manifestations, and so on. No more than 10 or 15 minutes should be utilized for this purpose.

An example of how Rorschach cards can help reveal underlying impulses not brought out by regular interviewing methods is illustrated in a severely depressed man with a controlled, obsessional character whose passivity and inability to express aggression resulted in others taking advantage of him at work and in his marriage. When questioned about feelings of hostility or aggression, he denied these with some pride. The following were his responses to the Rorschach Cards.

1. Two things flying at each other.
2. Something sailing into something.
3. Two figures pulling something apart; two adults pulling two infants apart.
4. Animals' fur spread out. X-ray (*drops card*)
5. Flying insect, surgical instrument forceps.
6. Animal or insect split and flattened out.
7. X-ray fluoroscope of embryo, adolescents looking at each other with their hair whipping up in the wind.
8. Two animals climbing a tree, one on each side; female organs in all of these cards.
9. Fountain that goes up and spilling blood.
10. Underwater scene, fish swimming, crabs. Inside of a woman's body.

The conflicts related to aggression and being torn apart so apparent in the responses became a principal therapeutic focus and brought forth his repressed anger at his mother.

Select the Symptoms, Behavioral Difficulties, or Conflicts that You Feel are Most Amenable for Improvement

The selection with the patient of an important problem area or a disturbing symptom on which to work is for the purpose of avoiding excursions into regions that, while perhaps challenging, will dilute a meaningful effort. Thus, when you have decided on what to concentrate, inquire of the patient if in his or her opinion these are what he or she would like to eliminate or change. Agreement is important that this chosen area is significant to the patient and worthy of concentrated attention. A patient who complains that the selection is too limited should be assured that it is best to move one step at a time. Controlling a simple situation or alleviating a symptom will help strengthen the personality, and permit more extensive progress.

Thus the focal difficulty around which therapy is organized may be depression, anxiety, tension, or somatic manifestations of tension. It may be a situational precipitating factor or a crisis that has imposed itself. It may be a disturbing pattern or some learned aberration. It may be a pervasive difficulty in relating or in functioning. Or it may be a conflict of which the patient is aware or only partially aware.

Once agreement is reached on the area of focus, the therapist may succinctly sum up what is to be done.

Th. Now that we have decided to focus on the problem [*designate*] that upsets you, what we will do is try to understand what it is all about, how it started, what it means, why it continues. Then we'll establish a plan to do something about it.

Example 1. A symptomatic focus

Th. I get the impression that what bothers you most is tension and anxiety that makes it hard for you to get along. Is it your feeling that we should work toward eliminating these?

Pt. Yes. Yes, if I could get rid of feeling so upset, I would be more happy. I'm so irritable and jumpy about everything.

Example 2. A focus on a precipitating event

Th. What you are complaining most about is a sense of hopelessness and depression. If we focused on these and worked toward eliminating them, would you agree?

Pt. I should say so, but I would also like to see how I could improve my marriage. It's been going downhill fast. The last fight I had with my husband was the limit.

Th. Well, suppose we take up the problems you are having with your husband and see how these are connected with your symptoms.

Pt. I would like that, doctor.

Example 3. A dynamic focus

Whenever possible the therapist should attempt to link the patient's symptoms and complaints to underlying factors, the connections with which the patient may

be only dimly aware. Carefully phrased interpretations will be required. It may not be possible to detect basic conflicts, only secondary or derivative conflicts being apparent. Moreover, the patient may not have given the therapist all the facts due to resistance, guilt, or anxiety. Or facts may be defensively distorted. It is often helpful (with the permission of the patient) to interview, if possible, the spouse or another individual with whom the patient is related after the first or second interview. The supplementary data obtained may completely change the initial hypothetical assumptions gleaned from the material exclusively revealed by the patient.

Nevertheless, some invaluable observations may be made from the historical data and interview material that will lend themselves to interpretation for defining a focus. Thus a patient presenting great inferiority problems and repetitive difficulties in work situations with supervisors, who as a child fought bitterly with an older sibling, was told the following: "It is possible that your present anxiety while related to how you get along with your boss touches off troubles you've carried around with you for a long time. You told me you always felt inferior to your brother. In many cases this sense of inferiority continues to bother a person in relation to new substitutive older brothers. It wouldn't be mysterious if this were happening to you. What do you think?" This comment started off a productive series of reminiscences regarding his experiences with his brother, a focus on which resulted in considerable understanding and betterment of his current relationships.

More fundamental nuclear conflicts may be revealed in later sessions (for example, in the above patient an almost classical oedipal conflict existed), especially when transference and resistance manifest themselves.

Considering the short span of a session it would be most propitious to concern ourselves exclusively with issues related to a dynamic theme. It is obviously impossible to do this when so many urgent reality issues impose themselves during the alloted time. The duty of the therapist is to sift out issues that truly must be discussed (one cannot concentrate on early love objects when the patient's house is burning down) separating them from issues utilized for defensive resistance or indulgence of transference gratifications. Nevertheless, where our goal is personality reconstruction we must utilize every session to best advantage even when pressing reality matters require attention. What the therapist readies himself or herself to do is to listen to the patient's legitimate immediate concerns and establish a bridge to dynamic issues in order to show how a basic theme weaves itself through every aspect of the patient's existence including the immediate reality situation and the relationship with the therapist.

Undoubtedly the relationship with the therapist offers the best focus from the standpoint of understanding personality distortions and their maladaptive consequences. In long-term approaches treatment may be considered incomplete unless adequate consideration is given to transference and countertransference issues. In short-term therapy the press of time and the need to deal with the immediate stressful concerns of the patient may tend to push this focus onto the back burner. At the end of the assigned limited number of sessions, transference phenomena may have received hardly any attention. This is all the more reason for sensitizing oneself to any relationship happenings that offer an opportunity for exploration. When such happenings do occur, or when the therapist discerns transferential distortions from dreams and acting-out, proper interpretation may make a deep imprint on the patient. Even in sessions limited to five or ten treatment hours, when one hits upon some transferential propitious happenings and

explored them later on, the discussion is often considered by the patient a high point in therapy. Obviously, we can expect no miracles from such a brief interchange, but if the patient's resistance is not too great, it can have an important influence.

Define the Precipitating Events

It is essential that we identify clearly the precipitating factors that led to the patient's present upset or why the patient came to treatment at this time.

Th. It seems as if you were managing to get along without trouble until your daughter told you about the affair she is having with this married man. Do you believe this started you off on the downslide?

Pt. Doctor, I can't tell you the shock this was to me. Janie was such an ideal child and never was a bit of a problem. And then this thing happened. She's completely changed, and I can't understand it.

Sometimes the events are obscured or denied because the patient has an investment in sustaining situational irritants even while seeking to escape from their effects. Involvement in an unsatisfactory relationship with a disturbed or rejecting person from whom the patient cannot extricate is an example. It may be necessary to encourage continuing conversation about a suspected precipitant, asking pointed questions in the effort to help the patient see the relationship between symptoms and what may have considered unrelated noxious events. Should the patient fail to make the connections, the therapist may spell these out, asking pertinent questions that may help the patient grasp the association.

Evolve a Working Hypothesis

After the first session the therapist should have gathered enough data from the present and past history, from any dreams that are revealed, and from the general attitude and behavior of the patient to put together some formulation about what is going on. This is presented to the patient in simple language, employing concepts with which the patient has some familiarity. This formulation should never be couched in dismal terms to avoid alarming the patient. Rather a concise, restrained, optimistic picture may be painted making this contingent on the patient's cooperation with the therapeutic plan. Aspects of the hypothesis should ideally bracket the immediate precipitating agencies with what has gone on before in the life history and, if possible, how the patient's personality structure has influenced the way the patient has reacted to the precipitating events.

A woman experiencing a severe anxiety attack revealed the precipitating incident of discovering her husband's marital infidelity. As she discussed this, she disclosed the painful episode of her father's abandoning her mother for another woman.

Th. Is it possible that you are afraid your husband will do to you what your father did to your mother?
Pt. (*breaking down in tears*) Oh, it's so terrible I sometimes think I can't stand it.
Th. Stand his leaving you or the fact that he had an affair?
Pt. If it could end right now, I mean if he would stop, it (*pause*).
Th. You would forget what had happened?
Pt. (*pause*) Yes—Yes.
Th. How you handle yourself will determine what happens. You can see that your present upset is probably linked with what happened in your home when you were a child. Would you tell me about your love life with your husband?

The focus on therapy was thereafter concerned with the quality of her relationship with her husband. There were evidences that the patient herself promoted what inwardly she believed was an inevitable abandonment.

The therapist in making a tentative thrust at what is behind a problem should present formulations in simple terms that the patient can understand. The explanation should not be so dogmatic, however,

as to preclude a revision of the hypothesis at a later date, should further elicited material demand this. The patient may be asked how he or she feels about what the therapist has said. If the patient is hazy about the content, the confusion is explored and clarification continued.

For example, a patient with migraine is presented with the hypothesis that anger is what is creating the symptom. The patient then makes a connection with past resentments and the denial defenses that were erected, which apparently are still operative in the present.

Th. Your headaches are a great problem obviously since they block you in your work. Our aim is to help reduce or eliminate them. From what you tell me, they started way back probably in your childhood. They are apparently connected with certain emotions. For example, upset feelings and tensions are often a basis for headaches, but there may be other things too, like resentments. What we will do is explore what goes on in your emotions to see what connections we can come up with. Often resentments one has in the present are the result of situations similar to troubles a person had in childhood.
Pt. I had great pains and trouble fighting for my rights when I was small—a bossy mother and father who didn't care. I guess I finally gave up.
Th. Did you give up trying to adjust at home or work?
Pt. Not exactly. But fighting never gets anywheres. People just don't listen.

Make a Tentative Diagnosis

Despite the fact that our current nosological systems leave much to be desired, it may be necessary to fit the patient into some diagnostic scheme if for no other reason than to satisfy institutional regulations and insurance requirements. There is a temptation, of course, to coordinate diagnosis with accepted labels for which reimbursement will be made. This is unfortunate since it tends to limit flexibility and to invalidate utilizing case records for purposes of statistical research. Even though clinical diagnosis bears little relationship to preferred therapeutic techniques in some syndromes, in other syndromes it may be helpful toward instituting a rational program.

Convey the Need for the Patient's Active Participation in the Therapeutic Process

Many patients, accustomed to dealing with medical doctors, expect the therapist to prescribe a formula or give advice that will operate automatically to palliate the problem. An explanation of what will be expected of the patient is in order.

Th. There is no magic about getting well. The way we can best accomplish our goals is to work together as a partnership team. I want you to tell me all the important things that are going on with you and I will try to help you understand them. What we want to do is to develop new, healthier patterns. *My* job is to see what is blocking you from achieving this objective by pointing out some things that have and are still blocking you. *Your* job is to *act* to put into practice new patterns we decide are necessary, you telling me about your experiences and feelings. Psychotherapy is like learning a new language. The learner is the one who must practice the language. If the teacher did all the talking, the student would never be able to carry on a conversation. So remember you are going to have to carry the ball, with my help of course.

Make a Verbal Contract With The Patient

There should be an agreement regarding the frequency of appointments, the number of sessions, and the termination date.

Example 1. Where Limitation of the Number of Sessions is Deemed Necessary in Advance

Th. We are going to have a total of 12 sessions. In that time we should have made an impact on your anxiety and depression. Now, let's consult the calendar. We will terminate therapy on October 9, and I'll mark it down here. Can you also make a note of it?
Pt. Will 12 sessions be enough?

Th. Yes. The least it could do is to get you on the road to really working out the problem.
Pt. What happens if I'm not better?
Th. You are an intelligent person and there is no reason why you shouldn't be better in that time.

Should the therapist dally and compromise confidence in the patient's capacity to get well, the patient may in advance cancel the termination in his or her own mind to an indeterminate future one.

Example 2. When the Termination Date is Left Open

Th. It is hard to estimate how many sessions we will require. I like to keep them below 20. So let us begin on the basis of twice a week.
Pt. Anything you say, doctor. If more are necessary, OK.
Th. It is really best to keep the number of sessions as low as possible to avoid getting dependent on them. So we'll play it by ear.
Pt. That's fine.

The appointment times may then be set and the fee discussed.

Utilize Whatever Techniques are Best Suited to Help the Patient with Immediate Problems

After the initial interview, techniques that are acceptable to the patient, and that are within the training range and competence of the therapist, are implemented, bearing in mind the need for activity and flexibility. The techniques may include supportive, educational, and psychoanalytically oriented interventions and a host of adjunctive devices, such as psychotropic drugs, hypnosis, biofeedback, behavioral and group approaches, and so on, in whatever combinations are necessary to satisfy the patient's immediate and future needs. An explanation may be given the patient about what will be done.

Th. At the start, I believe it would be helpful to reduce your tension. This should be beneficial to you in many ways. One of the best ways of doing this is by teaching you some relaxing exercises. What I would like to do for you is to make a relaxing casette tape. Do you have a casette tape recorder?

Pt. No, I haven't.

Th. You can buy one quite inexpensively. How do you feel about this?

Pt. It sounds great.

Th. OK. Of course, there are other things we will do, but this should help us get off to a good start.

Many therapists practicing dynamic short-term therapy ask their patients to reveal any dreams that occur during therapy. Some patients insist that they rarely or never dream or if they do, that they do not remember their dreams.

Th. It is important to mention any dreams that come to you.

Pt. I can't get hold of them. They slip away.

Th. One thing you can do is, when you retire, tell yourself you will remember your dreams.

Pt. What if I can't remember?

Th. Keep a pad of paper and a pencil near the head of your bed. When you awaken ask yourself if you dreamt. Then write the dream down. Also, if you wake up during the night.

In some patients brief group therapy may be decided on. This is an active, goal oriented ahistorical, current-life approach, with emphasis on decision making and patient responsibility with modeling, feedback, and stress on behavioral practice (Imber et al. 1979; Marcovitz & Smith, 1983).

Study the Patient's Reaction and Defense Patterns

The utilization of any technique or strategem will set into motion reactions and defenses that are grist for the therapeutic mill. The patient will display a range of patterns that the therapist can study. This will permit a dramatic demonstration of the patient's defenses and resistances in actual operation rather than as theories. The patient's dreams and fantasies will often reveal more than actions or verbalizations, and the patient should continually be encouraged to talk about these. The skill of the therapist in working with and interpreting the patient's singular patterns will determine whether these will be integrated or will generate further resistance. Generally, a compassionate, tentative type of interpretation is best, sprinkling it if possible with a casual light humorous attitude. A patient who wanted hypnosis to control smoking appeared restless during induction:

Th. I noticed that when I asked you to lean back in the chair and try relaxing to my suggestions, you were quite uneasy and kept on opening your eyes. What were you thinking about?

Pt. (*emotionally*) My heart started beating. I was afraid I couldn't do it. What you'd think of me. That I'd fail. I guess I'm afraid of doctors. My husband is trying to get me to see a gynecologist.

Th. But you kept opening your eyes.

Pt. (*pause*) You know, doctor, I'm afraid of losing control, of what might come out. I guess I don't trust anybody.

Th. Afraid of what would happen here, of what I might do if you shut your eyes? (*smiling*)

Pt. (*laughing*) I guess so. Silly. But the thought came to me about something sexual.

While the Focus at all Times is on the Present, be Sensitive to How Present Patterns Have Roots in the Past

Examination in dynamic short-term therapy of how the patient was reared and the relationship with parents and siblings is particularly revealing. An attempt is made to note established patterns that have operated throughout the patient's life of which the current stress situation is an immediate manifestation. This data is for the therapist's own consumption and should not be too exhaustive, since the patient if encouraged to explore the past may go on endlessly, and there is no time for this. At a propitious moment, when the patient appears to have some awareness of connections of the past with the present, a proper interpretation may be made. At that time a relationship may be cited among genetic determinants, the existing personality patterns, and the symptoms and complaints for which therapy was originally sought.

Watch for Transference Reactions

The immediate reaching for help encourages projection onto the therapist of positive feelings and attitudes related to an idealized authority figure. These should not be interpreted or in any way discouraged since they act in the interest of alleviating tension and supporting the placebo element. On the other hand, a *negative* transference reaction should be dealt with rapidly and sympathetically since it will interfere with the therapeutic alliance.

Th. [*noting the patient's hesitant speech*] You seem to be upset about something.

Pt. Why, *should* I be upset?

Th. You might be if I did something you didn't like.

Pt. (*pause*) No—I'm afraid, just afraid I'm not doing what I should. I've been here six times and I still have that panicky feeling from time to time. Do other patients do better?

Th. You seem to be comparing yourself to my other patients.

Pt. I—I—I guess so. The young man that came before me. He seems so self-confident and cheerful. I guess I felt inferior, that you would find fault with me.

Th. Do you think I like him better than I do you?

Pt. Well, wouldn't you, if he was doing better than I was?

Th. That's interesting. Tell me more.

Pt. I've been that way. My parents, I felt, preferred my older brother. He always came in on top. They were proud of his accomplishments in school.

Th. So in a way you feel I should be acting like your parents.

Pt. I can't help feeling that way.

Th. Don't you think this is a pattern that is really self-defeating? We ought to explore this more.

Pt. (*emotionally*) Well, I really thought today you were going to send me to another doctor because you were sick of me.

Th. Actually, the thought never occurred to me to do that. But I'm glad you brought this matter out because we will be able to explore some of your innermost fears about how people feel about you.

Examine Possible Countertransference Feelings

If you notice persistent irritability, boredom, anger, extraordinary interest in or attraction to any patient, ask yourself whether such feelings and attitudes do not call for self-examination. Their continuance will almost certainly lead to interference with a good working relationship. For example, a therapist is treating an unstable middle-aged female patient whom he regards as a plumpish, sloppy biddy who sticks her nose into other people's affairs. He tries to maintain an impartial therapeutic stance, but periodically he finds himself scolding her and feeling annoyed and enraged. He is always relieved as the session hour comes to an end. He recognizes that his reactions are countertherapeutic, and he asks himself if they are really justified. The image of his own mother then comes to his mind, and he realizes that he had many of the same feelings of exasperation, displeasure, and disgust with his own parent. Recognizing that he may be transferring in part some of these attitudes to his patient whose physical appearance and manner remind him of his mother, he is better able to maintain objectivity. Should self analysis, however, fail to halt his animosity, he may decide to send the patient to another therapist.

Countertransference may also be a sensitive instrument in dynamic psychotherapy toward understanding of projections from the patient of aspects of inner conflict of which the patient may be incompletely aware.

Constantly Look for Resistances That Threaten to Block Progress

Obstructions to successful therapeutic sessions are nurtured by misconceptions about therapy, lack of motivation, needs to maintain certain benefits that accrue from one's illness, and a host of other sources, conscious and unconscious. Where resistances are too stubborn to budge readily or where they operate with little awareness that they exist, the few sessions assigned to short-term therapy may not suffice to resolve them. One way of dealing with resistances once they are recognized is to bring them out openly in a noncondemning manner. This can be done by stating that the patient may hold on to them as defenses, but if this is so, he or she must suffer the conseqeunces. A frank discussion of why the resistances have value for the patient and their effects on treatment is in order. Another technique is to anticipate resistances from the patient's past modes of adaptation, dreams, and the like, presenting the patient with the possibility of their appearance and what could be done about them should they appear. The therapist should watch for minimum appearances of resistance, however minor they may be, that will serve as psychological obstructions. Merely bringing these to the attention of the patient may help dissipate them.

Pt. I didn't want to come here. Last time I had a terribly severe headache. I felt dizzy in the head. (*pause*)

Th. I wonder why. Did anything happen here that upset you; did I do anything to upset you?

Pt. No, it's funny but it's something I can't understand. I want to come here, and I don't. It's like I'm afraid.

Th. Afraid?

Pt. (*Pause; patient flushes.*) I can't understand it. People are always trying to change me. As far back as I can remember, at home, at school.

Th. And you resent their trying to change you.

Pt. Yes. I feel they can't leave me alone.

Th. Perhaps you feel I'm trying to change you.

Pt. (*angrily*) Aren't you?

Th. Only if *you* want to change. In what way do you want to change, if at all?

Pt. I want to get rid of my headaches, and stomachaches, and all the rest of my aches.

Th. But you don't want to change to do this.

Pt. Well, doctor, this isn't true. I want to change the way *I* want to.

Th. Are you sure the way *you* want to change will help you get rid of your symptoms?

Pt. But that's why I'm coming here so you will tell me.

Th. But you resent my making suggestions to you because somehow you put me in the class of everybody else who you believe wants to take your independence away. And then you show resistance to what I am trying to do.

Pt. (*laughs*) Isn't that silly, I really do trust you.

Th. Then supposing when you begin to feel you are being dominated you tell me, so we can talk it out. I really want to help you and not dominate you.

Pt. Thank you, doctor, I do feel better.

In brief therapy with patients who possess a reasonably strong ego, confrontation and management of the patient's untoward reactions to challenges may be dramatically effective. Managing the patient's reactions will call for a high degree of stamina, sensitivity, and flexibility on the part of the therapist, an ability to cope with outbursts of anger and other disturbing reactions, and knowledge of how to give reassurance without retracting one's interpretations. However, because judgments about what is happening are made on fragmentary data, it is apt to create justifiable anger and resistance where a therapist is wrong about an appraisal of the problem. This is less the case in long-term therapy where the therapist has a firmer relationship with the patient and is more certain about the dynamics.

Give the Patient Homework

Involve the patient with an assignment to work on how the symptoms are related to happenings in the patient's environment, to attitudes, to fallacies in thinking, to disturbed interpersonal relationships, or to conflicts within oneself. Even a bit of insight may be a saving grace. As soon as feasible, moreover, ask the patient to review his or her idea of the evolution of the problem and what the patient can do to control or regulate the circumstances that reinforce the problem or alleviate the symptoms. Practice schedules may be agreed on toward opposing the situations or tendencies that require control. The patient may be enjoined to keep a log regarding incidents that exaggerate the difficulties and what the patient has done to avoid or resolve such incidents. The patient may also be given some cues regarding how one may work on oneself to reverse some basic destructive personality patterns through such measures as acquiring more understanding and insight, rewarding oneself for positive actions, self-hypnosis, and so on. These tactics may be pursued both during therapy and following therapy by oneself.

For example, the following suggestion was made to a patient who came to therapy for help to abate migraine attacks:

Th. What may help you is understanding what triggers off your headaches and makes them worse. Supposing you keep a diary and jot down the frequency of your headaches. Everytime you get a headache write down the day and time. Even more important, write down the events that immediately preceded the onset of the headache or the feelings or thoughts you had that brought it on. If a headache is stopped by anything that has happened, or by anything you think about or figure out, write that down, and bring your diary when you come here so we can talk about what has happened.

Suggestions on homework assignments may be found in Chapter 53.

Keep Accenting the Termination Date if One was Given the Patient

In preparing the patient for termination of therapy, the calendar may be referred to prior to the last three sessions and the pa-

tient reminded of the date. In some patients this will activate separation anxiety and negative transference. Such responses will necessitate active interpretation of the patient's past dependency and fears of autonomy. Evidences of past reactions to separation may help the patient acquire an understanding of the underpinnings of present reactions. The therapist should expect a recrudescence of the patient's symptoms as a defense against being on one's own and as an appeal for continuing treatment. These manifestations are dealt with by further interpretation. *Do not promise* to continue therapy even if the patient predicts failure.

Pt. I know we're supposed to have only one more session. But I get scared not having you around.

Th. One of our aims is to make you stronger so you won't need a crutch. You know enough about yourself now to take some steps on your own. This is part of getting well. So I want you to give yourself a chance.

Many patients will resent termination of therapy after the designated number of sessions have ended. At the middle point of therapy, therefore, the therapist may bring up this possibility. The therapist should search for incidents in the past where separations have created untoward reactions in the patient. Individuals who were separated from their parents at an early age, who had school phobias produced by inability to break ties with the mother, and who are excessively dependent are particularly vulnerable and apt to respond to termination with anxiety, fear, anger, and depression. The termination process here may constitute a prime focus in therapy and a means of enhancing individuation.

Th. We have five more sessions, as you know, and then we will terminate.

Pt. I realize it, but I always have trouble breaking away. My wife calls me a holder-oner.

Th. Yes, that's exactly what we want to avoid, the dependency. You are likely to resent ending treatment for that reason. What do you think?

Pt. (*laughing*) I'll try not to.

Th. Well, keep thinking about it and if you have any bad reactions let's talk about it. It's important not to make treatment a way of life. By the end of the five sessions, you should be able to carry on.

Pt. But supposing I don't make it?

Th. There you go, see, anticipating failure. This is a gesture to hold on.

Pt. Well, doctor, I know you are right. I'll keep working on it.

Terminate Therapy on the Agreed-upon Date

While some therapists do not consider it wise to invite the patient who has progressed satisfactorily to return, others find it a helpful and reassuring aid for most patients to do so at the final session. I generally tell the patient to write to me sometime to let me know things are coming along. In the event problems develop that one cannot manage by oneself, the patient should call for an appointment. Rarely is this invitation abused and if the patient does return the difficulty can be rapidly handled, eventuating in reinforcement of one's understanding.

Th. This is, as you know, our last session. I want you now to try things out on your own. Keep practicing the things I taught you—the relaxation exercises [*where these have been used*], the figuring out what brings on your symptoms and takes them away, and so forth. You should continue to get better. But setbacks may occur from time to time. Don't let that upset you. That's normal and you'll get over the setback. In fact, it may help you figure out better what your symptoms are all about. Now, if in the future you find you need a little more help, don't hesitate to call me and I'll try to arrange an appointment.

Actually relatively few patients will take advantage of this invitation, but they will feel reassured to go out on their own knowing they will not be abandoned. Should they return for an appointment, only a few sessions will be needed to bring the patient to an equilibrium and to help learn about what produced the relapse.

Stress the Need for Continuing Work on Oneself

The matter of continuing work on oneself after termination is very much underutilized. Patients will generally return to an environment that continues to sponsor maladaptive reactions. The patient will need some constant reminder that old neurotic patterns latently await revival and that one must alert oneself to signals of their awakening. In my practice I have found that making a relaxing tape (a technique detailed on p. 1019) sprinkled with positive suggestions of an ego-building nature serves the interest of continued growth. In the event the patient has done well with homework during the active therapy period, the same processes may continue. Institution of a proper philosophical outlook may also be in order prior to discharge. Such attitudes may be encouraged as the need to isolate the past from the present, the realization that a certain amount of tension and anxiety are normal, the need to adjust to handicaps and realistic irremediable conditions, the urgency to work at correcting remediable elements in one's environment, the recognition of the forces that trigger one's problems and the importance of rectifying these, and the wisdom of stopping regretting the past and of avoiding anticipating disaster in the future. It must be recognized that while the immediate accomplishments of short-term therapy may be modest, the continued application of the methods the patient has learned during therapy will help bring about more substantial changes.

Arrange for Further Treatment if Necessary

The question may be asked regarding what to do with the patient who at termination shows little or no improvement. Certain patients will require long-term therapy. In this reference there are some patients who will need help for a prolonged period of time; some require only an occasional contact the remainder of their lives. The contact does not have to be intensive or frequent. Persons with an extreme dependency character disorder, borderline cases, and schizophrenics often do well with short visits (15 to 20 minutes) every 2 weeks or longer. The idea that a supportive person is available may be all that the patient demands to keep him or her in homeostasis. Introducing the patient into a group may also be helpful, multiple transferences diluting the hostile transference that so often occurs in individual therapy. A social group may even suffice to provide the patient with some means of a human relationship. Some patients will need referral to another therapist who specializes in a different technique, for example, to someone who does biofeedback, behavioral therapy, hypnosis, psychopharmacology, or another modality.

Th. Now, we have completed the number of sessions we agreed on. How do you feel about matters now?

Pt. Better, doctor, but not well. I still have my insomnia and feel discouraged and depressed.

Th. That should get better as time goes on. I should like to have you continue with me in a group.

Pt. You mean with other people? I've heard of it. It scares me, but I'd like to do it.

Where the patient is to be referred to another therapist, he or she may be told:

Th. You have gotten a certain amount of help in coming here, but the kind of problems you have will be helped more by a specialist who deals with such problems. I have someone in mind for you who I believe will be able to help you. If you agree, I shall telephone him to make sure he has time for you.

Pt. I'd like that. Who is the doctor?

Th. Dr. _____. If he hasn't time, I'll get someone else.

CRISIS INTERVENTION

Every individual alive is a potential candidate for a breakdown in the adaptive equilibrium if the stressful pressures are sufficiently severe. A crisis may precipitate around any incident that overwhelms one's coping capacities. The crisis stimulus itself bears little relationship to the intensity of the victim's reaction. Some persons can tolerate with equanimity tremendous hardships and adversity. Others will show a catastrophic response to what seems like a minor mishap. A specifically important event, like abandonment by a love object, can touch off an explosive reaction in one who would respond much less drastically to bombings, hurricanes, cataclysmic floods, shipwreck, disastrous reverses of economic fortune, and major accidents. The two important variables are, first, the *meaning* to the individual of the calamity and, second, the *flexibility of one's defenses,* that is, the prevailing ego strength.

The immediate response to a situation that is interpreted as cataclysmic, such as the sudden death of a loved one, a violent accident, or an irretrievable shattering of security, is a dazed shock reaction. As if to safeguard oneself, a peculiar denial mechanism intervenes accompanied by numbness and detachment. This defensive maneuver, however, does not prevent the intrusion of upsetting fantasies or frightening nightmares from breaking through periodically. When this happens, denial and detachment may again intervene to reestablish a tenuous equilibrium, only to be followed by a repetition of fearsome ruminations. It is as if the individual is both denying and then trying somehow to acquire understanding and to resolve anxiety and guilt. Various reactions to and defenses against anxiety may precipitate self-accusations, aggression, phobias, and excessive indulgence in alcohol or tranquilizers. Moreover, dormant past conflicts may be aroused, marshalling neurotic symptomatic and distorted characterologic displays. At the core of this confounding cycle of denial and twisted repetitive remembering is, first, the mind's attempt to protect itself by repressing what had happened and, second, to heal itself by reprocessing and working through the traumatic experience in order to reconcile it with the present reality situation. In an individual with good ego strength this struggle usually terminates in a successful resolution of the crisis event. Thus, following a crisis situation, most people are capable after a period of 4 to 6 weeks of picking up the pieces, putting themselves together, and resuming their lives along lines similar to before. People who come to a clinic or to a private practitioner are those who have failed to achieve resolution of stressful life events.

In some of these less fortunate individuals the outcome is dubious, eventuating in prolonged and even permanent crippling of functioning. To shorten the struggle and to bolster success in those who otherwise would be destined to a failing adaptation, psychotherapy offers the individual an excellent opportunity to deal constructively with the crisis.

In the psychotherapeutic treatment of crisis situations (crisis therapy) the goal is rapid emotional relief—and not basic personality modification. This does not mean that we neglect opportunities to effectuate personality change. Since such alterations will require time to provide for resolution of inner conflicts and the reshuffling of the intrapsychic structure, the most we can hope for is to bring the patient to some *awareness* of how underlying problems are related to the immediate crisis. It is gratifying how some patients will grasp the significance of this association and in the post-therapy period work toward a betterment of fundamental characterologic distortions. Obviously, where more than the usual six-session limit of crisis-oriented therapy can be offered, the greater will be the possibility of demonstrating the operative dynamics. Yet where the patient possesses a motivation for change—and the existing crisis often stimulates such a motivation—even six sessions may register a significant impact on the psychological status quo.

Crisis Therapy

Selection of techniques in crisis therapy are geared to four variables (Wolberg, 1972). The first variable we must consider relates to *catastrophic symptoms that require immediate handling.* The most common emergencies are severe depressions with strong suicidal tendencies, acute psychotic upsets with aggressive or bizarre behavior, intense anxiety and panic states, excited hysterical reactions, and drug and alcoholic intoxications. Occasionally, symptoms are sufficiently severe to constitute a portentous threat to the individual or others, under which circumstances it is essential to consider immediate hospitalization. Conferences with responsible relatives or friends will then be essential in order to make provision for the most adequate resource. Fortunately, this contingency is not now employed as frequently as before because of modern somatic therapy. Consultations with a psychiatrist skilled in the administration of somatic treatments will, of course, be in order. Electroconvulsive therapy may be necessary to interrupt suicidal depression or excitement. Acute psychotic attacks usually yield to a regimen of the neuroleptics in the medium of a supportive and sympathetic relationship. It may require almost superhuman forebearance to listen attentively to the patient's concerns, with minimal expressions of censure or incredulity for delusional or hallucinatory content. Panic reactions in the patient require not only fortitude on the part of the therapist, but also the ability to communicate compassion blended with hope. In an emergency room in a hospital it may be difficult to provide the quiet objective atmosphere that is needed, but an attentive sympathetic doctor or nurse can do much to reassure the patient. Later, frequent visits, even daily, do much to reassure a frightened patient who feels himself or herself to be out of control.

Less catastrophic symptoms are handled in accordance with the prevailing emotional state. Thus during the first stages of denial and detachment, techniques of confrontation and active interpretation of resistances may help to get the patient talking. Where there is extreme repression, hypnotic probing and narcoanalysis may be useful. On the other hand, where the patient is flooded by anxiety, tension, guilt, and ruminations concerning the stressful events, attempts are made to reestablish controls through relaxation methods (like meditation, autogenic training, relaxing hypnotherapy, and biofeedback), or by pharmacological tranquilization (diazepam, Xanax), or by rest, diversions (like social activities, hobbies, and occupational therapy), or by behavioral desensitization and reassurance.

Once troublesome symptoms are brought under reasonable restraint, attention can be focused on the second important variable in the crisis reaction, *the nature of the precipitating agency.* This is usually in the form of some environmental episode that threatens the individual's security or damages the self-esteem. A developmental crisis, broken love affair, rejection by or death of a love object, violent marital discord, persisting delinquent behavior and drug consumption by important family members, transportation or industrial and other accidents, development of an incapacitating or life-threatening illness, calamitous financial reverses, and many other provocative events may be the triggers that set off a crisis. It is rare that the external precipitants that the patient holds responsible for the present troubles are entirely or even most importantly the cause.

Indeed, the therapist will usually find that the patient participates actively in initiating and sustaining many of the environmental misfortunes that presumably are to blame. Yet respectful listening and questioning will give the therapist data regarding the character structure of the patient, the need for upsetting involvements, projective tendencies, and the legitimate hardships to which the patient is inescapably exposed. An assay of the existing and potential inner strengths in relation to the unavoidable stresses that must be endured and identification of remediable problem areas will enable the therapist better to focus the therapeutic efforts. Crucial is some kind of cognitive reprocessing that is most effectively accomplished by interpretation. The object is to help the patient find a different meaning for the upsetting events and to evolve more adequate ways of coping.

The third variable, *the impact on the patient of the family system,* is especially important in children and adolescents as well as in those living in a closely knit family system. The impact of the family may not be immediately apparent, but a crisis frequently indicates a collapsing family system, the end result of which is a breakdown in the identified patient's capacities for adaptation. Crisis theory assumes that the family is the basic unit and that an emotional illness in any family member connotes a disruption in the family homeostasis. Such a disruption is not altogether bad because through it opportunities are opened up for change with potential benefit to each member. Traditional psychotherapy attempts to treat the individual patient and often relieves the family of responsibility for what is going on with the patient. Crisis theory, on the other hand, insists that change must involve more than the patient. The most frequently used modality, consequently, is family therapy, the object of which is the harnessing and expansion of the constructive elements in the family situation. The therapist does not attempt to halt the crisis by reassurance but rather to utilize the crisis as an instrument of change. During a crisis a family in distress may be willing to let a therapist enter into the picture, recognizing that it cannot by itself cope with the existing emergency. The boundaries are at the start fluid enough so that new consolidations become possible. The family system prior to the crisis and after the crisis usually seals off all points of entry. During the crisis, before new and perhaps even more destructive decisions have been made, a point is reached where we may introduce some new perspectives. This point may exist for only a short period of time; therefore it is vital that there be no delay in rendering service.

Thus a crisis will permit intervention that would not be acceptable before nor subsequent to the crisis explosion. One deterent frequently is the family's insistence on hospitalization, no longer being able to cope with the identified patient's upsetting behavior. Alternatives to hospitalization will present themselves to an astute therapist who establishes contact with the family. Some of the operative dynamics may become startlingly apparent by listening to the interchanges of the patient and the family.

The most important responsibility of the therapist is to get the family to understand what is going on with the patient in the existing setting and to determine why the crisis has occurred now. There is a understandable history to the crisis and a variety of solutions may have been tried. The therapist may be curious as to why these measures were attempted and why they failed, or at least why they have not succeeded sufficiently. The family should be involved in solutions to be utilized and should have an idea as to the reasons for this. Assignment of tasks for each member is an excellent method of getting people to work together and such assignments may be quite arbitrary ones. The important thing is to get every member involved in some way. This will bring out certain resistances which may have to be negotiated. Trades may be made with the object of securing better cooperation. Since crisis interven-

tion is a short-term process, it should be made clear that visits are limited. This is to avoid dependencies and resentments about termination.

The fourth variable is often the crucial factor in having initiated the crisis situation and consists of *unresolved and demanding childhood needs, defenses and conflicts* that obtrude themselves on adult adjustment, and compulsively dragoon the patient into activities that are bound to end in disaster. These would seem to invite explorations that a therapist, trained in dynamic psychotherapeutic methodology, may be able to implement. The ability to relate the patient's outmoded and neurotic modes of behaving, and the circumstances of their development in early conditionings, as well as the recognition of how personality difficulties have brought about the crisis, would be highly desirable probably constituting the difference between merely palliating the present problem and providing some permanent solution for it. Since the goals of crisis intervention are limited, however, to reestablishing the precrisis equilibrium, and the time allotted to therapy is circumscribed to the mere achievement of this goal, one may not be able to do much more than to merely point out the areas for further work and exploration. Because crisis therapy is goal limited, there is a tendency to veer away from insight therapies organized around psychodynamic models toward more active behavioral-learning techniques, which are directed at reinforcing appropriate and discouraging maladaptive behavior. The effort has been directed toward the treatment of couples, of entire families, and of groups of nonrelated people as primary therapeutic instruments. The basic therapeutic thrust is, as has been mentioned, on such practical areas as the immediate disturbing environmental situation and the patient's disruptive symptoms, employing a combination of active procedures like drug therapy and milieu therapy.

The few sessions devoted to treatment in crisis intervention certainly prevent any extensive concern with the operations of unconscious conflict. Yet a great deal of data may be obtained by talking to the patient and by studying the interactions of the family, both in family therapy and through the observations of a psychiatric nurse, caseworker, or psychiatric team who visit the home. Such data will be helpful in crisis therapy planning or in a continuing therapeutic program.

In organizing a continuing program the therapist must recognize, without minimizing the value of depth approaches, that not all persons, assuming that they can afford long-term therapy, are sufficiently well motivated, introspective, and possessed by qualities of sufficient ego strength to permit the use of other than expedient, workable, and goal-limited methods aimed at crisis resolution and symptom relief.

Techniques in Crisis Intervention

The following is a summation of practical points to pursue in the practice of crisis intervention.

1. *See the patient within 24 hours of the calling for help* even if it means canceling an appointment. A crisis in the life of an individual is apt to motivate one to seek help from some outside agency that otherwise would be avoided. Should such aid be immediately unavailable, one may in desperation exploit spurious measures and defenses that abate the crisis but compromise an optimal adjustment. More insidiously, the incentive for therapy will vanish with resolution of the emergency. The therapist should, therefore, make every effort to see a person in crisis preferably on the very day that help is requested.

2. At the initial interview *alert yourself to patients at high risk for suicide*. These are (a) persons who have a previous history of attempting suicide, (b) endogenous depression (history of cyclic attacks, early morning awakening, loss of appetite, retardation, loss of energy or sex drive), (c) young drug abusers, (d) alcoholic female patients, (e) middle-aged men recently widowed, divorced, or separated, (f) elderly isolated persons.

3. *Handle immediately any depression in the above patients.* Avoid hospitalization if possible except in deep depressions where attempts at suicide have been made recently or the past or are seriously threatened now. Electroconvulsive therapy is best for dangerous depressions. Institute antidepressant medications (Tofranil, Elavil, Sinequan) in adequate dosage where there is no immediate risk.

4. *Evaluate the stress situation.* Does it seem sufficiently adequate to account for the present crisis? What is the family situation, and how is it related to the patient's upset? What were past modes of dealing with crises, and how successful were they?

5. *Evaluate the existing support systems available to the patient* that you can utilize in the therapeutic plan. How solid and reliable are certain members of the family? What community resources are available? What are the strengths of the family with whom the patient will live?

6. *Estimate the patient's ego resources.* What ego resources does the patient have to depend on, estimated by successes and achievements in the past? Positive coping capacities are of greater importance than the prevailing pathology.

7. *Help the patient to an awareness of the factors involved in the reaction to the crisis.* The patient's interpersonal

relations should be reviewed in the hope of understanding and reevaluating attitudes and patterns that get the patient into difficulty.

8. *Provide thoughtful, empathic listening and supportive reassurance.* These are essential to enhance the working relationship and to restore hope. The therapist must communicate awareness of the patient's difficulties. The patient should be helped to realize what problems are stress related and that with guidance one can learn to cope with or resolve.

9. *Utilize tranquilizers only where anxiety is so great that the patient cannot make decisions.* When the patient is so concerned with fighting off anxiety that there is no cooperation with the treatment plan, prescribe an anxiolytic (diazepam, Xanax). This is a temporary expedient only. In the event a schizophrenic patient must continue to live with hostile or disturbed parents who fail to respond to or refuse exposure to family therapy, prescribe a neuroleptic medication and establish a way to see that medications are taken regularly.

10. *Deal with the immediate present and avoid probing of the past.* Our chief concern is the here and now. What is the patient's present life situation? Is trouble impending? The focus is on any immediate disruptive situation responsible for the crisis as well as on the corrective measures to be exploited. Historical material is considered only if it is directly linked to the current problem.

11. *Avoid exploring for dynamic factors.* Time in therapy is too short for this. Therapy must be reality oriented, geared toward problem solving. The goal is restoration of the precrisis stability. But if dynamic factors like transference produce resistance to

therapy or to the therapist, deal rapidly with the resistances in order to dissipate them. Where dynamic material is "thrown" at the therapist, utilize it in treatment planning.

12. *Aim for increasing self-reliance and finding alternative constructive solutions for problems.* It is essential that the patient anticipate future sources of stress, learning how to cope with these by strengthening adaptive skills and eliminating habits and patterns that can lead to trouble.

13. *Always involve the family or significant others in the treatment plan.* A crisis represents both an individual and a family system collapse, and family therapy is helpful to alter the family system. A family member or significant friend should be assigned to supervise drug intake where prescribed and to share responsibility in depressed patients.

14. *Group therapy can also be helpful* both as a therapy in itself and as an adjunct to individual sessions. Contact with peers who are working through their difficulties is reassuring and educational. Some therapists consider short-term group therapy superior to individual therapy for crises.

15. *Terminate therapy within six sessions if possible and in extreme circumstances no later than 3 months after treatment has started to avoid dependency.* The patient is assured of further help in the future if required.

16. *Where the patient needs and is motivated for further help for purposes of greater personality development after the precrisis equilibrium has been restored, institute or refer for dynamically oriented short-term therapy.* In most cases, however, further therapy is not sought and may not be needed. Mastery of a stressful life experience through crisis intervention itself may

be followed by new learnings and at least some personality growth.

SUPPORTIVE, BEHAVIORAL AND EDUCATIONAL APPROACHES IN SHORT TERM THERAPY

By far the most common measures utilized in short-term therapy are supportive, behavioral, and educational approaches that aim at symptom relief and problem solving. These are employed without compromising the possibility that some reconstructive personality alterations may serendipitously germinate over time. The therapist assiduously avoids probing for unconscious conflicts or developmental difficulties in childhood, or issues of transference and resistance except where they interfere with the conduct of therapy. A focus on problems in the here-and-now is agreed on by patient and therapist, and the number of sessions may be set in advance. These usually are limited to from 6 to 10, but may sometimes be extended to 25 sessions. Upon agreement the therapist actively pursues the focus with selective inattention to and refusal to be diverted by peripheral aspects no matter how important they may seem. The theme is "get in fast and get out fast." This usually precludes dealing with extensive dynamic factors. In the few sessions that constitute the treatment plan, all that may be reasonably expected is resolution of a current problem situation and restoration of the patient to a previous optimal level of functioning.

The fact that we have so many different techniques for the same emotional problem can be confusing. What may help is a system approach that considers behavior an integrate of coordinated individual systems that are tied together like links in a chain. I have tried to illustrate this in Table 57-1, which can help in the selection of a therapeutic focus and preferred treatment modality. Because of time restrictions one will want to select the one method or combination of methods that is most applicable to the prevailing difficulty. Thus if the patient complains about fatiguability, loss of appetite and weight, listlessness, diminished libido, and insomnia, and it becomes apparent that he or she is suffering from a depressive disorder, one may consider organizing the therapeutic thrust around the biochemical link and supplying an antidepressant medication. This would not preclude working with other links in the behavioral chain if these are implicated. If the patient suffers from a great deal of tension with gastrointestinal irritability and bouts of high blood pressure, the therapist may want to manage the somatic link with relaxation therapy or biofeedback while searching for coordinate etiological factors. A conditioned phobic complaint, e.g., fear of entering elevators or other enclosed spaces, would invite a working with the conditioning link through behavioral approaches such as in vivo desensitization. While recognizing that personality factors associated with intrapsychic conflict are probably present, one would have to bypass the intrapsychic link unless such factors constituted the primary complaint, or if personality problems were operating as resistance to symptom-oriented interventions. In the latter case dynamic therapy would be considered. Should the patient have a severe marital problem one would deal with the interpersonal link through couple therapy. In the event stress could not be eliminated because of intolerable environmental circumstances, the therapist would focus on situational difficulties, and institute the proper therapy associated with the social link. If the assessment of the problem points to the philosophic link because of noxious attitudes and belief systems (which can be as pathogenic as virulent viruses and bacteria), one would attempt to detoxify thinking

Table 57-1
Therapeutic Focus, Goals, and Selection of Modality

(A) COMPLAINT FACTOR (target symptoms)	(B) SYNDROMES	(C) AREAS OF PATHOLOGY	(D) GOALS	(E) THERAPEUTIC FOCUS (implicated links)	(F) APPLICABLE FIELDS	(G) EFFECTIVE THERAPEUTIC MODALITIES

Depression
Hyperactivity
Hallucinations
Severe anxiety
Panic attacks
Impulsivity and inattention
Binge eating
Obsessions and compulsions
Phobias
	1. Major depression
	2. Bipolar disorder
	  a. depressed
	  b. manic
	3. Atypical depression
	4. Schizophrenic disorder
	5. Schizophreniform disorder
	6. Generalized anxiety disorder
	7. Panic disorder
	8. Attention deficit disorder
	9. Bulimia
	10. Obsessive-compulsive disorder
	11. Agoraphobia
		Neurotransmitter systems	Restoring balance in neurotransmitter systems	Biochemical link	Biochemistry	1. 2a, 7, 9, 11:
						  Antidepressants
						  Interpersonal therapy
						  Cognitive therapy
						2. Lithium
						3. MAO inhibitors
						4. 5. Neuroleptics
						6. Anxiolytics
						8. Psychostimulants
						10. Clomipramine
						1. ECT [for uncontrollable suicidal gestures and excitement]
						4. Hospitalization, rehabilitation

Poor emotional and impulse control; incoordination; personality change; tension; defective	Organic brain syndrome Organic mental disorder [primary degenerative dementia; multi-infarct dementia]	Neuronal masses of brain	Resolving affective and autonomic dysregulations	Neurophysiological link	Neurophysiology	Pharmacotherapy Relaxation therapy Psychosocial therapies Counseling

information processing; paranoid attitudes; neurological impairments; delirium; amnesia; dementia	Substance-induced intoxications [alcohol, amphetamine, barbiturate, cannabis, cocaine, opioid, PCP, other]		Removal of abused toxic substances		Toxicology	
Physical complaints of various organ systems [e.g. severe pain; headache; indigestion; backache; hypertension; colitis, etc.]	Organic physical disease	Implicated organ systems	Relieving or resolving organic and functional pathology	Somatic link	Medicine Psychiatry	Medicinal & surgical interventions; Relaxation therapy, biofeedback; Supportive psychotherapy; Individual & group counseling
Conditioned behavioral disturbances and poor adjustment following an identifiable psychosocial stressor; Depression; jitteriness; conduct disorder [truancy; vandalism; reckless driving; fighting] work or academic failure; phobic avoidance	Adjustment disorder [with depressed mood; with various emotional features; with disturbances of conduct; with academic or work inhibitions; with withdrawal; with atypical features]; Phobic disorders	Conditioned anxieties	Reconditioning anxiety responses	Conditioning link	Learning theory	Behavior therapy; Hypnosis; Cognitive therapy

(continued)

Table 57-1 (*continued*)

(A) COMPLAINT FACTOR (target symptoms)	(B) SYNDROMES	(C) AREAS OF PATHOLOGY	(D) GOALS	(E) THERAPEUTIC FOCUS (implicated links)	(F) APPLICABLE FIELDS	(G) EFFECTIVE THERAPEUTIC MODALITIES
Anxiety; panic attacks; obsessions; compulsions; depression; somatic symptoms; sensory and motor disturbances; fugue states; mutiple personality; depersonalization; sexual deviations; sexual dysfunction; phobias	Panic disorder Generalized anxiety disorder Obsessive-compulsive disorder Dissociative disorder Conversion disorder Dysthymic disorder Psychosexual disorder Agoraphobia Simple phobia Social phobia Posttraumatic stress disorder	Unconscious conflicts	Recognition, understanding, and resolution of conflicts	Intrapsychic link	Psychoanalytic theory	Psychoanalysis Psychoanalytically oriented therapy Hypnoanalysis Guided imagery
Disturbed relationships with people [paranoidal, oppositional, hostile, defensive, stubborn, power driven, hypersensitive, eccentric, seclusive, aggressive, indifferent, excitable, irrational, overactive,	Personality disorder [paranoid, schizoid, schizotypal, histrionic, narcissistic, antisocial, borderline, avoidant, dependent, compulsive, passive-aggressive, atypical] Substance abuse/depen-	Interpersonal-relationships Developmental arrest [impaired separation-individuation]	Personality maturation Improved relationships with authority and peers Enhanced self-esteem	Developmental interpersonal link	Developmental theory Psychoanalytic theory Role theory Group dynamics Social psychology	Psychoanalytic psychotherapy Psychodrama Group therapy Marital [couples] therapy Family therapy Rehabilitation

Target symptoms (A)	Syndromes (B)	Responsible areas of pathology (C)	Goals in therapy (D)	Implicated link (E)	Fields of interest (F)	Therapeutic modalities (G)
exhibitionistic, exploitative, self-centered, impulsive, explosive, manipulative] Antisocial behavior Academic problems Occupational problems Marital problems Family problems Substance abuse and dependence	dence [alcohol, barbiturates, other hypnotics, opioids, cocaine, amphetamine, PCP, hallucinogens, cannabis, tobacco] Identity disorder Adjustment disorders		Improved identity		Self psychology Object relations theory Systems theory	Environmental manipulation Milieu therapy Social casework Counseling Social therapy Rehabilitation therapy
Situational problems [e.g. education, health, housing, neighborhood, finances, cultural differences, pollution, international tensions]	Phase of life problem Environmental problem Occupational problem Adjustment problem	Environmental stress	Rectification of or adaptation to environmental stress	Social link	Sociology Anthropology Economics Political science	
Distorted values and standards Maladaptive belief systems	Multiform adaptational difficulties	Cognitive distortions	Reeducation Cognitive restructuring	Philosophical-spiritual link	Philosophy Theology Metapsychiatry	Cognitive therapy Education Existential therapy

Target symptoms (A) characteristic of different syndromes (B) may often be expediently resolved by dealing directly with specific responsible areas of pathology (C). Goals in therapy here (D) are directed at such distortions. Looking at behavior as a chain of interrelated systems (biochemical, neurophysiological, somatic, conditioned, intrapsychic, developmental-interpersonal, social-environmental, philosophic-spiritual) a suitable focus is on the implicated links of this chain (E). Distinctive fields of interest (F) and special theories related to each link inspire a number of therapeutic modalities (G) that may be preferred approaches in certain syndromes even though through feedback interventions bracketed to other links may also be effective.

patterns through cognitive therapy. Unless this is done, disturbed cognitions can poison relationships with people and vitiate the self-image.

We can console ourselves in a minor way. No matter what technique is employed, if the therapist is skilled in its use, has faith in its validity, and communicates this faith to the patient, and if the patient accepts the technique and absorbs this faith, he or she will be influenced in some positive way. The therapist anticipates that in resolving a difficulty related to one disturbed link in the behavioral chain, this will influence by feedback other links. Thus, if neuroleptics are prescribed for a schizophrenic patient with a disturbing thinking disorder, the impact on the biochemistry will register itself positively in varying degrees on the patient's neurophysiology, general behavior, intrapsychic mechanisms, interpersonal relations, social attitudes, and perhaps even one's philosophical outlook. Applying behavior therapy to a phobia will in its correction influence other aspects from the biochemical factors to spiritual essences. Modifying disturbed interpersonal relations through group or interpersonal therapy, correcting environmental difficulties through therapeutic counseling, and altering belief systems through cognitive therapy will have an effect throughout the behavioral continuum. This global response, however, does not in the least absolve therapists from trying to select the best method within their range of skills that is most attuned both to the patient's immediate concerns and unique learning aptitudes.

Be this as it may, there are some general principles that are applicable to most patients. First, one starts therapy by allowing the patient to unburden verbally, to tell his or her story uninterruptedly, interpolating comments to indicate understanding and empathy and to keep the patient focused on important content. Second, the therapist helps the patient arrive at some preliminary understandings of what the difficulty is all about. Third, a method is selected that is targeted on the link that is creating greatest difficulty for that patient-biochemical, physiological, behavioral, interpersonal, social or philosophic. Fourth, as therapy progresses the therapist tries to show the patient how he or she is not an innocent bystander and that the patient, in a major or minor way may be involved in bringing trouble on him or herself. Fifth, the therapist deals with any resistances that the patient develops that block an understanding of the problem and the productive use of the techniques employed. Sixth, the therapist tries to acquaint the patient with some of the disturbed attitudes carried around by the patient that can create trouble for him or her in the future, how they developed, how they operate now, and how they may show up after he or she leaves therapy. Seventh, the patient is given homework that is aimed at strengthening oneself enough so that problems may be minimized or prevented from occurring later on. Within this broad framework there are, of course, wide differences on how therapists with varying theoretical orientations will operate. By and large, however, psychotherapists with adequate training should anticipate satisfactory results with the great majority of their patients utilizing this format.

Employing whatever techniques or group of techniques are indicated by the needs of the patient and that are within the scope of one's training and experience, the therapist may be able to achieve the goals agreed on in a rapid and effective way. Where the therapist has become aware of the underlying dynamics, it may be necessary to mention at least some salient aspects and to enjoin the patient to work on these by oneself after treatment has ended. On the other hand, the therapist may not be able to achieve desired goals unless interfering dynamic influences that function as resistance are dealt with during the treatment period because the patient is blocked by such resistance toward making progress.

Dealing with Environmental Factors

In practically every emotional problem an improvement in well-being motivates the individual to alter circumstances of living. This comes about as the patient recognizes that he or she does not have to exist under conditions of stress and deprivation. Demoralized by the inner turmoil, the patient may have hopelessly accepted a bad environmental plight as inevitable. In desperation surcease may be sought through involvement in situations that offer asylum, but the patient then gets into predicaments that turn out to be a greater blight than boon. The patient may even masochistically arrange matters so that he or she can suffer as if to pay penance for pervasive guilt feelings. Over and over we observe the phenomenon of people, distraught with inner conflict, deliberately attempting to give this objectivity by immersing themselves in outside vexations that consume their attention and concern.

In the course of therapy, it is essential to help the patient break the grip of forces that are hurtful or depriving by identifying them and pointing out their effects. Unless the patient has a basic understanding of the role he or she plays in supporting difficulties of which the patient bitterly complains, wresting from one jam will only result in arranging for another in a very short time.

Generally, it is better for the patient to figure out for oneself what can be done to straighten out his or her life. However, active suggestions may have to be given if the patient cannot devise a plan of action alone, and, toward this end, the therapist may suggest available resources that can aid the patient in this particular need. For instance, a patient who has withdrawn from activities may be encouraged to participate in sports, hobbies, and social recreations, the thera-

pist guiding the patient to groups where such diversions may be found. The patient's economic situation may have to be supplemented through opportune expediencies to supply funds for medical and dental care. A husband, wife or child may be ill, and the pressures on the patient will require alleviation through referral to appropriate clinics or agencies. Better housing may be essential to remedy overcrowding or to remove the patient from neighborhoods where there is exposure to prejudice, threats to life, and crime. A handicapped child may require assignment to a special rehabilitative clinic. A child failing at school may need psychological testing. An aging parent with nothing else to do to occupy his or her time may rule a household with an iron fist and be responsible for an impending break-up of a family. Appropriate outlets may have to be found to consume the oldster's energies. Adoption of a child may be the best solution for a childless couple who are anxious to rear a boy or girl. A patient who has moved from another town may feel alone and estranged and need information about recreational and social facilities in the community. These and countless other situations may require handling in the course of short-term psychotherapy.

The therapist, may, of course, be as puzzled as the patient regarding how to fill an existing need. He or she may not know the suitable resources. The chances are, however, that resources do exist if a proper search is launched. A voluntary family agency, or the family agency of the religious faith of the patient, may be able to act as the initial information source, as may a Council of Social Agencies, Welfare Council, Community Council, local or State health or welfare department or children's agency like a Children's Aid Society. Public health nurses and social workers are often cognizant of immediate instrumentalities in the community, and it may be appropriate to call in a social worker to work adjunctively with the therapist as a consultant.

Perhaps the most pressing problems will concern the patient's relationships with members of the immediate family. Pathological interactions of the various family members are the rule, and the patient may be imprisoned by the family role. Indeed, the patient may not be the person in the family who needs the most help; he or she may be the scapegoat or the member with the weakest defenses. Active assistance may have to be given the patient in resolving family crises. For example, a woman sought help for depressive spells accompanied by sporadic lower abdominal spasms. Although she rationalized her reasons for it, it soon became apparent that she resented deeply a situation that she had brought upon herself. Her sister's son who was getting a Master's degree at college needed his thesis typed. The patient casually offered to help and soon found herself working steadily against a deadline, typing several drafts of a two hundred page manuscript. This she did without compensation and with only minimal appreciation from her sister and nephew. Yet the patient felt obligated to continue since she had promised to complete the thesis. Periodically she would abandon her typewriter when her abdominal cramps became too severe; but her guilt feelings soon drove her back to work. Encouraged by the therapist's appraisal of the unfairness of the situation, the patient was able to discuss with her nephew, with reasonable calmness, her inability to complete his manuscript. This precipitated a crisis with her sister who credited the patient's defection to ill-will. After several sessions were focused on the role she had always played with her exploitative sister, the patient was able to handle her guilt feeling sufficiently to desist from retreating from her stand. A temporary break with her sister was terminated by the latter who apologetically sought to restore the relationship which assumed a much more wholesome tenor.

It may at times be necessary to see other family members to enlist their cooperation. Patients rarely object to this. For instance, a patient though married was being victimized by an over-concerned and dominating mother who visited her daily and assumed control over the patient's household. It was obvious that the patient's protests masked a desire to maintain a dependent relationship with her mother. She refused to get into a fight with her mother or to offend her by requesting that she stay away. She claimed that her mother never would understand her protest to be left alone; her mother was the one person concerned over the patient's depression and helplessness. This was why she commandeered the role of housekeeper in her daughter's home. The patient was urged to discuss with mother her need to become more independent and to take over increasing responsibility. It was pointed out that some of her depression and helplessness were products of her refusal to accept a mature status. The more she depended on her mother, the more inadequate she felt. This situation sponsored a retreat from self-reliance. It was important to urge her mother to stay away from her apartment. I then suggested to the patient that I have a talk with the mother. The presumed purpose as far as the mother was concerned was to get as much historical data as possible. Her parent readily acquiesced and the interview centered around the patient's great sensitivity as a child and her lack of confidence in herself. Feeling myself to be in rapport with the woman, I pointed out to her how urgent it was to help her daughter grow up. I suggested that it might be difficult to resist her daughter's pleas for help, but that it was vital that she do so in order to stimulate her daughter's independent growth. Nor should she come to her child's rescue when the latter made mistakes. It was important for her daughter to make her own decisions and to take the consequences of her blunders. As a matter of fact the more mistakes she made, the more she would learn. The mother agreed to assist me in helping her daughter, and her cooperation in restricting visits to weekly intervals, as a guest not as a housekeeper, was a principal factor in my being able to bring the patient to a much more self-confident adjustment.

Psychotherapy may have to be prescribed for one or more members of the patient's family in order to alter a family constellation that is creating difficulties for all. In our search for pathology we are apt to overlook the fact that every family unit contains healthy elements which if released can aid each of its constituent members. Instead of or in addition to individual therapy family therapy may best be employed. If family therapy is decided on, sessions may be held with as many of the family group as possible. Each person must be made to see how he or she is deprived and depriving, punished and punishing, and exploited and exploiting. Even a few sessions with this intimate group may serve to release feelings and attitudes that may rejuggle the family equation sufficiently to permit the emergence of healthy trends.

Managing Dependency

Most persons in trouble at the start of therapy feel helpless and want to lean on an idealized parental agency. Being permitted to do so relieves their fear and lessens their anxiety. Whether the therapist realizes it or not he or she will be a target for the patient's dependency yearnings, no matter if one tries to be detached and passive, or actively supportive, reassuring or persuasive. Gratification of dependency needs is hoped to be a temporary measure that is ideally followed by developing independence as mastery is restored. This is accompanied by such signs as a decrease in sensitivity,

diminished tendencies to over-react to stimuli, a greater ability to handle criticism, a channeling off into more constructive channels of rage, a better management of feelings of rejection, an avoidance of destructive competition, a reduction of personal overambitiousness, and a correction of distorted ideas about one's world. There are no miracles regarding such developments. They come about as the patient is helped to overcome the symptoms, to solve problems, and to evaluate more rationally an immediate environmental situation that will then enable the patient to make better and less neurotic decisions. Basic personality patterns may not undergo alteration although methods of living around them may be handled more easily. Over time the therapist may hopefully discern some reconstructive changes if the patient has some awareness of underlying personality distortions and has motivation to change these. Engaging in additional dynamic therapy may expedite these changes.

DYNAMIC SHORT-TERM PSYCHOTHERAPY

Where the therapist has decided to deal with the intrapsychic link in the behavioral chain with the object of reconstructive personality change, one would have to consider that patterns of behavior will generally follow a sequence of conditionings that date back to childhood. Many of the patterns have become firmly fixed, operate automatically, and, while the circumstances that initiated them no longer exist, and the memory traces are firmly embedded in the unconscious, they continue to display themselves often to the dismay of the individual and the consternation of those around him or her. Thus, where defiance in childhood was a prerequisite to expressing assertiveness in relation to overly restrictive and moralistic parents, defiant, recalcitrant, aggressive, or hostile outbursts may be essential before assertiveness can be released. Where self-worth was measured in terms of vanquishing a sibling or parent and proving oneself better than these adversaries, compulsive competitive activities may preoccupy the individual to an extraordinary degree. Where sexual feelings were mobilized by parental provocations, strokings, spankings, enemas, observation of adult sexual activities, or precocious stimulation in varied kinds of sex play, engagement in similar activities, or the exploitation of phantasies about such activities, may be requirements for the release of sexual feeling. These impulses may become organized into perversions. Recrudescence into adult life of unusual behavior is often explicable on the basis of the linkage of adult needs with outmoded anachronistic patterns. Such behavior is usually rationalized when it is manifestly out of keeping with the reality situation.

The individual is, more or less, at the mercy of personality distortions, since the experiences that produced them are sealed off from awareness by repression and are thus not easily available to conscious deliberation or control. The patient is driven by needs, drives and defenses that clash with the demands of society on the one hand and with personal values on the other.

Since the patient carries the burdens of conflict, which impose extraordinary pressures, he or she will be prone to overreact to stressful circumstances in the environment, particularly when these create insecurity or undermine self-esteem. If one's coping mechanisms falter, one may become overwhelmed by a catastrophic sense of helplessness and by shattering of feelings of mastery. This contingency may bring the frightening experience of anxiety with which one will have to deal with whatever mechanisms of defense can be mustered. Often these revive early defenses, which at one time were employed in childhood, but which are now worthless, since though

temporarily allaying anxiety, they foster complications that further tend to disorganize the individual in dealings with life.

One must not underestimate the importance of promptings developed in childhood that have been relegated by repression to the dubious oblivion of the unconscious. These underpinnings of personality—the drives and defenses of childhood—assert themselves throughout the life of the individual.

Thus a man, undermined by an overprotective mother who crushed his autonomy and emerging feelings of masculinity, may have sufficient ego strength to rise as an adult above his devalued self-image, by pushing himself into positions of power and achieving monetary success. To all outward appearances he may appear masterful, strong, and accomplished. Yet his feeble inner promptings to make himself dependent register themselves in passive impulses with homosexual phantasies. He will drive himself into compromising relationships with men, promoting fierce competitiveness, needs for identification with their strength, paranoidal outbursts and perhaps desires for sexual contact when under the influence of alcohol. Understandably, the individual will function under a great hardship being in almost constant conflict, with little awareness of what is going on inside of himself.

Essentially the process of therapy that is rooted in the dynamic theoretical model consists of utilizing the relationship situation with the therapist as a means of helping the patient to gain an understanding of himself in regard to how his current reactions and interpersonal involvements are related to formative experiences in his past. An attempt is made to bring him to an awareness of unconscious needs, drives and value systems, as well as their origin, significance and contemporary manifestations through special techniques introduced by Freud, such as exploration of dreams. The resistances to unveiling these repressed ingredients are dealt with by interpretation. In the course of working with the patient, the therapist will observe the development of attitudes toward him that reflect early disturbed feelings toward authority (transference). Repeated in the medium of the therapeutic relationship ultimately will be some important incidents that resemble traumatic experiences with past authorities.

It goes without saying that the therapist must have the education, understanding and the personality stability to cope with the patient's projections in order to help the patient gain an awareness of his unconscious maneuvers. The therapist may tend to become frustrated by some patients. He or she may feel enervated by the acting-out, demandingness, hostility, criticial attitudes, and unreasonableness of the patient who will watch carefully for the therapist's reactions. Should the therapist respond in ways similar to actions of the parents, the therapeutic process will tend to stop. Actually, the patient will probably engineer the situation so that certain traumatizing experiences can be reenacted with the therapist. If the therapist acts in a therapeutically positive manner the contrast to the past actions of the parents helps the patient gain a different conception of what rational authority is like. The hope is that eventually the patient will, because of new understanding, begin to relate to the therapist in a way different from the habitual responses to authority. Thus, the patient will utilize the therapeutic situation as a vehicle for the evolution of constructive attitudes towards oneself and others. New capacities as a person will develop, as will lessened severity of conscience, greater assertiveness and independence, and an ability to express basic drives in relation to the standards of a group.

The particular way of working will depend on the experience and skill of the therapist. One cannot, as a rule, due to lack of time, employ the time-honored devices of free-association, passivity, and anonymity. Nor should the couch be the preferred posi-

tion. Transference reactions are dealt with rapidly with the objective of avoiding a transference neurosis. While the latter may release the deepest conflicts, there is no time available for the essential working-through. If a transference neurosis develops without intention, this must be dissipated as soon as possible because of its interference with therapy. Resistance is managed by active interpretations.

To help the patient gain a better understanding of inner drives, the therapist utilizes focused interviewing, structures a broad picture of the existing dynamics, and encourages the patient to fill in the details through concentrated self-observation. If the therapist knows how to employ them, dreams can be advantageously utilized. For example, a patient in the early part of therapy experienced an unaccountable recrudescence of symptoms that discouraged him greatly. Productions were relatively sterile, and, since there was currently no concentration on depth material, and no explanation for the relapse on the basis of unusual environmental difficulties, I assumed that he was resisting talking about matters that bothered him. He denied having any particular feelings toward me, but, when I specifically inquired about dreams, he recalled the following:

"I'm in a room where there is a performance going on, like a theatre. But I'm not paying attention to it. A quite heavy, unattractive, chunky man is there carrying a large gun, like a machine gun. This man—he and I are emotionally involved, but there is no connotation of physical sex. He gets up and leaves, and I follow. He said he was told by his doctor that day—I don't know how he put it—that he had a heart attack. He began to cry. It meant the end of everything between us. Life was not absolutely desolate for me. He was losing everything, but I was detached and unconcerned. The heart attack meant I would be free of him. Then later in the night I had a second dream involving you. A law suit is going on, something like a trial. You are the lawyer. You are cross examining people. I am disappointed in your performance, the way you handle the cross examination—jumping around, no logic. (*Patient laughs*) You make a reference to making money. I feel let down. All you want is to make money—calculating.''

The portion of the session that follows brings out what was bothering the patient—a transference response in which he was equating me with his inadequate greedy father from whom he desired escape.

Dr. You must have had some feelings about me that upset you. (*Pause. Patient laughs*)

Pt. That day you took off on ethics. I felt you were taking off on something I had no desire to talk about. Also when I talked about the law suit I had contemplated and the lawyer handling the case, (*The patient was involved in a minor civil suit*) you said: "You act precipitously." I felt you misunderstood me because I don't act precipitously. I nullify action by indecision. You spoke strongly.

Dr. Yes.

Pt. I guess I seek perfection from you, like I do from my girl friend. When you make a grammatical error, I dwell on it all day.

Dr. You seem to have a need for a powerful, accepting, perfect person in whom you can put your trust, and you get infuriated when that person shows any weakness. (*Interpreting the patient's feeling as a response to not finding the idealized authority figure.*)

Pt. I see that, but this doesn't have to be that way.

Dr. Why do you think it *is* that way?

Pt. I don't know. (*pause*)

Dr. What about your ever having had a perfect person around? Have you?

Pt. Jesus, no. I wish I had. My father was cruel and weak. I couldn't depend on him. He left my mother and me. I felt helpless and dependent on my mother. (*The patient's father had abandoned his mother when the patient was a boy.*)

Dr. Maybe you hoped that a strong man would come into your life some day?

Pt. I always wanted one. Even now I get excited when I see such a person.

Dr. Perhaps you felt I was going to be such a person? (*Patient laughs.*)

Pt. This is a false outlook on life. I'm not in bondage. I'm not a slave. This is all a lot of crap.

Dr. What about bondage to me? In the dream you escape when the man claims to be sick.

Pt. I do feel I need you, but seeing you puts me in bondage. But I don't dare let myself feel angry toward you. Only toward my girl friend.

Dr. Perhaps that's why you had a return of your symptoms. The feelings of being trapped

with me, in a dependency, with an inadequate father figure at that. (*Interpreting the patient's symptoms as a product of conflict.*)

Pt. Yes, yes, I am sure of it.

It is quite possible that the patient may have been able to work through his transference without the use of dreams. However, I felt that handling his dream short-circuited this process.

There is no substitute for experience in doing dynamic short-term therapy. The seasoned therapist will be able to attune himself or herself sensitively to what is going on, gauging the the manner of making an interpretation, and moving from challenge to support in response to the immediate reactions of the patient. It is difficult to outline specific rules that apply to every case since no two therapists will develop the same relationships with any one patient. And a patient will play different roles with different therapists, depending upon where in his or her characterologic scheme the patient happens to fit the therapist. Almost anything can happen in a therapeutic situation, but if the therapist is flexible, sensitive, and empathic mindful of the basic processes of psychotherapy, and aware of existing neurotic impulses as they are mobilized in a relationship with the patient, one should be able to bring the average patient to some understanding of basic problems within the span of a short-term approach. In long-term therapy, sooner or later, the patient's symptoms, the current precipitating factor, the immediate conflicts activated in the present disorder, the underlying personality structure, deeply repressed conflicts originating in childhood, the relationship with parental agencies, and the defensive mechanisms will slowly become defined and correlated. The working-through process proceeds on all levels of the psychic organization, and no aspect of personality or environment is usually considered unimportant in the painstaking investigative design.

In dynamic short-term therapy, we

cannot afford the leisurely pace that so extensive a proceeding requires. It is essential to focus on areas that will yield the highest dividends. Generally these deal with problems of immediate concern to the patient. While aspects that trouble the patient topically may not actually be the most important elements of the disorder, they do engulf the attention. Skill as a therapist is revealed in the ability to establish bridges from the immediate complaints to more basic personality difficulties. Only when a continuity has been affirmed between the immediate stresses and the conflictual reservoirs within the personality, will the patient be able to proceed working on more substantial issues. Focusing on what the patient considers to be mere corollaries to the pain, before having shown the patient that they are actually the responsible mischief makers, will usually turn out to be an unproductive exercise. It would be as if in a business faced with bankruptcy we were to advise delay in regulating office expenditures in favor of studying the economic picture of the world at large. The perturbations of management could scarcely be allayed with remote objectives when what immediately occupies them is the anxiety of meeting the weekly payroll. Were one to consider the day-to-day survival needs, and tangentially relate current operations to more comprehensive, and ultimately more important, general business factors, greater cooperation would be secured.

The particular problem area to be attacked at first in dynamic short-term therapy is, therefore, more or less of the patient's own choosing. Often this deals with the *precipitating stress situation* an exploration of which may alleviate tension and serve to restore the individual to an adaptive balance. Here an attempt is negotiated to identify the immediate trouble source, and to relate it to the patient's subjective distress. An endeavor is made at working-through, at least partially, of the difficulties liberated by the stress situation. These, de-

rivatives of enduring and fixed underlying core conflicts, are handled as autonomous sources of anxiety. Historical material is considered only when it is bracketed to the current problems. Not only may the patient be brought back to emotional homeostasis rapidly, particularly when seen immediately after the stress situation has set in, but inroads may be made on deeper conflicts.

A bright young man of eighteen applied for therapy on the basis that he was about to fail his last year of high school. What worried him was that he would not receive a certificate and could, therefore, not enter college. His parents were no less disturbed than the patient at his impending educational debacle. While his first three years of high school work had yielded passable grades, these were far below his potential as revealed by an intelligence test. What was even more provoking was that in his college entrance examinations he had scored lowest in his class. He had also been unable to secure a passing grade in his midterm examinations. Embarrassed and manifestly upset, he expressed a futile attitude during the initial interview about better ability to study. What kept happening to him was that his mind wandered. When he forced himself to read his assignments, he could not retain what he read. The prospect of repeating his last year at school was a severe blow to his pride. He envisaged accepting a position as a general helper at a local gasoline service station.

No comment was made to discourage him from stopping school. Instead my retort dealt with the wisdom of adjusting one's career to one's intellectual capacity. If it were true that he was unable to keep up with his class because of his inferior mental ability, it might be very appropriate to accept a less ambitious career status. Why burden oneself with impossibilities? The patient then spent the remainder of the session trying to convince me that his intelligence quotient was in the upper ten percentile. This was most extraordinary, I admitted. Perhaps there were emotional reasons why he had to fail.

During the next few sessions we feverishly explored his fears of competitiveness, his desire to remain the favorite child in his family, his dependency on his mother, his impulse to frustrate and punish his father for pushing him to satisfy a personal selfish ambitiousness, and his dread to leave home and to pursue an independent life. The meaning of his need to fail soon crystallized in his mind. He realized that it required an effort to avoid educational success, that he was actually trying to fail in order to retain the pleasures of irresponsible childhood.

No moral judgments were expressed as to the virtues of these aims. If he really wanted to be a child, if he desired to hurt himself in order to get back at his parents, if he had the wish to retreat from being as good as any of his colleagues, this was within his rights as a person. However, he had to realize that he was doing this to himself. Angrily he protested that such was not at all the case. He was convinced that his parents did not want him to grow up; they lamented losing their older children when they went to college. They wanted him to be dependent. Why then should he go along with their designs and nefarious intentions; why should he be the "fall guy"? The rage he vented at his parents was followed shortly by a recognition of his own dependency desires and his fear of growing up. As we explored this he discovered that there was a clearing of his mind and a greater dedication to his studies. His successful final examinations were a fitting climax to his fifteen sessions of therapy. Letters that I received from the patient from an out-of-town college, and a follow-up visit one year later, revealed measures of personality growth hardly consistent with the relatively short period that he stayed in treatment.

Another early focus in therapy is on *distressing symptoms*. The patient is only too eager to talk about these. Their explora-

tion may lead to a discovery of provocative anxieties and conflicts that initiate and sustain them. The importance of giving some meaning to disturbing or mysterious complaints cannot be overemphasized. So long as a symptom remains unidentified, it is like an autonomous and frightening foreign body. To label it, to explain its significance, gives the individual a measure of control helping one to restore one's sense of mastery. This enables one to function better, since, in finding out some reasons for the symptoms, one can utilize one's energies to correct their source.

Generally, the presenting symptom is explored thoroughly in the context of the question: "How is the symptom related to the individual's personality structure as a whole?" For example, a man comes to therapy undermined by uncontrollable bouts of anxiety. The history reveals that the first attack followed a quarrel with his wife. From the character of his relationship with his mother, his Rorschach responses, and his dreams it is apparent that he basically is a dependent individual who is relating disagreeably to his wife. The symptom of anxiety is explicable on the basis of his releasing hostility toward the parental substitute and fearing abandonment and counterhostility. Our focus shifts then from his symptom to his personality structure in operation.

Other areas of focus may present themselves, for instance transference and resistance manifestations which, when they appear, will occupy the therapist's attention to the exclusion of any other concern. But here, too, when such reactions arise, they should be integrated with the general theme of the patient's personality functioning.

All persons possess blind spots in understanding of themselves. Many of these are due to gaps in education; some are distortions promoted by parents and friends; some are perversions of factual data; some are misrepresentations initiated and sustained by misguided education. During therapy some of these falsifications will require greater clarification. In assuming a role geared toward clarification, the therapist disclaims being an oracle of wisdom, but that there are some facts of which he or she is confident. If the therapist is not sure of the stand, ideas may be offered with some reasonable reservations, since it may turn out that they are wrong.

In short-term therapy, the interpretation of unconscious motives prior to their eruption into awareness is generally avoided. This is because the therapist may not in a brief contact feel sure of one's ground, and because one does not wish to stir up powerful resistances that will negate the therapeutic efforts. Interpretations deal with immediately discernable feelings and personality reactions. However, it is sometimes possible for an extremely experienced psychoanalytically trained therapist, who has established good rapport with a patient, to interpret in depth, albeit in a reassuring way. It may be possible also to utilize confrontation, which in some cases may be very productive with a dramatic impact on the patient. For example, a young man in a state of anxiety with uncomfortable somatic accompaniments reveals great fear of standing next to strong looking men in the subway. His dreams repetitively picture him fleeing from men with destructive weapons. The therapist, on the basis of his experience, and his intuitive feelings about the patient's problem, concludes that the patient is concerned about homosexual impulses. The therapist has, in the first few interviews, won the confidence of the patient. He decides to interpret the patient's inner conflict. The following is from a recording of the interview:

Dr. You know it is very common for a person who has lost confidence in himself to assume he isn't masculine. The next thing that happens is that he gets frightened of being beat up, hurt, attacked and even sexually assaulted by strong men. He begins to feel that he is more feminine than masculine. The next thing he be-

gins to assume is that he is homosexual and this scares the devil out of him. (*pause.*)

Pt. Yes, yes. Isn't he? I mean how does one know?

Dr. I get the impression this is something that is bothering you.

Pt. I get caught in this terrible fear. I feel I'm not a man and that I'll do something terrible.

Dr. You mean like letting yourself get involved sexually with a man?

Pt. Not exactly, but when I have a few drinks, I find myself looking at the men with muscles and it scares the hell out of me.

Dr. When you have a few drinks, you *might* get sexually aroused. This is not uncommon. But what makes you think you are a homosexual?

Pt. I know I'm attracted to women and I enjoy being with women. But I constantly compare myself to other men and I come out the low man on the totem pole.

Dr. So the problem is your position in relation to other men, and your feelings about yourself. This seems to me to be your real problem. You've probably had a low opinion of yourself as far back as you can remember. What do you feel about what I have said?

Pt. (Obviously flustered) I . . . I . . . I think you're right (blushes). (*In this interchange the patient has been given an opportunity to face his inner phantasies and to give them another interpretation than that he is a hopeless homosexual. The emotional relief to the patient was manifest even in one interview.*)

Unless the therapist is on firm ground psychodynamically, and has developed a good working relationship, probings in depth are apt to pose a hazard. They may create great anxiety, or they may provoke resentment and resistance. The best rule is to preserve a good relationship with the patient by testing the patient's reactions to a few interpretations in depth that are presented in a casual and tentative manner.

A patient with an obsessive fear of being hurt, injured and cut, and thus of coming to an untimely death, had so gentle and obsequious a manner with people that I was convinced he was concealing profoundly destructive tendencies. On one occasion when he was discussing his fear of death, I said: ''A problem like yours may be touched off by a number of things. I had one patient who imagined himself to be a killer. This scared him so that he had to push the idea out of his mind. Instead he substituted fears of being hurt or killed. This happens over and over again. Whether or not the same thing is happening to you, I don't know. But if so there may be reasons for it. In the case of the man I treated, he confused being assertive with being aggressive and murderous.''

This initiated an exploration into the patient's childhood. There was little question that he had felt overprotected and thwarted in various ways, particularly in exploratory activities. Quarreling, fighting and even disagreeing with others were considered to be evil and ''against God's will.'' My indirect interpretation was accepted and utilized. Where an interpretation is premature or wrong, or where the patient's ego resources are unable to sustain its implications, one may on the other hand, react badly. The therapist then will have to retrieve the situation, working toward the reestablishment of a positive relationship.

The interpretation of a transference reaction is especially helpful when correct. An adolescent boy treated his visits with me as a casual incident in his routine, refusing to talk about himself and waiting for me to do something dramatic to remove his facial tic. At one visit I remarked, ''You just won't say anything about yourself and your feelings. I get the impression that you don't trust me.'' The patient's reaction was a startled one. He blushingly revealed that he was embarrassed at his thoughts. He never was able to be frank with his family. Whenever he divulged any secrets to his brothers or his parents, they were immediately revealed to the whole family to his great embarrassment. When I retorted that there must be something about coming to see me that made him feel sheepish, he admitted wanting to ask me for some ''sex books'' to explain masturbation and sex. Perhaps, I replied, he felt I might get the idea he wanted to stimulate himself pornographi-

cally with this literature. He blushed furiously at this, whereupon I reassured him that there was nothing to be ashamed of, that a strong sexual interest at his age was normal, and that I certainly would reveal nothing about our conversations to his parents. After all, what we talked about was between ourselves. This maneuver had the effect of releasing a flood of memories of incidents in which his confidence had been betrayed. Our sessions thereafter took a new direction with the patient participating actively. I repeatedly assured him that his parents or family would never know about the content of our talks.

In some cases, it may be expedient to present the patient with a general outline of personality development, particularly what happens with delayed separation individuation, inviting the patient to see which elements apply to him or her. I have found that this is occasionally helpful where insufficient time is available in therapy to pinpoint the precise pathology. Patients are usually enthusiastic at first at having received some clarification, and they may even acknowledge that segments of the presented outline relate to themselves. They then seem to lose the significance of what has been revealed to them. However, much later on follow-up many have brought up pertinent details of the outline and have confided that it stimulated thinking about themselves.

For instance, a man whose depression was set off by his losing face at work when a younger colleague was advanced ahead of him, came to therapy in an extremely discouraged state and with little motivation to inquire into his patterns of adjustment. Deep resentments were apparent from the violent responses to the Rorschach cards, and from his dreams, which centered around destruction and killing. When I commented that it would be natural for him to feel angry under the circumstances, he countered with the remark that he had written advancement off years ago, that he bore no resentment toward his victorious colleague, and that he was resigned to getting the "short end of the stick." From childhood on he was the underdog in the family, and he was accustomed to this role. Apparently, I retorted, he was not as resigned as he imagined himself to be, otherwise he would not have reacted to the present situation with such despair. Maybe he had not written himself off as a permanent underdog. Then I sketched an outline that followed along lines that I have used on other patients with minor variations. This deals with derivative conflicts much closer to awareness than the nuclear conflicts from which they come that are too deeply repressed to be available in the short period devoted to therapy. The following is from an audio tape that I made with the patient's consent:

"I believe I have a fair idea of what is going on with you, but I'd like to start from the beginning. I should like to give you a picture of what happens to the average person in the growing up process. From this picture you may be able to see where you fit and what has happened to you. You see, a child at birth comes into the world helpless and dependent. He or she needs a great deal of affection, care, and stimulation. The child also needs to receive the proper discipline to protect him or her. In this medium of loving and understanding care and discipline, where one is given an opportunity to grow, to develop, to explore, and to express oneself, independence gradually increases and dependence gradually decreases, so that at adulthood there is a healthy balance between factors of dependence and independence. Let us say they are equally balanced in the average adult; a certain amount of dependence being quite normal, but not so much that it cripples the person. Normally the dependence level may temporarily go up when a person gets sick, or insecure, and independence will temporarily recede. But this shift is only within a narrow range. However, as a result of bad or depriving experiences in childhood, and from your history this seems to have happened to you to some extent (*the patient's father, a salesman was away a good deal of the time and his older brother brutally intimidated him.*), the dependence level never goes down sufficiently and the independence level stays low. Now what happens when a person in adult life has excessive dependency and a low level of independence? Mind you, you may not show all the things that I shall point out to you, but try to figure out which of these do apply to you.

"Now most people with strong feelings of dependence will attempt to find persons who are stronger than they are, who can do for them what they feel they cannot do for themselves. It is almost as if they are searching for idealized parents, not the same kind of parents they had, but much better ones. What does this do to the individual? First, usually he becomes disappointed in the people he picks out as idealized parental figures, because they never come up to his expectations. He feels cheated. For instance, if a man weds a woman who he expects will be a kind, giving, protective, mother figure, he will become infuriated when she fails him on any count. Second, he finds that when he does relate himself to a person onto whom he projects parental qualities, he begins to feel helpless within himself; he feels trapped; he has a desire to escape from the relationship. Third, the feeling of being dependent, makes him feel passive like a child. This is often associated in his mind with being non-masculine; it creates fears of his becoming homosexual and relating himself passively to other men. This role, in our culture, is more acceptable to women, but they too fear excessive passivity, and they may, in relation to mother figures, feel as if they are breast-seeking and homosexual.

"So here he has a dependency motor that is constantly operating, making him forage around for a parental image who will inevitably disappoint him. (*At this point, the patient interrupted and described how disappointed he was in his wife, how ineffective she was, how unable she proved herself to be in taking care of him. We discussed this for a minute and then I continued.*) In addition to the dependency motor, the person has a second motor running, a resentment motor, which operates constantly on the basis that he is either trapped in dependency, or cannot find an idealized parental figure, or because he feels or acts passive and helpless. This resentment promotes tremendous guilt feelings. After all, in our culture one is not supposed to hate. But the hate feelings sometimes do trickle out in spite of this, and on special occasions they gush out, like when the person drinks a little too much. (*The patient laughs here and says this is exactly what happens to him.*) If the hate feelings do come out, the person may get frightened on the basis that he is losing control. The very idea of hating may be so upsetting to him that he pushes this impulse out of his mind, with resulting tension, depression, physical symptoms of various kinds, and self-hate. The hate impulse having been blocked is turned back on the self. This is what we call masochism, the wearing of a hair shirt, the constant self-punishment as a result of the feedback of resentment. The resentment machine goes on a good deal of the time running alongside the dependency motor.

"As if this weren't enough, a third motor gets going along with the other two. High dependence means low independence. A person with low feelings of independence suffers terribly because he does not feel sufficient unto himself; he does not feel competent. He feels nonmasculine, passive, helpless, dependent. It is hard to live with such feelings, so he tries to compensate by being overly aggressive, overly competitive, and overly masculine. This may create much trouble for the person because he may try to make up for his feelings of loss of masculinity. He may have phantasies of becoming a strong, handsome, overly active sexual male, and, when he sees such a figure, he wants to identify with him. This may create in him desires for and fears of homosexuality which may terrify him because he does not really want to be homosexual. Interestingly, in women a low independence level is compensated for by her competing with men, wanting to be like a man, acting like a man, and resenting being a woman. Homosexual impulses and fears also may emerge as a result of repudiation of femininity.

"A consequence of low feelings of independence is a devalued self-image with starts the fourth motor going. The person begins to despise himself, to feel he is weak, ugly and contemptible. He will pick out any personal evidence for this that he can find, like stature, complexion, physiognomy, and so on. If he happens to have a slight handicap, like a physical deformity or a small penis, he will focus on this as evidence that he is irretrievably damaged. Feelings of self-devaluation give rise to a host of compensatory drives, like being perfectionistic, overly ambitious and power driven. So long as one can do things perfectly and operate without flaw, he will respect himself. Or, if he is bright enough, and his environment favorable, he may boost himself into a successful position of power, operate like a strong authority and gather around himself a group of sycophants who will worship him as the idealized authority, whom in turn the individual may resent and envy while accepting their plaudits. He will feel exploited by those who elevate him to the postion of a high priest. "Why," he may ask himself, "can't I find somebody strong I can depend on?" What he seeks actually is a dependent rela-

tionship, but this role entails such conflict for him that he goes into fierce competitiveness with any authority on whom he might want to be dependent. (*The patient nods and keeps saying "Yes, yes."*)

"So here we have our dependency operating first; second, resentment, aggression, guilt, and masochism; third, drives for independence; and, fourth, self-devaluation and maneuvers to overcome this through such techniques as perfectionism, overambitiousness and power strivings, in phantasy or in reality.

"To complicate matters some of these drives get sexualized. In dependency, for instance, when one relates to a person the way a child or infant relates to a parent, there may be experienced a powerful suffusion of good feeling which may bubble over into sexual feeling. There is probably a great deal of sexuality in all infants in a very diffuse form, precursors of adult sexuality. And when a person reverts emotionally back to the dependency of infancy, he may re-experience diffuse sexual feelings toward the parental figure. If a man relates dependently to a woman, he may sustain toward her a kind of incestuous feeling. The sexuality will be not as an adult to an adult, but as an infant to a mother, and the feelings for her may be accompanied by tremendous guilt, fear, and perhaps an inability to function sexually. If the parental figure happens to be a man instead of a woman, the person may still relate to him like toward a mother, and emerging sexual feelings will stimulate fears of homosexuality. (*If the patient is a woman with sexual problems, the parallel situation of a female child with a parental substitute may be brought up: A woman may repeat her emotions of childhood when she sought to be loved and protected by a mother. In body closeness she may experience a desire to fondle and be fondled, which will stir up sexual feelings and homosexual fears.*) In sexualizing drives for independence and aggressiveness, one may identify with and seek out powerful masculine figures with whom to fraternize and affiliate. This may again whip up homosexual impulses. Where aggressive-sadistic and self-punitive masochistic impulses exist, these may, for complicated reasons, also be fused with sexual impulses, masochism becoming a condition for sexual release. So here we have the dependence motor, and the resentment-aggression-guilt-masochism motor, and the independence motor, and the self-devaluation motor, with the various compensations and sexualizations. We have a very busy person on our hands. (*At this point the patient revealed that he had become impotent with his wife and had experienced homosex-*

ual feelings and fears which were upsetting him because they were so foreign to his morals. What I said was making sense to him.)

"In the face of all this trouble, how do some people gain peace? By a fifth motor, that of detachment. Detachment is a defense one may try to use as a way of escaping life's messy problems. Here one withdraws from relationships, isolates himself, runs away from things. By removing himself from people, the individual tries to heal himself. But this does not usually work because after a while a person gets terrified by his isolation and inability to feel. People cannot function without people. They may succeed for a short time, but then they realize they are drifting away from things; they are depriving themselves of life's prime satisfactions. Compulsively, then, the detached person may try to reenter the living atmosphere by becoming gregarious. He may, in desperation, push himself into a dependency situation with a parental figure as a way out of his dilemma. And this will start the whole neurotic cycle all over again.

"You can see that the person keeps getting caught in a web from which there is no escape. So long as he has enough fuel available to feed his various motors and keep them running, he can go on for a period. But if opportunities are not available to him to satisfy his different drives, and if he cannot readily switch from one to the other, he may become excessively tense and upset. If his tension builds up too much, or if he experiences great trouble in his life situation, or if his self-esteem gets crushed for any reason, he may develop a catastrophic feeling of helplessness and expectations of being hurt. (*The patient here excitedly blurted out that he felt so shamed by his defeat at work that he wanted to atom bomb the world. He became angry and weak and frightened. He wanted to get away from everything and everyone. Yet he felt so helpless he wanted to be taken care of like a child. He then felt hopeless and depressed. I commented that his motors had been thrown out of gear by the incident at work and this had precipitated excessive tension and anxiety.*)

"When tension gets too great, and there seems to be no hope, anxiety may hit. And the person will build up defenses to cope with his anxiety, some of which may succeed and some may not. For instance, excessive drinking may be one way of managing anxiety. Fears, compulsions, physical symptoms are other ways. These defenses often do not work. Some, like phobias, may complicate the person's life and make it more difficult than before. Even though ways are sought to deal with anxiety, these prove to be self-defeating.

"Now we are not sure yet how this general outline applies to you. I am sure some of it does, as you yourself have commented. Some of it may not. What I want you to do is to think about it, observe yourself in your actions and relations to people and see where you fit. While knowing where you fit will not stop the motors from running, at least we will have some idea as to with what we are dealing. Then we'll better be able to figure out a plan concerning what to do."

Self-observation should be encouraged and this will help the "working-through" process without which insight can have little effect. It is important then even though a patient can spend limited time in treatment that he or she gain some awareness of the source of the problems. This ideally should establish the complaint factor as a parcel of a much broader design, and should point to the fact that self-defeating patterns are operating that are outcroppings of elements rooted in past experiences. Once the patient gets the idea that these troubles are not fortuitous, but are events related to definite causes—perhaps carryovers of childish needs and fears—he or she will be more apt to utilize energies toward resolving difficulties rather than expending them in useless resentment and self-recriminations. Insight may operate primarily as a placebo force at first, but if it enables the individual to relate significant forces in development to day-to-day contemporary functioning, this may enable the patient to establish inhibitory controls, and even to structure life along more meaningful and productive lines.

Because the degree of insight that can be inculcated in the patient in a short period of therapy is understandably limited, some therapists circumscribe the area of inquiry. Sifneos, for example, organizes interpretations around oedipal problems, Mann around issues of development, others around separation and grief. Whatever the focus, resistances will tend to sabotage self-understanding. Though the patient may seek to get rid of anxiety and disturbing symptoms, though possessing incentives to be assertive and independent, though wishing to be fulfilled happily and creatively, he or she is a prisoner of one's conditionings that tend compulsively and confoundingly to repeat. Moreover, there are virtues derived from a perpetuation of neurotic drives: symptoms do tend to give the patient temporary protection from anxiety; secondary gains operate that supply the individual with spurious dividends for the illness; normality poses dangers more disagreeable than being well. To work through resistances toward complete understanding, and to put insight into practice with corrective personality change, is a prolonged procedure that will have to go on outside of therapy, perhaps the remainder of the individual's life.

What will be needed is a form of discipline to approach the task of self-understanding toward liberation from destructive patterns. In order to get well the patient will have to acquire the strength to renounce patterns that have personal values. Even though awareness is gained into the need to renounce certain ways of behaving, the patient may prefer to hang onto a preferred though neurotic way of life despite the inevitability of suffering. The patient may also become resentful to the therapist for not reconciling irreconcilable objectives of achieving the fruits of victory without bothering to till the soil and plant the seed, and of retaining neurotic patterns while avoiding the accompanying pain.

For example, a female patient seeks love from men at the same time that she is extremely competitive with them. To outdo and outshine them has intense values for her. When she fails to vanquish them, she becomes infuriated; when they stop short of giving her the proper affection, she goes into despair. Her lack of insight into her ambivalence toward men is startling in view of the fact that she is capable of advising her friends in *their* affairs of the heart. From her history it is suspected that her problem stems in part from her competitiveness with an older brother against

whom she was pitted by her mother, who herself was in rivalry with her passive husband. Yet the patient loved and admired her brother. What bothers the patient is that she can never hold onto a strong male; only weak and passive men seek her out, for whom she has only contempt.

Within six sessions of therapy the patient became aware of her two antagonistic drives, to give affection and to defeat men. An inkling of her strong competitiveness with men also filtered through. She acknowledged how contradictory her motives were, but this had no effect whatsoever on her behavior. Indeed, she became embittered with and repudiated my suggestion that until a change occurred in her rivalrous attitudes toward men, she could not expect that they would respond to her, nor would she be able to realize the love she desired. She countered with the statement that she was looking for a man with "guts" who could fight back and make her feel like a woman.

Ordinarily, one would anticipate that a problem of this severity could be resolved only in prolonged treatment, preferably with the setting-up and working-through of a transference neurosis. For many reasons long-term therapy was not feasible, and after eighteen sessions treatment was terminated with symptomatic relief, but with no alteration of her patterns with men. What I enjoined her to do was to practice principles of self-observation, which I encourage in all patients who have a desire to achieve more than symptomatic change. Follow-up visits over a 10-year period have revealed deep and continuing changes with a successful marriage to a man she respects with whom she has enjoyed raising two children.

Post-Therapy
Self-Observation

Among the areas around which post-therapy self-observation is organized are the following:

1. *Relating outbursts of tension, anxiety and symptom exaggeration to provocative incidents in the environment and to insecurities within the self.* The patient may be told: "Whenever you get upset, tense or anxious, or whenever your symptoms get disturbing, ask yourself: 'What is going on? What has upset me?' Keep working at it, thinking about matters until you make a connection between your symptoms and what has provoked them." If the patient has gotten clues about the operative dynamics from the treatment experience, he or she will be in a position to pinpoint many of the current upsets. Even if the assigned determinants are not entirely complete, the fact that the patient attempts to identify the sources of trouble will help to overcome helplessness and to alleviate much tension.

2. *Observing circumstances that boost or lower feelings about oneself.* The patient is instructed to watch for incidents and situations that boost morale or that are deflating to the ego relating these, if possible, to operations of inherent personality assets and liabilities. For instance, when first forming a relationship with a person, a feeling of peace and contentment may follow on the assumption that the relationship will magically resolve problems. A realization may then dawn that such inordinate expectation can sponsor a parade of troubles since it is based on neurotic dependency. If, on the other hand, the patient experiences greater self-esteem in doing something constructive through personal efforts, the resulting feeling of independence and self-growth may encourage further efforts in this direction.

3. *Observing one's relationship with people.* The patient is encouraged to ask oneself: "What tensions do I get with people? What kind of people do I like or dislike? Are these tensions with all people or only with certain kinds of people? What do people do to upset me and in what ways to I get upset? What do I do to upset them or to upset myself when I am with them? What do I do and what do they do that tends to make me angry? What problems do I have with my parents, my mate, my children, my boss, associates at work, authorities, people in general?" Whatever clues are gathered about habitual reaction patterns will serve to consolidate an understanding of one's general personality operations.

4. *Observing daydreams or dreams during sleep.* The patient may be reminded, if during therapy he or she has learned that dreams have a meaning, that one may be able to get some valuable data about oneself from phantasies or dreams. The patient may be instructed: "Make a note of any daydreams or night dreams especially those that repeat themselves. Try to remember them and to figure out what they mean." How valuable this exercise may be is illustrated by the case of a young man with fears about his masculinity who developed stomach pains the evening of a blind date that forced him to cancel his appointment. Unable to understand why his pains disappeared immediately after the cancellation, he asked himself to remember any dreams that night. The dream he recalled was this: "My father had his arm around my mother and kept me from her. I felt guilty." He was so enthusiastic that he had made a connection between the incident of the blind date and his oedipal problem that he telephoned me to say he was going to challenge his putting women into the role of his mother by seeing his date through another evening. This he was able to do. Obviously not all patients will be able to utilize their dreams in self-observational practices.

5. *Observing resistances to putting one's insights into action.* The patient is ad-

vised that every time understanding is applied to the challenging of a neurotic pattern, this will tend to strengthen one. "You will eventually get to a point where you will be able to block destructive or self-defeating actions before they get you into trouble. But expect some resistance, tension and fear. When you stall in doing what you are supposed to do, ask yourself why? What are you afraid of? Then deliberately challenge your fear and see if you can overcome it."

By a studied application of the above principles of self-observation, the patient may be able to achieve considerable personality growth after treatment has stopped. Gradually one may become aware of patterns that have to be revised before interpersonal horizons can be expanded. Understandably, this process is slow. First, the individual realizes that symptoms do not occur at random, but rather are related to life situations and relationships with people which stir up tensions, hostilities, and anxieties. This leads to a questioning of the types of relationships that are habitually being established. It may seem incredible to the patient that other ways of behaving are possible. Even partial acceptance of this premise may spur an inquiry into origins of existing attitudes toward people and toward oneself. A continuity may be established between present personality traits and past conditionings. The "blueprint" of the personality that was tentatively sketched while in treatment becomes more solidly outlined, and essential revisions in it are made. The patient sees more clearly the condi-

tions under which early fears and conflicts originated to paralyze functioning. In the course of this investigation one may recover memories long forgotten, or may revive feelings associated with early recollections that have been repressed. There is an increasing facility to master the anxiety associated with the past. He or she begins to doubt that life need be a repetition of past happenings and becomes increasingly convinced that it is unnecessary to inject past attitudes into present situations. Tenuously, against resistance, the patient tests new responses, which in their reward help gradually to extinguish old reactions. Throughout this reconstructive process, the old patterns keep coming back, particularly when the individual feels insecure or self-esteem becomes undermined. The recognition that one is trying to regress as a security measure assists in reversing the reatreat. More and more one expresses a claim to a new life, the right to be more self-expressive. The ego expands; the conscience gets less tyrannical; inner promptings find a more healthy release; relationships with people undergo a change for the better.

There is, of course, no guarantee that these productive developments will take place in all cases. Nor can any estimate be made as to how long a period change will require after therapy has ended. But persistence in the practice of self-observation, and active challenging of neurotic patterns, are prime means of achieving reconstructive results. Where the patient has been taught self-relaxation or self-hypnosis, one may advantageously employ these techniques to catalyze self-observation.

58
Handling Emergencies in Psychotherapy

Although emergencies are not common in the practice of the average therapist, preparation for their proper management, should any occur, makes good sense, since mishandling can be destructive to the patient and ruinous to one's reputation, apart from the medico-legal complications that can ensue. Not only will the therapist have to palliate the patient's turmoil, but will also have to cope with the concerns of the patient's family, as well as the anxieties within oneself. To retain objectivity and composure in the face of ominous happenings will tax the resources of the most stable therapist. Responsibility should therefore be shared with a skilled consultant psychiatrist, especially if the therapist is a nonmedical person.

Crucial decisions are essential in emergencies. Knowing when to pacify, when to confront, when to enjoin, when to direct, when to order, when to notify relatives or friends, when to hospitalize, when to prescribe medications, how to evaluate existing stress situations, how to appraise useful support systems, how to gauge available ego strengths, how to bring the patient to an awareness of factors that keep the crisis alive, when to involve the family in the treatment plan, and the solution to other troublesome points requires expertise in crisis intervention practiced in the medium of an empathic relationship.

Among such possible emergencies are suicidal attempts; psychotic attacks; excitement, overactivity, and antisocial behavior; panic states; acute alcoholic intoxication; acute barbiturate poisoning; hallucinogenic and other intoxications; severe psychosomatic symptoms; and intercurrent incurable somatic illness.

SUICIDAL ATTEMPTS

Suicide ranks among the 10 most common causes of death among adults and among the three most common causes among adolescents. Statistics underestimate its true incidence due to flaws in reporting. Most (90 percent) of suicidal attempts are unsuccessful. This is because they are ill conceived and reflect the ambivalence of the perpetrator. Usually they constitute a gesture that communicates a plea for life. About 70 percent of successful suicides are among adults, most occurring in the syndrome of major depression and in alcoholics experiencing periodic depressed states. A disproportionate number of suicides are found among professional persons such as lawyers, physicians, dentists, and military men. The therapist should be alerted to a number of warning signs.

1. Symptoms of severe depression especially in males over the age of 55, social isolation, recent divorce or widowhood, unemployment, alcohol or drug abuse, and physical illness of a chronic or painful nature are predisposing factors.
2. At any age those who have made serious suicidal attempts, or where there is a history of suicide or of affective disorder in the family, these should be considered danger signals.
3. Dysthymia (reactive depression) resulting from broken or unhappy love affairs, disharmony in marriage, serious fights with parents among the young, bereavements in the elderly, and severe physical ailments may initiate a suicidal attempt. Likewise, personality problems of a psychopathic or hysterical nature with poor impulse control and peaks of violence and aggression may register themselves in suicidal gestures or in suicidal equivalents like reckless driving and dangerous sports.
4. Most likely to commit successful suicide are severe depressions during early stages of treatment when retardation and indecisiveness are replaced by a slight release of energy. Here prescribed psychotropic drugs and hypnotics may be massively incorporated.

Even in well-conducted psychotherapy vague suicidal threats may be expressed by some patients to the effect that they would be better off dead but they are too cowardly to try suicide. Where such statements lack the tone of conviction, it is best for the therapist not to subject the patient to concentrated interrogation around the matter of suicide. The therapist's expressed concern may frighten the patient badly resulting in loss of self-confidence. It may be found that the patient is trying to prove something or to hurt someone with a suicidal threat. Actually, an individual is responsible for his or her own actions, and cannot be watched 24 hours per day to prevent executing a threat if this is what is urgently wanted. The family of the patient may also be helped to resist being blackmailed by suicidal threats.

The following signs, symptoms, and situations, however, do point to a potential suicidal risk in a patient:

1. Loss of appetite, severe weight loss, insomnia, listlessness, apathy, persistent expressions of discouragement and hopelessness, loss of sexual desire, extreme constipation, hypochondriac ideas, continuous weeping, and general motor retardation which are present at the start or appear in the course of therapy.
2. Irrespective of diagnosis, any patient who has made a suicidal attempt in the past, or who has a history of severe depression, or who is taking antihypertensive and other medications and drugs that are having a depressive effect.
3. A patient who, during therapy, insistently threatens suicide.
4. Dreams of death, mutilation, and funerals.

Where during treatment, the patient talks *openly and seriously* about a desire to "end it all," it is important not to change the topic or to reassure the patient unduly. Rather, a frank talk about the reasons why the patient feels that suicide is the best recourse gives the patient an opportunity to investigate hidden feelings. This will enable the therapist to determine whether the threat is real, whether it is casually made as a dramatic gesture, whether it is a hostile stab at the therapist, or whether it constitutes an appeal for reassurance. Under no circumstances should the therapist minimize the importance of the threat, cajole the patient, or administer a verbal attack. Arguing with the patient is generally useless. Where the threat seems ominous, the therapist might make helpful statements to the effect that suicide *seems* to be a way out of difficulty, but it actually accomplishes nothing; that there may be other solutions than suicide that are not now apparent; and that suicide is a final act that cannot be undone and that it could always be resorted to later on if the patient so wishes. The attitudes conveyed to the patient in such statements are respect for one's right to self-determination and a reminder that one is not giving oneself an opportunity to explore more constructive actions. Talking frankly about suicide often serves to rob it of its awesome or appealing quality. Where suicide seems imminent in spite of anything the therapist can do or where an abortive attempt is actually made, there is no alternative than to advise responsible relatives to get the patient hospitalized immediately in a closed ward of a psychiatric hospital.

Suicide prevention centers do exist in the larger cities, and they have been used by depressed individuals and their families in crises. How effective these centers are in preventing suicide has not been evaluated adequately. Their impact may be minimal because individuals intent on suicide do not generally call in. Suicide centers do, however, serve a purpose if no more than to act as a referral source.

Hysterical Personalities

Suicidal attempts in hysterical personalities are common and consist of histrionic gestures calculated to impress, frighten, or force persons with whom the patient is in contact to yield attention and favors. Such attempts are incited by motives for display rather then by genuine desires to take one's life. Dramatic performances of an ingenious nature are indulged, during which there is a superficial slashing of the wrists, or feigned unconsciousness with stertorous breathing while placing an empty bottle of sleeping pills alongside the bed, or the gulping of tincture of iodine, or the impetuous opening of gas jets. Feverish demonstrations of suffering and martyrdom continue after the patient is restrained or "revived," until convinced of having emphasized protests sufficiently. The danger of these pseudosuicidal maneuvers is that the patient's judgment may not be too good during dramatic overacting and one may accidentally go too far and commit suicide even though this was not the original intent.

In treating hysterical cases with suicidal threatenings, we must demonstrate to the patient that we are neither intimidated by nor angry at the actions of the patient. Interpretation of the purpose of the patient's frenzied behavior should be made in terms of the broader neurotic patterns.

Psychopathic Personality

Of a related but more serious nature are the suicidal attempts of the psychopathic personality. During episodes of excitement, violence, deep remorse, excessive drinking, or temporary psychotic outbreaks, the psychopaths may slash the wrists or take an overdose of sleeping pills. The desire for self-punishment and death are genuine, though temporary. When their attempt has been aborted and they have been hospitalized, such patients recover rapidly, evidence no further suicidal impulses, and express great remorse at their folly. Yet, a short time later, under propitious circumstances, the attempt will be repeated, with further contrition and promises of abstention. Interpretation of the episode is essential, but it usually fails to act as a deterrent to the patient's actions. When the suicidal episodes are motivated by disturbed interpersonal relationships, as, for instance, a broken love affair or rejection by a love object, the continued exploration of the patient's feelings and patterns is indicated. In addition, the therapist may have to increase the frequency of visits and insist on being telephoned when the patient is tempted to indulge in suicide.

Where the patient persists in this impulsive suicidal behavior, after seeming to have acquired insight into operative patterns, the therapist may have no other alternative than to tell the patient that treatments will have to be discontinued. It may be suggested that the patient may perhaps want to start treatment with another therapist. This may give enough of a jolt to the patient to ensure insistence on the therapists continuing, based on the promise that all further suicidal attempts will be abandoned. Whether or not the therapist concedes to the patient's wishes to continue treatment will depend on how the therapist feels about the patient. Unfortunately, with some psychopaths the threat of discontinuance of therapy may be the only force that can control their explosive conduct. Even here the effect may be temporary.

Schizophrenia

In some types of schizophrenia suicide is a grave possibility. It is most common in acute, excited catatonic states, particularly those associated with panic. Hallucinations may drive certain patients to mutilate or kill themselves. Fear of homosexual attack or of being persecuted may also force some paranoidal individuals to suicide. The methods of self-destruction employed in schizophrenia may be bizarre, including such mutilations as disembowelment and genital amputation.

The handling of the suicidally inclined schizophrenic patient is organized around administering ample sedation, communicating with the family so that they may assume some responsibility, and arranging for transportation and admission to a mental hospital. Electric convulsive therapy is often indicated. Chlorpromazine (Thorazine), thioridazine (Mellaril), perphenazine (Trilafon), or haloperidol (Haldol) in ample dosage (see the section on somatic therapy in Chapter 56) are indicated.

Pathologic Depressions

Depressed episodes may occur in people due to loss of security, status, or a love object; however, the depression is rarely of such depth as to inspire a desire to take one's life. Where the depressed state is extreme, suicide is always a possibility. Among the most vulnerable pathologic depressive conditions are major depression, bipolar depression, depressions in alcoholics, involutional depression, senile depression, and depressions in organic brain disease.

To manage a patient with a pathologic depression, certain palliative measures are helpful. The handling of diet with the inclusion of stimulating and appetizing foods and the prescription of tonics and vitamins may be indicated in anorexia. In mild depression, a stimulant like Ritalin may be useful temporarily to activate the patient during the day, while sedation may be required at night for insomnia. Here small amounts of a mild hypnotic like chloral hydrate (Noctec) may be prescribed to prevent the patient from accumulating a lethal quantity. In more severe depressions, the patient's family or a reliable friend should be contacted and acquainted with the potential dangers. Where the patient remains at home while in a deep depression, a trustworthy adult person should be in constant attendance. The patient should not be permitted to lock oneself into a room, including the bathroom. Sleeping pills, tranquilizers, poisonous drugs, razor blades, rope, and sharp knives and instruments should be removed. Window guards are necessary if there is a chance that the patient may destroy oneself by leaping through a window. Hospitalization on a closed ward with constant supervision by efficient nurses or attendants may be essential. The treatment of choice is electroconvulsive therapy, which may prove to be a lifesaving measure. Antidepressants are second best where the patient refuses ECT, but the patient must be watched carefully since the early "lift" from the medication may give enough energy to try suicide. Psychotherapy during severe depression is generally confined to supportive measures, as insight approaches tend to stir up too much anxiety.

Fear and guilt feelings are common in the therapist who will usually be in a dilemma about hospitalization. It is urgent that a nonmedical therapist secure a consultation with a psychiatrist to share responsibility, to prescribe ECT or proper medications, or to arrange for hospitalization should the patient need it and is willing to consider it. Although a desperate patient can terminate life in spite of any safeguards, there is a lesser chance in a hospital setting, particularly when ECT is immediately started. Usually there is little problem in decision making when the patient has made an unsuccessful attempt. Here relatives and neighbors rush the patient to an emergency hospital service, or the police are brought into the picture and arrange for admission and perhaps for transport of the patient.

Difficulties in decision are greater in the event a patient has mildly threatened to take his or her life, but makes no active gesture to do so, and has no history of past suicidal attempts. Under these circumstances the therapist may have to utilize the greatest interviewing skills (Murray, 1972). The patient may be told that the ultimate responsibility for one's life is one's own. "You probably won't believe this, but you *will* get over this depression and will feel better. Right now it is natural for you to imagine your suffering will continue indefinitely. It will not." Here it is assumed that the patient is started on a regime of antidepressant drugs (e.g. Tofranil, Elavil, Sinequan) in adequate dosage (see the section on somatic therapy in Chapter 56). In the great majority of patients a frank empathic talk will tide them over the crisis.

It is often important to see the patient frequently and to telephone between sessions to maintain as close a tie as possible.

Miscellaneous Suicidal Conditions

Sometimes a therapist is consulted by the parents or friends of a child or adolescent who has made a suicidal attempt. Examination may fail to reveal hysteria, depression, or schizophrenia, especially when the child is noncommunicative to the point of mutism. It is possible here that the child is internalizing destructive feelings. Young drug abusers are particularly vulnerable. Because the youth is nonmotivated for therapy and resents having been taken to a psychiatrist, it may be difficult to treat the patient. By following the rules outlined in Chapter 32. Dealing with Inadequate Motivation, and by indicating to the patient that he or she seems to be angry at someone, it may be possible to establish rapport.

A 14-year-old girl, for example, who had made a suicidal attempt by swallowing 50 aspirin tablets was brought in for a consultation. Refusing to talk except in monosyllables, it was difficult to carry on an interview. The therapist finally remarked, "You must have been awfully angry at someone to have done this to yourself." The patient blanched, then brought her hands to her face and started compulsive sobbing, which went on for 15 minutes. Intermittent were outbursts in the form of protestations of how "bad" she was for feeling the way she did about her mother. Ventilation of her resentment produced immediate emotional relief and established sufficient contact with the therapist to start psychotherapy.

Should a suicidal attempt have been made, the immediate injuries will have to be treated and artificial respiration instituted if necessary. If concentrated oxygen is available, it should be given. In asphyxiation with gas or from fumes of an automobile 50 cc of 50 percent glucose, injected intravenously, may help prevent cerebral edema. Intramuscular adrenalin (epinephrine), 0.5 to 1.0 cc of 1:1000 concentration, may also be administered.

If suicide was attempted with poisons or drugs, identification of these will permit selection of the proper antidote. Patients who are not unconscious and who have not taken corrosives or petroleum products may be induced to vomit by tickling the pharynx with a finger or spoon, and by giving them a glass of water containing 1 tablespoonful of salt or 1 teaspoonful of powdered mustard or soap suds. This should be repeated several times if necessary and followed by a gastric lavage with 1 quart of water containing 1 tablespoonful of (a) "universal antidote," or (b) 2 parts burnt toasts to 1 part strong tea and 1 part milk of magnesia, or (c) table salt. Next, a neutralization of the specific poison with the antidote is attempted and demulcents (flour, starch, gelatin in a paste, or 12 beaten eggs mixed with milk) are given. Finally, the poisons remaining in the intestinal tract are removed by administering magnesium sulfate (Epsom salts: 30 g in a glass of water). Suicidal attempts with barbiturates are handled by inducing emesis, administering "universal antidote," and preventing shock with measures to be described in a later part of this chapter, under Acute Barbiturate Poisoning.

The Telephone Threat

Where a patient telephones the therapist and states that he or she is about to take a lethal dose of medication (or engage in another kind of suicidal act) the therapist should try to keep communication going especially around any incident that has inspired the impulse to die. The patient's name should be repeated to firm up the sense of identity and some constructive action may be suggested as well as a reminder that the therapist wants to help as

much as possible, and that others care for the patient and want to help. If the patient has already taken the lethal pills or opened a gas jet the address should be obtained while the patient is kept talking on the telephone. Another person should be dispatched (perhaps by a note written by the therapist during an interval when the patient is talking) to call the police, trace the call if the patient refuses to say where he or she is, and immediately send an ambulance to escort the patient to an emergency room.

PSYCHOTIC ATTACKS

In the course of psychotherapy anxiety may be released that is beyond the endurance of certain patients. A psychotic episode occurring during treatment may be the product of too early or too avid an attack on resistances and defenses in a patient with fragile ego strength. It may be the consequence of a transference neurosis that gets out of control. A good psychotherapist is capable of gauging the ego strength of the patient and of introducing supportive measures should signs of shattering appear. Nevertheless, even good psychotherapists may be unable to control the outbreak of psychosis in vulnerable patients. The quality of the working relationship is a crucial factor. Some therapists are capable of operating sensitively and empathetically with potentially psychotic and even overtly psychotic patients. Other therapists, particularly those who are unable to manage their countertransference, may be unable to work with infantile dependent personality disorders, with borderline, or with psychotic patients. They may have to transfer patients who show tendencies toward psychotic outbursts once the treatment process is under way.

Symptoms that lead one to suspect beginning ego disintegration during psychotherapy are feelings of unreality, depersonalization, excessive daydreaming, ideas of reference, paranoidal ideas, bizarre somatic sensations, motor excitement, uncontrollable sexual and hostile impulses, propensity for perversions, heightened interest in toilet activities, compulsive talking, fears of castration, and fleeting hallucinations and delusions. These symptoms may appear individually or in combination. For a while the patient may maintain a good grasp on reality, recognizing the unusual or irrational nature of his or her ideas, impulses, and acts. Later on, distortions of reality may occur in the form of fixed delusions and hallucinations, perhaps accompanied by panic reactions, suicidal tendencies, and violent aggression. The first step is to identify any immediate stress factor that is upsetting the patient. Is it in the current life situation? If so, the patient should be helped to resolve the problem or to extricate satisfactorily from it. Is it a consequence of what is happening in therapy? Transference reactions are extremely common, and in a patient with weak ego strength this may pitch protective defenses overboard. Such reactions in stronger patients may be concealed and evidence of them manifested only in acting-out or in dreams. Getting the patient to talk about feelings in regard to the therapist, with proper clarification and interpretation, may restore the patient's equilibrium. It may be necessary to increase the patient's visits during a period of emotional turmoil.

Second, if the precipitating factor cannot be identified, an attempt should be made to get the patient to speculate as to some cause for the trouble. The preferred explanation may then be used as a focus around which interviewing is organized to explore the patient's suppositions or to discover more cogent etiologic factors.

Third, where the support offered through psychotherapy does not restore the patient to an equilibrium in a short time, a neuroleptic drug, like Thorazine (chlorpromazine), Haldol (haloperidol), Stelazine (trifluoperazine), or Permitil (fluphenazine),

in proper dosage may be prescribed. Too frequently, inadequate doses of medication are used. A nonmedical therapist will have to bring a psychiatrist who knows drug therapy into the picture.

Should a psychotic attack take place it may be handled within the therapeutic situation by a therapist who has a warm feeling for the patient, who is not disturbed by the existing symptoms, and who is capable of modifying the approach so as to bring about the restoration of repressive barriers. The fact that a psychosis has precipitated is usually indicative of something having gone amiss in the therapeutic relationship. If one can admit to oneself the possibility of errors in handling and if one is able to restore the patient's feelings of trust and confidence, such a therapist may be capable of bringing the retreat from reality to a halt. In line with this objective it is best to discontinue probing for conflictual areas and to keep the content of the interview focused on current reality problems. The relationship with the therapist should be kept on as positive a level as possible, the therapist assuming a helpful active role. Under no circumstances should the therapist express alarm at or condemnation toward any of the patient's misconceptions. Listening attentively to the patient's productions, the therapist counters with reality, suggesting that perhaps things seem to be as they are because the patient has been so upset. If disturbing transference is at the basis of the patient's turmoil, measures to lessen transference, described in Chapters 42 and 46 may be invoked. Should the patient require more support, the frequency of interviews may be increased.

Where these practices fail to bring relief to the patient, it is likely that the therapeutic relationship has deteriorated and the patient may have to be referred to another therapist. The referral can be upsetting to the patient, and he or she is apt to consider it a further manifestation of rejection or an indication of failure. The therapist may explain that the patient's specific problem will probably be helped more by another therapist with a slightly different approach. If the patient is incapable of thinking rationally and if the difficulties are potentially dangerous to oneself and others, a reliable family member should be asked to assume some responsibility in the matter of referral. Should the patient object to the therapist's making contact with the family, the therapist may, if the situation is sufficiently dangerous, have to communicate with the family irrespective of the patient's wishes.

Where self-injury, suicide, homicide, violent aggression, ruinous spending, criminality, or other disasters are possible, hospitalization may be mandatory. If the therapist is a nonmedical person, a consulting psychiatrist should be called in. Discussion may convince the patient to enter an institution voluntarily. Hospitalization will, however, have to be accomplished against the wishes of the patient where one is dangerous to oneself or others and sees no need for confinement. In the event that one is actively resistant and must be hospitalized, intravenous sodium Amytal to the point of deep sleep will permit transport to an institution without the need for physical restraint. A physician should be in attendance in the ambulance that transports the patient in order to handle such emergencies as respiratory paralysis.

The therapist will have to arrange the details of hospital admission in cooperation with the patient's family and, in addition, may have to explain the reasons for hospitalization to them in a reassuring way. In doing this, the therapist may experience some guilt and anxiety, as if accountable for the patient's collapse. It is important, however, not to castigate oneself for what has happened nor to confess to failure; rather, the family may be informed that the patient's personality structure has been unable to stand inner tensions and that the patient has temporarily broken down. A period of hospitalization is necessary to restore equilibrium.

The specific treatment rendered in the hospital will depend on the severity and type of psychosis. In acute excitement or depression with exhaustion it will be necessary to sedate the patient adequately, to correct dehydration by injecting fluids and salts parenterally, and to administer electroconvulsive therapy or intensive drug therapy, whichever is indicated. In milder excitements or depressions sedatives and hospitalization alone may suffice to restore the patient's stability. It is important that the person assigned to look after the patient avoid arguing with or "psychoanalyzing" the patient, no matter what the provocation, since this will upset the patient even more.

Postoperative reactions after extensive surgery are not uncommon and probably occur in persons who have been maintaining a tenuous emotional homeostasis. For example, a considerable number of cases of psychosis have been reported following open heart surgery. Even in less major procedures, a temporary massive outbreak of pathology (brief reactive psychoses) may occur in unstable personalities. One sees this in some patients receiving hemodialysis for chronic kidney failure. The clinical picture in postoperative reactions will vary. syndromes may resemble organic brain upsets (confusion, disorientation, memory loss), acute schizophrenia (delusions, hallucinations), or affective disorders (depression, agitation, mania).

EXCITEMENT, OVERACTIVITY, AND ANTISOCIAL BEHAVIOR

States of excitement and overactivity developing during psychotherapy are signs of acting-out or manifestations of ego shattering.

During acting-out the patient may engage in destructive, antisocial, or unusual sexual behavior. In attempting to understand acting-out, one's first suspicion is that the patient is protecting the self from awareness of transference by projecting it away from the therapist. Hostile or aggressive outbursts, delinquency, criminality, marked promiscuity, and perverse sexuality are often products of hostile and sexual impulses toward the therapist that the patient is unable to acknowledge. It is natural to react emotionally when a patient becomes antagnostic toward the therapist. Counteraggression, even though verbal, will only stir the patient up more. Recognizing one's own fear of violence, as well as the pot of anger one may be trying to control that always seeks some kind of release is vital. One should try to get the patient to verbalize anger and outrage without being judgmental and without trying to justify untenable conditions against which the patient is rebelling. If the patient's reaction is an aspect of negative transference, this may be interpreted, but the patient should not be made to feel guilty for his or her behavior. If the patient is responding to some outside stimulus, one should ask oneself: "How would I feel if I were in the patient's situation?" Since the other side of violence is fear, one should try to find out what frightens or upsets the patient and try to act empathic, supportive and reassuring. A simple statement such as "I don't blame you for being upset," may do much to quiet the patient. By acting composed, the therapist may be able to calm the patient. If fear is shown, this may engender more fear and violence in the patient.

MANAGING DANGEROUS PATIENTS

When a patient is being treated who makes a substantial threat against an identifiable third person, the therapist should first assess the degree of dangerousness and possibilities of acting-out as indicated by past history and present lack of impulse control. Then if violence is felt to be possible, a course of action to protect potential victims should be evolved. Documenting one's decisions in the case record is important. It may be that hospitalization, medication, and intensified psychotherapeutic interventions will eliminate the possibility of actualizing the threat. Nonmedical therapists should seek the help of a psychiatrist where a dangerous situation impends. In some cases, confidentiality will have to violated and the intended victim notified. A considerable literature has accumulated around the California Tarasoff case (Appelbaum, 1985; Beck, 1982; Monahan, 1981; Dix 1981; Stone, 1976) that initiated the ferment about dangerousness in patients.

The best way to resolve acting-out is to explore the patient's feelings and attitudes toward the intended victim, to determine which of these are rooted in realities and which are irrational carryovers from the past, and to see if concealed transference is at the basis of the patient's aggression. As long as the patient is unaware of and cannot verbalize proclivities toward the therapist, the patient will continue to "blow off steam" outside of therapy. Skillful use of the interviewing process that brings out verbalizations related to the transference may put a halt to the patient's destructive patterns.

Sometimes it is difficult or impossible to get the patient to analyze transference and in this way to terminate acting-out. The therapist here may attempt to deal with this obstruction by (1) stimulating transference, through devices already described, in order to make its manifestations so obvious that the patient cannot help but talk about his or her feelings, or (2) controlling acting-out by increasing visits to as many as daily sessions and by the assumption of a prohibitive, authoritative role. If these measures fail to help the situation, therapy will have to be terminated with transfer to another therapist.

Excitement and antisocial behavior that occur as a result of ego shattering may be dealt with after identifying the cause of the present difficulty. A struggling patient may have to be restrained and 5 mg of Haldol injected into the nearest available muscle. Rapid neuroleptization may be essential (Schwarcz, 1982). Supportive techniques are generally indicated, and the patient may have to be put on a regimen of Haldol (2–5 mg), Thorazine (25–100 mg), or Valium (10 mg), repeated at intervals until adequate sedation occurs. If the decline continues, the therapist had best transfer the patient to another therapist, since the therapist is probably unable to control the situation. Where a dangerous psychotic condition develops, the patient's family will have to be apprised of it, for hospitalization will in all likelihood be necessary. Where violent rages or excitement continue, an organic cause such as temporal lobe lesions including epilepsy should be ruled out. It is not usual that a dangerously disturbed or assaultive patient will have to be handled in one's office, but if this is unavoidable common sense dictates that the therapist should be reasonably protected. This means that where a patient is potentially dangerous to oneself or to others, he or she should be sent to a hospital or place where adequate treatment can be given and protection is available if necessary. In emergency units in general hospitals, sufficient personnel should be available to restrain the patient. (at best four accessory persons are needed, one for each limb should restraint be essential) The attitude of the therapist is a most important factor, an easygoing, calm manner being reassuring for a patient. Since most violence is a consequence of fear, a quiet, secure atmosphere surrounding the consulting room is desirable. Angry threats directed at a disturbed patient merely aggravate the fear and create further violence.

More can be accomplished with calming demeanor than with drugs, which, of course, also should be administered where necessary. Once communication is established with the patient and the patient has confidence that he or she will not be hurt, psychotherapy may be possible under the usual office conditions.

INTENSE ANXIETY ATTACKS

Severe anxiety sometimes breaks out in the course of psychotherapy. It may become so overwhelming that the patient feels helpless in its grip. One's coping resources have seemingly come to an end, and one can no longer crush the fear of imminent disintegration. Demands on the therapist then may become insistent, and the patient will bid for protection and comfort.

The handling of intense anxiety reactions will require much fortitude on the part of the therapist. By assuming a calm, reassuring manner, the therapist provides the patient with the best medium in which to achieve stability. Accordingly, the therapist will have to tolerate the emotions of the patient, conveying a feeling of warmth, understanding, and protectiveness while respecting the patient's latent strengths that have been smothered by the turmoil. Upbraiding the patient for exhibiting foolish fears and attempting to argue away anxiety serve to stimulate rather than to reduce tension.

The best means of handling acute anxiety is to permit the patient to verbalize freely in an empathic atmosphere. Helping the patient to arrive at an understanding of the source of the anxiety, whether it be environmentally oriented or rooted in unconscious conflict, transference, resistance, or the too abrupt removal of existing defenses, promises the quickest possibility of relief. The triad of emotional catharsis, insight, and reassurance operates together to permit of a reconstitution of defenses against anxiety.

Where anxiety is intense, it is usually impossible to work with the patient on an insight level. Here, supportive measures will be necessary to restore the habitual defenses. If the patient is living under intolerable environmental circumstances, a change of environment may be indicated to lessen harsh pressures on him. In the event that anxiety has followed intensive mental probing, a holiday from exploration may be necessary, with a focusing on casual or seemingly inconsequential topics. A patient who has spent many sleepless nights tossing about restlessly or, once asleep, has awakened periodically with frightening dreams may benefit from a benzodiazepine like Valium (5 or 10 mg) orally. In highly disturbed patients 10 mg of Valium intramuscularly or intravenously may be given. The use of sedatives during the day is to be minimized, if possible, to forestall the sedative habit. If anxiety continues, the frequency of sessions may be increased and the patient may be assured that he or she can reach the therapist at any time in the event of a real emergency. Referral to an experienced psychiatrist skilled in the somatic therapies may be necessary.

Excessive anxiety in psychoneurotic patients is best handled psychotherapeutically, increasing the frequency of sessions if necessary. Where this fails to bring relief, several sessions devoted to "narcosuggestion," that is, reassurance and suggestion under intravenous Pentothal or Amytal (see Narcotherapy, Chapter 56), may be tried. Oral Librium (25 mg. 3 to 4 times daily) or Valium (10 mg, 3 to 4 times a day) may restore the individual's composure, following which the drugs are diminished, then discontinued. Where anxiety is out of control and constitutes an emergency, 50 to 100 mg of intravenous Librium, repeated in 4 to 6 hours if necessary and followed by oral Librium, may be helpful. Some patients respond better to barbiturates than to tranquilizers. In acute anxiety pentobarbital (Nembutal) ¾ to 1½ gr, or secobarbital (Seconal) ¾ to 1½ gr may dissipate symptoms in about 30 minutes. Some patients prefer to take ¼ to ½ gr of phenobarbital sodium every 3 or 4 hours. Barbiturate administration is to be halted as soon as possible because of the danger of habituation.

In borderline or psychotic patients it is wise to institute drug treatments immediately. Haldol, Thorazine, or Mellaril in adequate dosage (see Table 56-3) may bring anxiety to a halt.

These measures will rarely fail to control severe anxiety in borderline or psychoneurotic patients. In the rare case where they fail, and especially where a transference neurosis is present and cannot be resolved, the patient may have to be referred to another therapist or a short period of hospitalization may be required.

PANIC STATES

The treatment of panic states is more difficult than the management of anxiety. Here the patient is victimized by a wild, unreasoning fear that plunges one into disorganized thinking and behavior or drives one to the point of immobilization. Suicide is always a grave possibility. Admission to an emergency unit in a hospital may be essential, the therapist giving the admission doctor pertinent information about the patient.

Where a patient in panic is seen for the first time, the therapist will be somewhat in a dilemma. The initial step in the management of a panic state with a strange patient is attempting to promote calm by quiet, empathic listening in a quiet atmosphere. Thereafter prescribed a tricyclic antidepressant or MAO inhibitor may be all that the therapist may want to do at the moment. Reassuring the belligerent individual that one is belligerent because one is frightened may have a dramatic effect. Often little more will be needed than to display interested attention and to express sympathy at appropriate times. Sorting out the problem in this way will give the therapist clues about appropriate therapeutic steps to take, whether medication or hospitalization necessary (emergency units unfortunately do not usually have a secluded place where quiet interviewing can take place). Where the patient is out of contact with reality, is suicidal, or is aggressively excited, however, he or she will require rapid sedation or tranquilization and probably hospitalization.

Diagnosis is important. The patient may be psychotic as a result of a functional ailment like schizophrenia. Or the patient may be manifesting a toxic psychosis as a result of taking too many drugs or because of a physical ailment. Giving the patient more medication in the latter instances will merely compound the injury. Information about the patient from relatives or friends is highly desirable, even indispensable, in ruling out drug intoxication or physical ailments, such as cardiovascular illness, diabetes, etc., that may be responsible for delirium.

If drug intoxication is ruled out, drug therapy is the treatment of choice for schizophrenic or manic excitements. Rapid tranquilization is indicated to reduce social consequences of morbidity. Not everybody agrees with this, however. In young schizophrenics who are having a first attack there are some who believe that they should be allowed spontaneously in a protected environment to reach a baseline. Thus, Mosher and Feinsilver (1973) state, "We believe that the inner voyage of the schizophrenic person, which is induced by environmental crisis, has great potential for natural healing and growth, and we therefore do not attempt to abort, rechannel, or quell it before it has run a natural course." Whether one heeds this advice or not will depend on the existing social support systems on which the patient will depend. A congenial hospi-

tal regimen with empathic nurses and attendants is helpful. On the other hand, and particularly in older patients or those who have had a previous minimum absence from work and their families, it may be vital to avoid prolonged disability and unemployment which can operate as stress factors after the schizophrenic episode is over.

Restoration to a nonpsychotic state is possible within a few hours employing powerful neuroleptic drugs that act on the limbic system and influence the psychotic thinking process. The drug often chosen is haloperidol (Haldol) given intramuscularly. The first dose is 5 mg, then 2–5 mg every 30 minutes until the patient is sedated; the blood pressure should be monitored to avoid hypotension. The objective is to get the maximum therapeutic impact with a minimum of side effects (dystonia, akithesia, and other Parkinsonian symptoms). If the patient falls asleep after the first 5 mg injection, he or she is probably suffering from a toxic psychosis like drug intoxication (e.g., alcoholism), and Haldol is stopped.

Some therapists still prefer chlorpromazine (Thorazine) which is given intramuscularly in 25 to 75 mg dosage according to the size of the patient and degree of disturbance. If the systolic blood pressure standing is below 95, the Thorazine is discontinued; the patient's head is lowered and the feet elevated. If the blood pressure is maintained satisfactorily, the drug is given every hour until control of the excitement is achieved. The dosage is either increased or decreased depending on how the patient responded to the previous dose. The intramuscular medication is discontinued should the patient fall asleep or quiet down sufficiently. The choice of being subsequently seen on an outpatient basis or immediately hospitalized will depend upon whether the patient is dangerous to oneself or others, the attitude of the family, hospital resources in the community, and the patient's cooperativeness.

What dosage of drug orally for ensuing 24-hour periods will be required can be estimated by multiplying the intramuscular dosage of Thorazine that it has taken to tranquilize the patient by 2⅔ (Ketal, 1975). With Haldol one may give the same dose orally as was given intramuscularly. If the patient is too sedated, this can be reduced. Patients should be seen daily or every other day to make sure that they do not slip back.

Drowsiness and hypotension with Haldol are less than with Thorazine. Extrapyramidal side effects are more common, however. Where such side effects occur with Haldol or other antipsychotic drugs, 1 to 2 mg of Cogentin by mouth (or intravenously if emergent) or 50 mg of Benadryl by mouth or intravenously may be given. Continuance of the drug for several days is indicated. Reassurance of the patient and the family are important. To avert the pyramidal symptoms, some therapists give Cogentin prophylactically, but others do not recommend this.

Where intramuscular injection is not possible or urgent, oral medications are used. Here 10 to 20 mg of Haldol may be given in liquid concentrate form for the first day; if no response, this is raised to 40 mg the second day and 60 mg the third day until an effect is achieved. Or Thorazine in liquid concentrate form of 50 to 150 mg dose may be given and regulated according to response.

Intravenous sodium Amytal (up to 15 gr) will put the patient into narcosis. If panic continues following this, the patient may require hospitalization on a closed ward. Electroconvulsive treatments will also often interrupt the excitement. As many as 2 ECTs daily may be needed for a few days, followed by one treatment daily, until equilibrium is established. Where delirium and confusion appear in elderly patients or those with respiratory and cardiovascular disorders, Thorazine may be given for restlessness and paraldehyde or chloral hydrate for insomnia. Should epileptic seizures develop and continue (status epilepticus), intravenous sodium Amytal, phenobarbital sodium parenteral, or diphenyl hydantoin (Dilantin) may be administered.

In hospital settings "sleep therapy" is occasionally instituted, especially in psychotic patients, where panic cannot be arrested through other means (Azima, 1958). Here sleep, which lasts 20 to 24 hours a day, is induced by giving the patient a combination of 100 mg (1.5 gr) Seconal, 100 mg Nembutal, 100 mg sodium Amytal, and 50 mg of Thorazine. The patient is aroused three times daily, and the dosage of medication is regulated according to the degree of wakefulness. Good nursing care is urgent; indeed, without it sleep therapy is hazardous. During the waking period the pulse rate, blood pressure, temperature, and respiration are recorded; the patient is gotten out of bed, washed, and fed. Daily 2000 cc of fluid and at least 1500 calories in food are supplied, while vitamins are administered parenterally. A half-hour prior to meals 5 units of insulin are injected to stimulate the appetite. Milk of magnesia is supplied every other day if necessary, and a colonic irrigation is given should a bowel movement not occur in 2 days. Catherization is performed if the patient does not urinate for 12 hours. The bed position of the patient must be changed every 2 hours, and should the patient's breathing become shallow, oxygen and carbon dioxide are administered. Sometimes ECT is instituted with sleep therapy, either daily during the first waking period or three times weekly. In this way a deep regression is induced. The average treatment duration is 15 to 20 days. Rehabilitative therapy must follow the sleep-treatment episode.

In manic reactions, after the acute psychotic disturbance is brought under control, lithium therapy may be started. Where panic has occurred as a result of battle conditions or civil catastrophes, a withdrawal from the stressful situation for a few days may be necessary. This should not be prolonged to avoid chronicity in cases where the patient will have to function in an unstable atmosphere.

Once the panic state has subsided psychotherapy is essential to forestall further attacks.

TOXIC DRUG PSYCHOSES

Mixed drug intoxications are common and may constitute important emergencies. It is difficult, if not impossible, to determine what substances the patient has imbibed since even he or she may not know their true nature, purchased as they have been from dubious sources. Knowledge of the local drug scene may be of some help, at least in screening out certain possibilities. The kinds of drugs utilized vary in different parts of the country. They include amphetamine, barbiturates, meprobamate, alcohol, phencyclidine, THC, nonbarbiturate hypnotics (like Doriden, Quaalude), marijuana, morning glory seeds, nutmeg, LSD, mescaline, codein, DMT, STP, MDA, psylocybin, and a variety of mescaline and amphetamine combination compounds.

In many cases adequate therapy can be administered only in a hospital, which unfortunately may not provide the quiet, relaxed atmosphere that excited patients need. Gastric lavage is limited to instances where the drug was recently taken. After a number of hours it is relatively useless. Hemodialysis is valuable for certain drugs and not for others. In all cases maintenance of an airway, of respiration, and of the cardiovascular apparatus is fundamental.

If the nature of the drug that has been taken is known, for example, from the blood or urine analysis, it may be possible to prescribe certain antagonistic medicinal agents. Thus, if amphetamine is the culprit, Thorazine or other neuroleptic or antipsychotic drugs can be given. If the patient has taken STP or LSD, antidotes may block some sympathomimetic effects without in-

fluencing the hallucinogenic aspects. As yet there is no totally effective antagonist for these hallucinogens. Indeed, Thorazine is contraindicated in STP toxicity because of the hypotensive and convulsive potentiating effect, which can be dangerous. Mildly excited patients may respond to a mild tranquilizer like Valium given parenterally.

Global nystagmus is a frequent symptom in drug psychosis and may serve as a valuable diagnostic indicator. Disorientation, confusion, and hallucinations are common, of course. Because, in the average toxic patient, the kinds of drugs that the patient has been taking are difficult to diagnose, it is best to err on the side of caution in administering antipsychotic drugs. Some of the effects of the substances the individual has been taking, like THC (the pure extract of marijuana), may be reinforced by antipsychotics. After reassuring the patient that recovery will soon occur, he or she may be given 10 to 20 mg of Valium intramuscularly. If there is no improvement in the patient after a few hours and no anticholinergic symptoms, such as a lowering of blood pressure and rapid pulse, a major antipsychotic, such as 5 mg of Haldol or 4 mg of Navane or Trilafon, may be given. These drugs have a marked antipsychotic effect without too great sedation. Where an opiate drug is suspected, an airway is introduced, the heart monitored, fluids introduced intravenously with 50 cc of 50 percent dextrose, 2 mg of naloxone (Narcan) and 100 mg thiamine.

Handling the "Bad Trip"

Individuals experimenting with hallucinogenic drugs, including marijuana and amphetamines, may occasionally experience a frightening journey away from reality and need emergency intervention. In the street vernacular such an experience is referred to as a "bad trip." Hallucinations may be vivid, and there may be an inability to communicate. Such reactions may be inspired by an overdose of drug or may be the consequence of something frightening that the patient perceives or imagines in the environment or even may occur with small dosage in schizophrenic patients. The atmosphere in which the "bad tripper" is treated is important. It should be as quiet as possible. Sending the person to an emergency hospital unit may induce more panic. The therapist or person managing the patient should be reassuring and gentle and never question the patient about the experience, for this may tend to stir the patient up. One should be asked to concentrate one's attention on something in reality, like an object in the room, in order to shift the focus from one's inner life. Rarely are physical restraints or drugs necessary, except when the patient becomes violent. Valium (10 mg intramuscularly, repeated if necessary) is helpful in the latter instance.

The treatment of severe amphetamine psychosis is similar to that of schizophrenic psychosis, namely, prescribing Thorazine or Haldol intramuscularly. In the case of LSD, psylocybin, or marijuana intake with a psychoticlike response, the therapist should stay with the patient while reassuring that the reactions are temporary and will pass in a few hours. Valium (5–10 mg) or Librium (25–50 mg), or a short-acting barbiturate, may be helpful. Where not successful and panic increases, Thorazine intramuscularly may be utilized with all of the precautions outlined under the section on Panic States. Great caution must rule the use of phenothiazines because of the danger of lowering the blood pressure too much, especially where phencyclidine (PCP) has been injested. In the event of overdose of sleeping medications containing scopalamine, Thorazine should be avoided. Valium may be utilized as may physostigmine (2–4 mg).

The most frightening consequence of a toxic drug absorption is a status epilepticus, a constant series of seizures without the patient regaining consciousness in between. Here one must establish an adequate airway, particularly being sure that the patient's tongue does not block respiration. Diazepam (Valium) 5 to 10 mg intravenously followed by 200–400 mg of phenobarbital intravenously, or reinjecting Valium alone every 10 to 15 minutes for up to one hour (maximum of 40 mg per hour for adults). Phenobarbital (100–200 mg intramuscularly) is also commonly utilized after a single seizure to prevent status epilepticus. It may be given intravenously (200–400) very slowly. A respirator should be available in the event respiration stops. Phenobarbital may thereafter be given intramuscularly (100–200 mg) every 2 to 6 hours up to 1 g of the drug in 24 hours. The next day the patient may be started on Dilantin (200 mg intramuscularly).

Acute Alcoholic Intoxication

Pathological intoxication sometimes presents itself as a psychiatric emergency. The reactions range from stupor or coma to excited, destructive, combative, homicidal, or suicidal behavior. Comatose states are best treated in a hospital where a neurological study may be made to rule out other causes of unconsciousness, such as apoplexy, brain concussion, status epilepticus, cerebral embolism or tumor, subdural hematoma, toxic delirium, uremic or diabetic coma, and carbon-monoxide or morphine poisoning. Where alcoholic intoxication exists, a hospital with a 24-hour laboratory service permits of the testing of blood sugar and carbon-dioxide levels required for the administration of insulin and dextrose. Nursing care is important. The patient must be turned from side to side regularly and the head lowered to prevent aspiration pneumonia. The pulse, respiration, and blood pressure are recorded every half hour. Oxygen is given by tent or nasal catheter where respiration is depressed. Intravenous sodium chloride should be injected in amounts of 250 cc every 3 or 4 hours.

Where the patient is conscious and gag reflexes are present, a gastric lavage may be provided, external heat applied, and strong coffee administered by mouth or rectum. Intramuscular caffeine and sodium benzoate (0.5–1.0 g) may be dispensed every hour until the patient is alert. Intravenous dextrose solution (100 cc of 50 percent dextrose) may be introduced and repeated, if necessary, every hour, and 10 to 20 units of insulin may be provided, repeated in 12 hours. Thiamine hydrochloride (100 mg) intravenously is also a useful medicament.

Excited reactions, including acute alcoholic intoxication, alcoholic hallucinosis, and delirium tremens are treated by intramuscular injection of Haldol (5 mg), or Navane or Trilafon (4 mg), or Thorazine (25–50 mg) repeated if necessary. Many psychiatrists use Librium intramuscularly or intravenously (50–100 mg) or Valium (10–20 mg) repeated, if necessary, in 2 to 4 hours, for alcoholic agitation and impending or active delirium tremens or hallucinosis. Dextrose (100 cc of a 25 percent solution), thiamine hydrochloride (100 mg), and 20 units of insulin are given routinely. Morphine and rapid acting hypnotics (Nembutal, Seconal) are contraindicated; however, sodium Amytal (0.5–1.0 g) is sometimes administered intravenously (1 cc per minute) to quiet a violently disturbed patient. Ample fluids should be given intravenously to combat acidosis and dehydration (approximately 3000 cc daily, containing magnesium and potassium minerals). Other drugs include thiamine hydrochloride (20–50 mg), intramuscularly, and nicotinamide (niacinamide, 100 mg), intravenously, substituted in several days by oral thiamine hydrochloride; vitamin C (100 mg), caffeine and sodium benzoate (0.5 g every 4 to 6 hours for 4 to 6 doses) for stimulation, saline laxatives to promote proper elimination, and Compazine (10 mg intramuscularly) for uncontrollable nausea and vomiting. Milk and eggnog may be offered the patient; if not tolerated, 10 percent dextrose and sodium chloride solution intravenously may be required. The need to protect the patient from convulsions is urgent in delirium tremens and here anticonvulsant therapy (e.g., diphenylhydantoin) may be necessary.

Acute Barbiturate Poisoning

The popularity of barbiturates as sedatives has resulted in a relatively large incidence of barbiturate poisoning. Patients who have developed a sedative habit may accidentally take an overdose of barbiturates, or the drugs may be purposefully incorporated with suicidal intent. Sometimes the patient, having swallowed a lethal dose, will telephone the therapist informing of his or her act. At other times relatives or friends will chance on the patient before respiratory paralysis has set in.

The usual therapy consists of immediate hospitalization, if possible, and the institution of the following measures:

1. Establishing an airway, such as with an endotracheal tube with suction of secretions.
2. Administration of oxygen, or artificial respiration if necessary, using a mechanical resuscitator.
3. Early gastric lavage carefully administered.
4. Fluids given parenterally (5 percent glucose); in extreme hypotension, plasma injected intravenously.
5. Stimulants—vasopressors like Neosynephrine (2–3 mg) if blood pressure is low or L-norepinephrine (4 mg/L of 5 percent glucose solution).
6. Turning the patient hourly with head slightly lower than feet. (Trendelenburg position)
7. Catherization of the bladder if necessary.
8. Prophylactic antibiotics.
9. Hemodialysis with an artificial kidney, if available, or peritoneal dialysis.

10. Digitalis for heart failure.
11. Avoidance of analeptics.

Clemmesen (1963) has described the treatment of poisoning from barbiturates in Denmark, where the incidence of attempted suicide has always been relatively high. A special intoxication center helps control the clinical condition day and night. The pulse, respiration, temperature, blood pressure, and hemoglobin are monitored every 2 or 4 hours; each day the barbiturate acid content of the blood is determined, as is plasma chloride and bicarbonate, blood urea, and serum protein. The gastric contents are *not* aspirated unless the drug was taken within the past 4 or 5 hours, and the pharyngeal and laryngeal reflexes are present. Gastric lavage is avoided. The Trendelenburg position is maintained during the first few days to prevent aspiration of gastric contents. Patients are moved to a different position in bed every 2 hours. There is intensive slapping of the chest and suction of secretion from the air passages. Procaine penicillin (2 million units × 2) are injected each day as a prophylactic against infections. Fluids of 2–3 L are given parenterally. Shock, if present, is managed by blood transfusion and perhaps by drugs such as norepinephrine. Complications, such as pulmonary edema, pneumonia, and atalectasis are treated. Stimulation with analeptics is avoided. In the absence of pronounced hypotension, pulmonary edema, and reduced renal function, after the clinical condition is under control, osmotic diuresis and alkalinization by infusions of urea and electrolyte solutions reduce the duration of coma two to four times. Of 92 patients with severe barbiturate poisoning, 85 recovered with this treatment approach.

Poisoning from overdose of nonbarbiturates or tranquilizers like the benzodiazepines, may be managed in essentially the same way, although these drugs are somewhat safer than barbiturates. Amphetamine and pressor amines are contraindicated, although norepinephrine may be given. Should inordinate restlessness or tonic and clonic convulsions follow excessive phenothiazine intake, careful administration of sodium Amytal may be helpful, recognizing the potentiation possibility. Cogentin or Artane may also be valuable.

SEVERE PSYCHOSOMATIC SYMPTOMS

There are a number of psychosomatic symptoms for which the patient initially seeks treatment, or that develop suddenly in therapy, that may be regarded as emergencies. Most of these are hysterical conversion or dissociative reactions, such as blindness, seizures, fugues, vomiting, aphonia, amnesia, paralysis, astasia-abasia, violent contractures, and anorexia nervosa. The patient may be so disabled by the symptom that he or she will be unable to cooperate with any attempted psychotherapeutic endeavor. Immediate removal of the symptom may thus be indicated. Such removal need not block the later use of more ambitious therapeutic measures. In the course of symptom removal, efforts may be made to show the patient that the symptoms are rooted in deeper personality problems, the correction of which will necessitate exploration of conflictual sources.

Hypnosis is an ideal adjunctive technique to expedite the emergency relief of hysterical symptoms. Once symptom removal has been decided upon, it is necessary to determine whether to attempt the removal at one session or whether to extend therapy over a period of several weeks. The severity of the symptom, its duration, the nature of the patient's personality, and the aptitude for hypnosis have to be considered. The approach is an individual one, and suggestions must be so framed that they will conform with the patient's personality, the type of symptom, and its symbolic significance. It is essential to adapt one's language to the patient's intelligence and education. Many failures in symptom removal are due to the fact that what the hypnotist is trying to convey is not clearly understood by the patient.

If hypnotic removal of the symptom at one session is decided upon, sufficient time must be set aside to devote oneself exclusively to the problem. As many as 2 to 3 hours may be necessary. A new patient may be encouraged to discuss past history and symptoms in order for the therapist to determine the patient's reaction to the illness as well as to gain clues to the patient's attitudes, motivations, and personality structure. Accenting of the patient's protestations of how uncomfortable he or she is, the therapist may emphasize that there is no reason why, if the patient has the motivation, the symptom cannot be overcome.

An optimistic attitude is important because many patients are terrified by their illness and have convinced themselves of the impossibility of cure. However, a cure should not be promised. The patient may be told that hypnosis has helped other people recover and that it can help him or her, too, if one will allow oneself to be helped.

The patient may be informed that it is necessary to test individual responses to suggestion; there is no need to concentrate too hard on what is said because, even though attention wanders, suggestions will get to the subconscious mind and produce desired reactions. An urge to rid oneself of suffering stimulates the desire to relax and follow suggestions. No indication is given the patient at this time that the symptom will be removed in its entirety, since the symptom may have hidden values and resistance may occur if the patient suspects that its immediate loss is at hand.

Hypnosis is then induced, and confidence in the ability to follow suggestions is built up by conducting the patient through light, medium, and, finally, if possible, deep trance states. Where the patient has a symptom that consists of loss of a physical function, it may be expedient to suggest that the therapist does not want the patient now to use the part. This is done in order to associate malfunction with the hypnotist's command instead of with a personal paralysis.

The next step in treatment is to get the patient, if so desired, to discuss under hypnosis reactions to the illness and what is happening in the immediate life situation.

In some patients active participation is encouraged. A reasonable explanation is given for the suggestions that will be made. The patient may even be encouraged to veto suggestions should there be any suspicion that they are against one's best interests or if there is no real desire to follow them. Active participation is encouraged in patients with relatively good ego strength who shy away from too authoritarian an approach.

Symptom removal by suggestion is far more effective where it is demonstrated to the patient that one has not lost control over one's functions, and hence is not the helpless victim of symptoms that cannot be altered or removed. This is achieved by showing the patient, while in a trance, that it is possible to create on command such symptoms as paralysis, spasticity, and anesthesia. Once the patient responds to these suggestions the important influence that the mind had over the body is stressed. Then a symptom identical with the patient's chief complaint is suggested in some other part of the body. Should the patient respond successfully, a partial removal of the symptom in the original site is attempted. For example, where there is a paralyzed arm, the suggestion is made that the fingers will move ever so little. Then paralysis of the other arm, which has been artificially produced, is increased in intensity, while a strong suggestion is made that the patient will find that function is restored to the ailing part. In the case of a paralyzed arm it is suggested that the hand will move, then the arm, and, finally, that the paralysis will disappear altogether.

The fact that symptoms can be produced and removed so readily on suggestion may influence the patient to accept the fact that one is not powerless and that one can exercise control over the body.

In order to protect the patient, should the symptom have a defensive function, some residual symptom that is less disabling than the original complaint can be suggested. It is hoped that the residual symptom will take over the defensive function. For instance, in the case of a paralyzed arm, paralysis of the little finger may be induced, and a suggestion may be given the patient that the finger paralysis will have the same meaning as the arm paralysis and that the finger paralysis will remain until the patient understands fully the reasons for the original paralysis and no longer needs the paralysis. In the event of an extensive anesthesia, numbness of a limited area may be suggested as a substitute.

Posthypnotic suggestions are next given the patient to the effect that the restored functions will continue in the waking state, except for the induced residual symptom. An activity may then be suggested that brings into use the ailing part; the patient finally being awakened in the midst of this action.

These suggestions are repeated at subsequent visits, and, if desired, the patient is taught the technique of self-hypnosis so that suggestive influences may continue through one's own efforts.

Although removal of the patient's symptom at one sitting may be possible and desirable in certain acute disabling hysterial conditions, it is usually best to extend therapy over a longer period. Suggestions are carried out very much better where the patient is convinced that one has been hypnotized and that hypnosis can have a potent influence on one's functions. It may, therefore, be advisable to delay giving therapeutic suggestions until the patient achieves as

deep a trance as possible and gains confidence in the ability to experience the phenomena suggested. The employment of therapeutic suggestions at a time when the patient lacks confidence in his or her ability to comply, and where faith in the therapist is not sufficient may end in failure and add discouragement and anxiety to the patient's other troubles.

A deep trance seems to increase therapeutic effectiveness in most patients. Where only a light trance is possible, the patient may not be able to get to a point where he or she becomes assured of the capacity to control the symptom.

All suggestions must be as specific as possible and should be repeated several times. The therapist should build, as completely as possible, a word picture of what the patient is supposed to feel or to do.

The lighter the trance, the less emphatic should the suggestions be. In extremely superficial hypnotic states the patient may be instructed that there is no need to concentrate too closely on the suggestions of the therapist, but rather to fixate attention on a restful train of thought. This technique is based on the idea that the patient's resistances can be circumvented. A logical explanation may be presented of why suggestions will work, along such lines as that the mind is capable of absorbing and utilizing suggestions even though some resistance is present.

If the patient is in a medium or deep trance, suggestions should be framed as simply as possible. The patient, especially when in deep hypnosis, should repeat the suggestions to be followed. Otherwise the therapist will not know whether the commands have been understood. Somnambules, may be instructed to carry out instructions even though they do not remember that these were formulated by the therapist. It is also a good idea in somnambulistic patients to give them a posthypnotic suggestion to the effect that they will be unresponsive to hypnotic induction by any person except the therapist. This will prevent the patient from being victimized by an amateur hypnotist who may very well undo therapeutic benefits.

If facts important in the understanding of the patient's condition are uncovered in hypnosis, these may or may not be brought to the patient's attention, depending upon their significance and upon the ability of the patient to tolerate their implications. It is best to make interpretations as superficial as possible, utilizing knowledge one has gained in working with the patient to guide him or her into activities of a creative nature that do not stir up too much conflict.

Termination of hypnosis by having the patient sleep for a few minutes before interruption is advantageous. The patient is instructed to continue to sleep for a designated number of minutes, following which he or she may awaken. The period of sleep may range from 2 to 15 minutes. Where the patient is able to dream on suggestion, this period may profitably be utilized to induce dreams either of a spontaneous sort or of a nature relevant to the particular trends elicited during the trance.

There is no set rule as to how much time to devote to hypnosis during each session. Except for the initial induction period, the trance need not exceed one-half hour. Ample time should be allowed to take up with the patient problems both before and after hypnosis. Reaction to the trance may also be discussed. Prejudice against symptom removal continues in force. On the whole, it is unjustified. Needless to say, more extensive psychotherapeutic measures will be necessary to insure lasting relief.

INTERCURRENT INCURABLE SOMATIC ILLNESS

The incidence of an intercurrent incurable physical illness constitutes an emergency in some patients. Development of certain conditions, such as multiple sclerosis, brain tumor, Hodgkin's disease, cancer, cerebral hemorrhage or thrombosis, or a coronary attack, will make it necessary for the therapist to take stock of the reality situation and perhaps to revise therapeutic goals. Essential also is a dealing with the emotional impact of the intercurrent illness on the individual. Insight therapy may have to be halted, and supportive approaches implemented.

Where the person is suffering from a nonfatal illness and where there is a possibility of a residual disability, as in coronary disease, apoplexy, tuberculosis, and various neurologic disorders, an effort must be made to get the patient to accept the illness. A desensitization technique may be utilized, encouraging the patient to discuss the illness and to ventilate fears concerning it. The need to recognize that this illness does not make one different from others, that all people have problems, some of which are more serious than one's own, that it is not disgraceful to be sick, may be repeatedly emphasized.

Persuasive talks may be given the patient to the effect that the most important thing in the achievement of health is to admit and to accept the limitations imposed on one by one's illness. This need not cause the patient to retire in defeat. One will still be able to gain sufficient recognition and success if one operates within the framework of the handicap. It is most important for self-respect that one continue to utilize remaining capacities and aptitudes, expanding them in a realistic and reasonable way. Many people suffering from a physical handicap have been able to compensate for a disability in one area by becoming proficient in another.

In patients who tend to regard their disability as justifying a completely passive attitude toward life, an effort must be made to stimulate activity and productiveness. The dangers of passivity and dependency, in terms of what these do to self-respect, are stressed. The person is encouraged to become as self-assertive and independent as the handicap will allow.

Where it is important for the patient to relax and to give up competitive efforts, persuasive or cognitive therapy may be combined with a reassuring, guidance approach aimed at externalizing interests along lines that will be engaging, but not too stimulating. The cultivation of a different philosophy toward life, directed at enjoying leisure and looking with disdain on fierce ambitious striving, will often help the patient to accept this new role.

Tension may be alleviated by Librium, and Valium; nausea, by Compazine; severe pain in dying patients, by regular administration of narcotics such as heroin. Intractable and unbearable pain that does not respond to the usual analgesics and to hypnosis may require psychosurgery (lobotomy). The practice of permitting a terminal patient to die with dignity (passive euthenasia) without being burdened with useless and desperate artificial means and heroic measures is becoming more and more accepted (Fletcher MI, 1974; Jaretzki, 1975). Interesting also is the publication called *A Living Will* (Euthenasia Education Council, 1974). Antidepressant drugs are often valuable for reducing pain as well as depression.

In progressive, incurable, and fatal ailments there may be a temptation to stop therapy on the basis that nothing more can be done for the patient. Actually, the patient may need the therapist more than before the ailment had developed. Where the patient has no knowledge of the seriousness of the condition, as, for instance, inoperable cancer, the decision of whether or not to reveal fully the calamity is a grave one that will influence the degree of suffering in the remaining days of one's life. In many cases it is unwise to burden one with the full seriousness of the condition. Statements may be made to the effect that a condition exists that the physician has classified as one that will get worse before it gets better. There is an obligation, of course, not to withhold facts from the patient, but honesty can be tempered with optimistic uncertainty. Many persons cling to a straw extended to them by an authority and maintain a positive attitude to the end. This is especially important in an illness such as AIDS where the degree of suffering may be influenced by the hopeful outlook that a cure may eventually be discovered through research.

In other patients it is sometimes practical to inform them, particularly if they already more than suspect it, that they have a progressive ailment. They may be assured that everything will be done to reduce pain and suffering and to keep up their good health as much as possible. Persuasive suggestions to face the remaining months with calmness and courage may be very reassuring. The patient may be told that while one's life span is limited, one may extend and enjoy it by the proper mental attitude. A guidance approach helps reduce the disturbing effect of environmental factors and permits the patient to divert interests toward outlets of a distracting nature. Where the patient is so disposed, he or she may be encouraged to cultivate religious interests in which one may find much solace.

The patient's time may be so arranged so as not to sit in utter desolation waiting for death. One may also be taught the technique of self-hypnosis to induce relaxation, diminish tension, reduce pain, and promote a better mental outlook. Mendell (1965) states that patients respond to his statement: "You are not alone. The struggle is not over. You don't have to worry that what can be done is not being done. I am with you and aware of what you are undergoing. I am with the forces that are to help you, and if anything develops, I will bring it to you immediately." An attitude should be inculcated in the patient that one has fulfilled one's task well and that it is now time to let oneself relax. Such an attitude may permit of the peaceful, even happy, acceptance of the end of life. Actually, few dying patients do not appreciate the imminence of death, even though their psychological defenses tend to deny it. The therapist may keep emphasizing that the patient, through courage, is doing much for his or her family. What the patient needs is someone to understand and to help mobilize existing resources, to listen closely with respect and not pity, to display a compassionate matter-of-factness, and above all to help him overcome the fear of isolation. The greatest problem in working with the dying patient is the therapist's own feeling of helplessness, guilt, and fear of death.

The work of Cicely Saunders, Director of St. Christopher's Hospice (Liegner, 1975) is evidence that for dying patients a great deal can be done toward making their last days comfortable, painless, and free from anxiety. Administration of medications ("polypharmacy") to render the patient symptom-free has been routine at St. Christopher's. Diamorphine (heroin) every 4 hours orally, Thorazine and its derivatives, and other medications that are indicated for special conditions, such as dexamethasone for brain metastases and increased intracranial pressure, may be given during the day and night. The physical atmosphere should be clean, cheerful, and comfortable. The members of the staff must be supportive and participate in working through the stress of separation anxiety. Discussion about incurability and dying are not avoided, and the fact is accented "that death is a continuum of life and is not to be feared." Under these conditions the patients may respond to the passing of another patient with little dread or fear.

If the patient who knows that he or she is dying can be shown that the acceptance of death is a positive achievement rather than resignation to nothingness, much will have been accomplished in making the remaining days more tolerable. Understanding the patient's anxiety, guilt feelings, and depression through empathic listening may be extremely reassuring. Helping members of the patient's family to deal with their hostility and despair may also be an essential part of the therapist's task. Cautioning them on the futile search for expensive and nonexistent cures may, incidentally, be in order. At all times the focus is on relieving the patient's physical pain and distress, on making one comfortable in one's home, and on assuaging mental turmoil. If this is done, peace will usually follow. A good relationship with the patient's family during the last days will help them to an acceptance of the reality of death and lessen the pain of bereavement.

Where death has occurred, the therapist may be called on to render help to the bereaved. Different members of the family will respond with their distinctive reactions to the incident. The detached and presumably adjusted member may actually need more support than the one who is ostensibly upset and manifestly grief stricken. Since members are bound to respond to the emotional tone of those around them, the manner and mode of communication of the therapist will influence the healing process. Cooperativeness, understanding, sympathetic listening, and an expressed desire to help can inspire friendship and trust in the therapist. As Beachy (1967) has pointed out, it is unwise to whitewash the facts of suffering and death or to try to evade the evolving emotional reactions, however unreasonable they may seem. A completely open, factual manner that is not falsely oversolicitous is best, and where needed, the continued care and attention of a clergyman or other supportive person may be advisable. The value of therapy with groups of terminally ill patients makes this modality one that should be considered in selected cases (Yalom & Greaves, 1977).

Readings on this subject may be found in Aldrich (1963), Cassem (1974), Christ (1961), G.W. Davidson (1975), Eissler

(1955), Feifel (1959), J. Fletcher (1972), GAP Symposium (1965), Gerson & Bassuk (1980), Kennedy (1960), Krupp & Kligfeld (1961), Kubler-Ross (1969), Langer (1957), Makadon et al. (1984), Morgenthau (1961), Pack (1961), Reeves (1973), P.S. Rhoads (1965), Rund & Hutzler (1983), Saul (1959), A. Schwartz (1961), Standard & Nathan (1955), Tagge et al. (1974), Wahl (1960), A.F.C. Wallace (1956), Weisman (1985), Worcester (1935), Worden (1982), and Zilboorg (1943).

59
Stress and its Management

A common denominator in all mental illness is stress, which is a trigger that can set off many deleterious physical and psychological reactions. It is a potent precipitant of emotional disorders and therefore of vital concern to the psychotherapist.

In the course of daily living a certain amount of stress is unavoidable. To an extent this is constructive since it "oils up" the physiological mechanisms essential to adaptation, much as a machine requires periodic use to prevent the constituent parts from drying up and rusting. People often seek ways of stressing themselves temporarily with some pleasurable excitement like competitive sports and games, or exposing themselves to mildly frightening experiences like horror movies or murder mysteries. This not only helps keep the various body organs and systems in tune, but also enables the fight-or-flight mechanisms of the organism to hold themselves in preparation for some more-than-normal stressful emergency.

What we are concerned with in mental health practice are not these adaptive responses to everyday stress, but the effects on the individual of stressful events to which a proper adaptation cannot be made. Specifically we want to know what to do for the patient who is being victimized by abnormal and incapacitating stress reactions, and more importantly, how to modulate or remove the stressful stimuli that are causing the problems.

PHYSIOLOGICAL CONSEQUENCES OF STRESS

It is estimated that stress reactions are a major factor in the etiology of physical illness like heart disease, stomach ulcers, and even cancer to name a few. Knowledge of the involved physiology may be helpful in understanding how this comes about. Simply put, what stress does, as Selye (1956) has shown, is to activate a massive conditioned nonspecific reaction to prepare for appropriate coping with an actual or anticipated threat. The psychological component of this response is part of our animal heritage having evolved over millions of years as a survival mechanism in the face of danger. Once a situation is *perceived* and *evaluated by* the brain as dangerous, several subcortical centers come into play. Two systems are primarily involved that ordinarily operate to regulate the normal functions of the body. Both depend on complex chemical compounds (hormones) in the hypothalamus. One of these hormones, cortisol, is so essential to life that its concentration in the blood must be steadily maintained within narrow limits. Cortisol is vital in preparing the body physically to overcome a threatening stress stimulus. What cortisol does is break down aminoacids from muscle and connective tissue into glucose to supply the body with energy. In addition, it regulates cell metabolism, stabilizes plasma membranes, elevates the mood, and has an antiinflamatory effect. This over a short-term period is helpful in dealing with stress. But if excessive cortisol manufacture continues over an extensive period, which is the case in prolonged and continued stress or chronic intermittant stress, cortisol starts doing damage. It breaks down too much muscle tissue, produces clotting failure, weakens bone structure encouraging fractures, depresses the body's immune reactions causing susceptibility to infection, and sometimes produces bizarre behavior. In recent years it has been discovered that another brain hormone liberated by the same adrenal steroid feedback mechanism responsible for cortisol is beta-endorphin, which has a pain-killing morphinelike action, but that in too great concentration, that is when stress is prolonged, may also have an unwholesome effect.

Additionally important to body function is the second system, the sympathetic nervous system and the catecholamine hormones epinephrine and norepinephrine released by the adrenal medulla. In short-term stress this system is activated to increase cardiac output, help respiration by dilating the bronchioles, distribute blood from the inside of the body to muscles and the heart, lessen fatigue, increase alertness and facilitate energy supplies by liberating glucose from muscles and liver and releasing fatty acids from fat deposits. This is all to the good in dealing with temporary stress, but if this action goes on over an extended period, physiological damage can occur in the form of hypertension, gastric ulcers, cardiac arrhythmia, and other organ malfunctions. Increased plasma cholesterol and elevated low density lipoprotein may predispose to atherosclerosis and coronary insufficiency.

SOURCES OF STRESS

Sources of stress are legion and it would be an insuperable task to list all of them since they vary with each individual. On an environmental level we need merely to catalogue the kinds of problems social agencies deal with to realize that endless troubles stressfully plague human beings apart from cataclysms of climate, war, accidents, and catastrophic physical illness, which after all are not too common in the lives of most people. Noteworthy for the majority are tensions caused by difficult interpersonal relationships with families, spouses, authorities and peers, bereavements, material or fancied threats to the safety, security, and life of the individual such as violent assaults, rape, serious accidents and illnesses, blows to self-esteem, undermining of autonomy and identity, anger that is blocked in expression, and the inability to fulfill important personality needs which may in susceptible persons become stress sources. The origins of many of these difficulties are rooted in past conditionings. Incomplete separation-individuation, devalued self-esteem, accumulating hostilities, guilt feelings, and personality drives that interfere with harmonious interactions are a few of the surviving anachronisms and traits that generate troubles.

Belief systems sometimes contribute anomalous sources of stress even though the individual recognizes their irrational source. Authentic cases of death may follow the breaking of a taboo or the spells cast on a victim by shaman, voodooist witch doctor or medicine man. Among civilized people, a deep conviction of hopelessness, with expectation of death may bring on irrecoverable illness with loss of appetite and a wasting away, with a calm acceptance of one's inevitable doom. Years ago Walter Cannon wrote about how supernatural fear can bring about a fatal outcome, and he pointed out the fact that some surgeons refused to do a major operation on a patient who was terrorized by the conviction that he or she would not survive.

There are additionally a plethora of aversive events and factors in daily life that can have a cumulative stressful effect. The individual may to some extent be aware of the damage these mischief-mongers cause and may force himself or herself to tolerate them, either on the basis that the problems are insoluble and there is no escape, or because one feels destined to endure them. More often there is no awareness of the damage they cause and years may go by before the victim realizes that something is wrong and can no longer go on physically or emotionally.

A good deal of literature has been published on selective areas of stress a most interesting contribution having been made by Holmes and Rahe (1967) who developed a Social Rehabilitation Rating Scale designating areas of stressful changes in one's life situation in hierarchical order, assigning to them "life change units" from 100 to 11. At the top of the list, the first three items are the death of a spouse, divorce, and marital separation. These are followed by a large number of other damaging incidents, with somewhat lesser scores. The authors found that a total of 200 or more life change units in a year was matched by an increased incidence of myocardial disease, infections, peptic ulcer, and assorted psychiatric disorders.

Bereavement as a stress source commonly occurs with the death or permanent departure of a person with whom there has been a close relationship (parent, spouse, child, lover). It may develop with removal from one's home, neighborhood, or work situation as in relocation and retirement. The reaction of grief may appear immediately after the critical separation incident, or manifest itself following weeks or months. The classic investigation of Erich Lindemann (1944) revealed five main reactions: (1) somatic symptoms (physical distress, shortness of breath, muscular weakness, tension, subjective discomfort); (2) preoccupation with the image of the lost object; (3) guilt (self-accusations for the situation); (4) hostile reactions (anger at being abandoned; irritability at people in general); (5) behavioral alterations (restlessness, forcing oneself feverishly into activities; enhancement of dependency, feelings of unreality, imitation of attitudes and behavior of a deceased through identification). Reaction formations such as forced cheerfulness or stoicism may mask some of these symptoms.

Grief that follows a lost home precipitates similar reactions to those resulting from the death or permanent departure of a valued person (Fried, 1963). Clearance of urban slum areas, the devastation caused by tornadoes and floods, invasion, and the massive destruction of war has resulted in forced relocation and massive bereavement and personal suffering. The sense of loss of intimacy with one's surroundings, disruption of customary social networks, absence of familiar groups of people, results in a sense of disorientation, the fragmentation of identity, and a grieving for the lost familiar neighborhood.

Retirement, without adequate preparation or training for postretirement activities and hobbies can impose stressful burdens on a person whose sense of importance, worth, and self-esteem has been contingent on gainful employment. Lacking methods of restoring feelings of being needed the individual may respond with despair, depression, and a longing for return to the previous status. The sense of grief and bereavement parallel those that follow the loss of an important love object.

Why bereavement and separation have such intense effects on people has engaged the attention of many observers. It is the belief of some that these are tangentially related to the fear of death that exists on some level in all people. No satisfactory formula has ever been evolved to neutralize this death fear in spite of such expediencies as belief in immortality, reincarnation, soul survival, and the like. There are those who contend that fear of dying cannot be avoided since it is a biological and evolutionary phenomenon residing within the structure of man. There are others who believe that such fear is not biological, but rather bound to the peculiarities of human development. At its core is the infant's primitive reaction to object loss precipitated by separation from the mother. No matter how secure the individual may seem, the terror of abandonment-separation-death slumbers ominously in the unconscious and symbolically fastens itself to later separation experiences and to any bereavement contingency that threatens personal physical and emotional security. Obviously the more wholesome the rearing of the child, and the more stable the personality structure, the better the coping tactics in dealing with separation. But even in well adjusted individuals the repressed death obsession may awaken with severe deprivations and life-threatening crises. In unstable persons, fears of annihilation can appear explosively with minor separations and insignificant losses which are interpreted as threats to one's integrity.

Terminal cancer patients and those experiencing severe myocardial disease may be realistically confronted with the imminence of death; such patients often barricade themselves from the terror of dying by denial mechanisms, a conspiracy entered into by visiting persons who, dealing with their own anxieties of mortality, try to flourish a false facade of hope. Slips of speech and disturbing dreams only too pointedly indicate the patient's distrust of such denial maneuvers.

We cannot dismiss the fact that constitutional factors sometimes enter into the generation of stress through hypersensitive biochemical and neurophysiological systems that fire off excessively with even minor stimuli. Nor can we neglect cultural elements that endow certain events with a portentous meaning. *The meaning the individual imparts to any stimulus, external or internal, will determine its stressful potential.* The most insidious sources of stress issue from unconscious conflicts, the individual attempting to rationalize inner turmoil by attributing it to outside sources. Indeed, disturbing stressful situations may deliberatedly be created to provide objectivity for one's inner feelings.

REACTIONS TO STRESS

Research on stress has shown, sometimes to the exasperation of the experimentor, that the severity of the stresses bear little relationship to the intensity of the resultant physiological and behavioral disruption, even in the same experimental subject at different times. A number of intervening variables appear to be operative, some of which are confoundingly elusive. What is of primary importance is the cognitive set that imparts special meaning to the stressor. The reaction of any individual to stress is regulated by the sense of one's own vulnerability and the perception of one's capacity to cope with, adjust to, or overcome the source of trouble. Mastery of a stress situation in the past akin to the present one, is a positive factor, while failure is a negative element in determining stress tolerance. Most individuals will react to a life-endangering situation with fear or panic. But a suicidally inclined soul, intent on self-destruction, or a religious martyr, who expects rewards in heaven, may actually promote a life-terminating event. Highly motivated, well doctrined soldiers exposed to skilled prebattle morale building will enter stressful combat with fierce enthusiasm. Soldiers who do not know what they are fighting for are deplorably handicapped during combat.

Are there any personality measures that can tell us how an individual will react to stress? Coping adequacy is related to flexibility of defenses, one predictive measure being the stability of the individual in the face of previous life crises. Andreasen et al. (1972) studied hospitalized burn patients, and found that patients with adjustment difficulties prior to the burn and those with premorbid psychopathology coped poorly with their injury. In an interesting piece of research on physiological and psychological responses to stress, Katz et al. (1970) have shown that "the ego's defenses are obviously able to buffer the individual from threat with great efficiency" and, even to block expected biochemical reactions. So far no reliable test has been found that can measure defenses and that can predict what an individual will do under certain stressful circumstances. Responses are highly specific. In this author's practice, both amateur and seasoned actors on screen, stage, and TV have been seen whose stage fright prior to the opening night performance approached shock reactions, yet with the arrival of doomsday, before a live audience, performed brilliantly with scarcely a whisper of anxiety. On the other hand, the author has seen composed, self-confident individuals including some veterans, decorated for bravery in battle, fall apart when asked unpreparedly to make a speech before a group. No prior psychological test could have predicted these transformations.

Cultural attitudes often determine reaction patterns. For instance, tolerance of pain and the ability to disregard it stoically may be considered virtuous in some societies, contrasting with the complaining, demanding, groaning, angry responses found in other cultural groups. As Zborowski (1977) has stated, stress in part is "a cultural experience in perception as well as in interpretation, and as such is responded to by behavior and attitudes learned within the culture in which the individual is brought up." Such philosophical defenses as a penchant to accept adversity as inevitable, the endorsing of a fatalistic attitude that man is destined to suffer pain and discom-

fort, and confidence in faith and prayer as ultimate means of gaining protection through the divine order can greatly subdue reactions to stressful stimuli. Accordingly, stress is subject to the psychological embellishments of the responder who draws on inherent physiological and psychological sensitivities. In individuals with a tendency to depression, stress often functions as an important precipitant. Controlled studies have shown that stressful life events precede the outbreak of major depressions in predisposed individuals. Other syndromes than depression may be precipitated by stress, and it is a challenging hypothesis that predispositions to a specific response may exist in such persons. Brown and Birley (1968) found that 60 percent of patients suffering from a schizophrenic episode had experienced strong stressful situations some weeks prior to the onset of the illness. Only 19 percent of the control group were similarly affected. Past conditionings also provide a fertile paradigm for behavioral patterns. Thus an individual victimized as a child by the abandonment or death of a parent may respond to mild separations in adult life intensely, even catastrophically.

Where physiological responses to stress continue over a period of time, we may expect complications of physical illness and organ damage (Rahe & Arthur, 1977). What inspires the choice of organ afflicted is still hard to say. On the surface we would assume that the weakest link in the physiological chain would break down under the stressful pounding. This then would be a matter of hereditary weakness of an organ system, or previous damage to the organ wrought by a past illness or pathological assault. Because chronic stress affects immunological reactivity and predisposes to autoimmune reactions, some authorities believe that nonspecific damage can occur, postulating as one example rheumatoid arthritis. However, here too a genetic predisposition cannot be ruled out.

Many authorities believe that variant personality typologies generate different degrees of stress and show different modes of coping with adversity. While most authorities downplay the thesis of Alexander (1950) that the organ disrupted by stress is determined by the basic character structure, there may be some tendency in certain dependent, "orally" disposed individuals whose dependent need is frustrated, to oversecrete digestive juices as if they seek to incorporate food, which from infantile associations is equated with love. Continued gastric hyperacidity may thus result in peptic ulcer. Special personality constellations are believed to activate selected organ systems. A hard driven, time-hungry, competitive, restless personality, type A personality described by Friedman and Rosenman (1959, 1974), is said to be predisposed to coronary disease. There seems to be some experimental evidence for this. Van Egeren and his coworkers (1983) found that social stresses, like competitive rivalry and goal frustration affected the ventricular myocardium differently in type A than the less driven, calmer type B persons. Computer analysis of the electrocardiograms revealed in type A persons a statistically significant depression of the ST segment and a reduction of T wave and R wave amplitude. There are additional studies that show that type A individuals in comparison with type B individuals have more frequent arrhythmias, and increased sympathetic adrenergic responses (rises in blood pressure, accelerated heart rate, and mobilization of epinephrine and norepinephrine) to stress which provide added evidence for greater liability to cardiac illness in type A individuals.

Attempts have been made to correlate other personality typologies with diabetes, ulcerative colitis, cancer, asthma, migraine, and arthritis. One example is the study of a large group of patients with chronic insomnia in different parts of the country (Kales et al, 1983). A consistent pattern was the handling of stress and conflicts, especially about aggression, by internalizing rather than expressing emotions, which apparently promoted physiological disturbances during sleep.

Important to differentiate in evaluating this complex data are physical manifestations of conversion reactions that fulfill defensive psychological needs and are products of the voluntary sensorimotor system. Here the physical symptom (e.g., paralysis, anesthesia, etc.) constitutes a symbolic communication coached in body language. We are inevitably led to the conclusions that organ choice is multifactorial and must be individually evaluated.

Physiological reactions to stress that result in organ damage are obviously inimical to adequate coping. Psychological defenses similarly may be maladaptive. The adequacy of the coping method depends on a number of factors, principally whether the defense employed succeeds in halting the deleterious effect of the stress response on the physiological level, and whether, on a psychological level, it compromises the present or future adjustment of the individual. A stressed executive earning a large salary and enjoying tenure in an organization can achieve temporary peace of mind by resigning his or her position, but in the long run may be cutting one's own throat and become even more severely stressed while waiting for the meager unemployment check in line with other job hopefuls. Studies indicate that adequate methods of coping include humor, anticipation, rationalization, and philosophizing (Ford 1975; Vaillant, 1971).

MANAGEMENT OF STRESS

There is enough research evidence* to make plausible the following facts about stress: (1) the impact of a stressful event,

---

* A good bibliography on stress research may be found in McGrath JE (ed): Social and Psychological Factors in Stress. New York: Holt, Rinehart and Winston, 1970; and McGrath, JE: Settings, measures and Themes: An integrative review of some research on social-psychological factors in stress. In Monat A, Lazarus RS (eds): Stress and Coping. New York: Columbia University Press, 1977, pp. 67–76.

physical or social-psychological is modulated by the expectations, perception, and the unique meaning given the stressor by the subject; (2) the reaction of any individual to stress is regulated by a sense of one's own vulnerability, and the perception of the capacity to cope with, adjust to, or overcome the source of the trouble. (3) Mastery in the past of a stress situation akin to the present one, is a positive, failure a negative factor in determining stress tolerance; (4) graded exposure to a stressful situation, with mastery of some aspects, tend to desensitize the subject to the effects of the stressor; (5) stressful reactions following failure to cope with a threat, or missing the mark on an assigned task, encourage deterioration of responses at later trials; (6) verbalization about one's feelings, and the presence of people who the individual trusts, increases tolerance of stress, reducing psychological and psychosomatic symptomatology. These research findings, paralleling what common sense would tell us, form the basis around which the management of stress can be organized.

The first step in management is to identify the operative stressors. If they are purely environmental, a counseling approach may do more good than depth-oriented psychotherapy. In most cases, however, it is rare that external stressors are not reinforced by the motivational connivance of the patient who may even have initiated the troubles and then subversively sustains them. Here attempts to deal with the stressors by counseling and millieu therapy will be blocked by the emotional needs of the patient. Should this happen, the therapist will have to institute an approach focused on rectifying the personality operations of the patient.

Initiation of an effective treatment program will depend on the condition of the patient when first seen. A four-part "stress response syndrome" (Horowitz, 1976) is commonly experienced by persons exposed to an acute traumatic event such as bereavement, surgery, a serious accident, a catastrophic blow to security or self-esteem, or anything that is interpreted as an irretrievable loss. The first phase is characterized by an initial shock reaction with a dulling of perception and feelings of unreality. Second, there is an attempt at denial in order to push out painful emotions related to the incident. The person may act and talk as if nothing has happened, or there may be a minimization of the incident. Following this, a third phase occurs with gradual intrusive feeding into consciousness of the true significance of the event and an experiencing of previously blocked emotions like pain and deprivation. This may alternate with bouts of emotional withdrawal when anxiety is too strong. Fourth, the change in life status that the traumatic event makes inevitable is accepted. This working-through cognitive processing phase may go on for years. It may never be completed being interrupted by images and phantasies of the lost object or previous stabilizing life situation. Patients react uniquely to each phase in accordance with their personality needs and neurotic defenses.

During the first phase of the reaction, therapy is best focussed on terminating, if possible, any identifiable stressful stimuli. This may necessitate removing the patient physically from the stress source provided such rescue will not complicate matters. Where it is essential to live with and adapt to a stressful environment, the person will need to desensitize to its effects and develop ways of modifying or eliminating its most hurtful elements. A relationship with an empathic, knowledgeable person here is most important and the degree of directiveness, support and empathic reassurance must be titrated against the existing confusion, helplessness, and disorganization. In severe reactions, psychotherapy may be necessary. Hypnosis and the *temporary* administration of an anxiolytic medication may be helpful. The objective is to bring the patient back to a realistic appraisal of the situation. If possible, one should avoid anxiolytics especially in addictive personalities. Should they have to be prescribed, their use must be terminated as rapidly as possible so that the patient does not become dependent on them.

By the time the patient presents for help to a psychotherapist he or she will undoubtedly have made some attempts at self-regulation and environmental manipulation through control, attack, or escape measures. These will show up in manifestations of denial, detachment, displacement, projection, and rationalization. Such defenses are implemented with the aim of dealing with, neutralizing or removing the perceived threat. An insidious escape measure is the use of mind-altering drugs (sedatives, tranquilizers, alcohol, marijuana, cocaine), which will complicate therapy. As soon as some stabilization occurs and the relationship with the therapist is sufficiently firm, resort to substance use or abuse will need to be terminated and this may require aggressive handling. Other untoward defenses are acting out manifestations, outbursts of anger and violence, masochistic activities, unusual sexual practices, withdrawal, and restless agitation. Complications may have ensued as a result of these responses, which, though disturbing and requiring handling, should not sidetrack the therapist's pursuit of mediating the initiating stress.

If the patient is in the denial phase of the stress reaction, during which an attempt is being made by the patient to blot out the presence of the threat by acting as if it did not exist or by minimizing it as through humor or joking, the therapist will have to alter the approach. Without withholding support and reassurance, denial is countered by continued careful confrontations interpreting the purpose behind the patient's disputative maneuvers. In acute stress reactions denial may be so severe as to practically paralyze the person. Phobias and conversion symptoms may be pressed into

service to avoid reminders of the stressful situation. Amnesia, fugue states, delirious attacks, tremors, paralysis, sensory disturbances and paralyzing phobias may develop and constitute the immediate reason why the patient comes to treatment. Repression is never complete and periodically the repressed stressful experience or conflict will feed back into consciousness stimulating bouts of anxiety. So long as denial exists, this back and forth movement will continue. It is essential here to dose the patient with increments of the disavowed or repressed material through confrontation and interpretation of existing fantasies, dreams, and behavioral distortions. Where denial is extreme, hypnosis and narcosynthesis may be of some help in breaking through the resistance, but will require administration by a professional skilled in their use.

The next phase of therapy may well be the most difficult one since it requires a working through of the insights gained in treatment and putting these into corrective practice. During this phase there will be periods of anxiety and depression as the patient reexperiences the trauma, as well as repressive renunciatory interludes.

Therapy is usually performed under a handicap because of continued stubborn distrust of one's environment and of authority in general. This promotes detachment, easily aroused anger, and reluctance to engage in psychiatric or psychological treatment. Where therapy is attempted, the transference may become so ambivalent as to interfere with treatment.

Enjoining the patient to verbalize feelings, the temporary use of medication, and perhaps exposure to hypnosis may open the way to establishing a relationship with the therapist who is then in a better position to institute counseling, cognitive therapy, or dynamically oriented psychotherapy. Should transference still interfere with treatment, group therapy may be tried which, because transference is split and more diffused, may be better tolerated than individual treatment in these highly stressed individuals.

While less dramatic than acute gross stress reactions, but no less devastating in their effects are *chronic stresses of an intermittent nature*. Stress here is due either to an environment from which the individual cannot or will not escape and to which one responds adversely, or to disturbed relationships with significant others like parents, siblings, spouse, children, employer, etc. Usually personality problems are basic and are subsidized by intrapsychic conflicts which sponsor such defenses as projection, fantasy, dissociation and obsessive rumination that interfere with adequate coping.

A prime goal in dealing with chronic intermittent stress is evolving defenses aimed at a more constructive adaptation and, if possible, the elimination of the sources of tension. Of vital importance is the shoring up of morale, which has usually become vitiated because of the long period of suffering. Regular relaxing exercises, meditation, or self-hypnosis can help a person avoid resorting to tranquilizers, hypnotics, alcohol and smoking.

Attitudes can influence one's physiological and psychological responses. For example, in physical illness an optimistic outlook, the will to live, faith in one's physician, commitment to achievement and conviction of recovery help stimulate the immunological system, speed healing in surgery, shorten physical illness, and, according to some recent research, even inhibit the growth of cancer cells. On the other hand, abandoning hope, giving up one's claim on life, a belief that one is doomed, apathy, and the unwillingness to fight puts a damper on recovery, heightens tension, and hastens death. Norman Cousins (1976) has written an excellent article on the value of a positive outlook. In all cases of stress some form of cognitive therapy is usually called for, which adds an important dimension to the other interventions being employed. In working with such terminal ailments as AIDS this boosting of morale is especially important.

Attitude change through cognitive therapy may also be helpful in prolonged and obdurate *bereavement reactions* aiding in the resolution of grief. The grief work seems to be essential in liberating the individual from the bondage of the cherished object, preparing for a different outlook, and the development of new relationships. What interferes most with a working through of the separation crisis is denial of one's true feelings in the attempt to insulate oneself from painful stress. It may require a good deal of effort on the part of any helping person to gain the individual's confidence, counter the hostility, and break through the wall of detachment that prevents the victim from enduring the pain essential in coming to grips with the loss.

The development of a relationship with some trusted person or counselor is almost mandatory to help the individual acknowledge and accept feelings and to begin to move toward other relationsips. Discussions of misgivings, guilt feelings, idealizations, and memories encourage emotional catharsis. In most cases improvement will come about within a period of about 6 weeks. Where there is denial of one's feelings of guilt and pain, the somatic symptoms, restlessness, insomnia, and nightmares may go on for a prolonged period. A kind of paranoidal distrust often prevents the individual from getting close to people and it will require a good deal of tactful persuasion to promote resumption of close social contacts. The most extreme reaction to bereavement is precipitation of a deep depression with suicidal ideas or actual attempts to kill oneself. One usually encounters a history of previous depressive incidents in such extreme reactions. Antidepressive medications and, where suicide is a possibility, ECT may be required.

A question often asked is how much social support should be rendered in dealing with the effects of stress? In most cases where the stressful situation overwhelms the coping capacities of the victim, social support bolsters up the reserve of the individual. However, it should be withdrawn as soon as possible lest it reinforce helplessness and dependency. In chronic stress especially one should avoid operating as a good genie taking over responsibilities that should be handled by the patient. Indeed there is evidence, as shown by work with cancer patients that supportive activities for patients not undergoing chemotherapy or radiation treatments may "increase negative mood and decrease self-perceptions of worth, mastery, acceptance of the patient role, and acceptance of death." (Revenson et al, 1983). The very rendering of social supports in some persons acts as a stress source (Dunkel-Schetter & Wortman, 1982; Brickman et al, 1982).

Another question relates to the value of prevention. There is a good deal of evidence that anticipating impending stress may be helpful in dealing with it when it comes. For instance according to a study at the Harvard Medical School retirement is a risk factor in coronary heart disease (Gonzales, 1980). Job-related dissatisfactions are also a risk factor that may lead to a decision to leave one's work as the lesser of two evils. Cultivating proper attitudes toward retirement may prove to be a saving grace. A conception of retirement as a worthy reward for years of dedicated work helps overcome the stressful conviction that it is a punishment for growing old. Where the individual faces an inevitable loss, behavioral practice sessions with role playing and encouraging the person to verbalize feelings may serve a valuable purpose. On the basis of the theory that people can adapt to any stress if they acquire adequate coping facilities, training in stress management may be a priority item in those in high-risk situations (Meichenbaum et al, 1975; Ford, 1975; Vaillant, 1971). Despite unsubstantiated claims of psychological cures rendered by exercises like running and calisthenics, there is evidence that regular exercise and other measures to improve physical fitness help individuals cope better with a high proportion of life changes like divorce, death of a loved one, and switching jobs (Science News, Vol. 130, August 2, 1986).

If an impending stressful event is anticipated such as subjection to major surgery, the expected death of a spouse or family member suffering from an incurable illness, fearful reactions to forced retirement, etc., there is no substitute for counseling sessions with a respected person who is able to supply realistic information in advance and reassuringly to handle the individual's anxieties and concerns. High morale is an important factor in stress coping, and it is best obtained by proper prior preparation or realistic indoctrination. Excessive fears or denial of concern are both conducive to poor coping. Studies show that "A moderate amount of anticipatory fear about realistic threats is necessary for the development of effective inner defenses for coping with subsequent danger and deprivation." (Janis, 1977). During counseling or psychotherapy, contingencies are assessed, resources and supports assayed, and appropriate options and adaptations reviewed.

60
Psychotherapy in Special Conditions

The principles of psychotherapy that have been outlined and the technical procedures that have been delineated apply to all emotional problems and conditions irrespective of clinical diagnosis. It may be possible, with the proper working relationship and the adroit use of appropriate techniques, to approach the goal of some personality reconstruction in any symdrome. Experience, however, has shown that certain conditions make extensive therapeutic objectives difficult to achieve. Experience also indicates that they seem to respond favorably to specific techniques or combinations of methods. In this chapter we shall consider the problems and technical modifications encountered in the treatment of neurotic, psychophysiological, personality, and psychotic disorders.

ANXIETY DISORDERS (ANXIETY NEUROSIS, PHOBIC NEUROSIS, ANXIETY STATES)

Some anxiety is a universal human experience considered by existentialists as basic to the nature of existence. It is common to all physical and emotional ailments in which the problems are conceived of as a threat. Anxiety usually generates a host of defenses marshalled to neutralize its effects. Some defenses, however, contribute to greater maladaptation than the anxiety experience itself, for example, recourse to avoidance behavior, inhibitions of function, or overindulgence in drugs and alcohol. When anxiety becomes excessive, it is regarded as a pathological syndrome to which several labels are applied, such as panic disorder, agoraphobia, generalized anxiety disorder, social phobia, simple phobia, obsessive-compulsive disorder, and posttraumatic stress disorder. Except for the anxiety, the specific features of these syndromes are fashioned by the unique personality and cognitive styles of the patient, by family dynamics, and by variable features in the environment. Although anxiety as a symptom is found in many disorders such as depression, schizophrenia, and organic brain disease, the panic, phobic, obsessive-compulsive, and generalized anxiety disorders constitute a distinctive and discrete assembly of entities (Lesser & Rubin, 1986) that are probably biologically based and affect only approximately 8 percent of the population.

Panic Disorder Without Agoraphobia (DSM-III-R Code 300.01) Panic Disorder With Agoraphobia (DSM-III-R Code 300.21)

The identifying feature of this disorder is that intensive anxiety and catastrophic feelings of impending doom are apt to erupt unexpectedly or in relation to situations that realistically should not be threatening. Faintness, trembling, dizziness, heart palpitations, sweating, depersonalization, chest pain, and paresthesias overwhelm the individual and cause him or her to seek safety at home or in a doctor's office. If the condition repeats itself under the same conditions, phobic defenses may be organized, leading to anticipation of the attacks and further discomfort. The patient may resort to alcohol and barbiturates. Panic disorder must be differentiated from symptoms of certain physical conditions such as hypoglycemia, hyperthyroidism, and pheachromocytoma and from panicky attacks in patients with depression, schizophrenia, somatization disorder, and organic brain disorder. There is some evidence that early separation anxiety is a precursor to the condition and that a genetic predisposition may exist.

In treating the condition it should be kept in mind that appeals to reason have little effect and that insight will be deluged and rendered worthless by the flood of anxiety that overwhelms the individual. The best therapeutic focus is on the biochemical and conditioning links in the behavioral chain. When panic attacks have diminished or disappeared, cognitive therapy may be valuable, and if unconscious conflictual elements are suspected, psychoanalytically oriented psychotherapy may be attempted.

Drug therapy with antidepressants (see Table 56-1, p. 968) gives us a choice of three classes of medication: tricyclics, MAO inhibitors, and a benzodiazepine antidepressant, alprazolam. Each has its advantages and disadvantages. Tricyclics, such as imipramine (Tofranil), are the most common medications used, but they may require as long as 8 weeks before a substantial response occurs. Moreover, anticholinergic side effects, such as dry mouth, blurred vision, and rapid heart beat, may upset some patients. Tofranil is started with 10 to 25 mg daily to reduce the patient's fear of side effects. Gradually, over a 2-to-4-week period, the dose is raised to 100 to 200 mg/day. If in 8 to 12 weeks the response is poor, the dose may be increased to 300 mg. Should tachycardia and heart palpitations frighten the patient, a beta blocker such as propranolol (Inderal) may be tried. A MAO inhibitor such as phenelzine (Nardil) requires restrictions of diet and avoidance of certain medicaments that some patients find inconvenient. The beginning dose is 15 mg/day, increased by 15 mg every 3 to 4 days until 60 mg are taken daily. The medication should be given in the morning and at noon to avoid possible insomnia. If after 8 to 12 weeks the effect is not impressive, the dose may be raised to 75 to 100 mg. If a side effect of muscle twitching occurs, 150 to 300 mg of vitamin B_6 should be given. One should never go from a regime of tricyclic therapy (which was not effective) to MAO inhibitors without stopping medication for 2 weeks. Alprazolam (Xanax) works within 1 to 2 weeks but may produce some drowsiness, and, taken over a long period, it can be addictive. It is started with 0.25 or 0.5 mg two or three times daily, increased every 3 days by one pill to 4 mg/day. A combination of Xanax 1–3 mg/day and propanolol (Inderal) 40–160 mg/day has resulted in an almost total relief of both panic attacks and anticipatory anxiety (Sheki & Patterson, 1984). Patients, especially those on tricyclics and MAO inhibitors, should be informed that medications require weeks to take effect. The results will depend on consistency in taking the medications.

Some patients absolutely refuse to take

these medications. For these patients, relaxation therapy, systematic desensitization and then in vivo desensitization should be employed. In any case the latter therapies are almost indispensable even when drug therapy has controlled the panic. Moreover, if other links in the behavior chain are pathologically implicated, therapies bracketed to these links may productively be employed (see table 57-1). Thus group, couple, and family therapy are valuable if serious interpersonal problems exist; milieu therapy to resolve environmental difficulties; cognitive therapy for rectification of faulty attitudes, self-statements, and belief systems; and dynamically oriented, psychotherapy for personality difficulties of long standing that act as sources of continuing anxiety. In most cases psychotherapy will be needed, with a focus on interpersonal problems, such as marital conflict.

Generalized Anxiety Disorder (DSM-III-R Code 300.02)

Symptoms of a generalized anxiety reaction include restlessness, jitteriness, sighing, fidgetiness, sweating, heart pounding, sensations of tingling in the extremities, gastrointestinal symptoms, urinary frequency, a lump in the throat, flushing, great apprehensiveness, anticipation of catastrophes, fear of losing control, death fears, edginess, irritability, fatigue, and insomnia. The anticipatory expectations relate to unrealistic events or those in which possibilities are not sufficient to justify the patient's massive emotional response. In this way the anticipated happenings may be distinguished from a fear reaction that is stimulated by realistic threatening circumstances. Fears of death, disease, violence, sexual perversions, and so on are often at the basis of undifferentiated excessive anxiety, which may readily be activated by minimal unfortunate or threatening outside events, for instance, sickness in the family, the discovery on physical examination of a

minor organic ailment, or an unfortunate environmental happening. The rapid heartbeat, rise in blood pressure, chest pains, and distress in breathing may convince the victim that he or she is suffering from cardiac illness, initiating persistent visits to practitioners and specialists who may diagnose the condition as "psychosomatic," the functional nature of which the patient usually fails to believe.

Most patients with generalized anxiety are so upset by their symptoms that relief from suffering constitutes their only motivation. Because they feel helpless and frightened, they are apt to demand an authoritative, directive relationship in which they are protected and through which they seek to obtain immediate symptomatic relief. To abide by these demands, the therapist may decide to employ emergency measures, which prove temporarily successful in abating anxiety. Some measures will help bring the individual to a point where the anxiety is reduced and spontaneous reparative forces come into play (see Supportive Therapy, Chapter 9). Such supportive treatment may be all that is needed to eliminate suffering, especially if the basic ego structure is reasonably sound and has broken down under the impact of severe external stress. Palliative measures may alleviate anxiety in these cases even if the problems are internally inspired. Should supportive tactics prove to be successful, most patients will lose their incentive for further help and be content to function in their symptom-free state, even though it may be impermanent. If treatment is unsuccessful, they may lose confidence in the therapist and go elsewhere in search of relief.

It is important, therefore, to persuade the patient to accept more than supportive therapy. This may prove to be a greater task than the therapist has bargained for. Because repression is a chief defense against sources of anxiety, the patient may be unwilling to challenge habitual coping mechanisms, even though they are inadequate in dealing with the difficulty.

Treatment of pathological anxiety reactions must be adapted to their intensity, the needs and motivations of the patient, and the readiness to accept help. We now have a battery of medications that are successful in dealing with anxiety on a symptomatic level. It is always best to see if one can abate anxiety through psychosocial measures before resorting to medications, because, unless the sources of the anxiety are handled with the object of modifying or removing them, the patient will be tempted to use pills as a way of life. This is particularly important when employing the benzodiazepine drugs, which, though relatively safe and less addictive than barbiturates, are still subject to abuse. Alternatively, we may focus on vulnerable links in the behavioral chain (see Table 57-1) and use interventions that have proven helpful in dealing with these links. For example, we may in interviewing a woman with anxiety recognize that many of the patient's problems are organized around ambivalence toward a spouse. To subdue the patient with drugs, acting as if the marital situation can be bypassed, will not help the patient come to grips with the source of her trouble. Marital therapy would not preclude our dealing with any other pathogenic links in the behavior chain with suitable coordinate interventions. If she was so demoralized by anxiety that she could not use psychosocial treatments effectively, we could add anxiolytics to our therapeutic interventions.

Among the most suitable anxiolytics for achieving symptomatic stabilization in from 1 to 6 weeks are alprazolam (Xanax), 0.75 to 4.0 mg/day, diazepam (Valium), 4.0–40 mg/day, lorazepam (Ativan), 2–6 mg/day, oxazepam (Serax), 30–180 mg/day, and clorazepate (Tranxene), 15–60 mg/day. Elderly patients require a reduced dose. The actual dose is titrated to the patient's response, starting with the smallest dose and working up. We can expect some relief in from 1 to 2 weeks, with optimal effect after 6 weeks.

A new anxiolytic that undoubtedly will receive extensive testing is buspirone (BuSpar). This medication has been found to be as effective as the above drugs and to produce less drowsiness and sedation (Cohn & Wilcox, 1986).

Phobic Disorders (Phobic Neurosis, Anxiety Hysteria)

As a defense designed to control anxiety, the phobic reaction constitutes one of the most common syndromes that the psychotherapist must handle in everyday practice. When we consider the structure of a phobia, we must recognize that a maze of primary and auxiliary phenomena embrace this defense. First, the phobia, apart from the simple conditioned fear reaction, is generally a facade that conceals an underlying, earlier causative factor. Second, it is a manifestation that protects the individual from constant and intense anxiety. Third, a phobia gradually changes in its dimensions by generalizing to stimuli that are more and more remote from the initiating phobic excitant. Fourth, as the phobia spreads and circumscribes the individual's activities, the person feels increasingly undermined, self-confidence is progressively shattered, self-image is more and more devalued, and the individual may become depressed and even phobophobic. Loss of mastery revives regressive defenses and needs, including childish dependency promptings, which, if gratified, further contribute to feelings of helplessness.

Agoraphobia (DSM-III-R Code 300.22)

The most common and paralyzing phobia is agoraphobia, which usually manifests as a fear of being alone or of being adrift and helpless in public places such as shopping centers, transportation vehicles, tunnels, bridges, and elevators. In many cases the phobic reaction follows one or more experiences of severe panic while away from home. Safety is sought within the confines of one's home, and the individual becomes housebound, venturing out only in the company of a spouse, parent, or other member of the family. There is both great dependency on and hostility toward the protective agent whose own neurotic needs to control may be gratified by the patient's helplessness. In this way a mutual neurosis is nurtured and kept alive amid hypocritical protests on both sides. Therapy for agoraphobia is directed principally at the panic against which the agoraphobia is the defense. In vivo desensitization and other adjuncts, such as the antidepressants described above for panic disorders, are also indicated. If the marital or family relationship is symbiotic, marital and family therapy are indispensable. Experience teaches that unless the family member most intimately involved with the patient is also in therapy, he or she will experience disrupted homeostasis and try to undermine the patient's treatment.

Social Phobia (DSM-III Code 300.23)

Here the individual is fearful of exposing himself or herself to the scrutiny, judgment, and possible condemnation of others. Such people justify avoiding situations where their "nervousness," shyness, weakness, inferiority, or ineptitude will be detected. In the extreme form, patients apply judgmental criteria to themselves and develop a fear of manifesting any failings even when they are alone. A common fear of such individuals is of shaking, spilling food, belching, or showing other peculiarities in behavior while eating with one or more people. Stage fright is a frequent form of social phobia found in countless numbers of people, including experienced performers. Erythrophobia, or fear of blushing, and insistence that people can detect expressions on one's face that will be mis-

interpreted as a sign of "craziness," nymphomania, or homosexual interest are peculiarly resistant to reasoning even when colored movies display the patient in close-ups with normal facial expressions under varied circumstances. The patient may seem to be close to a paranoidal condition here but lack other symptoms that would justify this diagnosis. Secondary depression sometimes accompanies social phobia, stimulated by the patient's conviction of helplessness in being able to do anything about his or her reaction.

Therapy for social phobia is organized around behavior therapy, particularly desensitization, with repeated exposure to the phobic situation. Too early attempts at in vivo desensitization or flooding are not recommended since the patient may panic and thus reinforce the phobia. Assertiveness training, relaxation therapy, hypnosis, and systematic desensitization using imagery can prepare the individual for exposure to the phobic stimulus that he or she dreads. Cognitive therapy may help deal with attitudinal distortions. Group therapy and psychodrama can also be of great value in giving the individual opportunities for performance desensitization and reality testing. The benzodiazepines (e.g., Valium, Atavan) may sometimes be employed as a preliminary form of treatment. They subdue anxiety, but there is always the danger that they will become a primary shield and lead to habituation. Of value for stage fright is 40 mg of propranolol (Inderal) taken shortly before performance. It helps control the shaking, rapid heart beat, and palpitations but does not dull the mind or interfere with muscular coordination, frequent consequences of tranquilization with anxiolytics. Psychoanalytic therapy has not proven to be of much help in the usual run of social phobias, in part because most patients with social phobias are not motivated to receive such intensive help and are unable to tolerate the anxiety inherent in altering ego-syntonic personality distortions.

Analysis of pre-Oedipal stresses, in a more supportive object-relations format, is sometimes successful with motivated patients who have not responded to other therapies.

Simple Phobias (DSM-III-R Code 300.29)

Phobias of insects, dogs, mice, bats, snakes, lightning, heights, swimming, closed spaces, air travel, and the like may be conditioned-avoidance responses that are patterned after parental phobias or that followed upon anxiety-provoking experiences with the objects or situations in question (near drowning, air crash, etc.). They may yield to behavior therapy with imagery, desensitization, relaxation exercises, and gradual exposure, first to pictures of the phobic objects and situations, then to imitation objects (toys, insects, mice, etc.), and finally to in vivo desensitation and implosive therapy, perhaps at first in the presence of the therapist. A claustrophobic patient, for example, may lock oneself in a closet in the therapist's office for gradually increasing periods. Group behavior therapy with participants suffering from the same or similar phobias can accelerate treatment, especially during the phase of in vivo desensitization.

Sometimes, however, simple phobias turn out to be not so simple. In such cases anxiety over one's unconscious dangerous drives have been displaced onto external objects and situations that have become disguised symbols of the repudiated inner drives (Oedipal strivings, perverse sexual cravings, hostility, etc.). For example, a person may avoid knives and other potentially lethal objects as a defense against repressed anger. Because of its apparent protective quality, the phobia may become fixed, the patient manifesting the greatest obstinacy in facing it. The treatment of choice is dynamic psychotherapy, which in the most stubborn cases will necessitate setting up and resolving a transference neurosis using the technique of classical analysis. In some cases hypnoanalysis may expedite therapy, but this requires a subject capable of entering a somnambulistic trance (Wolberg, 1964a).

Obsessive-Compulsive Disorder (DSM-III-R Code 300.30)

In obsessive-compulsive disorders ideas, usually with obscene, violent, necrophobic, or thanatophobic content, flood the mind and liberate aversive feelings of guilt, shame, and anxiety. The phenomenon sometimes takes the form of an inner voice that commands the person to do antisocial acts. Attempts to neutralize these ego-alien thoughts may in some cases provoke certain compulsive movements or rituals, which, seemingly absurd to an observer and even to the patients themselves, temporarily relieve the painful feelings. Attempts to control or resist obsessive ideas and the compulsions they inspire generally are in vain and may even activate the obsessions. Compulsive acts that oppose rational conduct may be executed in secret. Obsessives usually chastise themselves for their weakness and betrayal of common sense. Fears of losing control, of becoming psychotic, and figuratively or literally of being possessed by demons complicate the picture and add to the victim's misery (Nemiah, 1985).

The etiology of the disorder is still obscure. There are indications that a biochemical factor of some kind exists in this illness perhaps related to serotonin imbalances. Hypothesized also is an affiliation with depression, since many patients exhibit biological markers of an affective disorder. Some authorities postulate that there are anatomical abnormalities in the cingulate gyrus and hippocampus. Though psychological mechanisms in obsessive-compulsive disorders offer themselves luxuriously to psychoanalytic inquiry, psychoanalysis and psychoanalytic therapy have failed to bring about hoped-for results in alleviating obsessive and compulsive symtoms.

Clinically, several types of obsessive patients are commonly seen (Insel, 1983). The largest number are those who fear contamination and who then indulge in washing or scrubbing rituals. Such "washers" may, to their dismay, spend a good deal of their time in the bathroom. A second large group are the "checkers," who have to check repeatedly that they have completed an act because they fear that dereliction may bring harm to themselves or others. A third group are the "stallers," who may take forever to execute a simple task; for example, the completion of normal activities such as dressing or eating may take hours. A fourth group are the "worriers," who are preoccupied with Cassandra-like fears of evil acts and catastrophes that are about to happen; usually patients do not perform rituals to neutralize them. Although each patient exhibits the unique traits of his or her personality structure, obsessive persons demonstrate remarkably similar behaviors in every country the world over.

Many therapies have been unsuccessfully employed to bring relief to these suffering and handicapped individuals. Of all treatments, behavior therapy has scored the greatest successes in controlling obsessive and compulsive symptoms (Rachman et al, 1973; Rachman, 1976; Wilson TG, 1976; Marks et al, 1975; Marks, 1981; Foa et al, 1985). The most effective method (scoring up to 80 percent benefit) is in vivo desensitization with practice sessions of (1) deliberate prolonged exposure (45 minutes to 2 hours) to thoughts, fantasies, and situations that inspire disturbing symptoms; and (2) coordinate blocking of compulsive responses (hand washing, checking, ritualistic behavior) that have temporarily served to neutralize anxiety in the past. In implementing this approach, which consists of 10 to 20 sessions, graded exposure to increasingly intense stimuli from 45 minutes to 2

hours and the absolute blocking of responses for long periods (sometimes for days) requires a motivated patient willing to endure the anxiety and suffering that such restrictions entail.

Obviously the patient will protest vociferously and express dread of being exposed to dangers. It will require tact, understanding, and great persuasion, utilizing the working relationship skillfully, to convince a patient to try this intervention.

The treatment protocol evolved by Stekete and Foa (1985) for exposure and response prevention details the sequence of treatment and contains useful appendices and a case study that illustrates the application of specific procedures. Approximately 3 to 6 hours are spent in gathering information and in treatment planning. The patient is then given a full explanation as to what to expect. The scenes to be used in imagery (flooding), the situations to be met in in vivo desensitization, and the responses and rituals to be prevented are delineated. A decision is made as to whether the patient's home or a hospital is to be used, and the aides (family members, friends, nurses) to assist the patient in the assignments are chosen. Since massed sessions produce better results, a minimum of 3 sessions weekly are given. The total number of sessions are between 15 and 20. At each session the first few minutes are spent in discussing what has happened since the last visit. Next, the patient is exposed to the target thoughts and fantasies and is enjoined to try to fantasize that he or she is actually in the imagined situation. Every 10 minutes, levels of anxiety are monitored. This exercise, which lasts from 1 to 2 hours, is at first highly anxiety provoking, but eventually the anxiety lessens. In advance of the sessions, a series of five graded upsetting scenes are prepared to be presented in low to high order, and each is used until the anxiety diminishes greatly or is gone. After this exposure, the patient is confronted by the therapist with the situations he or she fears most (touching dirt, being prevented from checking a gas stove, etc.) and the therapist models normal behavior (e.g., touching dirt and refraining from washing). Projected slides, pictures, movies, or video recordings may be used to convey the feared situations (funerals, homosexuality, etc.) if the actual situation cannot be confronted. In the case of "washers," no washing of hands is allowed (sometimes for as long as several days), and only a brief shower is permitted every fifth day. In the last few sessions, the patient is instructed as to normal modes of behavior. Thus "washers" are enjoined to wash their hands only before meals, after bathroom use, and after handling especially dirty objects. Following the intense treatment period, a self-exposure maintenance program (practiced at least weekly) is prescribed as a preventive measure. When necessary, interpersonal skills training, assertiveness training, marital therapy, and family therapy may be prescribed. A follow-up self-help group may be valuable. Only when absolutely essential should hospitalization be prescribed since many provocative situations are likely to be absent in a hospital setting.

As accessory therapy, relaxation exercises may periodically be employed for tension relief (Jacobson, 1974; Benson, 1974). Another technique that some patients find useful is "thought stoppage" (Wolpe, 1958). Here thoughts to be controlled are identified and deliberately practiced at the same time as one shouts "Stop" and perhaps coordinately bangs one's hand against one's thigh. Or one may wear a rubber band around the wrist and flick it to deliver a painful stimulus. Attention should then be diverted elsewhere. Systematic desensitization (Wolpe, 1958) may also occasionally be effective if tension is high. The patient may be enjoined to engage in regular practice sessions of fantasies, such as being exposed to extremes (often to a most ridiculous degree) of his or her symptoms and perhaps their consequences. The logotherapeutic technique of paradoxical intension (*q.v.*) is a form of this type of therapy. At home the patient may be requested to engage in such varied tension-relieving exercises as keeping a diary record of accomplishments (such as response resistance or blockage) and his or her reactions.

Because depression has been so frequently observed in obsessive patients, a variety of drugs have been tried, including clonidine, loxapine, and the tricyclic antidepressants. The latter class of drugs has proven especially beneficial both for their antidepressant and antiobsessional effects (Mavissakalian et al, 1985). Clomipramine (Anafranil) in particular has proven to be valuable and in many cases has enabled an intractable patient to become cooperative. This medication appears to have a specific antiobsessional effect that is distinct from its antidepressive property (Singh & Sexena, 1977). I have found clomipramine almost indispensable in working with some obsessive-compulsive patients since by muting symptoms motivation is greatly improved. The initial dose of clomipramine (which is available in Canada, Mexico, and Europe and may soon be released in the United States) is 25 mg three times daily, increased to 150 mg/day as required (maximum dose 200 mg and 300 mg for hospitalized patients). Adolescent and elderly patients should be given 20–30 mg daily, increased by 10 mg daily, if necessary, depending on response and tolerance. A history of glaucoma, liver damage, or blood dyscrasias or pregnancy contraindicates treatment. Use of a MAO inhibitor drug following the use of clomipramine necessitates a delay of 14 days, the same as for any other antidepressant drug. Anticholinergic effects as with other antidepressants, are to be expected. In some cases a combination of clomipramine and clonopin reinforces the beneficial effect. Physical examinations and blood tests should be done periodically. The combination of clomipramine and in vivo desensitization is at this date the best treatment for the symptomatic relief of obsessive-compulsive illness.

Any therapist who believes that the relief of obsessions and compulsions in the obsessive patient is all that is necessary is, however, in for an unpleasant surprise. Although dealing with the biological and conditioning links in the behavioral chain is important, this will not resolve all the problems encountered by the patient any more than relieving painful and distracting hemorrhoids will cure a coordinate sinus condition. Additional implicated links in the behavioral chain (see Table 57-1) require attention since the troubles they cause will sometimes cry out for help. In certain patients, symptom alleviation enhances the chances for a reasonable adjustment, including the usual evasions and compromises essential in our society. Other patients may find their liberated energies merely intensify their interpersonal, environmental, and intrapsychic problems. Here interventions related to these areas of trouble are indicated. Counseling, interpersonal therapy, group therapy, marital therapy, family therapy, and milieu therapy are indicated for dealing with difficulties in special areas. Cognitive and dynamic approaches enable the individual to give a more authentic meaning to his or her symptoms than the misinterpretations usually assigned to them (such as that he or she is destined to psychosis, sexual perversion, cancer, murderous acting-out, etc.). Recognition that fantasies and impulses are manifestations that possess a symbolic significance and that they do not have to be taken literally can be reassuring to many patients, even if it is not completely curative.

The great problem is not only how to deal with the unexpected outbursts of nascent anxiety, which become particularly pronounced when obsessional ideas periodically break loose, but, more significant, how to manage the hostile, disturbing char-

acter structure that is a component of the disorder in many patients.

Obsessive-compulsive neurosis does not respond to insight therapy as well as do other neurotic syndromes. It can be done, of course, but the therapist must be extremely skilled in handling the transference and must have much fortitude to tolerate the vicissitudes that will come up in the course of treatment. Years of futile probing into the unconscious and careful unravelment of the sources and meanings of rituals may accomplish little. The obsessional personality is an expert in "one-upmanship." He or she engages in a verbal tug-of-war, must get in the last word, undermines psychotherapy as a process, and derogates the ability of the therapist to provide help. Yet obsessional patients bitterly complain that they are not being helped. What is important in therapy is to deal with the immediate transactions between therapist and patient and to prevent the patient from entering into gambits through which he or she can conspire to wrest control from the therapist. The therapy for compulsive-obsessive personality disorders must, therefore, take into account the patient's dependence, profoundly hostile impulses toward people, need for detachment, tendency to "isolate" intellect from feeling, and the magical frame of reference in which the patient's ideas operate. Salzman (1966) points out that the obsessive-compulsive defense of persistent doubting, negativism, unwillingness to commit oneself, and striving for perfection, omnipotence, and omniscience are attempts to control the universe and to guarantee one's safety, security, and survival. This defense acts as a block to constructive learning. Free association and concern with past memories are used as a screen behind which the obsessional person conceals his or her coping maneuvers. According to Salzman (1983), what is essential in working with obsessional patients is to be continually aware of their obstructive personality characteristics; their defensiveness, which causes them to reject the therapist's observations; their need for control; their striving for perfection; and their doubt, ambivalence, and tendency to obfuscate issues. This calls for great activity on the part of the therapist, a focus on the present, a need to deal with the patient's grandiosity, continual reexamination of issues so as to facilitate working-through, and "risk-taking" by the therapist.

Most therapists find working with the patient on an analytic level a most difficult and frustrating experience. Classical analysis is usually ineffective and therapy can become interminable as the patient and therapist become locked into a sadomasochistic relationship, very much like a bad marriage, that can go on for years. This does not mean that one has to cast a dynamic approach to the winds. I have found it helpful with many obsessive cases to work dynamically with derivative rather than nuclear conflicts, showing the patients, how the characterological distortions of dependency, hostility, low feelings of independence, devalued self-esteem, and tendencies toward detachment operate in producing disruptions in their relationships with people and their attitudes toward themselves. Patients must be shown how their personality characteristics inevitably create the stress and generate the anxiety that initiate many of their disruptive defenses. Although a patient may seemingly accept such explanations and interpretations, they will at first have little effect on his or her behavior. The therapist will have to demonstrate the workings of the patient's dynamics in his or her everyday life over and over again until a tiny chink occurs in the patient's defensive armor. Most penetrating will be the elucidation of how the patient's personality problems display themselves in the transference with the therapist. A tremendous amount of dogged perseverance will be necessary which can

tax the tolerance of the most empathic therapist. Countertransference must be watched assiduously and used as constructively as the therapist can manage given the undisciplined, resistive, and helter-skelter behavior of the patient. Therapists who have the stamina and forebearance to work with their patients beyond the profits of symptom relief toward alteration of the character structure will have to resign themselves to the battle conditions of tempestuous long-term therapy, which, while unnerving in the beginning, may very well prove worthwhile in the end. Some helpful leads may be found in the section in this chapter on the therapy of personality disorders. The articles by Barnett (1972), E. K. Schwartz (1972), Salzman (1966, 1983), and Suess (1972) contain interesting pointers.

The prognosis for obsessive-compulsive neuroses will depend upon the severity of the condition and the residual ego strength. It will also depend upon the length of time the patient has been ill. In some cases obsessive-compulsive patterns appear to be of relatively recent duration, the compulsive difficulty having developed as a result of external pressures and problems to which the patient could not adjust. The prognosis for these patients is much more favorable than it is for patients who have been ill since puberty. Some psychiatrists recommend that patients who do not respond to medications, behavior therapy, and psychotherapy and whose anxiety and suffering become unendurable ultimately submit to leucotomy, which, in some cases, will control symptoms when everything else fails. Tippin and Haun (1982) report that more than 69 of 110 obsessive patients who had modified leucotomy operations were symptom-free or improved and needed no further treatment. Understandably, this radical form of therapy will be resisted and should not be used except under extraordinary circumstances.

Posttraumatic Stress Disorder (DSM-III-R Code 309.89)

Under unusually harsh and catastrophic conditions of stress, therapists may confront reactions of great physiological and cognitive severity, beyond what we encounter in the face of such adversities as bereavement, marital conflict, chronic illness, and other calamities (see Chapter 59). These conditions include such natural disasters as earthquakes, floods, hurricanes, famine, transportation and industrial accidents, rape, assault, torture, and bombings. For the most part, posttraumatic stress disorders are mainly consequent to the disasters of war. Especially prominent is combat fatigue among soldiers of the participating armies. The most common reaction is an anxiety state characterized by tension, emotional instability, somatic symptoms, insomnia, and nightmarish battle dreams. Less common are conversion, depressive, and psychophysiological reactions. Acute temporary psychoticlike episodes may also occur.

Knowledge of the dynamics of war neurosis made certain preventive measures possible in World War II. Soldiers who had had training that had made them feel they could defend themselves under all circumstances, who had been shown that they had adequate weapons of attack, who had confidence in their leaders, and who had obtained sufficient indoctirnation and morale building were best prepared to resist a breakdown. An important element in prevention was group identification. Cooperation with others was essential, and the individual had to be made to feel that he was part of a team and that he had enough of an idea of the battle situation and the planned strategy so that he would not be caught by surprise.

The incidence of war neuroses is proportionate to shattered morale and to feelings of isolation from fellow soldiers. An organized body of men fighting for a cause that they consider just can best overcome war stress and hardship.

Adequate information regarding the significance of the conflict, assignment to units with congenial companions, fair discipline, commanding officers who merit respect, periodic relief from duty in the combat zone, and confidence in the assigned weapons all contribute to better morale and greater stress tolerance. Teaching soldiers that fear is normal and that one can function with it may be reassuring. A history of previous emotional disorders, an unstable family situation, and poor socioeconomic conditions in civilian life are usually though not always bad prognostic signs. Some solders maladjusted in civilian life relish the conditions and even dangers of army life. Upon termination of army service, having adjusted adequately up to this time, a certain number of such individuals are unable to adjust to civilian life. A phenomenon that was noted among officers and enlisted personnel in Korea and Vietnam was separation anxiety, which developed when the end of their service was near and the solder had to leave his companions. This occurred even among soldiers in combat units. The group identification which held the individuals together was reluctantly given up.

In spite of preventive attempts, stress reactions of varying degrees of intensity may occur, particularly in response to precarious conditions of combat. A more vulnerable soldier may manifest panicky reactions during which thinking gets disorganized, nonproductive somatic symptoms become pronounced, and behavior tends to become maladaptive, exposing the individual to even more danger. In combat situations during fierce shelling, for example, the soldier may flee safety areas and run wildly away, exposing himself to shrapnel and gunfire. Overwhelming stress may produce a temporary shocklike reaction followed by what seems to be recovery.

Even the most stable combatants are

apt to exhibit a good deal of muscle tension, faintness, giddiness, tachycardia, palpitations, shaking, and tremors during an engagement. The bravest soldier will experience fear, which prevents him from throwing caution to the winds. In many cases gross stress reactions are brought on by killings, fatigue, loss of sleep, hunger, and cold over a prolonged period. Homesickness, uncertainty about the future, physical discomfort, and sexual deprivation may be as traumatic as actual engagement in combat. Reactions will usually follow responses to past situations of acute stress. One of the most important factors in subduing these reactions is good leadership, including thoughtful directing of activities toward maintaining morale.

Experience in treating gross stress reactions in the last war indicated that removing soldiers from forward areas to hospitals in the rear tended to aggravate the difficulty. Good results were obtained when treatment was organized around the expectation of returning to duty. It has been observed that an aversive attitude toward "nervousness" and "weakness" by frontline troops acts as a deterrent to neurotic combat reactions. Expectations that a soldier who "breaks down" will be moved away from the battle zone, released from the army, and perhaps compensated for his disability encourage neurotic symptoms. Group identification tends to reassure the individual and bolster morale. The need to be accepted by the group is one of the most important safeguards against "breaking down." A soldier removed from his unit and sent to a hospital is a candidate for psychological disability, which will stir up guilt feelings and devalued self-esteem. The security of the hospital setting paradoxically prevents him from making a rapid recovery. During the last war, rest outside of a hospital, good food, and the opportunity to verbalize fears and other feelings to a reassuring person proved most successful. Tranquilization, narcosyntheses, and hyp-nosis in serious cases were employed with rapid success in susceptible subjects. Combat exhaustion, if treated early, did not necessarily result in neurosis. A moderate anxiety state cleared up in 24 hours with rest, reassurance, and some tranquilization if needed. It was assumed that the soldier would go back to the front. Where there was reluctance to return to battle duty, appeals to patriotism, courage, and "not letting one's buddies down" often built up the person's courage and determination. Encouragement to verbalize fear and disgust was vital, since the soldier in this way released tension and discovered that others shared his anxieties.

The value of respecting the soldier's "gripes" in building morale has long been recognized. The role of the leader is important, too, and an intrepid commanding officer has always been of great service. It is amazing how often a change in attitude in a soldier can prevent neurotic collapse. Under constructive leadership, a soldier has the best chance of pulling himself together and of dealing with his need to protect himself from danger while discharging his duties honorably to preserve acceptance from his peers.

In many cases an incubation period ensues during which what Kolb (1982) has termed "secondary reflective cognitive consequences of the catastrophic experiences" surface in the form of survival guilt, shame, and heightened sensitivity to stimuli directly or remotely resembling the initial stressful assault. Mardi Horowitz (1976), in pointing out this reaction, has emphasized the importance of existential threat as a basic cognitive factor in posttraumatic states.

The posttraumatic reaction may occur within 6 months of the trauma (the acute subtype) or after 6 months and even after several years (the chronic or delayed subtype). Often it develops after the individual has become stabilized and has resumed habitual functioning. Reactions here draw upon latent personality strengths and on the degree of repression that has sealed off appropriate emotional reactions to the offensive stressor. After the individual has apparently digested the implications of what has happened, he may respond with depression, bouts of anxiety, restlessness, aggression, guilt feelings, obsessions, insomnia, nightmares, fugue states, and amnesia, which may continue indefinitely. In the majority of cases, however, an adaptation is made, even though certain symptoms continue, and, after a period of adjustment, these symptoms may become fixed. In some instances detachment, aggression, startle reactions to noise, muscle tension, tremors, depression, insomnia, battle nightmares, psychosomatic complaints, and bouts of anxiety may be very difficult to handle. In serious cases, outbursts of violence, detachment, and paranoia may interfere with a constructive social adjustment, Guilt feelings about one's behavior in the army, particularly related to the killings and personal feelings of cowardice, may sponsor a good deal of recrimination and self-punishment.

Therapy for posttraumatic stress disorders may require some time, especially if alcohol or drugs have been employed to quiet the symptoms. Even when these are brought under control, a good deal of working-through of the guilt feelings may be required. Hendon et al. (1983) have evolved a useful questionnaire as a first step, along with an excellent outline for a five-session evaluation of the problem. Most important, a provision should be made for continuing therapy after the initial sessions have opened the door to suppressed feelings. Working through such feelings is important. Otherwise the patient will be left in a more vlunerable state than before. Once a treatment is started, exploration of the meaning of the combat experiences and the devices the veteran uses in covering up his guilt and pain are in order.

Treatment of stress reactions in civilian life (hurricanes, floods, explosions,

mass bombings, etc.) should be started as soon as possible, since delay permits the neurosis to become more highly organized and allows the secondary gain element to take hold. First aid helps victims of disasters to return to proper functioning in a short time. Preventive measures are of incalculable value if a disaster is anticipated and potential victims are apprised of dangers as well as suitable protective and ameliorative actions that may be taken. Practice drills under simulated disaster conditions, faithfully repeated, help to establish appropriate patterns if and when emergencies occur.

Responses of people to both unexpected and expected dangers will vary depending on the specific meaning of the danger situation to them and their residual stabilities and habitual coping mechanisms in the face of stress. They will also respond uniquely to any warning signals. Among the gravest dangers to the group are the wildly uncontrolled panic reactions of a few unstable individuals, which can have a contagious influence on the rest of the group. If the leader knows in advance which members are apt to manifest unrestrained fear, he or she may select them in advance and assign them definite tasks so as to divert their energies.

Even with drills, exercises, and warning signals, the impact of a disaster is bound to provoke immediate reactions of anxiety and confusion. These, however, should soon be replaced by adaptive responses encouraged during the practice sessions. As soon as the violent impact of the disaster has subsided, organized activities will take place. Working together and helping the more physically and emotionally disabled has a profoundly reassuring effect. People who are unable to compose themselves may need special treatment. For example, a person who shows blind panic will require firm restraining by two or three people to avoid spreading panic throughout the group. Drug therapy may be necessary as described in the section on dealing with panic reactions in emergencies (see Chapter 58).

In treating disaster victims whose neurotic or psychotic responses do not subside with the termination of the emergency, the first principle is to permit them to verbalize feelings; the second, to accept their reactions, no matter how unreasonable they may seem. Supportive therapy coupled with sedation or tranquilization will usually suffice to restore the person to his or her previous state. Imagery plays an important part in working through these disorders (Horowitz MJ, 1970, 1976; Brett 1985) and may serve as a productive therapeutic vehicle, especially in hypnosis.

If a patient has a continuing stress reaction that threatens to become chronic, narcotherapy (*q.v.*) and hypnotherapy (*q.v.*) are often effective for purposes of symptom removal. In instances where anxiety is extreme, one may utilize an "uncovering" type of technique. Here hypnosis and narcotherapy are also of help. The recovery of amnesias, and the reliving of the traumatic scene in action or verbalization, may have an ameliorative or curative effect.

While hypnotherapy and narcotherapy accomplish approximately the same results, the emotions accompanying hypnotherapy are often much more vivid, and the cartharctic effect consequently greater, than with narcotherapy. There are other advantages to hypnosis. The induction is usually brought about easily without the complication of injections and without posttherapeutic somnolence. Additionally, hypnotic suggestions are capable of demonstrating to the patient more readily his or her ability to gain mastery of functions. On the other hand, narcotherapy is easier to employ and does not call for any special skills.

If it is essential to remove an amnesia, the patient is encouraged under hypnosis or narcosis to talk about the events immediately preceding the traumatic episode and

to lead into the episode slowly, reliving the scene as if it were happening again. Frequently the patient will approach the scene and then block, or he or she may actually awaken. Repeated trance inductions often break through this resistance. Also, it will be noted that the abreactive effect will increase as the patient describes the episode repeatedly. Apparently the powerful emotions that are bound down are subject to greater repression than the actual memories of the event.

Hadfield's (1920) original technique is still useful. The patient is hypnotized and instructed that when the therapist's fingers are placed on the patient's forehead, the patient will picture the experiences that caused the present breakdown. This usually produces a vivid recollection of the traumatic event with emotions of fear, rage, despair, and helplessness. The patient often spontaneously relives the traumatic scene with a tremendous cathartic effect. If the patient hesitates, the therapist must encourage a detailed description of the scenes dominating the patient's mind. This is the first step in therapy and must be repeated for a number of sessions until the restored memory is complete. The second step is the utilization of hypnosis to readjust the patient to the traumatic experience. The experience must be worked through, over and over again, until the patient accepts it during hypnosis and remembers it upon awakening. Persuasive suggestions are also given, directed at increasing assurance and self-confidence. After this the emotional relationship to the therapist is analyzed at a conscious level to prevent continuance of the dependency tie.

Horsley (1943) has mentioned that when the ordinary injunctions to recall a traumatic scene fail, several reinforcing methods can be tried. The first has to do with commanding the patient to remember, insisting that he or she will not leave the room until memory is completely restored for the traumatic events. The second method is that of soothing, coaxing, and encouraging a total recall ("You are about to remember the troubled scenes that will remind you of your experiences.") If this is unsuccessful, the patient is told that although the memory has not yet come through, it will upon awakening reveal itself in any way the patient sees fit. Instruction to recall more details in a dream the same or the next night is given.

Various hypnoanalytic procedures, such as dramatization, regression and revivification, play therapy, automatic writing, and mirror gazing, may be utilized to recover an obstinate amnesia (Wolberg, 1964a). The reaction of patients to the recall of repressed experiences varies. Some patients act out the traumatic scene, getting out of bed, charging about the room, ducking to avoid the attacking objects and people. Other patients live through the traumatic episode without getting out of bed. Some individuals collapse with anxiety; they should be reassured and encouraged to go on. If the patient voices hostility, he or she should be given an opportunity to express grievances and dislikes. Clarification of feelings of injustice may afford considerable relief.

It must be remembered that the object in therapy is to dissipate feelings of helplessness and of being menaced by a world that the patient no longer trusts. The sense of mastery and the ability to readjust oneself to life must be restored. The best reactions to hypnosis are obtained when it is executed as close in time to the trauma as possible. This may prevent organization of the condition into a chronic psychoneurosis. Follow-up therapy is essential, with integration on a waking level of the material brought up during the trance. If the anxieties relating to the disaster have precipitated hysterial, phobic, compulsive, and other reactions characteristic of the ways that the patient has dealt with anxiety in everyday life, long-term insight therapy will usually be required.

In chronic stress reactions, treatment is difficult because of the high degree of organization that has taken place and because of the strong secondary gain element involving monetary compensation and dependency. The recovery of amnesias should always be attempted, but even where successful, this may not at all influence the outcome. An incentive must be created in the patient to function free of symptoms, even at the expense of forfeiting disability compensations, which in comparison to emotional health may be shown to be diminutive indeed. (See also Chapter 59; Crisis Intervention, Chapter 57; and pertinent parts of Chapter 58 on emergencies.)

DISSOCIATIVE DISORDER (HYSTERICAL NEUROSIS, DISSOCIATIVE TYPE)

Dissociative disorders manifest themselves in disturbances of consciousness, memory, and identity. In *multiple personality disorder (DSM III-R Code 300.14)* a dramatic interruption of the habitual personality is periodically produced by the intrusion of a seemingly foreign personality or personalities that inspire variant behaviors often at odds with the usual patterns of the individual. In *psychogenic fugue (DSM-III Code 300.13)* the person wanders off away from home with the assumption of a new identity and amnesia for the previous identity. In *psychogenic amnesia (DSM-III Code 300.12)* disturbances in recall are characteristic. These blank spots may occur without identifiable cause or may follow an accident or catastrophic incident. In *depersonalization disorder (or depersonalization neurosis) DSM-III-Code 300.60)* the reality sense is impaired with feelings of detachment from oneself.

The basic defense employed in dissociation reactions is repression. Therapeutic techniques are best organized to resolve the repression and deal with inner conflicts. Transference analysis, especially the working through of a transference neurosis, is ideally suited to therapy of this disorder, but may not be possible for practical reasons and because of patient resistance. When transference analysis cannot be used, a less intensive psychoanalytically oriented psychotherapy may be employed. From the viewpoint of mere handling and removal of symptoms, hypnosis is classically of value. Although hysterical symptoms can often be eliminated in relatively few hypnotic sessions, the dramatic, infantile, and self-dramatizing personality constellation associated with this reaction will require prolonged psychotherapy, preferably along reconstructive lines. Unfortunately, even though insight therapy is accepted by the patient, a great many impediments will become manifest during the course of treatment in the form of intellectual inhibitions and other devices to reinforce repression.

Whereas insight therapy is the best treatment for this condition, circumstances of obstinate resistance, faulty motivation, and profound secondary gain may prevent any other than a supportive approach.

Symptom removal by authoritative suggestion, with or without hypnosis, is occasionally indicated, particularly where the symptom produces great personal discomfort and interferes with the individual's social and economic adjustment. Some symptoms serve a minimal defensive purpose in binding anxiety. The inconvenience to the patient of such symptoms is an important incentive toward their abandonment. If the symptom constitutes a plea for help, love, and reassurance on the basis of helplessness, the therapist, by ordering cessation of symptoms, virtually assures the patient of support and love without the need to utilize symptoms for this purpose. Should the patient sense that his or her demands are not being fulfilled, a return of symptoms or histrionic acting out may be expected.

Although some symptoms vanish with a strong authoritarian suggestive approach, one must not overestimate the permanency of the apparent cure since the original moti-

vations that sponsored the symptom are not altered in the least and a relapse is always possible. Consequently, whenever the therapist can do so, the patient should be prepared for future therapy by explaining the purposeful nature of the symptom and its source in unconscious conflict.

Since hysteria often represents a reaction to unpleasant circumstances that stimulate inner conflicts, a guidance approach is sometimes utilized in appropriate cases to adjust the patient to environmental demands from which he or she cannot escape and to help the patient modify existing remediable situational difficulties. It may be possible to get a hysterical individual to make compromises with the environment so that he or she will not be inclined to overreact to current stresses. Here, too, an attempt must be made to acquaint the person with the fact that the symptoms, though inspired by external difficulties, are actually internally sponsored. Once the patient accepts this fact, therapy along insight lines may be possible.

The treatment of hysteria through hypnotic symptom removal and by guidance therapy are least successful if the symptom serves the purpose of providing intense substitutive gratification for sexual and hostile impulses.

Difficulty will also be encountered if the symptom tends to reinforce the repression of a traumatic memory or conflict, as in amnesia. The extent of amnesia varies. It may involve a single painful experience in the past, or it may include a fairly wide segment of life. It may actually spread to a point where the person loses his or her identity and forgets the past completely. Amnesia serves the defensive purpose of shielding the individual from anxiety. The intractibility of an amnesia, consequently, is related to the amount of anxiety bound down and to the ego resources that are available for coping with the liberated anxiety. The fear of being overcome by anxiety may be so great that an impenetrable block to recall will exist despite all efforts to reintegrate the person to past memories. Indeed, the fear of uncovering a memory may be so strong that the person will resist trance induction.

When resistance to hypnosis is encountered, a light barbiturate narcosis, either oral or intravenous (see the section on Narcotherapy), may remove the block. A trance, once induced, is deepened, and a posthypnotic suggestion is given the patient that he or she will henceforth be responsive to hypnosis without narcosis.

It must again be emphasized that, although certain hysterical symptoms may be treated rapidly through short-term supportive treatment, the basic personality problems associated with the hysterical disorder require a considerable period of reconstructive therapy.

SOMATOFORM DISORDERS

A number of psychophysiological autonomic and visceral disorders are included in this category, namely, somatization disorder, somatoform pain disorder, hypochondriasis (or hypochondriacal neurosis), body dysmorphic disorder, and conversion disorder (hysterical neurosis, conversion type). In *somatization disorder (DSM-III-R Code 300.81)*, the patient presents a variety of somatic complaints resulting in frequent consultations with physicians. Despite batteries of negative tests, and medical reassurance that no organic basis exists for the symptoms, the patient is never fully convinced that this is so. Such "psychosomatic" or "psychophysiological" manifestations are complicated by a depressive and anxiety overlay, which adds to the suffering of the individual. An exaggerated form of this symptomatology is found in *hypochondriasis (or hypochondriacal neurosis) DSM III-R Code 300.70*. Here the symptoms, though intense, are still not of a delusional nature, and some appeal to reason is possible. A special condition in this category is preoccupation with presumed defects in the appearance of one's face and body in the absence of any real anomaly *(body dysmorphic disorder [dysmorphobia])* that may drive the victim to a succession of plastic surgeons for correction that never comes about. Where pain for over six months constitutes the complaint factor and persists in the absence of organic pathology, we may be dealing with a *somatoform pain disorder (DSM-III-R Code 307.80)*. This must be differentiated from a *conversion disorder (or hysterical neurosis, conversion type (DSM-III-R Code 300.11)*, which usually takes the form of a neurologic disease (paralysis, aphonia, visual disorder, anesthesia, astasia-abasia, and hysterical contractions) or of such morbidities as persistent vomiting, false pregnancy (pseudocyesis) and other peculiar symptoms that are basically symbolic manifestations of inner conflict. In many conversion syndromes a casual attitude (la belle indifférence) accompanies the outwardly alarming symptoms. Somatoform disorders are often rooted in disturbances in the personality organization; some are engendered by defects in the earliest contacts of the infant with the mother. The personality structure of the patient, consequently, contains dependent, hostile, and masochistic elements that tend to obstruct a good working relationship. Because the ego is more or less fragile, anxiety, mobilized by the transference and by interpretation, may be intolerable. Insight therapy may, therefore, have to be delayed in favor of discreet supportive techniques during which the patient is permitted to relate dependently to the therapist.

The negative elements of the relationship with the therapist must constantly be resolved, and the therapist must be alert to hostile manifestations, which the patient will perhaps try to conceal. Once a good working relationship is established, exploration of inner strivings, needs, and conflicts with cautious interpretations may be attempted. Most patients with somatoform disorders find it difficult or impossible to think abstractly, however, and revelations of conflict seem to do little good. They cannot seem to describe their affects and to relate their fantasies, and they fail to respond to free association and interpretation (Nemiah, 1971). Exaggeration of the patient's physical symptoms is a common sign of resistance. When symptoms increase in intensity, the patient may be tempted to leave therapy. Tratment is generally a long-term proposition, since the deep personality problem associated with the symptoms resolves itself slowly. Essentially, therapy may follow the design for the management of personality disorders (q.v.).

A constant danger during insight therapy is the unleashing of excessive quantities of anxiety, usually the result of too speedy symptom removal or too rapid dissipation of defenses. Often the somatic disturbance represents the most acceptable avenue available to the patient for the discharge of anxiety and hostility. Because the ego has been unable to handle these emotions on a conscious level, the mechanism of repression is invoked. When coping devices are threatened without a coordinate strengthening of the ego and the person becomes prematurely aware of unacceptable conflicts and strivings, there is definite danger of precipitating a crisis. The patient may release such intense anxiety that he or she will employ symptomatic contingencies to bind this emotion. The patient may, for instance, develop depressive or compulsive symptoms or display detachment and other characterological defenses. Anxiety may, nevertheless, get out of hand and shatter the ego in fragile personalities even to the point of precipitating a psychosis. In hysterical conversion disorders symptoms may astonishingly be temporarily dissipated by strong authoritative commands as during hypnosis. Little impact is registered on the underlying personality distortions.

It may be impossible to do more for the patient than to give supportive therapy. For instance, persuasion and guidance may enable the patient to organize his or her life around the defects and liabilities, to avoid situations that arouse conflict and hostility, and to attain, at least in part, a sublimation of basic needs. The object here is to bolster the ego to a point where it can handle damaging emotions more rationally as well as to improve interpersonal relationships so that hostility and other disturbing emotions are not constantly being generated. In some instances such therapies help to liberate the individual from the vicious cycle of neurosis, facilitating externalization of interests, increasing self-confidence, and indicating ways of discharging emotions. Minor tranquilizers, such as Librium and Valium, may be administered periodically if symptoms are especially harsh. Considerable relief from symptoms may be obtained through relaxation exercises, meditation, hypnosis, and biofeedback (see Chapter 56, pages 965–972). Behavior therapy works better than dynamic psychotherapy.

The therapeutic relationship is kept at as positive a level as possible, an attempt being made to show the patient that the symptoms are not fortuitous, but that a causal relation exists between symptoms and difficulties in dealing with life. The circumstances under which symptoms become exaggerated are investigated with the objective of determining areas of failure in interpersonal functioning. Once a pattern is discerned, its significance and origin are explored. Finally, the patient is encouraged to put into action the retrained attitudes toward life and people. In some cases sufficient ego strength may be developed to make psychoanalytically oriented psychotherapy possible.

Where the patient is coordinately under the care of an internist, cooperation between the therapist and internist will improve the results.

PERSONALITY DISORDERS

Personality problems plague every human being. They are an inevitable consequence of cultural and family abberations that cannot help but influence child-rearing practices. The great majority of people manage to live with and around disturbing personality problems and to make a reasonable adjustment to everyday pressures and responsibilities. When problems become intolerably distressful, however, maladjustment may ensue.

Personality disorders encompass a heterogeneous group of traits, tendencies, and patterns of behavior that impair social and occupational functioning. Some of these disorders have a long history dating back to childhood. In the DSM-IIIR classification a number of syndromes fit this description: (1) Disruptive Behavior Disorders (conduct disorder, attention-deficit hyperactivity, oppositional-defiant disorder), (2) Anxiety Disorders of Childhood (separation anxiety disorders, avoidant disorders of childhood or adolescence, overanxious disorder), (3) Eating Disorders (Anorexia nervosa, bulimia nervosa, pica, rumination disorder of infancy), (4) Gender Identity Disorders (gender identity disorder of childhood, transsexualism, (5) Tic Disorders, (6) Disorders of Elimination, (7) Other Speech Disorders, (8) Other Disorders (reactive attachment disorder, stereotyping/habit disorder, elective mutism, identity disorder). Some of these disorders may in history-taking be identified as early manifestations of the pathology for which the patient now seeks help. In many, perhaps most cases, we have problems in tracing the histories of personality disorders because the individual usually forgets, conceals, distorts, or rationalizes early difficulties.

Urgent, inflexible, "ego-syntonic," and resistive to change, personality disorders interfere drastically with adjustment. There may be some awareness of the nature of the problem but it cannot seem to be controlled.

When a patient presents for therapy, the complaint is generally a disturbing symptom or a stressful event that has upset the habitual equilibrium. Most patients do not see the connection between their personality operations and their symptoms at the beginning of therapy. A too early em-

phasis on such a connection will tend to be confusing. It is important to consider that personality is the machinery through which the individual regulates his or her relationships with life and people. Individuals regard their traits as integral a part of themselves as their skin, and a premature effort to peel away traits that are disruptive will be staunchly resisted. Why this is so is not difficult to understand. During development, the individual evolves defenses to cope with stresses brought about by hurtful or depriving circumstances. Such defenses endure as a way of life far beyond their period of usefulness. They become welded into the intrapsychic structure, and the original events that initiated them are repressed and more or less relegated to unconscious oblivion. In adult life, they nevertheless continue to operate insidiously, independent of reality. Individuals may even attempt to create conditions that will justify their reactions, as if they seek to master a challenge and to complete the unfinished business of their past.

Treatment with the goal of some reconstructive change is a long-term proposition. It cannot be completed in 6 or 20 or even 40 sessions. It requires detailed work during which the patient is brought to an awareness of the nature of his or her problem and its investment in past history. Once some insight is achieved, the working-through process slowly takes place, aided by homework away from the therapist's office in the crucible of life experience itself. Permanent change may require several years of dedicated treatment. A sequence of operations usually takes place: (1) the disorder is clearly identified; (2) the consequences of the patient's behavior are delineated; (3) motivation to alter offensive patterns are developed; (4) exploration of the origins and purpose of the disorder may be required; (5) modes of rectification of attitudes and a reconditioning of behavior are designed; and (6) termination of treatment is carefully structured.

In the treatment of a personality disorder, we may accordingly execute the following *baseline interventions:*

1. *The patient is brought to an awareness of the traits he or she pursues that create problems.* Detection of these traits will not be difficult from the case history as revealed by the patient, from reports of informants if these are available, and particularly from the patient's attitudes and behavior toward therapy and the therapist. Some patients are at least partially aware of their maladaptive patterns; some appear to be oblivious to their nature and the effect on themselves and others. One cannot jump in immediately and vigorously confront the patient with his or her self-defeating attitudes and corrosive conduct unless a good working relationship has been established. The patient will either not listen or will assume he or she is being unfairly attacked and misunderstood. But as soon as the therapist feels that a reasonably sound therapeutic relationship exists, confrontation blended with empathic understanding may be necessary and invaluable. If repression acts like an interfering block of concrete, analysis of dreams, transference, and acting-out may be helpful in expediting awareness. Interpretations must be carefully titrated to the patient's ego strength and level of anxiety.

Interpreting character drives in a way that will be therapeutic is an art because reactions to interpretations of anger, offensiveness, denial, disbelief, or detachment can have a negative effect on the therapeutic alliance.

One way of softening the negative impact of interpretations is to couch them in universal terms. In this way, one hopes to avoid a disintegration of the therapeutic relationship. For example, the following statements were offered patients:

(Strong dependency traits in a man) "Many people come through a difficult childhood with scars that burden them. Because of an unfulfilled early life, they try to make up for satisfactions they failed to get by looking for and getting dependent on a better, more idealized parent figure. Could it be that you are reaching for a more fulfilling relationship, which you believe your wife is not supplying?"

(Masochistic tendency) "There is really nothing so unusual in the way you are reacting. People who are angry at what has happened to them often are very guilty and may seek to punish themselves for even feeling angry."

(Detachment) "It is only natural that when a person feels hurt there is a need to escape from one's feelings. Sometimes not feeling emotions or physically getting away from people is an effective defensive maneuver. But there are penalties one pays for detachment."

(Perfectionism) "Doing things perfectionistically is one way people have of protecting themselves. The only trouble is that nobody can ever be perfect, and if perfection is a goal one always has to suffer."

By avoiding confronting the patient directly with a character defect, one may obliquely be able to penetrate defenses. Once the patient acknowledges a problem openly, confrontation can then be more direct and personal. The therapist should watch the patient's reactions to interpretations to see whether the patient is strong enough to tolerate and make use of them. Initial reactions should not be taken at face value. As long as there is evidence that confirm the assumptions of the therapist, interpretations should carefully be woven into questions, continuously presenting these to the patient in the hope that the patient will eventually make the proper connections.

In the case of a man with untoward aggression, his acting-out patterns were vivid enough so that it required little from me to get him to realize that his behavior was problematic, although he attempted to justify and rationalize it. Interpretations fell on deaf ears, even though explanations were deliberately modulated. It was obvious that he defended against using them in the early phases of treatment.

2. *The aversive consequences of the patient's patterns are reviewed in detail.*

These are abundant and usually well-known to the patient, although he or she will ascribe them to being misunderstood or discriminated against. A wealth of excuses, resentments, and recriminations will drown the patient's judgment. The therapist will soon realize that no matter how severe the punishment is that follows untoward behavior, the patient is completely unable to control it. Indeed it may become evident, as happened in my patient, that he or she masochistically seems to welcome punishment.

3. *Detailed determination of the function of the disturbed patterns must be elaborated.* Here dynamic thinking is indispensable since the purpose behind the manifest symptomatology is often not explicable in terms of everyday logic. In our patient under discussion it became apparent through exploration of his dreams, associations, and behavior toward me that he was trying to mask underlying passivity, low feelings of independence, and a nonmasculine image he believed he was displaying to the world. Blustering verbal attacks and an appearance of belligerence served the purpose of presenting a macho front. He had guilt feelings about homosexual fantasies but apparently never acted them out. Interest in women was high, and he enjoyed heterosexuality. He was, however, unable to establish an enduring relationship with any one woman. Discussions about his irrational fantasies created motivation to inquire further into their nature.

4. *In some cases it is important to explore the origins of the personality disorder in past formative relationships.* Memories of early determining experiences are usually blurred and their connection with present-day behavior obscure. As therapy proceeds, some memories and connections become clearer. The transference may reveal significant feelings toward early care-taking agencies that are being projected toward present-day authorities. The most dramatic revelations will occur when an actual transference neurosis precipitates. A few motivated patients may be susceptible to the classical analytic technique, which will most reliably produce a transference neurosis. Countertransference, if studied assiduously, may also yield data about some of the patient's projected unconscious processes. One occasionally finds that the patient's behavior is molded by identification with a parental figure and that the patient is acting-out the hidden designs of these figures with the therapist, or outside persons (projective identification). In many cases a modified analytic approach, dealing with derivatives of nuclear conflicts, is all that is possible. Presentation of a schema such as outlined in Chapter 44 may enable the patient to reconstruct past experiences and to assign to his or her personality patterns a more significant meaning. This will help establish better controls.

Our patient became aware of his continuing dependency, his futile search for an idealized maternal figure, his delayed separation-individuation, his resentment of women as symbols of the controlling and castrating mother, his feelings of low independence and masculinity, and his compensatory strivings for more effective affirmation of his masculinity through power drives, aggression, and fantasies of penis acquisition via homosexual fantasies. These insights fascinated him but still were not sufficient to cure his personality disorder. It did provide him with motivation to want to halt some expressions of self-defeating aggression.

5. *The acquisition of more constructive modes of reacting to provocative stim-*

uli may be expedited through the employment of cognitive and behavioral techniques. Here the patient may keep a diary of successes and failures in controlling his or her symptoms under various circumstances. Cognitive therapy helps rectify faulty self statements. Assertiveness training, group therapy, and psychodramatic role playing may aid in the reconditioning process if the patient is unable to achieve greater control through simple homework practice. These adjunctive measures were all employed with our patient because of his continuing resistance. Many patients will not need all of these measures.

6. *As soon as the patient manifests some control over his or her patterns and substitutes more productive behavioral alternatives, termination of therapy is in order, with injunctions given to continue homework practice.* A 5-year follow-up of our patient revealed continuing assertiveness without need for aggression, as well as gratifying signs of personality maturity.

7. *Severe chronic personality disorders do not lend themselves to a "quick fix."* Reinforcements in the environment keep their patterns alive, and resistances to change interfere with progress. Some cases of personality disorders, antisocial personality disorder, and very severe borderline personality disorder, for example, may require treatment in an institution staffed by personnel sufficiently well trained to deal with encrusted characterological patterns that will not yield to anything other than reconditioning in a therapeutic milieu.

The above outline of therapy for personality disorder is a barren description of treatment that of necessity extends over a long period and that requires innovative management. While treatment focuses ide-ally on intrapsychic and interpersonal links in the behavioral chain, difficulties related to other links may claim priority and need to be treated with special techniques, as well as the baseline interventions described above (see Table 57-1). Diagnosis of personality disorder is usually made on the basis of the most obnoxious or maladaptive traits that are being exhibited. Blatant and unpalatable, these may mask other less disagreeable but equally important personality distortions. Not uncommonly, two or more diagnostically distinct personality disorders may appear in the same person. The classification of character types into diagnostic entities is convenient but faulty to the extent that traits shift and vary with prevailing needs and existing stresses imposed on the individual. Accordingly, at irregular times, different impulses and demands may appear that will inspire a complex array of defenses and reaction formations and suggest many different classifications. Nevertheless, distinctive diagnostic categories are listed in the DSM classification system.

Paranoid Personality Disorder (DSM-III-R Code 301.00)

Individuals with this disorder, which rarely produces sufficient discomfort to bring an individual to therapy for the personality problem alone, exhibit an unwarranted sensitivity to actions in the environment that they believe are designed to annoy, humiliate, or take advantage of them. Such suspicions are impervious to reason. Most persons with this disorder come to treatment for symptoms such as depression, anxiety, phobias, and other manifest disturbances. Only when the therapist gains their confidence will they reveal some of their peculiar ideas. When attempts are made to bring logic into the picture to prove the ideas incredulous, the relationship may begin to disintegrate. Indeed, these patients may consider the therapist allied to their enemies. It is difficult to convince them that they are trying to preserve themselves by building an impenetrable wall between themselves and others and that secrecy, guardedness, jealously, lack of humor, and involvement with fantasies of being humilitated and downgraded are symptoms of a disorder.

The best way to manage therapy with the paranoidal individual is to listen respectfully to his or her qualms and not argue about them. When the patient expresses concern about being threatened and humiliated by others, the therapist might say: "Anyone who is going through what you are is bound to be upset." One deals with the patient's emotional turmoil and does not try to ridicule or belittle his or her twisted cognitions.

Because of the vulnerability of the relationship with the therapist, the patient is apt to regard criticism as a blow to his or her self-esteem, initiating depression, rage, or anxiety. Criticism is interpreted as evidence that the therapist does not approve of him or her. The patient is apt to intellectualize the entire therapeutic process, using knowledge either as resistance or as a means of fortifying against change. Despite all logic, the patient strives to wedge therapy into the framework of his or her distorted attitudes toward life. Feelings of rejection and distrust are exhibited, and at the slightest challenge from the therapist, defenses crumble, leaving the patient in a state of anger and despair. The patient may then show a psychic rigidity that refuses to yield to reason or entreaty.

Some therapists attempt to gain the goodwill of paranoidal patients through a form of strategic therapy in which they act as if the patient's ideas are factual and even become a partner in the patient's bizarre schemes. This may work at first to solidify the relationship since the patient may accept the therapist as an exceptional friend who does not ridicule his or her ideas and judgments. Unless the therapist is an excellent actor, the acutely sensitive patient will detect a fraudulent note in the play-acting maneuvers.

Some patients achieve relief from severe symptoms such as depression with antidepressants, and eventually are able to accept the therapist as a sincere friend who wants to help rather than harm. They may then begin to express some doubts about their suspicions. At this point, one may institute cognitive therapy carefully designed so as not to convey the impression that the patient is peculiar or psychotic.

Dependent Personality Disorder (DSM-III Code 301.60)

The character trait of extreme dependency sponsors relegation of responsibilities to other persons and avoidance of decision making. The individual allows a spouse or parent to arrange the most simple matters and has little incentive to promote action on his or her own. The dependence is actually one manifestation of a widespread deficit in separation-individuation, the product of faulty early development. Inability to transcend the dependency stage of development results in severe damage to the self system, including evolvement of compensations and reaction formations such as those described in Chapter 44. An inability to manage the ordinary stresses of life may result in adaptive breakdowns, with ensuing anxiety, depression, phobias, and other neurotic difficulties.

Treatment poses special problems. Dependent persons often show up for treatment not because they feel a need for change but rather because parents, marital partners, or friends insist that something be done for them. Visits to the therapist in such cases are a mere formality. Such patients expect that no change will occur and will be resistant to any effort to get them to participate in the treatment process. The limit of their cooperativeness is to expose themselves to the therapist during the allotted hour.

Dependent patients seek to establish themselves with the therapist in ways that resemble the infant's imposition on the parents. They do not seem to be interested in developing resources within themselves. Rather, they desire to maneuver the therapist into a position where constant favors will be forthcoming. They will abide by any rules of therapy in order to obtain this objective, even to the apparent absorption of insight. It is most disconcerting, therefore, to learn that assimilated insights are extremely superficial and that the patients are less interested in knowing what is wrong than in perpetuating the child–parent relationship. They actually seem incapable of reasoning logically, and there is an almost psychotic quality to the persistence of their demands for support and direction. Sometimes the residual hostility is expressed in aggressiveness, which is usually masked by passive maneuvers such as procrastination, obstinacy, recalcitrance, and stubbornness, hence the term "passive-aggressive character disorder."

Interpretations of the patient's dependency are usually regarded as chastisement. He or she will assume that any attempt to put responsibility on his or her shoulders is a form of ill will expressed by the therapist. The patient will demonstrate reactions of disappointment, rage, anxiety, and depression and will repeat these reactions in spite of lip service to the effect that he or she wants to get well.

In treating a dependency reaction, it is essential to recognize that hostility is inevitable in the course of therapy. The demands of dependent people are so insatiable that it is impossible to live up to their expectations. Only when such people begin to experience themselves as people with constructive assertiveness and independence are they able to function with any degree of well-being. This goal, unfortunately, may in some instances never be achieved.

Supportive therapy that propitiates the patient's dependency needs is of extremely temporary effect. It is advisable, where possible, to promote a therapeutic approach in which the individual learns to accept responsibility for his or her own development in the hope that the patient will utilize this opportunity to grow.

There are some individuals, however, whose self-structure has been so crushed that they will resist any attempt to make the therapeutic situation a participating one. Here the treatment program may have to be directed at a limited therapeutic goal. The therapist will then have to become resigned to educating the patient to function with his or her dependency strivings with as little detriment as possible.

Behavior therapy is sometimes very helpful. Conditionings are organized so that the patient is rewarded for making his or her own decisions. It is to be expected that the patient will resent this vigorously, accusing the therapist of refusing to accept responsibility. The therapist may then explain that pandering to the patient's demands for support and making decisions for him or her only tends to infantilize the patient. It would make the patient more dependent and more unable to develop to a point where he or she could fulfill himself or herself productively and creatively. The therapist does not wish to shirk responsibility but withholds directiveness out of respect for the patient's right to develop. Although patients may still resent the therapist's intent, they may finally understand that unless they begin to make their own decisions, they will never get to a point where they are strong within themselves. Behavioral assertive training may prove helpful.

Some patients who seemingly are fixated on a dependent level may, with repeated reinforcements and assertiveness training, finally begin to accept themselves as having the right to make their own choices and to develop their own values. Unflagging persistence, however, is the keynote. In therapy the patient will exploit every opportunity to force the therapist to assume a directive role. Nevertheless, when the patient sees that the therapist has his or her welfare at heart, he or she may be able to develop more independence and assertiveness. The shift in therapy from a directive to a nondirective role calls for considerable skill, and it must be tempered to the patient's incentives and ego strength. Unless such a shift is made at some time, psychotherapy will probably be interminable, and the patient will continue on a dependent level requiring the ever presence of the therapist or some other giving person as a condition to security.

Should it become apparent that one cannot work along participating lines and that the patient's only objective is to become dependent on the therapist, visits may be cut down to 15- to 20-minute sessions once weekly or bimonthly, and/or the patient may be referred to a supportive social or reeducative group with periodic fulltime sessions when required.

Obsessive-Compulsive Personality Disorder (Compulsive Personality) DSM-III-R Code 301.40

Compulsive personalities are obsessed with orderliness, preoccupied with trivia, irritatingly perfectionistic, immovably obstinate, overconscientious, and addicted to work and what they consider demanding daily responsibilities. They have little time for leisure and enjoyment, and their relationships with people are often organized around manipulations for their own ends. Lack of confidence in themselves forces many of these individuals to engage "experts," whose advice they rarely follow, to instruct them in "what to do." Maintenance of control becomes a preoccupation, and every thought and action is measured carefully so they will not be caught off guard. Occasionally, particularly in emergencies and under the impact of great stress, controls may shatter and behavior becomes impulsive and disorganized. It be-

comes apparent then that forced control at all times is a means of preventing the possibility of being destroyed by unpredictable disasters. Because of the fears of making mistakes, some compulsives ruminate about alternative solutions and find it difficult to arrive at decisions. They then ask for advice, which they question and doubt, and make a nuisance of themselves pilloring people with questions. Feelings of warmth and tenderness are subordinated to cold intellectualizations and formal stiffness in manners. The more adjusted compulsive persons are cautious, conscientious, conservative, and conforming solid citizens, and for this reason are often put in positions where punctilious work is demanded. Too frequently, the joy of living is sacrificed to a sense of responsibility. Certain cultures encourage and reward some compulsive traits that are considered desirable, not abnormal.

Though obsessive compulsive personality disorder seems related to obsessive-compulsive disorder, relatively few persons with compulsive personalities succumb to an actual neurosis. They come to therapy because their controlling defenses have failed to function, resulting in underlying fears of shattering. Symptoms of anxiety and depression constitute the complaint factor. Environmental stresses such as severe financial problems, physical illness, forced retirement, and marital difficulties may have taxed coping capacities.

If the individual has adequately adapted to the compulsive personality most of his or her life and if it has not been responsible for a serious physical ailment (such as cardiac disease in the compulsive Type A personality), the objective in treatment is restitution of the old personality controls. Resolution of identifiable environmental stress (via counseling, environmental manipulation, etc.) and medicinal management of symptoms related to the implicated biological links (anxiolytics, antidepressants, etc.) are instituted when indicated. Relaxation therapy is often of great value, and many of these patients are good subjects for hypnosis and biofeedback. Marital therapy may be employed. Cognitive therapy to change attitudes, as toward forced retirement, may be tried, but the patient's stubborn clinging to established belief systems may be difficult to overcome.

Because many of these patients are intellectually keen, some alteration of stubborn personality traits may be possible through persistent application of the "baseline interventions" described at the beginning of this chapter. Supplying the patient with a chart delineating how personality drives operate may prove helpful since this permits the patient to put his or her patterns into an ordered arrangement that can be studied as assigned homework.

Passive-Aggressive Personality Disorder (DSM-III-R Code 301.84)

Persons who display extraordinary resistance to demands being made on them in their education, work, and social relationships may be suffering from a passive-aggressive personality disorder. This diagnosis is, along with "atypical, mixed, or other personality disorder," a kind of wastebasket into which varied reaction patterns are dumped. One often gets the impression that many passive-aggressive individuals utilize their resistance as a form of aggression. They refuse to allow themselves to be "pushed around." In their way, their "forgetting," inefficiency, procrastination, and oppositional tendencies serve the purpose of supporting a spurious independence.

At the core of these traits is a severe developmental disturbance characterized by incomplete separation-individuation. The high level of dependence may be concealed or masked by projecting it onto a religious deity who is worshipped for hoped-for rewards in the present (e.g., winning at Lotto) or in the future (e.g., reserving an established seat in heaven). Where it is expressed toward a human target (i.e., parent, spouse, lover, authority, etc.), the individual will usually downgrade the strength, wisdom, and designs of his or her chosen host as failing to achieve the virtues of an idealized parental figure. Patients will project toward this person great though controlled hostility for failing them in their need and additionally will blame them for taking away their independence. Hostility may assume the form of aggression, scapegoating, or sadism toward others; or it may be fed back internally with self-punitive and other masochistic maneuvers. Low independence may produce self-criticism and a devaluated self-image, which may sponsor fantasies of being inferior, physically damaged, or sexually inadequate. Compensations take the form of perfectionism, overambitiousness, grandiosity, and compulsive drives to prove one's strength and power. Resorting to alcohol and drugs to overcome anxiety and depression may complicate the picture.

Therapy of patients with a passive-aggressive personality disorder is difficult because of the strong ego-syntonic nature of the associated traits and the ambivalent transference that is bound to emerge. One may deal with such symptoms as anxiety and depression on a short-term basis, but the basic personality structure will continue to stir up problems for the person. Implementation of the "baseline interventions" (page 1167) is desirable, recognizing that a dynamic long-term approach is essential to make any impression on the individual.

During the course of treatment the patient will seemingly modify attitudes toward the therapist, but in this alteration the therapist must search for areas of resistance. For instance, a submissive, ingratiating attitude, which is often a cover for a fear of abandonment, may, upon interpretation, be replaced by an apparently sincere attempt to search for and to analyze inner problems. The therapist may, if the patient is observed closely, detect in this new attitude a fraudulent attempt to gain security by complying with what the patient feels is expected of him or her. While the patient appears to be analyzing his or her problem, the real motive is to gain security by adjusting to what he or she considers are the demands of the therapist. In this way the process of therapy itself becomes a means of indulging the neurosis.

In analyzing resistances, their sources in infantile attitudes and conditionings usually become apparent. Eventually it is essential to bring the patient to a realization of how the machinery with which he or she reacts to the world now is rooted in early conceptions and misconceptions about life. The interpretation of passive-aggressive character strivings does not suffice to change their nature, for they are the only way the patient knows of adjusting.

A breakdown of character strivings often brings out in sharp focus the repressed needs and impulses from which the strivings issue. When the patient becomes cognizant of what produces insatiable destructive interpersonal attitudes, he or she has the best chance of taking active steps toward their modification.

In certain cases, particularly if there are time limitations, the only thing that can be accomplished is to compromise with the existing disorder in as painless a manner as possible. Environmental manipulation may be necessary to take pressures off the patient. The patient may be shown how to adjust to the reality situation. For instance, if a woman has a strong striving for perfectionism that drives her incessantly into positions that she cannot handle with her intellectual and physical equipment, she may be shown how she can confine herself to a project that she can master proficiently. Whereas the scope of her operations may be limited, she can indulge her perfectionistic strivings in a circumscribed way, gaining some measure of gratification in this. If she is inordinately dependent on strong people, it may be pointed out that she can maintain a certain freedom of action in spite of the fact that she has to lean on authority. If she has an insatiable need to dominate, avenues for its toned-down exercise may be suggested. This approach, of course, merely panders to the patient's neurosis, but it may be the only practical approach for the time being; in many cases it will make the patient's life immeasurably more tolerable.

Whenever possible, patients should be brought to an awareness of the nature, genesis, and dynamic significance of their passive-aggressive character trends. They should be encouraged to observe how mercilessly they operate in everyday life and to scrutinize why they cannot change their attitudes toward people. Desirable as this may be, a shift in therapeutic orientation toward insight may stir up a hornet's nest in the relationship with the therapist.

Though character trends in the passive-aggressive person are constantly shifting, they are usually interrelated and the fusion makes for a picture that is unique for each individual. Behavior is not the static product of a group of isolated trends; rather, it is a complex integrate of a number of drives. The product of this intermingling differs from any of the component strivings. That is, if the person is compulsively modest, is fired by perfectionism, is quiet at some times and arrogant and aggressive at others, some of these traits will tend to neutralize and some to reinforce each other. Nevertheless, for treatment purposes, we should consider them part of a conglomerate and not deal with them as isolated and distinctive entities.

Power Patterns

While not listed as a separate personality disorder in DSM-III-R, compensatory power impulses predominate in some individuals. Here all that seems to matter in life is forcefulness and strength. The feelings and rights of other people are disregarded. There is a blind admiration for everything invincible. The person is contemptous of softness and tenderness, and self-esteem is seemingly dependent on the ability to be dominant. As in dependency, the dynamic force behind the power impulse is a profound sense of helplessness and an inability to cope with life with the available resources. A motive behind the power drive is to coerce people to yield to one's will, which provides bounties of various sorts.

The treatment of power drives is oriented toward building up frustration tolerance and increasing the capacity to withstand tension without resorting to aggression. A reeducative or behavioral approach may be effective in helping these patients develop inner restraints capable of controlling their impulses. It is essential to be firmer in working with this type of pattern than with either dependency or detached reactions. These patients must be constantly reminded that there are limits beyond which they cannot go and that they must face responsibility for their actions. The dynamic significance of their power drive must be constantly pointed out, particularly its use as a means of shoring up the patient's devalued self-image. Patients should be encouraged to make efforts toward the expansion of their personal resources so as to minimize the need for power ploys.

A man may display unprovoked aggression whenever he tries to assert himself or when he feels deprived. Figuratively, he uses an elephant gun to kill a sparrow. He rationalizes his behavior to the effect that people pay no attention unless one forces them to do so. Behind this attitude is a feeling of helplessness and a fear of being rejected or attacked when one expresses one's rights. Consolidated is the conviction that one must display an image of strength and invulnerability to prevent exploitation. When people back away from his violence, this proves to the patient that they are unwilling to pay attention to his reasonable demands. He then becomes all the more angry, demanding, and forceful. The end result of his obnoxious conduct is that he is rejected and cannot hold a job even though he is intelligent and highly qualified. Depression forces him to seek psychiatric help. In therapy we can deal rapidly with the complaint factor of depression by prescribing an antidepressant medication, which in a few weeks may dissolve his malaise. If this is all he wants from therapy, the patient will then terminate treatment secure in the belief that he is cured and that he can now set off to find a new job. Undoubtedly the pattern will repeat itself because his illness has not been dented, let alone resolved. To go beyond mere symptom relief to correction of personality deficits will entail an extensive carefully planned stretch of psychotherapy.

If dependency and power drives are fused, the individual may be shown how he functions in a dual manner, seeking security from stronger people by shows of helplessness or wresting security from them by force and aggression. The chief resistance the therapist will encounter is transference, which may not be resolvable until the patient connects his reactions to historical developmental data.

Schizoid Personality Disorder (DSM-III-R 301.20)

The schizoid personality disorder is organized around the defense of detachment. The individual is often referred to as a "loner" or "isolate" with whom it is difficult to establish a relationship. There is a consuming flatness of mood with an inability to resonate through the spectrum of normal feelings from happiness to sorrow to anger. People who seek to establish contacts with schizoid personalities complain that they are withdrawn, isolated, and "standoffish" ("I'd like to shake him into reacting and feeling"). Daydreaming and living in fantasy are common. The schizoid personality disorder must be differentiated from the schizotypal personality disorder, which is closer to schizophrenia and in which there are distortions in thinking (ideas of reference and influence, depersonalization, peculiar fantasies, and paranoidal notions), odd manner of speaking, and episodes of eccentric behavior.

Such isolated and detached individuals, who shy away from establishing close interpersonal relationships and yet maintain a good hold on reality, rarely come to therapy for the disorder itself. If, however, the need for a relationship of some kind becomes pressing or, more likely, the individual is caught in a relationship from which there is no escape, anxiety may occur and motivate the victim to seek professional help. The disorder, with its features of coldness, aloofness, and absence of concern with and indifference to the feelings of others, is a protective screen and consequently resists therapeutic alteration.

Detachment may be the means elaborated by the individual to protect himself or herself from intense dependency strivings. A close relationship poses dangers of being overwhelmed, for in it the patient may envisage a complete giving up of his or her independence. Detachment may also be a technique of avoiding injury or destruction that the patient believes will occur when he or she comes close to a person. Finally, it may be a method by which the patient protects himself or herself from fears of attacking and destroying others.

In treating a detached patient, one must anticipate that there will be difficulty for a long time in establishing a close relationship, since this tends to mobilize fears of injury and inspires the building of a protective wall. Much active work will be required in detecting and dissolving resistances to change. The detached patient often has a tendency to intellectualize the entire therapeutic process. The patient will particularly shy away from expressing feelings because he or she will conceive of them as dangerous.

Great hostility is bound to arise, which may be disconcerting principally because it is usually unexpressed or liberated in explosive outbursts. The therapist must realize that hostility is a defense against interpersonal closeness. It is extremely important that the therapist be as tolerant toward the patient's provocations as possible. The patient will probably attempt to goad the therapist into expressions of counteraggression to justify attitudes toward people as untrustworthy and withdrawal from the world because it is potentially menacing.

Sometimes the patient may be encouraged to participate in social activities, competitive games, and sports. Commanding, restrictive directions should, however, be avoided. With encouragement, detached people may begin to relate to others. In groups they drift cautiously from the periphery to the center as they realize that they will not be injured in a close interpersonal relationship. Group therapy may sometimes be most rewarding in certain detached, schizoid individuals, as long as no pressure is put on them to participate. Social groups with a wide range of activities may be prescribed.

A common reaction in the therapy of schizoid personalities is anxiety, which is manifested by disturbing nightmarish dreams or by actual anxiety attacks. The reaction will usually be found when the patient experiences for the first time real closeness or love toward the therapist. The emotions terrorize the patient and cause him or her to fear injury of an indefinable nature. It is essential to deal with this reaction when it occurs by giving the patient as much reassurance and interpretation as is necessary. Detached patients whose defenses have crumbled may go into a clinging dependent attitude when they realize the full weight of their helplessness. Supportive therapy may have to be given here, in an effort to provide the patient with an experience in which he or she receives help without being domineered or smothered with cloying affection. Should anxiety become too disturbing, anxiolytic medications may temporarily be prescribed.

Schizotypal Personality Disorder (DSM-III-R Code 301.22)

The schizotypal personality disorder is closer to schizophrenia than the schizoid personality disorder. Emotional instability, peculiarities of ideation, involvement with superstition and magical thinking, and perhaps bizarre preoccupations as with clairvoyance and "out-of-body" experiences convey a feeling of strangeness and a psychoticlike tinge, although a definite psychosis is not present. Ideas of reference, fragmentary illusions, and odd mannerisms may be present. The patient often seeks therapy because of depression, anxiety, and depersonalization that have come on spontaneously or as a result of a stressful experience. Insight into cognitive dysfunctions is lacking, and motivation is confined to achieving freedom from disturbing symptoms. It is futile to reason with or to argue these patients out of their peculiarities of thinking and oddities of behavior. Therapy should be confined to dealing supportively with symptoms while establishing a friendly helping relationship. Anxiolytic, antidepressant, and carefully administered neuroleptic treatment in small doses may be indicated.

Narcissistic Personality Disorder (DSM-III-R Code 301.81)

In recent years an interest in the dynamics and therapy of narcissistic subjects has been revived. Scrutiny of the earliest phases of ego development have led to a number of hypotheses on how the disorder evolves and its influence on treatment (Kohut, 1971). Attempts have been made, with variable results, to differentiate narcissistic reactions from borderline cases and schizophrenia, which are distinctive ailments even though a strong bond exists among these entities. Problems in all three have occurred in the primary stages of separation and individuation. Object relationships, as a result, become distorted and shallow and are oriented around how they can enhance the individual's status and interests. Fusion and dependency are basic themes; love objects are inbued with both terrifying and grandiose qualities. In therapy the transference reaction, which is essentially narcissistic, encourages regressive episodes with fear of the loss of the love object, paranoidal symptoms, and a fear of mutililation. The regression is never as deep in narcissistic personalities as in borderline or schizophrenic patients.

Therapists experience much difficulty in treating the character disorder of excessive narcissism. Persons with this problem seem to have such a need for personal admiration that they conceive of therapy as a means of making themselves more worthy of praise.

Unlike the mature person who gains security from cooperative endeavors in attitudes of altruism and sympathy, narcissistic individuals concentrate most of their interest on themselves. Self-love may actually become structured into grandiose strivings, omnipotent impulses, and megalomania. Although the image of the individual appears to be bloated, analysis readily reveals how helpless and impoverished he or she actually feels. There is danger here of precipitating depression or excitement by presenting insights prematurely. The shock-aborbing capacity of the ego must always be weighed, and interpretations must be given in proportion to the available ego strength. In markedly immature individuals little development may be expected other than a somewhat better environmental adaptation through guidance techniques.

Many of these patients often band together in Bohemian groups, posturing and posing, displaying a haughty defiance of convention, garbing themselves in outlandish dress, arranging their hair out of keeping with the accepted style as a way of expressing their exaggerated exhibitionistic, omnipotent, sadistic, and masochistic impulses. Language for them serves to release tension and not as a genuine means of communication. As long as they impulsively discharge their tension and anxiety in acting-out, they will not be too uncomfortable. "They are hunting eternally for satisfactory and secure models through which they may save themselves by a narcissistic identification. On the surface it appears later as a scattered, superficial pseudo competitiveness" (Greenacre, 1952). There is little motivation for therapy, which is usually sought not by the person but by a concerned parent or friend who is shocked or frightened by the patient's behavior. Under these circumstances psychotherapy proceeds under a great handicap, the patient generally breaking appointments or manifesting such resistance that the therapist's tolerance is put under the severest test. The only incentive that the patient has for treatment is to please the parent or referral agency, usually to avoid the catastrophe of having his or her allowance cut off. If the person is unable to release tension because of the absence of or removal from environmental resources, anxiety may then come to the surface. Symptomatic discomfort will then act as a motive for help.

Classical psychoanalysis is disappointing in its results with narcissistic patients, but if a semblance of a relationship can be maintained, a modified analytic approach, perhaps drawing inspiration from object relations theory or self-psychology (see Chapter 11) may be useful. Some guidelines for therapy are found in the section on borderline personality disorder that follows.

Borderline Personality Disorder (DSM-III-R Code 301.83)

From the numbers of papers and books published and the frequency of seminars given, borderline patients have replaced white rats as the prime research subjects in the psychological field. Research has yielded some interesting hypotheses about the origins and the dynamics of borderline personality disorder, but it has not definitively established reliable ways of managing the difficult and fragile groups of patients embraced by this diagnostic category. Characteristic is a fluctuating assembly of symptoms that markedly cause subjective distress and impair social and occupational functioning. These include lack of impulse control leading to patterns of unstable and impulsive behavior that seemingly make no sense and involve the patient in difficulties with authority and peers. There are shifts in mood ranging from feelings of emptiness and boredom to temper outbursts and violent bouts of anger that are inappropriate and occasionally lead to quarreling, fighting, suicidal attempts, and other destructive activities. There may be confusion about one's identity in relation to self-image and gender. Fluid, unexpected changes in attitudes, moral precepts, values, and belief make it difficult to reason with and securely adapt to the person. Sometimes, especially when under great stress, transient, quickly recoverable, psychotic episodes occur. Characterologically, the individual manifests dependency, immaturity, detachment, and a wide variety of shifting traits.

Unlike the mature personality whose coping mechanisms are reality-oriented, the borderline patient retains and employs the archaic defenses that were evolved during infancy and childhood in relationship to parental agencies. Prominent among these are projection, displacement, withdrawal, autism, dissociative processes (splitting of the ego), denial, and hysterical and obsessive-compulsive maneuvers. These combine with a fragmentary delusional system that is repressed but used as a coping device whenever the patient is under extraordinary stress. The existence of this system may be exposed during narcosynthesis or with the administration of small quantities of the psychotomimetic drugs.

Borderline patients are sometimes falsely classified as schizophrenics. Gunderson et al. (1975) have shown that there is little justification for this, since borderline patients do not exhibit distinguishing schizophrenic symptoms and differ in the quality of the thought disorder. Kernberg (1974) has described the personality organization of the borderline as one in which there is ego weakness with primitive mechanisms of defense, such as splitting, denial, omnipotence, devaluation, and early projective tendencies; a shift toward primary process thinking that may come through only in projective testing; and pathological internalized object relations. Kohut (1971) has expounded on the early traumatic disturbances in the relationship with the archaic idealized self-object and the damage to the maturing personality that continues because of this trauma. Fixation to aspects of archaic objects fashions the regression that occurs during analytic therapy.

The psychotherapy of borderline personality disorder is a long and difficult procedure, largely because of the fragile character of the patient–therapist relationship (Eisenstein VW, 1951; Bychowski, 1950). Borderline patients often seek help on an emergency basis when a crisis occurs or when symptoms such as anxiety and depression become intolerable. Some recognize that their interaction with people is disturbed and that they are unable to make a satisfactory social and occupational adjustment. At the start of therapy the therapist may be regarded as a curative deity who will rapidly dissolve the patient's troubles.

This idea rapidly vanishes when immediate cure is not forthcoming. Disturbing transference reactions then interfere with the patient's ability to cooperate with treatment routines. There seems to be a deficit in the quality of the "observing ego," that part of the self that can judge one's pathological maneuvers. This interferes with establishing a trustful and realistic therapeutic alliance and encourages disturbing transference. How to deal with these reactions is a matter of controversy. Therapists such as Kernberg (1975) believe that the best method is to attempt reconstructive personality change by encouraging regression, by allowing the transference to build up, and then to interpret it. Others like Zetzel (1971) and H. Friedman (1975) have a dimmer view about the possibilities of reconstructive change in borderline patients and are firm in their belief that all that can be done is to keep transference under control and improve adaptation. Still others try pragmatically to move from one to the other paradigm as required. There are advocates and dissenters who support or ridicule each of these three viewpoints.

Disagreements about the most suitable approach probably occur because borderline disorders are constituted by a wide variety of patients who genetically, constitutionally, developmentally, and experientially are different. Moreover, patients are exposed to therapists whose training, skills, philosophies, and personalities may or may not provide a good match. No hard and fast rules about preferential treatment choice can therefore be made for all cases, but a flexible approach may be rewarding (Katz S, 1982).

Most therapists are dubious about curing patients with borderline pathology. They therefore adopt the course of supporting the defensive structure by avoiding unconscious conflict, minimizing concentration on the past, and providing symptom relief in the medium of a benevolent relationship with as much setting of limits as situations warrant. They will then adopt interventions that deal expediently with remediable pathology related to pathological links in the behavioral chain, for example, psychopharmacology for severe anxiety and depression, relaxation exercises for tension, desensitization techniques for phobias, behavioral therapy for impulsivity and self-destructiveness, environmental manipulation for situational disturbances, and cognitive therapy for distortions in thinking. They will veer from counseling, reassurance, confrontation, education, and concern with dynamics within the limits of their training and as required by the immediate needs of their patients. Therapy is usually conducted on a once- or twice-a-week basis. Modifications in method include the following:

1. Establishing a warm supportive relationship is of paramount importance.
2. Time restrictions in the session must be elastic.
3. A long testing period is to be expected. It may often be very difficult for the patient to make a relationship with the therapist.
4. Environmental manipulation may be inescapable.
5. Working with the patient's family to reduce pressure on the patient is frequently indicated.
6. The interview focus is on reality, the patient's relapse into daydreaming or delusion being interpreted as a reaction to fear or guilt.
7. Avoiding the probing of psychoticlike material is advisable.
8. Active reassurance and advice giving may be necessary.
9. Directive encouragement is given to the patient to participate in occupational therapy, hobbies, and recreations.
10. Neurotic defenses are supported and strengthened.

11. Challenging or disagreeing with the patient's distorted ideas is delayed until a good relationship exists.
12. The patient may at the start of therapy be told what to expect during therapy, especially that at times he or she may be upset with the therapist for not doing more for him or her. The patient may want to quit therapy. If the patient does quit, he or she is welcome to return (Katz, 1982).
13. Therapy may last a long time, perhaps the rest of the patient's life.

The importance of keeping the relationship with the therapist as nondistorted and productive as possible with a minimum of acting-out is paramount. When necessary, there is a search for maladaptive defenses and, when there is evidence of interference with transference, (1) elaboration of how they influence the patient's relations with others, (2) confrontation and interpretation of defenses that sponsor a negative transference, (3) the setting of limits in the therapeutic situation, and (4) the employment of modalities such as hospitals, and foster homes when needed. Combined individual and group psychotherapy for the borderline patient has special advantages and a specific function. It is at present used widely for borderlines in private offices, clinics, and institutions where insight into the necessity for treatment and an ability to relate to a therapeutic situation remain at least partially intact.

While the one-to-one relationship of individual therapy satisfies dependency needs, the borderline patient also feels threatened by it. Many of these patients profit in a group therapeutic setting where they feel less dependent and the therapist appears less powerful. In the security of the group the members relate to each other and to the "democratic" authority figure of the therapist with more freedom and less anxiety than in any other situation. The group atmosphere facilitates expression of one's feelings. It makes interaction and with it socialization desirable and rewarding. The all-or-none conflict that leads to emotional inhibition and withdrawal out of fear of one's own destructive impulses is worked through under the protective leadership of the therapist and by testing the reality of anticipated dire consequences following expression of one's emotions. In the social situation of the therapy group, with its graded anxiety-releasing potential and the opportunity for reality testing, the borderline patient may find his or her first constructive experience in human relationships and may grasp a glimpse of understanding into the positive sides of socialization.

In working with dynamic vectors, care must be taken to prevent the patient's anxiety from getting too extreme. It is better to deal with the secondary elaborations of nuclear conflicts (derivative conflicts) as reflected in personality interactions (see Chapter 44) than with the nuclear conflicts directly. This may be especially useful if the patient displays evidence of obstructive transference and resistance and has enough of an "observing ego" to handle interpretations. Some of the techniques of A. Wolberg described later in this section may be helpful here. Management of counter-transference is a most vital part of therapy because in trying to understand one's untoward feelings and reactions the therapist can obtain important clues regarding basic conflicts that are being extruded through projective identification.

The prescription of psychotropic drugs may be indicated if the patient urgently requires calming or depression is bogging him or her down. Here one must recognize that the reports by patients of benefit may not coordinate with that of outside observers. Drugs may be poorly tolerated in borderlines, and even minor side effects may tempt the patient to discontinue medications. Haldol (Soloff et al, 1986) and Navane (Serban & Siegal, 1984) in moderate doses may be useful for anxiety and emotional instability as well as for psychoticlike symptoms. MAO inhibitors, such as Nardil, have been recommended for depressions associated with experiences of rejection (Klein DF, 1977). Benzodiazepines (Xanax, Valium, Ativan) may occasionally be useful for strong anxiety, recognizing the potential for abuse and that they may stimulate destructive actions. Tegretol in some cases has lowered tendencies toward impulsivity. Lithium has also been used when emotional instability was extreme (Rifkin et al, 1972).

Psychological testing for borderline patients has its advantages. Frieswyk (1982) believes that testing is especially valuable when manifestations of borderline pathology are subtle. We may detect "potential for acting-out, depressive mood swings, suicide, psychotic decompensation, as well as circumstances most likely to evoke untold reactions." We are helped to estimate the patient's capacities for a therapeutic alliance and "potential responses to different treatment modalities."

Short-term hospitalization may be required during critical phases of adjustment, particularly when the patient encounters rejection in a close relationship, is fired from a job, is involved in an accident, or during family crises. When serious regression has been stirred up by negative transference, an explosive reaction or suicidal gesture may require control in a protective setting. A halfway house sometimes is all that is required. The therapist must guard, however, against the patient's desire to use hospitalization as a repetitive escape device.

Reconstructive Psychotherapy

Borderline patients have traditionally been considered unsuitable candidates for psychoanalysis, but in recent years, inspired by the work of such analysts as Kernberg (1975), Gunderson et al., (1975), Masterson (1976), Kohut (1971), Rinsley (1980), and others, and under the influence of object relations theory, certain modifications in psychoanalysis have been introduced geared toward the hitherto considered impossible goal of reconstructive change. Unfortunately, the writings of some of the innovators have been vertiginous and difficult to understand. Moreover, there are fundamental disagreements regarding the best way to implement psychoanalytic psychotherapy.

Although true classical psychoanalysis is generally contraindicated, some analysts agree with Kernberg that regression should be promoted in order to activate pathological object and self representations and their projection onto the analyst in the transference. Consequently, the therapist is enjoined to be technically neutral and noninterfering. Primitive transference, which rapidly precipitates, should immediately be interpreted in here-and-now terms. Suggestive and manipulative techniques are best avoided, but the patient's condition may necessitate some structuring of daily routines. The therapist is empathic but must be as noninterfering as possible, activities should be confined to clarification and interpretation and external arrangements left to others. Genetic reconstructions cannot be made early in treatment because self and object representations are too fuzzy and undifferentiated and projective identification and splitting are too imminent. Later in therapy when there is a better differentiation and part-object relations have given way to more mature (whole-object) relations, genetic reconstructions may be effective. This form of treatment is long-term, with session frequency no less than three times weekly. Because primitive transferences may activate psychotic processes, hospitalization may be necessary to protect the patient and others. If the patient's defenses are sufficiently strong to prevent acting-out, therapy may proceed outside of a hospital, perhaps with day-hospital arrangements, and if living with a disturbed family is intolerable, in a foster home. This modified analytic approach, known also as "expressive psychotherapy," may not be possible if the patient's secondary gains through exploitation of the illness are too powerful and milieu distortions are so strong as to necessitate constant environmental manipulation. Social isolation may also be too prominent, ego weakness too intense, and antisocial tendencies too dangerous. In addition, there may be too little motivation, too low economic wherewithal, too poor psychological mindedness, and too limited capacity for introspection to recommend this kind of treatment. Finally, the therapist may have too little training and sophistication in the use of the requisite techniques and too little confidence in their effectiveness to give the method a fair trial.

A large group of analysts question the value of expressive psychotherapy with its promotion of regression as the principal technique and think that it may pose dangers for the patient. They believe that the therapist must be more active and maintain an openly empathic front and provide a reassuring "holding," limit-setting, structured environment irrespective of the intensity of disturbance of the patient. This group, following the leads of "self-psychology," has evolved an elaborate concept of the "self-object" and of personality development that encourages a conception of the borderline patient as less of a laboratory of pathological strivings that require activation and interpretation in an atmosphere of technical neutrality and more of a creation of faulty conditioning and inadequate development with deficits that must be repaired in a nurturant relationship. The patient is helped to tolerate his or her transference reactions and then to replace destructive and angry feelings that emerge in the transference. Only very much later is interpretation utilized.

A modified analytic approach that has proven effective with some borderline patients is illustrated by the work of Arlene Wolberg (1952, 1959, 1960). She recommends that reconstructive treatment must be slowly and carefully organized because of the ever-present projective frame of reference and the danger of throwing the patient into anxiety that will force the patient to use his or her delusional system as a defense, thus pushing the patient over the border into an active psychosis. Freud's account of his management of the patient described in his paper "An Infantile Neurosis" contains tactics that may be used with borderline patients: "The patient . . . remained . . . unassailably entrenched behind an attitude of obliging apathy. He listened, understood, and remained unapproachable. His shrinking from an independent existence was so great as to outweigh all the vexations of his illness. Only one way was to be found of overcoming it. I was obliged to wait until his attachment to myself had become strong enough to counterbalance this shrinking, and then played off this one factor against the other" (*Collected Papers*, Vol. III, pp. 477–478). In view of the degree of sadomasochism in the borderline patient, the treatment process must take into account the severe anxiety to which such patients are constantly subjected, the peculiar composition of the ego, which tends to be organized around oppositional tendencies (sadism), stubborn negativism, the need of the patient to fail in certain situations, the passivity, the projective framework, the psychoticlike transference, and the characteristic failure of the various defensive structures. Special techniques are needed.

The first phase of treatment must involve what A. Wolberg (1960, 1973) has called "projective techniques." These are methods of coping with the sadomasochism of the patient, the acting-out tendencies, the denial and dissociative mechanisms, the autism (fantasy life), and the negativism so that the therapist does not become embroiled with the patient in a sadomasochistic relationship. Three projective techniques are recommended: (1) "the use of the other," (2) "attitude therapy," and (3)

"ego construction," i.e., reinforcement of the patient's constructive ego trends.

In the "use of the other" the therapist takes advantage of the tendency of borderline patients to deny their own feelings and ideas and to project them onto others. When they speak of "others," therefore, they are actually talking about themselves in a masked way to avoid anxiety. Should the therapist do what is ordinarily done with neurotic patients, i.e., interpret the projection and confront the patient with the defense, borderline patients will be unable to organize themselves and to utilize the interpretation constructively. Instead they will become more resistive and deny the validity of the interpretation, incorporating the interpretation into their sadomasochistic operations by beating themselves with it and advancing it as another reason to hate themselves or, on the other hand, by becoming paranoid against the therapist and using the interpretations as a rationalization for the distrust. The relationship with the therapist is bound to disintegrate under these circumstances; a transference neurosis may precipitate out abruptly; psychotic manifestations may emerge. For these reasons the therapist must preserve the projective defenses of the patient and always (at least during the early stages of treatment) talk about the motives and maneuvers of the "others," allowing the patient to make personal connections or to deny them as he or she wishes. Such a method will help cement a positive relationship with the patient. Dreams are handled in the same way, never pointing an accusing finger at the patient. Fantasies that have motivated the acting-out are analyzed in a manner similar to dreams: the therapist does not challenge or confront the patient. One merely explores. One does not justify or reassure the patient, even though one acts empathic.

The "others" in the interpersonal encounters are analyzed by conjecturing as to why they feel and act as they do and what their motives could possibly be. The therapist does not charge the patient with the fact that he or she is like the "others." Eventually when the working relationship consolidates, the patient will acknowledge this. When the first statements are made by the patient that "this is like me," the therapist simply agrees and does not pursue it further. Each time that the patient says "this is like me," the therapist agrees that is *might* be true. Should the patient repeatedly bring up the consociation, the therapist may suggest that this is a pattern worth exploring. The therapist may query, "How does the pattern operate? It is not too obvious in the sessions. This could be worth exploring."

"Attitude therapy" is a projective device used to point up the patient's patterns of operation within any given interpersonal relationship. Inevitably he or she will bring up details of a personal encounter that are highly prejudiced and contain a paranoidal flavor. Accurate accounts will be resisted since this will reveal the patient's acting-out proclivities that mobilize his or her guilt. The therapist must not be put off by the patient's maneuvers; the therapist keeps asking for details, but not to the point where the patient becomes overly defensive. In such a case the therapist discontinues questioning, indicating that it is causing too much anxiety in the patient. When other incidents are reported, however, questioning is begun again.

Eventually the patient's true attitudes and feelings, which contain fragments of the fantasies motivating the acting-out, will be revealed. The therapist may then say, "Incidents like this can be very upsetting." As the patient brings up accounts of further encounters, definite patterns will emerge. Eventually the therapist will be able to help the patient consolidate his or her thoughts, attitudes, feelings, and behavior in these situations. The interpretations are in the form of broad statements that in a roundabout way, through focusing, indicate a connection between thoughts, feelings, fantasies, anxieties, and patterns of acting-out behavior. Questions are posed in such a manner that the patient makes the associations. If the therapist offers the patient an interpretation before he or she is ready for it, i.e., before the patient has mentioned the possibility several times, then the therapist may become involved in the patient's obsessive mechanisms. The patient will weave the therapist into the warp and woof of his or her fantasy life and chew on the information instead of using it to work out the problem.

In the technique of "positive ego construction" the therapist is the projective object, taking positive trends in the patient's ego and reflecting them back to the patient as if they were the therapist's own. This is because borderline patients cannot accept good things about themselves or utilize their own constructive thinking without excessive anxiety. Such patients are guilty about their positive trends since they have been taught by their parents to disbelieve them; they have been encouraged to fail in certain ways in order to play the roles consigned to them. Success constitutes a greater threat than failure in specific areas. To reduce their guilt but not to analyze it is one of the purposes of this technique. For instance, if a patient brings in the tale of having applied for a job and having bungled the interview by purposefully saying that he could not qualify because of lack of skills, and if he then reflects back on what happened with the remark, "I should have told him that I know enough about this work to be able to learn the special details rapidly, which is the truth," the therapist may respond in a qualified positive way: "It is definitely *my* opinion that you know enough about this work to able to learn the special details rapidly." Thus the phrases the patient has uttered are repeated as the therapist's own ideas. The phrases may also be reorganized and the same thing said in different words. For example, the patient states: "Probably I feel I don't deserve the job." The therapist does not reply with the conventional, "Why not?" Instead the comment may be, "I've thought of this too. Many people I've worked with feel guilt when a good opportunity presents itself. They shouldn't have to feel this way, but they do."

Role playing may also be employed to rehearse with the therapist what the patient *might* have said, the patient and therapist interchanging roles of patient and employer. After a certain number of incidents have been "role played," a patient may wonder why he or she acts this way. The therapist then replies, "This is an important thing for us to figure out." The therapist does not give the patient the answers when questioned, "Why?" Rather the therapist indicates that the two must seek answers together; this is a cooperative effort between two people who have come to an agreement on certain points.

After the patient is able to accept responsibility for his or her own actions without developing intense anxiety or manifesting the usual defenses, the treatment may take on a form similar to that of working with a neurotic patient. Should the patient become excessively anxious, projective techniques, as outlined above, should be used.

Avoidant Personality Disorder (DSM-III-R Code 301.82)

The determining feature of avoidant personality disorder is possession of a markedly devaluated self-esteem. This produces a defensive reaction of avoidance of any stimulus that points to this defect. Avoidant individuals safeguard against criticism, rejection, humiliation, failure, and social derogation by withdrawal tendencies and refusal to take chances or to expose themselves to any activities that threaten to bring out their inferiority and personal shortcomings. Ungratified needs for love, acceptance, and recognition sponsor frustration, anger, self-debasement, and other masochistic tendencies. Unlike the schiz-

oid personality, who displays some of the same tendencies, the avoidant personality has not given up desires for success and good social relations, and in fact retains an unquenchable thirst for these bounties.

During psychotherapy, the thrust should be toward encouraging exposure to challenges and to activities that promise self-enhancing rewards. In addition to the baseline interventions (see page 1167), the following are recommended:

1. Behavioral assertiveness training to enable the patient to accept challenges and to put his or her best foot forward;
2. In vivo desensitization in situations that are usually avoided;
3. Group therapy and psychodrama to provide a platform for the practice of assertive behavior; and
4. Cognitive therapy to correct false attitudes and inhibiting self-statements.

Histrionic Personality Disorder (DSM-III-R Code 301.50)

The need for histrionic and dramatic displays characterize the histrionic personality disorder. A strong narcissistic tinge colors attitudes and interpersonal relationships. The individual, while evincing a superficial though exaggerated show of affection for and concern with others, is actually self-centered, seeking to impress the immediate audience with his or her charm and talents. Emotional instability with periods of screaming, crying, and explosive carrying-on break out when wishes are not granted or actions are disapproved. The irritability, egocentricity, demandingness, and irresonsibility of such persons result in rejection, which is apt to stimulate retaliatory rage and paranoidallike recriminations. Such behavior is usually forgiven because of the individual's skilled show of remorse and clever seductiveness, only to be repeated at the next frustrating episode. Dependency patterns are common. The histrionics typically fasten onto hosts whose lives they make a continuing episode of crises. Suicidal threats and abortive attempts at destroying themselves are prominent chapters in the book of theatrical displays.

Therapy is usually sought when a spouse or lover seriously threatens to abandon the person unless the latter begins therapy or analysis. With astonishing rapidity, the therapist becomes the object of the patient's displays, seductiveness, and acting-out, since transference is easily mobilized in these patients. Treatment is usually unsuccessful because motivation to change is shallow and insincere. As long as the patient has another human subject to fasten onto, the referring agency is temporarily relieved of the burden. If a therapeutic relationship can be established and the therapist does not allow countertransference to distort a professional stance, some of these patients may be helped with long-term dynamic psychotherapy.

Antisocial Personality Disorder (DSM-III-R Code 301.70)

Allied to narcissistic character disorders is an antisocial personality manifested by poor frustration tolerance, egocentricity, impulsivity, aggressiveness, antisocial acting-out, an inability to profit from experience, undeveloped capacities for cooperative interpersonal relationships, poorly integrated sexual responses, and urgent pleasure pursuits with an inability to postpone gratification. Many such patients lied, fought, stole, and were truants during childhood and resorted to severe substance abuse during adolescence. Vagrancy, sexual promiscuity, and criminality are hallmarks of the disorder in adults. Because of the indelible warping in ego formation, goals in therapy, as with the narcissistic personality, are geared toward symptomatic relief rather than character change.

Modification of destructive and antisocial behavior is, of course, desirable but usually visionary. Recognition of acting-out, the circumstances and needs that initiate it, and the way that the patient draws other people into his or her maneuvers are not too difficult. Doing something to prevent this behavior is another matter.

Most authorities agree that the management of an antisocial personality is most difficult. All approaches have yielded meager results. In many cases the only thing that can be accomplished is manipulation of the environment to eliminate as many temptations as possible that stimulate the patient into expressing his or her vicarious impulses.

If an antisocial individual can establish a relationship to a person, the latter may be able, as a kind but firm authority, to supervise and somehow restrain the patient's actions. Hypnosis may reinforce this authoritative relationship but the patient will usually continue to test the powers of the therapist who acts as a repressive moral force and as a pillar of support. The patient may get to the point where he or she will turn to the therapist for guidance when temptation threatens. Suggestions are couched in terms so as to convince the patient that he or she is actually wiser and happier for resisting certain activities that, as he or she knows from past experience, are bound to have disastrous results. On the basis of a guidance relationship, the patient may be instructed in the wisdom of postponing immediate gratifications for those that in the long run will prove more lasting and wholesome. The patient is taught the prudence of tolerating frustration and the need to feel a sense of responsibility and consideration for the rights of others. Not that these lessons will be immediately accepted or acted on, but constant repetition sometimes helps the patient to realize that it is to his or her best interest, ultimately, to observe social amenities and to exercise more self-control.

Experience demonstrates that it is possible to modify to some extent the immature explosive reactions of the patient by an extensive training program, particularly in cooperative group work where the individual participates as a member toward a common objective. Adequate group identifications are lacking in these people, and the realization that ego satisfactions can accrue from group experiences may create a chink in the defensive armor. In cases where the individual comes into conflict with the law and incarceration is necessary, a program organized around building up whatever assets the individual posssesses, particularly in a therapeutic community, may, in some instances, bring success. In young patients vocational schools that teach a trade may contribute to self-esteem and provide a means of diverting energies into a profitable channel. Should group therapy be deemed necessary, the constituent members ideally should be antisocial personalities with problems similar to those of the patient. The group leader should ideally be an antisocial personality who has recovered and gained respectability. Even if therapy seems successful, intervals of acting-out are to be expected.

PSYCHOACTIVE SUBSTANCE-INDUCED DISORDERS

Alcoholism (Alcohol Abuse) [DSM-III-R Code 305.00]; Alcohol Dependence [DSM-III-R Code 303.90]

People with alcohol dependence rarely come to psychotherapy because they want to quit drinking of their own accord. They are usually pushed into it because of aversive circumstances that their drunkenness has created. A wife threatens her husband with divorce unless he stops his irresponsible tippling. An employer gives an old employee a last chance to get off the bottle by personally arranging a consultation with a therapist. A drunken driver is about to lose his license and his lawyer insists that it is a good strategy to be in treatment. A judge suspends sentence on a person who has committed a crime while drunk on the condition that he do something about his alcoholic habit. A physician has frightened the drinker or his family with the announcement that alcoholic liver disease will result in incurable cirrhosis. In many cases the principal reason alcoholics seek help is for symptoms of anxiety, depression, blackouts, and insomnia or for stressful environmental conditions with which they cannot cope even under the influence of alcohol or other abusive substances. Alcoholics will often fail to mention their proclivity to drink until the therapist asks how much they drink. Alcoholics will usually minimize the amount they consume and derogate the idea that they cannot hold their liquor. They do this not because they want to deceive the therapist, but because *they are unable to stop their habit* and want to ensure its continuity without paying the penalty with which they are now confronted. The therapist will then realize that the complaint factor may be a secondary complication and that the basic problem is that the patient is poisoning himself and ruining his life with drink. The therapist will recognize also that unless the alcoholic stops drinking completely psychotherapy will have little effect. If the individual is only psychologically and not physiologically dependent on alcohol, it may be possible with psychotherapeutic help to wean the person from drink. If the pattern has progressed to the point where there is a physical need for alcohol, the problem may be an insuperable one unless motivation is created to achieve complete abstinence. Without this motivation, therapeutic efforts will be useless.

Because motivating drinkers to give up alcohol and other abused substances is so difficult, alcoholism has become, world over, one of the most serious and prevalent problems that threatens society today. The more than 10 million alcoholics in the United States affect the lives of 40 million family members. The economic loss to the nation amounts to $120 billion annually. Alcoholism accounts for a great many illnesses with fatal consequences. It is the fourth leading cause of death. Liver disease, gastritis, an increased risk of acquiring certain cancers, toxic interactions with other drugs, nutritional deficiencies, birth defects, hypertension, sluggishness of the cardiac musculature, interference with hypothalamic and pituitary hormones, and various other calamities shadow the existence of the indiscrete drinker. In addition, there are the ever-too-abundant psychological ravages that interfere with adaptive functioning which affect work, marriage, family, and social relationships, create accident proneness, and otherwise disrupt one's personal life. These problems are too well known to require elaboration here. In sum, alcoholism is the most commonly abused and most dangerous drug habit today.

The fact that alcoholism has traditionally been regarded as a moral failing rather than a disease with genetic associations has led families to regard it as a stigma and a disgrace. In recent years, however, this attitude has changed. The courageous revelation by First Lady Betty Ford of her struggle with alcoholism has helped enormously to give people a more authentic outlook at this crippling and potentially fatal malady. Recognition that alcoholism can be treated has led to the introduction of a number of regimes that try to approach the illness from a scientific perspective. Acceptance of modern treatments give the alcoholic patient almost a 75 percent chance of returning to productive life. The fact that one-half to three-quarters of all referrals to recently created employee assistance programs are for alcohol misuse has stimulated industry and unions to develop services for alcoholically impaired employees. Many deterrents exist, however, (JAMA, 1983). First, there is the matter of confidentiality and the patient's right to privacy. Revealing the nature of the difficulty can threaten advancement if not termination of one's job. Second, follow-up studies on treated alcoholics are thwarted by federal confidentiality regulations. Third, there is difficulty in coordinating the accumulated information so that it can be distributed effectively and utilized in medical curricula and by specialists. Fourth, reliable cost-effective methods of assessing new treatment programs must still be developed.

Aggressive programs, such as one at General Motors Corporation, have proven not only that such programs have economic advantages for a company, but also that they enable the company to retain valued employees and thus minimize staff turnover. Three- to 4-week care in institutions practicing a variety of interventions have proven so popular that freestanding inpatient and residential facilities for alcoholism and substance abuse have multipled. Medically supervised programs and "Care-Units" now exist that provide hospital-based medical care, as well as educational and psychological counseling for patients and their families. On some units offering multimodel programs some staff members are themselves recovered alcoholics who, because they have gone through similar experiences and "speak the language" of alcoholics, can often provide better role models than professionals.

A common treatment format includes at the start medical detoxificiation in a hospital. When the patient is able to do so, he or she attends daily group and individual psychotherapy and counseling sessions as well as recreation therapy. Weekly family seminars with patients and their families are held to discuss mutual problems and to explore changes that are essential in the future. Films are shown, literature distributed, and workshops are held to enrich education about the nature and consequences of alcoholism. An aftercare program acts as a bridge to the community to prepare the individual for the habitual stresses he or she will face without alcohol. These treatment units are located in differents part of the country, and information about them may be obtained from local social service agencies.

Getting off alcohol, it is now recognized, is not the end-all of therapy. It is the beginning. What one must do in addition is maintain sobriety and ideally deal with the sources of the drinking problem. Here we come back to the problem of motivation. It is hard enough to get an alcoholic to want to try to stop drinking and enter a unit that will enable him or her to get off alcohol; it is even more difficult to get the alcoholic to do something about the conditions that have created the drinking problem.

Creating Motivation for Abstinence

As mentioned previously, the first step in therapy is to create a sincere desire to remove from one's life the toxic substances that one uses to subdue anxiety. Initial resistance to the idea of accepting help is common and confounding. It is especially a problem in elderly alcoholics, whose denial mechanisms are abetted by their need to flaunt independence. Motivating an individual to accept that he or she needs to give up alcohol to feel better requires a good deal of patience and skill.

The following points and caveats may be of help:

1. When the average alcoholic applies for therapy, he or she usually expresses or suggests a secret hope of learning to drink normally and to "hold my liquor like anyone else." This may be possible in anxiety drinkers following abatement of their neurosis; it is not possible in the case of real alcoholics.
2. Although some persons believe that alcoholics can be cured by weaning them gradually from the bottle and that they may learn to engage in social drinking without exceeding their capacity, experience has shown that success is possible only where alcohol is completely and absolutely eliminated from an individual's regime. The object in therapy is complete elimination of all alcoholic beverages, including wine and beer.
3. The treatment of alcoholism not only embraces the removal of the desire for alcohol; it also involves restoration of the patient to some adaptational equilibrium. Without such restoration, the person will become pathologically depressed, and tension will drive him or her to drink no matter what pressures are exerted.
4. In the anxiety drinker any attempt to force or shame the person into sobriety will interfere with the therapeutic relationship. A useful rule is not to make the diagnosis of alcoholism for the patient but to give the patient information so that he or she makes the diagnosis or at least genuinely asks for help. It is fruitless to design a treatment program for an alcoholic unless he or she is ready to accept the need for help.
5. Never accuse the patient of being an alcoholic, this will stimulate defiance and denial. The patient will accept any other diagnosis except alcoholism. One may tell the patient that some people are chemically unable to tolerate alcohol and that it acts like a poison to their bodies. Many patients will accept that they are "allergic" to alcohol more easily than that they are psychologically unable to control their drinking.
6. Emphasize that it is difficult to break the habit without professional help because the body has become chemically dependent on alcohol and requires medical and psychological interventions to control the effects of withdrawal.
7. Never pressure a patient into giving

up alcohol. Explain its effects on the body and tell the patient to be the judge of whether he or she wants to try to give it up.

8.   If the patient asks what the signs of alcoholic dependency are, one may simply say: "If you can't get through the day without a drink, you may want to do something about it. This indicates that the body is asking for help."

9.   Warn the patient that he or she may need some support to stop drinking. The best support is an AA (Alcoholics Anonymous) or similar group. If the patient claims he or she is not an alcoholic and does not see the reason to go to an AA group, tell him or her that people with a wide assortment of problems other than drinking are helped by such groups. Deal with the patient's resistance.

10. You may not be able to do very much with an alcoholic without AA or a similar group as a helping adjunct.

11. Avoid psychoanalytic probing or any other insight therapy until the patient is off alcohol; such treatment will do no good. The triad of confrontation, empathy, and proferred hope is the best technique for breaking down denial mechanisms and other resistances (Whitfield, 1980).

12. A patient may be able to start and continue in psychotherapy without becoming an inpatient in a hospital or treatment unit if he or she has sufficient motivation to join a supportive group such as AA and is able to detoxify himself or herself.

Detoxification

A large number of patients who have no serious physical illness can be detoxified at home or preferably at a local detoxification center, usually without drugs (Whitfield, 1980). A pleasant atmosphere is important. The patient being ambulatory, introductory group sessions are initiated, and distracting group activities are arranged. Drug-free detoxification, if it can be done, has advantages; it is shorter, less expensive, can be executed by nonmedical personnel, avoids dependence on drugs, and helps the patient remember the unpleasant withdrawal experience, which acts as an aversive stimulus in the face of temptation. Any medications that are needed except anxiolytics and energizers should be continued. If the patient is uncomfortable, however, benzodiazepines such as Librium or Ativan may be prescribed during the first few days and then discontinued. A strong multivitamin, 50–100 mg of thiamine, and 1 mg of folate should be given daily. If withdrawal seizures have occurred in the past, 300 mg of phenytoin (Dilantin) should be given daily for 5 days. Where an anxiolytic is deemed necessary for more than a few days BuSpar may be used since this medication produces tranquilization with no apparent abuse liability and no withdrawal syndrome reported at the end of therapy.

Conditioned reflex therapy is not as popular as it was in past years. It requires hospitalization in a special unit when it is used. A popular model is to administer an emetic paired with alcohol. Apomorphine is given for purposes of conditioning if there is no disease of the kidney or liver and the patient has not recently been on Antabuse. The patient then receives several glasses of warm water flavored with his or her favorite alcoholic beverages. Several spasms of vomiting may occur. Suggestions are made that the patient will be able to control his or her drinking by disliking all alcoholic beverages; in this way a person's health is restored. This treatment is repeated on successive or alternate days. Salt should be added to the diet to compensate for the salt lost in vomiting. The conditioning method is expensive, and statistics on its usefulness are still unclear.

Some behavior therapists attempt detoxification by training the patient in behaviors that are incompatible with excessive drinking (Miller, 1977). The patient is taught substitutive behaviors in situations that operate as cues for drinking. Thus assertive training (Alberti & Emmons, 1973) may be instituted to enable the individual to express personal rights and feelings without his or her customary recourse to alcohol. Relaxation training and systematic desensitization teaches the patient to master anxiety-provoking situations that lead to drinking. Because troubled marriages are sometimes at the basis of an alcoholic's drinking, couples may be instructed in the use of mutual positive reinforcing behavior with contingency contracting (Stuart, 1969). A variety of other operant approaches have also been employed (Cohen et al, 1972; Azrin, 1976). "Covert sensitization" utilizes imagery to pair a desire for alcohol with nausea (Elkins, 1980). Hypnosis has also been employed (Katz RC, 1980).

If a patient continues to drink or whatever approach is tried proves only partially effective, he or she should be counseled, best in the presence of the spouse, to take a vacation and go to a treatment unit for help. There are many such units, some good, some not so good. The Yellow Pages of the telephone directory lists them under "Alcohol Information and Treatment," but finding units in this way will require investigating their qualifications. They should be hospital based, state certified, and approved by the Joint Commission for the Accreditation of Hospitals (JCAH). There are more than 100 "care units" around the country. They should have a rounded-out program from detoxification to aftercare. The reason concentrated therapy in a closed unit is necessary is that the alcoholic, despite his or her show of independence, is very dependent and needs people around all the time, as well as activities to divert his or her mind. Boredom easily sends the patient to drink. The alcoholic cannot fill the day with suffi-

cient activities at home or at work. Stresses associated with everyday routines may be too anxiety provoking. A complete change of scene in a well-run unit is needed to get these patients off to a fresh start.

In heavy drinkers, detoxification will precipitate abstinence reactions in 12 to 24 hours. Shaking and agitation may frighten these patients, delirium tremens may kill them unless they get proper treatment. Librium, 50–100 mg intravenously, repeated as necessary in 2 to 4 hours, or Ativan intramuscularly, 0.05 mg/kg up to 4 mg, may be required. Emergency reactions will need speical interventions (see Chapter 58, "Handling Emergencies in Psychotherapy"). It usually requires 3 to 5 days to detoxify an alcoholic, and up to 3 weeks if other addictive substances have been taken, which is very common. Coincident with and subsequent to detoxification, a multimodal program of counseling, education, group work, and recreational therapy is implemented. Family counseling and therapy are employed as needed. The patient is prepared to continue in an Alcoholics Anonymous or similar group in the area in which he or she lives, and the spouse and family are referred to Al-Anon (Anthony, 1977). The telephone number for Al-Anon is listed in the telephone directory or may be obtained from Alcoholics Anonymous, also listed in the directory.

A considerable number of alcoholics take abuse substances in addition to alcohol. Among the most popular of these drugs are sedative-hypnotics such as barbiturates (Nembutal, Seconal), nonbarbiturate hypnotics. (Noludar, Placidyl), opiates (heroin, illicit methadone), and stimulants (dexedrine, cocaine). After being detoxified from alcohol, the alcoholic may experience symptoms of withdrawal from the other abused substances, which may also require therapy. In some cases the primary problem was the abuse of substances other than alcohol, and alcohol was taken to reinforce the effects of or to deaden withdrawal symptoms from the drugs. Because of the ease and relatively low cost of alcohol, the drinking continued, resulting in alcoholism.

Not uncommon are manifestations of such syndromes as major or bipolar depression, panic disorder, agoraphobia, impulse control disorder, and psychogenic pain, which appear after detoxification has rendered the patient alcohol free. In many cases the primary problem was the syndrome, whose symptoms the individual has tried to control with alcohol. In such cases corrective interventions will be needed.

Once the patient is free from the mind-befogging effects of alcohol, he or she more easily becomes aware of how drinking has interfered with his or her life and happiness. The patient may still have symptoms of anxiety and depression; stress situations will still exist at home and at work; or a personality problem may continue to interfere with proper adaptation. The patient will continue to need care and psychotherapy for these problems. During the period of hospitalization the therapist will have telephoned the patient once or twice or, better still, if possible, would have visited. In this way, continuity of treatment is maintained.

Postabstinence Therapy

When the patient returns for psychotherapy, he or she may be able to accept the diagnosis of alcoholism. The patient is told that alcoholism is a treatable disease like diabetes for which one cannot be blamed. However, it must be watched and taken care of the rest of one's life. While the patient is better now, care must be taken not to slip back into old habits. This is best prevented by going regularly to an AA group and by continuing in psychotherapy. A common question is "Can I ever resume normal drinking?" The answer is a categorical no. Alcoholism like diabetes is a life-long disease and resuming drinking (even one drink) will activate it again." The patient is told that the recovery rate is high if a person follows a good treatment plan. Doing this is the patient's own responsibility. Nobody else can do it for the patient.

If the patient, in spite of this talk, cannot seem to avoid tippling, he or she should be put on Antabuse (disulfiram) after discussing the urgent need for this helping agent. The average daily dose of the drug is 250 mg (with a range of 125 mg to 500 mg), although sometimes more is needed. The patient must be completely off alcohol when it is started. The patient should be instructed that the drug is harmless unless he or she drinks, and that "going off the wagon" will make him or her violently and even dangerously sick. Antabuse will protect the patient from temptation, so taking it daily is important. Ayerst Laboratories puts out a patient education booklet entitled "Now that You're on Antabuse." After one or two years of abstinence, the patient, in conference with the therapist, spouse, or close family member and AA group leader, may experiment with going off Antabuse, provided the patient is able to cope with life and with crises adequately, is relating well with people, and most important, continues in the AA group. Antabuse is most helpful in older motivated individuals who need to control psychological stressors that invite drinking. Contraindicated for Antabuse use are illnesses such as diabetes, cardiac disease, and cirrhosis of the liver. Antabuse is not suitable for schizophrenics and patients with schizoaffective reactions and markedly unstable impulse disorders. It is best to arrange for a relative or a trusted person at work to supervise the regular and uninterrupted taking of Antabuse to maintain a constant level of the drug in the bloodstream. With too small doses of Antabuse, the patient may be able to override its effect with alcohol resumption.

Psychotherapy

The psychotherapeutic treatment of an alcoholic is vital, since true alcoholics never get over the threat of relapsing into drinking. During the period when they are well, they become nondrinking alcoholics. For many, attendance at AA is necessary all their lives. Older members eventually become leaders and helpers, ministering to the more vulnerable alcoholics. In this way, by identification, nondrinking alcoholics help themselves. Immediately after detoxification, individual therapy is needed in addition to the supportive AA group experience. The danger of relapse during the first 6 weeks after stopping drinking is real and the patient should be seen as frequently as possible during this period. Vulnerable patients who need supervision may be taken care of in a halfway house.

Designing a treatment program for the nondrinking alcoholic is dependent on what pathogenic links in the patient's behavioral chain require treatment. Basic to any treatment program is, to repeat what has been said before, continuing membership in AA or a similar group. Some alcoholics terminate the group program and are able to remain abstinent. For most, however, a good group is indispensable indefinitely as an anchor to sobriety. Psychotherapy for patients who do not have severe marital, family, or environmental problems can be short term, but group membership should continue without interruption.

Many alcoholics suffer from an underlying depression, which should not be too difficult to diagnose. A major depression may require antidepressant therapy with tricyclics or other drugs. A bipolar depression may need Lithium therapy. A neurotic depression is best helped by cognitive, interpersonal, or other form of verbal therapy. Some borderline cases may need carefully controlled neuroleptic therapy. Panic disorders and agoraphobia should be treated with behavioral approaches and antidepressants; and sedative-hypnotics assiduously avoided. Anxiety and tension are ubiquitous complaints, and the individual may importunately petition for some medications to relieve it. This request should not be treated lightly, but the patient must be reminded that the benzodiazepine drugs may be as harmfully addictive for him or her as alcohol. It is therefore best to use other tension-relieving approaches, such as relaxing exercises (a relaxing tape may be made), biofeedback, hypnosis and meditation, as well as physical exercise. Joining a YMCA or YWCA or other athletic club, running (if it is physically permissible), and swimming are often helpful. Where an anxiolytic is absolutely necessary, buspirone (BuSpar) may be employed.

Searching out and finding existing causes of stress and anxiety in the patient's work, marital, or family situation will necessitate appropriate interventions. In examining the work situation, a battery of vocational lists may disclose that the patient's interests and aptitudes are in a direction other than the existing work. The patient may then be guided to develop along the lines indicated by the tests. Marital difficulties are best approached with marital therapy and family problems with family therapy. Environmental stress will require counseling and environmental manipulation. Consultations with a social agency for recommendations of suitable resources can save a great deal of time. Any existing remediable elements in the patient's environment that may be creating conflict for the patient should be straightened out with the aid of a social worker if necessary. In spite of expressed optimism, the patient is unable to handle frustration, and any objective source of difficulty may suffice to promote tension that will produce a craving for drink. An inquiry into the patient's daily routine and habits may be expedient. Often one finds a gross defect in the person's diet.

Alcoholic overindulgence has been coincident with a depletion in dietary intake and with vitamin deficiency. Bad food habits may persist. Prescribing a well-balanced diet with sufficient calories and with supplementary vitamin B is important. The patient should also be encouraged to appease his or her hunger whenever he or she feels a need for food. Hitherto the patient has propitiated hunger pains by drinking alcohol. He or she may be surprised to observe that eating three square meals a day can remove much of the craving for liquor.

The numerous difficulties a patient has experienced through increasing inability to control drinking, the general condemnation of society, and the disdain of family all contribute toward a depreciation of self-esteem. It is difficult to rebuild self-esteem by reassurance, but an effort must be made to underscore repeatedly that the patient has many residual assets that can be expanded. Because alcoholics become negligent about their appearance, it is essential to rebuild interest in their personal care. Appearing neat and well groomed usually has a bolstering effect upon the person. Alcoholic women may be directed toward taking care of their complexions and hair by going to a beauty parlor. Whatever interest the patient shows in hobbies or external recreations should be encouraged. Patients must be reminded that they are not hopeless cases and that they have many good qualities that they have neglected. Their guilt may be continuously appeased by showing them that their alcoholic craving is part of an illness and that it will be possible to substitute something much more constructive for it.

Teaching the alcoholic to handle frustration will require considerable effort. The patient must be brought around to a realization that everyone has frustrated feelings and that an important job in life is to exercise control. Because of what has happened, the patient is apt to misinterpret any disappointment as a sign of personal failure. It is mandatory that the patient build up a tolerance of frustration, even though willful effort must be extended in this direction. Behavioral therapy may enable the patient to adjust better to many frustrating situations.

Since frustration is usually accompanied by gastric distress, it may stimulate a desire for drink. The patient, therefore, may be advised to carry, at all times, a piece of chocolate or candy. Whenever he or she feels frustrated or under any circumstances a craving for drink develops, he or she can partake of this nourishment. Hot coffee, cocoa, and milkshakes are also good for the same purpose. As the patient gains more self-respect, greater and greater amounts of frustration may be tolerated.

Many misconceptions and faulty self-statements plague the alcoholic, and clarification, persuasion, as well as cognitive therapy are usually in order. In many cases the basic difficulty is a personality disorder. There is no one predisposing personality problem. The character trait of dependency is often prominent, although the patient may try to conceal it. Dependency makes for a host of difficulties that have been outlined previously. Treating a personality disorder usually necessitates using a modified psychoanalytic approach, which is a long-term procedure (see Personality Disorders). If the patient is motivated and it is done properly, however, the reconstructive effects can be most gratifying.

Other Abused Substances

A miscellaneous group of psychoactive substances other than alcohol are used in all societies for mildly stimulating, tension-relieving, or recreational purposes. Among these are caffeine and tobacco. Only if the incorporation of such substances is beyond the individual's tolerance level, or if they impair social or occupational functioning, or produce abnormal physical and psychological changes, or if habituation upsets the individual or those around the individual, may help be sought from a psychotherapist. When the individual is unable to control the intake of a substance, he or she is suffering from what is commonly called a *substance abuse disorder*. If there is physiological dependence on the drug, it is regarded as a *substance dependence disorder*.

Although noxious substances such as alcohol and tobacco, which are consumed legally by average citizens, can have a pathological impact, minor abuse of these substances is generally disregarded. Serious addictions that lead to lives of crime and other social evils are of much greater concern to society. Prominent disorders encountered other than alcohol abuse and alcohol dependence are cocaine abuse, opioid abuse and opioid dependence, barbiturate and other sedative-hypnotic dependence, amphetamine and other sympathomimetic drug abuse and dependence, hallucinogen abuse (such as with cannabis, phencyclidene, and psychedelic drugs), and tobacco dependence.

The chief objective of this growing stable of substances is to reduce tension, anxiety, and depression and to stimulate feelings of tranquility and euphoria. The search for these rewards has brought forth a host of substances, some of which for years have languished unnoticed in chemical laboratories. Periodically, "revolutionary" drugs appear on the streets which are said to produce heaven on earth. Peace of mind, the ability to love unambivalently, the painless acquisition of deep insights, and other astonishing bounties have never before been promised as they are today. Such a drug was MDMA, dubbed "Ecstacy" by its habitues, who claimed results in minutes never before obtained with other substances. Word travels fast among aspirants looking for lasting euphoria, and before long Ecstacy became the promising gate to a new life. But like other miracle drugs, disillusionment rode on the wings of reality:

changes were short-lived, and episodes of disinhibition and psychosis destroyed the fantasy of harmlessness. Like other hallucinogens, its abuses led to its scientific discreditment and prohibition. Since then, other substances have taken its place. The latest "miracle drug" is "crack," a reincarnation of time-honored cocaine.

Cocaine Abuse (DSM-III-R Code 305.60) and Cocaine Dependence (DSM-III-R Code 304.20)

"The psychic effect of cocaine of .05 to .1 gram consists of exhilaration and lasting euphoria, which does not differ in any way from the normal euphoria of a healthy person. . . . One senses an increase of self-control and feels more vigorous and more capable of work. . . . One is simply normal and soon finds it difficult to believe that one is under the influence of any drug at all."

These words of Sigmund Freud describe what the founder of psychoanalysis observed during his own dalliance with the champagne of illicit substances, which now has become a public health and safety menace. Cocaine is rapidly becoming the major drug problem in this country because of its intense euphoric impact, ready availability on the street, and ease of administration. Snuffing (snorting) small amounts rapidly produces heightened alertness, feelings of well-being, and self-confidence, which last only a short time. Intravenous injections, ("freebasing") and smoking the concentrated refined drug ("crack") have a strikingly exaggerated effect, but the aftermath of this "high" are uncomfortable physical symptoms. Headache, palpitations, stereotyped movements, confusion, incoherence, rambling, nausea, vomiting, perspiration, chills, tachycardia, skin paresthesias ("insects crawling"), anxiety, trembling, and depression enjoin the addict to dose again. Overactivity, impaired judgment, and other behavioral abnormalities may occur. Recovery within 24 hours is usual unless the individual gets a "fix," initiating a new cycle of exhilaration followed by more unpleasant symptoms. Cocaine addiction is associated with weight loss, insomnia, irritability, and paranoid ideas. It may lead to violent activities and crime. With continued use of large amounts of the drug, psychotic attacks may eventuate, resembling amphetamine psychosis. Serious physical ailments also intervene, especially when the addict habitually combines cocaine with opiates ("speedballs"). Cardiac abnormalities, brain seizure, and pulmonary dysfunction may be followed by respiratory arrest and even death. The cocaine abuser may try to calm anxiety with Valium, but continued physical suffering soon motivates the addict to search for funds to buy relief, often resulting in thievery. The power of the drug is described by Grinspoon and Bakalar (1985): "Cocaine, along with some amphetamines, is the drug most eagerly self-administered by experimental animals under restraint; they will kill themselves with voluntary injections." Human beings seem to be no less hedonistic, and cocaine addiction is spreading at an alarming rate. At a national information and treatment referral service, for example, more than 1000 telephone calls (the number is 800-COCAINE) are received daily and more than $50 billion for the purchase of cocaine are spent annually by abusers of the drug.

Management of acute symptoms of abstinence is urgent to prevent the individual from dosing again with cocaine. Anxiety and restlessness may yield to 10 to 20 mg of Valium or Librium, repeated as necessary. This, of course, is a temporary measure and as soon as some control is established, more permanent therapeutic measures, including residential care, counseling, and psychotherapy, should be initiated. If an overdose of cocaine has been taken, forced oxygen inhalation and muscle relaxants are given, and for convulsions, sodium pento-

thal (25–50 mg) is injected intravenously. In the event anxiety and tachycardia are especially strong, 1 mg of Inderal (propanolol) is sometimes injected intravenously every minute for up to 10 times. There is some evidence that bromocriptine (Parlodel), a dopamine agonist, may represent a new adjunctive treatment for cocaine abuse.

Opioid Abuse (DSM-III-R Code 305.50) and Opioid Dependence (DSM-III-R Code 304.00)

An occupational hazard for physicians, and pharmacists because of their easy accessibility, a component of pleasure seeking among psychopaths and sociopaths, a means of proving their masculinity among adolescents belonging to gangs, an unfortunate consequence of their prolonged use for pain or anxiety, opiates (particularly heroin) constitute a growing menace to the population. Harsh penalties for the possession and sale of these drugs make their cost so high that the average addict must steal and engage in other criminal activities to secure a constant supply. The addict consequently becomes a social menace. Because he or she neglects his or her physical health, the addict suffers from disease and premature aging. Suicide is common as an escape from pain when drugs are not available.

Among the numerous narcotic opioid drugs in use today are heroin, morphine, hydromorphone (Dilaudid), oxycodone (Percodan), nalbuphine (Neubain), meperidine (Demerol), alphaprodine (Nisentil), anileridine (Leritine), methadone (Dolophine), propoxyphene (Darvon), pentazocine (Talwin), propiran (Dirame), levorphanol (Levo-Dromovan) and butorphanol (Stadol). The most frequent abusers of these drugs are teenagers, who are introduced to addiction by their peers.

The action of these drugs mimics the effect of built-in pain relievers released by the brain (endorphins and enkaphalins). Both the artificial and natural analgesics can be neutralized by certain substances such as naloxone, naltrexone, nalorphine, and cyclazocine, which block the effects of the addictive drug.

Generally, narcotic drug addition is not a simple matter of physical dependence. It is a manifestation of a long-standing personality problem that has many forms, addiction being one of the symptoms. It is not only a consequence of social and economic deprivation, although many users of drugs come from areas of poverty and destitution; it also occurs among the wealthier classes. Juvenile drug users are (1) seriously disturbed youngsters with a delinquent orientation to life who, because of a lack of cohesiveness, supervision, and discipline in their homes, drift toward renegade gangs to supply them with a sense of belonging and, through antisocial actions, to bolster up a stunted sense of identity; (2) adolescents in schools, whose peers induce them to experiment or who are depressed, bored, defiant, or simply seeking excitement. Drugs provide them with an answer to the tensions and anxieties of growing up. The pleasure rewards of drug intake followed by the violent discomfort of abstinence make drugs the central interest in the life of the addict. It requires a good deal of money to satisfy the drug need. This sum is generally obtained through crimes against property and by "pushing" drugs, selling them at profit to other addicts.

The treatment of the drug addict with any of our present methods is frustratingly unsuccessful, principally because the addict traditionally lacks the motivation for cure; the presence of narcissistic, immature, schizoidlike personality patterns that stir up incessant inner conflict and interfere with an adaptation to reality; and the existence of a home environment that imposes burdens for which the addict can find no solution. The following guidelines, nonetheless, may be useful:

1. The treatment of addiction to narcotic drugs is best achieved in a specialized institution where withdrawal symptoms can be handled and there is close supervision to prevent the addict from obtaining drugs. If the financial condition forbids hospitalization in a private institution, it is advisable to ask the patient to apply for voluntary admission or commitment to a U.S. Public Health Service hospital at Lexington, Kentucky, or Forth Worth, Texas (Council on Pharmacy and Chemistry, 1952).

2. Withdrawal or detoxification, which takes 4 to 12 days, is best accomplished with methadone, which may be administered orally (Dole and Nyswander, 1965). According to Fraser and Crider (1953) and H.A. Raskin (1964), 1 mg of methadone is equivalent to 2 mg heroin, 4 mg morphine, 1 mg Dilaudid, 20 to 30 mg Demerol, and 25 mg codeine. The dosage of methadone must be titrated to the tolerance of the patient. Too concentrated a dosage may produce respiratory depression, circulatory depression, shock, and cardiac arrest. Generally, detoxification treatment is administered daily under close supervision, does not exceed 21 days, and may not be repeated earlier than 4 weeks following the preceding course. A single oral dose of 15 to 20 mg of methadone will usually control withdrawal symptoms. This may have to be repeated if symptoms are not suppressed. A usual stabilizing dose is 40 mg per day in single or divided doses. After 2 or 3 days the dosage is decreased at a daily or 2-day interval. Hospitalized patients generally are reduced by 10 to 20 percent each day; ambulatory patients require a slower reduction. In cases of great physical debilitation, a high caloric diet, vitamins, hydrotherapy, massage, and glucose infusions are helpful. It is important to prevent all visitors and other persons

not concerned with treatment from seeing the patient who is hospitalized since drugs may be smuggled in as a result of pitiful pleas to relieve his or her suffering. Patients who have been taking low doses of an opioid and who have a good relationship with the therapist may be given Clonidine, 0.1 to 0.3 mg, three or four times daily for detoxification purposes instead of methadone. Patients must be watched for excessive lowering of blood pressure and for excessive sedation. The relapse rate is high once a patient leaves the hospital. Theoretically, a drug antagonist such as naloxone, cyclazocine, and naltraxone should prevent resumption of the habit. Practically, patients can be induced to start, but they rarely continue on the drug antagonist, and in one study 94 percent gave up the medication within 9 months. Librium, Thorazine, Trilafon, or Sodium Amytal may be taken to alleviate distress. Hypnotherapy has served to make some patients more comfortable. A prolonged period of hospitalization is best. Follow-up studies have shown that a high percentage of addicts released before 4 months become readdicted within 6 months.

3. While many drug addicts do well in a sheltered, drug-free environment, a return to the pressures and conflicts of their everyday world rekindles tensions, escape from which will be sought in drugs. An aftercare program is mandatory. Some authorities advocate legislation to force the addict to obtain aftercare services.

4. Aftercare is best administered in a day–night hospital or halfway house where the addict may spend a good part of his or her time, be exposed to the forces of group dynamics, and obtain a full range of social, rehabilitative, vocational, recreational, and psychotherapeutic services geared to his or her needs. The aftercare of drug-free addicts poses many hazards and disappointments principally because of their immature, hypersensitive personalities, their low level of frustration, and their inability to find adequate ways of dealing with their needs and tensions. A return to drugs is easily initiated by one disturbing experience.

5. An aftercare rehabilitation and guidance center is not enough. Rather, *constant care and supervision* are required, with daily interactions with some person (social worker, minister, rehabilitation worker, or psychotherapist). An adequate drug-control program must be so organized as to meet the individual patient's changing needs. Medical, psychiatric, social, educational, and rehabilitative services are part of this program; and unless these are closely coordinated, treatment can become both chaotic and ineffective. Methadone maintenance programs by themselves are inadequate without the additional services of counseling, vocational training, and psychotherapy.

Psychotherapy of the opioid addict is usually unsuccessful unless all the measures outlined above supplement the treatment program. In a 12-year follow-up study of addicts who had achieved abstinence, it was found that recovery is possible among delinquent addicts provided there is compulsory supervision and a discovery by the addict of gratifying alternatives to drugs (Vaillant, 1966). Since a considerable number of the patients are borderline or schizophrenic, they must be handled with methods attuned to sicker patients.

Addicts sometimes consult psychiatrists asking that they be given an opiate for renal or gall bladder colic or some other emergent condition that requires temporary narcotic administration. Signs of the addiction include the presence of needle marks on the arms, legs, hands, abdomen, and thighs or physical signs of withdrawal.

Other marks of opioid intoxication are constricted pupils, euphoria, dysphoria, apathy, motor retardation, slurred speech, drowsiness, and memory and attention impairment. Withdrawal symptoms (sweating, diarrhea, tachycardia, insomnia, eye watering, running nose, and yawning) may rapidly be brought on in an addict by injecting naloxone (Narcan) as an antidote to morphine, heroin, and similar narcotics. The presence of an opiate may also be detected from chemical analysis of the urine.

Because it is impractical to treat addition unless the drug intake is completely brought under control, the therapist should insist on hospitalization as a preliminary step in the treatment program. During aftercare, a small number of addicts will have sufficient ego strength to respond to reeducation, behavior therapy, or psychotherapy. But, it must be emphasized, psychotherapy unreinforced by a prolonged, perhaps perpetual program of rehabilitation is, as a rule, unsuccessful. An important deterrent in treating a drug addict by psychological means is countertransferential resentment and strong sympathy with the addict, which interfere with the therapist's capacity to show both tolerance and firmness when necessary. The addict's acting-out tendencies and low level of frustration will upset the equilibrium of the most stable therapist.

Some authorities, disappointed with the results of all treatment methods, advocate supplying addicts legally with drugs to keep them in balance, in this way eliminating the illegal supply outlets. Other authorities argue against dispensing drugs, saying that the factor of increasing tolerance enjoins the addict to expand the dose required to secure the desired effect. Having obtained the limit prescribed from the physician or clinic, the addict will return to the illegal market and continue to be exploited by drug peddlers, resorting to crime for funds as usual.

For this reason, methadone mainte-nance therapy has become the most common approach for chronic opioid dependence. Patients come to a methadone maintenance clinic (which is controlled by federal regulations) for their daily (up to 40 mg) methadone and after 3 months are given a supply (100 mg) to take home. Progress is monitored by interviews and urine testing. During the first few months of methadone maintenance some side effects may occur, such as sexual dysfunction, sweating, and constipation. Eventually, tolerance of methadone develops and patients feel more comfortable. We are dealing with a difficult population, however, and violent outbursts may be expected, especially among unstable personalities around such issues as take-home supplies of methadone. Some patients continue to seek opioids in addition to methadone (Maddun & Bowden, 1972; Newman, 1976), and some use alcohol and sedative-hypnotics. But many are helped toward a more productive life; criminality lessens, employability increases, and general adaptation is better (Cushman, 1972; Sharoff, 1966). Even some patients who have complicated psychotic and personality problems are helped with adequate counseling and psychotherapy to stabilize with methadone. A few who are not too ill emotionally may achieve complete abstinence from drugs provided environmental stress can be controlled. The preferred objective, of course, is to render the individual completely free of all abused substances as well as methadone. This may be possible in some cases. In other cases abstinence is obtained by administering an opioid antagonist which the addict continues to take much as some alcoholics rely on Antabuse to help keep them dry.

Among the newer treatments for heroin control in addition to methadone is methadyl acetate, a synthetic congener of methadone. Methadyl acetate appears to be equal to methadone in its rehabilitative efficacy, but its duration of action is from 48 to

72 hours, so it can be dispensed three times weekly instead of daily. It may be useful for a certain subgroup of the addict population (Senay et al, 1977).

There are some incurable addicts who are "well-adjusted and leading useful, productive and otherwise exemplary lives which would probably be upset by removing their drugs. They are contented with their present states, do not desire treatment and would resist change. The wisdom of disturbing them is to be questioned, for the result socially and economically might be destructive and bad" (NY Academy of Medicine, 1963). This applies also to elderly addicts with healed lesions of various sorts.

Some addicts seem highly motivated to rehabilitate themselves but require a drug other than methadone and a narcotic antagonist to sustain them in resisting narcotics. Neuroleptics are helpful in certain situations, particularly if psychotic symptoms threaten. Roskin (1966) believes that the schizophrenic addict uses narcotics as a tranquilizer in the throes of severe schizophrenic decompensation. The schizophrenic addict, in his opinion, has a better prognosis than the pure acting-out addict. "If a drug addict seeks help on his own volition, it may be suspected that he is a schizophrenic." Neuroleptic drugs, therefore, and the supportive relationship with the therapist are helpful replacements for narcotics in the adjustment of the schizophrenic addict. Patients with primary and bipolar depression will require antidepressants.

As mentioned before, clonidine has been used as a detoxifying agent (Mark et al, 1980; Charney et al, 1981) to wean addicts completely off opioid substances and methadone. This is followed by administration of a substance like naltrexone (Resnick et al, 1974). Naltrexone (Traxan) is a non-addicting narcotic antagonist that has fewer side effects than the older cyclazocine (Martin WR et al, 1965; Jaffe and Brill,

1966) and naloxone (Narcan) (Zaks et al, 1971). Blocking the euphoric effects of opioids, naltrexone acts somewhat in the same way with narcotic addicts as Antabuse does with alcoholics (i.e., by reducing motivation for drugs). The patient must be narcotic free when it is started. After detoxification and the slow reduction of methadone to where it is completely withdrawn and when 7 to 10 days of freedom from all opioids and methadone has been verified (sustained by urine tests), naltraxone (50 mg) is administered daily. Charney et al. (1982) have described use of a combination of naltraxone and clonidine as a "safe, effective, and extremely rapid method for treating the methadone withdrawal syndrome."

Motivated addicts also have been helped in groups by relating themselves to other addicts who have broken the habit. The most successful experiment is that of Synanon under whose care the addict deliberately places him- or herself (Casriel, 1962; Gould, 1965; Walder, 1965). Part of the Synanon idea includes an intensive leaderless form of group therapy—usually three times weekly—during which each member is expected to reveal his or her feelings truthfully, and to lay bare fears and hates. "At Synanon we snatch off all the covers of our dirty little secrets. Then we stand there naked for everybody to see" (*Life Magazine,* 1962). Groups with a leader also exist, ideally consisting of three male and three female addicts and one ex-addict ("Synanist"). The Synanist acts as moderator who utilizes insight into himself or herself for interpretations. The Synanist also employs such tactics as ridicule, cross-examination, and hostile attack to stir up involvement and activity. Another device, used with a new addict is the "haircut," in which four of five significant members of the Synanon family structure "take one apart," criticizing actions and performances to date. While the "haircut" may be a verbally brutal experience, it is usually quite effective. "When the word gets around that 'haircuts' are being given, people seem to get in line. . . . Many of the people who have experienced these 'haircuts' reported a change in attitude or a shift in direction almost immediately." Lectures are given daily by one of the more experienced members. The members support each other and come to each other's aid when temptation threatens to disrupt drug abstinence. Each member is also expected to perform household tasks according to ability, which gives the addict a sense of participation. Additionally, "a concerted effort is made by the significant figures of the family structure to implant spiritual concepts and values that will result in self-reliance. Members are urged to read from the classics and from the great teachers of mankind—Jesus, Lao Tse, Buddha. These efforts have been successful to a rather surprising degree. The concept of an open mind is part of a program to help the addict find himself or herself without the use of drugs" (Dederich, 1958). As soon as the addict is adjusted to the new environment, he or she is encouraged to get a job on the outside, to contribute some salary to the group, and to continue living at the Synanon house. Dropout rates, however, are high.

The Synanon idea, which essentially depends for its force on group dynamics, is being adopted in some correctional institutions. The lack of communication between the inmates of an institution and the authorities who run it has always posed a problem. To circumvent this, the people chosen to work with offenders are themselves ex-offenders who have modified their own deviant behavior. Offenders, alcoholics, and drug addicts seem to respond to a leader who, like themselves, has gone through criminal, alcoholic, or drug addiction experiences, who talks their language, and who, in having achieved resocialization, becomes a model with whom new identifications may be made. Such a leader usually approaches his or her work with an evange-

licallike zeal to point out new directions in life from which he or she cannot be outmaneuvered by specious arguments. Another technique that has come into recent use with drug addicts is the "marathon group" of continuous group interaction for 2 or more days with short periods of rest.

Residential treatment centers like Synanon have been developing in different parts of the country. An example is Daytop. Therapeutic communities, such as Odyssey House and Phoenix House (DeLeon et al, 1972; Densen-Gerber, 1973), have provided a refuge for some addicts and beneficial effects are usually maintained for as long as a patient is an active member.

Coincident psychiatric problems found among drug abusers are, in order of frequency, affective disorders, especially major depression; alcoholism; personality disorders, principally antisocial personality; and anxiety disorders. Schizophrenia sometimes may be seen, but paranoidal conditions are more common. Therapy, such as Doxepin for depression, Antabuse for alcoholism, and neuroleptics for schizophrenia, should be instituted if necessary. About one-quarter of opioid addicts take other substances, such as barbiturates, benzodiazepines, cocaine, cannabis, amphetamines, and alcohol. This accents the need to work with many variables that influence continuance of the drug habit. Therapists looking for an ideal model of therapy should consider detoxification with methadone as a preliminary step toward complete abstinence, the use of an antagonist such as naltrexone as safeguard against resumption of the drug habit, and treatment in therapeutic communities of drug-free day-care centers, with the use of behavioral, cognitive, and, in a few cases, modified analytic therapy according to the needs and aptitudes of the patient (see Summary, page 1209).

The following readings on narcotic addiction are recommended: Dole and Nyswander (1965, 1966), A.M. Freedman

(1966), A.M. Freedman and Sharoff (1965), Mueller (1964), Nyswander (1956), Ray (1961), Sabath (1964), Seevers (1968), Senay (1983), Stimson and Oppenheimer (1982), U.S. Department of Health, Education, and Welfare (nd), Verebey (1982), and Wikler (1980).

Sedative, Hypnotic, or Anxiolytic Dependence (DSM-III-R Code 304.10) and Abuse (DSM-III-R Code 305.40)

Dependence on *barbiturates* was once as serious an addiction problem as dependence on narcotics is now. Barbiturates in overdose are lethal and constitute one of the chief means of suicide. They are especially dangerous when taken with alcohol. Sometimes suicide is unintentional if an individual, because of sluggish thinking or chronic intoxication, forgets he or she took pills and swallows additional ones.

In 1962, a survey by the Food and Drug Administration revealed that more than a million pounds of barbituric acid derivatives were available in the United States (Committee on Alcoholism & Addiction, 1965). This 1-year inventory is enough to supply two dozen 1.5-gm doses to every man, woman, and child in the country. The survey led to the conclusion that "any patient whose psychological dependence on a barbiturate drug has reached a degree sufficient to constitute drug abuse has some form of underlying psychopathology." He or she is "directly comparable to the opiate-dependent person." There are no specific syndromes involved; practically all diagnostic categories are represented. Since federal restrictions have been placed on the sale of barbiturates, benzodiazepines have largely taken their place.

Short-acting barbiturates (Pentothal, Seconal, Amytal) are particularly addicting "They are as truly addicting as heroin or morphine and give the individual and his physician an even greater problem" (U.S. Department of Health, Education, & Welfare, nd). Like alcohol, they are intoxicating, produce confusion, lack of coordination, and emotional instability. Sudden or complete withdrawal of barbiturates from an addicted person usually results in convulsions and sometimes in a temporary psychosis like delirium tremens. Death may follow.

A sizable class of barbiturate addicts are middle-aged and older people who have been given barbiturates for insomnia and have consumed pills for years. This leads to hazy thinking, poor judgment, memory loss, emotional instability, and diminished motor skills.

The most common barbiturates sold illegitimately are secobarbital (Seconal), known on the street as "reds," pentobarbital (Nembutal), dubbed "yellows" or "nembies," and amobarbital secobarbital (Tuinol), called "double-trouble" or "tooies." Sometimes inveterate addicts, especially alcoholics and amphetamine users ("speed freaks"), inject barbiturates ("downers") intravenously ("pill popping") and use them interchangeably with heroin and amphetamines ("uppers"). Behavior is affected markedly and may include episodes of violent disruptive outbursts.

Any person who has taken an overdose intentionally or unintentionally should be rushed to a hospital for immediate treatment. While waiting for the ambulance, vomiting should be induced and the airways kept clear to prevent strangling. The person should be prevented from slipping into unconsciousness. Withdrawal from the drug is essential, but complete immediate withdrawal is dangerous. The patient must be put back on barbiturates to counteract abstinence symptoms and then phased into withdrawal. No more than 0.1 gm should be withdrawn daily, and physiological signs should be monitored throughout withdrawal (Ewig, 1966). The daily intake is reduced over a 1- to 3-week period. Librium or Valium may be given temporarily to control agitation, tremor, and insomnia. Supportive restoration of electrolyte balance, vitamins, and intravenous fluids are in order (see Chapter 58 on Emergencies). Hospital admission and proper nursing care are mandatory. Physical dependence on minor tranquilizers (Miltown, Librium, Valium) will also be followed by abstinence symptoms, convulsions, and occasionally even death if withdrawal is abrupt, and emergency measures as for barbiturate overdose should be employed. Continuing aftercare, as with narcotic addiction, will be necessary. Caution in prescribing tranquilizers and sedative drugs with dependence-producing properties is essential in "dependence-prone" persons (Bakewell and Wikler, 1966).

Methaqualone (Quaalude) has had some use in recent years as an agent to counteract insomnia, but it has been abused, especially by young people who take one or two pills, sometimes with wine, to produce relaxation and euphoria. It has a reputation for being an aphrodisiac. Depersonalization and various physical symptoms are common adverse effects. Convulsions, delirium, and death may occur with overdose. Other nonbarbiturates that may be overused are glutethimide (Doriden), ethinamate (Valmid), ethchlorvynol (Placidyl), and methprylon (Noludar). Emergency treatment for overdose is similar to that for barbiturate intoxication. While benzodiazepines (Valium, Librium, Xanax, etc.) are much safer than sedative-hypnotics, addiction can occur when they are taken over an extended period. After a month or so, even therapeutic doses may produce a tolerance. Since withdrawal symptoms are apt to occur, a gradual slow reduction of the medication is necessary. If large doses of benzodiazepines have been taken and withdrawal was abrupt, convul-

sions are possible and Dilantin (hydantoin) is indicated.

Amphetamine or Similarly Acting Sympathomimetic Abuse (DSM-III-R Code 304.40) and Dependence (DSM-III-R Code 305.70)

Addiction to *amphetamine* and similar-acting sympathomimetic stimulants has been growing in this country. It is used by students to prod them into greater alertness, by pleasure seekers in search of "kicks," and by those who habitually try to supress their appetites to control overweight. Such addiction results in serious physical effects, the disorganization of the personality, and can even precipitate outright paranoid psychoses (Lemere, 1966) that resemble paranoid schizophrenia. Other symptoms are impaired judgment, aggressive behavior, and lack of coordination. Tolerance to the drug causes the abuser to increase the dosage for a euphoric effect, sometimes to 20 times the original dose. The intake of large amounts of amphetamine may cause a delirium. Attempts at withdrawal produce a letdown or "crash," with depression, physical symptoms, and aggressive behavior that usually send the addict out for a "fix." Amphetamines have been implicated in increasing numbers of automobile accidents and crimes of violence (Medical Society of the County of New York, 1966). Treatment of the individual who takes only 2 or 3 tablets a day requires quick withdrawal and administration of ammonium chloride to bring the pH to the acid side. Though withdrawal is not as urgent in these cases as in persons who take large amounts, there is always the danger that the intake will be increased. Mandatory withdrawal for persons who consume large quantities of amphetamine substances should be carried out in a hospital. The drug is removed abruptly, and the withdrawal effects are treated with intramuscular neuroleptics such as Haldol and, if necessary, barbiturates at night. These are especially indicated if amphetamine-barbiturate mixtures have been used (Connell, 1966). Depression may need to be treated with antidepressant medication such as tricyclics. Aftercare is as important as it is for narcotic addiction, and psychotherapy may be an essential part of the rehabilitative program.

Cannabis Abuse (DSM-III-R Code 305.20) and Cannabis Dependence (DSM-III-R Code 304.30)

Marijuana (cannabis) continues to be a popular substance, especially among students in school and young people in middle- and upper-income groups. The drug is neither as innocuous as is claimed by its friends nor as destructive as contended by its foes. It is a hallucinogen with varying potentials for toxicity depending on the host and the conditions under which it is taken. Generally, marijuana ("joints," "dope," "pot") is smoked experimentally on only random occasions and the hallucinogenic ingredient is in too low a dose to create any real difficulties. Some authorities say that harmful physical and psychological effects of prolonged marijuana use have not been consistently demonstrated and are minimal compared with the ravages of alcohol intake. Emotionally disturbed persons will, however, continue to indulge in concentrated efforts to experience euphoria by using the most potent substances such as hashish and purified THC, which can cause greater mischief, including depersonalization, paranoidal ideas, anxiety, depression, tachycardia, and apathy. The abuse potential of marijuana is high. There is, nevertheless, no evidence that the use of marijuana is associated with crimes in the United States (Medical Society of the County of New York, 1966). Nor is there evidence that the drug is a narcotic or that it is truly addicting. Yet, in its usual form, it *is* a mild hallucinogen and may, in some susceptible persons, promote panic and aggressive behavior. Moreover, the impaired judgment under the influence of the drug interferes with skilled activities such as driving. Some people with severely disturbed personality problems may proceed from marijuana intake to a heroin habit, although the exact correlation between marijuana and subsequent heroin addiction has not been established. Pressure to legalize marijuana understandably has brought forth heated debate and controversy. Arguments pro and con related to the harmlessness of marijuana do not suffer from a dearth of misinformation. Research has had little effect on bias and the polarization of opinions.

Phencyclidine (PCP) or Similarly Acting Arycyclohexylamine Abuse (DSM-III-R Code 305.90) and Dependence (DSM-III-R Code 304.50)

Phencyclidine (PCP, "angel dust," "crystal," "Peace Pill") and similar substances such as ketamine (Ketalar) and TCP may be taken orally and intravenously, as well as by smoking and inhalation (Cohen, 1977). Effects are rapid and consist of euphoria, grandiosity, hallucinations of color and sound, and slowing of the time sense. Agitation, vomiting, anxiety, nystagmus, elevated blood pressure, ataxia, muscular twitchings or rigidity, anaesthesia, paranoidal ideas, and other symptoms may follow. Delirium can occur with large doses (20 mg or more). Hospitalization and administration of antipsychotics such as haloperidol (Haldol) may be helpful as an emergency measure.

Indulgence of other hallucinogens has been increasingly reported. The use of dimethyltryptamine, psilocybin, bufotenine, peyote, mescaline, charas, morning glory seeds, and nutmeg sometimes produces variant problems, and glue sniffing among youngsters of school age can become disturbing (Jacobziner, 1963). LSD, which was popular in the past, was obtained from amateur chemists or from organized criminal groups. Usually 100 to 600 micrograms were ingested by individuals on a sugar cube for the purpose of "taking a trip," which was embarked on once or twice a week. Large doses (more than 700 micrograms) were ingested to produce more intense psychotic experiences. Psychotic episodes persisted for days or weeks and, in schizoid personalities, for months or even years, requiring hospitalization. The use of these hallucinogens has diminished in favor of such drugs as cocaine.

Nicotine Dependence (DSM-III-R Code 305.10)

According to the World Health Organization approximately one million persons die of cigarette-related diseases each year the world over and approximately one-third this number (350,000) in the United States alone. This is not because of misuse or abuse of cigarettes since "no safe use for this product exists; every cigarette smoked is intrinsically harmful to health. . . . even when used normally and as intended" (JAMA, 1986). The National Institute on Drug Abuse has warned that nicotine in tobacco is "a powerful addictive drug. . . . six to eight times more addictive than alcohol." In the United States, medical care and cost productivity associated with cigarette smoking total approximately $65 billion per year.

Promotional advertising linking cigarettes to a healthy and athletic life style nevertheless continue in force. To a large extent, adolescents and children fail to comprehend the dangers of the habit, which they continue as adults. Billions of dollars of profit pour into the coffers of the cigarette companies annually. In the meantime the ravages of cigarette smoking promote heart disease, emphysema, cancer of the lung, cancer of the upper respiratory tract, as well as other debilitating and fatal diseases. These are amply detailed in medical journals, although most of the cigarette-smoking public overlook or minimize medical warnings. But some request help.

Cure of the smoking habit is a difficult task, especially if smoking serves the purpose of alleviating tension. Educational campaigns, psychotherapy, and pharmacological aids have all yielded limited success (Ford & Ederer, 1965). Mark Twain's comment, "It's easy to quit smoking; I've done it hundreds of times," is tragically the experience of most inveterate smokers who try to force themselves to give up tobacco. Group therapy with smokers, anesthetic lozenges, astringent mouth washes, anticholinergic drugs, vitamins, tranquilizers, stimulants, sensory deprivation, systematic desensitization, aversive conditioning, stimulus control, and lobeline as a nicotine replacement may produce temporary withdrawal from tobacco, but the relapse rate is high—75 to 80 percent. The entire process of smoking becomes for the inveterate user of tobacco an adjustment mechanism serving to satisfy specific needs: appeasing and reducing tension, providing a facade of nonchalance and poise, controlling anger, overcoming embarrassment in upsetting interpersonal situations, providing mouth and oral gratifications, acting as a substitute for overeating. Giving up smoking leaves a hollow in the life of the tobacco addict, mobilizes tension, and deprives the addict of a powerful adaptational tool.

In many cases smokers will openly or indirectly reveal that they are convinced that they will be unable to stop. In one case I was consulted by a professional man with Berger's disease, an illness in which smoking is dangerous. When he was admitted to a hospital for the beginning of gangrene of a toe, he had strapped cigarettes across his back to conceal them from the nurses and attendants, knowing that they would remove any cigarettes on his doctor's orders!

The "I can't" resistance ("I don't have what it takes," "My life is too unsettled now," "I'm not strong enough," etc.) is a means of reducing anxiety stemming from the conflicting desires of wanting to smoke and wanting to maintain one's defensive gratifying prop (Clark R, 1974). The defeatist belief is a way of denying this conflict. In applying for help, there is a forlorn hope that someone other than the patient can control his or her smoking. The resistance if unresolved will defeat any applied therapeutic efforts. The fact that smoking continues in spite of treatment convinces the individual that he or she is hopeless and provides an excuse for continued smoking. The idea that the smoker has exposed himself or herself to therapy appeases the guilt. "I know it's bad for me, but I don't care, it doesn't matter, I'm not going to think about it." In working with any smoker, therefore, this resistance should be tackled at first. The therapist should verbalize the nature of the resistance and explain its purpose. Smokers should be encouraged to stop pretending that they are doing all they can to overcome the habit. At the same time the therapist should express confidence that they *can* quit smoking if they want to and work toward kindling the patients' faith in themselves.

It is important in treating individuals who want to give up smoking to keep in mind that immediate abstinence is possible with many techniques. As with any other addiction, resumption of the habit will usually follow within the first year unless the needs that led to smoking originally are adequately fulfilled.

The first step in smoking control is to ask the patient why he or she feels he or she should give up tobacco at this time. The patient will probably have been warned by a physician to stop the habit because it is a health risk. Such warning usually has fallen on deaf ears. The habit is compelling and insidious. The patient may be told that he or she, like many others, can succeed by recognizing the *positive* value of abstinence. Some therapists give the patient a typewritten form that says something along the following lines:

Overcoming the tobacco habit may be achieved with a minimal amount of suffering if you follow these principles:

1. First, prepare a written or typewritten list of the *benefits* you will gain in giving up tobacco, such as that your health will improve, and that you will feel more vigorous, look better, lose the offensive tobacco odor, save money, and respect yourself more for abandoning a self-destructive habit.

2. Choose a time to quit when you are under the least stress or tension. *Then quit completely.* Shred or destroy every cigarette or cigar in your possession. Give away your lighter and ashtrays.

3. Discomfort during the next few days is to be expected but will disappear within 2 weeks. Such discomfort may be minimized by (a) reading the list you have prepared once in the morning when you get up and at bedtime and more often if you desire; (b) practicing relaxing exercises at least twice daily (meditation, self-relaxation, self-hypnosis, listening to a relaxing audiotape); (c) oral substitutes like Nicorette gum or smoke-free cigarettes (Favor) *if you need it* to stop physical reactions. Keep sugarless candies, carrot sticks, and menthol-filled plastic fake cigarettes on hand to take to work or use at social functions; (d) tell your friends that you are quitting smoking for health reasons and ask them, please, if they can, not to smoke in your presence for the next few weeks; (e) during the first 24 hours of abstinence expect to feel some muscle cramps, fatigue, headaches, or nausea as nicotine disappears from your body.

Expect periodic cravings for a cigarette. Push your mind away from the thought and busy yourself with some activity; take a long walk, write letters, or do other activities; (f) spend as much time as you can in smokeless surroundings such as libraries and theaters; (g) cultivate a hobby (golf, swimming, tennis, bridge).

4. Your eating habits may need to be changed because in giving up tobacco you are apt to crave sweets and more food. Drink 6 to 8 glasses of water daily; keep water, some fruit juice, or a diet soda near you while watching television and sip it to appease your appetite. Avoid spicy foods, and minimize the intake of alcohol and coffee, which can stimulate a desire for tobacco and increase your appetite. Do not despair if you gain a few pounds; you will lose weight after the craving for cigarettes disappears.

5. In about 2 weeks you will have conquered a good deal of the tobacco desire, but the rest of your life fight off the impulse to take even one puff. When nicotine has completely left your body, the joy and vigor you will feel will more than compensate for the loss of this dangerous habit.

In many cases, these simple suggestions may suffice. If they do not, more extensive measures may be needed. Among the chief methods for getting the smoker off tobacco are behavior modification, hypnosis, and group approaches.

Behavior modification methods are fashioned after the techniques used to overcome overweight and obesity (see page 1230). An investigation is launched into the history of the smoking habit, how many cigarettes are consumed daily and under what circumstances, when the frequency increases, what puffing on a cigarette does for the individual, what efforts have been made to stop in the past, and why the individual wants to give up smoking now. Behavior modification techniques are then devised to replace reaching for a cigarette with other activities, thus providing a nonsmoking routine for the patient (Bernstein & McAlister, 1976). Holding a sizable sum of money in escrow that is forfeited with the taking of even one puff of a cigarette within 6 months may be effective beyond any other technique.

Therapists acquainted with the hypnotic technique will find hypnosis a useful adjunct. Many ways of employing hypnosis have been described, with varying claims of success (Crasilneck & Hall, 1968; von Dedenroth, 1968; Spiegel H, 1970; Watkins H, 1976). In my own experience I have found that hypnosis can help eliminate sources of tension, especially after the smoking habit has been broken. The initial visits should, if possible, be frequent. Suggestions are made in the trance to the effect that the patient will develop a *desire* to stop smoking and that he or she will grow so strong that neither temptation nor tension, no matter how intense, will deviate him or her from the resolve to give up tobacco. This achievement will be rewarded by a feeling of well-being and strength that will be greater with each day of continued abstinence. It is strongly suggested that the patient will, in relinquishing smoking, be able to control his or her appetite so as not to overeat. Dictated tape recordings, made by the therapist, which the patient plays at home twice daily (see section on Induction of Hypnosis, page 1019) often help to reinforce suggestions and to reduce tension. They are especially useful if the patient cannot come for frequent reinforcing sessions. Self-hypnosis, facilitated by the recording, will also prove to be of value.

Should the patient inquire about other oral gratifications, such as gum chewing or allowing a hard piece of candy to dissolve in the mouth, "permission" for this may be given if it is not overindulged. Some patients who have a need to defy authority will, rather than return to smoking, engage in these harmless oral activities beyond what they believe is permitted. In this way the tobacco habit may become more readily extinguished. The gum chewing and candy indulgence are gradually given up on their own. Because nicotine addiction drives smokers back into the habit, nicotine in a flavored chewing gum (Nicorette) is sometimes prescribed to ease the physical craving for nicotine. The gum may be helpful during the first few weeks of quitting smoking (Russell et al, 1982). Other common methods that may be used to get individuals off cigarettes (Schwartz I, 1977) are rapid concentrated smoking inhalation and group approaches (supportive and behavioral). The latter prove especially valuable when behavior modification and self-control methods are combined. Powell and Arnold (1982) have described a multiple-treatment design for coronary-prone men that achieved a 50 percent smoking cessation rate at the end of one year, which is about double the usual reported rate of abstinence. Their "Stop Smoking Program" consisted of four consecutive 1½-hour sessions, Monday through Thursday, composed of highly structured activities along the following lines:

1. Stimulus control (altering the antecedents leading to smoking);
2. Relaxation training (deep breathing with pleasant imagery);
3. Thought stopping (see page 870) to eliminate thoughts about reaching for a cigarette;
4. Eating management (avoiding food and eating situations that stimulate a desire to smoke);
5. Substituting props (such as sugar-free candy);
6. Rehearsal of suitable nonsmoking behaviors;
7. "Cognitive coping" to associate positive thoughts with quitting smoking.

In addition, mild aversive stimulation (pairing smoking with pain stimulation to reduce the appeal of tobacco) was employed in some cases. Three once-weekly meetings were held after the formal 4-day program. A manual containing persuasive "pep" talks was supplied, and a counselor telephoned the patient to inquire about progress and to encourage maintenance of abstinence. At the start of therapy, return of part of the patient's fee is promised (contingency contracting) if abstinence is maintained after three to six months, thus providing further motivation to stop the habit.

Smoking cessation programs have been prepared by the American Cancer Society (1971) and by Dananer and Lichtenstein (1978). An innovative behavior modification program, "Quit-by-Mail," using a home computer has been devised by Schneider (1984). Participants mail out weekly correspondence detailing their progress and problems, and their questions are addressed in pointed computerized responses. It has shown some promise.

Regardless of the methods employed to produce abstinence, many patients need continuing help to deal with the stress and other factors that promote a craving for cigarettes. The nature of such help will have to be designed for specific problems: environmental factors through environmental manipulation, marital difficulties through marital therapy, family problems through family therapy, faulty attitudes through cognitive therapy, and so on. The continued use of self-relaxation techniques, indulgence in interesting diversions and absorbing hobbies, and graded regular physical exercise are valuable. Should excess tension develop as a result of unusual stress, a minor tranquilizer (Valium, Librium) prescribed for only a short period may be required to ease a patient through the crisis. Patients' feelings of well-being in ridding themselves of the tobacco habit, their enhanced physical stamina as a result of eliminating nicotine from their bodies, and the approval they sense from their therapist and friends for their "courage" will, one hopes, suffice in maintaining abstinence. If smoking persists, more extensive therapy will be needed.

A "nonsmoking kit" of pamphlets written for children, adolescents, and parents may be obtained at a small cost from the Superintendent of Documents, U.S. Government Printing Office, Washington, D.C., 20402.

Summary of Treatment Approaches in Substance Abuse

The treatment of substance abuse is a difficult task as attested to by the worldwide pessimism about the prognosis for this disorder. Dropouts from therapy are more the rule than the exception, and noncompliance with therapeutic routines tax the patience of the most empathic therapist. The therapist has to be more active in approaching substance abusers than is customary, especially at the start of treatment. In an attempt to deal with resistance, the therapist should call when the patient misses a session. Continued noncompliance with routines that have been set up and failure to execute homework assignments may require more aggressive tactics (Marlatt & Gordon, 1985). The maintenance of discipline, so important in acquiring essential nondrinking and nondrug-taking skills, requires that therapists refuse to be lied to or manipulated, since these merely reinforce the patient's self-destructive patterns. The patient does not, however, have the substitutive skills to deal with stress at the beginning of therapy, so the therapist will have to tolerate an occasional relapse at the start. Such relapse provides an opportunity to review what has produced it. The manner of its management by the therapist can be important in consolidating the therapeutic relationship.

Treatment outcomes in substance abuse are dependent on the severity of the psychopathology (McLellan et al, 1983; Woody et al, 1984; Woody et al, 1986). Supportive therapy and drug counseling may suffice for patients who are not too psychiatrically disturbed. Those with a moderate degree of pathology may be helped, often substantially, by additional psychotherapy. But severely psychiatrically handicapped individuals will show a poor outcome whatever the intervention.

A growing problem in the treatment of substance abuse is that more and more people are increasingly using combinations of substances for purposes of recreation, relaxation, control of disturbing psychological and physical symptoms, and the ever-constant search for euphoria ("pharmacodynamic elation"). A recent estimate placed the figure of polydrug use at 84 percent of all substance abusers. The choice of alcohol, tranquilizers, sleeping pills, marijuana, cocaine, amphetamines, opioids, and other substances makes for mixtures whose effects are unpredictable and that pose many health hazards. Detoxification programs will have to deal with the fact that polydrug use can lead to dangerous withdrawal reactions. For this reason, detoxification, which is basic to the start of any organized treatment program, should be done in a hospital or residential center that has adequate facilities. The incidence of withdrawal and abstinence reactions makes mandatory the use of staff members in these units who are experienced in emergency treatments, and the management of problems specific to the substances that are being abused.

Temporary administration of substitute narcotics such as methadone in the opioid addiction, and small doses of barbiturates in barbiturate abuse, can prevent convulsions and other dangerous physical reactions. Thereafter, phased slow withdrawal, while monitoring physiological responses, is mandatory. The use of oxygen, neuroleptics, and, if they exist, specific drug antagonists (e.g., naltraxone in opioid addiction) can also be better controlled in an institutional setting. Most important, abused substances must not be made secretly accessible in institutional surroundings.

Once the patient is detoxified, the next step is to keep him or her off alcohol and drugs. Here, psychosocial treatments are instituted. The largest handicap in using such therapies is lack of cooperation. Most addicts or alcoholics are brought to a psychotherapist by frantic parents, spouses, or friends. The patients, despite verbal declarations, are not fully committed to staying off drugs, or, if they have "hit bottom" and suffered the after affects of a "binge," their commitment soon vanishes when they recover. If the therapist can establish a relationship with the patient, confrontation may be possible and some motivation stimulated. Despite considerable skepticism, it has been shown that *properly* conducted treatment for alcohol and drug abuse can be effective along a wide range of parameters, including, in overcoming the habit, finding employment, reducing criminal behavior, and enhancing psychological functioning (McLellan et al, 1982).

In formulating a proper treatment plan, the therapist should be aware of a number of essential factors:

1. The patient's enthusiasm for therapy, however, sincere, may be short-lived, giving way sooner or later to what seem to be self-destructive impulses. Extreme physical dependence is inescapable with habitual use of opiates, barbiturates, and alcohol. There is some physical dependence and considerable psychological dependence with the long-term use of amphetamines. Psychological dependence is present with marijuana, tobacco, and hallucinogens, but only moderate physical dependence unless dosage has been high. Great tolerance is soon established with opiates, amphetamines, and hallucinogens; somewhat lesser tolerance with the barbiturates, alcohol, and tobacco.

2. The addict is convinced that drug indulgence, better than anything else, enables him or her to overcome despair, dissatisfaction, depression, and anxiety.

3. Drug abstinence achieved outside of an addict's habitual environment may not last long after the addict returns to his or her customary surroundings.

4. Since single addictions are rare, removal of one substance does not lessen the craving for others. Indeed, it may provoke the addict to try new experiments with other potentially exciting or calming materials.

5. Detoxification and "cure" of the desire for drugs has little effect on underlying pathological personality problems, only one manifestation of which is the thrust toward drug intake. Other manifestations will require psychosocial interventions. These may yield meager results, and prolonged care (1–2 years) in a therapeutic community like Synanon and Phoenix House may be needed to achieve a social adjustment.

6. A support group (Alcoholics Anonymous, Narcotics Anonymous, Cocaine Anonymous) of some kind will be necessary, sometimes for the remainder of the individual's life, as a source of reassurance, education, and companionship and as a "port in the storm" when troubles at home or at work brew or the inevitable cravings for a "fix" or drink return. The best support groups are patterned around the precepts of groups that have proven valuable, such as Alcoholics Anonymous or Synanon, and are composed of peers with similar substance abuse problems. Preferably, some of the leaders have suffered from and conquered similar problems.

A professional person should be available for supervision and consultation. Periodic urine and serum drug screens should be employed if possible to detect early defection from abstinence. The choice of a proper group cannot be overemphasized because bad leadership and the presence of too disturbed or offensive members can negate the positive benefits of group participation. In large cities, resources for finding good groups are usually ample. In smaller communities, groups in neighboring towns may need to be explored. The therapist may enlist the assistance of social agencies for this purpose. Other community reinforcement resources—social, athletic, and so on—may be available to provide leisure-time positive reinforcements. Caution is needed in their selection, however, since social (or heavier-than-social) drinking may be the norm in some of these groups. One cannot protect the patient from the presence of alcohol. It is everywhere, being consumed freely in and out of homes. The patient must be able to resist any goading and encouragement to "have a short one." Most patients learn to cope with this pressure by restricting themselves to plain soda and lime or soft drinks.

7. Marital therapy and family therapy are usually conjunctively needed for marital and family problems, and stress factors in the environment will call for counseling and environmental manipulation.

8. Nondrug management of tension and stress are important because the use of any anxiolytics or hypnotic-sedatives after the first week following detoxification is contraindicated. Here, relaxing exercises, self-hypnosis, and meditation may be taught individually and in groups. Cognitive therapy should be employed to rectify faulty philosophies and attitudes. Proper physical exercise daily and instructions regarding diet to overcome and prevent nutritional deficiencies are necessary. Education in self-care may be needed if there is a pattern of habitual neglect.

9. Depression is one of the most common symptoms of substance abuse, and if it is intense may require antidepressants, such as amitriptyline (Elavil) or sinequan (Doxepin). Psychotic ideation and behavior may necessitate antipsychotic drugs such as haloperidol (Haldol), trifluoperazine (Stelazine), or thiothixene (Navane). Some alcoholics need Antabuse, and some opioid addicts off methadone do well with naltrexone (Trexan) to offset impulsive drug use.

10. Once abstinence is sustained by faithful attendance at a support group, and environmental stresses have been mediated through counseling, the therapist should consider whether individual psychotherapy would be valuable. Depth therapy, focused on unconscious conflict and the acquisition of insight into early conditionings, has failed notoriously with this class of patients. Some analysts believe that this is because substance abusers possess an arrested personality and are so handicapped by infantile omnipotence that they cannot make a proper transference to the therapist. Any transferences that do develop are bound to reflect distortions that developed in the original family that are now ego-syntonically indelible. Their revival will prove antitherapeutic. Treatment programs that have proven successful have taken into account the patient's disturbed character structure but have dealt with it in ways other than through insight. They have approached the need on the part of the

patient to engage masochistically in unrewarding behaviors by reconditioning responses through a social learning paradigm. The model of treatment described below (12 to 15) can be adapted to both alcohol and substance abuse (McGrady 1983, 1985; Miller WR et al, 1980; Miller PM, 1982).

11. Preaching the evils of drug and alcohol intake, and its effects on oneself or one's family, does not work. What the patient must achieve is the conviction that he or she can be happier over a longer period without the abused substances than with them. One hopes that through positive reinforcements the patient will acquire this conviction during the early stages of abstinence. Every satisfactory experience of social and vocational adjustment should be rewarded by praise or other reinforcer to encourage a better life style. Designed programs will vary because of differences in personal needs and environmental opportunities, as well as specific responses to reinforcers. What is universally important is a job, occupation, or diversion to engross the individual a good part of the day; boredom is a leading source of stress. If the patient is unemployed, involvement in a hobby (music, art work, occupational therapy, etc.) or organized work-adjustment or volunteer program may have to precede finding paid work. Some substance abusers, especially adolescents, turn with vigor to religion or esoteric philosophies (Zen, Yoga, etc.), which supply them with a meaning for existence that they have sought through spurious chemically induced "insights." This should not be discouraged unless it is overdone and counterproductive.

12. The actual treatment process starts with identification of the stimuli that initiate alcohol or drug intake. This necessitates consideration of all the disturbing factors in the patient's personal, marital, family, and social life. Elements that further reinforce or that punish the drinking or drug response in the present situation are examined. This intensive study of external and internal stimuli that inspire the taking of drugs or alcohol is done with the object of determining ways of modifying or eliminating these stimuli or of finding better modes of dealing with them, cognitively, emotionally, and behaviorally. The treatment interventions that will be used will depend on the resources available, the readiness of the patient to accept them, and the skill of the therapist in implementing them.

13. Vital to the success of any program is motivation to stop the bad habit of resorting to the abused substance. If the patient does not have adequate coping skills, the best resolve will go down the drain as soon as he or she experiences strong anxieties or stress. Further, depression may have been masked by alcohol or drug intake. Insidious also are the ubiquitous desires for pleasure, and need to escape from responsibilities in living and from the pressures of inner conflicts. Because the patient minimizes the bad consequences of his or her habit and exaggerates his or her ability to control it, efforts toward abstinence may be minimal. The therapist may work on the patient's false assumptions through cognitive therapy, by providing reasons why the patient will be better off dealing with pressures and problems in more suitable ways. Some therapists hand the patient a list of the negative consequences of drinking that the patient has previously identified and ask the patient to read the list several times a day as homework. Training in self-relaxation techniques and a relaxing ego-building audiocassette tape may be valuable. Some patients will require assertive-

ness training over a period of many months.

14. The therapist must keep searching for stimuli that provoke the patient. Dealing with such mischief mongers directly is an important part of treatment. A prime source of stress here is a family member or spouse who nags, attacks, criticizes, and acts-out his or her problems through the medium of the patient. Counseling of the spouse on an individual or group basis may be important. Marital therapy or family therapy may be indicated, and self-help organizations such as Al-Anon should be sought out. Family members who have been battered by the patient's substance abuse may discover in these group settings better ways of dealing with the patient's difficulties.

Help in the acquisition of new stress-resolving skills and strategies is an important part of the therapy program. The patient is enjoined to search for "triggers" that initiate drinking or drug taking (e.g., an invitation to have a drink, fatigue, stressful events, receiving bad news, perceiving good news, engaging in "happy hour," etc.) and to explore nonalcoholic and nondrug responses to these triggers. The effects of a drink or other substances are then discussed in depth: talking too much, acting foolishly or brashly, guilt, self-disgust, feeling bad physically, a hangover, and so on. Instead of stopping the desire for drugs or drink, these aversive consequences may be shown to act as stressful triggers that initiate more substance abuse. So a chain reaction ties the patient into his or her destructive habit. One strategy to break the chain is to teach the patient to think *immediately* of the negative consequences the moment an impulse, invitation, or other trigger brings up the desire for a drug or drink. Some therapists ask the patient to prepare and carry around a card for each day of the week and to write down the cues that stimulate a desire for indulgence as well as what the patient did about it. Honesty in recording is stressed, and if a slip occurs the exact amount of drug or drink that was taken must be written down.

Alternative ways of dealing with triggers are encouraged. Insofar as doing something about the environments that tempt the habit, two ways of management are possible. The first consists of reducing environmental temptation, such as avoiding parties where conviviality demands imbibing alcohol, marajuna, or cocaine for good cheer. The second way is deliberate exposure, necessitating in vivo desensitization practice in some situations. Actually, alcohol and recreational drug taking are so much a part of the subculture that one cannot avoid exposure. Patients are constantly confronted with temptation, and it is best to deal with such challenges while in therapy.

Even with all the skills, the therapist will need dedication and concern to deal with substance abusers. Some patients will fail to achieve complete abstinence. Recourse to alcohol and drugs may constitute a preferred way of life. There seems to be little one can do with these patients to stimulate the motivation essential for sobriety or drug abstinence. In these cases, the therapist can perhaps act as a good friend and counselor who is available when the patient needs help with a crisis, to arrange for detoxification if necessary, and to get the patient back to work and acceptable functioning. The therapist need not consider himself or herself a failure in such cases but instead recognize that for some patients neither God nor man can do more than the patient wills.

15. It may be possible with a certain number of patients who have been off abused substances for a while to approach underlying personality conflicts, being aware that such probings may produce untoward transference reactions that will serve as stress stimuli. There are, however, a few patients who have the curiosity and the residual ego strength needed to reach for reconstructive goals.

16. The following self-help groups may be contacted:

Narcotics Anonymous
World Service Office, Inc.
P.O. Box 622
Sun Valley, CA 91352
and
World Service Office, Inc.
16155 Wyandotte St.
Van Nuys, CA 91406-3423

Nar-Anon Family Group Headquarters, Inc.
P.O. Box 2562
Palos Verdes Peninsula, CA

Families Anonymous
P.O. Box 344
Torrance, CA 90501
Telephone: 213-775-3211

Pills Anonymous
P.O. Box 473
Ansonia Station
New York, NY 10023

SEXUAL DISORDERS*

A complex aggregate of physiological, psychological, and environmental factors enter into the sexual reaction. The capacity or incapacity for responsiveness to sexual needs and the distorted or perverted forms of their expression are largely products of

---

* See also the section on sexual therapy in Chapter 56.

---

past conditionings. Interfering emotions may relate to defects in early training and education (e.g., prohibition of masturbation), to transferential projections (e.g., incestuous feelings toward parental figures), to carryovers of later childhood experiences (e.g., fearsome and humiliating seductions), and to unsatisfactory adult human relationships (e.g., a hostile or nonresponsive partner). Resulting anger and fear are anathema to proper sexual functioning. These affects are not always clearly perceived by the individual suffering from sexual difficulties. Indeed, their existence may be completely denied, and even if the early initiating circumstances are remembered, the emotions relating to them may be shielded under a coat of nonfeelingness. This anesthesia influences sexual behavior, distorting the perception of sexual stimuli or altering the manifestations of the sexual drive. Joining this conspiracy are defects in the self-image prompted by disturbances in personality development and by prolonged exposure to humiliating happenings.

The most common phenomena influencing sexual behavior are premature ejaculation and impotence in the male and nonorgasmic response, frigidity, dyspareunia, vaginismus, and conflicts about infertility in the female (Practitioners Conference, 1957; Kleegman, 1959; Geijerstam, 1960; Hastings DW, 1960; Mann EC, 1960; Nichols, 1961). The degree of failure of response may range from total disinterest in sex and inability to derive any sensation from autoerotic stimulation, to prurience under special circumstances (e.g., singular dreams, fantasies, and fetishes), to orgasmic response to certain acts (e.g., rape, "bondage," humiliation, pain, or sadistic acting-out), to selective reaction to the embraces of a specific love object, to excited behavior with a variety of sexual objects, to constant preoccupation with sexuality (e.g., nymphomania and satyriasis). People are "turned on" by a host of stimuli that are unique to their personalities and early conditioning experiences. Objects and circumstances accompanying the first sexual arousal may be indelibly imprinted and may motivate acutal or symbolic revival for sexual feeling thereafter. Later sexual expression may host consequences dependent on the significance of guilt-ridden experiences (e.g., relaxation and exhilaration or self-punitive mechanisms, like anxiety, migraine, and gastrointestinal symptoms). It is understandable that with the complex array of operative contingencies, a vast assortment of patterns will be displayed by different people and at different times prior to, during, and after the sexual act. The degree of orgasmic reaction will also vary individually, from mild release to violent, ecstatic excitement and even unconsciousness.

Sexual Dysfunctions (DSM-III-R Codes for Hypoactive Sexual Desire, 302.71; Sexual Aversion Disorder, 302.79; Female Sexual Arousal Disorder, 302.72; Male Erectile Disorder, 302.72; Inhibited Female Orgasm, 302.73; Inhibited Male Orgasm, 302.74; Premature Ejaculation, 302.75; Dyspareunia, 302.76; Vaginismus, 306.51)

A diagnostic assessment of any sexual problem is vital to determine what kind of treatment is necessary. It is important to determine which of four phases of sexual response is implicated. Is the disorder one of inhibited desire or inability to maintain excitement and genital tumescence, to control or achieve orgasm, or to achieve postorgasmic relaxation and well-being? (Kaplan & Moodie, 1984; Lief 1981). Distinguishing these phases of sexual response is important because different mechanisms and neural pathways are operative in each and different therapeutic interventions may be called for. For example, inhibited sexual desire may be the product of guilt about and repression of sexuality produced by over-moralistic promptings in childhood with consequent fantasies or needs for self-punishment, indulgence in rape or bondage fantasies, and sexual masochism as a condition for the release of sexual feeling. Conquest of these developmentally sexual inhibitions may inspire the individual to imagine or act-out violently and sometimes sadistically (sexual sadism) and to use antisocial behavior as a way of subduing or symbolically destroying the conscience or projected guilt representations. Guilt feelings and masochistic self-punishment usually follow these releases but rarely eliminate them. Treatment when sought will require psychotherapy, preferably dynamically oriented, and behavioral approaches later should sexual functioning continue to fail. Inhibited sexual desire may also be associated with the release triggers that open the gates to sexual feeling, such as fetishism, transvestism, zoophilia, pedophilia, exhibitionism, and voyeurism, which must be approached psychotherapeutically, although prognosis for recovery in these ailments is guarded. Sexual desire can be deadened by ailments such as depression, as well as by antihypertensive, antidepressant, tranquilizing and other medications. These interferences require specific correction. Finally, one's relationship with a marital partner may be pathological (e.g., incestuous) or so seeped in ongoing hostility as to deaden all thoughts of sex. Here marital therapy and dynamic psychotherapy may be essential. Appropriate treatment for all these conditions requires accurate diagnosis. In the case of inhibited sexual excitement with frigidity and impotence, once organic (endocrinopathics, diabetes, arteriosclerosis, etc.) and medical factors (antihypertensive and beta-adrenergic drugs, alcohol, tranquilizers, etc.) have been ruled out, behavioral sex therapy may be effective in itself, especially if the onset of the dysfunction has been recent or the causes minor. If personality difficulties exist or anxieties and phobias are strong, however, coordinate psychotherapy may be necessary. The same may be said for inhibited female and male orgasm, premature ejaculation, dyspareunia, and functional vaginismus. If postorgasmic relaxation and well-being are a concern, such treatment as cognitive therapy to alter meaning systems and dynamic psychotherapy to explore conflicts may be useful (Wasserman et al, 1980). If an antidepressant is found necessary for depression, bupropion (Wellbutron) has been found less associated with sexual dysfunction than other antidepressants.

Unfortunately, there has been a tendency on the part of some professionals to project their own experiences into their opinions of what constitutes "normal" sexuality instead of dealing with it as a broad spectrum of behavioral repertoires that cannot rigidly be circumscribed in terms of "healthy" and "pathological." Thus, there are writers who insist that oral contacts are abnormal, that manual genital stimulation is immature, and that orgasm derived in any other way than through penetration of the penis in the vagina is aberrant if not perverse. These injunctions reinforce any prevailing misconceptions that a patient may be harboring and add to guilt feelings.

Brief sex therapy (see pages 1036–1046) may be eminently successful in modifying or curing some milder sexual disturbances. In an inspired setting, away from everyday problems and pressures, a couple has the best opportunity for loosening up their inhibitions, relaxing their defenses, and under the prompting of new permissive authorities acquiring better habits of sexual response. Interpersonal hostilities are quietly subdued under these circumstances, and new and more constructive communicative patterns are set up. After therapy is terminated, the real test occurs. Can the improved functioning be sustained in the couple's habitual setting? There is always a possibility that reinstitution of customary pressures and responsibilities may restore tensions and break down the new communication patterns. It would, therefore, seem vital to continue to see the couple after the instruction period is over to help resolve developing problems.

The key to successful sexual therapy is the therapist. One's personality, one's casualness, one's flexibility, one's empathy, one's understanding, one's sense of humor, and one's capacity to communicate all influence the techniques. In many couples the strong defenses and resistances to the directives of the therapeutic authority are apt to create frustration and anger in the therapist. The therapist has to know how to deal with the patient's reactions in an easy-going way without taking offense. The therapist actually needs the skills of a good communicator. It is not possible to adopt a passive analytic stance with this type of treatment.

The short period of therapy can provide a biopsy of the prevailing pathology between the two people. If the pathology is not too severe, if healthy defenses are present, if reasonable flexibility of adaptation prevails, new sexual habits may be maintained. On the other hand, if the sexual difficulty is a reflection of a personality problem, there may still be some improvement sexually but the personality difficulties will have to be dealt with by more intensive methods.

For example, an impotent single man comes to therapy harboring deep hostile feelings toward women, stemming from a high level of dependency that one may historically trace to his being overprotected by a dominant mother figure—by no means an uncommon condition in problems of impotency. The immediate precipitating factor for the impotency in our present patient, let us imagine, was sexual association with a dominant, demanding woman who somehow undermined his confidence in himself. Let us also hypothesize that, through behavior therapy and in relationship with a cooperative and nondominant woman, the patient is restored to potency. Lacking recognition of his inner drives and needs, however, he may soon lose interest in what he would consider "uninteresting weak females" and seek out domineering women with whom he could act out his dependency and hostility. Without speculating too much, we would probably witness in a new relationship with a controlling woman a revival of his symptom. A thorough understanding of the problem, however, may help him not only to try to desensitize himself to domineering women, but also to manage more assertively their specific domineering traits. By seeing that he was projecting attitudes toward his mother into his contemporary relationships, he might better be able to deal with "strong" women. The evolvement of firmer controls may enable him to relate even to manipulating women without fear. Or, realizing his choice of women as a weakness he must overcome, he may decide to restrict his sexual contacts to more passive types, while handling his impulse to goad them into domineering roles.

A complicating factor in many patients is that the sexual function in the human being is often employed as a vehicle for the expression of varied strivings, interpersonal attitudes, and needs. Thus, sexual behavior may embrace, among other things, impulses to hurt or to be hurt, to humiliate or to be humiliated, and to display or to mutilate oneself.

When impotence results from vascular surgical procedures, an implant or a recently developed surgical procedure may be effective (Zorgniotti, 1987).

Paraphilias (DSM-III-R Codes for Exhibitionism, 302.40; Pedophilia, 302.20; Sexual Masochism, 302.83; Sexual Sadism, 302.84; Transvestist Fetishism, 302.81; Voyeurism, 302.82)

Among the more serious and less prevalent sexual disorders are those that relate to gender identity and the paraphilias. An assorted group of problems are embraced under the term *transsexualism*. Here there is conflict about one's anatomic sex and a desire to exchange it for genitals of the opposite sex. Assumption of a role consonant with the desired sex identity are compelling, and occasionally submission to surgery to amputate the undesired sex organs is yielded to. The cross-dressing here is distinguished from transvestism in that in the latter there is no desire to rid oneself of one's genitals. The cross-dressing appears to act as a stimulus for sexual excitement, which in most cases is expressed heterosexually. A *gender disorder of childhood* is characterized by a repudiation of one's sexual identity and a frantic need to act like a member of the opposite sex. The little boy plays with dolls and desires to dress like a girl; the little girl engages in male activities and may deny not having a penis. In the paraphilias there is a compulsive need to utilize imagery or to engage in unusual acts in order to stimulate sexual desire, such as specific items of clothing (*fetishism*) or animals (*zoophilia*); to be humilated, bound, and beaten (*sexual masochism*); to inflict pain or humilation on the sexual object (*sexual sadism*); to exhibit one's genitals to strangers (*exhibitionism*); to spy upon and observe people in situations of undress or intercourse (*voyeurism*); and to engage in sex (usually mingled with aggression) with a child (*pedophilia*). Neurotic and personality disorders often coexist with these sexual distortions.

These conditions are among the most difficult of all syndromes to treat. Because of the intense pleasure values inherent in the exercise of the perversions and the fact that they fulfill deep needs other than sexual, the patient is usually reluctant to give them up. Although there may be a desire to overcome certain disagreeable symptoms, such as anxiety or tension, the motivation to abandon the coveted sexual expression may be lacking. Because of the lack of incentive, resistance often becomes so intense as to interfere with the therapeutic process.

There is, nevertheless, a growing conviction that sexual deviations are pathological conditions that sometimes may be helped by psychotherapy. The specific approach to perversions will vary with the theoretical orientation of the therapist (Bieber I, 1962; Bychowski, 1961; Deutsch H, 1965; Fried, 1962, Lorand, 1956; Marmor, 1965; Nunberg, 1955; Ovesey, 1954, 1955a & b; Ovesey et al, 1963; Saul & Beck, 1961; Stark, 1963).

Some authorities speculate that a genetic defect complicated by conditionings in childhood makes certain preliminary fantasies or acts mandatory for sexual feeling and performance in adult life. The origin of many of these conditionings are forgotten, repudiated, and repressed, although the individual is mercilessly bound to special stimuli (fetishistic, masochistic, sadistic, etc.) to release his or her sexuality. In many instances the sexual disturbance reflects improper identity. If normal masculine identification is lacking (an overly possessive controlling mother, intimidation by an overwhelming father, passive indulgence by a weak father) tendencies toward effeminacy may develop in a male. Lack of a feminine and motherly mother who can act as a feminine model may divert a girl from female identification. Under these circumstances, the sexual direction may be altered.

Whether all forms of homosexuality should be classified as abnormal is a moot point about which there are differences in opinion among professionals. Under pressure of some groups, the trustees of the American Psychiatric Association (amidst considerable controversy) officially ruled that the term "homosexuality" be replaced in the Statistical Manual of Mental Disorders by the phrase "ego-syntonic homosexuality" to avoid the stigma of being classified as a disorder. Ego-dystonic homosexuality was a diagnosis applied only to those homosexuals who were in conflict with their sexuality. In justification of this move, we do find many homosexuals who are happy and adjusted, and some studies reveal that symptoms and behavioral disorders among this group are no more frequent than among heterosexuals.

Under these circumstances, it is argued, homosexuality might for some individuals be regarded as a manifestation of a preferred normal life style rather than as a distortion of sexuality. On the other hand, there are those who continue to accent the point that analysis of even so-called well-adjusted homosexuals indicates without question that they have a developmental block in the evolution of the sexual drive. In appraising the pathological nature of homosexuality, we do have to consider the fact that many homosexuals suffer from the abuse and discrimination heaped on them by society, without which they would probably be able to make a better adjustment.

Homosexuals who apply for therapy are in a special category when they are ostensibly disturbed and upset about their sexual behavior. They may seek therapy for their symptoms, but they may not be motivated to change their sexual orientation. A therapist's forceful attempts to induce change under these circumstances will usually fail. If there are strong conflicts about homosexuality and a sustained and powerful desire for heterosexuality, dynamic psychotherapy or psychoanalysis may succeed in a certain number of cases (Bieber I, 1962) in changing their sexual orientation. Adolescents disturbed about homosexuality may well benefit from some brief counseling along the lines suggested by Gadpaille (1973), which may help lessen their identity problems.

Sometimes homosexual preoccupations in a conflicted individual become so uncontrollably compulsive as to cause the person to act out impulses in a destructive and dangerous manner. Masochistic and sadistic drives are usually operative here. The problem is that the person can easily jeopardize one's safety by becoming involved with psychopathic individuals or by getting into trouble with the law. Such a person may seek from psychotherapy not so much stoppage of homosexual activity as the opportunity to direct one's behavior into less dangerous channels.

Traditional psychotherapy, unfortunately, has had little to offer such applicants; neither insight nor appeals to common sense influence the driving determination to involve themselves in exciting trouble. A form of therapy still in the experimental state is aversive behavioral treatment. Some behavior therapists recommend that if patients are insistent on being forced to stop their behavior, and if sufficiently motivated, they may be able to endure exposure to a series of slides that are sexually stimulating to them but are rewarded with a painful electric shock through electrodes attached to the fingertips (Feldman & MacCulloch, 1965). In a technique evolved by McConaghy (1972) the male patient selects 10 slides each of a nude adolescent and of young men and women to which he feels some sexual response. At each session three male slides are shown for 10 seconds. A 2-second shock is delivered during the last second of exposure, with the level of shock as unpleasant as the patient can stand. Following this, a slide of a woman is turned on for 20 seconds without accompanying shock. Variable intervals between 3 to 5 minutes pass between showing the three sets of male and female slides. Sessions are given three or more times the first week and are gradually reduced in frequency over the following few months. In female patients the shocks would be delivered with the slides of women, and no shocks would be delivered with the male slides. Again, unless the incentive to control one's homosexual activities is high, this treatment is doomed to failure.

The treatment of sexual perversions, such as sadism, masochism, voyeurism, and exhibitionism, must be organized around removing blocks to personality development in order to correct the immature strivings that are being expressed through the sexual perversion. Fears of adult genitality and of relating intimately and lovingly to persons of the opposite sex must be resolved before adequate sexual functioning is possible. The only rational approach is, therefore, reconstructive in nature. Lack of motivation may, however, inhibit the patient from entering into reconstructive treatment. Additionally, ego weakness and disintegrative tendencies are often present in sexual perversions and act as further blocks to deep therapy. For these reasons the therapeutic objective may have to be confined to the mere control of the perversion and to its possible sublimation. Behavior modification has been utilized here. The therapist may have to function as a supportive, guiding authority who helps the patient to lead a more restrained life.

In treating perversions, the therapist must be prepared for a long struggle. Resistances are, as has been mentioned, usually intense, and the patient will repeatedly relapse into the sexual deviation. The patient should not be blamed, reproved, or made to feel guilty for this. Rather, he or she must be helped to see the purposes served by the perversion and to appreciate why the need to express it becomes more overwhelming at some times than at others. While the ultimate outlook is not as favorable as in some other problems, there is no reason why patients who become motivated for, and who can tolerate reconstructive therapy, cannot achieve satisfactory results.

SPEECH DISORDERS (DEVELOPMENTAL ARTICULATION DISORDER (DSM-III-R Code 315.39), EXPRESSIVE LANGUAGE DISORDER (DSM-III-R Code 315.31), RECEPTIVE LANGUAGE DISORDER (DSM-III-R Code 315.31); CLUTTERING, 307.00; STUTTERING, 307.00)

Functional speech problems, which are sometimes arbitrarily called "stuttering" or "stammering," are the consequence of the lack of coordination of various parts of speech wherein the speech rhythm becomes inhibited or interrupted. Associated are vasomotor disturbances, spasm, and incoordination of muscle groups involving other parts of the body. The speech difficulty is initiated and exaggerated by certain social situations, so that the individual is capable of articulating better under some circumstances than others. This is confirmed by the fact that the person is usually able to sing and to talk without difficulty to himself or herself and to animals. Some authorities insist that since there is no actual pathology of the speech apparatus, it may be a grave misnomer to label stuttering a speech disorder. Rather it might be conceived of as a manifestation of total adaptive dysfunction.

Martin F. Schwartz (1974) of Temple University has presented evidence that stuttering is produced by an inappropriate vigorous tightening of the larynx (contraction of the posterior cricoarytenoid) triggered off by subglottal air pressures required for speech. Psychological stress reduces the action of the usual supramedullary inhibiting controls of the involved muscle. To correct this, the patient must place the larynx in an open and relaxed position, which helps keep the air pressure in the voice box low. One-way mirrors and videotape equipment are used to coach the patient. The therapy is still in the experimental stage but a "reasonable expectation of perhaps a 90 percent success rate with stutterers given the proper therapeutic implementation" may be expected within 2 or 3 months (Pellegrino, 1974). Should the therapy prove itself to be this successful, it will undoubtedly replace the traditional treatment methods.

The counseling of parents of a stuttering child is important in the total treatment plan. Generally, parents react with dismay, frustration, and guilt feelings in relation to their child, many assuming that they are responsible for the problem. At the onset of counseling the parents should be told that we are still unsure of what produces a stuttering child and that worry about complicity in it is not as important as doing something about it. There are, however, things they can do that may help the problem. Constant emphasis on mistakes and subjecting the child to drilling helps aggravate the nonfluency by making the child more self-conscious and aware of his or her failings. The stuttering child requires a great deal of demonstrated love and affection, and the parents must be enjoined to go out of their way to give these. It is essential also that they encourage the child to express feelings openly no matter how badly the child enunciates these and that they control themselves if the child bumbles along in front of friends and relatives. This does not mean that proper discipline should not be imposed, even punitive measures for outrageous behavior, since discipline is an important learning tool for healthy growth. There is in some families a tendency to infantalize and to overprotect a stuttering child. This must be avoided, and the child should be expected to manage whatever responsibilities one of his or her age must assume. The role of the father is important in providing proper guidance and companionship. Since tension in the home contributes to the child's disturbance, it may be necessary to institute marital therapy or family therapy before appreciable improvement can be expected.

Therapy with a child therapist, particularly one experienced in speech difficulties, may have to be prescribed for the manifestly disturbed child or one who has been undermined by the speech problem. These children are exposed to ridicule, teasing, and social ostracism by their classmates. They shy away from talking and presentations in class, resulting in an undermining of self-esteem.

The usual treatment of adult stuttering proceeds on two different levels: correction of the improper speech habit and the handling of the deeper emotional problem that originally initiated and now sustains the difficulty. A guidance approach and social skills training are used toward achieving the first objective (Brady, 1984).

The second goal is obtained through a persuasive, reeducative and, where possible, reconstructive approach. Therapy involves correcting patent difficulties in the environment that stir up the person's insecurity, and dealing with disturbing inner conflicts. Since the character disturbance in stutterers is usually extensive, therapy is bound to be difficult, prolonged, and, in many cases, unsuccessful insofar as alteration of the underlying personality disorder is concerned. The most that can be done for many stutterers is symptomatic relief in the form of speech correction.

Speech training may do as much harm as good. It is valuable only as a means of building up confidence in the individual's powers to articulate. Unfortunately, it may psychologically have the opposite effect since it overemphasizes will power and control and concentrates the stutterer's attention on the mechanics of speech rather than on what is being said. Instead of becoming less conscious about the speech difficulty, the person becomes more involved with it, thus intensifying the problem. This is not to say that proper exercises in diaphragmatic breathing, phonetics, and articulation are of no value in certain patients. Sometimes, with these methods, a symptomatic recovery may take place in mild cases. In severe cases, however, they are relatively ineffectual, and, especially if the person makes a voluntary effort to stop stuttering, the severity of the speech problem may increase. Rhythmics and eukinetics are sometimes helpful. Training methods, when used, should be employed by a therapist experienced in speech techniques.

In supportive approaches with stuttering adults certain evasions and defenses are sometimes taught to tide the stutterer over situations in which he or she must talk. Drawling, speaking in a rhythmic manner or in a sing-song tone, utilizing distracting sounds like "ah" or a sigh prior to articulation, employing a gesture or engaging in some motor act like pacing or rubbing a watch chain, purposeful pauses, and a variety of other tricks are used. These are entirely palliative and must be considered escapes rather than therapeutic devices.

A persuasive approach is sometimes helpful. The first step in therapy consists of convincing the patient that because of disappointing experiences, he or she has come to overemphasize the speech function. To the stutterer it constitutes an insignia of aggrandizement and defamation. Self-esteem has become linked with the performance of speech. Because of this the stutterer concentrates attention on the manner of talking more than the content of what is being said. While the speech problem is understandably disturbing, it is probably not regarded with the same emphasis by others. People suffering from stuttering overcome it more easily when they stop running away from acknowledging it. The best tactic is to face the situation and even admit it. As soon as this is done the person will be more at ease and the speech will improve.

A talk such as the following may be indicated:

Th. There is nothing disgraceful about stuttering. Avoiding social situations because of fear of ridicule merely serves to exaggerate the sense of defeat. It is necessary to regard stuttering in the same light as any other physical problem. If you stop being ashamed of it, and do not concern yourself with embarrassing others, people will notice your speech less and less. As you become more unconcerned about *how* you talk, you will concentrate on *what* you say. Keep concentrating on what you say, and pay no attention to how it sounds. Fear and embarrassment exaggerate your speech difficulty, so make yourself act calm and you will feel calm, and your speech will improve.

The next stage of therapy draws on some reeducative techniques and consists of demonstrating to the patient how he or she becomes upset and loses the sense of calmness in some situations. There will be no lack of material since the patient will bring to the therapist's attention many instances in which his or her stuttering becomes exaggerated. Examining the patient's emotional reactions to these situations as well as his or her fantasies give the therapist clues as to the dynamic elements involved in the patient's speech disorder. These may be pointed out to the patient in terms that conform with his or her existing capacities for understanding. The aim is to show the patient that the speech difficulty appears when he or she loses the capacity to remain relaxed and when, for any reason whatsoever, emotional instability develops.

In some cases it will be advisable to refer the patient to a good speech therapist. The therapeutic approach that appears most successful comes from the work of Van Riper (1971), and Wendell Johnson (1946). This aims at the elimination of anxieties about stuttering, which is considered a learned reaction to conscious fears of speech or fluency failure. Patients are enjoined to adopt an "objective attitude" by facing the fact squarely and, instead of avoiding displaying their stuttering, talking about the speech handicap to others, deliberately meeting all fearful and difficult speaking situations, and articulating in the best way they can, utilizing, if necessary, the evasions, defenses, and tricks that are so often employed by stutterers. Exposure to various speaking challenges while maintaining as objective an attitude as possible is also advised.

Specifically, patients are taught to open up, in as casual and objective and even humorous a way as possible, the speech problem with others, even if the listeners do not know that they have a speech problem. Clearing the atmosphere in this way will put both the listeners and themselves at ease. They are asked to observe how others falter and make mistakes in speaking and by this to realize that normal fluency is imperfect and quite variable. They are requested to observe how certain listeners react to what they say and to check their observation with those of others present. In this way they will discover that they project their personal fears and prejudices onto other people. Most important they are requested to give up running away from fearsome words that cause stuttering and to utter them deliberately, particularly in situations in which they have stumbled over them while remaining emotionally detached and not caring how the listener reacts. Role playing may be used here to prepare the patients for such stints. They are requested to discuss their experiences with the therapist at the next session. The patient is reminded to try to cultivate a calm, unemotional tone of voice. They may practice this with a friend or with members of the family. One-half hour each day is devoted to reading aloud from a book, jotting down those words that are difficult to pronounce. They may then practice enunciating words several times during the day. Some persons find it helpful to talk for a short time daily in front of a mirror, watching their facial movements as they utter sounds. Along with these reconditioning techniques, environmental therapy may be used, geared toward an expansion of the assets of the individuals and a remedying of liabilities in themselves and their situations.

If these techniques do not yield desired results, patients may be taught ways of postponing word attempts, of starting difficult words or of releasing themselves from blockages. They may also be taught a substitutive stuttering pattern, deliberately prolonging or repeating themselves in an unhurried, tenseless way. For instance, Van Riper's cancellation technique enjoins stutterers to pause immediately after they experience a stuttering block and to ask themselves what they did (pressed their lips together? pushed the tongue against the roof of their mouth? felt panic? diverted their gaze from the listener?). They are then to cancel their failure by "stuttering" on the same word deliberately in a new way with prolonged relaxation, maintaining eye contact with the listener. This starts a reconditioning process so that the stutterers may begin to change their behavior during the fist attempt and then to manipulate preparatory sets prior to the attempt "to facilitate the production of a 'fluent' pattern of stuttering" (Bloodstein, 1966; Van Riper, 1971).

Three important adjuncts in speech therapy are behavior therapy, self-hypnosis, and group therapy. Assertiveness training may be extremely important. Other behavioral approaches can be quite valuable (Brady, 1968) particularly utilizing a metronome. In metronome-conditioned speech retraining (MCSR) a miniaturized electronic metronome* is worn behind the ear like a metronome (Brady, 1971, 1972). This may be especially helpful when patients are confronted with a speaking engagement. The metronome allows the speaker to pace the speech. Prior to the use of the ear metronome, the therapist may expose the patients to an ordinary desk metronome, such as used in piano practice. At first as few as 40 beats per minute may have to be used, the patient pronouncing one syllable for each beat. As soon as the patients are fluent in pronouncing several syllables at this speed, the rate is gradually increased to 90 to 100 per minute. A metronome should be procured for practice at home, at first alone, then when feeling confident, with a friend or parent in the room; then with more than one person present. Pauses are introduced to some beats and then more than one word to each beat. What can be helpful is practicing while fantasizing progressively more anxiety-provoking scenes. When reaching a satisfactory fluency, the patients practice with the miniature metronome and then utilize the fluency outside the home, at first in low-stress situations and then in high-stress situations. Should difficulty be experienced under some conditions, they may reduce the speed of the metronome and speak more slowly. Gradually, as the patients gain confidence, they may practice speaking without turning on the metronome, first in low then higher stress situations.

Another method is to listen to a transistor radio, using earphones while talking to a cassette tape recorder. The radio is played so loudly that one's voice is not heard. At first this is done after practicing relaxation. Then situations of increasing anxiety are imagined. The patient articulates feelings and thoughts at the same time and particularly pronounces his or her name and the words over with which difficulties have been experienced. As the stutterer gains confidence in speaking, he or she may turn the radio off while speaking, turning it back on should nonfluency return.

Persuasive autosuggestions in a self-induced trance reinforce the patient's desires for self-confidence and assertiveness. Group therapy in which the patient comes into contact with other persons suffering from speech problems removes the sense of isolation. The fact that companions experience the same trepidations as the patient does help the patient reevaluate his or her reaction. An opportunity is provided to speak and to recite in a permissive setting. The identification with the group, along with the growing confidence in the ability to speak fluently, may have a most positive effect on speech performance.

As the patient begins to experience improvement in his or her interpersonal relationships, the speech problem will plague the patient less and less. Utilizing the speech group as a bridge, one may be able

---

* A metronome known as a "Pacemaker" is made by Associated Auditory Instruments, Inc., 6796 Market Street, Upper Darby, Pennsylvania 19082.

to integrate with other groups and to consider oneself on an equal plane with its constituent members. In some cases reconstructive therapy may be possible to deal correctively with the personality disorder (Barbara, 1954, 1957, 1958, 1963). This, however, is associated with many vicissitudes as Glauber (1952) has pointed out.

In situations of strong anxiety, such as speaking before a group, some therapists advise taking 40 mg of Inderal shortly before the assignment, which will cut down on the anxiety without impairing cognition.

SLEEP DISORDERS (DYSSOMIAS)

Among the sleep disorders are the *Dyssomias,* which include primary insomnia, hypersomnias, and sleep–wake schedule disorders, and the *Parasomnias* identified as dream anxiety disorders (nightmare disorder), sleep terror disorder and sleepwalking disorder. By far, Primary Insomnia DSM-III-R Code 307.42 is the most common sleep disorder encountered in practice.

Insomnia is a ubiquitous symptom which more than one-third of the population experiences periodically. In most cases episodic sleeplessness is accepted philosophically, especially if it does not interfere too much with everyday functioning. In some persons, however, it is a persistent phenomenon for which help may be sought. Causes are heterogeneous, ranging from physical ailments, to depression, to environmental crises, to psychiatric stress. Sometimes insomnia is a consequence of prolonged consumption of hypnotics and sedatives, in which case the buildup of tolerance inspires wakefulness.

Patterns of insomnia are individual: (1) some people find it difficult to fall asleep but once slumber occurs do not awake until morning; (2) some fall asleep easily but awake in a few hours, fall asleep again, and go through the sleep-awakening cycle several times during the night; (3) some doze off readily but awaken at 4 to 6 A.M. and then cannot return to sleep; (4) others sleep throughout the day lightly, fitfully, restlessly, and get up in the morning as exhausted and tired as when they went to bed.

In recent years, research in sleep laboratories and clinical experience has yielded important information that is valuable in treatment planning (Kales, 1984). The following points are important to consider:

1. Insomnia is not as ruinous to health as the victim imagines. People can go without sleep for even several days without being damaged physically or becoming psychotic.
2. The amount of sleep required for optimal alertness the next day varies with the individual. Not everybody needs 8 or 9 hours; some persons do well with $4\frac{1}{2}$ or 5 or 6 hours. Aging lowers the requirements to as little as 4 hours in some people, and older people normally sleep lightly.
3. People generally underestimate the hours of true sleep they get. Thus, many subjects on testing in sleep laboratories will show no sleep disturbance yet will complain of insomnia.
4. Insomnia is only a symptom. Its causes can be diverse. In all cases, treating the causes if possible is primary: Physical ailments such as coronary artery disease, which produces nocturnal anginal pain; duodenal ulcer, which stimulates gastric acid especially at night, driving the person to seek antacids; prostatic enlargement, which produces arousal because of the frequency of urination; bronchial asthma; hypothyroidism, sleep apnea, myoclonus, and other physical conditions that cause discomfort and pain requiring proper medical or surgical help. Depression may need

antidepressive medications; anxiety re-actions often do well with simple relax-ation therapy; environmental distur-bances may be helped with counseling and milieu therapy; and psychiatric stress necessitates psychotherapy and behavior therapy.

5. Certain medications such as beta block-ers and tranquilizers can make a person feel sleepy and fatigued during the day, which may falsely lead a person to think he or she is not getting enough sleep. Other substances may actually cause insomnia. These include Dexe-drine, Ritalin, Tenuate, Proludin, and coffee, tea, soft drinks containing caf-feine, and alcohol taken late in the day or evening. Steroids, Inderal, and other beta blockers, may also create prob-lems.

6. Once insomnia develops for any reason an added deterrent to sleeping well is anticipating being awake during the night and suffering fatigue and exhaus-tion as a consequence. This whips the person into a state of self-defeating al-ertness.

7. Markedly irregular hours of retiring in-terfere with the bodies built-in time clock. People who go to bed late at night usually, often to their dismay, wake up at their regular morning hour.

8. Hypnotic drugs used over a long period lose their effectiveness and therefore are for short-term (no longer than 3 to 4 weeks) or periodic use. Continued em-ployment creates tolerance and addic-tion without added benefits. With-drawal of these drugs, taken over a period, produces a "surge" of dream-ing, jitteriness, and more insomnia. Such withdrawal must be done slowly and in some cases may require hospi-talization to deal with unpleasant se-quelae.

9. Over-the-counter sleep medications contain methapyrilene and/or scopola-mine. Prolonged use is neither safe nor effective at current dosage levels.

The treatment of insomnia will depend upon whether or not it is acute, the provoc-ative factors that keep the patient awake, and the degree of addiction to hypnotic drugs.

Acute temporary periods of insomnia produced by situational stress are usually readily handled by reassuring the patient that sleeping less than his or her usual quota will not cause damage, by permitting the patient to verbalize his or her fears and resentments, and perhaps by prescribing a hypnotic substance for 1 to 3 nights if nec-essary. Short-term insomnia due to work and family problems, bereavement, or ill-ness requires education about insomnia, helping the development of proper sleeping habits, and, if necessary, prescription of a benzodiazepine hypnotic for no more than 3 weeks.

The treatment of chronic insomnia is a more difficult matter, largely because the patient has established faulty habits and has probably incorporated the insomnia into his or her neurotic superstructure. The primary treatment is behavioral (Hauri, 1979), and hypnotics should be avoided if possible.

The therapy for established insomnia starts with exploring its history and mani-festations, the patient's attitudes toward it, what he or she has done about it in the past, and what is maintaining it in the present. In many cases the demoralization of the pa-tient will have to be dealt with by supplying scientific facts about insomnia to displace as much as possible unfounded myths and fears. If the patient has not had a good physical examination in the past, he or she should be asked to get one to rule out any organic causes. The patient should also be asked to keep a diary of his or her sleeping habits and working schedule for at least 24 hours, including bedtime routines, use of medications, sleep disruptions, and daytime fatigue, which may or may not yield important clues.

The next procedure is to instruct the patient in proper sleeping habits. These can serve as effective alternatives to drugs. Among measures to be recommended are the following:

1. Rearranging sleeping habits.
2. Reassuring the patient about sleep needs.
3. Getting the patient to accept insomnia.
4. Teaching the patient relaxing exercises.
5. Treating hypnotic drug dependence.
6. Prescribing medication.

Rearranging Sleeping Habits

(1) The patient should attempt to establish a regular bedtime, avoiding naps during the day. If sleep does not come easily, one may try relaxing exercises (or deep breathing, audiotapes, self-hypnosis, or meditation) or imagery with object counting ("counting sheep"). Should sleep not follow, one should go to another room to read or watch television until drowsiness develops instead of tossing around. (2) excessive smoking and drinking should be eliminated. (3) In some patients a change of mattresses should be made from hard to soft or vice versa, attention being paid to the bedcovers so that the patient is neither over- nor underheated, to the wearing of more comfortable night apparel, and to the regulation of the room temperature. Simple as this may sound, it may be all that is required. (4) A change in position during sleep may be indicated if the patient is in an uncomfortable repose. Superstitions such as that one must not sleep on the left side because the heart may be damaged, should, if this position is a preferred one, be corrected. Patients with asthma or orthopnea are more comfortable propped up in bed rather than lying prone. An elevation of the head and upper trunk is sometimes a preferred position. In married persons a change

from a double to twin beds, or the reverse, may be considered. (5) A bedtime snack (warm milk, sandwich, cocoa) is reassuring to some people, as is a glass of beer or ale or a small tumbler of sherry, port, or an aperitif. (6) Tea or coffee should be excluded from the evening meal and not taken before going to bed. (7) Reading in bed concentrates the attention away from inner concerns. Television programs selected before bedtime should not be too stimulating. (8) Daily exercise and a brisk walk in the evening followed by a hot bath are recommended by some. (9) Should the patient desire to experiment with it, an oscillating mattress is available in "sleep shops" or department stores that rhythmically rocks some people to sleep. (10) Ear plugs, anti-snore masks, and eye shades may be used to control situations disturbing to sleep. If necessary, one may sleep in a separate room away from a snoring partner. (11) Making up for lost sleep during weekdays by sleeping longer over weekends or on holidays can be disruptive to establishing proper sleeping patterns. Regular wake-up times should be observed even after a poor night's sleep.

Reassuring the Patient About Sleep Needs

The individual's estimate of how much sleep he or she must have for health reasons is usually far above his or her true physiological requirements. As people get older, sleep needs decrease. A reduction of deep sleep stages (III and IV) is normal. Because lighter stages (I and II) occur, older people get the feeling they do not sleep a wink. They also awaken several times during the night and fall asleep again, which is normal. If the patient can be convinced that merely reposing in bed and not forcing oneself to sleep is not damaging to one's health and if the patient can develop the philosophy "If I sleep, so much the better; if not, it doesn't matter," he or she may be able to stop worrying himself or herself into wakefulness. The patient may be told that merely lying in bed and relaxing are usually sufficient to take care of the physiological needs. If the patient does not sleep as much as he or she believes is necessary, no real harm will befall the patient. Of course, he or she may be driven to distraction by worrying about not sleeping. Worry will actually cause the insomniac more difficulty than not sleeping.

Relaxing Exercises

Progressive muscle relaxation with deep breathing exercises and self-hypnosis are valuable adjuncts in insomnia. The techniques of relaxation and self-hypnosis have been outlined previously in this volume (q.v.). They may advantageously be taught to the patient. Repeated suggestions are made that he or she will be able to "turn one's mind off," to focus on a pleasant scene, and to feel himself or herself getting more and more drowsy and relaxed. This may reestablish the sleep rhythm more effectively than any other measure. A useful pamphlet on ways to approach sleep may be prescribed for the patient (Better Sleep, 1963). An interesting article called "The science of sleep," by Joan Arehart-Treichel (1977) in Science News, may be recommended, as may the book by Coates and Thoresen (1979).

Acceptance of Insomnia

Several unusual methods of controlling sleep have emerged that may be suited for certain patients. One technique deliberately restricts the hours spent in bed fruitlessly attempting to fall asleep. Persons appear to "sleep better if they spend fewer, rather than more hours, in bed" (JAMA, 1985). Subjects are enjoined to stay awake later but to arise at their customary times. They are not permitted to nap during the daytime. Another method that has been employed with patients who drive themselves frantic during the day with the fear that they will not be able to sleep that night is

paradoxical intention (Ascher and Efran, 1978, Ascher et al. 1980). Here suggestions are given that the person "try to remain awake as long as possible, rather than attempt to fall asleep." A rapid reduction of sleep onset latency can result.

Should insomnia continue to be distressing, referral to a sleep disorder clinic may be considered. Such may be the case in phase-shift sleep-wake (in which the patient seems to be able to sleep only during the daytime and is awake at night). Chronotherapy, a specialized procedure, is best done in such clinics.

Some therapists try to get insomniacs to accept their insomnia as something with which they can learn to live. Indeed, insomniacs may, as Modell (1955) has pointed out, successfully exploit their symptom. Once they are convinced they need less sleep physiologically than their mind dictates, patients may be encouraged to accomplish something useful during their waking hours at night. Instead of tossing about fitfully in bed and brooding about problems, they may read or write in bed. Or they may get up, take a shower, and, for an hour or two, apply themselves to useful work, particularly work that worries them if it goes undone. They may then return to bed.

Drug Treatment

Prescription of a hypnotic should be given only when behavioral or psychosocial therapy fails to relieve sleeplessness. In cases of depression, antidepressants may eliminate the insomnia. If stress exists, the only logical intervention is to deal with its sources. Hypnotics temporarily given for no more than 3 weeks, and preferably less, may be of great help. If there is a history of alcohol or drug abuse, hypnotics should not be prescribed because the patient will almost invariably refuse to give them up or, worse still, will take them with alcohol or other depressants, which may be fatal. When hypnotics have been used for more than 2 weeks, withdrawal should be gradual to avoid rebound sleeplessness or such neurological symptoms as twitching.

Many substances have been used, abused, and then discarded in humans' quest for a harmless substance that can hasten and sustain sleep. We still do not have such a substance, but currently the benzodiazepines, the least harmful, though still not perfect, solution, have replaced alcohol, bromides, opiates, barbiturates, ethclorvynol, glutethimide, and methaqualone as the most frequently prescribed drug for insomnia. Chloral hydrate is still employed by some as a safe and effective hypnotic.

Taken occasionally when stress distracts the normal sleep tendency, hypnotic benzodiazepines are useful aids. When taken regularly as sleep insurance, all hypnotics eventually betray their purpose by fostering cognitive and psychomotor impairments. Without a pharmacological "straight jacket," the individual anticipates a sleepless night with the feared consequence of not being able to function well or at all the next day. On the other hand, if benzodiazepines are not prescribed, a stressed individual may resort to alcohol or more dangerous drugs that cannot be monitored.

The most popular benzodiazepines employed as hypnotics are the long-acting flurazepam (Dalmane), with a half-life of about 100 hours, the short-acting temazepam (Restoril), with a half-life of 9.5 to 12.5 hours, and the ultrashort-acting triazolam (Halcion), with a half-life of only 1.6 to 5.4 hours. Diazepam (Valium), 2 to 5 mg (and up to 10 mg), is an old standby; it has a half-life of several days. Lorazepam (Ativan), 2 to 4 mg, is also popular and has a shorter half-life of up to 18 hours. Doxepin (Sinequan), 25 to 50 mg, is another choice. It is a dibenzoxepin tricycle compound used in depression and hence less prescribed for insomnia although it may be effective in some cases.

The drug to use will depend on the type of insomnia the patient is suffering. In transient situational stress with a carry over of anxiety during the day, Valium (2 to 5 mg) is a good alternative, especially if one wants its anxiety-reducing effects (with its accompanying slight hangover) to continue through the daytime. Dalmane has its advocates. Its sedative effects continue in the daytime because of its long half-life. Here one starts with a 15-mg dose but informs the patient that it is more effective on the second, third, or fourth night of consecutive use than on the first night. Should 15 mg fail to work after a week, 30 mg may then be given. In severe chronic insomnia one may start initially with the 30-mg dosage. Elderly persons who require daytime alertness and good psychomotor performance are best given 0.125 mg of Halcion, which may be increased to a limit of 0.25 to 0.5 mg. Halcion (0.25 to 0.5 mg) is also valuable for persons with jet lag or who awaken in the middle of the night and need a short boost to fall back to sleep. Restoril (15 to 30 mg) is also tolerated well by young and old and is especially suited to those who anticipate sleep difficulties. For early-morning awakening, doxepin (25 to 50 mg) is sometimes quite effective. The amino acid L-tryptophane has been shown to reduce sleep latency without distortions of psychological sleep (Hartmann, 1977), but it has not been consistently used as a hypnotic because of its mild effect.

Should these medications fail and it is judged that the patient truly needs a stronger temporary hypnotic, the choice of drug will depend upon whether short action is desired (i.e., 3–4 hours), in which case pentobarbital (Nembutal) 1.5 grains (100 mg) is prescribed; intermediate action (i.e., 4–6 hours) will require butabarbital (Butisol); 1.5 grains or long action (i.e., 6–8 hours) for which 1.5 grains of phenobarbital will be necessary. Sometimes a combination drug is used such as Tuinol (1.5 grains), which contains Seconal and Amytal, for short and intermediate action. Should a "hangover" result the next morning, the doses should be halved. Under no circumstances should a stimulant such as amphetamine be prescribed to alert the patient the next day since a vicious sedating-stimulating habit may be established. The nonbarbiturates are also popular. Among these chloral hydrate is preferred (7.5–15 grains). This is available in capsule form (Noctec), which consists of $3\frac{3}{4}$ or 7.5 grains of chloral hydrate and is taken in doses of one to two capsules nightly; or in syrup form, which contains 7.5 grains of chloral hydrate per teaspoonful. Other nonbarbiturates are also occasionally employed but must be used with caution. These include Placidyl (500 mg), Doriden (500 mg), and Noludar (300 mg).

The use of hypnotics should be confined to at most 3 weeks because beyond this time habituation is likely. If long-term use is anticipated, the patient may be enjoined to skip medication several times during the week. Many patients are comfortable with a hypnotic every 3 days, which enables them to catch up on their desired quota of sleep. In spite of everything that can be done to deal with the causes of insomnia, it may be impossible to stop it. This is especially the case if the patient has an intractable medical condition with pain and debility. In these cases, the therapist may have to prescribe long-term periodic hypnotic medication as adjunctive therapy.

When hypnotic drugs have been used over a long period, they usually become less effective and REM sleep is markedly reduced. Therapy is much more difficult since the patient will resist going off hypnotics. Should drugs be abruptly withdrawn, disturbing rebound insomnia will eventuate. The brief snatches of sleep that do occur are interrupted by a rebound in REM sleep, upsetting dreams, and nightmares. Consequently, slow withdrawal is necessary (a good rule is reducing by one nightly dose every 5 or 6 days). The patient should be warned about the possibility of a temporary increase in insomnia, vivid dreams, and nightmares. Relaxation exercises or self-hypnosis are prescribed or biofeedback employed if the therapist has the apparatus. Other principles outlined above should be followed.

In absolutely refractory insomnia, multidimensional treatment in an inpatient psychiatric unit may be most helpful.

EATING DISORDERS

Overweight and Obesity (Psychological Factors Affecting Physical Condition, DSM-III-R Code 316.00)

The pursuit of thinness has become an obsession, especially in prosperous societies, but often it is a futile gesture. Obesity is a refractory condition whose cure rate is less than for many kinds of cancer. If grossly excessive, overweight leads to many physical disabilities, but even more important to untold hours of self-reproach and suffering on the part of even its less overweight victims. Recent studies have shown that such physiological factors as fat cells that are enlarged in size and number and a low metabolic rate are prominent among some obese persons. These factors, probably genetically determined, make it difficult and for some individuals impossible to lose weight even on a prescribed low-calorie diet. There is also a small group of persons who have serious personality problems dating back to infancy and early childhood associated with an overvaluing of oral activities, in whom overeating becomes a compulsive mechanism that defies all methods of control except long-term psychotherapy (Bruch 1957, 1961, 1973; Caldwell, 1965). Even here the food compulsion may defy correction. Most overweight persons do not fit into these subtypes of obesity, however, and may be helped by modern methods of treatment to lose weight for cosmetic if not health reasons.

The basic therapy that has been commonly employed is behavior modification that takes into consideration the prevailing eating patterns of the patient (Stunkard 1972, 1985, Craighead et al, 1981). Detailed questioning is essential regarding not only the kinds and preparation of foods the patient prefers to eat, but also the time of day when overeating occurs, the availability of the food, the exact circumstances under which the appetite is stimulated, propensity for sweets, late-evening snacking, social pressures, and so on. What is essential is control of environmental eating cues that excite temptation. Once these factors are identified, the patient is instructed in how to rearrange eating routines and given homework assignments to practice the new orientation.

Standard forms of therapy involve (1) following a diet of around 800 to 1000 calories daily, carefully recording the food consumed, (2) keeping a chart, daily or weekly, of one's weight, (3) eating meals preferably at home with no distractions such as radio, television, or reading, (4) chewing each mouthful of food very slowly and spending at least 20 minutes at each meal, (5) forbidding snacking between meals, (6) food shopping from a list of essential items and no more, (7) exercising daily and walking rather than riding, and (8) being rewarded with money or gifts for losing weight and being penalized by a fine for gaining weight. Such programs are often executed in groups for a number of sessions, among which Weight Watchers and Overeaters Anonymous are especially popular.

Except for a small group of physiologically and psychologically handicapped persons, overweight individuals who follow the principles of these programs will lose considerable poundage. The real problem is maintenance, because most people are constantly plagued with temptation and sooner or later will abandon their new eating styles. Fantasies of the good life—the tinkle of beautiful crystal, the feel of fine silver, and the smell and taste of gourmet cooking will haunt the most dedicated soul. And, in an incredibly short time, to the great consternation of the dieter, the old weight has been restored. Anyone who operates under the illusion that weight loss is simply a matter of discipline and diet and that a few behavioral strategies can dissolve fat and ensure permanent weight loss will be subject to disappointment.

For many people, food is a pacifier. It alleviates tension and acts as a means not only of gratifying hunger and securing great pleasure but of quelling anger and restoring one's adaptive equilibrium. The driving impact of hunger is kept alive by inner forces of which the individual may not be entirely aware. This fact has led to a broadening of behavioral strategies to include cognitive elements. We are interested not only in what the patient does but in the thoughts and impulses that stir up the craving for food and especially for those foodstuffs that are fattening.

In some cases, particularly if physiological factors exist and constant dietary attempts have led to failure, the individual should not be forced to reduce. The lesser of two evils is to accept one's body size and try to lessen the overconcern with achieving thinness. Society does discriminate against overweight people, and even those who are mildly plump get to hate their bodies and to despise themselves for loss of willpower. Psychotherapy may not be able, especially with short-term methods, to get to the provocative psychological factors responsible, and the most we will be able to accomplish is to help people to stop tormenting themselves with their obsessional dieting preoccupations.

If a patient comes to therapy principally for help for emotional and adjustment problems and obesity is a secondary concern, the focus at first will be on the primary complaint factor. In the course of therapy, the patient may bring up the matter of overweight, in which case techniques may be used similar to those used when obesity is the initial complaint. Generally the patients will already have experimented with weight-loss measures on their own. The therapist may inquire about those that have proven temporarily successful. In some cases no more has to be done than to encourage the patient to continue on these diets and to join Weight Watchers, Overeaters Anonymous, or similar groups. Commercial weight-loss clinics must be selected carefully since some employ potentially dangerous drugs, have minimal medical supervision, and neglect essential exercise, which is an important ingredient in a good program. In treating the average adult who is less than 40 percent overweight and who probably does not possess serious psychological problems, some clarification about diets will usually be necessary. Though the patient has been exposed to years of dietary information and may profess to know all about dieting, there are usually large gaps in knowledge that have been filled with old wives' tales about food and feeding as well as faddist whimsies extracted from magazines and newspapers. Information on what constitutes a good dietary regime (7 calories per pound of ideal weight with proper protein, mineral, and vitamin content) that can act as the basis of a living diet to be followed faithfully may have to be supplied. In some patients alcohol, taken to appease tension, constitutes a block to dieting. One ounce of drink of any spirit contains about 135 calories. An average martini has as many calories as three slices of bread! Considering that several highballs or cocktails supply 500 to 750 calories and that the appetite is in addition stimulated by alcohol, food control for the drinker becomes a nonexistent entity. The matter of exercise will also require explanation. A 250-pound man climbing 20 flights of stairs will lose the equivalent of one slice of bread. Exercise firms up muscles, but it cannot take off sufficient poundage without strict dieting. When suggesting a proper diet, the therapist may have to give the patient a basic nutritional list of essential daily foods. This consists of a helping of fresh fruit twice daily; a small helping of cooked vegetables; a salad; lean broiled meat, fish, or fowl twice daily; a glass of milk or cheese twice daily; 2 to 3 eggs weekly; and little or no alcoholic beverages (Tullis, 1973). Fats, nuts, candy, cake, and all desserts are to be avoided. Low-calorie salad dressings, low-calorie sweeteners, and sugar-free drinks may be permitted.

A report released by researchers in a study supported by the National Institutes of Health has lauded the substitution of fats in the diet with 60 mg of sucrose polyester per day. This reduces caloric intake by 23 percent (*JAMA*, 1982) and contributes to weight loss. Meals should be taken at regular hours with no snacking allowed.

In most cases, however, the lack of success with these routine methods will necessitate an aggressive therapeutic program on either an individual or group basis. Assessment should include an evaluation of the patient's goals. Sometimes these are unrealistic, for example, if the patient expects to lose 20 pounds in 4 weeks. The patient's dietary and eating habits should be recorded as well as any stress factors of which the patient is aware. Many patients believe that they can lose weight by having little or no breakfast and skimping on lunch. In this case, most of the eating occurs at nighttime, when a ravenous appetite is set loose. Some patients desire medications that will act as appetite suppressants. Information should be supplied that experience with these chemical adjuncts has been disappointing. Their effect is temporary at best, and when they are discontinued, the patient is worse off than at the beginning.

An evaluation of social support systems is vital since many tensions are the product of social isolation and lack of family and group contacts. Because the relationship with the spouse is especially important, the spouse should become a vital part of the treatment program from the start. As the patient loses or fails to lose weight, the attitudes of the spouse will influence what happens, and the spouse's relationship with the patient may change for the better or worse. Not infrequently, the spouse will subtly encourage the patient to go off the diet as body changes in the latter occur. Obesity may be a way of locking the patient into a neurotic relationship that the spouse needs for his or her personal stability. There may be fear that greater physical attractiveness will motivate the patient to abandon the spouse or make the spouse attractive sexually to others or seek activities away from home. Some men find obese wives more sexually stimulative and thus may discourage weight loss in their wives. These additional reasons for sabotage of the patient's therapy make the husband's presence at some of the sessions a desirable part of the treatment program.

It is obvious that motivation to lose weight is crucial to the success of any treatment program for obesity. Certain patients come to therapy with the expectation that some miracle will happen and that their appetites for food will somehow disappear as a result of magical tactics like hypnosis (Krogar, 1970; Stanton, 1975). Because motivation to participate actively in the assigned program is essential, an initial screening process may be used. Patients are told that unless they are ready to follow the routines prescribed, they are not ready for the program. They are then given a few routines to follow during the first and second session, such as keeping a record of their weight and their food intake each week.

Simple tactics such as chewing food very slowly, putting the fork down between bites, sitting in the same place for each meal, and avoiding distractions like television while eating may be advised. Should the patients fail to do these simple things nor be disciplined enough to lose at least 2 pounds during the first 2 weeks of therapy, it is doubtful that the more burdensome

tasks that come later will be executed. Such reluctant patients may be told bluntly that they are not yet ready for the program the therapist has to offer. Motivation may sometimes be helped by imposing financial penalties for nonattendance at sessions (Brownell & Foreyt, 1985). At the University of Philadelphia and Baylor College of Medicine, for example, patients are required to deposit $100 in addition to a treatment fee of $200. If the patient attends at least 80 percent of the sessions, the deposit is returned.

Included in the weight-reducing directives are definite instructions regarding routine exercise. Physical exercise is prescribed not so much for its weight-reducing potential, which is low, but for its general effect on the well-being of the patient, which reflects back on the patient's ability to follow a sensible weight-loss maintenance regime. Morever, exercise helps prevent the loss of essential muscle tissue and the lowering of the basal metabolic rate as dieting proceeds. The therapist must be firm about insisting that graded exercises be carried out daily. Most obese patients will resist exercising for many reasons, including shame of exposing their bulky bodies to others and the torpor that excessive poundage imposes on them.

According to some authorities on obesity (Stunkard, 1984; Garrow, 1981), different degrees of obesity call for different approaches. Mildly obese people (30–40 percent overweight) are best helped with behavioral methods. Moderately obese people (40–100 percent overweight) require a very low-calorie diet as well as behavior modification. Severely obese people (more than 100 percent overweight), which is rare, may need an intestinal bypass operation after having failed with a very low-calorie diet and behavior modification. Such intractable cases usually display a combination of basic defects in metabolism and poor motivation, which results in lack of cooperation. A "short-circuit" procedure (ileal bypass) results in a reduction of the length of the small bowel lowering the abosrptive surface for nutrients. While weight loss occurs, serious malabsorption, diarrhea, gallstones, and susceptibility to infections may impair health. The operation is consequently done as a last resort.

It is important to remember that weight will rapidly be regained if a reducing diet is markedly different from the diet the individual will return to later. Some nutritionists therefore advise patterning a diet around the patient's customary one but substituting nonfattening for fattening items, eliminating high-calorie foods, and introducing more vegetables, fruits, and cereals. It is essential that the organization of a dietary regime take into account the need for the person to continue to eat healthful foods to maintain his or her ideal weight. How fast one should lose weight is also important. Obese people want to reduce rapidly. They have previously tried to do this with crash diets. This has not worked because returning to previous food habits nullified their accomplishment. The rate of weight loss during the active period of dieting is best maintained at a low level, perhaps no more than 1 to 1 $\frac{1}{2}$ pounds weekly, which gives the individual a chance to reorganize food habits. If however, obesity is pronounced, if morale demands it, and especially if the metabolism of the individual is sluggish, a drastic reduction of food intake (to 400 to 700 calories) or outright semistarvation (Genuth et al, 1974) *under medical supervision* may be undertaken to foster the loss of 3 to 5 pounds weekly. Naturally, there is great danger here of rapid return to the original weight once professional supervision if terminated.

In recent years a very low-calorie diet mainly of protein (lean meat, fish and fowl, vitamins and minerals) has been popularized for patients who are at least 40 pounds overweight. Patients have initial physical examinations and are seen regularly by their physicians for checkups and laboratory tests. Supervision is essential, and if the patient adheres to the diet, and in addition receives behavior modification, impressive weight loss is possible in most cases. Unless a continuing maintenance program exists, however, relapses are the rule. Satisfactory maintenance may often be achieved when patients are continuously supervised, preferably in a group setting.*

Weight-loss maintenance is a key issue and, as has been mentioned, the involvement of a spouse at the point when the patient has lost enough weight to make a difference in appearance may spell the difference between a successful and poor outcome. Most patients will require personal individual or group therapy for a year. Thereafter, some patients do better in a continuing group, but this is not always the case. The patient should be forewarned to contact the therapist should there be danger of slipping back into the old habits. Any stress situations are apt to cause a patient to overeat to appease tensions. Often fantasies of gourmet foods may tempt or upset the patient. Patients who have irreverent thoughts about luscious foods must be taught to correct self-statements that keep undermining their resolve. The emphasis in such a cognitive approach must be on their strengths not weaknesses. Hunger may be explained as a good sign, indicating that the patient is consuming excess body fat. Mastering hunger then becomes a virtuous act of caring about themselves and safeguarding health, longevity, and appearance.

One should not overlook the damaging psychological consequences of having been overweight. Obese people often have a depreciated self-image and believe their bodies to be misshapen, grotesque, and

* An interesting treatment manual describing a behavioral approach to obesity has been prepared by Brownell. Information on it may be obtained by writing to Dr. Kelly D. Brownell, Department of Psychiatry, University of Pennsylvania, 133 South 36th Street, Philadelphia, PA 19104.

contemptible. They sustain a loathsome hatred of themselves. This is most often the case in juvenile obesity in which extraordinary efforts may be made to conceal body fat. Some of these residues remain even after weight loss. Or an attractive body may confront the individual with new challenges, for example, coping with sexual gestures from members of the opposite sex which they are not equipped to handle. Continued psychotherapy may then be in order.

Psychoanalysis and psychoanalytic therapy have little impact on the isolated symptom of obesity. Correcting disturbed personality factors may, however, have an impact on overeating patterns. When successful, they can significantly improve the quality of life of their beneficiaries in a broad spectrum of behaviors.

Anorexia Nervosa (DSM-III-R Code 307.10)

Anorexia Nervosa usually invites desperate expediencies. In their anger, anguish, and dismay, patients and therapists may take recourse in such measures as cajolery, bribes, tube feedings, and even electroconvulsive therapy. These may have an immediate ameliorative effect, but since they circumvent the core problems they ultimately aggravate self-starvation. Anorexia nervosa mainly affects young adolescent girls of well-to-do families who defend their avoidance of food with a captious logic that does not yield to common-sense arguments. Even though they are emaciated, they still insist on losing weight by restricting food intake, forcing themselves to vomit, and driving themselves mercilessly in forced exercise. Sometimes obsessive-compulsive behavior takes place. Interludes of binge eating (bulimia) and vomiting are followed by self-hatred. If some motivation exists, behavior therapy by itself sometimes brings temporary benefits (White JG, 1964). Follow-up studies, however, have been discouraging, with re-

lapse and alarming substitutive symptoms being the rule rather than the exception (Bruch, 1973). The malady appears to be on the increase throughout the world, as the pursuit of thinness remains a chief obsessive concern.

Theories of its cause range from genetic predisposition, to hypothalamic dysregulation, to exaggerated dopamine activity, to an affective disorder, to reaction to psychosexual conflict, to an extraordinary stressful experience. Psychological studies often reveal an erstwhile "perfect" child struggling to maintain her stature with abstemious relentlessness. Basic is the search for identity and a struggle for independence and control. Paradoxically, short-lived bouts of uncontrollable eating binges further undermine the anorexic's self-esteem and incite an exaggerated refusal to eat. A pathological distortion of the body image is universal.

Therapy is thus understandably difficult. It hinges on two objectives: (1) improving nutrition (the use of high-calorie diet is sometimes helpful but must not be forced (Maxmen et al, 1974); and (2) rectifying the instrumental psychological causes. In mild cases, where the family warfare is not too extreme, treatment may be achieved at home. In most instances, separation from the home environment (usually with hospitalization) is mandatory in order to remove the patient from the highly charged family situation and from the aversive entourage surrounding the prevailing eating atmosphere. The relationship with the therapist is primary, with a minimum of pressure employed. Focus on food stuffs and calories is avoided.

Certain medications have a positive effect on anorectic patients. The most important of these is the antidepressant group, such as amitryptiline (Elavil), which is started in a low dose and worked up to 150 mg daily. Another drug with antidepressant qualities is cyproheptadine (Periactin). Chlorpromazine (Thorazine) has also been used with good results in some cases. Behavior modification is used freely to reinforce corrective eating patterns. If family difficulties are prominent, family therapy can be helpful. Psychoanalysis in the classical from has not been found to be too useful, one reason being the lack of motivation for depth therapy. A modified form of dynamic therapy reinforced by family therapy (Liebman et al, 1974) and supportive measures has yielded the most encouraging results and has helped to rectify identity problems, temper cognitive distortions, and expand autonomy and self-control in relation to eating habits. Continuing psychotherapy with the patient, and perhaps family therapy, is required after hospitalization (Bruch, 1973, 1975).

Bulimia Nervosa (DSM-III-R Code 307.51)

The episodic unrestrained incorporation of large quantities of food, which sometimes occurs along with anorexia nervosa, is also an isolated pattern that is increasingly being encountered in adolescent girls of normal weight. Occasionally it occurs in obese people who seemingly resent the strictures of dietary control, and periodically indulge themselves in compulsive eating. A recent survey of tenth-grade students has also revealed an alarming number of children who engage in binge-purge activities (Killen et al, 1986). The activity is usually followed by guilt feelings, self-recrimination, and forced vomiting. Laxatives and diuretics are taken for the purpose of trying to regulate weight. A good deal of secrecy may accompany the habit, spasms of wild food intake being confined to stealthy visits to the refrigerator or to the privacy of one's room, where sweets and other goodies have been stowed away. Depression accompanies the disorder either as a primary or secondary factor. Indulgence in such substances as barbiturates and amphetamines may sometimes occur. Periods of frantic dieting are often pursued. Concern with one's body and appearance mingled with distortions of the body image make for a peculiar picture, although in all other respects the individual appears normal. Most victims of this illness do not spontaneously seek therapy, but they may be referred by concerned parents or friends.

The association of bulimia and depression is an interesting one. A disproportionate number of bulimics have a positive dexamethasone suppression text, reflecting a relationship between bulimia and major affective disorder (Hudson et al, 1983a). A number of reports have detailed the successful treatment of bulimia with tricyclic antidepressants such as imipramine (Hudson et al, 1983b) and MAO inhibitors, such as phenelzine (60–90 mg daily) (Walsh et al, 1982).

The fact that binge eating may be controlled by antidepressants does not reduce the impulse to engage in this abnormal food activity. For this reason, individual therapy plus short-term therapy groups should be held with a focus on nutrition, expanding self-esteem, and finding alternatives to binge eating and purging. Indeed, some studies show that a multifaceted group approach produces results equivalent to the taking of antidepressants. Connors et al. (1984) has shown that utilization of a treatment approach incorporating education, self-monitoring, goal setting, assertiveness training, relaxation, and cognitive restructuring can lead to significant attitudinal and behavioral change. Following the initial improvements with antidepressants and with brief group therapy, prolonged dynamic psychotherapy may be needed if personality disorders require restructuring.

HABIT DISORDERS

A number of symptomatic complaints are commonly encountered among patients that serve either as a prime reason for seeking therapy or become so distracting that they obstruct the therapeutic effort. Their resolution consequently will concern the psychotherapist, who, having satisfactorily managed to overcome them, may proceed with any underlying personality problems of which the symptoms are a surface manifestation. Many of the techniques for habit modification come from the behavioral field. The effectiveness of reinforcement therapy has been validated even with chronic psychotic patients (Gottfried & Verdicchio, 1974).

Functional Enuresis (DSM-III-R Code 307.60)

Once urologic or general causes for enuresis (a good physical examination is a necessity) are eliminated (for instance, local irritation around the meatal or urethral area, phimosis, adherent clitoris, balanitis, cystitis, urinary tract infections, pinworms, diabetes, cerebral dysrhythmia, and systemic diseases), its sources in psychological conflict may be explored. If the patient is not mentally defective or of borderline intelligence, the presence of enuresis probably indicates improper habit training, emotional immaturity, or conflicts related to sexuality or aggression (Bakwin, 1961). Frequently enuresis has positive values for the individual as a masturbatory equivalent. In some instances it represents a form of aggression against the parents or against the world in general. Often it signifies an appeal for dependence on the basis of being a childish, passive, helpless person. In this context, enuresis may symbolize for the boy castration and the achieving of femininity. In girls it may connote aggressive masculinity and symbolic functioning with a penis.

For children a record is kept of dry and wet nights, the former being rewarded by praise and the record marked with a star. Rewards like ice cream may also be used. When the child wets, he or she should be responsible for changing the bed clothes and for seeing that they are washed. One-third of the children presenting with enuresis may be cured by this regimen alone (McGregor HG, 1937).

Strong emotional stress sometimes produces enuresis in persons who are ordinarily continent. This was brought out during World War II when certain soldiers subjected to the rigors of induction or warfare displayed the regressive symptom of bedwetting. Most soldiers who showed this symptom had a history of early bedwetting or of periodic attacks of the disorder prior to induction.

In treating enuretic children, they may first be requested to empty their bladder at bedtime; then awakened 2 hours later and induced to urinate again. This interval may gradually be prolonged, and, if enuresis stops, the evening awakening may be discontinued after 6 months. Positive praise and encouragement are given the children when they control their bladder; however, there should be no scolding or punishment for wetting. Exciting play or activity prior to bedtime is best curtailed, and fluids restricted after four o-clock. Coffee, tea, cocoa, sweets, salts, and spices should be avoided. Sedatives, amphetamine, methyl testosterone, anticonvulsants, belladonna, and other substances have been administered with varying results. Imipramine (Tofranil) has been used (Poussaint & Ditman, 1964; Stewart MA, 1975) one-half hour before bedtime and the results have been promising. The dose is 25 mg for children of 4 to 7 years, 35 mg for children of 8 to 11 years, and 50 mg for children older than 11 years. Countering improvement are side effects in certain cases. Friedell (1927) obtained an 80 percent cure rate with intramuscular injections of sterile water. W. A. Stewart (1963) described how Zulliger cured a young man of 19 with lifelong enuresis in one session by convincing the patient that he, the therapist, sided with the patient against his father. The fact that so many treatments have yielded positive results indicates the presence of a strong suggestive and placebo element in the management of enuresis (English OS & Pearson, 1937; *Hospital Focus,* 1964).

Enuresis developing in an adult is usually a regressive phenomenon connoting a desire to return to a childish adaptation and a defiance of the adult world.

The treatment of enuresis will depend upon whether one wishes to deal with the symptom as an entity, disregarding the emotional undercurrents, or to work with the intrapsychic structure in hopes that the symptom will eventually resolve itself (Pierce, 1975). Focusing on the symptom as preliminary to working with more fundamental dynamic factors is preferred by many since the symptom is an undermining element that robs the individual of self-confidence and vitiates interest in searching for conflictual sources. Accordingly, concomitant counseling and carefully conducted psychotherapy should, if possible, be employed.

A rapid effective conditioning technique, which, according to the British journal *Lancet* (1964), brings a relief yield of 75 percent, involves a buzzer or bell which sounds off when there is wetting of the bed (Mowrer & Mowrer, 1938). There are advocates and critics of this method. Sidetracking the issue of whether symptom removal is rational or irrational (Winnicott, 1953; Eysenck, 1959) or whether the buzzer treatment is a form of classical or operant conditioning (Lovibond, 1963), this approach to enuresis in controlled studies has been shown to be superior to other therapies (Werry, 1966). While the relapse rate is about 30 percent, relapses respond rapidly to a second course of treatment. There is little evidence that symptom substitution or precipitation of a neurosis develops with the removal of enuresis; on the contrary, the emotional well-being seems benefited (Baller & Schalock, 1956; Behrle et al, 1956; Bostock & Schackleton, 1957; Gillison & Skinner, 1958; Lovibond, 1963; Werry, 1966). The apparatus consists of two foil electrodes separated by thin gauze placed under the child. The covering over the electrodes should be as thin as possible. Parents and child are reassured there will be no shock, and the child is to prepare the bed and set the alarm. Should the alarm go off, he or she must get up and go to the bathroom. On return the child is to remake the bed and reset the alarm. Eventually the child will awaken before the alarm goes off. Should the child fail to awaken when the alarm sounds, the parents should awaken the child and see to it that he or she goes to the bathroom. A 90 percent cure is reported in 6 months (Dische, 1971). An improved form of apparatus is the Mozes Detector invented and used in Canada and tested at the Toronto Hospital for Sick Children with impressive results (*Medical World News,* 1972). Another conducting apparatus consists of a moisture pad worn inside the underwear (jockey pants or stretch-type bikini). The reported success rate is more than placebo. It may be obtained through Nite Train'r Enterprises, P.O. Box 282, Newberry, Oregon 97132.

Hypnotherapy is sometimes a useful adjunct (Stanton, 1979). Elsewhere (Wolberg LR, 1948), a full recording of the hypnotic treatment of enuresis is described. Actually, there is no single hypnotic method suitable for all patients; the specific suggestions and strategems will depend upon the problems and personality characteristics of the patient. One method is to train the patient to enter as deep a trance state as possible. In the trance, an attempt is made to show the patient that he or she is able to produce various phenomena, such as paralysis and muscle spasm, and that he or she can shift or remove these by self-suggestions. Fantasies related to the most pleasurable thing that can happen to a person are obtained for the purpose of reinforcing the conditioning process later on. The patient is then requested to experience a sensation of slight bladder pressure such as occurs immediately prior to urination.

As soon as he or she feels this sensation, it will inspire a dream or will make his or her hand rise to the face, which will cause the patient's eyes to open and to awaken. Even though no dream or hand levitation occurs, it is suggested that the patient's eyes will open, nevertheless. At that moment he or she will experience an urgency to get out of bed. Going to the bathroom will be associated with a feeling similar to that accompanying the fantasy of the best thing that can happen to a person. These suggestions are repeated a number of times.

The next stage in therapy is teaching the patient to control sensations that arise inside the bladder so that urine can be retained without needing to awaken until morning. Suggestions to this effect are given the patient as soon as he or she establishes a habit of getting out of bed and going to the bathroom. The positive relationship with the therapist may be utilized as a reinforcing agent in reconditioning, praise and reassurance being offered when suggestions are followed.

In patients who have expressed a willingness to undergo dynamic psychotherapy, conditioning procedures may be delayed until they are deemed absolutely necessary. This is because the symptom may disappear as the origins of bedwetting are explored, and the unconscious fantasies associated with it clarified. There is, however, no reason why psychotherapy cannot be combined with a conditioning approach.

Nail Biting and Hair Plucking

Nail biting and finger sucking are common outlets for tension in preadolescence and adolescence and may persist as a neurotic symptom into adult life. Among other things,, nail biting serves as a substitutive release for masochistic, sadistic, and repressed masturbatory needs. If no other serious emotional problems coexist, the treatment may be symptomatic (Pierce, 1975),

or therapy may be focused on outer emotional factors that generate tension, particularly environmental family problems. Most nail biters have little motivation for real psychotherapy, seeking mere measures of control because of embarrassment about their habit. They are usually unaware that the nail-biting symptom has a meaning, and they are often puzzled by the persistence of the urge to chew their fingertips.

If psychotherapy is resisted, the therapist may have no alternative but to treat the symptom. Hypnosis may be useful here. In hypnosis, strong authoritarian suggestions are made to the effect that the patient will have a desire that grows stronger and stronger to give up the childish habit of nail biting. Patients who put their fingers into their mouths will discover that their fingernails taste disgustingly bitter. They may even develop nausea with the mere desire to bite the nails. Daily hypnotic sessions are best, but since this is usually impractical, a tape recording may be made that the patient may use twice daily (see Induction of Hypnosis, Chapter 56, page 1019). Some therapists teach the parents of nail biters to activate the machine while the child is asleep to reinforce suggestions through sleep conditioning. Self-hypnosis may be employed in an adult. If these tactics fail, aversive conditioning (*q.v.*), a small shocking apparatus or a heavy rubber band around the wrist that can be painfully snapped may be tried (Bucher, 1968). A strong desire to control the symptom must be expressed by the patient and cooperation secured.

An assessment of the patient's problems will determine whether further reeducative or reconstructive therapy is indicated after the nail biting is brought under control.

Hair plucking (trichotillomania) (DSM-III-R Code 312.39) of the head, eyelashes, eyebrows is often a manifestation of a severe personality problem, often of an obsessive-compulsive or schizoid nature. It may serve as an outlet for revenge and self-punishment, and it is often accompanied by frustration, guilt feelings, and remorse. Psychotherapy is notoriously ineffective in dealing with this symptom. Hypnosis and particularly aversive conditioning may score some successes.

AFFECTIVE DISORDERS (MOOD DISORDERS, DSM-III-R Codes/BIPOLAR DISORDERS: bipolar disorder manic [296.4X]; bipolar disorder depressed [296.5X]; bipolar disorder mixed [296.6X]; cyclothymia [301.13]; DEPRESSIVE DISORDERS: major depression, single episode (296.2X); major depression recurrent [296.3X]; dysthymia [or depressive neurosis] 300.40; Atypical Disorders: Bipolar Disorder not otherwise specified [296.70]; Depressive disorder not otherwise specified [311.00]).

Depression is a generic term that embraces a variety of syndromes ranging from normal grief at the passing of a loved one, to reactions of prolonged distress out of proportion to the intensity of the traumatic stimulus, to paralyzing inhibition and retardation arising spontaneously from endogenous sources, to psychotic manifestations with intense melancholia and nihilistic, somatic, or paranoid delusions or hallucinations. A number of syndromes are classified under the category of affective disorders. At the top of the scale in intensity are *major depressive disorder* and *bipolar disorder*. The latter is characterized by alternating moods of elation and depression and is constituted by three subtypes: (1) *bipolar disorder, manic,* in which expansiveness and overactivity are dominant; (2) *bipolar disorder, depressed,* in which sadness and retardation are prominent; and (3) *bipolar disorder, mixed,* in which one or the other

mood occurs within a short span. *Cyclothymic disorder* is a mixed affective disorder of lesser intensity. Depressive reactions that often follow psychosocial stress and promote sleep disturbance, fatiguability, social withdrawal, and ahedonia are classified as *dysthymic disorder* (depressive neuroses, reactive depression). Atypical features of a mixed reaction merit the diagnosis of *atypical bipolar disorder;* or if the mood is primarily depression without the usual characteristics of a major depression or dysthmic disorder, they are regarded as signs of an *atypical depression.* Shadings of depression with schizophrenic symptoms have been called *schizoaffective disorder.*

According to some researchers, bipolar and unipolar disorders are two distinct entities. There is some controversy about the precipitating factors that activate a bipolar disorder. In some cases, stress seems to initiate an attack. In other cases, endogenous causes are implicated that appear to have little relation to environmental or inner conflictual sources. Typical of the manic phase are euphoria, irritability, grandiosity, hyperactivity, pressure of speech, and flight of ideas. After recovery and a varying interval of relative calm, a depressive phase may intervene, marked by sluggishness, retardation, loss of appetite, insomnia, and somatic distress. Symptoms vary in intensity from being so mild and under control that the illness is overlooked to being floridly psychotic. It is important to distinguish major depressive disorder from bipolar disorder. To establish the unipolar diagnosis, there must be at least three episodes of depression without a manic episode. Atypical symptoms may confuse the diagnosis, such as when mania masks itself as a personality problem in spurts of creative overactivity and productiveness and depression is concealed by dry humor and a smiling countenance. The search for biological markers goes on, but the Dexamethasone Suppression Test (DST), the TRH Stimulation Test, catecholamine metabolite levels, urinary phenylacetic acid levels, and sleep EEG studies are still inconclusive.

Depressive Reactions

Depression is one of the most common syndromes encountered in psychotherapeutic practice. Approximately 20 to 26 percent of women and 8 to 12 percent of men will be affected by at least one episode of depression in their lifetimes. Symptoms of this illness vary, but most often it is manifested by listlessness, fatiguability, loss of interest in practically all activities, diminution of the sexual drive, disturbances in appetite and sleep, feelings of worthlessness, self-reproach, and, in severe cases, psychomotor agitation or retardation and suicidal ideas or impulses. Bipolar depressions are characterized by periodic manic phases with swings toward hyperactivity. In most severe depressions, psychotic ideation is not uncommon. Once a depression occurs, there is a 40 to 50 percent likelihood of a second attack, and in the majority of these cases, subsequent attacks are possible. The person may then be plagued by recurrent depressions throughout his or her life. Some depressions seem to persist over a period of years with varying degrees of intensity; others apparently disappear; still others disappear only to recur at some time later.

Depression is a common reaction to separation and bereavement. It may become especially intense after the loss of an important person, such as a spouse, parent, child, or love object, inspiring grief and mourning. In most people the depression, after a period, is resolved. Its continuance or appearance and persistence when there is no adequate stimulus to account for it has a pathological significance and may require clinical intervention. Sometimes depression accompanies a severe physical illness, particularly if its chronic quality makes the person feel hopeless or proper functioning is impaired. Thus cancer, crippling arthritis, Parkinson's disease, cardiac failure, and other enduring medical and neurological ailments may sustain a prolonged depression. Aging, with its effect upon one's health, appearance, memory, and work capacities, is an especially provocative depressive stimulus. Substance abuse and detoxification (alcohol, amphetamines, barbiturates, narcotics, etc.) are frequently followed by a spell of depression that drives the person to more drinking or drug indulgence. The intake of certain medicinal agents such as antihypertensives (Reserpine, Diuril, Hygroton, etc.) and beta blockers (Inderal, Corgard, etc.) may also produce depression.

Depression sometimes merges with anxiety, making it difficult to distinguish the two. Confusing also is "masked depression" that is camouflaged by such somatic symptoms as headache, backache, facial and limb pains, dysuria, dyspareunia, dysmenorrhea, and sundry other complaints. A puzzling relationship exists between certain psychiatric syndromes and depression. Some observers consider conditions such as anorexia nervosa, bulimia, panic attacks, and obsessive-compulsive neurosis to be manifestations of neurotransmitter abnormalities akin to those of depressive illness, and, most important, they are relieved by antidepressants. Depression in childhood often takes the form of somatic illnesses such as headaches and abdominal pain mingled with a dysphoric mood. Aggressive and hyperactive children may also actually be suffering from depression. Depression among the elderly is common and is accompanied by relatively frequent somatic concerns, memory and cognitive deficits, and occasional paranoid delusions.

The diagnosis of depression is not difficult to make with a good clinical interview. Some physical ailments, however, mask themselves as depression. Gianninni et al. (1978) list 91 such ailments, and Hall (1980) lists almost as many. Consequently, a physical examination and laboratory tests should be done on all depressed patients. Similarly, substance abuse may produce depressive symptomatology and if suspected will justify urine and blood drug abuse screens. Some clinicians recommend the Dexamethasone Suppression Test if there is a problem in differential diagnosis. The DST can identify at least 50 percent of severe depressions (major depressive disorder) but is less accurate in detecting mild to moderate depressions. Certain medical problems, commonly prescribed medications, and some psychiatric disorders can distort DST results, and a negative DST does not rule out severe depression. At this stage, therefore, the test should not be employed as a routine diagnostic procedure although it still has some utility in research.

In reactive or neurotic depression (dysthymic disorder) some ostensible blow to security or self-esteem seems to set off the depressive pattern. The stress stimulus may be loss of a love object, of status, or of worldly goods. The meaning to the individual of the traumatic incident is the key to whether or not depression will result. The depressed patient organizes his or her thinking around the precipitating incident. If a love object has died or abandoned the patient, he or she is preoccupied with the image of the departed one. If status is impaired, the patient considers that he or she is "a nothing." Loss of worldy goods sparks off a poverty complex. The question is still not completely answered as to why some people respond with depression to a crisis in their lives, whereas others marshall their adaptive resources and overcome the vacuum created by the incident. Dynamically, reactive depression is related to (1) feelings of loss of a love object (expressed as feelings of isolation and emptiness), (2) a feedback of hostility blocked from external expression (expressed in self-deprecatory comments) in a masochistic maneuver, and (3) a converted form of anxiety (here anxiety and depression may alternate, depres-

sion apparently serving as a means of dealing with anxiety).

Major depressive disorder and bipolar disorder spring from biological disturbances presumably hereditary in nature and can develop periodically without identifiable exogenous or internal conflictual provocations. Social and psychological disruptions consequent to such biological depressions in turn can aggravate the symptoms. Depression in such conditions is often ushered in by feelings of loss of self-confidence, the absence of initiative, and fatiguability. The depressive mood itself may not be apparent; it is often covered by an overlay of hollow humor in what has been called the "smiling depressions." As the depression deepens, loss of appetite, insomnia, diminution of the sexual drive, and a general anhedonia (lack of gratification in the pursuit of pleasure strivings) follow. There are difficulties in attention and concentration and variations in mood, the intense depression during the morning lifting as the evening approaches. Interference with work and interpersonal relationships follow. Extreme suffering and regression to early dependency with masochistic behavior then develops in the course of which suicidal thoughts, impulses, and acts may erupt.

Principal goals in therapy consist of the following:

1. Removal of symptoms and a relief of suffering.
2. Revival of the level of adaptive functioning that the patient possessed prior to the outbreak of the illness.
3. Promotion, if possible, of an understanding of the most obvious patterns that sabotage functioning and interfere with a more complete enjoyment of life.
4. In motivated patients, recognition of conflictual patterns and exploration of their meaning, origins, and consequences.

5. Provision of some way of dealing with such patterns and their effects in line with a more productive integration.

Unfortunately, depressions are singularly resistive to treatment in that the mood change imposes a barrier to three of the most important elements in therapy: faith, hope, and trust. Lost is the expectancy of geting well that so often powers the machinery of cure. Gone is the feeling that someone cares, so essential in establishing a therapeutic relationship. Yet beneath the isolation and hopelessness, the depressed individual seeks a restoration of his or her ties with humanity. The person resists relationships, and then credits the feelings of isolation to the fact that he or she is unloved.

Among the therapeutic measures that are most effective are the following:

1. *Establish as rapidly as possible a relationship with the patient.* This is precarious as has been mentioned before. Yet winning the patient over in spite of inertia, gloom, sluggishness, despair, hostility, and self-recriminations is urgent. Depressed patients are insatiable in their demands for help and love. No matter how painstaking are the therapist's attempts to supply their demands, they will respond with rage and aggression, often accusing the therapist of incompetence or ill will. The patients should, nevertheless, be approached with the attitude that the therapist understands and sympathizes with their suffering. Such measures as active guidance and externalization of interests may be attempted. The basis of treatment is a warm relationship between the patient and the therapist. The relationship that the patient establishes with the therapist will, however, be extremely vulnerable. Much leniency and tolerance are needed, and an attempt must be made to show that the therapist realizes the depth of the pa-

tient's fears and misgivings. This, however, is more easily said than done, since the depressed patient has a distrustful nature.

Distrust springs from the fusion of hate with love. Hostile feelings generate guilt that may be so disabling that the person will want to discontinue treatment. The slightest frustration during therapy, such as the unavoidable changing or canceling of an appointment, may be equivalent to rejection and will mobilize a tremendous amount of anxiety. Under the surface there is always fear of abandonment, and there is a tendency to misinterpret casual actions. The patient seeks reassurance but may resent its being called psychotherapy.

The aim in treatment is to develop and reinforce all positive elements in the relationship. This will involve much work, since the attitudes of the patient are so ambivalent that he or she will feel rejected no matter what the therapist does. It is best to let the positive relationship take root in any way it can without attempting to analyze its sources.

One of the means of maintaining the relationship on a positive level is by communicating empathy and by avoiding arguments. It is essential to convey to the patient nonverbally the idea that he or she is liked and that the therapist is a friend in spite of anything that happens. An attitude of belittling, harshness, ridicule, or irritation must be avoided. The therapist must maintain an optimistic outlook and express the sentiment that although the patient may not believe it now, he or she *will* get over the depression in a while.

Hypnosis may be of help for some of the milder depressions as a means of establishing a relationship primarily as an avenue toward inducing relaxation and toward giving persuasive suggestions to stabilize the person. A number of depressed patients appear to thrive under hypnotic therapy, probably because it appeals to their dependency needs.

2. *Use drug therapy when necessary.* Benzodiazepines such as Valium and Xanax may be of help in patients with mild depressions, especially those associated with anxiety, in elevating the mood and supplying energy. Simple mild depression occasionally is helped by methylphenidate (Ritalin) but should be taken for no more than 3 weeks. More severe inhibited depressions may be approached with imipramine (Tofranil) (100–200 mg daily), while agitated depressions appear to respond better to amitriptyline (Elavil) (100–200 mg daily) combined, if anxiety is especially strong, with Librium (30–40 mg). In very severe anxiety 20–25 mg 3 or 4 times daily may be given. The effects of the latter drugs may not be felt for several weeks. The MAO inhibitors (Nardil, Parnate) are also of some value, especially for atypical or neurotic depressions. Bupropion (Wellbutrin) is an antidepressant with a minimal effect on sexual functioning. Some experimental drugs for depression are being tested, which have low side effect profiles. These include idazoxan and S-adenosylmethionine.

   If side effects are intolerable, some of the newer depressive agents may be tried, such as trazodone (Desyrel) and maprotiline (Ludiomil). Mellaril has been employed for depressions of the schizoaffective type. If a schizoid element is present, a phenothiazine drug (Trilafon, Stelazine) may be combined with Tofranil and Elavil. In bipolar depressions, lithium has been given, but in almost one-third of cases it is ineffective or produces bad side effects or sparks of manic attacks. Alternative therapies have been tried, including anticonvulsants such as carbamazepine (Tegretol), valproic acid, (Depakene), tryptophan, thyroid medications, calcium channel blocking agents, and propanolol. Carbamazepine has been increasingly employed because, unlike combined tricyclic-lithium and neuroleptic-lithium treatments, it does not encourage more rapid cycling. Haldol and Navane are often used for psychotic depressions. Depression during medical illness often responds well to triglycerides. (See also Chapter 56, Somatic Therapy (pp. 984–987 for a detailed description of antidepressant medications.)

   If drugs are used, patients should be told about the side effects to encourage the continuation of the medications in spite of them. Side effects are the chief reason why antidepressants are discontinued. The need for sleep may be reduced without harmful effect, and the patient may, if not forewarned, take excessive hypnotics. Constipation and weight gain may occur and require remedial measures. Mouth dryness may be counteracted partly by chewing gum or glycerin-based cough drops. Postural hypotension of a severe nature may be handled by advising the patient not to arise suddenly, to avoid standing unmoving in one place, and for women to wear elastic stockings and a girdle. Neuralgias or jactitation of the muscles may require 50 mg vitamin B_6 and 100 micrograms of vitamin B_{12} twice daily. Coffee intake should also be reduced. The troublesome insomnia in depression is best handled by chloral hydrate (Noctec, $7\frac{1}{2}$ gm) or the benzodiazepine hypnotics (see Insomnia). The patient may be given a mimeographed form about the side effects of drugs (see Appendix T). In older people, antidepressants such as Elavil may be effective, but the dose after the age of 60 must be cut down to 25–100 mg daily. Tetracyclic antidepressants are useful in this group because of the minor anticholinergic and cardiovascular effects. Maprotiline, for example, may be started with 25 mg to 50 mg daily, increasing by 25 mg every third day until 75 to 100 mg is reached, which can then be given in a single-evening dose. Some drugs have been introduced to reduce intolerable anticholinergic effects, e.g. bethanechol, and cyclic tremor, e.g. propranolol.

3. *Administer electroconvulsive treatments immediately in severe depressions, or if there is any danger of suicide.* Electroconvulsive treatments are superior to any of the present-day drugs. (See section on Electroconvulsive Therapy in Chapter 58.) The effect is rapid, 8 ECTs generally eliminating the depression; however, more treatments may be required. In very severe agitated depression, 2 ECTs daily for 2 or 3 days may be followed by 1 ECT daily, and then by treatments twice or three times weekly. Following ECT, energizing drug therapy may be instituted (Tofranil, Elavil) and, if agitation continues, Thorazine or Trilafon can be prescribed. Unilateral ECT may be employed if even temporary memory loss cannot be countenanced. The superiority of ECT over drug therapy for psychotic depression is without question.

4. *Hospitalize patients with severe depression.* Mild depression may be treated at home, preferably under the supervision of a psychiatrically trained attendant or nurse, or, better still, and especially if family problems exist, the patient should be admitted to a rest home. Isolation from parents and friends, bed rest, and constant care by a motherly attendant may prove very beneficial. Because of anorexia, efforts should be made to bolster the diet with high caloric and high vitamin intake in the form of small but frequent feedings.

In severe cases of malnutrition, a few units of insulin before meals may be helpful. If the depression is more than mild, hospitalization is advisable. Suicidal attempts in depression are made in almost one-third of the cases, and deaths resulting from these attempts occur with great frequency. The patient's complete loss of interest in himself or herself makes mandatory the establishment of definite daily routines, such as a hospital can best supply. Electroconvulsive therapy, the treatment of choice, can best be instituted in a hospital setting, and, if the patient requires tube feeding, nursing care is available.

5. *Institute psychotherapy as soon as feasible.* Psychotherapy is usually ineffective during extremely depressed phases. The only thing that can be done is to keep up the patient's morale. Patients should not be forced to engage in activities that they resist because this may merely convince them of their helplessness and inability to do anything constructive. If there is little suicidal risk, patients should be encouraged to continue their work, if they feel at all capable of managing it, since inactivity merely directs their thinking to their misery. In many cases, contact should be regulated with the patient's family and environment. This is necessary since the family of depressed patients often chides them for "not snapping out of it" and constantly reminds them that they must make up their mind to get well. The family members may be told that recovery is more than a matter of will power, and they must be urged to avoid a nagging and critical attitude.

6. Sleep deprivation therapy is still in an experimental state with varied reports attesting to its efficacy (King 1980), uncertainty of benefit (Pflug 1976), and possible worsening of the depression (Vogel et al, 1973). Different proce-

dures have been employed, including sleep deprivation for only one night totally, one night weekly, several nights weekly, and partial sleep deprivation in which the patient is awakened repeatedly during sleep.

Exactly how to conduct psychotherapy is difficult to say. Much depends on the training and skill of the therapist and his or her ability to establish a therapeutic alliance (Arieti, 1978). In general, during the acute depressed stage a supportive, reassuring manner is best, shying away from probing for unconscious material, which may increase anxiety and heighten the possibility of suicide. The patient is given an opportunity to verbalize his or her fears and feelings. Guidance, support, reassurance, and persuasion are used. The patient is told that no matter how bad things seem and how depressed he or she feels, patients with depression recover. There are, however, steps that can be taken to speed recovery: It is essential that the patient get involved in his or her usual activities to the extent that available energy will allow, but not beyond this. Because initiative may be lacking, the patient may require a daily routine for retiring, arising, meals, working, and social and recreational contacts. One difficulty encountered is dealing with the tendency for denial regarding the severity of the problem and the need for treatment. Regardless of the therapy employed, the countertransferences of the therapist are apt to be brought into play and will have to be handled appropriately. The tendency of the patient to employ the therapist as a replacement for an object of loss has to be handled with tact and understanding, avoiding rejecting the patient without supporting too enthusiastically a dependency relationship and without draining oneself too much with givingness and empathy.

Dealing with the depressed patient calls for a good deal of optimism, support graded to the patient's requirements, and need to control the tendency to be overprotective and overly reassuring. The patient must be made to feel that the therapist understands him or her and will do everything possible to help. The self-limited nature of depression should be repeatedly pointed out and the patient reminded that eventually he or she will feel much better, as others before have. Depressive ideas should never be ridiculed or accepted at face value. The therapist should point out that the situation is not as hopeless as it seems. If the patient harbors suicidal thoughts, a frank aereation of these feelings should be encouraged. It may be essential to extract a promise from the patient that he or she will not try suicide. If suicide is more than a passing fancy immediate ECT is necessary. A physical basis (biochemical, for example) for the depression may be presented and the patient told that there are medications that can help. "When an emotion of depression develops everything seems gloomy, but this will pass." Much of the benefit from psychotherapy is due to the relationship with the therapist. Appreciation of the therapist as a person who cares is important in securing cooperation. Family therapy may be indicated to manage guilt feelings in the members and to educate them regarding factors that can create a more harmonious relationship with the patient. Marital therapy can also be important, as may group therapy and behavioral therapy. Termination of therapy will have to be managed carefully because of the depressed person's sensitivity to loss. Adequate time must be given prior to terminating psychotherapy to allow for the working through of grief and rage reactions, which if neglected may spark off another round of depression. If a transfer to another therapist has to be made, the therapist must be careful not to give the patient the impression he or she is being rejected and pushed off into the hands of substitutes, which may be interpreted as another object loss and precipitate a deeper depression.

In depressions that have followed in the wake of actual or fantasied loss of a love object we may expect a rapid, positive transference as a means of object replacement. The substitution, however, is often rooted in magical expectations with desires for a giving, loving, nurturing, and omnipotent object reincarnation. The immediate reaction may be a temporary lifting of one's spirits, an overidealization of the therapist, and a stimulation of hope and anticipation that all will be well.

Inevitably, as the relationship with the therapist develops, the patient becomes aware of some failings in the therapist, a realization that the therapist is not the all-giving, all-powerful figure he or she imagined. What will emerge then is hostility and a feeling that the therapist has failed in anticipated obligations. The patient may try to vanquish his or her hopelessness by repressing doubts about the therapist, and passively submitting to the therapist with a sadomasochistic dependency. The hostility is usually suppressed by guilt feelings or in response to disapproving or attacking maneuvers on the part of the therapist. Depression may then return in full force or even become greater than before. Yet the patient will cling desperately to the therapist out of fear of undergoing another object loss.

The countertransference of the therapist will determine the fate of these transferential shifts, the proper handling of which will enable the patient to work through the termination phase of therapy. This involves resolution of the separation and grief reactions associated with loss of the love object that had initiated the depression. Some impact may also be scored on the original separation traumas sustained during the developmental years that sensitized the patient to later object loss.

Klerman has described a brief interpersonal psychotherapy (IPT) (12–16 weeks) for ambulatory, nonbipolar, nonpsychotic depressed patients aimed at symptom relief and enhanced interpersonal adjustment, rather than at personality change. The treatment is organized around the premise "that clarifying and renegotiating the (interpersonal) context associated with the onset of symptoms is important to the person's recovery and possibly to the prevention of further episodes" (Klerman et al, 1984b). A procedural manual (Klerman et al, 1984a) designating the rationale and techniques has been prepared and the method tested against some other treatments for depression. IPT rests on the assumption that depression issues out of stress induced by life events, especially social adjustment and interpersonal relations. Predisposing to the depressive reaction are personality factors, especially those involving self-esteem and the handling of guilt and anger. Therapy consists of exploring immediate interpersonal difficulties and then clarifying and modifying them. Alteration of maladaptive perceptions is attempted without delving into unconscious conflict or childhood antecedents or developing and exploring transference. Four interpersonal precipitants are particularly dealt with, namely, grief, role disputes, role transitions, and interpersonal deficits. Controlled studies have shown that IPT significantly lessens symptoms and after 6 to 8 months, social impairments. The final appraisal of IPT awaits further replication studies.

Cognitive therapy for depression can also be helpful and in some cases is superior to drug therapy. In cognitive therapy an attempt is made to rectify conceptual distortions in order to correct the ways that reality is being experienced. Interviewing techniques analyze defects in a patient's views of the world (cognitive assumptions or "schema"), methods of stimuli screening and differentiation, and the erroneous ideas that mediate destructive response patterns. Homework assignments reinforce the patient's ability to deal constructively and confidently with adaptive tasks. The treatment is short term, consisting of approximately 20 sessions on a twice-a-week basis. Cognitive therapy for depression is organized around a number of assumptions (Rush & Beck, 1978; Rush et al, 1977). As a consequence of early events, the patient retains a "schema" that makes him or her vulnerable to depression. Among such events is the death of a parent or other important person. What results is a "prepressive cognitive organization." Operative here is a global negative attitude on the part of the patient. Thus the patient misconstrues situations to a point where "he has tailored facts to fit preconceived negative conclusions" (Rush, 1978).

Depressed patients regard themselves as unworthy and assume this is because they lack essential attributes to merit worthiness. They assume their difficulties will continue indefinitely in the future, that failure is their destiny. These characteristics constitute the "cognitive triad" in depression. In treatment these patients are enjoined to keep a record of aspects of their negative thinking whenever this occurs and to connect these episodes with any associated environmental events that trigger them off. The simple quantifying of any symptoms—in this instance negative thinking—tends to reduce them. Whenever the patient during a session brings up a negative thought, the therapist asks the patient to reality-test it and then to do this away from therapy. Through this means patients are helped to see how they make unjustified assumptions ("arbitrary inferences"), how they magnify the significance of selected events ("magnification,") and how they use insignificant situations to justify their point of view ("overgeneralization"). Other "cognitive errors" are identified, such as how offensive details are used out of context while ignoring more important constructive facts ("selective abstraction"), how circumstances and thoughts that do not fit in with negative "schemas" are bypassed ("minimization"); how unrelated events are unjustifiably appropriated to substantiate their ideas ("personalization"). The patient is encouraged to review his or her record of thoughts, to identify

past events that support his or her faulty schemas. Point by point, the therapist offers alternative interpretations of these past events. By so doing, the therapist hopes that sufficient doubt will develop in the patient so that he or she will engage in experimental behaviors, recognizing the fallaciousness of his or her hypotheses, and arrive at different, less destructive explanations for events. A marital partner or family may also be involved in cognitive therapy to reinforce correction of distorted negative meanings.

Step by step the patient is encouraged to undertake tasks that he or she hitherto had considered difficult ("graded task assignment") and to keep a record of his or her activities ("activity scheduling") and the degree of satisfaction and sense of mastery achieved ("recording a mood graph"). Discussions in therapy focus on the patient's reactions to his or her tasks and tendencies at minimization of pleasure and success. Homework assignments are crucial. These range from behaviorally oriented tasks in severe depression to more abstract tasks in less severe cases oriented around correcting existing schemas. Should negative transference occur, it is handled in the manner of a biased cognition. (See also pages 154 and 877.)

The material elicited during the periods of active depression, both as to mental content and as to the character of the relationship with the therapist, may yield important clues to the inner conflicts of the patient. Although notes may be made for later reference, all confrontive interpretations during the active period should be suspended. Only during a remission can interpretive work of any depth be helpful. In most cases interpersonal and cognitive therapies are useful, but depth therapy is avoided in patients with major depressive disorder. Some patients with dysthymic disorder spontaneously express a desire to know more about their illness. Here, a dynamic insight approach may be used. Many patients, however, show an unwillingness to go into their difficulties and resist insight therapy. Having recovered, they are convinced they are well, and they desire no further contact with the therapist. Without the "wish" to get well, little can be accomplished in the way of reconstructive psychotherapy.

Following recovery, the patient should be guided regarding the possibility of further depressions. If the patient has been on medications, half to two-thirds of the effective dose should be continued for at least 4 months. An excellent discussion on therapies helpful for severely depressed suicidal patients may be found in the paper by Lesse (1975). Insofar as prophylaxis is concerned lithium presents promise. Controlled studies have shown that lithium can substantially reduce the long-term morbidity of both unipolar and bipolar disorders. Unipolar patients with endogenous and psychotic features, a family history of depression, and minor disturbance in personality respond well. Prophylactic treatment should be started after 3 episodes in unipolar depression and after the second episode in bipolar depression. Lower lithium plasma levels (0.45–0.6 mEq/l) are maintained best to reduce side effects.

Manic Reactions

The immediate objective in manic reactions is to quiet the patient. This is best achieved with neuroleptics, such as chlorpromazine (Thorazine), which must be administered in ample dose (up to 1600 mg daily or more). In wild excitements, intramuscular injections (25–50 mg repeated in an hour if necessary) are indicated, followed by oral administration. (See also Chapter 58 on Emergencies.) Dangerous overactivity may call for electroconvulsive therapy (ECT). This may be given twice daily for 3 or 4 days, followed by a treatment every other day. Following this, Thorazine or other neuroleptics may be substituted. Lithium carbonate (see Chapter 56 on Pharmacotherapy) has been employed with considerable success for recurrent manic states. The most effective treatment for mania is reported by Black et al., (1987) to be ECT. Almost 70 percent of patients who did not respond to lithium had marked improvement with ECT.

Psychotherapy is usually ineffective in most manic conditions. The patient's attention is too easily diverted; acting-out is too unrestrained; emotions are too explosive. Because of this, hypomanic and manic patients are extremely difficult to manage in the office. They will seek to involve the therapist in all of their fantastic plans. They will make demands which, when unfulfilled, will release great hostility or aggression. They will try to overwhelm and dominate those around them, and they may become uncontrollable when their wishes are not gratified.

One of the chief reasons for hospitalizing overexcited manic patients is to prevent them from involving themselves and other people in projects that issue out of their overconfidence. Because they are inclined to be erotic, they must be protected from sexual indiscretions and from a hasty marriage that they may contract on the crest of an ecstatic wave. Another reason for early hospitalization is that some manic cases will go into a state of delirium when they are not treated intensively at the start. These delirious attacks may be fatal if they give rise to exhaustion, dehydration, and hypochloremia. Sedation, tranquilization, and electroconvulsive therapy are most easily administered in a hospital setup.

SCHIZOPHRENIC DISORDERS (Types and DSM-III-R Codes: Catatonic 295.2X, Disorganized 295.1X, Paranoid 295.3X, Undifferentiated 295.9X, Residual 295.6X)

Schizophrenia, in spite of the massive amount of accumulated data, remains psychiatry's greatest challenge (Bleuler E, 1950; Bleuler M, 1984; Arieti, 1959, 1974;

Redlich & Freedman, 1966; Cancro, 1985). The question of whether it is a special disease entity or a unique way of experiencing is still being debated. Although it affects less than 1 percent of the population, its devastating influence on the patients and its cost to society are astronomical. Efforts to understand it along neurophysiological, biochemical, genetic, psychosocial, epidemiological, psychoanalytic, existential, anthropological, cultural, and communicative lines have been heroic. But many aspects of the illness are still unclear. Neither biochemical nor analytic-psychological investigations have brought us closer to its real essence.

While we do not have a complete picture regarding the etiology and pathology of schizophrenia, it is reasonable to assume from all the available evidence that a genetic factor exists. For one thing, the fact that the concordance ratio for schizophrenia is three times greater in monozygotic than in dizygotic twins suggests a hereditary component. But the finding that in 50 to 75 percent of monozygotic twins one member *does not* become schizophrenic when the other twin develops the disease indicates that a genetic deficit is not enough to produce schizophrenia. Nongenetic constitutional factors must also be considered, for example, flaws through damage to the brain during intrauterine life or as a result of birth trauma. In short, while schizophrenia appears to be a genetically determined disease, its phenotypical expression is, at least in part, influenced by life experience.

Among the life experiences that have a destructive impact is the use of the child by the parents as a foil for their own neuroses. When parents are themselves emotionally unstable and mentally confused, they are unable to provide sensible and temperate learnings. The child thus receives training in irrationality, as Lidz (1973) has remarked. Communication patterns are distorted and the child is exposed to contradictory messages. There is defective gender identity and a crushing of the child's efforts

at autonomy. The parents offer poor role models for the child. The consequence of the personality deficits that eventuate out of these conditionings is a deficiency in ways of interpeting reality and of handling and resolving stressful life events.

Of all speculations advanced to account for the outbreak of schizophrenia, the stress hypothesis seems to many to be the most feasible. Postulated here is the idea that stress activates in the schizophrenic individual anomalous biochemical and neurophysiological mechanisms as a result of faulty enzyme action. It is avowed that the end product of this action is hyperactivity of catecholamines, especially dopamine, as well as the release of pathological psychotogenic metabolites, resulting in a disorganization of brain function. Some authorities have also conjectured the existence of increased numbers of dopamine brain receptors to account for dopamine hyperactivity. In some cases, computed tomography shows ventricular enlargement in the brain, which has been correlated with such negative symptoms as emotional flattening, social withdrawal, and lack of energy.

When we search for stress sources that may have precipitated a schizophrenic breakdown we often find it to be environmental events that have a special traumatic meaning for the individual. Perhaps the most powerful sources of stress are disturbed family interactions, and there is ample evidence of difficulties in families of schizophrenic patients. A provocative question is why all members of a family in which there is a schizophrenic member are not affected with schizophrenia. The answer is that there is no such thing as the same environment for all family members, even for identical twins. Some are more protected than others; some are chosen for projective identification by a mother or father; some are scapegoated, or subjected to contradictory demands, or exposed to discriminatively defective communication signals. The consequence is an interference in the character organization, making for conflicts that in themselves become sources of tension. The stresses that impose themselves on the individual therefore are environmental difficulties from without and disturbances from within (biochemical and cognitive). Such stresses may become critical at certain periods in the developmental cycle (as during adolescence) and when pressures and demands both from without and within exceed the individual's coping capacities.

Many schizophrenic patients were exposed to *selective illogic* in early development, which made for irrational thinking around specific areas. The consequence is that the patient can think seriously about certain subjects and disjointedly about other subjects. He or she can deal better with selected stresses and be completely unable to manage other stresses to which he or she is singularly sensitive.

Among the deficits that emerge from a difficult childhood are an overwhelming sense of helplessness, a defective self-image, and overpowering hostilities. These impulses are handled by defenses organized around different levels of reasonableness. Helplessness may be managed by either a dependent clinging to some magical protective figure or movement, or by denial manifested in compulsive independence. Ambivalence toward objects will make for varied responses to people and be so disturbing to the individual that he or she will become apathetic and detached from people to avoid being rejected, hurt, or completely engulfed in a relationship. A defective self-image gives rise to a host of coping devices, ranging from inferiority feelings on one end to grandiosity on the other. The hostility may be turned outward in sadistic attitudes and aggression, or turned inward in the form of masochistic self-punishment. In part, reactions are the product of a massive biochemical upset set off by stressful stimuli with which the individual cannot cope. Impulses are fed through neurophysiologi-

cal channels disorganized by these biochemical alterations. This produces changes in the transmission messages in the subcortex, ultimately influencing thought processes. Because of the existing pockets of irrationality, the manifestations of these impulses and the defenses that control them may in cases of extreme distortion become highly and even psychotically symbolized and distorted. Thus dependency may be expressed by feelings of being influenced and manipulated by powerful or protective or malevolent agencies or machines. A devalued self-image may take the form of being accused by voices of emitting a foul odor or of having changed into an animal. Or it may be neutralized by the defense of a grandiose delusion. Hostility may be acted out directly in terms of paranoidal delusions and of violence toward persecutory enemies. Periods of rationality may alternate with those of irrationality, and the nature of the symbols may vary. When emotional stability is restored, pathological manifestations may temporarily vanish, only to reappear under the further impact of stress.

Most people who are able physiologically to deal with stress are threatened with periodic irrationalities but are able to process these cognitively and to control them without distorting reality. Yet psychoticlike impulses may appear in fantasy or in dreams. Other persons maintain their stability by circumscribing and isolating areas of psychotic or psychoticlike thinking or behavior, for example, by paranoidal ideation which serves as an outlet for hostility. This defense permits them to function and to maintain some adaptive capacity. Still other persons decompensate temporarily under the impact of stress and show overt psychotic behavior from which they rapidly recover (*schizophreniform disorder*). If there is a specific genetic vulnerability, however, the cognitive distortion may be extensive and prolonged, resulting in the syndrome of schizophrenia.

The onset of schizophrenia varies. Often it is insidious, becoming apparent only in late adolescence or in early adult life. The individual shows behavioral changes such as isolation and withdrawal and may drop out of school or quit work. Emotionally the schizophrenic may be unstable and depressed and resort to drugs or alcohol for relief. Unhappy at home, the schizophrenic may run away, seeking out groups of other isolated children or young adults with whom he or she may establish an unstable affinity. Affiliations are shallow, ideation more or less fragmented, the self-image devalued, and the boundaries between reality and fantasy blurred. The expression of needs is chaotic, and often fulfilled only in fantasy. Omnipotent, grandiose, and paranoidal ideas prevail. There is constant moving about as the person seeks some refuge in relationships that eventually are distrusted and abandoned. There is repeated experimenting with disorganized ways of regaining control, solving problems, bolstering security, and enhancing self-esteem.

Once a genetic vulnerability exists, the individual always is at high risk. The avoidance, removal, or palliation of environmental situations that have a stress potential for the person, the identification and mediation of faulty behaviors through psychotherapy, the building of self-esteem through positive achievements and productive work, the presence of accepting role models with whom the patient can identify, the utilization of support systems where necessary, and the administration of neuroleptics when a breakdown threatens may bring the individual back to his or her customary equilibrium.

The big problem for the therapist at this early stage is that the patient has little or no motivation for treatment. He or she distrusts people and resists any kind of close relationship, the vehicle through which psychotherapy is done. If treatment is attempted, it will take all the tact and resourcefulness a therapist can muster to keep a patient coming for sessions in the face of his or her detachment, suspiciousness, fear, and hostility. The therapist should try to avoid giving commands and orders because the patient will resist them. Nor should any mention be made of the need for or direction of change. Clues as to focus are gathered from what the patient is interested in and wants to deal with. No judgments should be expressed about the patient's behavior or dynamics except when the patient asks. Even then, interpretation must be carefully and reassuringly made. Attempts to alter the patient's attitudes, to plan goals, and to offer suggestions on how best to manage one's personal affairs will usually be resisted. Breaking of and lateness in coming for appointments call for great flexibility in time arrangements. The therapist concentrates on ways of solidifying the relationship with the patient and on introducing some reality into the patient's perceptions of what is happening to him or her. In spite of remedial interventions, the schizophrenic process may proceed to an adaptive breakdown that defies all efforts at resolution. An external precipitating factor may or may not be apparent, but a search for it should be instituted.

Removing the Stress Source: Hospitalization

If the patient's psychosis has been precipitated by an *overwhelming* external traumatic situation, simple environmental manipulation may help, if not suffice, to bring the patient back to his or her prepsychotic level of adaptation. Most schizophrenic reactions, however, are associated with such great weakness of the ego that the person is unable to withstand even average pressures. There is variation in the degree of stress that can be tolerated. In some, ordinary responsibilities of living and relating to people cannot be mediated. Environmental manipulation may not suffice to restore the patient because he or she senses menace everywhere, even in the most obviously congenial atmosphere. There is faulty information processing.

Fears rooted in past inimical conditionings and damaging conflicts seem to generate anxiety continuously and prevent the ego from emerging from its regressed level. The patient erects a wall of detachment and isolation as a protection from further hurt; it is this wall that interferes so drastically with any attempted therapy.

If the patient feels threatened in his or her present environment in spite of efforts at regulation, if his or her responses constitute a potential source of danger to the patient and others, and if the patient cannot be treated satisfactorily in the existing milieu, temporary hospitalization may be inevitable. The employment of psychotropic drugs and consultation with the patient's family in an effort to get them to be less critical, hostile, demanding, and demonstratively emotional toward the patient may enable the patient to adapt outside of an institutional setting. There will still be acute emergencies, however, for which no other alternative is available than hospitalization, either on the psychiatric ward of a general hospital or in a mental institution.

On the other hand, there are certain disadvantages to hospitalization. The most insidious feature of "institutionalization" is that the patient's tendencies to regress will be reinforced enormously by any lack of stimulation in the hospital. As one of a large group of patients, the individual may lose his or her identity. The patient becomes dilapidated in appearance and oblivious to customary habit routines. There may be little in the environment to encourage latent desires for growth and development. This unfortunate feature is due, to a large extent, to the overcrowding of institutions and to the lack of enlightenment and education of the personnel. The motives governing an employee's choice in working in an institution may not be those helpful to restoring the patient to active participation in society.

That hospitalization can prove to be a stimulating rather than a retarding influence is illustrated in institutions with a progressive administration and well-trained personnel. Selected occupational therapy and crafts, carefully chosen to meet the patient's interests and aptitudes, can help prevent the abandonment of reality. Exercises, games, entertainment, dancing, music, social affairs, and group discussions can also be of inestimable benefit. When it is practiced in an empathic setting, group therapy of a short-term nonpsychoanalytic nature (Parloff, 1986) may be helpful. The benefits of such therapy help convince the patient that he or she is not considered hopeless, in this way building up a feeling of confidence in the therapist and in oneself. It is probable that the old-time Aschner treatment for schizophrenia, with its emphasis on detoxification, stimulation, exercise, baths, sweats, venesection, catharsis, emesis, and hormone therapy, was mostly psychological in effect. At any rate, hospitalization should be regarded as a temporary measure, and the patient should be moved back into the community as soon as possible.

Milieu Therapy

Regulation of the environment so that it is therapeutically constructive, meaning that it provides stress relief and gratifying experiences, is important in treating schizophrenia. Occupational, recreational, and social therapy may be gainfully instituted in a hospital or outpatient setting. The atmosphere of a day-and-night hospital, halfway house, or community rehabilitation or recreational center also lends itself to environmental control and social skills training. A total therapeutic community program (e.g., with a suitable group) may prove rewarding. Settlement in the community and encouragement to engage in productive work is much better for the patient than assignment to the barren hinterlands of a mental hospital ward.

As part of a milieu therapy program, family therapy and individual psychotherapy with other members of the family may put a halt to many destructive stimuli within the household. Schizophrenia, more and more, is being regarded as a manifestation of family pathology. Relationship distortions are not only with the mother, but also with the father and other significant persons in the family constellation (Wynne et al, 1958; Bowen, 1960; Lidz & Fleck, 1960). The importance of the "double bind" as a basis for schizophrenia has been underscored by Bateson, Jackson, Haley, and Weakland (1956). These authors, describing the family interactions in schizophrenia, contend that the "victim" who succumbs to schizophrenia is exposed to (1) a repetition of prescriptive themes or experiences, (2) conflicting injunctions in relation to these "themes" with threats of punishment for disobedience, and (3) further restricting "commands" that prevent the "victim" from escaping the field of communication.

The "victim" arrives at a perception of his or her life as based on a number of key double-bind interactions with family members. For example, a mother's reaction of hostility to her boy may be concealed by overprotecting him. The child may be aware of this deception, but to retain her love, he cannot communicate this knowledge to her. "The child is punished for discriminating accurately what she is expressing, and he is punished for discriminating inaccurately—he is caught in a double-bind." Incongruence between what is said and what is intended is the essence of the faulty communicative process: " . . . the more a person tries to avoid being governed or governing others, the more helpless he becomes and so governs others by forcing them to take care of him" (Haley, 1959a & b, 1961). Family relationships alternate be-

tween overcloseness and overdistance; the members become intrapsychically "fused" so that differentiation of one from the other is often impossible. A psychosis may constitute a mirror image of the patient's unconscious. These factors have focused attention on family therapy as a preferred approach in schizophrenia (Midelfort, 1957; Boszormenyi-Nagy & Framo, 1965). Family psychotherapy increases the chances of breaking the schizophrenic's communication "code" (Jackson J, 1962).

Psychotherapy

Psychotherapy with schizophrenics is an art that graces few therapists. In the face of the patient's stubborn resistance, suspiciousness, withdrawal tendencies, and inability to communicate appropriately, most therapists are apt to throw their hands up in surrender. Yet there are a few experiences as gratifying to a therapist as providing an empathic bridge to reality for a withdrawn patient. It is difficult to define the qualities a therapist must possess for such a successful eventuality. I once asked Frieda Fromm-Reichmann what she considered the most desirable characteristic for work with schizophrenics. She repied, "Humility, persistence, sensitivity, compassion, and [she added drolly] a good deal of masochism." It is only human to respond with frustration at repeated therapeutic efforts that slide off the patient with little or no apparent effect. But I am convinced that when such efforts are sustained, with warmth and sincerity, they ultimately will be rewarded.

In my training as a psychiatrist I spent 13 years of my early career working in a state hospital, principally with schizophrenics. Those were the days before psychotropic drugs, and the only tools available to the therapist (other than wet packs and hydrotherapy) were his or her skills in establishing a meaningful relationship with patients. No matter how severely withdrawn the patients were from external stimuli (and sometimes our catatonic citizens retained their frozen, statuelike behavior for years), it seemed obvious to me that they craved and needed consistent and kindly communication, even though this seemed to register no impact on them. When some of the patients "spontaneously" emerged from their deathlike repose, it astonished me to hear them recount in minutest detail some of the things they had observed going on around them, with virtual playbacks of my one-way conversations with them. They particularly recalled the little kindnesses bestowed upon them by the nursing staff and myself, which I am now convinced had a more penetrating effect on them than the most mighty of miracle drugs.

Even wild paranoidal individuals seemed to respond to quiet sympathy and lack of retaliation for their abuses. I remember one of the most disturbed patients I had ever encountered, a middle-aged, distraught and disheveled, hallucinating woman, who accosted me the first day I was put in charge of the disturbed ward on which she had been sequestered for more than 10 years. Blood-curdling shrieks and cries for the police came from her at the first sight of me as I walked through the ward protected by a bodyguard of nurses and attendants. She identified me positively as her tormentor—the man who had for years been making indecent proposals to her and who had been sending electrical impulses up her rectum and genitals. It was all my bodyguard could do to keep her from assaulting me.

Despite the daily indignities that she heaped on me, I took pains each day briefly to talk quietly to her, expressing my concern at her upset and assuring her that if there were anything I could do to help her, I would be happy to do it. Her response was stereotyped—anger, vilification, and occasionally expectoration. On one occasion as

I left her, she managed to find a flower pot, which she hurled at me, barely missing my head. Slowly, after many months, her response to my consistent reassurances became more attenuated, although she daily repeated her resentment that I had the temerity to persist in talking to her when I was the last person on earth she wanted to see.

And then something dramatic happened. On one occasion I was in a hurry to get ward rounds over with to attend a special meeting, and I breezed through the ward without talking to her. Her reaction was electric. She became more highly disturbed than before, upbraiding the nurses for their neglect in directing me away from her, and accusing me of having no respect for her and her feelings. The next morning, for the first time, I was able to talk to her without fear of bodily harm. We spoke quietly about matter-of-fact subjects, and although she was still psychotic and hallucinating, she spoke calmly and with good sense about many matters, apparently enjoying her exchanges with me. Shortly thereafter, the patient became ill with lobar pneumonia and was transferred to the acute medical unit. Sick as she was, she refused to allow anyone except myself to treat her. With persuasion, I convinced her that she could trust the regular staff members of the unit. Upon her recovery from pneumonia, she returned to her old building and was transferred to a quiet, open ward.

My final victory occurred when the patient requested that I cut her toenails! Since her admission she had not trusted anyone to get near her feet. Her nails had become thickened like horns, and I had to borrow special shears from the tool shop to do a half-decent job. To my delight and surprise, the patient recovered from her psychosis and was able to leave the hospital. I am not certain what other forces were responsible for the patient's improvement, but I am convinced that the relationship I developed with her was a prime vehicle in bringing her back to a reasonable contact with the world.

The ability to enter into the patient's life and to share his or her anguish and despair, to refrain from making demands that would ordinarily seem justified, to persist in showing friendship and respect in the face of outrageous and irresponsible behavior may ultimately win out. To carry out this formidable task, a therapist needs to possess a good deal of stamina and an undaunted optimism that the healthy elements in a sick human being will eventually bubble through. Obviously, the average custodial unit and the average therapist are not equipped to render ideal psychotherapeutic care for these vulnerable human beings. Because some therapists can engage effectively with schizophrenics and others cannot, the literature on psychotherapy in schizophrenia is ambivalent. For example, May's 1968 research indicates that psychotherapy had little to offer schizophrenics in comparison with medication. The Massachusetts Mental Health Center study by Grinspoon, Ewalt, and Shader (1972) also cast doubts on the value of psychotherapy. The studies by Rogers et al. (1967) and case reports of Vaillant, Semrad, and Ewalt (1964), Kayton (1975), and McGlashan (1983) are more optimistic. May's research was flawed, however, by the use of only inexperienced therapists and supervisors who were dubious about the use of psychotherapy with schizophrenics. The other studies could also be criticized for faulty design and controls.

There are many pitfalls in working psychotherapeutically with schizophrenics, not the least of which is provoking and nurturing a hostile dependency that cannot be resolved. Transference is frequently a problem, and if it is not dealt with in the early stages, it may evolve into a disturbing transference neurosis or transference psychosis. No less troublesome are the therapist's irritation and anger at the patient, which is understandable considering the vexations inherent in dealing with the patient's obstinacy, querulousness, uncooperativeness, contentiousness, belligerence, and detachment. Such emotions on the part of the therapist must be controlled. Countertransference mismanaged can interfere with the therapist's objectivity and ability to provide an empathic relationship.

While there may be some advantage to working exclusively with psychotherapy in the few instances when the psychotherapist is especially dedicated and skilled in working with schizophrenics (Laing, 1960, 1967; Arieti, 1974), the vast majority of therapists find antipsychotic drugs most helpful, if not indispensable if a thinking disorder exists. Drugs are capable of keeping many chronic schizophrenics operating so that they can reasonably maintain their responsibilities, of preventing them from regressing to a state of work disability, and of restoring their capacity to communicate. The disadvantages that drugs impose by masking defenses are more than offset in many cases by their ability to make hospitalization unnecessary and to foster better cooperation with the therapist. Nevertheless, one must keep in mind the possibility of untoward side effects and sequelae such as tardive dyskinesia.

The immediate objective of psychotherapy in schizophrenia is to enhance the adaptive reserves of the patients so that they will be able to come to a rapid equilibrium, to discern their chief sources of stress, and either to help resolve or remove themselves from them as expeditiously as possible. While the schizophrenic's vulnerability will not be eradicated, the patient may be strengthened so that he or she does not shatter so readily upon exposure to stressful stimuli. In extremely uncooperative and withdrawn patients, behavior therapy, employing operant conditioning, has been used with some success (see Chapter

51). When the patient becomes accessible, formal psychotherapy may begin. Sometimes supportive and reeducative group therapy is utilized adjunctively with individual therapy; at times, it constitutes the sole psychotherapeutic modality.

The key to the treatment of schizophrenia lies in the ability to establish some sort of contact with the patient. Most schizophrenics desperately fear relationships with people and erect various obstacles to any interpersonal threat. The withdrawal from reality and the archaic type of thinking and symbolism enhance the individual's isolation, since there is no common means of communication. Yet, beneath the surface, the patient yearns for a friendly and loving relationship. The patient wards it off, however, because he or she has been injured by past interpersonal contacts. He or she does not wish to encounter further rebuffs. The patient's apathy, detachment, and expressed hostility and aggression are means of protection from the desire for a closer union with people. Establishing rapport with the patient is in line with two objectives: first, to reintegrate the patient in more intimate relationships with people to where he or she can obtain at least partial gratification of personal needs without fear of abandonment or injury and, second, to bring the patient back to the realistic world by proving that reality can be a source of pleasure rather than pain.

The technique of developing rapport varies with the patient. A great deal of activity is essential. In very sick patients whose productions are seemingly irrelevant and incoherent, a careful analysis of the productions will disclose a language that is very meaningful to the patient. The ability to show the patient that his or her words and gestures are understood may be the first constructive step. Sullivan (1931) has stressed the need to communicate understanding of the patient's language and gestures as a means of solidifying the interpersonal relationship. To do this, it may be necessary to talk to the patient on his or her own regressed level. J. M. Rosen (1947, 1962) has interpreted the utterances of the patient in terms of their symbolic meaning and has been able to develop a relationship with some of his patients through this method. Entering into the psychotic world of the patient, Rosen and his followers attempt to make contact by intensive daylong sessions, overwhelming the patient with direct interpretations of his or her unconscious. How valid these interpretations are may be challenged, but the fact that the patient is showered with attention and is shocked with statements coached in harshly frank and sometimes sexually explicit terms may in a relatively short time bring the patient out of his or her regressed state. This approach has been practiced in foster homes, where the patient is provided with a therapeutic environment throughout the day and night. It is, consequently, an expensive form of therapy and one that can be indulged by a limited clientele. Moreover, follow-up studies are not encouraging.

Employing symbolic objects, Sechehaye (1951) evolved a nonverbal method of communicating with a regressed schizophrenic girl. This was necessary, Sechehaye believed, because the primary trauma occurred before the stage of verbal language. For example, only by realizing that apples symbolized mother's milk was it possible to offer the patient love through drinking "the good milk from Mummy's apples." In ways similar to this, the therapist may gather clues to essential needs and conflicts from the bizarre symbolic thought content, translating it the same way as if it were a dream. Cryptic as these utterances may be, they contain important messages that may well be heeded by the sensitive therapist, who will answer them in ways that indicate to the patient that his or her plaints are recognized and acknowledged.

Using an existential approach as well as family therapy, Laing (1960) and Laing and Esterson (1971) have explored the despair of patients, siding with them against their families and the environment and, in this way, establishing intimate contact. The relationship is utilized as a vehicle for recasting patients' concepts of themselves. The approaches of Harry Stack Sullivan (Mullahy, 1967, 1968), Frieda Fromm-Reichmann (Ballard, 1959), Otto Will (1967, 1970), and Harold Searles (1960, 1966) also make worthwhile reading.

In patients, therapy may consist of nothing more than sitting with them, without prodding them to express themselves. The very fact that the therapist refrains from probing their trends, avoids discussing the causes of their breakdown, and accepts them as they are may help these patients to regard the therapist as a less threatening force than other people. In many cases therapy may consist of working with the patient at occupational projects and playing games, such as cards, checkers or chess. Sometimes a more positive approach is made to the patient by giving him or her food, such as milk, candy, and cake. For a long time it may seem that these gratuities are the only reason that the patient desires to see the therapist. In querying the patient after recovery, however, one becomes convinced that the patient actually had a desire for closeness and was testing the therapist constantly.

Any relationship that the patient is able to establish with the therapist is at first bound to be extremely unstable. The schizophrenic individual feels very vulnerable and helpless. His or her level of frustration tolerance is inordinately low. Schizophrenics are distrustful, suspicious, and inclined to misinterpret the motives of the therapist in accordance with their inner fears and prejudices. They feel incapable of coping with life and resent the intentions of the therapist to return them to reality, which holds unbounded terrors. Schizophrenics fear injury and frustration from people, and it may be months, sometimes years, before

they are willing to accept the therapist as a friend. Even then they will sense rejection and neglect in the most casual attitude. Anxiety with a temporary return to regression will interrupt therapy repeatedly, and it must be handled by a consistently reassuring and friendly manner. Violent reactions may punctuate treatment from time to time, especially when the patients sense that liking the therapist will force them to leave the relative security of their reality retreat.

Fromm-Reichmann (1939) has commented on the unpredictable nature of the schizophrenic's relationship to the therapist. A sympathetic, understanding, and skillful handling by the therapist of the relationship is far more important than an intellectual comprehension of the operative dynamics. She ascribes difficulties in therapy to the fact that the therapist is unable to understand the primitive logic and magical reasoning that governs schizophrenic thinking.

Unless we analyze our own reactions repeatedly, our sense of frustration may arouse strong aggression that will interfere with treatment. It is manifestly impossible to treat any psychotic person if one does not genuinely like him or her. If we are able to regard the actions of the patient as essentially childlike, we shall best be able to understand the patient's outbursts. Cold logic fails miserably in explaining the reactions of the schizophrenic. Despite his or her age, the patient seeks an infantile relationship to the therapist and desires unlimited warmth, understanding, protection, and help. He or she seeks a mothering affiliation rather than a give-and-take encounter between two equals. At the same time, the patient distrusts the therapist and resents his or her own helplessness in seeking nurturing.

The therapist should try to be as sympathetic and reassuring as possible, approaching the patient casually and informally and conveying an interest in him or her and in matters of immediate concern. Sometimes it is desirable to encourage the patient by touching a shoulder or arm as a gesture of friendship. I have found that I have been able to establish a relationship in a remarkably short time by offering to show the patient how to relax his or her tensions, utilizing a simple hypnotic relaxing technique (*q.v.* page 1019). Even frightened patients can be helped, but, obviously, they must be willing to cooperate. The therapist may say, "It's been rather tough on you, and you can't avoid being upset by all that has happened. If you'd like, I can show you how to relax yourself, which should make you feel a lot better." Patients who respond positively are asked to make themselves comfortable in their chair and to shut their eyes while relaxing suggestions are made.

It is important not to cross-examine the patient or subject the patient to questioning. An attitude of acceptance without reserve is best while conveying sincere interest in his or her needs and problems. Sicker patients will usually flood the therapist with their irrational ideas and delusions. One way of handling this situation is to focus as much as possible on matter-of-fact reality items. This is not as difficult as it sounds, although the therapist must avoid giving the impression of being bored with or disbelieving the patient's irrational concerns.

Probing for conflicts is taboo, as is the lying-down couch position. Only when the patient brings up topics for discussion is it desirable to discuss them, but this should be done in as a matter-of-fact way as possible. This does not mean that depth interpretaions are always to be avoided; they may be made once the therapist–patient relationship is solidified and the patient brings up a conflictual topic and shows some awareness of its nature. It may be reassuring to the patient to have a dynamic explanation for some distressing problems. This may relieve the patient of the mystery of what is happening to him or her.

Therapy in schizophrenia must, in summary, be oriented around the immature ego of the patient. The patient's emotional reactions to people, like those of an infant, are unstable and ambivalent. Schizophrenics are easily frustrated and feel rejection without ostensible cause. They are unreasonable and demanding. Their concept of reality is unreliable; they often confuse inner mental processes with outside reality. They may assume that the person on whom they depend is omniscient and will supply their every demand, expressed or unexpressed. They will react with hostility if they are not granted what they believe to be their due. Alone, their egos are so weak that they are unable to tolerate complete responsibility. They need help and support, and yet fear and resist assistance.

Federn (1943) has advised enlisting the aid of a relative or friend, preferably a motherly person who can look after the patient. He stressed that schizophrenics should not be allowed to depend on their own resources. They should at all times be surrounded by an atmosphere of love and warmth. Their stability and strength grow as a result of positive identifications with loved ones. If they are at all able to develop to self-sufficiency, their independence will grow best in the soil of this positive identification. The hope is to bring them to a point where they can function satisfactorily without the aid of a parental figure. In many cases the latter stage of self-sufficiency is never attained, and all one can do is adapt the individual to reasonable social functioning while attached to some kindly person.

The need to surround schizophrenic patients with a favorable atmosphere necessitates work with their families or with people with whom they live. This is essential to relieve the burden induced by demands and responsibilities that the patient imposes on the members. Often the inertia and apathy of the patient stir up resentment on those present, and when the patient is aware of their hostility, he or she may retreat further from reality. Considerable work with the patient's relatives may be required before they are sufficiently aware of the dynamics of the patient's reactions and before they are willing to aid the therapist in the treatment plan.

The chief emphasis in treatment in chronic schizophrenia must be on the creation of a human relationship with the patient that has pleasure values for him or her. Only by this means will the patient relinquish the safety and gratification of regression and, utilizing the relationship with the therapist as a bridge, return to reality. The handling of treatment, however, requires considerable tact. No matter how detached the patient is, he or she is extremely sensitive to everything that the therapist says or does. An avoidance of situations that evoke anxiety in the patient is essential. This is often a very difficult task because the most casual remark may stir up powerful emotions.

The patient may choose to remain silent throughout the treatment hour and will appreciate it if the therapist refrains from challenging refusal to talk. It is expedient with such a mute patient to point out occasionally that perhaps there is abstinence from talking because of a belief that the therapist is interfering or because there is fear of what he or she might say. The patient may feel more at ease with such remarks and may finally break through the silence.

In most cases schizophrenic patients at first will feel alone, helpless, and misunderstood. They resent the intrusion of the therapist into their private lives and believe that the therapist, like everyone else, is unable to understand them. The initial task is to show them that their impulses and wishes are respected and that they are not required to comply with demands that are unreasonable. Usually in all of their previous interviews they have been bombarded with questions about their breakdown, and, even when they have responded to these ques-

tions in a more or less frank manner, they have sensed disapproval. The fact that the therapist accepts them as they are may eventually build up their self-respect and strengthen the desire to return to reality.

Constantly, during treatment, the patient may react with detachment or withdrawal or may subject the therapist to a testing period during which he or she is recalcitrant and hostile. The purpose may be to find out whether the therapist is the kind of person who can be trusted or whether the therapist, like all other people in his or her experience, makes unfair stipulations or react to expressed hostility with counterhostility. The patient may believe that what the therapist demands is that a person be "good." This "goodness" means to the patient that it is urgent to comply with standards that all other people impose. At first he or she will act as if the therapist actually expects unyielding submission to these standards, threatening the patient with rejection or aggression if he or she resists. The testing period may be a trying one for the therapist, since it may continue for many months during which the patient constantly rejects the therapist's friendship. When the patient realizes that the therapist does not expect compliance with certain things, that the therapist sides with the patient against unreasonable demands made by the family, the patient may begin to regard the therapist in a new light.

The beginning of a feeling of closeness can precipitate panic; the patient may try to run away from therapy, or he or she will exhibit aggression toward the therapist. The ability to see the patient through this stage may finally succeed in breaking down the patient's reserve and in establishing for the first time an identification with a person based upon love. There exists within schizophrenics a psychic tug of war between the spontaneous forces of mental health that drive them to seek gratifying relationships with people and the security of their regressed state that harbors them from the imagined dangers of a hostile world. The therapist's attitudes will determine which of these impulses will triumph.

The method of handling the treatment hour is of signal importance. It is best not to cross-examine these patients because they may interpret this as censure. They must be convinced that the therapist does not want to invade and remove them from their private world, but rather seeks to participate in it with them. This does not mean assuming a cloying sweetness during sessions, because the patient will be able to see through this. It must be expected that the patient's attitudes will be ambivalent. He or she may profess little interest in the interview, yet resent its termination at the designated time. There may be attempts to defy or to provoke the therapist or refuse to cooperate. If the therapist becomes ill and cannot keep an appointment, the patient may react with rage and refuse to continue treatments. If the therapist is unavoidably late for an appointment, peevishness can occur. The patient may resent the therapist's taking any vacation or assigning another person as an assistant. Where customary routines have to be interrupted, it is best to prepare the patient far in advance and, if necessary, to enlist the help of family members with whom the patient has an attachment. If the patient becomes hostile toward the therapist, every attempt must be made to explore why there is suspicion the therapist has failed. Should the patient persist with hostility and insist on seeing another psychotherapist, these wishes should be respected, for it is futile to do any work with a patient while being governed by feelings of resentment.

Once a positive relationship has been established, it is necessary to cherish it carefully. Nothing must jeopardize the relationship. For example, the patient must never be led to feel that cherished delusions are ridiculous. Any fanciful feelings and attitudes must be respected at all times. It is unnecessary to reinforce these attitudes by agreeing with them; but they should be accepted as something that the patient believes in sincerely. It may be impressed on the patient, however, that there might possibly be another explanation for a certain experience than the one that he or she supports. All probing for dynamic material must assiduously be avoided at this point. This is one of the most frequent errors in the handling of psychotic patients. It is also an error to interrogate the patient regarding previous mental upsets.

Because the aim in the psychotic patient at first, at least, is to increase repression, since the ego is already too weak and permits the filtering through of disturbing unconscious material, such techniques as free association are to be discouraged. Rather, the patient should be enjoined to talk about everyday reality happenings. In general, the past had best be avoided, and the patient may be aided in any expressed desire to regard it as a "bad dream" or something that should be forgotten. Under no circumstances should a positive relationship with the therapist be analyzed. If the patient exhibits inhibitions or phobias, these too should be respected, since they probably have protective values. All resistances the patient uses to repress psychotic material must be reinforced, although the symbolisms employed may sometimes be interpreted to the patient. Unlike the treatment of neurosis, analysis of resistances should be avoided to prevent the release of the unconscious content that will upset the patient more. When the patient brings up delusional material or symptoms and spontaneously talks about the connection with traumatizing circumstances in his or her past, an effort may then be made to explain in uncomplicated terms how these manifestations originated. The rule never to dissolve resistance does not apply to resistances to getting well or to integrating more closely with the therapist and with reality.

These impediments should be analyzed and removed if possible. Guilt feelings may be met by reassurance and hostilities dealt with in a manner that does not put responsibility or blame on the patient.

One of the ways in which a positive relationship with the therapist may be used is to try to show the patient that his or her thoughts and ideas often appear to be realistic but that it is necessary always to differentiate between what seems to be real and what actually is real. In the patient's case, too these may have been confused, even though there is no question of doubt in his or her mind that the two states are identical. An excellent sign of restoration of ego strengh is the ability of schizophrenic patients to recognize the irrational nature of their ideas while they were in an upset condition.

While some patients achieve a fairly good grasp of reality and tend to return to their prepsychotic habitude, and even to tolerate relationships with other people along the lines of the close attachment they establish with the therapist, it may be necessary to continue the treatment process to prevent a relapse. The problems of some patients are kept alive because they harbor bloated ambitions of what they should accomplish in life. Their grandiose expectations inevitably lead to constant frustration. Under such circumstances it is essential to help the patient modify exorbitant goals through the careful use of the therapeutic relationship. It may be possible, for instance, to convince the patient that it is better to devote his or her life to the attainment of happiness in the immediate present than to strive for things in the unknown future. Character disturbances may exist that make relationships with people fraught with anxiety. An active manipulation of the patient's environment through consultation with interested family may enable the patient to function more comfortably. Attempts should also be made to motivate the patient gradually toward making contacts with other people.

In spite of such corrective measures, hostility, tension, and anxiety may constantly be created by inner cognitive, affective, and autonomic derangements. The intensity of untoward emotions may again tend to shatter the patient's ego. The danger of another schizophrenic collapse may, therefore, be imminent. *It is best here, as mentioned before, not to attempt probing for conflicts until the patient evinces an interest in understanding his or her own problems.* Schizophrenic persons are remarkably intuitive and can grasp the dynamics of their disorder better than most neurotics. This is probably because they live closer to their unconscious and because ego barriers to deep impulses and fears are not so strong. It is for this reason that one must proceed very carefully in analyzing the patient's deepest impulses (Bychowski, 1952; Eisenstein VW, 1952; Fromm-Reichmann, 1952; Bruch, 1964). Haley (1961) has outlined some excellent suggestions for the practical handling of schizophrenics. Other suggestions, namely the use of projective techniques, may be found in the section on the treatment of the borderline patient (p. 1183).

Although the therapist assumes a directive role, it is the patient who is expected to uncover the meaning of ongoing communications (Bruch, 1964). This fact has been stressed by many therapists working with schizophrenics, particularly Sullivan (1962), Fromm-Reichmann (1954), and Lidz and Lidz (1952). In this way the therapist avoids bombarding the patient with useless interpretations or confronting the patient with a road map of his or her unconscious that will lead the patient nowhere. Inevitably, the relationship between therapist and patient will begin to stir up feelings and impulses that the patient will have to clarify with the help of the therapist. For example, if the patient identifies the therapist with his or her mother, interpreting this may mean little. Exploring in what way the therapist *acts* like a mother may, on the other hand, become meaningful.

The realization of unconscious guilt, hostility, and erotism has a dual effect on the psychic apparatus. On the one hand, it floods the ego with destructive emotion; on the other, by forcing a more realistic cognition, it attempts to liberate the psyche from incessant conflict. In this way the dynamic probing is like a two-edged sword; the ego has to be traumatized by the liberated emotions before it is able to mobilize defenses less destructive to the person than regression. In neurosis and character disorders this may prove helpful. In schizophrenia however defenses are so fragile and ego so weak that it collapses under the impact of emotion before it can adapt itself in a more adequate manner. This is always a danger in psychotic and prepsychotic conditions. All interpretations must, therefore, be very cautiously applied. Reconstructive techniques should be abandoned if any excitement or great hostility develops, for only when the patient is positively attached to the therapist will it be possible to bear the suffering brought out by a realization of the deeper stirrings within.

Summary of general psychotherapeutic rules in schizophrenia:

   a. *Establishing a relationship.*

1. The initial task is to establish a relationship and not to collect information. Asking the patient if he or she hears voices or believes someone is against him or her is a poor tactic. Nor should the patient be grilled about previous attacks or hospitalizations. The therapist should act attentive and reassuring. Sitting behind a desk is not as good as facing the patient directly. Walking with the patient, having coffee together, and touching the patient occasionally are not contraindicated.

2. Do not argue, cajole, or try to reason with a delusional or hallucinating patient, no matter how absurd the ideas or fantasies may seem. Not only will the effort be useless, but it may also convince the patient that you are aligned with the forces of evil against him or her. Listen respectfully to what the patient has to say. If he or she complains about something and if you must make a comment, simply say reassuringly, "This must be upsetting you."

3. If the patient is perturbed or agitated, one may say: "I certainly understand how upset you must feel, If such a thing happened to other people they'd be upset too."

4. If the patient prefers to remain silent, accept this, and do not try to bully or shame the patient into talking.

5. If an upset patient asks you for help in allaying tension or anxiety, you may reassure the patient that you will do everything you can. If the patient is not taking medications, ask if he or she would like to have some medicine to quiet the restlessness. You also may suggest teaching the patient how to relax his or her tensions. If he or she responds positively, utilize relaxing exercises or relaxing hypnosis. This may rapidly expedite the relationship.

6. Give the patient regular sessions, and be sure you keep the appointment times. If you will be late for a session, notify the patient in advance if possible and tell him or her you will make up the lost time. Anticipate the patient's breaking appointments and being tardy. If this happens do not chide the patient—merely say you missed him or her.

7. Bizarre behavior or attitudes may

strike the therapist as humorous. To succumb to ridicule or laughter may shatter the chances of a relationship.

b. *The treatment process*. I have found the following 20 suggestions useful in working with schizophrenics:

1. Any activity that can bolster the patient's self-esteem should be supported. This includes the patient's grooming and clothing habits and positive achievements of any kind. These should be talked about and encouraged; the patient should be praised for even slight accomplishments in work, hobbies, and creative activities.

2. The best way to handle delusional or hallucinatory material is to listen respectfully and never ridicule or make light of them. One may even act as if uninterested in the hope of discouraging the frequency of these pathological responses. On the other hand, reasonable talk should command alert attention and active responses in an effort to reinforce rationality. If the patient is disturbed by what he or she brings up, the therapist may agree that if matters were as the patient reported, anybody would be disturbed. Then the therapist may gently offer an alternative explanation as a possibility, not pressing the point if the patient does not agree.

3. No matter how truculent, neglectful, disrespectful, or hostile the patient acts toward the therapist (even if the patient throws a tantrum), punitive, scolding, or rejecting responses should never be indulged. The patient may be merely testing the therapist. Nor should the therapist encourage any regressive behavior or talk to or treat the patient as if he or she were a child. In other words, irrespective of how "crazy" the patient acts, he or she should be treated with dignity and respect as an adult. After their recovery, many patients talk about how they appreciated the therapist's manner.

4. For a long time direct interpretation may have to be delayed and projective techniques used instead. The therapist may by illustration make comments such as: (to a patient in despair at being rejected) "*Most* people feel hurt if people neglect them"; (to a patient with fantasies of death and killing) "It often happens that when a person feels angry he may imagine that the person he is angry at will hurt him, or will die"; (to a woman who felt her looks repelled men) "I knew a woman once who felt she was so ugly, no man would want her and she would get furious if a man wanted to date her because she believed he was teasing her." These comments illustrate how one does not directly confront the patient with his or her actions, but uses other individuals as examples. The patient may or may not then pick up the implications. If the patient applies what is being said, the interpretations can be made more directly.

5. With paranoidal patients who have fixed delusions, disagreeing with these delusions will put the therapist in the class of all other persons who have tried to argue the patient out of what he or she believes to be true. Thus, a therapeutic relationship may never get started. Yet, to support the patient's delusion completely may not be wise. Here the therapist may give credence to the patient's right to believe what he or she knows to be true and express an interest in all the facts that have led to the patient's conclusions. One should not directly support the patient's conclusions but merely state: "I can understand how facts like these lead you to feel the way you

do.'' For example, a patient felt he was being pursued by the Mafia, who wanted to steal his business away from him. As evidence, he cited seeing an automobile with New Jersey license plates in the area of his apartment. He was sure he was being watched and followed by New Jersey gangsters who were out to kill him. His complaints to the police and district attorney were greeted with amused disdain. Instead of challenging the patient, I asked him to be sure to keep a diary of all of his daily observations that pointed to his persecutions. At every visit he would bring many sheets of written matter containing detailed rambling "observations," which I would greet as interesting and important and which I promised I would later read in studied detail after our visit. I would then put the material aside and we would talk about his other interests and daily activities, avoiding the psychotic area as much as possible. The volume of the reports gradually dwindled to a single sheet and then stopped altogether, the patient apologizing for his neglect in bringing in this material. With the cessation of his reports he began to concern himself with immediate problems in his daily life and work and soon lost interest in the Mafia delusion.

6. The management of transference reactions will call for fortitude on the part of the therapist. The range of how the patient regards the therapist is great: God, mother, father, sibling, the devil, seducer, lover, persecutor, friend. Dependency reactions must be expected and these release other impulses and defenses such as sexuality, hostility, masochism, devalued self-esteem, and detachment. Different phases of these reactions express themselves at varying times and the patient will try to involve the therapist

in his or her schemes. The therapist must resist acting out with the patient and becoming countertransferentially rejecting, seductive, overprotective, or punitive. Yielding to the patient's importunate transferential demands will breed more irrationality. Yet, an honest careful explanation of why it is impossible to fulfill the patient's demands must be given so that the patient does not feel rejected as a person.

Expressed hostility will be especially difficult to handle, since it can be like a never-ending spring issuing out of depths that have no bottom. So long as it remains on a verbal level, the therapist may be able to tolerate it, realizing that some of the rage is in the way of a test, some a means of warding off a threatened close relationship with the therapist, some a belated effort to resolve a needed breaking away from the maternal figure, some a rebellious desire to assert and be oneself. We may suspect that the patient retains a ray of hope that the therapist will handle the patient's anger and not respond in an expected retaliating way that would justify a continued withdrawal. If the therapist can stand this test, feelings of unthreatened love and closeness may bubble through. On the other hand, should rage take the form of expressed violence that does not cease when met by a calm and self-assured manner on the part of the therapist, and by statements that the patient should try not to lose control, it will require firm but kindly and considerate action or physical restraint to protect the patient, the therapist, and others. The patient should later be given an explanation for the preventive action. The therapist here must act in a composed but determined way without giving the impression of retaliating for the patient's behavior. One way of diluting transference reactions is by involving the patient in some group activity—a hobby, social group, or therapeutic group.

7. If there is no desire to work intensively with the patient (which will happen in a majority of psychotic patients), visits are gradually lessened in frequency once improvement is stabilized but never discontinued completely. Rather, the patient is given the option of seeing the therapist once in two weeks, then once a month, and then at longer intervals.

8. False promises should never be made to a patient because they will inevitably be broken and with this the therapeutic relationship may terminate. Nor should deception be utilized as a way of escaping a difficult situation because here too the patient somehow will divine the deceit. Sometimes it is necessary to withhold the true facts temporarily from the patient since the patient may not be prepared to deal with them but may be able to handle them later when his or her ego gets stronger. Whatever explanations or interpretations are given the patient, these should be coached in frank but reassuringly optimistic terms.

9. Whether to engage in deeper insight therapy is a decision one must reach after working with the patient for a long period, seeing how he or she handles interpretations and observing the buildup of ego strengths. Schizophrenics live close to their unconscious and are often first in arriving at insights themselves. Whether such insights can help the patient is another matter. When stress becomes too strong, the patient will collapse, insight or no insight.

10. The greatest use of therapy is to increase the patient's stress tolerance, and this means doing a careful assay of current and future stressors, preparing and helping the patient to cope with them. Behavior therapy can be of great value when properly employed (Agras, 1967).

11. Avoid language the patient cannot understand. If possible, use the dialect of the patient.

12. Point out in a nonaccusatory and nonjudgmental way patterns the patient exploits that can prove harmful and that tend to make others withdraw. The message should be given in as reassuring a manner as possible, reflecting the therapist's confidence in the patient's ability to change.

13. Avoid interpreting the dynamics of the patient's symptoms. Without a firm working relationship with the patient and evidences of his or her trust, this will be counterproductive. Do not belittle or ridicule the patient's delusions, no matter how foolish they may seem.

14. Do not take notes while with the patient. This will enhance suspiciousness, especially if there is some paranoidal tendency. Notes can be made after the patient leaves.

15. Credit the patient's disturbed behavior, if he or she shows it, to the fact that he or she is being frightened and upset and not to the fact that the patient is a difficult violent person. The patient may be responding to the environment as dangerous and will need reassurance and support, not condemnation.

16. Before prescribing medications, explain why drugs are useful in quieting a person down, helping one sleep, and so on.

17. As soon as the patient's symptoms subside, reduce medications to as low a level as will control symptoms. When the relationship becomes firm, the medications may even be discontinued. If symptoms reappear, drug dosage may be increased.

18. Start family therapy as soon as the patient quiets down, building a relationship with the family and counseling them as to steps each member can take to improve communication. Establish a contact with the most stable family member, who will act as a liaison. Instruct this member when to increase medications. Invite this member to telephone you if problems occur.

19. There is no reason why patients cannot be taught to medicate themselves when they feel their equilibrium threatened. Having the proper medications on hand and utilizing such medications to quiet and stabilize oneself can often nip a psychotic break in the bud.

20. Flexibility in approach is the keynote of good therapy with schizophrenics.

General rules such as I have cited here are useful but they will have to be adapted to each patient and modified according to individual reactions. Similarly, the use of aftercare services will depend on what special needs each patient has and the availability of services in the community in which the patient lives.

Somatic Therapy

The introduction of neuroleptics has introduced a new and more hopeful outlook in the therapy of many schizophrenics. Phenothiazines (e.g., Thorazine, Mellaril, Prolixin), butyrophenones (e.g., Haldol), thioxanthenes (e.g., Navane), and dihydroindolones (e.g., Moban) in proper dosage may, when indicated, rapidly resolve psychotic states and render the individual more accessible to social demands. (The choice and dosage of neuroleptics have been outlined extensively in the section on Pharmacotherapy in Chapter 56).

Useful as they have proven to be, neuroleptics unfortunately have their drawbacks since, apart from the side effects and serious sequelae (e.g., tardive dyskinesia) with prolonged employment, they tend to discourage the application of psychologically based therapies. Too frequently, young people suffering an initial psychotic break are saturated with massive amounts of drugs, which, while restoring homeostasis, prevent them from integrating the significance of the psychotic experience, which may, with the help of an empathic therapist, have a beneficial impact on their future development. This in no way minimizes the value of the neuroleptics, but it does necessitate some restraint in their use. With rare exceptions in the initial stages of therapy, patients with acute schizophrenia manifesting thought disorders will need neuroleptics. Once the patient's symptoms are brought under control and environmental stress factors regulated, the patient should be slowly taken off drugs but rehabilitative and psychosocial therapies continued. Should the patient decompensate again, medications may be resumed, although a considerable number of patients can be managed solely with counseling, milieu therapy, group therapy, family therapy, and other psychosocial treatments. Only if stress factors in the environment cannot be controlled satisfactorily or the stress from internal sources is unmanageable will the patient require prophylactic drug therapy. If neuroleptics are resorted to after the acute phase is over, interruptions of drug intake with drug holidays are in order. While the utilization of insulin coma therapy has practically disappeared, some authorities still believe it has a utility in younger patients who have been ill for less than 6 months. Electroconvulsive therapy is also considered to be helpful under certain conditions, such as when a severe depression develops during a schizophrenic episode.

Aftercare

The aftercare of hospitalized schizophrenic patients constitutes a serious problem because of the large numbers of such persons in the community as a consequence of deinstitutionalization and the high rate of relapse. Good facilities for aftercare rehabilitative services are lacking in most communities. Those that are available provide the patient with an important means of retarding relapse because of the many modalities offered and the opportunities for patients to establish relationships with a case manager and rehabilitation counselor. If organized services are not available, some patients are able to take advantage of self-help groups such as Recovery, Inc., and Schizophrenics Anonymous. Different therapies are required at different stages of a schizophrenic illness. The proper choice of interventions can best be assured in an organized outpatient setting. Long-term social, behavioral, and problem-solving groups are of special importance, Additionally, social skills training, psychoeducation, supervision of maintenance drugs, resocialization techniques, work adjustment counseling, family therapy, and a variety of other activities geared to the special needs of patients can help many attain stability and lead more rewarding lives. We have seen this happen repeatedly in the Social Rehabilitation Clinic of the Postgraduate Center for Mental Health. What is outstandingly absent are residential facilities where patients without families and those whose homes are too riddled with stressors can be securely housed. But what is even more confounding is that those patients who most need rehabilitation services do not seek them for many personal reasons, including fear of new strange surroundings and of being sent back to a mental institution.

Chronically ill patients, especially when they are hospitalized for a long period and then deinstitutionalized, lose their independent living and practical problem-solving skills, so essential for adaptation. Rehabilitative procedures designed to equip the individual to live independently and cooperatively in the community are important and pitifully lacking in programs of deinstitutionalization.

Examples of how chronic mentally disabled patients may be trained in community living skills have been described in the literature (Hersen & Bellack, 1976; Trower et al, 1978; Wallace et al, 1980). More recently, Wallace et al. (1985) have detailed a program organized into 10 modules designed to teach conversational skills, vocational rehabilitation, medication management, self-care and grooming, personal recordkeeping, how to find and maintain housing, leisure/recreational skills, food preparation, use of public transportation, and money management. How to obtain the necessary resources to implement the skills taught in each module is also included in the training, as well as how to adapt oneself to unexpected or unsatisfactory outcomes for the performance of the different community survival skills and problem solving under various contingencies. Such a program calls for staff who are empathic, resourceful, and capable of tolerating small increments of progress with difficult clients who are confronted with unique personal, environmental, motivational, and other deficits. The use of role playing, modeling, rehearsal, feedback, reinforcement, and homework assignments must regularly be employed as part of the training in social and independent living skills.

Some therapists believe that work rehabilitation is "more powerful than drugs, psychotherapy, social therapy or any other kind of intervention" (Greenblatt, 1983). The vital role of sheltered workshop programs in the rehabilitation of the mentally ill has been amply demonstrated (Black & Kase, 1986). Though a sheltered workshop is a valuable modality, we must realize that some patients will probably never be able to return to a normal competitive work role. Short-term hospitilization should be available should this be necessary. The psychiatric unit in a general hospital is adequate for this purpose. Psychotherapy on some level, ranging from supportive to behavioral, will be most effective if the above priorities are adequately fulfilled.

The use of maintenance medications as a routine procedure in aftercare has undergone challenge in recent years (Marder & May, 1986). Neuroleptics, once regarded as the greatest advance in the treatment of schizophrenia, have now become more conservatively evaluated in aftercare programs. They have not altered the long-term outlook of the disease; some patients do refuse to take the medications; some fail to respond to them; and there are side effects, some of which may be permanently disabling (e.g., tardive dyskinesia). All in all, neuroleptics are more carefully and selectively employed; acute active symptomatology such as excitement, for example, (hallucinations and delusions) responds best to drugs. On the other hand, their influence on symptoms such as withdrawal, apathy, and anhedonia is minimal. Prescribed prudently, drugs are an important asset, especially in patients with a poor prognosis whose ability to adapt to a stressful environment is enhanced through a regulated drug maintenance program. Contrarily, for patients with a good prognosis, neuroleptics may be detrimental. One of the problems produced by long-term maintenance neuroleptic therapy in aftercare is that the sensitivity of the dopamine receptors is so increased that any withdrawal of the drug causes a rebound of symptoms. On the whole, good psychosocial treatment is still the preferred approach in the average case of chronic schizophrenia. Psychosocial treatments operate under a handicap if the environment is irreparably stressful, and in this case one may be forced to employ supplementary drug maintenance to avoid a critical psychotic break.

A compromise solution for the maintenance drug dilemma considers that patients who have recovered from an attack of schizophrenia be withdrawn from medications and then watched carefully for symptoms of relapse, which may be detected at least for a week before the break occurs. These consist of tension, loss of appetite, problems in concentrating and sleeping, withdrawal tendencies, and depression. If these symptoms appear, appropriate pharmacotherapy is immediately instituted along with psychosocial treatment and family therapy, the intensity of such interventions being titrated to the seriousness of the patient's condition. In many cases the relapse may be aborted by these measures (Herz et al, 1982; JAMA, 1984).

In some patients continuing external or internal stress will put the individual on the brink of a relapse. In these cases, maintenance drug therapy will be needed. Some patients spontaneously take medications or increase the dose when their tensions increase or when they feel reality slipping away. But most patients will go off drugs if they are not closely supervised. Cooperation of the family is necessary to ensure that the patient takes the medications. Periodic visits to an outpatient clinic may help the patient maintain the proper drug balances and arrange for drug holidays.

One of the great problems in aftercare is that the schizophrenic is so often used as a foil to hold his or her parents or the rest of the family together. Even when a patient has been removed from a home where there is highly expressed emotion or continuing criticism, the family will not let go. As long as a vehicle for projection exists in the form of a sick child or young adult, hostility and other disturbed feelings are focused on the assigned target and disguised by overconcern. The patient's illness becomes a valuable investment, and signs of recovery threaten the tenuous family balance. A sabotage of treatment may then be expected. Under such circumstances it is vital to get the parents or the entire family into couples, family, or individual treatment to safeguard the patient's treatment. The combination of family treatment and medication has been shown to lower the relapse rate greatly (Hogarty et al, 1986).

Rehospitalization

Rehospitalization for severe psychotic disorganization may be mandatory not only to provide the patient with an atmosphere of protection and to dispense therapeutic measures, but to get the patient away from the family and other environmental stressors that may have initiated the relapse and tend to sustain it.

More and more patients are being admitted for treatment of acute attacks to selected wards of a general hospital rather than to mental institutions. To an extent this is due to the regulations governing compensation by insurance companies and other third-party payment resources. It is due also to the growing deemphasis on institutionalization in mental hospitals. One disadvantage is that payments for hospitalization may be restricted to a limited number of days. This encourages massive tranquilization to bring the patient speedily out of the psychotic state, resulting in discharge before the patient has had an opportunity to establish a relationship with a therapist who may carry on treatment in the posthospital period. What is sorely needed are units strong on psychosocial treatment in which the patient can live for 5 or 6 weeks. This provides the patient with sufficient time to work through his or her experience, in part at least, and to consolidate a continuing therapeutic plan.

To prevent another relapse as much as possible, the home to which the patient returns must be relatively free from stress. If members of the patient's family continue to be hostile, unconcerned, or disturbed, the chances of a further relapse are great. Under such conditions, the patient, if possible, should be housed elsewhere. If this is not feasible, provision should be made to get the patient out of the house, to a day hospi-

tal or rehabilitation unit, for instance, for a good part of the day. Maintenance drug therapy is more essential for these patients than for those whose families are loving and understanding. In either instance, psychosocial treatment is important.

Continued hospitalization over a long-term period may be required for certain patients and is preferable to depositing those lacking in social skills in a furnished room where they will languish in psychotic isolation, refusing to participate in social rehabilitation programs on an outpatient basis and, if they are on maintenance drugs, eventually giving them up.

Prognosis for Schizophrenia

Among patients discharged to families with high degrees of emotion, we can expect a rate of relapse of about 68 percent within the first year of discharge. Maintenance drug therapy will cut this high relapse rate to about 41 percent. A controlled study by Hogarty et al. (1986) has shown that adding psychoeducation and other family-oriented treatments for families, as well as social skills training for patients, lowers this figure to 20 percent. In households where the high degree of emotion has been reduced, the relapse rate has been brought down to negligible percentages. Beyond the first year, the relapse rate rises even among treated patients and families, probably because many schizophrenic patients have psychobiological deficits in dealing with what would be ordinary life experiences for those not affected by the disorder. Internal stress factors include faulty information processing and inherent affective and autonomic dysregulations that over a period of time can override maintenance drug and psychosocial therapies, although the latter interventions may, as indicated above, reduce the relapse rate.

The outlook for chronic schizophrenics is not nearly as gloomy as it was once believed to be. In Third World countries, where schizophrenics are more socially accepted in the community and family and where they do not suffer rejection, discrimination, and degradation for manifesting their symptoms, the illness runs a relatively benign course. In Western industrial countries, however, patients do not have opportunities for appropriate work, social acceptance, or means of improving their status or integrating into community life. These deficiencies tend to interfere with emergence from the psychotic illness and to promote retreat from relationships so characteristic of this group of patients (Warner, 1985). But even in the United States, long-term studies have shown that many patients released from institutions somehow, after years have gone by, adjust to the outside world and even do productive work, marry, and have children. A 30-year longitudinal study by a group of researchers from Yale University and the University of Vermont have shown that "one-half to two-thirds of 82 subjects released from a State mental hospital and rehabilitation program in the mid-1950's now live in the community, care for themselves, act as productive citizens involved with their families and friends, and show few or no signs of schizophrenia" (*Psychiatric News, 1985*). Other long-term studies of 1400 schizophrenics observed over two decades have revealed that more than half are significantly improved or recovered. This argues for a change in our traditional pessimistic attitude about chronic schizophrenia toward a more favorable outlook.

Psychosurgery

Psychosurgery has been prescribed with variable results for seriously ill schizophrenic patients who have failed to show improvement after 2 or 3 years on psychotropic drugs and psychotherapy. This form of treatment is said to yield the best results where the prepsychotic personality was fairly well integrated, there is no emotional deterioration, and the patient's current symptoms include tension, restlessness, motor activity, combativeness, and destructiveness. Catatonic and paranoid reactions respond best; hebephrenic reactions poorly. After schizophrenia has existed for 10 years or more, psychosurgery is rarely of value. (See the section on Psychosurgery in Somatic Therapy.)

MISCELLANEOUS PSYCHOTIC REACTIONS

A number of other categories of psychotic disorder are included in DSM-III-R Codes: *schizophreniform disorder (295.40), brief reactive psychosis (298.90), atypical psychosis (298.90), schizoaffective disorder (295.70)*, and *induced psychotic disorder (297.30)*. There are also a number of organic mental disorders in the form of dementias arising in the senium and presenium, as well as a host of psychoactive substance-induced organic mental disorders, and those associated with physical disorders or conditions.

In *schizophreniform disorder* the duration of the illness is less than 6 months; there is a rapid onset and a high degree of confusion and emotional turmoil, but there is also a good likelihood of recovery to premorbid functioning. A *brief reactive psychosis* must be differentiated from schizophrenia. Here the psychosis follows a strong stressful environmental stimulus and there is recovery within 2 weeks. If no such psychological stress has occurred and there is still a psychosis (disturbed behavior, hallucinations, delusions, associational disorganization, etc.) that disappears in less than 2 weeks, the diagnosis of *atypical psychosis* is often given. The diagnosis of *schizoaffective disorder* is more difficult to make since it is a wastebasket for combinations of affective and schizophrenic symptomatology in the form of mood-incongruent psychotic features that do not fit into any of the other categories.

Induced psychotic disorder occurs when a dominant psychotic person, the primary patient, influences others in the family to display the same delusional beliefs. One form of this disorder is *folie à deux* involving two persons. The intensity of the psychotic symptoms in these conditions may necessitate hospitalization during which antipsychotic drugs are administered. In schizoaffective disorder antidepressants and lithium may additionally be needed and, if medications are ineffective, occasionally ECT.

Symptoms of psychosis may occur with various organic brain diseases of neurological origin or as a toxic effect of drugs (alcohol, hallucinogens, etc.). Among the most common of these neurologically based disorders is primary degenerative dementia, especially Alzheimer's and Pick's diseases, which are characterized by progressive deterioration of intellectual, social, and occupational functioning. Multi-infarct dementia presents similar symptoms, combined with focal neurological disease and cerebrovascular residues. Impulsiveness, poor judgment, memory loss, and personality problems create difficulties for the patient and those around the patient. A variety of other organic brain syndromes may be seen in which the symptoms are delirium and dementia, clouding of consciousness, disturbances in psychomotor activity, memory impairment, aphasia, and other disturbances of the higher cortical functions. Persistent delusions and hallucinations, appearing in a normal state of consciousness, may also develop as a consequence of organic illness and are diagnosed according to the symptoms (organic delusional syndrome, organic hallucinosis, organic personality syndrome). Management of these conditions depends on the symptoms. Restlessness and uncontrollable hostility may be helped by Thorazine or Mellaril (10–50 mg or more in divided doses). Sometimes a beta-adrenergic blocker like Inderal (60 mg daily) or an antidepressant like Desyrel (200–400 mg daily) may be found useful. Delirous overactivity, confusion, agitation, and paranoidal excitement call for antipsychotics (Haldol, 5 mg, or Navane, 4 mg, intramuscularly) repeated as needed. Cogentin (1–2 mg) intramuscularly to offset extrapyramidal complications is sometimes coordinately given as a precautionary measure. Intravenous benzodiazepines (Valium, 10 mg; or Librium, 50 mg; or Ativan, 2 mg) repeated every 2 hours until symptoms are under control are often preferred as an alternative. When the delirium has abated, oral medications may be employed. A search for causes of both delirium and dementia is imperative, and, when found, specific and nonspecific therapies should be instituted. Supportive and directive psychotherapy may be required, bolstered by antianxiety, antipsychotic, and antidepressive medications as needed. Needless to say, family counseling will usually be adjunctively required.

61

Supervision of the Psychotherapeutic Process

Supervision of the work of the beginning therapist is an essential requirement in the learning process (Greben, 1985). Without supervision it will be difficult or impossible for the therapist to translate theoretic knowledge into effective practice, to work through blocks in understanding, and to develop skills to a point where the therapist can help patients achieve the most extensive goals. Supervision, then, in psychotherapy is essentially a teaching procedure in which an experienced psychotherapist helps a less experienced individual acquire a body of knowledge aimed at a more dexterous handling of the therapeutic situation.

LEARNING PRINCIPLES IN SUPERVISION

Adequate learning necessitates, first, an appropriate presentation of data in terms meaningful to students, second, the incorporation of this data by the students, and third, the ability of the latter to organize experiences cognitively and to generalize from them to related aspects of their work.

The first requirement presupposes an ability on the part of the teacher to develop an empathic understanding with the students and to discern what aspects of the available material are pertinent to their immediate needs and to the teaching task. The second essential assumes the existence of motivation, an adequate intellectual capacity to integrate the information, and the relative absence of anxiety. The third requisite entails the presence of a synthesizing function of the ego that enables students to examine themselves critically, to give up old modes of conceptualizing, and to apply themselves to new creative tasks. Helpful is alertness and ability of the teacher to keep the relationships on a level where transference resistances do not interfere with this process. Helpful also is detection of the students' specific learning problems and the evolvement of techniques designed especially to deal with these problems.

Unfortunately, there are many interferences with the expeditious learning of psychotherapy, not the least of which is the ambiguity of the concepts that constitute the marrow and lifeblood of the psychotherapeutic process. It is difficult to authenticate techniques that are universally applicable. A method that works in one case may not be effective in another; it may produce good results for one therapist and a string of failures for another with a different kind of personality; it may be highly productive at a certain phase of treatment and backfire in the same patient at another phase. What appears to be necessary is more research into the actual procedures of teaching psychotherapy. Christine McGuire (1964) has pointed out that much of the ongoing clinical teaching is conducted in a manner that runs counter to basic principles about learning long known to educators and psychologists. A professional coach who sends his or her players out to complete a number of practice games with instructions on what to do and who asks them to provide at intervals a verbal description of how they had played and what they intend to do next would probably last no more than one season. Yet this is the way much of the teaching in psychotherapy is done. What is lacking is a systematic critique of actual performances as observed by peers or supervisors. This is not to say that an account, highly screened as it may be, of what a therapist says he or she has done with a patient may not lend itself to a dynamic learning relationship. The account, however, is most valuable when it is compared to what the supervisor has actually observed in a live session between the student and patient through a one-way mirror or in viewing a videotape of the session.

A sensitive question relates to the validity of using data in teaching psychotherapy drawn from the teaching of related disciplines. Can the information, for example, derived from such areas as social work supervision, the psychology of learning, communication theory, and programmed instruction be applied to psychotherapy? On the surface the reply would be "yes." Yet there are special problems in the teaching of psychotherapy that force a qualification to this answer.

An individual who masters a complex skill proceeds through a number of learning phases, namely (1) the acquisition and retention of certain factual information, (2) the development of ways of using this information in a practical way, and (3) the evolvement of a capacity of altering this information when new situations arise that call for different approaches. In psycho-

therapy modern methods of acquiring information embrace exposure to didactic materials through fact-finding learning (lectures, reading, and observation of therapy performed by expert therapists through a one-way mirror, videotapes, and sound movies) and problem-solving learning (programmed instruction and role playing with immediate feedback). Practical applications of what has been learned are inherent in observing the consequences of treatment techniques by actually *doing* psychotherapy under supervision, by listening to audiotapes and watching videotapes of one's own performances, by observing others performing in psychotherapy through a one-way mirror, or viewing videotapes of their actions, and by clinical conferences and case seminars. The creative employment of psychotherapy with the development of methods designed for the special problems of each patient are consequences of continued supervision and prolonged experience. Through such a program of scholarship, searching inquiry, observation, and experiment, a body of organized knowledge is eventually developed in the matrix of sophisticated theory.

Research into teaching method indicates that the effectiveness of teaching is increased "when the teacher accepts a teacher's responsibility for directing learning, providing every opportunity and inducement for the student to accept a larger responsibility for his own education, and holding out always his and their goal the maximum achievement of which they are both capable" (Hatch and Bennet, 1960). Fundamental is a spirit of inquiry that provides the motivational fuel for the powering of proper learning (Matarazzo, 1971). This is the most sustained when the content of teaching is related to the needs and educational level of the students.

Once teaching goals have been explicated in operational terms and the most effective methods have been designed to help the students achieve these goals, the effectiveness of learning experiences must be tested through the students' demonstrating how much they have mastered. Reliable methods of recording and measuring performance are needed here. This should be more than a matter of clinical impressions, for, as McGuire (1964) has pointed out, these "are no more acceptable in a scientific study of the educational efficacy of a training program than they are in a scientific appraisal of the therapeutic efficacy of a new drug." The crucial obstruction is, of course, the current relatively undeveloped methods of evaluation. In psychotherapy, where the clinical data may be interpreted in endless ways and where criteria of competence are so vague, evaluation techniques are still more pedantic than precise. Yet it must be agreed that, however tenuous they may seem, measures of competence must be constructed to require students to demonstrate that they can perform in a desired way. Both the continuous case conference and supervision offer means of approaching the thorny problem of evaluation. Important leads may perhaps be taken from the study of the evaluation of the teaching of psychiatry at the undergraduate level in the film test series developed at the University of Rochester, the University of Nebraska, and the University of Pittsburgh. At the postgraduate level a number of interview films have been developed—for instance, those at Temple University Medical School, which may be used to test clinical judgment and problem-solving skills and which can be adapted to the evaluation of different training programs.

PSYCHOANALYTIC CONTRIBUTIONS

Some outstanding work on supervision has been done in the field of social work (Towle, 1954). But the area that has commanded greatest interest for many psychotherapists has been psychoanalytic supervision (Balint, 1948; Benedek 1954, 1972; Blitzstein & Fleming 1953; Bruner, 1957; Dewald, 1969; Ekstein, 1953; Gitelson, 1948; Kubie 1958(a); Sloane, 1957). The early publications of Ekstein and Wallerstein (1958), Fleming (1963), and Fleming and Benedek (1964) are still considered valuable. The latter authors, using electrically recorded sessions of students with patients and their supervisors, developed a project to investigate "the processes of interaction between communicating systems in the teaching–learning relationship" that involved the triadic dimensions of supervisor, student-analyst, and patient. Assessment of students brought into play a complicated network of motivations in the supervisor, for instance, the preconceived expectations of students, the supervisor's own investment in teaching, and the defensive reactions to students' resistances. "Our experience demonstrated again and again the necessity for a supervisor to listen to and evaluate himself in interaction with his student; and it is our opinion that the more aware a supervisor is of the various aspects of his educational role, the more effective he will be as an object for identificatory learning and as a developer of students in general."

These and later data from studies of supervision of the psychoanalytic process (Chessick, 1985; Buckley et al. 1982; Gauthier, 1984; Glass, 1986) require a reconciliation with treatment situations of greater activity and more limited goals, as in the less intensive dynamic, reeducative, and supportive therapies (Sandell, 1985; Winokur, 1982).

It is almost inevitable that psychotherapists will be influenced by unconscious processes in their patients. Patients who have incorporated parental messages and repudiated their presence may through projective identification accuse the therapist of the very impulses that they deny within themselves. More insidiously the projections may not be direct, but the therapist will become aware of them through countertransference, perhaps reflected in dreams or fantasies (Langs, 1979). Failure to understand what is happening may provoke defensiveness and hostility. Moreover, the therapist may with some patients develop transference, which can lead to antitherapeutic acting out manifested by smothering overprotectiveness, aggressiveness, or sexual misbehavior. One of the supervisor's prime duties is to be alert to such transferential and projective identification interferences and, when they occur, help the supervisees recognize them. This is a tricky task because the supervisor will in so doing be playing the role that should be assumed by the supervisor's therapist, if there is one. What may result is that the supervisees will begin developing more irrational transferences toward the supervisor and, if the supervisor does not watch it, the supervisory teaching process may become converted into a prolonged therapeutic venture with the focus away from the learning of psychotherapy and the welfare of the supervisees' patients.

FUNCTIONS OF SUPERVISION

All participants in the supervisory process bring to it a separate agenda. The supervisees are interested in learning how to do good psychotherapy, and perhaps in achieving certification or earning a degree. The supervisor seeks to demonstrate competence as a senior clinician while teaching the students a skill and contributing to their growth. The institution that sponsors the treatment desires that standards imposed by licensing and regulatory bodies be meticulously followed. The paying agencies insist that records and documentation be carefully maintained and available for auditing. The central members of the conglomerate, the patients, seek the most effective help to reduce their problems and want to be assured that their therapy is going well. Such aims may be contradictory,

and the supervisor will deftly have to weave through the tangle of these self-oriented objectives and bureaucratic rules. There may be difficulty in deciding where loyalties should be placed. Good supervisors are able to fuse the disparate elements into a serviceable amalgam. Skills *can* be taught while considering the welfare of the patient, the needs of the student, and the rules of the institution. Coordinately the supervisor will have to deal with personal frustrations and countertransference, with the students' transferences and resistances to learning, with the intransigence and arbitrariness of the school or agency, and, by remote control, with the anxieties of the patient.

The traditional type of supervision, unfortunately, has become so contaminated with overseeing, directorial, and inspective functions that it has frequently been diverted from its teaching objective. This has particularly been the case in agency work, where the supervisor, as part of the administrative body, is responsible for the quality of service rendered to clients. Many difficulties arise here because the supervisor serves in a dual role—as an overseer and a teacher.

As overseer, the supervisor may be so concerned with maintaining the standards of the agency that he or she may not be able to exercise the kind of tolerance and patience required in a teacher. For instance, under press of responsibility, the supervisor is likely to ''jump in'' and interfere with the treatment plan set up by the supervisees, the execution of which, while perhaps less expert than a plan devised by the supervisor, would prove of greatest learning value to the supervisees. Because the students' status is dependent on evaluations by the supervisor, the process of supervision in agencies is apt to become extremely trying. A parallel situation develops when the supervisees are in training at a psychotherapeutic or psychoanalytic school and their careers are dependent on the evaluation by the supervisor. Similarly, if the supervisees are staff members of a clinic, the supervisor as part of the administration may subordinate the teaching role to over-concern with the total case load. This shift in emphasis cannot help but influence adversely the quality of training received; this is inevitable whenever the training is oriented around circumscribed goals set up in relation to specific kinds of service for which the clinic is responsible. Much less complicated is the supervision of psychotherapists in private practice, who choose a supervisor principally to expand technical skills, not being dependent on the supervisor for an evaluation that may destroy their careers or eliminate their means of livelihood.

In schools or clinics, the supervisor will usually operate as a teacher, an evaluator, an administrator, and a policymaker.

Teaching

The first responsibility of the supervisor is observation of the total functioning of therapists to help in the supervisees' educational growth. Toward this end, it may be essential to bring the supervisees to an awareness of how they have failed to live up to therapeutic potentialities, either because of insufficient knowledge or because of neurotic character problems that inject themselves into the psychotherapeutic relationship. It is incumbent on the supervisor, among other things, to help the supervisees (1) to gain knowledge that is lacking, (2) to achieve an awareness of their own character problems that may interfere with the establishment and maintenance of a therapeutic relationship, and (3) to overcome resistances to learning.

Evaluating

A second responsibility of the supervisor is an evaluation of the capacities and progress of the supervisees for the purposes of determining professional development and current skills as a therapist. Evaluation involves a number of areas, including theoretic understanding, therapeutic aptitudes, and the kinds of relationships that are established with patients and the supervisor.

Administration and Policy Making

The third responsibility of the supervisor lies in the helping of administration and policy making of the school or clinic under whose aegis the program is being conducted. The supervisor recommends modifications of the therapeutic and teaching programs that may influence adversely the training and the work of the therapists as well as the patients' responses to treatment.

To summarize, supervision in psychotherapy is fundamentally a teaching process in which a more experienced participant, the supervisor, observes the work of less experienced participants, the supervisees, with the aim of helping the supervisees acquire certain essential therapeutic skills through better understanding of the interventions involved in mental illness and through resolution of personality factors that block performance of effective psychotherapy. Supervision embraces a sharing of experiences; not only those gathered in the relations between therapist and patient, but also those occurring in the relationship between the supervisor and supervisees.

Qualifications of a good supervisor are the following:

1. Ability to function expertly as a psychotherapist.
2. Ability to function effectively as a teacher.
3. Ability to accept the supervisees unconditionally, without contempt, hostility, possessiveness, and other unwarranted attitudes and feelings.

Supervisory problems may roughly be divided into five categories of problems:

orientation, recording, technical performance, learning and termination of supervision.

PROBLEMS IN ORIENTATION

Differences in Theoretic Orientation

Important and often irreconcilable differences occur in the theoretic background and orientation of the supervisor and the supervisees, a product usually of varying kinds of preclinical training. Illustrative of such differences are the following:

1. The relative weight to be placed on constitutional as compared with experiential factors in the genesis of neurosis.
2. The importance of biologic as contrasted with sociologic factors.
3. The respective emphasis on past childhood experiences and on current environmental hardships.
4. The degree of stress placed on unconscious conflict as the focus of neurotic and behavioral difficulties.
5. The extent of acceptance of the Oedipus complex, castration fears, and penis envy as universal phenomena.
6. The primacy of sexual over other drives and behavioral disorders.
7. The significance of character structure in creating and sustaining emotional disturbance.
8. The relative emphasis of conditioning theory in accounting for anxiety.
9. The value of short-term as compared to long-term approaches and of psychoanalytic versus behavioral and cognitive therapy.

The most effective supervisor is one who respects the right of therapists to their own ideas and opinions, yet who realizes that some of these may interfere with good psychotherapy.

Differences in Communication

Since communication is the basis of the supervisory relationship, it is important that verbalizations and concepts be understood by both supervisor and supervisees. Assuming that there are no important language differences, problems in communication are frequently related to differences in terminology.

A poignant objection to psychology by scientists in other fields is that it is partial to neologisms. Tendencies to use unconventional and complex terms have been one of the strongest barriers in a rapproachment with other sciences. Both supervisor and supervisees may be victimized by dedication to an esoteric terminology. Translation of complex terms into concepts with which supervisor and supervisees are conversant is vital to a mutual understanding and to the establishment of a common frame of reference.

Difference in Method

Another problem in supervision relates to differences in method—that practiced by the supervisor and that accepted or practiced by the supervisees. Such differences may involve various matters, such as the most desirable number of treatment sessions per week, whether or not to employ routine history taking and psychological workups, the use of free association, the emphasis on dream material and the manner of its employment, the use of the couch, the degree of activity in the interview, the extent to which a transference neurosis is permitted to develop, and the adjuncts to be used during therapy. Resolution of serious differences in method is to be expected in the course of good supervision.

Considerable flexibility will be required in methodologic approaches, particularly when the therapists are expected to handle, in the practice for which they are being trained, a wide assortment of clinical problems. Supportive of the principle of technical eclecticism is the fact that no single approach is applicable to all types of emotional difficulties. Some problems seem to respond better to certain kinds of therapeutic intervention than to others.

Differences in Goals

Problems may arise between supervisee and supervisor on the basis of varying concepts of what makes for success in psychotherapy. Is success in therapy the achievement of complete resolution of all blocks in personality maturation with effective functioning in all areas of living? Or is success to be graded in terms of optimal development within the practical limitations imposed on individuals by their existing motivations, ego strength, and environmental pressures from which they cannot reasonably escape?

Reasonableness dictates that though a responsibility exists in bringing patients to the most extensive personality reconstruction possible, there are circumstances that block this. A modest treatment objective may be the only possible alternative. Supervisees trained in the tradition that therapeutic change falling short of complete reconstruction is spurious, however, may look askance at the supervisor who considers goals in terms of optimal functioning within realistic limitations. Or conversely, the supervisor may be unwilling to accept goal modification and may downgrade changes that fall short of absolute psychosocial maturity and then blame the supervisees for not being able to do the impossible.

PROBLEMS IN RECORDING AND REPORTING

Careful listening to the supervisees' accounts, to the manner of reporting, to evasions and points of emphasis, to slips of speech, and to casual off-the-record references to feelings about patients help the supervisor to evaluate the therapeutic work of the supervisees.

In making this appraisal, the supervisor must take into account that the role being played by the supervisees with the supervisor, and the attitudes harbored, are not a reliable index of what the supervisees actually do with patients. With patients, supervisees are operating in an entirely different setting than with the supervisor, with whom they are in a more subordinate status, more vulnerable, and more capable of being challenged or criticized. They may respond to the supervisor with fear, detachment, resentment, and other character patterns related to feelings about authority. Therefore, it may not be possible for supervisees to communicate to the supervisor their true capacities to be spontaneous, empathic, and responsive such as may occur with patients in the relatively secure atmosphere of one's office.

For instance, a therapist presented material to her supervisor in a cocky, superior manner, reflecting a somewhat contemptuous attitude toward the patient about whom she talked. It soon became obvious to the supervisor, however, in listening to tape recordings of actual treatment sessions, that hostile feelings were not manifest in the therapist's responses nor in her manner with the patient. Hostility, marshalled by transference feelings toward the supervisor, was seeping into the supervisory session and was influencing the nature of the reporting.

Neurotic feelings toward the supervisor may thus distort therapists' presentation of material. Pertinent data may be deleted, irrelevant items may be introduced, and secondary elaboration may destroy the value of the presentation. Fear of exposing deficiencies, of appearing ridiculous, and of incurring the displeasure and contempt of the supervisor are among the more common causes of poor reporting.

Anxiety to please the supervisor, to

hold back differences of opinion, and to suppress transferential displays so as not to antagonize the supervisor may interfere with factual reporting. The supervisees may fear revealing what is happening in treatment so as not to appear incompetent.

Some of the difficulties in reporting may be obviated by insisting on process recording in which there is a verbatim account of both patients' and therapists' verbalizations. Process recording has the advantage of presenting a reasonably cogent picture of what is going on, since the tendency toward distortion or deletion will be minimized. There are certain objections to this method, however, in that the supervisees may be unable to record simultaneously while doing good therapy or because patients protest not being able to make good contact with someone immersed in writing. Furthermore, no matter how careful an attempt to record, the students will be unable to include everything that is said. There will then be a tendency to curtail the material, consciously or unconsciously eliminating elements that cause them to feel that they are revealing themselves unfavorably. In intensive supervision, in which one case is being presented over a long period of time, the supervisor may, nevertheless, have to insist on process recording until convinced of the therapist's ability to report correctly in a more abbreviated way. (See Appendix K for a case outline.)

Perhaps the most effective type of recording is done with a video machine. These machines are now sufficiently improved and modest in price to become an almost indispensable item of equipment for supervision. This use is described and illustrated by Maguire et al. (1984) and Morgan (1984). Videotaping is valuable not only to the supervisor but also for playback to patients, who observe and listen to themselves communicating (Geocaris, 1960); Gutheil et al. 1981). Video recording is also helpful for playback to the supervisees,

who may learn as much by self-observation as from the supervisor (Moore et al, 1965; Beiser, 1966). Moreover, the supervisor may profit from self-observance in supervisory operation. Audio recordings on tape are cheaper but less effective. For purposes of record keeping and for later transcription, however, audiotapes are sufficient. Few patients object to the use of machine recorders, and once the fears about revealing themselves have been overcome, the supervisees can function freely.

The value of video recording cannot be overestimated. It gives a most factual picture of what has actually gone on in the session, not only in content, but also in revealing bodily movements, intonations, and subvocal utterances that cannot be communicated in written types of recording. The method enables the supervisor to observe aspects of the interviewing process that are handled well or poorly. It helps to understand how the different kinds of content are dealt with, whether the supervisees exaggerate, minimize, or negate the importance of certain types of material. It permits observation of how the therapist responds to unreasonable demands of patients, to hostilities and other transference manifestations that are developing in the relationship. It enables the supervisor to study how techniques are being implemented. The difference between the written or verbal account and what actually went on, which is revealed in observing and listening to a playback, is often so astonishing as to leave little question about the value of this kind of recording (Gutheil et al., 1981; Maguire, 1984; Morgan, 1984).

For instance, one supervisee's verbal account made no mention of hostile feelings in the patient, to which the therapist was responding by shifting the topic of discussion and by complacent, reassuring utterances whenever the patient introduced a slightly antagonistic remark. The supervisee was totally unaware of his diversionary responses, but in the playback he could not escape what had happened. Another supervisee reported a progressively deepening depression in a borderline patient. The process recording related that the patient talked incessantly about how she had been neglected, particularly by a mother preoccupied with outside activities, and a detached father. The supervisee, in her recorded responses, appeared to be saying the right things. A session of the supervisee working with the patient, which was recorded on videotape, however, demonstrated that the therapist had placed her chair so that she was not facing the patient; she was in effect detaching herself from her and repeating the patient's childish trauma. Correction of this position, with the closer interaction that the face-to-face placement encouraged, rapidly brought the patient out of the depression and accelerated progress.

The advantage of watching students performing with patients behind a one-way mirror and of recording the session on videotape so that it may be played back for the students is incalculable, since immediate feedback is possible. Parenthetically, a session in which the supervisor treats a patient, observed by students through a one-way mirror or by watching a video recording, is helpful in pointing out techniques that are difficult to describe verbally. Understandably, it will be impossible to use recordings at every supervisory session due to lack of time. Several recorded sessions presented during each six months of supervision will usually suffice to measure the therapist's progress, and in themselves will justify the use of the video machine. A unique device described by Boylston and Tuma (1972) is "bug in the ear," a receiver placed in the therapist's ear through which a supervisor gives instructions via a transmitter from behind a one-way mirror.

From the standpoint of research, recordings, videotapes, or sound film recordings of interviews permit the researcher to approach the problems of both process and outcome evaluation with greater objectivity (Davidman, 1964; Kubie, 1950b; Strupp, 1960).

Although the students' written notes and observations about therapeutic work are valuable (Beckett, 1969; Bush, 1969; Moulton, 1969), they are rendered more significant by studying the inclusions, omissions, and exaggerations in video recordings of the same sessions. As Schlessinger (1966) points out, different kinds of data are dealt with in both types of recording, each of which has a different potential for teaching but which is by no means mutually exclusive.

Recently, computer programs have been made available that have been found useful by some therapists, for example, Harless's Computer-assisted Simulation of the Clinical Encounter (Harless, 1971, 1972), which deals with diagnostic problem solving. Elaborations of this computer-assisted instruction involving typical psychotherapeutic situations will probably have a significant impact on some students since, as Hubbard and Templeton (1973) have pointed out, they can expose students to a wide variety of clinical problems, provide modes of practice and diagnostic skills in a simulated therapy setting, and permit early feedback by a consensus of experts in the field. The authors predict, because of such technological instruction, that a different role for teachers is possible. Helfer and Hess (1970) and Lomax (1972) have published interesting material on related new trends in teaching.

PROBLEMS IN TECHNICAL PERFORMANCE

The supervisees will experience trouble in various areas in the process of psychotherapy. These difficulties are the consequence either of lack of understanding, experience and skill, or of negative countertransference. They will have to be handled by the supervisor in relation to their origin and function. Most common are the following problems:

1. Difficulties in the conduct of the initial interview.
2. Inability to deal with poor motivation.
3. Inability to clarify for the patients misconceptions about psychotherapy.
4. Inability to extend warmth and support to the patients or to establish a good initial contact with them.
5. Inability to define for the patients goals in therapy.
6. Inability to structure the therapeutic situation adequately for the patients.
7. Inability to recognize and to handle manifestations of transference in the therapeutic relationship—specifically, dependence, sexual feelings, detachment, hostility, and aggression.
8. Lack of knowledge about how to explore and to bring to awareness conflicts that mobilize anxiety in the patients (in insight therapy).
9. Lack of sensitivity and perceptiveness to what is going on in therapy.
10. Lack of technical skill in the implementation of free association, dream interpretation, and analysis of the transference (in insight therapy).
11. Inability to deal with resistances in the patients toward verbal exploration of their problems.
12. Tendencies to avoid problems of the patients that inspire anxiety in the therapist.
13. Tendency to probe too deeply and too rapidly at the start.
14. Impatience with resistances toward the acquisition of insight (in insight therapy).
15. Faulty techniques of presenting interpretations.
16. Frustration and discouragement at the patients' refusal to use insight in the direction of change.
17. Tendency to push the patients too

hard or too rapidly toward normal objectives.
18. Fear of being too directive, with resultant excessive passivity.
19. Lack of understanding of how to create incentives for change.
20. Lack of understanding in dealing with forces that block action.
21. Lack of understanding about how to help the patients master anxieties surrounding normal life goals.
22. Inability to scale down therapeutic goals when modification of objectives is mandatory.
23. Lack of understanding about how to implement the translation of insight and understanding into action.
24. Inability to deal with resistance toward abandoning primary and secondary neurotic aims.
25. Inability to deal with resistance toward normality.
26. Inability to deal with resistance in the patients toward activity through their own resources.
27. Tendencies to overprotect or to domineer the patient.
28. Inability to assume a nondirective therapeutic role.
29. Lack of understanding about how to deal with the refusal on the part of the patients to yield their dependency.
30. Lack of understanding of how to handle the patients' fear of assertiveness.
31. Lack of understanding about how to analyze dependency elements in the therapist–patient relationship.
32. Lack of understanding about how to terminate therapy.

Good supervisors exercise tolerance for the specific style of activity of the supervisees. They realize that irrespective of intensive training and exposure to specific schools of psychological thought, basic personality patterns of the supervisees will infiltrate the treatment situation. These cannot help but influence the techniques that have been learned. Some modification of learned techniques will always occur, particularly those that are not compatible with the therapists' style or personality structure. The supervisees will probably never be able to duplicate the exact style of the supervisor, nor vice versa, since they are individuals and relate to patients in their own unique ways. Yet certain basic principles in psychotherapy must not be violated, no matter what kinds of relationships are established and what types of techniques are employed. By defining the broad bounds of psychotherapy, and by elucidating on the fundamental principles to which every therapist must adhere, the supervisor may help the supervisees perfect skills yet maintain spontaneity, which is a most cherished characteristic in the psychotherapist.

PROBLEMS IN LEARNING

A number of propositions are involved in the learning of psychotherapy that may be expressed as follows:

1. All learning necessitates a substitution of new patterns for old. This requires a working through of blocks that constantly impede the acquisition of new patterns. Sometimes the struggle is minimal; sometimes it is intense.

2. The manner in which learning proceeds is unique for individuals both in relationship to the rate of learning and the methods by which material is absorbed and integrated. Some people learn by leaps and bounds, others by cautious, precarious crawling. Many variants expedite or interfere with learning in different people. What is taught to individuals has to be accepted by them in their own terms.

3. Learning involves both an understanding of theory as well as its integration and translation into effective action. The instruction leading toward

an understanding of theory is vested in the instructors and teachers with whom the supervisees have had preliminary training. The instruction for execution of theory into practice is vested in the clinical supervisors.

4. Little learning is possible without a motivation to learn. This motivation must be sufficiently intense to overcome the difficulties that are inherent in all learning. It is assumed that the supervisees have sufficient motivation—in terms of desire to be psychotherapists—to expose themselves to the ordeals of the learning process.

5. Anxiety is present in all learning. Its sources are related to fear of change and the desire to cling to familiar patterns as well as to resistance in altering basic accepted attitudes and behavior tendencies.

6. Some resistances to learning are present in all people in response to anxiety. The kind and the degree of resistance will vary with each individual. Most common are lack of attention, lack of retention, amnesia, and simulated stupidity. In addition, resistance may take the form of dependency, submissiveness, self-depreciation, ingratiation, arrogance, grandiosity, resentment, aggression, and detachment. These are products of specific neurotic character problems but there also may be a universality of expression of such trends in certain cultures, reflecting accepted attitudes toward education and toward the authorities that are responsible for education.

7. Resistances to learning must be overcome before learning can proceed. The attitudes of the supervisor are crucial here. The supervisor's tolerance, flexibility, and capacity to extend warmth, support, and acceptance toward the supervisees, irrespective of the errors that the latter make, pro-

motes the most effective medium for the handling of resistance.

8. Learning is thus facilitated by a warm working relationship between supervisor and supervisees. It is impeded by hostility that develops in this relationship. A primary focus, then, in the supervisory process is the existing relationship between students and teacher, with thorough ventilation of negative feelings before these exert a corrosive influence on the learning process. The supervisees must be encouraged to express disagreements, criticisms, or feelings in relation to the supervisor. The supervisees must also be able to accept criticism, and this will be possible where there is a good rapport with the supervisor.

9. As a general rule, learning blocks are resolved during the first few months of supervision. An inability to master such blocks after several months indicates a severe problem that necessitates incisive investigation.

10. In learning, the supervisees have a backlog of past experiences on which to build. They cannot be expected to progress any faster than would be warranted by the degree of this experience, no matter how hard the supervisor may push; severe demands will be a hindrance.

11. As a rule, in the early stages of learning, the supervisees will feel resentful, unsure, and certain of failure. They will want to be told how to function—indeed, will demand that the supervisor demonstrate exactly what to do. The supervisor must accept the presence of dependency and yet treat the supervisees as equals. The setting of supervision is best permissive, the supervisees being given the feeling that they are free to act, experiment, and make mistakes. Mistakes are to be expected since even expert therapists make them.

12. Learning how to become a therapist is a tedious process enhanced by the active participation in the learner's growth. It is facilitated by selected case studies that serve a specific purpose in filling in gaps in experience, as well as by assigned readings and recommended courses. At all times, critical thinking is to be encouraged.

13. Learning is more an educational than a therapeutic process, and the focus in good supervision is on supervisees' work rather than their personal problems. It is essential that supervisees be treated as adults and not as problem children.

14. Learning is expedited by successes, and it is impaired by failures. Provision should be made for some successes that will reinforce learning. If supervisees encounter repeated failures, damage will be done to their learning capacity. The supervisor should therefore be encouraging and commendatory of any successes that are scored.

PROBLEMS IN TERMINATION OF SUPERVISION

The relationship that supervisees establish with the supervisor will, in general, proceed through various phases, including the establishing of rapport, the understanding of problems that occur in relationship to the supervisor, the translation of this understanding into corrective action, and, finally, the ending phase in which supervisees develop the capacity to carry on, on their own, with working through of the dependence on the supervisor.

If the supervisor has an authoritarian personality structure, it may be difficult to operate on equal terms with the supervisees. The supervisor will want to continue to make decisions, to utter judgments, and to offer interpretations, consciously or unconsciously resenting the supervisees' right to self-determination. Under these circumstances the ending of supervision may impose great hardships on both supervisor and students.

On the other hand, the greater the dependency needs in the supervisees, the more difficult it will be to countenance termination. An inability to resolve dependence on the supervisor indicates severe characterologic problems for which the supervisees may require further therapeutic help.

During the terminal phases of supervision the supervisor, in anticipation of the trauma of separation, may assume a nondirective role, insisting that the supervisees be more active and figure things out entirely alone. One may expect that the supervisees will respond to such nondirectiveness with anxiety and hostility and that there will be an attempt to force the supervisor to abandon this passive role. If the supervisor is persistent, however, justifying the passivity displayed on the basis of a respect for the supervisees' growth process, the latter will eventually be convinced of the rationale of the supervisor's behavior.

TECHNICAL DETAILS OF SUPERVISION

Preclinical Training of the Therapist

Before supervision begins, the supervisor will desire information about the preclinical training of the prospective supervisees. Questions that may arise include these: Is the theoretic background of the supervisees adequate for functioning in psychotherapeutic practice? Have the required courses been taken and the essential reading done? Has this theoretic material been integrated satisfactorily? Do the supervisees have the personality qualities that will

make for a good therapist? How profound an understanding do the supervisees have of their own emotional and interpersonal processes? Will the supervisees be able to resolve or to control the expression of hostility, detachment, sexual interest, overprotection, rejection, and other strivings on the part of the patient that will be inimical to the psychotherapeutic relationship? Can it be reasonably assumed that the supervisees are sufficiently adjusted to life now, so that they will not use the therapeutic situation and the experiences of the patient to live through vicariously certain frustrated ambitions, dependencies, and hostilities? Do the supervisees have a capacity to empathize with people, to feel warmth toward them and to communicate it? Is there the capacity to be resolute and firm on occasion, capable of insisting on certain essential actions during the therapeutic process? How much experience have the supervisees had in psychotherapy? What kinds of cases have been treated and with what results? Has there been previous supervision, and if so, with whom and for how long? Do the supervisees believe such supervision has been beneficial?

There is general agreement that the prospective psychotherapist requires an extensive amount of preclinical training. A review of training that is being given in most of the recognized schools reveals a close similarity in prescribed courses and requirements. These include the following:

1. Courses in basic neuropsychiatry, normal psychosocial development, psychopathology, psychodynamics, techniques of interviewing, techniques of psychotherapy, dream interpretation, child psychiatry, group psychotherapy, and behavior modification.
2. Clinical conferences and continuous case seminars that have been attended regularly.
3. Readings in psychiatric literature of

sufficient scope to provide the students with a good background in history, theory, and practice.

4. Ideally, enough personal psychotherapy or psychoanalysis to provide the students, first, with an opportunity to achieve self-understanding through self-observation, studying their own emotional conflicts, the genesis and projection of such conflicts into present functioning; and, second, to liberate themselves sufficiently from personal problems and character disturbances that interfere with the establishment and maintenance of a therapeutic interpersonal relationship.

Should the supervisees be lacking in any of these basic requirements, the supervisor must help find ways of making up these deficiencies. (See Appendix L, for a form that supplies the supervisor with essential information.)

The Beginning Stages of Supervision

The first contact of the supervisor with the supervisees is in the nature of an exploratory talk. At this time there may be a discussion of the supervisees' preclinical training, and arrangements may be made as to the hours, frequency of visits, and the method of recording and presentation. The supervisees may be given preliminary orientation as to what will be involved in supervision and how supervisory sessions may best be used. Arrangements may be made for the handling with the supervisor of any emergency situations that may occur during the course of supervision.

In the early months of supervision, a period of disillusionment is to be anticipated. Supervisees will be brought face to face with practical problems in implementing therapy that may be at variance with what has been learned from books. Student therapists often are upset by the fact that the specific kinds of problems that provoke their patients may be precisely those that are disturbing to themselves. They may be exposed to certain situations that develop in treatment that have a violent impact on them and tax their own capacities for adjustment. It is incumbent upon the supervisor to extend to the supervisees during this period a good deal of warmth and understanding. The primary focus in early supervision is the relationship between supervisor and supervisees, since little progress will be possible until good rapport exists.

Later Phases of Supervision

In supervision the supervisor seeks to ascertain whether or not the supervisees are living up to their potential. If not, the sources of this lack must be diagnosed. For instance, the problem may relate to deficiencies in the kind of preclinical training received, or in the assimilation of educational materials presented in training. It may be due to an absence of perceptiveness or to insensitivity about what is going on in the therapeutic situation. It may be the product of personality problems that prevent the supervisees from establishing a meaningful contact with patients.

The areas in which supervisees need help will soon become apparent. In the main, technical problems break down into difficulties in diagnosis, conduct of the initial inverview, use of interviewing techniques, understanding of the operative dynamics, detection and handling of transference, awareness and mastery of countertransference, dealing with resistance, use of interpretations, and termination of therapy.

The task of the supervisor here is not to tell supervisees what to do but rather to teach them how to think through solutions for themselves. Toward this end, it will be essential to ask questions and to structure problems so that the supervisees can come to their own conclusions. Learning problems are to be diagnosed and handled along lines indicated previously. Modes of improving sensitivity are described by Fielding and Mogul (1970).

In the course of supervision, supervisees are bound to show transference manifestations. The supervisor will also have emotional attitudes toward the supervisees. Both positive and negative feelings will have to be subjected to close scrutiny to permit development of empathic yet objective attitudes. Furthermore, the supervisor will have to maintain a certain amount of tension in the supervisory sessions to expedite activity.

The beginning supervisor, particularly, may respond to supervision with untoward feelings. There may be a tendency to be pompous and overbearing and to overwhelm supervisees with material. The supervisor is apt to feel irritable when supervisees do not learn rapidly or defy suggestions and criticisms, even though these are offered in a constructive way. The supervisor may be provoked when there is persistence in errors that are so obvious that they scarcely need identification. Such attitudes on the part of the supervisor will, of course, interfere with learning. An honest self-questioning by the supervisor will often reveal tendencies that stifle the development of supervisees. It must be emphasized again that some countertransference is always present and that it need not be destructive to the teaching objective, provided that the supervisor is capable of understanding his or her feelings and of modifying and correcting them before they get out of control.

Disagreements between the supervisor and supervisees are inevitable, even desirable. All learning inspires resistance. Supervisees will voice protests in changing habitual patterns. They are bound to be critical. Actually, they cannot change unless they are given an opportunity to voice and to work through their criticisms. The

supervisor may be offended by such challenging reactions, but will best be able to respect the supervisees' right to their own opinions, realizing the unavoidable learning struggle that is involved.

Essential for learning is an open mind to new ideas. Some students have already settled their opinions about psychological theory and process and seal themselves off from fresh points of view. What they seek from the supervisor is a confirmation of their frozen ideologies. Similarly, there are supervisors so rigidly wedded to their credos that they insist on their students becoming a mirror image of themselves. Vital for learning in the supervisory process, then, are participants who are willing to collaborate, share experiences, and, if necessary, change. Students must be able to countenance exposure of deficiencies in psychotherapeutic performance. The supervisor must be able constructively to bring students to an awareness of these deficiencies and to provide students with an appropriate means of rectifying them.

Illustrative of some of the problems are the following comments of a supervisor:

I have a supervisee who is a chatterbox and who is highly defensive about any comment I make—even a casual comment on the dynamics is interpreted as a criticism of her. Her defense is to interrupt, challenge me, justify herself, etc., without permitting me to finish what I have to say. Often, by the end of the session, I find that I have been able to tell her very little. I have been debating with myself whether to take up the problem with her directly, which might merely provoke additional defensiveness, to pull back and tell her virtually nothing until she complains about it to me, or to go on as I have but being very supportive until she feels less threatened.

These are the remarks of a student:

The trouble with my supervisor is that he is constantly trying to force his point of view on me. I would think that he would know I can't do things exactly how he does them. I would like to have him help me work better with my good points and to help me eliminate my bad points. When I show him what I believe is a gain in my patient, he usually criticizes it as merely defensive, a new resistance.

In both of these illustrations effective learning is being blocked by problems that are influencing the relationship between student and supervisor. The supervisory encounter is far more complex than that of a simple teaching contingency. It embraces unconscious processes that may require mutual exploration. In any of the social sciences where professionals function as investigative or therapeutic tools, there are bound to be differences in theoretical assumptions and methodological approaches. These differences may interfere with the manner in which individuals communicate themselves to other professionals. Even within the same school, problems in communication may be vast. They are particularly annoying in the psychotherapeutic learning and teaching situation.

The supervisor is constantly involved in a process of self-analysis while relating to supervisees and examining personal reactions, both transferential and reality determined. There is recognition that students will be carrying out therapy with their own personalities and not with the personality of the supervisor. Students may not be able to perform exactly the way the supervisor performs, nor will students be able to deduce from interactions with patients all of the nuances that are apparent to the supervisor. A tremendous amount of tolerance and acceptance will be required from the supervisor that may tax the latter's patience and bring countertransference into play. Although the supervisor serves as a model for the student, it must be a flexible model and not one that demands a clone. These conditions should readily be acceptable to anyone who possesses the sophistication that is a prerequisite for becoming a supervisor, understanding from experience that there is no single accurate way of providing therapy. There are many ways. What can be taught is a broad framework of psychotherapy with a buttressing up of those elements of

the students' functioning that permit good therapeutic process, while expurgating interfering elements.

'Intensive' versus 'Technical' Supervision

In practice, two general types of psychotherapeutic supervision may be defined. The first type, "intensive" supervision, consists of the "continuous-case" type of reporting with a single patient, preferably from the initial interview to termination, using video recordings if possible. This enables the supervisor to help supervisees in all phases of treatment by observing operations with one patient over a long-term period. "Intensive" supervision is the most effective kind of teaching for beginning therapists.

The second type of supervision, arbitrarily called "technical" supervision, may be further divided into two subtypes. The first, or "case-load" supervision, which is usually prescribed especially for beginning therapists in a clinic, covers the general progress and specific difficulties being encountered in the entire case load of the supervisees. This might be considered a kind of administrative supervision. The second subtype, which we may, for want of a better name, call "special-problem" supervision, is handled in a manner similar to a clinical conference. Any pressing problem in diagnosis, psychodynamics, or technical management may be presented, and the discussion is centered around the specific difficulty encountered by the supervisees.

The latter kind of supervision is more highly advanced than other types and presupposes more experience on the part of the supervisees. It may also be effectively practiced in a group of no more than three or four therapists, who participate in the discussion with the supervisor. Each therapist may be given the privilege of presenting material on successive sessions. In practice, this proves to be a highly provocative teaching device, provided all the supervisees are on approximately the same level.

The Evaluation of the Supervisee

Evaluation is a means of helping supervisees develop skills through a continuous assay of strengths and weaknesses. As such, it becomes part of the teaching method, pointing to areas in which more development is needed and helping in a positive way to promote such development. Criteria of evaluation may be along the following lines:

1. Method of presentation, and recording ability.
2. Theoretic understanding.
3. Diagnostic ability.
4. Integration of theory into practice.
5. General therapeutic aptitudes, sensitivity, empathy, and capacity for critical thinking.
6. Kinds of relationships that the supervisees establish with patients and the skill in handling these relationships.
7. Type of relationship that the supervisees have with the supervisor and the use made of the sessions.
8. Types of relationships that the supervisees establish with colleagues and personnel of the clinic, if any, with which they are affiliated.
9. Supervisees' good points and special skills.
10. Supervisees' deficiencies.
11. General learning ability and the progress that has been made in learning.
12. Positive recommendations for increasing learning, including recommended readings, prescribed courses, and preferred kinds of cases to be assigned.

Yardsticks of expected progress have never been set. Arbitrarily, a rough gauge such as the following may be useful to indicate minimal levels of achievement:

End of first six months of supervision: Ability to make diagnoses, ability to keep patients in therapy.

End of first year: Ability to understand what promotes, aggravates, and helps emotional illness; capacity to establish good rapport with patients.

End of one and one-half years: Recognition of personal problems in therapeutic functioning.

End of second year: Ability to overcome most personal problems in therapeutic functioning.

End of two and one-half years: Ability to function without serious mistakes.

End of three years: Ability to do good psychotherapy.

Evaluation imposes burdens on both supervisor and supervisees. The supervisor may not want to criticize out of fear of hurting or offending the supervisees. The latter, in turn, may feel humiliated at having weak points exposed. The manner in which evaluation is presented, and the purpose for which it is used, will largely determine the reactions of the supervisees. If understanding is clear that there will be periodic evaluations, say every six months, to point out the areas in which the greatest or least development has been made, the experience can prove to be an aid to learning.

The evaluation conference may be set up in advance, and supervisees and supervisor may prepare their observations for mutual discussion and consideration. At the conference a common understanding must be reached. If a written evaluation must be sent to the head of a clinic or school, agreement on as many points as possible is best achieved in advance of sending the report.

The point at which the supervisor certifies the student therapists as competent to do psychotherapy will vary with the kind of therapy for which the students are being prepared. Table 61-1 shows an outline for evaluation for certification that has been

Table 61-1
Outline of Evaluation for Certification

Technical Skill	Personality of the Therapist	Direction of Growth and Promise	Supervisor-Supervisee Relationship	
1. Diagnostic skill.	1. Ways of relating to the patient.	1. Continuing ability to learn from patients.	1. Ease with which supervisor can work with supervisee.	Add any statement you wish to make about your evaluation.
a. Ability to establish diagnosis and tentative psychodynamics after one or two sessions with the patient.	a. Genuine interest in and empathy for the patient.	a. Continuing improvement in recognition of similarities and dissimilarities in various patients.		
b. After six weeks, the ability to describe the patient's character manifestations and how they will most likely work out in relation to the therapist.	b. Readiness and capacity to relate emotionally to the patient in a healthy way, that is,	b. Awareness that one does not know everything about the psychodynamics of one's patients (accepts the fact that one does not know all the answers).		
c. After six weeks, ability to write an organized case report including diagnosis, psychodynamics and estimate of rate of progress.	(1) To disengage from neurotic involvements.	2. Recognition of areas in which one is competent as well as those in which one needs to learn more.		
2. Treatment planning.	(2) Be aware when it is productive to express feelings, positive and negative.	3. Ability to develop own individual style without needlessly imitating an idealized supervisor.		
a. Formulation of a plan of treatment consistent with some theoretical orientation.	(3) Be able to estimate the attitudes and role that are assumed in the therapeutic sessions (awareness of roles that may hurt the patient, such as putting up a front, being managerial, rigid, detached, overconcerned, not showing respect).	4. Progressive diminution of countertransference reactions.		
b. Estimation of areas of difficulty.		5. Continuing interest in scientific problems of personality (diagnosis, prognosis, and psycho-		
c. Estimation of which stage of therapy a patient is in				

(continued)

Table 61-1 (*continued*)

Technical Skill	Personality of the Therapist	Direction of Growth and Promise	Supervisor-Supervisee Relationship
and formulation of what to do accordingly. d. Estimation of when the patient is ready to discuss transference. e. Judgment in management and timing of interpretations and communications. 3. Session-to-session handling of the patient. a. Perception and understanding of continuity and discontinuity of communications of the patient within a session and from session to session. b. Recognition of manifestations of resistance. c. Judgment about when to give ego support and ability to do so. 4. Skill in handling the middle phases of therapy. a. Judgment in the use of dreams in the best interests of the patient's therapy. b. Judgment in the use of transference in the patient's best interest. c. Awareness and use of countertransference. d. Ability to recognize acting-	c. Appraising factors in the previous experience of the patient. (1) Sorting out real hardships from neurotic ones in the life of the patient. (2) Appraising what might have gone on in a previous therapy. (3) Being alert to grievance collecting. d. Speaking in terms natural to the patient; using technical language only when necessary. e. Ability to use values judiciously, especially when therapist's value judgments differ from those of the patient. f. Ability to learn by mistakes. 2. Ways of relating to supervisor. a. Ability to communicate therapy sessions and problems meaningfully to the supervisor. b. Relative freedom from defensiveness in relation to what is going on in therapy with a patient.	dynamics) and psychotherapeutic techniques. 6. Estimate by supervisor(s) as to how the therapist will function when on his or her own and in a new status. a. Will the therapist continue in supervision or consult when there is a need? b. Will the therapist feel free to exchange problems with colleagues? 7. After certification will the therapist work in the community, such as teach, do research, work in some organization or clinical setting, or participate in professional activities?	

out and to help the patient recognize this either in what patient does in the session or between sessions, including the desire to terminate therapy prematurely.

5. Skill in handling emergencies, including the recognition of the severity of a crisis.

6. Skill in handling problems of termination.
   a. Recognition of when termination should be planned for.
   b. Preparation of the patient for this.

c. Respect for and honesty toward the supervisor.
d. Use of supervisory sessions in order to learn.
e. Tolerance for new point of view other than one's own.
f. Ability to discuss one's own evaluation in a mature way.

3. Ways of relating to the administration.
   a. Reliable in relation to requirements (e.g., paper work).
   b. Reliable in relation to class attendance.
   c. Reliable in making arrangements for supervision.
   d. Reliable in relation to patient load.
   e. Honesty in relation to administration.
   f. Reasonable consideration for clerical personnel.

4. Ways of relating to colleagues.
   a. Respect for colleagues in different disciplines.
   b. Ability to cooperate with colleagues on related cases (husband and wife, child and parent).
   c. Mature attitudes, in classroom and professional meetings, toward presenting of case material by colleagues.

used at the Postgraduate Center for Mental Health.

Administrative Responsibilities

If the supervisor and supervisees are associated with the same clinic, the supervisor will have further responsibilities. For instance, the supervisor may participate in an analysis of administrative or intake policies, making recommendations toward alteration of old, or the devising of new, policies. The object here is the elimination of influences that are destructive to the patients' therapy or to the therapists' functioning. If supervision is part of a school training program, the supervisor will also probably be engaged in an analysis of administrative and pedagogic procedures in the program. This will include methods of choice of students, modification of curricula, introduction of new courses, and proposed changes in instructors or instructional methods. Routine meetings among the supervisors, or between supervisors and the supervisory head, will cover discussion of such problems in detail, with the introduction of whatever current difficulties the supervisor is having with supervision and routine evaluations of the progress shown by the different supervisees.

SUPERVISION AS AN INTERPERSONAL RELATIONSHIP

The supervisory relationship is one to which supervisees react with mingled attitudes of admiration, jealousy, fear, and hostility. Admiration and jealousy are usually inspired by the supervisor's superior knowledge, training, and status. Fear of the supervisor is often the product of the therapists' helplessness in the face of an authority, who, they feel, may judge them unfairly and destroy their careers and livelihood in the event they fail to live up to expecta-

tions. Hostility issues from many sources. On the one hand, it is the product of dependency on the supervisor, which is especially inevitable at the beginning of supervision. Dependency yearnings that are mobilized are usually accompanied by expectations that these yearnings will be frustrated. Feelings of being victimized by these dependency needs, and the threats imposed by these needs on independence and assertiveness, inspire further resentment. The very acceptance of supervision implies to some supervisees a kind of subordination that imposes burdens on adjustment, particularly when independence has become the keynote in the students' life struggles. The supervisees, in addition, resent demands that they believe the supervisor makes on them. The restrictions imposed on the students, the criticisms directed at their functioning, deliver blows to their narcissism and contribute to further fears of loss of self.

Supervision will thus produce feelings in the supervisees that are related to neurotic attitudes toward authority. Difficulties may come out openly in the form of verbalizations or behavioral acting-out. They may also be concealed behind a barrage of defenses that reflect supervisees' habitual covert patterns in their dealings with authority.

The supervisor, in turn, will respond in supervision with untoward feelings toward the supervisees, many of which are the product of neurotic attitudes toward subordinates. In a flush of omnipotence, a patronizing attitude may be displayed toward the supervisees, with presentation of ideas as if they were irrevocable pronouncements. Contempt may be expressed for the relatively inferior knowledge, skill, or status of the supervisees. Hostility may appear when supervisees challenge the supervisor's opinions or theories. The growth or advance of the supervisees may be resented from a desire to keep them on a subordinate level, in an effort to preserve superiority.

Accordingly, successes of the supervisees may be threatened with chariness of praise, so important in learning. Such attitudes are rarely expressed directly. They may be cloaked in solicitous, ingratiating behavior with overkindliness and overattentiveness. Or they may show up as disinterest, offering the supervisees little help or reassurance. Searles (1955) and Benedek (1972) have written on the use of the supervisor's feelings and "intuition" as a way of gaining understanding into the problems of supervisees.

The supervisory process will thus arouse varied feelings and attitudes in both supervisor and supervisees that are inimical to learning. Sufficient resolution of such deterrants must occur before progress is possible. As a general rule, assuming that the participants are mature people capable of facing their feelings and communicating with one another, differences should be satisfactorily resolved. Problems may persist in some cases, however.

The supervisor may be tentative, indecisive, irritable with the students, overprotective, and patronizing, all of which put a damper on the students' need to express criticism and verbalize doubts. Lack of interest in the students and their growth acts as a damper to learning.

In supervisees, character problems show up in the form of many resistances, some of which persist with an amazing tenacity. Among these are attitudes of conformity and a seeming absorption of every gesture and utterance of the supervisor. This spurious kind of admiration is accompanied by a constant repetition of mistakes, as if all knowledge is shed immediately after leaving the supervisor's office. There may be a continuing fear of losing one's independence by yielding to the supervisor's dictates and demands. Resisting learning then becomes for the supervisees a means of retaining identity.

Another kind of resistance is the need to dominate and to take control by out-su-

pervising the supervisor. In such cases, the supervisees overwhelm the supervisor with material, edit reports—even falsifying material—to impress the supervisor. Belittling and derisive attitudes and feelings may exist toward the supervisor that are only indirectly expressed and that serve to protect the supervisees from fancied exploitation and injury.

On the other hand, those supervisees with many personal problems may become so terrified about what is happening in the relationship with the supervisor as to seek reassurance, affection, and support in sundry ways. One way is to become helpless and hopeless, assume a defenseless attitude, and seek from the supervisor various panaceas for difficulties. In making such demands, the student-therapist may express lack of confidence in resolving developing problems in an attempt to force the supervisor to shoulder all obligation for decisions. Self-devaluation may follow in the wake of this attitude, much of which is an effort to avoid criticism and to forestall responsibility.

Resistance to learning may also be expressed in the form of hostility. The patterns that hostility takes are legion, depending upon the individuals' habitual modes of dealing with this emotion. When supervisees find it hard to express rage, their response may be depression and discouragement. One individual may seek to terminate supervision on the basis that he is completely incapable of learning. Another may mask her hostility with dependence, with feigned amiability, and with strong gestures to force the relationship with the supervisor into social channels. In instances where the student-therapist is capable of expressing her hostility openly, she may become defiant, challenging, and overcritical. She may develop feelings of being exploited, misunderstood, and humiliated, and she may attempt to find evidence for these feelings by misinterpreting what goes on between herself and the supervisor. She may become suspicious about the supervisor's abilities, training, and personal adjustment. She may enter into active competition with the supervisor, bringing in materials, quotations, and references from authoritative works to challenge the supervisor or to nullify suggestions the latter has made. In some instances, the supervisee may actually become uncooperative, negativistic, and even defiant. In other instances, hostility is masked by apathy and detachment. Here one will get the impression that the supervisee, while presenting material and listening to the comments of the supervisor, is mentally "off in the clouds."

Supervisees may also try to ward off the supervisor by discursive talk about superficial topics or by self-interpretations that are expressed with great vehemence. This attempt to disarm the supervisor by spurts of productivity has little corrective value for the supervisees, since it is motivated by an effort to belittle the supervisor rather than to learn.

Other resistances take the form of an inability to think clearly and an incapacity to express one's ideas. There may be an insistence by the supervisees that there is great development that is not supported by facts, and though self-confidence and assertiveness may be expressed, these will be found to be without substance. Another defense is an attempt to seduce the supervisor with gifts, lavish praise, and compliments. The overvaluation of the abilities of the supervisor may be boundless, and an unwary supervisor is apt to respond to these devices with omnipotent feelings.

Assuming that the supervisor is capable of controlling or of resolving countertransference, can help be rendered the supervisees to overcome such varied resistances to the supervisory relationship?

One must remember that supervision is a student–teacher, rather than a patient–therapist, relationship. Emotional problems stirred up in supervisees during work with patients cannot entirely be handled by the supervisor in the setting of supervision. Although the outcome of supervision may be therapeutic for supervisees, the goal is toward more adequate functioning in psychotherapy rather than the helping of personal neurotic difficulties. Naturally, the supervisor does point out neurotic problems that express themselves in resistance to learning and in countertransference in the hope of dispelling blocks in functioning. Since some of the problems that supervisees experience with the supervisor may be similar to those being experienced with their patients, working them out with the supervisor is bound to have some salubrious effect on overall therapeutic functioning. It is assumed that most supervisees have had sufficient personal psychotherapy, or are sufficiently integrated emotionally, to be able to resolve blocks through their own resources in the supervisory setting. The supervisor will have to handle those aspects of feeling and attitude that impede the acquisition of therapeutic skills. This experience, as has been mentioned, may prove itself to be therapeutic for supervisees, but, if this occurs, it is a byproduct of the chief objective—the learning of psychotherapy. Should the supervisor's effort to help supervisees resolve difficulties fail, referral for personal psychotherapy may be advisable, which the supervisor may also benefit from receiving if personal problems in the existing relationship with particular supervisees cannot be worked through. In the event mutual trust and respect do not develop between supervisor and certain supervisees and no progress in learning has occurred after these avenues have been tried, transfer to another supervisor may be necessary.

These difficulties are not uncommon in a school or clinic. They are attenuated, though not entirely obliterated, when a therapist in private practice chooses and pays for a supervisor who does not need to render reports to the school or clinic.

Among the recommended readings on

supervision are Alonson (1935), Arlow (1963), Blumenfield (1982), Caligor (1983), Collins (1962), DeBell (1963), Ekstein and Wallerstein (1958), Fleming (1961, 1963, 1967), Fleming and Benedek (1966), Grinberg (1970), Grotjahn (1955), Hess (1980), Kris (1956), Langer et al. (1964), Langs (1979), Schuster (1972), Solnit (1970), Steinhelber (1984), Szasz (1958), Towle (1954), and Windholz (1970).

62
Questions Therapists Ask About Psychotherapy

Sundry questions plague the individual doing psychotherapy. Answers to these questions are not easily provided, since there are many ways of accomplishing the same task in psychotherapy, some of which are suitable for one therapist and wholly inappropriate for another. In this chapter a number of common questions, posed by therapists participating in case seminars conducted by the writer, and not answered completely in the text of this book, are considered. The answers given to these questions are, of course, not absolute and will require modification in terms of the individual's unique experience and specific style of working.

Q. If a patient attacks you verbally at the initial interview, how would you handle the situation?

A. An aggressive outburst in the first interview is clearly an indication of great insecurity or fear in the patient. Patients will generally rationalize the hostility on one basis or another. A way of handling the situation is to accept the patients' hostility and to inform the patients that under the circumstances, you do not blame them for being angry. As a matter of fact, it would be difficult for them to feel any other way. If possible, an effort should be made to bring the meaning of the aggressive outburst to the patients' awareness. If this can be done, it may alleviate their tension and initiate more positive feelings toward the therapist.

Q. How do you handle patients who come to see you while they are being treated by another therapist?

A. This situation occasionally happens and will have to be managed diplomatically. There are a number of reasons why patients find it necessary to consult a second therapist. They may be in a state of resistance, and their visit constitutes an attempt at escape from, or a gesture of hostility toward, their therapists. Or the patients may sense that they are unable to relate to their therapists, or that their therapists are unable to relate to them, and they are reaching out for a new, better therapeutic relationship. In either instance, one must respectfully listen to the patients and focus particularly on the specific meaning of their consultation with you. Under no circumstances should one participate in criticism of the other therapists, no matter what outlandish activities are ascribed to them by the patient. On the contrary, one should be alerted to transference manifestations and attempt to clarify any misconceptions or irrational attitudes about the patients' therapists that present themselves. The ultimate result of the interview may be emotionally cathartic for patients, and they may return to their therapists with insight into their resistance. Should there be reason for your considering treating the patients, and if they had not informed their therapists about the prospective consultation with you, it will be important to emphasize the need to discuss the situation with their therapists. The patients may be told that for ethical reasons it will be impossible to start treatments with them unless both they and their therapists agree that a transfer is indicated. In the event the patients have, when they consult you, discontinued treatment with their therapists, the visit may, of course, be conducted as an initial interview.

Q. Is it permissible to treat one's friends or relatives?

A. It is extremely difficult to be therapeutically objective with friends and relatives. Nor will they be able to establish the proper kind of relationship with you. For these reasons, if they need treatment they are best referred to another therapist.

Q. How far can the therapist go in making interpretations at the beginning of therapy?

A. An experienced therapist may discern important dynamics in the first interview or shortly thereafter. To interpret these to patients may be harmful. A strategic moment must be waited for—which may come many months later—before revealing to patients what the therapist already knows. New therapists, in their enthusiasm, frequently violate this rule, as do experienced therapists with strong narcissistic leanings who attempt to demonstrate to patients how much they know about them.

Q. What causes violent feelings that are stirred up in patients after the first interview?

A. These may be caused by transference or by something the therapist has done in error.

Q. Are mistakes that a therapist makes in psychotherapy irretrievably destructive?

A. Even the most experienced psychotherapist makes mistakes in the conduct of therapy. There are many reasons for this, including the fact that the therapeutic relationship is so complex that the therapist cannot see all of its facets. Such mistakes are not too important if the working relationship with patients is a good one.

Q. Are the various psychotherapeutic approaches ever used together?

A. Practically all forms of psychotherapy purposefully or inadvertently employ a combination of approaches. Even in formal psychoanalysis one may, at times, be unable to avoid suggestion and reassurance. Persuasive and other supportive influences may by design enter into insight therapy from time to time, and disturbing environmental factors may deliberately have to be handled in order to promote maximal progress. Wittingly or unwittingly, then, no approach is used in isolation. Rather, it is blended with other approaches, made necessary on occasion by the exigencies of the therapeutic situation.

Q. Does one ever start off using one approach and then, in the course of treatment, switch over to another approach?

A. This is very frequently the case. One may start off with an approach aimed at a supportive or palliative goal. In the course of treatment it may become apparent that no real improvement will be possible unless one deals with underlying causative factors. One will consequently have to motivate the patient toward accepting therapy aimed at more extensive goals. On the other hand, one may begin reconstructive treatment and, in the course of administering this, discover that circumstances make less extensive goals desirable. A supportive approach may therefore become advisable.

Q. Should patients be required to pay for their own treatment?

A. Some patients will get more out of therapy if they feel in some way responsible for its payment. This does not mean that they will not benefit from treatment financed for them if they cannot afford it. With the increasing incidence of third-party payments (insurance, Medicare, Medicaid), a considerable body of experience shows that good psychotherapy is possible even though patients do not pay for it themselves. In child and adolescent therapy, parents or guardians assume responsibility for fees, and this fact does not denigrate the therapeutic effort. When therapy is given free, and no payment is made for it by any party, some patients are handicapped in expressing any feelings toward the therapist that they believe will cause offense. A perceptive therapist can detect this reluctance and deal with it to promote freedom of expression.

Q. How is the matter of fees best handled?

A. The matter of setting a fee satisfactory to both therapist and patient, and of agreeing on the manner in which payments are to be made, is part of the reality that therapy imposes on patients. Many therapists gauge their fees according to patients' ability to pay. In setting a fee, it is important that the therapist consider the patient's capacity to carry the financial responsibility over the estimated treatment period. Unless this is done, both therapist and patients will find themselves in a difficult situation later on. Though grading the patients' fees according to the patients' ability to pay over the estimated time period of treatment, the therapist must be assured that the fee is adequate. Should the therapist accept a fee too low to meet personal obligations, the therapist will feel insecure. Resentment or anxiety may occur that will impose a destructive influence on the therapeutic relationship. Once a fee is set, it is difficult and unfair to raise it unless patients' financial situation has improved. Often a neurotic problem interferes with the work capacity and productivity of patients. At the start of therapy, patients' earning ability will therefore be minimal. Once therapy gets under way, patients may be able to earn a great deal more money. Under such circumstances, discussing with them the raising of a fee is justifiable, and an adjustment of fees upward usually will be acceptable. On the other hand, financial reverses may occur during the course of therapy. In such instances a reduction of fee may be required.

Q. What do you do when patients neglect payment of fees?

A. Lack of punctuality in the payment of fees may be a manifestation of temporary financial shortage, a problem related to money or to giving, or an indication of resentment toward, and desire to frustrate the therapist. Should patients disregard the payment of bills for a considerable period, the matter may merit inquiry and therapeutic handling. If the therapist has neurotic problems in relation to money, he or she may evidence marked anxiety when payments are not being made on time. The therapist may consequently tend to overemphasize the importance of punctuality in payments and may introduce the matter of finances completely out of context with the material that concerns the patients. On the other hand, the therapist may be negligent on the matter of payments and may fail to bring to the patients' awareness possible avoidance of a responsibility that is part of reality. Unless justified by financial reverses, the accumulation of a debt creates hardships for patients that may be harmful to their relationships with the therapist.

Q. If you discover that patients' finances are greater than those reported at the beginning of therapy, would you boost the fee?

A. Financial arrangements with patients may have been made on the basis of a reported low income. If patients have purposefully concealed their finances from the therapist, this deception will, in all probability, later create guilt and tension. The therapist may assure patients that there must have been reasons for falsification of income. Understandably, careful handling is necessary to avoid mobilizing further guilt. In the event the set fees require adjustment because of patients' larger income, this matter must be discussed thoroughly with the patients, no change of fees being made except on mutual agreement. If the patients' fees are arbitrarily raised without their complete cooperation, grave difficulties may be anticipated in the therapeutic relationship.

Q. Should the therapist ever visit patients in their home?

A. Only in the event of a crisis or serious incapacitating illness or accident when it is impossible for the patients to come to the therapist's office and when it is urgent to administer psychotherapy.

Q. What do you do when patients talk too much and don't allow the therapist to speak?

A. If patients are focused on an important area and doing good therapeutic work, one does not interrupt. If they are talking about irrelevant things or their rambling seems to be resistance, one interrupts and focuses on pertinent topics. If this does not help, one may question the reason for rambling, or perhaps attempt its interpretation.

Q. Is there not a similarity between friendship and a working relationship?

A. Only peripherally. The therapeutic relationship is a professional one. Implicit in it is the absolute promise of confidentiality, the recognition that the time span is a limited one, and that termination of the relationship will eventually come about.

Q. What do you do if patients have been in negative transference for a long time and this continues no matter what the therapist does?

A. First the therapist might undertake self-examination to see if he or she is provoking these feelings. If the therapist is sure there is nothing in the therapeutic situation that is stirring up the patient, analysis of possible projections by the patients into the present relationship of negative attitudes toward important past personages may be undertaken. If this does not help, the therapist may go back to the first phase of therapy and actively try again to establish a working relationship with the patients.

Q. What is the relative merit of focusing on past, as compared with present life difficulties in reconstructive therapy?

A. In reconstructive psychotherapy, some controversy exists as to the relative importance of material that deals with the past and material relating to the present. Extremists of both points of view argue the merits of their particular emphasis. On the one hand, there are those who regard the present problems of individuals as a peripheral product of personality disturbances arising out of insecurities in childhood. These insecurities have undermined self-esteem and blanketed sexual and aggressive drives with a mantle of anxiety. Environmental difficulties and current situational distortions stir up hardships for individuals by agitating past problems. Dealing with provocative current situations may restore the individuals' equilibrium. This stability is, however, precarious due to the continued operation of immature strivings. Although harmony may be reconstituted, the recurrence of environmental stress will promote a new breakdown in adaptation. It is fruitless, therefore, always to concentrate on the present since the roots of the difficulty, imbedded in the past history, will remain firmly entrenched. On the other hand, there are therapists who are opposed to an emphasis on the past. It is claimed that individuals repeat in present-day patterns their important childhood disturbances. A concern with the present must of necessity involve a consideration of the past. To discuss the past in detail results in a mere raking over of dead historical ashes; though interesting material may be exposed, it may bear little relationship to current happenings. A dichotomy may then be set up between the past and the present, without unifying the two. As irreconcilable as these two viewpoints appear, they are not so disparate as the proposed arguments would seem to indicate. In psychotherapeutic practice one constantly uses current life experiences as vehicles for discussion, for it is in the present that individuals live and feel. Yet, a consideration of the past is mandatory in understanding what is happening in the present. Current life experiences may be regarded as reflecting the past through the use of present-day symbols. It is therefore necessary to blend the past and the present and to focus on whichever element is of immediate importance.

Q. Is it ever permissible to assign "homework" to patients?

A. This can be very rewarding, particularly if patients are not too productive and do not work industriously at therapy. Asking them to keep a kind of diary, writing out their reactions, observations, and dreams between sessions, may get them to approach treatment more seriously. Each interview may be organized around discerning and exploring basic patterns that are revealed in the patients' notes or observations. Patients should leave every session with a general problem to focus on until next session. They may then work on this problem, observing themselves and their reactions, noting which environmental or interpersonal situations tend to aggravate or moderate it. This "homework" may catalyze the patients' thinking and get them to assume more responsibility for treatment.

Q. If patients want information about a subject like sex, do you give it to them?

A. First find out why they ask for information and then give it to them or assign appropriate reading.

Q. Should all patients have a physical examination prior to psychotherapy?

A. All patients about to enter psychotherapy should have a good physical examination and, if the practioner deems necessary, a thorough neurological examination performed by a competent neurologist. The findings will be negative in the vast majority of patients, but the occasional case of early cancer, brain tumor, or other operable maladies that are detected will justify the precaution of routine physicals.

Q. How would you handle patients who appear to have read just about everything on the subject of psychiatry and keep citing the opinions of different authorities that may or may not agree with your point of view?

A. Some patients may have read more on psychiatry than you, but this does not mean that they have integrated what they have read. As a matter of fact, they will probably tend to use the knowledge they have gained in resistance, by intellectualizing what goes on, or by criticizing the technique or formulations of the therapist. At some point in therapy it may be necessary to mention to such patients that, while their reading has given them a good deal of information, this information may be a hindrance to therapy rather than a help. No two problems of an emotional nature are alike, and facts patients have read applying to other people surely do not exactly apply to themselves. They can be fair to themselves only by observing their feelings and attitudes, without speculating what these must be like on the basis of readings. Sometimes it may be necessary to be very blunt and to tell patients that it is important for them to forget what they have read since this seems to interfere with their spontaneity.

Q. What do you do when patients ask a question the therapist is unable to answer?

A. The therapist may say that the question cannot be answered at this time but will be later when the answer becomes more clear.

Q. Is it ever justifiable to lie to patients?

A. Lies eventually reveal themselves and shatter the patients' trust and confidence in the therapist. Truthfulness is, consequently, the keynote in therapy. In an effort to be truthful, however, one should not reveal things to patients that may be harmful to them. It may be essential, therefore, if their security and health are menaced, to avoid answering certain questions directly. If, for instance, patients show symptoms of an impending psychosis, and are dangerously tottering between sanity and mental illness, and if they are frightened by the upsurge of archaic unconscious material to a point where they believe themselves to be insane, it may be harmful to tell them that they are approaching a psychosis. Rather, they may, if they question the therapist, be told that their preoccupation with becoming insane is more important then the symptoms they manifest. These are evidence of great insecurity. Whenever the patients asks a direct question, an honest answer to which may be upsetting in view of existing ego weaknesses, the patients may be asked why they ask this question, and their concern may be handled without upsetting them with a straight reply. It is important to remember that truthfulness must not be confused with necessary caution in divulging information and interpreting prematurely. If patients are insistent on a complete answer to their questions, it may be helpful to point out that therapy involves a mutual inquiry into a problem and an avoidance of premature judgments. One must patiently wait until enough evidence is available before being certain of one's observations. The answer to questions will soon become evident, both to the patients and to the therapist. If for any reason the patients cannot perceive the truth, the therapist will point out why it is difficult for them to understand what is happening. The patients will eventually develop confidence in the fact that the truth will not be withheld but that ideas must be checked and double-checked for their validity before they can be communicated.

Q. Sometimes it is necessary to break an appointment with patients. How can this best be done?

A. Appointments should, if possible, never be broken without adequate notice being given to the patients. Unless this is done, the relationship may be injured and a great deal of work may be necessary to undo the damage. If circumstances make it necessary to break an appointment, the therapist or the therapist's secretary should telephone the patients, explain that an emergency has developed that necessitates a a revision of the therapist's schedule, and that, consequently, it will be necessary to make a new appointment or to skip the present appointment. In instances where the therapist is ill, or expects to be away from the practice for an indefinite period, patients may be informed that the therapist will get in touch with them shortly to set up a new appointment. If a reasonable explanation is given, there will probably be no interference with the working relationship.

Q. How would you handle patients' resentment because you do not keep appointments on time?

A. The patients' resentment may be justified. Because of ambivalent feelings, patients usually have difficulties trusting any human being completely. The therapist must, therefore, give patients as little basis for distrust as possible, always explaining the reasons for unavoidable irregularities in appointment times so patients will not assume that the therapist is irresponsible. Giving patients an allotted amount of time is part of a reality to which both patients and therapist must adjust. When appointments are forgotten by the therapist, or patients have to sit around and wait for the therapist because the therapist has not finished with a preceding patient, resentments will develop that may interfere with therapy. Of course, there will be occasions when the therapist cannot help being late for a session. Emergencies with a preceding patient may develop, and the therapist may have to run over in time into the next session. Under such circumstances an explanation must be given patients to the effect that an emergency occurred that could not be avoided and that necessitated a delay in starting the session. To impress on patients the fact that they are not being exploited, they may be told also that time taken from their sessions will be made up. In the event a mistake has been made in patients' appointments, and the patients appears for their session at a time allotted to another patient, they must be taken aside and given an explanation to the effect that an unfortunate error in scheduling has occurred that resulted in the patients' being given the wrong appointment time. Another appointment should then be given the patients, during which any resentment resulting from the errors may be handled.

Q. If you are unable to understand what is going on dynamically in a case you are treating, what do you do?

A. Occasions will arise when the therapist may be unable to discern exactly what is going on in treatment. Should this continue for long, it may be indicative of such blocks as unyielding resistance in the patients or of countertransference. In either instance, where the therapist is disturbed by what is happening or where progress is blocked, one or more supervisory sessions with an experienced psychotherapeutic supervisor may be helpful in resolving the difficulty.

Q. When do you increase the frequency of sessions?

A. During the course of therapy it may be necessary to increase the number of sessions weekly for the following reasons: (1) an upsurge of intense anxiety, depression, or hostility that the patients cannot themselves control; (2) violent intensification of symptoms; (3) severe resistance that interferes with progress; (4) negative transference; (5) unrestrained acting-out that requires checking; (6) threats of shattering of the ego unless constant support is given; and (7) when the therapist wishes to stimulate transference to the point of creating a transference neurosis.

Q. When would you decrease the number of sessions weekly?

A. A decrease in the number of weekly sessions is indicated (1) when patients are becoming too dependent on the therapist, (2) when alarming transference reactions are developing which one wishes to subdue, (3) when patients have a tendency to substitute transference reactions for real life experiences, and (4) when patients have progressed sufficiently in therapy so that they can carry on with a diminished number of visits.

Q. How important is adhering to the exact time of a session?

A. From the standpoint of scheduling, adhering to a set time may be necessary. The usual time is between 45 to 60 minutes. But shorter spans, as low as 15 minutes, can be effective in some patients, and certain situations can arise that require extending the scheduled time.

Q. Is advice-giving taboo in reconstructive therapy?

A. Generally. One must keep working on the patients' resistances to the solving of their own problems. The ultimate aim is self-assertiveness rather than reliance on the therapist. On rare occasions, however, advice-giving may be unavoidable.

Q. Should the therapist ever insist on patients' engaging in a specific course of action?

A. Only when it is absolutely necessary that patients execute it and its rationale is fully explained to and accepted by patients.

Q. Should the therapist ever try to forbid patients from making crucial decisions during therapy?

A. Although important changes in life status, like divorce or marriage, may best be delayed until patients have achieved stability and greater personality maturity, it is obviously difficult for the therapist to "forbid" patients to make any decisions. Patients may be reminded that it is important not to take any drastic steps in altering their life situations without discussing these thoroughly with the therapist. If the therapist believes the decisions to be neurotic, the decisions may be questioned, presenting interpretations if necessary. In the event patients decide, nevertheless, to go through with a move that is obviously impetuous, it means that they are still at the mercy of neurotic forces they cannot control, that their insight is not yet sufficiently developed, or that they have to defy or challenge the therapist. The therapist may have no other alternative than to let patients make a mistake, provided the patients realize that they have acted on their own impulses. It is important not to reject patients or to communicate resentment toward them for having made a move against advice. Only when patients are about to take a really destructive or dangerous step is the therapist justified in actively opposing it.

Q. What do you do if patients bring in written material for you to discuss?

A. Occasional written material may be important, but if large quantities are brought in, this practice should be discouraged.

Q. What would you do if patients refuse to talk spontaneously session after session but offer to write out their ideas?

A. If this is the only way patients will communicate, it should be accepted. An attempt must be made, however, to handle the patients' resistance to talk at the same time that they are encouraged to bring in written comments.

Q. What do you do if patients say they fear they will kill someone?

A. One should not reassure the patients or minimize what they say. Rather, they may be told that there are reasons why they feel so upset that they believe that they will kill someone. They may then be encouraged to explore their impulses and fears. If the patients are psychotic or destructively dangerous, hospitalization may be required. If acting-out is likely, the intended victim should be notified.

Q. Should the therapist permit patients to express hostility or aggression openly in the therapeutic situation?

A. Any overt behavioral expressions of hostility or aggression are forbidden, although verbalization of these emotions or impulses is permissible, even indispensable.

Q. Do you ever reassure patients during insight therapy?

A. Reassurance should be kept at a minimum. Gross misconceptions, however, will require reassuring correction, or patients may be in an emotional crisis which needs mitigation. Reassurance should never be given patients when they are in a negativistic state, since this may produce an effect opposite to what is intended.

Q. Are fleeting suicidal thoughts arising in patients during treatment important?

A. Suicidal thoughts are not uncommon during therapy. They often serve a defensive purpose, acting as a kind of safety valve. Vague ideas of suicide may be entertained as a way of ultimate escape from suffering in the event life should become too intolerable. In most instances such ideas are fleeting and are never put into practice no matter how bad conditions become. They are handled therapeutically in the same way that any fantasy or idea might be managed. It is important not to convey undue alarm when patients talk about suicide as an escape fantasy. To do so will frighten patients or cause them to use suicidal threats against the therapist as a form of resistance. Rather, the therapist may listen respectfully to patients and then state simply that there may be other ways out of their situation than suicide. Suicide is an irrevocable act. More suitable ways of coping with the situation will present themselves as they explore their difficulty. If, however, the patients have, in the past, made attempts at suicide, fleeting suicidal thoughts must be taken very seriously. A careful watch is indicated since the attempt may be repeated. Any evidence of hopelessness or resentment that cannot be expressed as such must be explored and resolved if it is possible to do so. Should resolution be impossible and should the danger of suicide continue to lurk, hospitalization may be required. Suicidal thoughts in patients who are deeply depressed must be considered as dangerous, and the patients must be handled accordingly.

Q. What do you do when patients you are treating telephone and insist on seeing you that very day?

A. If possible, this request should be respected, provided the situation is an emergency. Should the therapist be unable to arrange for an appointment, or for a partial appointment, a promise may be made to telephone the patients at a specified time that day to discuss the situation with them. As early an appointment as possible may be arranged.

Q. What would you say to those patients who ask whether they may telephone or write to you whenever they desire?

A. Lack of time will obviously make it difficult for the therapist to answer telephone calls or to read all the material that patients wish to communicate in writing. The therapist may handle a request on the part of patients to telephone by saying simply that it is much better to take up matters during a session, since the limited time

available during telephone conversations may create more problems than are solved. In response to excessive written communications, the therapist may remark that verbalization is to be preferred to writing. Patients may be informed that when emergencies occur, they may feel free to telephone the therapist. If a crisis has developed, patients may be given specific times at which they may call or may be told that the therapist will telephone them at a certain hour. It is usually best to keep such telephone calls at a minimum and to increase the sessions of the patients should a more intensive contact be required.

Q. How would you handle patients who are insistent that you inform them of your whereabouts at all times so that they can get in touch with you?

A. One would deal with this the way any other symptom in a neurosis would be handled. Patients may be told that it is important to find out why they need to know the therapist's whereabouts. It may be that they feel so helpless and insecure that they must be convinced that the therapist will not desert them or deny them help in the event of a catastrophe. Patients may be assured that the therapist will, in the instance of a real emergency, always be happy to talk with them but that it is important to understand what is behind the patients' insecurity in order that they be able to overcome their feelings of helplessness.

Q. In the event patients in psychoanalysis who have been using the couch position manifest anxiety and ask to sit up, would you encourage this?

A. Anxiety may be the product of penetration of unconscious material into preconsciousness, or it may indicate a feeling of isolation from or a fear of the therapist. Encouraging patients to continue their verbal associations on the couch may enable them to gain awareness of important feelings or conflicts. If anxiety becomes too great, however, their request to assume the sitting-up, face-to-face position should be granted. This will generally permit a restoration of stability, especially if supportive measures are coordinately employed.

Q. Should patients be encouraged to use the couch in psychotherapy?

A. In most cases this is not indicated or advisable. The possible exception is in formal psychoanalysis in which free association is employed.

Q. What do you do when patients have reached a stalemate in therapy? They are com-

pletely unproductive, and any attempts of the therapist to mobilize activity and to resolve resistance fail.

A. Group therapy with alternate individual sessions often stimulates activity, as may several sessions of hypnosis or narcotherapy. Continued resistance may justify a vacation from therapy, or, as a last resort, transfer to another therapist.

Q. When is psychotherapy likely to become interminable?

A. Patients whose personalities have been so damaged in early childhood that their personalities have never allowed for a satisfactory gratification of needs or for an adequate defense against stress may feel they require a continuing dependent relationship to function. Transference here is organized around maneuvering the therapist into a parental role. There is strong resistance to a more mature relationship. If the therapist enters into the patient's design, due to needs to play parent, therapy is apt to become interminable.

Q. What does dreaming indicate when it becomes so excessive that it takes up the entire session?

A. If patients deluge the therapist with dreams, the therapist should suspect that the dreams are being used as resistance, perhaps to divert the therapist from other important material.

Q. Which dreams that patients present should one consider of great importance?

A. Repetitive dreams and those with an anxiety content may be of great importance.

Q. What do you do when patients constantly bring up important material several minutes before the end of a session, leaving no time to discuss it?

A. This is usually a manifestation of anxiety. It may be handled by mentioning to patients the fact that the material they have brought up sounds important and should be discussed at the next session. If patients do not spontaneously bring it up, the therapist may do so, handling whatever resistances arise.

Q. How would you handle parents who bring a child to you for therapy, and you are impressed by the fact that the parent needs treatment more than does the child?

A. It may be important to determine how much motivation the parents have for therapy and their level of understanding. Should the parents be unaware of how they participate in the child's neurosis, it may be necessary to inform them that the treatment of their child will require

seeing the parents also, both to determine what is going on at home and to help the parents understand how to handle developing problems. In this way the parents themselves may be brought into a treatment situation.

Q. Are interviews of any value with the patients' families or with other people important to adult patients?

A. The therapist may frequently get information from people close to patients that the patients themselves has been unable to convey. Often a conference reveals distortions in the patients' attitudes and behavior that are not based on reality. One or more interviews with important family members may thus be useful. Furthermore, if patients are unable to correct disturbed environmental situations by themselves, the cooperation of a related person as an accessory may be helpful. If patients are reacting destructively to a relative who then responds in a counterdestructive manner, if demands on patients by relatives are stirring up problems in the patients, if relatives are opposing patients' therapy—and it is obvious, help, financial and other, is needed—an interview with the relative, aimed at the clarification of these issues, may yield many dividends. These relatives may require reassurance to neutralize their guilt about the patients. Sometimes relatives can be prepared for contingencies that may arise in therapy, such as rebelliousness and hostility directed at them by the patients. An explanation that such occurrences are inevitable in treatment, and that they are part of the process of getting well, may forestall retaliatory gestures. The patients' needs for independence and assertiveness may be explained for the benefit of relatives who unwittingly overprotect the patients. Statements to the effect that the patients will get worse before they get better and that it will require time before results are apparent often prevent discouragement and feelings of hopelessness among concerned relatives. Because a therapeutically induced change in the patients' attitudes brought about by therapy may impose new and unaccustomed burdens on people with whom the patients live or associate, preparing these people for the change may avoid a crisis. An interpretation of the patients' actions in dynamic terms will often relieve relatives' guilt and lessen their resentment. For instance, if an adolescent is beginning to act cantankerous and resistive, an explanation to the parent that this behavior is to be expected at the patient's time of life, as a gesture toward cutting the umbilical cord of dependency, that all adolescents are often difficult to live with, and that parents are bound to feel resentful at the behavior of their offspring, may foster greater tolerance. Or a wife distraught at her husband's inattentiveness may be helped to realize that her spouse is responding not specifically to her as a person, but rather to her as a symbol of some actual past or fantasied personage against whom the patient had to build a wall of detachment. This insight may help avoid the creation of the very situations that would drive her husband deeper into isolation.

Q. How would you approach patients should you decide a conference with a relative is necessary?

A. The patients may be told that in psychotherapy the therapist may want to have an occasional conference with a relative or other person close to the patients. The purpose is to get to know the relatives and their attitudes. Following this, the therapist may say, "I wonder how you would feel if I thought it necessary to talk with _____ [*mentioning name of person*]?" The patients may acquiesce; they may question the need for such a conference; or they may refuse indignantly to permit it. If patients are insistent that no contact be made, their desire should be respected. Important material concerning the relative will undoubtedly be forthcoming and may constitute the material of later interviews.

Q. If an interview with family members or other significant people is decided on, are there any rules one should follow?

A. Experience has shown that a number of precautions are necessary when it is decided to contact the family. First, the patients' consent should always be obtained, the only exception being where they are dangerously psychotic or suicidal. Second, confidential material revealed by patients must never be divulged, since the breach of confidence will usually be flaunted at the patients even if the relatives promise to keep the revelations to themselves. Third, in talking to the relatives or friends, the therapist will often have a temptation to blame, to scold, or to enjoin them to change their ways or attitudes toward the patient. Distraught, confused, frustrated, and filled with guilt and indignation, the relatives will expect the therapist to accuse them of delinquencies toward the patients. Permitting them to talk freely, sympathizing with their feelings, and encouraging them to express their ideas about the situation will tend to alleviate their tension. It is important to try to establish a rapid working relationship with them, if this is at all possible. Once they realize that the therapist is sympathetic toward them, they will be more amenable toward accepting interpretations, and

more cooperative in the treatment plan. Indeed they may, if they have been hostile to the patients' therapy or to the therapist, become helpful accessories. Fourth, should they telephone the therapist, they must be told that it is best that the patients be informed about the call, although the specific details need not be revealed. Fifth, if the patients are insistent on knowing what went on in the conference or conversation with the therapist, they may be told that the conversation was general and dealt with many personal and other problems, as well as their relationships with the patients. Sixth, it may be necessary to see these relatives or friends more than once, perhaps even periodically. Seventh, the therapist should not participate with the patients in "tearing down" family members, nor should the members be defended when the patients launch an attack. A sympathetic, impartial attitude is best.

Q. Under what conditions would you advise relatives of patients to get psychotherapy?

A. If the patients are in close contact with neurotic relatives and they are being traumatized by the relatives, psychotherapy may be advised, provided the therapist has a sufficiently good relationship with the relatives to make this recommendation. Therapy may also be advised when a change in the patients' condition makes a new adjustment by the relatives necessary. For instance, a frigid wife, living with an impotent husband, may, as a result of psychotherapy, on the basis of experiencing sexual feelings, make sexual demands on her husband that the latter will be unable to fulfill. For the husband to make an adjustment, he may require psychotherapy.

Q. Is it permissible to treat several members of the same family?

A. The situation often becomes complicated, but it can be done. Whether or not simultaneous treatment is possible will depend on the therapist's ability to handle the inevitable complications. Reconstructive individual therapy with several members of the same family is not easily managed. Treating all or a number of family members together in a group (family therapy) may result in better family adjustment. Marital problems are often advantageously handled in joint marital therapy.

Q. How should one act when one meets patients on the street or at a social affair?

A. A professional therapeutic relationship requires reducing social contacts to a minimum. Occasions will, however, arise when the therapist will run into patients on the street, in public places, or at private social affairs. This may prove embarrassing to both therapist and patients. One cannot handle such situations by running away from them. Once the therapist is recognized by patients, the former may greet them cordially and then proceed with activities as usual. Understandably, at private gatherings, one's spontaneity will have to be curtailed to some extent. The patients' reactions to seeing the therapist in a different role may have to be handled with them during the ensuing sessions.

Q. Should you expect all your patients to like you?

A. Except for very sick patients, a satisfactory resolution of prejudices, suspicions, and resentments will occur relatively early in therapy, leading to a good working relationship. Periodically, however, the patients' feeling about the therapist will be punctuated by hostility, issuing either out of transference or out of an inadvertent error in the therapist's handling of the patients. Analysis and resolution of hostilities as they develop should bring the relationship back to a working level.

Q. If patients continue to dislike you no matter what you do, should you discontinue therapy?

A. A continued dislike is usually indicative of either errors in therapeutic management or of transference that the patients cannot resolve. As long as the dislike persists, little progress can be expected in treatment. Should the patients' feelings persist, the therapist may have to suggest the possibility of transfer to a different therapist. This must be done in such a way that the patients realize that the transfer is being recommended out of consideration for their welfare and not because the therapist rejects them. As a general rule, very few patients will need to be transferred because of persistent negative feelings. If a therapist encounters this problem frequently, the chances are that he or she is doing something in the therapeutic situation that is inspring the dislike of patients. The therapist should, therefore, seek supervision with an experienced psychotherapist who may be able to help in understanding what is happening.

Q. How should you act to displays of crying or rage on the part of patients?

A. One generally permits these to go on without reassurance until the meaning of the reaction is explored and determined. If the reaction is dangerous to patients or to others, it should be controlled by supportive measures.

Q. Should the therapist engage in a confessional, confiding about his or her life to the patient in an effort to show the patient that the therapist also has some personal frailties?

A. This can be very destructive to the relationship, especially at the beginning of therapy. Patients may use any revelations made as a confession of the therapist's weakness and ineptness and may then decide to discontinue treatment. Patients will usually discover enough frailties in the therapist spontaneously without being alerted to them.

Q. Should you ever admit to patients that you may be wrong about certain things?

A. It is important to admit an error when this is obvious to patients and they question the therapist about it.

Q. If patients ask you if you are ill or tired, would you admit it?

A. If it is true, it may be important to confirm the patients' observation, adding that you do not believe this will interfere with your ability to work with them.

Q. What happens in insight therapy if the therapist's personality is authoritarian?

A. If the authoritarianism of the therapist interferes with the patients' ability to express hostility, and with their assertiveness, it will probably limit therapeutic goals.

Q. Is it possible that a therapist may develop a deep hate for certain patients?

A. If a circumstance like this develops in therapy, there is something seriously wrong with the therapist or the technique used. It is not possible for the therapist to like all patients to the same degree, nor is it possible to avoid disliking some patients temporarily in certain phases of treatment. When this happens, the therapist must resolve the untoward feeling before it interferes with therapeutic progress. If this is not possible, the therapist should transfer the patients to another therapist and perhaps seek personal psychotherapy.

Q. Does a therapist ever fall in love with patients?

A. If such a situation develops, it is a manifestation of countertransference that will seriously interfere with the therapist's essential objectivity. Failure to analyze such a feeling and to resolve it will make it necessary to transfer these patients to another therapist.

Q. Does a therapist ever develop sexual feelings for patients?

A. It is possible that certain patients may arouse sexual feelings in the therapist. If this happens, such feelings must be subjected to self-analysis and resolved.

Q. Should not the conduct and attitudes of the psychotherapist be as passive and noncommittal as possible?

A. The idea that the therapist should remain

detached and completely passive stems from the notion that this attitude will best demonstrate to patients how they automatically project onto the therapist attitudes and feelings that are rooted in past relationships. Not having done anything to incite their attitudes, the therapist is in a better position to interpret transference. The passive, detached attitude also is believed to avoid dependency and to throw the patients on their own resources. Experience shows, however, that the projections of patients, which are sparked by past distortions in interpersonal relationships, will emerge whether the therapist is passive or active. Patients with hostility problems will thus develop hostility toward the therapist who acts detached as well as toward one who acts accepting. If patients have dependency problems, they will get dependent on the most passive therapist. Rather than cripple the spontaneity of the therapist in the dubious quest of interpreting transference phenomena, or of mobilizing assertiveness, it is best for the therapist to act natural and not to assume artificial passivity if the therapist is not normally a passive person. Such an assumption may signify rejection to patients and, in mobilizing hostility, may interfere with the working relationship.

Q. Are not warmth and emotional support necessary for some patients?

A. Yes, especially when the patients' adaptive resources are at a minimum. Unfortunately, some therapists have been reared in the tradition of passivity and nondirectiveness to a point where they provide for patients a sterile, refrigerated atmosphere that, in seriously sick patients, is anathema to a working relationship.

Q. Is the assumption of a studied role by the therapist of any help in insight therapy?

A. It has been recommended by some authorities that the therapist play a deliberate role in insight psychotherapy that is at variance with the therapist's usual neutral, though empathic, position. Such role playing, however, may inspire intense transference that the therapist may be unable to control. As a general rule, the therapist should not transgress the defined role of a professional person who seeks to enable patients to help through selfunderstanding. An exception to this rule is an extremely experienced and skilled therapist who is thoroughly acquainted with the existing dynamics operative in a patient and who, by dramatizing a part and becoming actively involved in the patients' lives, strives to expedite change. Such activity is not without risks, but it may, in some cases, produce brilliant results. On the whole, deceptive role playing is not to be recommended.

Most patients quickly perceive the artificiality in the assumed part played by the therapist.

Q. What about role playing to provide patients with corrective emotional experiences?

A. One of the reasons that role playing with that aim is frowned on is that it is sometimes employed with incomplete evidence about what requires correction. Premature assumptions about factors responsible for patients' pathology, and about the dynamics of existing interactions with others, may be nothing more than guesswork. To act merely on such impressions is not only unscientific but also may be counterproductive. What could be most propitious is to observe patients in their actual life settings to study their interactions with people and examine their dreams, fantasies, and verbal associations. Since it is not possible to be with patients 24 hours a day and to observe them in their habitual environments, therapists have to rely only on fragmentary observations within the therapeutic situation. Some therapists believe that the therapist is playing a designed role with the patient in any case and that a specifically designed role offers the greatest opportunity for taking advantage of the limited time available. My own feeling about the active providing of patients with corrective emotional experiences is that good therapy in the medium of nonjudgmental and empathic attitudes, as well as reasonably accurate interpretations of transference, will do this without the therapists' disguising their true selves by playacting in a deceptive manner. This is not to depreciate artificial role playing when it is needed to practice more desirable responses or to probe repudiated attitudes and fantasies. But here the patients are aware that no deception is being employed and that the therapist is not putting on a false front by engaging in theatrical maneuvers.

Q. If the therapist acts consistently permissive and accepting, will this not in itself eventually reduce the patients' irrational responses to authority?

A. The behavior of the therapist, no matter how well controlled will, to some degree, always be subject to distortion in terms of the patients' conceptual framework, which, in turn, is based on their previous experiences with authority. This is not to say that gross deviations of behavior on the part of the therapist will not bring about appropriate reality-determined responses. A brusque, disinterested, detached, or hostile manner will produce untoward reactions in most patients. It must not be concluded, however, that absolutely correct activity and behavior will always bring about good responses, since patients may interpret the therapist's actions as a hypocritically conceived lure.

Q. Should deprivations ever by imposed on patients?

A. Occasionally, it is necessary to enjoin patients to deprive themselves of certain sources of gratification to help the exploratory process. Thus, patients with destructive sexual acting-out tendencies may be urged to control their sexual impulses so that tensions may accumulate that will facilitate an analysis of their problem. If patients are shown the reason for their need to give up certain pleasure promptings, they will be less inclined to resent the therapist.

Q. How would you handle overanxious and completely unreasonable patients who act more like children than adults?

A. It is essential to remember that though patients may be chronologically adults, emotionally they may not have progressed beyond a childhood level. One may expect, therefore, childish tantrums, ambivalent feelings, unrestrained enthusiasms, and other reactions. If one can respect patients despite their unreasonableness, one will best be able to help them.

Q. What do you do when your relationship with patients starts getting bad?

A. All other tasks cease, and one must concentrate on bringing the relationships back to a satisfactory level. It is useless to explore patterns, to interpret and to engage in any other interviewing tasks so long as good rapport is absent. Essentially one must go back to the first phase of therapy and focus on reestablishing a working relationship.

Q. Why is the handling of transference important in reconstructive therapy?

A. Since much of the suffering of patients is produced by destructive transference involvements with people, part of the therapeutic task in reconstructive therapy is to put a halt to such reactions and to replace them with those that have a foothold in reality. If, for instance, patients respond automatically to authority with violent hate, as a result of an unresolved hatred toward a parent or sibling, their reactions may have a disorganizing effect on their total adjustment. Patients usually do not appreciate that this response to all authority is undifferentiated. They may not even be aware of their hate, which, considered to be dangerous in expression, becomes internalized with psychosomatic or depressive consequences. Liberation from such reactions is essential before patients can get well. This can best be insured in therapy by bringing them to an awareness of their projec-

tions. Several means are available to the therapist in executing this goal. First, on the basis of functioning in the role of an objective and impartial observer, one may help patients realize how many of their reactions outside of therapy have no reality base. Second, by watching for instances of transference toward the therapist, one may demonstrate to patients, often quite dramatically, the nature of those projections that constitute basic patterns.

Q. What is the difference between "transference," "transference neurosis," "parataxic distortions," and "positive relationship?"

A. Stereotyped early patterns, projected into the relationship with the therapist, were called by Freud "transference reactions." When these became so intense that patients acted out important past situations, this was known as a "transference neurosis." No satisfactory name was given to repetitive early patterns occurring with people outside of the therapeutic situation until Sullivan invented the term "parataxic distortions," which included all stereotyped patterns that developed inside or outside of therapy. A "positive relationship" usually refers to a good working relationship with minimal transference contamination.

Q. Isn't the accepted idea of transference as a manifestation of purely infantile or childish attitudes or feelings a restricted one?

A. Probably. A broader concept of transference would consider it to be a blend of projections onto the therapist of attitudes and feelings that date back to infancy and childhood, as well as more current attitudes that have had a formative influence on, and have been incorporated into, the character structure.

Q. Do all patients have to go through a transference neurosis in order to achieve very deep, structural personality changes?

A. There is much controversy on this point, but experience shows that some patients can achieve extensive personality growth without needing to live through a transference neurosis.

Q. What activities on the part of the therapist encourage neurotic transference responses?

A. Dependency may be stimulated in patients by such therapist activities as overprotecting patients, making decisions for them, and exhibiting directiveness in the relationship. Sexual feelings in patients may be provoked by seductive behavior displayed toward the patients, by socializing with the patients, and by physical contact of any kind. Fearful attitudes and hostile impulses may be mobilized if the therapist acts excessively passive, detached, authoritarian, overprotective, hostile, pompous, or belligerent. It must, however, be remembered that transference may arise without any provocation whatsoever on the part of the therapist. This is the case when needs are intense and can be voiced and expressed due to the permissiveness of the therapeutic relationship.

Q. What is the best way of handling transference?

A. There is no best way; methods depend on the kind of therapy done and the therapeutic goals. Transference may not be explored or handled in supportive therapy. In reeducative therapy it may be immediately interpreted in an effort at resolution whenever it becomes apparent as resistance. In some types of reconstructive therapy it may be allowed to develop until it becomes so disturbing that the patients themselves achieve awareness of its irrational nature. In Freudian analysis it may be encouraged to the point of evolution of a transference neurosis.

Q. Are so-called "transference cures" ever permanently effective?

A. Structural personality changes rarely occur. A "transference cure," however, may permit patients to relate better to their life situations. This facilitates the development of more adaptive patterns that can become permanent.

Q. How does countertransference lead to an improper assessment of neurotic traits in patients?

A. Countertransference may cause the therapist to make incorrect interpretations of the patterns exhibited by patients. Thus, the therapist may, if welcoming hostile outbursts, regard these as manifestations of assertiveness rather than as destructive responses. If the therapist relishes a submissive, passive attitude on the part of patients, he or she may credit this to cooperation and to the abatement of neurotic aggression rather than to a neurotic need for compliance.

Q. Should you ever emphasize positive aspects of the patients' adjustment?

A. Therapists too often tend to regard patients as a respository of pathologic strivings, emphasizing these to a neglect of constructive traits, mention of which is very important in reinforcing constructive behavior.

Q. Is acting-out always a bad sign?

A. No. It may be a transitional phase in therapy indicative of a shift in the psychic equilibrium. Thus repressed, fearful individuals, realizing that they have been intimidated by an archaic fear of physical hurt for assertiveness, may become overly aggressive and act-out their defiance of authority as a way of combating their terror. Proving themselves to be capable of this

expression without experiencing the dreaded punishment may enable them to temper their outbursts. In the same way, sexually inhibited people may become temporarily promiscuous, almost as if liberation from fear is tantamount with indulgence in sexual excesses. Incorporated also in the acting-out process are unresolved impulses and conflicts, in relation to early authorities, that have been mobilized by the transference. When the therapist becomes aware of acting-out, it is important that it be discouraged in favor of verbalization. As verbalizations replace impetuous acts and as understanding progresses, a more rational solution is found for neurotic drives and impulses.

Q. How do the value prejudices of therapists interfere with treatment?

A. Whether intentional or not, therapists will accent in the interview attitudes and feelings that are in line with their value systems, and will minimize those that are opposed to it. If, for instance, therapists have a problem in their relationships with authority, manifesting submission and ingratiation, they may overvalue these traits. They may then tend to discourage assertiveness or aggressiveness when patients seek to take a stand with authority. Therapist may credit this philosophy to "good common sense" and justify it in terms of the benefits that accrue. This may seriously inhibit patients from working through neurotic feelings toward authority. On the other hand, if therapists themselves react to authority with aggression and hostility, they may inspire defiance or promote aggressive attitudes toward authority figures, which may seriously endanger the patients' security.

Q. What do you do with patients who break or cancel appointments consistently?

A. This can be a disturbing problem since consistency in attendance is vital to good therapy. Should confrontation and discussion fail to resolve this problem, the therapist may suggest discontinuance of therapy. If, as in a clinic, the therapist is obliged to see patients irrespective of the latter's motivation, the therapist may insist on the patients' calling for an appointment when they want to be seen. In this way the burden of stopping therapy is put on the patients, and if there is any motivation at all, the patients may "shape up."

Q. Shouldn't therapists be trained in all therapeutic approaches?

A. The most effective therapists are those who can implement whatever therapies are indicated, whether these are of a supportive, reeducative, or reconstructive nature. If therapists have a broad understanding of various therapeutic procedures, know how to execute them, and are sufficiently flexible in personality so as not to be tied to a single treatment process, they will score the greatest therapeutic successes. This, however, is an idealistic situation. Most therapists learn only one kind of technique, which enables them to handle only a certain number of problems—those which are amenable to their technique. They may also be limited by their character structure so as to be unable to use certain techniques. For instance, a therapist may be an essentially passive person and, on this account, be unable to employ the directiveness and authoritativeness of approach essential for symptom removal, reassurance, guidance, persuasion, environmental manipulation, and other supportive therapies. On the other hand, the therapist may be so extremely authoritarian and dogmatic that patients may not be allowed to make misakes, work out their own problems, or establish their own sense of values, so essential in reconstructive therapy.

Q. Is there any consistency in therapeutic focus among therapists appraising the same patients?

A. A therapist's judgment concerning existing core problems involves speculations that are not always consistent with what another therapist may hypothesize. Given the same data, different therapists will vary in choosing what is significant. In a small experiment I conducted, three experienced therapists trained in the same analytic school witnessed the first two sessions conducted by a fourth colleague through a one-way mirror. Each therapist, including myself, had a somewhat different idea of what meaningful topic was best on which to focus. But such differences, in my opinion, are not significant. Even if one strikes the patient's core difficulties tangentially, one may still register a significant impact and spur patients on toward a better adaptation. After all, reasonably intelligent patients are capable of making connections and even of correcting the misperceptions of a therapist when a good working relationship exists and the therapist does not respond too drastically with wounded narcissism when challenged or corrected.

Q. Is not insight a basic factor in all therapies?

A. Insight on some level is helpful in all therapies. Even in supportive therapy, an understanding of the existing environmental encumbrances may eventually lead to a correction of remediable difficulties or to an adjustment to irremediable conditions. In reeducative therapy knowledge of the troublesome consequences of

existing behavioral patterns may ultimately sponsor a substitution with more wholesome interpersonal relationships. In reconstructive therapy insight into unconscious conflicts, and their projected manifestations into everyday life, encourages patients toward actions motivated more by the demands of reality than by the archaic needs and fears of their childhood. Obviously, insight alone is not equivalent to cure.

Q. What is the difference between the level of insight effectuated in reeducative therapy and the kind in reconstructive therapy?

A. In reeducative therapy an inquiry is conducted into conscious and preconscious drives, impulses, feelings, and conflicts with the object of suppressing or changing those that disorganize behavior and of encouraging others that expedite adjustment. In reconstructive therapy the exploratory process deals with the more unconscious drives and conflicts. Due to the intensity of repression, one must implement the inquiry through examination of, and the inculcation of insight into, derivatives from the unconscious as revealed in verbal associations, dreams, fantasies, slips of speech, and transference. The object in reconstructive therapy is to liberate individuals as completely as possible from anachronistic values, attitudes, strivings, and defenses and to remove blocks to personality growth.

Q. What is the best kind of therapy to use when the sole object is symptom relief or mere control of certain obnoxious personality traits?

A. The objective in the treatment effort may be limited to the restoration of habitual controls to individuals, to the mediation of any continuing environmental stress, and to the modification of strivings and goals that are inimical to the patients' well-being or that are beyond their existing potentialities. Through the use of supportive and conditioning techniques, and by fostering an awareness of some of their character distortions and strivings, these objectives may be accomplished in a satisfactory way. There are, however, some conditions when character structure is so disturbed, and when elaborated crippling mechanisms of defense are so tenacious, that even the objective of mere symptom relief presupposes an extensive exploration of aspects of personality that have been repressed. This will necessitate recontructive approaches.

Q. Is it possible to do reconstructive therapy on the basis of once-a-week sessions?

A. The effectiveness of therapy is dependent upon factors more important than the number of times each week patients are seen. Reconstructive therapy is possible in some patients on the basis of sessions once weekly; it is not possible in others. Great skill is required to bring about reconstructive changes when there are long intervals between visits. When a transference neurosis is to be created, four to five sessions weekly will be needed.

Q. What is the difference between an apparent and a permanent recovery as related to reconstructive therapy?

A. An apparent recovery is mere restoration to the premorbid level with the strengthening of the defensive techniques that have served, prior to illness, to maintain the ego free from anxiety. A permanent cure involves a real alteration of the ego to a point where those compromising defensive attitudes and mechanisms are no longer necessary to keep it free from anxiety. Under these circumstances, individuals are capable of gratifying their basic needs and strivings without undue conflict. Recovery in psychotherapy is permanent only insofar as it produces a real change in the character structure of individuals and a reorientation of their relationships with others and themselves. Due to the operation of resistances that blanket offending impulses, and because of repressions that keep from awareness the most important problems of the individual, reconstructive psychotherapy offers the greatest chance of overcoming a severe emotional difficulty.

Q. What would you consider an acceptable minimal goal in reeducative therapy?

A. The least we can do for patients is to bring them to as great an awareness of their problems as is reasonably possible, to enable them to lead as useful, happy, and constructive lives as they can with their personality and environmental handicaps, to help them overcome remediable life difficulties and adapt to irremediable ones, and adjust their ambitions to their existing capacities.

Q. What is the difference between a "normal" and "neurotic" person?

A. "Normality" is a social designation that embraces characteristics not entirely consonant with a definition of mental health. Average "normal" people in a culture possess many neurotic drives that are sanctioned and perhaps encouraged by society. Although these drives nurture some anxieties, "normal" individuals are still capable of functioning and of making a satisfactory social adjustment. If people are no longer able to adjust themselves and begin to manifest excessive anxiety and maladaptive mechanisms of defense, they may be classified as "neurotic." In therapy the objective may be to restore the individual's social adjustment and

their "normal" neurotic tendencies. A more extensive objective, however, would be a correction of all neurotic traits, even those condoned as "normal," which is more idealistic than realistic.

Q. If ideal goals of complete reconstruction are impossible, what would be reasonably good goals in reconstructive therapy?

A. It is manifestly impossible for any one individual to reach the acme of emotional maturity in every psychic and interpersonal area. One may decide that a satisfactory result has been achieved when patients lose their symptoms, abandon their disturbing neurotic patterns, deal with their difficulties spontaneously without needing help from the therapist, manifest productivity and self-confidence, show absence of fear following expression of assertiveness, and exhibit an improvement in their interpersonal relationships with increased friendliness and respect and lessened suspiciousness, detachment, aggression, and dependency.

Q. In interviewing patients, should a therapist disclose intimate personal facts as a way of positively influencing the therapeutic relationship?

A. Studies of the effects of self-disclosure on the part of the therapist are inconclusive insofar as their influence on the relationship is concerned. The results cannot be predicted in advance. Depending on their personalities, patients may respond to a therapist's revelations positively ("My therapist is marvelously human," "He does not present himself as a flawless god," "She trust me by revealing these intimacies") or negatively ("This person has such weaknesses that I'm not sure she can help me," "If he can't help himself, how can he help me?").

Some research studies do indicate that therapist self-disclosure facilitates patient self-disclosure and greater therapist trustworthiness (Bierman, 1969; Sermat and Smyth, 1973). My personal view is to use self-disclosure very sparingly and only when it does not point to severe neurotic problems in the therapist. It may, for example, be employed to show how a therapist handled a problem or situation akin to that confronting patients, thus enhancing modeling.

Q. How do therapists' personalities influence their techniques?

A. Therapists eventually evolve their own therapeutic method, which is a composite of the methods they have learned, the experiences they have had, and their specific personality traits. For instance, analytically trained therapists, inclined by personality to be authoritarian, may be unable to maintain the traditional silence and passivity demanded by classical psychoanalysis. To do so robs them of spontaneity; it provokes tension and prevents them from exhibiting the kind of relaxed objectivity that is most helpful in treatment. They may find it necessary to abandon passivity and to permit themselves to participate more actively in the treatment process. Their patients will perhaps respond to this change in a gratifying way and react more positively than when the therapists were behaving in a stultified manner. This success may encourage the therapists to be themselves, and they will probably find that their results continue to justify their alteration of technique. For them, then, the shift is justified since it liberates them from acting in an artificial, inhibited way. Yet other therapists may not be able to do the same thing; for instance, those who by personality are more retiring, quiet, and unobtrusive. For them the passive technique will probably work well; to attempt to force activity would be as artifical as to expect active therapists to assume a feigned passivity.

Q. How do you explain the misunderstanding that exists among the different schools of psychiatry and psychology?

A. In so virgin a territory as the uncharted psyche, a diversity of theories, interpretations, and methods may be expected. A great deal of animosity has, however, unfortunately come to the surface among groups with divergent points of view. Splinter societies have erupted, justifying their break with the parent body on the basis of discrimination and lack of academic freedom in the older organization. Sparked at first by the impulse to create groups possessed of scientific liberalism, a number of the splinter organizations have, upon achieving independence, then practiced the same intolerant bigotry that initiated their secession, developing their own dogmas and rejecting original thinking among the members. Such entrenched and reactionary attitudes are to be condemned in any scientific group.

Q. Should a good therapist be able to cure or help all patients?

A. No matter how highly trained the therapist may be, some patients will be able to be helped more than others. There will be certain patients therapists will not be able to treat—patients whom other therapists may successfully manage. On the other hand, therapists will probably be able to cure some patients with whom other therapists have failed. Therapists will make some mistakes during the course of ther-

apy with all of their patients, but these mistakes need not interfere with ultimate beneficial results. Finally, therapists will be rewarded by a large number of successes, but they will also have their quota of failures.

Q. Does it follow that psychoanalytically trained therapists will do better therapy than those who have not been analytically trained?

A. It is fallacious to assume that nonanalytically trained therapists are incapable of doing many kinds of psychotherapy as well as those who have been analytically trained. If therapists plan to do reconstructive psychotherapy, however, using dream interpretation, transference, and resistance, they will be helped by sound training in reconstructive therapy, including a personal analysis.

Q. Must the therapist be completely free from neurosis?

A. It is doubtful that any person in our culture is entirely free from neurosis, no matter how much personal psychotherapy has been undergone. To do psychotherapy, however, therapists must be sufficiently free from neurosis so that their own personal problems do not divert the relationship from therapeutic goals.

Q. Will personal psychotherapy or psychoanalysis guarantee good functioning on the part of an adequately trained therapist?

A. In most instances it will. Serious personality difficulties may in some cases not be resolved to a point where individuals will be able to function as therapists, however, although they might work satisfactorily in some other field. In other words, where their egos have been so damaged through a combination of constitutional predisposition and traumatic life experiences, individuals may not, even with extensive psychotherapeutic help, be able to achieve that kind of personality flexibility, objectivity, sensitivity, and empathy that are prerequisite for functioning as an effective psychotherapist.

Q. Why should not psychotherapy or psychoanalysis be able to resolve the neurotic problems of psychotherapists, since they actually are not as sick as most patients and should benefit greatly from psychotherapeutic help?

A. The motivation to carry out psychotherapy, which is what inspires many therapists to seek personal therapy, may not be sufficient to enable therapists to endure and to work through the anxieties underlying their character distortions. For instance, the individuals may, prior to their determination to become therapists, have been functioning in a more or less detached manner, removing themselves from disturbing interpersonal situations periodically when these had become too difficult to handle. Under ordinary circumstances, and in average relationships, they would be able to function quite effectively with this kind of a defensive attitude. This detachment, however, may seriously affect their capacity to operate in a therapeutic interpersonal relationship, in which they will constantly be brought into contact with critically disturbed people who will seek to extract from them constructive responses they may be unable to give. A tremendous amount of personal psychotherapeutic work may be required before therapists will be able to give up their detachment as an interpersonal defense. If they do not have sufficient anxiety to incite them, however, to seek new modes of adjustment, they may not have the incentive to tolerate the great amount of work and suffering that will be involved in effecting a reconstructive change in their own personalities. Consequently, in their personal therapy, they will keep warding off the deepest character change and may go through their treatment without significant modification of their detachment. The fact that many therapists have exposed themselves to extensive personal therapy or psychoanalysis and have emerged from it without any basic character changes is no indictment of psychotherapy. Rather, it is an indication of how difficult it is to treat certain kinds of emotional disturbance without adequate motivation. In other words, the desire to become a psychotherapist is not in itself sufficient motivation to promote deep character change.

Q. What can therapists do whose personality problems interfere with their executing good psychotherapy even after they has gotten extensive personal therapy and supervision?

A. If a qualified supervisor finds that the supervisees' problems are interfering with their therapeutic effectiveness, the supervisees may be advised to seek further personal psychotherapy. Should no change occur, it may be necessary for the therapists completely to give up psychotherapy as a career. They should not regard this as a personal defeat or as a sign of devaluated status, since they will probably be able to function very effectively in another role. For example, psychiatrists may decide to do diagnostic, institutional, or other kinds of work that do not bring them into an intimate therapeutic relationship with patients. Caseworkers can confine activities to an agency organized around areas other than therapeutic services. Psychologists can restrict functions to diagnostic testing, research, vocational guidance, and counseling.

Q. Don't you believe that every therapist should learn the principles of preventive mental health in addition to knowing how to do psychotherapy?

A. Mental health needs are only partially served by an exclusive program of psychotherapy. This is because the impact of emotional problems on the lives of people so often reflect themselves in disturbances in work, family, marital, interpersonal, and social relations without causing collapse in adaptation characteristic of neuroses. The providing of help for these preclinical problems requires an ability to consult with, and to supervise, community workers and professionals such as social workers, teachers, nurses, physicians, psychologists, correctional workers, and ministers, who are unable to handle such problems alone. It is advisable that every therapist be acquainted with the principles of preventive mental health and know how to communicate well with community agencies and the ancillary professions.

Q. What do you do if you make an outlandish error like forgetting patients' ages or marital status?

A. Being human, therapists will, from time to time, unintentionally commit some blunders. They may forget patients' ages, details about their families, or items in the history that patients have already recounted. Distracted, the therapist may even forget the patients' first names. Sometimes a more flagrant blunder may occur, such as calling patients by the wrong name, or asking them if they have dreamed recently, when they already have in the first part of the interview recounted a dream. Should such slip-ups happen, there is no need to conceal them or to be too apologetic. Therapists may merely say: "Of course, you told me this" (or "I know this") or "It just temporarily slipped my mind." Patients will not make too much of such errors if a good relationship exists. At any rate, it may, if it seems indicated, be important to explore the patients' feelings immediately upon commission of a mistake.

Q. Should psychiatrists do physical examinations if necessary?

A. Psychiatrists will probably not be as skilled in diagnosis as the internists to whom they can refer patients needing medical treatment. A physical examination in any therapy other than psychoanalysis, however, theoretically need not interfere with the therapeutic process, if the patients' reactions to it are examined and explored. It may bring many interesting and important feelings to the surface.

Q. Should two therapists, each working on separate members of the same family, confer?

A. A conference may be helpful to clarify

the patient's interactions with the other member and to check on data significant to both. Usually, however, this is not routine. If it is done, each therapist should be mindful of personal competitiveness with and need to impress the other therapist and of defensiveness regarding the patient's progress.

Q. *What is multiple therapy, and does it have a use?*

A. Multiple therapy is the treatment of a single patient or a group by two or more therapists. It is preferred by some therapists in the management of difficult patients, such as psychotics and psychopaths. Differences in opinion and transference reactions between the therapists will require careful handling, sometimes within and sometimes outside of the therapeutic session. There may be advantages in employing multiple therapy in cases that do not respond to conventional treatment.

Q. *Does not behavior therapy circumvent transference and other resistances?*

A. Behavior therapy possesses ingredients that are common to all psychotherapies. Inaugurated almost immediately is a relationship, patients responding to the therapist as an idealized authority who holds the key to their well-being. The trinity of faith, hope, and trust, while not openly expressed, are aspects that cannot be avoided. The placebo element is as much a component of behavior therapy as it is of any other kind of treatment. Factors of motivation and dyadic group dynamics undoubtedly come into play and act as accelerants or deterrants to progress. If readiness for change is lacking, one might expect a negative result in behavior therapy. Subtly, transference will be set into motion, no matter how assiduously the behavior therapist attempts to avoid it, and resistances of various kinds will rear their obstructive heads at almost every phase of the therapeutic operation. Some behavior therapists refuse to acknowledge the presence of these intercurrent elements, though this obviously will not negate their influence.

Q. *If psychological tests indicate that particular patients are very sick, shouldn't you approach them carefully in therapy, and isn't this a sign that your goals have to be superficial ones?*

A. One may be forewarned about the strength of the individuals' egos from psychological tests, but this should not prejudice the treatment process. One of the disadvantages of testing is that it puts a label on patients the therapist may be reluctant to remove, even though the therapist's clinical judgment disagrees with the test findings. The therapeutic relationship is a better index of how deep one may go in therapy and the extensiveness of goals to be approached than any psychological test or battery of tests.

Q. *Isn't it difficult at present to develop a real science of mind because of the many divergent ideas about psychodynamics?*

A. The subject of psychodynamics opens up many founts of controversy because authorities with different orientations have different ways of looking at psychopathological phenomena. Irrespective of orientation, one can always find data that seems to substantiate one's particular point of view. The same interview material may thus be variously interpreted by several observers. Some regard it as confirming their theory that neurosis is essentially a clash between instinctual strivings and the environment. Others as enthusiastically demonstrate cultural forces as the primary provocative agent. Still others may find in the material evidence that neurosis is fostered by disturbances in the integrative functioning of the ego. Such divergent ideas are not too serious; they are to be regarded as the inevitable forerunners of a real science of mind. In the study of the uncharted psyche, theories in abundance were bound to emerge, supporting many rifts and controversies. Fortunately, the beginnings of amalgamation are occurring, an honest effort to blend the findings of the various schools into a body of knowledge shorn of prejudice and bias.

Q. *Is it possible for a therapist to be supervised by several different supervisors who espouse different theoretical viewpoints?*

A. Unavoidable, particularly in an eclectic atmosphere, is the fact that student therapists will be supervised by several supervisors whose approaches reflect wide theoretical differences. It is to be expected that these divergencies will mobilize insecurity in students who are seeking a definite structure in theory and process. The function of the good supervisor is to help students see that different views merely expose contrasting aspects of the same phenomenon. These muliform facets may seemingly conflict with each other, though they are actually constitutents of a unified whole. One must handle the students' disappointments that everything does not harmonize and fit together into a master plan. Should their anxiety prove too great, students may need special, even psychotherapeutic, help. Appreciating that other points of view exist is one of the most important contributions of the supervisor. Only a supervisor who is sufficiently secure not to regard differences in approach as interferences and can view them as a challenge toward further scientific inquiry will be able to render the kind of help that students need and have a right to expect.

Q. Can dependent patients progress in therapy beyond the goal of achieving freedom from symptoms?

A. It is sometimes contended that if patients seek guidance and an authoritarian relationship in therapy their mental set will prohibit their entering into the participatory mode of activity essential for deeper therapy. Their desire for paternalism, it is said, will block essential collaboration. This is not always correct. The majority of patients, even those who have read tomes on psychoanalysis, seek a relationship with a strong, idealized parental figure who can lift them out of their distress. The stronger the anxiety, the greater the expectation. The task of the therapist is to promote a shift in motivation toward expanding the patients' inner resources and working cooperatively with the therapist. A fundamental task in all therapy is to promote the conviction in patients that they have the inner resources to resolve feelings of helplessness. Good technique in psychotherapy takes this factor into account. Understandably, there are some characterologically dependent souls and borderline patients so inwardly damaged that they will need a dependency prop in order to function. No amount of therapeutic work will deviate them from this aim. But even here the therapist owes it to the patients to make an effort to promote greater self-sufficiency. Patients may diagnostically be written off as candidates for reconstructive psychotherapy in view of the depth of their disturbance, their habitual infantile relationships with people, wretched past conditionings with emotionally ill parents, uncontrollable acting-out propensities, paranoic ideas, and so forth. On this basis, a supportive relationship is provided the patients, only to find that they press for deeper self-understanding. Yielding to this pressure, the therapist may institute reconstructive treatments, helping some to rise out of their dependent morass and to use their understanding toward great self-actualization.

Q. Are there any diagnostic signs that will indicate how patients will actually respond to psychotherapy?

A. Very few diagnostic or other rules can be laid down to anticipate patients' responses to therapy. The only true test is the way patients take hold of the opportunity offered them in psychotherapy to approach their lives from a different perspective. Trial interpretations may be in-stituted to determine how patients will respond in the relationship. Will they deny, resist, fight against, or accept the interpretation, and will they act on it?

Q. What is the effect on patients of passivity in the therapist?

A. Passivity on the part of the therapist may produce frustration and anxiety, which, if not too intense, may mobilize patients to think things through for themselves and to act on their own responsibility. Should excessive hostility and anxiety be engendered, however, or should patients interpret the therapist's passivity as rejection or incompetence, it may have a paralyzing effect on their progress. This is particularly the case when patients, in their upbringing, have been victimized by a neglectful or uninterested parent who put too much responsibility on their immature shoulders. The therapeutic situation then will merely tend to recapitulate the early traumatizing experience and reinforce the sense of rage and helplessness.

Q. Should a trial period be instituted in psychotherapy to see how patients will react?

A. Freud [1913] originally recommended that a trial period of a week or two be instituted to see if patients are suitable for psychoanalysis. A trial period is more or less inherent in all psychotherapeutic endeavors. Patients and therapists mutually survey one another to see whether they feel comfortable and confident about working together. Patients test therapists. Does the therapist like them? Does the therapist have confidence in them? Does the therapist trust them? The therapist subjects patients to an empirical scrutiny. Can he or she interact with the patients? Are the patients properly motivated, and if not, how can incentives be developed? Are patients operating under misconceptions about treatment? How far will they be able to go in therapy—toward symptom relief? Toward reconstructive personality change? The therapist may, during this trial phase, make a few interpretations to test the patients' receptivity, flexibility, and capacities for change. At the same time that ground rules are established; a working hypothesis is laid down, and the beginnings of treatment are instituted. Reformulations of this early hypothesis will have to be made periodically in accord with the patients' reactions, resistances, and rate of movement.

Q. Shouldn't therapists always remain neutral?

A. Therapists as human beings have feelings, values, prejudices, and needs. They will reveal these to patients sooner or later, if not verbally then nonverbally, both directly in their interpretations and indirectly in their silences, pauses, content of questions, and emphasis. While ideally therapists should avoid prejudicial pronouncements, they should not deceive themselves into thinking that they can always maintain a neutral stand. Nor is this desirable. It may be quite suitable to apply value pressure where it is needed and sometimes, as in patients' acting-out proclivities, it is the only tactic that makes sense. Though maintaining the philosophy that patients have an inalienable right to their points of view, decisions, and behavioral twistings and turnings, therapists do not need to accept the validity of some ideas and actions. There is no such thing as true "neutrality" in therapists. Otherwise they would not care whether patients remained sick or got well. Therapists have opinions and prejudices. They will display these in one way or another, if not one day then the next.

Q. Are there differences among psychoanalysts regarding the use of activity as opposed to passivity in psychoanalysis?

A. Polemics have been organized around the matter of activity versus passivity. On the one hand there are purists like Glover who defend the sanctity of the passive classical procedure. There are nonpurists, like Franz Alexander, who insist that the rejection of activity can only lead to therapeutic stagnation. Activity is generally eschewed in the classical technique on the basis that it tends to produce a refractory and insoluble as opposed to an ameliorative transference neurosis (Mitchell, 1927). Since the time of Ferenczi (1950b, 1950c) who instituted "active" approaches, many analysts have introduced manipulations that to Glover (1964) exceed the limits of pure analytic practice on the basis that "deliberately adopting special attitudes and time restrictions for special cases changes the character of therapy in these cases, converting it into a form of rapport therapy." Although such methodological innovations may produce excellent results and even be the best therapy for cases inaccessible to the customary technique, they should not be confused with "psychoanalysis" in which one analyzes and does not manipulate the transference. Supporting rigidity in approach, Glover avows that "flexibility in both psychoanalytic theory and practice has in the past been a frequent preamble to abandonment of basic principles." Passivity and the adoption of a "blank screen" are advocated as the best of deliberately nurtured attitudes to reduce complications. On the other hand, there are analysts who disagree with Glover, recommending modifications in method

from the manipulation of the transference to the open exhibition of interest in and modulated demonstrations of affection toward the patient (Bouvet, 1958; Eissler, 1958; Nacht, 1957, 1958). Commenting on the fact that few cases of simple transference neurosis are seen in practice, Lorand (1963) points out that psychoanalytic technique today "is quite different from that of earlier periods of analysis." Unless active interference is used in certain cases, for example in character disorders and infantile patterns of behavior, the analysis may stagnate or break down. Obviously, it is impossible at all times to adhere to the basic rules of psychoanalysis. Directiveness and active interference are sometimes essential, especially during stages of resistance "where the standard technical methods are of little help." Such variations in technique within the framework of classical psychoanalysis may be used to further therapeutic progress. The "dosing" of interpretations may also be necessary to activate the unconscious, to eliminate defenses as well as to prevent their too ready emergence. In a past contribution, Glover (1955) himself considered *complete* neutrality a myth and wondered whether adhering to the rule of not making important decisions was really desirable. When deviations from classical technique are in order, however, they must, he insisted, be dictated by the needs of the situation and not by countertransference. In practice, modification of analytic rules is frequently necessary. But whether we should label such deviations as "psychoanalysis" is another matter. There would seem to be some justification in restricting the term "psychoanalysis" to the classical technique and to entitle procedures incorporating modifications and active interventions as "modified psychonanalysis" or "psychoanalytically oriented psychotherapy."

Q. What is the theory behind cognitive therapy, and does it have utility?

A. The theory underlying cognitive therapy is that people are dragooned into maladaptive actions by distortions in thought that they can both understand and control; within themselves they possess capacities for awareness of such understanding and solution of their difficulties. Therapeutic techniques organized around this hypothesis are directed toward correcting deformities in thinking and developing alternative and more realistic modes of looking at life experiences. It is said that this is a much more direct approach to problems than other approaches since it draws on patients' previous learning encounters. Interventions are aimed at rectifying misconceptions and conceptual flaws that are at the basis of individuals' difficulties. This technique involves explorations of the stream of consciousness with the object of modifying the ideational content associated with the symptoms. Among the basic assumptions here are that the quality of therapists' thinking will inevitably influence the prevailing mood and that the *meaning* of a stimulus to patients is more important than the nature of the stimulus itself.

There is a good deal of overlap of cognitive therapy with behavior therapy. Albert Ellis (1962, 1971) in his rational–emotive therapy pioneered cognitive appraoches in a behavioral set-

ting. Meichenbaum (1977) attempts to blend cognitive–semantic modification with behavioral modification. Aaron T. Beck (1976) has written extensively on cognitive therapy and has claimed advantages for it in treating depression over all other therapeutic methods, including drug therapy. A new magazine, *Cognitive Therapy and Research* (Plenum), is devoted to explicating the role of cognitive processes in human adaptation and adjustment. Whether cognitive therapy is useful for therapists depends on their skill and conviction and the special learning capacities of individual patients.

63
Recording in Psychotherapy

Satisfactory recording is conducive to good psychotherapy. It acts as discipline for the beginning therapist. It is helpful even to experienced therapists, facilitating the following of the progress of a case and helping in the rendering of a report. It is indispensible for purposes of research (Wolberg, LR, 1964b).

Except in those clinics where an ample budget provides dictating facilities and secretarial services, records of patients receiving psychotherapy are apt to be pitifully sparse. To some extent this is due to the absence of an organized routine recording system. Additionally, note taking during the treatment session is distracting to therapists and annoying to some patients. Of utmost value, therefore, would be a recording system that is both simple to follow and not too disturbing to patients.

Most patients expect that some kind of record will be kept. They usually accept note taking during the initial interview and do not object to occasional notes being written during later sessions. If objections are voiced, these may be dealt with by an explanation to the effect that the keeping of a record is helpful in following patient's progress. Should the patient continue to object to notes being taken during sessions because this is much too distracting, or should the practice distract the therapist, a note may be entered into the record following each session. If fear is expressed that confidential material may be read by another person, the patient may be informed that under no circumstances will the record be released, nor any information divulged, even to the patient's family physician, unless the patient gives written permission for this. Excellent outlines and suggestions for recording may be found in the books by Menninger (1952b) and Beller (1962).

CASE RECORD

The case record should minimally contain the following data: (1) statistical data sheet, (2) initial interview, (3) daily progress notes, (4) monthly progress notes, (5) termination note, (6) summary, and (7) follow-up note.

Statistical Data

Basic statistical data include the following:

1. Patient's name
2. Address, home and business telephone
3. Age
4. Sex

5. Marital status, how long married, previous marriages, ages and sex of children
6. Age and occupation of mate
7. Education
8. Occupation, salary, sources of income if unemployed
9. Military record
10. Referral source

These data may be entered on a separate sheet or on a form (see Appendix A), or the first sheet of the initial form interview (see Appendix C). A more complete statistical form, which is useful in clinics, is illustrated in Appendix B.

Sometimes the patient may be asked to fill out certain questionnaires to help get statistical data without taking up too much of the therapist's time. Short forms are included under Appendix D, which is a Personal Data Sheet, and Appendix E, which is a Family Data Sheet. In using these forms, the Personal Data Sheet is given to the patient to fill out immediately prior to the initial interview. The Family Data Sheet is filled out after the therapist has accepted the patient for treatment.

Initial Interview

The data to be included in the recording of the initial interview are the following:

1. Chief complaint
2. History and development of complaint
3. Other symptoms and clinical findings
4. Patient's attitudes toward family members
5. Previous emotional upsets
6. Previous treatment
7. Estimate of existing insight and motivation
8. Tentative diagnosis
9. Tentative dynamics
10. Disposition of the case

A convenient initial interview form is included under Appendix C, the first sheet of which is for statistical data.

Daily Progress Notes

At the end of each session, the date and a brief note, which may consist of no more than one sentence, should be entered on a progress note sheet. This should contain the dominant theme of the session. Other entries may include the following:

1. Present state of symptoms or complaints (absent, improved, the same, worse)
2. How the patient feels (anxious, placid, depressed, happy)
3. Important life situations and developments since last visit and how they were handled
4. Content of the session
5. Significant transference and resistance reactions
6. Dreams

Since the wording of the patient's dreams is important, it is best to write dreams down during the session while they are related by the patient.

Appendix F is a convenient form for progress notes.

Monthly Progress Notes

A summarizing monthly progress note is of value in pulling together the events of the month. This may be a succinct recapitulation of what has been going on in treatment. In clinics where supervision of the total caseload is essential, a monthly progress summary (such as illustrated under Appendix G), which is routinely reviewed by the supervisor, may make for a more efficient kind of reporting.

Termination Note

A termination note is important and contains the following:

1. Date of initial interview.
2. Date of termination interview.
3. Reason for termination.

4. Condition at discharge (recovered, markedly improved, moderately improved, slightly improved, unimproved, worse)
5. Areas of improvement (symptoms, adjustment to environment, physical functions, relations with people)
6. Patient's attitude toward therapist at discharge
7. Recommendations to patient
8. Diagnosis

A termination form will be found under Appendix H.

Summary

The summary should contain the following information though curtailed.

1. Chief complaint (in patient's own words)
2. History and development of complaint (date of onset, circumstances under which complaint developed, progression from the onset to the time of the initial interview)
3. Other complaints and symptoms (physical, emotional, psychic, and behavior symptoms other than those of the complaint factor)
4. Medical, surgical, and, in women, gynecologic history
5. Environmental disturbances at onset of therapy (economic, work, housing, neighborhood, and family difficulties)
6. Relationship difficulties at onset of therapy (disturbances in relationships with people, attitudes toward the world, toward authority, and toward the self)
7. Hereditary, constitutional, and early developmental influences (significant physical and psychiatric disorders in patient's family, socioeconomic status of family, important early traumatic experiences and relationships, neurotic traits in childhood and adolescence)
8. Family data (mother, father, siblings, spouse, children—ages, state of health, personality adjustment, and patient's attitude toward each)
9. Previous attacks of emotional illness (as a child and later). When did patient feel completely free from emotional illness?
10. Initial interview (brief description of condition of patient at initial interview, including clinical findings)
11. Level of insight and motivation at onset of therapy (how long ago did the patient feel that treatment was needed? for what? awareness of emotional nature of problem, willingness to accept psychotherapy)
12. Previous treatments (when did the patient first seek treatment? what treatment was obtained? any hospitalization?)
13. Clinical examination (significant findings in physical, neurologic, psychiatric, and psychologic, examinations)
14. Differential diagnosis (at time of initial interview)
15. Estimate of prognosis (at time of initial interview)
16. Psychodynamics and psychopathology
17. Course of treatment:
    (a) Type of therapy employed, frequency, total number of sessions, response to therapist
    (b) Significant events during therapy, dynamics that were revealed, verbatim report of important dreams, nature of transference and resistance
    (c) Progress in therapy, insight acquired, translation of insight into action, change in symptoms, attitudes, relationships with people
18. Condition upon discharge (areas of improvement, remaining problems)
19. Recommendations to patient
20. Statistical classification

A summary form with spaces for the above items will be found under Appendix I.

Follow-up Note

A note on follow-up visits, or the inclusion of follow-up letters from patients, helps the therapist to evaluate the effectiveness of treatment. A follow-up letter may be mailed out 1, 2, and 5 years after therapy. A form letter such as the following may be used:

Dear _____:

In the past year I have wondered how things were progressing with you. Would you drop me a note telling me how you feel, and indicating any new developments. You may perhaps want to comment on your experience in treatment and how this was of help to you.

Sincerely yours,

_____

Case Folder

A manila folder is advisable to hold the case record of the patient. The name of the patient is written on the flap, and, if the patient is being treated in a clinic, the case number is also entered. Some therapists prefer a folder that has several pockets that may be used for correspondence in relationship to the patient, as well as for detailed notes. Under Appendix J, there is a folder the writer has found useful in private practice as well as in clinic practice. Printed on the front of an ordinary folder are spaces for entry of the date of each visit, payments made, and certain items that are pertinent to the treatment of the patient. It is a simple matter of only a few seconds to check on the total number of visits, the number of broken or cancelled appointments, the payments that have been made, and the dates of completion of the statistical data sheet, initial interview, monthly progress notes, consultations (psychiatric, medical, psychological, and casework) if these were obtained, tests administered by the therapist, or others, termination note, summary and follow-up notes. There is space also for entry of supervisory sessions if these were obtained in relation to the patient. Printed on

the back of the folder are lines for entry of dates for more visits if the space on the front of the folder is not sufficient.

Miscellaneous Enclosures

Included in the case record, in addition to the above data, are other notations and forms used by the therapist, such as psychological test results, notes on medical and other consultations, detailed notes made by the therapist, written comments and notes by the patient (see Appendix S), and correspondence in relation to the patient.

The flexibility of computers in selection, orderly storage, and rapid recovery of data—beyond the capacities of human performance—puts them in the forefront as instruments for research in the mental health field, not only for the calculating of results in experiments designed around specific hypotheses but also in delineating trends and significant information and in generating new hypotheses (Cappon, 1966). Computer programs capable of carrying out principle components factor analysis with varimax rotation may measure clinical change with greater objectivity and probable reliability than other methods (Cole, 1964). By proper programming it may be possible to ask computers to make decisions between alternate futures, thus expediting the predictability of human behavior.

Electrical Recording in Psychotherapy

The employment of videotape recorders (see also Videotape Recording) has also introduced a new dimension into psychotherapeutic recording, with vast potential for teaching and the expediting of treatment (Alger and Hogan, 1969; Berger MM, 1970; Czajkoski, 1968; Danet, 1969; Melnik and Tims, 1974; Stoller, 1967, 1969; Torkelson and Romano, 1967). Therapists, viewing themselves interacting with their patients, may learn as much as they do in a good supervisory session (Geocaris, 1960; Beiser, 1966; Moore, FJ, et al., 1965). The initial shock value of seeing oneself performing inadequately, however, usually induces one to change for a limited time only. Therapists will soon adapt themselves to their television image unless there is a reworking of the material by a supervisor to reinforce learning. Observance by the supervisor of therapists in actual operation with patients is feasible by videotape, the contrast between what the therapists' reports of what they believe has been going on and the recorded events lending itself to emotional learning in the students. Supervisors also may be able to sharpen their own techniques in supervision by videotaping some of their supervisory sessions. Finally, beginning therapists may learn the process of interviewing and the management of various stages in treatment by watching videotapes (or sound movies) of expert therapists working with patients.

Although useful, written records and sound tape recordings alone are limited in bringing about an awareness on the part of patients of incongruous or paradoxical communication patterns. Sound films (Scheflen, 1963) and videotapes are more useful. Alger and Hogan (1966), employing videotape recordings in conjoint marital therapy, have pointed out that many levels of communication, as well as discrepancies between levels, become readily apparent to patients watching themselves immediately after interacting during a session. Differences between the televised actions and remembered responses are beneficially registered on patients. In individual therapy the videotaped interview may help patients see themselves as others see them. This is an excellent way of demonstrating to patients how they communicate. Use of the playback technique has proven valuable for many syndromes, including speech problems and alcoholism. A view of themselves in a drunken state may help motivate some

alcoholics to stop drinking. Videotaping may be of value in group and family therapy.

Obviously, it is impossible to record all of the treatment sessions of patients even if therapists possess the proper equipment. Apart from the expense of recording materials and the problem of storage of the recordings, transcription of serial recorded sessions is costly. Occasional recordings that are saved until they have served their purpose will, however, be found valuable. From a practical viewpoint, audiocassette tape recordings may serve the purpose of preserving the verbal interactions of patients and therapists. Although not nearly as valuable as videotapes, they are less expensive and are easily transcribed.

If therapists are not resistive to recording sessions, generally there will be relatively little difficulty in gaining patients' permission and cooperation. The apparatus is placed unobtrusively (it must not be concealed) in the room. When patients enter the room (usually when recordings are to be made, it is best to introduce this possibility to the patient at the initial interview), they may be approached in a way somewhat similar to this:

Th. Hello, I'm Dr. _____ .

Pt. Hello.

Th. Won't you sit down in this chair so we can talk things over?

Pt. Yes, thank you.

Th. (pointing to the tape recorder) Don't mind this machine. Sometimes I record an important session during therapy. It saves me the need to write everything down, so I can pay attention better to what is said.

Pt. I see.

Th. (smiling) Does this scare you?

Pt. Oh, no, if it's useful, I've never been recorded.

Th. Of course, what is recorded is completely confidential between us, but if you object for any reason, we don't really have to record.

Pt. No, I don't mind.

Th. If, for any reason, it interferes in any way or bothers you, tell me and I'll turn it off.

Pt. All right, I really don't mind.

Th. All right then, would you like to tell me about your problem so we can decide the best thing to do for you?

The recorder may be turned on at this point, or, if it has been on, no further attention should be paid to it. During later sessions it may be started prior to the patients' entering the room, so that the first comments may be recorded. If the recording is to be used for teaching purposes or transcribed for publication, a signed release is usually necessary. If, for any reason, patients object to the machine, it should immediately be turned off and not used again unless the patients' permission has been obtained.

64
Computers in Clinical Practice

Recording is being revolutionized by advances in computer technology. Machines can never replace the heuristic propensities of humans. But machines can supplement decision making and contemplative facilities by sorting, storing, categorizing, and retrieving vast amount of information with astonishing rapidity, efficiency, and accuracy. As new developments in switching, information theory, and automatic coding techniques become incorporated into computers, the machines' capabilities will undoubtedly be expanded to include preparation of software programs for instructions fed into the machines. For 30 years, computers have been indispensable instruments in medicine, aiding in diagnosis by categorizing and analyzing symptoms and physical findings (Brodman and van Woerhom, 1966).

New means of cataloging, storing, and dealing with complex variables have made it possible to employ the modern computer in psychiatric hospital systems Glueck and Stroebel, 1975b; (Laska et al., 1967) and even statewide systems (Sletten et al., 1970). In clinical practice, attempts have been made to computerize data regarding the history of patients, their mental status, and symptom clusters in an attempt to aid in diagnosis, prognosis, progress evaluation, and treatment outcome (Colby et al., 1969; Spitzer and Endicott, 1969). The making of computer diagnosis has been especially challenging and has attracted an increasing number of experimenters (Glueck and Stroebel, 1969; Maxwell, 1971). Glueck and Stroebel (1975b) have estimated that classification-assignment techniques are now available to permit accuracy in diagnostic labeling comparable to that of expert clinicians with an accuracy nearing 100 percent, but they point out that there is a lack of ability "of any classification system to achieve more than 70 to 75 percent interrater reliability in the prediction of psychopathological criteria."

Some attempts have also been made to refine computerized analysis of the electroencephalographic and neurologic findings, and innovative tactics have been evolved for various other types of data recording. The development of automated files help expedite the tabulation and retrieval of diagnostic, treatment, progress, and disposition information. Simple and effective methods for computer programming immeasurably help administrators, auditors, researchers, and ultimately clinicians by simplifying the massive amount of memoranda included in the traditional case record, enabling the scanning of essential elements of a case without needing to spend endless hours looking for pertinent facts.

The programming of computers to process the data of psychotherapy requires that therapists reduce the complex interpersonal transactions that take place to mathematical symbols that can be coded. Because the full encoding of human pursuits is not now, and probably never will be, complete, only limited parameters can be assigned to the circuitry of electronic computers. A number of interesting experiments have been reported. For instance, Colby (1963) has described the simulation of a neurotic process by a computer, and Bellman (1957, 1961) has, through dynamic programming, attempted to contribute insights into the interviewing process. A computer-assisted simulation of the clinical encounter is described by Harless and his associates (1971, 1972) and Hubbard and Templeton (1973).

More mundane operations that are being performed by computers include work with psychiatric records and other data related to the patient's history, symptomatology, and responses to therapy that may speedily and systematically be "memorized," synthesized, and retrieved. Feeding into the machine the recorded history, the psychological test results, and the symptoms of the patient, computers will quickly process these facts against the statistics of relative possibilities of diagnosis, prognosis, and treatment approaches (Rome et al., 1962; Swenson et al., 1963).

In clinical practice, attempts have been made to computerize data regarding the history of patients, their mental status, and symptom clusters in an attempt to aid in diagnosis, prognosis, progress evaluation, and treatment outcome (Colby et al., 1969; Spitzer and Endicott, 1969). The making of computer diagnosis has been especially challenging and has attracted an increasing number of experimenters. Classification-assignment techniques are now available to permit an accuracy in diagnostic labeling estimated as comparable to that of expert clinicians.

For the most part, computers in psychiatry have been used mainly in clinics, hospitals, and group practices for purposes of office automation. In this capacity they have improved productivity greatly, providing access to satellite offices and to vast data banks. For word processing, data processing, electronic mail, record keeping, billing, accounts payable, accounts receivable, preparation of insurance forms, and other office functions they are proving indispensable. This is invaluable when extensive reporting is necessary to qualify for third-party payments and in response to demands for better accountability and quality of care. A number of computer service bureaus now exist to provide fiscal-administrative help to mental health facilities in line with these demands. Software packages are available that help streamline office management, accounting, scheduling, billing, insurance form preparation, and on-line inquiry.

With the evolvement of efficient, low-cost microcomputers, clinicians are increasingly using computers for data organization and management of their practices. The possibilities are enormous and, for certain functions—as when vast amounts of data must be recorded, processed, stored, retrieved and printed—there is no equal to the efficiency of a computer. Whether computerization can be cost-effective for the therapist in solo practice is another matter. Simple office tasks such as billing and the balancing of checkbooks can be done more rapidly by hand. Although patient records take a good deal more time to process in a computer, they can be meticulously kept and easily and accurately updated. The preparation of reports and manuscripts can efficiently be accomplished through word processing. Programs such as Word Perfect and Microsoft Word, once mastered, can be a godsend for a therapist writing a paper. If a literature search on a certain topic is necessary, a communications program using a modem enables rapid access of data bases that will produce in minutes a print-out equivalent to days of painstaking exploration in a library. The National Library of Medicine has a computerized literature retrieval service, MEDLARS (Medical Literature Analysis and Retrieval System), consisting of 20 data bases that are accessible from terminals at more than 2000 U.S. institutions. Among the most commonly used component is MEDLINE, which has about four million references to journal articles and books. An area that is now being developed is artificial intelligence, with the goal of answering questions beyond the MEDLAR system that are often diagnosis related and "perform at the level of a human expert in the area that they're programmed for" (JAMA 252: 2337, 1984). Other commercial databank services for literature searches include SCIMATE, Knowledge Index, BRS Catalogue, and Psychoinfo Database, the latter developed by the American Psychological Association and which has more than four million references and abstracts. In research, the computer is irreplaceable for statistical analysis, data management, graphics plotting, creation of tables, and indexing references.

Apart from word processing and research, the clinician may find sundry other uses for the computer. Among the software programs now in use are ones for automated history taking, clinical records management, patient interviewing, mood assessment, treatment planning, medication monitoring, outcome monitoring, projective testing, and patient–therapist simulation. Therapists may through rating scales be helped in estimating the mental status of patients, evaluating prognosis, predicting outcome, making a diagnosis, assigning special treatments, and tracking progress in therapy (Glueck and Stroebal, 1980).

The question arises as to whether computers can improve quality control of patient care. In medical practice this has been shown to be feasible (Pollak, 1985). In psychiatry this also is possible in some areas.

Thus, where psychotropic medications are prescribed, anticipated cross-reactions with miscellaneous drugs the patients habitually take for existing physical ailments—as well as tabulation of dosage, complications, and side effects—can be expeditiously accessed. Sophisticated software programs oriented around the DSM-3 classification system may be helpful in diagnosis and thus in the selection of appropriate treatment. As a diagnostic helpmate, computers are acceptable to patients and do at least as good a job as clinicians and at lower cost (Sawyer, 1966; Scharfstein, et al., 1980). A number of programs are also available for diagnostic psychological testing. Automated testing with the Minnesota Multiphasic Personality Inventory (MMPI), Beck Depression Scale, and Strong Campbell Interest Inventory permits rapid administration and scoring with as good patient compliance as with traditionally administered tests. Moreover, the level of accuracy is relatively high in culturally diverse clinical settings (Ensel, 1980; Labeck et al. 1983; Green, 1982; Colligan and Offord, 1985). The application of a computerized information system to the psychotherapeutic care of individual patients and families is obviously more complicated. Psychiatric problems involve much more complex data than do medical conditions. For example, in nephrology the data base consists of limited physical signs, symptoms, laboratory findings and relevant therapeutic information. In any psychiatric problem, however, there is a host of interrelated biochemical, neurophysiological, intrapsychic, interpersonal, social, and philosophic systems, each of which is tremendously complex and influences treatment progress.

Computers have been programmed to give clinicians reliable information about such variables as symptom change, work and social adjustment, sexual functioning, and risk of suicide (Greist et at., 1973).

Computer interviewing is efficient, reliable, accurate, and highly acceptable to most patients. Up to 85 percent of markedly disturbed patients may be interviewed by computers at the time of admission to a hospital (Erdman et al., 1981). A number of programs lend themselves to consultation, performing as effectively as clinicians in making clinical decisions. For example, Greist et al. (1973) have evaluated an on-line computer program that makes predictions about suicide risks that are more accurate than those of clinicians. A number of computer software programs have been designed to meet the needs of handicapped people. Thus successes have been secured in cerebral palsy, learning disabilities, and hyperactive and autistic children to improve attention and performance. Computers are increasingly being used in psychoeducation to dispense information about topics such as birth control and sex, and it is often easier and less embarrassing for patients to learn via computer rather than a human lecturer. If therapists are looking for silent, nonarguing cotherapists, they may find it in computer programs such as BARRY which engages patients in dialogue; this can be of help in monitoring the depth of depression and adherence to the medication schedule. Computers can be programmed to help interview patients regarding substance abuse (alcohol, tobacco, drugs) in a relatively relaxed atmosphere.

By interacting with the computer, clinicians can obtain or substantiate DSM-III diagnoses with a high degree of reliability. Facilitating this is the software program "Psychiatric Diagnostic Assistance." Helpful also in making clinical decisions are such programs as MYCIN, CADUCEUS, AND PUFF. A rapid screening for most mental disorders is now possible (Carr et al., 1981; Fischer, 1974). Attitudes, beliefs, and intimate important bits of information may be revealed by patients to the computer in many cases more readily than to a human interviewer (Greist and Klein, 1981) which is an important aid in treatment planning. Suggested treatment programs already exist in relation to agoraphobia, obsessive-compulsive neurosis, and depression, and more are being developed. Computerized information regarding new psychotropic drugs, changes in administration of existing medications, and side effects and their management can be a valuable aid in pharmacotherapy. The best known data bases for drug information (interactions, contraindications, warnings) are Medline, International Pharmaceutical Abstracts, and the University of Wisconsin Lithium Information Center. Other uses for computers are the updating of available pamphlets, books, and other materials for bibliotherapy and psychoeducation; information regarding social, recreational, and therapeutic resources in the community; and location of self-help groups. Computer-elicited case histories have been shown to be more than 90 percent accurate and reveal data of importance in the management of patients, some of which were not divulged to human interviewers (Carr et al., 1983; Greist et al., 1973, 1977; Lang et at., 1970).

Experiments with computers to enhance psychotherapeutic operations have resulted in the development of a number of interactive programs. Computer mediated psychotherapy systems are to an extent organized around the symbolization of the computer as another human being with which one can interact. People often do this with animals who as pets substitutively serve an important but limited interpersonal function. The computer can become much more anthropomorphized than an animal when it is programmed to communicate in language the person can understand. The earliest example of a computer therapist is provided by ELIZA, a program devised by Weizenbaum (1966, 1976) a Massachusetts Institute of Technology computer scientist, which simulated a Rogerian non-directive therapist (Colby, et al. 1966). If we observe subjects "talking" to ELIZA we can see how easily transferential phenomena can be elicited, and we may speculate about the usefulness of computers as therapeutic instruments for cognitive and value change above and beyond their proven educational value (DeMuth, 1982).

Attempts have been made to do this (Colby, 1980; Rokeach, 1975; Cole et al., 1976; Friedman, 1980; Spero, 1978; Hedlund, 1979; Selmi et al., 1982; Trappi, 1981; Wagman, 1980; Wegman and Kerber, 1980; and Zarr, 1984). The concensus of opinion by these authors is that despite the threat of dehumanization, there will be important future uses for the computer as an adjunct in organized psychotherapy programs. Caution nevertheless dictates not to compare the brainpower and skill of a computer to that of well-trained and empathic therapists. Granted that some computer behavioral, cognitive, and relaxation programs may be conveniently and economically administered, computers have not yet reached the stage where they have made psychotherapists obsolete.

Computer fantasy games, fashioned after the popular computerized games for youngsters, Dungeons and Dragons, and Adventure (Adams, 1980; Clarke and Schoech, 1984) have been developed for child and adolescent patients which allow them to control the actions of characters on the display monitor with whom the patients identify (Allen, 1984). Children may even construct the main characters in the game—identifying them with the angels and monsters in their own inner world—give them names, and design their dodges and achievements. A tremendous amount of material becomes available to the therapist through such modern play therapy and this can provide an opportunity to question, encourage, and support the children in working through fantasies, needs, and defenses. The responses of the children may be saved on disk for later replay, to procure associations, to invite more reality oriented revisions, and to improve decision making.

The program ELIZA and the interactive fantasy games devised for children with emotional problems open up the vast possibilities of the computer as a way of influencing behavior that can serve as an adjunct to psychotherapy. As has been mentioned before, the computer can never replace the professional who provides the warmth and empathy of a skilled human relationship (Spero, 1978) but in some ways it can do selective tasks better—for example, educational reinforcement. Required is appropriate software prepared by creative innovators. Some leads in this direction have been provided by a number of experimenters. Reitman (1985) has described a self-help program for impotence oriented around cognitive restructuring that has produced excellent results. Thirty-eight other programs of psychoeducation, sex education for children, sex therapy for varied sexual problems, and therapy for couples' problems are being developed. Lang et al. (1970) have developed a program for desensitization of phobias that has produced results equal to that of a clinician. Schneider (1984) has devised a four-week "Quit-by-Mail" antismoking program with clients treated at home who mail to the author's clinic diary sheets of smoking control progress and responses to smoking questionnaires. These data are entered into a computer, and a personalized reply, prepared by the computer, is mailed back to clients. Initial successes have been encouraging.

Because verbal psychoeducation is an important aspect of a well-organized psychotherapy schema, it has been more and more incorporated into some therapeutic designs. It is, however, costly and inefficient when it is employed by therapists themselves especially in short-term psychotherapy where time is limited. Bibliotherapy has been of some use in providing supplementary readings, but often these cover a subject too diffusely and do not zero in on the specific problems of patients.

It is posited that improved computer methods will revolutionize education with replacement of present-day teaching technologies by computer systems that permit active personalized conversational dialogue between student and instrument, thereby eliminating the highly inefficient lecture techniques that reduce the student to an immobilized, passive, and resistant receiving station. An actual attempt in this direction, the teaching of interviewing by employing a suitably programmed computer to simulate an initial psychiatric interview, has met with some success (Bellman et al., 1963, 1966). Here trainees assume the role of therapists, and the computer, properly programmed, replies as patients would respond. The computer may be programmed to represent a range of problems and patients. Jaffe (1964) has described specific techniques for interview analysis through the aid of computers with special methods of coding interpersonal phenomena; such computers have potential research applications. Wedding (1984) has developed a technique of mailing letters to patients after the third or fourth session that reiterate and elaborate many of the points brought out in therapy—occasionally even anticipating points to be made in the future. A personalized letter typed on the computer is merged with psychoeducational data and specific instructions relevant to the problems of the patient avoiding irrelevant and counterproductive information. The planning of vocational and educational counseling can be vastly enhanced through the use of a computer in an automated "Educational and Vocational Guidance System" (Murray, 1984). A modem provides a telecommunications link between the computer and a data base, such as the "Guidance Information System" of TSC, a Houghton Mifflin Company. The advantages of computer-assisted instruction for patients over written materials and verbal educational methods have repeatedly been demonstrated.

The interactional aspects of computer instruction permit learners to proceed at their own pace, minimizing the transference reactions common in interviewing that may interfere with learning, getting immediate feedback to data provided by the computer, allowing for greater flexibility in learning, and providing great stores of relevant information. A tremendous amount of literature has accumulated detailing the advantages and drawbacks of computer-assisted information systems (Flynn and Kuczeruk (1984), Misselt (1980), Schoech (1982).

Microcomputers are being used in remedial training for correction of memory, perception, concept formation, and problem-solving deficits resulting from brain impairment (Kurlychek and Gland, 1984). Rehabilitation professionals are also employing computers to assist their work with handicapped learning-disabled children and adults. Patients who have suffered a stroke may be asked to acquire and use an inexpensive computer in their homes for cognitive rehabilitation (Brady, 1984). Programs are available to enhance attention, initiation/inhibition skills, cognitive discrimination, and differential responses.

These examples of computer use in psychotherapy merely provide an inkling of what the future has in store for this remarkable instrument. Zarr (1984) has pointed out the need for enthusiasm and belief in computers' effectiveness as a requirement in computer-mediated psychotherapy. He also believes that the best uses are in brief and focused therapy, especially of a cognitive behavioral type. Excellent accounts of future trends in uses of computers in mental health may be found in the books by M. D. Schwartz (1984) and Crawford et al. (1980).

The optimistic reports are to some degree offset by some emerging problems. For example, attempts made to develop checklists of symptoms and levels of function to enhance psychiatric record keeping have been thwarted by both technical difficulties and resistance by clinicians who find it difficult to accept computers. The old hardware problems that involved a batch-mode use of mainframe systems with difficult-to-manage punched cards have more or less been eliminated by the use of interactive mainframe and microcomputer systems. A number of problems have not yet been resolved, however, such as the programming of computers to simulate clinicians' summaries of input data, or to make inferences about diagnosis, prognosis, and treatment. What appears essential is refinement of the data that are most suitable for psychiatric summary statements.

Prevailing complaints are that the need to adhere to a preset and rigid reporting system that requires the skills of a human clinician cannot be subtly managed by a computer. Moreover, because the variables of human behavior are so complex and diverse, the computer reports to date have failed to differentiate patients who present even dissimilar clinical pictures. Sometimes a failure occurs in entering key pieces of information, and this results in wrong diagnoses. Gradually, greater sophistication is entering computer usage, but there still remain the difficulties of clinical compliance and acceptance.

Among the reasons computers do not enjoy greater popularity among clinicians than they do are the difficulties inherent in mastering them. Not only must users learn a new language, acquire typing skills, and technical know-how but also plow through complicated reading. Many instructional manuals are not monuments of conceptual clarity or good writing. It takes a great deal of time and patience to master operations that are more complex than simple word processing. Learning to develop new computer programs is difficult, but if interest is there are and time of no essence, the effort can be rewarding. Examples of such use is provided in an article by Klepac (1984). The complexity of the data elicited in psychotherapy makes it difficult to organize data for purposes of computerization, although

some preliminary attempts have been made toward providing greater regularity in this direction. Mergenthaler (1985), for example, describes an attempt to integrate information technology following guidelines of fundamental research in psychoanalysis.

Therapists first entering the world of computers may be bewildered by the vast variety of hardware equipment and software programs available. It is best in purchasing a computer to deal with a reliable agency locally to which a machine may be returned for repair or adjustment if necessary. The most popular computers are IBM instruments, or IBM-compatible clones that are less expensive; in the latter case, purchasers must be sure that repair facilities will not be too difficult to find. Apple (including MacIntosh) computers are excellent, but buyers should ascertain beforehand that any software purchased is suitable for these machines. If possible, a computer with at least 640 K of RAM (memory) and a hard disk should be purchased, but 256 K of RAM and two drives for floppy disks may be adequate for most purposes. A monochrome monitor is eminently suitable, but some therapists prefer a color monitor, even though this is more expensive, because color makes some interactive programs more interesting. A good dot-matrix printer will be needed for speed and, if desired, near–letter-quality printing. A stand to support the printer and covers for the fanfold paper rounds out the basic equipment. Accessory purchases can include a modem (with at least 1200-band speed) for accessing outside data bases and equipment for use with compact disks.

Elaborations of computer programs are proceeding at an enormous pace, covering the entire field of practitioners', interests. Thus software programs, such as psQ "Practice Partner" (psyQ systems, 1730 Rhode Island Ave., N. W., Washington, D.C. 20086) and "Insight Billing Software" (Applied Innovations, Inc., South Kingstown Office Park, Wakefield, RI 02879) are sold with the object of managing the paperwork requirements of mental health practitioners in relation to preparation of billings, daily schedules, accounts receivable, insurance forms, and special reports.

Some programs exist that prepare a DSM-III diagnosis as required by third-party payers. In the "P.D.M. 2000 computerized Diagnostic Interview Schedule" (p.r.n. systems, 222 N. Midvale Blvd., Suite 1, Madison, WI 53705) patients are interviewed on a computer, the data are processed, and a "clear, concise, and documented written report of suggested DSM-III diagnoses" is offered. A "computerized textbook" is available in "Decision Base," which diagnoses all DSM-III disorders, takes histories, and programs other functions (P.W. Long, M.D., II 1206-750 West Broadway, Vancouver, B.C., V5Z Canada). One program, MORTON, administers the Beck Depression Inventory for diagnostic purposes. Tests such as the MMPI are executed with a written narrative describing the personality dynamics and interpreting the scale scores. (Behaviordyne, Inc., 994 San Antonio Road, P.O. Box 10994, Palo Alto, CA 94303-0997; Applied Innovations, Inc., South Kingstown Office Park, Wakefield RI 02879). A computerized stress-inventory program generates a stress profile for diagnostic purposes and suggests changes (Preventive Measures, Inc., 1115 West Campus Road, Lawrence, KS 66044). A "Chronic Pain Battery" screens for psychopathology (Pain Resource Center, Inc., P.O. Box 2836, Durham, NC 27705). "Q Fast" converts questionnaires and surveys into interactive computer programs useful for practioners and researchers who administer tests, and "Psychostat" is a complete statistical package (Stat Soft, 2833 East 10th St. Suite 4, Tulsa, OK 74104).

The "Gordon Diagnostic System" administers game-like tasks for diagnostic and treatment recommendations for attention-deficit disorders and hyperactivity (Gordon Systems, P.O. Box 746, DeWitt, NY 13214). Software programs are being developed for automating test-report writing, statistical analysis of data, projective drawing tests, diagnostic screening batteries for children and adults, and many other purposes. A number of other microcomputer software programs are designed for initial evaluations, session summaries, treatment planning, termination and discharge, summaries, child and adolescent diagnostic screening, intelligence test interpretation, and Rorschach data summary and report (Psychologistics, Inc. P.O. Box 3896, Dept. A, Indialantic, FL 32903).

For therapists interested in research, a statistical analysis package is available (Walonick Associates, 6500 Nicolet Ave. S., Minneapolis, MN 55423). "PsycINFO" has prepared a compact disk (which will require special equipment) providing summaries of the world's literature in psychology from more than 1400 journals. For quick, convenient searches there is "PsycLIT" (The American Psychological Association, 1400 North Uhle Street, Arlington, VA 22201). The use of microcomputers to provide direct access to databases has increased markedly in the past few years. It is not unusual for clinicians to keep terminals in their offices and also in their homes. New user-friendly computer literature search systems are available from various sources. BRS/Saunders Colleague is a medical literature and information-retrieval service accessible 22 hours daily containing both bibliographic and full-text references. Some of the data bases are MEDLINE, Medical and Psychological Previews, PsycInfo, Excerpta Medica, the full text of the *American Journal of Psychiatry* and also of the *Comprehensive Textbook of Psychiatry*, 4th edition. Colleague, another data base, can be menu driven or accessed by direct commands (BRS/Saunders, 555 East Lancaster Avenue, St. Davids, PA 19087.) KNOWLEDGE INDEX is DIALOG's after-hours, simplified search service, available weekends and evenings. It is intended for the weekend user and the at-home user. Its data bases include Mental Health Abstracts, MEDLINE, and PsycInfo (available through local DIALOG offices or DIALOG Information Services, Inc., 3460 Hillview Avenue, Palo Alto CA 94304). Health-sciences librarians can provide further information.

Some periodicals that may be of interest to therapists are (1) *Computers in Psychiatry/Psychology* (26 Trumbull Street, New Haven, CT 06511; quarterly, $40 a year), (2) *Computer Use in Social Science,* (CUSS Network, Graduate School of Social Work, University of Texas, Box 19129, Arlington, TX 76019; quarterly, $10 a year). Recommended books are (1) J. D. Lieff, *How to Buy a Personal Computer Without Anxiety.* Cambridge, Mass., Ballinger Publishing Co., 1980; (2) J. D. Lieff, Computer Applications in Psychiatry. Washington, DC, American Psychiatric Press, Inc., 1987; (3) M. D. Schwartz: *Using Computers in Clinical Practice,* New York, Haworth Press, 1984. To use telecommunications for accessing data bases, a subscription to systems such as "Source" or "Telenet" is recommended. Mental

health software catalogues may be obtained from (1) American Association for Medical Systems (AAMSI, 1101 Connecticut Avenue N.W., Suite 700, Washington, DC 20036); (2) Psychological Software Specialists, 1776 Fowler, Suite P, Richland, WA 99352; (3) Computers in Psychiatry/Psychology 26 Trumbull Street, New Haven, Connecticut, 06511; and (4) National Health Information Clearinghouse, Dept. GGG, P.O. Box 1133, Washington, DC 20013. Recommended reports and articles are (1) M. D. Schwartz: "Resources for Computer Users." *Hospital & Community Psychiatry* 35:537-539, 1984; (2) J. L. Hedlund et al.: *Computers in Mental Health: A Review and Annotated Bibliography.* NIMH Clearinghouse, Room 15C-17, 5600 Fishers Lane, Rockville, MD 20857; (3) J. H. Johnson: Computer Technology and Methodology in Clinical Psychology. Psychiatry and Behavior Medicine, Vol. 13, No. 4, Aug. 1982; (4) *Applying Computers in Social Service and Mental Health Agencies: A Guide to Selecting, Equipment, Procedures, and Strategies.* Administration in Social Work, N.Y., Haworth Press, 1981.

65
Psychotherapy During Childhood, Adolescence, and Old Age

There are critical stages in the development of personality in which crucial incidents and experiences have a destructive impact that are not registered during another period. The stages of weaning, habit training, bodily exploratory activities, entry into school, puberty and adolescence, marriage, pregnancy, child rearing, and retirement and old age pose special problems that influence psychotherapeutic interventions when these are needed.

CHILD AND ADOLESCENT THERAPY

Psychopathology in children must at all times be viewed against the backdrop of developmental norms. Moreover, it must be considered in relation to existing family and social distortions that deprive children of needs essential to their growth or subject them to rejection, violence, or overstimulation with which they cannot cope. Among common noxious influences are parental absence, rejection, seduction, overprotection, or cruelty. Contemporary disruptions in family life, such as a detached and disinterested father, subjection to television bombardments of violence and sexuality, poverty, lack of intimate family ties, and

racial conflicts at school, exaggerate the normal problems inherent in growing up. Fears of separation, resistance to socialization, defiance of discipline, sibling rivalry, and Oedipal crises may also interfere with the resolution of developmental disturbances. Emotional difficulties in childhood usually express themselves in symptoms of excessive irritability, hyperkinesis, fearfulness, daydreaming, obsessions, compulsions, bed-wetting, or excessive masturbation. Sleep, speech, eating, and learning disturbances are common, as are psychophysiological manifestations such as tics, spasms, vomiting, diarrhea, headaches, asthma, ulcers, and colitis.

During the first three years of life, excessive and continuous crying unrelieved by attention from the mother signals a state of unresolved tension (Cramer, 1959). Inordinate rocking, thumb sucking, head rolling, sleeplessness, food refusal, vomiting, retention, soiling, temper tantrums, ritualistic behavior, defiance, stammering, and unusual aggression often indicate disturbances in the child's environment, particularly in the relationship with the mother. In a small number of instances, these are manifestations of organic physical or neurological ailments.

During the fourth and fifth years extravagant fears, nightmares, excessive masturbation, and enuresis reflect sexual identity difficulties. Overactivity, tantrums, negativism, and destructiveness constitute another type of patterning for conflicts developed during this period. Such difficulties are often nurtured by sexual and hostile acting-out in parents and by their seductive use of the child to satisfy their own neurotic needs.

Neurosis during the sixth to ninth years of life frequently manifests itself in failing adjustment at school, the outcroppings taking the form of school phobias, truancy, aggression toward fellow pupils and teachers, and learning disabilities. Outright neurotic symptoms may appear in other types of phobias, tics (blinking, grimacing, jerking of the head and extremities), stammering, compulsions, and conversion phenomena. Excessive withdrawal and daydreaming or aggressiveness and antisocial activities (e.g., stealing, exhibitionism, fetishism, peeping) interfere with social adjustment. Frank, unbound anxiety may erupt. Eventuating psychophysiological disturbances may derange various organ functionings.

In the preadolescent (latency) stage, between nine and twelve, there may be enhanced aggressiveness, fighting with siblings and friends, and occasional depressive states stimulated by disappointments and failures.

During adolescence, potential problems incorporate the full spectrum of psychopathology from behavior disorders to psychoneuroses to psychoses. The emotional disorders that are most common in adolescence, however, are adjustment difficulties, personality disturbances, scholastic failure, school phobia, enuresis, psychosomatic complaints, delinquency, anorexia, bulimia, and identity disorders.

In the tumultuous growth period of adolescence, with the extensive alterations in the physical, biochemical, and emotional makeup characteristic of this epoch, therapists must, in judging the degree of disturbance, take into consideration the normal anxieties and concerns that plague individuals.

Adolescents have a need for both uniqueness and difference, a desire to conform and a fear of being different from others of their age and sex. Strong and strange impulses dominate the body as the sexual glands mature and the adolescent comes under the influence of erotic thoughts and feelings. New demands are made by family and community; no longer is the youth considered a child. Swings into independence and aggressiveness are followed by refuge in childish dependency and passivity. The need for recognition vies with the impulse to defy. Drives for success and prestige are paramount, while conflict rages over issues of religion and death. A fluctuating sense of values and confusion in identity add to the adolescent's turmoil.

Constructive solutions will be needed. The adolescent must first dissipate dependency ties sufficiently to enter into a more assertive and independent attitude toward the world. This is especially necessary in a society where the burden of one's own support and ultimately that of one's family will fall on the individual's shoulders. Second, the adolescent must learn to control sexual feelings so that there will be a proper balance between restraint and expression. Evolvement of adequate sexual role identification is mandatory. Third, one must change from the subordinate manner of a child to the dominant habitude of a grownup, to feel equal with other adults. Fourth, one must develop a cooperative attitude toward authority, without feeling victimized or excessively hostile. Fifth, one must learn to be assertive and creative and to assume leadership on occasion, without ulterior motives of control or power. A proper educational and career choice must be made.

In primitive cultures the adolescent struggle is less intense than in civilized societies because there is much more continuity in the behavior patterns of child and adult. Primitive economies are less complex and consequently afford an easier and earlier emancipation from parental support. Child marriage and premarital intercourse are more or less condoned. This sanction affords the growing child an outlet for energies. Civilized societies impose barriers against which the adolescent will struggle. While relatively mature biologically, the adolescent cannot become economically self-sufficient until well along in adult life. A large proportion of today's young people are forced by the requirements of their chosen careers to enter into a long and expensive period of study that must be financed by their parents.

Hostility and resentment are frequently the outcome of the conflict between the impulse to break dependency ties and the need for material help and support. Although adolescents feel an urge to lash out at their parents, most realize that such action will result in retaliatory measures that threaten personal security. In addition, the hostile urge clashes with some of the adolescent's ideals. Thus a youth is at the mercy of many ambivalent and conflicting values and goals. Sometimes the child is driven by contradictory impulses reflecting both the secret sexual and delinquent wishes of one or more parents that they have projectively and covertly conveyed to their offspring, as well as guilt feelings of the parents that have prevented the parents from personally expressing these impulses. The child here acts as a messenger for the parents, who stealthily relish the exploits of their offspring and then heap blame on the child.

Under the best of circumstances the adolescent period is a chaotic one and is characterized by a recrudescence of problems that had their origin in childhood and were never adequately resolved. Often parents have not been aware of these problems, and they are dismayed and frightened by the eruption of severe behavioral disturbances in a previously exemplary child. The early adolescent (12 to 15 years) is plagued by regressive thrusts that conflict with the new growth demands of this stage. The child ambivalently veers between submission and rebellion, sociability and isolation, friendships and enmities, overactivity and retreat, depression and overexcitement. Delinquency and acting-out are common. The struggle in this period is a process of resolution of sexual identity, object ambivalence, and needs for separation and individuation. In middle adolescence (14 to 17 years) there is some resolution of sexual conflicts with greater ability to relate. Narcissistic defenses alternate with more mature coping mechanisms. Homosexual episodes, depersonalization, anxiety, and runaway tendencies may occur. In late adolescence (17 to 21 years) separation-individuation accelerates, object choice solidifies, identifications strengthen. Identity crises, depression, and adjustment difficulties continue, however, often encouraged by available peer groups involved in sexual and deviant exploits.

In summary, *adjustment reactions* to growing up are a normal byproduct of socialization. They occur in all children. The reactions become exaggerated in those who are subjected to extraordinary stress, or whose developmental needs are not being met by parents, or who are being grossly mismanaged, improperly disciplined, or subjected to cruel and abusive treatment. The constitutional makeup of the child will influence the severity of reactions and the ability to cope with the stress being experienced. The responses of the parents to the child's reactions will also influence the outcome. If they are kindly and caring adults, capable of maintaining control of the situation and their own emotions, the child may be helped through the critical adjustment years. If they are not so equipped, minor maladjustment reactions may explode into severe behavior disorders that can persist and influence adversely later stages of the child's development. The ultimate outcome may be a pathological neurotic or psychotic reaction for which treatment will be needed.

General Principles of Child and Adolescent Therapy

Choice of techniques in child therapy is complicated by a wide variety of available interventions. These are usually determined more by predilections of the clinician than by precise diagnostic assessments. This, in the words of Harrison (1979), has produced a state of "undisciplined chaos" in the field. Experience is the mother of compromise and the great leveler of differences in therapeutic operation. For example, whereas in past years there was a tendency to segregate behavioral from psychodynamic approaches, a fusion of these methodologies has more and more dominated the practices of many child therapists. Family therapy, with its transactional system orientation, has become an indispensable mode and is often executed coordinately with behavioral–psychodynamic–medicinal approaches and environmental therapy. It seems obvious that therapists cannot neglect any links in the behavioral chain among children any more than they can neglect them in adults, and this will necessitate the use of interventions designed to influence different zones of pathology. With the present knowledge, therapists can match a number of syndromes with appropriate interventions provided a proper diagnosis can be made.

The basic rule in treating disorders in childhood is providing an adequate climate in which developmental needs are met, opportunities for impulse gratification supplied, and proper discipline and restraints imposed. Alterations of the milieu are usually required and the cooperation of the parents and family may be essential even to the point of exposing them to individual or family therapy. Unless this is done, work with the child alone may prove to be fruitless, the parents and other family members sabotaging the child's efforts at adjustment. Indeed a sick child may be the vehicle for holding a family together.

Therapeutic interventions will accord with the accepted theoretical model. Thus, if deviant behavior is regarded as originating through reinforcement of unhealthy patterns by the family, treatment tactics will be organized around modifying the consequences of such patterns through behavior therapy (Ross, A, 1972). Should a psychoanalytic family interaction model be adopted, a search for pathogenic conflicts and their resolution through insight and working-through in the patient–family–therapist relationships will be embarked on. If constitutional organic neurological factors are considered most significant, developmental and language lags that interfere with the normal timetable in the evolution of essential functions will be looked for. Prescription of medications and the institution of adequate training routines will follow.

The existence in childhood of relatively undeveloped personality functions, strivings for independence and mastery that inevitably conflict with dependency yearnings, heightened motor activity and fantasy life, lowered frustration tolerance, greater needs for discipline, and extraordinary plasticity of the developing ego will require innovations in therapy technique. Environmental manipulation, crisis intervention (q.v.), family therapy (q.v.), drawings (q.v. art therapy), the use of play materials (q.v. play therapy), and the employment of greater activity and supportiveness with efforts at symptom control are more or less standard aspects of child treatment. The key to management is a proper diagnosis with assessment of the potential of the child as well as the role the mother and family will play in organizing a therapeutic milieu.

The majority of child therapy clinics

use therapeutic methods that stress the interpersonal therapeutic relationship, focus on the presenting problems, and encourage therapist activities of a friendly, active, and supporting nature to provide a corrective experience for the child. Psychotherapy is considered a new and unique growth experience that is family centered with the focus of concern on the child (F. H. Allen, 1962, 1963).

In mental health clinics for children that emphasize careful evaluation, diagnosis, and treatment planning, both the child and parent are given attention. Thus at the beginning of therapy, parents require help in expressing their feelings about the plans being made for therapy. Prior to bringing their children into a treatment situation, parents are aided in ventilating their hopes, doubts, and fears. Discussions consider the part they can play in preparing their offspring for treatment. In these early interviews the role distortions of the parents with each other and their children usually become apparent. It is essential to involve both parents, when possible, in the planning to avoid distorting the family drama further. The beginning phase of treatment with children is diagnostic for the therapist. The therapist witnesses how the children react to a unique experience of acceptance and empathy, their degree of accessibility, the content and manner of their communications, and the ways that they express or conceal feeling. At the start, children will probably perceive the therapist as they do other adults—hostile, dogmatic, overprotective, or omnipotent. Expectations, fears, and desires for magical cure are sooner or later projected onto the therapist. Recognizing this the therapist encourages the child to express and then to test out misconceptions in the hope of inspiring a more realistic life orientation. Dealing with the child's need to transform the therapist into a good or bad parent, steady maintenance of one's identity helps to provide for the child a truly differentiating experience.

But even in the first interview a therapeutic process may begin. Winnicott (1969), using the child's drawings, has demonstrated that therapists can score a significant imprint on the child and increase their understanding in just one interview.

Emerging from this diagnostic phase is a therapeutic plan determined by the children's physical condition, the evaluative studies of the psychologist, the ability of the children to form a relationship with the therapists, and the cooperation of the parents. A definite schedule is set up, usually once weekly, the children and parents having separate and sometimes concurrent appointments. In a team plan different team members may see the parents and the children.

Changing paradigms of therapy have placed an accent on *child behavior therapy*. Its briefness, ease of administration, and effectiveness in behavior and habit disorders have enabled therapists to help some children, particularly those who because of deficiencies in motivation, cooperation, intelligence, and verbal skills have not been able to use traditional interview and play techniques. The focus is on altering the environmental circumstances that initiate and support deviant patterns. No effort is made to probe for conflicts or to promote insight. There is little emphasis on the importance of the child–therapist relationship except to establish sufficient rapport to enhance the acceptance of social reinforcement. The traditional diagnostic categories are not considered of great importance.

Initially, a behavioral assessment is made of the problem, consisting of an exact description of its nature, its history, its frequency, the circumstances under which symptoms occur, the reactions of the parents or teachers, and the consequences to the children. Many pertinent techniques on behavior therapy are delineated in Chapter 51. The selective method used with particular children will depend on the specific behavior to be altered. Bijou and Redd (1975) have outlined some useful methods. Monitoring procedures are set up to provide data about progress, and parents are trained in proper responses, and at home to act as accessory behavior therapists.

Thus, in children who have tendencies that are upsetting to others (such as pushing, fighting, hitting), a program may be organized that grants rewards (candy, a token or points exchangeable for something the children like to receive or do, praise) for each instance of desirable social behavior. Coordinately, an aversive contingency may be employed whenever the obnoxious behavior occurs, for example, removal of the children from the room for a period and placement in a room without toys. Or the children may be penalized for conduct by taking away some tokens or points.

If children are psychologically withdrawn or show shy or phobic behavior, they are rewarded with praise and attention when they manifest sociable and nonphobic behavior. They are ignored when they do not. Reinforcements are gradually spaced and delayed, and requirements for reinforcement gradually are made more stringent to shape behavior. Modeling appropriate behavior may be utilized both for the children and the parents, the latter observing how the therapist responds through a one-way mirror if one is available. Systematic desensitization may also be employed. Thus, a school phobia is treated by gradual introduction to the school environment for slowly increasing periods, each success being rewarded.

The acquisition of new and desirable behavior repertoires will call for contingent positive reinforcement for initial improvements then for increasing intensities of the new behavior. Inappropriate normal responses (e.g., of speech, conduct) may gradually be extinguished and displaced to suitable situations by adequate reinforcements.

These operant techniques are also applicable to hospitalized adolescent patients.

Their effectiveness is illustrated by the experience in the Adolescent Service of the Boston State Hospital (Lehrer et al., 1971). A token economy is tailored to individual needs or problems. Patients are given points that can be redeemed for money, school attendance, and participation in various activities. Points buy food (hot dogs, pizza, hamburgers, soda, or ice cream). Then patients are permitted to play a jukebox, games (pinball, table tennis, board games) as well as purchase various items in a special teenage lounge that has a soda fountain and grill. Points are also exchangeable for parties, dances, camping expeditions, and so on. Points are taken away for infraction of the rules. Serious violations, such as assaultiveness and abuse of property, lead to restriction of all activities until the patients have worked out with a psychologist strategies for controlling their behavior and proper point payment for any damages that they have done to property.

Some therapists use the findings of dynamic psychology to conceptualize the development and problems of children. The therapeutic focus of *child psychoanalysis* follows this model and brings to the children's awareness the anxieties, unconscious wishes, and defenses that produce their difficulties. Since children do not respond to therapy as adults do, classical technique must be modified taking into account the children's tendencies to project problems onto the environment and the lack of motivation for therapy. The parents and other important members of the family also have to be brought into the therapeutic situation through parent guidance, family therapy, or individual therapy in accordance with what is required in each individual case. Because children express themselves most readily in play, play therapy is seen as an important tool for probing conflicts and for interaction with therapists. The analysis of children's problems was originally explicated by Sigmund Freud in his "Analysis of a Phobia in a Five-Year-

Old Boy.'' The two main orientations that emerged were those of Anna Freud (1928, 1945, 1946) and Melanie Klein (1932, 1961). According to Anna Freud, children as young as three years of age may be analyzed. Free association and the couch position, however, cannot be employed. Instead the children's activities in movement, play, and random talk are used for interpretation, as are stories, dreams, and the children's reactions to the therapist. Caution in making interpretations is essential since the egos of children are not as firmly developed as those of adults. Generally children do not develop a transference neurosis, instead reflecting more of the immediate situation than the past. The cooperation of the parents should be enlisted as an adjunct to their children's treatment but no attempt is made to offer direct advice. In Melanie Klein's technique, children as young as two may be treated. Unlike Anna Freud's method, the deepest interpretations to fantasies revealed by children in play are given, starting with the first interview. These are concerned with Oedipal wishes, awareness of parental intercourse, the desire to destroy the mother's body, and the desire to incorporate the father's penis. Since the reality situation is not considered significant, the cooperation of the parents is not sought; indeed, it is considered an unnecessary inconvenience. In recent years the formulations of self-psychology (Kernberg, 1980; Kohut, 1977; Mahler, 1968) have been applied to work with the more seriously disturbed children and adolescents (Marohn et al., 1980). Interesting descriptions of the psychoanalytic process in children may be found in the writings of Aichorn (1936), Blos (1962, 1970), Bornstein (1949), Erikson (1963), Fraiberg (1965), Gyomroi (1963), Isaacs (1930), and Winnicott (1958). There is some disagreement among analysts regarding how thoroughly the unconscious should be probed. Instead of an expressive–exploratory

approach it may be decided to employ a supportive–educative–suppressive type of therapy to bolster repression of offensive conflicts and active promotion of more constructive behaviors. Here combinations of therapies are commonly used such as environmental manipulation, promotion of emotional release, family therapy, educational techniques, behavior therapy, and play therapy as means of maintaining communication and releasing fantasies that may be explored. Examples of play therapy are Winnicott's (1977) squiggle game and Gardner's (1971) storytelling methods detailed in a number of books published by Creative Therapeutics of Craskill, N.J. In play therapy, psychotherapists may employ psychodynamic concepts and in essence integrate psychoanalytic with behavioral, educational, family, and environmental–manipulative approaches, an integration which is probably for the majority of cases the most rational mode of operation.

Children and adolescents are less motivated for therapy than adults and a good part of the time may have to be spent by therapists developing a relationship with the recalcitrant youngsters. Children are more likely than adults to project their difficulties onto the environment, acting out their needs and conflicts while avoiding inner exploration and self-observation and inhibiting the constructive use by the therapist of transference as a therapeutic tool. On the other hand, the children's natural use of play as a form of communication enables trained therapists to harness some of the bubbling energies that seem so chaotic. Working with the material elicited during play therapy calls for a great deal of skill, particularly in knowing how and when to interpret defenses, conflicts, and the underlying impulses (Harrison et al., 1984; Fraiberg, 1965). In adolescents the capacity for self-observation is somewhat more developed than in children. This is balanced by the ambivalence and confusion of identity that are hallmarks of this developmental period. Because adolescents tend to project their conflicts and to act out explosively at times, therapists may have to abandon their preferred roles as participant observers and intervene when the acting-out assumes dangerous proportions.

Technical modifications are necessary in adolescents that take into account the identity struggles going on within them (Esman, 1983). Because adolescents are so resistive to receiving help of any kind, an empathic, active, nonchallenging approach is more effective than a confrontational one, which inexperienced therapists are tempted to employ, especially when the adolescents test them by acting-out. Periodically, therapists may have to substitute game playing for interviewing. Patients may find it difficult during puberty or early adolescence to discuss sexual concerns, and to lessen anxiety, therapists of the same sex may be preferable. Between 15 to 17, adolescents are somewhat less in a tumult and become more amenable to an exploratory approach, but here the relationship with therapists must be sufficiently firm to support this effort and to handle the adolescents' inevitable countertransference reactions. Therapists who have had difficulties in their own adolescence are likely to adopt an antitherapeutic stance in working with patients exhibiting defiance, or resistance. Short-term psychotherapy may be especially suited to adolescents (Proskauer, 1971; Rosenthal and Levine, 1971) focused on certain problems that patients choose to handle. Because children's and adolescents' pathology occurs before the maturational cycle is complete, because dependency on parents and family is still high and economically necessary, involvement of the parents and/or family is, as has been mentioned before, essential for good therapy. Family therapy is especially of value when dysfunctional transactional family processes exist, when scapegoating of patients is sus-

pected, when the patients' difficulties are related to a pathological family structure, and when urgent intervention is required as a consequence of a family crisis (Berlin, 1970; Williams, 1973). Adolescents with borderline problems may require a special approach using some of the insights from object relations theory (Masterson, 1972).

Attempts to use more formal psychoanalytic therapy in late adolescence are more successful than in earlier years. A search is made for fixations and problems in the infantile period and in early childhood that reappear in direct or disguised forms as well as the defenses against regression, castration anxieties, and superego guilt. From these therapists may better understand how hitherto adjusted children become converted into disorganized, willful, or violent adolescents. Youthful patients are, however, usually resisting participants in probing noxious early experiences and reactions, not seeing the connection with what is happening in the present.

Gladstone (1964) describes three major groupings of adolescents for whom different treatment approaches are applicable. The first group consists of acting-out character problems and offenders who will require extreme therapist activity to promote a relationship, a firm setting of limits, and a constant emphasis on human values and their communication in the relationship. In another study, Gladstone points out how this may be done. The second group includes neurotic disorders and dependency problems. Here observant and interested objectivity is offered patients, emotional catharsis is encouraged, there is a probing of underlying conflicts toward insight, and there is a minimum of interference from therapists in working out the conflicts. Illustrations of such tactics are provided by Josselyn (1952, 1957). The third group is composed of withdrawn schizoid reactions. With such patients are best employed supportive techniques, experience sharing, continuous correction of distorted perceptions with efforts at reality testing, and educational correction and filling in of learning deficits. Silber (1962) gives examples of these procedures.

Group therapy (*q.v.*) with children has been described by Slavson (1949, 1952) and has become an accepted way of dealing with problems in childhood, both as a principal therapy and as an adjunct to individual therapy. Of note, too, are Moreno's methods of using psychodramatic play with groups of children (Moreno, 1965).

The size of children's groups must be kept below that of adult groups (Geller, 1962). For instance, in the age group six years and under, three children constitute the total. Both boys and girls can be included. Single-sex groups are those (1) from 6 to 8 years, which optimally consist of 3 to 5 members; (2) from 8 to 12 years, which may have 4 to 6 members; and (3) from 12 to 14 years, which also have 4 to 6 members. Mixed-sex groups at the oldest age level are sometimes possible. Play therapy is the communicative device up to 12 years, the focus being on feelings and conflicts. It is obvious that the ability to communicate is a prerequisite here. Beyond 12, discussions rather than play constitute the best therapeutic medium. Techniques include confrontation, analysis of behavior in the group, and dream and transference interpretation. Both activity (during which acting-out may be observed) and discussions are encouraged at various intervals. Interventions of the therapist should be such so as not to hamper spontaneity. Discussion is stimulated by the therapist, and silences are always interrupted. Ideally, individual therapy is carried on jointly with group therapy, particularly at the beginning.

Group therapy may be helpful for adolescents even though resistance is prominent. Identity crises and confusion respond better to group treatment than to any other approach (Rachman, AW, 1972a & b). The therapist must function in roles other than that of psychotherapist—for example, as guide counselor and teacher (Slavson, 1965). A behavioral group approach is often helpful, for example, with disturbed adolescents in a hospital, such as was previously described, as well as in a residential setting (Carlin and Armstrong, 1968). The introduction of several young adults of ages 21 to 24 helps foster healthier transference reactions and provides identification models. The therapist amid the impulsive behavior in the group (which is spontaneous among adolescents) cautiously introduces interpretations.

Some therapists find a cotherapist (preferably of the opposite sex) useful (Evans, 1965; Godenne, 1965). Countertransference phenomena that often occur in cotherapy include excessive attraction to young patients of the opposite sex, fear of "liking too much" certain patients of the same sex (due to homosexual fears), projection of feelings and frustrated impulses in relation to the therapists' own mates onto the cotherapists or patients of the opposite sex, competition with the patients of the opposite sex for the cotherapists, competition with the cotherapists for the group's admiration and support, and transfer of emotions originally felt for children of the therapists onto members of the group.

The *drug therapy* of children with behavior disorders, schizophrenia, and chronic brain syndromes has included the use of a number of substances (Fish, 1963, 1965, 1966). The most important drug influence has been registered on psychomotor excitement, a control of which reduces other symptoms, such as perceptual and thought disorders. As a result of being calmed down, the children may become amenable to group activities, educational offerings, and psychotherapy (Fish, 1960a & b).

Generally no drug is given until it is proven that environmental manipulation and psychotherapy have had no effect on the prevailing symptoms. Diphenhydramine (Benadryl 12.5–25 mg 3 or 4 times daily; average dose 100–200 mg daily, maximum dose 300 mg) is valuable in behavior disorders with hyperactivity in children over 20 pounds of weight and in anxiety reactions in children under 10 years of age. Since it produces drowsiness, it may be employed as a bedtime sedative. Other drugs that can be used are chlordiazepoxide (Librium) for children over 6 years of age, 5 mg 2 to 4 times daily, increased if necessary to as much as 10 mg 2 to 3 times daily; and diazepam (Valium), 1 to 2.5 mg 3 or 4 times daily, increased gradually as needed and tolerated for anxiety. Promethazine (Phenergan) for severely disturbed children (Bender and Nichtern, 1956) acts as a sedative when 25 mg is given at bedtime or 6.25 mg to 12.5 mg is given three times daily. Phenothiazines may be tried for primary behavior disorders, as well as schizophrenia and organic brain disease where milder therapies are ineffective. Chlorpromazine (Thorazine, 1 mg per pound of body weight daily, or 50–100 mg daily) is used in excited states; should an emergency necessitate intramuscular injection, 0.25 mg per pound of body weight every 6 to 8 hours as needed are given. Trifluoperazine (Stelazine, 0.15 mg per pound of body weight daily, or 1–15 mg daily) is used sometimes in apathetic, withdrawn children. Taractan (in children over 6 years of age) in dosage of 10 to 100 mg daily, Navane (in adolescents) in dosage of one to 40 mg daily, Haldol (in adolescents) 0.5 to 6 mg daily, and Moban (in adolescents) in dosage of 10–50 mg daily may be tried, in that order, where phenothiazines are ineffective. Haldol may be effective also in tic disorders and Tourette's disease. The employment of Ritalin and Dexedrine will be described later in drug therapy for attention-deficit disorders. Barbiturates should not be given to children. Should hypnotics become necessary, Benadryl or chloral hydrate may be used. The latter is prescribed as Noctec syrup

(each teaspoon equals 500 mg) in a single dose depending on body weight up to a total of 750 mg. In depressive disorders in adolescents where psychosocial treatments have failed, imipramine (25–75 mg daily) may be tried, recognizing that cardiovascular symptoms may occur. MAO inhibitors are not recommended. Antidepressants have also been found useful in separation-anxiety disorder, attention-deficit disorder with hyperactivity, enuresis, and obsessive-compulsive disorder (Rancurello, 1986). The use and dosage of imipramine (Tofranil) in enuresis is described in the section on habit disorders. The use of stimulant drugs in attention-deficit disorders is detailed later in this chapter.

The Management of Aggression

The management of aggression constitutes an important aspect of working with children. Methods of handling aggression range from extreme permissiveness—even to the undesirable extent of allowing physical attacks on the therapist—to rigid disciplinary measures and physical restraint.

Aggression is representative of many diverse conditions. It may be a reaction to frustration of a fundamental need or impulse. It may be a means of coping with overwhelming inner fears stirred up by terror of a menacing world. In the detached child it may signify an averting of close relationships with people; in the child with power strivings, a way of gaining control; and in the masochistic youngster, a technique of provoking others to a point where they retaliate in kind. In some children it is the only form of relationship to another human being that they know, and it constitutes a frenzied appeal for companionship or help. Aggression may be a camouflage for a deep feeling of inner helplessness, and as such it is motivated by the conviction that the only way to escape hurt is to overwhelm others. It may be a manifestation in compulsively dependent children of disappointment in the adults to whom they cling, on the basis that the children's whims are not being satisfactorily gratified or because more favors are being shown to others than to themselves. Before adequate therapy can be instituted, it is essential to know the symbolic significance of aggression to the children and the situations under which it is most likely to appear.

A number of children who exhibit behavior problems in the form of direct or subversive aggression never seem to have developed an inner system of moral restraint or the ability to tolerate an average amount of frustration. Neglected children—those reared without proper guidance or discipline or those brought up by parents who themselves fear aggression and are consequently unable to take a stand with the child—frequently develop a defective repressive mechanism that is incapable of inhibiting rage or of directing it into socially approved channels. Such children usually have no fear of, or respect for, authority. They are narcissistically oriented and use aggression as a coercive tool to force others to yield to their will. There is little contrition or guilt associated with their destructive acts, and the children usually take the attitude that people or objects on which they vent their rage are worthy of its consequences. Retaliatory measures have little deterrent influence and actually may incite the children to further bouts of aggression.

In treating children showing this form of aggression, a permissive environment is worse than useless. This is because a sympathetic tolerance of the children's rage plays into the children's contemptuous attitudes toward authority. Actually, the children themselves see no necessity for change, and a permissive atmosphere merely perpetuates aggressive strivings.

The ideal objective in these children is to build up a superego capable of exercising control of their inner impulses. Much as growing infants develop a conscience from external restraints and prohibitions, so the children with diminutive superegos need discipline to nourish this impoverished portion of their personality. A kindly but firm expression of disapproval, and even irritation in response to destructive behavior, are much more rational approaches than its sanction or tolerance. The children must be taught that there are limits to their conduct beyond which they cannot go, that they have responsibilities for their daily acts that they must face, that definite things are expected of them, and that they have to live up to these expectations. When, in the therapeutic setting, limits to the children's conduct are first established, the children are apt to react violently; but as firm discipline continues, they will themselves discover that they are much more comfortable knowing that there are boundaries beyond which they cannot go. This is not to say that they yield themselves readily to such circumscription of their freedom. The usual reaction is to engage in a prolonged struggle with the therapists to break down the limits imposed on behavior.

The therapeutic situation differs from any previous atmosphere because the children soon begin to feel in it a warmth and expectation such as they have never before experienced. Indeed, while in the realistic world their impulses have brought them a measure of gratification they have also isolated them from people. They gradually begin to understand that therapists are adults who are not threatened by their aggression and do not yield to it or withdraw love even in the face of the most provoking tantrum.

As the children continue therapy, affection for the therapist gradually increases. Eventually, the children seem to go through a stage in development similar to that of the normal evolution of the conscience, namely, they feel it essential to win the therapists' approval and love. Whereas punishment and threats of abandonment have had little influence on the children's aggression, the fear of losing the approval of the only adults who have become significant to them has an extremely potent effect on the ability to inhibit rage. Needless to say, the process during which the children reintegrate themselves with authority, in which they identify themselves with loving adults and seek to win the latter's love and approval, is a long and tedious one. But the conscience, even in normal children, never develops precipitiously; rather it extends over a period of years. One must not get too discouraged if the youthful patients have temporary setbacks in relationships with authority, including therapists.

There is another type of aggression in the form of a power striving that resembles the aggression in children with an undeveloped superego, but it has an entirely different dynamic significance and calls for a radically different kind of approach. The superego, instead of being diminutive, is hypertrophied and takes on a terrifying and punitive aspect. The image of authority is that of a fearful and destructive force that can overpower and mutilate the children if they yield to its control. The way that the children cope with their helplessness is by overwhelming others with their power drive and aggression.

The object in therapy here is not so much to reinforce and solidify the superego, but rather to undermine it and replace it with one that does not threaten the children for the exercise of their impulses or functions. It is consequently necessary to tolerate aggression as much as is possible within reasonable limits of safety and decorum. Unlike the case of the first type of aggression, a permissive environment is essential. The permissive atmosphere at first often incites power-driven children to exaggerated acts of aggression. These seem to be defensive techniques by such children to avoid yielding their vigilance against authority.

Power-driven children often have diffi-culty in expressing softness, love, or tenderness. These emotions conflict with their self-ideals, and this is especially the case in children reared in environments where toughness and strength are the only admirable qualities in life. During therapy in a permissive situation, such children gradually begin to let down their guard. One sees them working cautiously with creative materials, and there often emerges from deep within the children a great deal of esthetic feeling that has been buried previously under a crust of hardness. The amount of anxiety that accompanies the expression of tender emotions is amazing. As the attitude toward authority gradually undergoes a change, the children usually find it more permissible to enjoy softer impulses. In a hospital ward, for example, many children who have been egocentric and destructive may be seen, after a while, making active attempts to help the crippled and defenseless children in dressing, in their habit training, and in other routines. During the period when I was in charge of a boys' ward in a large mental hospital that housed violent and intractable boys who had not been able to get along in any other setting, I noticed this phenomenon repeatedly.

Another form of aggression frequently encountered is that in dependent children, who cling to the therapist or to other children in a submissive and ingratiating way. The aggression is stimulated by a feeling in the children that they have not received a sufficient amount of attention or love. The demands of dependent children are often so inordinate that it is impossible to live up to their expectations. There is involved an element of magical wish fulfillment, and rage occurs when wishes are not authomatically granted. There is another important reason for aggression in the dependent child, and this emerges from their conviction that independence is being crushed by the people upon whom they lean. As long as dependency remains the keynote of living, assertiveness, activity, and creative self-fulfillment are constantly subdued. Great hostility may be underneath the outer core of submissiveness and ingratiation, and the children may regard the adults who care for them as overpowering beings who prevent them from attaining to self-sufficiency. This is one reason why aggression is precipitated without any apparent cause in those children who receive unlimited privileges and favors. It is essential for personnel who deal with children to understand this, because the eagerness of adults to overprotect dependent children may actually rob the children of the necessity of participating actively in their own growth.

Dependent children may burn up their energy cajoling or forcing others to carry them, because they feel too helpless to accomplish things through their own efforts. Therefore, a program must be instituted in which the children learn to accept responsibility for daily routines of living. Self-growth is attained primarily through achievement. It is understandable that the children will exhibit episodes of aggression when they sense that others insist that they stand on their own feet. It is important not to yield to the children's aggression when it is obvious that the children are trying to force the therapist to care for them.

Finally, it is necessary to consider the aggression exhibited by shy and detached children. Such children are usually referred to a clinic or to a hospital because of neurotic symptomatology, psychosomatic complaints, or severe psychoses. Aggression, here, is at first not expressed, and the outward behavior of the children is usually of a compliant and innoculous nature. Detached children are threatened constantly by life and by people. They maintain their safety either by submitting to others or by building a defensive chasm that separates them from the world. In individual play therapy they will sit quietly awaiting instructions with little show of spontaneity. In a group of other children they will isolate

themselves and play alone. They possess an enlarged and punishing superego as well as a great undermining of self-esteem. Beneath the shell of compliance are great quantities of hostility that they fear expressing openly. The object in treatment is to get them to mingle intimately with other children, to engage in competitive activities freely, and to express their aggression without counteraggression on the part of surrounding adults. This necessitates an extremely permissive environment.

Detached children are driven by a spontaneous force to assert themselves with other children and with adults, but their efforts in a normal environment are usually frustrated. In the permissive environment of the clinic or hospital these children gradually experiment with self-expressiveness. In play therapy they may reach a point where they break through their reserve and begin working with pliable materials that they can manipulate or destroy. Later on, they may begin to penetrate from the periphery of the group to its center, participating in activities that bring them into contact with others.

As the children realize that they will not be hurt in closer relationships with others, they may engage gradually in mild competitive activities. Later, they may actually take a stand in life, defending their own rights and demands. At this point a tremendous amount of aggression is released, and they may become very destructive or assaultive. The aggression frequently is in the nature of a test to provoke adults around them into acts of retaliation in order to prove to themselves that their previous concepts of the world as menacing were justified. Furthermore, as the permissive environment begins eating away at their repressive images of authority, they may begin experiencing feelings of love toward the therapist. They may become so overwhelmed with terror out of fear of getting close to anyone they may direct their aggression at the therpist with little external provocation. Therefore, some tolerance of the children's aggression is therapeutically indicated.

Aggressive acting-out children have been helped by behavioral reinforcement programs. Rewarding desired behaviors with complete ignoring of unacceptable behavior has resulted in significant improvement. Working with parents and teachers to educate them regarding the meaning of the disturbed behavior is indispensable as a way of helping the children retain their gains. If behavior therapy does not help the problem, a program of psychotherapy (which may be a long-term one) with the children and parents will be required.

The Hyperkinetic Child (Attention-Deficit Hyperactivity Disorder (DSM-III-R Code 314.01)

Whenever therapists encounter an aggressively hyperkinetic child, it is important to rule out organic syndromes that may manifest themselves purely as a behavior disorder (Wender, P, 1971). Symptoms of aggression, frustration intolerance, hyperactivity, and disturbed behavior occurring prior to 6 years and even 10 years of age may be a consequence of damage to the brain brought about by such etiological factors as a high forceps delivery, severe infantile infectious illness (e.g., whooping cough, measles), and frequent spells of high fever without apparent cause (Levy, S, 1966). Before making a diagnosis, however, it will be necessary to rule out ordinary physiologic hyperactivity, reactive and neurotic behavior disorders, childhood schizophrenia, and mental retardation. Childhood depression also may mask itself in hyperactive and psychosomatic reactions (headache, abdominal pain). A rule of thumb has been applied to the effect that if children do not have enough control over

themselves to sit still while watching their favorite television programs, an organic brain problem should be suspected. In true hyperactivity of organic origin there is a limited attention and concentration span, emotional lability along with impulsiveness, an inability to delay gratification, and poor frustration tolerance. Minor neurological signs and an abnormal electroencephalogram may be present. Often a learning disability is the reason children are referred for treatment. Because of sadistic, uncontrollable behavior, the children may be ostracized by other children and may be excluded from school. This undermines self-esteem and sponsors paranoidal ideas and more violent behavior.

Therapy is difficult and prolonged and is best administered by child therapists, preferably those who have had experience with hyperactive children. Work with both children and parents is essential. The latter must be counseled and educated regarding the nature of the problem and the need to refrain from applying the labels of "good" and "bad" to the children. It is often difficult for parents to accept the diagnosis of organicity and to control their desperate fears and guilt feelings. The cooperation of a neurologist may be helpful. Tutoring for special learning difficulties may be essential, as may exercise programs to improve motor skills. A comprehensive treatment approach is thus best. Feighner and Feighner (1974) describe one such program consisting of a complete evaluation of the child, pharmacotherapy, behavior modification, curriculum counseling, training for parents and teachers, parent–child interaction videotaping, and feedback sessions while coordinating the treatment of the children with the family.

Drug therapy is usually symptomatically effective, the object being to stimulate the braking mechanisms of the brain to inhibit the motor overactivity. The drug that is most popular is methylphenidate (Ritalin), which is used in children over six years of age. Before breakfast and before lunch, 5 mg is given, gradually increasing by increments of 5 to 10 mg weekly up to a total of 60 mg if necessary. Usually 20 to 40 mg will be effective. If there is no improvement in one month, the drug should be discontinued. Other drugs that may be employed are the amphetamines. Dextroamphetamine (Dexedrine) may be given to children over three years of age as tablets or elixir. In children of 3 to 5 years, 2.5 mg is given daily, increased at weekly intervals by 2.5 mg until an optimal response occurs. In children over six years of age, 5 mg is given once or twice daily, raised weekly in increments of 5 mg until the best response is obtained, which is usually below 40 mg. Pemoline (Cylert) is an alternative drug and is given in dosages of 37.5–112.5 mg. All of these medications may be reduced or discontinued over weekends or during school vacations. After the patients reach puberty, the drugs may not be needed at all. Hyperactive children in a classroom setting may be helped by the stimulant drugs Dexedrine and Ritalin to control their behavior by improving attention and completion of classroom assignments. Behavior therapy is also effective in reducing fighting and quarrelsomeness, improving frustration tolerance, and controlling temper outbursts. Much of the behavior therapy can be done at home, the parents being trained in operant-reinforcement techniques. Target behaviors to be controlled are listed, their frequency and provocative stimuli charted, and contingent positive reinforcements of appropriate conduct and negative reinforcements of misbehaviors consistently applied (Safer and Allen, 1976). Self-instructional, self-control training may also be possible in some children (Meichenbaum and Goodman, 1971).

Coordinately, other adjunctive modalities previously mentioned should be employed. Parent groups meeting in six weekly sessions have proven beneficial.

Reading materials should be assigned to parents, such as the article by M. A. Stewart (1970). Teacher groups also have their use. Play therapy, contact with teachers, videotape sessions with the parents to play back interactions, remedial tutoring, and special exercises are other useful techniques.

In the medium of their relationship with their therapists, the children are encouraged to explore their feelings and attitudes. The poor impulse control and the motor incoordination of the children during treatment may stir up countertransference reactions in the therapist, at home in the parents, and at school in the teachers. A passive neutral attitude will create insecurity in the children. On the other hand, counteraggression will add fuel to the fire. A firm, kindly attitude is best. Should the children become violent, they should physically be removed from the disturbing situation so as not to perpetuate their behavior. Slowly, with proper management, mastery of behavior may be established, and there will be an ability to cope with increasingly challenging situations.

Hyperactive reactions may occur in situations other than in minimal brain dysfunction and present the same symptoms as the latter—for example, in children with unsocialized aggressive behavior, anxiety disorder, sociopathic personality disorder, and psychosis. In such cases stimulant drugs may not be effective or may actually exaggerate the symptoms. Appropriate diagnosis is essential in treatment planning. Individual, family, group, and behavioral approaches are productively employed in these conditions, but stimulant medications are definitely contraindicated.

Residual–attention-deficit disorder in adults, characterized by emotional lability, restlessness, and impulsive outbursts that are not due to schizotypal or borderline personality disorders also respond to methylphenidate (Ritalin) and pemoline (Cylert) (Wender et al., 1985).

Juvenile Delinquency (Childhood or Adolescent Antisocial Behavior, DSM-III-R Code Y 71.0)

A famous writer presented the problem of juvenile delinquency in these words: "Our youth now love luxury. They have bad manners, contempt for authority, disrespect for older people. Children nowadays are tyrants. They no longer rise when their elders enter the room. They contradict their parents, chatter before company, gobble their food, and tyrannize their teachers." These are the words of Socrates, written in the fifth century B.C. In the thousands of years that have passed since Socrates, we are not only still grappling with how to control youth's defiance of convention, but also with serious infractions of law that are represented by offenses of violence, stealing, fire setting, vandalism, dangerous drug use, rape, and other crimes.

Delinquency among children who belong to asocial gangs is common in economically depressed areas. Here a cultural-transmission theory has been posited by such authorities as Tannenbaum (1938) and Topping (1943). Other authorities insist that the quality of family life is what is of greater etiological significance. Susceptible children are those from families in which there is no cohesiveness, no clear-cut authoritative model with which to identify, and little or no constructive supervision and discipline (Glueck and Glueck, 1950). Delinquent groups are powered by forces in opposition to the social world. (Cohen, AK, 1955). Collective solutions are evolved that, though antisocial, gain mutual support and identification. Work with delinquents, therefore, must take into account both the disruptive family organization and the deprived environment from which they come. Therapeutic directions are milieu oriented. These focus on a broad community approach, enlisting the aid of religious leaders, social agencies, and police groups. Ec-onomic help, counseling, and casework for the delinquents' families and rehabilitative group work with the delinquents themselves are given within the strictures of the available personnel and budgetary restraints of the involved community. Individual psychotherapy generally fails unless comprehensive environmental approaches are employed. A peer group can be the treatment of choice. Nevertheless, the need for individual therapy with a therapist who can act as a role model should not be minimized. Therapists directing adolescent groups require training and experience in working with adolescents.

Delinquency does not confine itself to children from deprived and lower socioeconomic families. It affects upper- and middle-class groups as well. A. M. Johnson and S. A. Szurek (1952) have shown that the inability of parents to set limits due to poorly integrated impulses and "superego lacunae" (Johnson, AM, 1949), and the goading of children to act out unconscious perverse and hostile parental strivings that were unresolved in the parents' own relationships with parental figures, produced delinquent behavior. "It is possible, in every case adequately studied, to trace the specific conscience defect in the child to a mirror image of similar type and emotional charge in the parent" (Johnson AM, 1959). A specific superego defect may thus be created in the children that reflects the parental flaw. Szurek (1942) insists that many cases of psychopathic personality are products of unconsciously determined promptings from both mothers and fathers that encourage amoral and antisocial behavior. The child "victims" chosen are the recipients of subtle insinuations and suggestions that may often, even though the parents are not aware of their presence or implications, be detected by a good clinician during an interview. Indeed, psychotherapy with delinquents may have to be focused on the parents rather than the children since they will tend to undermine the children's treatment should the children stop responding to their messages.

Modifications of technique are obviously very much in order in working with a family neurosis, and this was years ago pointed out by Aichhorn (1936). Aichhorn's methods, employed during the residential treatment of delinquent adolescents, inspired the founding of special residential units organized around providing emotionally corrective experiences (Brady S, 1963; Redl, 1959). Bettelheim (1950), E. Glover (1956), Noshpitz (1957), Szurek (1949), and Szurek, Johnson, and Falstein (1942), among others, have introduced methods that have proven of value in dealing with the problems of delinquent children and their families.

The treatment of delinquency is eminently unsuccessful, however, no matter what strategies are utilized. This is in large part due to the effect on the people handling the children. The children's expectation of rejection and punishment promote rampancy and rowdyism, to which the human targets of this turbulence respond with retreat, outrage, and often brutality. The self-fulfilling prophecy of the children that they will be hurt creates a feeling of hopelessness and distrust. They move from one situation to another with the same result. Ultimately, the children may be placed in a *residential treatment unit* organized around the philosophy of a structured therapeutic community (Alt, 1960; Balbernie, 1966, Noshpitz, 1975). Various orientations exist among different centers. Thus, a center may operate as a school, casework agency, or hospital with appropriate personnel such as teachers, caseworkers, nurses, and physicians. Psychotherapy of a group and behavioral nature is usually available in such units depending on the philosophies and skills of the therapists.

Residential centers have increased in numbers, but unfortunately not in quality. An exception is the unit in England known as Finchen Manor described by Langdell (1967), which was organized for selected multiproblem families. An effective unit requires a special design. (*Roche Report,* 1966). Most present-day units are not well organized or operated effectively for ideal management of delinquent children. Moreover, residency is too short term, less than the minimum of two years usually required for any change to register. In addition, there is a lack of coordinated services (provision for educational and vocational opportunities, outlets for aggression, need for privacy, and an absence of well-trained staff and other personnel who are both caring and capable of maintaining adequate control. Too often the aggression of the children leads to rememdies of isolation, punishment, and drug treatment, which, while temporarily effective, do not alter the existing difficulty. A pertinent problem in some settings is the insistence in retaining the medical model in the institution, which is an inappropriate one for children (Linton, 1973). Here the responsible psychiatrists, clinical psychologists, and psychiatric caseworkers are not in as intimate contact with the children as would be child-care workers, teachers, and other people who can be intimately related to the children's daily life and behavior. A reeducational model that involves total milieu planning is more appropriate than a medical model. It has been recommended that a different type of professional is needed for residential units, one who has received comprehensive training designed for the tasks that he or she will pursue. In France, Denmark, and the Netherlands, for example, a new discipline is evolving concerned with mediating child problems ("education orthopedagogue").

A great deal of the failure in treatment is also due to the paucity of aftercare services once the children leave the residential unit. Little continuity usually exists between the residential center and the environment to which the children are returned, which continues to impose on them the original traumas and deprivations. *Intensive home therapy* by medical and nonmedical personnel has been employed with some success (Dornberg et al., 1968). Therapist activities will vary from guidance and support to formal marital or family therapy depending on the needs of the family. The home therapists usually work under the supervision of the child therapists who are in charge of the program. Among the conditions for which home therapy is especially indicated are the presence of a psychotic parent at home, refusal of children or parents to accept office treatment, the dealing with double and multiple binds, adverse reactions of a mother to a baby or her pregnancy, and projective mechanisms in parents that activate the children's disturbed behavior.

A *day care center* constitutes a useful modality for some children, particularly those who manifest such problems as severe withdrawal, lack of object relationships, impulse control, and blocked language use (Westman, 1979). Reinforcements are provided for constructive conduct (North, 1967). Day-care treatment often avoids prolonged hospitalization, providing the children with a therapeutic environment for many hours a week while remaining a part of their families. A disadvantage is the low therapist-to-child ratio, which is ideally one to one. One way of meeting this dilemma is to train ancillary workers, some of whom can be recruited as part of a corps of volunteers.

Learning and Reading Developmental Disorders

A host of academic skill disorders exist under the umbrella of specific developmental disorders that have distinctive DSM-III-R Codes. These include *developmental arithmetic disorders (315.10), developmental expressive writing disorders (315.80), developmental reading disorder (315.00), developmental expressive language disorder (315.31), developmental receptive language disorder (315.31), and developmental articulation disorder (315.39)*.

Learning and reading disabilities are the commonest single immediate causes for the referral of children to guidance clinics (Rabinovitch, 1959, Silver, 1975). In prescribing appropriate treatment, psychological tests are in order to ascertain the general intelligence and to assess the potential, achievement level, developmental readiness, and degree of emotional disturbance; neurological examinations are recommended to rule out brain injury and aphasic disorders. Generally there is a close relationship between learning disabilities and emotional disturbance, but the presence of emotional illness itself does not presuppose that there will be failure in school work. A psychological inability to learn or to read is often a symptom that serves a specific purpose, such as to punish the parents, to defy authority, to refuse to grow up, to avoid competition, or to punish oneself. Anxiety that emerges from the children's school failures adds to their inability to attend and to concentrate on work. Even when the problem is organically determined, as when there is damage to the associational patterns controlling visual–motor functioning, such anxiety may act as a prime disorganizing factor. The treatment of learning and reading difficulties will depend upon their cause. Problems rooted in organic brain disorders will require retraining, using visual, auditory, and kinesthetic approaches (Kephart, 1955; Strauss, AA and Lehtinen, 1947; Strauss, AA and Vernon, 1957). Disabilities provoked by emotional factors will call for psychotherapy, aided, if necessary, by special tutoring and remedial reading.

School Phobias (Separation-Anxiety Disorder, DSM-III-R Code 309.21)

A school phobia is really a family problem and usually involves an immature, indulgent, or highly controlling mother who has been unwilling to separate herself from the child. A prephobic conditioning occurs prior to the school years. Children who have been reared with the idea that the world is an unsafe place, and that a mother is necessary to protect them and make things safe, are particularly vulnerable when thrust into the strange environment of a school. Often the mothers are unaware of their own dependent needs and of their ambivalence toward their own mothers, which they are projecting onto the children.

Once realistic causes for fear have been ruled out, such as stressful situations within the school itself, juvenile terrorists who threaten or attack the child, a disturbed teacher, identifiable handicaps such as reading disabilities and other cognitive dysfunctions, or childhood depression, treatment may be started. The first step is to insist that the parents be firm with the children to the effect that school must be attended. Sometimes the children will have developed a host of somatic complaints (headaches, "stomach trouble," intestinal cramps) to reinforce the stay-at-home position. After a physical examination has revealed no organic problem, the parents will have to handle their fear that they will damage their children by insisting on school attendance. They must be persuaded of the fact that the longer the children stay away from class the more difficult it will be for the children to return. The school personnel may have to be brought into treatment planning to bolster the parents' resolve that the children must go to school even if the children complain and act ill in class.

Some family therapy with the parents is usually necessary to apprise them of their own involvement in the situation (in terms of their personal history and problems) and to give them support in the handling of the children's recalcitrance. The parents have to bring the children to school at first, and therapists should be available on the telephone to render assistance to these flagging parents who are wilting under the children's intransigence. Occasionally, behav-

ioral desensitization is helpful as an adjunct (Eysenck, 1960a).

If the children's fear is associated with children who terrorize or threaten, this will have to be handled with the school authorities. Should the problem be the children's classroom teachers who are disturbed, the children may do better in another class. Coordinately, psychotherapy may be needed for the children, as well as the parents, and sometimes they may all be seen together. If the children have a serious emotional problem, such as depression, intensive therapy may be required and perhaps some antidepressant medications. The parents may have to continue in long-term therapy after the children's symtoms have come under control to work through their own dependency problems.

Psychotic Children

Apart from *autistic* disorder (DSM-III-R Code 299.00) no generally recognized subtypes are classified in the existent group of "pervasive developmental disorders". In the past they have been loosely lumped in the categories of Atypical Development, Symbiotic Psychosis, Childhood Schizophophrenia, and Childhood Psychosis.

The treatment of psychotic children is organized around a design that takes into consideration "the severity of the psychological impairment, the creation of a therapeutic relationship, the formulation of realistic expectations, and the maintenance of therapeutic agility" (Shafii, 1979). Psychoanalytic approaches are of greater use in exploring the dynamics than in contributing to practical management. This will necessitate flexible combinations of pharmacology, behavioral techniques, family therapy, and milieu therapy. Drug treatment has many drawbacks but in active psychotic states it may be essential. What has to be kept in mind is that children require relatively higher doses of psychoactive medication in relation to their weight than do adults and adolescents, that low dosage exposes children to risk with little chance of benefit, and that medications may result in unforeseeable long-term complications. When deemed necessary, neuroleptics such as chlorpromazine (Thorazine) and haloperidol (Haldol) may be employed with overactive children. Haldol is especially valuable in children with tics and Tourette's disease. Operant conditioning techniques may be indispensable in psychotic children, and especially with autistic children, in whom they may establish some measure of social conformity and reality-based behavior.

Residential treatment of children and adolescents is sometimes essential in youngsters who are out of control and who constitute a danger to themselves or others (Wolberg, LR, 1959). Psychotic children particularly will need hospitalization (Gralnick, 1966) as may severe cases of anaclitic depression (Spitz, RA, 1946), certain delinquencies (Aichhorn, 1936), and severe psychosomatic and organic conditions (Rapaport, HG, 1957).

Childhood schizophrenia (Bender, 1947; Despert, 1948), early infantile autism (Kanner, 1959), and the "symbiotic psychosis syndrome" (Mahler, 1952) are characterized by profound disturbances of behavior on every level of functioning—physiological, psychological, and interpersonal. Withdrawal tendencies and problems in communication make treatment extremely difficult. Therapy aims at establishing a better integrity of body image, a sense of entity and identity, a consolidation of object relationships, and a restoration of defective developmental ego functions (Mahler et al., 1959). Therapists provide for the patients auxiliary egos and encourage a living through of those developmental phases that were thwarted in the patients' actual growth experience. An interesting account of such a working-through with a schizophrenic in an intensive relationship is described by Sechehaye (1956). Due to the primary process nature of the children's behavior and communication, it may be difficult to comprehend the meaning of their verbalizations and actions. Here therapists may have to serve an educational function.

Emergencies

Sometimes emergencies arise in children that the psychotherapist may be called on to resolve. Usually they are the climax of a long preceding period of maladjustment to which the parents may have been oblivious or indifferent. They are differentiated from the normal developmental crises that call for minimal interventions since they may be the means to conflict resolution. Acute disturbances in adolescents may occur as a result of identity crises. Here a quiet youngster may suddenly become aggressive and destructive. Often we find this among adolescents who have been forced to be "good." As they enter into the turmoil of adolescence they break through their passivity by outbursts of aggressiveness. On the other hand, aggressive and violent behavior, as toward people, may be the result of a psychosis, which will call for entirely different management. To put a youngster with an identity crisis into a psychiatric institution as a result of the crisis will only contribute to the identity confusion.

True emergencies will call for accurate assessment of underlying causes. A detailed history of the children's development and interviews with the parents and perhaps teachers and other significant adults is in order. The therapeutic plan will then be discussed with these people. The plan may follow a crisis interventional model.

One of the most common emergencies is *running away* from home (Jenkins RL, 1973). It is estimated that there are 600,000 to 1 million runaway children yearly in the United States. Often the elopement is to communes of peers who encourage drug and promiscuous sexual indulgence. Some runaways are normal children escaping from a situation of intolerable stress or complete rejection. Some seek constructively to effectuate separation-individuation, which is impossible in a home that continues to infantilize them.

The effect of this gesture may be disturbing to the families, but it calls for an examination of their role in blocking the children's personality growth. Since over 90 percent of cult members leave the group within two years, patience, understanding, and resumption of communication with the children are essential.

Some schizophrenic children resort to disorganized runaway tendencies and may be accepted in a group that seeks to protect them, though they in fact offer little. Commonly, running away is a delinquent response, all the more dangerous since the children may be attracted to delinquent gangs that wreak havoc in the community. Diagnosis is important since *why* the children run away will determine the kind of treatment that must be instituted. In all runaway problems, work with the families as well as the children is mandatory.

Another emergency is a *suicidal attempt,* which most frequently occurs in teenagers between 15 to 19 years of age. These are often impulsive in nature, precipitated by disproportionately minor provocative incidents that, for the youths, are interpreted as of major importance. What is behind the attempt (conflict over sexual impulses, self-punishment for forbidden impulses or thoughts, projected aggression against a parent or sibling, frustrated dependency, persecutory delusions, toxic drug reaction, hopelessness, depression) will require persistent probing. Whether or not hospitalization will be needed must be assessed. At any rate, environmental rearrangements may be required along with therapy for the children and at least counseling for the parents.

The easy accessibility of *drugs* during period of school attendance or during leisure hours has, particularly in adolescents, produced emergencies brought on both by the discovery of the indulgence by parents and by an overdose of the intoxicating substance. Although casual temporary experimentation with such drugs as marijuana may not be too significant, substances such as amphetamines, barbiturates, codeine, and heroin can lead to serious emergencies and addiction. The use of mind-expanding drugs, such as LSD, substances in glue (glue sniffing), and gasoline is also fraught with dangerous consequences. Usually, combinations of drugs have been taken, and their exact identification is difficult when the children are admitted to a detoxification center, since they themselves usually will not know what they have imbibed. Behind the taking of such destructive drugs may be efforts to escape from depression, boredom, stresses of separation-individuation, and impulses of aggression. Often the only signs that these youngsters exhibit are anxiety, excitement, and overactivity. The temptation for clinicians is immediately to use sedatives. Without knowing whether or not drugs have been taken, and their nature, it is dangerous to contribute to the drug toxicity by adding other substances to an already overloaded nervous system. In recent years there has been a shift from hallucinogenic and tranquilizing drugs to alcohol, and it may be anticipated that cases of acute alcoholic toxicity will be increasing among adolescents. After successful detoxification, a psychotherapeutic program, often prolonged, will be required.

In *car crash cases* where one youngster is killed and another survives with minor injuries, it is often helpful in the emergency room for the doctor or nurse to communicate to the survivor that it is common in such cases to feel guilty and, if this happens, to recognize that it will eventually be gotten over. Allowing the youth to verbalize feelings while listening sympathetically may be important. Sedatives should not be offered since refuge may henceforth be found in drugs. The parents should also be informed regarding the turmoil the child is likely to experience and to anticipate it.

In the event of *death of a parent* the surviving parent should be encouraged to talk about the departed member openly with the children and not to cover the matter up by denying the validity of the pain that the children are bound to suffer. A great area of prevention can be instituted in the emergency room when an adult with a coronary attack is brought dead on arrival. The surviving parent may have no opportunity to see any other professional people than the personnel in the emergency room, who should try to explain how best to guide the children through their grief. A few minutes spent with the parent explaining the need not to cover matters over with a pall of silence may prevent a great deal of misery, particularly among adolescents.

Other emergencies include school phobias, anorexia nervosa, parental beating of the child (the battered child), sexual and other violent assaults, and deaths in the family. These will call for special handling and perhaps extended treatment (Morrison, 1975).

In the U.S., where the divorce rate is almost 50 percent and father absence (due to separation, abandonment, or divorce) is approaching a national epidemic, the breakup of the family may be considered another crisis in child development. Recent studies (Mallerstein and Kelly, 1982) indicate that the effects of divorce are persistent and pervasive for children as well as their parents, with stress, anxiety, and depression lasting as long as five years after the event. Particularly vulnerable are children under six years of age, when the presence of the father during the Oedipal phase plays a critical role in healthy development. Both mothers and children need special support to weather this crisis. The stress provoked by separation and divorce may need to be dealt with through special counseling, crisis intervention, divorce mediation, and psychotherapy.

PSYCHOTHERAPY IN OLD AGE

As people mature they are confronted with ravages of aging that make a mockery of the advertised joys of the golden years. Eyes, ears, teeth, joints, heart, and other organs gradually deteriorate and physical energies slowly give way. These burdens are increased by the death of loved ones, as well as the detachment of children who insist on leading overly independent lives. Loss of the great ego supports of job and professional position, along with disillusionment with the false promises of retirement, add to the strains of loneliness and devalued self-esteem. The elderly are subject to multiple personal losses due to their longevity (Goodstein, 1985). As medical advances add years to peoples' lives, diseases of aging (arthritis, cardiac ailments, kidney disease, arteriosclerosis, cataracts, cancer) and associated infirmities complicate the existence of the elderly person. But even more devastating are the ravages of fear and insecurity. Little wonder, then, that depression and growing old are so often inseparable.

Women experience such consequences of aging somewhat later than men do. They must, however, endure the disabling illnesses of their aging mates, whose enhanced dependency needs and importunate demands for attention may make them difficult to manage. For the spouse of a depressed, phobic, hypochondriacal, paranoidal, or mentally deteriorating partner, individual or group psychotherapy may be vital to the couple's welfare.

The loss of a mate through death or divorce during the elderly years is especially traumatic, and bereavement reactions not too uncommonly terminate in suicide. Therapeutic help is often focused on crisis intervention followed by continuing psychotherapy of a combined counseling and supportive nature. The ideal philosophy on which bereavement therapy should be based is that although, in the words of Nemiah (1984), humans do "have a built-in-clock, and are programmed to a destiny to which we all must yield," a happy and fulfilling existence can still be enjoyed in the years remaining.

The assumption that the elderly cannot benefit by psychotherapy, that their dulled cognition and blunted memory are permanently gone, has been proven false (Cath, 1982). Therapy will require an empathic immersion by therapists into the relationship and the ability to deal with countertransference that often involves the therapists' own terror of growing old. There is resistance also on the part of therapists to being viewed as objects of idealized identification.

The employment of environmental support systems is vital as an adjunct to psychiatry. Unfortunately, our culture fails to provide adequate roles for the many old people who retire or who, because of their age, are pushed aside by younger and more energetic citizens. In making efforts at facilitating adjustment, counseling and casework methods may help resolve problems of housing, finances, health, occupation, socialization, and recreation. Proper information and guidance may be all that an older person requires to continue to maintain self-respect and to shore up feelings of self-sufficiency. In many cases more will be needed. Community health centers for the aged are increasingly being demanded that consider the common problems of medical care, housing, transportation, finances, nutrition, job training, recreation, and hospitalization. Preparation for retirement is urgent, and some enlightened industrial groups have taken responsibility for development of educational and social-action programs to ready their executives and employees for termination of their jobs. The

economic burden of medical care has for many been lightened by Medicare, but the rising costs of delivery of health-care services are creating many budgetary problems. The economic, legislative, and administrative bodies of government are accordingly constantly being reminded of the growing problems of dealing with the aged.

A shift in living arrangements alone may eliminate a host of difficulties. Any changes must obviously take into account both the person's desire to live in familiar surroundings and the practical needs of one's situation. Dwelling units especially designed for the elderly have become increasingly popular, and retirement villages containing medical, recreational, and rehabilitative services are available.

Many aged people are needlessly condemned to the wretchedness of nursing homes or the segregation of poorly run retirement communities. In some cases private-home placement may be a more suitable solution, supplemented with the facilities of community centers that have programs for the aged. On the other hand, if individuals are unable to care for themselves, a hospital or old-age nursing or convalescent home may be what is required.

Finding suitable work for an active older person may restore vitality, interest, and self-esteem. It is totally unrealistic to assume that leisure alone can bring contentment to those who have been occupied productively all of their lives. Nor is it sensible for the community to turn people out to pasture who have acquired skills and knowledge that cannot easily be duplicated.

The problems of retirement make preretirement counseling an important preventive measure. New adaptations will be required. Spouses should be prepared for irritation at being with each other full time. Role playing is helpful in preparing the retirees for what is inevitable—time on their hands, a feeling that they are out of the mainstream of life and "has beens." A search for new meanings to existence will be needed.

Education in an aging society is an important aspect of a comprehensive program. Properly implemented, it supplies information to the older person regarding the physical changes in the body and new emotional requirements that take place with ongoing years. It clarifies confusion about sexuality. It furnishes guidelines for continued creativity and vocational usefulness. It encourages enjoyment of positive assets and minimization of liabilities. Programs of adult education to prepare individuals for aging and to help develop new leisure-time interests must include instruction for people working with older people about various phases of geriatrics. The booklet, *Planning for the Later Years,* issued by the U.S. Department of Health, Education and Welfare (Washington, D.C., U.S. Government Printing Office) contains some excellent suggestions for health maintenance, nutrition, emotional adjustment, housing and living arrangements, retirement income, work, and legal problems. It may be profitably read by the aging person. Other reading materials for the aged or their relatives are given elsewhere in this volume (see the section on old age in the Addenda, Selected Texts). For professional persons the writings of Weinberg (1975), Butler and Lewis (1973), Rossman (1971), and Simon and Epstein (1968) and the pubications *Medical World News, Geriatrics* (1973) and *Psychiatric Annals,* (vol. 2, no. 10 and 11, 1972) are recommended.

Among the most useful measures are the development of appropriate recreational facilities in churches, schools, community centers, and the various old-age institutions that encourage hobbies, handicrafts, dancing, lectures, and discussions. Social participation increases morale and counteracts withdrawal and deterioration.

The above measures designed to meet the diversified needs of older people may avert or delay the development of untoward senile reactions. The most common of these are confusional syndromes that come on suddenly, particularly when individuals are moved to unfamiliar surroundings or subjected to situations to which they cannot adjust. Old people have a tendency to prowl around at night and during the day to wander away from home. Providing them with activities to occupy their minds tends to keep them more focused on reality.

Perhaps the most difficult problem in providing a solution to the elderly in family setings is the inability of children to accept the inevitable change in role that will be demanded of them as their parents become more helpless and dependent. The psychotherapists consulted by the families will usually have to involve the entire families in the treatment plan, helping children to face the physical and emotional changes in their parents, and educating them about the need for becoming substitute parents for their own parents in response to the latter's developing dependency needs. What the aged person often requires is "a surrogate-protector in much the same way that he approached a parent as a child. . . . It is possible for the therapist to use this delegated authority to foster and maintain an illusion that the patient has found a protector and one who will satisfy many psychological needs" (Goldfarb AI, 1964).

Mental disorders in elderly people are characterized by a superimposition of psychological reactions (usually depression and paranoidal projections) on an organic substrate. Assessment of the degree of organic involvement is essential in outlining an appropriate program of therapy. This will require clinical observation, laboratory tests, and an electroencephalogram. Once the degree of affective and organic components implicated is estimated, a comprehensive treatment plan includes physical care, rehabilitation, drugs, and psychotherapy. With good supervision the vast majority of unstable older people may be treated outside of a hospital. Geriatric day treatment is both therapeutic and cost effective (Roche Report (March 15, 1982). Transfer to a mental institution causes great anxiety and agitation and may shorten life. If home conditions are unsuitable or upsetting, institutionalization may be inevitable, and, if proper facilities can be found, the last years of life may be made tolerable if not enjoyable.

Depression is the most common symptom in the elderly. Frequently it is misdiagnosed as dementia, memory loss, or other presumed organic conditions, which disappear when the depression clears up. Depression in the elderly is accompanied by frequent somatic concerns, memory or cognitive defects, and occasionally, paranoidal ideas that may expand into delusions. The treatment of depression in old age differs in some respects from that in younger years (Charatan, 1975). Modest treatment goals are pointed toward symptom relief employing a directive, supportive approach with frequent brief sessions rather then infrequent long ones.

If drugs are needed, it must be remembered that elderly people are extraordinarily sensitive to psychotropic medications, which may produce untoward and sometimes dangerous side effects even with lowered dosage. Pressure to prescribe medications is brought to bear by relatives because of disturbing symptoms such as confusion, somatic complaints, insomnia, nocturnal wandering, behavior disturbance, and especially, depression. Adverse side effects are common especially when cardiovascular, kidney, and other ailments exist, and when various drugs employed to control these ailments interact with the psychotropic substances. Yet psychotropics properly employed can be useful. For example, depression may be the basis of an elderly person's confusion, impaired memory, and personality change. A misdiagnosis of organic brain disease fosters hopelessness and "giving up" by the patient. Here antidepressants may be valuable, with selection of those drugs that produce a minimum of sedation and cardiotoxic and anticholinergic effects, such as trazodone (Desyrel) nortriptyline (Pamelor), desipramine (Norpramin), and monamine oxidase inhibitors (e.g., Nardil). Neuroleptics like thioridazine (Mellaril) or chlorpromazine (Thorazine) should be used with awareness of their anticholinergic side effects. If sedation must be avoided, haloperidol (Haldol) or fluphenazine (Prolixin) may be selected. The anticholinergic effects of antidepressants and antipsychotics (constipation, blurred vision, dry mouth, difficulty urinating) may be very annoying and can be minimized by choosing the least anticholinergic agents available. A good antianxiety drug is alprazolam (Xanax), which has a half-life of eight hours; it may also be used as a hypnotic and mild antidepressant. Oxazepam (Serax) and Lorazepam (Ativan) are preferred to diazepam (Valium). Other good hypnotics for elderly insomniacs are temazepam (Restoril) with a half-life of about nine hours and triazolam (Halcion), whose half-life is very short (3 to 4 hours). Temazepam has been shown to mix well with other drugs used by the elderly. Since low blood pressure and ataxia, which lead to falls and disabling injuries and fractures, are often caused by psychotropic drugs, patients must be warned to take special precautions in footwear and walking. Absorption of drugs is delayed when taken with food. Medications should, therefore, be given on an empty stomach at least 30 to 60 minutes before retiring. In treating depression in the elderly, it should be kept in mind that depression can be produced or exaggerated by medications taken for cardiovascular disease, such as reserpine (Serpasil), methyldopa (Aldomet), and beta blockers, e.g., propranolol (Inderal). Substitutes for such medications may have to be found. Severe depressions may require electroconvulsive therapy (ECT) after a thorough physical examination, blood count, urinalysis, electrocardiogram, and x-ray of the chest and spine show no contravening abnormalities. A total of 8 to 10 biweekly treatments is best.

Insomnia may require chloral hydrate (Noctec), Dalmane, Restoril, or Halcion. Barbiturates should be given sparingly, if at all, and central analeptics should never be given in confusional states. There are many other substances in use whose virtues are mixed (Hollister, 1975). These include the cerebral dilators Pavabid, Cyclospasmol, Vasodilan, and Riniacol, the ergot alkaloids (Hydergine), and procaine (Gerovital), although the latter can produce a mild antidepressant effect. Small doses of stimulants such as Ritalin sometimes help fatigue and mild depression. Vitamin supplements are often used, but a balanced diet should eliminate the need for heavy vitamin intake.

The conditions requiring psychotherapy in geriatric patients include all of those in younger groups as well as syndromes arising with the deteriorative, metabolic and systemic disturbances of old age. Relationship and interpretative therapies are employed in combination as needed (Goldfarb AI, 1955, 1959; Meerloo, 1955). The question arises as to whether reconstructive changes in the elderly can be achieved through alteration of the basic character structure and development of new potentialities. Or must therapists be content with a holding operation, with symptom relief and better adaptation in areas of living in which the patients are failing, with at best a reorganization of attitudes and value? Elderly people with a basically good ego structure and in whom organic brain damage is minimal may, if sufficiently motivated, be brought to some reconstructive change (Yesarage and Karasu, 1982). Generally, however, significant alterations in character structure are not to be anticipated. Psychotherapy serves to alleviate the anxieties of aging individuals, providing a means for

emotional catharsis, reassuring them about their physical condition, helping them deal with depression, grief, and the death of family members and friends, assuaging frustrated sexual feelings, correcting misinformation, managing problems of retirement and difficulties in living alone, mollifying paranoidal projections, and convincing them that their basic needs will be met because somebody cares. Chronically ill patients who live in fear of death appreciate friends and counselors. In psychotic states, psychotherapy may be coordinated with drug therapy even in those with brain damage (Hader, 1964). Short sessions (10 to 15 minutes weekly or bimonthly) may be all that is required. This usually suffices to support dependency needs and to give patients a feeling of being protected.

Group therapy and group discussions are ideally suited to the needs of elderly people, fostering group belongingness, reducing the sense of isolation, and enabling people to deal with feelings of separation and fears of loss and death (Cooper, 1984). The goals in group methods are to support existing personality strengths, inculcate knowledge of human behavior, expand tolerance and flexibility toward individual differences, accept a changing role in life, deal with personal prejudices, facilitate group cooperation, and promote better interpersonal relationships (Burnside, 1970; Goldfarb AI and Wolk, 1966; Klein WH et al., 1966).

One of the problems, however, is getting older people to break through their isolation and join a group. Often individuals will come to an outpatient clinic in search of help for somatic complaints and will resent being referred to a psychiatrist. A well-explained referral, however, will often be accepted, such as that physical problems and suffering always give rise to tensions that make it difficult or impossible for a physical problem to heal and that group therapy often will help resolve tensions and aid the healing process. Most patients experience great relief as a result of group therapy. This may ameliorate somatic complaints as well as mollify problems of living. Through group interactions the virtues of continuing work, sexual, and exercise activities are discussed and encouraged and social isolation is reduced. Many "organ deficits" vanish when personal life interests and social activities are restored (Levenson, 1982).

66
Failures in Psychotherapy

Psychotherapy was never designed to cure everybody. With present techniques, therapists are able to effectuate symptomatic improvement in almost all patients, behavioral changes in the majority, and complete cure in some. The fact that reconstructive alterations are possible is an encouraging sign, however, since it contradicts the commonly accepted adage that human nature cannot be changed. With continued empirical research the understanding of personality will undoubtedly be advanced, and with more clinical experience therapeutic methods should become enriched. In the meantime, therapists may follow the old Chinese proverb, "It is better to light one candle than to curse the darkness."

Failures in psychotherapy, apart from the employment of improper interventions, are generally the product of mismanagement of the therapeutic relationship. Most commonly, patients are pushed toward reconstructive goals that are beyond their competence and motivation. Also some may seek extensive personality change even though they are incapable of achieving more than symptom relief.

No matter how ambitiously therapists may pursue treatment, they are confronted with limitations in all patients in their potential for growth. Three kinds of patterns may be clinically observed. First, there are promptings so deeply imbedded in the personality matrix that they seem to pursue an autonomous course. No amount of insight or authoritative pressure seems capable of modifying their expression or lessening their force. These tendencies are rooted in conditionings sustained during early childhood, perhaps in the preverbal period before the individuals were able to conceptualize experiences. They may, if sufficiently intense, disorganize adult adjustment. For instance, separation from a mother for extended periods during infancy may sponsor profound feelings of distrust. Apathy, depression, pressing drives for oral gratification, suspicion regarding the motives of people, and a view of the world as menacing may survive in traits that distort the most bountiful reality in later years. The ego, structured on an infirm basis, sustains disintegrative proclivities. In most people, however, symptomatic residues of early conditionings, though present, are not so pronounced. Minor as the symptoms are, they still defy change and energize maladjustment.

A second group of patternings develops somewhat later, which are remembered, at least in part, and can be verbalized. Serving spurious neurotic functions, they may in execution promote conflict. this group of patternings is subject to some control through willful inhibition once the individuals appreciate the nature and consequences of their inclinations. While these strivings may continue to press for expression, their mastery by patients becomes an important goal. Many of these strivings are rooted in needs and drives that, in promoting anxiety, are repressed. Their recognition, if the individuals are sufficiently motivated, may enable them to bring these forces under control and, in fortunate instances, to eliminate them completely.

For example, a girl whose assertiveness during the second and third years of life was inhibited by parents wedded to the doctrine that children are to be seen and not heard may discover that when she mobilizes sufficient aggression and rage she can get her own way. "Hell-raising" then becomes a pattern essential to the expression of assertiveness. Recognition that her aggression is resented by her colleagues, and insight into the sources of her affiliation of assertiveness with aggression, may enable her to experiment with modes of assertive display dissociated from acting-out. A boy fondled seductively by a parent may become too stimulated sexually and detach from his sexual feelings. Intimate relationships in adult life may precipitate an incestuous association that inhibits sexual expression. Awareness of the roots of his difficulty may enable the individual to experiment sexually with the objective of establishing new habit patterns. A host of pathological conditionings may, as Freud pointed out, invest the sexual and aggressive drives, and the person may develop inhibitions of function or distorted and perverse modes of expression. Burdened by essentially childish needs, he or she may be fixated in activities that survive as outlets for sex or aggression. To gratify these drives, a toll must be paid in currencies of insecurity and damaged self-esteem. This group of neurotic promptings, with proper therapy—should the individual strongly desire it—may undergo modification. The patient thus either learns to live with handi-

caps, once they are understood more thoroughly, or is better able to control them. With reconstructive therapy an individual may be able to develop more mature ways of managing sexual and aggressive feeling and behavior.

A third group of patterns present in all people is relatively flexible. This group is not subject to severe repression and does not press for release against all reason. Developing both during early and late childhood and in adult life, the group constitutes the bulk of the individuals' coping maneuvers. These, the most malleable of tendencies, may be influenced most significantly in therapy.

Disappointment in psychotherapy is often registered when, after an ambitious, carefully designed and prolonged program of treatment, patients continue to resist giving up the first set of patterns and must exercise their will power constantly to keep the second group in check. Faulty habit patterns, disorderly study and work activities, conditioned phobias, and many maladaptive attitudes and values are among such tendencies. All human beings are so constituted that no amount of therapy, as practiced today, can alter some personality components, since they have become so firmly entrenched that they function like organic fixtures. Yet, properly designed psychotherapy offers individuals a substantial opportunity to rectify many destructive personality traits and to achieve a measure of happiness that, prior to treatment, was outside their grasp.

UNTOWARD REACTIONS DURING PSYCHOTHERAPY

The bulk of patients in psychotherapy move along well. Obstructions in progress and inimical emotional outbursts are readily handled. There are conditions, however, that pose hazards even for experienced psychotherapists. Personality structures in which emotional instability is ingrained, having existed since early childhood, will in all probability erupt with greater bursts of violence, responding with insurgency and defying control. Impartial as they may try to be, therapists will be drawn into the patients' onslaught and may be unable to maintain an even tenor, either yielding to unreasonable demands or counterattacking in retaliation. The greatest incidence of untoward reactions in psychotherapy occurs when the relationship between therapists and patients is faulty. Inexperience and improper conduct of treatment, as well as countertransference, account for a large percentage of unfortunate results, although it is unclear how these take place. The work of Bergin (1963, 1971) and Strupp & Hadley (1977) accents the need for further research into deterioration effects and reasons for failures in psychotherapy.

It may not be amiss to mention the virtue of therapists' seeking consultation or supervision for a case that is not going well. This will necessitate courage and honest self-confrontation in facing the fact that they may be acting nontherapeutically with a patient or be employing interventions that do not satisfy the patient's needs. Talking things out with a colleague will often break through the current obstruction and promote satisfactory future movement.

Constituting treatment failure is the emergence during therapy of certain disturbed reactions. These are most apt to erupt when the customary defenses of the individuals are challenged or blocked, as in reeducative and reconstructive therapy; however, they may break loose in certain patients as a consequence of mere contact with the therapists, however supportive therapists may try to be. Thus, borderline patients who are maintaining a delicate balance in holding onto reality are particularly vulnerable to close interpersonal relationships. Even ordinary human encounters stimulate undue tension and conflict. Underlying morbid traits—kept under control by tenuous defenses—may emerge, often with explosive violence. Depressive mani-

festations may deepen into suicidal attempts; psychopathic aberrations may be acted out in total disregard of consequences; feelings of unreality and depersonalization may spread into an outright psychosis. During any kind of psychotherapy with borderline patients, the course of treatment is customarily stormy, punctuated by fluctuations in the sense of reality. The patients may interpret the relationship as an assault on their integrity, particularly if the therapists are excessively authoritarian or have unresolved hostile or sexual difficulties that filter through in manner and speech. Borderline patients sensitively divine these from the tiniest cues (Schmideberg, 1959). Emotional crises constitute the usual climate in which therapy is conducted.

Problems are also commonly encountered in the treatment of somatoform disorders, characterized by intensified recrudescence of symptoms. When such eruptions are minor, there is no great danger; however, severe outbreaks of somatic disturbance may occur, such as a thyroid crisis, violent asthmatic attack, or fulminating ulcerative colitis that may lead to death. Suicide is also a possibility. The most disturbing reactions occur in patients who have habitually had a tenuous relationship with other people and a fragile self-image since childhood. "These individuals easily react . . . with a violent frenzied emotional flood, or with destructive violence at times turned in on themselves, or with a more complete withdrawal and inaccessibility. Any of these reactions may be fused with various disturbances of organ function (oral, excretory, circulatory, and also genital) and may reach the point of abandoning adequate contact with reality" (Mittelman, 1948b).

Patients suffering from brain injuries are apt, during psychotherapy, to manifest outbreaks of euphoric, paranoidal, sexually aggressive, or suicidal behavior (Weinstein and Kahn, 1959). Probing procedures employed in manic-depressive psychosis and involutional psychosis may release great anxiety and resentment and activate latent suicidal drives (Arieti, 1959). A treatment relationship in dependent individuals who mask their hopelessness by a thin overlay of indifference may precipitate a deep depression when the patients realize the realistic limitations in the degree of closeness possible with the therapists. Exploratory activities in reactive depressions, are notorious for exciting intense anxiety (Muncie, 1959).

Paranoid reactions respond adversely to almost any kind of human contact. Thus individuals who are burdened with self-doubt and suspicion may in a relationship of even moderate intensity find themselves responding with strong mechanisms of denial and projection. Ego defenses may then shatter, with emergence of oversensitivity, estrangement, preoccupation, distrust, suspicion, fears of physical and sexual attack, litigious tendencies, homosexual impulses, delusional jealousies, and grandiose delusions (Cameron N, 1959). Schizophrenics who interpret psychotherapy as an intrusion on their privacy often will be provoked into fearful or aggressive reactions. Personality disorders manifest diverse reactions to therapeutic contacts. Urgent dependency needs may be projected onto the therapists, with excessive clinging, release of intense erotic feelings, and liberation of resentment at the inevitable frustration. Detachment with needs for control may be threatened by the patients' belief that yielding to another person implies a trap from which there is no escape. Masochistic promptings may enjoin the individuals to torture themselves with luxurious symptoms. Homosexual strivings kept in check prior to treatment may suddenly appear, promoting panic. Impulsive characters may exhibit acting-out proclivities without warning, engaging in outlandish and dangerous activities (Michaels, 1959).

Antisocial personalities may when challenged respond with excited and even psychotic behavior. Alcoholics and drug addicts are notoriously treacherous, indulging in defiant and occasionally destructive practices. Some patients with conversion reactions display alarming conduct when an attempt is made to alleviate or reduce their symptoms. A psychotic disorder of a depressive or paranoidal type may supervene (Abse, 1959). In obsessive reactions, frightening extremes of anxiety and rage may from time to time be released, along with guilt feelings and expiatory self-punishment, the therapists being accused of promoting the appearance of these symptoms (Rado, 1959).

RISKS OF PSYCHOTHERAPY

Difficulties will also develop as a consequence of the new adaptations forced on individuals as a result of removal of the problem for which they originally sought help. Sometimes a neurotic disorder constitutes the best compromise individuals can make with life and with themselves. Although they may complain bitterly about the disabling effects of their condition, when they are relieved of it, they may expose themselves to new circumstances that will or will not terminate happily. This, of course, is something for which practitioners cannot be held responsible. There is no crystal ball with which to predict the ultimate outcome of any problem. The responsibility of therapists is to help patients overcome an illness and to enable them to make a constructive future adjustment.

The end issues, however, may leave much to be desired, under which circumstances therapy may be scored as a failure. Thus a patient with migraine gets insight into the fact that she is complying, with strong internalized rage, to the authoritative demands of a widowed mother who seeks to infantilize her only child as an outlet for her controlling needs. Therapy helps the patient to liberate herself from her mother. The latter, unable to accept her daughter's freedom, commits suicide. The ensuing guilt, recriminations, and depression in the patient make her regret having started psychotherapy. An obese girl, helped to diet by psychological treatments, finds herself attractive to men. Unable to cope with the sexual demands made on her by her admirers, she responds with panic. A patient with frigidity dramatically overcomes her sexual indifference. Responding passionately to a seductive male, her episode terminates in pregnancy and the birth of an illegitimate child, which complicates her life detrimentally.

It is often impossible to foresee and to forestall future calamities that follow even traditional medical and surgical treatments. Thus the relieving of anginal pain, through prescription by an internist of a vasodilator, may encourage a cardiac patient to overtax the heart through physical efforts beyond one's endurance, initiating a massive coronary attack. Plastic surgery often exposes patients to responsibilities that their devalued self-image is unable to countenance, sometimes initiating many adverse reactions.

Another example would be refusing to treat travel phobias by psychotherapy to protect patients from the possibility of an airplane crash; this would constitute a foolish if not irresponsible shirking of therapists' duty. The best course to follow is to attempt to anticipate possible consequences of therapy and to work with patients until a reasonable stabilization is reached in their life situations.

FAILURES IN RECONSTRUCTIVE THERAPY

There are certain patients in whom long-term reconstructive treatment is not only useless but constitutes a definite hazard. Such patients, in good faith, enter into treatment with well-trained psychoana-lysts, and after years of futile probing reach a desperate dead end. In many instances the hope of cure enjoins patients to engage a succession of therapists, each espousing a well-documented theoretical system that promises success but ultimately results in failure.

If a hard look is taken at what has been happening, it is often found that the therapists have become incorporated by the patients into their neurotic schemes. It becomes obvious that what the patients are seeking from treatment is not cure, but satisfaction of dependency needs, a relief from the suffering that their conflicts foster, but which they refuse to relinquish, and replacement of amputated aspects of themselves that, with present knowledge, are far beyond the power of science to supply. Freud, astute clinician that he was, recognized that not all people were ready for the long-term pull of psychoanalysis when he advised that only individuals able to develop a transference neurosis be treated with his method. Although the diagnostic boundaries are diffuse, empirically it is possible to designate the kinds of conditions in which failures are common with reconstructive therapy.

The most unacceptable of candidates are patients who seem to be unable to get along on their own. These individuals are possessed of such great fragility in their defenses that they tend to fall apart in the face of even reasonable stress. Often they protect themselves from hurt by restricting needs and circumscribing the zones of their interpersonal operations. Yet their helplessness enjoins them to fasten themselves to some host who, they insist, must supply them with love, support, and other intangible bounties. Such unfortunate individuals have been so damaged in their upbringing that no amount of help, affection, discipline, entreaty, supplication, or castigation seems to repair their hurt. They tend to find and fasten themselves to individuals, movements, and institutions from whom and from which they hope to gain sustenance and strength. They act like exsanguinated people in need of perpetual transfusions.

Diagnostically these individuals spread themselves over a wide nosologic spectrum. They include schizophrenics, borderline patients, alcoholics, drug addicts, and antisocial personalities. They may have obsessive-compulsive, depressive, phobic, and somatoform disorders. Essentially they are characterologically immature, never having achieved inner freedom and independence. It is as if they have become marooned on an island of infantile affect. Outwardly they may present a facade of assurance, but inwardly they are anchored to pitifully dependent moorings.

When such individuals enter psychotherapy, they soon sweep therapists into the orbit of their dependent designs. The grim objective of making therapists idealized parent figures is not diverted in the least by therapists' technical skills, astute observations, lucid interpretations, management of countertransference, encouragement of emotional catharsis, transference revelations, expert unraveling of dream symbolisms, the uncovering of forgotten memories, free association, structured interviews, firm directiveness, punishment, kindness, support and reassurance, suggestion, hypnosis, drugs, or by any other method therapists may exploit or devise. Therapists who are deceived by the earnestness with which patients dedicate themselves to the therapeutic task will credit the patients' lack of progress to the obstinacy of the patients' resistances, which, the therapists imagine, will eventually be resolved. And the patients, coasting along on the premise that time itself brings the cherished gift of unconscious motive or memory, will become increasingly helpless and will then supplicate for greater professions of dedication from the therapists. The liberated hostility serves no purpose other than to make the mutual lives of patients and therapists miserable in a futile tug of war.

With expanded public education and the exciting promises of fulfillment through psychotherapy, more and more individuals—unable to gratify their pathological dependency promptings in their habitual relationships, or through religion, or by affiliation with special movements—have flocked to the office of therapists seeking the elusive pot of gold that never quite materializes. And because hope springs eternal, the therapeutic diggings go on for years in the vain quest of bringing up treasure that somehow, according to legend, must eventually be exposed. Both patients and therapists enter into this undeliberate deception only marginally aware that the quest is a useless one and that what the patients really seek from therapy is supportive aliment for their emptiness.

The great danger in long-term reconstructive psychotherapy is not only its becoming a never-ending placebo to such characterologically dependent individuals who would otherwise find an object of faith outside of therapy, but, more insidiously, its activation of latent dependency needs in those who have managed their lives, prior to treatment, with a modicum of independence and assertiveness. As treatment continues, the defenses, organized around avoiding dependency, break down and are swept away. This contingency is useful, of course, in patients who have a solid enough core to reconstitute themselves. Indeed, unless the shaky superstructure is removed, the defective underpinnings cannot be strengthened to support more adequate defenses. But what happens in individuals who do not have the materials, let alone the tools, to rebuild their lives? That which once served to carry them through daily chores, albeit not as mature as might be ideal, no longer can be used. The patients have thrown away their crutches, and their legs are now too weak to propel them in any direction. The specter of patients being damaged by prolonged therapy is one that unfortunately haunts every psychotherapist.

Can therapists, by proper diagnosis, select patients for reconstructive therapy more appropriately, eliminating those who are subject to the dependency hazard? Are there ways that poor therapeutic risks can be spotted in advance? Psychotherapists find themselves in a quandary because morally and ethically they are committed to helping people develop and grow no matter how sick. A corollary may, therefore, be appended to the questions: When poor therapeutic risks are detected, are there effective treatments?

Before an attempt is made to answer these questions, the qualities of a good therapeutic risk for protracted reconstructive treatment should be designated. For individuals to benefit from reconstructive therapy, the following conditions should prevail.

1. The presence of a personality disorder serious enough to justify the sacrifices inherent in an extended period of treatment.

2. The presence of symptoms or behavioral difficulties that are intensely annoying to the patient.

3. An ability to accept the conditions related to time and finances, and cooperation to undergo techniques that probe the unconscious.

4. The presence of rigid resistances that cannot be resolved by less ambitious approaches.

5. A level of dependency that is not too high.

6. The ability to tolerate anxiety without severe disintegrative reactions.

7. The presence of some flexible defenses, ample enough to support the patients when anxiety is mobilized.

In advance of starting an actual therapeutic program, there are a few prognostic indicators that may be of value. If the patients have been seriously maladjusted since childhood—have failed to achieve goals ordinary for their age levels; have not had a good relationship with at least one person in the past; are not psychologically minded; are prone to severe acting-out; have been in psychotherapy for a number of years, particularly with a series of therapists without achieving benefits; have been institutionalized in a mental hospital; or manifest symptoms of schizophrenia, manic-depressive psychosis, organic brain disease, severe compulsion neurosis, antisocial personality, alcoholism, drug addiction, severe psychosomatic illness, or obstinate sexual perversion—trouble is likely. Projective psychological testing is helpful diagnostically, but it may not reveal much in relation to the outcome.

The best clues will be supplied by the psychotherapeutic experience itself. If patients show favorable responses to interpretations, evidenced by constructive reactions inside and outside of therapy, and particularly an ability to implement insight in the direction of change, therapists may be encouraged. Material from free associations, dreams, and transference reactions will reveal much that is not apparent on the surface. These are usually good indicators of therapeutic movement. If patients respond catastrophically to interpretations, or if they do not respond at all, if they manifest few or no transference reactions or the transferences are too violent, if acting-out persists in spite of interpretation, if their associations and dreams consistently reveal no constructive developments—these are warnings that danger may shadow continued intensive explorations.

TREATMENT OF POOR THERAPEUTIC RISKS

When signs indicate patients are poor therapeutic risks, the objective will be to bring them to homeostasis as rapidly as possible with short-term supportive and reeducative approaches. It may be useful to confront patients frankly with the realities of their situation. Remarks may be couched in terms such as these:

Th. You have problems that date way back in your life. It will require some time to reverse these completely. There may be some things we may not be able to alter entirely because they go so far back and are so firmly welded into your personality that they may not budge. But you can still live a comfortable and happy life. Now one of the problems in a situation like yours is that you feel helpless to do things by yourself. You will then get very dependent upon me, and it will set you back. For this reason we will keep our treatment short. Please don't feel that I am neglecting you if I encourage you to do things on your own.

These directives obviously will pass over patients' heads. Even though they may appear to agree intellectually, emotionally they will continue to press for a long-term dependent relationship. In some cases they will really need to be dependent on someone or something the rest of their lives since they cannot get along by themselves. If this is a possibility, therapists may still acquaint patients with the dynamics of their problems in the hope of enlisting their reasonable egos as allies. By showing patients the relationship of their dependency to other elements of their personalities, of how and why they get angry, of what they do with their anger, of how they undermine their self-esteem, of why they detach, they are given a reality explanation for manifestations that they have hitherto considered to be mysteriously ordained.

If patients persist in retaining therapists as their dependency agents—and there are many patients who are able to afford this luxury and some therapists who are willing to play such an exhausting role—therapists may graciously accept the post and inform the patients of willingness to treat them and work with them on their daily problems. The therapist may add, however, that the situation will be very much as in diabetes, where insulin must be taken constantly. There are some emotional problems that are like diabetes and that will require help on a regular basis. Patients need not be ashamed if this is their situation.

There is hardship in working at depth under these circumstances. The patients will merely regurgitate their insights and recite their dynamics like a catechism. The best practice is to settle back with the patients and handle their immediate reactions with logical, persuasive arguments, attempting to inculcate in them a philosophy of living that will help them to accept their limitations and difficulties with grace. At the same time, deep material is interpreted whenever it is propitious to do so. Should the patients rail at the therapist and objurgate him or her for failing to transform them, the therapist must try to control the patients' frustrated feelings. A simple reply is best here: "Maybe it is impossible for you to change." This may have a startling effect on patients for the good, often shaking them out of their therapeutic lethargy.

Recognizing that there are patients who will require aid the rest of their lives and cognizant of the ever-expanding waiting lists, therapists may attempt to provide these sicker patients with a dependency prop that does not require a tie-up of services. For instance 15-, 20-, or 30-minute sessions may be all that is needed. Medications are prescribed intermittently if necessary, and the patients may be encouraged to join groups. Group approaches offer advantages to patients, since they help them to diffuse transference. Within any group, patients generally will select one or two people as their dependency target, but they know they can draw on the group at large when necessary. It is helpful, therefore, to encourage joining various activity groups, such as social and discussion groups. These may eventually replace the therapists as the prime supportive mainstay.

67
The Psychotherapist in Community Mental Health

There is a story about a unique way of diagnosing mental illness developed in a small community in Scotland. The "suspected" person is placed in a basement room that has a water tap. The faucet is turned on to flood the floor, the person is handed a mop and asked to dry the floor. If he or she continues to dry the floor without turning off the faucet, the diagnosis of "madness" is confirmed. This droll story is sometimes used to illustrate the situation of mental disturbances in the community. By concentrating efforts on managing the pressing disorders of the mentally and emotionally ill, therapists often lose sight of the fact that they coordinately fail to turn off the faucet in the polluted social system that is pouring out more patients than can be treated.

Such a statement assumes that enough is known about what causes emotional illness and that there are means to remedy the causes to turn off the faucet. Such assumptions are only partially true, but there certainly is sufficient knowledge at the present time, if not to dry the floor, to keep the basement from being flooded. The point is that such knowledge is not being used, nor does our society yet support with adequate economic and other means its implementation.

On the debit side it must be admitted that what was posited 20 years ago as "community mental health" is still a relatively unchartered field that embodies a variety of theoretical systems and methodological approaches. Designs for essential services vary with the characteristics and problems of the community being accommodated, with the needs of the individuals and agencies who constitute the consumers or the client systems, and with the philosophies and training of the personnel staffing the center or clinic that is executing the program. The problem areas for reform potentially are limitless, and, obviously, a rigid selection of zones of involvement will be in order. These range from clinical services for severe emotional problems, to counseling or casework for circumscribed personal and environmental difficulties, to educational projects for the public geared to preventive objectives, to training programs for allied professionals and paraprofessionals, to hospitalization and day care facilities for the mentally ill, to rehabilitative and work adjustment programs for the handicapped, to consultation aids to organizations or groups in the community.

There are many existing models in community mental health that deal with how these services may be integrated, and many more will undoubtedly be developed with changing politico-socioeconomic conditions. Caplan (1974) in explicating some of these models states that "since we are grappling with a highly complex multifactorial field, no single model can be expected to do more than focus our attention and pattern our expectations about one aspect of the field." What would be applicable in one community does not necessarily conform with the special problems and conditions of another community. Mental health workers must consequently maintain flexibility and use whatever models seem pertinent, always altering these as new accomodations become necessary. At the Postgraduate Center for Mental Health in New York City we have worked in different communities and with almost 500 different agencies, institutions, and community groups in cities and counties in New York, New Jersey, and Connecticut. We have found that rigid adherence to any one model of operation can cripple a program and that a great deal more innovative flexibility is required than in working with individual and group psychotherapy.

There are times in the career of most psychotherapists when they are called on to apply their mental health skills to the social system. For example, a local school is experiencing an extraordinary increase in droupouts. A community is being plagued with an epidemic of misdemeanors and crimes perpetrated by juvenile delinquents. A center is being organized to provide recreational and rehabilitative services for older people, and the founders insist that it be oriented around sound mental health principles. A social agency wants to know how to start a mental health clinic. A group of ministers needs help in doing more effective pastoral counseling. Vocational rehabilitative workers request a course in the psychiatric and psychological aspects of work readjustment. A parent–teacher's association desires a lecture on child develop-

ment illustrated by a good film. A fraternal society is setting up a series of discussion groups dealing with family life education and needs a discussion leader. The roles that psychotherapists will be expected to play in servicing any of these requests go beyond those they conventionally assume in the clinic or their office. They must take on among other responsibilities those of educator, public health expert and mental health consultant. If they have had the traditional residency and post-residency training, they will not be equipped to do this, the focus of their education being more on clinical than on community functions.

It is beyond the scope of this book to explicate the details of community mental health or the full operations of the mental health specialist. Ample literature exists on these subjects. Mannino, MacLennan, and Shore (1975) have compiled an excellent reference guide to the consultation literature as well as a serviceable list of films and tapes. A full bibliography may be found in *Community Mental Health and Social Psychiatry,* prepared by Harvard Medical School and the Psychiatric Service of the Massachusetts General Hospital (Cambridge, Harvard University Press, 1962), and *Community Mental Health, Selected Reading List 1961–1965* (Canada's Mental Health Supplement No. 50; November–December, 1965), as well as Bellak et al. (1969, 1972, 1975) Bindman (1966), Braceland et al. (1975), Hume (1966), and NIMH (1967–1970). Nevertheless, some guidelines will be indicated in this chapter that therapists may find of practical value.

Assume for illustration that a therapist receives a letter requesting a consultation from the director of a boys' club that has been organized around activities, such as carpentry and other handicrafts, for adolescents from deprived economic areas. The presenting problem is poor staff morale, which the director credits to the fact that the staff members feel themselves to be ineffectual in dealing with psychiatric problems. Delinquency and drug addiction among many of the boys, for example, continue unabated. The director believes that a course on psychopathology would be good for the staff and may help them to function more efficiently. The therapist replies affirmatively to the letter and sets up an appointment with the director. Prior to the conference, the therapist may make several assumptions:

1. The director's diagnosis of what is needed, namely a course on psychopathology, may or may not be what is required to resolve the problem.
2. In entering into the picture, the consultant (therapist) most likely will find among different levels of the administration, supervisory group, and staff workers, as well as among the recipients of the service (the adolescents) a hotbed of interlocking psychopathological constellations. The consultant will, with full justification, be tempted to prescribe psychotherapy for the most disturbed individuals. To do this would probably prove fatal. Limited finances, absent motivation, and the dearth of treatment facilities render psychotherapy impractical. Solutions other than therapy will be required.
3. A series of conferences will be needed with the director, the supervisors, and the staff individually and collectively to determine what they believe is wrong and to observe the way that they interact with one another in the work situation.
4. A series of conferences with the adolescents, particularly the leaders, may be desirable at some time once the picture has crystallized.
5. The entry of the consultant into the organization will probably stir up initial anxiety and resistance on all levels of the organization that will require handling.
6. Being involved in the dynamics of a so-cial system, the consultant will have to keep communication channels open between the administrative, supervisory, and staff levels of the organization. The boundaries of the consultant's operations will require explicit definition; i.e., the director may need to be informed about what is going on but may not have to be involved in the project itself; written communications will have to be sent by the consultant to the director outlining what decisions are reached and what the consultant proposes to do; written agreement to proposals must be received by the consultant; a liaison person must be appointed by the director to represent the administration; and a decision must be made in joint conference who the consultant will work with in the project.

With these assumptions in mind, the consultant and director set up an appointment to meet in the consultants office. The director appears to be an intelligent, interested, and knowledgeable person, a social worker who has had considerable experience in the field of group work. The director is very active in community affairs and has affiliations with many community organizations. The director is sociable and relates well. The consultant, inquiring about the program, discovers that 1000 boys are being worked with who live in the area of the club. During the summer the club runs a camp outside of the city. The activity program is managed by a staff of expert crafts people who have had no mental health orientation. The initial impression of the consultant is that if the staff had some mental health information, they may be able to use this in their work with the adolescents. For instance, many of the boys are expressing the usual defiant gestures of adolescents, and some of the staff, the consultant believes, are responding with feelings of not being appreciated. Moreover, a good number of the adolescents have severe character disturbances and are engaging in antisocial activities that may be upsetting the staff. Clarification about the dynamics would, therefore, seem indicated.

The consultant makes an appointment to visit the club and arranges to meet with the staff and supervisory groups individually. Several meetings are also held jointly with the staff supervisors and director. It soon becomes obvious to the consultant that the relationship of the staff and supervisors with the director leaves much to be desired. They consider the director an autocrat who overrides their decisions and who does not allow them freedom in their work. They respond to this by sullen withdrawal and disinterest in their duties. Most of the staff believe that they might learn something constructive from a course in mental health principles and practices. The consultant, however, is convinced that little will be accomplished until better relationships are established among the personnel. The director is not at all aware of personal shortcomings in managing the staff or of their hostile reactions to this management. From the way the director had communicated in the initial conference, the consultant could not diagnose what was wrong until the work situation and the ongoing interactions had been observed.

In discussion with the staff, the following plan is elaborated: (1) a group process to enable the staff to verbalize feelings and to become aware of self-sabotaging reactions that paralyze their functions and interfere with their relationships with the adolescents, (2) conferences with the director to give the director an opportunity to express feelings and to test the director's flexibility, (3) group meetings with the staff, supervisors, and director, during which they are encouraged to discuss how they feel about one another in their work roles. Such sessions help the director play a more cooperative role with the staff and encourage them to talk to the director about their "gripes."

The consultant does not consider the staff participants as "patients" for very good reasons. First, they do not regard themselves as patients; second, the consultant is principally concerned with their work problems and not their neuroses; and third, group process, employing principles of group dynamics, is the instrumentality that will be used, not probing techniques into defenses and unconscious conflicts. The upshot may be therapeutic for all participants, but this is a byproduct. The focus is on conscious feelings in relation to the staff's ongoing interactions. Improved morale results in the staff taking greater interest in the boys, even taking them on outings. The effects are registered in dramatic improvements in behavior both within and outside the club.

Another example of how a therapist-consultant may respond to a community need is contained in the request of a suburban psychiatric clinic for staff training in psychotherapy. Upon visiting the clinic, the consultant finds that the problem confronting the clinic is that all of the available time of the staff members is occupied in treating a stationary caseload that does not seem to be going anywhere. The waiting lists are long; intake has more or less been frozen for months due to the absence of available therapeutic hours.

Examining the records of the kinds of patients being treated, the consultant finds that most of them are chronic cases: borderlines, or dependent-personality patients who have fastened themselves onto their therapists and have settled into what is turning out to be a permanent niche. The director of the clinic believes that what is required is more sophisticated training of the staff in depth approaches so that the basic inner problems of their patients may be influenced, in this way "curing the patients" and resolving the stalemate. An interview with the staff reveals frustration and demoralization because of disappointment that they are unable to effectuate cures and because of pressures on them to open up more time for new patients.

The consultant sets up conferences with the staff members, and what is finally decided is the following: (1) establishment of a special clinic for sicker patients organized around drug therapy and no more than 15-minute supportive interview sessions once weekly or bimonthly, (2) transfer of the bulk of patients to this clinic, (3) development of a social rehabilitative unit in a neighboring church recreational center to which the patients may be referred for adjunctive social programs, (4) organization of a group therapy clinic and training of the staff in group therapeutic techniques, (5) concentration on short-term therapy as standard for the clinic and staff training in brief psychotherapy, (6) since this plan is long-term, requiring a period of years for its full development, a training program in group therapy and short-term therapy, for which the consultant will help recruit appropriately qualified trainers, (7) work by the consultant, if possible, with this group over the 3 or 4 years of transition, since there will be much staff anxiety that will require handling.

A third example will illustrate how psychotherapists engage in community work. A therapist-consultant is called into a school to determine why so large a percentage of the students are failing their college entrance examinations. Upon studying the school program, and after conferences with the principal, the teachers, and some of the students, the consultant comes to the conclusion that what is needed in the school is a school psychologist who can help students with problems in school and personal adjustment. An expanded budget is presented by the principal to the school board, some of whose members accuse the principal of being lax in running the school. They then oppose the recommendations. A group of irate taxpayers organizes itself into a political-action body and argue that a psychologist in the school will "make the students crazy" or give them "new-fangled foolish ideas about sex." The principal of the school is greatly disturbed and realizes that the community will not accept a psychologist to serve the high school population. The consultant and the principal discuss the problem with the teachers, and it is decided that an educational program is needed for the community. The help of the PTA is enlisted, and an educational program is planned. A series of community lectures is organized employing mental health films, with discussion groups following the lectures around problems of child development and family life. There results a change in attitude, and the psychologist is accepted into the school system.

It will be seen from these illustrations that the operations of community mental health specialists go beyond those of mere psychotherapist. If they are to live up to community responsibility, psychotherapists will need skills not now developed in the traditional residency and postresidency programs. It so happens that by the nature of education and background, psychotherapists may not know as much about the community and their proper role in it as do certain professionals, such as community organizers, public health officers, and other social scientists. Yet the knowledge of human dynamics and of the irrational forces that prompt people and groups qualifies psychotherapists to understand the disorganizing emotional cross-currents that operate in society. What therapists need, as has been mentioned before, is the acquisition of a completely new set of professional talents in addition to psychotherapy, since psychotherapy as such may not be suited to the client group or will require reinforcement with other techniques.

The lines along which this supplementation may be organized is perhaps best conceptualized in an ecological model of community mental health that draws upon theories and techniques from clinical psychiatry, social science, and public health.

Since one objective is the control en masse of emotional disturbance, it is essential to bring into the orbit of techniques methods that not only influence individuals but also families and other groups. A network of coordinated services is consequently employed that acts independent of psychotherapy. By the very nature of the work, psychotherapists who work in the community must collaborate with other professionals in the fields of education, medicine, nursing, welfare, correction, law, religion, and other disciplines. This does not mean a watering down of psychotherapy when it is indicated in individual cases; however, the limitations of psychotherapy in dealing with community problems must be acknowledged. Essential is a broadening of the base of operations to include every measure—psychological and sociotherapeutic—that can help people relate better and function better.

Actually, present knowledge of dynamics and psychopathology has widened the horizons of illness to include deviant behavior in addition to the traditional neurotic and psychotic syndromes. With this insight has come the need to provide services for disorders up to recently not considered within the province of psychotherapeutic concern. As a consequence, it has been necessary to blend therapeutic methodologies with educational, social, and rehabilitative approaches and to modify ideas and methods within the context of the communities' medical and social organizations.

Alterations in line with community need inevitably includes psychotherapy. In extending the benefits of psychotherapy to the masses, however, it becomes necessary to adapt psychotherapeutic tactics to abbreviated objectives. Short-term psychotherapy devoid of ambiguous abstractions and amorphous theoretical concepts that applies itself to the immediate problems of patients becomes essential. The effect of these modified treatment techniques can be both reparative and reconstructive, although goal compromise may be necessary to meet the practical needs of the millions who require aid. Attention to the populations that are now being unserved or underserved, such as the chronically mentally ill, the aged, children, minorities, alcoholics, and substance abusers, is particularly urgent.

In addition to psychotherapy, the total involvement of the community and its resources in a comprehensive program is unavoidable. One form particularly suited for sicker patients is the "therapeutic community" (Edelson, 1964; Kraft, AM, 1966). The therapeutic community is actually an old concept, dating far back in history. But the ways in which therapeutic communities have operated have varied with the level of our understanding of group and interpersonal processes. Mental heaalth specialists will need to know how to help each member of the community achieve as maximal a development as is within the individual's potential.

Because emergencies in the lives of people most commonly motivate them to seek help, some mental health centers have largely devoted their efforts to working with crises. According to Caplan and Grunebaum (1972), the folowing points are essential crisis intervention:

1. Timing: Intensive and frequent visits during the first 4 to 6 weeks are mandatory, rather than spacing interviews at weekly intervals over a long-term period.

2. Family orientation: The integrity of the family should be preserved to help support the member in crisis. Interviews with the family at its home may be required.

3. Avoiding dependency: Undue dependency is avoided by dealing with the current situation rather than focusing on past problems.

4. Fostering mastery: All efforts are made to encourage understanding of a problem and modes of coping with it effectively. This may require intensive short-term education.

5. Outside support: Enlisting the help of available outside support (friends, clergy, and other agencies) facilitates treatment.

6. Goals: The objective is to improve adjustment and immediate coping with the current situation rather than "cure." Trained nonprofessionals may be useful in carrying out the therapeutic plan.

Helping people to deal constructively with crises necessitates less a focus on etiology than on encouraging exiting health-promoting forces of an interpersonal and social nature that are present or latent. Caplan (1974) points out appropriately that capacities for adaptation of individuals are bolstered by help from their social networks, "which provide them with consistent communications of what is expected of them, supports and assistance with tasks, evaluations of their performance, and appropriate rewards." Although the intensity of stress and the existing ego strength of individuals is important, the quality of the support that the individuals get from their group is even more important in adjusting to the noxious effects of an environment or in coping with crises. Supportive groups are many, the individuals involving themselves consistently with some of these such as in work, church, and political or recreational associations; or groups may be selected and utilized only in times of need, such as self-help groups, physicians, social workers, ministers, lawyers, nonprofessionals, mental health aides, and concerned friends who have had and perhaps conquered problems similar to those of the individuals. These helping aids may be exploited spontaneously by the individuals or,

if a community is lacking in them, organized and stimulated by a knowledgeable professional. Where they exist and the individuals isolate themselves from them, the task of community mental-health workers may be to motivate the clients to make use of them or to deal with the resistances against their use. Adequate support programs are vital in any comprehensive program of community mentalhealth (Caplan and Killilea, 1976).

COMMUNITY PSYCHIATRY

The reduction of psychiatric morbidity through preventive, rehabilitative, and therapeutic measures is the objective of "community psychiatry" or "social psychiatry." Elaboration of community-based treatment and aftercare services draws upon principles of public health and incorporates epidemiological and biostatistical precepts even though psychiatric techniques are ultimately employed. An ample body of literature has accumulated on community psychiatry: Bellak (1964, 1974); Bernard (1954, 1960); Carstairs (1962); Clausen and Kohn (1954); J. V. Coleman (1953); Columbia University School of Public Health (1961); Dax (1961); Dohrenwend et al. (1962); Duhl (1963); Dunhan and Weinberg (1960); Faris and Dunham (1939); Felix (1957, 1961); Forstenzer (1961); L. K. Frank (1957); H. Freeman and Farndale (1963); GAP (Reports 1949, 1956b; Symposium, 1965); Goldston (1965); Greenblatt et al. (1957); Gruenberg (1957); Hanlon (1957); Harvard Medical School (1962); Hume (1964, 1965, 1966); M. Jones (1952); I. Kaufman (1956); Kupers (1981); Lager and Zwerling (1983); Lamb (1984); Lebensohn (1964); Leighton (1960); Leighton et al. (1957, 1963); Lemkau (1955); Lin and Standley (1962); Milbank Memorial Fund (1956, 1957, 1959); Mintz and Schwartz (1964); NIMH (1961); Pepper et al. (1965);

Plunkett and Gordon (1960); Redlich and Pepper (1963, 1964); Rennie and Woodward (1948); Ruesch (1965); Stainbrook (1955); Talbot (1984); Weston (1975); and WHO (1960).

PREVENTIVE PSYCHIATRY

Originally, therapy was focused on caring for seriously impaired mental patients. The emphasis on prevention, however, has shifted attention to patients with less severe emotional ailments, i.e., the psychoneuroses, the character disorders, the minor addictions, and even the milder adjustment problems. Caplan (1965) stressed that it was essential to accept responsibility "for helping those of all ages and classes who are suffering from disorders of all types, wherever they occur in the community." His statement makes clear why therapeutic services shifted away from the desperately mentally ill: there just was not enough money to go around.

A public health model of prevention divides such a program into primary, secondary, and tertiary categories (Caplan, 1964; Zusman, 1975). In *primary prevention,* attempts are made both to modify the environment and to reinforce constructive elements within individuals to aid in their coping capacities and to reduce the incidence of mental disorder. In *secondary prevention,* the aim is to diagnose and to treat patients with existing mental disorders to lower the severity and duration of morbidity. In *tertiary prevention,* the object is to rehabilitate people with emotional difficulties so that they may make some kind of adaptation to their environment.

Efforts at prevention require knowledge of community organization and planning as well as cooperation with other productive community programs that are operative within the community. There are relatively few psychotherapists who have gone beyond their clinical training to ac-

quire required skills to work at prevention. But even if mental health workers have had adequate knowledge and training, there are regressive forces within the community that will resist change and will even attempt to restore the prior pathogenic elements once change is effectuated. Indeed, there are professionals who insist that the present-day community mental health movement is geared predominantly toward social control and toward preserving the politico-economic system and that change will be possible only by the assumption of a radical position, with mental health centers becoming politically involved while using methods that reach large masses of people (Kunnes, 1972). Advocated is turning over the control of policies and priorities of services to the citizenry of the community, the "consumers." On the other hand, it is pointed out by oppositionists that where such a radical position has been taken, the results have been sadly wanting and that, therefore, a more conservative stance is to be preferred. Therapists can only do for a community what it is willing to accept. This should not dampen enthusiasm about what can be accomplished or discourage efforts at public education that can reduce the resistance threshold.

Primary prevention, though "the most desirable and potentially most effective approach to a solution of the problem of mental disorder in our communities, is clearly more a hope than a reality" (Caplan and Grunebaum, 1972). "In regard to preventive programs there seems to be no empirical evidence that any program is capable of preventing abnormal behavior." The provision of adequate health, housing, police, sanitation, educational, welfare, social, and recreational facilities requires outlays of public funds so vast that any effective provision would threaten other priorities. Increasing taxation and the issuing of bonds to bolster flagging budgets have acted like time bombs that threaten fiscal solvency. Accepting the fact that primary prevention is still a dream, some community mental-health operations have served quite successfully to supply services for secondary and tertiary prevention.

THE COMMUNITY MENTAL HEALTH CENTER

Broadening the base of services to the mentally ill and emotionally disturbed and focusing on early treatment and ambulatory services result in a minimal disruption of personal, family, work, and social life. Essentially, therapists function most effectively as consultants both for the management of individual cases and for the development and implementation of programs. Therapists' major areas of competence, diagnosis and treatment, is of great value here.

Two patterns of community psychiatry appear to be emerging. The first is organized around the community mental-health center, which aims at decentralization, regionalization and local service and is not too intimately related to other health services. The second is the integration of psychiatric srvices centered around the general hospital, which has consultative, outpatient, inpatient, round-the-clock care facilities but which is relatively isolated from community welfare and educational services.

The assembly under one umbrella of *all* services for the mentally ill was one of the recommendatons of the National Congress of Mental Illness and Health, held by the American Medical Association Council on Mental Health in 1962 (NIMH: *The Comprehensive Community Mental Health Center,* Public Health Service Pamphlet No. 1137, 1964; see also *Community Mental Health Advances,* Public Health Services Publication No. 1141). The Joint Commission on Mental Illness and Health, in its report to Congress in 1961, also emphasized the need for community services as a way of prevention and treatment to avert

the debilitating effects of long hospitalization. The Joint Commission recommended expanded services in the community, a shift of focus from mental hospital institutionalization to smaller inpatient units as well as increased community care, a concentration on prevention and rehabilitation, greater cooperation among the different professions toward improving mental health research and treatment, and a more intimate coordination of hospital and community resources (*Action for Mental Health: Joint Commission on Mental Illness and Health.* New York, Basic Books, 1961). These recommendatons fostered the organization of community mental health centers that promised the following:

1. Inpatient services, including a 24-hour emergency service
2. A day hospital
3. Outpatient clinic services for adults, children, and families without a waiting period
4. Partial hospitalization for day care and night care
5. Consultation services
6. Diagnostic services
7. Rehabilitative services of an educational, vocational, and social nature
8. Precare and aftercare services, such as placement in foster homes and halfway houses
9. Training of all types of mental health personnel
10. Research and evaluation

These instrumentalities were not to be under one roof or one sponsorship but were to be administered so that a continuity of care was achieved (Downing et al., 1966; Dorsett and Jones, 1967; McKinley et al., 1966; NIMH, 1963a & b).

The concentration of services around a general hospital was recommended by some authorities, and a selected annotated bibliography was prepared by the National Institute for Mental Health detailing how a hospital may function as a psychiatric resource (*The Community General Hospital as a Psychiatric Resource,* Public Health Service Publication No. 1484, Public Health Bibliography Series No. 66).

The experience of implementing the community mental health center program has not been an entirely happy one. Glasscote et al. (1969) believed that the flaw was in the timetable: "Lack of experience, lack of staff, and lack of definition have all played a role, but they have been less of a problem than bad timing." The urgency to spend allocated funds for construction of community mental health centers over a two-year period encouraged the building of centers prior to planning how they would be used in comprehensive statewide designs. Problems also developed in providing for adequate staffing, a prime key to the adequate operation of a center. Psychiatrists, who were in preponderance, now find themselves in the minority in comparison to psychologists, social workers, and nurses. Much of the fault in fulfilling the original purpose of Congress in creating the program lay in the fact that providing for the mental health needs of all people in all parts of each state with adequate preventive, screening, diagnostic, therapeutic, rehabilitative, consultative, educational, research, and training services was a too ambitious, and perhaps unrealistic, goal that awaited a good deal of experiment over many years before it could be even minimally fulfilled. This is perhaps why unfavorable publicity and reports of failure of the community mental health programs have appeared in the literature. For instance, Ralph Nader (*Medical Tribune,* 1972) has claimed that the programs in action have perpetuated a two-class system of care that is sterile in ideas and operations. An overcommitment to broad social problems at the expense of the immediate needs of clients "wastes professional staff and is both expensive and unfruitful, thus causing public disillusionment and endangering the whole community psychiatry program" (Wachpress, 1972). Under the circumstances it is remarkable that many community mental health centers have functioned as well as they have (*New York Times,* 1972). It is hoped that profiting from what has happened in the past, with adequate governmental funding and more sophisticated staffing, the centers may ultimately bring to fruition some of Congress's original goals. It is hoped, too, that aftercare programs for patients discharged from mental hospitals will become better financed and organized so that readmissions to hospitals are less necessary. Some of the statistics are presented as impressive. The number of hospital beds for mental patients has been more than halved, and the average stay has been reduced from 8 years to 17 months. Without adequate support systems in the comuity, however, the benefits of deinstitutionalization are questionable.

EXPANDED FUNCTIONS OF THE PSYCHOTHERAPIST

Since diagnostic and treatment resources cannot be deployed for relatively large groups of patients, and patient–therapist contact being limited, other modes of contact are necessary. Preventive methods entail the detection and remedying of *social forces* and *environmental pressures* that have a potentially pathogenic effect. Consequently it is advisable to include in the treatment plan "the active manipulation of the organizational aspect" of patients' lives (Caplan, 1965). This often requires the offering of individual or group consultation to administrators and others in an organization. Advice may be given affecting any phase of organizational functioning, including policy making. In expanding operations, therapists will, as has been mentioned before, have to go beyond habitual clinical theoretical models.

Community work foists onto therapists responsibilities that differ from those of traditional psychotherapy and are in line with the new tools being used (i.e., consultation, in-service training, and general public education). Guiding people in the organization (executives, foremen, staff workers) with problems is complicated. Exploiting the theory and practice of community psychiatry, the practical implementation of community research methodology, the planning of services in line with the most efficient use of resources, and the development and administration of community programs are functions that will require specialized training beyond that of the psychiatric residency. Such training will undoubtedly be organized in the future as part of a career program and may be as eagerly sought after as psychoanalytic training had been for the past generations of psychotherapists. One design of training was a model offered at the Columbia Presbyterian Medical Center, which was organized and carried out jointly by the Department of Psychiatry and the School of Public Health and Administrative Medicine through an interdepartmental Division of Community Psychiatry (Columbia University, 1961; Bernard, 1960, 1965). Other training programs have been at the Johns Hopkins School of Hygiene and Public Health (Lemkau, 1955), at Harvard (Caplan, 1959), and at Berkeley (Bellak, 1964). There are some who believe that it is possible to teach community psychiatry in a traditional residency training program (Daniels and Margolis, 1965). Some favor the Community Mental Health Center (Sabshin, 1965). Others have developed programs in relationship to state and local health departments and university, state, and private training centers (Kern, 1965).

Comprehensive Training in Community Mental Health

There is disparity in ideas of who should be trained in community psychiatry and community mental health. Some authorities believe that psychiatrists should have the priority; others believe that psychiatric nurses, clinical psychologists, and clinical social workers are fully capable, with training, of learning skills in community psychiatry (Hume, 1966). Community mental health is, according to Lemhkau (1965), of medical concern, but it is not identical or coincident with psychiatry. It is much broader: it is a commuity-wide responsibility that sponsors the concept that "the program is to be under professional and lay auspices, and that mental health is promoted and fostered not solely through medical treatment, but also through a variety of institutions and agencies with numerous disciplines joining in the effort."

The multidisciplinary accent on community mental health has exacerbated rivalries and hostilities among the disciplines involved whenever adequate financing for services has become available. With expanded funding, arguments of who can practice—and under what auspices and supervision—will perhaps be as vehement as in the practice of psychotherapy. With added information about epidemiology and biostatistics, and with a greater public health orientation, trained psychotherapists in any of the professions can very well adapt to a community-based design for the mentally ill and, if creative and experienced, may be able to organize, direct, and execute projects of public educaton in mental health. To do consultation, however, and the in-service staff training and education of allied professionals (ministers, nurses, social workers, physicians, rehabilitation workers, speech therapists, and teachers) in therapeutic techniques (counseling, group process, and so on), even experienced therapists will need to fulfill certain requirements. They will preferably, following their residencies, have completed postgraduate work in a psychoanalytic or psychotherapeutic training center. They will ideally also have completed a structured course in community mental health that draws upon the public health and behavioral science fields. Work in community projects under supervision will have taught them the fundamentals of mental health consultation and how to gear teaching methods to the needs of the different professionals who handle people experiencing problems. It is hardly conceivable that a mental health consultant and professional trainer can be on a level below that of supervising psychotherapist.

One of the chief difficulties for most psychotherapists launching into the field of mental health is that, with the possible exception of social workers, their training, experience, and hence conceptual framework is largely clinical. Although this framework may operate effectively in psychotherapy, it does not apply to many, perhaps most, of the problems encountered in the community. An ideal community mental health worker should in part be a sociologist, anthroplogist, psychologist, educator, political scientist, community organizer and planner, psychoanalyst, psychiatrist, physiologist, social worker, historian, pubic health specialist, biologist, social philosopher, researcher, and administrator. Since no therapist has or will ever have a complete combination of skills relating to the above professions, therapists will have to accommodate existing talents to a complex, difficult, and constantly changing community atmosphere, utiizing themselves as constructively as possible while preserving the open mind of a student and scholar who is in constant search for new information and knowledge. Training is helpful within a community mental health center to equip therapists with the specialized abilities required to work in the community. When therapists have the motivation and are fortunate enough to live in an area where there is a training course in community mental health, the experience may be very profitable.

The kind of training that is most suited for community mental health specialists is, in addition to psychotherapy, experience with group processes and group dynamics, research design and methods, community organization and planning, communication techniques, teaching, various rehabilitation procedures, administration, and legal and legislative processes. A knowledge of public health objectives and measures is also helpful. It is rare that an individual can be interested in all of these fields. Generally therapists concentrate on a special area, such as mental health education, but comprehensive knowledge will enhance functioning even though greatest weight is given one kind of activity. Work in such fields as rehabilitation, law enforcement, industry, recreation, and religion, requires an extensive repertoire of techniques. The broader the education of therapists, the more effective they will be as consultants.

Since substantial therapeutic impact may be made during periods of crisis, contact with individuals in trouble may be of incalculable help if therapists have fundamental information about how to recognize an emotional problem, how to interview, how to conduct themselves constructively in therapeutic relationships, and how to make referrals. Educating such individuals presupposes an understanding of teaching method.

TECHNIQUES IN COMMUNITY MENTAL HEALTH

Mental Health Consultation

Consultation is a basic tool of mental health specialists. It consists of an interaction between a specialist or consultant and one or more consultees (usually agency professionals) aimed at the mental health components of their work, including program and practices of the consultee organization. In the course of such consultation the consultee is also, according to Gerald Caplan, "being educated in order that he will be able in the future to handle similar problems in the same or other clients in a more effective manner than in the past" (U.S. Public Health Service, 1962).

Mental health consultation must be differentiated from psychotherapy, supervision, professional education, in-service training, and collaboration (Haylett and Rapaport, 1964). In psychotherapy, the interaction is with patients toward resolving symptoms and strengthening personality assets; in consultation, the relationship is with consultees and is geared toward enhancing their knowledge and skills. In supervision, supervisors assume an administrative in addition to an educative role; in consultation, consultants do not play an administrative authority role. In professional education, students are schooled in a skill that equips them to enter a certain profession; in consultation the consultees have already fulfilled the minimum requirements for their profession. In in-service training, the focus is on improving competence in the tasks for which therapists have been hired; in consultation new tasks are envisioned to expand the consultees' functions in mental health areas.

Consultation is usually offered to individuals in key administrative and supervisory positions to maximize the effect and reach the greatest numbers of people, i.e., the working staffs. It is generally done at the consultees' place of work unless consultants possess or arrange for special facilities.

Stages of consultation may be divided into a beginning or "entry" phase, a problem-solving phase, and a termination phase. It is assumed that the consultee is acquainted with the consultant or the consultant's work and is oriented regarding the nature of consultation services. If not, a preparatory interpretive meeting or group of meetings may have to be arranged. A contract is drawn up either verbally or, preferably, in the form of an exchange of letters. The consultant and consultee agree on details about participating personnel,

the extent of time of the project, and physical arrangements. It may be necessary to clarify the consultant's role—for instance, that services are not given directly to the consultee's clients. The next phase is that of problem solving, which is the core of the consultation process. Here the consultee's motivations and readiness for change mingle with the consultant's skill, experience, and capacity to handle emotional aspects of the relationship. This interaction will determine the rapidity with which movement and change are registered. The final phase is that of a mutually agreed upon termination.

The methods employed by the mental health consultant will have to be adapted to the special needs and problems of the agency, group, or individual who is seeking help. Generally, methods derived from the clinical model, i.e., therapeutic work with individuals, are not too applicable to consultation. As an example, suppose that the specialist is engaged by a social agency as a consultant in making their functions more effective. The first step is the "entry process" into the agency—"consultee system," or "client-system" as R. Lippitt et al. (1958) call it. This entails a proper diagnosis of the problem determined by setting up a series of meetings with key personnel. The objective is to help the consultee arrive at an understanding of what is needed and which aspects of the problem to approach immediately and which later on. A problem-solving plan is evolved, and the consultant then focuses on facilitating and enhancing the problem-solving skills of the individuals who will execute the plan. Communication channels are opened up between the various levels of the agency (executive, supervisor, and staff) to handle the effects of feedback, and resistances to change and to learning. The consultant then continues to work with the agency until the plan is proceeding satisfactorily. If the agency is large, the consultant may restrict efforts just to training the supervisory staff, expanding their information and skills so that they may by themselves manage and continue the program that has been instituted. The consultant may have to use some research techniques and engage in 9 or 10 group conference sevices, getting details of work habits, studying records, and becoming familiar with the functions of the organization. Then attention may be directed to training. If the consultant cannot personally enter into the problem-solving process, help may be obtained from the proper outside resources for this task. Finally, the consultant withdraws from the agency or "consultee system" (Wolberg A and Padilla-Lawson, 1965).

Considerable numbers of writings have accumulated detailing theory and method in mental health consultation. Recommended readings are the following: Argyris (1961); Berlin (1956, 1960, 1964); Bindman (1959, 1960, 1966); Boehme (1956); Brashear et al. (1954); Caplan (1961b, 1963, 1964, 1970); L. D. Cohen (1966); J. V. Coleman (1947); Cooper and Hodges (1983); Covner (1947); Croley (1961); Davies (1960); W. E. Davis (1957); GAP (1956a); Garrett (1956); Gibb (1959); Gibb and Lippitt (1959); Gilbert (1960); Gilbertson (1952); Glidewell (1959); Gordon DE (1953); Greenblatt (1975); Halleck and Miller (1963); Kazanjian et al. (1962); Lamb and Peterson (1983); Leader (1957); Lifschutz et al. (1958); G. Lippitt (1959); R. Lippitt et al. (1958); Maddux (1953); Malamud (1959); Mannino et al. (1975); Mental Hygiene Committee (1950); Nunnally (1957); K. B. Oettinger (1950); Parker (1958, 1962); L. Rapaport (1963); Rogawski (1979); M. J. Rosenthal and Sullivan (1959); San Mateo County (1961); G. S. Stevenson (1956); Valenstein (1955); A. Wolberg and Padilla-Lawson (1965); Zander (1957).

More specifically, the entry phase is characterized by an exploration during conferences of the manifest problems and needs of the consultee. During this phase relationships will be established. If possible, a personal interview is arranged by the consultee for the consultant with the head of the agency to affirm the agency's support for the project. Answers are needed to the following:

1. What is the structure of the agency, including the history, budget, and financing?

2. What is the organizational structure involving the personnel in the agency? What are the authority lines and policy-making bodies?

3. What are the supervisory policies?

4. Are there any apparent personality problems of, and conflicts in relation to, the leadership?

5. Are there any apparent conflicts in policies and aims?

6. What are the existing functions of the agency and are these being fulfilled?

7. What are the proposed future functions, if any, and are these realistic?

8. What is the community setting in which the agency operates? Are there conflicts between policies and functions of the agency and the community? What are the areas of community support and the areas of opposition? (For example, a school may wish to focus its resources and energies on the most gifted children who are showing learning blocks. The parents' association may be pressing for better tutoring to prepare the students for college boards. Some community organizations, courts, and social agencies, in contrast, may be insistent that juvenile delinquents and retarded children receive special attention, which will conflict with a program for brighter students.)

9. What is the community organization; is there now or will there be a duplication of services? Is there cooperation with other agencies?

10. What are the existing and anticipated conflicts regarding programming and policy changes?
11. What were the previous experiences of the agency with consultants?

During the next (problem-solving) phase of the consultation there is an ordered gathering of informaation about the consultee system, including needs and difficulties. A true working relationship begins to develop. Diagnostic assessments are made and a plan of action is agreed upon. It will be essential for consultants to educate the consultees in handling anxieties and resistances. A periodic review of services and problems may be required and role limitations defined. It is to be expected that some untoward reactions will crop up among the staff, supervisors, and adminision when program changes are proposed or implemented. Great tact must be exercised in dealing with these. It may that the staff's proposals for change may not be consonant with the personal philosophies of the administrator, in which case exploratory conferences will be necessary.

In the course of problem solving, tranference and countertransference will come into evidence. The consultants' own analysis and experience as psychotherapists will help the consultants deal with these contingencies. Obviously, psychotherapy will not be done; however, inimical reactions may tactfully be interpreted on the "here-and-now" level. Temptation to fall back on clinical methods must be resisted. If the consultees recognize an emotional problem in themselves and request help for this, the consultants may offer advice about resources. Plunging in blindly and trying to get consultees to accept personal therapy without their desire for this may destroy the working relationship.

What is discouraging to most consultants is the slowness with which attitude change can be brought about. Personality difficulties among the personnel in an agency are the greatest deterrents to change and constructive action, and consultants will have to work with these obstructions painstakingly. Honest, frank communication in the matrix of a working relationship is the best way of dealing with emerging resistances and problems. Consultants must expect that some of the intrusions proffered will be challenged and that discrimination may be exercised that will not always be in the consultants' favor. Questions consultants ask about the organization and its functions may arouse suspicions of "trespassing" and may mobilize guilt feelings in those who fear that their negligence in duty will be discovered. Some may resent being told how to do their jobs. The consultants during conferences should convey no implication of blame or criticism, no "eyebrow lifting." A casual reassuring manner is best punctuated by occasional approving remarks for praiseworthy tasks the consultees are doing. Attempts should be made to build up confidence and trust, realizing that no matter how meritorious or urgently changes are needed, they are bound to be resisted. Even a poorly functioning organization has achieved a shaky equilibrium, which will be defended.

Among the rules to follow are these:

1. Do not be hasty with advice. Community problems are complex and a thorough exploration will be essential before conclusions are valid.
2. Consider carefully the ideas and opinions of the people with whom you are working.
3. Expect power groups to try to involve you; avoid taking sides.
4. Try to see all aspects of a question if there is conflict. Verbalize how the opponents must feel. Let them offer suggestions regarding proposed courses of action.

Table 67-1

A Multilevel, Multisystem, Method for the Study of Problems of Organizations and the Individual Functioning in these Organizations as They Attempt the Solution of Problems: A Mental Health Consultation Technique—Directives to the Consultant

---

Part 1. Definition of Problem

Succinctly formulate the chief problem for which the study is undertaken based on the subjective estimation of the problem by members from three levels of the organization. (administrative, supervisory, and line staff). The statement must include what the problem means to the organization and to the individuals functioning in the setting. Important administrative, supervisory, and staff members should be interviewed.

Part 2. Detection, Identification, and Description of the Problem

A. Study of the individuals in the organization who have the particular problem or who are affected by it.
  1. Study formal records.
  2. Study anecdotal records.
  3. Study questionnaires that have been answered by the individuals requesting the study.
  4. Direct interviews with three or four individuals affected by this problem.
  5. Study the work records of individuals affected by this problem in relation to skill, absenteeism, illness.
B. Study peer groups in three levels of the organization, (administrative, supervisory, and staff personnel) members of which are affected by the problem.
  1. Hold a series of four group discussions with peers from each organizational level and answer these questions:
     (a) How does each individual react in the group?
     (b) Can the members communicate?
     (c) Do subgroups form as the discussion proceeds?
     (d) Are some members disruptive?
     (e) Are any of these group members emotionally disturbed?
     (f) Does this disturbance cause trouble in the group?
     (g) Does the emotional difficulty affect work roles?
C. Study of the organization in relation to this particular problem.
  1. What is the function of this organization?
  2. Study the institutional records for the purpose of determining how the problem affects the operation of the organization.
  3. What disposition has been made of the problem up to the present?
  4. How seriously does the problem affect the organization?
  5. Has the problem affected individuals in a destructive way?
  6. What institutions or organizations or agencies in the community is this organization responsible to with respect to this problem?
  7. Is this trend or problem a unique one that exists only in this organization? Or does it exist in all organizations? Or only in some? Specify.
  8. What efforts have been made to reverse this trend? And what techniques have been used? By whom? Where?
  9. Typical day in the organization with respect to this problem.
  10. Group discussion with at least four or more individuals on the supervisory level with respect to the information collected to date.
  11. Is there any discrepancy between the ideas of the supervisors and those of the staff with respect to the problem?
  12. Are there subgroups within the organization that are competing or are antagonistic to one another?
  13. Is the consultative process threatening to individuals within the organization, and do they build up resistance to it? Illustrate.

Part 3. Analysis of Data

A. What are the motivations of the individuals who requested the consultation?
B. Where are the main pressures in the organization?
C. What groups of individuals need additional skills?
D. Can the supervisory staff give the members of the group the appropriate training for the skills, or do they themselves need further education?
E. Can you determine the point at which information is acceptable and at which it can be integrated by the supervisors and by the staff?
F. Are other resources than skills of the consultant needed to assist in the retraining of the staff?
G. Is there conflict between workers and supervisors? Between supervisors and administrators?
H. Are there intra-agency clashes between departments? Among people due to lack of role boundary? Due to personality problems?
I. What are the main problems as you see them according to the analysis of the data? List.
J. Will the changes in role by training or retraining cause dislocation of a temporary nature in the organization?

Part 4. Planning and Decision Making

A. What plan do you suggest?
B. How will you explain this plan to the administration? To the supervisors? To others who may have to be informed?
    1. Illustrate the types of communication that you will use with the above categories in the social organization.
C. Where do you anticipate that resistance will occur and for what reasons?
    1. Can anything be done to counteract this?
D. What is the nature of your relationship with the members of the organization with whom you will have to work? Explain.
E. Steps in working out the plan.
    1. List the steps you will take to carry out the plan.
    2. How will this reverse the trend or help the problems that you have found?
        (a) Document this plan and the rationale for the steps you are taking with theoretical concepts from the literature.
    3. What are the specific techniques you will employ?
    4. What do you anticipate as a result of the carrying out of this plan?

5. Try to exhibit tact and to retain a sense of humor.

The withdrawal phase of consultation will take place after the problem for which the consultants was retained has been solved, or prior to its solution by mutual consent. An evaluation of the service and plans for future cooperation (e.g., reports, personal contact) are made.

It is apparent that the consultants will need to know something about community organization and planning for mental health, social planning, organizational management, administration, public relations, public health, individual and group dynamics, research, law, teaching, supervision, social psychology, cultural anthropology, sociology, and political action.

At the Postgraduate Center for Mental Health in New York City, an interdisciplinary specialty program trained psychiatrists, psychiatric social workers, and clinical psychologists to function as community mental health consultants only after they had completed a postgraduate psychoanalytic training program (which requires an average of 4 years of didactic courses, personal psychoanalysis, and intensive supervision) and who thereafter spent an additional 2 years, part time, in active consultative work in the community under supervision (Hamburger, 1976; Wolberg A, and Padilla-Lawson, 1962). In practically all cases, students have become so interested in community work that they have participated substantially as community workers after completing their course in addition to operating as therapists in private practice. The model for the consultation process taught has been developed and organized in part around the paradigms of G. Lippitt (1959) and Gibb and R. Lippitt (1959), which emphasize systems theory and group dynamics, and in part around concepts of a mental health "multilevel-planning-activity group (MPAG)" developed by A. Wolberg and Padilla-Lawson (1959), an outline of which is given in Table 67-1.

To apply themselves most effectively in the community, therapist-consultants will have to fulfill a number of roles. Ideally, they should be able to plan, develop, and implement programs for prevention of mental illness, for reduction of psychiatric morbidity, for training of mental health personnel, for agency evaluation and reorganization, for education of professionals (e.g., physicians, teachers, ministers, lawyers, correctional workers) who deal with people blocked in learning, work, and interpersonal and social relationships, for upgrading of skills of institutional staffs (e.g., schools, industry, social agencies), and for public education in mental health. Obviously, neither the consultants' backgrounds nor available time will enable consultants to be equally effective as community mental health consultant, professional trainer, and public health educator. Consequently, it will be necessary to restrict efforts to areas within the consultants' competence while acquiring further training that will equip consultants to play an expanded mental health role. Thus if zones of interest and ability are in the field of treatment, adminis-

tration, research, or teaching, therapist-consultants will most likely seek out and be sought for selective projects in line with this expertise.

In some of these projects the consultants will become involved in organizing, administrating, and supervising a variety of other services, some of which they can do better than others. These include preventive care, home treatment, walk-in clinics, admission procedures, partial hospitalization, work programs, social rehabilitation, planning development of the locus of care, rural program development, metropolitan mental health center development, legal issues in establishment and operation, record keeping and research, and so on (Grunebaum H, 1970).

The Training of Mental Health Personnel

Mental disorders constitute a major public health problem resulting not only in syndromes that totally incapacitate a large section of the population, but also, in their early stages and incipient forms, directly or indirectly influencing the happiness and efficiency of every individual alive. Because of the ubiquity of the problem, psychotherapists are being increasingly drawn into programs of training on federal, state, and local levels. The broadening of vistas of mental health to penetrate into every nook and cranny of the community and diffusion of psychological knowledge into programs of education, correction, health, and welfare have resulted in an enlistment of psychotherapists toward planning programs and participating in their development in accordance with the needs, readiness, and practical limitations existing in a specific area of the country. Psychotherapists are also playing a vital role in the recruitment of mental health personnel.

In view of the great shortage of mental-health workers, training programs are being sponsored with federal and state support, which include not only professional groups such as general practitioners, nurses, social scientists, health officers, health educators, ministers, teachers, social workers, occupational therapists, recreational therapists, speech therapists, and vocational counselors, but also subprofessional and technical personnel such as psychiatric aides and paraprofessionals. While it is difficult to estimate the precise personnel requirements, it is safe to assume that at least twice the number of mental health professionals will be needed to cope even minimally with the existing demand for services. In recognition of these needs, the Surgeon General's Ad Hoc Committee on Mental Health Activities (NIMH, 1962) encouraged the in-service training in mental health of professional personnel in organizations that deal with problems confronting human beings on every level of functioning, the introduction of mental health courses in schools of public health, more intensive exposure of psychiatric residents to social science and public health methods, and support for the training of greater numbers of high-level professional mental health personnel, particularly for work in community mental health programs.

In designing a training program for an agency or organization, the therapist-consultant will need to use some of the processes of consultation. This may be illustrated by a problem presented to the Postgraduate Center by the casework staff of the case study unit of one of the bureaus of a school system (Wolberg A, 1964). The staff was concerned with the need to learn new techniques to approach the hard-to-reach children expressing their emotional problems in poor school attendance. Home visits, referrals to community agencies, supervision of the children, consultation with community agencies, and appearances in court constituted the work done by the social work staff. After a series of confer-

ences of the consultees with the casework staff, it was agreed that some of the children might benefit from group approaches. It was decided to organize a training program to teach the social workers the group-counseling method within casework process.

Four broad phases in this program were planned: (1) Six to eight exploratory sessions with the case study supervisors of the bureau and the consulting supervisory staff of the Postgraduate Center to discuss typical cases handled by the bureau, with the hope (a) of developing a set of criteria for the choice of clients who would participate in the groups and (b) of developing group techniques appropriate to this situation. (2) A regular 15-session seminar in group process for the case-study supervisory staff of the bureau and for the three caseworkers who were to handle the first three trial groups. (3) Three consultants assigned to the first trial groups were to teach the caseworkers how to use group dynamic methods in handling their groups of children, and to teach the supervisors how to supervise this group process. Other supervisors and social workers were to observe the supervision of the worker. This phase was to continue for 2 or 3 years in a progressively diminishing manner as the bureau staff acquired greater skills. (4) In 4 or 5 years the project was to be expanded to train social workers in the bureau to assume responsibility for a citywide group program in the schools. After this the Postgraduate Center was to withdraw and the consultation program was to be terminated. According to the plan, each caseworker (attendance teacher) carried 2 groups of 8 children each, weekly, over a period of 1 semester (15 weeks), in addition to the caseworker's regular work. The objective was not to make group therapists out of the social workers, but to adapt group methods to casework procedure to enhance the mental health of the children.

Table 67-2

Mental Health Consultation Guide for Multisystem Consultation Method

Within an Organization Tensions are Expressed on	Expressions of Problems Found upon Entry into an Organization	Psychological, Social, and Health Factors Contributing to Organizational Difficulties
Individual Level: by Executives Supervisors Staff	Lack of clarity in goals Inability to achieve objectives Lack of skills (inadequate training) Rigidity; confused hierarchy Inability to change practices Apathy, boredom, and lack of interest in work Procrastination, lack of initiative Sense of hopelessness Inability to undertake responsibility Self-excusing	Characterologic, neurotic, and psychotic difficulties Frequent illnesses Alcoholism Delinquency and crime Drug addiction Chronic disease Absenteeism Other
Internal Relationships Level by individuals who belong to subgroups involved with agency philosophy, policy making, and establishing rules and regulations. Management in relation to owners, stockholders, and boards of trustees Intramanagement relationships Administrative actions Staff–management relationships Staff interaction Staff–client relationships	Inadequte administration Cluttered and inoperative channels of communication: divisive techniques; unclear administrative channels; lack of coordination of activities Confusion in giving and taking orders Interdisciplinary and departmental conflicts (prestige, control, status, and authority problems) Unqualified staff Conflicts between policy makers and those who carry out policy Lack of participation in group process Fear of democratic process and need for authoritarian system Inadequate system of rewards and recognition for personal achievement Inadequate personnel practices, training programs, and counseling Vague and conflicting aims Inadequate programming for goal achievement Inadequate board of trustees, owners, or corporate personnel	Projection of difficulties onto others Hostility, aggression, or compulsive competitiveness Acting-out of sadomasochistic fantasies Withdrawal Obsessive doubting, indecisiveness Resistance to change Recurrent frustrations in work effort Conflicting interpersonal relations Unconscious sabotaging Paranoid feelings (griping, complaining, undermining) Laissez-faire attitudes
External Relationships Level by individuals who are working with Organized Professional Groups Labor Religious organizations Civic organizations Political groups Business groups Press Government	Difficulties in obtaining cooperation of community leaders Inadequate interagency cooperation on programs Failure in communication with groups Failure in obtaining acceptance from professional groups Difficulty in obtaining acceptance of community groups Inability to reduce conflicts with groups in the community Poor image of performance and role of organization Inadequate techniques to deal with community criticism and pressures	Failure of staff and/or organization to satisfy standards acceptable to the community Failure of staff to meet standards of professionals in the community Inadequate service Failure to meet community needs

Consequences to Organization	Consultation Activity Aimed at Problem Resolution; Consultant Assists Staff toward	Recommendations and Plans
Inadequate service	Presenting of problems through case method	Programming for individual counseling, psychotherapy, and/or referral sources
Loss of work due to high rate of lateness and absenteeism	Discussing staff studies and staff understanding of problems presented by individuals	
	Collecting of information on staff attitudes based on opinions expressed	Clarification of roles
		Clarification of duties
	Observing of interaction of staff members (in framework of group dynamics)	Clarification of supervisory practices
	Making inferences as to problems presented and their analysis and evaluation	
Organizational goals not achieved due to inappropriate planning and programming	Discussing of organizational chart to obtain clarification of lines of authority and channels through which decisions are made and implemented	Changes in staff orientation and role
Inadequate supervision and controls; unclear responses and practices	Identifying needs and problems of staff and making inferences as to kinds of and intensity of problems in the organization; establishing the expertness of staff and agency resources to cope with the problems	Education for new roles through training
Inability of staff to meet requirements of job		Adaptation of mental health information and techniques to the needs of the organization and its goals and practices
High turnover of qualified people	Exchange of ideas	
Duplication, errors, minimization of benefit from skills of expert staff	Handling feedback from communication	
Difficulty in rendering service		
Failure on collaboration efforts		
Low morale		
Low prestige	Interpreting goals and purposes to community	Joint programs with agencies
Confused public image	Organizing sevices useful to the district in which the organization exists	Community education
Lack of community acceptance		Consultation services
Difficulty in raising funds or obtaining credit	Public relations	Work in professional societies
	Fund raising (for non-profit organizations)	Explicit public relations programs that are educational as well as informative
Difficulty in obtaining adequate staff	Changes in board membership	
	Programming in relation to other organizations	Reporting of work done

The value of this program was proven by the marked improvement by the participant children in actual school attendance (complete cessation of absenteeism in 53 percent, marked reduction in 20 percent), in scholastic achievement, in attitudes toward school, and in general attitudes toward their classmates and adults. The school personnel expressed enthusiasm regarding the results of the program. A total of 25 attendance teachers was trained to manage groups, most of whom became supervisors and in turn began to train others.

Training programs must be tailormade, designed for the specific needs of the professionals who are seeking further tutelage, taking into consideration their present education and the functions that they intend to fulfill. Generally, a consultation process will be required to assess what the training requirements are and the best means of executing the proposed goals. It is essential that the training equip the individuals to work more effectively within their particular profession and not be geared to making the "trainees" psychotherapists. Didactic lectures are secondary to case discussions and supervised work with clients. A group process is often helpful for the the professionals themselves, enabling them to become aware of some of their personal problems and resistances.

Public Education in Mental Health

The great need for public education in mental health was pointed out by Braceland (1955): "public information on what constitutes illness and health is a hodgepodge of folklore, information, and misinformation." He appropriately warned, moreover, that the techniques and particularly the use of mass propaganda methods may present a distorted picture of any public health problem. Data about mental and emotional disease may easily arouse fears and anxieties. The ineffectiveness of intensive educational programs using a wide variety of materials is, unfortunately, not too uncommon an experience, established attitudes rarely being changed. Braceland affirmed the need to avoid calling attention to the ravages of mental illness; rather it is essential, he noted, to stress hope and the promise of recovery with early diagnosis and treatment "to reassure rather than to threaten or frighten" and "the audience . . . spared technical language and abstruse, complex material that they are not prepared to handle." What requires emphasis is normal behavior, the fluctuations in emotional well-being, the universality of anxiety and some of its common manifestations, the determining (but not necessarily irreversible) influences of past experiences, the impact of social and cultural factors on personality development and functioning, the psychological needs at various developmental phases, the stress situations that create emotional insecurity at different age periods, and a description of how emotions influence humans toward unrealistic goals and immature behavior.

Mass approaches to public education in mental health must await the development of television and radio programs as well as the kinds of press reporting and magazine writing that does not emphasize the destructive, dramatic, and violent aspects of mental illness and emotional disturbance. If the sponsors of programs and the controlling forces in the publication field were to apply the organizational and creative skills they use to sell advertised products, they undoubtedly would be able to adapt mental health materials that would change attitudes. This would necessitate a shift in the content of mass media away from preoccupations with violence and disturbed relationships among people.

In the meantime, mental health workers may have to confine themselves to the influencing of small, motivated groups who need and ask for special kinds of information. Materials pertinent to the topics of interest may be procured, and leads regarding appropriate films, pamphlets, plays, and other audiovisual and graphic aids may be obtained, from such educational organizations as the Mental Health Materials Center, 30 E. 29th St., New York, NY 10016. There is a useful Public Health Service Publication (No. 218, Washington, D. C., 1960) titled *Mental Health Motion Pictures: A selective Guide*. A film guide, *Index to 16 mm Educational Films,* is published by NICEM, University of Southern California, National Information Center for Educational Media, University Park, Los Angeles, CA 90024. The Library of Congress publishes a catalogue of motion pictures and filmstrips on many educational topics. Films may also be obtained from Psychological Cinema Register, Audiovisual Service, Pennsylvania State University, University Park, PA 16802; and New York University Film Library, Washington Square North, New York, NY 10003. If audio materials alone would be sufficient, a catalogue with a full listing may be obtained from The Center for Casette Studios, 8110 Webb Avenue, North Hollywood, CA 91605; and from Xerox University Microfilms, 300 North Zeeb Road, Ann Arbor, MI 48106.

In the section on Bibliotherapy (p.

1046), books, pamphlets, and films on different subjects written for the general public will give educators ideas of content and methods of presentation.

A brief outline of suggested methods of working with films and conducting discussion groups follows.

SUGGESTIONS ON METHODS OF INTRODUCING AND DISCUSSING MENTAL HEALTH FILMS (OR VIDEOTAPES)

1. *General.* Mental health films presented to lay groups are mainly informational in objective. This means that the discussion leaders function as "experts." They must make the largest contributions elaborating on the theme of the film and clarifying the questions brought up by the audience. Nevertheless, audience participation must be encouraged. This can be done by stimulating discussion on several points illustrated by the film.

   Many members of the audience will identify with characters in the film. Consequently, the tone of the discussion must always be sympathetic and reassuring. *Never* belittle or ridicule any character; *never* say a condition is hopeless or incurable.

2. *Previewing the film.* If possible, preview the film, preferably at least an hour before the actual showing. Make a notation in writing of the following: (a) What is the theme of the film? (b) What three or four points does it illustrate? The discussion that follows the film may be organized around these points.

   If a preview of the film is not possible, study the *leader's guide* issued with the film, if there is such a guide, at least an hour before the showing. Make notations in writing of the film theme and of several psychiatric points that are illustrated.

   If a preview of the film is not possible and if there is no leader's guide, make a mental note of the theme and points raised while watching the film at the actual showing.

3. *Starting the class or meeting.* The class or meeting must be started sharply on time. Latecomers will probably come on time at the next meeting if this is done.

4. *Introducing the film.* There are two methods of introducing the film: Method 1—Give a brief lecture (10 to 15 minutes) on the general topic illustrated by the film, indicating which points the audience is to observe. Method 2—Describe the film briefly (1 to 5 minutes), indicating the general theme and the points the audience is to watch for especially.

5. *Film showing.* Arrangements will probably have been made with a projector operator so that the film is ready for showing on a signal from you. Since breakdowns in equipment are common, you should determine in advance if the projector is in good working order. Do this also with the videotape recorder if a tape is to be shown.

6. *Discussing the film.* After reviewing the film, you may proceed along several lines:

   a. *Lecture.* If there is to be a lecture, this should last no more than 15 minutes. The points in the film are introduced in the context as illustrative material. Following this, the meeting is opened to discussion.

   b. *Presentation of the salient points of the film.* The chief points illustrated by the film are mentioned, following which there is discussion.

   c. *Asking pertinent questions about*

the film. The points illustrated by the film are presented as questions. This is a very good way to get audience participation.

7. *Handling group situations.*
   a. *Group failing to participate.* When the group fails to enter into the discussion, ask one or two provocative questions. If no one responds, call on one member of the group.
   b. *A member arguing too much.* Simply say, "I understand your reaction; perhaps other people here would like to comment on it." The group usually has a way of subduing the the disturbed member. If this does not work, invite the person to discuss matters with you after the meeting.
   c. *One member talking too much.* At a pause in his talk, cut the person off with a summarizing statement and direct a question at someone else.
   d. *A member persisting on talking off the subject.* Cut the person off with the statement, "That is interesting, and we may come back to that later." Direct a question at someone else.

8. *Terminating meeting.* The meeting should be terminated after about one hour of discussion, or lecture and discussion. A brief summary is sometimes helpful, as is assignment of reading material.

SUGGESTIONS ON CONDUCTING A DISCUSSION GROUP

1. *General.* A discussion group provides the participants with perhaps the best opportunity for learning. Sharing ideas and experiences promotes an exchange of information. Verbalizing attitudes and doubts helps to resolve resistances and learning blocks. Furthermore, the discussion group may serve a therapeutic function, enabling individuals to gain a measure of assuredness in expressing their ideas and opinions and in working through fears, hostilities, and other disabling attitudes in relation to a group.

2. *Physical arrangements.*
   a. *Size of group.* The ideal size of the group ranges from 6 to 10 people. This number makes it possible for all members to contribute actively. In exceptional or unavoidable instances, a larger group may be handled, though this will involve some sacrifice in individual activity.
   b. *Position of chairs.* Seating arrangement is important to avoid your being placed in too prominent a position, which is apt to stifle discussion. Members may be seated facing you and one another around a table, or, if this is impractical, in chairs placed in a circle or semicircle. It goes without saying that proper ventilation, comfortable lighting and where smoking is permitted ash trays add to the relaxed atmosphere that is most conducive to good discussion.
   c. *Length of discussion sessions.* This will vary depending on the circumstances, but a good average is $1\frac{1}{2}$ hours.
   d. *Starting the session on time.* The session should begin on time. Latecomers will probably come on time at the next session if this is done.

3. *The first session.*
   a. Once members are seated, a good way to start is to ask members to introduce themselves to the group by stating their names, disciplines, (if they have one, and the organization, if any, with which they are associated. This serves to "break

the ice'' and to introduce an air of informality into the atmosphere.

b. Next introduce the general subject to be discussed and relate it to the interests of the group members. A distributed outline designating material to be considered is a very helpful adjunct.

c. If essential information needs to be conveyed to the members before discussion begins, a short talk is in order. If desired, introduce an auxilliary lecturer, or a movie, filmstrip, or other audiovisual aid. Make this preliminary presentation as brief as possible.

d. Following this, begin the discussion. If there is any doubt in the minds of the members about procedure, inform them that no one will be called on formally, that anyone may speak up whenever desired, and that members should limit their comments to 2 or 3 minutes at most.

e. Encourage the group to participate by any of the following methods:

(1) Ask a provocative question relating to the outline or to the material under discussion.

(2) If there are two points of view on a topic germane to the discussion, call for a show of hands of those who share the different viewpoints. Then ask a question as to why one or the other point of view is taken.

(3) Select a topic related to the general subject and ask if there is anyone in the group who has had experience with this topic.

(4) Using a blackboard, list the different opinions or ideas of the members about a topic, or possible approaches to the topic. Group these into specific categories, and then ask questions about the various listings.

4. *Subsequent sessions.* At the start of each subsequent session, you may summarize the salient points about the previous session and then bring up the topic for the present session. If new information is to be introduced, this may be done by, for example, assigned readings, written reports from the members, an informative talk by an expert, or films.

5. *Activity of the leader.* Your function as leader in a discussion group is to help the members verbalize their ideas and integrate their thinking about a specific subject. Your role is to participate in the discussion only when the members stop talking, when they deviate from the topic under consideration, or when they are not able to think things through for themselves. Such participation does not mean delivering a lecture, giving advice, or showing off knowledge.

To fulfill this function, there must be respect for all the members in the group and for their opinions, resistances, and resentments. The fact must be accepted that the learning process requires time and that people must resolve their doubts and suspicions before they can accept ideas, no matter how logical these may seem. This will necessitate great tolerance and the ability to handle aggression that is projected by some members toward the group and toward you. Required is an informal manner and a sense of humor. Essential also is an ability to talk the same down-to-earth language as the group, eschewing complicated formulations and avoiding impressing the members with abstruse talk.

From time to time, clarify the material presented, particularly conflicting issues, and summarize the contributions that have been made by the members. If certain points are not covered, ask questions about these. Never argue, belittle, or disagree with anyone. If you have a contribution to make yourself, make it briefly, saying, "This is what I have come to believe," or "This is what is generally believed."

6. *Handling special situations.* This is, on the whole, handled as done in this category under the section on discussing films.

   a. *Group fails to participate.* When the group fails to enter into discussion, ask one or two provocative questions. If no one responds, call on one member of the group. If, after this person comments, nobody else volunteers, say, "Perhaps someone has a different slant on this."

   b. *A member arguing too much.* Simply say, "I can understand your reaction; perhaps other people here would like to comment on it." The group usually has a way of subduing the disturbed member. If this does not work, invite the person to discuss matters with you after the meeting.

   c. *One member talking too much.* At a pause in this talk, cut the person off with a summarizing statement and direct a question at the group.

   d. *A member persisting on talking off the subject.* Cut the person off with the statement, "That is interesting, and we may come back to that later." Direct a question at the group.

   e. *A side argument developing between two or more members.* Rap on the table or chair and say, "May I interrupt please. Perhaps others here would like to comment on this question that is causing controversy." If this does not stop the argument, or if the argument

spreads, say, "Obviously there are several points of view; perhaps I can help integrate them." Attempt then to explain why the differences exist and how they can be resolved. If no resolution is possible, say, "Let us think about this matter further, and we may have a chance to come back to it later." Following this, ask another question, directing the discussion into another channel.

   f. *One member constantly interrupting the comments of others.* Firmly say to the person at each interruption, "X [the person interrupted] has not finished talking, let us permit X to continue." If this does not stop the person from interrupting, say, "There is something that is bothering you, and it may be helpful for you to see me after the session." Arrange then to have a talk or talks with the person, and if the disruptive activity does not halt, suggest that the person drop out from the group.

   g. *Side conversations.* Rap on the table or chair and say, "Please let us all concentrate on what is being said."

   h. *The discussion straying too far afield from the subject.* Say, "This is interesting, but how does it apply to the subject we are discussing?"

   i. *A member refusing to budge from an opinionated and obviously erroneous point of view.* Do not take issue directly. Merely say, "Perhaps Y would like to bring in source material next time to back up that point of view." Then pass on to another person.

   j. *A member refusing to participate.* Respect the person's silence. After a number of sessions, if the person asks to speak, respond positively immediately. Rarely you may say,

"Perhaps Z may want to comment on this subject." If the person indicates no or remains silent, gloss this over with, "Not at this time; well, perhaps later."

k. *Lags in the discussion.* Point out the differences in ideas or opinions that have been presented, and ask how these differences may be reconciled.

l. *Unnecessary repetition.* Summarize what has been said, point out important aspects and highlights; then introduce a different question.

7. *The recorder and observer.* In some discussion groups it is helpful to appoint a volunteer who will record the salient features of the discussion for purposes of transcription or for summarization at the end of the present or at the beginning of the next session. Another volunteer, an observer, may be appointed to record the activity or passivity of the various members and leaders, the interpersonal reactions, and perhaps the dynamics of the group process, if trained in dynamics, which may also be prepared at the end of the session or at the beginning of the next session.

8. *Summarizing the discussion.* Before the session ends, it may be helpful to summarize the discussion, mentioning the salient points that have been covered, relating the material to what has gone on in previous sessions, restating differences of opinion, tying together topics that have not been coordinated, and adding suggestions about procedure and areas of future exploration. It is essential that the summary contain the conclusions of the group rather than your own conclusions. If the group conclusions are in your opinion inadequate or erroneous, a statement may be made to the effect that further discussion on the subject will open up areas that may yield important data.

9. *Reading assignments and reports.* Assigned readings, and verbal or written presentations by the members, are helpful as teaching aids. They serve also to introduce new material for group consideration. Suggestions regarding readings may be obtained in the Bibliotherapy section in Chapter 56.

VI

Addenda

Selected Texts for Special Situations and Problems

The literature in the field of psychotherapy flourishes with ever increasing contributions from all divisions of the behavioral sciences. Accordingly, the selection of recommended reading becomes progressively more difficult as new books and periodicals accumulate. The present section contains a representative sampling of the most popular texts among students and reviewers. A more complete bibliography explicating specific topics will be found in the various chapters of this book. Obviously it will be difficult or impossible for any therapist to read or even to acquire all the recommended texts, which will undoubtedly be found on the shelves of any good psychiatric library. Readers, nevertheless, will be able discriminately to cull from the suggested lists items that suit their interests and needs. New books, as well as revisions, will undoubtedly appear as time goes by. Nevertheless, many of the present texts will in all probability continue to survive as classics.

The lists of books that follows has been divided into 50 main categories. To make it easier for readers to find the particular section or sections that are of interest to them, Addenda Table 1 gives the subject organization of the texts recommended.

Addenda Table 1
Content of Recommended Texts

(continued)

REFERENCE WORKS

Dictionaries and Glossaries

1. American Psychiatric Association: A Psychiatric Glossary (5th ed). Boston, Little, Brown, 1980
2. Campbell RJ: Psychiatric Dictionary (5th ed). New York, Oxford University Press, 1981
3. English HB, English AC (eds): A Comprehensive Dictionary of Psychological and Psychoanalytic Terms: A Guide to Usage. New York, Longmans, Green, 1958
4. Goldenson RM (ed): Longman Dictionary of Psychology and Psychiatry. New York, Longman, 1984
5. Harré R, Lamb R (eds): The Encyclopedia Dictionary of Psychology. Cambridge, MA, MIT Press, 1983
6. Moore BE, Fine BD (eds): A Glossary of Psychoanalytic Terms and Concepts (2d ed). New York, American Psychoanalytic Association, 1968
7. Walrond-Skinner S: Dictionary of Psychotherapy. New York, Methuen, 1986

Encyclopedias

8. Corsini RJ (ed): Encyclopedia of Psychology, 4 vols. New York, John Wiley, 1984
9. Eidelberg L (ed): Encyclopedia of Psychoanalysis. New York, Free Press, 1968
10. Eysenck HJ (ed): Encyclopedia of Psychology, 3 vols. New York, Continuum, 1980
11. Freud S: Standard Edition of the Complete Psychological Works of Sigmund Freud, 24 vols. Strachey J (trans). London, Hogarth, 1964
12. Minahan A (ed): Encylcopedia of Social Work, (18th ed), 3 vols. Silver Spring, MD, NASW, 1986
13. Wolman BJ (ed): International Encyclopedia of Psychiatry, Psychology, Psychoanalysis, and Neurology, 13 vols. New York, Van Nostrand Reinhold for Aesculapius Publishers, 1977

HISTORY

14. Altschule MD: Roots of Modern Psychiatry (2d ed). Orlando FL, Grune & Stratton, 1965
15. Ehrenwald J (ed): History of Psychotherapy: From Healing Magic to Encounter. New York, Jason Aronson, 1976
16. Ellenberger HF: The Discovery of the Unconscious: The History and Evolution of Dynamic Psychiatry. New York, Basic Books, 1970
17. Fine R: A History of Psychoanalysis. New York, Columbia University Press, 1979
18. Hunter R, Macalpine I: Three Hundred Years of Psychiatry, 1535–1860. Hartsdale, New York, Carlisle Publisher, 1982. (Reprint of 1963 ed.)
19. Jones E: The Life and Work of Sigmund Freud, 3 vols. New York, Basic Books, 1953–1957
20. Inhelder B, Chipman HH: Piaget and His School: A Reader in Developmental Psychology. New York, Springer-Verlag, 1976
21. Misiak H, Sexton VS: History of Psychology: An Overview. Orlando FL, Grune & Stratton, 1966
22. Quen JM, Carlson ET (eds): American Psychoanalysis: Origins and Development. New York, Brunner/Mazel, 1978
23. Zilboorg G, Henry GW: A History of Medical Psychology. New York, Norton, 1941

MENTAL FUNCTIONS

Perception

24. Boff KR, Kaurman L, Thomas JP (eds): Handbook of Perception and Human Performance, 2 vols. New York, John Wiley, 1986
25. Bruner JS, Krech D (eds): Perception and Personality: A Symposium. Greenwood, 1968
26. Geldard F: The Human Senses (2d ed). New York, John Wiley, 1972
27. Heil J: Perception and Cognition. Berkeley, CA, University of California Press, 1983
28. Savage CW (ed): Perception and Cognition: Issues in the Foundations of Psychology, Vol. 9. Minneapolis, University of Minnesota Press, 1978

Cognitive Processes (See also 27, 28)

29. Lindsay PH, Norman DA: Human Information Processing (2d ed). Orlando FL, Academic Press, 1977

30. Sanford AJ: Cognition and Cognitive Psychology. New York, Basic Books, 1986

Conditioning and Learning

31. Bachrach AJ: Psychological Research: An Introduction (4th ed). New York, Random House, 1980
32. Domjan M, Burkhard B (eds): The Principles of Learning and Behavior. Monterey, CA, Brooks-Cole, 1981
33. Honig WK, Staddor J (eds): Handbook of Operant Behavior. New York, Prentice-Hall, 1977
34. Mazur JE: Learning & Behavior. Englewood Cliffs NJ, Prentice-Hall 1986
35. Mowrer OH: Psychology and Language of Learning. New York, Plenum, 1980
36. Skinner BF: Science and Human Behavior. New York, MacMillan, 1953

Thinking and Reasoning

37. Bowers JS, Meichenbaum D: The Unconscious Reconsidered. New York, John Wiley, 1984
38. Evans J (ed): Thinking & Reasoning: Psychological Approaches. Boston, Routledge & Kegan, 1983
39. Mandler JM, Mandler G: Thinking: From Association to Gestalt. Westport, CT, Greenwood, 1982
40. Mayer RE: Thinking, Problem Solving, Cognition. New York, W. H. Freeman, 1983

Intelligence

41. Brody EB, Brody N (eds): Intelligence: Nature, Determinants, and Consequences. Orlando, FL, Academic Press, 1976
42. Cancro R (ed): Intelligence: Genetic and Environmental Influences. Orlando, FL, Grune & Stratton, 1971
43. Eysenck HJ, Fulker DW (eds): The Structure & Measurement of Intelligence. New York, Springer-Verlag, 1979
44. Wolman BB (ed): Handbook of Intelligence: Theories, Measurements, and Applications. Somerset, NJ, John Wiley, 1986

Creativity

45. Arieti S: Creativity: The Magic Syntheses. New York, Basic Books, 1980
46. Stein M: Stimulating Creativity: Vol. 1, Individual Procedures. Orlando FL, Academic Press, 1974

Motivation

47. Bolles RC: Theory of Motivation (2d ed). New York, Harper and Row, 1975
48. Maslow AH: Motivation and Personality (2d ed). New York, Harper & Row, 1970 (paperback)
49. Weiner B: Theories of Motivation: From Mechanism to Cognition. Chicago, Rand McNally, 1974

Attitudes, Beliefs, and Values

50. Ajzen I, Fishein M: Understanding Attitudes and Predicting Social Behavior. Englewood Cliffs, NJ, Prentice-Hall, 1980
51. Maslow AH (ed): New Knowledge in Human Values. New York, Harper & Row, 1959 (paperback, 1970)
52. Morris C: Varieties of Human Value. Chicago, University of Chicago Press, 1959 Reprint from UMI (paperback, 1973)
53. Reich B, Adcock C: Values, Attitudes, and Behavior Change. New York, Methuen, 1976
54. Rokeach M: Beliefs, Attitudes, and Values: A Theory of Organization and Change. San Francisco, Jossey-Bass, 1968

Sleep and Biological Rhythms

55. Aschoff J (ed): Handbook of Behavioral Neurobiology: Biological Rhythms. New York, Plenum Press, 1981
56. Hartmann E: The Functions of Sleep. New Haven, CT, Yale University Press, 1973
57. Kleitman N: Sleep and Wakefulness. Chicago, University of Chicago Press, 1963
58. Webb WB (ed): Biological Rhythms, Sleep and Performance. New York, John Wiley, 1982
59. Wehr TA, Goodwin FK (eds): Circadian Rhythms in Psychiatry. Pacific Grove, CA, 1983
60. Williams RL, Karacan I: Pharmacology of Sleep. New York, John Wiley, 1976

PERSONALITY DEVELOPMENT

61. Erikson EH: Childhood and Society (2d ed). New York, Norton, 1963
62. Erikson EH: Identity and the Life Cycle:

Selected Papers. Psychological Issues, Monogr 1: Vol. 1, No. 1. New York, International Universities Press, 1967

63. Glidewell JC: The Social Context of Learning and Development. New York, John Wiley, 1977

64. Hall CS, Lindzey G: Theories of Personality. New York, John Wiley, 1978

65. Knobloch H, Pasamanick B (eds): Gesell and Amatruda's Developmental Diagnosis (3rd ed). New York, Harper & Row, 1974

66. Piaget J, Inhelder B: Psychology of the Child. New York, Basic Books, 1969

SOCIAL PSYCHOLOGY

General

67. Brehm SS: The Application of Social Psychology to Clinical Practice. New York, Halstead/Wiley, 1976

68. Lindzey G, Aronson E (eds): Handbook of Social Psychology, (3rd ed), 2 vols. New York, Random House, 1985

69. Wechsler H, Solomon L, Kramer BM (eds): Social Psychology and Mental Health. New York, Holt, 1970

Communication

70. Altheide DL: Media Power. Beverly Hills, CA, Sage Publications, 1985

71. Giles H, St. Clair RN (eds): Recent Advances in Language, Communication, and Social Psychology. Hillsdale, New Jersey, L Erlbaum, 1985

72. Harper RG, Wiens AN, Matarazzo JD: Nonverbal Communication: The State of the Art. New York, John Wiley, 1978

73. McLaughlin ML (ed): Communication Yearbook 9. Beverly Hills, CA, Sage Publications, 1985

Group Dynamics

74. Anzieu D: The Group and the Unconscious. Boston, Routledge & Kegan, 1984

75. Cartwright D, Zander A (eds): Group Dynamics: Research and Theory (3rd ed). New York, Harper & Row, 1968

76. Kreeger L (ed): The Large Group: Dynamics and Therapy. Itasca, IL, Peacock, 1975

77. Payne R, Cooper CL: Groups at Work. New York, John Wiley, 1981

78. Zander A: Motives and Goals in Groups. Orlando FL, Academic Press, 1971

Interactional Process

79. Argyle M: Social Interaction. New York, Methuen, 1973

80. Bales RF: Interaction Process Analysis: A Method for the Study of Small Groups. Chicago, University of Chicago Press, 1951

81. Hare PA: Social Interaction and Creativity in Small Groups. Beverly Hills, CA, Sage, 1981

EXPERIMENTAL PSYCHOLOGY

82. Borkowski JG, Anderson DC: Experimental Psychology: Tactics of Behavioral Research. Glenview, IL, Scott, Foresman, 1977

83. Hearst E (ed): The First Century of Experimental Psychology. Hillsdale, NJ, Lawrence Erlbaum, 1984

84. Murchison C (ed): The Foundations of Experimental Psychology. Watkins Glen, NY, Century House Publishing, 1984. (Reprint of 1929 ed.)

85. Zinser O: Basic Principles of Experimental Psychology. New York, McGraw-Hill, 1984

INDUSTRIAL AND ORGANIZATIONAL PSYCHOLOGY

86. Russ TF, et al: Mass Unemployment: Plant Closing & Community Mental Health. Beverly Hills, CA, Sage, 1983

87. Cooper CL, Robertson I (eds): Annual Review of Industrial & Organizational Psychology, Vol. 1. New York, John Wiley, 1986

88. Drenth PJ, et al (eds): Handbook of Work and Organizational Psychology, 2 vols. New York, John Wiley, 1984

89. Dunnette MD (ed): Handbook of Industrial and Organizational Psychology. New York, John Wiley, 1983

90. Lauffer A: Careers, Colleagues, and Conflicts: Understanding Gender, Race, and

Ethnicity in the Workplace. Beverly Hills, CA, Sage Publications, 1985

91. Levinson H, et al: Organizational Diagnosis. Cambridge, MA, Harvard University Press, 1972

EDUCATIONAL PSYCHOLOGY

92. Belkin GS: Perspectives in Educational Psychology. Dubuque, IA, William C. Brown, 1979

PHYSIOLOGICAL PSYCHOLOGY

93. Andreassi JL: Psychophysiology: Human Behavior & Physiological Response. New York, Oxford University Press, 1980

ANTHROPOLOGY

94. Abel TM, Metraux R, Roll S: Psychotherapy and Culture, (rev ed). Albuquerque, NM, University of New Mexico Press, 1987

95. Helman C: Culture, Health, and Illness: An Introduction for Health Professionals. Boston, Wright-PSG, 1984

96. Jahoda G: Psychology & Anthropology: A Psychological Perspective. Orlando FL, Academic Press, 1982

97. Le Vine RA (ed): Culture and Personality: Contemporary Readings. Chicago, Aldine, 1974

98. Malinowski B: Scientific Theory of Culture. Chapel Hill, NC, University of North Carolina Press, 1944

99. Marsella AJ, White GM: Cultural Conception of Mental Health and Therapy. Boston, Reidel, 1982

100. Tseng WS, McDermott, JF: Culture, Mind and Therapy. New York, Brunner/Mazel, 1981

SOCIOLOGY

General

101. Coser LA, Rosenberg B: Sociological Theory, New York, Macmillan, 1982

102. Eaton WE: Sociology of Mental Disorders. New York, Praeger, 1986

103. Goldman MS, Rabow J, Platt G (eds): Studies in Psychoanalytic Sociology. Melbourne, FL, Krieger Publishing, 1986

Social Theory

104. Collins R: Max Weber: A Skeleton Key. Beverly Hills, CA, Sage Publications, 1985

105. Jones RA: Emile Durkheim: An Introduction to Four Major Works. Beverly Hills, CA, Sage Publications, 1985

106. Merton RK: Social Theory and Social Structure. New York, Free Press, 1968

107. Turner JH: Herbert Spencer: A Renewed Appreciation. Beverly Hills, CA, Sage Publications, 1985

Social and Family Problems (See also 208)

108. Bell RR: Contemporary Social Problems. Chicago, Dorsey, 1981

109. Gelles RJ, Cornell CP: Intimate Violence in Families. Beverly Hills, CA, Sage Publications, 1985

110. Scanzoni L, Scanzoni J: Men, Women and Change: A Sociology of Marriage and Family. New York, McGraw-Hill, 1981

Social Behavior

111. Homans GC: Social Behavior: Its Elementary Forms, (rev ed), Orlando FL, Harcourt Brace Jovanovich, Inc., 1974

112. Shaver P (ed): Self, Situations, and Social Behavior: Review of Personality and Social Psychology 7. Beverly Hills, CA, Sage Publications, 1985

Family Interaction (See also 208, 592, 617)

113. Hanson SMH, Bozett FW (eds): Dimensions of Fatherhood. Beverly Hills, CA, Sage Publications, 1985

114. Kantor D, Lehr W: Inside the Family. San Francisco, Jossey-Bass, 1976

115. Lewis RA, Salt RE (eds): Men in Families. Beverly Hills, CA, Sage Publications, 1985

116. Parsons T, Bales RF: Family Socialization and Interaction Process. New York, Free Press, 1955

117. Pleck JH: Working Wives, Working Hus-

bands. Beverly Hills, CA, Sage Publications, 1985

118. Walsh F: Normal Family Processes. New York, Guilford Press, 1982

Bureaucracy

119. Bennis WG (ed): American Bureaucracy (2d ed). New Brunswick, NJ, Transaction Books, Rutgers-The State University, 1972

120. Blau P: The Dynamics of Bureaucracy, (rev ed), Chicago, University of Chicago Press, 1973 (paperback)

Social Stratification

121. Beeghely L: Social Stratification in America. New York, Random, 1978

122. Bendix R, Lipset SM (eds): Class, Status & Power: A Reader in Social Stratification. New York, Free Press, 1966

Social Class and Mental Illness (See also 592)

123. Freeman HL (ed): Mental Health and the Environment. New York, Churchill Livingstone, 1985

124. Hollingshead AG, Redlich FC: Social Class and Mental Illness: A Community Study. New York, John Wiley, 1958

125. Myers JK, Bean LL: A Decade Later: A Follow-Up of Social Class and Mental Illness. New York, John Wiley, 1968

Ethnic Relations (See also 147, 894)

126. Clazer N, Moynihan DP (eds): Ethnicity: Theory & Experience. Cambridge, MA, Harvard University Press, 1975

Discrimination (See also 894)

127. Becker G: The Economics of Discrimination, (rev 2d ed), Chicago, University of Chicago Press, 1971 (paperback)

128. Gilman SL: Difference and Pathology: Stereotypes of Sexuality, Race, and Madness. Ithaca, New York, Cornell University Press, 1985

Crime & Delinquency (See also 238, 437–441)

129. Lundman RJ: Prevention and Control of Juvenile Delinquency. New York, Oxford University Press, 1984

130. Rutter M, Giller H; Juvenile Delinquency: Trends and Perspectives. New York, Guilford, 1983

131. Savitz LD, Johnston N: Contemporary Criminology. New York, John Wiley, 1982

132. Vito GF, Wilson DG: The American Juvenile Justice System. Beverly Hills, CA, Sage Publications, 1985

Aggression, Homicide, and Suicide (See also 131)

133. Baron RA: Human Aggression. New York, Plenum, 1977

134. De Catanzaro D: Suicide and Self-Damaging Behavior: A Sociobiological Perspective. Orlando FL, Academic Press, 1981

135. Durkheim E: Suicide. New York, Free Press, 1966

136. Goldstein AP, Carr EG, Davidson WS, Wehr P: In Response to Aggression. New York, Pergamon Press, 1981

137. Henry AF, Short JF Jr (eds): Suicide and Homicide: Some Economic, Sociological and Psychological Aspects of Aggression, (reprint of 1954 ed). Salem, NH, Ayer, 1977

138. Mednick SA, Christianson KO: Biosocial Basis of Criminal Behavior. New York, Gardner Press, 1977

139. Toch H: Violent Men, Revised Edition. Cambridge, MA, Schenkman Publishing, 1980

140. Wolfgang M, Weiner NA (eds): Criminal Violence. Beverly Hills, CA, Sage Publications, 1982

Military

141. Carlton D, Schaerf C (eds): The Arms Race In the Nineteen Eighties. New York, St Martin's, 1982

142. Egendoff A, Kadushin C, Laufer R, Rothbart G, Sloan L: Legacies of Vietnam: Comparative Adjustment of Veterans and their Peers. Washington, DC, Center for Policy Research, Inc. U.S. Government Printing Office, 1981

143. Thomas L: The Medical Implications of Nuclear War: Institute of Medicine/National Academy of Sciences. Washington, D.C., National Academy Press, 1986

Adoption

144. Benet MK: The Politics of Adoption. New York, Free Press, 1976
145. Churchill SR, et al: No Child Is Unadoptable: A Reader on Adoption of Children with Special Needs. Beverly Hills, CA, Sage, 1979
146. Curto J: How to Become a Single Parent: A Guide for Single People Considering Adoption or Natural Parenthood Alone. Englewood Cliffs, NJ, Prentice-Hall, 1983
147. Day D: The Adoption of Black Children. Lexington, MA, Lexington Books, 1979
148. Joe B: Public Policies Toward Adoption. Washington, D.C., Urban Institute, 1979

SOCIOBIOLOGY

149. Barash DP: Sociobiology and Behavior. New York, Elsevier, 1982
150. Chagnon N, Irons W (eds): Evolutionary Biology and Human Social Behavior: An Anthropological Perspective. North Scituate, MA, Duxbury, 1979
151. Lifton RJ: The Broken Connection. New York, Simon and Schuster, 1979
152. Wilson EO: Sociobiology: The New Synthesis. Cambridge, MA, Harvard University Press, 1975

ECONOMICS

153. Becker GS: The Economic Approach to Human Behavior. Chicago, University of Chicago Press, 1978
154. Brenner MH: Mental Illness and the Economy. Cambridge, MA, Harvard University Press, 1973
155. Fineman S: White Collar Unemployment: Impact and Stress. New York, John Wiley, 1983
156. Haefner H (ed): Estimating Needs for Mental Health Care: A Contribution of Epidemiology. New York, Springer-Verlag, 1979
157. Mechanic D: Mental Health and Social Policy (2d ed). Englewood Cliffs, NJ, Prentice-Hall, 1980
158. Piven F, Cloward RA: Regulating the Poor: The Functions of Public Welfare. New York, Random House, 1972

POLITICAL SCIENCE

159. Glass JM: Delusion: Internal Dimensions of Political Life. Chicago, University of Chicago Press, 1985
160. Kraus S, Perloff RM (eds): Mass Media and Political Thought: An Information-Processing Approach. Beverly Hills, CA, Sage Publications, 1985
161. Lindgren HC: Leadership, Authority and Power-Sharing. Melbourne, FL, Krieger Publishing, 1982
162. Macmanus S, Bullock C, Freeman D: Governing a Changing America. New York, John Wiley, 1984
163. Winter HR, Bellows TJ: People and Politics: An Introduction to Political Science. New York, John Wiley, 1985

EDUCATION

164. Dewey J: Democracy and Education. New York, Free Press, 1966
165. Hosler VN, Fadely JL: Holistic Mental Health for Tomorrow's Children: For Teachers and Mental Health Workers. Springfield, IL, CC Thomas, 1981
166. Kremer B: Mental Health in the Schools (2d ed). Boston Way, Lanham, MD, University Press of America, 1981

ETHOLOGY

167. Corson SA, Corson EO: Ethology and Nonverbal Communication in Mental Health: An Interdisciplinary Biopsychosocial Exploration. New York, Pergamon, 1980
168. Darwin C: Expression of Emotions in Man and Animals. Chicago, University of Chicago Press, 1965
169. Davey GCL: Animal Models of Human Behavior: Conceptual, Evolutionary and Neurobiological Perspectives. New York, John Wiley, 1983

170. Hinde RA: Ethology. London, Collins, 1982
171. Lorenz KZ: The Foundations of Ethology. New York, Springer-Verlag, 1981

HUMAN BEHAVIOR AND ADAPTATION

172. Dollard J: Frustration and Aggression. New Haven, Yale University Press, 1939
173. Serban G (ed): Psychopathology of Human Adaptation. New York, Plenum, 1976
174. Symonds PM: Dynamics of Human Adjustment. Westport, CT, Greenwood, 1946
175. Vaillant GE: Adaptation to Life. Boston, Little, Brown, 1977

RELIGION

176. Byrnes JF: The Psychology of Religion. New York, Free Press, 1984
177. Robinson LH: Psychiatry and Religion: Overlapping Concerns. Washington, D.C., American Psychiatric Press, 1986

PHILOSOPHY

178. Hook S (ed): Psychoanalysis, Scientific Method and Philosophy; a Symposium. New York, New York University Press, 1986
179. Maslow AH: The Farther Reaches of Human Nature. New York, Viking Press, 1971

HUMAN LIFE CYCLE—NORMAL DEVELOPMENT AND PROBLEMS OF ADJUSTMENT

General

180. Erikson EH: Identity and the Life Cycle: Selected Papers. Psychological Issues, Monogr 1: Vol. 1, New York, International Universities Press, 1967
181. Greenspan SI, Pollock GH (eds): The Course of Life, 3 vols, Rockville, MD.
National Institute of Mental Health, 1980 (o.p.)
182. Lidz T: The Person: His and Her Development Throughout the Life Cycle (rev ed), New York, Basic Books, 1976
183. Miller JG: Living Systems. New York, McGraw-Hill, 1978
184. Munroe RH, et al: Handbook of Cross-Cultural Human Development. New York, Garland Publishing, 1980
185. Wolman BB (ed): Handbook of Developmental Psychology. Englewood Cliffs, NJ, Prentice-Hall, 1982

Men and Women (See also 110, 117, 495, 553)

186. Cancro R, Taintor Z (eds): Towards a New Psychology of Women and Men: A Special Issue of Journal of Psychiatric Education. New York, Human Sciences Press, 1984
187. Howell E, Bayes M: Women and Mental Health. New York, Basic Books, 1981
188. Maccoby EE (ed): The Development of Sex Differences. Stanford, CA, Stanford University Press, 1966
189. Masters WH, Johnson VE: Homosexuality in Perspective. Boston, Little, Brown, 1979
190. Solomon K: Men in Transition. New York, Plenum Press, 1982
191. Miller JB: Toward a New Psychology of Women. Boston, Beacon Press, 1986

Infancy and Childhood (See also 66, 231, 342, 343, 588, 689, 692, 695)

192. Brim OG, Kagan J (eds): Constancy and Change in Human Development. Cambridge, MA, Harvard University Press, 1980
193. Call JD, Galenson E, Tyson RL (eds): Frontiers of Infant Psychiatry, New York, Basic Books, 1983
194. Greenspan, SI: Psychopathology and Adaptation in Infancy and Early Childhood: Principles of Clinical Diagnosis and Preventive Intervention. Clinical Infant Reports No. 1. New York, International Universities Press, 1981
195. Josselyn IM: Psychosocial Development of Children, (2d ed). Milwaukee, WI, Family Service America, 1978

196. Noshpitz J, Cohen RL (eds): Basic Handbook of Child Psychiatry, Vol. 1. New York, Basic Books, 1979
197. Ollendick TH, Hersen M (eds): Handbook of Child Psychopathology. New York, Plenum Press, 1983
198. Osofsky JD: Handbook of Infant Development. New York, John Wiley, 1979
199. Powell GJ (ed): Psychosocial Development of Minority Group Children. New York, Brunner-Mazel, 1983
200. Tyson RL, Call JD, Galenson E: Frontiers of Infant Psychiatry. Vol. 2. New York, Basic Books, 1984

Adolescence (See also 129, 130, 590)

201. Csikszentmihalyi M, Reed L: Being Adolescent. New York, Basic Books, 1984
202. Esman AH (ed): The Psychology of Adolescence: Essential Readings. New York, International Universities Press, 1975
203. Group for the Advancement of Psychiatry: Power and Authority in Adolescence. The Origins and Resolutions of Intergenerational Conflict. GAP Report No. 101. New York, Group for the Advancement of Psychiatry, 1978

Adulthood (See also 360)

204. Blumstein P, Schwartz P: American Couples. New York, Morrow, 1983
205. Colarusso CA, Nemiroff RA: Adult Development: A New Dimension in Psychodynamic Theory and Practice. New York, Plenum Press, 1981
206. Levinson D: The Seasons of a Man's Life. New York, Knopf, 1978
207. Vaillant G: Adaptation of Life. Boston, Little Bryson & Co, 1977

Family and Alternate Life Styles

208. Aldous J: Family Careers: Developmental Change in Families. New York, John Wiley, 1978
209. Bernard J: The Future of Marriage. New Haven, CT, Yale University Press, 1982
210. McCubbin H, Dahi B: Marriage and Family: Individuals and Life Cycles. New York, John Wiley, 1985

Old Age (See also 633)

211. Butler RN, Lewis MI: Aging and Mental Health: Positive Psychosocial and Biomedical Approaches, (3rd ed). St. Louis, C. V. Mosby, 1982
212. Kimmel DC: Adulthood and Aging: An Interdisciplinary, Developmental View, (2d ed). New York, John Wiley, 1980

Dying and Death (See also 410)

213. Hansen J: Death and Grief in the Family. Rockville, MD, Aspen Systems, 1984
214. Kubler-Ross E: Death: The Final Stage of Growth. Englewood Cliffs, NJ, Prentice-Hall, 1974
215. Raphael B: The Anatomy of Bereavement. New York, Basic Books, 1983
216. Schowalter JE (ed): The Child and Death. New York, Columbia University Press, 1983
217. Wass H, Corr CA (eds): Childhood and Death. New York, Hemisphere Publishing, 1984

FIELDS OF PSYCHIATRY

Clinical Psychiatry (See also 13, 14, 18, 274, 277–285, 897, 898)

218. Arieti Silvano (ed): American Handbook of Psychiatry, 7 vols. New York, Basic Books, 1974–1986
219. Cavenar JO (ed): Psychiatry, 3 vols. New York, Lippincott, 1986
220. Gregory I, Smeltzer DJ: Psychiatry: Essentials of Clinical Practice. Boston, Little, 1983
221. Kaplan HI, Sadock BJ (eds): Comprehensive Textbook of Psychiatry. Baltimore, Williams and Wilkins, 1984
222. Kaplan HI, Sadock BJ (eds): Study Guide and Self Examination: Review for Modern Synopsis of CTP/IV. Baltimore, Williams & Wilkins, 1985
223. Keller PA, Ritt LG (eds): Innovations in Clinical Practice: A Source Book (4 vols.). Sarasota, FL, Professional Resource Exchange, 1985
224. Kolb L, Brodie HK (eds): Modern Clini-

cal Psychiatry. Philadelphia, W. B. Saunders, 1982

225. Masserman JH (ed): Current Psychiatric Therapies. Orlando FL: Grune & Stratton. (Annually since 1961)

226. Sacks M, Sledge WH, Rubinton P (eds): Core Readings in Psychiatry: An Annotated Guide to the Literature. New York, Praeger, 1984

227. Sullivan HS: Conceptions of Modern Psychiatry. New York, Norton, 1966 (paperback)

228. Trethowan WH, Sims AC: Psychiatry. Philadelphia, PA, W. B. Saunders, 1983

Infant & Child Psychiatry (See also 193, 194, 196, 408, 415–424, 596, 597, 629, 644, 652, 760, 808, 813, 817, 820)

229. Barker P, Battezati M, Donini I: The Residential Psychiatric Treatment of Children. New York, John Wiley, 1974

230. Call JD, Galenson E, Tyson RL (eds): Frontiers of Infant Psychiatry. New York, Basic Books, 1983

231. Greenspan SI: Psychopathology and Adaptation in Infancy and Early Childhood: Principles of Clinical Diagnosis and Preventive Intervention. (Clinical Infant Reports: Series of the National Center for Clinical Infant Programs, no.1.) New York, International Universities Press, 1981

232. Noshpitz JD (ed): Basic Handbook of Child Psychiatry, 5 vols. New York, Basic Books, 1979–1986

233. Ollendick T (ed): Handbook of Child Psychopathology. New York, Plenum Press, 1982

234. Rutter M (ed): Developmental Neuropsychiatry. New York, Guilford, 1985

235. Shaffer D, Ehrhardt A, Greenhill L (eds): The Clinical Guide to Child Psychiatry. New York, Free Press, 1984

236. Thomas A, Chess S, Birch HS: Temperament and Behavior Disorders in Children. New York, New York Universities Press, 1968

Adolescent Psychiatry (See also 259, 351)

237. Esman AH (ed): Psychiatric Treatment of Adolescents. Madison, CT, International Universities Press, 1983

238. Lewis DO (ed): Vulnerabilities to Delinquency. New York, Spectrum Publications, 1981

239. Masterson JF: The Psychiatric Dilemma of Adolescence. New York, Brunner/Mazel, 1984

240. Steinberg D (ed): The Adolescent Unit. Somerset, NJ, John Wiley, 1986

Adult Psychiatry

241. Gulledge DA: Adult Psychiatry Case Studies. New York, Med Exam, 1981

Geriatric Psychiatry

242. Busse E, Blazer DG (eds): Handbook of Geriatric Psychiatry. New York, Van Nostrand Reinhold, 1980

243. Raskin A, Jarvik LF (eds): Psychiatric Symptoms and Cognitive Loss in the Elderly: Evaluation and Assessment Techniques. Washington, D.C., Hemisphere Publishing, 1979

Hospital Psychiatry (See also 261–263)

244. Hackett TP, Cassem N: MGH Handbook of General Hospital Psychiatry. Littleton, MA, PSG Publishing, 1987

245. Harbin HT (ed): The Psychiatric Hospital and the Family. New York, SP Medical & Scientific Books, 1982

246. McCord WJ: Psychopathology and Milieu Therapy: A Longitudinal Study. Orlando FL, Academic Press, 1982

247. Sederer LI (ed): Inpatient Psychiatry: Diagnosis and Treatment. Baltimore. Williams and Wilkins, 1986

248. Yalom ID: Inpatient Group Psychotherapy: Its Place and Use in Acute Psychiatric Settings. Philadelphia, Lippincott, 1983

Psychopharmacology (See also 385, 810–820)

249. Gilman AG, Goodman LS, Gilman A (eds): The Pharmacological Basis of Therapeutics. New York, MacMillan, 1980

250. Grahame-Smith DG, Hippius H, Winokur G (eds): Clinical Psychopharmacology. Amsterdam, Excerpta Medica, 1982

251. Physicians Desk Reference (PDR). Ora-

dell, NJ, Medical Economics Co, Inc. 1987 (an annual)

252. Youdim MBH, Lovenberg W, Sharman DF, Lagnado JR (eds): Essays in Neurochemistry and Neuropharmacology. New York, John Wiley, 1978

PSYCHIATRIC EMERGENCIES
(See also 399, 607–610, 786)

253. Bassuk EL, Birk AW (eds): Emergency Psychiatry: Concepts, Methods and Practices. New York, Plenum Press, 1984

254. Glick RA, et al: Psychiatric Emergencies. Orlando FL, Grune & Stratton, 1976

255. Guggenheim FG, Weiner MF (eds): Manual of Psychiatric-Consultation and Emergency Care. New York, Jason Aronson, 1984

256. Lieb J: The Crisis Team: A Handbook for the Mental Health Professional. New York, Harper Medical, Lippincott, 1973

257. Slaby AE, et al: The Handbook of Psychiatric Emergencies (3rd ed). New York, Medical Examination, 1984

258. Walker JI et al: Psychiatric Emergencies: Intervention and Resolution. Philadelphia, Lippincott, 1983

259. Klerman GL (ed): Suicide and Depression Among Adolescents and Young Adults. Washington, D.C., American Psychiatric Press, 1986

260. Roy A: Suicide. Baltimore, Williams & Wilkins, 1986.

HOSPITALIZATION (See also 244–248)

261. Grob GN: Mental Institutions in America: Social Policy to 1857. New York, Free Press, 1973

262. Maxmen JS, Tucker GJ, LeBow M: Rational Hospital Psychiatry. New York, Brunner/Mazel, 1974

263. Peszke MA: Involuntary Treatment of the Mentally Ill. Springfield, Ill, CC Thomas, 1975

PARTIAL HOSPITALIZATION

264. Barofsky I, Budson RD (eds) The Chronic Psychiatric Patient in the Community.

New York, SP Medical and Scientific Books, 1983

265. DiBella GA, Weitz GW, Poynter-Berg D, Yurmark JL: Handbook of Partial Hospitalization. New York, Brunner/Mazel, 1982

266. Henisz JE: Psychotherapeutic Management in the Day Program: Practices in Day Hospital Psychiatry. Springfield, IL, CC Thomas, 1984

267. Zigler E, Gordon E: Day Care: Scientific and Social Policy Issues. Boston, Auburn House, 1982

268. Budson RD: Psychiatric Halfway House: A Handbook of Theory and Practice. Pittsburgh, University of Pittsburgh Press, 1978

269. Dibella GA, et al: Handbook of Partial Hospitalization. New York, Brunner/Mazel, 1982

270. Luber RF (ed): Partial Hospitalization: A Current Perspective. New York, Plenum Press, 1979

ADMINISTRATIVE PSYCHIATRY

271. Barton WE, Barton GM: Mental Health Administration. New York, Human Sciences Press, 1983

272. Talbott JA, Kaplan SB (eds): Psychiatric Administration: A Comprehensive Text for the Clinician-Executive. Orlando, FL, Grune & Stratton, 1983

BIOLOGICAL PSYCHIATRY (See also 305, 307, 378, 395, 515, 802)

273. Andreasen NC: The Broken Brain: The Biological Revolution in Psychiatry. New York, Harper & Row, 1984

274. Berger PA, Brodie HK (eds): American Handbook of Psychiatry, (2d ed), vol. 7. Biological Psychiatry. New York, Basic Books, 1986

275. Kalinowsky L, et al: Biological Treatment in Psychiatry. Orlando, FL, Grune & Stratton, 1982

276. Passonneau JV, Hawkins RA, Lust WD, Welsh FA (eds): Cerebral Metabolism and Neural Function. Baltimore, Williams & Wilkins, 1980

277. Van Praag HM: Handbook of Biological Psychiatry. New York, Marcel Dekker, 1981

CONSULTATION-LIAISON PSYCHIATRY

278. Guggenheim FG (ed): Psychological Aspects of Surgery, (Advances in Psychosomatic Medicine: Vol. 15)>. Basel, Switzerland, S. Karger, 1985
279. Hollingsworth CE (ed): Pediatric Consultation Liaison Psychiatry. New York, SP Medical and Scientific Books, 1982
280. Howells A (ed): Modern Perspectives in the Psychiatric Aspects of Surgery. New York, Brunner/Mazel, 1976
281. Institute of Medicine Series on Mental Health Services in General Health Care. Washington, DC, National Academy of Sciences, 1979
282. Pasnau RO (ed): Consultation-Liaison Psychiatry. Orlando, FL, Grune & Stratton, 1975
283. Reiffel J, et al: Psychosocial Aspects of Cardiovascular Disease: The Life-Threatened Patient, the Family & the Staff. New York, Columbia University Press, 1980
284. Slaby AE, Glicksman AS: Adapting to Life-Threatening Illness. New York, Praeger, 1985
285. Wise TN, Freyberger H (eds): Consultation Liaison Throughout the World. New York, Karger, 1983

ETHNOPSYCHIATRY

286. Tseng W, McDermott JF: Culture, Mind and Therapy: An Introduction to Cultural Psychiatry. New York, Brunner/Mazel, 1981

ETHOLOGICAL PSYCHIATRY

287. McGuire MT, Fairbanks LA (eds): Ethological Psychiatry: Psychopathology in the Context of Evolutionary Biology. Orlando, FL, Grune & Stratton, 1977

FORENSIC PSYCHIATRY (See also 344, 345)

288. American Psychiatric Association: Issues in Forensic Psychiatry. Washington, D.C., American Psychiatric Press, 1984

289. Blinder M: Psychiatry in the Everyday Practice of Law. Rochester NY, Lawyers Cooperative Publishing, 1982
290. Gutheil T, Applebaum P: Clinical Handbook of Psychiatry & the Law. New York, McGraw-Hill, 1982
291. Simon RL: Clinical Psychiatry and the Law. Washington, DC, American Psychiatric Press, 1987
292. Wright F, et al (ed): Forensic Psychology & Psychiatry. (Annals of the New York Academy of Sciences: Vol. 347. New York Acad. Science, 1980
293. Slovenko R: Psychiatry and Law. Boston, Little, 1973

GENERAL SYSTEMS THEORY AND PSYCHIATRY (See also 183)

294. Gray W, Duhl FJ, Rizzo ND (eds): General Systems Theory and Psychiatry. Seaside, CA, Intersystems, 1981

ETHICS AND PSYCHIATRY

295. Bloch S, Chodoff P (eds): Psychiatric Ethics. New York, Oxford University Press, 1985
296. Hartmann H: Psychoanalysis and Moral Values. New York, International Universities Press, 1960
297. Levine M: Psychiatry and Ethics. New York, Braziller, 1972
298. Rosenbaum M: Ethics and Values in Psychotherapy: A Guidebook. New York, Free Press, 1981

PSYCHOSOMATIC MEDICINE (See also 758)

299. Adler R (ed): Psychoneuroimmunology. Orlando FL, Academic Press, 1981
300. Alexander F: Psychosomatic Medicine. New York, Norton, 1965
301. Dunbar F: Emotions and Bodily Changes. New York, Columbia University Press, 1954
302. Grinker RR: Psychosomatic Concepts (rev ed). New York, Jason Aronson, 1973
303. Hill O (ed): Modern Trends in Psychosomatic Medicine. London, Butterworth, 1970

304. Lipowski ZJ, Lipsitt DR, Whybrow PC: Psychosomatic Medicine: Current Trends and Clinical Applications. New York, Oxford University Press, 1977
305. Weiner H: Psychobiology and Human Disease. New York, Elsevier, 1977
306. Wittkower ED, Warnes H (eds): Psychosomatic medicine: its clinical applications. New York, Harper & Row, 1977
307. Young SH, et al: Psychobiological Aspects of Allergic Disorders. New York, Praeger, 1986

GENERAL MEDICINE AND PSYCHIATRY (See also 517, 549, 550, 781, 906, 907)

308. Dubovsky SL, Weissberg M: Clinical Psychiatry in Primary Care, (3d ed). Baltimore, Williams & Wilkins, 1986
309. Shepherd M, et al: Psychiatric Illness in General Practice, (2d ed). New York, Oxford University Press, 1981

MEDICAL SCIENCES OTHER THAN PSYCHIATRY

Behavioral Medicine (See also 516)

310. Pomerleau OF, Brady JP (eds): Behavioral Medicine. Theory and Practice. Baltimore, Williams & Wilkins, 1979
311. West LJ, Stein M (eds): Critical Issues in Behavioral Medicine. Philadelphia, Lippincott, 1982

Endocrinology (See also 511, 513)

312. Beaumont PVJ, Burrows GD (eds): Handbook of Psychiatry. Amsterdam, Elsevier Biomedical Press, 1982

Genetics (See also 42, 847)

313. Kallmann FJ: Heredity in Health and Mental Disorder. New York, WW Norton, 1953
314. Lewin B: Genes. New York, John Wiley, 1983

315. Schmitt FO, Bird SJ, Bloom FE (eds): Molecular Genetic Neuroscience. New York, Raven Press, 1982
316. Vogel F, Motulsky AG: Human Genetics: Problems and Approaches. New York, Springer-Verlag, 1986

Neuroanatomy

317. Chusid JG: Correlative Neuroanatomy and Functional Neurology (19th ed). Los Altos, CA, Appleton & Lange, 1985
318. Willis WD, Grossman RG: Medical Neurobiology: Neuroanatomical and Neurophysiological Principles Basic to Clinical Neuroscience. St. Louis, CV Mosby, 1981

Neurology (See also 446–452)

319. Adams RD: Principles of Neurology, (ed 3). New York, McGraw-Hill, 1985
320. Baker AB, Baker LH (eds): Clinical Neurology, 3 vols. Philadelphia, Harper & Row, 1984 (Looseleaf: rev. annually)
321. Benson DF, Blumer D (eds): Psychiatric Aspects of Neurologic Disease. Orlando, FL, Grune & Stratton, Vol 1, 1975, Vol 2, 1982
322. Katzman R, Terry RD: The Neurology of Aging: Philadelphia. FA Davis, 1983
323. Lechtenberg R: Psychiatrist's Guide to Diseases of the Nervous System. New York, John Wiley, 1982
324. Lee SH, Raokcug: Cranial Computed Tomography. New York, McGraw-Hill, 1983
325. Mayo Clinic: Clinical Examinations in Neurology. Philadelphia, W. B. Saunders, 1981
326. Weiner WJ: Psychiatric Aspects of Neurologic Disease. Philadelphia, Lippincott, 1986
327. Wells CE, Duncan GW: Neurology for Psychiatrists. Philadelphia, F. A. Davis, 1980
328. Wiederhelt WE (ed): Therapy for Neurologic Disorders. New York, John Wiley, 1982

Neuropathology and Pathophysiology

329. Hirano A: A Guide to Neuropathology. New York, Igaku-Shoin, 1981

Neurophysiology (See also 509)

330. Glass DC (ed): Neurophysiology and Emotion. New York, Rockefeller, 1967
331. Krieger DT, Hughes JC (eds): Neuroendocrinology. Sunderland, MA, Sinauer Associates, 1980
332. Klawans HL, Weiner WJ: Textbook of Clinical Neuropharmacology. New York, Raven Press, 1981
333. Somjen GG: Neurophysiology: The Essentials. Baltimore, MD, Williams & Wilkins, 1983

Neurosciences

334. Kandel ER, Schwartz JH (eds): Principles of Neural Science. New York, Elsevier, 1981
335. National Institute of Mental Health. The Neuroscience of Mental Health. Washington, D.C., American Psychiatric Press, 1985
336. Wood JH, Brooks BR (eds): Frontiers of Clinical Neuroscience. Baltimore, Williams & Wilkins, 1984

Nutrition

337. Wurtman RJ, Wurtman JJ (eds): Nutrition and the Brain. New York, Raven Press, 1983

Pediatrics (See also 442, 596)

338. Prugh DG: The Psychological Aspects of Pediatrics. Philadelphia, Lea & Fabiger, 1983

FIELD OF CLINICAL PSYCHOLOGY

General (See also 8, 21, 899–901)

339. Barlow DH (ed): Clinical Handbook of Psychological Disorders: A Step-by-Step Treatment Manual. New York, Guilford, 1985
340. Walker CE: Handbook of Clinical Psychology: Theory, Research and Practice, 2 vols. Chicago, Dorsey, 1983

341. Weiner IB: Clinical Methods in Psychology (2d ed). New York, John Wiley, 1983

Child Psychology (See also 20)

342. Mussen P (eds): Handbook of Child Psychology (4th ed), 4 vols. New York, John Wiley, 1983
343. Walker CE, Roberts MC (eds): Handbook of Clinical Child Psychology. New York, John Wiley, 1983

Forensic Psychology (See also 288–293)

344. Blau TH: The Psychologist as Expert Witness. New York, John Wiley, 1984
345. Curran WJ, et al: Forensic Psychiatry and Psychology. Philadelphia, Davis, 1986

FIELD OF CLINICAL SOCIAL WORK

Training and Supervision

346. Mishne J: Psychotherapy and Training in Clinical Social Work. New York, John Wiley, 1978
347. Munson, CE (ed): Social Work Supervision. New York, Free Press, 1979
348. Wiedeman GH, Hatison S (eds): Personality Development and Deviation: A Textbook for Social Work. New York, International Universities Press, 1975

Clinical Work (See also 12, 902, 903)

349. Garrett A: Interviewing: Its principles and methods, (3rd ed). New York, Family Service Association of America, 1982
350. Hidalgo H, et al: Lesbian and Gay Issues: A Resource Manual for Social Workers. Silver Spring, MD, National Association of Social Workers, 1985, Random House, 1981
351. Mishne JM: Clinical Work with Adolescents. New York, The Free Press, 1986
352. Shulman L: The Skills of Helping: Individuals and Groups (2nd ed). Itasca, Il. Peacock Publishers, 1984
353. Turner FJ (ed): Differential Diagnosis and

Treatment in Social Work (3rd ed). New York, Free Press, 1983

FIELD OF PSYCHIATRIC NURSING (See also 904, 905)

354. Lego S: The American Handbook of Psychiatric Nursing. Philadelphia, Lippincott, 1984
355. Topalis M, Aguilera D: Psychiatric Nursing. St. Louis, Mosby, 1978

PSYCHOPATHOLOGY (See also 246, 372, 377, 461, 513, 766, 888)

356. Davis DR: Introduction to Psychopathology (4th ed). New York, Oxford University Press, 1984
357. Millon T, Klerman G (eds): Contemporary Directions in Psychopathology. New York, Guilford, 1986
358. Nemiah J: Foundations of Psychopathology. New York, Jason Aronson, 1973
359. Sahakian WS: Psychopathology Today: The Current Status of Abnormal Psychology, (3rd ed). Itasca, IL, Peacock Publisher, 1986
360. Zigler E, Glick M: A Developmental Approach to Adult Psychopathology. Somerset, New Jersey, John Wiley, 1986

DIAGNOSIS AND TESTING

361. Anastasi A: Psychological Testing. New York, Macmillan, 1982
362. Bellak L, Goldsmith L: The Broad Scope of Ego Function Assessment. New York, John Wiley, 1984
363. Deutsch F, Murphy WF: The Clinical Interview, 2 vols. Vol 1: Diagnosis; Vol 2: Therapy. New York, International Universities Press, 1967
364. Diagnostic and Statistical Manual of Mental Disorders DSM-III-R. Washington, D.C. American Psychiatric Association, 1987
365. Frances A, Clarkin J, Perry S: Differential Therapeutics in Psychiatry; the Art and Science of Treatment Selection. New York, Brunner/Mazel, 1984
366. Gill MM, Newman R, Redlich F: The Initial Interview in Psychiatric Practice.

New York, International Universities Press, 1954
367. Goodwin DW, Guze SB: Psychiatric Diagnosis (3rd ed). New York, Oxford University Press, 1984
368. Hersen M, Turner SM (eds): Diagnostic Interviewing. New York, Plenum Press, 1985
369. Kahn RL, Cannell CF: The Dynamics of Interviewing. Melbourne, FL, Krieger, 1983, (reprint of 1957 ed)
370. Leff JP, Isaacs AD (eds): Psychiatric Examination in Clinical Practice. St. Louis, C. V. Mosby, 1981
371. MacKinnon RA, Yudofsky ST: Manual for Psychiatric Evaluation. Philadelphia, Lippincott, 1986
372. Millon T, Klerman GL (eds): Contemporary Directions in Psychopathology: Toward the DSM-IV. New York, Guilford, 1986
373. Perry S, et al: A DSM-III Casebook of Differential Therapeutics: A Clinical Guide to Treatment Selection. New York, Brunner/Mazel, 1985
374. Roberts JK: Differential Diagnosis in Neuropsychiatry. New York, John Wiley, 1984
375. Spitzer RL, et al: DSM-III Case Book: A Learning Companion to the Diagnostic and Statistical Manual of Mental Disorders. Washington, D.C., American Psychiatric Association, 1981
376. Sullivan HS: The Psychiatric Interview. New York, Norton, 1954 (paperback)
377. Turner SM, Hersen M: Adult Psychopathology and Diagnosis. New York, John Wiley, 1984
378. Usdin E, Hanir J (eds): Biological Markers in Psychiatry and Neurology. Oxford, Pergamon Press, 1982

MENTAL AND EMOTIONAL DISORDERS

Affective Disorders (See also 739)

379. Arieti S, Bemporad J: Severe and Mild Depression: The Psycho Therapeutic Approach. New York, Basic Books, 1978
380. Baldessarini RJ: Biomedical Aspects of Depression and Its Treatment. Washington, D.C., American Psychiatric Press, 1983

381. Ban TA, Gonzalez R, Jablensky AS, Sartorius NA, Vartanian FE (eds): Prevention and Treatment of Depression. Baltimore, University Park Press, 1981

382. Beck AT, Rush AJ, Shaw BF, Emery G: Cognitive Therapy of Depression. New York, Guilford, 1979

383. Belmaker RH, Van Praag HM (eds): Mania: An Evolving Concept. New York, Spectrum, 1980

384. Davis JM, Maas JW (eds): The Affective Disorders. Washington, D.C., American Psychiatric Press, 1983

385. Gardos G, Casey DE (ed): Tardive Dyskinesia and Affective Disorders. Washington, D.C., American Psychiatric Press, 1984

386. Gaylin W (ed): Psychodynamic Understanding of Depression. New York, Jason Aronson, 1983

387. Greenacre P (ed): Affective Disorders. New York, International Universities Press, 1961

388. Klerman G, et al: Interpersonal Psychotherapy of Depression. Philadelphia, Lippincott, 1984

389. Paykel ES: Handbook of Affective Disorders. New York, Guilford, 1982

390. Post R, Ballenger J (eds): Neurobiology of Mood Disorders. Baltimore, Williams & Wilkins, 1984

391. Zales MR (ed): Affective and Schizophrenic Disorders. New York, Brunner/Mazel, 1983

Alcoholism

392. Brown S: Treating the Alcoholic: A Developmental Model of Recovery. Somerset, NJ, John Wiley, 1985

393. Gitlow SE, Peyser HS (eds): Alcoholism: A Practical Treatment Guide. Orlando FL, Grune & Stratton, 1980

394. Goodwin DW: Alcoholism: The Facts. New York, Oxford University Press, 1981

395. Kissin B, Begleiter H (eds): The Biology of Alcoholism, 7 vols. New York, Plenum Press, 1983

396. Zimberg S (ed): Practical Approaches to Alcoholism Psychotherapy (2d ed). New York, Plenum Press, 1985

Anxiety Disorders

397. Beck AT, Emergy G: Anxiety Disorders and Phobias: A Cognitive Perspective. New York, Basic Books, 1985

398. Beech HR: Obsessional States. London, Methuen, 1974

399. Everly GS Jr, Rosenfeld R: The Nature and Treatment of the Stress Response. New York, Plenum Press, 1981

400. Figley CR (ed): Trauma and Its Wake: The Study and Treatment of Post-Traumatic Stress Disorder. New York, Brunner/Mazel, 1985

401. Insel TR (ed): New Findings in Obsessive-Compulsive Disorder. Washington, D.C., American Psychiatric Press, 1984

402. Jenike MA: Obsessive-Compulsive Disorders: Theory and Management. Littleton, MA, PSG Publishing, 1986

403. Keiser L: The Traumatic Neurosis. Philadelphia, Lippincott, 1968

404. Mavissakalian M, Turner SM, Michelson L (eds): Obsessive-Compulsive Disorder: Psychological and Pharmacological Treatment. New York, Plenum Press, 1985

405. Neuman R (ed): Anxiety Disorders of Childhood. New York, Guilford, 1985

406. Pasnau RO (ed): Diagnosis and Treatment of Anxiety. Washington, D.C., American Psychiatric Press, 1984

407. Tuma AH, Maser J (eds): Anxiety and the Anxiety Disorders. Hillsdale, NJ, L. Erlbaum, 1985

Attention Deficit Disorders

408. Wender PH: Minimal Brain Dysfunction in Children. New York, Wiley-Interscience, 1971

Bereavement (See also 212, 822)

409. Bowlby J: Attachment and Loss III: Sadness and Depression. New York, Basic Books, 1980

410. Gonda TA, Ruark JE: Dying Dignified: The Health Professionals Guide to Care. Menlo Park, CA, Addison-Wesley, 1984

411. Kutscher A, Carr A, Kutscher L (eds): Principles of Thanatology. New York, Columbia University Press, 1986

412. Parkes CM: Bereavement. New York, International Universities Press, 1972

413. Schoenberg B, Carr AC, Peretz D, Kutscher AH (eds): Loss and Grief: Psychological Management in Medical Practice. New York, Columbia University Press, 1970

414. Schoenberg B (ed): Bereavement Counseling: A Multidisciplinary Handbook. Westport, CT, Greenwood Press, 1980

Developmental Disabilities
(See also 404)

415. Aram DM, Nation JE: Child Language Disorders. St. Louis, C. V. Mosby, 1982
416. Ceci SJ (ed): Handbook of Cognitive, Social & Neuropsychological Aspects of Learning Disabilities, 2 vols. Hillside, NJ, L. Erlbaum, 1986
417. Doehring D, Trites R, Patel P, Fiedorowicz C: Reading Disabilities. Orlando FL, Academic Press, 1981
418. Eisenson J, Ogilvie M: Communicative Disorders in Children. New York, MacMillan, 1983
419. Fundudis T, Kelvin I, Garside RG: Speech Retarded and Deaf Children: Their Psychological Development. Orlando FL, Academic Press, 1979
420. Lewis M, Taft LT (eds): Developmental Disabilities: Theory, Assessment and Intervention. New York, SP Medical & Scientific Books, 1986
421. Mauser AJ: Assessing the Learning Disabled: Selected Instruments, the Diagnostician's Handbook. Novato, CA, Academic Therapy Publications, 1981
422. Myklebust HR (ed): Progress in Learning Disabilities. Orlando, FL, Grune & Stratton, 1983
423. Pavadis GT, Fisher DF: Dyslexia. New York, John Wiley, 1986
424. Wender PH: Minimal Brain Dysfunction in Children. New York, Wiley-Interscience, 1971

Dissociative Disorder

425. Bliss EL: Multiple Personality, Allied Disorders, and Hypnosis. New York, Oxford University Press, 1986
426. Hilgard ER: Divided Consciousness. New York, John Wiley, 1977
427. Janet P: L'Automatismo Psychologique. Paris, Félix Alcan, 1889
428. Kihlstrom J (ed): Functional Disorders of Memory. Hillsdale, NJ, Lawrence Erlbaum Associates, 1979
429. Prince M: The Dissociation of a Personality. New York, Longmans, Green, 1906

Eating Disorders

430. Agras WS: Eating Disorders. Elmsford, NY, Pergamon Press, 1987
431. Bruch H: Eating Disorders: Obesity and Anorexia Nervosa and the Person Within. New York, Basic Books, 1973
432. Darby PL, Garfinkel PE, Garner DM, Coscina DV: Anorexia Nervosa: Recent Developments. New York, Allen R. Liss, 1983
433. Garner DM, Garfinkel PE (eds): Handbook of Psychotherapy for Anorexia Nervosa and Bulimia. New York, Guilford, 1985
434. Neuman PA, Halvorson PA: Anorexia Nervosa and Bulimia: A Handbook for Counselors and Therapists. New York, Van Nostrand Reinhold, 1983
435. Stunkard AJ (ed): Obesity. Philadelphia, W. B. Saunders, 1980
436. Stunkard AJ, Stellar E: Eating and Its Disorders. New York, Raven Press, 1983

Impulse Control Disorders

437. Alvarez A: The Biggest Game in Town. Boston, Houghton Mifflin, 1983
438. Lewis D: Vulnerability to Delinquency. New York, Spectrum Publications, 1981
439. Lewis NDC, Yarnell H: Pathological Firesetting. New York, Nervous and Mental Disease Publishing Co, 1951
440. Wishne HA: Impulsive Personality. New York, Plenum Press, 1977
441. Wolfgang M, Weiner NA (eds): Criminal Violence. Beverly Hills, CA, Sage Publications, 1982

Mental Retardation

442. Levine MD, WB Carey, Crocker AC, Gross RT (eds): Developmental Behavioral Pediatrics. Philadelphia, W. B. Saunders, 1983
443. Matson JL, Mills D: Assessing the Mentally Retarded. Orlando, FL, Academic Press, 1983
444. Menolascino FJ, Stark JA (eds): Handbook of Mental Illness in the Mentally Retarded. New York, Plenum Press, 1984
445. Szymanski LS, Tanguay PE (eds): Emotional Disorders of Mentally Retarded Persons. Baltimore, University Park Press, 1980

Organic Mental Disorders
(See also 633)

446. Benson DF, Blumer D: Psychiatric Aspects of Neurologic Disease. Orlando FL, Grune & Stratton, Vol 1, 1975; Vol 2, 1982

447. Freemon FR: Organic Mental Disease. New York, SP Medical & Scientific Books, 1981
448. Katzman R, Terry R: The Neurology of Aging. Philadelphia, F. A. Davis, 1983
449. Lishman WA: Organic psychiatry: The Psychological Consequences of Cerebral Disorder. Oxford, England, Blackwell, Philadelphia, Lippincott, 1978
450. Mortimor JA, Schuman LM: The Epidemiology of Dementia. New York, Oxford University Press, 1981
451. Strub RL, Black FW: Organic Brain Syndromes. Philadelphia, F. A. Davis, 1981
452. Walsh KW, Mills D: Understanding Brain Damage: A Primer of Neuropsychological Evaluation. Orlando, FL, Academic Press, 1985

Pain Syndrome (See also 505, 506, 514)

453. Brena SF, Chapman SL (eds): Management of Patients with Chronic Pain. New York, SP Medical and Scientific Books, 1983
454. Hendler NH, Long DM, Wise TN (eds): The Diagnosis and Treatment of Chronic Pain. Boston, John Wright/PSG, 1982
455. Smith WL, Merskey H, Gross SC (eds): Pain, Meaning and Management. New York, SP Medical and Scientific Books, 1980
456. Stimmel B: Pain, Analgesia, and Addiction. The Pharmacological Treatment of Pain. New York, Raven Press, 1983
457. Wall PD, Melzack R, Mills D (eds): Textbook of Pain. Orlando, FL, Academic Press, 1984

Paranoid Disorders

458. Meissner W: Paranoid Process. New York, Jason Aronson, 1978
459. Retterstol N: Prognosis in Paranoid Psychosis. Springfield, IL, 1970
460. Swanson DP, Bohnert PJ, Smith JH: The Paranoid. Boston, Little, Brown & Co. 1970

Personality Disorders (See also 25)

461. Cameron N, Rychlak JF: Personality Development and Psychopathology: A Dynamic Approach (2d ed). Boston, Houghton Mifflin, 1985
462. Frosch JP (ed): Current Perspectives on Personality Disorders. Washington, D.C., American Psychiatric Press, 1983
463. Grinker RR, Werble B: The Borderline Patient. New York, Jason Aronson, 1977
464. Gunderson JG: Borderline Personality Disorder. Washington, D.C., American Psychiatric Press, 1984
465. Hartocollis P (ed): Borderline Personality Disorders: The Concept, the Syndrome, the Patient. New York, International Universities Press, 1977
466. Kernberg OF: Severe Personality Disorders: Psychotherapeutic Strategies. New Haven, Yale University Press, 1984
467. Kernberg OF: Borderline Conditions and Pathological Narcissism. New York, Jason Aronson, 1975
468. Lion JR: Personality Disorders: Diagnosis and Management (2d ed). Baltimore, Williams & Wilkins, 1981
469. Meissner WW: The Borderline Spectrum: Differential Diagnosis and Developmental Issues. New York, Jason Aronson, 1984
470. Millon T: Disorders of Personality DSM-III: Axis II. New York, John Wiley, 1981
471. Salzman L: The Obsessive Personality. New York, Science House, 1968
472. Stone MH: The Borderline Syndromes: Constitution, Personality, and Adaptation. New York, McGraw-Hill, 1980
473. Wishne HA: Impulsive Personality. New York, Plenum Press, 1977
474. Wolberg AR: Psychoanalytic Psychotherapy of the Borderline Patient. New York, Thieme-Stratton, 1982

Schizophrenic Disorders (See also 391, 763)

475. Arieti S: Interpretation of Schizophrenia. New York, Basic Books, 1974
476. Bellack AS (ed): Schizophrenia: Treatment, Management, and Rehabilitation. Orlando FL, Grune & Stratton, 1984
477. Bellak L (ed): Disorders of the schizophrenic syndrome. New York, Basic Books, 1979
478. Bleuler E: Dementia Praecox or the Group of Schizophrenias. New York, International University Press, 1950
479. Curran JP, Monti PM (eds): Social Skills Training: A Practical Handbook for Assessment and Treatment. New York, Guilford, 1982

480. Goldstein MZ: Family Involvement in the Treatment of Schizophrenia, Washington, D.C., American Psychiatric Press, 1986

481. Liberman RP, Falloon IRH, Wallace CJ: The Chronically Mentally Ill: Research and Services. New York: SP Publications, 1983

482. McFarlane WR (ed): Family Therapy in Schizophrenia. New York, Guilford, 1983

483. Pao PN: Schizophrenic Disorders: Theory and Treatment from a Psychodynamic Point of view. New York, International Universities Press, 1979

484. Shapiro SA: Contemporary Theories of Schizophrenia: Review and Synthesis. New York, McGraw-Hill, 1981

485. Strauss JS, Bowers M, Downey TW, Fleck S, et al (eds): The Psychotherapy of Schizophrenia. New York, Plenum Press, 1980

486. Warner R: Recovery from Schizophrenia. New York, Methuen, 1985

487. Zales MR (ed): Affective and Schizophrenic Disorders. New York, Brunner/Mazel, 1983

Sexual Life Styles and Disorders (See also 188, 189, 350, 589, 595, 728–730)

488. Bayer R: Homosexuality and American Psychiatry: The Politics of Diagnosis. New York, Basic Books, 1981

489. Bell A, Weinberg M, Hammersmith S: Sexual Preference. Bloomington, Indiana University Press, 1981

490. Brownmiller S: Against Our Will: Men, Women, and Rape. New York, Simon & Schuster, 1975

491. Green R: From "Sissy Boys to Gay" Men? A Fifteen Year Puzzle. New Haven, Yale University Press, 1983

492. Kaplan HS: The Evaluation of Sexual Disorders: Psychological and Medical Aspects. New York, Brunner/Mazel, 1983

493. Lothstein LM: Female-to-Male Transsexualism. London, Routledge and Kegan Paul, 1983

494. Masters WH, Johnson VE: Human Sexual Inadequacy. Boston, Little, Brown, 1970

495. Money J, Ehrhardt AA: Man and Woman, Boy and Girl. Baltimore, Johns Hopkins University Press, 1972

496. Money J, Musaph H (eds): Handbook of Sexology. Amsterdam, Excerpta Medica, 1977

497. Murstein BI: Love, Sex, and Marriage Throughout the Ages. New York, Springer-Verlag, 1974

498. Stoller RJ: Sex and Gender. New York, Science House, 1968

499. Tietz C: Induced Abortion: A World View. New York, Population Council, 1981

Sleep/Wake Disorders

500. Guillaminault C: Sleeping and Waking Disorders: Indications and Techniques. Reading, MA, Addison-Wesley, 1982

501. Kales A, Kales JD (eds): Evaluation and Treatment of Insomnia. New York, Oxford University Press, 1984

502. Kellerman H (ed): The Nightmare: Psychological and Biological Foundations. New York, Columbia University Press, 1986

503. Mendelson WB, Gillin JC, Wyatt RJ: Human Sleep and Its Disorders. New York, Plenum, 1977

504. Williams RL, Karacan I: Sleep Disorder: Diagnosis and Treatment. New York, John Wiley, 1978

Somatoform Disorders

505. Bellissimo A, Tunks E: Chronic Pain: The Psychotherapeutic Spectrum. New York, Praeger, 1984

506. Brena SF, Chapman SL (eds): Management of Patients with Chronic Pain. New York, SP Medical and Scientific Books, 1983

507. Ford CV: The Somatizing Disorders: Illness as a Way of Life. New York: Elsevier, 1983

508. Krohn A: Hysteria—The Elusive Neurosis. New York, International Universities Press, 1978

509. Levy S (ed): Biological Mediators of Stress and Disease: Neoplasia. New York, Elsevier/North Holland, 1982

510. Ladee GA: Hypochondrical Syndromes. Amsterdam, Elsevier, 1966

511. Martin JD, Reichlin S, Brown G: Clinical Neuroendocrinology. Philadelphia, F. A. Davis, 1977

512. Roy A: Hysteria. New York, John Wiley, 1982

513. Sachar EJ (ed): Hormones, Behavior, and Psychopathology. New York, Raven Press, 1976

514. Saper JR: Headache Disorders: Current Concepts and Treatment Strategies. Boston, John Wright/PSG, 1983
515. Weiner H, Hofer MA, Stunkard AJ (eds): Brain, Behavior, and Bodily Disease. New York, Raven Press, 1981
516. West LJ, Stein M (eds): Critical Issues in Behavioral Medicine. Philadelphia, Lippincott, 1982
517. Whitlock FA: Psychophysiological Aspects of Skin Disease. London, W. B. Saunders, 1976

Speech, Voice & Hearing

518. Bloodstein O: Speech Pathology: An Introduction. Boston, Houghton Mifflin, 1979
519. Peterson EW (ed): Deafness and Mental Health: Emerging Response. (Readings in Deafness Monograph: No. 12). Silver Spring, MD, American Deafness & Rehabilitation Association, 1985
520. Skinner PH, Shelton R: Speech, Language, and Hearing: Normal Processes and Disorders. New York, John Wiley, 1985
521. Speech Foundation of America: Self-therapy for the Stutterer: One Approach. Memphis, TN, Speech Foundation, 1978

Stress (See also 399, 400, 607, 608, 786, 893)

522. Figley CR, McCubbin HI (eds): Stress and the Family: Coping with Catastrophe, Vol 2. New York, Brunner/Mazel, 1983
523. Henry JP, Stephens PM: Stress, Health and the Social Environment: A Sociobiologic Approach. New York, Springer-Verlag, 1977
524. Levi L (ed): Society, Stress and Disease: Working Life. New York, Oxford University Press, 1979
525. McCubbin HI, Figley CR (eds): Stress and the Family: Coping with Normative Transitions (Vol 1). New York, Brunner/Mazel, 1983
526. Selye H: Stress in Health and Disease. Reading, MS, Butterworth, 1976
527. Selye H: Selye's Guide to Stress Research. New York, Van Nostrand Reinhold, 1980

Substance Abuse (See also 625)

528. Grinspoon L: Marijuana Reconsidered. Cambridge, MA, Harvard University Press, 1977
529. Grinspoon L, Bakalar JB: Cocaine: A Drug and Its Social Evolution. New York, Basic Books, 1977
530. Grinspoon L, Bakalar JB: Psychedelic Drugs Reconsidered. New York, Basic Books, 1977
531. Institute of Medicine: Marijuana and Health. Washington, D.C. National Academy Press, 1982
532. Kaufman E, Kaufman P (eds): Family Therapy of Drug and Alcohol Abuse. New York, Gardner Press, 1979
533. Levinson JH, Ruiz P (eds): Substance Abuse: Clinical Problems and Perspectives. Baltimore, Williams & Wilkins, 1981
534. Marlatt GA, Gordon JR (eds): Relapse Prevention Maintenance Strategies in the Treatment of Addictive Behaviors. New York, Guilford, 1986
535. Miller WR (ed): Addictive Behaviors. New York, Pergamon, 1980
536. Petersen LC, Stillman RC (eds): Phencyclidine (PCP) Abuse: An Appraisal. NIDA Research Mongr. 21, Washington, D.C. U.S. Government Printing Office, 1978
537. Pickens RW, Heston L: Psychiatric Factors in Drug Abuse. Orlando, FL, Grune & Stratton, 1979
538. Senay EC: Substance Abuse Disorders in Clinical Practice. Littleton MA, John Wright, 1982
539. Shaffer H, Burglass ME (eds): Classic Contributions in the Addictions. New York, Brunner/Mazel, 1981
540. Spitz HI, Rosecan JS: Cocaine Abuse. New York, Brunner/Mazel, 1987
541. Stimson GV, Oppenheimer E: Heroin Addiction: Treatment and Control in Britain. London, Tavistock, 1982
542. Szara SI, Ludford JP (eds): Benzodiazepines: A Review of Research Results, 1980. NIDA Research Mongr 33, Washington, D.C. U.S. Government Printing Office, 1980
543. United States Public Health Service. Smoking and Health—Report of the Advisory Committee to the Surgeon General of the Public Health Service. Washington,

D.C., U. S. Government Printing Office, 1964

544. Verebey K (ed): Opioids in Mental Illness. Theories, Clinical Observations, and Treatment Possibilities. New York, Academy of Science, 1982

545. Washton AM, Gold MS (eds): Cocaine: A Clinician's Handbook. New York, Guilford, 1987

546. Wesson DR, Smith DE: Barbiturates: Their Use, Misuse, and Abuse. New York, Human Sciences Press, 1977

Miscellaneous Disorders

547. Cholden LS: Psychiatrist Works with Blindness. New York, American Foundation for the Blind, 1958

548. Coping with AIDS: Psychological and Social Considerations in Helping People with HTLV-III Infection. Rockville MD, National Institute of Mental Health, 1986

549. Goldberg R, Tull RM: The Psychosocial Dimensions of Cancer: A Practical Guide for Health-Care Providers. New York, Free Press, 1983

550. Nichols S, Ostrow DG: Psychiatric Implications of Acquired Immune Deficiency Syndrome. Washington D.C., American Psychiatric Press, 1984

PSYCHOTHERAPEUTIC MODALITIES

General Diagnostic and Therapeutic Methods (See also 7, 10, 13, 225, 226, 363, 365, 373, 376, 761, 762, 873)

551. Abt EL, Stuart IR (eds): The Newer therapies: A Sourcebook. New York, Van Nostrand Reinhold, 1981

552. American Psychiatric Association. Commission on Psychiatric Therapies. The Psychiatric Therapies. In two parts: Part I The Somatic Therapies, Part II, The Psychosocial Therapies. Washington D.C., American Psychiatric Press, 1984

553. Brodsky AM, Hare-Mustin RT (eds): Women and Psychotherapy: An Assessment of Research and Practice. New York, Guilford, 1980

554. Carmichael HP: Prospects and Proposals: Lifetime Learning for Psychiatrists. Washington D.C., American Psychiatric Association, 1972

555. Corsini R (ed): Current Psychotherapies (3rd ed). Itasca IL, Peacock, 1984

556. Frances A, Clarkin J, Perry S: Differential Therapeutics in Psychiatry: The Art and Science of Treatment Selection. New York, Brunner/Mazel, 1984

557. Garfield SL, Bergin AE (eds): Handbook of Psychotherapy and Behavior Change (3rd ed). New York, John Wiley, 1986

558. Griest J, Jefferson J, Spitzer R (eds): Treatment of mental Disorders. New York, Oxford University Press, 1980

559. Hales RE, Yudofsky SC. The American Psychiatric Press Textbook of Neuropsychiatry. Washington D.C. American Psychiatric Press, 1987

560. Hales RE, Frances AJ: Psychiatry Update: American Psychiatric Association Annual Review. Washington D.C., American Psychiatric Press. (Annual; beginning with vol 4, 1985, CME Supplement available)

561. Havens LL: Making Contact: Uses of Language in Psychotherapy. Cambridge MA: Harvard University Press, 1986

562. Kaslow FW (ed): Psychotherapy with Psychotherapists. New York, The Haworth Press, 1984

563. Keller PA, Ritt LG (eds): Innovations in Clinical Practice: A Source Book, 4 vols. Sarasota FL, The Professional Resource Exchange, 1982

564. Lewis JM, Usdin G (eds): Treatment Planning in Psychiatry. Washington D.C., American Psychiatric Association, 1982

565. Lovinger RJ: Working with Religious Issues in Therapy. New York, Jason Aronson, 1984

566. Meeks JE: The Fragile Alliance: An Orientation to the Out-patient Psychotherapy of the Adolescent (2d ed). Huntington NY, Krieger, 1980

567. Millman HL, Huber JT, Diggins DR: Therapies for Adults. San Francisco, Jossey Bass, 1982

568. Nemiroff R, Colarusso C (eds): The Race Against Time: Psychotherapy and Psychoanalysis in the Second Half of Life. New York, Plenum Press, 1985

569. Reiker PP, Carmen EH (eds): The Gender Gap in Psychotherapy: Social Realities

and Psychological Processes. New York, Plenum Press, 1984

570. Weiner IB: Principles of Psychotherapy. New York, Wiley, 1975

571. Weiss L: Dream Analysis in Psychotherapy. New York, Pergamon Press, 1986

572. Wolberg LR: The Technique of Psychotherapy, 2 vols. Orlando FL, Grune and Stratton, 1988

Behavior Therapy (See also 339, 646, 765)

573. Annual Review of Behavior Therapy: Theory and Practice. New York, Guilford Press, (1973)

574. Bellack AS, et al: International Handbook of Behavior Modification and Therapy. New York, Plenum Press, 1982

575. Fensterheim H, Glazer HI (eds): Behavioral Psychotherapy: Basic Principles & Case Studies in an Integrative Clinical Model. New York, Brunner/Mazel, 1983

576. Hersen M, Bellack AS (eds): Handbook of Clinical Behavior Therapy with Adults. New York, Plenum Press, 1985

577. Hersen M, Last CG (eds): Behavior Therapy Casebook. New York, Springer, 1985

578. Hersen M, Van Hasselt VB (eds): Behavior Therapy with Children and Adolescents: A Clinical Approach. Somerset NJ, John Wiley, 1986

579. Kanfer FH, Phillips S: Learning Foundations of Behavior Therapy. New York, John Wiley, 1970

580. Lazarus AA (ed): Casebook of Multimodal Therapy. New York, Guilford, 1985

581. Turner SM (ed): Behavioral Theories and Treatment of Anxiety. New York, Plenum Press, 1984

582. Wolpe J: The Practice of Behavior Therapy (3rd ed). Elmsford, New York, Pergamon Press, 1982

Child and Adolescent Therapy (See also 229–240)

583. Adams PL: A Primer of Child Psychotherapy (2d ed). Boston, Little, Brown, 1982

584. Chess S, Hassibi M (eds): Principles and Practice of Child Psychiatry. New York, Plenum Press, 1978

585. Fontana VJ: The Maltreated Child: The Maltreatment Syndrome in Children (4th ed). Springfield IL, CC Thomas, 1978

586. Glenn J (ed): Child Analysis and Therapy. New York, Jason Aronson, 1978

587. Group For the Advancement of Psychiatry. The Progress of Child Therapy. New York, Group for the Advancement of Psychiatry, 1982

588. Harrison SI, McDermott JF Jr (eds): New Directions In Childhood Psychopathology, (2 Vols.). New York, International Universities Press, 1982

589. Kempers, Kempe CH: The Common Secret: Sexual Abuse of Children and Adolescents. New York, Freeman, 1984

590. Malmquist CP: Handbook of Adolescence: Psychopathology, Antisocial Development, Psychotherapy. New York, Jason Aronson, 1985

591. Noshpitz JD: Basic Handbook of Child Psychiatry. New York, Basic Books, 1979

592. Provence S, Naylor A: Working with Disadvantaged Families and Their Children. Scientific and Practice Issues. New Haven CT, Yale University Press, 1983

593. Schaefer CE, et al: Family Therapy Techniques for Problem Behaviors of Children and Teenagers. San Francisco, Jossey Bass, 1984

594. Schaefer CE, O'Connor KJ (eds): Handbook of Play Therapy. Somerset NJ. John Wiley, 1983

595. Sgroi SM: Handbook of Clinical Intervention in Child Sexual Abuse. Lexington MA, D. C. Heath, 1982

596. Werry JS: Pediatric Psychopharmacology: The Use of Behavior Modifying Drugs in Children. New York, Brunner/Mazel, 1978

597. Wiener JM: Psychopharmacology in Childhood and Adolescence. New York, Basic Books, 1977

Client-Centered Therapy

598. Rogers C: Client-Centered Therapy: Its Current Practice, Implications, and Theory. Boston, Houghton Mifflin, 1951

599. Levant RF, Shlien JM: Client-Centered Therapy and the Person-Centered Approach: New Directions in Theory, Research and Practice. Westport CT, Praeger, 1984

600. Wexler DA, Rice LN: Innovations in Cli-

ent-Centered Therapy. New York, John Wiley, 1974

Cognitive Therapy (See also 382)

601. Beck AT: Cognitive Therapy and Emotional Disorders. New York, International Universities Press, 1976
602. Beck AT, Emery G: Anxiety and Phobias: A Cognitive Approach. New York, Basic Books, 1984
603. Meichenbaum D: Cognitive-Behavior Modification: An Integrative Approach. New York, Plenum Press, 1977
604. Weiner ML: Cognitive–Experiential Therapy: An Integrative Ego Psychotherapy. New York, Brunner/Mazel, 1985
605. Williams J, Mark G: The Psychological Treatment of Depression: A guide to the Theory and Practice of Cognitive–Behavior Therapy. New York, Free Press, 1984

Confrontation Therapy

606. Adler G, Myerson PG (eds): Confrontation in Psychotherapy. New York, Jason Aronson, 1973

Crisis Intervention

607. Horowitz MJ: Stress Response Syndrome. New York, Jason Aronson, 1976
608. Horowitz MJ: Stress Response Syndromes and Brief Psychotherapy. Strecker Mongraph Series No. 14. Philadelphia Institute of the Pennsylvania Hospital, 1977
609. Lester D, Brockopp GW: Crisis Intervention and Counseling By Telephone. Springfield IL, Thomas, 1976
610. Parad HJ: Crisis Intervention. Selected Readings. New York, Family Service Association, 1965

Existential Psychotherapy

611. Bugental JF: Psychotherapy and Process: The Fundamentals of an Existential-Humanistic Approach. New York, Random, 1978
612. Misiak H, Sexton VS: Phenomenological, Existential and Humanistic Psychologies. Orlando FL, Grune & Stratton, 1954
613. Ofman W: Affirmation and Reality. Los Angeles, Western Psychological Services, 1976
614. Sonneman V: Existence and Therapy. Orlando FL, Grune & Stratton, 1954
615. Wann T (ed): Behaviorism and Phenomenology. Chicago, University of Chicago Press, 1964
616. Talom ID: Existential Psychotherapy. New York, Basic Books, 1980

Family & Marital Therapy (See also 480, 482, 532, 593, 759)

617. Ackerman NW: The Psychodynamics of Family Life: Diagnosis & Treatment of Family Relationships. New York, Basic Books, 1972 (paperback)
618. Bowen M: Family Therapy in Clinical Practice. New York, Jason Aronson, 1978
619. Guerin PJ, Fay LF, Burden S, Kautto JG: The Evaluation and Treatment of Marital Conflict. New York, Basic Books, 1986
620. Gurmin AS, Kniskern DP (eds): Handbook of Family Therapy. Orlando, FL, Grune & Stratton, 1981
621. Hoffman L: Foundations of Family Therapy: A Conceptual Framework for System Change. New York, Basic Books, 1981
622. Jacobson NS, Gurman A (eds): Clinical Handbook of Marital Therapy. New York, Guilford, 1986
623. Minuchin S, Fishman HC: Family Therapy Techniques. Cambridge, MA, Harvard University Press, 1981
624. Paolino T, McGrady B (eds): Marriage and Marital Therapy. New York, Brunner/Mazel, 1978
625. Richman J: Family Therapy for Suicidal People. New York, Springer, 1986
626. Sholevar GP (ed): The Handbook of Marriage and Marital Therapy. New York, SP Medical & Scientific Books, 1981
627. Satir VM: Helping Families Change. New Jersey, Aronson, 1976
628. Strean HS: Resolving Marital Conflicts: A Psychodynamic Perspective. Somerset, NJ, John Wiley, 1985
629. Zilbach JJ: Young Children in Family Therapy. New York, Brunner/Mazel, 1985

Geriatric Therapy (See also 242, 243, 451)

630. Atkinson RM (ed): Alcohol and Drug Abuse in Old Age. Washington, D.C. American Psychiatric Press, 1984
631. Brink TL: Geriatric Psychotherapy. New York, Human Sciences Press, 1979
632. Busse EW, Blazer DG (eds): Handbook of Geriatric Psychiatry. New York, Van Nostrand Reinhold, 1980
633. Cole JO, Barrett JE (eds): Psychopathology in the Aged. New York, Raven, 1980
634. Reisberg B (ed): Alzheimer's Disease: The Standard Reference. New York Free Press, 1985

Gestalt Therapy

635. Perls F: Gestalt Therapy Verbatim. Moab, UT, Real People Press, 1969
636. Smith WWL (ed): Growing Edge of Gestalt Therapy. New York Brunner/Mazel, 1976

Group Therapy (See also 248, 795)

637. Bion WR: Experiences in Groups. New York, Basic Books, 1961
638. Caligor J, Fieldsteel ND, Brok AJ: Individual and Group Therapy: Combining Psychoanalytic Treatments. New York, Basic Books, 1984
639. Durkin H: The Group in Depth. New York, International Universities Press, 1966
640. Grotjahn M, Freedman CTH (eds): Handbook of Group Therapy. New York, Van Nostrand Reinhold, 1983
641. Kadis A: Practicum of Group Psychotherapy (2d ed). New York, Harper-Row, 1974
642. Kaplan HI, Sadock BJ (eds): Comprehensive Group Psychotherapy (2d ed). Baltimore, MD, Williams & Wilkins, 1983
643. Kissen M (ed): From Group Dynamics to Group Psychoanalysis: Therapeutic Applications of Group Dynamic Understanding. New York, Halsted, 1976
644. Rose SD: Treating Children in Groups. San Francisco, Jossey Bass, 1972
645. Rosenbaum M, Berger MM (eds): Group Psychotherapy and Group Function (2d ed). New York, Basic Books, 1975
646. Sank LI, Shaffer CS: A Therapist's Manual for Cognitive Behavior Therapy in Groups. New York, Plenum Press, 1984
647. Seligman M: Group Counseling and Group Psychotherapy with Special Populations. Austin TX, Pro Ed, 1982
648. Yalom ID: The Theory and Practice of Group Psychotherapy (3rd ed). New York, Basic Books, 1985

Hypnosis

649. Crasilneck HB, Hall JA: Clinical Hypnosis—Principles and Applications. Orlando, FL, Grune & Stratton, 1985
650. Edmonsten WE: The Induction of Hypnosis. New York, John Wiley, 1986
651. Erickson MH: The Collected Papers of Milton H. Erickson, E Rossi (ed), 4 vols. New York, Irvington, 1980
652. Gardner GG, Olness D: Hypnosis and Hypnotherapy with Children. Orlando, FL, Grune & Stratton, 1981
653. Spiegel H, Spiegel D: Trance and Treatment: Clinical Uses of Hypnosis. New York, Basic Books, 1978
654. Wester WC II, et al: Clinical Hypnosis: A Multidisciplinary Approach. Philadelphia, Lippincott, 1984
655. Wolberg LR: Hypnoanalysis (2d ed). Orlando, FL, Grune & Stratton, 1964
656. Wolberg LR: Medical Hypnosis, 2 vols. Orlando, FL, Grune & Stratton, 1948

Morita Psychotherapy

657. Reynolds DK: Morita Psychotherapy. Berkeley, University of California Press, 1976

Psychoanalysis

Historial Aspects (See also 14–22, 673

658. Adler A: The Individual Psychology of Alfred Adler: A systematic Presentation in Selections from His Writings, (edited and annotated by Heinz L. Ansbacher & Rovena R. Ansbacher). New York, Basic Books, 1956
659. Ferenczi S: Further Contributions to the Theory and Techniques of Psychoanalysis. London, Hogarth, 1960
660. Freud A: Writings of Ana Freud, 8 vols.

Madison CT, International Universities Press, 1973–1981

661. Freud S: Standard Edition of the Complete Psychological Works of Sigmund Freud, 24 vols. Strachey J (trans). London, Hogarth, 1964

662. Horney K: New Ways in Psychoanalysis. New York, Norton, 1964

663. Jung CG: Psychology of the Unconscious. New York, Dodd, Mead, 1931 (Orig 1916)

664. Rank O: Will Therapy and Truth and Reality. New York, Knopf, 1979 (paperback)

665. Reich W: Character Analysis. New York, Farrar, Strauss & Giroux, 1972, (paperback)

666. Stekel W: Technique of Analytical Psychotherapy. New York, Liveright, 1950

667. Sullivan HS: The Interpersonal Theory of Psychiatry. New York, Norton, 1953

Introductory Aspects (See also 9, 178, 707)

668. Brenner C: An Elementary Textbook of Psychoanalysis (rev. ed). New York, International Universities Press, 1955

669. Eagle MN: Recent Developments in Psychoanalysis: A Critical Evaluation. New York, McGraw-Hill, 1984

670. Fenichel O: Psychoanalytic Theory of Neurosis. New York, Norton, 1945

671. Kubie L: Practical and Theoretical Aspects of Psychoanalysis. (rev ed.), New York, International Universities, 1975

Freudian Psychoanalysis

672. Shapiro D: Neurotic Styles. New York, Basic Books, 1965

673. Wyss D: Psychoanalytic Schools from the Beginning to the Present. New York, Jason Aronson, 1973

Clinical Use of Dreams

674. Altman LL: The Dream in Psychoanalysis, (rev. ed.) New York, International Universities Press, 1975

675. Bonine W: The Clinical Use of Dreams. New York, Basic Books, 1962

676. Freud S: The Interpretation of Dreams. J. Strachey (ed). New York, Basic Books, 1955

677. Gutheil EA: The Handbook of Dream Analysis. New York, Liveright, 1951

Techniques of Psychoanalysis

678. Glover E: The Technique of Psychoanalysis (rev ed). New York, International Universities Press, 1968

679. Greenson RR: The Technique and Practice of Psychoanalysis, Vol. 1. New York, Basic Books, 1971

Ego Psychological Approaches

680. Blanck G, Blanck R: Ego Psychology. New York, Columbia University Press, 1974

681. Hartmann H: Ego Psychology and the Problem of Adaptation. New York, International Universities Press, 1958

682. Kris E: Selected Papers of Ernst Kris. New Haven, Yale University Press, 1975

683. Loevinger J: Ego Development: Conceptions and Theories. San Francisco, Jossey Bass, 1976

684. Loewenstein RM: Practice and Precept in Psychoanalytic technique: "selected papers of Rudolph M. Loewenstein; with an introduction by Jacob A. Arlow. New Haven, Yale University Press, 1982

Object Relations Approaches

685. Balint M: Primary Love, and Psycho-analytic technique. New York, Liveright, 1965

686. Fairbairn WRD: Psychoanalytic studies of the personality. London, Tavistock, 1952

687. Guntrip HSS: Psychoanalytic Theory, Therapy, and the Self. New York, Basic Books, 1971

688. Klein M: The Writing of Melanie Klein, 4 vols. New York, Free Press, 1984

689. Isaacs SSF: Social Development in Young Children. New York, Schocken Books, 1972

690. Kernberg O: Borderline Conditions and Pathological Narcissism. New York, Jason Aronson, 1975

691. Kohon G (ed): The British School of Psychoanalysis: The Independent Tradition. New Haven, Yale University Press, 1985

692. Mahler M, et al: Psychological Birth of the Human Infant. New York, Basic Books, 1975

693. Mahler MS, Furer M: On Human Symbiosis and the Vicissitudes of Individuation. New York, International Universities Press, 1968

694. Segal H: Introduction to the Work of Melaine Klein. New York, Penguin, 1980
695. Spitz R: The First Year of Life: A Psychoanalytic Study of Normal and Deviant Development of Object Relations. New York, International Universities Press, 1965
696. Winnicott, DW: Collected papers: Through Paediatrics to Psychoanalysis. London, Tavistock, 1958

Self Analytic Approaches

697. Goldberg A: The Psychology of the Self. New York, International Universities Press, 1978
698. Goldberg A: Advances in Self Psychology. New York, International Universities Press, 1980
699. Kohut H: The Analysis of the Self. New York, International Universities Press, 1971
700. Líchtenberg JD, Kaplan S (eds): Reflections on Self Psychology. Hillsdale NJ Analytic Press, 1983
701. White MT, Weiner MB: The Theory and Practice of Self Psychology. New York, Brunner/Mazel, 1986

Existential Analysis

702. Boss M: Psychoanalysis and Daseinalysis. New York, Basic Books, 1963
703. May R, Angel E, Ellenberger H: Existence: A New Dimension in Psychiatry and Psychology. New York, Basic Books, 1958
704. May R: Existential Psychology (2d ed). New York, Random, 1961
705. Misiak, H, Sexten VS: Phenomenological, Existential and Humanistic Psychologies. Orlando, FL, Grune & Stratton, 1973
706. Ruitenbeck HM (ed): Psychoanalysis and Existential Philosophy. New York, Dutton, 1962

Case Material

707. Dewald PA: The Psychoanalytic Process: A Case Illustration. New York, Basic Books, 1972
708. Freud S: Fragment of an analysis of a case of hysteria, pp 13–146; Analysis of a phobia in a five-year-old boy, pp 149–189; Notes upon a case of obsessional neurosis, pp 293–383, Psycho-analytic notes upon an autobiographical account of paranoia (dementia paranoides), pp 387–470.

In Collected Papers. Vol. 2, London, Hogarth, 1952
709. Gardiner M (ed): The Wolf Man by the Wolf Man. With the Case of the Wolf-Man by Sigmund Freud, with a supplement by Ruth Mack. Brunswick, New York, Basic Books, 1971
710. Niederland WG: The Schreber Case: Psychoanalytic Profile of a Paranoid Personality. New York, Quadrangle, 1974
711. Rosenbaum M, Muroff M (eds): Anna O. Fourteen Contemporary Reinterpretations. New York, Free Press, 1985
712. Wolberg LR: Hypnoanalysis (2d ed). The Case of Johann R. Orlando, FL, Grune & Stratton, 1964

Psychoanalytically Oriented Psychotherapy (See also 751)

713. Alexander F: Psychoanalytic Therapy: Principles and Application. Omaha, University of Nebraska Press, 1980
714. Chessick RD: Technique and Practice of Intensive Psychotherapy. New York, Jason Aronson, 1983
715. Dewald PA: Psychotherapy: A Dynamic Approach, (2d ed). New York, Basic Books, 1970
716. Fromm-Reichman F: Principles of Intensive Psychotherapy. Chicago, University of Chicago Press, 1960 (paperback)
717. Giovacchini P (ed): Tactics and Techniques in Psychoanalytic Therapy, 2 vols. Vol. 1: Tactics and Techniques, 1972. Vol. 2: Countertransference, 1975. New York, Jason Aronson
718. Goldman GD, Milman DS (eds): Psychoanalytic Psychotherapy. Reading MA, Addison-Wesley, 1978
719. Langs R: The Technique of Psychoanalytic Psychotherapy, 2 vols. New York, Jason Aronson, 1973–1974

Psychodrama

720. Moreno JL: Psychodrama. Beacon NY, Beacon House, 1947
721. Yablonsky L: Psychodrama: Resolving Problems Through Role-Playing. New York, Gardner Press, 1981

Rational-Emotive Therapy

722. Ellis A: Humanistic Psychotherapy—The Rational-Emotive Approach. New York, McGraw-Hill, 1974

723. Ellis A, Bernard ME (eds): Clinical Applications of Rational–Emotive Therapy. New York, Plenum Press, 1985

Reality Therapy

724. Glasser W: Reality Therapy: A New Approach to Psychiatry. New York, Harper-Row, 1975

Sex Therapy

725. Hetrick ES, Stein TS: Innovations in Psychotherapy with Homosexuals. Washington, D.C. American Psychiatric Press, 1984
726. Kaplan HS: The New Sex Therapy. New York, Brunner/Mazel, 1974
727. Kaplan HS: The Illustrated Manual of Sex Therapy. New York, Quadrangle, 1975
728. Marmor J (ed): Sexual Inversion. New York, Basic Books, 1965
729. Masters WH, Johnson VE: Human Sexual Response. Boston, Little, Brown, 1966
730. Masters WH, Johnson VE: Human Sexual Inadequacy. Boston, Little, Brown, 1970
731. Meyer JK, Schmidt CW, Wise TN (eds): Clinical Management of Sexual Disorders (2d ed). Baltimore, Williams & Wilkins, 1983

Short-term Therapy

732. Balint M: Focal Psychotherapy: An Example of Applied Psychoanalysis. London, Tavistock, 1972
733. Castelnuovo-Tedesco P: The Twenty-Minute Hour: A Guide to Brief Psychotherapy for the Physician. Washington D.C., American Psychiatric Press, 1986 (paperback)
734. Davanloo H (Ed): Short-term Dynamic Psychotherapy. New York, Spectrum, 1978
735. Horner AJ (ed): Treating the Oedipal Patient in Brief Psychotherapy. New York, Jason Aronson, 1985
736. Horowtiz M, et al: Personality Styles and Brief Psychotherapy. Philadelphia, Lippincott, 1984
737. Malan DH: Frontiers in Brief Psychotherapy: An Example of the Convergence of Research and Clinical Practice. New York, Plenum Press, 1976
738. Mann J, Goldman R: A Casebook in Time-Limited Psychotherapy. New York, McGraw-Hill, 1982
739. Rush AJ (ed): Short-term Psychotherapies for Depression: Behavioral, Interpersonal, Cognitive and Psychodynamic Approaches. New York, Guilford, 1982
740. Sifneos PE: Short-term Dynamic Psychotherapy, Evaluation and Technique. New York, Plenum Press, 1979
741. Strupp H, Binder JL: Time-limited Dynamic Psychotherapy (TLDP): A Treatment Manual. Nashville TN, Vanderbilt University, 1983
742. Tilley BW: Short-term Counseling: A Psychoanalytic Approach. New York, International Universities Press, 1984
743. Wolberg LR: Handbook of Short-term Psychotherapy. New York, Thieme-Stratton, 1980

Strategic Therapy

744. Erickson MH, Rossi E (eds): Collected Papers of Milton H. Erickson. New York, Halsted Press, 1980
745. Frankl V: The Doctor and the Soul: From Psychotherapy to Logotherapy. New York, Bantam Books, 1967
746. Haley J: Problem Solving Therapy. New York, Harper-Row, 1978
747. Haley J: Strategies of Psychotherapy. Orlando FL, Grune & Stratton, 1963
748. Rosen S: My Voice Will Go With You: The Teaching Tales of Milton Erickson. New York, WW Norton, 1982
749. Zeig JK: Ericksonian Approaches to Hypnosis and Psychotherapy. New York, Brunner/Mazel, 1982
750. Zeig JK (ed): Ericksonian Psychotherapy, Vol. 11: Clinical Applications. New York, Brunner/Mazel, 1985

Supportive Psychotherapy

751. Luborsky L: Principles of Psychoanalytic Psychotherapy: A Manual for Supportive-Expressive Treatment. Philadelphia, Lippincott, 1984
752. Werman DS: The Practice of Supportive Psychotherapy. New York, Brunner/Mazel, 1984

Transactional Analysis

753. Berne E: Games People Play: The Psychology of Human Relationships. New York, Grove Press, 1964
754. Harris T: I'm OK, You're OK: A Practical Guide to Transactional Analysis. New York, Harper & Row, 1969
755. Klein M: Lives People Live: A Textbook of Transactional Analysis. New York, John Wiley, 1980

Case Material (See also 241, 738)

756. Baruch DW: One Little Boy. New York, Dell, 1952 (paperback)
757. Davitz LJ: The Psychiatric Patients: Case Histories. New York, Springer, 1971
758. Grinker RR, Robbins FP (eds): Psychosomatic Case Book. New York, Blakiston, 1954
759. Gurman AS (ed): Casebook of Marital Therapy. New York, Guilford, 1986
760. Klein M: Narrative of a Child Analysis: The Conduct of Psycho-Analysis of Children as Seen in the Treatment of a Ten-Year-Old Boy. New York, Basic Books, 1961 (rev ed.) New York, Delacorte, 1975)
761. Kutash IL, Wolf A: Psychotherapist's Casebook. San Francisco, Jossey Bass, 1986
762. Lazarus AA (ed): Casebook of Multimodal Therapy. New York, Guilford, 1985
763. Sechehaye MA: Symbolic Realization: A New Method of Psychotherapy Applied to a Case of Schizophrenia. New York, International Universities Press, 1960
764. Stekel W: Compulsion and Doubt (rev ed), 2 vols. (Case Material.) New York, Liveright, 1949
765. Ullman LP, Krasner L (eds): Case Studies in Behavior Modification. New York, Holt, 1965
766. Zax M, Stricker G: Patterns of Psychopathology: Case Studies of Behavioral Dysfunction. New York, Macmillan, 1963

Adjunct Therapies

Activities Therapy

767. Mosey AC: Activities Therapy. New York, Raven, 1973

Art Therapy

768. Landgarten HB: Clinical Art Therapy: A Comprehensive Guide. New York, Brunner/Mazel, 1981
769. Rubin JA: The Art of Art Therapy. New York, Brunner/Mazel, 1984
770. Ullman E, Dachinger P (eds): Art Therapy: Art in Education, Rehabilitation and Psychotherapy. New York, Schocken, 1975
771. Wadeson H: Art Psychotherapy. New York, John Wiley, 1980

Bibliotherapy

772. Brown EF: Bibliotherapy and Its Widening Applications. Metuchen, New Jersey, Scarecrow Press, 1975
773. Rubin RJ: Using Bibliotherapy: A Guide to Theory and Practice. Phoenix, AZ, Oryx Press, 1978

Biofeedback

774. Basmajian JV (ed): Biofeedback: Principles and Practice for Clinicians. Baltimore, Williams & Wilkins, 1983
775. Birbaumer N, Kimmel HD: Biofeedback & Self-Regulation. NJ, L. Erlbaum, 1976
776. Gaarder KR, Montgomery S: Clinical Biofeedback: A Procedural Manual for Behavioral Medicine. Baltimore, Williams & Wilkins, 1981
777. Orne MT (ed): Task Force Report, No. 19: Biofeedback. Washington, D. C. American Psychiatric Association, 1980
778. Yates AJ: Biofeedback and the Modification of Behavior. New York, Plenum Press, 1980

Counseling (see also 349, 352, 413, 548, 609, 619, 647, 742, 911, 912)

779. Ard B: Counseling and Psychotherapy: Classics on Theories & Issues, rev ed. Palo Alto, CA, Science & Behavior Books, 1975
780. Brammer LM, Shostrom EL: Therapeutic Psychology: Fundamentals of Counseling and Psychotherapy, 4th ed. Englewood Cliffs, NJ, Prentice-Hall, 1982.
781. Coping with Aids: Psychological and Social Considerations in Helping People with HTL-III Infection. Rockville MD, National Institute of Mental Health, 1986
782. Curte J: How to Become a Single Parent: A Guide for Single People Considering Adoption or Natural Parenthood Alone.

Englewood Cliffs NJ, Prentice-Hall, 1983

783. Dennis H (ed): Retirement Preparation: What Retirement Specialists Need To Know. Lexington Mass, Lexington Books, 1984

784. Farnsworth DL: Psychiatry, the Clergy and Pastoral Counseling. Collegeville MN, St. Johns University Press, 1969

785. Freeman DR: Marital Crisis and Short-term Counseling: A Casebook. New York, Free Press, 1982

786. Figley CR, McCubbin HI (eds): Stress and the Family: Coping with Catastrophe, Vol 2. New York, Brunner/Mazel, 1983

787. Haynes JM: Divorce Mediation: A Practical Guide for Therapist and Counselors. New York, Springer, 1981

788. Kempe RS, Kempe CH: The Common Secret: Sexual Abuse of Children and Adolescents. New York, W. H. Freeman & Co., 1984

789. Kiev A: A Strategy for Handling of Executive Stress. Chicago, Nelson-Hall, 1974

790. L'Abate L, Milan M: Handbook of Social Skills Training and Research. New York, John Wiley, 1985

791. Lester D, Brockopp GW: Crisis Intervention and Counseling By Telephone. Springfield, IL, Thomas, 1976

792. President's Commission for the Study of Ethical Problems in Medicine and Biomedical and Behavioral Research. Screening and Counseling for Genetic Conditions. Washington D.C., U.S. Government Printing Office, 1983

793. Rubin RJ: Using Bibliotherapy: A Guide to Theory and Practice. Phoenix AZ, Oryx Press, 1978

794. Schoenberg B (ed) Bereavement Counseling: A Multidisciplinary Handbook. Westport, CT, Greenwood Press, 1980

795. Seligman M: Group Counseling and Group Psychotherapy with Special Populations. Austin, TX, Pro Ed, 1987

796. Shulman L: The Skills of Helping: Individuals and Groups. Itasca, IL, Peacock Publishers, 1986

Dance and Movement Therapy

797. Bernstein PL: Theory and Methods in Dance-Movement Therapy: A Manual for Therapists, Students, and Educators (2d ed). Dubuque IA, Kendall/Hunt, 1981

798. Espenak L: Dance Therapy: Theory and Application. Springfield IL, CC Thomas, 1981

Drama Therapy

799. Landy RJ: Drama Therapy: Concepts and Practices. Springfield IL, Thomas, 1986

Electroconvulsive Therapy

800. Abrams R, Esman WB (eds) Electroconvulsive Therapy: Biological Foundations and Applications. New York, SP Medical & Scientific Books, 1982

801. Fink M: Convulsive Therapy. Theory and Practice. New York, Raven Press, 1979

802. Kalinowsky LB, Hippius H, Klein HE: Biological Treatments in Psychiatry. Orlando FL, Grune & Stratton, 1982

Milieu Therapy (See also 246, 264–270, 823–825, 827, 829, 832, 857)

803. Barofsky I, Budson RD (eds): The Chronic Psychiatric Patient in the Community: Principles of Treatment. New York, SP Medical and Scientific Books, 1983

804. Canter D, Canter S: Designing for Therapeutic Environments. New York, John Wiley, 1979

Music Therapy

805. Schulberg CH: The Music Therapy Sourcebook: A Collection of Activities Categorized and Analyzed. New York, Human Sciences Press, 1981

Occupational Therapy (See also 826, 828)

806. Black BJ (ed): Work as Therapy and Rehabilitation for the Mentally Ill. New York, Altro Health and Rehabilitation Services, 1986

807. Mosey AC: Psychosocial Components of Occupational Therapy. New York, Raven, 1986

Pet Therapy

808. Levinson BM: Pet-Oriented Child Psychotherapy. Springfield, IL, CC Thomas, 1969

Poetry Therapy

809. Leedy JJ (ed): Poetry as Healer: Mending the Troubled Mind. New York, Vanguard, 1985

Psychopharmacological Therapy
(See also 249–252, 385, 456, 596, 597)

810. American Medical Association: Drug Evaluations (6th ed). Philadelphia, PA, Saunders, 1986
811. Baldessarini RJ: Chemotherapy in Psychiatry: Principles and Practice. Cambridge, MA, Harvard University Press, 1985
812. Bernstein JG: Handbook of Drug Therapy in Psychiatry. Boston, MA, John Wright-PSG, 1983
813. Campbell M, Green WH, Deutsch SI: Child and Adolescent Psychopharmacology. Beverly Hills, CA, Sage Publications, 1985
814. Goldsmith W: Psychiatric Drugs for the Non-Medical Mental Health Worker. Springfield, IL, CC Thomas, 1977
815. Grahams-Smith G, Hippius H, Winokur G (eds): Clinical Psychopharmacology. Amsterdam, Excerpta Medica Foundation, 1982
816. Hersen M (ed): Pharmacological and Behavioral Treatment: An Integrated Approach. Somerset NJ, John Wiley, 1986
817. Klein DF, Gittelman R, Quitkin F, et al: Diagnosis and Drug Treatment of Psychiatric Disorders: Adults and Children (2d ed). Baltimore MD, Williams & Wilkins, 1980
818. Lipton MA, DiMascio A, Killam KF (eds): Psychopharmacology: A Generation of Progress. New York, Raven, 1978
819. Schatzberg AF: Manual of Clinical Psychopharmacology, (1st). Washington D.C., American Psychiatric Press, 1986
820. Weiner JM (ed): Psychopharmacology in Childhood and Adolescence (2d ed). New York, Basic Books, 1985

Psychosurgery

821. National Commission for the Protection of Human Subjects of Biomedical and Behavioral Research: Psychosurgery: Report and Recommendations. Washington D.C. U.S. Government Printing Office, 1977
822. Valenstein ES (ed): The Psychosurgical Debate. San Francisco, W. H. Freeman, 1980

Recreational Therapy

823. Daubert JR, Rothert EA: Horticulture Therapy at a Psychiatric Hospital. Glencoe IL, Chicago Horticulture Society, 1981
824. Gunn S: Basic Terminollgy for Therapeutic Recreation and Other Action Therapies. Champaign IL, Stipes, 1975
825. Kraus R: Therapeutic Recreation Service (3rd ed). New York, Saunders College Publishing, 1983

Rehabilitation and Case Management *(See also 479)*

826. American Occupational Therapy Association: Handbook for the Division of Professional Development, Mental Health. Rockville, MD, American Occupational Therapy Association, 1981
827. Beigel DE, Naparstek (eds): Community Support Systems and Mental Health. New York, Springer, 1982
828. Cromwell FS (ed): Occupational Therapy Strategies and Adaptations for Independent Daily Living. New York, Haworth Press, 1985
829. Fine SB: Occupational Therapy: The Role of Rehabilitation and Purposeful Activity in Mental Health Practice. Rockville, Md, American Occupational Therapy Association, 1983
830. Fromstein RH, Churchill JC: Psychosocial Intervention for Hospital Discharge Planning. Springfield, IL, CC Thomas, 1982
831. Hollister WG, et al: Alternative Services in Community Mental Health: Programs and Processes. Chapel Hill, NC, University of North Carolina Press, 1985
832. Jones M: Maturation of the Therapeutic Community: An Organic Approach to Health and Mental Health. New York, Human Sciences Press, 1976
833. L'Abate L, Milan M: Handbook of Social Skills Training and Research. New York, John Wiley, 1985
834. Smith CJ: A Typology of Community Residential Services: Task Force Report Twenty-One. Washington, D.C., American Psychiatric Press, 1982

Relaxation Methods & Meditation *(See also 774–777)*

835. Benson H, Proctor W: Beyond the Relaxation Response. New York, Berkley Publishing Group/G. P. Putnam's Sons, 1985
836. Carrington P: Freedom in Meditation. Kendall Park NJ, Pace Education Systems, 1977

837. Goldstein J: The Experience of Insight: A Simple and Direct Guide to Buddhist Meditation. Boston, Shambhala, 1983 (paperback)

838. Jacobson E: You Must Relax, (5th ed). New York, McGraw-Hill, 1978

839. LeShan L: How to Meditate: A Guide to Self-Discovery. New York, Bantam, 1986 (paperback)

840. Smith JC: Relaxation Dynamics: Nine World Approaches to Self-Relaxation. Champaign, IL, Research Press, 1985

Self-Help

841. Gartner A, Riessman F: The Self-Help Revolution. New York, Human Sciences Press, 1983

842. Smith JC: Relaxation Dynamics: Nine World Approaches to Self-Relaxation. Champaign, IL, Research Press, 1985

843. Stuart RB (ed): Behavioral Self-Management Strategies, Techniques and Outcomes. New York, Brunner/Mazel, 1977

Videotherapy

844. Berger MM (ed): Videotape Techniques in Psychiatric Training and Treatment (2d ed). New York, Brunner/Mazel, 1978

RESEARCH IN PSYCHOTHERAPY
(See also 169)

845. APA Commission on Psychotherapies. Psychotherapy Research: Methodological and Efficacy Issues. Washington, D.C. American Psychiatric Association 1982

846. Bellack AS, Hersen M (eds): Research Methods in Clinical Psychology. New York, Pergamon Press, 1984

847. Fieve RR, Rosenthal D, Brill HC (eds): Genetic Research in Psychiatry. Baltimore, MD, Johns Hopkins University Press, 1975

848. Garfield SL, Bergin AE (eds): Handbook of Psychotherapy and Behavior Change (3rd ed). Somerset, NJ, John Wiley, 1986

849. Greenberg L, Piasof WM (eds): Psychotherapeutic Process: A Research Handbook. New York, Guilford, 1986

850. Guze S, Roth M (eds): Psychiatric Development, Advances and Prospects in Research and Clinical Practice. New York, Oxford University Press, 1983

851. Hanin I, Usden E: Animal Models in Psychiatry and Neurology. New York, Pergamon Press, 1977

852. Hersen M, Michelsen L, Bellack AS (eds): Issues in Psychotherapy Research. New York, Plenum Press, 1984

853. Karasu TB (ed): Psychotherapy Research: Methodological and Effectiveness Issues. Washington, D.C., American Psychological Association, 1981

854. Kendall PC, Butcher JN: Handbook of Research Methods in Clinical Psychology. New York, John Wiley, 1982

855. Stricker G, Keisner RH (eds): From Research to Clinical Practice: The Implications of Social and Developmental Research for Psychotherapy. New York, Plenum Press, 1985

SENSORY DEPRIVATION

856. Solomon P (ed): Sensory Deprivation. Cambridge, MA, Harvard University Press, 1961

857. Suedfeld P: Restricted Environmental Stimulation: Research and Clinical Applications. New York, John Wiley, 1980

858. Zubeck JP (ed): Sensory Deprivation: Fifteen Years of Research. New York, Appleton-Century-Crofts, 1969

COMMUNITY MENTAL HEALTH

Administration

859. American Psychiatric Association: Manual of Psychiatric Peer Review. Washington, D.C., American Psychiatric Association, 1981

860. Barton WE, Barton GM: Mental Health Administration: Principles and Practice. New York, Human Sciences Press, 1983

861. Feldman S (ed): The Administration of Mental Health Services (2d ed). Springfield, IL, CC Thomas, 1981

862. Williamson JW, Hudson JI, Nevins MN: Teaching Quality Assurance and Cost Containment in Health Care. San Francisco, Jossey Bass 1982

Centers and Clinics (See also 827, 831)

863. Biegel D, Naparstek AJ: Community Support Systems and Mental Health: Re-

search, Practice and Policy. New York, Springer Publication, 1982

864. Fairweather GW, et al: Creating Change in Mental Health Organizations. Elmsford, New York, Pergamon, 1974

865. Golann S, Eisdorfer C (eds): Handbook of Community Mental Health (2d ed). New York, Irvington, (in press)

866. Langsley DG, Berlin IN, Yarvis RM: Handbook of Community Mental Health. Garden City NY, Medical Examination Publishing Co, 1981

867. Manning FV, MacLennan DW, Shore MF (eds): The Practice of Mental Health Consultation, Washington, D.C., U.S. Government Printing Office, 1975

868. Melton GB, et al: Community Mental Health Centers and the Courts: An Evaluation of Community-Based Forensic Services. Lincoln, University of Nebraska Press, 1985

869. Schulberg HC, Killilea M (eds): The Modern Practice of Community Mental Health: A Volume in Honor of Gerald Caplan. San Francisco, Jossey Bass, 1982

Mental Health Consultation

870. Caplan G: The Theory and Practice of Mental Health Consultation. New York, Basic Books, 1970

871. Cooper S, Hodges W (eds): The Mental Health Consultation Field, Vol II, Community Psychology Series. Washington, D.C., American Psychological Association, 1983

872. Plog SC, Ahmed PI (eds): Principles and Techniques of Mental Health Consultation. New York, Plenum Press, 1977

Public Health

873. Kupers TA: Public Therapy: The Practice of Psychotherapy in the Public Mental Health Clinic. New York, Free Press, 1982

874. Lieberman EJ (ed): Mental Health: The Public Health Challenge. Washington, D.C., American Public Health Association, 1975

875. Wagenfeld MO, Lemkau PV (eds): Public Mental Health Perspectives and Prospects. (Studies in Community Mental Health). Beverly Hills, Sage, 1982

Deinstitutionalization (See also 803, 804, 830, 834)

876. Jones BE: Treating the Homeless: Urban Psychiatry's Challenge: Washington, D.C., American Psychiatric Press, 1986

877. Segal SP, Avirom U (eds): The Mentally Ill In Community-Based Sheltered Care: A Study of Community Care and Social Integration. New York, John Wiley, 1978

EPIDEMIOLOGY

878. Barrett J, Rose RM (eds): Mental Disorders in the Community: Findings from Psychiatric Epidemiology: Annual Proceedings of the American Psychopathology Association. New York, Guilford Press, 1986

879. Dohrenwend BP, Dohrenwend BS, Gould MS, Link B, Neugebauer R, Wunsh-Hitzig R: Mental Illness in the United States. New York, Praeger, 1980

880. Dohrenwend DP, Dohrenwend BS: Social Status and Psychological Disorder: A Casual Inquiry. New York, John Wiley, 1969

881. Eaton WW, Kessler LG (eds): Epidemiologic Field Methods in Psychiatry: The NIMH Epidemiologic Catchment Area Program. Orlando, FL, Academic Press, 1985

882. Haefner H: Estimated Needs for Mental Health Care: A Contribution of Epidemiology. New York, Springer-Verlag, 1979

883. Hoch PH, Zubin J (eds): Comparative Epidemiology in the United States. Orlando, FL, Grune & Stratton, 1961

884. Hollingshead AB, Redlich FC: Social Class and Mental Illness. New York, John Wiley, 1958

885. Kaplan BH, Cassel JC (eds): Family and Health: An Epidemological Approach. Chapel Hill NC, Institute for Research in Social Sciences, 1975

886. Kleinbaum DG, Kupper LL, Morgenstern H: Epidemiologic Research: Principles and Quantitative Methods. Belmont CA, Lifetime Learning Publications 1982

887. MacMahon B, Pugh TF: Epidemiology Principles and Methods. Boston, Little Brown & Co, 1970

888. Ricks DF, Dohrenwend BS (eds): Origin

of Psychopathology—Problems in Research and Public Policy. New York, Cambridge University Press, 1983

889. Srole L, Langnor JS, Michael ST, Opler MK, Rennie TAC: Mental Health in the Midtown Manhattan Study. New York, McGraw-Hill, 1962

INDUSTRIAL MENTAL HEALTH

890. Buss TF, et al: Mass Unemployment: Plant Closings and Community Mental Health. Beverly Hills, Sage, 1983
891. Cooper CL, Robertson I (eds): Annual Review of Industrial and Organizational Psychology, Vol. 1. New York, John Wiley, 1986
892. Drenth PJ, et al (eds): Handbook of Work and Organizational Psychology, 2 vols. New York, John Wiley, 1984
893. Kiev A: A Strategy for Handling Executive Stress. Chicago, Nelson-Hall, 1974
894. Lauffer A: Careers, Colleagues, and Conflicts: Understanding Gender, Race, and Ethnicity in the Workplace. Beverly Hills, CA, Sage Publications, 1985
895. Levinson H, et al: Organizational Diagnosis. Cambridge, MA, Harvard University Press, 1972

MENTAL HEALTH PERSONNEL

General

896. Copans S, Singer T: Who's the Patient Here? Portraits of the Young Psychotherapist. New York, Oxford University Press, 1978

Psychiatrists

897. Maxmen JS: The New Psychiatry: How Modern Psychiatrists Think about their Patients, Theories, Diagnoses, Drugs, Psychotherapies, Power, Training, Families, and Private Lives. New York, Morrow, 1985
898. Shepherd M (ed): Psychiatrists on Psychiatry. New York, Cambridge University Press, 1983

Clinical Psychologists

899. Kendall PC, Norton Ford JD: Clinical Psychology: Scientific and Professional Dimensions. Somerset, NJ, John Wiley, 1982
900. Walker CE (ed): Clinical Practice of Psychology: A Practical Guide for Mental Health Professionals. Elmsford, NY, Pergamon, 1981
901. Walker CE (ed): The Handbook of Clinical Psychology. Homewood IL, Dow-Jones-Irwin, 1983

Clinical Social Workers

902. Lieberman F (ed): Clinical Social Workers as Psychotherapists. New York, Gardner Press, 1982
903. Waldfegel D, Rosenblatt A (eds): Handbook of Clinical Social Work. San Francisco, Jossey Bass, 1983

Psychiatric Nurses

904. Critchley DL, Maurin JT (eds): The Clinical Specialist in Psychiatric Mental Health Nursing. New York, John Wiley, 1985
905. National Institute of Mental Health: Proceedings: Psychiatric Mental Health Nursing: Recruitment to the Speciality. Washington, D.C. U.S. Department of Health and Human Services, Grant No. 5 T0IMH 14408-05, 1982

Nonpsychiatric Physicians (See also 308, 309)

906. Freeman AM, et al: Psychiatry for the Primary Care Physician. Melbourne FL, Krieger, 1979
907. Thompson TL, Byyny RL (eds): Primary and Team Health Care Education. New York, Praeger, 1983

Teachers

908. Rosenthal R, Jacobson L: Pygmalion in the Classroom: Teacher Expectation and Pupils' Intellectual Development, (rev ed.) New York, Irvington, 1986
909. Salzberger-Wittenber I, Henry G: The

Emotional Experience of Learning and Teaching. New York, Methuen, 1983

910. Todd KR: Promoting Mental Health in the Classroom. Rockville MD, National Institute of Mental Health, 1980. For sale from Superintendent of Documents, U.S. Government Printing Office, Washington, D.C., 20402

Clergy

911. Clinebell H: Basic Types of Pastoral Care and Counseling, (rev ed.) Nashville, TN, Abingdon Press, 1984

912. Sipe AWR, Rowe CJ (eds): Psychiatry, Ministry and Pastoral Counseling. Collegeville, Minn, Liturgical Press, 1984

Paraprofessionals

913. Gershon M: The Other Helpers: Paraprofessionals and nonProfessionals in Mental Health. Lexington MA, Lexington Books, 1977

914. Robbins E: Psychiatric Technician's Handbook. (Allied Health Professions Monograph Ser.). St. Louis, MO, 1985

Volunteers

915. Group for the Advancement of Psychiatry: The Community Worker: A Response to a Human Need. New York. Group for the Advancement of Psychiatry, 1974

916. Hunt CJ, Paschall NC: Volunteers: Forming Effective Citizens Groups. New York, University Press of America, 1984

TEACHING AND SUPERVISION
(See also 347, 554, 909)

917. Ekstein R, Wallerstein RS: The Teaching and Learning of Psychotherapy rev ed. New York, Basic Books, 1972

918. Goodman S (ed): Psychoanalytic Education and Research: The Current Situation and Future Possibilities. New York, International Universities Press, 1977

919. Hess AK: Psychotherapy Supervision: Theory, Research and Practice. New York, John Wiley, 1980

920. Joseph ED, Wallerstein RS (eds): Psychotherapy, Impact on Psychoanalytic Training: The Influence of the Practice and Theory of Psychotherapy on Education in Psychoanalysis. New York, International Universities Press, 1982

921. Kaslow FW: Supervision, Consultation, and Staff Training in the Helping Professions. San Francisco, Jossey Bass, 1977

922. Yager J (ed): Teaching Psychiatry and Behavioral Science. Orlando, FL, Grune & Stratton, 1982

CONTINUING EDUCATION

923. Carmichael HP: Prospects and Proposals: Lifetime Learning for Psychiatrists. Washington, D.C., American Psychiatric Association, 1972

924. Hales RE, Frances AJ: Psychiatry Update: American Psychiatric Association Annual Review. Washington, D.C., American Psychiatric Press. (Annual; beginning with vol. 4, 1985, CME Supplement available)

925. Sholevar PG (ed): Child and Adolescent Psychiatry Continuing Education Review (2d ed). New York, Medical Examination, 1982

COMPUTERS IN CLINICAL PRACTICE

925a. Lief JD: How to Buy a Personal Computer without Anxiety. Cambridge, MS, Bellinger Publishing Co., 1980

925b. Lief JD: Computer Applications in Psychiatry. Washington, D.C. American Psychiatric Press, Inc., 1987

925c. Schwartz MD (ed.): Using Computers in Clinical Practice. New York, Haworth Press, 1984

Recommended Films, Audiotapes, and Videotapes

Films, audiotapes, and videotapes are excellent teaching vehicles that are useful for purposes of psychoeducation for lay audiences as well as for professional education. A good discussion leader will enhance their value. In this section films, videotapes, and audiotapes that relate to the topics discussed in these volumes are listed, along with pertinent details concerning their themes and where to obtain them. They are valuable adjuncts to any educational program. A single film or tape may be used to demonstrate different themes with a variety of audiences, serving as visual reinforcement for lectures or discussions. The prices given for rental or sales, obviously, will not necessarily remain the same in the future. Addenda Table 2 summarizes all the pro-

grams by subject area.* Space has prevented the listing of all available films, videotapes, audiotapes, and new items appear monthly, but a representative sample will be found in this section. Some items listed in the Third Edition of this book are still valuable. Though they are not available now from the distributors, they may be found through some rental sources. All rental sources and sales distributors have been abbreviated in the three sections. At the end of each section there is a complete listing of sources with their addresses and other pertinent information. Where films alone are listed, they also may be available in videocassette format; inquire of the distributor. The individual items under each heading have been arranged in the alphabetical order of titles. Methods of using mental health films have been suggested at the end of Chapter 67.

---

* Media are also listed alphabetically by subject in the general index.

1435

Addenda Table 2
Guide to Films, Audiotapes, and Videotapes

Subject Areas	Film No.	Audio No.	Video No.
History	926–931, 946, 1045, 1057, 1058	1085, 1195, 1216, 1219	1276, 1277
Mental Functions			
Perception	932, 953		
Cognitive Process	944		
Conditioning and Learning	933, 934		1433
Social Psychology			
Communications	935		
Group Dynamics	936		
Sociology			
Social and Family Problems	938, 939		
Crime and Delinquency	940		
Suicide and Homicide	990, 991		
Ethology	941–942		
Human Life Cycle— Normal Development and Problems of Adjustment			1278–1281
General	943–947		
Men and Women	948, 964, 1040		
Infancy and Childhood	949–958, 1003		1282–1287
Adolescence	959–960		1288, 1289
Adulthood	961, 962		1290
Family and Alternate Life Styles	963, 969		1291
Old Age	966–969		1292, 1293
Dying, Death, and Bereavement	970–973		1292–1303, 1358
Field of Psychiatry			
Child and Adolescent Psychiatry	974–985	1086, 1087, 1088, 1103, 1109, 1112, 1113, 1115, 1131, 1133, 1141, 1182, 1212	1304–1314, 1431, 1484
Geriatric Psychiatry			1424
Psychopharmacology			1315, 1316
Psychiatric Emergencies	986–991	1088–1095	1317–1322, 1414
Partial Hospitalization	992–994		
Hospitalization	977, 978, 995, 996		
Field of Psychiatric Nursing	997–999	1096, 1097 1098	
Forensic Issues			1323
Medical Sciences Other Than Psychiatry			
Neurology			1324
Psychophysiology			1325–1327
Psychopathology			1328–1331

Mental and Emotional
Disorders

Affective Disorders	1000–1002	1099–1103	1332–1342, 1491
Alcoholism	939, 1003, 1004	1104–1106, 1144	1343–1354, 1448
Anxiety Disorders	1005–1007	1107–1111, 1156, 1157	1355–1357
Behavioral Disorders	986, 988, 1008–1009	1184	1438
Bereavement	970, 973		1358
Child Abuse	938	1112, 1113	1359–1360
Developmental Disorders	1010, 1011		1499
Disabilities		1114–1116	1308
Dissociation Disorders		1117	
Eating Disorders	1012	1118–1123, 1148, 1188	1361–1364
Folie A Deux	1013		
Mental Retardation	1014, 1015		1365–1367
Obsessive-Compulsive Disorders	1016		1368–1370
Organic Mental Disorders		1124–1128, 1258	1368–1370
Pain Disorders			1371–1377, 1399
Personality Disorders	956, 1017–1021	1129–1136, 1149, 1240, 1253	1373–1377, 1399
Schizophrenic Disorders	1022–1027	1137, 1168, 1263, 1264	1378–1386, 1445
Sexual Life Styles and Disorders	984	1138, 1139, 1171, 1173, 1140	1387–1393
Sleep/Wake Disorders		1140	1394–1396
Somatoform Disorders			1397–1401
Speech, Voice, and Hearing Disorders	1028, 1029		
Substance Abuse Disorders	1030, 1031	1141–1145, 1150, 1153, 1188	1343–1349, 1402–1409
		1194, 1274	1410

Miscellaneous
Psychotherapeutic
Modalities

General Diagnostic and Psychotherapeutic Methods	1032–1034	1216–1241	1411–1425
Behavior Therapy	1035, 1036	1106, 1107, 1121, 1146–1153, 1155, 1190, 1220	1352, 1426–1436
Client-Centered Therapy	1037	1154, 1224	1437
Cognitive Therapy		1108, 1155–1160	1438, 1438a, 1438b, 1438c
Confrontation Therapy	1038, 1039		
Existential Analysis and Therapy		1161, 1162	

(continued)

Addenda Table 2 (continued)

Subject Areas	Film No.	Audio No.	Video No.
Family and Marital Therapy	1040–1044	1163–1177, 1219, 1230, 1231	1439–1455
Gestalt Therapy	1045–1053		1456–1457
Group Psychotherapy		1178–1184, 1230, 1231	1458–1463
Hypnosis	1054, 1055	1185–1194	1464–1469
Psychoanalysis	1056–1058	1195–1215, 1221	
Psychodrama			1470–1475
Psychotherapy (general)	1032–1034, 1059–1063	1101, 1102, 1216–1241, 1255	1411–1425
Rational-Emotive Therapy			1476–1480
Short-term Therapy		1192, 1224	1478–1480
Strategic Therapy		1235, 1242–1247	
Transactional Analysis and Therapy	1064–1066		1481
Case Material	975, 976, 1014, 1015, 1021, 1024, 1063, 1067, 1072, 1241, 1248	1241–1248	1309, 1435, 1436
Adjunct Therapies			
Art Therapy	1073, 1074	1249	1482–1484
Biofeedback		1249	1482–1484
Clinical Social Work	1075		
Counseling	1076	1249a	1485–1489, 1489a, 1489b
Dance and Movement Therapy	1078–1080		1490
Electroconvulsive Therapy		1250	1491
Milieu Therapy		1251–1253	
Music Therapy			1492
Occupational Therapy			1493
Psychopharmacological Therapy		1111, 1254–1265	1494–1497
Rehabilitation			1498–1502
Relaxation Methods		1266–1271	1503–1508
Self-help		1192, 1270 1272–1275	
Sensory Feedback Therapy			1509
Sexual Therapy			1387, 1388, 1390, 1392
Videotherapy			1510, 1511
Community Mental Health	1081–1083		1512
Deinstitutionalization			1513–1514
Teaching and Supervision	1084		1515–1517

FILMS*

History (See also Films 946, 1045, 1057, 1058)

926. Freud: The Hidden Nature of Man. (Western Civilization: Majesty and Madness Series.) 29 min, color, 16 mm, 1970. Order Source: IUAVC Rental: $17.75. Freud's revolutionary theories of the power of the unconscious.
927. Sigmund Freud: His Offices and Home, Vienna, 1938. 17 min, color, 1975. Distributor: UCEMC. Rental: $25. Depicts #19 Berggase, which was Freud's office and home for more than 45 years, using a series of celebrated photographs taken before he moved from Vienna to London in 1938 to escape Nazi persecution.
928. Dr. Carl Jung: Interview with Carl Jung on the shores of Lake Zurich touching on his life and work. Order Source: PSU.
929. Dr. Jean Piaget with Dr. Mabel Inhelder. Part 1. 40 min, color. Stages of cognitive development. Source: PSU.
930. Interview with Erick Fromm. Part II. 50 min. General approaches to Psychotherapy. Source: PSU.
931. Professor Erik Erikson. Part I. 50 min. The eight stages of psychosocial development. Part II. 50 min. Ego identity and identity crisis. Source: PSU.

MENTAL FUNCTIONS

Perception

932. Perception. (Psychology Series.) 17 min, b&w, 16 mm, nd. Produced by McGraw-Hill. Order Source NYUFL. Rental: $10.50. Basic principles of perception as an organizing process.

Cognitive Processes (See Film No. 944)

Conditioning and Learning

933. B. F. Skinner and Behavior Change: Research, Practice and Promise. 45 min, color, 1976. Order Source: PSUPCR.

---

* Many of the films listed here are also available as videotapes from the same distributors. Inquiries should be addressed to the distributor to check on availability.

Purchase $510.00. Rental: $23.50. Traces the development of modern behaviorism and its application. Dr. Skinner and others discuss theory, practical uses, and ethical/social implications of behaviorism. Onsite visits show applications of behavioral intervention in education, mental health, counseling, and medicine.
934. Moral Development. 27 min, color, 16 mm, 1973. Order Source: CRM and MCGH. Rental Source: IUAVC. Rental: $15.25. Examines two of the major theories in the field of moral development through a dramatization of Dr. Stanley Milgram's famous obedience experiment in which subjects are required electrically to shock the other participants.

Social Psychology

Communication

935. This is Marshall McLuhan: The Medium Is the Massage. 53 min, color, 16 mm, nd. Produced by NBC-TV. Order Source: NYUFL. Rental: $44. Presents McLuhan's basic ideas through pictorial techniques and his own comments as well as the reactions of others to his views. Examines the way in which all media of communication shape and alter society.

Group Dynamics

936. Group Dynamics: Groupthink. 22 min, color, 1973. Distributor: PSUPCR. Rental: $18. Offers examples of group decision-making processes that influenced such historical events as Pearl Harbor, the Korean War, and the Bay of Pigs, and describes how effective leadership can prevent a decision-making group from falling into "groupthink." (From the Behavior of Business Series.)
937. Group Leadership: The History of the Group Process Movement. 28 min, b&w, 16 mm, 1976. Order Source: UCEMC. Purchase: $225. Rental: $18.

Sociology

Social and Family Problems

938. Raised in Anger. 60 min, color, 1979. Distributor: UCEMC. Order Source: MEDIAG. Rental: $49. Documents the

extent, nature, and causes of child abuse in America, showing that it cuts across all socio-economic boundaries.

939. Soft Is The Heart Of A Child. 28 min, color, 1979. Distributor: UCEMC. Order Source: OC. Rental: $34. Drama illustrating a typical alcoholic family situation.

Crime and Delinquency

940. Hard Time. 27 min, color, 1980. Distributor: UCEMC. Source: MTI. Rental: $37. Shows the harsh reality of life in a maximum security prison.

Suicide and Homicide (See Film Nos. 990, 991)

Ethology

941. Konrad Lorenz. 25 min, color, 1979. Distributor: UCEMC. Order Source: MEDIAG. Rental $33. Intimate portrait of the Nobel Laureate, generally considered the founder of the science of ethology.

942. Mother Love. 26 min, b&w, 16 mm, nd. Produced by CBS. Order Source: NYUFL. Rental: $11. Testing by Harry F. Harolow of the reactions of newborn rhesus monkeys to unusual mother substitutes. Shows that the single most important factor is body contact and that deprivation causes deep emotional disturbances.

Human Life Cycle—Normal Development and Problems of Adjustment

General

943. Anna N.—Life History from Birth to Fifteen Years. The Development of Emotional Problems in a Child Reared in a Neurotic Environment. (Film Studies on Integrated Development: Interation Between Child and Environment Series.) 60 min, b&w, 16 mm, silent. nd. Produced by Margaret Fries, MD. Order Source: NYUFL. Rental: $11.

944. Cognitive Development. 26 min, color, 1973. Source: McGraw-Hill. UCEMC; Rental: $29. Explains Piaget's theory of maturational stages of development and contrasts it with learning-based theory and practice.

945. Growing Up Without Sight. 20 min, color, 16 mm. nd. Order Source: NYUFL. Rental: $12.50. Follows three blind children through a morning's experience in a day nursery for the blind. (Hampstead Child Therapy Clinic).

946. Erikson On Erikson: On Developmental Stages. 19 min, color, 16 mm, 1978. Order Source: PMF. Erik Erikson, his wife, and students at the Erikson Institute. Exchange thought on Erikson's Eight Stages of Man.

947. Everybody Rides the Carousel. 72 min, color, 16 mm, 1976. Source: UCEMC. Rental: $57. Animation illustrates Erik Erikson's Eight Stages Of Man theory. Vignettes trace personality development, emotional changes, and needs through the following stages: newborn, toddler, childhood, school age, adolescents, young adulthood, adulthood, old age.

Men and Women

948. The Sexes: What's the Difference. 28 min, color, 16 mm, 1972. Produced by Canadian Broadcasting Corp. Order Source: PSUPCR. Rental: $19.50. Surveys the research of leading child developmentalists: Dr. Jerome Kagan (Harvard), Dr. Eleanor Maccoby (Stanford), and Drs. Jeanne and Jack Block (National Institute of Mental Health) on the subject of inborn vs. learned male/female traits.

Infancy and Childhood (See also Film 1005)

949. Mother–Infant Interaction. Film 6: Resemblances in Expressive Behavior. 40 min, b&w, 16 mm, nd. Order Source: NYUFL. Rental: $14.50. Mother–infant interaction with different forms of maternal behavior.

950. Mother Love. (Film Studies of the Psychoanalytic Research Project on Problems in Infancy Series.) 20 min, b&w, 16 mm, silent. nd. Produced by Rene A Spitz, MD. Order Source: NYUFL. Rental: $8.50. Sale: $135.00. Impact of mother love on the social relations of a child.

951. A Study in Maternal Attitudes, 30 min, b&w, 16 mm, nd. Produced by NY Fund for Children. Order Source: NYUFL. Purchase: $165. Rental: $15.

952. Development of the Child: Infancy. 20 min, color, 16 mm, 1972. Source: HARR and MTI. Rental Source: IUAVC. Rental: $15.25. Examines behavior and cognitive patterns that are characteristic of the first 18 months of life. Discusses briefly the Harlow mother surrogate experiments.

953. Development of the Child: Cognition. 29 min, color, 16 mm, 1972. Source: BAYS and MTI. Rental Source: IUAVC. Rental: $16. Discusses thought processes in terms of perception, memory, evaluation, and reasoning. Presents an overview of Piaget's theory of intellectual development.

954. Genesis of Emotions. (Film Studies of the Psychoanalytic Research Project on Problems in Infancy Series. 30 min, b&w, 16 mm, silent. nd. Produced by Rene A Spitz, MD. Order Source: NYUFL. Rental: $9.50. Sale: $195. Earliest evidence of interpersonal interests.

955. Grief. (Film Studies of the Psychoanalytic Research Project on Problems in Infancy Series.) 30 min, b&w, 16 mm, silent, nd. Produced by Rene A Spitz, MD. Order Source: NYUFL. Rental: $8.50. Sale: $195. Effect upon infants of prolonged absence of the mother.

956. Overdependency. (Mental Mechanisms Series.) 32 min, b&w, 16 mm, n.d. Produced by NFB. Order Source: NYUFL. Rental: $11. A young man crippled by overdependency seeks psychiatric help.

957. Child's Play and the Real World. 16 min, color, 16 mm, 1974. Source: DAVSN. Rental Source: IUAVC. Rental: $13. The relevance of play in developing the childs self-awareness, thinking, and learning. Review and illustrates Piaget's three forms of play—sensorimotor play, symbolic play, and games with rules.

958. Normal Child. 25 min, b&w, 16 mm, 1967. Made by Margaret D Griffel, MD, Robert C Prall, MD. Jacques Van Vlack. Order Source: PSUPCR. Purchase: $125. Rental: $5.90.

Adolescence

959. Adolescence: The Winds of Change. 30 min, color, 1975. Source: PSUPCR. Rental $20. Presents physical, sexual, and cognitive changes in adolescents through interviews with adolescents and child development authorities John Conger, Jerome Kagan, and David Elkind.

Stresses the importance of parents in helping their children master the developmental tasks of adolescence, especially in today's complex, rapidly changing, and technologically sophisticated society. Directed by Glen Howard and Carolyn Ferris.

960. Adolescence: A Case Study. (Developmental Psychology: Infancy to Adolescence Series.) 29 min, color, 1978. Source: PSUPCR. Rental: $17.50. Explores the psychosocial development of a seventeen-year-old girl, Angie, who has reached the advent of formal thinking skills, is so preoccupied with matters of the moment that intellectual tasks often seem remote and inconsequential. Other vignettes, however, show Angie to be capable of sophisticated thought processes, to be slowly maturing to adulthood. Narrated by Beau Bridges.

Adulthood

961. Development Of The Adult. 29 min, color, 16 mm, 1978. Source: IUAVC. Rental: $16.50. Introduces current issues, questions, and research in the field of adult development. Examines various methodological approaches through discussions with leading American authorities in the field, including Bernice Neugarten, Paul Costa, Roger Gould, David Gutmann, and Daniel J. Levinson.

962. Responsible Assertion: A Model for Personal Growth. 28 min, video, color, 16 mm, 1981. Producer N. Baxley. Distributor: RESPRC. Purchase: $450 (16 mm) $460 (video). Introduces adult assertive behavior. Includes dramatizations of passive, aggressive and hostile behavior.

Family and Alternate Life Styles

963. Children of Divorce. 37 min, color, 1976. Source NYUFL. Distributor: UCEMC. Rental: $36. Documents the social, psychological, and economic problems experienced by children whose parents divorce.

964. Focus On Women. 28 min, color, 1980. Source: UN. Distributor: UCEMC. Rental: $35. Examines the traditional image of women as portrayed throughout the world and shows how women are working to change that image.

965. Guilty Madonnas. 55 min, color, 1981.

Distributor: McG-H. Source: UCEMC. Rental: $48. The psychological pressures and emotional problems faced by working mothers, showing how group day-care centers benefit both children and mothers.

Old Age

966. Aging-The Losses. 29 min, color, 1979. Source: PSUPCR. Rental: $21. Examines the losses of family and friends, as well as the changes in living arrangements, income, roles, and responsibilities, which are faced by the elderly. Stresses the need for nurses to help the elderly find ways of reinvesting their interests and energy.

967. To Live With Dignity. 29 min, color, 16 mm, 1972. Produced by Institute of Gerontology, University of Michigan, Wayne State University. Order Source: UCEMC. Purchase: $200. Rental: $22 per day ($5 each additional day over contracted period). Documentary of a 3-month project involving milieu therapy with 20 institutionalized elderly patients.

968. The Rights of Age. 28 min, b&w, 16 mm, nd. Produced by the Mental Health Film Board. Order Source: NYUFL. Rental: $12.50. Examination of a number of older people in need of physical, psychological, or legal assistance.

969. Trigger Films on Aging. 15 min, color, 16 mm, nd. Order Source: UMTVC. Purchase: $180. Rental: $25. Five very brief dramatized vignettes on various aspects of growing old.

Dying, Death and Bereavement

970. On Death and Dying. 58 min, color, 1974. Distributor: NYUFL. Source: UCEMC. Rental: $47. In-depth interview with Dr. Elisabeth Kübler-Ross, who discusses her experiences in helping the terminally ill face death.

971. Psychosocial Aspects of Death. 39 min, b&w, 16 mm, 1971. Source: IUAVC. Director Dr. Kenneth Gene Faris. Dramatized story of a leukemia patient, his pregnant wife, and a nursing student who is facing patient death for the first time.

972. All You Have to Do. 54 min, color, 16mm, 1981. Sources: MOBIUS and NFLC. Pat Logan, her husband, chil-

dren, best friend, and counselor discuss how Pat's contraction of terminal illness Hodgkins disease has changed their outlooks on life and death.

973. As Long As There Is Life. 40 min, color, 16 mm, 1979. HIETR, PIC. Cinema Verite documents a young cancer victim's last days of life at home under the care of her husband, sons and a hospice team. Continuation of hospice support is shown during the bereavement period.

Field of Psychiatry

Child and Adolescent Psychiatry

974. Autistic Syndrome Series. (Series in four parts.) 16 mm, b&w, sound, English narration, nd. Part I, 43 min. Sale: $230. Rental: $18. Part II, 42 min. Sale: $230. Rental: $18. Part III, 36 min. Sale: $195. Rental: $14.50. Part IV, 43 min. Sale: $230. Rental: $18. Produced by Stichting Film en Wetenschap-Universiaire Film, Utrech, the Netherlands; Scientific Hospital for Child Psychiatry, Utrecht, the Netherlands. Order Source: NYUFL. Purchase: Parts I,II IV, $200; Part III, $195. Rental: Parts I,II,IV, $15; Part III, $14.50.

975. A Boy Named Terry Egan. 53 min, b&w, 16 mm, nd. Order Source: GFL. Rental: $20 base service charge for 2 days. Shows a 9-year-old boy making measurable gain against autism. Comments by Bruno Bettelheim on behalf of the 80,000 autistic children in the country.

976. Natural History of Psychotic Illness in Children. 19 min, b&w, 16 mm, nd. Produced by Institute of Psychiatry, London (NYU). Order Source: NYUFL. Purchase: $160.00. Rental: $10.50. Describes the evolution of a psychotic child from infancy to adolescence, showing the change from normal to abnormal. The "behavior day" of a psychotic child fully documented.

977. Two-Year-Old Goes to Hospital. 50 min, b&w, 16 mm, 1952. Produced by James Robertson. Order Source: GFL. Sale: $230. Rental: $18 base service charge for 2 days. Research described sponsored by the World Health Organization in a project directed by John Bowlby, MD.

978. We Won't Leave You. 17 min, color, 16

mm, 1975. Made by Edward A Mason, MD. Order Source: MHTFP. Purchase: $195. Rental: $20. A film record about meeting the emotional needs of hospitalized young children.

979. Jane: Aged 17 months in Fostercare for 10 Days. 37 min, b&w, 16 mm, nd. Produced by James and Joyce Robertson, Tavistock Child Development Research Unit, London. Order Source: NYUFL. Sale: $220. Rental: $16.50 base service charge for 2 days. Emotional sequelae in an infant after a 10-day separation from her mother.

980. John: 17 months-Nine Days in a Residential Nursery. 45 min, b&w, 16 mm, 1969. Produced by James and Joyce Robertson. Order Source: NTUFL. Sale: $295. Rental: $23. Follows the daily increasing distress and deterioration as John is defeated in efforts to secure a "mother" while residing in a residential nursery during his mother's hospitalization.

981. The Neurotic Child. 28 min, b&w, 16 mm, 1968. Produced by MD Griffel, RC Prall, Eastern Psychiatric Institute. Order Source: PSUPCR. *Showing Restricted*. Purchase: $340. Rental: $15.50. Depicts a 7-year-old boy diagnosed as a psychoneurotic in clinical interview situation.

982. He Comes From Another Room. (Part of NIMH's Series. One to Grown on.) 28 min, color, 16 mm, 1974. Made by Ed Mason, MD. Order Source: NAVC. Purchase $295. Rental: $30. A sensitive documentary about integrating two emotionally disturbed children into a regular classroom.

983. Clinical Aspects of Childhood Psychosis. 55 min, b&w, silent, 16 mm, nd. Produced by the Institute of Psychiatry, London. Order Source: NYUFL. Purchase $165. Rental: $11.

984. Teenage Homosexuality. 11 min, color, video, 16 mm, 1980. Producer: CBSNEW. Distributor: CAROUF. Purchase: $210. Three female and two male high school students discuss their lives as homosexuals. Separate interviews with a mother and a psychiatrist explore additional aspects of the issue. YASD

985. Child Psychiatry: Modern Approaches. 59 min, color, 1985. Producer/Sponsor USNIH. Source: NAVC. Purchase:

$155. Dr. Rapoport of the National Institutes of Health provides a perspective on early development of mental disorders in children. She discusses the relationship between handicaps such as reading and language disorders, and behavior problems. Dr. Rapoport also explores new data in the epidemiology of childhood mental illness.

Psychiatric Emergencies

986. Crisis Intervention for the Acting-Out Patient. 30 min, video or 16 mm, color, 16 mm, 1980. Producer: FAIRVGH. Distributor: FAIRVGH. Purchase $275 (16 mm) $195 (video). Rental: $45 (16 mm) $40 (video). Demonstrates techniques to handle acting-out behavior from a patient. Illustrates how to identify anxiety, offer reassurance and alternatives, and encourage communication.

987. Psychological Response. 13 min, color, 1975. Source: PSUPCR. Rental: $12 Deals with human emotional responses in emergencies. Three people who were caught up in the tragedy of natural disasters recall their experiences and reactions, and a counselor attempts to help them assess their feelings and move toward a changed attitude about their guild.

988. Mental Illness. 14 min, video or 16 mm, color, Harper & Row Criminal Justice Media, 1980. Source: APA/H&CPS. Distributor: UIFC. This brief but comprehensive film illustrates several kinds of aberrant or violent behavior that might indicate mental illness and would require special handling.

989. Psychosis: A Family Intervention, #4 (Psychiatric emergency series). 13 min, color, 16 mm/video 1982. $250.00. Rental: $60.00; Order Source: POLMYR. Dramatizes a schizophrenic psychotic break.

990. Suicides. 16 mm, video, color, 1981. Distributor: UCLANI. Purchase: $450 (16 mm). $250 (video). Rental: $40 (16 mm). The psychological and social aspects of suicide are discussed by well-known authorities. Prevention is emphasized.

991. Suicides. 42 min, color, 16 mm, 1981. Source: Behavioral Sciences Media Laboratory, Neuropsychiatric Institute,

UCLA. Distributor: BSML; Purchase: $450. Rental: $40, Video-cassette: $250. This documentary film explores the complex and enigmatic world of suicide.

Partial Hospitalization

992. Back into the Sun. 27 min, b&w, 1957. Produced by the National Film Board of Canada. Source: PSUPCR. Rental: $13.50 The day hospital of the Allan Memorial Institute of Psychiatry in Montreal pioneered a new concept of mental treatment: Patients came for daytime treatment but returned to their homes at night and over weekends. Through the history of a woman patient, the use of drugs, interviews, occupational therapy, sociodrama, and group talks is shown.

993. Day Hospital, 22 min, b&w, 1965. Source: PSUPCR. Rental: $12 Dr. Joshua Bierer, English psychiatrist, tours the Malborough Day Hospital, located in a quiet residential section of London. Patients live out and come to the house for individual counseling, activity therapy, and group therapy. Includes patients' comments.

994. The Day Hospital. 22 min, b&w, 16 mm, nd. Produced by NYUFL. Order Source: NYUFL. Purchase: $160. Rental: $11 Portrays Marlborough Day Hospital, London, England, where nonresident patients come for such therapies as individual counseling activity therapy, electroshock, chemotherapy, and group therapy.

Hospitalization (See also Films 977, 978)

995. Bitter Welcome. 26 min, b&w, 16 mm, 1959. Order Source: NYUFL. Rental: $11 Describes the struggle of a discharged mental hospital patient to overcome the fears and prejudices of his fellow workers and to regain his place in the community.

996. Full Circle. 27 min, b&w, 16 mm, nd. Produced by the Mental Health Film Board. Order Source: NYUFL. Rental: $11 Describes the importance of the job situation to the well-being of the discharged mental patient; shows the role of the psychiatric ward of the hospital in preparing the patient to find and keep a job.

Field of Psychiatric Nursing

997. Psychiatric Nursing: The Nurse–Patient Relationship. 34 min, b&w, film & video, 1958. Source: WPIC. Designed to meet a specific need in psychiatric nursing education, this film emphasizes the importance of a therapeutic nurse–patient relationship in the care and treatment of hospitalized mental patients. The film traces a developing relationship between a psychiatric nurse and one of the many patients in her care. In following the frustrations as well as the achievements of a nurse in a typical state hospital situation, many of the basic techniques in psychiatric nursing are reviewed.

998. On Becoming A Nurse–Psychotherapist. 42 min, color, 1970. Source: UCEMC. Distributor: UCEMC. Purchase: $575 film/$400 videotape. Rental: $44. Dramatized case study of the experiences of Judy, a young nursing student with some training, as she learns to assume the role of nurse–psychotherapist.

999. Broken Appointment. 30 min, b&w, 16 mm, nd. Produced by MHFB. Order Source: NYUFL. Rental: $11 Describes the experience of a young public health nurse who discovers it is as important to understand a patient's feelings as well as to interpret physical symptoms.

Mental and Emotional Disorders

Affective Disorders

1000. Depressive States: I. (Mental Symptoms Series.) 12 min. b&w, 16 mm, 1952. Produced by the National Film Board of Canada. Order Source: NYUFL. Rental: $8.50. A demonstration of some manifestations of the agitated form of severe depression.

1001. Depressive States: II. (Mental Symptoms Series.) 11 min, b&w, 16 mm, 1952. Produced by the National Film Board of Canada. Order Source: NYUFL.

Rental: $8.50. The retarded form of depression and severe depression that has reached the point of attempted suicide.

1002. Manic State. (Mental Symptoms Series.) 15 min, b&w, 16 mm, nd. Order Source: NYUFL. Rental: $8.50. Hypomania.

Alcoholism (See also Film 939)

1003. Alcoholism: Life Under the Influence. Parts 1 and 2. 57 min, color, 1984. Produced by WGBH for the Nova Series. Source: PSUPCR. Rental: $35. Alcoholism has been called one of the nation's most widespread and least admitted diseases, and it is related to 90 percent of all physical assaults, half of all homicides, and a quarter of all suicides. Offers an interdisciplinary report on the disease of alcoholism and interviews therapists, researchers, and alcoholics.

1004. Different Alcoholics—Different Treatments. 16 mm, 1982. Order Source: CONFC. Features real patients talking about their problems and a consultant/narrator discussing treatment. Restricted to professional audience.

Anxiety Disorders

1005. Anxiety: Its Phenomenology in the First Year of Life. 29 min, b&w, silent, 16 mm, 1953. Producer: Rene A. Spitz, MD. Distributor: NYUFL. Rental: $8.50. Sale: $135. The phenomenology of anxiety, from birth to the end of the first year, with behavioristic observations of its manifestations.

1006. Anxiety: The Endless Crisis, Parts 1 and 2. 59 min, color, 1975. Produced by NET. From the "Thin Edge" series. Source: PSUPCR. Purchase: $635. Rental: $28. Examines a wide range of anxiety-producing situations from the momentary flashes of anxiety we all experience to extreme anxiety that can ultimately lead to death. Mental health authorities discuss the difference between state anxiety and trait anxiety. Physiological as well as mental reactions to anxiety are explained. Also discusses "fight or flight" response, performance anxiety and panic.

1007. A Pathological Anxiety (The Disordered Mind Series.) 28 min, b&w, 16 mm, nd.

Produced by Robert Anderson. Order Source: NYUFL. Rental: $12.50.

Behavioral Disorders (See also Films, 986, 988)

1008. Neurotic Behavior: A Psychodynamic View. 19 min, color, 16 mm, 1973. Order Source PSUPCR. Purchase: $345.00. Rental: $16.50.

1009. Neurotic Behavior: A Psychodynamic View. 20 min, color, 1973. Source: McG-H. Distributor: UCEMC. Rental: $29. Dramatized episode in the life of a 19-year-old college sophomore, linking his "neurotic" behavior to external anxiety and childhood memories.

Bereavement (See Film 990–993)

Child Abuse (See Film 938)

Disabilities (See Film 945)

Developmental Disorders

1010. Anybody's Child: Dyslexia Defined. 48 min, color, 1975. Source: MP. Distributor: UCEMC: Rental: $33. Examines the physical and emotional problems associated with dyslexia, a disability that interferes with a child's capacity to learn to read, write, and spell.

1011. Hidden Handicaps. 23 min, color, 1977. Source: McG-H. Distributor: UCEMC: Rental: $32. The causes, symptoms, and treatment potential of learning disabilities in children.

Eating Disorders

1012. Psychosomatic Conditions-Obesity. (Disordered Mind Series.) 28 min, b&w, 16 mm, nd. Produced by Robert Anderson. Order Source: NYUFL. Rental: $10. Case study in which a 13-year-old girl and her parents are made aware, through treatment, of the relationship between her unmet emotional needs and her overeating.

Folie A Deux

1013. Folie A Deux. (Mental Symptoms Series.) 15 min, b&w, 16 mm, nd. Order Source: NYUFL. Rental: $8.50. A psychosis developed first in the daughter and was then communicated to the mother.

Mental Retardation

1014. Lilly—A Story About a Girl Like Me. 14 min, color, 1977. Source: DAVF. Distributor: UCEMC: Rental: $24. Sensitive portrait of a 10-year-old girl with Down's syndrome. Shows her daily life and demonstrates how she develops when raised in a normal home.

1015. Mental Retardation: Part 1. 30 min, color, 1967. Produced by the Bureau of Handicapped Children, Wisconsin Department of Public Instruction. Source: PSUPCR. Rental: $16.50. Survey of the research, treatment, and types of mentally retarded and physically handicapped children. Emphasizes the importance of early recognition of symptoms and assesses chemical damage to the brain.

Obsessive-Compulsive Disorders

1016. Obsessive-Compulsive Neurosis. (The Disordered Mind Series.) 28 min, b&w, 16 mm, nd. Produced by Robert Anderson. Order Source: NYUFL. Rental: $12.50.

Personality Disorders (See also Film 956.)

1017. Interpersonal Behavior. 44 min, b&w, 1972. Produced by University of Mississippi Medical Center. Department of Psychiatry, Jackson, MS. Source: WPIC. Rental: $50. Discusses the types of interpersonal behavior that can be observed, such as behavior towards the examiner and specific attitudes. The attitudes portrayed in this program include: paranoid, schizoid, compulsive, explosive, antisocial, passive-aggressive, hysterican, and inadequate. Interviews with several patients with personality disorders with emphasis on the importance of making appropriate evaluations for diagnosis.

1018. A Psychopath (Disordered Mind Series.) 28 min, b&w, 16 mm, nd. Produced by Robert Anderson. Order Source: NYUFL. Rental: $12.50.

1019. A Coronary (The Disordered Mind Series.) 28 min, b&w, 16 mm, nd. Produced by Robert Anderson. Order Source: NYUFL. Rental: $12.50. Illustrates the relationship of the patient's personality to his attack.

1020. Neurotic Behavior: A Psychodynamic View. 19 min, color, 16 mm, 1973. Order Source PSUPCR. Purchase: $345.00. Rental: $16.50.

1021. Neurotic Behavior: A Psychodynamic View. 20 min, color, 1973. Source: McG-H. Distributor: UCEMC. Rental: $29. Dramatized episode in the life of a 19-year-old college sophomore, linking his "neurotic" behavior to external anxiety and childhood memories.

Schizophrenic Disorders

1022. Diagnosis of Childhood Schizophrenia. 35 min, b&w, 16 mm, nd. Produced by Brooklyn Juvenile Guidance Center, Inc. Narrator: Abraham A. Fabian. Order Source: NYUFL. Purchase: $195. Rental: $15.00.

1023. Schizophrenia: The Shattered Mirror. 60 min, b&w, film & video, 1966. Produced by NET. Source: WPIC. This is the first of two programs dealing with the seriously disturbed. This program concentrates on schizophrenia, a mental disease that is widespread, but about which little is known as to causes and cures. The documentary shows some of the ways psychiatrists and others are attempting to help people with schizophrenia.

1024. Victorian Flower Paintings: Pictorial Record of a Schizophrenic Episode. 7 min, color, 16 mm, 1968. Produced by Institute of Psychiatry, London. Order Source: NYUFL. Rental $12. This is a pictorial record of a schizophrenic episode in which the well-known distortions imposed by the illness are seen and described.

1025. Schizophrenia: Catatonic Type. (Mental Symptoms Series.) 11 min, 16 mm, nd. Produced by the National Film Board of Canada. Order Source: NYUFL. Rental: $8.50. A demonstration of characteristic symptoms of stuporous catatonia. Three male patients are presented.

1026. Schizophrenia: Hebephrenic Type. (Mental Symptoms Series.) 13 min, b&w, 16 mm nd. Produced by the National Film Board of Canada. Order Source: NYUFL. Rental: $8.50. Demonstrates the chief manifestations of hebephrenic schizophrenia. A male patient is presented.

1027. Schizophrenia: Simple-Type Deteriorated. (Mental Symptoms Series.) 11 min, b&w, 16 mm, nd. Produced by National Film Board of Canada. Order

Source: NYUFL. Rental: $8.50. Presents a characteristic picture of chronic simple schizophrenia. A female patient psychotic for more than ten years is presented.

Sexual Life Styles and Disorders
(See also Film 994.)

Speech, Voice & Hearing Disorders

1028. Identifying Speech Disorders: Language. 20 min, b&w, 16 mm, nd. Produced by Harper & Row. Order Source: NYUFL. Rental: $12. A variety of language disorders illustrated by individuals of different ages.

1029. Identifying Speech Disorders: Stuttering. 20 min, b&w, 16 mm, nd. Produced by Harper & Row. Order Source: NYUFL. Rental: $12

Substance Abuse Disorders

1030. Angel Death. 33 min, color, 1979. Source: FL. Distributor: UEMC: Rental $38. Study of the chornic and debilitating effects of angel dust.

1031. Hooked. 20 min, b&w, 16 mm, nd. Produced by Churchill Films. Order Source: NYUFL. Rental: $11. A vivid description of the experience of drug addiction provided by statements from young (ages 18–25) former addicts.

Psychotherapeutic Modalities

General Diagnostic and
Psychotherapeutic Methods
Psychotherapy

1032. Psychotherapy. 25 min, color, 16 mm, 1977. Order Source: ECLIP and MCG-H. Rental Source: IUAVC. Rental: $19. Provides an overview of the three significant elements in the basic psychotherapy process: Providing a safe relationship for the patient, working through feelings and ideas, and developing new attitudes and patterns of behavior.

1033. Psychotherapy. 26 min, color, 1977. Source: McG-H. Distributor: UCEMC. Rental: $35. Introduction to the basic concepts and processes that underlie most psychotherapeutic techniques. Dramatizes several patient–therapist sessions to illustrate the goals of psychotherapy.

1034. Three Approaches to Psychotherapy. 16 mm, b&w, Part 1, Carl Rogers, 48 min, Part 2, Frederick Perls, 32 min; Part 3, Albert Ellis, 37 min. Source: NYUFL. Three part series depicting one patient undergoing therapy with therapists of different orientations.

Behavior Therapy

1035. Behavioral Therapy Demonstration. 32 min, color, 16 mm, 1969. Produced by the Eastern Pennsylvania Psychiatric Institute. Order Source: PSUPCR. *Showing Restricted.* Purchase: $440. Rental: $25. Dr. Joseph Wolpe demonstrates his behavioral method of therapy. Following an interview with a young woman who suffers from extreme anxiety in social situations, Dr. Wolpe identifies the situations eliciting anxiety and offers an assessment of their relative effects. The subject is given initial training in deep muscle relaxation, and during relaxation her reactions to imaginary anxiety-eliciting situations are tested.

1036. Broad Spectrum Behavior Therapy in a Group. 29 min, b&w, 16 mm, 1969. Produced by A Lazarus, MD, J Van Vlack. Order Source: PSUPCR. Showing Restricted. Purchase: $410. Rental: $15.50. Similarities and differences between conventional group psychotherapy and Lazarus' brand of group behavior therapy.

Client-centered Therapy

1037. Dialogues: Dr. Carl Rogers, Part 1. 49 min, color, 1971. Source: MACMFL. Distributor: UCEMC. Rental: $34. Wide-ranging interview with the psychologist, developer of client-oriented therapy and a founder of the human potential movement.

Confrontation Therapy

1038. Come Out, Come Out, Whoever You Are. 50 min, b&w, 16 mm, 1971. Order Source: UCEMC. Rental: $20. Confrontation therapy with long-term mental patients.

1039. Confrontation: A nurse and a drug addict. 9 min, color, 16 mm, 1971. Source: APA. In an actual incident on a hospital ward, a white, middle class nurse, who thinks of herself as liberal, unprejudiced, and understanding, is confronted by a minority-group addict who accuses her of racism, insensitivity, and authoritarianism. The film explores the dynamics of the situation and poses some key questions about approaches and attitudes toward the drug user.

Family and Marital Therapy

1040.   Between Man and Woman. 33 min, color, 16 mm, Order Source: PFI. Everett L. Shostrom discusses various marital roles people play. Professional actors demonstrate modes of reacting.

1041.   The Enemy in Myself. 50 min, b&w, 16 mm, nd. Made by Nathan Ackerman. Order Source: NAI. Rental: $40. Composite of four interviews with a family group over a period of 1½ years.

1042.   Family Therapy with Follow-up. 62 min, b&w, kinescope, 16 mm, 1972. Made by Gerald H Zuk, PhD, Jacques Van Vlack. Order Source: EPPI. *Restricted Use.* Rental: $15 Demonstration of problems of family interaction and discussion of methods of treatment.

1043.   Hillcrest Family: Studies in Human Communication, Assessment Series. (Series of two films.) color, 16 mm, 1968. Order Source: PSUPCR. A series of four separate interviews with the Hillcrest family, which has sought psychiatric help because of problems with the children. Discussion by each psychiatrist of his views on the dynamics of the family situation with a therapist who has been working with the family. *Showings Restricted.*

Assessment Interview 1: Dr Nathan W Ackerman. 32 min. Purchase: $435. Rental: $21.00

Assessment Consultation 1: Dr Ackerman. 12 min. Purchase: $150. Rental: $11.50

Assessment Interview 2: Dr Carl A Whitaker. 31 min. Purchase $425. Rental: $21.00

Assessment Consultation 2: Dr. Whitaker. 14 min. Purchase $175. Rental: $11.50

Assessment Interview 3: Dr Don Jackson. 32 min. Purchase: $440. Rental: $21.00

Assessment Consultation 3: Dr Jackson. 11 min. Purchase: $145. Rental: $11.50

Assessment Interview 4: Dr Murray Bowen. 28 min. Purchase: $400. Rental: $19.50

Assessment Consultation 4: Dr Bowen. 16 min. Purchase $220. Rental: $14.00

1044.   Trouble in the Family. (America's Crises Series.) 90 min, 1965. Source: UCEMC.

Explores family therapy, in which the family is treated as a unit. Subjects are from a middle class New England family with typical emotional problems. Extensive use of the one-way mirror technique records the candid reactions of the family. Scenes from 9 of the 13 therapy sessions are included in this film. Dr. Nathan W. Ackerman, Prof. of Psychiatry at Columbia, discusses the techniques of family therapy.

Gestalt Therapy

1045.   Fredrick Perls and Gestalt Therapy. #1: 39 min #2: 36 min, b&w, 16 mm, two reels. Produced by E. L. Shostrom. Order Source: PFI. Comprehensive overview on Gestalt Therapy. Latest summary of Perls' theories.

1046.   In The Now. The Individual Application of Gestalt Therapy. 45 min, b&w, 16 mm, nd. Produced by James S. Simkin, Ph.D. Source: PFI. A psychotherapy training film demonstrating the principles and techniques of Gestalt Therapy with three different subjects.

1047.   Gestalt Series. The Philosophy of the Obvious. 25 min. F. Perls. Two dreams illustrating the use of dreams in Gestalt Therapy. Source: PFI.

1048.   Group Therapy. 60 min, b&w, 16 mm, 1972. Order Source: GPF. Purchase: $295. Rental: $50.

1049.   Group Therapy. 60 min, b&w, 16 mm, 1972. Source: GPF. Social, psychological, and interpersonal aspects of a group session illuminating its dynamics.

1050.   Group Psychotherapy: The Dynamics of Change. 30 min, color, 16 mm, nd. Order Source: AMAFL. Order #05721. Rental: Free. Service Charge: $10. A pscyhoanalytically oriented group therapy session portraying some of the dynamics operative in the group process.

1051.   Tuesday Group. 14 min, 16 mm. Order Source: FEIL. Purchase: $159. Rental: $17.50–$32.50. Documents a group session of the aged suffering from acute emotional and physical deterioration. Shows therapeutic group work techniques for increasing interaction within the group.

1052.   Broad Spectrum Behavior Therapy In A Group. 30 min. Arnold Lazarus. Four sequences employing different techniques. Source: PSU.

1053.   Carl Rogers Conducts an Encounter

Group. 50 min. Demonstrating phases of the group process. Source: AACD.

Hypnosis

1054. Hypnotic Behavior. 20 min, b&w, 16 mm, nd. Produced by Association Films. Order Source: NYUFL. Rental: $9.50. A psychological film on common phenomena of hypnosis demonstrating, among others, induction of trance, abnormal illusions, awakening, posthypnotic amnesia, and execution of posthypnotic suggestion.

1055. The Use of Hypnosis in Psychotherapy. 30 min, b&w, 16 mm, 1976. Produced by James R. Hodge, MD, University of Akron. Order Source: JRH. *Restricted Use*. Rental: $35 plus mailing. Gives the physician or therapist an idea of what to expect in different levels of trance and also shows what he can do to help the patient.

Psychoanalysis

1056. Psychoanalysis. 30 min, b&w, 16 mm, 1964. Order Source: IUAVC. Rental Source: IUAVC. Purchase: $250. Rental: $12.50. Offers a dramatic portion in which two Chicago psychoanalysts enact episodes from several analytic sessions. Dr. Maria Piers explains the change in the patient's attitude as the treatment progresses.

(Freudian Psychoanalysis)

1057. Ernest Jones. 30 min, b&w, 16 mm, nd. Order Source: GFL. Rental: $20 base service charge for 12 days. Interesting sidelights on Freud and psychoanalysis.

(Jungian Psychoanalysis)

1058. Carl G Jung. 32 min, b&w, 16 mm, nd. Order Source: GFL. Rental: $20 base service charge for 2 days. Jungian ideas and theories.

Psychotherapy (See also Films 1032, 1033, 1034)

1059. Psychotherapy. 25 min, color, 16 mm, 1977. Order Source: ECLIP and MCGH. Rental Source: IUAVC. Rental: $19. Provides an overview of the three significant elements in the basic psychotherapy process: Providing a safe relationship for the patient, working through feelings and ideas, and developing new attitudes and patterns of behavior.

1060. Psychotherapy. 26 min, color, 1977. Source: McG-H. Distributor: UCEMC. Rental: $35. Introduction to the basic concepts and processes that underlie most psychotherapeutic techniques. Dramatizes several patient–therapist sessions to illustrate the goals of psychotherapy.

1061. Three Approaches to Psychotherapy II. (Series in three parts.) 48 min each, color, 16 mm film & videocassette, nd. Narrators: Drs. Carl R. Rogers, Everett L. Shostrom, Arnold A. Lazarus. Distributor: PFI. Purchase: $500 each. Rental: $50.00 each. Each film includes an introduction by the therapist and a description of his method of therapy, followed by an interview with the client Kathy, and finally, a summation by the therapist of the interview.

1062. Mental Confusion in the Elderly Series. 79 min, color, 16 mm, 1978. Order Source: NYUFL. Purchase: $300. Demonstrates the clinical assessment and management techniques for working with the mentally confused elderly. Titles are: "Mental Confusion in the Elderly," "Management and Diagnosis," "Management in the Community," and "Management in hospital."

1063. Man to Man. 30 min, b&w, 16 mm, nd. Produced by the Mental Health Film Board. Order Source: NYUFL. Rental: $11. Story of Joe Fuller who takes a temporary job in a state hospital and through a deep and moving relationship with one of his patients decides to stay permanently.

Transactional Analysis

1064. Changing Life Scripts. 30 min, color, 16 mm, 1973. Order Source: UMETHC and MMM. Rental Source: IUAVC. Rental: $16.50. Presents a combination of dramatized situations and group discussions to illustrate the concept of changing one's life plans or scripts in the concept of Transactional Analysis.

1065. Games People Play: The Theory. 30 min, b&w, 16 mm, nd. Produced by NET. Order Source: NYUFL. Rental: $11. Transactional analysis explained by Eric Berne.

1066. Games People Play: The Practice. 30 min, b&w, 16 mm, nd. Produced by

NET. Order Source: NYUFL. Rental: $11. A patient analyzed by Eric Berne during a group session at Berne's home.

Case Material (See also Films 975, 976, 1014, 1015, 1021, 1024, 1063, 1067–1072, 1241, 1248)

1067. Bold New Approach. 62 min, b&w, film, 1968. Produced by Mental Health Film Board. Distributor: NYUFL. Rental: $22. A psychiatrist presents several case histories of people (men, women and children) who can be treated in a comprehensive community mental health center. Discusses inpatient and outpatient treatment, day and night hospitals, emergency services, rehabilitation services, children's services, consultation services, preventive diagnostic and evaluation services that can be offered.

1068. Dreams So Real: Three Men's Stories. 30 min, video or 16 mm color. Oren Rudavsky, 1981. Source: APA. Distributor: UIFC. Three men who are making the difficult transition from mental hospital to community life take part in an unusual art therapy project, making animated films based on their own life experiences.

1069. Character Neurosis with Depressive and Compulsive Trends in the Making: A Life History of Mary from Birth to Fifteen Years. (Film Studies on Integrated Development Series.) 40 min, b&w, silent, 16 mm, nd. Produced by Margaret E Fries, MD, Paul J Woolf, MS. Order Source: GFL. Rental: $20 base service charge for 2 days. Shows how a child with superior biological capacity and an active congenital-activity type develops a neurosis through interactions with those in her environment.

1070. The Feeling of Rejection. (Mental Mechanisms Series.) 23 min, b&w, 16 mm, nd. Produced by the National Film Board of Canada. Order Source: NYUFL. Rental: $10. Case history of a young woman who learned in childhood not to risk social disapproval by independent action.

1071. Harold—A Character Disorder in the Making From Preconception to 32 Years. (Studies on Integrated Development: Interaction Between Child and Environment.) 36 min, b&w, silent, 16 mm, 1973. Produced by Margaret E Fries, MD, Paul J Woolf, MS. Order Source: NYUFL (also GFL). Rental: $11. Unique in that predictions at 7 weeks were revalidated at 32 years regarding physically healthy, active mode of adaptation, character disorder. Predictions based on his active healthy constitution interacting with a disturbed family.

1072. The Rat Man (Notes on a Case of Obsessional Neurosis.) 50 min, b&w, 16 mm, nd. Order Source: GFL. Rental: $20 base service charge for 2 days. A movie of Freud's case. The Rat Man. (This has been presented before the British and American Psychoanalytic Association.)

Adjunct Therapies

Art Therapy

1073. Art Therapy. 11 min, color, 1981. Produced by the American Art Therapy Association. Source: PSUPCR. Rental: $17.50. Presents an introductory overview of the field and shows artwork by patients who are participating in the therapy. Professional therapists discuss the assessment and treatment of clients in mental health, mental retardation, geriatric, medical, and educational settings.

1074. Art Therapy: Beginnings. 45 min, color, 16 mm, 1972. Order Source: AATA. Documents the philosophies of four art therapies, Naumburg, Ulman, Kwiatkowska, and Kramer and how their techniques can be used in mental health.

Clinical Social Work

1075. As Sick As They Say I Am. 35 min, 1967. Source: UCEMC. Rental: $28. Unedited interview with a 24-year-old "professional patient" in the psychiatric ward of a county hospital. He has a long history of voluntary outpatient and inpatient treatment and is facing commitment to a state hospital. This kinescope, intended for use in teaching social work methods, is valuable for teaching dysfunctional aspects of the client role and ways in which agency function and organization affect direction treatment. Restricted to professional education in recognized schools and colleges. Signed agreement required.

Counseling

1076. Focusing. 30 min, color, 16 mm. Order Source: PFI. Principles of focusing in counseling are demonstrated by Dr. Eugene Gendlin, the originator of this technique.

1077. Long Valley: A Study of Bereavement. 59 min, color, 1978. Source: NYUFL. Distributor: UCEMC. Rental: $47. Shows Dr. Colin Murray Parkes, a social psychologist and expert on counseling the bereaved, as he works with doctors, clergy, social workers, and the bereaved themselves.

Dance and Movement Therapy

1078. Dance Therapy: The Power of Movement. 30 min, color, 1983. Source: UCEMC. Distributor: UCEMC. Purchase: $470/$355 Rental: $39. Five therapists work with a variety of patients, from an emotionally disturbed young girl to the residents of a geriatric nursing home.

1079. Looking For Me. 29 min, b&w, 16 mm, 1968. Order Source: UCEMC. Sale: $375 film/$265 videotape. Rental: $28. Therapeutic benefits of patterned movement in working with three types of pupils-normal preschool children, emotionally disturbed children, autistic children and a group of adult teachers.

1080. Moving True. 19 min, b&w, 16 mm, 1973. Produced by Betty Shapiro. Order Source: CARC Purchase: $225. Rental: $40. The rationale and technique of dance therapy.

Community Mental Health

1081. Chain of Care. 38 min, b&w, 16 mm, 1962. Produced by MHFB. Order Source: NYUFL. Rental: $12.50. Shows patients in the various institutions that make up a coordinated statewide program of prevention, treatment, aftercare, and rehabilitation of mental illness.

1082. Community Mental Health. 32 min, b&w, 16 mm, nd. Produced by MHFB. Order Source: NYUFL. Rental: $11. Dramatizes the public health approach of the mental health center that is concerned with prevention and mental health promotion as well as treatment of disease.

1083. One Day a Week. 33 min, b&w, 16 mm, nd. Produced by CMC. Order Source: NYUFL. Rental: $12. The experience of a community psychiatrist on his visit to the Rodman Job Corps Center in Massachusetts, where he offers mental health consultation.

Teaching and Supervision

1084. Interstaff Communications. (Psychodrama in Group Process Series.) 42 min, b&w, 16 mm, nd. Produced by Dr. Ira Pauly (NYU). Order Source: NYUFL. Purchase: $335. Rental: $24. The use of psychodrama techniques to facilitate interstaff communications between a psychiatrist in charge of a psychiatric unit and his chief resident.

Film Sources:

AACD: American Association for Counseling and Development, 5999 Stevenson Ave, Alexandria, VA 22304. 703-823-9800

AATA: American Art Therapy Association, Business Office, 302 E Joppa Rd., Apt. 1902, Towson, MD 21204. 301-528-4147

APG: American Personnel and Guidance Association Film Department, 1607 New Hampshire Avenue N.W., Washington, D.C. 20009

AMAFL: American Medical Association Film Library, c/o Association Films, Inc., 600 Grand Avenue, Ridgefield, NJ 07657

APA: American Psychiatric Association, Hospital and Community Psychiatry Service, 1400 K Street, N.W., Washington, D.C. 20005

BSML: Behavioral Sciences Media Lab, Neuropsychiatric Institute, University of California, 760 Westwood Plaza, Los Angeles, CA 90024. 213-825-4321

CAROUF: Carousel Film & Video, 241 E 34 St. Rm 304, New York, NY 10016. 212-683-1660

CARC: Creative Arts Rehabilitation Center, 251 W 51 Street, New York, NY 10019. 212-246-3113

CONFC: Concord Films Council Ltd., 201 Felixstowe Road, Ipswich, Suffolk 1P3 9BJ, England

EPPI: Audio Visual Media, Eastern Pennsylvania Psychiatric Institute, Henry Ave & Abbottsford Avenue, Philadelphia, PA 19129

FEIL: Edward Feil Productions, 4614 Prospect Avenue, Cleveland, OH 44103

FINC: Films Incorporated, 733 Greenbay Road, Wilmette, Ill. 60691

GFL: Gittleson Film Library, The Chicago Institute for Psychoanalysis, 180 Michigan Avenue, Chicago, Ill 60601

GPF: Gibson Film Productions Ltd., 112–116 Courteney Pl, Wellington, New Zealand

HIETR: Hospice Institute for Education, Training, and Research, Inc., 765 Prospect Street, New Haven, CT 06511. 203-481-6231

INUAVC:
IUAVC: Indiana University, Audio-Visual Center, Bloomington, In 47405

JRH: James R. Hodge, MD., West Market Street, Akron, OH 44313

MHTFP: Mental Health Training Film Program, Harvard Medical School, 58 Fenwood Road, Boston, MA 02215

MOBIUS: MOBIUS International Box 315 Franklin Lakes, NJ 07417. 201-891-8240

NAI: Nathan Ackerman Institute, 149 E 78 Street, New York, NY 10021. 212-879-4900

NAVC:
NAC: National Audiovisual Center, Customer Services PJ, 8700 Edgeworth Dr, Capitol Heights, MD 20743-3701

NYUFL: New York University Film Library, 26 Washington Pl., New York, NY 10003. 212-598-6110

PFI: Psychological Films, Inc., 110 North Wheeler St, Orange, CA 92666. 714-639-4646

PMF: Parents Magazine Films, Inc., 685 Third Ave., New York, NY 10017. 212-878-8700

POLMYR: Polymorph Films, 118 South St., Boston, MA 02111. 617-542-2004

PSU: Pennsylvania State University,

PSUPCR: Psychological Cinema Register, 17 Willard Building, University Park, PA 16802

RP
RESPRC: Research Press, Box 317760, Champaign, IL 61820. 217-352-3273

UCEMC: University of California, Extension Media Center, 2223 Fulton St., Berkeley, CA 94720

UCLANI: University of California, Neuropsychiatric Institute, 2025 Zonal Ave., Los Angeles, CA 9003. 213-224-7044

UMTVC: University of Michigan, Audio-Visual Education Center, 416 Fourth St., Ann Arbor, MI 48109. 313-764-5360

USNIH: Department of Health, Education and Welfare, Public Health Service, National Institutes of Health

WPIC: Western Psychiatric Institute and Clinic-Audiovisual Center, 3811 O'Hara St., Pittsburgh, PA 15213, (Institutional Membership Available)

AUDIOTAPES

Most of the available audiotapes are in the convenient form of cassettes. These are distributed by a number of companies designated in the descriptions of the audiotapes in this section. Several companies issue cassettes regularly to subscribers. For example, Audio-Digest Foundation, Glendale, California (a subsidiary of the California Medical Association) has provided an annual subscription service on the subject of Psychiatry. Practical Review in Psychiatry, Educational Reviews, Inc. Birmingham, Alabama, has sent out a monthly cassette reviewing important articles in the current psychiatric literature. Activities at annual meetings of the various professional disciplines are often available on audio-cassettes, e.g. the American Psychiatric Association and the continuing education programs of certain institutions. Virtually thousands of audiocassettes are obtainable, but only representative samples can be included in this volume mostly on the different diagnostic syndromes and the psychotherapeutic modalities. Catalogs and complete lists of audiocassettes may be acquired from the various distributors.

History (See also Tapes 1195, 1216, 1219)

1085. Personal Perspectives on the Masters: Freud, Jung Adler, Margo Adler, Sophie Freud, Dieter Bauman (Conservation Hours), 1986. Audiocassette. Source: MHEF. Purchase $9.50.

Field of Psychiatry

Child and Adolescent Psychiatry (See also Tapes 1088, 1103, 1109, 1112, 1113, 1115, 1131, 1133, 1141, 1182, 1212).

1086. Children's Reactions to Object Loss (Part I), nd. 3 cassettes. Price: $33. Source: TEI. Moderator: Aaron H. Esman, MD. Overview: The Place of Object Loss in Development (Fred Pine, PhD). Children's Reactions to the Death of a Parent (Mrs. Ema Furman) Preparing Children to Cope with Loss and Grief (Robert A. Furman, MD).

1087. Children's Reactions to Object Loss (Part II), 1978. 3 cassettes. Source: TEI. Price: $33. Moderator: Aaron H Esman, MD. The Effects of Divorce on Children (Virginia Lawson Clower, MD); The Influence on Child Development of a Psychotic Parent (E James Anthony, MD.); Case Presentation (Henri Parens, MD).

Psychiatric Emergencies

1088. Adolescent Suicide, 1985. Speaker: Linda M. Rusch, RN, MS, CS. 1 cassette. Source: CF. Purchase: $7.50.

1089. Clinician Suicide: Detection and Prevention-Biologic and Genetic Aspects of Suicide, 1985. Speaker: Alec Roy, MD. 1 cassette. Source: CF. Purchase: $7.50.

1090. Countertransference in Working with Suicidal Patients, 1985. Speaker: Anita Mozgal, RN, BS. 1 cassette. Source: CF. Purchase: $7.50.

1091. New Concepts in Assessing and Treating Suicide Risk, 1985. Speaker: William M Hom, MD. 1 cassette. Source: CF. Purchase: $7.50.

1092. Suicide in the Elderly, 1985. Speaker: Nancy J Osgood, PhD. 1 cassette. Source: CF. Purchase: $7.50.

1093. Suicide Risk in Outpatient Therapy of Depressed Patients, 1985. Speaker: Harold L Goldberg, MD. 1 cassette. Source: CF. Purchase: $7.50.

1094. Therapeutic Approaches to the Suicidal Patient, 1985. Speaker: Ari Kiev, MD. 1 cassette. Source: CF. Purchase: $7.50.

1095. Treating Survivors: The Aftermath of Depression/Suicide, 1985. Speaker: Karen A Maxim, RN, MD. 1 cassette. Source: CF. Purchase: $7.50.

Field of Psychiatric Nursing

1096. The Nurse Psychotherapist and the Hospitalized Patient, 1986. Speaker: Suzanne Lego, RN, CS, PhD. 1 cassette. Source: CF. Purchase: $7.50.

1097. Therapeutic Techniques for Brief Encounters with the Hospitalized Patient, 1986. Speaker: Suzanne Lego, RN, CS, PhD. 1 cassette. Source: CF. Purchase: $7.50.

Forensic Issues

1098. Relevant Forensic Issues: Who's Fault Is It? 1985. Speaker: Jonas R. Rappeport, MD. 1 cassette. Source: CF. Purchase: $7.50.

Mental and Emotional Disorders (See also Tapes 1093, 1158, 1159, 1261, 1262, 1265, 1273)

Affective Disorders

1099. The Bipolar Self, 1979. 3 cassettes. Source: TEI. Price: $33. Ernest S Wolf, MD, Sheldon J Meyers, MD, Michael F Basch, MD, Paul H Ornstein, MD, Heinz Kohut, MD, Robert S Wallerstein, MD.

1100. Depression: Diagnosis and Treatment Update, 1983. Speaker: Samuel Gershon, MD. 1 cassette. Source: CF. Purchase: $7.50.

1101. Special Problems in the Psychotherapy of Depression (Part I), nd. 3 cassettes. Source: TEI. Price: $33. Moderator: Rebecca Z Solomon, MD, Hartford, CT. The Diagnosis of Depression from a Contemporary Psychoanalytic Perspective (Otto F Kernberg, MD) Psycho-dynamics of Depression (Stuart S Asch, MD, New York.) Treatment of Pathologic Reactions to Death (Vanik D Volkan, MD, Charlottesville, VA).

1102. Special Problems in the Psychotherapy of Depression (Part II), 1980. 3 cassettes. Source: TEI. Price: $33. Moderator: Rebecca Z Soloman, MD, Hartford, CT. Issues in the Treatment of the Depressed Woman (Malkah T Notman, MD, Boston.) Problems in the Psychotherapy of the Older Patient (Stanley H Cath, MD, Belmont, MA.) A Technique for the Treatment of Depression in the Physically Ill (Milton Viederman, MD, New York.).

1103. Child and Adolescent Depression: Clinical Diagnosis and Treatment Update, 1987. Speaker: Derek H Miller, MD. 1 cassette. Source: CF. Purchase: $7.50.

Alcoholism (See also Tape 1144)

1104. Alcohol and Family Violence, 1982. Speaker: Riley Regan, MSW, MH. 1 cassette. Source: CF. Purchase: $7.50.

1105. Alcoholism and the Elderly, 1985. Speaker: Sheldon Zimberg, MD. 1 cassette. Source: CF. Purchase: $7.50.

1106. Behavioral Therapy and Alcoholism: Clinical Approaches, 1983. Speaker: Terrence Wilson, PhD. 1 cassette. Source: CF. Purchase: $7.50.

Anxiety Disorders (See also Tapes 1156, 1157, 1257, 1272)

1107. Behavior Therapy for Anxiety, 1986. Speaker: Kenneth S Mathisen, PhD. 1 cassette. Source: CF. Purchase: $7.50.

1108. Cognitive Therapy for Anxiety, 1986. Speaker: Arthur Freeman, EdD. 1 cassette. Source: CF. Purchase: $7.50.

1109. Differential Diagnosis and Treatment of Childhood Anxiety, 1986. Speaker: Harold S Koplewicz, MD. 1 cassette. Source: CF. Purchase: $7.50.

1110. Differential Diagnosis and Treatment of Geriatric Anxiety, 1986. Speaker: Fred B Charatan, MD. 1 cassette. Source: CF. Purchase: $7.50.

1111. Newer Medication Strategies for Anxiety: The Pros and Cons, 1986. Speaker: R. Bruce Lydiard, PhD, MD. 1 cassette. Source: CF. Purchase: $7.50. (See also tapes 230, 231, 329, 344)

Behavioral Disorders (See tape 1438)

Child Abuse

1112. Evaluation and Treatment of Sexually Abused Children, 1986. Speaker: Paul L Adams, MD. 1 cassette. Source: CF. Purchase: $7.50.

1113. Childhood Sexual Abuse: Ramifications Through Adulthood, 1986. Speaker: Ronnie Zielenski. 1 cassette. Source: CF. Purchase: $7.50.

Disabilities

1114. Emotional Help for the Hearing Impaired, 1986. Speaker: Howard Dickman, PhD. 1 cassette. Source: CF. Purchase: $7.50.

1115. Therapeutic Techniques with Learning Disabled Children, 1986. Speaker: Harold Lubin, MD. 1 cassette. Source: CF. Purchase: $7.50.

1116. Blindness: The Psychiatric Aspects of Disability, 1986. Speaker: David W Hartman, MD. 1 cassette. Source: CF. Purchase: $7.50.

Dissociative Disorders

1117. The Psychophysiology of Multiple Personality, 1986. Speaker: Frank W Putnam, MD. 1 cassette. Source: CF. Purchase: $7.50.

Eating Disorders (See also Tapes 1148, 1188)

1118. Anorexia Nervosa: Theory and Therapy—A New Look at an old Problem, nd. 3 cassettes. Source: TEI. Price: $33. Pietro Castelnuouo-Tedesco, MD; Barton J Blinder, MD, Martin A Ceaser, MD, Mark J Gehrie, PhD, C Philip Wilson, MD, John Hitchcock, MD, Stephen E Risen, MD.

1119. Anorexia Nervosa and Bulima: Clinical Update, 1987. Speaker: William J Swift, MD. 1 cassette. Source: CF. Purchase: $7.50.

1120. Anorexia Nervosa—Cause, Diagnosis, and Treatment, 1980. Speaker: Arthur Crisp, MD. 1 cassette. Source: CF. Purchase: $7.50.

1121. Behavioral Treatment of Anorexia Nervosa and Obesity, 1980. Speaker: Kelly Brownell, PhD. 1 cassette. Source: CF. Purchase: $7.50.

1122. Common Features of Anorexia Nervosa and Adolescent Obesity, 1980. Speaker: Hilde Bruch, MD. 1 cassette. Source: CF. Purchase: $7.50.

1123. Panel A: Compulsive Eating-Obesity and Related Phenomena, 1985. 3 cassettes. Source: TEI. Price: $33. Pietro Castelnuovo-Tedesco, MD, Lawrence Deutsch, MD, Ira L Mintz, MD, Christopher V Rowland, MD, C Phillip Wilson, MD, Stephen L Post, MD, Lynn W Reiser, MD.

Organic Mental Disorders (See also Tape 1258)

1124. A Clinical Overview and The Staging of Alzheimer's Disease, 1984. Speaker: Barry Reisberg, MD. 1 cassette. Source: CF. Purchase: $7.50.

1125. Behavioral Manifestations and Other Neurologic Signs of Alzheimer's Disease, 1984. Speaker: Richard Mayeux, MD. 1 cassette. Source: CF. Purchase: $7.50.

1126. Drug Strategies Treating Alzheimer's Disease, 1986. Speaker: Gary Meneilly, MD. 1 cassette. Source: CF. Purchase: $7.50.

1127. Neuropsychological Testing Aspects of Dementia, 1984. Speaker: Marilyn S Albert, PhD. 1 cassette. Source: CF. Purchase: $7.50.

1128. The Differential Diagnosis of Dementia: Clinical Evaluation and Treatable Dementias, 1984. Speaker: William R Dublin, MD. 1 cassette. Source: CF. Purchase: $7.50.

Personality Disorders (See also Tapes 1149, 1240, 1253)

1129. DSM-III Personality Disorders: Diagnosis and Treatment. Allen Frances. 4 cassettes. Source: BMA. Purchase: $50.

1130. Borderline Personality Disorders: Research Issues and New Empirical Findings, nd. 3 cassettes. Source: TEI. Price: $33. Philip S Holzman, PhD, Arnold M Cooper MD, John E Gunderson, MD, Gerald L Klerman, MD, J Christopher Perry, MD.

1131. Issues in Psychoanalytic Treatment of a Borderline/Severely Neurotic Child, nd. 3 cassettes. Source: TEI. Price: $33. Peter Blos, Jr, MD, Jack Novick, PhD, Henri Parens, MD, Alan Zients, MD,

Robert Galatzer-Levy, MD, Mr. Steven Marans.

1132. Borderline Personality Disorders: Research Issues and New Empirical Findings, nd. 3 cassettes. Source: TEI. Price: $33. Philip S Holzman, PhD, Arnold M Cooper, MD, John E Gunderson, MD, Gerald L Klerman, MD, J Christopher Perry, MD.

1133. The Borderline and Severely Neurotic Child, nd. 3 cassettes. Source: TEI. Price: $33. Peter Blos, MD, Mr. Morton Chethik, Paulina F Kernberg, MD, Fred Pine, PhD, Robert M Galatzer-Levy, MD.

1134. Clinical Diagnosis of Pathological Gambling, 1983. Speaker: Rena Nora, MD 1 cassette. Source: CF. Purchase: $7.50.

1135. Current Clinical Treatment of Pathological Gamblers, 1983. Speaker: Robert L Custer, MD. 1 cassette. Source: CF. Purchase: $7.50.

1136. Shyness. What Is It? What To Do About It? PG Zimbardo. 1 cassette. Source: BMA. Purchase: $12.50.

Schizophrenic Disorders (See also Tapes 1168, 1263, 1264)

1137. The Diagnosis of Schizophrenia, 1985. Speaker: Robert Cancro, MD. 1 cassette. Source: CF. Purchase: $7.50.

Sexual Life Styles and Disorders (See also Tapes 1171, 1173)

1138. Toward the Further Understanding of Homosexual Men, nd. 3 cassettes. Source: TEI. Price: $33. Richard A Isay, MD, Richard C Friedman, MD, Stanley A Leavy, MD, Robert J Stoller, MD.

1139. Toward the Further Understanding of Homosexual Women, nd. 3 cassettes. Source: TEI. Price: $33. Adrienne P Applegarth, MD, Martha Kirkpatrick, MD, Robert J Stoller, MD, Carol Nadelson, MD, Abby Wolfson, PhD.

Sleep/Wake Disorders

1140. Sleep, Dreams and Nightmares: A Panel in Honor of Charles Fisher on his 75th Birthday, nd. 6 cassettes. Source: TEI. Price: $66. Ernest Hartmann, MD, Milton Kramer, MD, E. James Anthony, MD, Charles Fisher, MD, Philip S Holzman, PhD, Howard Shevrin, PhD, Rosalind Cartwright, PhD, Ramon Greenberg, MD.

Substance Abuse (See also Tapes 1150, 1153, 1188)

1141. Clinical Recognition and Treatment of Adolescent Addictions, 1987. Speaker: Pasquale Sarglotto, MEd. 1 cassette. Source: CF. Purchase: $7.50.
1142. Cocaine Abuse-Current and Innovative Treatments, 1985. Speaker: Herbert D Kleber, MD. 1 cassette. Source: CF. Purchase: $7.50.
1143. Cocaine Compulsion. Speakers: David E Smith, Lester Grinspoon. Audiocassette. Vol. 16, February, 1987. Source: ADF. Purchase: $138/yr annual subscription for series.
1144. Current Developments in the Diagnosis and Clinical Treatment of Alcohol Syndromes, 1982. Speaker: Barton A Harris, MD. 1 cassette. Source: CF. Purchase: $7.50.
1145. Drugs in the Workplace, 1984. Speaker: Mark S Gold, MD. 1 cassette. Source: CF. Purchase: $7.50.

Miscellaneous (See 1194, 1274)

Psychotherapeutic Modalities

General Diagnostic and Psychotherapeutic Methods (See also Tapes 1216–1241)

Behavior Therapy (See also Tapes 1106, 1107, 1121, 1155, 1190, 1220)

1146. The Basics of Behavior Analysis and Therapy. Joseph Wolpe (Workshop), 1986. Audiocassette. Source: MHEF. Purchase: 2 tapes $19.
1147. Behavioral Therapy for Medical Illnesses, 1986. Speaker: Philip G Levendusky, PhD. 1 cassette. Source: CF. Purchase: $7.50.
1148. Behavioral Techniques With Eating Disorders: What's Working? 1986. Speaker: Kelly D Brownell, PhD. 1 cassette. Source: CF. Purchase: $7.50.
1149. Borderline Personality Disorder: Behavioral Modification, 1986. Speaker: R Mac Turner, PhD. 1 cassette. Source: CF. Purchase: $7.50.

1150. Relapse Prevention and Addiction: Behavioral Approaches, 1986. Speaker Frederick Rotgers, PsyD. 1 cassette. Source: CF. Purchase: $7.50.
1151. Multimodal Therapy: Is it the Best of All Worlds? Arnold Lazarus (Workshop), 1986. Audiocassette. Source: MHEF. Purchase: 2 tapes $19.
1152. Multimodal Therapy: Current Concepts and Techniques, 1986. Speaker: Arnold A Lazarus, PhD. 1 cassette. Source: CF. Purchase: $7.50.
1153. Multimodal Training Aids for Controlling Smoking, Tension Headaches, and Insomnia. AA Lazarus. 3 cassettes (121 min). Source: BMA: Purchase: $40.

Client-Centered Therapy (See also Tape 1224)

1154. The Client-Centered Approach. Carl Rogers, Ruth Sanford (Workshop). 1986. Audiocassette. Source: MHEF. Purchase: 2 tapes $19.

Cognitive Therapy (See also Tape 1108)

1155. Cognitive Behavior Theory Series. 1 audiocassette. Distributor: BMA. Subject experts discuss the therapy, research, and case examples of common behavior problems.
1156. Cognitive Therapy of Anxiety. Aaron Beck, Stowe Hausner (Workshop), 1986. Audiocassette. Source: MHEF. Purchase: 2 tapes $19.
1157. Cognitive Therapy of Anxiety and Panic Disorders. First Inverview with Aaron T Beck, MD, nd. 58 min, 1 cassette, Cat. #287403. Source: BMA. Purchase: $12.50. In cognitive therapy, the initial interview is crucial, because the therapist attempts both to complete the diagnosis and to begin the process of change. Aaron T. Beck demonstrates his technique in beginning to treat an otherwise successful patient for debilitating panic attacks. By the end of the interview, he has made significant progress in helping the patient overcome her anxiety about social situations and her misinterpretation of physiological sensation.
1158. Cognitive Therapy of Depression. Aaron Beck, Stowe Hausner (Program No. L330), 1986. Audiocassette. Source: MHEF. Purchase: 2 tapes $19.

1159. Cognitive Therapy of Depression: Live Demonstration of Interview Procedures, nd. Speakers: Aaron T Beck, MD, Jeffrey E Young, MD. 56 min, 1 cassette. Cat. #2837. Source: BMA. Purchase: $12.50. This audio-program offers a rare opportunity to listen in as Beck works with a depressed patient. His sensitive intervention to overcome the patient's feelings of futility demonstrate the fundamental cognitive techniques. Commentary by Dr. Beck's colleague, Jeffrey Young, reveals the dynamics of the session.

1160. New Directions for Cognitive Therapy, 1985. Speaker: Arthur Freeman, EdD. 1 cassette. Source: CF. $7.50.

Existential Analysis and Therapy

1161. Existential-Humanistic Psychotherapy. James Bugental (Program No. L330), 1986. Audiocassette. Source: MHEF. Purchase: 2 tapes $19.

1162. Existential Psychotherapy. Ronald Laing (Live Demonstrations), 1986. Audiocassette. Source: MHEF. Purchase: $9.50.

Family and Marital Therapy (See also Tapes 1219, 1230, 1231)

1163. Family Therapy, 1985. Speaker: Carl S Whitaker, MD. 1 cassette. Source: CF. Purchase: $7.50.

1164. Family Systems Therapy. Murray Bowen (Program No. L330), 1986. Audiocassette. Source: MHEF. Purchase: 2 tapes $19.

1165. Strategic Family Therapy. 1986. Invited Address by Cloe Madanes (P. Watzawick, Disc). Audiocassette. Source: MHEF. Purchase: $9.50.

1166. My Many Voices: Personal Perspectives on Family Therapy. Invited Address by Salvador Minuchin (Zerka Moreno, Disc), 1986. Audiocasette. Source: MHEF. Purchase: $9.50.

1167. Using One's Own Personal Life Experience and Values in the Therapy of the Families of Others, 1984. Speaker: Harry Aponte, ACSW. 1 cassette. Source: CF. Purchase: $7.50.

1168. Family Therapy and Schizophrenia-Historical and Clinical Concepts, 1985. Speaker: Christian Beels, MD. 1 cassette. Source: CF. Purchase: $7.50.

1169. American Family: Current Perspectives. Six cassettes (60 min each). Distributor: HUPR. Purchase: $49.50. Presents well-known Harvard University faculty such as Robert Coles, Mary J. Bain and Robert S. Weiss from the disciplines of psychology, sociology, anthropology, business, history, education and medicine, discussing their own views of the changing structure and position of the contemporary American family in society.

1170. Contemporary Marriage: Challenge in Couple Therapy, 1986. Speaker: Daniel Goldberg, PhD. 1 cassette. Source: CF. Purchase: $7.50.

1171. Treatment of Inhibited Sexual Desire: A Couple's Perspective, 1986. Speaker: Gerald R Weeks, PhD. 1 cassette. Source: CF. Purchase: $7.50.

1172. Treating the Remarried, Those Living Together, and Their Families, 1984. Speaker: Clifford J Sager, MD. 1 cassette. Source: CF. Purchase: $7.50.

1173. Treating Couples with Intimacy and Sexual Problems, 1986. Speaker: David Treadway, PhD. 1 cassette. Source: CF. Purchase: $7.50.

1174. The Fear of Intimacy, 1986. Speaker: Laurie Klein Evans, MSW. 1 cassette. Source: CF. Purchase: $7.50.

1175. Perspectives on Deterioration in Marital Psychotherapy, 1986. Speaker: Daniel Goldberg, PhD. 1 cassette. Source: CF. Purchase: $7.50.

1176. Helping Couples Change, 1986. Produced by: Dr. Richard B Stuart. Set of 4 cassettes and 16-page *Practitioner Manual* in vinyl album. Source: RP. Purchase: $50.00/set. Tape 1—Social Learning Strategies for Marital Therapy; Tape 2—Clinical Demonstrations of a First Interview; Tape 3—Getting Your Marital Therapy off on the Right Foot; Tape 4—Client Guide for Problem Solving after Treatment. This noteworthy addition to the clinical literature amplifies basic concepts in the Stuart text. Cassettes 1 and 2 are designed for practioners, while cassettes 3 and 4 are for direct client use. The accompanying *Practitioner's Manual* contains detailed examples of evaluation and recordkeeping instruments.

1177. Divorce Mediation, 1986. Speaker: John Haynes, EdD. 1 cassette. Source: CF. Purchase; $7.50.

Group Psychotherapy (See also Tapes 1230, 1231)

1178. Supervision in Group Psychotherapy. Robert Goulding (Workshop), 1986. Audiocassette. Source: MHEF. Purchase: 2 tapes $19.

1179. Demonstration–Discussion Group: Starting a Psychotherapy Group for Couples. I. Alger. Source: AGPA. Purchase: 2 tapes, $20.

1180. Current Research in Group Therapy. E M Kahn, A Beck, L Peters, J Connelly, W Piper, L Greene, D Muth, J Rosenkrantz, V Tschuschke, J Oehler, L Braaten. Source: AGPA. Purchase: 2 tapes, $20.

1181. The Contribution of the Therapist in Group Therapy: Personal Resources, Interpretation and Leadership Behavior. N Edwards, A Yassky, S Scheidlinger, D Cooper, L Phipps, T Zastowny. Source: AGPA. Purchase: 2 tapes, $20.

1182. Group Psychotherapy with Adolescents. D Halperin, R Hochstedler, F Jozitis, M Sugar. Source: AGPA. Purchase 2 tapes, $20. Demonstration-Discussion Group- Understanding Family Life Cycles: Treatment Implications, A Serrano, J Zilbach. Source: AGPA. Purchase: 2 tapes, $20.

1183. A Group Psychotherapy Session-Four Psychotherapeutic Approaches. M Yeager, A Alonso, R Goulding, H Kibel, W Stone. Source: AGPA. Purchase: 2 tapes, $20.

1184. Anger Across the Ages: Group Therapy with Acting Out/Aggressive Clients from Adolescents to Elderly. R Ebert, C Atchison, M Hollander, K Katz, D McMurtry, N Neiberg. Source: AGPA. Purchase: 2 tapes, $20.

Hypnosis

1185. Introducing Hypnosis in Psychotherapy. A Gaito. 2 cassettes, 1986. Source: MHEF. Purchase: $19.

1186. Self-transformation Through the New Hypnosis. DL Araoz. 4 cassettes, 153 min. Source: BMA. Purchase: $50.

1187. Ericksonian Hypnotherapy. Jeffrey K Zeing (Program No. L330), 1986. Audiocassette, Source: MHEF. Purchase: 2 tapes $19.

1188. Ericksonian Approaches to Permanent Weight Reduction and Non-smoking. B Grodner, 1986. Source: MHEF. Purchase: $9.50.

1189. Hypnosis: Diagnostic Uses and Treatment Update, 1983. Speaker: Frederick J Evans, PhD. Source: CF. Purchase: $7.50.

1190. Ericksonian Hypnotherapy/Behavior Therapy: Weight Control in Groups. E Williams, 1986. Source: MHEF. Purchase: $9.50.

1191. The Language of Hypnosis. K Thompson, D Gordon, J Zeig. 2 cassettes, 1986. Source: MHEF. Purchase: $19.

1192. Clinical Hypnosis: Brief Treatment with Restructuring and Self-Management. H Spiegel, D Spiegel. 6 cassettes (337 mins). Source: BMA. Purchase: $75.

1193. Hypnotherapy with Specific Populations. D Araoz, R Crowley, J Mills, D Corydon Hammond. 2 cassettes, 1986. Source: MHEF. Purchase: $19.

1194. Hypnotherapy with Children in a Pediatric Practice. E Baumann. 2 cassettes. Source: MHEF. Purchase: $19.

Psychoanalysis (See also Tape 1221)

1195. Psychoanalytic Classics Revisited: Problems of Psychoanalytic Technique, nd. Produced by Otto Fenichel. 3 cassettes. Source: TEI. Price: $33. Arnold M Cooper, MD., Merton M Gill, MD, Leo Rangell, MD, Arthur F Valenstein, MD. (Paper ready by Arnold M Cooper, MD).

1196. The Relationship of Models of the Mind to Clinical Work: The Structural Hypothesis, nd. 3 cassettes. Price: $33. Source: TEI. Sydney E Pulver, MD, Charles Brenner, MD, J Alexis Burland, MD, Arnold Goldberg, MD, Albert Mason, MBBS, Martin Silverman, MD, Estelle Shane, PhD.

1197. The Relationship of Models of the Mind to Clinical Work, nd. 9 cassettes. Source: TEI. Price: $99. Jacob A Arlow, MD, Charles Brenner, MD, Arnold M Cooper, MD, Arnold Goldberg, MD, Edgar Levenson, MD, Robert Michels, MD, Arnold H Modell, MD, Sydney E Pulver, MD, William J Richardson, PhD, Arnold Rothstein, MD.

1198. Panel D: The Relationship of Models of the Mind to Clinical Work-Object Relations Theory, nd. 3 cassettes. Source: TEI. Price: $33. Robert Michels, MD, Otto F Kernberg, MD, Allan Compton, MD, Arnold H Modell, MD, Calvin F Settlage, MD, Ernest S Wolf, MD, John M Oldham, MD.

1199. Contemporary Problems of Psychoanalytic Technique, nd. 3 cassettes. Source: TEI. Price: $33. Harold P Blum, MD, Richard C Simons, MD, Mark Kantzer, MD, Leo Rangell, MD, Leo Stone, MD.

1200. The Relationship Between Psychoanalytic Theory and Technique, 1982. 3 cassettes. Source: TEI. Price: $33. Robert S Wallerstein, MD, Arnold D Richards, MD, Otto F Kernberg, MD, Paul H Ornstein, MD, Leo Rangell, MD.

1201. The Changing Vistas of Transference: The Effect of Developmental Concepts on the Understanding of Transference, 1981. 3 cassettes. Source: TEI. Price: $33. Morton Shane, MD, Calvin A. Colarusso, MD, Phillip J Escoll, MD, Melvin A Scharfman, MD, Calvin F Settlage, MD.

1202. Perspectives on the Superego-Part I and Part II, nd. 6 cassettes. Source: TEI. Price: $66. Arnold Rothstein, MD, Harold P Blum, MD, Charles Brenner, MD, Arnold Goldberg, MD, Otto F Kernberg, MD, Robert Michels, MD, Phyllis Tyson, PhD.

1203. The Significance of the Interpretation of Dreams in Clinical Work, 1985. 3 cassettes. Source: TEI. Price: $77. Paul A Bradlow, MD, Scott Dowling, MD, Alan J Eisnitz, MD, Philip J Escoll, MD, Robert D Gillman, MD, Wayne A Myers, MD, Joseph Nemetz, MD, Jerome D Oremland, MD, Paul H Ornstein, MD, Ethel S Person, MD, George H Pollock, MD, Leo Rangell, MD, Arnold Rothstein, MD, Martin H Stein, MD.

1204. The Significance of the Reconstruction of Trauma in Clinical Work, 1984. 9 cassettes. Source: TEI. Price: $99. Sander M Abend, MD, Harold P Blum, MD, Charles Brenner, MD, Arnold M Cooper, MD, Scott Dowling, MD., Sydney S Furst, MD, Eleanor Galenson, MD, Robert D Gillman, MD, Milton E Jucovy, MD, Joyce McDougal, D Ed, Anna Ornstein, MD, George H Pollock, MD, Sydney E Pulver, MD, Arnold Rothstein, MD.

1205. Construction and Reconstruction: Clinical Aspects, nd. 3 cassettes. Source: TEI. Price: $33. Homer C Curtis, MD, Arthur Malin, MD, Joseph D Lichtenberg, MD, Evelyne Schwaber, MD, Samuel Abrams, MD, Helen C Meyers, MD.

1206. Countertransference in Theory and Practice, 1984. 3 cassettes. Source: TEI.

Price: 33. Robert L Tyson, MD, Theodore J Jacobs, MD, Hans Loewald, MD, Harold P Blum, MD, Owen Renik, MD, Heiman van Dam, MD.

1207. Interpretation: Toward a Contemporary Understanding of the Term, nd. 3 cassettes. Source: TEI. Price: $33. Jacob A Arlow, MD, Arnold Rothstein, MD, Charles Brenner, MD, John E Gedo, MD, Roy Schafer, PhD.

1208. The Clinical Use of the Manifest Dream, nd. 3 cassettes. Source: TEI. Price: $33. Sydney E Pulver, MD, Owen Renik, MD, A Scott Dowling, MD, John E Mack, MD, Stanley R. Palombo, MD.

1209. Current Concepts of Object Relations Theory, 1977. 3 cassettes. Source: TEI. Price: $33. Mark Kanzer, MD, John E Gedo, MD, John B McDevitt, MD, Vann Spruiell, MD, Joseph D Lichtenberg, MD, William W Meissner, MD.

1210. The Technical Consequences of Object Relations Theory, nd. 3 cassettes. Source: TEI. Price: $33. Ernst A Ticho, PhD, Arnold D Richards, MD, Otto F Kernberg, MD, Selma Kramer, MD, James T McLaughlin, MD.

1211. Psychoanalytic Theories of the Self (Part I), nd. 3 cassettes. Source: TEI. Price: $33. Ernst A Ticho, PhD, Arnold D Richards, MD, William J Grossman, MD, Otto F Kernberg, MD, Leo Rangell, MD, Harold P Blum, MD.

1212. Conceptualizing the Nature of the Therapeutic Action of Child Analysis, 1978. 3 cassettes. Source: TEI. Price: $33. (Sponsored jointly with the Association for Child Psychoanalysis) Marjorie Harley, PhD, Lawrence M Sabot, MD, Samuel Abrams, MD, LeRoy J Byerly, MD, Samuel Weiss, MD, Samuel Ritvo, MD.

1213. Psychoanalysis of the Young Adult: Theory and Technique, Source: TEI nd. 3 cassettes. Price: $33. Theodore J Jacobs, MD, Sander M Abend, MD, Peter Blos, Sr, PhD, Melvin A Scharfman, MD, Samuel Ritvo, MD, Judith F Chused, MD.

1214. The Psychoanalysis of the Older Patient, nd. 3 cassettes. Source: TEI. Price: $33. George H Pollock, MD, Stanley H Cath, MD, Miss Pearl HM King, Earl J Simburg, MD, Nancy Miller, PhD.

1215. Psychoanalytic Contributions to Psychiatric Nosology, nd. Source: TEI. 3 cassettes. Price: $33. Robert S Wallerstein,

MD, Sol Altschul, MD, Robert Michels, MD, Richard C Simons, MD, Morris L Peitz, MD.

Psychotherapy (See also Tapes 1101, 1102, 1255)

1216. History of Psychotherapy. R May, C Rogers, T Szasz, G Whitaxer (Panels), 1986. Audiocassette. Source: MHEF. Purchase: $9.50.

1217. The Evolution of Psychotherapy: Future Trends (Invited Address by Lewis Wolberg (A Lazarus, Disc), 1986. Audiocassette. Source: MHEF. Purchase: $9.50.

1218. The Nature of the Psychotherapeutic Process. Invited Address by Judd Marmor (A Beck, Disc), 1986. Audiocassette, Source: MHEF. Purchase: $9.50.

1219. Psychotherapy-Past, Present and Future. Invited Address by Murray Bowen (James Masterson, Disc), 1986. Audiocassette. Source: MHEF. Purchase: $9.50.

1220. The Promotion of Scientific Psychotherapy: A Long Voyage. Invited Address by Joseph Wolpe (J Marmor, Disc), 1986. Audiocassette. Source: MHEF. Purchase: $9.50.

1221. The Evolution of the Developmental Object Relations Approach to Psychotherapy. Invited Address by James Masterson (J Haley, Disc), 1986. Audiocassette. Source: MHEF. Purchase: $9.50.

1222. The Evolution of Rational-Emotive Therapy and Cognitive Behavior Therapy, 1986. Invited Address by Albert Ellis (M Goulding, Disc). Audiocassette. Source: MHEF. Purchase: $9.50.

1223. Rogers, Kohut and Erickson: A Personal Perspective on Some Similarities and Differences, 1986. Invited Address by Carl Rogers, Ruth Sanford (M Polster, Disc). Audiocassette. Source: MHEF. Purchase: $9.50.

1224. Brief vs. Long-Term Therapy. M Goulding, J Marmor, J Masterson, P Watzlawick (Panels), 1986. Audiocassette. Source: MHEF. Purchase: $9.50.

1225. Going Behind the Obvious: The Psychotherapeutic Journey. Invited Address by Virginia Satir (E Polster, Disc), 1986. Audiocassette. Source: MHEF. Purchase: $9.50.

1226. A Feminist Perspective on Psychotherapy. Sophie Freud (Program No. L330), 1986. Audiocassette, Source: MHEF. Purchase: 2 tapes $19.

1227. Conceptualizing the Nature of the Therapeutic Action of Psychoanalytic Psychotherapy, 1978. 3 cassettes. Source: TEI. Price: $33. Robert S Wallerstein, MD, S Joseph Nemetz, Paul A Dewald, MD, Mardi J Horowitz, MD, Robert Michels, MD, Otto F Kernberg, MD.

1228. The Transference in Psychotherapy: Clinical Management (Part I), nd. 3 cassettes. Source: TEI. Price: $33. Moderator: Evelyne Schwaber, MD, Boston. Transference: An Introduction to the Concept (Robert Michels, MD, New York). A Developmental Approach to Transference: Diagnostic and Treatment Considerations (Arthur F Valenstein, MD, Boston). The Thwarted Need to Grow: Clinical-Theoretical issues on the Selfobject Transferences (Paul H Ornstein, MD, Cincinnati.)

1229. The Transference in Psychotherapy: Clinical Management (Part II), 1981. 3 cassettes. Source: TEI. Price: $33. Moderator: Evelyne Schwaber, MD, Boston. Pre-Oedipal influences in the Transference, with Particular Reference to Women (Eleanor Galenson, MD, New York.) An Interactional View of Transference (Merton M Gill, MD, Chicago.) Interpretation and Psychoanalytic Psychotherapy: A Clinical illustration (Jacob A Arlow, MD, New York)

1230. Group, Individual or Family Therapy I, M Goulding, V Satir, P Watzlawick, J Zeig (Panels), 1986. Audiocassette. Source: MHEF. Purchase: $9.50.

1231. Group, Individual or Family Therapy II, A Ellis, R Goulding, S Minuchin, Z Moreno (Panels), 1986. Audiocassette. Source: MHEF. Purchase: $9.50.

1232. Interviewing Techniques in Psychiatry, 1983. 12 sound cassettes (90 min. each): $1\frac{7}{8}$ ips + 1 guide, Prepared by McLean Hospital Facility for Continuing Education, Belmont, MA. Teaching hospital of Harvard Medical School: Audio/Visual Medical Marketing, Inc.

1233. Resistance. A Lazarus, J Masterson, E Polster, J Zeig (Panels), 1986 Audiocassette. Source: MHEF. Purchase: $9.50.

1234. Insight: Clinical Conceptualizations, 1980. 3 cassettes. Source: TEI.

Price: $33. Melvin A Scharfman, MD, KH Blacker, MD, Samuel Abrams, MD, E James Anthony, MD, Leonard L Shengold, MD, Helen H Tartakoff, MD.

1235. Paradoxical Strategies in Therapy, 1986. Speaker: Gerald R Weeks, PhD 1 cassette. Source: CF. Purchase: $7.50.

1236. Therapeutic Use of Humor. M Bowen, A Ellis, R Goulding, R Laing. (Panels). Audiocassette, 1986. Source: MHEF. Purchase: $9.50.

1237. Diagnosis and Treatment of DSM-III Personality Disorders. Audio, 4 audiocassettes and 90 page manual in Folio, 1986. Produced by Allen Frances. Source: GP. List Price: $50.

1238. Treatment Refusals: Causes and Cures, 1986. Speaker: Arnold Zeleznik. Source: 1 cassette. CF. Purchase: $7.50.

1239. Sex Role Issues in Psychotherapy, 1982. Speaker: Janet Wolfe, PhD. 1 cassette. Source: CF. Purchase: $7.50.

1240. Diagnosis and Treatment of DSM-III Personality Disorders. 1986. 4 audiocassettes and 90 page manual in Folio. Produced by Allen Frances. Source: BMA. Purchase: $50.

1241. Consultations on Neurotic Case Problems. Joseph Wolpe (Workshop). 1986. Audiocassette. Source: MHEF. Purchase: 2 tapes $19.

Short-term Therapy (See also 1192, 1224)

Strategic (Eriksonian) Therapy (See also Tape 1235)

1242. Foundations of Ericksonian Psychotherapy. H Lustig. 2 cassettes, 1986. Source: MHEF. Purchase: $19.

1243. Perspectives on Ericksonian Therapy. S Lankton. B O'Hanlon, R Havens. 2 cassettes, 1986. Source: MHEF. Purchase: $19.

1244. Ericksonian Approaches in the Treatment of Depression. 2 cassettes, 1986. Source: MHEF. Purchase: $19.

1245. Becoming an Ericksonian. H Lustig, S Rosen, C Zalaquett. 2 cassettes, 1986. Source: MHEF. Purchase: $19.

1246. Humor in Strategic Therapy. R Belson, 1986. Source: MHEF. Purchase: $9.50.

1247. Therapeutic Metaphor. D Gordon. 2 cassettes, 1986. Source: MHEF. Purchase: $19.

Case Material (See also Tape 1241)

1248. Monica: A Twenty-Five Year Longitudinal Study of the Consequences of Trauma in Infancy, nd. 5 cassettes. Source: TEI. Price: $55. George L Engel, MD, Franz K Reichsman, MD, A Scott Dowling, MD, Vivian Harway, PhD, D Wilson Hess, PhD, Milton Viederman, MD.

ADJUNCT THERAPIES

Art Therapy

1249. Combined Art Therapy and Psychotherapy: The Unique Benefits, 1983. Speakers: Francis F Kaplan, DA, ATR., Susanne Pitak, MPS. 1 cassette. Source: CF. Purchase: $7.50.

Counseling

The Family Living Series. Gerald R. Patterson, PhD & M.S. Forgatch. 1975. Part I–5 audiocassettes $49.95; Part II–3 audiocasettes $29.95. Distributor CP.

Instructing parents in skills for dealing with problems in children.

Electroconvulsive Therapy

1250. ECT: How it Works; Patient Selection, 1985. Speaker: Max Fink, MD. 1 cassette. Source: CF. Purchase: $7.50.

Milieu Therapy

1251. Developing and Maintaining the Therapeutic Milieu, 1984. Speaker: Donna Flanagan, RN, MS. 1 cassette. Source: CF. Purchase: $7.50.

1252. The Therapeutic Milieu: Therapy in a Residential Setting, 1986. Invited Address by Bruno Bettelheim (R Laing, Disc). Audiocassette, Source: MHEF. Purchase: $9.50.

1253. Milieu Issues in Treating the Borderline Patient, 1986. Speaker: Sheila Rousin Welt, RN, MS. 1 cassette. Source: CF. Purchase: $7.50.

Psychopharmacological Therapy
(See also Tape 1111)

1254. Advances in Neuroleptic Medication, 1984. Speaker: Ross J Baldessarini, MD. 1 cassette. Source: CF. Purchase: $7.50.

1255. Integrated Psychopharmacology and Psychotherapy, 1986. Speaker: David S Harnett, MD. 1 cassette. Source: CF. Purchase: $7.50.

1256. Informed Consent for Psychiatric Drug Therapy, 1985. Speaker: Joseph DeVaugh Geiss, MD 1 cassette. Source: CF. Purchase: $7.50.

1257. Medication Treatment of Phobias, 1984. Speaker: David Sheehan, MD. 1 cassette. Source: CF. Purchase: $7.50.

1258. Drug Strategies Treating Alzheimer's Disease, 1986. Speaker: Gary Meneilly, MD. 1 cassette. Source: CF. Purchase: $7.50.

1259. Prescribing for Geriatric Patients, 1985. Speaker: Carl Salzman, MD. 1 cassette. Source: CF. Purchases: $7.50.

1260. Pharmacologic Treatment of the Biologic Clock, 1986. Speaker: Charles A Czeisler, MD., PhD. 1 cassette. Source: CF. Purchase: $7.50.

1261. The Classical and Selective MAO Inhibitors, 1985. Speaker: J John Mann, MD. 1 cassette. Source: CF. Purchase: $7.50.

1262. Treatment of Psychotic/Delusional Depression, 1986. Speaker: Raymond Anton, Jr, MD. 1 cassette. Source: CF. Purchase: $7.50.

1263. Latest Developments in the Use of Anti-Psychotics, 1986. Speaker: Richard L Borison, MD, PhD. 1 cassette. Source: CF. Purchase: $7.50.

1264. Dosage Strategies in Schizophrenia, 1986. Speaker: Arthur Rifkin, MD. 1 cassette. Source: CF. Purchase: $7.50.

1265. The Usefulness of Antidepressant Plasma Levels and Cardiovascular Implications, 1985. Speaker: Alexander Glassman, MD. 1 cassette. Source: CF. Purchase: $7.50.

Relaxation

1266. Principles and Practice of Progressive Relaxation: A Teaching Primer. E Jacobson, F J McGuigan. 4 cassettes (214 min.) Source: BMA. Purchase: $50.

1267. Relaxation Training Program. T Budzynski. 3 cassettes (158 min.) Source: BMA. Purchase: $40.

1268. Relaxation Procedures. A Rappaport. 1 cassette. Source: BMA. Purchase: $12.50.

1269. Passive Muscle Relaxation. MS Schwartz, SN Haynes. 1 cassette. BMA. Purchase: $12.50.

1270. Meditation and Behavioral Self-Management. D Shapiro. 1 cassette. Source: BMA. Purchase: $12.50.

1271. Introducing Patients to Biofeedback Assisted Relaxation. 1 cassette. Source: BMA. Purchase: $12.50.

Self-help (See also Tapes 1192, 1270)

1272. Self-modification of Anxiety. Client Instructions. MR Goldfried. 1 cassette. Source: BMA. Purchase: $12.50.

1273. Combating Depression: Self-help Techniques. PM Lewinsohn. 1 cassette with instruction manual. Source: BMA. Purchase: $12.50.

1274. Self-Management Techniques for Controlling Insomnia. R Bootzin. 1 cassette with instruction manual. Source: BMA. Purchase $12.50.

1275. Auto-Induction Procedures for Relaxation. AJ Cannistraci. 1 cassette. Source: BMA. Purchase: $12.50.

AUDIOCASSETTE SOURCES

ADF: Audio Digest Foundation, 1577 E. Chevy Chase Dr., Glendale, CA 91206. (213) 245-8505 Back issue of audiocassettes are available. Twenty-four audiocassettes are sold on a two tape-per-month annual basis. Each tape bears 20 Category. 1 CMF credits.

AGPA: American Group, Psychotherapy Association, 25 East 21st Street 6th Floor, New York, NY 10010.

BMA: BMA Audio Cassettes Dept. 42, A Division of Guilford Publications, Inc, 200 Park Avenue South, New York, NY 10003. 1-800-221-3966 or (in NY) 212-674-1900

CF: Carrier Foundation, Belle Mead NJ, 08502. (201) 874-4000 ext. 4462

CP: Castalia Publishing Co. P.O. Box 1587, Eugene OR 97440

GP: Guilford Publications, 200 Park Avenue South, New York City, NY 10003. 212-674-1900

HUPR: Harvard University Press, Audiovisual Divn., 79 Garden Street, Cambridge, MA 02138. 617-495-3173

MHEF: The Milton H. Erickson Foundation, Inc., 3606 N. 24th Street, Phoenix, AR 85016. (602) 956-6196
Uncut and unedited from: The Evolution of Psychotherapy: A Conference. Phoenix Arizona, AR, December 11–15, 1985. These tapes may be purchased by professionals in health related fields with a minimum of a masters degree or graduate students of accredited programs. For quantity purchase contact the M.H.E. Foundation.

RP: Research Press, Box 3177, Dept. G., Champaign, IL 61821. 217-352-3273

TEI: Teach'em Inc., 160 E. Illinois Street, Chicago, IL 60611

VIDEOTAPES

Videotapes make excellent, if not indispensable, teaching supplements, particularly when directed by a good discussion leader. Both lay and professional audiences can benefit greatly from their use. An effort has been made to include as much information as possible about the tapes. Data for reel or tape width is indicated where it appears in producers' catalogues. Owing to lack of standardization in the industry, readers are advised to determine the compatability of desired videotape programs with existing videotape recorders in their possession. Many of the films mentioned in the previous section on films also are available in videotape format and inquiry may be made from the film distributors. In searching for a special topic please refer to the guide (Addenda Table 2, p 000). Listed videotapes as well as films and audiotapes constitute a mere sampling of the rich audiovisual resources that are increasingly becoming available to enhance training programs.

History*

1276.   Selye on Stress. Speaker: Selye, MD, PhD, DSc, 17 min, videocassette, color, nd. 3/4″ U-matic, 1/2″ Beta, 1/2″ VHS. Source: NCME. Purchase: $50. Rental: $20. The originator of the General Adaptation Syndrome updates his life work, emphasizing the clinical application of treatment based on this biological phenomenon.

1277.   The Story of Carl Gustav Jung. A 3 part series, each about 30 minutes, reviewing the early, late, and middle life of Jung, and detailing his contributions. Distributor: IV.

Mental Functioning

Conditioning and Learning (See also Videotape 1433)

Human Life Cycle

General

1278.   Maternal-Infant Bonding. Speaker: David A Kliot, M.D. 18 min, videocassette, color, nd. 3/4″ U-matic, 1/2″ Beta, 1/2″ VHS. Source: NCME. Purchase: $50. Rental: $20. Dr. Kliot explores the complex process of maternal-infant attachment. How the Leboyer "gentle birth" approach can be used in the safety of the modern delivery room.

1279.   Development of Gender Identity. 32 min, color, video, 1979. Source: BLU-HILL. Purchase: $200. Rental: $35. Dr. Betty Steiner, director of the University of Toronto's Gender Identity Clinic, defines and identifies gender identity, gender role, and gender identity confusion.

1280.   Sex Role Development 23 min. Distributor: IV.

---

* As mentioned previously the listed films on History may also be available in videotape form. Inquiry from the film distributors is recommended.

1281. And Father Makes Three: Paternal attitudes and adaptation. Edited by Dr. Clarice Kestenbaum and Dr. Llana Kochen. Videocassette, 3/4" tape or VHS, color, nd. Source: ER #42. Purchase: $300 plus postage. ER#42. This tape presents six young fathers being interviewed about various attitudes toward their newborn children and the changes fatherhood made in their lives. They discuss changes in self concept, relationship with their wives and their own parents, envy of their wives' maternal role, recollections of sibling rivalry and fantasies and expectations about their developing relationship with their children. Other programs on normal child development include:

ER#8- Child Development: the early years (30 minutes)

ER#9- Child Development: the middle years (28 minutes)

ER#10- Child Development: the adolescent girl (25 minutes)

ER#21- Mental Health Assessment Form (26 minutes)

ER#22- Child Development: the adolescent boy (22 minutes)

ER#41- Early Mother-Child Interaction (21 minutes)

Infancy and Childhood

1282. The Theory of Child Development. Speaker: Margaret Mahler, MD. 51 min, videocassette, 3/4" tape or VHS 1/2" tape. nd. Source: ER.#40 Purchase: $300 plus postage. The tape begins with a brief introduction by Dr. Mahler followed by a more elaborate introduction to Dr. Mahler's work given by Dr. John McDevitt and Dr. Anni Bergman. Following the introduction, film clips demonstrate the various phases of early child development as described by Dr. Mahler.

1283. The Psychological Birth of the Human Infant. Margaret Mahler and her coworkers present the raw data on the unfolding of the normal child's personality in interaction with the primary caretakers. 50 min. MRF.

1284. Child. A series of 30 min. tapes on child development. Part I: The first two months; Part II, 2–14 months; Part III; Part V: 4–6 years. Distributor: IV.

1285. Child Development: The Early Years. 30 min, 3/4" videotape. Produced by James

H Ryan. MD. Distributor: ER. Apply to ER for purchase information. The Electronic Textbook of Psychiatry. Accompanying script. Restricted Audience.

1286. Child Development: The Middle Years. 28 min, 3/4" videotape. Produced by James H Ryan, MD. Distributor: ER. Apply to ER for purchase information. The Electronic Textbook of Psychiatry accompanying script. Restricted Audience.

1287. Some Psychiatric Aspects of Infancy and Toddlerhood. Joseph Marcus, MD. 45 min, b&w, 1981. A brief review of research conducted in child development. Use of the Bayley Scales of Infant Development and the Ordinal Scale of Psychological Development is demonstrated. Produced with funding from the Harris Foundation and the University of Chicago Medical Center, Department of Psychiatry, 5841 S. Maryland Ave. Chicago, Ill. 60637.

Adolescence

1288. Child Development: The Adolescent Boy. 22 min, 3/4" videotape. Produced by James H Ryan. MD. Distributor: ER. Apply to ER for purchase information. The Electronic Textbook of Psychiatry accompanying script. Restricted Audience.

1289. Child Development: The Adolescent Girl. 25 min, 3/4" videotape. Produced by James H Ryan. MD. Distributor: ER. Apply to ER for purchase information. The Electronic Textbook of Psychiatry accompanying script. Restricted Audience.

Adulthood

1290. The Adult Years. 12 min, videocassette, color, 1976. Distributor: NAC. Focuses on the following concepts as they relate to the adult years: multiplicity of roles, productivity, the raising of offspring, physical and emotional changes and self-esteem. Source: NMAC.

Family and Alternate Life Styles

1291. Contracting-A Therapist's Aid to Family Counseling. 47 min, color, videocassette, 1975. Distributor: ARF. Purchase: $95. In this initial interview with a young married couple, obtaining a commitment from the spouses to work on their marital problems is a therapist's central goal.

Old Age

1292. Growing Old. Facts, myths, and treatment of aging. 16 min, Distributor: IV.
1293. Exploring Aging. 10 min, videocassette, ¾" or ½" VHS. Color, sound. 1982. Produced by Marilyn Whitley, RN, MA Source: UWP. Purchase: $125.00. The interview is ended by the interviewee giving advice to the rising health professional about care of the aged. The interview is bright and upbeat, and would best be used as an adjunct to lecture material that discussed not only the infirmities of old age, but the capabilities of America's senior population.

Dying, Death and Bereavement
(See also Tape 1358)

1294. The Grief Process: Children. Helping children cope with the death of a family member. 23 min. Distributor: IV.
1295. Living With Death: Unfinished Business. Helping the dying deal with guilt and pain. 30 min. Distributor IV.
1296. Living With Serious Illness, Death, and Bereavement. A set of programs dealing with: Part I: Cancer, Part II: Loss and Hope, Part III Coping strategies in cancer; Part IV: Emotional Issues in Terminal Illness, Part V: Support Systems, Part VI. Health Care Professionals, Part VII: The Grieving Process. Distributor: UWP.
1297. Part I: Cancer: This videocassette series presents one family's adaptive struggle in living with cancer. Candid discussions with Professor Vernon Bryant, School of Social Work, University of Washington, and his wife Anita, a psychologist, are preserved on tape based on their annual visits to classes on death and dying taught by Dr. Thomas R McCormick at the School of Medicine, University of Washington, Seattle, Washington 98195.
1298. Part 3: Coping with Cancer: Practical Strategies. 48 min, ¾" videocassette, b&w and color, sound. 1984. Purchase: $375. ½" VHS. Purchase: $365. This cassette begins with Dr. McCormick's summary of the five stages of response to a terminal illness: denial, anger, bargaining, depression, and acceptance.

Vern and Anita discuss the coping strategies they each employ to help make it through difficult times.

1299. Part 5: Support Systems: 35 min, ¾" videocassette, b&w and color, sound. 1984. Purchase: $275. ½" VHS. Purchase: $265. Dr. McCormick explores with Vern and Anita their various support systems. They discuss the mutual psychological and emotional support they feel from family, friends, the health care team, their professional work, and their religious faith.
1300. Part 7: The Grieving Process: 45 min, ¾" videocassette, b&w and color, sound. 1984. Purchase. $375. ½" VHS. Price $365. Part seven is different from the others in the series in that the edited portions are limited to the years after Vern's death. Returning to the class alone, Anita shares many of the physical, emotional, social, and psychological reactions that she has experienced, and continues to experience, during the time leading up to Vern's death and in the months following.
1301. Terminal Illness: Reactions of a Patient, His Family, Friends, and Physicians. Part I: Interviews with the Patient. 25 min, b&w, videocassettes, 1974. Produced by the Health Services Learning Resources Center and CCTV Services of the University of Washington, through the cooperation of Dr. Gary E. Leinbach, his family, friends, and physician. Source: UWP. Purchase: $125. Rental: $25.
1302. Learning to Live with Dying. 39 min, color. Distributor: NCME.
1303. Management of the Terminally Ill: The Family, with Elizabeth Kübler-Ross, MD. 16 min. Distributor: NCME.

Fields of Psychiatry

Child and Adolescent Psychiatry
(See also Tapes 1431, 1484)

1304. Child Psychiatry: Modern Approaches. Perspective in early development of mental disorders in children. 59 min. Distributor: NAC.
1305. Interviewing Children: Assessing Mental Status. G Lewis. 30 min, videocassette, b&w, 1978. Distributor: UMSM. Source: University of Maryland. An in-

tegrated approach for developing the interview skills required of health professionals in all disciplines involving the care of children, with emphasis on the clinical dynamics of the interview process. Sponsored by the Foundation for Clinical Research in Psychiatry, University of Maryland School of Medicine, Department of Psychiatry. Produced by Media Perspectives.

1306. The Challenge of Adolescent Medicine. Speakers: Robert Masland, MD, Estherann Grace, MD, Norman Spack, MD 51 min, videocassette, color, nd. 3/4″ U-matic, 1/2″ Beta, 1/2″ VHS. Source: NCME. Purchase: $50. Rental: $20. Using excerpts from six patient interviews, the telecourse faculty demonstrates and discusses the difficulties and peculiarities of dealing with adolescent patients. The problems of delayed puberty, sexual activity, and depression are emphasized and expanded upon in the accompanying workbook.

1307. Interviewing Children Sounds Easy, But . . . 24 min, 3/4″ videocassette, color, sound. 1979. Produced by Hugh J Lurie MD, and Eric Trupin, PhD. Source: UWP. Purchase $200. A psychiatrist supervisor and a medical student taking a psychiatry clerkship discuss the challenge of interviewing children during psychiatric evaluation. The tape shows, in detail, ways to begin and develop interviews with children, the steps of assessment, and specific diagnostic tools—such as kinetic family drawing and mutual storytelling—which will facilitate the evaluation process.

1308. Diagnosis of Learning Disabilities, with Dorothy L DeBoer, PhD, Lowell M Zollar, MD. 16 min, color. Distributor: NCME. Apply to NCME for subscription information.

1309. Modern Little Hans. Color, 1/2″ videocassette, 1974. Distributor: PCGC. Rental: $70. A series of excerpts and an analysis of an entire treatment sequence where the presenting problem is a patient with a fear of dogs.

1310. Playing Pretending: Spontaneous Drama with Children. Irwin, 20 min, B&W, 1973. Source: WPIC. Describes different forms of spontaneous drama (creative movement, puppetry and improvisation) with preschool and elementary school children.

1311. The Pleasure of Play. Irwin B Heisler. 12 min, videocassette, color, 1979. Source: WPIC. Demonstrates dramatic play therapy used in with handicapped preschool children learning to play and playing to learn.

1312. You Can Learn A Lot from A Lobster. The Family Puppet Interview. ES Portner. 28 min, videocassette, color, 1981. Source: WPIC. Puppets are used as a means of communication during the therapy session of a family with school-age children.

1313. Adolescent Psychiatry: Distinguishing Developmental From Pathological Behavior. Speakers: Graham B Blaine, Jr, MD, Richard Galdston, MD. 51 min, videocassette, color, nd. 3/4″ U-matic, 1/2″ Beta, 1/2″ VHS. Source: NCME. Purchase: $50. Rental: $20. Patients with common complaints and disorders of adjustment in adolescence are presented in this telecourse. Does the patient need advice and support, psychiatric treatment or hospitalization, or perhaps, greater parental tolerance?

1314. Moonstones. Produced by Donald C Fidler, MD; Jeffry J Andresen, MD; and Stanely G Alexander, University of North Carolina at Chapel Hill, 1982, revised 1985. 76 min. (two videotapes): Catalog number: 841-VI-146A/B. Source: HSC. Price: $350 for the two tapes, $175 to HSC members. Rental is available for 1–7 days for $60 per videotape, $40 per tape for consortium members. Rental videotapes are for one-time classroom use. This program dramatizes the progress of a relationship between a male psychiatry resident and his thirteen-year-old patient over a three-month period. The patient has been referred to the hospital for evaluation after raping a twelve-year-old girl at knifepoint. The program illustrates how a patient can have an emotional effect on a doctor and how the doctor-patient relationship can affect willingness to confront a patient's problems.

Psychopharmacology

1315. Consider This . . . Psychotropic Medications and Their Effects on Patients. 23 min, video, b&w, 1979. Order Source: KPC. Rental: $45. The need for frank communication between doctor and patient is demonstrated. A patient describes his experiences after not being informed of the possible side-effects of drugs prescribed to him.

1316. Interview with Yvon Dennis Lapierre, MD. Interviewer Dr. Savodnik. 30 min, videocassette, b&w, 1977. Source: WPIC. Dr. Lapierre is interviewed on the relationship between psychiatry and psychopharmacology.

Psychiatric Emergencies (See also Tapes 986, 987–990, 1414)

1317. Dealing with the Assaultive Patient. Speaker: Samuel W Perry, MD. 16 min, videocassette, nd. ¾″ U-matic, ½″ Beta, ½″ VHS. Source: NCME. Purchase: $50. Rental: $20. A number of acutely disturbed patients seen in emergency rooms is increasing at an alarming rate. A step-by-step approach to help subdue and treat the assaultive patient.

1318. Crisis Intervention Theory. 41 min, b&w, 1″ videotape, 1971. Distributor: TCL. Purchase $85. Rental: $25.

1319. Crisis Intervention Therapy. Distributor: TCL. Purchase: $85. Rental: $25. Three scenes acted out to illustrate the use of crisis intervention as therapy.

1320. Crises Intervention for the Acting-Out Patient. 30 min, color, 16 mm, video, 1980. Order Source: FAIRVGH. Purchase: $275 (16 mm), $195 (video). Rental: $45 (16 mm), $40 (video). Demonstrates techniques to handle acting-out behavior from a patient. Illustrates how to identify anxiety, offer reassurance and alternatives, and encourage communication.

1321. Suicide-Practical Diagnostic Clues. Speaker: Matthew Ross, MD. 13 min, videocassette, b&w, nd. ¾″ U-matic, ½″ Beta, ½″ VHS. Source: NCME. Purchase: $50. Rental: $20. Dr. Ross describes some signs that will help the practicing physician to spot the potential suicide.

1322. Suicide Prevention: The Physician's Role. Includes a summary by Karl Menninger, MD. Distributor: NCME. Apply to NCME for subscription information.

Forensic Issues

1323. Lawyer and the Mental Health Expert in the Courtroom. 50 min, color, video, 1980. Order Source: GUFC. Purchase: $200. Rental: $100. E.W. Beal, MD narrates taped portions of a direct and cross-examination of a psychiatrist in a child custody hearing.

Medical Sciences Other Than Psychiatry

1324. Essentials of the Neurological Examination, with Houston Merritt, MD. 50 min, ¾-in vodeotape. Produced by James H Ryan, MD. Distributor: ER. Apply to ER for purchase information. The Electronic Textbook of Psychiatry accompanying script. *Restricted Audience.*

Psychophysiology

1325. The Body Works: [The Brain]. The brain and its functions. 22 min. Distributor IV.

1326. The Brain. A series of eight 60 min tapes on brain function. Distributor: IV.

1327. The Hidden Universe: The Brain. Functions and malfunctions. 50 min. Distributor IV.

Psychopathology (See also Tapes 1365, 1367, 1415)

1328. The Brain [7]: Madness, genetic and stress factors in mental illness; pharmacologic controls. 60 min. Distributor: IV.

1329. Stress and Strain. 20 min. Distributor: IV.

1330. Stress: You Can Live With It. Describes the Type A personality. 26 min. Distributor, IV.

1331. Anxiety and Symptom Formation. 51: 46 min, ¾″ videotape. Produced by James H R MD. Distributor: ER. Apply to ER for purchase information. The Electronic Textbook of Psychiatry accompanying script. *Restricted Audience.*

Mental and Emotional Disorders

Affective Disorders

1332. Depression: More Than Just the Blues. 29 min, ½ VHS, color. Producer/Distributor PBSAV. Rental: $95. Purchase: $250. Source: WPIC. Provides a quick complete look at clinical depression for beginning level health professionals and prevention programs.

1333. Depression: A Life-Threatening Illness, Parts I and II. Speaker: F Theodore Reid, MD. Part I (50 min), in color Part II (41 min), in color, videocassettes, nd. 3/4″ U-matic. 1/2″ Beta, 1/2″ VHS. Source: NCME. Purchase: $50. Rental: $20. Eight patients who represent a spectrum of volatile depressive illnesses. Dr. Reid also demonstrates his approach to forming a no-suicide contract.

1334. The Depressed Patient. Moderator and Medical Consultant: Alan F Schatzberg, MD, Co-director, Affective Disease Program, McLean Hospital; Associate Professor, Department of Psychiatry, Harvard Medical School. 3 hrs, videocassette, 1984. Source: AMA. Purchase: $80 (Member Institutional), $100 (non-member). Rental: $40 (member), $50 (non-member). Reviews the breadth of the problem in the general population, the current concepts and terminology of depressive illness, and concepts of neurotransmission in relation to the modes of action of psychopharmacological agents. Discusses diagnosis, management and prognosis of the common types of depression.

1335. I Want To Die. Speaker: Henry D. Abraham, M.D. 19 min, videocassette, color, nd. 3/4″ U-matic, 1/2″ Beta, 1/2″ VHS. Source: NCME. Purchase: $50. Rental: $50. Physicians at a psychiatric clinic provide practical guidelines for evaluating and managing depressed and suicidal patients in your office. Diagnostic signs and symptoms to look for are highlighted.

1336. Dysthymic Disorder and Major Affective-Disorders (Case Numbers 1–4). 38 min, 1/2″ video, color, 3/4″ U-mat, 1984. Order Source: INURTS and INUAVC. Rental Source: IUAVC. Purchase: $170. Rental: $30. The cases can be used to Illustrate both contemporary and traditional ways in which the affective disorders have been subdivided.

1337. Manic-Depressive Illness. 31 min, video, b&w. New York State Psychiatric Institute, 1975. Source: APA. Ronald Fieve, MD, presents four patients who describe the high and low phases of their bipolar manic-depressive illnesses. Dr. Fieve summarizes the phenomenology of both phases and discusses the entity from a descriptive and biological standpoint. Restricted to professionals in training in the mental health sciences.

1338. Bipolar Affective Disorders (Case Numbers 5–8). 32 min, 1/2″ video, color, 3/4″ U-mat, 1984. Order Source: INURTS and INUAVC. Rental Source: IUAVC. Purchase: $170. Rental: $30. Illustrates the dramatic contrasts as patients vary between manic and depressed states.

1339. Interviewing the Manic Patient. 12 min, videocassette, 3/4″ or 1/2″ VHS. Color, sound, 1982. Source: UWP. Purchase: $150. In this simulated nurse-patient interaction, actresses engage in a verbal exchange as the "patient" is being admitted to the treatment setting. The tape would be best used as a supplement to lecture material on the subjects of management of patient behavior of mania, manipulation, and violence.

1340. Depression: Coping with Loss. 36 min, 3/4″ videotape. Produced by James H Ryan, MD. Distributor: ER. Apply to ER for purchase information. The Electronic Textbook of Psychiatry accompanying script. Restricted Audience.

1341. Depression: Retarded and Agitated Forms. 30 min, 3/4″ videotape. Produced by James H Ryan, MD. Distributor: ER. Apply to ER for purchase information. The Electronic Textbook of Psychiatry accompanying script. Restricted Audience.

1342. The Diagnosis and Treatment of Depression. (Three programs produced with the cooperation of the Council on Scientific Assembly of the American Medical Association.) (1) Masked Depression: The Interview and the Recognition and Delineation of Depression (30 min); (2) Biogenic Amine Theories of Depression (14 min); (3) Managing the Depressed Patient (34 min). Distributor: NCME. Apply to NCME for subscription information.

Alcoholism (See also Tape 1449)

1343. Alcoholism: Disease or Bad Habit? Speakers: Marc H Hollender, MD, John A Ewing, MD. 17 min, videocassette, color, nd. 3/4″ U-matic, 1/2″ Beta, 1/2″ VHS. Source: NCME. Purchase: $50. Rental $50. Whether you think of your alcoholic patient as sick or as weak-willed could have a major effect on your attitude and treatment of the individual. An exercise in examining your own prejudices and how they may compromise patient care.

1344. Early Diagnosis of Alcoholism. Speaker: Marvin A Block, MD. 24 min, videocassette, color, nd. ¾" U-matic, ½" Beta, ½" VHS. Source: NCME. Purchase: $50. Rental: $50. Dr. Block provides specific criteria by which one may judge the kind of alcoholism and the stage of the disease.

1345. Drinkers In Crisis. Speaker: Henry D Abraham, MD. 16 min, videocassette, color, nd. ¾" U-matic, ½" Beta, ½" VHS. Source: NCME. Purchase: $50. Rental: $50. The psychiatric emergency department at Mass. General. The Players: Walk-in alcoholics seeking help. The Plot: How to use an alcoholic's time of crisis to set the stage for short and long-term care.

1346. Alcoholism: A Chronic, Treatable Disease. Make the Diagnosis-Medical Consequences of Alcoholic Use—The Medical Emergency of Acute Detoxification-Psychological Effects and Approaches to Treatment. Speakers: Luther A Cloud, MD, Charles S Lieber, MD, Ernest P Noble, MD, PhD. 1 hr, videocassette, color, nd. ¾" U-matic, ½" Beta, ½" VHS. Source: NCME. Purchase: $75: Rental $50. This is a practical guide to the detection, medical consequences and treatment of alcoholism.

1347. Alcoholism: A Model of Drug Dependence. 20 min. IV.

1348. A Family Talks about Alcohol. Family coping with alcoholism. 25 min. Distributor: IV.

1349. The Young Alcoholic: A Family Dilemma. Treating teenage alcoholism. 30 min. Distributor: IV.

1350. Antabuse: A Second Chance for Choosing. 21 min. ARF.

1351. Detoxification: The Ontario Model. 25 min. ARF.

1352. Behavioral Management of Intoxicated and Disruptive Patients. 20 min. ARF.

1353. Alcoholism: Early Diagnosis and Management. Distributor: AMA.

1354. The Multiphasic Treatment of Alcoholism. Speakers: Albert N Brown-Mayers, MD, Edward E Seelye, MD, Leonard R Sillman, MD. 29 min, videocassette, color, nd. ¾" U-matic, ½" Beta, ½" VHS. Source: NCME. Purchase: $50. Rental: $20. Presenters show how residential alcoholic treatment works.

Anxiety

1355. Anxiety and Symptom Formation. 52 min, video, b&w. New York State Psychiatric Institute, 1975. Source: APA Distributor: UIFC. The subject of this videotape, part of the *Electronic Textbook of Psychiatry and Neurology* from New York State Psychiatric Institute, is a 42-year-old woman with anxiety, agoraphobic attacks, and both somatic conversion and an organic-neurological disorder. Restricted to professionals in training in the mental health sciences.

1356. The Anxious Patient. Moderator/Medical Consultant: Alan Schatzberg, MD, 3 hrs. videocassette, 1984. Source: AMA. Purchase: $110 (Member Institutional), $140 (non-member), Rental: $55 (member), $70 (non-member). Offers the clinician a sharper awareness of the ubiquitous and multiform character of anxiety; outlines the different levels of distress experienced by the anxious patient in both reality situations through intrapsychic conflicts. Reviews the most appropriate therapy for the more common presentations of anxiety, with particular attention to chemical agents and practical areas of psychological support within time constraints of daily medical practice.

1357. Phobias and Panic Disorder. 58 min. Distributor: NAC.

Behavioral Disorders (See also Tape 1438)

Bereavement

1358. Long Valley: A Study of Bereavement. 59 min, color, 1978. Source: FL. Distributor: UCEMC: Rental: $47. Shows Dr. Colin Murray Parkes, a social psychologist and expert on counseling the bereaved, as he works with doctors, clergy, social workers, and the bereaved themselves.

Child Abuse

1359. Child Abuse. Moderator and Medical Consultant, Eli H Newberger, MD, Assistant Professor of Pediatrics, Harvard Medical School, Director, Family Development Center, Children's Hospital Medical Center, Boston, Massachusetts. 3 hrs. videocassette, 1984. Source: AMA. Purchase: $40 (Member Institutional), $100 (non-member). Rental: $55 (Member), $70 (non-member). Examines the etiologic factors and manifestations of physical and psychological abuse of children. Reviews methods of clinical approach to both abused and abuser; highlights legal, social, and psychological aspects of child abuse, and emphasizes establishment of physician's leadership role as well as an effective liaison with community and social agencies in the management of child abuse.

1360.   Management of the Battered Child Syndrome. Speakers: C Henry Kempe, MD, Brandt F Steele, MD, Helen Alexander, Medical Social Worker. 18 min, videocassette, color, nd. 3/4" U-matic, 1/2" Beta, 1/2" VHS. Source: NCME. Purchase: $50. Rental: $20. Three experts offer some practical advice on coping with parents once child abuse has been diagnosed and the underlying problems identified.

Developmental Disorders (See 1499)

Disabilities (See Tapes 1308)

Eating Disorders

1361.   Anorexia Nervosa: Psychic Puzzle. Speaker: Lila E Nachtigall, MD. 17 min, videocassette, color, 3/4" U-matic, 1/2" Beta, 1/2" VHS. Source: NCME. Purchase: $50. Rental: $20. The anorexic-typically adolescent, female, and under stress. Dr. Nachtigall interviews and illustrates the management of representative patterns.

1362.   Bulimia. Presentation by Anita Stiegman of the symptomatology and health risks of bulimia, as well as coping strategies. 20 min. Distributor: RP.

1363.   Can You Treat Obesity in Children? Speaker: Platon J Collipp, MD. 18 min, videocassette, color, nd. 3/4" U-matic, 1/2" Beta, 1/2" VHS. Source: NCME. Purchase: $50. Rental: $20. Long-standing obesity, a health hazard in later life, can be stemmed in childhood and adolescence. Dr. Collipp shows how diet, group treatment, challenge and support have successfully removed 60 tons of Long Island baby fat.

1364.   Obesity and Overweight. Dietary, psychological, pharmacologic, and surgical treatment. Distributor: AMA.

Obsessive-Compulsive Disorders

1365.   Symptoms and Their Meaning. 30 min, videocassette, sd., col.; 3/4" 1980. (The Art and Science of Psychotherapy Series. The Treatment of the Obsessive Personality by Leon Salzman.) Pro-

duced by Health and Education Multimedia, Inc. Source: HEM.

1366.   The Phenomenology of Rituals, Phobias, Doubting, Magic, and Sex as a Performance. 30 min, videocassette, sd., col.; 3/4" 1980. (The Art and Science of Psychotherapy Series. The Treatment of the Obsessive Personality by Leon Salzman.) Produced by Health and Education Multimedia, Inc. Source: HEM.

1367.   Discussion of Symptoms as Pseudo-Solutions; The Psychoanalytic Approach. 30 min, 1 videocassette, sd., col.; 3/4 in. 1981. (The Art and Science of Psychotherapy Series. The Treatment of The Obsessive Personality by Leon Salzman.) Source: HEM.

Organic Mental Disorders

1368.   Dementia: A Clinical Approach. Moderator: John T Flynn, MD. Associate Professor of Clinical Medicine Cornell University Medical College. Medical Consultant: D Frank Benson, MD, Professor of Neurology School of Medicine University of Southern California. 2 hrs. videocassette, 1984. Source: AMA. Purchase: $80 (Member Institutional), $100 (non-member. Rental: $40 (member), $50 (non-member). Emphasizes that many treatable and/or curable physical and psychological diseases in the elderly produce intellectual impairment difficult to distinguish from irreversible brain disease. Encourages the early use of appropriate mental status examinations in arriving at differential diagnosis. Addresses drug therapy and social and familial factors contributing to the patient's quality of life.

1369.   Alzheimer's Disease: Clinical Recognition, Diagnosis, Staging, and Management. Speaker: Barry Reisberg, MD 60 min, videocassette, color, nd. 3/4" U-matic, 1/2" Beta, 1/2" VHS. Source: NCME. Purchase: $75. Rental: $50. In addition to demonstrating a new approach to recognizing the stages of the disease, Dr. Reisberg offers management guidelines involving the patient's family.

1370.   Living With Grace (Alzheimer's disease). 28 min, videocassette, documentary, nd. Source: UMSM. Purchase: $400. Rental: $100. Living with Grace explores the life of one woman suffering from Alzheimer's disease—her loss of memory, emotional mood swings, catastrophic reactions, and confusion. A five-month documentation presents her life at home with her caring husband, his efforts and their solutions so that their life can continue with dignity and meaning.

Pain Syndrome

1371. Pain: Mechanisms and Management. Moderator/Medical Consultant: Kathleen Foley, MD, Associate Professor of Neurology and Pharmacology, New York Hospital, Cornell Medical Center, Director, Pain Clinic Memorial Sloan-Kittering Cancer Center, New York, NY. Guest Faculty: William H Sweet, MD, DSc. DHc. Professor of Surgery, Emeritus, Harvard Medical School, Whilom Chief of Neurosurgical Service, Massachusetts General Hospital, Boston, Massachusetts. 5 hrs, videocassette, 1984. Source: AMA. Purchase: $150 (Member Institutional), $200 (nonmember). Rental: $74 (member), $100 (non-member). A Multidisciplinary guest faculty focuses on clinical applicability of major pain research developments; reviews progress in the individualized management of chronic pain due to benign or malignant disease; and considers patients' psychosocial experiences.

1372. Relief of Chronic Pain. 58 min. Distributor: AMF.

Personality Disorders

1373. Passive-Aggressive Personality. 25 min, video, b&w. New York State Psychiatric Institute, 1975. Distributor: ER. Segments of two interviews with a 40-year-old single male stock clerk who displays markedly passive-aggressive personality traits are presented. The narrator's comments include a discussion of issues in psychotherapy with this patient and with passive-aggressive individuals in general.

1374. Inferiority and Compensation. 35 min, 3/4″ videotape. James H Ryan, MD. Distributor: Apply to ER for purchase information. The Electronic Textbook of Psychiatry accompanying script. *Restricted Audience.*

1375. Narcissistic Personality Disorder: An Interview with a Senior Adult. Produced by Iris R Winogrand, PhD, Assistant Professor, Departments of Preventive Medicine and Psychiatry and Mental Health Sciences, Medical College of Wisconsin, 1984, revised 1985. 30 min, videotape. Catalog number: 841-VI-151. Source: HSC. Price: $350, $175 to HSC members. Rental is available for 1–7 days for $60 per videotape, $40 per tape for consortium members. Rental videotapes are for one-time classroom use. Ruth, a 73-year-old woman who explains in detail her self-image and her attitudes towards her personal and professional relationships. Some of the characteristic manifestations of narcissistic personality disorder that Ruth displays are an exaggerated self-importance, grandiosity, and an exaggerated level of demand for attention and admiration.

1376. Neurotic Behavior: A Psychodynamic View. 20 min, color, 1973. Source: McG-H. Distributor: UCEMC: Rental: $29. Dramatized episode in the life of a 19-year-old college sophomore, linking his ''neurotic'' behavior to external anxiety and childhood memories.

1377. The Treatment of the Borderline Patient. Harold F Searles MD. 1091–10912. A series of 12 tapes on definition, selection, transference, therapeutic techniques, and other aspects related to the borderline patient. Distributor: HEM.

Schizophrenic Disorders (See also Tape 1445)

1378. Paranoid Schizophrenia. 28 min, 3/4″ videotape. Produced by James H Ryan, MD. Distributor: ER. Apply to ER for purchase information. The Electronic Textbook of Psychiatry accompanying script. *Restricted Audience.*

1379. Schizophrenia: Hebephrenic-and Schizo-Affective Forms. 42: 30 min, 3/4″ videotape. Produced by James H Ryan, MD Distributor: ER. Apply to ER for purchase information. The Electronic Textbook of Psychiatry accompanying script. *Restricted Audience.*

1380. Schizophrenia: Thought Disorder and Social Isolation. Videotape. 23 min, 3/4″ videotape. Produced by James H Ryan, MD. Distributor: ER. Apply to ER for purchase information. The Electronic Textbook of Psychiatry accompanying script. *Restricted Audience.*

1381. Schizophrenic Language. 40 min, 3/4″ videotape. Produced by James H Ryan. MD. Distributor: ER. Apply to ER for purchase information. The Electronic Textbook of Psychiatry accompanying script. *Restricted Audience*.

1382. Schizophrenic Vulnerability and the Social Breakdown Syndrome. 25 min, 1 videocassette, color and b&w, ¾″ and ½″, 1975. Order Source: BLUHILL.

1383. Acute Undifferentiated Schizophrenia. 16 min, videocassette, b&w, 1969. Produced by the University of Mississippi Medical Center, 2500 North State Street, Jackson, Mississippi, 39216. Segments of two interviews with an acutely disturbed young male are presented to illustrate behavior characteristics of an acute undifferentiated form of schizophrenia. The patient expresses extreme anger and suspiciousness both verbally and physically. Restricted.

1384. Therapeutic Interaction with a Schizophrenic Patient. 10 min, videocassette, ¾″ or ½″ VHS. b&w, sound. 1982. Produced by Marilyn Whitley, RN, MA, Margaret L Larson, RN, MN, and Sarah Sweeny, RN, NM. Source: UWP. Purchase: $100. This simulated nurse–patient interaction was filmed in black and white as an appropriate symbol of interactions with schizophrenic patients. This videocassette would be best used as an adjunct to lecture material about schizophrenic behaviors and the appropriate therapeutic response to those behaviors.

1385. Schizophrenic Disorders (Case Numbers 9–12). 35 min, ½″ video, color, ¾″ U-mat, 1984. Order Source: INURTS and INUAVC. Rental Source: IUAVC. Purchase: $170. Rental: $30. Represents 'classic' patterns of schizophrenia, rather than difficult or ambiguous cases, emphasizing the heterogeneity of this general diagnostic category.

1386. The Psychotherapy of the Schizophrenic Patient (1042) Silvano Arieti, MD. 60 min. Distributor: AV/MD.

Sexual Life Styles and Sexual Disorders

1387. Primary Care For Sexual Dysfunction. Speakers: Don Sloan, MD, Michele Arthur, AASECT Certified Sex Therapist. 52 min, videocassette, color, nd. ¾″ U-matic, ½″ Beta, ½″ VHS. Source: NCME. Purchase: $50. Rental: $20.

How to uncover and confront the patient's problems, initiate short-term therapy, and treat or refer specific dysfunctions; premature ejaculation, and several types of female orgasmic problems.

1388. What Goes On At Sex Therapy Clinics. Speaker: Harold Lear, MD. 22 min, videocassette, color, nd. ¾″ U-matic, ½″ Beta, ½″ VHS. Source: NCME. Purchase: $50. Rental: $20. Dr. Lear and cotherapist Ann Welbourne, RN, show you-in a counseling session with a couple whose problem is the husband's premature ejaculation.

1389. The State of the Art of Sex Education, Therapy and Counseling (1051) Mary Calderone, MD. Impact of changing sex values and practices on individuals. Distributor: AV/MD.

1390. Common Sexual Problems and Their Management (1059). Helen Kaplan, MD. Updated socio-psycho-biological approach to the understanding, diagnosis and treatments of impotency, orgasmic dysfunction, premature and retarded ejaculation, vaginismus and problems of desire in non-psychiatric as well as psychiatric patients. 60 min. Distributor: AV/MD.

1391. Update on the Homosexualities (10510). Alan Bell, PhD. 60 min. Distributor: AV/MD.

1392. Impotence, with Philip A Sarrel, MD, Lorna Sarrel. 18 min, color. Distributor: NCME. Apply to NCME for subscription information.

1393. Male Homosexuality. 50 min, ¾″ videotape. Produced by James H Ryan, MD. Distributor ER. Apply to ER for purchase information. The Electronic Textbook of Psychiatry accompanying script. *Restricted Audience*.

Sleep/Wake Disorders

1394. Sleep/Wake Disorders. Medical Consultant: Elliot D Weitzman, MD, Director, Institute of Chronobiology, Professor of Neurology in Psychiatry and Neurology, Cornell University Medical College, White Plains, New York. 2 hrs. videocassette, 1984. Source: AMA. Purchase $80 (Member Institutional), $100 (nonmember). Rental: $40 (member), $50 (non-member). Reviews the clinical aspects of the more common sleep/wake disorders in relation to appropriate phases of normal sleep and circadian rhythm cycles; identifies salient clinical features of the more common disorders of sleep in individual patients, and establishes a differential diagnosis in the patient. Offers regimens of general health measures and pharmacologic treatment applicable to each patient's problem. Discusses referral of certain patients with persistent and unresolved sleep/wake problems for specialized study.

1395. "Doctor, I Can't Sleep Nights," with Julius Segal, PhD. 15 min, color. Distributor: NCME. Apply to NCME for subscription information.

1396. Disturbed Sleep: Five Case Problems. Speakers: Milton Kramer, MD, Robert Rakel, MD. 15 min, videocassette, color, nd. 3/4" U-matic, 1/2" Beta, 1/2" VHS. Source: NCME. Purchase: $50. Rental: $50.

Somatoform Disorders

1397. Problems And Pitfalls in Psychosomatic Medicine: Speakers: Roy R Grinker, MD, F. Theodore Reid, MD. 15 min, videocassette, color, nd. 3/4" U-matic, 1/2" Beta, 1/2" VHS. Source: NCME. Purchase: $50. Rental: $20. Drs. Grinker and Reid take up the problem of a young woman suffering from hypertension.

1398. Problems and Pitfalls in Psychosomatic Medicine: Peptic Ulcer. Speakers: Roy R Grinker, MD, F Theodore Reid, MD. 16 min. videocassette, color, nd. 3/4" U-matic, 1/2" Beta, 1/'" VHS. Source: NCME. Purchase: $50. Rental: $20. This program will show the non-psychiatric physician the way to handle psychosomatic conditions by citing a peptic ulcer patient as an example.

1399. Does Type A Personality Affect Your Heart? with Ray H Rosenman, MD. William B Kanner, MD, Campbell Moses, MD. 18 min, color. Distributor: NCME. Apply to NCME for subscription information.

1400. Influence of the Emotions on the Outcome of Cardiac Surgery: Diagnosis and Decision, with Janet A Kennedy, MD, Hyman Bakst, MD. 20 min. Distributor: NCME. Apply to NCME for subscription information.

1401. Influence of the Emotions on the Outcome of Cardiac Surgery: Psychological Categories, with Janet A Kennedy, MD, Hyman Bakst, MD. 24 min. Distributor: NCME. Apply to NCME for subscription information.

Substance Abuse Disorders (See also Tapes 1343–1349)

1402. Angel Death. 33 min, color, 1979. Source: FL. Distributor: UCEMC: Rental $38. Study of the chronic and debilitating effects of angel dust.

1403. Marijuana Alert: Research on effects of marijuana on the body and brain. 20 min. Distributor: IV.

1404. Substance Use Disorders: Diagnosis And Management. Speaker: Daniel T Teitelbaum, MD. 51 min, videocassette, nd. 3/4" U-matic, 1/2" Beta, 1/2" VHS. Source: NCME. Purchase: $50 Rental: $20. During this practical video presentation, you will participate in four patient cases and learn how to detect and differentiate between the problems and symptoms associated with dependency on cocaine, marijuana, alcohol, and analgesics.

1405. We Can't Go On Like This . . . Video Vignettes for Smoking Intervention Programs. Vignettes to be used antismoking groups to facilitate discussion and role playing. 32 min. Distributor: NAC.

1406. Current Trends in Therapy for Narcotic Addiction. (Series: Concepts and Controversies in Modern Medicine.) 29 min. b&w. Distributor: NAC. Apply to NAC for subscription information. Contrasts intensive psychotherapy with methadone treatment.

1407. Drug Abuse: Recognizing and Treating Acute Reaction to Amphetamines and Sedative Hypnotics, with David E Smith, MD. 19 min. Distributor: NCME. Apply to NCME for subscription information.

1408. Drug Abuse: Recognizing and Treating Acute Reactions to Hallucinogens, with David E Smith, MD. 19 minutes. Distributor: NCME. Apply to NCME for subscription information.

1409. Medical Problems of Adolescent Heroin Abuse, with Michael I Cohen, MD. 14 min, color. Distributor: NCME. Apply to NCME for subscription information. An in-depth interview conducted with a 14-year-old heroin addict under treatment.

Miscellaneous

1410. Psychiatric Problems of Intensive Care Units. Speaker: Donald S Kornfield, MD. 16 min, videocassette, color, nd. 3/4" U-matic, 1/2" Beta, 1/2" VHS. Source: NCME. Purchase: $50. Rental: $20. Patients with serious illness are prone to psychiatric problems. Can maximal care be maintained while preventing the ICU Syndrome?

Psychotherapeutic Modalities

General Diagnostic and Therapeutic Methods

1411: The Psychiatry Learning System. Authors: Patricia Randels, MD, Lorenz Villeponteaux, PhD, Luis Marco, MD, Darlene Shaw, PhD, Layton McCurdy, MD, 1982. Videocassette 3/4" U-Matic, 1/2" Betamax and 1/2" VHS. Source: HSC. Purchase: PLS is available for $3,000 ($1,800 for members) for one set of 22 videocassettes and text. Contents - 1. Assessments: 1. Psychiatric Evaluation. 2. Psychodynamic Considerations and Defense Mechanisms. 3. Psychological Evaluation. 4. Psychosocial Factors in Physical Illness. II. Disorders: 5. Organic Mental Disorders. 6. Substance Use Disorders. 7. Schizophrenic disorders, Paranoid Disorders and Psychoses not Elsewhere Classified. 8. Affective Disorders. 9. Anxiety Disorders. 10. Somatoform and Dissociative Disorders. 11. Psychosexual Disorders. 12. Impulse Control Disorders. 13. Personality Disorders. 14. Sleep Disorders. 15. Disorders of Infancy, Childhood and Adolescence. III. Treatments: 16. Psychopharmacology. 17. Psychosocial Treatments. 18. Behavioral Treatments. 19. Other Treatment Modalities. This system is a full course in diagnosis and recommended treatment modalities that was developed at the Medical University of South Carolina to replace 55 hours of lectures in the psychiatry rotation. The new edition consists of a completely revised, one-volume text (x + 969 pp.) indexed to 22 new, full-color clinical videotapes providing specific examples of diagnostic and therapeutic techniques and the symptoms and mechanisms of each category of disorder. Both text and tapes have been organized to be consistent with the APA's DSM III. Fifteen of the nineteen chapters are provided with supporting videotape, and at the end of each unit within the chapter the student is directed to the relevant portion of the appropriate videocassette.

1412. Psychotherapy. Overview of the basic processes and common elements in psychotherapy. 25 min. Distributor: IV.

1413. Psychiatric Interview Technique: Demonstration and Critique. 51 min, video, B&W. New York Psychiatric Institute, 1975. Source: APA. Distributor: UIFC. The purpose of this videotape is to demonstrate different approaches to the initial psychiatric interview. The basic interview, of a 25-year-old white male outpatient, is conducted by James H. Ryan, M.D., who has had no previous contact with the patient and, at the beginning of the interview is totally unaware of his problems. Interspersed throughout the interview are comments from two other psychiatrists, Roger MacKinnon M.D., and Robert Michels, MD, who discuss certain aspects of the exchange as it occurs. Restricted to professionals in training in the mental health sciences.

1414. Mental Illness. 14 min, video or 16 mm, color. Harper & Row Criminal Justice Media, 1980. Source: APA. Distributor: UIFC. This brief but comprehensive film illustrates several kinds of aberrant or violent behavior that might indicate mental illness and would require special handling.

1415. The Change. Produced by Donald C Fidler, MD, University of North Carolina at Chapel Hill, 1983, revised 1985. 34 min, videotape. Catalog Number: 841-VI-155. Source: HSC. Price: $350, $175 to HSC members. Rental is available for 1–7 days for $60 per videotape, $40 per tape for consortium members. Rental videotapes are for one-time classroom use. This discussion trigger videotape helps viewers experience the disorientation of a man approaching a psychological breakdown. Clinical signs and symptoms of psychopathological disturbances are also illustrated.

1416. Application of the Mental Status Exam. 12 min, videocassette, 3/4" or 1/2" VHS. Color, sound. 1982. Produced by Margaret L Larson, RN, MN, Marilyn Peddicord Whitley, RN, MA, and Ann M

Creery, RN, MS Source: UWP. Purchase: 150.00. This videocassette is a simulated interview between depressed female "patient" and a "nurse" in which the nurse makes a systematic mental status assessment.

1417. The Mental Status Exam: Practical Aspects For The Clinician. Speaker: Donald J Dalessio, MD. 23 min, videocassette, color, nd. 3/4" U-matic, 1/2" Beta, 1/2" VHS. Source: NCME. Purchase: $50. Rental: $20. A method for conducting an organized conversation with a mentally disturbed patient in order to determine in what area the dysfunction lies; emotional, neurologic, psychotic, systemic.

1418. Simulated Psychiatric Patient Interview. 90 min, 6 videocassettes, sd., col.; 3/4" 1976. Consists of six interviews, each of which may be purchased or rented separately. Can be used in conjunction with Basic Psychopathology: a programmed text. Produced by Instructional Media Service, Univ. of Southern California, School of Medicine. Source: UCLASM.

1419. A Bad Baseball. Produced by Donald C Fidler MD. University of North Carolina at Chapel Hill, 1983, revised 1985. 50 min, videotape. Catalog number: 8410V1-154. Source: HSC. Price: $350, $175 to HSC members. Rental 1-7 days for $60 per videotape, $40 per tape for consortium members. Rental videotapes are for one-time classroom use. This discussion trigger videotape follows a hypothetical patient through six pivotal sessions in the course of psychotherapy. It gives the viewer an introduction to a wide range of patient defenses. Guided by an instructor, viewers can also learn about accepted therapeutic procedures and hone their own psychotherapeutic techniques.

1420. Body Language in Diagnosis. Speaker: Gordon H. Deckert MD. 17 min, videocassette, color, nd. 3/4" U-matic, 1/2" Beta, 1/2" VHS. Source: NCME. Purchase: $50. Rental: $20. A psychiatrist shows how to obtain a wealth of information during the first five minutes of an office visit by observing how a patient walks, talks, and acts.

1421. Mechanisms of Defense, with LC Hanes, MD. 17 min. Distributor: NCME. Apply to NCME for subscription information.

1422. Strategies of Psychotherapy. Ca 45 min, videocassette, sd., col., 3/4", 1981. (Leaders in Psychiatry Series). Produced by Social Psychiatry Research Institute, 150 E. 69th St. NY, NY 10021 by Jay Haley and Richard Rabkin.

1423. Working With Nonverbal Behavior. Speaker: David A Steere, PhD. 60 min, videotape, color, nd. 3/4" U-matic, 1/2" Beta, 1/2" VHS. Source: BM. Purchase: $150 plus $5.00 for shipping. Seven persons in group treatment. This tape introduces specific methods for working with nonverbal behavior within the normal processes of individual, group, or family psychotherapy. Dr. Steere talks informally about the nature of movement behavior by clients when addressing important life conflicts, analyzes the specific patterns of posture and gesture of each group member, and identifies the three vantage points from which the psychotherapist may view nonverbal behavior.

1424. The Geriatric Patient. 15 min, 3/4" videocassette, color, sound. 1977. Produced by Hugh J Lurie, MD. Source: UWP. Purchase: $175. The eleven segments in this videotape production present a variety of poignant and dramatic situations intended principally for those who work with geriatric patients. The situations depicted are relevant to an understanding, assessment, and treatment of the elderly in their own homes and in residential care facilities. *The Geriatric Patient* is intended to stimulate discussion in three major areas-interviewing techniques, intervention strategies, and diagnostic issues.

1425. The Person in the Therapist. 60 min, 1 videocassette, sd., col.; 3/4", 1984. Interview with John Howells, MD. Presented by the Boston Family Institute, Brookline, Mass. Source: BFI.

Behavior Therapy (See also Tape 1352)

1426. One Step At A Time: An Introduction to Behavior Modification. 30 min. Distributor: IV.

1427. Token Economy: Behaviorism Applied. 21 min. Distributor: IV.

1428. Responsible Assertion: Group Assertion training with cognitive restructuring and behavioral rehearsal. 20 min. Distributor: RP.

1429. What Could I say. Common situations that require assertive responses. 18 min. Distributor: RP.

1430. Effective Behavioral Programming: Richard M. Foxx. Eight videotapes of a training program in behavioral intervention. A one-day free preview videocassette is available. Distributor: RP.

1431. Parents and Children: A positive Approach to Child Management. Richard M. Foxx. 24 min. Distributor: RP.

1432. The Multimodal Therapy Training Series. Arnold A Lazarus. Three tapes are available: I. The Assessment/Therapy Connection, 29 min, II Multimodal Marital Therapy. 22 min, III The Use of Bridging and Tracking to Overcome "Apparent" Resistance. 17 min. Distributor: RP.

1433. B F Skinner and Behavior Change. Issues and controversies generated by behavioral psychology. 45 min. Distributor: RP.

1434. Behavior Modification: Treatment or Coercion? Speakers: Bernard Towers, MB, ChB, James Q. Simmons III, MD. 33 min, videocassette, color, nd. ¾" U-matic, ½" Beta, ½" VHS. Source: NCME. Purchase: $50. Rental: $20. A lively discussion about medicine and society.

1435. Harry: Behavioral Treatment of Self-Abuse. 38 min, video, color and b&w, 16 mm, 1980. Order Source: RESPRC. Purchase: $495. Rental: $50. Documents a case of behavior modification that cures the self-injurious behavior of Harry, a 24-year-old mildly retarded person, institutionalized because of self-abuse.

1436. A Case of Social Anxiety. Joseph Wolpe. 1 hr. videocassette. Source: MHEF. Purchase: ½" $75, ¾" $90.

Client-centered Therapy

1437. The Client-Centered Approach. Carl Rogers, Ruth Sanford (includes a live demonstration) 3 hrs. Source: MHEF. Purchase: ½" $145, ¾" $230 (tapes).

Cognitive Therapy

1438. Cognitive Behavior Theory Series. 1 audiocassette. Distributor: BMA. Subject experts discuss the therapy, research, and case examples of common behavior problems.

1438a. Demonstration of the Cognitive Therapy of Depression: The First Interview. Aaron T. Beck, MD.

1438b. Demonstration of the Cognitive Theory of Depression: A Dramatization—Acute Exacerbation of Depression and Suicidal Wishes During Treatment. Aaron T. Beck, MD. 45 min. $120 deposit, $80 rental. Distributor: NC.

1438c. Dr. Beck with I.E.: Demonstration of Initial Interview with Depressed a Woman. Aaron T. Beck, MD. 28 min. $120 deposit, $80 rental, Distributor: NC.

Family and Marital Therapy

1439. Family Therapy. 28 min, ¾" videocassette, b&w, sound. 1977. Produced by the University of Washington School of Nursing, and by Marilyn Whitley, RN, MA, and Sissy Madden, RN. Source: UWASH. Purchase: $175. This tape demonstrates the use of communication techniques by a cotherapy team working with a dysfunctional family.

1440. Between you and Me: Salvador Minuchin, therapist aspects of treatment of an anorectic adolescent and her parents. 47 min. Distributor: PCGC.

1441. I'd Rather Forget It: Gordon Hodas and Nila Betof, therapists. Use of cotherapy and combination of pediatrics and psychotherapy in the treatment of a family with an asthmatic child. 45 min. Distributor: PCGC.

1442. Sisters and Parents: A Family Finds Options. Al Virginia Satir demonstrates problem-solving in a family. Distributor: BFI.

1443. Initial Interview. I. Alger. 27 min, videocassette, color, 1979. Source: Restricted WPIC. Initial Family Interview. I. Alger. Demonstrates entry into family system and therapist's making contact with each family member and learning from each the nature of the conflict.

1444. The Process of Family Therapy. Carl Whitaker. 60 min, videocassette, b&w, 1979. Restricted. Source: WPIC. Presents the work of Carl Whitaker, MD. during six consecutive family therapy sessions and a later follow up.

1445. Family Systems Therapy with Schizophrenia. 57 min, video, color, 1980. Distributor: GUFC. Purchase: $190. Rental: $90. One in a series of interviews with Murray Bowen, MD. discussing his illustrious career as a therapist and teacher of family systems therapy. Focuses on his work with schizophrenic families.

1446. Techniques in the Application of Systems Theory. PH. Meyer. 240 min, videocassette, color, 1981. Source: WPIC. Four part series applicable to Murray Bowen's family systems theory. Four Phases of Therapy: II. The Process of Change. III Resistance in Systems Therapy. IV The Application of Theory; the ways in which knowledge of theory guides.

1447. Constructing the Multi-Generational Family Genogram: Exploring A Problem in Context. Produced by Stephen Lerner, PhD. 30 min, videotape, color, nd. ¾" U-Matic, ½" Beta, ½" VHS. Source: BM. Purchase: $150 plus $5.00 for shipping. This videotape, by using the genogram, teaches the viewer how to diagram the multigenerational family system and presents a clinical case, which illustrates the valuable contributions the genogram can make to the understanding of a problem in context. Family patterns and themes pertaining to the presenting problem (and its solution), become clear from the questioning process based on the genogram, are described. This videotape stands out as a unique educational production.

1448. Alcoholism in the Family. 28 min, video, color, 1980. Order Source: HEALMS. Purchase: $125. Dramatizes a family therapy case study in which the son brought the family into therapy for a number of problems including the father's drinking.

1449. Contracting—A Therapist's Aid to Family Counseling. 47 min, color, videocassette, 1975. Distributor: ARF. Purchase: $95. In this initial interview with a young married couple, obtaining a commitment from the spouses to work on their marital problems is therapist's central goal. Making the Invisible Visible. Peggy Papp and the Nathan W Ackerman Family Institute. Distributor: NWAFI. Rental: $50. A demonstration of the use of sculpting as a therapeutic technique in an initial family interview. The basic dysfunctional triangle spatially staged and subsequently corrected.

1450. A Marital Therapy Consultation. Speakers: Florence Kaslow, PhD., Stephen Hawthorne, ACSW. 60 min, videotape, color, nd. ¾" U-Matic, ½" Beta, ½" VHS. Source: BM. Purchase: $150 plus $5.00 shipping. This videotape depicts the value of utilizing a guest-consultant for a marital session to: (1) verify or change the assessment and treatment plan; (2) break an impasse in therapy; (3) do a demonstration-teaching session for faculty, staff and trainees; (4) provide new data to the patients by intervening differently; and (5) provide a new therapeutic experience by (temporarily) creating a heterosexual co-therapy team so that the couple can benefit from relating to therapists of both sexes.

1451. A Couples Group Demonstration: A2. James Framo. Distributor: BFI.

1452. Behavioral Interviewing With Couples. John Gottman. 14 min. Distributor: RP.

1453. Communication Problems of Couples. Milton Berger, MD and Albert Scheffen, MD. Changing Faulty Communication patterns in couples. 60 min. Distributor: HEM.

1454. Couples Communication. Modes of improving communication. 21 min. Distributor: IV.

1455. Spouse Abuse: Who Is The Victim? Speakers: Elissa P Benedek, MD. 30 min, videotape, color, nd. ¾" U-matic, ½" Beta, ½" VHS. Source: BM. Purchase: $150 plus $5.00 for shipping. This tape combines interviews with professionals and abusing and abused spouses (played by actors) to answer these questions, and to highlight essential treatment issues. The initial overview reveals the gradually escalating pattern of violence in these couples.

Gestalt Therapy

1456. Gestalt Therapy. 56 min, b&w 1970. Distributor: TCL. Purchase: $85. Rental: $25.

1457. The use of Gestalt Techniques. M Poster. Live demonstration. 1 hr Videocassette. Source: MHEF. Purchase: ½" $75, ¾" $90.

Group Psychotherapy

1458. Clarifying Group Therapy. Speaker: F Theodore Reid, MD. 16 min, videocassette, nd. ¾" U-matic, ½" Beta, ½" VHS. Source: NCME. Purchase: $50. Rental: $20. Dr. Reid explains the dynamics of group therapy in comments running between videotaping of an actual session in progress. The group reaction to one member's termination of therapy demonstrates typical group interactions.

1459. Starting a Therapy Group, or Beginning a Psychodynamic Interactional Therapy Group for Adult Neurotics. 55 min, videocassette, sd., b&w, ¾″, 1980. Produced by McMaster University, School of Medicine, 1200 Main St. West Hamilton, Ontario, CA L8N3Z5.

1460. Redecision Group Therapy. R. Goulding, M. Goulding. 1 hr. videocassette. Source: MHEF. Purchase: ½″ $75, ¾″ $160.

1461. Video Replay In Group Psychotherapy (1011). Milton Berger. Demonstration of many uses of video replay. 50 min. Distributor: AV/MD.

1462. The Tuesday Group. A group session with severely emotionally and physically deteriorated elderly persons illustrating group work techniques. Distributor: FEIL.

1463. Dream Therapy. 60 min, b&w, 1″ videotape, 1969. Distributor: TCL. Purchase: $85. Rental $25. The use of therapeutic guided daydreams in group setting.

1464. Hypnosis to Alter Affect. J Barber. 1986. Videocassette. Source: MHEF. Purchase: ½″ $75, ¾″ $90.

1465. Enhancing Therapeutic Responsiveness. JK Zeig, 1986. Videocassette. Source: MHEF. Purchase: ½″, $75, ¾″ $90.

1466. Hypnosis for Enhancing Emotional Intimacy and Sexual Desire. DC Hammond, 1986. Videocassette. Source: MHEF. Purchase: ½″ $75, ¾″ $90.

1467. Naturalistic Hypnosis Without Erickson's Genius. DL Araoz, 1986. Videocassette. Source: MHEF. Purchase ½″ $75, ¾″ $90.

1468. Stimulating Critical Moments and Providing Therapeutic Alternatives: A Dual Induction Approach. RA Havens, 1986. Videocassette. Source: MHEF. Purchase: ½″ $75, ¾″ $90.

1469. Update on Hypnosis in Psychiatry and Medicine (1061) Herbert Spiegel, MD. 60 min. HEM.

Psychodrama

1470. Psychodrama: A Demonstration. L Moreno. 180 min, videocassette, b&w, 1977. Produced by WPIC. Demonstration of psychodrama technique.

1471. The Journey, A Review of Intimate Relations Through Role Reversal. Z Moreno. Videocassettes, 1 hr. Source: MHEF. Purchase: ½″ $75, ¾″ $90.

1472. Psychodrama. A three part series. Speaker: James Enners, Director of Psychodrama. St. Elizabeth's Hospital and U.S. Department of Health, Education and Welfare. Videocassettes, b&w, nd., ¾″, U-matic, ½″ Beta, ½″ VHS. Source: NCME. Each part purchase: $50, Rental: $20.

1473. Part I. This workshop in psychodrama, with patients and staff of the Hennepin County General Hospital, Minneapolis, demonstrates the methods used to initiate and stage psychodrama.

1474. Part II. The Play: In this section of a special three-part series, psychiatric patients at Hennepin County General Hospital participate in an actual psychodrama.

1475. Part III. The Critique: Members of the medical and nursing staffs discuss their impressions after having observed and participated in a psychodrama.

Rational Emotive Therapy

1476. Rational Emotive Therapy. Featuring Dr. Albert Ellis. 30 min, 16 mm film or videocassette, color, 1986. Source: RP. Film Purchase: $495. Film Rental: $55/3 days. Videocassette Purchase: ¾″ $495. VHS $495. Beta $495. (includes User's Guide). Presents an informative overview of Rational Emotive Therapy, which was developed by Dr. Albert Ellis in the 1950's. The film takes you into the Institute for Rational Emotive Therapy in New York City during a five-day practicum conducted by Dr. Ellis and the Institute's training staff. Unstaged counseling sessions show clear examples of techniques used in RET.

1477. The Practice of Rational-Emotive Therapy. Albert Ellis (includes a live demonstration) 3 hrs. 1986. Source: MHEF. Purchase ½″ $145, ¾″ $230 (3 tapes).

Short-term

1478. Short-term Therapy. The Three Phases of a Therapeutic Relationship. Cheryl L White, RNMS. 17 min, videocassette, color, 1975. Rental: $35. Purchase: $175. Order Source: UMMCML, 1975. Demonstrates the phases and interaction between nurse-therapist and client during the first-(initiation, fourth, (working) and seventh (termination) month of short-term therapy.

1479. Brief vs. Long-term Therapy. M Goulding, Marmor, Masterson, Watzlawick. 1 hr. Videocassette. Source: MHEF. Purchase: ½ hr. $75, ¾ hr $90.

1480. Psychiatric Interview Technique: The Brief Interview. 23 min, ¾″ videotape. Produced by James H Ryan, MD. Distributor: ER. Apply to ER for purchase information. The Electronic Textbook of Psychiatry accompanying script. *Restricted Audience*.

Transactional Analysis

1481. I'm OK, You're OK—Can Transactional Analysis Free the Child in Us? 20 min. Distributor: CNEMAG.

Adjunctive Therapies

1482. Group Art Therapy (1083). Lynne Berger ATR. and Milton Berger, MD. 60 min. Distributor: AV/MD.

1483. Group Projective Art Therapy. 60 min, 1″ videotape, 1969. Distributor: TCL. Purchase $85. Rental: $25.

1484. Art Therapy with an Emotionally Disturbed 16-Year-Old Boy. 44 min, 1971. Produced by Leah Freedman, Robert C Prall, MD, Jacques Van Vlack. Distributor: EPPI. Rental: $15.

Counseling

1485. Contracting a Therapist's Aid to Family Counseling. 47 min. ARF.

1486. Counseling the Post-Abortion Patient. Ronald J Pion, MD, Nathaniel N Wagner, PhD. 18 min. color. Distributor: NCME. Apply to NCME for subscription information.

1487. Applying Communication Theory to Work With Patients. (1021). Albert Scheflen, MD. Exercises to improve communication skills. 60 min. Distributor: AV/MD.

1488. Use of Video Tape in Counseling Skills in Training, 40 min, color, videocassette, 1975. Distributor: ARF. Purchase: $70. Demonstrates how videotape tools and techniques can be introduced into specialized counseling skills training.

1489. Interview with Rabbi Edwin Friedman. 25 min, videocassette, color, 1978. Source: WPIC. Presents rabbi's view of religious issue in therapy; theoretical formations about family and role of the therapist.

1489a. Time Out. Gerald R. Paterson, PhD. 38 minutes. Purchase-$125. Distributor CP. Teaching parents skills in the use of nonviolent punishment with children 5 to 12 years of age.

1489b. Parents and children Series. Carolyn Webster-Stratton PhD. 1987. 4 videocasettes: (1)Play, (2)Praise and Rewards, (3)Effective Limit Setting. (4)Handling Misbehavior. Purchase: $85 each cassette.

A researched and field tested videocassette training program that acts as a tool to teach parents how to make significant improvement in the behavior of children 2½ to 8 years of age. Distributor CP.

Dance and Movement Therapy

1490. Looking In Reaching Out: Learning to Become a Dance Therapist. 18 min, b&w, ½-in videotape, 1973. Distributor: ETC. Purchase: $50. Rental: $15.

Electroconvulsive Therapy

1491. Electro-Convulsive Therapy. Speakers: Lothar Kalinowsky, MD, Shepard Kantor, MD. 27 min, videocassette, ¾″, VHS, color, nd. Source: ER.#24 Purchase: $300 plus postage. Cassette demonstrates the use of electro-convulsive therapy. It begins with a discussion by Lothar Kalinowsky about the history of the development of ECT. Following Dr. Kalinowsky there is an interview with a depressed woman viewed during the course of her first treatment. The woman is seen again after her course of treatment when she is in a normal state of mind. Following the patient interview, Dr. Shepard Kantor gives a brief lecture on the indications for ECT and a statistical analysis of therapeutic results and side effects.

Music Therapy

1492. The Music Child-Demonstrator D Parry. 48 min, videocassette, b&w, 1976. Source: WPIC. Demonstrates the use of music therapy in treatment of the autistic and multihandicapped child in live sessions. Blue Ribbon Award at Am. Film Festival Supporter Mauric Falk Medical Fund.

Occupational Therapy

1493. An Occupational Therapist Evaluating Functional Living Skills in Psychiatry. 24 min, 1 cassette, sd., col; ¾ in & guide, 1978. Produced by University of Washington, Division of Occupational Therapy, Seattle. Source: HSLRC. Loan or sale.

Psychopharmacological Therapy

1494. A Recommendation for a More Rational Use of Antipsychotic Drugs. 2 ¾″ videocassettes, 1979. Producer USVAST. Sponsor: USVA. Title No. A02249/PN. Sale: $145. Discusses use of drugs administered for psychotic conditions. Antipsychotic drugs. 20 Min. Overview to the Series, 5 min.

1495. Lithium: Its Use In Depression. Speaker: Nathan S. Kline, MD. 14 min, videocassette, color, nd. ¾″ U-matic, ½″ Beta, ½″ VHS. Source: NCME. Purchase: $50. Rental: $20. Lithium, the current therapeutic perspective.

1496. Therapeutic Strategies In Tardive Dyskinesia. Speaker: Ronald M Kobayashi, MD. 16 min, videocassette, color, nd. ¾″ U-matic, ½″ Beta, ½″ VHS. Source: NCME. Purchase: $50. Rental: $20. Electronically animated graphics illustrate the latest findings about the underlying neurochemical imbalances of tardive dyskinesia.

1497. Common Interactions of Drugs Used to Treat Psychiatric Disorders. 59 min, 1 videocassette, sd., col.; ¾ in, 1983. CNCP (Drug Source: Interactions Series) by Edward A Hartshorn and Ann D Hollerbach.

Rehabilitation

1498. Life Skills Training Course. Teaching problem solving behaviors. Distributor: ARF.

1499. The Self-Management Training Program. Training sessions helping persons with a developmental disabilities manage their disruptive actions. 27 min. RP.

1500. Extended Family. 27 min, video, color, 1980. Order Source: MEDIA. Purchase: $95. Documents a family that provides a halfway home for women recently released from psychiatric facilities. Interviews family members and the young women about the program.

1501. The Fifty-First Minute. 30 min, video, color. Southwest Denver Community Mental Health Services, 1980. Source: APA. Distributor: UIFC. Placing an acute psychiatric patient with a family in the community rather than in a hospital has been found workable by the Southwest Denver Community Mental Health Services.

1502. We're On Our Way. 29 min, videocassette, color, 1984. Source: WPIC. Family members describing their loved ones who have a long-term mental illness. To be shown to professional audiences who have commitment to serving the mentally ill.

Relaxation Methods

1503. Taking Time to Relax. Exercises in Stress Reduction. 47 min, videocassette, color, 1981. Produced by: WPIC. Three parts; introduction, describing stress in general (7 min); stress reduction stretches and massages (32 min); and a guided relaxation (8 min).

1504. Less Stress in Five Easy Steps. D Gross VHS. Videotape. BMA $69.95. This highly entertaining videotape featuring Ed Asner gives you (and your clients) the needed to deal effectively with everyday stress. Techniques include self-monitoring methods, ventilation techniques, relaxation exercises, meditation, self-appreciation exercises.

1505. Biofeedback . . . Therapeutic Self-Control. Introduction to biofeedback . . . 60 min. Distributor: NAC.

1506. Stress-Related Disorders and Their Management Through Biofeedback and Relaxation Training. Kenneth Greenspan, MD. 90 min. Distributor: AV/MD.

1507. Progressive Relaxation Training. Donald T Shannon. 20 min. Distributor: RP.

1508. Taking Time to Relax. Exercises in Stress Reduction. 47 min, videocassette, color, 1981. Produced by: WPIC. Three parts; introduction, describing stress in general (7 min.); stress reduction stretches and massages (32 min.); and a guided relaxation (8 min.).

Sensory Feedback Therapy

1509. Sensory Feedback Therapy, with Joseph Brudny, MD. 18 min, color. Distributor: NCME Apply to NCME for subscription information.

Videotherapy

1510. The Message is the Medium. 43 min, ¾″ videocassette, color, sound, 1977. Produced by Hugh J Lurie, MD, Hope Shaw, and Douglas Vernon. Source: UWP. Purchase: 275. Provides detailed information about all aspects of video production as it applies to mental health, from the simplest single-camera system to the complex studio operation, and shows the production of a segment from storyboard to set.

1511. Perspectives on Mental Health. b&w, 10-part series. Produced by Ari Kiev, MD. Distributor: BLUHILL. Rental: Contact BLUHILL. Demonstration by Ari Kiev, pioneer in "videotherapy," of his techniques with a variety of patients. Indicated for training programs in psychotherapy.

Community Mental Health

1512. Rural Mental Health Practice. 23 min, ¾″ videocassette, color, sound. 1981. Produced by: UWASHCDMR. Purchase: $225. Interviews with four mental health professionals who have made the transition from urban to rural practice are presented in this program.

Deinstitutionalization

1513. Psychiatric Illness On Skid Row. Part 1. Speaker: Robert G Priest, MD. 14 min, videocassette, b&w, nd. ¾″ U-matic, ½″ Beta, ½″ VHS. Source: NCME. Purchase: $50. Rental: $20. First results of the psychiatric testing of residents of skid row hotels.

1514. Psychiatric Illness on Skid Row. Part II. "The Disease." Speaker: Robert G Priest, MD. 16 min, videocassette, nd. ¾″ U-matic, ½″ Beta, ½″ VHS. Source: NCME. Purchase: $50. Rental: $20. The incidence of schizophrenia, alcoholism, and other psychiatric disabilities among inhabitants of skid row hotels.

Teaching and Supervision

1515. Dramatic Mental Health Teaching. 25 min, ¼″ videocassette, color, sound, 1977. Produced by Hugh J Lurie, MD. Source: UWP. Purchase: $200. *Dramatic Mental Health Teaching* vividly demonstrates the two kinds of roles that actors can take to meet specific teaching needs. The fixed role illustrates particular interviewing situations that have been defined and rehearsed in advance. The improvisational role relies heavily on an interactive process with the interviewer or interviewer-trainee and the actor exploring their respective roles as they evolve during the session. Credibility for the viewer is enhanced by the use of health professionals as interviewers in the examples.

1516. Improving Psychiatric Supervision. 30 min, videocassette, color, 1981. A series of videotaped teaching simulations to dramatize issues facing supervisors, training program directors and residents. Produced by Educational Development for Psychiatric Education Project of the American Psychiatric Association. Source: APA.

1517. Changing Attitudes Toward The Chronically Mentally Ill: Videotaped Vignettes for Discussion. 6 min, videocassette, color, 1981. Consists of brief vignettes that focus on the feelings of frustrating therapeutic nihilism, and pessimism often found in the discussions of the treatment of the chronically mentally disabled. Vignettes and accompanying Discussion Leader's Guide provide structured opportunities for teachers of psychiatry or for groups of students to discuss attitudes, assumptions and frustrations in dealing with the chronically mentally ill. Ideal for variety of learning situations such as residency training, grand rounds, educational conferences. Produced for Psychiatric Educators Project of the American Psychiatric Association.

VIDEO

AMA:	American Medical Association, 535 North Dearborn St., Chicago, Ill. 60610
APA:	American Psychiatric Association, Hospital and Community Psychiatry Services, 1400 K Street, N.W., Washington, D.C. 20005
ARF:	Addiction Research Foundation, 33 Russell St., Toronto, Ontario, CA M552S1
AV/MD:	Audio Visual Medical Marketing, Inc., 850 3 Ave., New York, N.Y. 10022. 212-421-6900

BFI: Boston Family Institute, 251 Harvard St., Brookline, MA 02146

BLUHILL: Blue Hill Educational Systems, 52 S. Main St., Spring Valley, NY 10977

BM: Brunner/Mazel Publishers, 19 Union Square, New York, NY 10003

BMA: BMA Cassettes, 200 Park Avenue South, Dept #9, New York, NY 10003

BSML: Behavioral Sciences Media Lab, Neuropsychiatric Institute, University of California, 760 Westwood Plz., Los Angeles, CA 90024

CNCP: Medical University of South Carolina, College of Nursing, College of Pharmacy and the Health Communications Network, Division of Continuing Education, Charleston, S.C.

CNEMAG: Cinema Guild, Division of Document Associates, 1697 Broadway, New York, NY 10019

CP: Castalia Publishing Co. P.O. Box 1587, Eugene OR 97440

HSC: Health Science Consortium, 103 Laurel Avenue, Carrboro, NC 27510. (919) 942-8731

HSLRC: Health Science Learning Resources Center, University of Washington, Division of Occupational Therapy, Seattle, WA 98195

HUPR: Harvard University Press, Audiovisual Divn., 79 Garden St., Cambridge, MA 02138. 617-495-3173

INUAVC:
IUAVC: Indiana University, Audio-Visual Center, Bloomington, IN 74705

IV: Illinois Video, University of Illinois Film Center, 1325 So. Oak St., Champaign, Ill. 61820. 1-800-252-1357

ER: New York State Psychiatric Institute, Educational Research, 722 West 168 Street, New York, NY 10032

EPPI: Eastern Pennsylvania Psychiatric Institute, Henry Ave and Abbotsford Rd., Philadelphia, PA 12129

ETC: Educational Technology Center, Hunter College-CUNY, 695 Park Ave., New York, NY 10021

FAIRVGH: Fairview General Hospital, Audio-Visual Communication, Rm.

                AU 1, 18101 Lorain Ave., Cleveland, OH 44111. 216-476-7054

FEIL: Edward Feil Productions, 4614 Prospect Ave., Cleveland, OH. 44103

GP: Guilford Publications, 200 Park Avenue South, New York City, NY 10003. 212-674-1900

GUFC: Georgetown University Family Center, 4380 MacArthur Blvd. N.W., Washington, DC 20007. 202-625-7815

HEALMS:
HEM: Health and Education Multimedia, Inc., 451 E 83 St, New York City, NY 10028. 212-288-2297

KPC: Kingsboro Psychiatric Center, 681 Clarkson Ave, Brooklyn, NY 11203

McG-H: CRM/McGraw-Hill Films, 110 15th St., Del Mar, CA 92014

MEDIA: Media Productions, 31 High St, New Haven, CT 06520. 203-865-0356

MHEF: Milton Erickson Foundation, 3606 North 24 St., Phoenix, AZ 85016

MRF: Mahler Research Foundation Film Library, P.O. Box 315, Franklin Lakes, NJ 07417. 201-891-8240

NAC:
NAVC: National Audiovisual Center, Customer Services PJ, 8700 Edgeworth Dr., Capitol Heights, MD 20743-3701

NC: National Computer, P.O. Box 416, Minneapolis, MN 55440

NCME: The Network for Continuing Medical Education, One Harmon Plaza, Secaucus, NJ 07094. 201-867-3550

NWAIF: Nathan W. Ackerman Family Institute, 149 E 78 St., New York, NY 10028

NMAC: National Medical Audiovisual Center, Branch B2E17, Bldg. 38 A, 8600 Rockville Pike, Bethesda, Md. 20209. 301-496-4244

PCGC: Philadelphia Child Guidance Clinic, 34th St & Civic Center Blvd, Philadelphia, PA 19104

POLMYR: Polymorth Films, 118 South St., Boston, MA 02111. 617-542-2004

PR:
RESPRC: Research Press, Box 317760, Champaign, Il 61820. 217-352-3273

TCL: Telecommunications Central Library, Dept of Health, Camarillo

UCEMC: State Hospital, Box A. Camarillo, CA 93010
University of California, Extension Media Center, 222 Fulton St., Berkeley, CA 94720

UCLASM: University of California, School of Medicine, Instructional Media Service, Keith Bldg. Room 200 D, 2025 Zoanl Ave, Los Angeles, CA 90033. 213-224-7044

UMMCML: University of Michigan, Medical Campus, Media Library, R4440 Kreage 1, Box 56, Ann Arbor, MI 48109. 313-763-2074

UMSM: University of Maryland, School of Medicine, 32 E. Greene Street or West Baltimore St., Baltimore, MD 21201

USVAST: United States Veteran's Administration, Medical Center, St. Louis, Mo.

UWASH: University of Washington, School of Nursing, Seattle, Wash. 98195

UWASHCDMR: University of Washington, Child Development and Mental Retardation Center, Media Services, WJ10, Seattle, WA 98195

UWP: University of Washington Press, P.O. Box C-50096, Seattle, Washington 98145-5096

WPIC: Western Psychiatric Institute and Clinic Audiovisual Center, 3811 O'Hara St., Pittsburgh, PA 15213 (Institutional Membership Available). 412-624-2378

VII

Appendices and References

The following forms include all the information that appears on the forms used in actual practice; in order to make these reproductions conform to the page size of the book, however, the layout has had to vary from the original in some instances, and occasionally spacing between items has been considerably reduced. For example, some forms, which in reproduction here appear on one page, appear in practice on two pages, or two sides of one page. The actual forms are on standard 8½ × 11 inch sheets, with sufficient space between items to allow for complete entry of data.

APPENDIX A
  Statistical Data*

PATIENT'S NAME: Date:

ADDRESS: Interviewer:

TELEPHONE: BUSINESS PHONE: Referred by:

Informant (*if any*): Name and address:

With whom is patient now living? (*list people*)

Age of patient: Sex: Religion:

Education: Occupation: Salary:

If unemployed, sources of income:

Marital status: How long married?   Any previous marriages?

When?   Age of mate: Occupation of mate:

                                                         Salary of mate:

Military record:

Miscellaneous:

---

* Short form: To be filled out by therapist, initial interviewer, or intake worker in a clinic set-up.

APPENDIX B
  Statistical Data*

Patient's Name ——————————————————   Case No. ——————

1. GENERAL DATA:

    a. Age: Date of birth: b. Sex (M, F)

    c. Race (W, B, Y, R):   d. Religion:

    e. Birthplace:

    f. If foreign-born, date of arrival in U.S.A.:

    g. Naturalization dates: 1st Papers: 2nd Papers:

    h. Education:

    i. Occupation:

    j. Employed (yes, no):

    k. Salary:

    l. Yearly income, all sources:

    m. If unemployed, on what sources of income, or on what person is patient dependent, giving occupation and relationship to patient of this person:

    n. Military Service (yes, no); dates:

    o. Name and address of nearest relative or friend:

    p. With whom is patient living at present?

2. RESIDENTIAL DATA:

    a. Address:

    b. Character of residence: ( ) house ( ) apartment ( ) room; ( ) self-owned
        ( ) rented, rental cost:

    c. Place of legal settlement:

    d. Length of residence in this town or city:

    e. Length of residence in state:

    f. Home telephone no: Business telephone no.:

    g. Previous addresses (*giving dates*):

3. MARITAL STATUS:

    a. M, S, W, Div, Sep:

    b. Date of marriage:

    c. Date termination of marriage:

    d. Name of mate, if any:

    e. Dates of previous marriages, if any:

    f. Dates of termination of previous marriages and reasons:

    g. Names and ages of children:

4. FAMILY IDENTIFICATION DATA:

    a. Father's name: Living or dead?

    Age at present, or, if dead, age at death and year of death:

    Birthplace:

    If foreign-born, date arrival U.S.A.:   Citizenship:

    b. Mother's maiden name: Living or dead?

    Age at present, or, if dead, age at death and year of death?

    Birthplace:

    If foreign-born, date arrival U.S.A.:   Citizenship:

    c. Siblings (list names, ages, and sex):

5. SOCIAL SERVICE EXCHANGE (*for clinic patients*):

---

*Long form: Complete statistical data outline to be filled out by therapist or social worker.

APPENDIX C
Initial Interview

PATIENT'S NAME: Date:

ADDRESS: Interviewer:

HOME TELEPHONE: BUSINESS PHONE: Referred by:

Informant (*if any*): Name and address:

With whom is patient now living? (*list people*)

Age of patient: Sex: Religion:

Education: Occupation: Salary:

If unemployed, sources of income:

Marital status: How long married?   Any previous marriages?

When?   Age of mate: Occupation of mate:

                                                    Salary of mate:

Military record:

Miscellaneous:

(Use additional blank sheets if necessary indicating item number.)

1. CHIEF COMPLAINT (*patient's own words*):

2. HISTORY AND DEVELOPMENT OF COMPLAINT (*from onset to present*):

3. OTHER SYMPTOMS AND CLINICAL FINDINGS AT PRESENT:

☐ Tension
☐ Depressed
☐ Severe depression
☐ Suicidal
☐ Severe anxiety
☐ Hallucinations
☐ Delusions
☐ Dangerous
☐ Excited

☐ Physical symptoms
☐ Fatigue
☐ Exhaustion
☐ Headaches
☐ Dizziness
☐ GI Symptoms
☐ Sexual problem
☐ Impotency
☐ Homosexuality

☐ Phobias
☐ Obsessions
☐ Compulsions
☐ Excessive sedatives
☐ Excess alcohol
☐ Insomnia
☐ Nightmares
☐ Other symptoms (*specify*)
☐ Present medications (*dosage and how long taken*)

Description of above:

4. DREAMS (*patient's own words*):

5. FAMILY DATA (*health and personality of mother, father, siblings, spouse, children; and patient's attitudes toward them*):

6. PREVIOUS EMOTIONAL UPSETS (*from childhood to present illness*):

7. PREVIOUS TREATMENT (*including hospitalization*):

8. PSYCHOLOGIC TESTS:

9. TENTATIVE DIAGNOSIS:

10. TENTATIVE DYNAMICS:

APPENDIX C (continued)

11. TENTATIVE PROGNOSIS:

12. PATIENT'S RESPONSE TO INTERVIEWER: ( ) cooperative ( ) fearful
     ( ) suspicious ( ) hostile
13. INTERVIEWER'S RESPONSE TO PATIENT: ( ) positive ( ) ill-defined
     ( ) negative
14. PHYSICAL APPEARANCE: ( ) meticulous ( ) presentable ( ) untidy
     ( ) disheveled
15. PATIENT'S ESTIMATE OF PRESENT PHYSICAL HEALTH: ( ) satisfactory
     ( ) poor
16. COMMUNICATIVENESS: ( ) garrulous ( ) satisfactory ( ) underprodutive
     ( ) answers questions only
17. Insight and motivation:

( ) aware of a problem   ( ) desires to correct problem
( ) aware of emotional nature of problem   ( ) willing to accept psychotherapy
( ) accepts present therapist   ( ) accepts conditions of therapy
( ) can arrange time for therapy   ( ) can afford treatment

18. DISPOSITION:

FEE:
Initial interview
Testing
Therapy

( ) Case accepted	Hours Patient Can Come for Treatment:
( ) Case referred	
( ) Case closed	

( ) Emergency	( ) Appointment given patient	( ) Paid
( ) ℞ Urgent	( ) Notify patient of appointment	( ) Charge
( ) ℞ Not urgent	( ) Patient will call for appointment	( ) Send Bill

TYPE OF THERAPY:

CORRESPONDENCE REQUIRED:

RECOMMENDATIONS AND REMARKS:

---

* To be filled out by initial interviewer.

APPENDIX D
Personal Data Sheet*

Please fill out the following blank as completely as possible. This will save time and make it unnecessary to ask you routine questions. All material is confidential and will not be released except on your written request.

Name _____

Address _____

    (Will it be all right to write to you at the above address for billing, changes of appointment, etc? _____)

Home phone _____   Business phone _____

    (Can we call you at either of these? _____)

    In the event of a change in appointment, at what time can we reach you at either of these phones? _____

Age _____   Birthday _____   Sex (M, F) _____

Birthplace _____

If foreign-born, date of arrival in U.S.A. _____

If foreign-born, are you a citizen? _____

Approximately how long have you lived in this city? _____

Marital status (Single, married, Separated, Divorced) _____

If married, how long ago? _____   If separated or divorced, when? _____

If married more than once, list dates of marriage, length of time married, whether marriage terminated by divorce, annulment, death: _____

Number of ages of children, if any _____

Occupation _____   Approximate gross yearly salary _____

How long have you been doing your present kind of work? _____

If unemployed, source of income at present: _____

How far through school did you go? _____

Name and address of nearest relative or friend: _____

Any army service? _____

Whom are you living with at present? _____

Who referred you here? _____

How strongly do you want treatment for your problem? (*check*)
  ( ) very much ( ) much ( ) moderately ( ) could do without it, if necessary
  ( ) do not want treatment

APPENDIX D (continued)

What days and times can you come here for treatments? _____

If your answer to above is after 5 p.m., can you, if necessary, get away for an hour once weekly during the day? _____

If psychologic or other tests are necessary to help your condition, would you object to them for any reasons? _____

Do you know what psychotherapy is? _____

---

* To be filled out by patient.

APPENDIX E
Family Data Sheet*

NAME:

Please fill out the following blank as complete as possible. This will save time and make it unnecessary to ask you routine questions. All material is confidential and will not be released except on your written request.

1. List the first names of your father, mother, brother, and sisters, in chronologic order, and supply the following information about each:

List first names.	Age.	Live in what city?	If dead, what year and cause?	Marital status— M, Div, Sep, Wid	Do you see them often or write often to them? (yes, no)	Personality adjustment (good, fair, poor)	How do (or did) you get along with them (good, fair, poor)?
Father:							
Mother:							
Sisters:							
Brothers:							

2. If married, age of mate: _____ Are you living with spouse now? _____
   Occupation of spouse: _____
   Personality adjustment of spouse (good, fair, poor): _____
   How are you getting along with spouse (good, fair, poor)? _____

3. List all of your children of both present and previous marriages, by first names in chronologic order, giving the following information on each:

Name	Living or dead	Ages	Living with whom at present?	Check if by previous marriage	Personality adjustment (good, fair, poor)	How do you get along with child (good, fair, poor)?

* To be filled out by patient.

APPENDIX F

Examiner:	**Daily Progress Note***	Date:

PATIENT'S NAME:

At each visit enter (1) present state of symptoms or complaints (absent, improved, the same, worse), (2) how patient feels (anxious, placid, depressed, happy), (3) important life situations and developments since last visit and how they were handled, (4) generate content of session, (5) significant transference and resistance reactions, (6) dreams.

---

* On the standard form, this Daily Progress Note is given two full sides of an 8½ by 11 inch sheet, to allow for as complete a report as is required.

APPENDIX G
  Monthly Progress Summary**

Month covered in this report:

(Fill out this side and on back of sheet elaborate on any checked items as well as other items of importance, using additional sheets if necessary.)†

NAME OF PATIENT: NAME OF THERAPIST:

NUMBER OF SESSIONS THIS   TOTAL NUMBER OF SESSIONS TO
  MONTH: DATE:

PATIENT'S RESPONSE TO THERAPY:

1. *General progress to date:* ( ) excellent ( ) satisfactory ( ) poor
      Symptoms are: ( ) better ( ) the same ( ) worse

2. *Appointments:* ( ) comes on time ( ) comes early ( ) comes late

3. *Communicativeness:* ( ) satisfactory ( ) overproductive ( ) incoherent
      ( ) underproductive ( ) responds on to questions
      ( ) long periods of silence ( ) other, describe:

4. *Relationship with therapist:* Working relationship: ( ) good ( ) fair
      ( ) poor ( ) intense dependency ( ) sexual feelings ( ) fear
      ( ) detachment ( ) negativism ( ) hostility ( ) other, describe:

5. *Resistance:* ( ) low ( ) moderate ( ) strong ( ) interferes with progress
      ( ) "acting-out" tendencies

6. *Insight:* ( ) achieving insight ( ) curiosity about dynamics
      ( ) intellectual, but no emotional, insight ( ) resists insight

7. *Translation of insight into action:* ( ) excellent ( ) satisfactory ( ) poor

8. *Present symptoms:* (Describe any checked items on back.)

   ( ) new physical symptoms   ( ) sexual disturbance   ( ) intense anxiety
       or complaints   ( ) intense depression   ( ) hallucinations
   ( ) exaggerated old physical ( ) suicidal threats   ( ) delusions
       symptoms   ( ) suicidal attempts   ( ) excess alcohol
   ( ) work disability   ( ) overactivity   ( ) excess sedatives or drugs
   ( ) marked insomnia   ( ) destructive tendencies   ( ) other, describe:

9. *Severe environmental problems:* ( ) finances ( ) work ( ) family ( ) other

---

** This form will be found helpful in clinics where there is routine supervision of the entire case load. It is turned over monthly to supervisor.
  † The original Monthly Progress Summary is on one side of a sheet only.

APPENDIX G (continued)

REMARKS:

1. ( ) Supervisory Conference Needed: ( ) emergency foreseen
        ( ) dynamics not clear ( ) treatment going poorly
        ( ) patient wants to discontinue ( ) may need medication
        ( ) therapist considering closing ( ) other, describe:

2. ( ) Consultation Needed: ( ) with caseworker ( ) with psychologist
        ( ) with medical consultant ( ) with psychiatric consultant
        ( ) other, describe:

3. *Other* (describe briefly on back of sheet what has been going on in treatment during the last month):

APPENDIX H
Termination Note

1. NAME OF PATIENT: _____

2. DATE OF INITIAL INTERVIEW: _____

3. DATE OF TERMINAL INTERVIEW: _____

4. TOTAL NUMBER OF SESSIONS: _____

5. REASON FOR TERMINATION: (   ) planned termination
   (   ) withdrawal by patient (explain)

6. CONDITION AT DISCHARGE:
   (   ) a. *Recovered:* Asymptomatic with good insight
   (   ) b. *Markedly improved:*
          (   ) Asymptomatic with some insight
          (   ) Asymptomatic with no insight
   (   ) c. *Moderately improved:*
          (   ) Partial reduction of symptoms with good insight
          (   ) Partial reduction of symptoms with some insight
   (   ) d. *Slightly improved:* Partial reduction of symptoms with little or no insight
   (   ) e. *Unimproved*
   (   ) f. *Worse* (Describe)

7. AREAS OF IMPROVEMENT *(use back of sheet, if necessary):*
       a. Symptoms:

       b. Adjustment to environment: (work, community, etc.)

       c. Physical functions: (appetite, sleep, sex, etc.)

       d. Relations with people:

8. PATIENT'S ATTITUDE TOWARD THERAPIST AT DISCHARGE *(use back of sheet, if necessary):*
   (   ) friendly   (   ) indifferent   (   ) unfriendly

9. Would patient object to a follow-up letter inquiring about progress?
   (   ) Yes   (   ) No

10. RECOMMENDATIONS TO PATIENT AT DISCHARGE *(if any. Use back of sheet, if necessary):*

11. DIAGNOSIS AT DISCHARGE:

12. ADDITIONAL COMMENTS *(use back of sheet).*

APPENDIX I
Summary*

PATIENT'S NAME:

Date of Summary:		Therapist:
Prepared by:	Total Treatment Sessions:	Initial Interview Date

   I. CHIEF COMPLAINT:

  II. HISTORY AND DEVELOPMENT OF COMPLAINT:

  III. OTHER COMPLAINTS AND SYMPTOMS:

  IV. MEDICAL, SURGICAL, AND GYNECOLOGIC HISTORY:

  V. ENVIRONMENTAL DISTURBANCES (at onset of therapy):

  VI. RELATIONSHIP DIFFICULTIES (at onset of therapy):

  VII. HEREDITARY, CONSTITUTIONAL, and EARLY DEVELOPMENTAL INFLU-ENCES:

  VIII. FAMILY DATA:

  IX. PREVIOUS ATTACKS OF EMOTIONAL ILLNESS:

  X. INITIAL INTERVIEW (brief summary of condition of patient):

  XI. LEVEL OF INSIGHT AND MOTIVATION (at onset of therapy):

  XII. CLINICAL EXAMINATION (significant physical, neurologic, psychiatric, and psychologic findings):

---

   * Type this form, if possible. Use and attach additional blank sheets in the event space for any item to be sufficient, carrying over the same item number. *Note:* This form has been condensed to two pages which is ordinarily in four pages, with considerable space between items.

XIII.   DIFFERENTIAL DIAGNOSIS:

XIV.   ESTIMATE OF PROGNOSIS:

XV.   PSYCHODYNAMICS AND PSYCHOPATHOLOGY:

XVI.   COURSE OF TREATMENT (type of therapy employed, frequency, total sessions, significant events during therapy, nature of transference and resistance, progress in therapy, insight, change in symptoms, attitudes, and relationships with people):

XVII.   CONDITION ON DISCHARGE:

XVIII.   RECOMMENDATIONS TO PATIENT:

XIX.   STATISTICAL CLASSIFICATION:

APPENDIX J*

NAME OF PATIENT: NAME OF THERAPIST:
(L-Late; B-Broken;
C-Cancelled)

	DATE	L, B or C	BILLING
1			
2			
3			
4			
5			
6			
7			
8			
9			
10			
11			
12			
13			
14			
15			
16			
17			
18			
19			
20			
21			
22			
23			
24			
25			
26			
27			
28			
29			
30			
31			
32			
33			
34			
35			
36			
37			
38			
39			
40			
41			
42			
43			
44			
45			
46			
47			
48			
49			
50			
51			
52			
53			
54			

DATE	FORM
	Personal Data Sheet
	Family Data Sheet
	INITIAL INTERVIEW
	Personality Inventory
	Rorschach Responses
	Man-Woman Drawing
	Consultations:
	Psychiatric
	Medical
	Neurological
	Psychological
	Casework
	TERMINAL NOTE
	SUMMARY
	Transfer
	Follow-up 1 yr.
	Follow-up 2 yrs.
	Follow-up 5 yrs.
	Case Re-opened

MONTHLY NOTES

1		13		25	
2		14		26	
3		15		27	
4		16		28	
5		17		29	
6		18		30	
7		19		31	
8		20		32	
9		21		33	
10		22		34	
11		23		35	
12		24		36	

SUPERVISION

Date	Supervisor	Date	Supervisor
1		13	
2		14	
3		15	
4		16	
5		17	
6		18	
7		19	
8		20	
9		21	
10		22	
11		23	
12		24	

* Case folder. This form is printed on the front of a heavy manila correspondence folder, and the numbered list of appointments (left-hand column) is continued in two columns on the back of the folder program being made for 165 appointments. (The above reproduction has been reduced in size from a original 9 × 11¾ inch folder.)

APPENDIX K
Outline for Case Presentation

1. Age of patient.
2. Sex.
3. Marital status.
4. How long married?
5. Number and ages of children.
6. Age and occupation of mate.
7. Any previous marriages? When?
8. Religion.
9. Education.
10. Occupation.
11. Employed? Salary.
12. If unemployed, source of income.
13. CHIEF COMPLAINT (in patient's own words).
14. HISTORY AND DEVELOPMENT OF COMPLAINT (date of onset, circumstances under which complaint developed, progression from the onset to the time of the initial interview).
15. OTHER COMPLAINTS AND SYMPTOMS (physical, emotional, psychic, and behavioral symptoms other than those of the complaint factor).
16. MEDICAL, SURGICAL, AND, IN WOMEN, GYNECOLOGIC HISTORY.
17. ENVIRONMENTAL DISTURBANCES AT ONSET OF THERAPY (economic, work, housing, neighborhood, and family difficulties).
18. RELATIONSHIP DIFFICULTIES AT ONSET OF THERAPY (disturbances in relationships with people, attitudes toward the world, toward authority, and toward the self).
19. HEREDITARY, CONSTITUTIONAL, AND EARLY DEVELOPMENTAL INFLUENCES (significant physical and psychiatric disorders in patient's family, socioeconomic status of family, important early traumatic experiences and relationships, neurotic traits in childhood and adolescence).
20. FAMILY DATA (mother, father, siblings, spouse, children—ages, state of health, personality adjustment, and patient's attitudes toward each).
21. PREVIOUS ATTACKS OF EMOTIONAL ILLNESS (as a child and later. When did patient feel himself to be completely free from emotional illness?).
22. INITIAL INTERVIEW (brief description of condition of patient at initial interview, including clinical findings).
23. LEVEL OF INSIGHT AND MOTIVATION AT ONSET OF THERAPY (How long ago did the patient feel that he needed treatment? For what? Awareness of emotional nature of problem, willingness to accept psychotherapy).
24. PREVIOUS TREATMENTS (When did the patient first seek treatment? What treatment did he get? Any hospitalization?).
25. CLINICAL EXAMINATION (significant findings in physical, neurologic, psychiatric, and psychologic examinations).
26. DIFFERENTIAL DIAGNOSIS (at time of initial interview).
27. ESTIMATE OF PROGNOSIS (at time of initial interview).
28. PSYCHODYNAMICS AND PSYCHOPATHOLOGY.
29. COURSE OF TREATMENT (up to time of presentation).
    (1) Type of therapy employed, frequency, total number of sessions, response to therapist.
    (2) Significant events during therapy, dynamics that were revealed, verbatim report of important dreams, nature of transference and resistance.
    (3) Progress in therapy, insight acquired, translation of insight into action, change in symptoms, attitudes, and relationships with people.
    (4) Verbatim account of all or part of a typical session, if desired.
30. STATISTICAL CLASSIFICATION.

APPENDIX L
  Application Blank for New Staff Members*

NAME: ADDRESS:

AGE: MARITAL STATUS: TELEPHONE:

1. DEGREES (where obtained and dates—undergraduate and postgraduate):

2. DIDACTIC INSTRUCTION:

a. BASIC COURSES	WHERE TAKEN, YEAR, INSTRUCTOR
Psychosocial Development	
Psychopathology	
Psychodynamics	
Techniques of Interviewing	
Basic Neuropsychiatry	
Readings in Psychiatric Literature	
Techniques in Psychotherapy	
Clinical Conferences	
Continuous Case Seminars	
Child Psychiatry	
Group Psychotherapy	

b. What schools of psychotherapy or psychoanalysis have you attended as a mainculated student?

Dates:

Were you ever certified?
Have you been qualified by any Board?
Date of license, if any, to practice profession:
Membership in which professional societies?

3. PERSONAL PSYCHOANALYSIS OR PSYCHOTHERAPY:

When started:

With whom:

Number of sessions per week:

Total number of sessions:

Additional therapy:

4. CLINICAL EXPERIENCE *(indicate names of therapeutic centers, clinics, institutions, or agencies; date of affiliation; capacity in which you have functioned):*

5. CASE EXPERIENCE:

When did you begin practicing psychotherapy?

Can you estimate the total number of patients treated?

Can you estimate the total number of patient sessions to date?

Underline the kinds of problems you have handled: character disorder, psychopathic personality, anxiety neurosis, anxiety hysteria, conversion hysteria, obsessive compulsive neurosis, psychosomatic problem, alcoholism, drug addiction, borderline case, schizophrenia psychoneurotic depression, manic-depressive psychosis, involutional melancholia, paranoid condition, marital problem, childhood behavior problem, childhood psychoneurosis, childhood psychosis, convulsive disorder

6. SUPERVISED CLINICAL EXPERIENCE *(give names of supervisors, place of supervision, dates, total number of sessions with each supervisor):*

APPENDIX L (continued)

7. SUPERVISORY EXPERIENCE:

   Have you ever supervised therapists in psychotherapy?

   If yes, how many therapists?

   Total number of supervisory sessions:

   Have you ever had a course of instruction in psychotherapeutic supervision?

8. GROUP THERAPY:

   Have you ever done group therapy?

   If so, underline types: inspirational and supportive groups
   educational groups   discussion groups   analytic groups
   social and activity groups   psychodrama   other

                 Total number of group therapy sessions

9. PSYCHOTHERAPEUTIC TEACHING EXPERIENCE *(courses taught, dates, places):*

10. HAVE YOU EVER PUBLISHED ANY MATERIAL ON PSYCHOTHERAPY *(papers, pamphlets)?* If so, list:

---

   * This form is useful in determining the didactic and experimental equipment of an applicant for a clinic position.

APPENDIX M
Questions You May Have about Psychotherapy*

1. DO I NEED PSYCHOTHERAPY?

   If you have nervous symptoms such as tension, depression, fears, fatigue, and certain physical complaints for which your doctor finds no physical basis; if you find it difficult to get along in your work or in your relations with people; if you have a school, sex, or marital problem; or if you merely feel irritable, unhappy, and believe you are not getting the most out of life, psychotherapy will be of help to you.

2. HOW DOES PSYCHOTHERAPY WORK?

   Nervous symptoms and unwarranted unhappiness are the product of inner emotional troubles. In psychotherapy you are helped to understand your problems. In this way it is possible for you to do something constructive about solving them.

3. CAN PHYSICAL SYMPTOMS BE CAUSED BY EMOTION?

   Many physical symptoms are psychosomatic in nature, which means that they have an emotional or nervous basis. When you come to think of it, it is not really so strange that emotional strain or worry should produce physical symptoms. After all, every organ in your body is connected with your brain by nerve channels; and so it is logical that when your nervous system is upset by some crisis or conflict, you may feel the effects in various organs of the body.

4. IF I CANNOT SOLVE MY PERSONAL PROBLEMS WITHOUT HELP, DOES THAT MEAN THAT I HAVE A WEAK WILL OR AM ON THE WAY TO A MENTAL BREAKDOWN?

   No. Even if you have no serious symptoms, it is difficult to work out emotional problems by yourself because you are too close to them and cannot see them clearly. More and more people, even those with a great deal of psychologic knowledge, are seeking help these days because they realize this. The fact that you desire aid is a compliment to your judgment and is no indication that you are approaching a mental breakdown. Psychotherapy has helped countless numbers of people to overcome serious emotional symptoms and has enabled many others to increase their working capacities and to better their relationships with people.

5. WHAT KIND OF TREATMENT WILL I NEED?

   The kind of treatment best suited for you can be determined only by a careful evaluation of your problem by a professional therapist.

6. WHAT HAPPENS TO THE INFORMATION ABOUT ME?

   In scientific work records are necessary, since they permit of a more thorough dealing with one's problems. It is understandable that you might be concerned about what happens to the information about you, because much or all of this information is highly personal. Case records are confidential. *No outsider, not even your closest relative or family physician, is permitted to see your case record without your written permission.*

7. HOW CAN I HELP TO COOPERATE WITH THE TREATMENT PLAN?

   The general practitioner has medications; the surgeon works with instruments; the heart specialist has x-rays and delicate recording apparatus. But for the most part, the psychotherapist has only one aid besides knowledge—YOU. Your cooperation and trust in the therapist are essential. You must feel free to take up with your therapist anything about the treatment process that disturbs you or puzzles you in any way. By doing this you have the best chance of shortening your treatment and insuring its fullest success.

* Informational sheet that may be given the patient prior to the initial interview.

APPENDIX N
  Personal History Sheet*

Name _____   _____

            LAST   FIRST   DATE

This material is necessary for the completion of your records. In answering the questions use extra sheets if required, noting the number of the question that is being answered. This, as all other information, will be kept confidential. If you are particularly troubled by any question and do not desire to answer it, merely write in "Do not care to answer."

  1. How would you describe your health (excellent, good, fair, poor)?

      a. Physical _____
      b. Emotional _____

  2. What physical illnesses have you had? When?

  3. When was your last examination by a physician? _____

          For what condition? _____

  4. Have you in the last 2 years had

      a. Chest x-ray _____
      b. Urine examination _____
      c. Blood tests _____

  5. Have you ever been turned down for life insurance? _____

          If yes, why?

  6. Have you ever been in a hospital? _____ If yes:

          Name of hospital _____
          Nature of illness _____
          Date and length of hospitalization _____

  7. When was the last time you felt well both physically and emotionally for a sustained period? _____

  8. Have you received treatment for "nervous" or emotional difficulties? _____
      If so:

          Date _____
          Frequency of visits _____
          Nature of treatment _____
          Whom treated by _____

  9. Does your present job satisfy you?

          If not, in what ways are you dissatisfied?

 10. Do you think you could handle a job more difficult than those you have held? _____

          If yes, describe.

 11. What is your ambition?

 12. Do you make friends easily? _____ Do you keep them? _____

13. Are most of your friends of one sex? _____ Which? _____
14. Can you confide in your friends? _____

15. How is most of your free time occupied?

16. What medications are you taking at the present time?
    Dosage?

Check any of the following that apply to you:

( ) headaches	( ) depressed
( ) dizziness	( ) suicidal ideas
( ) fainting spells	( ) always worried about something
( ) palpitations	( ) unable to relax
( ) stomach trouble	( ) unable to have a good time
( ) no appetite	( ) don't like weekends and vacations
( ) bowel disturbances	( ) over-ambitious
( ) fatigue	( ) sexual problems
( ) insomnia	( ) shy with people
( ) nightmares	( ) can't make friends
( ) take sedatives	( ) can't make decisions
( ) alcoholism	( ) can't keep a job
( ) feel tense	( ) inferiority feelings
( ) feel panicky	( ) home conditions bad
( ) tremors	( ) financial problems

* To be filled out by the patient when indicated.

APPENDIX O
  Medical Form

RE: ————————————————————

DEAR DR. ———————————————— :

The above patient has given me (us) permission to ask you for the results of his recent physical examination. I would appreciate your filling out this form and returning it in the enclosed envelope: (The patient's signed released is attached.)

Head: EENT

Cardiovascular:

Pulmonary:

Genito-urinary:

Neurologic:

Additional:

Diagnosis:

From your findings is there any evidence of physical illness which requires treatment at this time?   NO ——— YES ———

If, yes, what medical treatment do you recommend?

Sincerely yours,

————————————————————
Address ————————————————
Telephone No. ———————————————

APPENDIX P

Physical, Neurologic, and Laboratory Examinations

(Check items in which abnormality exists and explain below.)

I. *Physical Examination:*

( ) Stature

( ) Nutrition

( ) Weight

( ) Skin

( ) Hair

( ) Scalp

( ) Eyes

( ) Nose

( ) Sinuses

( ) Ears

( ) Lips

( ) Mouth

( ) Tongue

( ) Gums and teeth

( ) Pharynx

( ) Tonsils

( ) Neck

( ) Thyroid gland

( ) Chest

( ) Breasts

( ) Lungs

( ) Heart

( ) Blood vessels

( ) Blood pressure

( ) Abdomen

( ) Hernia

( ) Genitals

( ) Muscles

( ) Bones

( ) Joints

( ) Spine

( ) Extremities

( ) Nails

( ) Lymphatic glands

( ) Other (explain below)

II. *Neurologic Examination:*

( ) Station

( ) Gait

( ) Tactile sense

( ) Pressure sense

( ) Temperature

( ) Pain

( ) Muscular sense

( ) Stereognostic sense

( ) Olfactory nerve

( ) Optic nerve

( ) Achilles reflex

( ) Ankle clonus

( ) Wrist, biceps, triceps
    reflexes

( ) Babinski reflex

( ) Oppenheim's reflex

( ) Gordon reflex

( ) Cremasteric reflex

( ) Oculomotor, trochlear, and
    abducens nerves

( ) Trigeminal nerve

( ) Facial nerve

( ) Auditory nerves

( ) Glossopharyngeal nerve

( ) Vagus nerve

( ) Spiral accessory nerve

( ) Hypoglossal nerve

( ) Knee jerk

( ) Abdominal and epigastric reflexes

( ) Sphincteric reflexes

( ) Motor disturbances

( ) Paresis

( ) Muscles weakness

( ) Hypotonia

( ) Tremors, tics, spasms

( ) Other (explain below)

APPENDIX P (continued)

III. *Miscellaneous Examinations:*

    ( ) Urinalysis   ( ) X-ray examination

    ( ) Blood analysis   ( ) Electrocardiogram

    ( ) Endocrine analysis   ( ) Electroencephalogram

                         ( ) Other (specify)

IV. *Summary of Physical, Neurologic, and Laboratory Examinations:* If examinations are essentially negative, check below. Explain items that have been checked above.)

    ( ) Physical examination negative

    ( ) Neurologic examination negative

    ( ) Miscellaneous examinations negative

APPENDIX Q
  Mental Examination

NAME OF PATIENT:

(Check the following and elaborate below.)

I. *Attitude and General Behavior:*

A. Physical appearance: ( ) disheveled ( ) untidy ( ) unkempt
B. Degree of cooperativeness: ( ) fair ( ) poor
C. General manner: ( ) mistrustful ( ) suspicious ( ) antagonistic ( ) negativistic
    ( ) defiant ( ) preoccupied
D. General activity: ( ) motor retardation ( ) hyperactivity ( ) stereotype
    ( ) mannerisms ( ) tics ( ) echolalia ( ) echopraxia ( ) perseveration
    ( ) compulsion

II. *Stream of Mental Activity:*

A. Accessibility: ( ) indifferent ( ) self-absorbed ( ) inaccessible
B. Productivity: ( ) voluble ( ) circumstantial ( ) flight of ideas
    ( ) under-productive ( ) retardated ( ) mute
C. Progression of thought: ( ) illogical ( ) irrelevant ( ) incoherent
    ( ) verbigeration ( ) blocking
D. Neologisms:

III. *Emotional Reactions:*

A. Quality of affect: ( ) elation ( ) exhilaration ( ) exaltation ( ) euphoria
    ( ) mild depression ( ) moderate depression ( ) severe depression
    ( ) apprehension ( ) fear ( ) anxiety ( ) irritability ( ) morbid anger
    ( ) apathy ( ) emotional instability
B. Appropriateness of affect: ( ) incongruity with thought content ( ) ambivalence
    ( ) emotional deterioration

IV. *Mental Trend—Content of Thought:*

A. Thinking disorders: ( ) phobias ( ) obsessive ideas ( ) psychosomatic complaints
    ( ) persecutory trend ( ) ideas of reference ( ) grandiose ideas ( ) depressive
    delusions ( ) nihilistic delusions ( ) hypochondriac ideas ( ) ideas of
    unreality ( ) deprivation of thought ( ) delusions of influence ( ) autistic
    thinking
B. Perceptive disorders: ( ) auditory hallucinations ( ) visual hallucinations
    ( ) olfactory hallucinations ( ) tactile hallucinations ( ) reflex, microptic,
    hypnagogic, or psychomotor hallucinations ( ) illusions

APPENDIX Q (continued)

V. *Sensorium, Mental Grasp, and Capacity:*

    A. Disorders of consciousness: ( ) confusion   ( ) clouding   ( ) dream state
        ( ) delirium   ( ) stupor

    B. Disorders of apperception: ( ) mild   ( ) severe

    C. Disorders of orientation: ( ) time   ( ) place   ( ) person

    D. Disorders of personal identification and memory: ( ) general amnesia
        ( ) circumscribed amnesia   ( ) confabulation   ( ) retrospective falsification
        ( ) hypermnesia

    E. Disorders of retention and immediate recall: ( ) mild   ( ) severe

    F. Disorders of counting and calculation: ( ) mild   ( ) severe

    G. Disorders of reading: ( ) mild   ( ) severe

    H. Disorders of writing: ( ) mild   ( ) severe

    I. Disorders in school and general knowledge: ( ) mild   ( ) severe

    J. Disorders in attention, concentration and thinking capacity: ( ) mild   ( ) severe

    K. Disorders in intelligence: ( ) inconsistent with education   ( ) mild   ( ) severe

    L. Disorders in judgment: ( ) mild   ( ) severe

    M. Disorders in insight: ( ) mild   ( ) severe

VI. *Summary of Mental Examination* (check and describe abnormality, if any):

    ( ) Mental examination essentially negative
    ( ) Disturbance in attitude and general behavior
    ( ) Disturbance in stream of mental activity
    ( ) Disturbance in emotional reaction
    ( ) Disturbance in mental trend—content of thought
    ( ) Disturbance in sensorium, mental grasp and capacity

APPENDIX R
  Authorization for Release of Medical Records

TO: _____

ADDRESS: _____

   I would appreciate your releasing to _____
all records or abstracts pertaining to my case. I herewith grant permission for this release.

SIGNED: _____

Witness: _____

Date: _____

APPENDIX S
  Progress Report*

NAME: DATE:

(At the beginning of each month, it would be helpful if you would write a brief report on how you feel and what you believe has been accomplished in the past month.)

Checking the following:

   The symptoms are complaints for which I sought treatment originally are: ( ) the same
( ) better   ( ) worse

   My understanding of my condition is: ( ) excellent   ( ) good   ( ) fair   ( ) poor

   I believe my relationship with my therapist to be: ( ) good   ( ) fair   ( ) in need of improvement

   I would consider my progress to be: ( ) excellent   ( ) good   ( ) fair   ( ) poor

ADDITIONAL COMMENTS:

---

* This sheet may be given monthly to selected patients for a progress report.

APPENDIX T
Antidepressant Medications: Special Instructions for Patients*

TYPE OF MEDICINE

These medications properly taken can relieve depression *immediately or take up to 4 weeks of continuous medication.* The percentage of success with these medications is very high, and if the patient cooperates by not skipping medication and not under or overdosing hospitalization is rarely (less than 5%) necessary. The average time for signs of recovery to appear is 1 to 4 weeks.

DOSAGE

It cannot be overstressed that the medication should be taken as prescribed and not skipped. It is common for depressed persons to be their own worst enemies and thus, on one pretext or another, not take the medication as prescribed or most frequently to skip doses or days.

SIDE EFFECTS

Almost all good modern medicines have some mildly undesirable or minor reactions which are usually unimportant. Do not become alarmed. Usually it is best to tell the doctor if you do get them.

1. Dryness of the mouth is probably most frequent. Ignore it, or chew gum, keep hard candy in the mouth, or take liquids often.
2. Blurring of vision—is usually due to a temporary enlargement of the pupil. If it bothers you a great deal or interferes with your work, tell the doctor.
3. Lowered blood pressure—*Do not stand suddenly.* If you should forget and stand suddenly after having been on the medicine for some time, you get nauseous or dizzy. If you are afraid of fainting, lie flat. Get an elastic bandage to wrap tightly around the abdomen (belly). The wrapping should be at least 8 inches wide. A tight girdle or similar support may be enough. An abdominal support purchased in a surgical supply house or drugstore is best. Put the support on before getting out of bed in the morning and continue to wear it daily until the doctor says you may stop. It is rarely necessary to wear elastic stockings or wrap elastic bandages around the legs to the hip. The belly support tightly and properly applied is usually adequate. If it is not, tell the doctor and have him check your blood pressure *in the standing position.* The doctor can also use additional medicines to raise your pressure.
4. Constipation—Your body can adjust to bowel movements occuring every 2–3 days, and, thus, if medication or depression does this, laxatives are not required. Do not take any laxative but mineral oil or milk of magnesia except the doctor's advice.
5. Minor and rare inconveniences—never reason for stopping medication.
   a. Sweating—excessive perspiration may occur in some persons. This is usually a sign that an adequate dosage is being used. Excessive sweating may also be caused by nervousness, so do not stop medication under these circumstances; discuss it with your doctor.
   b. Sleepiness—most fatigue and sleepiness is due to emotional problems. Rarely, temporary sleepiness of a week's duration is caused by medication. Under no circumstances stop the medication entirely because of this. Dose may be taken more toward bedtime, decreased with doctor's consent, or sleepiness will stop after a week on the medication.
   c. Shakiness—most shakiness is due to the emotional problem. Rarely is it due to medication. Discuss with this your doctor.
6. *IMPORTANT!* Most antidepressants will mix well with foods or other medicines. However, if you are treated by another doctor for anything, even a cold, you should remind him that you are taking an antidepressant or have been in the last two weeks.
   a. DO NOT USE ALCOHOL IN ANY FORM.
   b. Do not take any medication without the doctor's knowledge, especially over-the-counter medicines with the exception of aspirin, mineral oil, or milk of magnesia. In particular,

APPENDIX T

---

avoid cold and cough medicines, antihistamines, and reducing or sleeping medicine. It is also well to avoid coffee and "colas" as they increase nervousness.

7. *MOST IMPORTANT*—For those on MAO antidepressants only. If the doctor tells you that you are on an especially strong antidepressant, such as an MAO (monoamineoxidase inhibitor) for depression, then:

    a. Do not use alcohol in any form, especially chianti wine.

    b. Do not eat cheese, except cottage cheese.

    c. Do not eat prepared herring or similar products, no wax beans, or other foods that the doctor may prohibit.

DEPRESSION AND ITS FUTURE

Almost all people get the "blues" or are depressed for some period of time. You have a longer period of depression than is healthy. You may usually feel that there is no hope for you . . . that you're not worth taking the time and money to cure . . . that you're too tired to make any effort . . . or that you're the one person who can't be cured. Usually your concentration and memory have temporarily declined. You may have little feeling for those you have loved before, even in your own family, and you may have little interest in sex. These and some other things are characteristic of depression. *They respond easily to treatment—do not give up hope.*

---

* Reprinted from mimeographed sheets by permission of the author, Dr. Irwin Rothman.

APPENDIX U
Questions You May Have About Hypnosis

1. EXACTLY WHAT IS HYPNOSIS?
   Hypnosis is a state of altered consciousness that occurs normally in every person just before one enters into the sleep state. In therapeutic hypnosis we prolong this brief interlude so that we can work within its bounds.

2. CAN EVERYBODY BE HYPNOTIZED?
   Yes, because it is a normal state that everybody passes through before going to sleep. However, it is possible to resist hypnosis like it is possible to resist going to sleep. But even if one resists hypnosis, with practice the resistance can be overcome.

3. WHAT IS THE VALUE OF HYPNOSIS?
   There is no magic in hypnosis. There are some conditions in which it is useful and others in which no great benefit is derived. It is employed in medicine to reduce tension and pain that accompany various physical problems and to aid certain rehabilitative procedures. In psychiatric practice it is helpful in short-term therapy and also, in some cases, in long-term treatment where obstinate resistances have been encountered.

4. WHO CAN DO HYPNOSIS?
   Only a qualified professional person should decide whether one needs hypnosis or could benefit from it. In addition to other experience, the professional person requires further training in the techniques and uses of hypnosis before being considered qualified.

5. WHY DO SOME DOCTORS HAVE DOUBTS ABOUT HYPNOSIS?
   Hypnosis is a much misunderstood phenomenon. For centuries it has been affiliated with spiritualism, witchcraft, and various kinds of mumbo jumbo. It is a common tool of quacks who have used it to "cure" every imaginable illness, from baldness to cancer. The exaggerated claims made for it by undisciplined persons have turned some doctors against it. Some psychiatrists too doubt the value of hypnosis because Freud gave it up 60 years ago and because they themselves have not had too much experience with its modern uses.

6. IF HYPNOSIS IS VALUABLE, SHOULDN'T IT BE EMPLOYED IN ALL PSYCHOLOGICAL OR PSYCHIATRIC PROBLEMS?
   Most psychological and psychiatric problems respond to treatment by skilled therapists without requiring hypnosis. Where blocks in treatment develop, a therapist skilled in hypnosis may be able to utilize it effectively. But only a qualified professional person can decide whether this is necessary or desirable.

7. IS THE USE OF HYPNOSIS ENDORSED BY THE PROPER AUTHORITIES?
   Both the American Medical Association and the American Psychiatric Association have qualified hypnosis as a useful form of treatment in the hands of skilled doctors who have had adequate training and who employ it in the context of a balanced treatment program.

8. CAN'T HYPNOSIS BE DANGEROUS?
   The hypnotic state is no more dangerous than is the sleep state. But unskilled operators may give subjects foolish suggestions, such as one often witnesses in stage hypnosis, where the trance is exploited for entertainment purposes. A delicately balanced and sensitive person exposed to unwise and humiliating suggestions may respond with anxiety. On the whole, there are no dangers in hypnosis when practiced by ethical and qualified practitioners.

9. I AM AFRAID I CAN'T BE HYPNOTIZED.
   All people go through a state akin to hypnosis before falling asleep. There is no reason why you should not be able to enter a hypnotic state.

10. **WHAT DOES IT FEEL LIKE TO BE HYPNOTIZED?**

The answer to this is extremely important because it may determine whether or not you can benefit from hypnosis. Most people give up hypnosis after a few sessions because they are disappointed in their reactions, believing that they are not suitable subjects. The average person has the idea that he will go through something different, new and spectacular in the hypnotic state. Often he equates being hypnotized with being anaesthetized, or being asleep, or being unconscious. When in hypnosis, he finds that his mind is active; that he can hear every sound in the room; that he can resist suggestions if he so desires; that his attention keeps wandering, his thoughts racing around; that he has not fallen asleep; and that he remembers everything that has happened when he opens his eyes, and thus he believes himself to have failed. He imagines then that he is a poor subject, and he is apt to abandon hypnotic treatments. *The experience of being hypnotized is no different from the experience of relaxing and of starting to go to sleep.* Because this experience is so familiar to you, and because you may expect something startlingly different in hypnosis, you may get discouraged when a trance is induced. Remember, you are not anaesthetized, you are not unconscious, you are not asleep. Your mind is active, your thoughts are under your control, you perceive all stimuli, and you are in complete communication with the operator. The only unique thing you may experience is a feeling of heaviness in your arms and tingliness in your hands and fingers. If you are habitually a deep sleeper, you may doze momentarily; if you are a light sleeper, you may have a feeling you are completely awake.

11. **HOW DEEP DO I HAVE TO GO TO GET BENEFITS FROM HYPNOSIS?**

If you can conceive of hypnosis as a spectrum of awareness that stretches from waking to sleep, you will realize that some aspects are close to the waking state, and share the phenomena of waking; and some aspects are close to sleep, and participate in the phenomena of light sleep. But over the entire spectrum, suggestibility is increased; and this is what makes hypnosis potentially beneficial, provided we put the suggestibility to a constructive use. The depth of hypnosis does not always correlate with the degree of suggestibility. In other words, even if you go no deeper than the lightest stages of hypnosis and are merely mildly relaxed, you will still be able to benefit from its therapeutic effects. It so happens that with practice you should be able to go in deeper, but this really is not too important in the great majority of cases.

12. **HOW DOES HYPNOSIS WORK?**

The human mind is extremely suggestible and is being bombarded constantly with suggestive stimuli from the outside, and suggestive thoughts and ideas from the inside. A good deal of suffering is the consequence of "negative" thoughts and impulses invading one's mind from subconscious recesses. Unfortunately, past experiences, guilt feelings, and repudiated impulses and desires are incessantly pushing themselves into awareness, directly or in disguised forms, sabotaging one's happiness, health, and efficiency. By the time one has reached adulthood, he has built up "negative" modes of thinking, feeling, and acting that persist like bad habits. And like any habits they are hard to break. In hypnosis we attempt to replace these "negative" attitudes with "positive" ones. But it takes time to disintegrate old habit patterns; so do not be discouraged if there is no immediate effect. If you continue to practice the principles taught you by your therapist, you will eventually notice change. Even though there may be no apparent alterations on the surface, a restructuring is going on underneath. An analogy may make this clear. If you hold a batch of white blotters above the level of your eyes so that you see the bottom blotter, and if you dribble drops of ink onto the top blotter, you will observe nothing different for a while until sufficient ink has been poured to soak through the entire thickness. Eventually the ink will come down. During this period while nothing seemingly was happening, penetrations were occurring. Had the process been stopped before enough ink had been poured, we would be tempted to consider the process a failure. Suggestions in hypnosis are like ink poured on layers of resistance; one must keep repeating them before they come through to influence old, destructive patterns.

13. HOW CAN I HELP IN THE TREATMENT PROCESS?

It is important to mention to your therapist your reactions to treatment and to him or her, no matter how unfounded, unfair, or ridiculous these reactions may seem. Your dreams may also be important. If for any reason you believe you should interrupt therapy, mention your desire to do so to your doctor. Important clues may be derived from your reactions, dreams, and resistances that will provide an understanding of your inner problems and help in your treatment.

14. WOULDN'T HYPNOTIC DRUGS BE VALUABLE AND FORCE ME TO GO DEEPER?

Experience shows that drugs are usually not necessary. Often they complicate matters. If you should require medications, these will be employed.

15. WHAT ABOUT SELF-HYPNOSIS?

"Relaxing exercises," "self-hypnosis," and "auto-hypnosis" are interchangeable terms for a reinforcing process that may be valuable in helping your therapist help you. If this adjunct is necessary, it will be employed. The technique is simple and safe.

APPENDIX V

Relaxing Exercises

These exercises may be performed the first thing in the morning before getting out of bed. They may be repeated during the day if desired. They should always be done at night prior to retiring; relaxing suggestion will eventually merge into sleep. The total time for each session should be at least 20 minutes.

After shutting your eyes, proceed with the following steps:

1. Deep slow breathing for about 10 breaths.
2. Progressive muscle relaxation from forehead, face, neck to fingertips; from chest to toes, visualizing and purposefully loosening each muscle group.
3. Visualizing a wonderfully relaxed scene or simply a blank white wall.
4. Slow counting to self from 1 to 20 while visualizing the relaxed scene (or white wall).
5. Relaxing or sleeping from 1 to 2 minutes during which visualization of the relaxed scene continues.
6. Make the following suggestions to yourself (using the word "you").
   a. *Symptom relief* (disturbing symptoms, like tension, etc., will get less and less upsetting).
   b. *Self-confidence* (self-assuredness will grow).
   c. *Situational control* (visualize impending difficult situations and successful mastery of them).
   d. *Self-understanding* (make connections if possible between flare-ups of symptoms and precipitating events and inner conflicts).
7. Relax or sleep for several more minutes.
8. During daytime arouse yourself by counting from one to five.

At night do not arouse yourself; continue relaxing until sleep supervenes.

If sleep begins developing during the 4th step before the count comes to an end, interrupt counting and proceed immediately to suggestions (6th step above). Then continue with count and go as deeply as you wish. A racing of the mind and a tendency to distraction are normal. When this occurs force your attention back to the exercises.

Remember, you will not really be asleep during these exercises. You will be aware of your thoughts and of stimuli on the outside. If, for any reason, before you finish you want to bring yourself out of the relaxed state, tell yourself that at the count of 5 you will be out of it. Count from 1 to 5 and say to yourself: "Be wide awake now, open your eyes." If negative thoughts crop up, bypass them, and continue with the steps outlined above. *Results are rarely immediate.* It takes a while to neutralize negative suggestions you have been giving yourself all your life. So be patient. Persistence is the keynote to success.

References

Abbott FK, Mack M, Wolf S: The action of banthine on the stomach and duodenum of man with observations of the effects of placebos. Gastroenterology 20:249–261, 1952

Ables BS, Brandsma JM: Therapy for Couples: A Clinician's Guide for Effective Treatment. San Francisco, Jossey-Bass, 1977

Abraham K: Notes on the psychoanalytical investigation and treatment of manicdepressive insanity and allied conditions, in Selected Papers. New York, Basic Books, 1953

Abraham W: Common Sense About Gifted Children. New York, Harper & Row, 1958

Abrahams J: Maternal Dependency and Schizophrenia: Mothers and Daughters in a Therapeutic Group. Abrahams J, Varon E (eds). New York, International Universities Press, 1953

Abrams R: Daily administration of unilateral ECT. Am J Psychiatry 124:384–386, 1967

Abrams R: Recent clinical studies of ECT. Semin Psychiatry 4:3–12, 1972

Abrams R, Esman WB (eds): Electroconvulsive Therapy: Biological Foundations and Clinical Applications. New York, SP Medical Scientific Books, 1982

Abrams R, Fink M: Clinical experiences with multiple electroconvulsive treatments. Compr. Psychiatry 13:115–122, 1972

Abrams R, Taylor MA: Diencephalic stimulation and the effects of ECT in endogenous depression. Br J Psychiatry 129:482–486, 1976

Abramson HA: LDS-25 as an adjunct to psychotherapy with elimination of fear of homosexuality. J Psychol 39:127–155, 1955

Abramson HA: LSD-25 XIX. As an adjunct to brief psychotherapy with special reference to ego enhancement. J Psychol 41:199, 1956(a)

Abramson HA: LSD-25 XXII. Effect on transference. J Psychol 42:51, 1956(b)

Abramson HA (ed): The Use of LSD in Psychotherapy. New York, Josiah Macy, Jr, Foundation, 1960

Abramson HA: LSD in psychotherapy and alcoholism. Am J Psychother 20:414–438, 1966

Abroms GM: The new eclecticism. Arch Gen Psychiatry 20:514–523, 1969

Abroms GM: Who prescribes drugs? Paper presented at the May 1972 meeting of the American Psychiatric Association. Audiodigest cassette 1(1), 1972

Abse DW: Hysteria, in Arieti S (ed): American Handbook of Psychiatry, vol. 1. New York, Basic Books, 1959, pp 290–291

Abt LE: Acting out in group psychotherapy: A transactional approach, in Abt LE, Weissman SL (eds): Acting Out Theoretical and Clinical Aspects. New York, Grune & Stratton, 1965

Abt LE, Bellak L: Projective Psychology. New York, Grove, 1959, p 357

Ackerman NW: The family as a social and emotional unit. Bulletin of the Kansas Mental Hygiene Society 12:1–3, 7–8, 1937

Ackerman NW: The training of case workers in

psychotherapy. Am J Orthopsychiatry 19:14–24, 1949

Ackerman NW: Psychoanalysis and group psychotherapy. Group Psychother 3:204–215, 1950

Ackerman NW: Interpersonal disturbance in the family: Some unsolved problems in psychotherapy. Psychiatry 17:359–368, 1954

Ackerman NW: Five issues in group psychotherapy. Z Diagnost Psychol 5:167, 1957(a)

Ackerman NW: An orientation to psychiatric research on the family. Marr Fam Living 19:68–74, 1957(b)

Ackerman NW: Behavior trends and disturbances of the contemporary family, in Galdston I (ed): The Family in Contemporary Society. New York, International Universities Press, 1958(a)

Ackerman NW: The Psychodynamics of Family Life. New York, Basic Books, 1958(b)

Ackerman NW: Family-focused therapy of schizophrenics, in Sher SC, David HR (eds): The Out-Patient Treatment of Schizophrenia. Orlando FL, Grune & Stratton, 1960

Ackerman NW: The schizophrenic patient and his family relationships, a conceptual basis for family-focused therapy of schizophrenia, in Greenblatt M, Levinson DJ, Klerman GL (eds): Mental Patients in Transition, Steps in Hospital Community Rehabilitation. Springfield, Ill, Thomas, 1961

Ackerman NW: The psychoanalytic approach to the family. Fam Process 1:i, 1962

Ackerman NW: Family therapy in schizophrenia: Theory and practice. Int Psychiatry Clin 1:929–43, 1964

Ackerman NW: Rational of family therapy. Roche Report 2:1–9, 1965

Action for Mental Health: Final Report of the Joint Commission on Mental Illness and Health. New York, Basic Books, 1961

Adams S: Pirate's adventure. Byte, 5(12):192–212, 1980

Adler A: Study of Organ Inferiority and its Psychical Compensation. Washington, DC, Nervous & Mental Disease Publishing Co, 1917(a)

Adler A: The Neurotic Constitution. Glueck B, Lind JE (trans). New York, Moffat Yard, 1917(b)

Adler A: The Practice and Theory of Individual Psychology. Orlando FL, Harcourt, 1929

Adler A: The Education of Children. New York, Greenberg, 1930

Adler A: Social Interest: A Challenge of Mankind. London, Faber & Faber, 1938

Adler, Alexandra: Guiding Human Misfits, A Practical Application of Individual Psychology. New York, Philosophical Library, 1948

Adler CS, Adler SM: Biofeedback: Interface with the Unconscious. Proceedings of the Biofeedback Research Society, Boston, November 1972

Adler CS, Adler SM: Biofeedback, in Karsu TB (ed): The Psychiatric Therapies. Washington, DC, American Psychiatric Association, 1984, pp 589–618

Adler G: A treatment framework for adult patients with borderline and narcissistic personality disorders. Bull Menninger Clin 44:171–180, 1980

Adler G, Buie DH: The misuses of confrontation with borderline patients, in Masserman JH (ed): Current Psychiatric Therapies, vol. 14. Orlando FL, Grune & Stratton, 1974, pp 89–94

Adler G, Myerson PG: Confrontation in Psychotherapy. New York, Aronson, 1973

Adler KA, Deutsch D (eds): Essays in Individual Psychology: Contemporary Application of Alfred Adler's Theories. New York, Grove, 1959

Agras S, Jacob R: Hypertension, in Pomerleau OF, Brady JP: Behavioral Medicine. Baltimore, Williams & Wilkins, 1979

Agras WS: Behavior therapy in the management of chronic schizophrenia. Am J Psychiatry 124:144–243, 1967

Agrin A: The Georgian Clinic: A therapeutic community for alcoholics. Q J Stud Alcohol 21:113–124, 1960

Ahsen A: Basic Concepts in Eidetic Imagery. New York, Brandon House, 1968

Ahsen A: Eidetic Parents Test and Analysis. New York, Brandon House, 1972

Aichorn A: Wayward Youth. London. Putnam. 1936

Aichorn A: Waywood Youth, New York, Viking Press, 1948

Aitchison RA, Lukoff D, Elder JP, Ferris C: A review and critique of social skills training with schizophrenic patients. Schizophrenic Bull 6, 1980

Albert RS: Stages of breakdown in the relationship and dynamics between the mental patient and his family. Arch Gen Psychiatry 3:682–690, 1960

Alberti RE, Emmons ML: Your Perfect Right. San Luis Obispo Calif, Impact, 1973

Aldrich CK: Psychiatry for the Family Physician. New York, McGraw-Hill, 1955

Aldrich CK: The dying patient's grief. JAMA 184:329–331, 1963

Aldrich CK: An Introduction to Dynamic Psychiatry. New York, McGraw-Hill, 1966

Aldrich CK, Nighswonger C: Pastoral Counseling Casebook. Philadelphia, Westminister, 1968

Alexander ED: In-the-body travel—a growth experience with fantasy. Psychother: Theory Res Prac 4:319–324, 1971

Alexander F: Five-Year Report of the Chicago Institute for Psychoanalysis, 1932–1937. Chicago, the Institute, 1937

Alexander F: Psychoanalysis revised. Psychoanal Q 9:1–36, 1940

Alexander F: The brief psychotherapy council and its outlook. Proc Psychother Council 2:14, 1944

Alexander F: Fundamental of Psychoanalysis. New York, Norton, 1948

Alexander F: Psychosomatic Medicine, Its Principles and Application. New York, Norton, 1950

Alexander F: Psychoanalysis and psychotherapy. Am J Psychoanal 2:722–733, 1954

Alexander F: Psychoanalytic contributions to short-term psychotherapy, in Wolberg LR (ed): Short-Term Psychotherapy. Orlando FL, Grune & Stratton, 1965, pp 84–126

Alexander F, French TM, Bacon CL, Benedek T, Fuerst RA, Gerard, MW, Grinker RR, Grotjahn M, Johnson AM, McLean HV: Psychoanalytic Theory. New York, Ronald, 1946

Alexander L: Effects of psychotropic drugs on conditioned responses in man, in Rothlin E (ed): Neuropsychopharmacology. Amsterdam, Elsevier, 1961

Alexander L: Objective evaluation of antidepressant therapy by conditional reflex technique, in Franks CM (ed): Conditioning Techniques in Clinical Practice and Research. New York, Springer, 1964, pp 71–85

Alger I: The clinical handling of the analyst's responses. Paper presented at the New York Medical College, Department of Psychiatry, Symposium on Transference and Counter-Transference, October 1964

Alger I: Joint sessions: Psychoanalytic variations, applications, and indications, in Rosenbaum S, Alger I (eds): Psychoanalysis and Marriage. New York, Basic Books, 1967(a)

Alger I: Joint psychotherapy of marital problems, in Masserman, JH (ed): Current Psychiatric Therapies, vol. 7. Orlando FL, Grune & Stratton, 1967(b)

Alger I: Television image confrontation in group therapy, in Sager CJ, Kaplan HS (eds): Progress in Group and Family Therapy. New York, Brunner/Mazel, 1972, pp 135–150

Alger I, Hogan P: The use of videotape recordings in conjoint marital therapy. Paper presented at the Annual Meeting of the American Psychiatric Association. Atlantic City, NJ, May 13, 1966

Alger I, Hogan P: The use of videotape recordings in conjoint marital therapy. Am J Psychiatry 123:1425–1430, 1967

Alger I, Hogan P: Enduring effects of videotape playback experience on marital and family relationships. Am J Orthopsychiatry 39:86–96, 1969

Allen CM: Day Care Centers for School Children. New York, Child Welfare League of America, 1947

Allen DH: The use of computer fantasy games in child therapy, in Schwartz MD (ed): Using Computers in Clinical Practice. New York, The Haworth Press, 1984, pp 329–334

Allen EK, Hart, B, Buell, JS, et al: Effects of social reinforcement on isolate behavior of a nursery school child. Child Dev 35:511–518, 1964

Allen FH: Therapeutic work with children: A statement of a point of view. Am J Orthopsychiatry 4:193–202, 1934

Allen FH: Psychotherapy with children. New York, Norton, 1942

Allen FH: Child psychotherapy, in Masserman JH (ed): Current Psychiatric Therapies, vol. 2. Orlando FL, Grune & Stratton, 1962, pp 41–47

Allen FH: Positive Aspects of Child Psychiatry. New York, Norton, 1963

Allen WY, Campbell D: The Creative Nursery Center. New York, Family Service Association of America, 1949

Allinsmith W, Goethals GW: The Role of Schools in Mental Health. Joint Commission on Mental Illness and Health, Monogr Ser No 7, New York, Basic Books, 1962

Allport GW: The Individual and His Religion. New York, Macmillan, 1950

Alonso A: The Quiet Profession: Supervisors of Psychotherapy. New York, Macmillan, 1985

Alonso A, Rutan JS: The impact of object relations theory on psychodynamic group therapy. Am J Psychiatry 141:1376–1380, 1984

Alt H, Residential Treatment for the Disturbed Child. New York, International Universities Press, 1960

Altman KP: Psychodrama with blind psychiatric patients. J Visual Impairment and Blindness 75:153–156, 1981

Altschuler CM, Picon WJ: The social living

class: a model for the use of sociodrama in the classroom. Group Psychother, Psychodrama and Sociometry 33:162–169, 1980

Altshuler IM: Four years' experience with music as therapeutic agent at Eloise Hospital. Am J Psychiatry 100:792–794, 1944

Alvarez WC: Psychosomatic medicine that every physician should know. JAMA 135:705, 1947

American Association of Psychiatric Social Workers: Better social services for mentally ill patients, in Knee RI (ed): Proceedings of the Institute for Social Work in Psychiatric Hospitals, 1955

American Association of Schools of Social Work: Preprofessional Education for Social Work. New York, the Association, 1946

American Board of Examiners in Professional Psychology: Annual Report. Am Psychol 12:620–622, 1957

American Board of Examiners in Psychodrama, Sociometry and Group Psychotherapy: Examination Information Pamphlet, 1982 (Available from P.O. Box 844, Cooper Station, New York, New York 10276)

American Cancer Society, California Division: Stop smoking program guide. San Francisco, 1971

American Nurses' Association: Guidelines for the Establishment of Peer Review Committees. Developed by the Ad Hoc Committee on Implementation of Standards of Nursing Practice. Kansas City, Mo, the Association, 1973(a)

American Nurses' Association: Standards: Psychiatric-Mental Health Nursing Practice. Kansas City, Mo, the Association, 1973(b)

American Occupational Therapy Association: Occupational therapy: Its definition and functions. Am J Occup Ther 26:204, 1972

American Psychiatric Association: Newsletter 3(9), May 15, 1951

American Psychiatric Association: First aid for psychological reactions in disasters. Washington, DC, the Association, 1964

American Psychiatric Association, Committee on Nomenclature and Statistics: Diagnostic and Statistical Manual of Mental Disorders (2d ed). Washington, DC, the Association, 1968

American Psychiatric Association: Task Force Report: Psychiatric Education and the Primary Physician. Washington, DC, the Association, 1970

American Psychiatric Association: Discussion Guide on National Health Insurance. Washington, DC, the Association, 1974

American Psychiatric Association: Diagnostic and statistical manual of mental disorders (3rd ed). Washington, DC, American Psychiatric Association, 1980

American Psychiatric Association Commission on Psychotherapies: Psychotherapy Research: Methodological and Efficacy Issues. Washington, DC, the Association, 1982

American Psychiatric Association Task Force on ECT: Task Force Report 14: Electroconvulsive Therapy. American Psychiatric Association, Washington, DC, 1978

American Psychoanalytic Association: Conference on Psychoanalytic Education and Research—Position Paper. Commission II—The Ideal Institute. New York, the Association, February 1974

American Psychological Association: Ethical Standards of Psychologies. Washington, DC, the Association, 1953

American Psychological Association: Conference on Level and Patterns of Training in Psychology, Vail, Col, July 1973

American Psychological Association: APA Monitor June, July, November, December 1973

American Psychologist: Professional Standards and Accreditation. Proceedings of the 57th Annual Business Meeting of the American Psychological Association in Denver, Colorado 4:445, 1949

Anderson HH: Domination and integration, in: The social behavior of young children in an experimental play situation. Genet Psychol Monogr 19:341–408, 1937

Anderson HH: Domination and social Integration in the behavior of kindergarten children and teachers. Genet Psychol Monogr 21:287–385, 1939

Anderson HH, Anderson GL: An Introduction to Projective Techniques. Englewood Cliffs, NJ, Prentice Hall, 1951

Anderson HH, Anderson GL: Social development, in Carmichael L (ed): Manual of Child Psychology (2d ed). New York, Wiley, 1954

Anderson HH, Brewer JE: Dominative and socially integrative behavior of kindergarten teachers. Appl Psychol Monogr No. 6, 1945

Anderson HH, Brewer JE: Effects of teachers' dominative and integrative contacts on children's classroom behavior. Appl Psychol Monogr No. 8, 1946(a)

Anderson HH, Brewer JE, Reed, MF: Studies of teachers' classroom personalities: III. Follow-up studies of the effects of dominative and integrative contacts on children's behavior. Appl Psychol Monogr No. 11, 1946(b)

Anderson VV, Kennedy WM: Psychiatry in college—a discussion of a model personnel program. Ment Hyg 16:353–383, 1932

Andreasen NJ, Noyes R, Jr., Hartford CE: Factors influencing adjustment of burn patients during hospitalization. Psychosom Med 34:517–525, 1972

Andrews G, Harvey R: Does psychotherapy benefit neurotic patients? A reanalysis of Smith, Glass, and Miller data. Arch Gen Psychiatry 38:1203–1208, 1981

Andrews JS: Directive psychotherapy: Reassurance, in Watson RI (ed): Readings in the Clinical Method in Psychology. New York, Harper & Row, 1949, pp 654–673

Andronico MP, Guerney BG: The potential application of filial therapy to the school situation. J School Psychol 6:2–7, 1967

Angell JR: Mental hygiene in colleges and universities. Ment Hyg 17:543–547, 1933

Ansbacher HL, Rowena R: The Individual Psychology of Alfred Adler. New York, Basic Books, 1956

Ansbach HL, Rownea R: Superiority and Social Interest, Alfred Adler. Evanston, Ill, Northwestern University Press, 1964

Antebi RN: Seven principles to overcome resistances in hypnoanalysis. Br J Med Psychol 36:341–349, 1963

Anthonisen MR: The practice of the college psychiatrist. Dis Nerv Syst 3:175–184, 1942

Anthony M: Al-Anon. JAMA 238:1062–1063, 1977

Appel KE: Drawings by children on aids to personality studies. Am J Orthopsychiatry 1:129–144, 1931

Appel KE: Religion, in Arieti S (ed): American Handbook of Psychiatry, vol. 2. New York, Basic Books, 1959, pp 1777–1782

Appel KE, Lhamon ST, Myers JM, Harvey WA: Long-Term Psychotherapy, in Association for Research in Nervous and Mental Disease: Psychiatric Treatment. Research Pub 31. Baltimore, Williams & Wilkins, 1953, pp 21–24

Appel KE, Ormsby R, Myers JM: Family casework agencies, psychiatric clinics and the Joint Commission Report. Am J Psychiatry 121:839–846, 1965

Appelbaum PS: Tarasoff and the clinician: Problems in fulfilling the duty to protect. Am J Psychiatry 142:425–429, 1985

Appleton WS, Davis JM: Practical Clinical Psychopharmacology (2d ed). Baltimore, Williams & Wilkins, 1980

Appley MH: Motivation Threat Perception, and the Induction of Psychological Stress. Proceedings of the Sixteenth International Congress of Psychology in Bonn, W. Germany 1960 Amsterdam, North Holland Publishers (Abstract), 1962

Arehart-Treichel J: The science of sleep. Science News 111:203–207, 1977

Argyris C: Explorations in consulting-client relationships. Human Organization 21:121–133, 1961

Arieti S: Some basic problems common to anthropology and modern psychiatry. Am Anthrop 58:26–29, 1956

Arieti S: Manic-depressive psychosis, in Arieti S (ed): American Handbook of Psychiatry, vol. 1. New York, Basic Books, 1959(a), p 450

Arieti S: Schizophrenia, in Arieti S (ed): American Handbook of Psychiatry, vol. 1. New York, Basic Books, 1959(b), p 494

Arieti S (ed): American Handbook of Psychiatry, vol. 3. New York, Basic Books, 1966

Arieti S: Interpretation of Schizophrenia (2d ed). New York. Basic Books, 1974

Arieti S: A psychotherapeutic approach to severely depressed patients. Am J Psychotherapy 27:33–47, 1978

Arje FB: The fine arts as an adjunct to rehabilitation. J Rehab 26:28–29, 1960

Arlow JA: The supervisory situation. J Am Psychoanal Assoc 11:576–594, 1963

Arlow JA: Unconscious fantasy and disturbances of conscious experience. Psychoanal Q 38:1–27, 1969

Arlow JA, Kadis A: Finger painting in the psychotherapy of children. Am J Orthopsychiatry 16:134–146, 1946

Aron KW, Smith S: The Bristol psychiatric day hospital. J Ment Sci 99:564–571, 1953

Aronson ML: Acting-out in individual and group psychotherapy. J Hillside Hosp 13:43, 1964

Aronson ML: Technical problems in combined therapy. Int J Group Psychother 14:425, 1964

Aronson ML: Resistance in individual and group therapy. Am J Psychother 21:86–95, 1967

Aronson ML: A group program for overcoming the fear of flying, in Wolberg LR, Aronson ML (eds): Group Therapy 1974: An Overview. New York, Stratton Intercontinental, 1974, pp 142–157

Arsenian J, et al: An analysis of integral functions in small groups. Int J Group Psychother 12:421, 1962

Ascher LM, Efran JJ: Use of Paradoxical intention in a behavioral program for sleep onset insomnia. Consult & Clin Psychology 46:547–550, 1978

Ascher LM, Turner FM, Ralph M, et al: A comparison of two methods for the administration of paradoxical intention. Behav Res Ther 18:121–126, 1980

Aserinsky E, Kleitman N: Regularly occurring periods of eye motility and concomitant phenomenon during sleep. Science 118:273–274, 1953

Aserinsky E, Kleitman N: Two types of ocular motility occurring in sleep. J Appl Psychol 8:1–10, 1955

Ash WE, Mahoney JD: The use of conditioned reflex and antabuse in the therapy of alcoholism. J Iowa Med Soc 41:456–458, 1951

Ashbrook J: Judgment and pastoral counseling. J Pastoral Care 20:1–9, 1966

Aspy D, Roebuck FN: Researching person-centered issues in education, in Rogers CR (ed): Freedom to Learn for the 80's. Columbus, Ohio, Charles E. Merrill, 1983

Assagioli R: Psychosynthesis: A Manual of Principles and Technique. New York, Hobbs, Dorman, 1965

Association for Supervision and Curriculum Development: Fostering Mental Health in Our Schools, 1950 Yearbook. Washington, DC, National Education Association, 1950

Astor MH: Hypnosis and behavior modification combined with psychoanalytic psychotherapy. Int J Clin Exp Hypn 21:18–24, 1973

Astrup C: The effects of psychotherapy. Int J Psychiatry 1:152–153, 1965

ATE Yearbook: Mental Health and Teacher Education. Washington, DC, Association of Teacher Educators, 1967

Atkinson RC, et al: Public Employment Service in the United States. Chicago, Public Administration Service, 1938

Atwood, GE, Stolorow RD: Structures of Subjectivity. Hillside, NJ, Analytic Press, 1984

Auerbach AA: An application of Strupp's method of content analysis to psychotherapy. Psychiatry 26:137–148, 1963

Auerswald EH: "Interdisciplinary" vs "Systems" approach in the field of mental health. Paper presented at the 122d Annual Meeting of the American Psychiatric Association. Atlantic City, NJ, May 1966

Austin LN: Trends in differential treatment in social casework. J Soc Casework 29:203–211, 1948

Austin LN: Qualifications for psychotherapists, social caseworkers. Am J Orthopsychiatry 26:47–57, 1956

Austin LN: Diagnosis and treatment of the cli-

ent with anxiety hysteria, in Parad HJ (ed): Ego Psychology and Dynamic Casework. New York, Family Service Association of America, 1958

Avnet HH: Psychiatric Insurance: Financing Short-Term Ambulatory Treatment. New York, Group Health Insurance, 1962

Avnet HH: How effective is short-term therapy? in Wolberg LR (ed): Short-term Psychotherapy. Orlando FL, Grune & Stratton, 1965, pp 7–22

Axel M: Treatment of schizophrenia in a day hospital. Int J Soc Psychiatry 5:174–181, 1959

Axline VM: Play Therapy. Boston, Houghton Mifflin, 1947 (rev ed—New York, Ballantine, 1969)

Ayd FJ: The current status of major antidepressants. Washington, DC, American Psychiatric Association, February 1960, pp 213–222

Ayd FJ: A critique of antidepressants. Dis Nerv Syst 22:5–32, 1961(a)

Ayd FJ: Toxic somatic and psychopathologic reactions to anti-depressant drugs. J Neuropsychiatry 2(1):119, 1961(b)

Ayd FJ: Chlorpromazine: Ten years' experience. JAMA 184:173–176, 1963

Ayd FJ: The future of pharmacotherapy: New drug delivery systems. Int Drug Ther Newsletter 1973

Ayd FJ: Benzodiazepine withdrawal phenomena—new insights. Psychiatric Annals 14:133–134, 1984

Ayd FJ: Twenty-five years of combining antidepressants. The Psychiatric Times April 1986, p 9

Ayllon T, Azrin NH: The Token Economy: A Motivational System for Therapy and Rehabilitation. New York, Appleton-Century-Crofts, 1968

Ayllon T, Houghton E: Control of the behavior of schizophrenic patients by food. J Exp Anal Behav 5:343–352, 1962

Ayllon T, Michael J: The psychiatric nurse as a behavioral engineer. J Exp Anal Behav 2:323–334, 1959

Ayllon T, Michael J: The psychiatric nurse as a behavioral engineer, in Franks CM (ed): Conditioning Techniques in Clinical Practice and Research. New York, Springer, 1964, pp 275–289

Azima H: The effects of Vesprin in mental syndromes. Squibb Inst Med Res Monogr Ther 2:203, 1957

Azima H: Sleep treatment in mental disorders. Dis Nerv Syst 19:623–530, 1958

Azrin NH: Improvements in the community—

reinforcement approach to alcoholism. Beh Res Ther 14:339–348, 1976

Bach GR: Intensive Group Psychotherapy. New York, Ronald, 1954

Bach GR: Observations on transference and object relations in the light of group dynamics. Int J Group Psychother 7:64–76, 1957

Bach GR: The marathon group: Intensive practice in intimate interaction. Psychol Rep 18:995–1002, 1966

Bach GR: Marathon group dynamics: I. Some functions of the professional group facilitator. Psychol Rep 20:995–999, 1967(a)

Bach GR: Marathon group dynamics: II. Dimensions of helpfulness: Therapeutic aggression. Psychol Rep 20:1147–1158, 1967(b)

Bach GR: Marathon group dynamics: III. Disjunctive contacts. Psychol Rep 20:1163–1172, 1967(c)

Bach GR: Group and leader phobias in marathon groups. Voices 3:41–46, 1967(d)

Bach GR: Fight with me in group therapy, in Wolberg LR, Aronson ML (eds): Group Therapy 1974: An Overview. New York, Stratton Intercontinental, 1974, pp 186–195

Bachrach AJ: Experimental Foundations of Clinical Psychology. New York, Basic Books, 1962

Back KW: Beyond Words: The Story of Sensitivity Training and the Encounter Movement. New York, Russell Sage Foundation, 1972

Baer DM, Harris FR, Wolf MM: Control of nursery school children's behavior by programming social children's behavior by programming social reinforcement from their teachers. Paper presented at a meeting of the American Psychological Association, Philadelphia, August 1963

Bagchi BK: Mental Hygiene and the Hindu doctrine of relaxation. Ment Hyg 20:424–440, 1936

Bailey P: The great psychiatric revolution. Academic lecture. Am J Psychiatry 113:387, 1956

Baily P: Sigmund the Unserene: A Tragedy in Three Acts. Springfield, Ill, Thomas, 1965

Baker BL: Symptom treatment and symptom substitution in enuresis. J Abnorm Psychol 4:42–49, 1969

Baker EFW: The use of lysergic acid diethylamide (LSD) in psychotherapy. Can Med Assoc J 91:1200–1202, 1964

Bakewell WE, Wikler A: Symposium: Nonnarcotic addiction. Incidence in a university hospital ward. JAMA 196:710–713, 1966

Bakker CB, Bakker-Rabdau MK: No Trespassing, Explorations in Human Territoriality.

Corte Madera, Calif, Chandler & Sharp, 1973

Bakwin H: Enuresis in children. J Pediatr 58:806, 1961

Balbernie R: Residental Work with Children. Elmsford, NY, Pergamon, 1966

Baldwin AL, Kalkorn J, Breese FH: Patterns of parent behavior. Psychol Monogr 58, No. 3, 1945

Baldessarani RJ: Symposium: Behavior modification by drugs. I: Pharmacology of the amphetamines. Pediatrics 49: 694–701, 1972

Baldessarini RJ: Chemotherapy in Psychiatry. Cambridge, Harvard University Press, 1977

Baldessarini RJ: Chemotherapy in Psychiatry. Cambridge, Harvard University Press, 1984(a)

Baldessarini RJ: Drugs and the treatment of psychiatric disorders, in Gilman AG, Goodman LS (eds): The Pharmacological Basis of Therapeutics (7th ed). New York, Macmillan, 1984(b)

Bales RF: Interaction Process Analysis: A Method for the Study of Small Groups. Reading, Mass, Addison-Wesley, 1950

Bales RF: Small-group theory and research, in Mertin RK, Broom L, Cottrell LS Jr (eds): Sociology Today: Problems and Prospects. New York, Basic Books, 1958, pp 293–305

Balint M: The final goal of psychoanalytic treatment. Int J Psychoanal 17, 1936

Balint M: On the psychoanalytic training system. Int J Psychoanal 29:163–173, 1948

Balint M: Training general practitioners in psychotherapy. Br Med J 1:115–131, 1954

Balint M: The doctor, his patient and the illness. Lancet 1:683–688, 1955

Balint M: The Doctor, His Patient and the Illness. New York, International Universities Press, 1957 (2d ed—London, Pitman, 1964)

Balint M: The other part of medicine. Lancet 1:40–42, 1961(a)

Balint M: Psychotherapeutic Techniques in Medicine. London, Tavistock, 1961(b)

Balint M: The doctor's therapeutic function. Lancet 1:1177–1180, 1965

Balint M: Psychoanalysis and medical practice. Int J Psychoanal 47:54–62, 1966(a)

Balint M: Medicine and psychosomatic medicine: New possibilities in training and practice. Comp Psychiatry 9:267–274, 1968(a)

Balint M: The Basic Fault: Therapeutic Aspects of Regression. London, Tavistock, 1968(b)

Balint M: Research-seminars: Its implications for medicine. J R Coll Gen Pract 17:201–211, 1969

Balint M: Research in psychotherapy and the importance of the findings for psychoanalysis. Rev Med Psychosom Psychol Medicale 12:225–240, 1970

Balint M, Balint E: On transference and countertransference. Int J Psychoanal 20:223–230, 1939

Balint M, Balint E: Psychotherapeutic Techniques in Medicine. London, Tavistock, 1961

Balint M, Balint E, Gosling R, Heidebrand P: A Study of Doctors. Philadelphia, Lippincott, 1966(b)

Balint M, Hunt J, Joyce D, et al: Treatment of Diagnosis: A Study of Repeat Prescriptions in General Practice. Philadelphia, Lippincott, 1970

Balint M, Ornstein PH, Balint E: Focal Psychotherapy—An Example of Applied Psychoanalysis. Philadelphia, Lippincott, 1972

Ballard J: Long Way Through. Boston, Houghton-Mifflin, 1959

Baller WR, Gianareco JC: Correction of nocturnal enuresis in deaf children. Volta Rev 72:545–547, 1970

Baller WR, Schalock HD: Conditioned response treatment of enuresis. Except Child 22:233–236, 247–248, 1956

Bambrace F: Effects of chlordiazepoxide in severely disturbed outpatients. Am J Psychiatry 118:69, 1961

Ban TA, Levy L: Physiological patterns: A diagnostic test procedure based on the conditioned reflex method, in Franks CM (ed): Conditioning Techniques in Clinical Practice and Research. New York, Springer, 1964, pp 56–60

Bancroft FW, Pilcher C (eds): Surgical Treatment of the Nervous System. Philadelphia, Lippincott, 1946

Bandler R, Grinder J: The Structure of Magic: A Book About Language and Therapy, vol. 1. Palo Alto, CA, Science and Behavior Books, 1975

Bandura A: Social learning through imitation, in Jones MR (ed): Nebraska Symposium on Motivation. Lincoln, University of Nebraska Press, 1962(a), pp 211–269

Bandura A: Punishment revisited. J Consult Psychol 26:298–301, 1962(b)

Bandura A: Behavioral modification through modeling procedures, in Krasner L, Ullmann LP (eds): Research in Behavior Modification. New York, Holt, 1965(a)

Bandura A: Psychotherapy conceptualized as a social learning process. Unpublished paper, 1965(b)

Bandura A: Principles of Behavior Modification. New York, Holt, 1969

Bandura A: Social Learning Theory. Englewood Cliffs, NJ, Prentice-Hall, 1977

Bandura A: On paradigms and recycled ideologies. Cognitive Ther Res 2:79, 1978

Bandura A, Blanchard ED, Ritter J: Relative efficacy of desensitization and modelling approaches for inducing behavioral affective and attitudinal changes. J Personality Soc Psychol 13:172–199, 1969

Bandura A, Huston AC: Identification as a process of incidental learning. J Abnorm Soc Psychol 63:311–318, 1961

Bandura A, Lipsher DH, Miller PE: Psychotherapists' approach-avoidance reactions to patients' expression of hostility. J Consult Psychol 24: 1–8, 1960

Bandura A, McDonald FJ: The influence of social reinforcement and the behavior of models in shaping children's moral judgments. J Abnorm Soc Psychol 67:274–281, 1963

Bandura A, Rosenthal TL: Vicarious classical conditioning as a function of emotional arousal. J Pers Soc Psychol 1, 1965

Bandura A, Ross D, Ross SA: Transmission of aggression through imitation of aggressive models. J Abnorm Soc Psychol 63:575–582, 1961

Bandura A, Ross D, Ross SA: Imitation of film-mediated aggressive models. J Abnorm Soc Psychol 66:3–11, 1963(a)

Bandura A, Ross D, Ross SA: Vicarious reinforcement and imitative learning. J Abnorm Soc Psychol 67:601–607, 1963(b)

Bandura A, Ross D, Ross SA: A comparative test of the status envy, social power and secondary reinforcement theories of identificatory learning. J Abnorm Soc Psychol 67:527–534, 1963(c)

Bandura A, Walters RH: Adolescent Aggression, New York, Ronald, 1959

Bandura A, Walters RH: Social Learning and Personality Development. New York, Holt, 1963

Banks SA: Psychotherapy: Values in action, in Regan PF, Pattishal EG (eds): Behavioral Science Contributions to Psychiatry. Boston, Little, Brown, 1965

Barahal HS: Resistances to community psychiatry. Psychiatr Q 45:333–343, 1971

Barbara DA: Stuttering. New York, Julian, 1954

Barbara DA: Working with the stuttering problem. J Nerv Ment Dis 125:329, 1957

Barbara DA: Communication in stuttering. Dis Nerv Syst 9(47):1, 1958

Barbara DA: The psychotherapy of stuttering, in Masserman JH (ed): Current Psychiatric

Therapies, vol. 3. Orlando FL, Grune & Stratton, 1963

Barber TX: Hypnotic phenomena: A critique of experimental methods, in Gordon JE (ed): Handbook of Experimental and Clinical Hypnosis. New York, Macmillan, 1967

Barber TX: Hypnosis: A Scientific Approach. New York, Van Nostrand, 1969

Barber TX: An alternative hypothesis, in Fromm E. Shor RE (eds): Hypnosis: Research Development and Perspectives. Chicago, Aldine, 1972

Bard M, Berkowitz B: Training police as specialists in family crisis intervention. A community psychology action program. Community Ment Health J 3:315–317, 1967

Barendregt JT: A psychological investigation of the effects of psychoanalysis and psychotherapy, in Research in Psychodiagnostics. Paris, Mouton, 1961

Barendregt JT: The effects of psychotherapy. Int J Psychiatry 1:161–163, 1965

Barkas M: The treatment of psychotic patients in institutions in the light of psychoanalysis. Neurol & Psychopath 5:333–340, 1925

Barnett J: Therapeutic intervention in the dysfunctional thought processes of the obsessional. Am J Psychother 26:338–351, 1972

Baron S: Limitations of the teacher in guidance. Am J Psychother 6:104–110, 1952

Barret BH: Reduction in rate of multiple tics by free-operant conditioning methods, in Franks CM (ed): Conditioning Techniques in Clinical Practice and Research. New York, Springer, 1964, pp 303–314

Barrett EB: Strength of Will. New York, PJ Kennedy, 1915

Barrett EB: The New Psychology. New York, PJ Kennedy, 1925

Barrios AA: Posthypnotic suggestion as higher ordered conditioning: A methodological and experimental analysis. Int J Clin Exp Hypn 21:32–50, 1973

Barron F, Learly TF: Changes in psychoneurotic patients with and without psychotherapy. J Consult Psychol 19:239–245, 1955

Bartemeier LH: The attitude of the physician. JAMA 145:1122–1125, 1951

Bartemeier LH: Psychoanalysis and religion. Bull Menninger Clin 29:237–244, 1965

Barten HH: The coming of age of the brief psychotherapies, in Bellak L, Barten HH (eds): Progress in Community Mental Health, vol. 1. Orlando FL, Grune & Stratton, 1969

Barten HH: Brief Therapies. New York, Behavior Publications, 1971

Bartlett J, Bridges P, Kelly D: Contemporary indications for psychosurgery. Br J Psychiatry 138:507–511, 1981

Bartlett MR: A six-month follow-up of the effects of personal adjustment counseling of veterans. J Consult Psychol 14:393–394, 1950

Barton WE, Malamud W: Training the Psychitrist to Meet Changing Needs. Washington, DC, Port City Press, 1964

Baruch DW: Procedures in training teachers to prevent and reduce mental hygiene problems. Pedagog Semin J Genet Psychol 67:143–178, 1948

Basescu S: Existential therapy, in Deutsch A, Fishman H (eds): The Encyclopedia of Mental Health, vol. 2. New York, Franklin Watts, 1963, p 589

Basmajian JV (ed): Biofeedback: Principles and Practice for Clinicians (2d ed). Baltimore, Williams & Wilkins, 1983

Bates ES, Dittemore JV: Mary Baker Eddy, New York, Knopf, 1932

Bateson G: Panel review, in Masserman JH (ed): Individual and Familial Dynamics. Orlando FL, Grune & Stratton, 1959

Bateson G: Discussion of Samuel J. Beck's "Families of schizophrenic and of well children: method, concepts and some results." Am J Psychiatry 30:263–266, 1960

Bateson G: The challenge of research in family diagnosis and therapy, summary of panel discussion: I. Formal research in family structure, in Ackerman NW, Beatman FL, Sanford S (eds): Exploring the Base for Family Therapy. New York, Family Service Association, 1961

Bateson G, Jackson DD: A note on the double bind. Fam Process 1962. 2:154–161, 1963

Bateson G, Jackson DD, Haley J, Weakland JH: Toward a theory of schizophrenia. Behav Sci 1:251–264, 1956

Battle CC, Imber SD, Hoehn-Saric R, Stone AR, et al: Target complaints as criteria of improvements. Am J Psychother 20:184–92, 1966

Bauman G, Douthit VB: Vocational rehabilitation and community mental health in deprived urban areas. Paper presented at the 122d Annual Meeting of the American Psychiatric Association, Atlantic City, NJ, May 1966

Bavelas A: A mathematical model for group structure. Appl Anthrop 7(3):16–30, 1948

Bavelas A: Communication patterns in task-oriented group, in The Policy Sciences: Recent Development in Scope and Method.

Stanford, Calif, Stanford University Press, 1952, pp 193–202

Baynes HG: Mythology of the Soul: A Research into the Unconscious from Schizophrenic Dreams and Drawings. London, Bailliere, Tindall & Cox, 1939

Beachy WN: Assisting the family in time of grief. JAMA 202:559–560, 1967

Beatman FL: Family interaction: Its significance for diagnosis and treatment. Soc Casework 38:111–118, 1957

Beck AT: Cognition, affect, and psychopathology. Arch Gen Psychiatry 24:495–500, 1971

Beck AT: Cognitive Therapy and Emotional Disorders. New York, International Universities Press, 1976

Beck AT, Kovacs M: A new fast therapy for depression. Psychol Today 10(8):94, 1977

Beck AT, Rush AJ, Shaw BF, et al: Cognitive therapy of depression: a treatment manual. Unpublished manuscript. University of Pennsylvania, 1978

Beck AT, Rush AJ, Shaw BF, et al: Cognitive Therapy of Depression. New York, Guilford, 1979

Beck AT, Young JE: Depression, in Barlow D (ed): Clinical Handbook of Psychological Disorders. New York, Guilford, 1985

Beck JC: When the patient threatens violence: An empirical study of clinical practice after Tarasoff. Bull Am Acad Psychiatry Law 10:189–201, 1982

Beck RL, Delaney W, Kraft IA: Moving through resistance: A multimedia approach to family therapy using dance therapy, video feedback and behavioral observation, in Wolberg LR, Aronson ML (eds): Group Therapy 1975: An Overview. New York, Stratton Intercontinental, 1975, pp 49–62

Beck SJ: Rorschach's Test, 3 vols. Vol. 1, Basic Processes: vol. 2, A Variety of Personality Pictures: vol. 3, Advances in Interpretation. Orlando FL, Grune & Stratton, 1944, 1945, 1952

Beck SJ: The Rorschach Test: A multi-dimensional test of personality, in Anderson HH, Anderson GL (eds): An Introduction to Projective Techniques. Englewood Cliffs, NJ, Prentice-Hall, 1951

Becker A, Goldberg HL: Home treatment services, in Grunebaum H (ed): The Practice of Community Mental Health. Boston, Little, Brown, 1970

Becker E: The Denial of Death. New York, Free Press, 1973

Becker WC, Madsen CH, Jr, Arnold CR, Thomas, DR: The contingent use of teacher attention and praise in reducing classroom behavior problems. J Spec Ed 1:287–307, 1967

Beckett T: A candidate's reflections on the supervisory process. Contemp Psychol 5:169–179, 1969

Beecher HK: The powerful placebo. JAMA 159:1602–1606, 1955

Beecher HK: Research and the Individual: Human Studies. Boston, Little, Brown, 1970

Behanan KT: Yoga: A Scientific Evaluation. New York, Dover, 1937

Behnken P, Merrill E: Nursing care following prefrontal lobotomy. Am J Nursing 49:431, 1949

Behrle FC, Elkin MT, Laybourne PC: Evaluation of a conditioning device in treatment of nocturnal enuresis. Pediatrics 17:849–856, 1956

Beier EG: The Silent Language of Psychotherapy. Chicago, Aldine, 1966

Beiser HR: Self-listening during supervision of psychotherapy. Arch Gen Psychiatry 15:135–139, 1966

Belinkoff J: The effect of group psychotherapy on anaclitic transference. Am J Group Psychother 14:474–481, 1964

Belinkoff J, Resnick EV, Stein A, Alpert H, Bookhalter S, Bross R, Golub M, Wachtel A, Bralove R: The effect of group psychotherapy on anaclitic transference. Am J Group Psychother 14:474–481, 1964

Bell F, Moore RR: Let's Create Activities and a Philosophy for Creative Teaching. Bedford, Mass, Creative Classrooms, 1972

Bell JE: Family and group therapy as a treatment method. Am Psychol 8:515, 1953

Bell JE: Family group therapy. Pub Health Monogr No. 64, 1961

Bell JE: Recent advances in family group therapy. J Child Psychol Child Psychiatry 3:1–15, 1962

Bell NW, Vogel EF: The emotionally disturbed child as the family scapegoat, in Bell NW, Vogel EF (eds): The Family. New York, Free Press, 1960(a)

Bell NW, Vogel EF (eds): The Family. New York, Free Press, 1960(b)

Bellack AS, Hersen M: Behavior Modification: An Introductory Textbook. Baltimore, Williams & Wilkins, 1977

Bellak L: The use of oral barbiturates in psychotherapy. Am J Psychiatry 105:849–850, 1949

Bellak L: Psychiatry applied to medicine, surgery and the specialties, in Bellak L (ed): Psychology of Physical Illness. Orlando FL, Grune & Stratton, 1952

Bellak L: The Thematic Apperception Test and the Children's Apperception Test in Clinical Use. Orlando FL, Grune & Stratton, 1954

Ballak L: Handbook of Community Psychiatry and Community Mental Health. Orlando FL, Grune & Stratton, 1964

Bellak L: The role and nature of emergency psychotherapy. Am J Pub Health 2:58, 1968

Bellak L (ed): A Concise Handbook of Community Psychiatry and Community Mental Health. Orlando FL, Grune & Stratton, 1974

Bellak L, Barten HH (eds): Progress in Community Mental Health, 3 vols. Orlando FL, Grune & Stratton, vol. 1, 1969: vol. 2, 1972; Brunner/Mazel, vol. 3, 1975

Bellak L, et al: Psychiatric training program for nonpsychiatric physicians. JAMA 184:470–472, 1963

Bellak L, Small L: Emergency Psychotherapy and Brief Psychotherapy. Orlando FL, Grune & Stratton, 1965

Beller EK: Clinical Process. New York, Free Press, 1962

Bellman R: Dynamic Programming. Princeton, NJ, Princeton University Press, 1957

Bellman R: Adaptive Control Processes: A Guided Tour. Princeton, NJ, Princeton University Press, 1961

Bellman R, Friend MB, Kurland L: Psychiatric interviewing and multistage decision processes of adaptive type. The Rand Corp. RM-3732-NIH, June 1963

Bellman R, Friend MB, Kurland L: Simulation of the initial interview. Behav Sci 11:389–399, 1966

Bellville, TP, Raths ON, Bellville CJ: Conjoint marriage therapy with a husband and wife team. Am J Orthopsychiatry 39:473–483, 1969

Ben-Avi A: Zen Buddhism, in Arieti S (ed): American Handbook of Psychiatry, vol. 2. New York, Basic Books, 1959, pp 1816–1820

Bender L: Art and therapy in the mental disturbances of children. J Nerv Ment Dis 86:249–263, 1937

Bender L: Childhood schizophrenia. Am J Orthopsychiatry 27:68, 1947

Bender L, Goldschmidt L, Siva-Sankar DV: Treatment of autistic schizophrenic children with LSD-25 and UML-491. Recent Adv Biol Psychiatry 4:170–177, 1962

Bender L, Nichtern S: Chemotherapy in child psychiatry. NY State J Med 56:2791–2796, 1956

Bender L, Woltmann AG: The use of puppet shows as a psychotherapeutic method for behavior problems in children. Am J Orthopsychiatry 6:341–354, 1936

Bender L, Woltmann AG: The use of plastic material as a psychiatric approach to emotional problems in children. Am J Orthopsychiatry 7:283–300, 1937

Benedek T: Countertransference in the training analyst. Bull Menninger Clin 18:12–16, 1954

Benedek T: Countertransference in the training analyst. Am J Psychiatry 129:156–160, 1972

Benedict R: Patterns of Culture. New York, Mentor, 1953

Benjamin JD: Psychoanalysis and nonanalytic psychotherapy. Psychoanal Q 16:169–176, 1947

Bennett AE, Eaton JT: The role of the psychiatric nurse in the newer therapies. Am J Psychiat 108:169, 1951

Bennett AE, Hargrove FA, Engle B: The Practice of Psychiatry in General Hospitals. Berkeley, University of California Press, 1956

Bennett IF: Clinical studies with phenothiazine derivatives in psychiatry, in Braceland FJ (ed): The Effect of Pharmacologic Agents on the Nervous System. Baltimore, Williams & Wilkins, 1957

Bennett LR: A therapeutic community. Nurs Outlook. 9:423–425, 1961

Bennett MJ: Focal psychotherapy—terminable and interminable. Am J Psychother 37:365–375, 1983

Benney C, Black BJ, Niederland WG: Rehabilitation of the mentally ill for the world of work. Proceedings of the Institute for the Rehabilitation of the Mentally Ill. New York, Altro Health and Rehabilitation Services, April 1962, pp 52–63

Benson H: The Relaxation Response. Morrow, New York, 1975

Benson H, Alexander S, Feldman CL: Decreased premature ventricular contractions through use of the relaxation response in patients with stable ischaemic heart-disease. Lancet, 2:380–382, 1975

Benson HB: Behavior Modification and the Child: An Annotated Bibliography. Westport, Conn., Greenwood Press, 1979

Benson H, Beary JF, Carol MP: The relaxation response. Psychiatry 37:37–46, 1974

Bentler PM: An infant's phobia treated with reciprocal inhibition therapy. J Child Psychol Pyschiatry 3:185–190, 1962

Berelson B (ed): The Behavioral Sciences Today. New York, Basic Books, 1963

Berg C: Psychotherapy—Practice and Theory. New York, Norton, 1948, pp 349–457

Berg IA: Measures before and after therapy. J Clin Psychol 8:46–50, 1952

Berger D: Guidance in the elementary school. Teachers Coll Rec 49:44–50, 1947

Berger MM: Nonverbal communication in group psychotherapy. Int J Group Psychother 8:161, 1958

Berger MM: Videotape Techniques in Psychiatric Training and Treatment. New York, Brunner/Mazel, 1969

Berger MM: Videotape Techniques in Psychiatric Training and Treatment. New York, Bruner/Mazel, 1970

Berger MM: Self-confrontation through video. Am J Psychoanal 31:48–58, 1971

Berger MM, Sherman B, Spalding J, Westlake R: The use of videotape with psychotherapy groups in a community mental heatlh service program. Int J Group Psychother 18:504–515, 1968

Berger SM: Conditioning through vicarious instigation. Psychol Rev 69:450–466, 1962

Berger RM, Rose SD: Interpersonal skill training with institutional elderly patients. J Gerontol 32:346–353, 1977

Bergin AE: The effects of psychotherapy: Negative results revisited. J Counsel Psychol 10:244–250, 1963

Bergin AE: Some implications of psychotherapy research for therapeutic practice. J Abnorm Psychol 71:235–246, 1966

Bergin AE: The deterioration effect: A reply to Braucht. J Abnorm Psychol 75:300–302, 1967

Bergin AE: The evaluation of therapeutic outcomes, in Bergin AE, Garfield, SL (eds): Handboook of Psychotherapy and Behavior Change: An Empirical Analysis. New York, Wiley, 1971, pp 217–270

Bergin AE, Lambert MJ: The evaluation of therapeutic outcomes, in Garfield SL, Bergin AE (eds): Handbook of Psychotherapy and Behavior Change: An Empirical Analysis (2d ed). New York, Wiley, 1978

Bergin II: Therapist patient matching, in Gurman AS, Razin AM (eds): Effective Psychotherapy: A Handbook of Research. New York, Pergamon, 1977

Bergler E: Homosexuality, Disease or Way of Life. New York, Collier, 1956

Berkowitz L: Aggressive cues in aggressive behavior and hostility catharsis. Psychol Rev 71:104–22, 1964

Berkowitz S: Some specific techniques of psychosocial diagnosis and treatment in family casework. Soc Casework 36:399–496, 1955

Berle B, Nyswander M: Ambulatory withdrawal treatment of heroin addicts. NY State J Med 64:1846–1848, 1964

Berlin IN: Some learning experiences as a psychiatric consultant in the schools. Ment Hyg 40:215–236, 1956

Berlin IN: Mental health consultation in schools as a means of communicating mental health principles. J Am Acad Child Psychiatry 30:827–828, 1960

Berlin IN: Learning mental health consultation. Ment Hyg 48:257–265, 1964

Berlin IN: Crisis intervention and short-term therapy: An approach in child-psychiatric clinic. J Am Academy Child Psychiatry 9:595–606, 1970

Berlin JI, Wycoff B: Human relations training through didactic-programmed instruction. Atlanta, Human Development Institute, 1964 (mimeo)

Berliner B: Short psychoanalytic psychotherapy: Its possibilities and its limitations. Bull Menninger Clin 5:204–213, 1941

Berman EM, Lief HJ: Marital therapy from a psychiatric perspective: An overview. Am J Psychiatry 132:583–593, 1975

Berman L: Countertransference and attitudes of the analyst in the therapeutic process: Psychiatry 12:159–166, 1949

Berman L: Some problems in the evaluation of psychoanalysis as a therapeutic procedure. Psychiatry 18:387–390, 1955

Bernal JD: Science in History. New York, Penguin, 1969

Bernard HW: College mental hygiene—decade of growth. Ment Hyg 24:413–418, 1940

Bernard HW: Psychiatric consultation in the social agency. Child Welfare 33:3–8, 1954

Bernard HW: A training program in community psychiatry. Ment Hosp 11:7–10, 1960

Bernard HW: Some aspects of training for cummunity psychiatry in a university medical center, in Goldston SE (ed): Concepts of Community Psychiatry: A Framework for Training. Pub Health Service Publ No. 1319. Bethesda, Md, National Institute of Mental Health, 1965, pp 57–67

Bernard HW: Mental Health in the Classroom. New York, McGraw-Hill, 1970

Berne E: The Mind in Action. New York, Simon & Schuster, 1947

Berne E: Transactional Analysis in Psychotherapy. New York, Grove, 1961

Berne E: The Structure and Dynamics of Organization and Groups. Philadelphia, Lippincott, 1963

Berne E: Games People Play. New York, Grove, 1964

Berne E: Principles of Group Treatment. New York, Oxford University Press, 1966

Berne E: Staff-Patient staff conference. Am J Psychiatry 125:3, 42, 1968

Bernfeld S: Sisyphos, or the Boundaries of Education. Vienna, Int Psa Press, 1925

Bernstein DA, McAlister A: The modification of smoking behavior: Progress and problems. Addictive Behaviors 1:89–102, 1976

Bertanlanffy L von: General System Theory; foundation, development, application. New York, Braziller, 1968

Best JA: Mass media, self-management, and smoking modification, in Davidson PO, Davidson SM (eds): Behavioral Medicine: Changing Health Life Styles. New York, Brunner/Mazel, 1980, pp 371–390

Bettelheim B: Love Is Not Enough. New York, Free Press, 1950

Bettelheim B, Sylvester E: A therapeutic milieu. Am J Orthopsychiatry 18: 191–206, 1948

Better Sleep Inc: Relax and Go to Sleep. Berkeley Heights, NJ, Better Sleep Inc, 1963

Betz BJ: Experiences in research in psychotherapy with schizophrenic patients, in Strupp HH, Luborsky L (eds): Research in Psychotherapy, vol. 2. Washington, DC, American Psychological Association, 1962, pp 41–60

Betz BJ: Studies of the therapist's role in the treatment of the scizophrenic patient. Am J Psychiatry 123:963, 1967

Beukenkamp C: Beyond transference behavior. Am J Psychother 10:467, 1956

Bhanji S, Roy GA: The treatment of psychotic depression by sleep deprivation: A replication study. Br J Psychiatry 127:222–226, 1975

Bibring E: The mechanism of depression, in Greenacre P (ed): Affective Disorders. New York, International Universities Press, 1953

Bibring E: Psychoanalysis and the dynamic psychotherapies. J Am Psychoanal Assoc 2:745–770, 1954

Bibring-Lehner G: A contribution to the subject of transference resistance. Int J Psychoanal 17:181–189, 1936

Bidder TG: Electroconvulsive Therapy (ECT) Psychopharmacology Module VII. Sepulveda, Calif, Veterans Administration Medical Center, May 1979

Bieber I: A critique of the libido theory. Am J Psychoanal 18:52–65, 1958

Bieber I: Homosexuality: A Psychoanalytic Study of Male Homosexuals. New York, Basic Books, 1962

Bieber TB: The emphasis on the individual in psychoanalytic group therapy. Int J Soc Psychiatry 2:275–280, 1957

Bieber TB: The individual and the group. Am J Psychother 13:635–650, 1959

Bierer J: A new form of group psychotherapy. Proc Roy Soc Med 37:208–209, 1943

Bierer J: A new form of group psychotherapy. Ment Health (London) 5:23–26, 1944

Bierer J: Therapeutic Social Clubs. London, Lewis, 1948

Bierer J: The Day Hospital. London, Lewis, 1951

Bierer J: Modern social and group therapy, in Harris NC (ed): Modern Trends in Psychological Medicine. London, Butterworth, 1958

Bierer J: Theory and practice of psychiatric day hospitals. Lancet 2:901–902, 1959

Bierer J: Day hospitals, further developments. Int J Soc Psychiatry 7:148–151, 1961

Bierer J: The Marlborough experiments, in Bellak L (ed): Community Psychiatry: The Third Psychiatric Revolution. Orlando FL, Grune & Stratton, 1963

Bierman R: Dimensions for interpersonal facilitation in psychotherapy and child development. Psychol Bull 72:338–352, 1969

Bijou SW, Redd WH: Behavior therapy for children, in Arieti S (ed): American Handbook of psychiatry (2d ed), vol. 5. New York, Basic Books, 1975, pp 319–344

Billings EG: A Handbook of Elementary Psychobiology and Psychiatry. New York, Macmillan, 1939

Bilmes M, Civin G: Psychiatric Education for the Non-Psychiatrist Physician. Community Project Publication. New York, Post-graduate Center for Mental Health, 1964

Binder JL: Modes of focusing in psychoanalytic short-term therapy. Psychother: Theory Res Prac 14:232–241, 1977

Bindman AJ: Mental health consultation: Theory and practice. J Consult Psychol 23:473–482, 1959

Bindman AJ: Bibliography on Consultation. Boston, Department of Mental Health, 1960

Bindman AJ: The clinical psychologist as a mental health consultant, in Abt L, Riess T (eds): Progress in Clinical Psychology. Orlando FL, Grune & Stratton, 1966, pp 78–106

Binger C: The Role of Training in Clinical Psychology in the Education of the Psychiatrist. Transactions of the First Conference. New York, Josiah Macy, Jr, Foundation, 1947, pp. 57–58

Bingham J: The Inside Story: Psychiatry and

Everyday Life. Redlich F (compiler). New York, Knopf, 1953

Binswanger L: Grundformen und Erkenntnis menschlichen Daseins. Zurich, Max Niehaus Verlag, 1942

Binswanger L: Ausgewählte Vorträge und Aufsätze, 2 vols. Bern, Switz, Francke, 1947, 1955

Binswanger L: Existential analysis and psychotherapy, in Fromm-Reichmann F, Moreno J (eds): Progress in Psychotherapy, vol. 1. Orlando FL, Grune & Stratton, 1956

Binswanger L: Sigmund Freud: Reminiscences of a Friendship. Gutermann (transl). Orlando FL, Grune & Stratton, 1957

Bion WR: Experiences in groups. Hum Relations 1:314–320, 1948; 2:487–496, 1948; 3:13–22, 1949; 4:295–303, 1949; 5:3–14, 1950; 6:395–402, 1950; 7:221–227, 1951

Bion WR: Group dynamics, in Kelin M, et al (eds): A Re-View in Psychoanalysis. New York, Basic Books, 1951, pp 440–447

Bion WR: Experiences in Groups, London, Tavistock, 1959; New York, Basic Books, 1961

Bion WR: Learning from Experience. London, Heinemann, 1962

Bion WR: Elements of Psycho-Analysis. London, Heinemann, 1963

Bion WR: Transformations. London, Heinemann, 1965

Bion WR: Second Thoughts. London, Heinemann, 1967

Bion WR: Attention and Interpretation. London, Tavistock, 1970

Bird HW, Martin PA: Countertransference in the psychotherapy of marriage partners. Psychiatry 19:353–360, 1956

Birdwhistell RL: Introduction to Kinetics. Louisville, Ky, University of Louisville Press, 1952

Birdwhistell RL: Contributions of Linguistic Kinetic Studies to the Understanding of Schizophrenia—An Integrated Approach. Auerbach A (ed). New York, Ronald, 1959

Birk L, et al: Behavior Therapy in Psychiatry. A Report of the APA Task Force on Behavior Therapy. Washington, DC, American Psychological Association, 1973

Bischoff A: Uber eine therapeutische verwendung der sogenannten "Weck-amine," in Der Behandlung Schizophrener Erregungszustande, Monatsschr Psychiat u Nuerol 121:329, 1951

Blachly PH: Recent developments in the therapy of addictions, in Masserman JH (ed): Current Psychiatric Therapies, vol. 12. Orlando FL, Grune & Stratton, 1972

Black BJ: The protected workshop in the rehabilitation of the mentally ill. Psychiatr Q Suppl 33:107–118, 1959

Black BJ: Psychiatric rehabilitation in the community, in Bellak L (ed): Community Psychiatry: The Third Psychiatric Revolution. Orlando FL, Grune & Stratton, 1963

Black BJ, Kase HM: Changes in programs over two decades, in Black BJ (ed): Work in Therapy and Rehabilitation for the Mentally Ill. New York, Altro Health and Rehabilitation Services, 1986

Black DW, Winokur G, Nasrallah A: Treatment of mania: A naturalistic study of electroconvulsive therapy versus lithium in 438 patients. J of Clin Psychiatry 48:132–139, 1987

Blackman N: Ward therapy—a new method of group psychotherapy. Psychiatr Q 16:660–666, 1942

Blackman N: The effects of group psychotherapeutic techniques on community attitudes. J Soc Ther 3:197–205, 1957

Blackwell B: Drug Therapy. N Engl J Med 289:249, 252, 1973

Blain D: The world around us. Roche Report 2:1–9, 1965

Blain D, Gayle RF: Distribution, form and extent of psychiatric consultation. JAMA 154:1266–1270, 1954

Blaine GH, et al: Music as a therapeutic agent. Ment Hyg 41:228–245, 1957

Blair BAS: The therapeutic social club. Ment Hyg 39;54–62, 1955

Blair O, et al: The value of individual music therapy as an aid to individual psychotherapy. Int J Soc Psychiatry 7:54–64, 1960

Blake RR: The other person in the situation, in Tagiuri R, Petrulio L (eds): Person Perception and Interpersonal Behavior. Stanford, Calif, Stanford University Press, 1958, pp 229–242

Blanchard EB, Theobald DE, Williamson DA, et al: Temperature biofeedback in the treatment of migraine headaches: A controlled evaluation. Arch Gen Psychiatry 35(5):581–584, 1978

Blanchard EB, Young LD: Clinical applications of biofeedback training: A review of evidence. Arch Gen Psychiatry 3:573–589, 1974

Blanchard EB, et al: Evaluation of biofeedback in the treatment of borderline essential hypertension. J Applied Behav 12(1):99–109, 1979

Blanton S, Peale NV: Faith Is the Answer. New York, Abington-Cokesbury, 1940

Blau A, Slaff B: A brief analysis of the nature of psychotherapy. NY State J Med 56:3319–3322, 1957

Blay NB: Group psychotherapy of married couples: Communications observed, in Wolberg LR, Aronson ML (eds): Group Therapy 1975; An Overview. New York, Stratton Intercontinental, 1975, pp 175–186

Bleuler E: Dementia Praecox or the Group of Schizophrenias. New York, International Universities Press, 1950

Bleuler M: What is Schizophrenia? Schizophr Bull 10:8, 1984

Blinder MG, Kirschenbaum M: The technique of married couple group therapy. Arch Gen Psychiatry 17:44–52, 1967

Blitzstein NL, Fleming J: What is a supervisory analysis? Bull Menninger Clin 17:117–129, 1953

Block MA: Rehabilitation of the alcoholic. JAMA 188:84–86, 1964

Blofeld J: The Zen Teaching of Huang Po, on the Transmission of Mind. New York, Grove, 1959

Blois MS: Clinical judgement and computers. N Engl J Med 303:192–197, 1980

Bloodstein O: The speech therapist's need for training in psychodynamic principles. Conference on Speech Therapy, Postgraduate Center for Mental Health, New York City, March 25, 1966

Bloom BL: Focused single-session therapy: Initial development and evaluation, in Budmen SH (ed): Forms of Brief Therapy. New York, Guilford, 1981, pp 167–216

Bloom JB, Davis N, Wecht CH: Effect on the liver of long-term tranquilizing medication. Am J Psychiatry 121:788–797, 1965

Bloomberg W: Developments in community psychiatry, in Masserman JH (ed): Current Psychiatric Therapies, vol. 7. New York, Grune & Stratton, 1967

Bloomquist ER: Marijuana. Beverly Hills, Calif, Glencoe Press, 1963

Blos P, Sr: On Adolescence: A Psycholanalytic Interpretation. New York, Free Press, 1962

Blos P, Sr: The Young Adolescent: Clinical Studies. New York, Free Press, 1970

Blum HP: The position and value of extra-transference interpretation. J Am Psychoanal Assoc 31:587–613, 1983

Blumenfield M (ed): Applied Supervision in Psychotherapy. Orlando FL, Grune & Stratton, 1982

Blumenfield M (ed): Clinical Perspectives on the Supervision of Psychoanalysis and Psychotherapy: A Guide to Teaching and Practice. New York, Plenum Press, 1983

Boag TJ: Further developments in the day hospital. Am J Psychiatry 116;801, 1960

Boas C Van Emde: Intensive group psychotherapy with married couples. Int J Group Psychother 12:142–153, 1962

Bodin AM: Family therapy, In Karasu TB (ed): Washington, DC, American Psychiatric Association, 1984, p 464

Boehme W: The professional relationship between consultant and consultee. Am J Orthopsychiatry 26:241–248, 1956

Bolte GL: A communications approach to marital counseling. Fam Coordinator 19:32–40, 1970

Bonime W: The liking and disliking of one's patients, in Schizophrenia in Psychoanalytic Office Practice. Orlando FL, Grune & Stratton, 1957

Bonime W: Intellectual insight, changing consciousness, and the progression of processes during psychoanalysis. Compr Psychiatry 2: 106–112, 1961

Bonime W: The Clinical Use of Dreams. New York, Basic Books, 1962

Bonime W: A psychotherpeutic approach to depression. Contemp Psychoanal 2:48–53, 1965

Bonstein I: Conditioning technique of psychoprophylactic preparation of the pregnant woman, in Psychoprophylactic Preparation for Painless Childbirth. London, Heinemann, 1958, pp 26–44. [Reprinted in Franks CM (ed): Conditioning Techniques in Clinical Practice and Research. New York, Springer, 1964]

Bookhammer RS, Meyers R, Schober C, Piotrowski Z: A five-year clinical follow-up study of schizophrenics treated by "direct analysis" (Rosen's) compared with controls. Paper presented at the 122d Annual Meeting of the American Psychiatric Association, Atlantic City, NJ, May 1966

Bootzin RR: Stimulus control treatment for insomnia, in Proceedings of the American Psychological Association. Washington, DC, American Psychological Association, 1972

Bootzin RR: Effects of self-control procedures for insomnia, in Stuart RB (ed): Behavioral Self-Management: Strategies and Outcome, New York, Brunner/Mazel, 1977

Borkovec TD, Boudewyns PA: Treatment of insomnia by stimulus control and progressive relaxation procedures, in Krumboltz J, Thoresen CE (eds): Behavioral Counseling Methods, New York, Holt, 1976

Borkovec TD, Fowles D: Controlled Investigation of the effects of progressive relaxation and hypnotic relaxation on insomnia. J Abnorm Psychol 82: 153–158, 1973

Bornstein B: The analysis of a phobic child, in Eissler RS, et al (eds). The Psychoanalytic Study of the Child, vol. 3/4. New York, International Universities Press, 1949, pp 181–226

Borus JF: Psychiatry and the primary care physician, in Kaplan HI, Sadock BJ (eds): Comprehensive Textbook of Psychiatry (4th ed). Baltimore, Williams & Wilkins, 1985, pp 1302–1308

Boss M: Psychoanalyse und Daseinsanalytik. Bern and Stuttgart, Hans Huber, 1957

Boss M: Psychoanalysis und Daseinsanalysis. New York, Basic Books, 1963

Bostock J, Schackleton M: Pitfalls in the treatment of enuresis by an electric awakening machine. Med J Aust 2:152–154, 1957

Boszormenyi-Nagy I: The concept of schizophrenia from the perspective of family treatment. Fam Proc 1:103–113, 1962

Boszormenyi-Nagy I, Framo JL: Intensive Family Therapy. New York, Harper & Row, 1965

Bott E: The Family and Social Network. London, Tavistock, 1957

Bottome P: Alfred Adler: A Biography. New York Putnam, 1939 (Alfred Adler: A Portrait from Life. New York, Vanguard, 1957)

Boulougouris JC, Marks IM: Implosion—a new treatment for phobias. Br Med J 2:721–723, 1969

Bouvet M: Technical variations and the concept of distance. Int J Psychiatry 39, 1958

Bowen M: A family concept of schizophrenia, in Jackson DD (ed): Etiology of Schizophrenia. New York, Basic Books, 1960

Bowen M: Theory in the practice of psychotherapy, in Guerin PJ (ed): Family therapy: Theory and Practice. New York, Gardner Press, 1976

Bowen M: Family Therapy in Clinical Practice. New York, Jason Aronson, 1978

Bowen M, Dysinger R, Basmania B: Role of fathers in families with a schizophrenic patient. Am J Psychiatry 115:1017–1020, 1959

Bowen M, et al: Study and treatment of five hospitalized family groups each with a psychotic member. Paper presented at the American Orthopsychiatric Association, Chicago, March 1957

Bower EM: Early Identification of Emotionally Handicapped Children in School. Springfield, Ill, Thomas, 1960; 2d ed, 1970

Bower TGR: A Primer of Infant Development. San Francisco, W. H. Freeman & Co. Publishers, 1977

Bowers KS: Hypnosis for the seriously curious. Monterey, Calif, Brooks/Cole, 1976

Bowers KS, Bowers PG: Hypnosis and creativity, in Fromm E, Shor RE (eds): Hypnosis: Research Developments and Perspectives. Chicago, Ill, Aldine, 1972

Bowers MK, et al: Counseling the Dying. New York, Thomas, Nelson, 1964

Bowers S: Social Work Year Book. Hodges MB (ed). New York, American Association of Social Workers, 1951

Bowlby J: Some aspects of the first relationship. Note on Dr. Lois Murphys' paper. Int J Psycho-Anal 45–46, 1964

Bowlby J: Attachment and loss, "Attachment, vol. 1. New York, Basic Books, 1969

Bowman KM, Simon A, Hine CH, et al: A clinical evaluation of tetraethylthiuramdisulphide (antabuse) in the treatment of problem drinkers. Am J Psychiatry 107:832–838, 1951

Boylston WH, Tuma JM: Training of mental health professionals through the use of the "bug in the ear," Am J Psychiatry 129:124–127, 1972

Braceland FJ: Present status of preventive psychiatry. JAMA 159:1187–1190, 1955

Braceland FJ: Comprehensive psychiatry and the mental hospitals. Ment Hosp 8:2–7, 1957

Braceland FJ, et al: Yearbook of Psychiatry and Applied Mental Health. Chicago, Year Book Medical Publishers, 1975

Braceland FJ, Stock M: Modern Psychiatry: A Handbook for Believers. New York, Doubleday, 1963

Bracy OL: Using computers in neuro-psychology, in Schwartz MD (ed): New York, The Haworth Press, 1984 pp 257–267

Bradford LP, Gibb JR, Benne KD: T-Group Theory and Laboratory method: Innovation in Re-Education. New York, Wiley, 1964

Bradley C: Benzedrine and dexedrine in the treatment of children's behavior disorders. Pediatrics 5:24, 1950

Brady JP: Brevital-relaxation treatment of frigidity. Behav Res Ther 4:71–77, 1966

Brady JP: A behavioral approach to the treatment of stuttering. Am J Psychiatry 125:843–848, 1968

Brady JP: Metronome-conditioned speech retraining for stuttering. Behav Ther 2:129–150, 1971

Brady JP: Behavior therapy of stuttering. Folia Phoniat (Basel, Switz) 24:355–359, 1972

Brady JP: Social skills training for psychiatric patients. I: Concepts, methods, and clinical results. Am J Psychiatry 141:333, 1984

Brady JP: Behavior therapy, in Kaplan HI, Sadock BJ (eds): Comprehensive Textbook of Psychiatry. Baltimore, Williams & Wilkins, 1985, pp 1365–1373

Brady JP, Luborsky L, Kron RE: Blood pressure reduction in patients with essential hypertension through metronome-conditioned relaxation: A preliminary report. Behav Ther 5:203–209, 1974

Brady JP, Lind DL: Experimental analysis of hysterical blindness, in Franks CM (ed): Conditioning Techniques in Clinical Practice and Research. New York, Springer, 1964, pp 290–302

Branch HCH: Should the medical student be trained to refer or to handle his own psychiatric patients. Am J Psychiatry 121:847–851, 1965

Brashear AD, et al: A community program of mental health education using group discussion methods. Am J Orthopsychiatry 24:554–562, 1954

Brennan EC: College students and mental health programs for children. Am J Public Health 57:1767–1771, 1967

Brenner C: Some comments on technical precepts in psychoanalysis. J Am Psychoanal Assoc 17:333–352, 1969

Bremner JD, Abrahams LM, Crupie JE, McCawley A, et al: Multicenter double-blind comparison of nomifensine and imipramine for efficacy and safety in depressed outpatients. J Clin Psychiatry 45:56–59, 1984

Brett EA, Ostroff R: Imagery and posttraumatic stress: An overview. Am J Psychiatry 142:417–424, 1985

Breuer J, Freud S: Studies in Hysteria. Washington, DC, Nervous & Mental Disease Publishing Co, 1936

Brick M: Mental hygiene value of children's art work. Am J Orthopsychiatry 14:136–146, 1944

Brickman P, Rabinowitz VC, Karuza J, Coates D, et al: Models of helping and coping. Am Psychologist 37:368–384, 1982

Brill NQ: Psychologists' useful role in medicine requires supervision of a physician. Modern Med, June 15, 1957, p 207

Brill NQ, Beebe GW: A follow-up study of war neuroses. VA Med Monogr. Washington, DC, Veterans Administration, 1955

Brill NQ, Glass JF: Hebephrenic schizophrenic reactions. Arch Gen Psychiatry 12:545–550, 1965

Brim OG: Family structure and sex-role learning of children, in Bell NW, Vogel EF (eds): The Family. New York, Free Press, 1960

Brister CW: Pastoral Care in the Church. New York, Harper & Row, 1964

Britton C: Casework techniques in child care services. Soc Casework 36:3–13, 1955

Brockbank R: Analytic group psychotherapy, in Massermann JH (ed): Current Psychiatric Therapies, vol. 6. Orlando FL, Grune & Stratton, 1966, pp 145–156

Brodman K, et al: The Cornell Medical Index: An adjunct to medical interview. JAMA 140:530–534, 1949

Brodman K, Van Woerhom AJ: Computer-aided diagnostic screening of 100 common diseases. JAMA 197:901–905, 1966

Brody MW: Observations on Direct Analysis; The Therapeutic Technique of John Rosen. New York, Vantage, 1959

Brody MW: Prognosis and results of psychoanalysis, in Moyer JH, Nodine JH (eds): Psychosomatic Medicine. The first Hahnemann Symposium. Philadelphia, Lea & Febiger, 1962

Brody S: Simultaneous psychotherapy of married couples, in Masserman JH (ed): Current Psychiatric Therapies, vol. 1. Orlando FL, Grune & Stratton, 1961, pp 139–144

Brody S: Community therapy of child delinquents, in Massermann JH (ed): Current Psychiatric Therapies, vol. 3. Orlando FL, Grune & Stratton, 1963, pp 197–204

Bromberg W: Advances in group therapy, in Masserman JH (ed): Current Psychiatric Therapies, vol. 1. Orlando FL, Grune & Stratton, 1961, pp 152–158

Brook A, Bleasdale JK, Dowling SJ, et al: Emotional problems in general practice: A sample of ordinary patients. J Coll Gen Pract 11:184–194, 1966

Brooks GW: Opening a rehabilitation house, in Greenblatt M, Simon B (eds): Rehabilitation of the Mentally Ill. Washington, DC, American Association for the Advancement of Science, 1959, p 127

Brooks GW: Rehabilitation house. NY State J Med 60:2400–2403, 1960

Brown BS, Wienckowski LA, Stoltz SB: Behavior Modification: Perspective on a Current Issue. DHEW Publ No. (ADM) 75-202. Bethesda, Md, National Institute of Mental Health, 1975

Brown GI: Human Teaching for Human Learning. New York, Viking, 1971

Brown GW, Birley JLT: Crises and life changes and the onset of schizophrenia. J Health Soc Behav 9:203–14, 1968

Brown JAC: Freud and the Post-Freudians. New York, Penguin, 1964

Brown S, Yalom ID: International group therapy with alcoholics. J Stud Alcohol 38(3):426–56, 1977

Brown W, Jaques E: Product Analysis Pricing. Carbondale. Southern Illinois University Press, 1964

Brown W, Jaques E: Glacier Project Papers. Carbondale. Southern Illinois University Press, 1965

Brownell KD, Foreyt JP: Obesity, in Barlow DH (ed): Clinical Handbook of Psychological Disorders. New York, Guildford Press, 1985

Brownell KD, Colletti G, Ernsner-Hershfield R, et al: Self-control in school children: stringency and leniency in self-determined and externally imposed performance standards. Beh Ther 8:442–455, 1977

Browning JS, Houseworth JH: Development of new symptoms following medical and surgical treatment for duodenal ulcer. Psychosom Med 15:328–336, 1953

Bruch H: The Importance of Overweight. New York, Norton, 1957

Bruch H: Conceptual confusion in eating disorders. J Nerv Ment Dis 133:46–54, 1961

Bruch H: Psychotherapy with schizophrenics, in Kolb LC, Kallmann FJ, Polatin A (eds): International Psychiatric Clinics, vol. 1. Boston, Little, Brown, 1964

Bruch H: Eating Disorders: Obesity, Anorexia Nervosa and the Person Within. New York, Basic Books, 1973

Bruch H: Learning Psychotherapy: Rational and Ground Rules. Cambridge, Harvard University Press, 1974(a)

Bruch H: Perils of behavior modification in treatment of anorexia nervosa. JAMA 230:1419–1422, 1974(b)

Bruch H: How to treat anorexia nervosa. Roche Report 5(8), 1975

Bruder EE: Ministering to Deeply Troubled People. Englewood Cliffs, NJ, Prentice-Hall, 1963

Bruner JS: Going beyond the information given, in Contemporary Approaches to Cognition. Cambridge, Harvard University Press, 1957

Bruner JS: Towards Theory of Instruction. Cambridge, Harvard University Press, 1966

Bruno FJ: Trends in Social Work as Reflected in the Proceedings of the National Conference of Social Work. New York, Columbia University Press, 1948

Bruyn GW, deJong UJ: The Midas-syndrome. An inherent psychological marriage problem. Am Imago 16:251–262, 1959

Bry A (ed): Inside Psychotherapy. New York, Basic Books, 1972, pp 57–60

Bry T: Varieties of resistance in group psycho-

therapy. Int J Group Psychother 1/2:106–114, 1951

Bry T: Acting-out in group psychotherapy. Int J Group Psychother 3:42–48, 1953

Buber M: I and Thou, New York, Scribner, 1937

Buber M: Das Problem des Menschen. Heidelberg, Schneider, 1948

Buber M: Lecture, March 17, 1957, Washington, DC, as reported in Newsletter (William Alanson White Institute) 5(2), April 1957

Buchanan DR: Psychodrama: A humanistic approach to psychiatric treatment for the elderly. Hosp Community Psychiatry 33:220–223, 1982

Buchanan DR: Psychodrama, in Karasu TB (ed): The Psychiatric Therapies. Washington, DC, American Psychiatric Association, 1984, pp 783–799

Buchanan DR, Dubbs-Siroka J: Psychodramatic treatment for psychiatric patients. J National Assn Private Psychiatric Hosp 11:27–31, 1980

Bucher BD: A picket portable shocking device with application to nailbiting. Behav Res Ther 6:389, 1968

Buck JN: Administration and Interpretation of the H-T-P Test (House-Tree Person). Richmond, Va. VA Hospital, August 1950

Buckley P, Conte HR, Plutchik R, Karasu TB, et al: Learning dynamic psychotherapy: A longitudinal study. Am J Psychiatry 139:1607–1610, 1982

Buda B: Utilization of resistance and paradox communication in short-term psychotherapy. Psychother Psychosom 20:200–211, 1972

Budson RD: The psychiatric half-way house. Psychiatr Ann 3:65–83, 1973

Budzynski TH, Stoyra JM, Adler C: Feedback-induced muscle relaxation: Application to tension headache. J Behav Ther Exp Psychiatry 1:205–211, 1970

Buehler RE, Patterson GR, Furniss JM: The reinforcement of behavior in institutional settings. Behav Res Ther 4:157–167, 1966

Bullard DM: Psychoanalysis and Psychotherapy. Selected Papers of Frieda Fromm-Reichmann. Chicago, University of Chicago Press, 1959

Bullis HE, O'Malley EE: Human Relations in the Classroom. Course 1. Wilmington, Delaware State Society for Mental Hygiene, 1947

Bullis HE, O'Malley EE: Human Relations in the Classroom. Course II. Wilmington, Delaware State Society for Mental Hygiene, 1948

Burgess AW: Psychiatric Nursing in the Hospital and Community (3d ed). Englewood Cliffs, NJ, Prentice-Hall, 1981

Burke JD, White AH, Havens LL: Matching patient and method. Arch Gen Psychiatry 35:177–186, 1979

Burke JL, Lee H: An acting-out patient in a psychotic group. Int J Group Psychother 14:194, 1964

Burns D, Brady JP: The treatment of stuttering, in Goldstein A, Foa EB (eds): Handbook of Behavioral Interventions. New York, Wiley & Sons, 1980

Burnside IM: Group work with the aged: Selected literature. Gerontologist 10:241–246, 1970

Buros OK: The Fourth Mental Measurements Yearbook. Highland Park, NJ, Gryphon, 1953

Burrow T: Social images versus reality. J Abnorm Soc Psychol 19:230–235, 1924

Burrow T: The laboratory method in psychoanalysis. Its inception and development. Am J Psychiatry 5:345–355, 1926(a)

Burrow T: Our mass neurosis. Psychol Bull 23:305–312, 1926(b)

Burrow T: Our social evasion. Med J Rec 123:793–795, 1926(c)

Borrow T: Psychoanalytic improvisations the personal equation. Psychoanal Rev 13:173–186, 1926(d)

Burrow T: The Social Basis of Consciousness: A Study in Organic Psychology Based upon a Synthetic Societal Concept of the Neurosis. New York, harcourt, 1927(a)

Burrow T: The group method of analysis. Psychoanal Rev 14:268–280, 1927(b)

Burrow T: The physiological basis of neurosis and dream. A societal interpretation of the sensori-motor reactions reflected in insanity and crime. J Soc Psychol 1:48–65, 1930

Burrow T: A phylogenetic study of insanity in its underlying morphology. JAMA 100:648–651, 1933

Burrow T: Kymograph records of neuromuscular (respiratory) patterns in relation to behavior disorders. Psychosom Med 3:174–186, 1941(a)

Burrow T: Neurosis and war. A problem in human behavior. J Psychol 12:235–249, 1941(b)

Burrows WG: Human sexuality: A program for sex education in the public school system. Psychosomatics 11:31–35, 1970

Bursten B: A diagnostic framework. In't Rev Psychoanalysis 5(1):15–32, 1978

Burtness JH, Kildahl JP (eds): New Community in Christ. Minneapolis, Augsburg, 1963

Burton A: A commentary on the problem of human identity. J Existentialism 5(19), 1965

Burton A: Encounter: The Theory and Practice of Encounter Groups. San Francisco, Jossey-Bass, 1969

Burton A: Operational Theories of Personality. New York, Brunner/Mazel, 1974, p 406

Bush G: Transference, countertransference and identification in supervision. Contemp Psychol 5:158-162, 1969

Butler RN, Lewis MI: Aging and Mental Health: Positive Psychological Approaches. St Louis, Mosby, 1973

Bychowski G: The rebirth of a woman: A psychoanalytic study of artistic expression and sublimation. Psychoanal Rev 34:32–57, 1947

Bychowski G: Therapy of the weak ego. Am J Psychother 4:407, 1950

Bychowski G: Psychotherapy of Psychosis. Orlando FL, Grune & Stratton, 1952

Bychowski G: The ego and the object of the homosexual. Int J Psychoanal 13:255–260, 1961

Cade JFJ: Lithium salts in the treatment of psychotic excitement. Med J Aust 2:349–352, 1949

Cairns RB: The influence of dependency inhibition on the effectiveness of social reinforcers. J Personal 29:466–488, 1961

Caldwell J: Lifelong obesity—a contribution to the understanding of recalcitrant obesity. Psychosomatics 6:417–426, 1965

Cairns D, Thomas L, Mooney V, et al: A comprehensive treatment approach to chronic low back pain: The spouse as a discriminative cue for pain behaviors. Pain 6:243–252, 1980

Calef V, Weinshel EM: The new psychoanalysis and psychoanalytic revisionism. Psychoanal Q 48:470–491, 1979

Caligor L, Bromberg P, Meltzer J (eds): Clinical Perspectives on the Supervision of Psychoanalysis and Psychotherapy: A Guide to Teaching and Practice. New York, Plenum Press, 1983

Caligor J, Fieldsteel ND, Brok AJ: Individual and Group Therapy. Combining Psychoanalytic Treatments. New York, Basic Books, 1984

Call AP: Power Through Repose. Boston, Little, Brown, 1891

Calvin AD, Clifford LT, Clifford B, et al: Experimental validation of conditioned inhibition. Psychol Rep 2:51–56, 1956

Cameron DE: The day hospital: An experiment of hospitalization. Mod Hosp 3:64, 1947

Cameron DE: General Psychotherapy. Dynamics and Procedures. Orlando FL, Grune & Stratton, 1950, pp 270–288

Cameron DE: The conversion of passivity into normal self-assertion. Am J Psychiatry 108:98–102, 1951

Cameron DE: Psychotherapy in Action. Orlando FL, Grune & Stratton, 1968

Cameron DE, MacLean RR, et al: Special areas involving hospital-community relations, the day hospital. Ment Hosp 9:54–56, 1958

Cameron DE, Sved S, Solyom L, Wainrib B: Ribonucleic acid in psychiatric therapy, in Masserman JH (ed): Current Psychiatric Therapies, vol. 4. Orlando FL, Grune & Stratton, 1964

Cameron N: Paranoid conditions and paranoia, in Arieti S (ed): American Handbook of Psychiatry. New York, Basic Books, 1959, pp 508–539

Cameron N, Margaret A: Behavior Pathology. Boston, Houghton Mifflin, 1951

Cammer L: Treatment methods and fashions in treatment. Am J Psychiatry 118:447, 1961

Campbell D: Counseling service in the day nursery. Family, March 1943

Campbell JH, Rosenbaum CP: Placebo effect and symptom relief in psychotherapy. Arch Gen Psychiatry 16:364–368, 1967

Campbell RJ: Facilitation of short-term clinic therapy, in Masserman JH (ed): Current Psychiatric Therapies, vol. 7. Orlando FL, Grune & Stratton, 1967

Canada's Mental Health: Suppl No. 36. Preventive Psychiatry: If Not Now—When? April 1963

Canada's Mental Health: Suppl No. 44, Prevention of Mental Illness and Social Maladjustment. November–December 1964

Canada's Mental Health: Vol. 13, Community Mental Health. November–December 1965

Cancro R: Experience with a new rapid-acting antidepressant: Amoxapine. Adv Biochem Psychopharmacol 32:121–124, 1982

Cancro R: History and overview of schizophrenia, in Kaplan HI, Sadock BJ (eds): Comprehensive Textbook of Psychiatry (4th ed). Baltimore, Williams & Wilkins, 1985, pp 631–642

Cancro R, Fox H, Shapiro L (eds): Strategic Interventions in Schizophrenia. New York, Behavioral Publications, 1974

Cannabis: A Report of the Commission of Inquiry Into the Non-Medical Use of Drugs. Ottawa, Information Canada 1972

Cannon W: "Voodoo" death. Am Anthropologist 44:169–181, 1942

Cantor MB: Karen Horney on psychoanalytic technique: Mobilizing constructive forces. Am J Psychoanal 17:118–199, 1967

Cantor MB: Personal communication. 1976

Cantor N: The Dynamics of Learning. Buffalo, NY, Foster & Stewart, 1946

Cantor P: The effects of youthful suicide on the family. Psychiatr Op, 12:6–11, 1975

Caplan G: An approach to the education of mental health specialists. Ment Hyg 43:268–280, 1959

Caplan G: Prevention of Mental Disorders in Children. New York, Basic Books, 1961(a)

Caplan G: An Approach to Community Mental Health. Orlando FL, Grune & Stratton, 1961(b)

Caplan G: Types of mental health consultation. Am J Orthopsychiatry 33:470–481, 1963

Caplan G: Principles of Preventive Psychiatry. New York, Basic Books, 1964

Caplan G: Community psychiatry, introduction and overview, in Goldston SE (ed): Concepts of Community Psychiatry: A Framework for Training. Pub Health Service Pub No. 1319. Bethesda, Md. National Institute of Mental Health, 1965

Caplan G: The theory and Practice of Mental Health Consultation. New York, Basic Books, 1970

Caplan G: Support Systems and Community Mental Health: Lectures on Concept Development. New York, Behavioral Publicaions, 1974

Caplan G, Grunebaum H: Perspectives on primary prevention: A review, in Gottesfeld H (ed): The Critical Issues of Communinity Mental Health. New York, Behavioral Publications, 1972

Caplan G, Killilea M: Support Systems and Mutual Help. Orlando FL, Grune & Stratton, 1976

Cappon D: Results of psychotherapy. Br J Psychiatry 110:35–45, 1964

Carlin AS, Armstrong HE: Rewarding social responsibility in disturbed children: A group play technique. Psychother: Theory Res Prac 5:169–174, 1968

Carmichael DM: A psychiatric day hospital for convalescent patients. Ment Hosp 11:7, 1960

Carmichael DM: Community aftercare services, in Masserman JH (ed): Current Psychiatric Therapies, vol. 1. Orlando FL, Grune & Stratton, 1961, pp 210–215

Carmichael HT< Masserman JH: Results of treatment in a psychiatric outpatients' department. JAMA 113:292–298, 1939

Carr AC, Ancill RJ, Ghosh A, Margo A: Direct assessment of depression by microcomputer: A feasibility study. Acta Psychiatrica Scandinavica 64:415–422, 1981

Carr AC, Ghosh A, Ancill RJ: Can a computer take a psychiatric history? Psychol Med 13:151–158, 1983

Carr M: School Phobia. Can Counselor 4:41–45, 1970

Carrera RN: Observable difference between rolfed and unrolfed bodies. Psychother: Theory Res Prac 11:215–218, 1974

Carrington P: Freedom in Meditation. New York, Doubleday, 1977

Carrington P: Releasing. New York, William Morrow & Company, Inc. 1984. (Releasing tapes: Pace Educational Systems, Inc. P.O. Box 113, Kendall Park, NJ 08824)

Carrington P, Ephron HS: Clinical use of meditation, in Masserman JH (ed): Current Psychiatric Therapies, vol. 15. Orlando FL, Grune & Stratton, 1975

Carroll EJ: Treatment of the family as a unit. Pa Med J 63:57–62, 1960

Carroll HA: Mental Hygiene: The Dynamics of Adjustment. Englewood Cliffs, NJ, Prentice-Hall, 1963

Carstairs GM, et al: The Burden on the Community. The Epidemiology of Mental Illness: A Symposium. London, Oxford University Press, 1962

Cartwright D: Emotional dimensions of group life, in Raymert ML (ed): Feelings and Emotions. New York, McGraw-Hill, 1950

Cartwright D: Annotated bibliography of research and theory construction in client-centered therapy. J Consult Psychol 4:82, 1957

Cartwright D, Lippitt R: Group dynamics and the individual. Int J Group Psychother 7:86–101, 1951

Cartwright D, Zander A (eds): Group Dynamics: Research and Theory (2d ed). Evanston, Ill, Row, Peterson, 1960 (3d ed–New York, Harper & Row, 1968)

Cartwright DS: Patient self-report measuring in Waskow IE, Parloff MB (eds): Psychotherapy Change Measures. Washington, DC, DHEW Publ No. (ADM) 74-120, 1975

Casey GA: Behavior rehearsal: Principles and procedures. Psychother: Theory Res Prac 10:331–333, 1973

Casey JF, Lindley CJ: Recent advances in Veterans' Administration psychiatry, in Masserman JH (ed): Current Psychiatric Therapies, vol. 2. Orlando FL, Grune & Stratton, 1962, pp 233–246

Casriel D: So Fair a House: The Story of Synanon, Englewood Cliffs, NJ, Prentice-Hall, 1962

Casriel D: A Scream Away from Happiness. New York, Grosset & Dunlap, 1972

Casriel D, Deitch D: The Marathon: Time Extended Group Therapy, in Masserman JH (ed): Current Psychiatric Therapies, vol. 8. Orlando, FL, Grune & Stratton, 1968

Cassem NH: Confronting the decision to let death come. Crit Care Med 2:113, 1974

Castelnuovo-Tedesco P: The twenty-minute hour: An experiment in medical education. N Engl J Med 266:283, 1962

Castelnuovo-Tedesco P: The Twenty-Minute Hour. Boston, Little, Brown, 1965

Castelnuovo-Tedesco P: Decreasing the length of psychotherapy: Theoretical and practical aspects of the problem, in Arieti S (ed): The World Biennial of Psychiatry and Psychotherapy, vol. 1. New York, Basic Books 1971, pp 55–71

Castelnuovo-Tedesco P, Greenblatt M, Sharef M: Paraprofessionals: A discussion. Psychiatr Op 8:13–21, 1971

Catanzaro RJ: Telephone therapy, in Masserman JH (ed): Current Psychiatric Therapies, vol. 11. Orlando FL, Grune & Stratton, 1971

Cath SH: Psychoanalysis and psychoanalytic psychotherapy of the older patient. J Geriatric Psychiatry 15:43–53, 1982

Cautela JR: Covert sensitization. Psychol Rep 20:459–468, 1967

Cautela JR: Covert conditioning, in Jacobs A, Sachs LB (eds): The Psychology of Private Events. New York, Academic Press, 1971

Cautela JR, Kastenbaum RA: A reinforcement survey schedule for use in therapy, training and research. Psychol Rep 20:1115–1130, 1967

Cautela JR, Upper D: The process of individual behavior therapy, in Herson RM, Eisler RM, Miller PM (eds): Progress in Behavior Modification, vol. 1. Orlando FL, Academic Press, 1975

Cautela JR, Wisocki PA: The thought stoppage procedure: Description, application, and learning theory interpretations. Psychol Record 9:255–264, 1977

Cerletti V, Bini L: Electric shock treatment. Bull Acad Med Rome 64:36, 1938(a)

Cerletti V, Bini L: Un nuevo metodo de shockterapie "L'elettro-shock." Bull Acad Med Roma 64:136–138, 1938(b)

Chalfen L: Use of dreams in psychoanalytic group psychotherapy. Psychoanal Rev 51:461, 1964

Chambers DW: Storytelling and Creative Drama. Dubuque, Iowa, Brown, 1970

Chance E: A study of transference in group psychotherapy. Int J Group Psychother 2:1–40, 53, 1952

Chance E: Families in Treatment. New York, Basic Books, 1959

Chandler AL, Hartman MA: LSD-25 as a facilitating agent in psychotherapy. Arch Gen Psychiatry 2:286, 1960

Chaney EF, O'Leary MR, Marlatt GA: Skill training with alcoholics. J Consult Clin Psychol 46:1092–1104, 1978

Chapman LS, Chapman JD: Genesis of popular but erroneous psychodiagnostic observations. J Abnorm Psychol 72:193–204, 1967

Charatan FB: Depression in old age. NY State Med 75:2505–2509, 1975

Charney DS, Riordan CE, Kleber HD, et al: Clonidine and naltrexone: A safe, effective, and rapid treatment of abrupt withdrawal from methadone therapy. Archives of General Psychiatry 39:1327–1332, 1982

Charney DS, Sternberg DE, Kleber HD, Heninger GR, et al: The clinical use of clonidine in abrupt withdrawal from methadone. Arch of Gen Psychiatry 38:1273–1277, 1981

Chein I, Gerard DL, Lee RS, Rosenfeld E: The Road to H. New York, Basic Books, 1964

Chessick RD: How Psychotherapy Heals. New York, Science House, 1969

Chessick RD: Why Psychotherapists Fail. New York, Science House, 1971

Chessick RD: Psychoanalytic listening II. Am J Psychotherapy 39:30–48, 1985

Child GP, Osinski W, Bennett RE, Davidoff E: Therapeutic results and clinical manifestations following the use of tetraethylthiuramidisulphide (antabuse). Am J Psychiatry 107:774–780, 1951

Chittenden GE: An experimental study in measuring and modifying assertive behavior in young children. Monogr Soc Res Child Devel No. 1, Ser No. 31, 1942

Chodoff P: Medical insurance and private psychiatric practice. Psychiatr Ann 4:45, 1974

Christ AE: Attitudes toward death among a group of acute psychiatric patients. J Gerontol 16:56–69, 1961

Christensen C: The minister—a psychotherapist. Pastoral Psychol 17:31–39, 1966

Christmas JJ: Group methods in training and practice. Nonprofessional mental health personnel in a deprived community. Am J Orthopsychiatry 34:410–419, 1966

Church RM: The varied effects of punishment on behavior. Psychol Rev 70:369–402, 1963

Chwelos N, Blewett DB, Smith B, Hoffer A: Use of d-lysergic acid diethylamide in the treatment of alcoholism. Q J Study Alcohol 20:577–590, 1959

Ciancilo PJ: Children's literature can affect coping behavior. Personnel Guid J 43:897–903, 1965

Clancy HG, McBride G: Therapy of childhood autism in the family, in Masserman JH (ed): Current Psychiatric Therapies, vol. 12. Orlando FL, Grune & Stratton, 1972

Clarizio HF (ed): Mental Health and the Educative Process. Chicago, Rand McNally, 1969

Clark DH: Administrative Therapy: The Role of the Doctor in the Therapeutic Community. New York, Barnes & Noble, 1971

Clark DH, Cooper LW: Psychiatric half-way hostel. Lancet 1:588–590, 1960

Clark DH, Kadis AL: Humanistic Teaching. Columbus, Ohio, Merrill, 1971

Clark PN: Human development through occupation: A philosophy and conceptual model for practice. Am J Occup Ther 1:1–10, 1922

Clark R: The "I can't" resistance to quitting smoking. Int Ment Health Res Newsletter 14:9–10, 1974

Clarke AM, Clark ADB: Early Experience: Myth and Evidence. London, Open Books, 1976

Clarke B, Schoech D: A computer-assisted therapeutic game for adolescents: initial development and comments, in Schwartz MD (ed): Using Computers in Clinical Practice. New York, The Haworth Press, 1984, pp 335–353

Clarkin JF, Frances A: Selection criteria for the brief psychotherapies. Am J Psychother 36:166–180, 1982

Clausen JA, Kohn MA: The ecological approach in social psychiatry. Am J Soc 60:140–151, 1954

Clawson G, Peasley E: Nursing care in insulin therapy. Am J Nurs 49:621, 1949

Clebsch W, Jaekle C: Pastoral Care in Historical Perspective. Englewood Cliffs, NJ, Prentice-Hall, 1964

Clements CC: Acting out vs acting through: An interview with Frederick Perls, MD. Voices, 4:66–73, 1968

Clemmesen C: The treatment of narcotic poisoning. Med Sci 14:74–82, 1963

Clinebell HJ, Jr: The challenge of the specialty pastoral counseling. Pastoral Psychol 15:17–28, 1964

Clinebell HJ, Jr: The future of the specialty of pastoral counseling. Pastoral Psychol 16:18–26, 1965

Clinebell HJ, Jr: Basic types of Pastoral Counseling. Nashville, Tenn, Abingdon, 1966

Clinebell HJ, Jr: The Mental Health Ministry of the Local Church. Nashville. Tenn. Abingdon, 1972(a) (published in 1965 as Mental Health Through Christian Community)

Clinebell HJ, Jr: Is pastoral counseling a credible alternative in the ministry? J Pastoral Care 26:272–275, 1972(b)

Coates TJ, Thoresen CE: How to Sleep Better: A Drug-free Program for Overcoming Insomnia. Englewood Cliffs, NJ, Prentice–Hall, 1979

Cockerill E, et al: A Conceptual Framework for Social Casework. Pittsburgh, University of Pittsburgh School of Social Work, 1952

Cofer CN, Appley MH: Motivation, Theory and Research. New York, Wiley, 1964

Cohen AK: Delinquent Boys: The Culture of the Gang. New York, Free Press, 1955 (paperback, 1971)

Cohen LD: Consultation as a method of mental health intervention, in Abt L, Riess B (eds): Progress in Clinical Psychology. Orlando FL, Grune & Stratton, 1966, pp 107–128

Cohen M: Counter-transference and anxiety. Psychiatr J Stud Interpers Proc 15:231, 1952

Cohen M: The therapeutic community. Psychiatry 20:173–175, 1957

Cohen M, Liebson IA, Faillace LA: A technique for establishing controlled drinking in chronic alcoholics. Dis Ner Syst 33:46–49, 1972

Cohen S: Lysergic acid diethylamide: Side effects and complications. J Nerv Ment Dis 130:30–40, 1960

Cohen S: Angel Dust. JAMA, 238:515–516 1977

Cohen S, Eisner BG: Use of LSD in a psychotherapeutic setting. Arch Neurol Psychiatry 81:615, 1959

Cohn JB, Wilcox CS: Low sedation potential of buspirone compared with alprazolam and lorazepam in treatment of anxious patients: A double-blind study J Clin Psychiatry 47:409–411, 1986

Cohn RC: A group-therapeutic workshop on countertransference. Int J Group Psychother 11:284–296, 1961

Colbert J: On the musical effect. Psychiatr Q 37:429–436, 1963

Colby KM: Energy and Structure in Psychoanalysis. New York, Ronald, 1955

Colby KM: Computer simulation of a neurotic process, in Tomkins SS, Messick S (eds): Computer Simulation of Personality. New York, Wiley, 1963

Colby KM: Computer psychotherapists, in Sidowski, et al (eds): Technology in mental health care systems. Norwood, NJ, Ablex Publishing corp., 1980, pp 109–116

Colby KM, Watt JB, Gilbert JP: A computer model of psychotherapy. Preliminary communication. J Nerv Ment Dis 142:148–152, 1966

Cole EB, Johnson JH, Williams TA: When psychiatric patients interact with computer terminals: Problems and solutions. Beh Methods and Instrumentation 8:92, 1976

Cole JO: Evaluation of drug treatments in psychiatry, in Hoch PH, Zubin J (eds): The Evaluation of Psychiatric Treatment. Orlando FL, Grune & Stratton, 1964, p 24

Coleman JS: The Adolescent Society: The Social Life of the Teacher and Its Impact on Education. New York, Free Press, 1961

Coleman JV: Psychiatric consultation in casework agencies. Am J Orthopsychiatry 17:533–539, 1947

Coleman JV: Mental health education and community psychiatry. Am J Orthopsychiatry 23:265–270, 1953

Colligen RC, Offord KP: Revitalizing the MMPI: The development of contemporary norms. Psychiatric Annals 15:558–568, 1985

Collins FL. Jr: Behavioral medicine, in Michelson L, Hersen E, Turner SM (eds): Future Perspectives in Behavior Therapy. New York, Plenum, 1981

Columbia University School of Public Health and Administrative Medicine. Mental Health Teaching in Schools of Public Health. New York, Columbia University Press, 1961

Committee on Alcoholism and Addiction and Council on Mental Health: Dependence on barbiturates and other sedative drugs. JAMA 193:673–723, 1965

Committee on Alcoholism and Addiction and Council on Mental Health: Dependence on amphetamines and other stimulant drugs. JAMA 197:1023–1027, 1966

Commission on Preventive Psychiatry of the Group for the Advancement of Psychiatry: Promotion of Mental Health in the Primary and Secondary Schools: An Evaluation of Four Projects. Rep No. 18. Topeka, Kans. the Group, 1951

Commission on Teacher Education: Helping Teachers Understand Children. Washington, DC, American Council on Education, 1945

Committee on Clinical Psychology of the Group for the Advancement of Psychiatry: The Relation of Clinical Psychology to Psychiatry. Rep No 10. Topeka, Kans, the Group, July 1949

Committee on the Function of Nursing: A Program for the Nursing Profession, Ginzberg E (ed): New York, Macmillan, 1949

Committee on Nomenclature and Statistics of the American Psychiatric Association: Diagnostic and Statistical Manual Mental Disorders. Washington, DC, the Association, 1952

Committee on Private Practice, Division of Clinical Psychology, New York State Psychological Association: The Clinical Psychologist in the Private Practice of Psychotherapy in New York State. New York, the Association, 1963

Committee on Psychiatric Nursing and the Committee on Hospitals of the Group for the Advancement of Psychiatry: The Psychiatric Nurse in the Mental Hospital. Rep No. 22. Topeka, Kans, the Group, May 1952

Committee on Psychiatric Social Work of the Group for the Advancement of Psychiatry: Circular Letter No. 21. Topeka, Kans, the Group, 1946

Committee on Psychiatric Social Work of the Group for the Advancement of Psychiatry: The Psychiatric Social Worker in the Psychiatric Hospital. Rep No. 2. Topeka, Kans, the Group, January 1948

Committee on Psychiatric Social Work of the Group for the Advancement of Psychiatry: Psychiatric Social Work in the Psychiatric Clinic. Rep No. 16. Topeka, Kans, the Group, September 1950

Committee on Training in Clinical Psychology of the American Psychological Association: Recommended graduate training program in clinical psychology. Am Psychol 2:548, 1947

Conant MA: Progressive therapy for herpes simplex. Med Op 3:12, 1974

Condon WS, Sander LW: Neonate movement is synchronized with adult speech: Interventional participation and language requisition. Science 183:99–101, 1974

Conference Group on Psychiatric Nursing Practice of the American Nurses' Association: Facing up to Changing Responsibilities. Kansas City, Mo, the Association, 1963

Conference Group on Psychiatric Nursing Practice of the American Nurses' Association: Psychiatric Nursing, Kansas City, Mo, the Association, 1966

Conigliaro V: Counseling and other psychological aspects of religious life. Rev Religion 24:337–362, 1965

Conn JH: A psychiatric study of car sickness. Am J Orthopsychiatry 8:130–141, 1938

Connell PH: Amphetamine Psychosis. Maudsley Mongr No. 5. London, Oxford University Press, 1958

Connell PH: The day hospital approach in child psychiatry. J Ment Sci 107:969–977, 1961

Connell PH: Clinical manifestations and treatment of amphetamine type of dependence. JAMA 196:718–723, 1966

Connors ME, Craig LJ, Stuckey MK: Treatment of bulimia with brief psychoeducation group therapy. Am J Psychiatry 141:1512–1516, 1984

Conte WR: Occupational therapy in the psychoses, in Masserman JH (ed): Current Psychiatric Therapies, vol. 2. Orlando FL, Grune & Stratton, 1962, pp 227–232

Conze E: Buddhism, Its Essence and Development. New York, Philosophical Library, 1951

Conze E (ed): Buddhist Texts through the Ages. New York, Philosophical Library, 1954

Conze E: Buddhist Wisdom Books. London, Allen & Unwin, 1958

Coogler OJ: Structured Mediation in Divorce Settlement: A Handbook for Marital Mediators. Lexington, Mass, Lexington Books, 1978

Cook TD, Campbell DT: Quasi-experimentation: Design Analysis Issues for Field Settings. Chicago, Rand McNally, 1979

Cooper AJ: A case of fetishism and impotence treated by behaviour therapy. Br J Psychiatry 109:649–652, 1963

Cooper DE: Group psychotherapy with the elderly: Dealing with loss and death. Am J Psychotherapy 38:203–228, 1984

Cooper JE: A study of behavior therapy in thirty psychiatric patients. Lancet 1:411–415, 1963

Cooper LM: Hypnotic amnesia, in Fromm E, Shor RE (eds): Hypnosis: Research Developments and Perspectives. Chicago, Aldine, 1972

Cooper S, Hodges W (eds): The Mental Health Consultation Field, vol. 2. Community Psychology Series, Washington, DC, American Psychological Association, 1983

Corsini RJ: Methods of Group Psychotherapy. New York, McGraw-Hill, 1957

Corsini RJ: Role playing in Psychotherapy: A Manual. Chicago, Aldine, 1966

Corsini RJ: The behind-the-back encounter, in Wolberg LR, Schwartz EK (eds): Group Therapy 1973: An Overview. New York, Stratton Intercontinental, 1973, pp 55–70

Corsini, RJ: Handbook of Innovative Psychotherapies. New York, Wiley, 1981

Cosin LZ: The place of the day hospital in the geriatric unit. Int J Soc Psychiatry 1:33–40, 1955

Costello CG: The essentials of behavior therapy. Can Psychiatr Assoc J 8:162–166, 1963

Cottle WC: Beginning Counseling Practicum. Orlando FL, Grune & Stratton, 1973

Coué E: La Maitresse de Soi-Même Par L'Autosuggestion Consciente. Paris, Oliven, 1936

Coulter G: Exercise as group therapy. Staff (Am Psychol Assoc) 3:6–7, 1966

Council of the American Psychiatric Association: Principles Underlying Interdisciplinary Relations Between the Professions of Psychiatry and Psychology. Washington, DC, the Association, 1964

Council on Pharmacy and Chemistry: What to do with a drug addict. JAMA 149:1220–1223, 1952

Cousins N: Anatomy of an illness as perceived by the patient. New Engl J Med 295:1458–1463, 1976

Covner BJ: Principles of psychological consulting with client organizations. J Consult Psychol 11:227–244, 1947

Cowen EL, et al: A preventive mental health program in the school setting: Description and evaluation. J Psychol 56:307–356, 1963

Cox RH: Do pastoral counselors bring a new consciousness to the health professions? J Pastoral Care 26:250, 1972

Craft M: Treatment of depressive illness in a day hospital. Lancet 2:149–151, 1958

Craft M: Psychiatric day hospitals. Am J Psychiatry 116:251, 1959

Craighcad LW, Stunkard AJ, O'Brien RM: Behavior therapy and pharmacotherapy for obesity. Arch Gen Psychiatry 38:763, 1981

Cramer JB: Common neuroses of childhood, in Arieti S (ed): Handbook of American Psychiatry, vol. 1. New York, Basic Books, 1959, pp 798–815

Crane GE: Prevention and management of tardive dyskinesia. Am J Psychiatry 129:466–467, 1972

Crank HH: The use of psychoanalytic principles in outpatient psychotherapy. Bull Menninger Clin 4:35, 1940

Cranswick EH, Hall TC: Desoxycortone with ascorbin acid in mental disorder. Lancet 1:540, 1950

Crasilneck HB, Hall JA: The use of hypnosis in controlling cigarette smoking. South Med J 61:999–1002, 1968

Crasilneck HB, Hall JA: Clinical Hypnosis:

Principles and Applications. New York, Grune & Stratton, 1975, pp 167–175

Crawford AL, Buchanan B: Psychiatric Nursing—A Basic Manual. Philadelphia, Davis, 1963

Crawford JL, Vitale S, Robinson J (eds): Computer Applications in Mental Health. Cambridge, Harvard University Press, 1980

Creer TL, Kotses H: Asthma: psychologic aspects and management, in Middleton E., Jr. Reed CE, Ellis EF (eds): Allergy: Principles and Practice (2d ed). St. Louis, Mosby, 1983

Crisp AH: "Transference," "symptom emergence," and "social repercussion" in behavior therapy: A study of fity-four treated patients. Br J Med Psychol 39:179–196, 1966

Critchley DL, Maurin JT: The Clinical Specialist in Psychiatric Mental Health Nursing. New York, Wiley, 1985

Crocket R, Sandison RA, Walk A (eds): Hallucinogenic Drugs and Their Psychotherapeutic Use. Springfield, Ill, Thomas, 1963

Croley HT: The Consultive Process. Contin Educ Mongr No. 1. New York, American Public Health Association, 1961

Cronbach LJ: Essentials of Psychological Testing (2d ed), New York, Harper & Row, 1960

Cronbach LJ: Designing Evaluations. Stanford, Calif. Stanford Evaluation Consortorium, 1978

Crow HJ, Cooper R, Phillips DG: Progressive leucotomy, in Masserman JH (ed): Current Psychiatric Therapies, vol. 3. Orlando FL, Grune & Stratton, 1963

Crowley RM: Harry Stack Sullivan: His Contributions to Current Psychiatric Thought and Practice. Nutley, NJ, Hoffman-LaRoche, 1971

Crutcher HB: Foster home care, in Arieti S (ed): American Handbook of Psychiatry, vol. 2. New York, Basic Books, 1959, pp 1877–1884

Csapo M: Peer models reverse the "one bad apple spoils the barrel" theory. Teaching Excep Children 4:20–24, 1972

Cumming J: A psychiatrist looks at the psychiatric nurse. Psychiatr Op 9:22–25, 1972

Cumming J, Cumming E: Ego and Milieu, Theory and Practice of Environmental Therapy. New York, Atherton Press, 1962

Cumming RG: Casebook of Psychiatric Emergencies: The "On Call" Dilemma. Baltimore, University Park Press, 1983

Cummings NA: Prolonged (Ideal) versus short-term (realistic) psychotherapy. Professional Psychology 8:491, 1977

Cummings NA, Follett WT: Psychiatric services and medical utilization in a prepaid health plan setting (Pt 2) Medical Care 5:31, 1968

Cummings NA, Kahn BT, Sparkman B: Psychotherapy and medical utilization. Paper presented at the conference on Protecting the Emotionally Disabled Worker, University of California Extension Center, San Francisco, June 11, 1963

Curran CA: Counseling in Catholic Life and Education. New York, Macmillan, 1952

Curran D: The problem of assessing psychiatric treatment, Lancet 2:1005–1009, 1937

Curran FJ: Art techniques for use in mental hospitals and correctional institutions. Ment Hyg 23:371–378, 1939

Curran JP, Monti, PM, Corriveau DP: Treatment of schizophrenia, in Bellack AS, Hersen M, Kazdin AE (eds): International Handbook of Behavior Modification and Therapy. New York, Plenum, 1982

Cushman PJ: Methadone maintenance treatment of narcotic addiction. NY State J Med 72:1752–1755, 1972

Cutner M: Analytic work with LSD-25. Psychiatr Q 33:715–757, 1959

Czajkoski EH: The use of videotape recordings to facilitate the group therapy process. Int J Group Psychother 18:516–524, 1968

Dahlberg CC: LSD as an aid to psychoanalytic treatment, in Masserman JH (ed): Science and Psychoanalysis. Orlando FL, Grune & Stratton, 1963(a)

Dahlberg CC: Pharmacologic facilitation of psychoanalytic therapy, in Masserman JH (ed): Current Psychiatric Therapies, vol. 3. Orlando FL, Grune & Stratton, 1963(b)

Dahlstrom, WG, Walsh GA, Dahlstrom LE: MMPI Handbook, vol. 1. Clinical Applications (rev ed). Minneapolis, University of Minnesota Press, 1972

Danet BN: Videotape playback as a therapeutic device in group psychotherapy. Int J Group Psychother 14:433–444, 1969

Daniels RS, Margolis PM: Community psychiatry training in a traditional psychiatric residence, in Goldston SE (ed): Concepts of Community Psychiatry: A Framework for Training. Pub Health Service Pub No. 1319. Bethesda, Md, National Institute of Mental Health, 1965, pp 69–77

Danaher BG, Lichtenstein E: Become an Ex-smoker. Englewood Cliffs, NJ, Prentice-Hall, 1978

Davanloo H (ed): Short-term Dynamic Psychotherapy. New York, Spectrum, 1978

Davidman D: Evaluation of psychoanalysis: A clinician's view, in Hoch PH, Zubin J (eds): Evaluation of Psychiatric Treatment. Orlando FL, Grune & Stratton, 1964, pp 32–43

Davidoff E, Best JL, McPheeters HL: The effect of Ritalin (methylphenidylacetate hydrochloride) on mildly depressed ambulatory patient. NY State J Med 57:1753, 1957

Davidson GW: Living with Dying. Minneapolis, Augsburg, 1975

Davidson HA: The effects of psychotherapy. Int J Psychiatry 1:171–173, 1965

Davidson PO, Davidson SM (eds): Behavioral Medicine: Changing Health Life-styles. New York, Brunner/Mazel, 1980

Davidson JR, Douglass E: Nocturnal enuresis: A special approach to treatment. Br Med J 1:1345–1347, 1950

Davies SP: Toward Community Mental Health. New York, New York Association for Mental Health, 1960

Davis DR: Introduction to Psychopathology (2d ed). New York, Oxford University Press, 1966

Davis JA: Education for Positive Mental Health. NORC Monogr Soc Res. No. 5, Chicago, Aldine, 1966

Davis JE: Play and Mental Health. New York, Branes & Noble, 1938

Davis JE: An introduction to the problem of rehabilitation. Ment Hyg 29:217–230, 1945

Davis JE, Dunton WR: Principles and Practice of Recreational Therapy for the Mentally Ill. New York, Barnes & Noble, 1946

Davis WE: Psychiatric consultation—the agency viewpoint. Child Welfare 36:4–9, 1957

Dax EC: Asylum to Community. Melbourne, Aust, Cheshire, 1961

DeAmicis LA, Goldberg DC, Lo Piccolo J, Friedman JM, et al: Three year follow-up of couples evaluated for sexual dysfunction. J of Sex & Marital Therapy 10:215–218, 1984

Dean SR: Self-help group psychotherapy: Mental patients rediscover will power. Int J Soc Psychiatry 17:72–78, 1970–1971

DeBell D: A critical digest of the literature on psychoanalytic supervision. J Am Psychoanal Assoc 11:546–575, 1963

DeCharms R, Levy J, Wertheimer M: A note on attempted evaluation of psychotherapy. J Clin Psychol 10:233–235, 1954

Dederich CE: Synanon Foundation. Paper presented before the Southern California Parole Officers, October 1958

deGroat AF, Thompson GG: A study of the distribution of teacher approach and disapproval among sixth-grade children. J Exp Educ 18:57–75, 1949

Dejérine J, Gaukler E: Psychoneurosis and Psychotherapy. Philadelphia, Lippincott, 1913

DeJulio, Steven S, Lambert MJ, et al: Personal satisfaction as a criterion for evaluating group success. Psychological Reports 40(2):409–410, 1977

Dekker D, Pelser HE, Groen J: Conditioning as a cause of asthmatic attacks: A laboratory study, in Franks CM (ed): Conditioning Techniques in Clinical Practice and Research. New York, Springer, 1964, pp 116–131

Dekker D, Pelser HE, Green J: Conditioning as a cause of asthmatic attacks: Laboratory study. J Psychosom Res 2:97–108, 1957

Delay J, Deniker P: Apport de la clinique à la connaissance de l'action des neuroleptiques, in Bordeleau JM (ed): Extrapyramidal System and Neuroleptics. Montreal, Editions Psychiatriques, 1960, p 301

Delay J, Deniker P: Méthodeschimiothérapiques en psychiatrique: Les noveaux medicaments psychotropes. Paris, Masson et Cie, 1961

Delay J, Hart JM: Utilisation en thérapeutique psychiatrique d'une phenothiazine d'action centrale élective. Ann Med Psychol (Paris) 110(2): 112, 1952

DeLeon G, Beschner GM (eds): The Therapeutic Community. Washington, DC, U.S. Department of Health, Education and Welfare, 1976

DeLeon G, Holland S, Rosenthal MS: Phoenix House criminal activity of dropouts. JAMA 222:686, 1972

DeLeon G, Mandel W: A comparison of conditioning and psychotherapy in the treatment of functional enuresis. J Clin Psychol 22:326–330, 1966

Demarest EW, Teicher A: Transference in group therapy. Psychiatry 17:187–202, 1954

Dement W: The effect of dream deprivation. Science 31:1705–1717, 1960

Dement W: REM sleep linked to psychophysiological changes. Roche Report 3:1–8, 1966

Dement W, Kleitman N: The rleation of eye movements during sleep to dream activity: An objective method for the study of dreaming. J Exper Psychol 53:339–346, 1957

DeMuth P: Psychological Diary. Cleveland, Psychological Systems, 1982

Denber HCB (ed): Research Conference on Therapeutic Community. Springfield, Ill, Thomas, 1960

Denber HCB, Merlis S: Studies on mescaline. I. Action in schizophrenic patients. Psychiatr Q 29:421, 1955

Denker PG: Results of treatment of psychoneurosis by the general practitioner: A follow-up study of 500 cases. NY State J Med 46:2164–2166, 1946

Densen-Gerber J: We Mainline Dreams: The Odyssey House Story. New York, Doubleday, 1973

Deri, S: Introduction to the Szondi Test. Orlando FL, Grune & Stratton, 1949

Derogatis LR, Lipman RS, Covi L: SCL-90: An outpatient psychiatric rating scale. Psychopharmacol Bull 9:13–27, 1973

DeRosis L: The existential encounter in group psychoanalysis. J Psychoanal Groups 1:38–46, 1964

DeRubeis RJ, Hollon SD: Behavioral treatment of affective disorders, in Michelson L, Hersen M, Turner SM (eds): Future Perspectives in Behavior Therapy. New York, Plenum, 1981

Despert JL: Technical approaches used in the study and treatment of emotional problems in children. Psychiatr Q 2:267–95, 1937

Despert JL: Delusional and hallucinatory experiences in children. Am J Psychiatr 104:528, 1948

Deutsch D: Group subgroup and individual therapy combined to treat the family. Roche Report 3:3, 1966

Deutsch F: The associative anamnesis. Psychoanal Q 8:354–381, 1939

Deutsch F: Applied Psychoanalysis. Orlando FL, Grune & Stratton, 1949(a)

Deutsch F: Applied Psychoanalysis. Selected Objectives of Psychotherapy. Orlando FL, Grune & Stratton, 1949(b)

Deutsch F: Correlations of verbal and nonverbal communication in interviews conducted by the associative anamnesis. 21:123–130, 1959

Deutsch F, Murphy WF: The Clinical Interview. Vol. 1, Diagnosis—A Method of Teaching Associate Exploration. Vol. 2, Therapy—A Method of Teaching Sector Psychotherapy. New York, International Universities Press, 1955 (1967)

Deutsch H: Neurosis and Character Type. Clinical Psychoanalytic Studies. New York, International Universities Press, 1965

Deutsch M: A theory of cooperation and competition. Hum Relations 2:129–152, 1949(a)

Deutsch M: The effects of competition on the group process. Hum Relations 2:199–223, 1949(b)

Deutsch M: Mechanism, organism, and society. Phil Sci 18:230–262, 1951

Dewald PA: Psychotherapy—A Dynamic Approach. New York, Basic Books, 1964

Dewald PA: Learning problems in psychoanalytic supervision. Compr Psychiatry 10:107–121, 1969

Dewald PA: The process of change in psychoanalytic psychotherapy. Arch Gen Psychiatry 35:535–542, 1978

Dewald PA: Elements of change and cure in psychoanalysis. Archives of Gen Psychiatry 40:89–95, 1983

Dickel HA: The physician and the clinical psychologist. JAMA 195:121–126, 1966

Dicks HV: Experience with marital tensions seen in the psychological clinic. Br J Med Psychol 26:181–197, 1953

Diehl HS, Baker AB, Cowan DW: Cold vaccines, further evaluation. JAMA 115:593–594, 1940

Dies RR: Group psychotherapy: Reflections on three decades of research. J Applied Behav Science 15:361–374, 1979

Dies RR, Hess AK: An experimental investigation of cohesiveness in marathon and conventional group psychotherapy. J Abnorm Psychol 77:258–262, 1971

Diethelm O: Treatment in Psychiatry. Springfield, Ill, Thomas, 1950, p 177

DiFuria G, et al: A milieu therapy program in a state hospital. Neuropsychiatry 17:3–10, 1963

Dince PR: Psychotherapy for the Difficult-to-Engage Adolescent (Cassette Recording No. 5). Glendale, Calif. Audio-digest Foundation, vol. 10, March 9, 1981

Dinkmeyer D: Developing Understanding of Self and Others. Play Kit and Manual, 1. Circle Pines, Minn, American Guidance Service, 1970

Dische S: Management of enuresis. Br Med J 3:33–36, 1971

Dittes JE: Extinction during psychotherapy of GSR accompanying "embarrassing" statements. J Abnorm Soc Psychol 55:187, 1957(a)

Dittes JE: Galvanic skin responses as a measure of patient's reaction to therapist's permissiveness. J Abnorm Soc Psychol 55:295–303, 1957(b)

Dix GE: *Tarasoff* and the duty to warn potential victims, in Hofling CK (ed): Law and Ethics in the Practice of Psychiatry, New York, Brunner/Mazel, 1981

Dixon HH, Dickel HK, Coen RA, Hangen GO: Clinical observations on tolserol in handling anxiety tension states. Am J Med Sci 220–23, 1950

Dohrenwend BP, Bernard VW, Kolb LC: The orientation of leaders in an urban area toward problems of mental health. Am J Psychiatry 118:683–691, 1962

Dole VP, Nyswander M: A medical treatment, for diacetyl-morphine (heroin) addiction. JAMA 193:646–650, 1965

Dole VP, Nyswander M: Rehabilitation of heroin addicts after blockade with methadone. NY State J Med 66:2011–2017, 1966

Dole VP, Nyswander M: Heroin addiction: A metabolic disease. Archives of Internal Med 120:19–24, 1967

Doleys DM, Merdith RL, Ciminero AR (eds): Behavioral Medicine: Assessment and Treatment Strategies. New York, Plenum, 1982

Dollard J, Miller NE: Personality and Psychotherapy. New York, McGraw-Hill, 1950

Dolliver RH: Personal sources for theories of psychotherapy. J Con Psychol 12:53–59, 1981

Domhoff B: Night dreams and hypnotic dreams Int J Clin Exper Hypnosis 12:159–168, 1964

Doniger S (ed): Religion and Human Behavior. New York, Association Press, 1954

Donnelly J: Psychosurgery, in Kaplan HI, Sadock BJ (eds): Comprehensive Textbook of Psychiatry (4th ed). Baltimore, Williams & Wilkins, 1985, pp 1563–1569

Donnelly J: The incidence of psychosurgery in the United States 1971–1973. Am J Psychiatry 135:1475–1480, 1978

Donner L, Guerney BG, Jr: Automated group desensitization for test anxiety. Behav Res Ther 7:1–13, 1969

Dorfman W: Masked depression. Dis Nerv Sys 22(5):Pt2. 41, 1961

Dornberg N, Rosen B, Walker T: A home training program for young mentally ill children. New York, League School for Seriously Disturbed Children, 1968

Dorsett CH, Jones C: Architectural Aspects for the Community Mental Health Center. Bethesda, Md. Community Mental Facilities Branch. National Institute of Mental Health, 1967

Downing JJ, et al: Planning Programming and Design for the Community Mental Health Center. Western Institute for Research in Mental Health, 1966

Drabman RD, Jarvie GJ, Hammer D: Residential child treatment, in Hersen M, Bellack AS (eds): Behavior Therapy in the Psychiatric Setting. Baltimore, Williams & Wilkins, 1978

Draper G: The concept of organic unity and psychosomatic medicine. JAMA 124:767–771, 1944

Dreikurs R: Techniques and dynamics of multiple psychotherapy. Psychiatr Q 24:788–799, 1950

Dreikurs R: Psychology in the Classroom. New York, Harper & Row, 1957

Dressel PL: Some approaches to evaluation. Personnel Guid J 31:284–287, 1953

Driscoll GP: Child Guidance in the Classroom. New York, Columbia University Press, 1955

DuBois P: The Psychic Treatment of Mental Disorders. New York, Funk & Wagnalls, 1909

DuBois P: Education of Self. New York, Funk & Wagnalls, 1911

Duhl LJ (ed): The Urban Condition. New York, Basic Books, 1963

Dulcan MK: The psychopharmacologic treatment of children and adolescents with Attention Deficit Disorder. Psychiatric Annals, 15:69–80, 1985

Duncan M: Environmental therapy in a hospital for maladjusted children. Br J Delinq 3:248–286, 1953

Dunhan HW, Weinberg SK: The Culture of the State Mental Hospital. Detroit, Wayne University Press, 1960

Dunkel-Schetter C, Wortman CB: The interpersonal dynamics of cancer, in Friedman HS, DiMatteo MR (eds): Inter-personal Issue in Health Care. New York, Academic Press, 1982

Dunlap K: Habits: Their Making and Unmaking. New York, Liveright, 1932

Dunn J: Distress and Comfort. Cambridge, Harvard University Press, 1977

Dunton WR: Occupation Therapy. Philadelphia, Saunders, 1915

Dunton WR: Prescribing Occupational Therapy (2d ed). Springfield, Ill., Thomas, 1945

Dupont H (ed): Educating Emotionally Disturbed Children: Readings. New York, Holt, 1969

Durham JD, Hardin SB: The Nurse Psychotherapist in Private Practice. New York, Springer, 1986

Durkin H: The analysis of character traits in group therapy. Int J Group Psychother 1:133–143, 1951

Durkin H: Group dynamics and group psychotherapy. Int J Group Psychother 4:56–64, 1954

Durkin H: Acting out in group psychotherapy. Am J Orthopsychiatry 24:644, 1955

Durkin H: Towards a common basis for group dynamics. Group and therapeutic processes in group psychotherapy. Int J Group Psychother 7:115, 1957

Durkin H: The Group in Depth. New York, International Universities Press, 1964

Durkin H: Current problems of group therapy in historical content, in Wolberg LR, Aronson ML (eds): Group Therapy 1974: An Overview. New York, Stratton Intercontinental, 1974, pp 116–141

Durkin H: The development of systems theory and its implications for the theory and practice of group therapy, in Wolberg LR, Aronson ML (eds): Group Therapy 1975: An Overview. New York, Stratton Intercontinental, 1975, pp 8–20

Durkin H, et al: Acting out in group psychotherapy. Am J Psychother 12:87–105, 1948

Durkin H, Glatzer HT: Transference neurosis in group psychotherapy: The concept and the reality, in Wolberg LR, Schwartz EK (eds): Group Therapy 1973: An Overview. New York, Stratton Intercontinental, 1973, pp 129–144

Dyckman JM, Cowan PA: Imaging vividness and the outcome of *in vivo* and imagined scene desensitization. J Consult Clin Psychol 48:1155–1156, 1978

Dykes HM: Evaluation of three anorexiants. JAMA 230:270–272, 1974

Dymond RF: Adjustment changes in the absence of psychotherapy. J Consult Psychol 19:103–107, 1955

Earp JD: Psychosurgery: The position of the Canadian Psychiatric Association. Can J Psychiatry 24:353–365, 1979

Eaton A: Some implications and effects of intragroup acting out of pregenital conflicts. Int J Group Psychother 12:435, 1962

Ebaugh FG: Evaluation of interviewing techniques and principles of psychotherapy for the general practitioner. J Omaha Med-West Clin Soc 9:29–35, 1948

Ebersole GD, Leiderman PH, Yalom ID: Training the nonprofessional group therapist. A controlled study J Nerv Ment Dis 149(3):37–44, 1969

Edelson M: Ego Psychology. Group Dynamics and the Therapeutic Community. Orlando FL, Grune & Stratton, 1964

Edelson SM, Taubman MT, Lovaas OI: Some social contexts of self-destructive behavior. J Abnor Child Psychology 11(2):299–312, 1983

Edmonson BW, Amsel A: The effects of massing and distribution of extinction trials on the persistence of a fear-motivated instrumental response. J Comp Physiol Psychol 47:117–123, 1954

Edward C: Craze for God. Englewood Cliffs, NJ, Prentice-Hall, 1979

Efron R: The conditioned inhibition of uncinate fits, in Franks CM (ed): Conditioning Techniques in Clinical Practice and Research. New York, Springer, 1964, pp 132–143

Egan MH: Home treatment—an addition to our continuum of therapies, in Masserman JH (ed): Current Psychiatric Therapies, vol. 7. Orlando FL, Grune & Stratton, 1967

Ehrenwald J: New Dimensions of Deep Analysis. London, Allen & Unwin, 1954

Ehrenwald J: Neuroses in the Family and Patterns of Psychosocial Defense. New York, Hoeber, 1963

Einstein A: Ideas and Opinions. New York, Crown, 1954

Eisenbud J: Psychology of headache. Psychiatr Q 11:592–619, 1937

Eisenbud J: Psi and Psychoanalysis. Orlando FL, Grune & Stratton, 1970

Einstein S: Psychoanalytic education—a critical view from within. Psychiatr Op 9:31–36, 1972

Eisenstein VW: Differential psychotherapy of borderline states. Psychiatr Q 25:379–401, 1951

Eisenstein VW: Differential psychotherapy of borderline states, in Bychowski G, Despert JL (eds): Specialized Techniques in Psychotherapy. New York, Basic Books, 1952

Eisenstein VW: Neurotic Interaction in Marriage. New York, Basic Books, 1956

Eisler RM, Hersen M, Miller PM: Effects of modeling on components of assertive behavior. J Behav Ther Exp Psychiatry 4:1–6, 1973(a)

Eisler PM, Hersen M, Miller PM: Components of assertive behavior. J Clin Psychol 29:295–299, 1973(b)

Eisler PM, Hersen M, Miller PM: Shaping components of assertive behavior with instructions and feedback. Am J Psychiatry 131:12, 1974

Eisner BG: Notes on the use of drugs to facilitate group psychotherapy. Psychiatr Q 38:310–328, 1964

Eisner BG, Cohen S: Psychotherapy with LSD. J Nerv Ment Dis 126:127–528, 1958

Eissler KR: The Psychiatrist and the Dying Patient. New York, International Universities Press, 1955 (paperback, 1970)

Eissler KR: Citation in Lowenstein R: Remarks on some variations in psycho-analytic technique. Int J Psychoanal 39:203, 1958

Eissler KR: Medical Orthodoxy and the Future of Psychoanalysis. New York, International Universities Press, 1965

Ekstein R: On current trends in psychoanalytic training, in Lindner R (ed): Explorations in Psychoanalysis. New York, Julian, 1953, pp 230–265

Ekstein R: Report of the panel on the teaching of psychoanalytic technique. J Am Psychoanal Assoc 8:167–174, 1960

Ekstein R: Concerning the teaching and learning of psychoanalysis. J Am Psychoanal Assoc 17:312–332, 1969

Ekstein R, Motto RL: From Learning for Love to Love of Learning. New York, Brunner/Mazel, 1969

Ekstein R, Wallerstein R: The Teaching and Learning of Psychotherapy. New York, Basic Books, 1958 (rev ed, 1972)

Ekstein R, Wallerstein R 1964

Eliasberg WG: Psychotherapy in cancer patients. JAMA 147:525, 1951

Elkin M: Short-contact counseling in a conciliation court. Soc Casework 43:184–190, 1962

Elkins RL: Covert sensitization treatment of alcoholism: Contributions of successful conditioning to subsequent abstinence maintenance. Addict Beh 5:67–89, 1980

Ellen F: A psychiatric nurse's experience in community nursing. Perspect Psychiatr Care 3(6), 1965

Ellis A: Outcome of employing three techniques of psychotherapy. J Clin Psychol 13:344–350, 1957

Ellis A: Neurotic interaction between marital partners. J Consult Psychol 5:24–28, 1958(a)

Ellis A: Rational psychotherapy. J Gen Psychol 59:35–49, 1958(b)

Ellis A: Reason and Emotion in Psychotherapy. New York, Lyle Stuart, 1962

Ellis A: An answer to some objections to rational-emotive psychotherapy. Psychotherapy 2:108–111, 1965

Ellis A: A weekend of rational encounter, in Burton A (ed): Encounter. San Francisco, Jossey-Bass, 1970

Ellis A: An experiment in emotional education. Educ Tech 11:61–64, 1971

Ellis A: My philosophy of psychotherapy. J Contemp Psychol 6:13–18, 1973

Ellis NR, Barnett CD, Pryer MW: Operant behavior in mental defectives: Exploratory studies. J Exp Anal Behav 3:63–69, 1960

Ellsworth PB: PARS V Community Adjustment Scale. Roanoke, Va, Institute for Program Evaluation, 1974

Ellsworth RB: Consumer feedback in measuring the effectiveness of mental health programs, in Struening EL, Guttentag M (eds): Handbook of Evaluation Research, vol. 2. Beverly Hills, Sage Publications, 1975

Elwood RS: Religious and Spiritual Groups in Modern America. Englewood Cliffs, NJ, Prentice–Hall, 1973

Emmelkamp PMG, Kwee, KG: Obsessional ruminations: A comparison between thought-stopping and prolonged exposure in imagination. Behav Res Ther 15:441–444, 1977

Endicott NA, Endicott J: Improvement in untreated psychiatric patients. Arch Gen Psychiatry 9:575–585, 1963

Endicott J, Spitzer RL, Fleiss RL, Cohen J: The global assessment scale. Arch Gen Psychiatry 33:766, 1976

Ends EJ, Page CW: A study of three types of group psychotherapy with hospitalized male inebriates. Q J Stud Alcohol 13:263–277, 1957

Enelow AJ, Adler L: Psychiatr skills and knowledge for the general practitioner. JAMA 189:91–96, 1964

Engel GC: The biopsychosocial model and medical education. N Engl J Med 306: 802–805, 1982

English HB: Three cases of the "conditioned" fear response. J Abnorm Soc Psychol 24:221–225, 1924

English HB, English AC: A Comprehensive Dictionary of Psychological and Psychoanalytical Terms. New York, McKay, 1958, p 169

English OS: Who should be trained for psychotherapy? in Hoffman FH (ed): Teaching of Psychotherapy. International Psychiatry Clinics. Boston, Little, Brown, 1964, p 281

English OS, Hamper WW Jr, Bacon CD, Settlage CF: Direct Analysis and Schizophrenia: Clinical Observations and Evaluation. Orlando FL, Grune & Stratton, 1961

English OS, Pearson GHJ: Common Neuroses of Children and Adults. New York, Norton, 1937, p 119

Enright JB: An introduction to Gestalt techniques, in Fagan J, Shepherd IL (eds): Gestalt Therapy Now. Palo Alto, Calif, Science & Behavior Books, 1970

Ensel RR: Validity of computer generated MMPI reports in psychiatric patients. Arch Psychiatr Nervenkr 229:165–167, 1980

Epstein L, Feiner AH: On the growing interest in countertransference: The therapist's contribution to treatment. Contemporary Psychoanalysis 15:489–513, 1979

Epstein LH, Cluss PA: A behavioral medicine perspective on adherence to long term medical regimens. J Consult Clin Psychol 50:950–971, 1982

Epstein NB, Vlok LA: Research on the results of psychotherapy: A summary of evidence. Am J Psychiatry 138:1027–1035, 1981

Erdman HP, Greist JH, Klein MH, Jefferson JW, et al: The computer psychiatrist. Beh Res Methods & Instrumentations 13:393–398, 1981

Erickson CE: A Basic Test for Guidance Workers. Englewood Cliffs, NJ, Prentice-Hall, 1947

Erickson MH: The investigation of a specific amnesia. Br J Med Psychol 13:143–150, 1933

Erikson EH: Dramatics Production Test, in Murray HA, et al (eds): Explorations in Personality. New York, Oxford University Press, 1939, pp 552–582

Erikson EH: Studies in the interpretation of play, in Tomkins SS (ed): Contemporary Psychopathology. Cambridge, Harvard University Press, 1944

Erikson EH: Ego development and historical development, in Eissler RS, et al (eds): Psychoanalytic Study of the Child. New York, International Universities Press, 1946, pp 359–396

Erikson EH: Childhood and Society. New York, Norton, 1950, 1963

Erikson EH: Sex differences in the play configuration of preadolescents. Am J Orthopsychiatry 21:667–692, 1951

Erikson EH: Identity and the Life Cycle. New York, International Universities Press, 1959

Erickson MH: A study of experimental neurosis hypnotically induced in a case of ejaculation praecox. Br J Psychol 15:34–50, 1935

Erickson MH: Development of apparent unconsciousness during hypnotic reliving of a traumatic experience. Arch Neurol Psychiatry 38:1282–1288, 1937

Erickson MH: The successful treatment of a case of acute hysterical depression by a return under hypnosis to a critical phase of childhood. Psychoanal Q 10:583–609, 1941

Erickson MH: Hypnotic investigation of psychosomatic phenomena: A controlled experimental use of hypnotic regression in the therapy of an acquired food intolerance. Psychosom Med 5:67–70, 1943

Erickson MH, Hill LB: Unconscious mental activity in hypnosis-psychoanalytic implications. Psychoanal Q 13:60–78, 1944

Erickson MH, Kubie LS: The permanent relief of an obsessional phobia by means of communications with an unsuspected dual personality. Psychoanal Q 8:471–509, 1939

Erickson MH, Rossi E (eds): Innovative Hypnotherapy. Collected Papers of Milton II. Erickson on Hypnosis. New York, Irvington, 1980

Eron LD: Prescription for reduction of aggression. Am Psychologist 35(3):244–252, 1980

Erwin E: Behavior Therapy: Scientific Philosophical and Moral Foundations. New York, Cambridge University Press, 1978

Erwin E: Psychoanalytic therapy: The Eysenck argument. Am Psychol 35:435–443, 1980

Esdaile J: Hypnosis in Medicine and Surgery. New York, Julian, 1957

Esman AH: The Psychiatric Treatment of Adolescents. New York, International Universities Press, 1983

Esquibel AJ, et al: Hexafluorodiethyl ether (Indokolon): Its use as a convulsant in psychiatric treatment. J Nerv Ment Dis 126:530, 1958

Eustace CG: Rehabilitation: An evolving concept. JAMA 195:1129–1132, 1966

Euthanasia Education Council: A Living Will. New York, the Council, 1964

Evan WM, Miller JR: Differential effects on response bias of computer vs. conventional administration of a social science questionnaire: An exploratory methodological experiment. Behav Sci 14(3): 216–227, 1969

Evans FJ: In-patient analytic group therapy of neurotic and delinquent adolescents. Some specific problems associated with these groups. Psychother Psychosom 13:265–270, 1965

Evans FJ: Hypnosis and sleep, in Fromm E, Shor RE (eds): Hypnosis: Research Developments and Perspectives. Chicago, Aldine, 1972

Evans FJ, Reich LH, Orne MT: Optopinetic nystagmus, eye movements, and hypnotically induced hallucinations. J Nerv Ment Dis 152:419–431, 1972

Everstine DS, Everstine L: People in Crisis: Strategic Therapeutic Interventions. New York, Brunner/Mazel, 1983

Ewig CF: Newer sedative drugs that can cause states of intoxication and dependence of barbiturate type. JAMA 196:714–717, 1966

Eymiew A: Le Gouvernement du soi-même. Paris, Perrin, 1922

Eysenck HJ: The effects of psychotherapy: An evaluation. J Consult Psychol 16:319–324, 1952

Eysenck HJ: A reply to Luborsky's note. Br J Psychol 45:132–133, 1954

Eysenck HJ: The effects of psychotherapy: A reply. J Abnorm Soc Psychol 50:147–148, 1955

Eysenck HJ: The Dynamics of Anxiety and Hysteria. London, Routledge, 1957

Eysenck HJ: Learning theory and behavior therapy. J Ment Sci 105:61–75, 1959

Eysenck HJ: The effects of psychotherapy. In Eysenck HJ (ed): Handbook of Abnormal Psychology: An Experimental Approach. London, Pitman, 1960(a) pp 697–725

Eysenck HJ: Behaviour Therapy and Neuroses. Elmsford, NY, Pergamon, 1960(b)

Eysenck HJ: Conditioning and personality. Br J Psychol 53:299–305, 1962

Eysenck HJ: The outcome problem in psychotherapy: A reply. Psychother 1:97–100, 1964

Eysenck HJ: The effects of psychotherapy. Int J Psychiatry 1:99–142, 1965

Eysenck HJ: The Effects of Psychotherapy. New York, International Science Press, 1966

Eysenck HJ: The non-professional psychotherapist. Int J Psychiatry 3:150–153, 1967

Eysenck HJ: A mish-mash of theories. Int J Psychiatry 9:140–146, 1970

Eysenck HJ: Psychotherapy and the experimental approach. J Contemp Psychol 6:19–27, 1973

Ezriel H: A psychoanalytic approach to the treatment of patients in groups. J Ment Sci 96:774–779, 1950

Ezriel H: Notes on psychoanalytic group therapy: II. Interpretation and research. Psychiatry 15:119–126, 1952

Ezriel H: Role of transference in psychoanalytic group psychotherapy and other approaches to group treatment. Acta Psychother 7:101, 1959

Ezriel H: Psychoanalytic group therapy, in Wolberg LR, Schwartz EK (eds): Group Therapy 1973: An Overview. New York, Stratton Intercontinental, 1973, pp 183–210

Fabing HD, Hawkins JR, Moulton JAL: Clinical studies on alpha-(2-piperidyl) benzhydrol hydrochloride, a new antidepressant drug. Am J Psychiatry 111:832, 1955

Fagan J, Shepherd IL: Gestalt Therapy Now. Palo Alto, Calif, Science Behavior Books, 1970

Fairbairn WRD: Prolegomena to a psychology of art. Br J Psychol 28:288–303, 1938(a)

Fairbairn WRD: The ultimate basis of aesthetic

experience. Br J Psychol 29:167–181, 1938(b)

Fairbairn WRD: Endopsychic structure considered in terms of object-relationships. Psychoanal Q 5:54, 1946(a)

Fairbairn WRD: Object-relationships and dynamic structure. Int J Psychoanal 17:30, 1946(b)

Fairbairn WRD: An Object-Relations Theory of the Personality. New York, Basic Books, 1954

Farau A: Fifty years of individual psychology. Compr Psychiatry 3:242–254, 1962

Farber L: Casework treatment of ambulatory schizophrenics. Soc Casework 39:9–17, 1958

Faris R, Dunham HW: Mental Disorders in Urban Areas. Chicago, University of Chicago Press, 1939

Farndale J: The Day Hospital Movement in Great Britain. Elmsford, NY, Pergamon, 1961

Farnsworth DL: Mental Health in College and University. Cambridge, Harvard University Press, 1957

Farnsworth DL, Blaine GB Jr (eds): Counseling and the College Student. Boston, Little, Brown, 1970

Farnsworth DL, Braceland F: Psychiatry, the Clergy and Pastoral Counseling. Collegeville, Minn, St. John's University Press, 1969

Farrell MP: Transference dynamics of group psychotherapy. Arch Gen Psychiatry 6:66–76, 1962

Faucett EC: Multiple-client interviewing: A means of assessing family processes. Soc Casework 43:114–120, 1962

Fay A: Clinical notes on paradoxical therapy. Psychotherapy: Theory, Research, and Practice 13:118–122, 1976.

Feather BW, Rhoads JM: Psychodynamic Behavior Therapy. Arch Gen Psychiatry 26:496–511, 1972

Federn P: Psychoanalysis of psychosis. Psychiatr Q 17:3–17, 470–487, 1943

Federn P: Principles of psychotherapy in latent schizophrenia. Am J Psychother 1:129–145, 1947

Feifel H (ed): The Meaning of Death. New York, McGraw-Hill, 1959, pp 251–258

Feighner AC, Feighner JP: Multimodel treatment of the hyperkinetic child. Am J Psychiatry 131:459–462, 1974

Fein LG: The Changing School Scene: Challenge to Psychology. New York, Wiley, 1974

Feld M, Goodman JR, Guido JA: Clinical and laboratory observations on LSD-25. J Nerv Ment Dis 126:176, 1958

Feldman MP, MacCulloch MJ: The application of anticipatory-avoidance learning to the treatment of homosexuality. Behav Res Ther 2:165–183, 1965

Feldman PE: Psychotherapy and chemotherapy (amitriptyline) of anergic states. Dis Nerv Syst 22(5): Sect 2, 27, Suppl, 1961

Feldman Y: A casework approach toward understanding parents of emotionally disturbed children. Soc Casework 3:23–29, 1958

Felix RH: The dynamics of community mental health, in Panel Discussion on Creating a Climate Conducive to Mental Health, National Health Forum, Cincinnati, 1957

Felix RH: Second report on the relations between medicine and psychology. NY State District Branch Bull (American Psychiatric Association) December 1960

Felix RH: A comprehensive community mental health program, in Felix RH (ed): Mental Health and Social Welfare. New York, Columbia University Press, 1961

Fellows L, Wolpin M: High school psychology trainees in a mental hospital, in Guerney BG (ed): Psychotherapeutic Agents: New Roles for Nonprofessionals, Parents and Teachers. New York, Holt, 1969

Felsenfield N, et al: The Training of Neighborhood Workers. Washington, DC, Institute for Youth Studies, 1966

Fenichel O: Ten Years of the Berlin Psychoanalysis Institute, 1920–1930.

Fenichel O: Problems of Psychoanalytic Technique. Albany, NY, Psychoanalytic Quarterly, 1941

Fenichel O: The Psychoanalytic Theory of Neurosis. New York, Norton, 1945, p 582

Fensterheim H: Help without Psychoanalysis. New York, Stein & Day, 1971

Fensterheim H: Behavior therapy: Assertive training in groups, in Sager CS, Kaplan HS (eds): Progress in Group and Family Therapy. New York, Brunner/Mazel, 1972, pp 156–169

Ferenczi S: The Further Development of the Active Therapy in Psychoanalysis (1921). Further contributions to Psychoanalysis. London, Hogarth, 1950(a)

Ferenczi S: Contra-Indications to the "Active" Psychoanalytical Technique (1926). Further Contributions to Psychoanalysis. London, Hogarth, 1950(b)

Ferenczi S: The Elasticity of Psycho-Analytical Technique (1928). Further Contributions to Psychoanalysis. London, Hogarth, 1950(c)

Ferenczi S: The Future Development of the Active Therapy in Psychoanalysis (1921). Further Contributions to Psychoanalysis. London, Hogarth, 1950(d)

Ferenczi S: Further Contributions to the Theory and Technique of Psychoanalysis. New York, Basic Books, 1952 (London, Hogarth, 1960)

Ferenczi S: Present-day Problems in Psychoanalysis (1926), in Balint M (ed): The Problems and Methods of Psychoanalysis. New York, Basic Books, 1955(a)

Ferenczi S: The elasticity of psychoanalytic technique (1928), in Balint M (ed): The Problems and Methods of Psychoanalysis. New York, Basic Books, 1955(b)

Ferenczi S, Rank O: The development of psychoanalysis. Washington, DC, Nervous & Mental Disease Publishing Co, 1925

Ferreira AJ: The "double bind" and delinquent behavior. Arch Gen Psychiatry 3:359–367, 1960

Ferster CB: Positive reinforcement and behavioral deficits of autistic children. Child Dev 32:426–456, 1961

Ferster CB: Positive reinforcement and behavioral deficits of autistic children, in Franks CM (ed): Conditioning Techniques in Clinical Practice and Research. New York, Springer, 1964, pp 255–274

Ferster CB: Classification of behavioral pathology, in Ullman LP, Krasner L (eds): Behavior Modification Research. New York, Holt, 1965

Ferster CB, DeMyer MK: The development of performance in autistic children in an automatically controlled environment. J Chronic Dis 13:312–345, 1961

Feshbach S: The stimulating versus cathartic effects of a vicarious aggressive activity. J Abnorm Soc Psychol 63:381–385, 1961

Festinger L: Wish expectation and group performance as factors influencing level of aspiration. J Abnorm Soc Psychol 37:184–200, 1942

Festinger L: The role of group belongingness is a voting situation. Hum Relations 1:154–181, 1947

Fiddler GS: The role of occupational therapy in a multi-discipline approach to psychiatric illness. Am J Occupat Ther 6:1, 1957

Fiedler FE: A comparison of therapeutic relationships in psychoanalytic, non-directive, and Adlerian therapy. J Consult Psychol 14:436–445, 1950(a)

Fiedler FE: The concept of an ideal therapeutic relationship. J Consult Psychol 14:239–245, 1950(b)

Fiedler FE: Factor analyses of psychoanalytic non-directive and Adlerian therapeutic relationships. J Consult Psychol 15:32–38, 1951

Fiedler FE: Quantitative studies on the role of therapist's feelings toward their patients, in Mowrer H (ed): Psychotherapy: Theory and Research. New York, Ronald, 1953, pp 296–315

Fielding B, Mogul D: Sensitivity training of psychotherapists. Int Ment Health Res Newsletter 12:5, 1970

Fierman LB: Myths in the practice of psychotherapy. Arch Gen Psychiatry 12:412, 1965

Filmer BG, Hillson JS: Some child therapy practices. J Clin Psychol 15:105–106, 1959

Finesinger JE: Psychiatric interviewing. I. Some principles and procedures in insight therapy. Am J Psychiatry 105:187–195, 1948

Fink M: Convulsive Therapy: Therapy and Practice. New York, Raven Press, 1979

Fink M, Abrams M: Selective drug therapies in clinical psychiatry: Neuroleptic, anxiolytic and antimanic agents, in Freeman AM, Kaplan HI (eds): Treating Mental Illness. New York, Atheneum, 1972

Fink P, Goldman M, Levick M: Art therapy: A new discipline. Pa Med 70:61, 1967

Finney BC: Some techniques for teaching psychotherapy. Psychother: Theory Res Prac 5:115–119, 1968

Fischer J, Gochros HL: Planned Behavior Change: Behavior Modification in Social Work. New York, Free Press, 1975

Fischer M: Development and validity of a computerized method for diagnosis of functional psychoses. Acta Psychiatrica Scandinavica 50:243–258, 1974

Fish B: Drug therapy in child psychiatry: Psychological aspects. Compr Psychiatry 1:55–61, 1960(a)

Fish B: Drug therapy in child psychiatry: Pharmacological aspects. Compr Psychiatry 1:212–227, 1960(b)

Fish B: Evaluation of psychiatric therapies in children. Paper presented at the American Psychopathologic Association meeting, February 1962

Fish B: Pharmacotherapy in children's behavior disorders, in Masserman JH (ed): Current Psychiatric Therapies, vol. 3. Orlando FL, Grune & Stratton, 1963, pp 82–90

Fish B: A topology of children's psychiatric disorders. I. Its application to a controlled evaluation. J Am Acad Child Psychiatry 4:32–52, 1965

Fish B: Treatment of children, in Kline NS, Lehman HE (eds): Supplement to International Psychiatric Clinics, vol. 2, no. 4. Boston, Little, Brown, 1966

Fisher C: Hypnosis in treatment of neuroses due to war and to other causes. War Med 4:563–576, 1943

Fisher C: REM and NREM nightmares. Int Psychiatry Clin 7:183–187, 1970

Fisher SH: The recovered patient returns to the community. Ment Hyg 42:463–473, 1958

Fisher SH, Beard JH: Fountain House: A psychiatric rehabilitation program, in Masserman JH (ed): Current Psychiatric Therapies, vol. 2. Orlando FL, Grune & Stratton, 1962, pp 211–218

Fisher SH, Beard JH, Goertzel V: Rehabilitation of the mental hospital patient: The Fountain House program. Int J Soc Psychiatry 4:295–298, 1960

Fishman HC: A study of efficacy of negative practice as a corrective for stammering. J Speech Dis 2:67–72, 1937

Fitzgerald RO: Conjoint marital psychotherapy: An outcome and follow-up study. Fam Process 8:260–271, 1969

Flach FF, Regan PF: Chlorpromazine and related phenothiazine derivatives, in Flach FF, Regan PF (eds): Chemotherapy in Emotional Disorders. New York, McGraw-Hill, 1960

Flade JK: Milieu therapy for the mentally ill. J Rehab 27:12–13, 1961

Fleck S: Family dynamics and origin of schizophrenia. Psychosom Med 22:333–344, 1960

Fleischl MF: The understanding and utilization of social and adjunctive therapies. Am J Psychother 26:255, 1962

Fleischl MF: Specific problems encountered in social rehabilitation. Am J Psychother 18:660, 1964

Fleischl MF, Waxenberg SE: The therapeutic social club, a step toward social rehabilitation. Int Ment Health Res Newsletter 6(1), 1964

Fleischl MF, Wolf A: Techniques of social rehabilitation, in Masserman JH (ed): Current Psychiatric Therapies, vol. 7. Orlando FL, Grune & Stratton, 1967

Fleming J: Observations on the use of finger painting in the treatment of adult patients with personality disorders. Char Personal 8:301–310, 1940

Fleming J: What analytic work requires of an analyst: A job analysis. J Am Psychoanal Assoc 9:719–729, 1961

Fleming J: Evolution of a research project in psychoanalysis, in Gaskill HS (ed): Counterpoint. New York, International Universities Press, 1963

Fleming J: Teaching the basic skills of psychotherapy. Arch Gen Psychiatry 16:416–426, 1967

Fleming J, Benedek T: Supervision: A method of teaching psychoanalysis. Psychiatr Q 33:71–96, 1964

Fleming J, Benedek T: Psychoanalytic Supervision. Orlando FL, Grune & Stratton, 1966

Flescher J: On different types of countertransference. Int J Group Psychother 3/4:357–372, 1953

Flescher J: The economy of aggression and anxiety in group formation. Int J Group Psychother 7:31, 1957

Fletcher J: Indicators of humanhood: Tentative profile of man. Hastings Center Rep 2:1, 1972

Fletcher MI: The Adult and the Nursery School Child. Toronto, University of Toronto Press, 1974

Flowers JV, Booraem CD: Stimulation and role playing methods, in Kanfer FH, Goldstein AP (eds): Helping People Change (2d ed). New York, Pergamon, 1980

Flumerfelt JM: Referring your patient to a psychiatrist. JAMA 146:1589–1591, 1951

Flynn JP, Kuczeruk T: Computer-assisted instruction for the private practitioner, in Schwartz MD (ed): Using Computers in Clinical Practice. New York, The Haworth Press, 1984, pp 395–416

Foa EB, Emmelkamp PMG (eds): Failures in Behavior Therapy. New York, Wiley, 1983

Foa EB, Steketee GS, Ozarow BJ: Behavior Therapy with obsessive-compulsives: From theory to treatment, in Mavissakalian M, Turner SM, Mickeston LE (eds): Obsessive-Compulsive Disorders: Psychological and Pharmacological Treatments. New York, Plenum, 1985

Foa EB, Steketee G, Turner RM, et al: Effects of imagined exposure to feared disasters in obsessive-compulsive checkers. Behav Ther 18:449–455, 1980

Folsom GS: The music therapist's special contributions. Ment Hosp 14:638–642, 1963

Folstein MF, Folstein SE, McHugh PR: Mini-mental state: A practical method for grading the cognitive state of patients for the clinician. J Psychiatr Res 12:189–198, 1975

Ford CV: The Pueblo Incident: Psychological response to severe stress, in Sarason IG, Spielberger CD (eds): Stress and Anxiety, vol. 2. New York, Wiley, 1975, pp 229–242

Ford S, Ederer F: Breaking the cigarette habit. JAMA 194:139–142, 1965

Fordyce WE: Behavioral Methods for Chronic Pain and Illness. St. Louis, Mosby, 1976

Fordyce WE, Fowler RS, Lehmann JF, et al: Operant conditioning in the treatment of chronic pain. Arch Phys Med Rehabil 54:399–408, 1973

Forem J: Transcental Meditation: Maharishi Mahesh Yogi and the Science of Creative Intelligence. New York, Dutton, 1973

Forstenzer HM: Problems in relating community programs to state hospitals. Am J Pub Health and the Nation's Health 51:1152–1157, 1961

Foster LE: Religion and psychiatry. Pastoral Psychol 1:7–13, 1950

Foulkes D: Psychology of Sleep. New York, Scribner, 1966

Foulkes SH: Introduction to Group Analytic Psychotherapy; Studies in the Social Integration of Individuals and Groups. London, Heinemann, 1948, pp 10–18, 28–31; Orlando FL, Grune & Stratton, 1949

Foulkes SH: Group-analytic dynamics with specific reference to psychoanalytic concepts. Int J Group Psychother 7:46, 1957

Foulkes SH: Group processes and the individual in the therapeutic group. Br J Med Psychol 34:23, 1961

Foulkes SH: Therapeutic Group Analysis. New York, International Universities Press, 1964

Foulkes SH, Anthony EJ: Group Psychotherapy. New York, Penguin, 1957, pp 31–43, 76–87

Fox R: Psychotherapeutics of alcoholism, in Bychowski G, Despert JL (eds): Specialized techniques in Psychotherapy. New York, Basic Books 1952, pp 239–260

Fox R: Antabuse as an adjunct to psychotherapy in alcoholism. NY State J Med 57:1540–1544, 1958

Fox R: No "sure" therapy for alcoholism. Med News, pp 14–15, July 14, 1961

Fox R: A multi-disciplinary approach to the treatment of alcoholism. Paper presented at the 122d Annual Meeting of the American Psychiatric Association, Atlantic City, NJ, May 1966

Foxx RM, Azrin NH: Restitution: A method of elimination of aggressive-disruptive behavior of retarded and brain-damaged patients. Behav Res Ther 10:15–27, 1972

Fraiberg SH: Psychoanalytic Principles in Casework with Children. New York, Family Service Association of America, 1954

Fraiberg S: A comparison of the analytic method in two stages of child analysis. Am Academy of Child Psychiatry 4:387–400, 1965

Framo JL: The theory of the technique of family treatment of schizophrenia. Fam Process 1:119–131, 1962

Framo JL: Marriage therapy in a couples group. Semin Psychiatry 5:207–217, 1973

Framo JL, Green RJ: Bibliography of Books Related to Family and Marital Systems Theory and Therapy. Upland, Calif., American Association for Marriage and Family Therapy, 1980

Frances A, Clarkin J, Perry S: Differential Therapeutics in Psychiatry. New York, Brunner/Mazel, 1984

Frank GH: The literature on counter-transference: A survey. Int J Group Psychother 34:441–452, 1953

Frank JD: Problems of controls in psychotherapy as exemplified by the Psychotherapy Research Project of the Phipps Psychiatric Clinic, in Rubenstein EA, Parloff MB (eds): Research in Psychotherapy. Washington, DC, American Psychological Association, 1959

Frank JD: Persuasion and Healing: A Comparative Study of Psychotherapy. Baltimore, Johns Hopkins Press, 1961, pp 65–74 (rev ed, 1973)

Frank JD: The effects of psychotherapy. Int J Psychiatry 1:150–152, 1965

Frank JD: Psychotherapy: The restoration of morale. Am J Psychiatry 131:271–274, 1974

Frank JD: The present status of outcome studies. J Consult Clin Psychol 47:310–316, 1979

Frank JD: Biofeedback and the placebo effect. Biofeedback Self Regul 7:449–460, 1982

Frank JD: Psychotherapy, the transformation of meaning. J Royal Society of Medicine 79:341–346, 1986

Frank JD, Gliedman LH, Imber SD, et al: Patient's expectancies and relearning as factors determining improvement in psychotherapy. Am J Psychiatry 115:961–968. 1959

Frank JD, Nash EH, Stone AR: Immediate and long-term symptomatic course of psychiatric outpatients. Am J Psychiatry 120:429–439, 1963

Frank LK: Research for what? J Soc Issues, Suppl Ser 10, 1957

Frankel BL, Buchbinder R, Snyder F: Ineffectiveness of electrosleep in chronic primary insomnia. Arch Gen Psychiatry 29:563–568, 1973

Frankel FH: Electroconvulsive therapy, in Karasu TB (ed): The Psychiatric Therapies. Washington, DC, American Psychiatric Association, 1984

Frankl VE: Arztliche Seelsorge. Vienna, Deuticke, 1948

Frankl VE: The Doctor and the Soul: An Introduction to Logotherapy. New York, Knopf, 1955

Frankl VE: The spiritual dimension in existential analysis and logotherapy. J Indiv Psychol 15:157–165, 1959

Frankl VE: Beyond self-actualization and self-expression. J Existen Psychiatry 1(1):5–20, 1960

Frankl VE: Basic concepts of logotherapy. Confin Psychiatr (Basel, Switz) 4:99–109, 1961(a)

Frankl VE: Logotherapy and the challenge of suffering. Rev Existen Psychol Psychiatry 1:3–7, 1961(b)

Frankl VE: From psychotherapy to logotherapy in Walters A (ed): Psychology. Westminister, Md, Newman, 1963(a)

Frankl VE: Existential dynamics and neurotic escapism. Paper presented at the Conference on Existential Psychiatry, Toronto, Canada, May 6, 1962. J Existen Psychiatry 4:27–42, 1963(b)

Frankl VE: Fragments from the logotherapeutic treatment of four cases, in Burton A (ed): Modern Psychotherapeutic Practice. Palo Alto, Calif, Science & Behavior Books, 1965

Frankl VE: Logotherapy and existential analysis—a review. Am J Psychother 20:252–260, 1966

Frankl VE: Psychotherapy and Existentialism. New York, Washington Square Press, 1967

Franks CM: Conditioning Techniques in Clinical Practice and Research. New York, Springer, 1964

Franks CM: Behavior therapy, psychology and the psychiatrist. Am J Orthopsychiatry 35:145–151, 1965

Franks CM: Behavior Therapy: Appraisal and Status. New York, McGraw-Hill, 1969

Franks CM: Can behavior therapy find peace and happiness in a school of professional psychology? J Clin Psychol 28:11–15, 1974

Franks CM, Wilson GT: Annual Review of Behavioral Therapy, Theory, and Practice, vol. 3. New York, Brunner/Mazel, 1975

Franks CM: On conceptual and technical integrity in psychoanalysis and behavior therapy: Two fundamentally incompatible systems, in Arkowitz H, Messer SB (eds): Psychoanalytic and Behavior Therapy: Are They Compatible? New York, Plenum, 1984

Franks CM, Wilson GT, Kendall PC, Brownell KD: Annual Review of Behavior Therapy:

Theory and Practice, vol. 10. New York, Guilford Press, 1985

Fraser HF, et al: Degree of physical dependence induced by secobarbital or pentobarbital. JAMA 166:126–129, 1958

Fraser HF, Grider JA, Jr: Treatment of drug addiction. Am J Med 14:571, 1953

Freedman AM: Drug Therapy in Behavior Disorders. Baltimore, Saunders, 1958

Freedman AM, Sharoff R: Crucial factors in the treatment of narcotics addiction. Am J Psychother 19:397–407, 1965

Freedman DA: Various etiologies of schizophrenia. Dis Nerv Syst 19:1–6, 1958

Freedman DX: On the use and abuse of LSD. Arch Gen Psychiatry 18:330–347, 1968

Freedman DX, Gordon RP: Psychiatry under siege: Attacks from without. Psychiatr Ann 3(11):23, 1973

Freedman MB, Sweet BS: Some specific features of group psychotherapy and their implications for selection of patients. Int J Group Psychother 4:355–368, 1954

Freeman FS: Theory and Practice of Psychological Testing (3d ed). New York, Holt, 1962

Freeman H, Farndale J (eds): Trends in the Mental Health Services. New York, Macmillan, 1963

Freeman RW, Friedman I: Art therapy in a total treatment plan. J Nerv Ment Dis 124:421–425, 1956

Freeman WJ, Watts JW: Psychosurgery. Springfield, Ill, Thomas, 1942

French JRP, Jr: The disruption and cohesion of groups. J Abnorm Soc Psychol 36:361–377, 1941

French JRP, Jr: Organized and unorganized groups under fear and frustration. University of Los Angeles Stud Child Welf 20:299–308, 1944

French LM: Psychiatric Social Work. London, Commonwealth Fund, 1940

French TM: The Integration of Behavior. Vol. 1, Basic Postulates. Chicago, University of Chicago Press, 1952

French TM, Fromm E: Dream Interpretation: A New Approach. New York, Basic Books, 1964

Freud A: Introduction to the Technique of Child Analysis. Washington, DC, Nervous & Mental Disease Publishing Co, 1928

Freud A: Psychoanalysis for Teachers and Parents. Stuttgart, Hippocrates Press, 1930

Freud A: The Ego and the Mechanisms of Defense. London, Hogarth, 1937

Freud A: Indications for child and analysis, in Eissler RS, et al (eds): The Psychoanalytic Study of the Child, vol. 1. New York, International Universities Press, 1945, pp 127–149

Freud A: The Psychoanalytical Treatment of Children: Technical Lectures and Essays. London, Imago, 1946

Freud A: Normality and Pathology in Childhood. New York, International Universities Press, 1965

Freud A, Burlingham DT: Infants Without Families. New York, International Universities Press, 1944

Freud S: Introduction to Pfister's the Psychoanalytic Method, in Standard Edition, vol. 12. London, Hogarth, 1913, pp 329–331

Freud S: A General Introduction to Psychoanalysis. New York, Boni & Liveright, 1920

Freud S: On psychotherapy, in Collected Papers, vol. 1. London, Hogarth, 1924(a), p 249

Freud S: On the history of the psychoanalytic movement, in Collected Papers, vol. 1. London, Hogarth, 1924(b), p 287

Freud S: Papers on technique, in Collected Papers, vol. 2. London, Hogarth, 1924(c)

Freud S: Turnings in the ways of psychoanalytic therapy, in Collected Papers, vol. 2. London, Hogarth, 1924(d), p 392

Freud S: The Future of an Illusion. London, Hogarth, 1928

Freud S: The Ego and the Id. London, Hogarth, 1927

Freud S: Three Contributions to the Theory of Sex. Washington, DC, Nervous & Mental Disease Publishing Co, 1930

Freud S: New Introductory Lectures on Psychoanalysis. New York, Norton, 1933

Freud S: On narcissism, in Collected Papers, vol. 4. London, Hogarth, 1934, pp 30–59

Freud S: The Problem of Anxiety. New York, Norton, 1936 (1926 transl)

Freud S: Analysis terminable and interminable. Int J Psychoanl 18:373–405, 1937

Freud S: Three Contributions to the Theory of Sex, in The Basic Writings of Sigmund Freud. New York, Modern Library, 1938(a)

Freud S: The Interpretation of Dreams, in The Basic Writings of Sigmund Freud. New York, Modern Library, 1938(b)

Freud S: The Ego and Id. London, Hogarth, 1947 (orig publ 1923)

Freud S: An Outline of Psychoanalysis. New York, Norton, 1949, pp 63–64

Freud S: Analysis terminable and interminable, in Collected Papers, vol. 5. London, Hogarth, 1952, pp 316–357

Freud S: Psychoanalysis (1922), in Collected Papers, vol. 5. London, Hogarth, 1952, p 125

Freud S: Postscript to a discussion on lay analysis (1927), in Collected Papers, vol. 5. London, Hogarth, 1952, pp 205–214

Freud S: Mourning and Melancholia (1917), in Standard Edition, vol. 14. London, Hogarth, 1955

Freud S: The Interpretation of Dreams. New York, Basic Books, 1959: Wiley, 1961 (orig publ 1900)

Freud S: Analysis of phobia in a 5-year-old boy, in Collected Papers, Vol. 5. New York, Basic Books, 1959, p. 125

Freud S: Resistances to Psychoanalysis, in Standard Edition, vol. 19. London, Hogarth, 1961

Freund K: Some problems in the treatment of homosexuality, in Eysenck HJ (ed): Behavior Therapy and the Neuroses. Elmsford, NY, Pergamon, 1960, pp 312–325

Freudlich D: Primal experience groups. A flexible structure. Int J Group Psychother 26:29–41, 1976

Freyhan FA: Schizophrenia. Initial separation rates for first admissions: Comparison of selected cohorts, 1908–58, in Rothlin E (ed): Neuro-psychopharmacology, vol. 2. Amsterdam, Elsevier, 1961, p 192

Freytag FF: The Hypnoanalysis of an Anxiety Hysteria. New York, Julian, 1959

Fried E: On Love and Sexuality. New York, Grove, 1962

Fried E: Some aspects of group dynamics and the analysis of transference and defenses. Int J Group Psychother 15:44–56, 1965

Fried M: Grieving for a lost home, in Duhl, LJ (ed): The Urban Condition. New York, Basic Books, 1963 pp 151–171

Friedell A: A reversal of the normal concentration of urine in children having enuresis. Am J Dis Child 33:717–721, 1927

Friedman AS: Family therapy as conducted in the home. Fam Process 1:132–145, 1962

Friedman DE, Silverstone JT: Treatment of phobic patients by systematic desensitization. Lancet 1:470–472, 1967

Friedman E: Nursing aspects of the treatment of lobotomized patients. Bull Menninger Clin 14:138, 1950

Friedman HJ: Patient-expectancy and symptom reduction. Arch Gen Psychiatry 8:61–76, 1963

Friedman HJ: Psychotherapy of borderline patients: The influence of theory on technique. Am J Psychiatry 132:1048–1052, 1975

Friedman JM, Hogan DR: Sexual dysfunction: Low sexual desire, in Barlow D (ed): Clinical Handbook of Psychological Disorders. New York, Guilford Press, 1985, pp 417–461

Friedman M, Rosenman RH: Association of specific over behavior patterns with blood and cardiovascular findings. JAMA 169:1286, 1959

Friedman M, Rosenman RH: Type A Behavior and Your Heart. New York, Knopf, 1974

Friedman RM: The use of computers in the treatment of children. Child Welfare 59:152, 1980

Friedman SB, Chodoff P, Mason JW, Hamburg DA: Behavior observations on parents anticipating the death of a child. Pediatrics 32:610–625, 1963

Frieswyk S: Treatment planning for borderlines: Why test? NAPPH Journal 13:17–20, 1982

Fromm E: Uber Methods and Aufgabe einer analytischen Sozialpsychologie. Ztschr. Soziale I, 1932

Fromm E: Authoritat and Familie, in Horkheimer M (ed): Socialpsychologischen. Paris, Alcan, 1936, pp 77–135, 230–238

Fromm E: Escape from Freedom. New York, Holt, 1941

Fromm E: Man for Himself. New York, Holt, 1947

Fromm E: Psychoanalysis and Religion. New Haven, Yale University Press, 1950

Fromm E: The Sane Society. New York, Holt, 1955

Fromm E: The Forgotten Language. New York, Harper & Row, 1959(a)

Fromm E: Sigmund Freud's Mission. New York, Harper & Row, 1959(b)

Fromm E: Value, psychology and human existence, in Maslow AE (ed): New Knowledge in Human Values. New York, Harper & Row, 1959(c)

Fromm-Reichmann F: Transference problems in schizophrenia. Psychoanal Q 8:412, 1939

Fromm-Reichmann F: Principles of Intensive Psychotherapy. Chicago, University of Chicago Press, 1950

Fromm-Reichmann F: Notes on the development of the treatment of schizophrenics by psychoanalytic psychotherapy, in Bychowski G, Despert JL (eds): Specialized Techniques in Psychotherapy. New York, Basic Books, 1952(a), pp 159–179

Fromm-Reichman F: Psychoanalysis and psychotherapy, in Bullard DM (ed): Selected Papers. Chicago, University of Chicago Press, 1952(b)

Fromm-Reichmann F: Psychoanalytic and general dynamic conceptions of theory and of therapy. J Am Psychoanal Assoc 2:711–721, 1954

Fuerst RW: Problems of short-time psychotherapy. Am J Orthopsychiatry 8:260, 1938, 8:260, 1938

Fulkerson SE, Barry SR: Methodology and research on prognostic use of psychological tests. Psychol Bull 58:177–204, 1961

Fultz AF: Music therapy. Psychiatr Op 3:32–35, 1966

Furst W: Homogeneous versus heterogeneous groups. Int J Group Psychother 1:120–123, 1950

Fry WF, Heersema P: Conjoint family therapy: A new dimension in psychotherapy, in Kadis AL, Winick CH (eds): Topical Problems of Psychotherapy, vol. 5. New York, Karger, 1965, pp 147–153

Gaarder KR, Montgomery PS: Clinical Biofeedback: A Procedural Manual. Baltimore, Williams & Wilkins, 1977

Gadpaille WJ: Observations on the sequence of resistances in groups of adolescent delinquents. Int J Group Psychother 9:275–286, 1959

Gadpaille WJ: Adolescent concerns about homosexuality. Med Asp Hum Sex 17:105–106, 1973

Galanter M, Rabkin P, Rabkin J, Deutsch A, et al: The "Moonies": a psychological study of conversion and membership in a contemporary religious cult. Am J Psychiatry 136(2):165–170, 1979

Galdston I: The problem of medical and lay psychotherapy. The medical view. Am J Psychother 4:421, 1950

Galdston I: An existential analysis of the case of Miss L. Paper presented at the Mid-Winter Conference on Existential Psychiatry, New York, December 15, 1963

Gambrill ED, Richey CA: An assertive inventory for use in assessment and research. Behav Ther 6:547–549, 1975

Gans RW: Group therapists and the therapeutic situation: A clinical evaluation. Int J Group Psychother 12:82–88, 1962

Gantt WH: The conditioned reflex function as an aid in the study of the psychiatric patient, in Franks CM (ed): Conditioning Techniques in Clinical Practice and Research. New York, Springer, 1964, pp 25–43

GAP Report No. 8: An Outline for Evaluation of a Community Program in Mental Hygiene. New York, Group for the Advancement of Psychiatry, 1949

GAP Report No. 34: The Consulting Psychiatrist in a Family Service Agency. New York, Group for the Advancement of Psychiatry, 1956(a)

GAP Report No. 35: The Psychiatrist in Mental Health Education. New York, Group for the Advancement of Psychiatry, 1956(b)

GAP Report No. 73: Psychotherapy and the Dual Research Tradition. New York, Group for the Advancement of Psychiatry, 1969

GAP Report No. 77: Toward Therapeutic Care—A Guide for Those Who Work with the Mentally Ill (2d ed). New York, Group for the Advancement of Psychiatry, 1970

GAP Report No. 93: The Community Worker: A Response to Human Need. New York, Group for the Advancement of Psychiatry, 1974

GAP Symposium No. 10: Urban America and the Planning of Mental Health Services. New York, Group for the Advancement of Psychiatry, 1964

GAP Symposium No. 11: Death and Dying: Attitudes of Patient and Doctor. New York, Group for the Advancement of Psychiatry, 1965

GAP Symposium No. 12: The Right to Die. New York, Group for the Advancement of Psychiatry, 1973

Gardner E: Newsletter. Psychiatric Society of Westchester, October 1965

Gardner G: Conflicting Needs and Models in Respect to the Delivery of Mental Health Service for Children. Washington, DC, National Institute of Mental Health, 1974

Gardner GE: Training of clinical psychologists. Round Table, 1951. The development of the clinical attitude. Am J Orthopsychiatry 22:162–169, 1952

Gardner RA: Therapeutic Communication with Children: The Mutual Storytelling Technique. New York, Science House, 1971

Garfield SL: Research on client variables in psychotherapy, in Bergin AE, Garfield SL (eds): Handbook of Psychotherapy and Behavior Change: An Empirical Analysis. New York, Wiley, 1971

Garfield SL: Research problems in clinical diagnosis. J Consult Clin Psychol 46:596–607, 1978

Garfield, SL, Bergin AE (eds): Handbook of Psychotherapy and Behavior Change: An Empirical Analysis (2d ed). New York, Wiley, 1978

Garner HH: Brief psychotherapy. Int J Neuropsychiatry 1:616, 1965

Garner HH: Psychotherapy: Confrontation Problem-Solving Techniques. St Louis, Green, 1970

Garrett A: Counseling Methods for Personnel Workers. New York, Family Welfare Association of America, 1945

Garrett A: Psychiatric consultation. Am J Orthopsychiatry 26:234–240, 1956

Garrett A: Modern casework: The contributions of ego psychology, in Parad HJ (ed): Ego Psychology and Dynamic Casework. New York, Family Service Association of America, 1958, pp 38–52

Garrison EA, Forward in Leninger MM (ed): Contemporary Issues in Mental Health Nursing. Boston, Little, Brown, 1973

Garrow JS: Treat Obesity Seriously: A Clinical Manual. London, Churchill Livingstone, 1981

Gartner A, Riessman F: Self-Help in the Human Services. San Francisco, Jossey-Bass, 1977

Gaston ET (ed): Music in Therapy. New York, Macmillan, 1968

Gauthier M: Countertransference and supervision: A discussion of some dynamics from the point of view of the supervisor. Can J Psychiatry 29:513–519, 1984

Gayle R, Neale C: Subshock insulin therapy. Dis Nerv Syst 10:231, 1949

Gediman HK, Wolkenfeld F: The Parallelism Phenomenon in psychoanalysis and supervision: Its reconsideration as a triadic system. Psychoanalytic Q 49:234–255, 1980

Gedo JE: A psychoanalyst reports at mid-career. Am J Psychiatry 136:646–649, 1979

Gedo JE: Reflection of some current controversies in psychoanalysis. J Am Psychological Assoc 28:363–383, 1980

Geertsma RH, et al: Auditory and visual dimensions of externally mediated self-observation. J Nerv Ment Dis 148:437–448, 1969

Geertsma RH, Reivich RS: Repetitive self-observation by videotape playback. J Nerv Ment Dis 141:29–41, 1965

Geijerstam G: The psychosomatic approach in gynecological practice. Acta Obst Gynecol Scand 30:346–390, 1960

Geist J, Gerber NM: Joint interviewing: A treatment technique with marital partners. Soc Casework 41:76–83, 1960

Gelb LA: Rehabilitation of mental patients in a comprehensive rehabilitation center. NY State J Med 60:2404–2411, 1960

Gelb LA, Ullman M: "Instant psychotherapy" in an outpatient psychiatric clinic—philosophy and practice. Paper presented at the 122d Annual Meeting of the American Psychiatric Association, Atlantic City, NJ, May 1966

Geller J: Parataxic distortions in the initial stages of group relationships. Int J Group Psychother 12:27–34, 1962

Gellhorn E, et al: Emotions and Emotional Disorders: A Neurophysiological Study. New York, Harper & Row, 1963

Gendro JM: The Roots and the Branches and Bibliography of Psychodrama, 1972–1980; and Sociometry, 1970–1980. Beacon, New York, Beacon House, 1980

Gendzel IB: Marathon group therapy and nonverbal methods. Am J Psychiatry 127:286–290, 1970

Gendzel IB: Marathon group therapy: Rationale and techniques, in Masserman JH (ed): Current Psychiatric Therapies, vol. 12. Orlando FL, Grune & Stratton, 1972

Gentry WD, Street AJ, Masur FT, Asken MJ: Training in medical psychology: A survey of graduate and internship training programs. Professional Psychology 12(2):224–228, 1981

Genuth SM, Castro JH, Vertes V: Weight reduction in obesity by outpatient semistarvation. JAMA 230:987–991, 1974

Geocaris K: The patient as a listener. Arch Gen Psychiatry 2:81–88, 1960

Geppert TV: Management of nocturnal enuresis by conditioned response, in Franks CM (ed): Conditioning Techniques in Clinical Practice and Research. New York, Springer, 1964, pp 189–195

Gershon S, Shopsin B: Lithium: Its Role in Psychiatric Research and Treatment. New York, Plenum, 1973

Gerson S, Bassuk E: Psychiatric emergencies: An overview. Am J Psychiatry 137:1–11, 1980

Gerty FJ: Roles and responsibilites in mental health planning. Am J Psychiatry 121:835–838, 1965

Gerty FJ, Holloway JW, Jr, MacKay EP: Licensure or certification of clinical psychologists. JAMA 148:271–273, 1952

Gerwitz JL: A learning analysis of the effects of normal stimulation, privation, and deprivation on the acquisition of social motivation and attachment, in Foss BM (ed): Determinants of Infant Behavior, New York, Wiley, 1961, pp 213–283

Giannini AJ, Black HR, Goettsche RL: Psychiatric, Psychogenic, and Somatopsychic Disorders Handbook. New York, Medical Examination Publishing, 1978

Gibb JR: The role of a consultant. J Soc Issues 15:1–4, 1959(a)

Gibb JR: Lippitt R (eds): Consulting with groups and organizations. J Soc Issues 15(11):2, 1959(b)

Gilbert R: Functions of the consultant. Teachers Coll Rec 61:117–187, 1960

Gilbertson EC, Williamson EM: The consultation process in public health nursing. Pub Health Nurs 44:146–147, 1952

Giles HH, McCutchen SP, Zeckiel AN: Exploring the Curriculum. New York, Harper & Row, 1942, p 5

Gill MM: Ego psychology and psychotherapy. Psychoanal Q 20:62–71, 1951

Gill MM: Psychoanalysis and exploratory psychotherapy. J Am Psychoanal Assoc 2:771–797, 1954

Gill MM: The analysis of the transference. J Am Psychoanal Assoc 27:263–288, 1979

Gill MM: Analysis of Transference I: Theory and Techniques. New York, International University Press, 1982

Gill MM, Brenman M: Treatment of a case of anxiety hysteria by a hypnotic technique employing psychoanalytic principles. Bull Menninger Clin 7:163–171, 1943

Gill MM, Brenman M: Hypnosis and Related States. New York, International Universities Press, 1959

Gill MM, Hoffman I: A method for studying the analysis of aspects of the patient's experience of the relationship in psychoanalysis and psychotherapy. J Am Psychoanal Assoc 30:137–167, 1982

Gill MM, Muslin ML: Early interpretation of transference. J Am Psychoanal Assoc 24:788, 1976

Gill MM, Newman R, Redlich FC: The Initial Interview in Psychiatric Practice. New York, International Universities Press, 1954

Gilliland EG: Uses of music therapy. Int J Group Psychother 14:68–72, 1961

Gilliland EG: Progress in music therapy. Rehab Lit 23:298–306, 1962

Gillison TH, Skinner JC: Treatment of nocturnal enuresis by the electric alarm. Br Med J 2:1268–1272, 1958

Ginott HG: Group Psychotherapy with Children. New York, McGraw-Hill, 1961

Ginott HG: Driving children sane. Today's Educ 62:20–25, 1973

Ginsburg EL: The Training and Function of a Psychiatric Social Worker in a Clinical Setting. Transactions of the First Conference. New York, Josiah Macy, Jr, Foundation, 1947, pp 31–40

Gitelson M: Clinical experience with play therapy. Am J Orthopsychiatry 8:466, 1939

Gitelson M: Problems of psychoanalytic training. Psychoanal Q 17:198–211, 1948

Gitelson M: The emotional position of the analyst in the psychoanalytic situation. Int J Psychoanal 33:1–10, 1952

Gitelson M: On the identity crisis in American psychoanalysis. J Am Psychoanal Assoc 12:451–476, 1964

Glad D: Operational Values in Psychotherapy. New York, Oxford University Press, 1959

Gladstone HP: A study of techniques of psychotherapy with youthful offenders. Psychiatry 25:147–159, 1962

Gladstone HP: Psychotherapy with adeolscents: Theme and variations. Psychiat Q 2:304–309, 1964

Gladstone RD: Do maladjusted teachers cause maladjustment? A review. J Except Child 15:65–70, 1948

Glass GV, Wilson VL, Gottman JM: Design and Analysis of Time-Series Experiments. Boulder, Colo, Laboratory of Educational Research, 1973

Glass J: Personal therapy and the student therapist. Can J Psychiatry 31:304–312, 1986

Glass LL, Kirsch MA, Parris FN, et al: Psychiatric disturbances associated with Erhard Seminars Training, I: A report of cases. Am J Psychiatry 134:245–247, 1977

Glass RM: Psychotherapy: Scientific art or artistic science. Arch Gen Psychiatry 41:525–526, 1984

Glasscote RM, Fishman ME: Mental Health on the Campus: A Field Study. Washington, DC, American Psychiatric Association, 1973

Glasscote RM, Sanders D, Forstenzer HM, Foley AR: The Community Mental Health Centers: An Analysis of Existing Models. Washington, DC, Joint Information Service of American Psychiatric Association and the National Association for Mental Health, 1964

Glasscote RM, Sussex JN, Cumming E, Smith LH: The Community Mental Health Centers: An Interim Appraisal. Washington, DC, Joint Information Service of the American Psychiatric Association and the National Association for Mental Health, 1969

Glasser W: Reality Therapy: A New Approach to Psychiatry. New York, Harper & Row, 1965

Glasser W, Zunin LM: Reality therapy, in Masserman JH (ed): Current Psychiatric Therapies, vol. 12. Orlando FL, Grune & Stratton, 1972

Glatzer HT: Transference in group psychother-apy. Am J Orthopsychiatry 22:449–509, 1952

Glatzer HT: Handling transference resistance in group psychotherapy. Psychoanal Rev 40:36, 1953

Glatzer HT: The relative effectiveness of clinically homogeneous and heterogeneous psychotherapy groups. Int J Group Psychother 6:258, 1956

Glatzer HT: Notes on the preoedipal fantasy. Am J Orthopsychiatry April 1959(a)

Glatzer HT: Analysis of masochism in group therapy. Int J Group Psychother 9:158–166, 1959(b)

Glatzer HT: Narcissistic problems in group psychotherapy. Int J Group Psychother 12(4), 1962

Glatzer HT: Practice of group psychotherapy based on classical psychoanalytic concepts. Am J Orthopsychiatry 34:395, 1964

Glatzer HT: Aspects of transference in group therapy. Int J Group Psychother 15:167–177, 1965

Glatzer HT, Pederson-Krag G: Relationship group therapy with a mother of a problem child, in Slavson SR (ed): The Practice of Group Therapy. New York, International Universities Press, 1947, p 219

Glauber IP: Dynamic therapy for the stutterer, in Bychowski G, Despert JL (eds): Specialized Techniques in Psychotherapy. New York, Basic Books, 1952, pp 207–238

Glick ID, Weber DH, Rubinstein D, et al: Family Therapy and Research: An Annotated Bibliography (2d ed). Orlando FL, Grune & Stratton, 1982

Glickman, L: Combined use of different antipsychotic drugs. JAMA 251:2657–2658, 1984

Glidewell JC: The entry problem in consultation. J Soc Issues 15:51–59, 1959

Gliedman LH, Nash EH, Imber SD, et al: Reduction of symptoms by pharmacologically inert substances and by short-term psychotherapy. Arch Neurol Psychiatry 79:345–351, 1958

Glover BH: The new nurse-therapist. Paper presented at the 122d Annual Meeting of the American Psychiatric Association, Atlantic City, NJ, May 1966

Glover E: Lectures on technique in psychoanalysis. Int J Psychoanal 8/9, 1927

Glover E: The therapeutic effect of inexact interpretations: A contribution to the theory of suggestion. Int J Psychoanal 12:397–411, 1931

Glover E: An Investigation of the Technique of Psychoanalysis. London, Bailliere, 1940

Glover E: Research methods in psychoanalysis. Int J Psychoanal 33:403, 1952

Glover E: The Technique of Psychoanalysis. New York, International Universities Press, 1955 (rev ed, 1968)

Glover E: Functional Group of Delinquent Disorders: On the Early Development of Mind. New York, International Universities Press, 1956

Glover E: Freudian or neo-Freudian. Psychiatr Q 33:97–109, 1964

Glover E: The effects of psychotherapy. Int J Psychiatry 1:158–161, 1965

Glover E, Fenichel O, Strachey J, et al: On the theory of therapeutic results of psychoanalysis. Symposium. Int J Psychoanal 18:125–

Glucksman M: Physiological measures and feedback during psychotherapy. Psychother & Psychosom 36:185–199, 1981

Glueck BC, Strobel CF: Biofeedback and meditation in the treatment of psychiatric illnesses, in Masserman JH (ed): Current Psychiatric Therapies, vol. 15. Orlando FL, Grune & Stratton, 1975

Glueck BC, Stroebel CF: Computers in Clinical Psychiatry, in Kaplan HI, Freedman BJ, Sadock BJ (eds): Comprehensive Textbook of Psychiatry. (3d ed) 1980, pp 548–565

Glueck S, Glueck ET: Unraveling Juvenile Delinquency. Cambridge, Harvard University Press, 1950

Glynn JD, Harper P: Behaviour in transvestism. Lancet 1:619, 1961

Godenne GD: Outpatient adolescent group psychotherapy. Am J Psychiatry 18:584, 1964

Godenne GD: Outpatient adolescent group psychotherapy. I. Review of the literature on use of co-therapists, psychodrama, and parent group therapy. Am J Psychol 19:40–53, 1965

Goertzel V, Beard JH, Pilnick S: Fountain House Foundation: Case study of an expatient club. J Soc Issues 16:54–61, 1960

Golan SE, Eisdorfer C: Handbook of Community Mental Health. New York, Appleton-Century-Crofts, 1972

Goldberg C: Peer influence in contemporary group psychotherapy, in Wolberg LR, Aronson ML (eds): Group Therapy 1975: An Overview. New York, Stratton Intercontinental, 1975, pp 232–241

Goldberg DP, Hobson RF, Margison F, et al: Evaluating the teaching of a method of psychotherapy. Br J Psychiatry 144:575–580, 1984

Goldberg HL: Home treatment. Psychiatr Ann 3:59–61, 1973

Goldberg HL, DiMascio A, Chaudhary B: A clinical evaluation of prolixin enanthate. Psychosomatics 2:173–177, 1970

Goldberg SC, Schultz SC, Schulz PM, Resnick RJ, et al: Borderline and schizotypal personality disorders treated with low-dose thiothixene vs placebo. Arch Gen Psychiatry 43:680–686, 1986

Goldenberg I, Goldenberg H: Family Therapy: An Overview. Monterey, Calif, Brooks/Cole, 1980

Goldfarb AI: Psychotherapy of aged persons. IV. One aspect of the psychodynamics of the therapeutic situation with aged patients. Psychoanal Rev 42:180–187, 1955

Goldfarb AI: Minor maladjustments in the aged, in Arieti S (ed): American Handbook of Psychiatry, vol. 1. New York, Basic Books, 1959, pp 378–397

Goldfarb AI: Management of aged patients who are mentally ill. Roche Report 1(7), 1964

Goldfarb AI, Wolk RL: The response of group psychotherapy upon recent admissions to a mental hospital. Paper presented at the 122d Annual Meeting of the American Psychiatric Association, Atlantic City, NJ, May 1966

Goldfarb W: Infant rearing and problem behavior. Am J Orthopsychiatry 13:249–265, 1943

Goldfried MR (ed): Converging Theories in the Practice of Psychotherapy. New York, Springer Publishing Company, 1982

Goldfried MR, Davison, GC: Clinical Behavior Therapy. New York, Holt, Reinhart & Winston, 1976

Goldiamond I: Fluent and nonfluent speech (stuttering): Analysis and operant techniques for control, in Krasner L, Ullman LP (eds): Research in Behavior Modification. New York, Holt, 1965

Goldman G: Reparative psychotherapy, in Rado S, Daniels GE (eds): Changing Concepts of Psychoanalytic Medicine. New York, Grune & Stratton, 1956, pp 101–113

Goldman RK, Mendelsohn GA: Psychotherapeutic change and social adjustment; A report of a national survey of psychotherapists. J Abnorm Psychol 74:164–172, 1969

Goldstein A, Wolpe J: Behavior therapy in groups in Kaplan HI, Sadock BJ (eds): Comprehensive Group Psychotherapy. Baltimore, Williams & Wilkins, 1971, pp 292–327

Goldstein AP: Patient's expectancies and nonspecific therapy as a basis for (un) spontaneous remission. J Clin Psychol 16:399–403, 1960

Goldstein AP: Therapist-Patient Expectancies in Psychotherapy. Elmsford, NY, Pergamon, 1962

Goldstein AP: Relationships-enhancement methods, in Kanfer FG, Goldstein AP (eds): Helping People Change (2d ed). New York, Pergamon, 1980

Goldstein AP, Heller K, Sechrest LB: Psychotherapy and the Psychology of Behavior Change. New York, Wiley, 1966

Goldstein AP, Wolpe J: Behavior therapy in groups, in Kaplan HI, Sadock BJ (eds): Comprehensive Group Psychotherapy. Baltimore, Williams & Wilkins 1971, pp 292–327

Goldstein SE: Marriage and Family Counseling. New York, McGraw-Hill, 1945.

Goldston SE (ed): Concepts of Community Psychiatry: A Framework for Training. Pub Health Service Pub No. 1319. Bethesda, Md, National Institute of Mental Health, 1965

Golton M: Private practice in social work, in Encyclopedia of Social Work, vol. 2. New York, National Association of Social Workers, 1971

Gomberg RM: Family-oriented treatment of marital problems. Soc Casework 37:3–10, 1956

Gommes-Schwartz B, Hadley SW, Strupp HH: Individual psychotherapy and behavior therapy. Annual Review of Psychology, vol. 29, 435–471, 1985

Gondor, EI: Art and Play Therapy. New York, Doubleday, 1954

Gonzales, ER: Retiring may predispose to fatal heart attack. JAMA 243:13–14, 1980

Good Education for Young Children. Flushing, NY, New York State Council for Early Childhood Education, 1947

Goodman G: An experiment with companionship therapy: College students and troubled boys—assumptions, selection and design, in Guerney BG (ed): Psychotherapeutic Agents: New Roles for Nonprofessionals, Parents and Teachers. New York, Holt, 1969

Goodman JA: Social work services for alcoholics and their families. California's Health, December 1, 1962

Goodman M: Ethical guidelines for encounter group leadership. A committee report for the New Jersey State Psychological Association, 1972

Goodman M, Marks M, Rockberger H: Resistance in group psychotherapy enhanced by the counter-transference reactions of the therapists. Int J Group Psychother 14:322, 1964

Goodman M, Marks D: Oral regression as manifested and treated analytically in group psychotherapy. Int J Group Psychother 13:3, 1963

Goodwin HM, Mudd EH: Marriage counseling, in Ellis A, Abarbanel A (eds): Encyclopedia of Sexual Behavior. New York, Hawthorn Books 1961 pp 685–695

Goodstein, RK: Common clinical problems in the elderly. Psychiatric Annals 15:299–312, 1985

Gordon DE: The function of the consultant. Nurs Outlook 1:575–577, 1953

Gordon T: Group Centered Leadership: A Way of Releasing the Creative Power of Groups. Boston, Houghton Mifflin, 1955

Gordon T, Grummon DL, Rogers CR, Seeman J: Developing a program of research in psychotherapy, in Rogers CR, Dymond RF (eds): Psychotherapy and Personality Changes. Chicago, University of Chicago Press, 1954, pp 12–34

Goshen CR: New concepts of psychiatric care with special reference to the day hospital. Am J Psychiatry 115:808, 1959

Gottesfeld H: The Critical Issues of Community Mental Health. New York, Behavioral Publications, 1972

Gottfried AW, Verdicchio FG: Modifications of hygienic behaviors using reinforcement therapy. Am J Psychother 28:122–128, 1974

Gottlieb H, Strite LC, Koller R, et al: Comprehensive rehabilitation of patients having chronic low back pain. Arch Phys Med Rehabil 58:101–108, 1977

Gottman JM, Markman HJ: Experimental designs in psychotherapy research, in Garfield SI, Bergin AE (eds): Handbook of Psychotherapy and Behavior Change: An Empirical Analysis. New York, Wiley, 1978

Gottschalk LA, Mayerson P, Gottlieb AA: Prediction and evaluation of outcome in an emergency brief psychotherapy clinic. J Nerv Ment Dis 144:77, 1967

Gough HG: A sociological theory of psychotherapy. Am J Soc 53:359–366, 1948

Gould I: Specialized group techniques with the narcotics addict. Paper presented at the Gracie Mansion Conference on Drug Addiction, New York City, February 4, 1965

Goulding RL: Four models of transactional analysis. Int J Group Psychother 26:385–392, 1976

Grad B: Some biological effects of the "laying on of hands": A review of experiments with animals and plants. J Am Soc Psychical Res 59:95–127, 1965

Graham SR: The effects of psychoanalytically oriented psychotherapy on levels of frequency and satisfaction in sexual activity. J Clin Psychol 16:94–95, 1960

Gralnick A: Psychoanalysis and the treatment of adolescents in a private hospital, in Masserman JH (ed): Science and Psychoanalysis, vol. 9. Orlando FL, Grune & Stratton, 1966, pp 102–108

Gralnick A, D'Elia F: A psychoanalytic hospital becomes a therapeutic community. Hosp Community Psychiatry, May 1969

Grant N, Jr: Art and the Delinquent. New York, Exposition Press, 1959

Gray W: Psychiatry and general systems—an introduction. Paper presented at the 122d Annual Meeting of the American Psychiatric Association, Atlantic City, NJ, May 1966

Greben SE: Dear Brutus: Dealing with unresponsiveness through supervision. Can J Psychiatry 30:48–53, 1985

Green BL, Gleser GC, Stone WN, et al: Relationships among diverse relationships of psychotherapy outcome. J Consult Clin Psychol 43:689, 1975

Green CJ: The diagnostic accuracy and utility MMPI and MCMI computer interpretive results. J Pers. Asses 46:359–365, 1982

Green DO, Reimer DR: The methohexitalmethylphenidate interview. Bull Menninger Clin 38:76–77, 1974

Green RJ: Therapy with hard science professionals. J Cont Psychother 8:52–56, 1976

Green RJ, Framo JL (eds): Family Therapy: Major Contributions, New York, International Universities Press, 1981

Green S: Psychoanalytic contributions in casework treatment of marital problems. Soc Casework 35:419–424, 1954

Greenacre P: Trauma, Growth and Personality. New York, Norton, 1952

Greenacre P: Certain technical problems in the transference relationship, in Blum HP (ed): Psychoanalytic Explorations of Technique: Discourse on the Theory of Therapy. New York, Internional Universities Press, 1980

Greenacre P, et al: Symposium on the evaluation of therapeutic results. Int J Psychoanal 29:7–33, 1948

Greenbaum H: Combined psychoanalytic therapy with negative therapeutic reactions, in Rifkin AH (ed): Schizophrenia in Psychoanalytic Office Practice. Orlando FL, Grune & Stratton, 1957, pp 56–65

Greenberg JR, Mitchell SA: Object Relations in Psychoanalytic Theory. Cambridge, Harvard University Press, 1983

Greenblatt M: Formal and informal groups in a therapeutic community. Int J Group Psychother 11:398–409, 1961

Greenblatt M: Rehabilitation: Some personal reflections. Psychiatric Annals 13:530–538, 1983

Greenblatt M: Mental health consultation, in Kaplan HI, Sadock BJ (eds): Comprehensive Textbook of Psychiatry (4th ed). Baltimore, Williams & Wilkins, 1985(a)

Greenblatt M: Volunteerism and the community mental health worker, in Kaplan HI, Sadock BJ (eds): Comprehensive Textbook of Psychiatry (4th ed). Baltimore, Williams & Wilkins, 1985(b)

Greenblatt M, Grosser GH, Wechsler H: Differential response of hospitalized depressed patients to somatic therapy. Am J Psychiatry 120:935–943, 1964

Greenblatt M, Levinson DJ, Williams RH (eds). The Patient and the Mental Hospital. New York, Free Press, 1957

Greenblatt M, Simon B: Rehabilitation of the Mentally Ill, Pub No. 58. Washington, DC. American Association for the Advancement of Science, 1959

Greenblatt M, York RH, Brown EL: From Custodial to Therapeutic Patient Care in Mental Hospitals; Explorations in Social Treatment. New York, Russell Sage Foundation, 1955

Greenblatt M, York RH, Brown EL: From Custoidal to Therapeutic Care in Mental Hospitals. New York, Russell Sage Foundation, 1957

Greene BL: Marital disharmony: Concurrent analysis of husband and wife. Dis Nerv Syst 21:1–6, 1960

Greene BL (ed): The Psychotherapies of Marital Disharmony. New York, Free Press, 1965

Greene BL: A Clinical Approach to Marital Problems: Evaluation and Management. Springfield, Ill, Thomas, 1970

Greene BL: Psychiatric therapy of marital problems: Modern techniques, in Masserman JH (ed): Current Psychiatric Therapies, vol. 12. Orlando FL, Grune & Stratton, 1972

Greene BL, et al: Treatment of marital disharmony where the spouse has a primary affective disorder (manic-depressive illness). I. General review—100 couples. J Marr Fam Counsel 1:82–101, 1975

Greene BL, Solomon AP: Marital disharmony: Concurrent psychoanalytic therapy of a husband and wife by the same psychiatrist (the triangular transference transactions). Am J Psychother 17:443–456, 1963

Greenson R: The Technique and Practice of Psychoanalysis. New York, International Universities Press, 1967

Greenspan S, Lourie R: Developmental structuralist approach to the classification of adaptive and pathologic personality organizations: Infancy and early childhood. Am J Psychiatry 138:725–735, 1981

Greenspoon J: in Dollard J, Miller NG (eds): Personality and Psychotherapy. New York, McGraw-Hill, 1950

Greenspoon J: The effect of two nonverbal stimuli on the frequency of members of two verbal response classes. Am Psychol 9:384, 1954(a)

Greenspoon J: The reinforcing effect of two spoken sounds on the frequency of two responses. Am J Psychol 68:409–416, 1954(b)

Greenspoon L, Bakalar JB: Psychedelic Drugs Reconsidered. New York, Basic Books, 1979

Greenwald H: The integration of behavioral, existential and psychoanalytic therapy into direct decision therapy. J Contemp Psychol 4:37–43, 1971

Greenwald H: Decision therapy. Personal Growth, No. 20, 1974

Greenwald H: Direct decision therapy, in Herink R (ed): The Psychotherapy handbook. New York, New American Library, 1980, pp 152–154

Greenwald JA: The ground rules in gestalt therapy. J Contemp Psychother 5:3–12, 1972

Greist JH, Gustafson DH, Stauss FF, et al: A computer interview for suicide-risk prediction. Am J Psychiatry 130:1327, 1973

Greist JH, Klein JH: Computers in psychiatry, in Arieti S: American Handbook of psychiatry (2d ed), vol. 7. New York, Basic Books, 1981

Greist JH, Klein MH, Gutman AS, Van Cura LJ: Computer measures of patient progress in psychotherapy. Psychiatry Digest 38:23, 1977

Griffiths R: A Study of Imagination in Early Childhood and Its Function in Mental Development. London, Routledge, 1935

Grinberg L: The problems of supervision in psychoanalytic education. Int J Psychoanal 51:371–304, 1970

Grinker RR: A demonstration of the transactional model, in Stein MI (ed): Contemporary Psychotherapies. New York, Free Press, 1961

Grinker RR: Psychiatry rides madly in all directions. Arch Gen Psychiatry 10:228–237, 1964

Grinker RR: Complementary psychotherapy—treatment of "associated" pairs. Paper presented at the 122d Annual Meeting of the American Psychiatric Association, Atlantic City, NJ, May 1966

Grinker RR, MacGregor H, Selan K, et al: Psychiatric Social Work: A Transactional Casebook. New York, Basic Books, 1961, pp 11–14

Grinker RR, Spiegel JP: Men Under Stress. Philadelphia, Blakiston, 1945

Grinker RR, Werble B, Drye RC: The Borderline Syndrome. New York, Basic Books, 1968

Grinspoon L, Bakalar JB: Psychedelic Drugs Reconsidered. New York, Basic Books, 1979

Grinspoon L, Bakalar JB: Drug dependence: Nonnarcotic agents, in Kaplan HI, Sadock BJ (eds): Comprehensive Textbook of Psychiatry IV. Baltimore, Williams & Wilkins, 1985, pp 1003–1015

Grinspoon L, Ewalt J, Shader R: Schizophrenia: Pharmacotherapy and Psychotherapy. Baltimore, Williams & Wilkins, 1972

Grobman J: The borderline patient in group psychotherapy: A case report. Int J Group Psychother 30:299–318, 1980

Groesbeck CJ: When Jung was the analyst: A review of "A Secret Symmetry" by A. Carotenuto. Psychol Persp 14:89, 1983

Groom D: Some applications of psychiatry in general medicine. JAMA 135:403, 1947

Gross M, Hitchman IC, Reeves WP, et al: Discontinuation of treatment with ataractic drugs, in Wortis J (ed): Recent Advances in Biological Psychiatry, vol. 3. Orlando FL, Grune & Stratton, 1961, p 44

Grosser, C: A polemic on advocacy: Past, present, and future, in Kahn AS (ed): Shaping New Social Work. New York, Columbia University Press, 1973

Grosz HJ: Psychiatric News, 7, (14), 1972, 1973

Grotjahn M: Brief psychotherapy on psychoanalytic principles. Illinois Psychiatry 2:1, 1942

Grotjahn M: The role of identification in psychiatric and psychoanalytic training. Psychiatry 12:141–151, 1949

Grotjahn M: The process of maturation in group psychotherapy and in the group therapist. Psychiatry 13:63–67, 1950

Grotjahn M: Special concepts of countertransference in analytic group psychotherapy. Int J Group Psychother 3:4, 407–416, 1953

Grotjahn M: Problems and techniques of supervision. Psychiatry 18:9–15, 1955

Grotjahn M: The efficacy of group therapy in a case of marriage neurosis. Int J Group Psychother 9:420–428, 1959

Grotjahn M: Psychoanalysis and the Family Neurosis. New York, Norton, 1960

Grotjahn M: Selected clinical observations from psychoanalytic group psychotherapy, in Wolberg LR, Aronson ML (eds): Group Therapy 1973: An Overview. New York, Stratton Intercontinental, 1973, pp 43–54

Grotjahn M: The Art and Techniques of Analytic Group Therapy. New York, Aronson, 1977

Grotjahn M, Freedman CTH (eds): Handbook of Group Therapy. New York, Van Nostrand Reinhold, 1983

Grotjahn M, Treusch JD. A new technique of psychosomatic consultations. Psychoanal Rev 44:176–92, 1957

Gruenberg EM: Application of control methods to mental illness. AM J Pub Health & Nation's Health 47:944–952, 1957

Grummon DL: Personality changes as a function of time in persons motivated for therapy, in Rogers CR, Dymond RF (eds): Psychotherapy in Personality Changes. Chicago, University of Chicago Press, 1954

Grunebaum H (ed): The Practice of Community Mental Health. Boston, Little, Brown, 1970

Grunebaum MG: A study of learning problems of children: Casework implications. Soc Casework 42: 461–468, 1961

Guerney BG, Jr: Filial therapy: Description and rationale. J Consult Psychol 28:304–310, 1964

Guerney BG, Jr (ed): Psychotherapeutic Agents: New Roles for Nonprofessionals, Parents and Teachers, New York, Holt, 1969

Guerney BG: Relationship Enhancement: Skill Training Programs for Therapy, Problem Prevention and Enrichment. San Francisco, Jossey-Bass, 1977

Guiora AZ, Hammann A, Mann RD: The continuous case seminar. Psychiatry 30:44–59, 1967

Gunderson JG, Carpenter WT, Jr, Strauss JS: Borderline and schizophrenic patients: A comparative study. Am J Psychiatry 132:1257–1264, 1975

Gunderson JG: A re-evaluation of milieu therapy for non-chronic schizophrenic patients. Schizophrenia Bull 6:64–69, 1980

Gunderson JG, Singer MT: Defining borderline patients. Am J Psychiatry 132:1–10, 1975

Gunderson JG, Will OA, Jr., Mosher LR: Principles and Practice of Milieu Therapy. New York, Aronson, 1983

Guntrip H: Schizoid Phenomena: Object Relations and the Self. New York, International Universities Press, 1969

Guntrip HJ: Psychoanalytic Theory, Therapy, and the Self. New York, Basic Books, 1971

Gurin G, Veroff V, Feld S: Americans View Their Mental Health, New York, Basic Books, 1960

Gurman AS, Kniskern DP (eds): Handbook of Family Therapy. New York, Brunner/Mazel, 1981

Gurman AS, Razin AM: Effective Psychotherapy: A Handbook of Research. New York, Pergamon Press, 1977

Gustin JC: Supervision in psychotherapy. Psychoanal & Psychoanal Rev 45:63–72, 1958

Gutheil EA: Psychoanalysis and brief psychotherapy. J Clin Psychopath 6:207, 1945

Gutheil EA: Music as an adjunct to psychotherapy. Paper presented at the Association for the Advancement of Psychotherapy. New York, February 27, 1953

Gutheil EA: Music as an adjunct to psychotherapy. Am J Psychother 8:94–109, 1954

Gutheil T, Mikkelsen BJ, Peteet J, Skilins D, et al: Patient viewing of videotaped psychotherapy. Part I. Psychiatric Q 53:219–226, 1981

Gutride ME, Goldstein AP, Hunter GF: The use of structured learning theory and transfer training in the treatment of chronic psychiatric inpatients. J Clin Psychol 30:277–279, 1974

Guze SB, Murphy GE: An empirical approach to psychotherapy: The agnostic position. Am J Psychiatry 120:53–57, 1963

Gyomroi EL: The analysis of a young concentration camp victim, in Eissler RS, et al (eds): The Psychoanalytic Study of the Child, vol. 18. New York, International Universities Press, 1963, pp 484–510

Haas LJ: Practical Occupational Therapy. Milwaukee, Bruce, 1946

Haber J, Leach A, Schudy S, Sideleau B: Comprehensive Psychiatric Nursing. New York, McGraw-Hill, 1982

Hadden SB: Counter-transference in the group psychotherapist. Int J Group Psychother 3:417, 1953

Hader M: Psychotherapy for certain psychotic states in geriatric patients. J Am Geriatr Soc 12:607–617, 1964

Hadfield JA: Functional Nerve Disease. London, Crichton-Miller, 1920

Hagelin A, Lazar P: The Flomp method. Int Ment Health Res Newsletter 15:1–8, 1973

Haggard EA, Hiken JR, Isaacs KS: Some effects of recording and filming on the psychoanalytic process. Psychiatry 28: 169–191. 1965

Hahlweg K, Jacobson NS: (eds): Marital Interaction: Analysis and Modification. New York, Guilford, 1984

Hain JD, Smith BM, Stevenson I: Effectiveness and processes of interviewing with drugs. J Psychiatr Res 4:95–106, 1966

Hald J, Jacobson E, Larsen V: Sensitizing effect on tetraethylthiuramdisulphide (antabuse) to ethyl alcohol. Acta Pharmacol Toxicol 4:285, 1948

Haley J: The family of the schizophrenic: A model system. J Nerv Ment Dis 129:357–374, 1959(a)

Haley J: An interactional description of schizophrenia. Psychiatry 22:321–332, 1959(b)

Haley J: Control in psychotherapy with schizophrenics. Arch Gen Psychiatry 5:340–353, 1961

Haley J: Family experiments: A new type of experimentation. Fam Process 1:265–293, 1962(a)

Haley J: Whither family therapy? Fam Process 1:69–103, 1962(b)

Haley J: Marriage therapy. Arch Gen Psychiatry 8:213–234, 1963(a)

Haley J: Strategies of Psychotherapy. Orlando FL, Grune & Stratton, 1963(b)

Haley J: An interactional description of schizophrenia, in Jackson D (ed): Communication, Family and Marriage, vol. 1. Palo Alto, Calif. Science & Behavior Books, 1968

Haley J: Uncommon Therapy: The Psychiatric Techniques of Milton H. Erickson. New York, Norton, 1973

Haley J: Problem-solving Therapy: New Strategies for Effective Family Therapy. San Francisco, Jossey-Bass, 1976

Haley J, Hoffman L: Techniques of Family Therapy. New York, Basic Books, 1967

Hall BH, Gassert RG: Psychiatry and Religious Faith. New York, Viking, 1964

Hall RCW: Psychiatric Presentations of Medical Illness. New York, SP Medical and Scientific Books, 1980

Hall RCW, Disook S: Paradoxical reactions to benzodiazepines. Br J Pharmacol 11 (Suppl 1) 99S–104S, 1981

Hall RCW, Gardner ER, Popkin MK, et al: Unrecognized physical illness prompting psychiatric admission: A prospective study. Am J Psychiatry 138:629–635, 1981

Hall RCW, Popkin MK, Devaul RA, et al: Physical illness presenting as psychiatric disease. Arch Gen Psychiatry 35:1315–1320, 1978

Hall RV, Lund D, Jackson D: Effects of teacher attention on study behavior. J Appl Behav Anal 1:1–12, 1968

Halleck SL: The Politics of Therapy. New York, Science House, 1971

Halleck SL: Future trends in the mental health profession. Psychiatric Opinion, 11:5–11, 1974

Halleck SL, Miller MH: The consultation; questionable social precedents of some current practice. Am J Psychiatry 20:164–169, 1963

Halpern J, Biner JR: A model for an output value analysis of mental health programs. Administration in Mental Health. DHEW Pub. No. (HSM 73–9050), Winter, pp 40–51, 1972

Halpern H, Lesser L: Empathy in infants, adults, and psychotherapists. Psychoanal Rev 47:32–42, 1960

Hamburg DA, Elliot GR, Parron DL: Health and Behavior: Frontiers of Research in the Behavioral Sciences. Washington, DC, National Academy Press, 1982

Hamburger B: Analysis of eleven school projects undertaken by community mental health consultants at the Postgraduate Center for Mental Health. Transnatl Ment Health Res Newsletter 18(2):2, 7–12, 1976

Hamilton DM, Vanney IH, Wall TH: Hospital treatment of patients with psychoneurotic disorders. Am J Psychiatry 99:243–247, 1942

Hamilton DM, Wall TH: Hospital treatment of patients with psychoneurotic disorders. Am J Psychiatry 98:551–557, 1941

Hamilton G: Theory and Practice of Social Casework. New York, Columbia University Press, 1940

Hamilton G: Psychotherapy in Child Guidance. New York, Columbia University Press, 1947

Hamilton G: Psychoanalytically oriented casework and its relation to psychotherapy. Am J Orthopsychiatry 19:209–223, 1949

Hammer LI: Family therapy with multiple therapists, in Masserman JH (ed): Current Psychiatric Therapies, vol. 7. Orlando FL, Grune & Stratton, 1967

Hammer LI, Shapiro I: Multiple therapist impact on family therapy. Paper presented at the 23rd Annual Conference of the American Group Therapy Association, 1965

Hammond DC: Myths about Erickson, etc. Please add 26(4):236–245, 1984

Hammons HG (ed): Hereditary Counseling. New York, Hoeber, 1959

Handlon JH: The effects of psychotherapy. Int J Psychiatry 1:169–171, 1965

Hanlon JG: The role of the mental health service in the local health department. Pub Health Rep 72:1093–1097, 1957

Hanrahan M, Gitlin B, Martin J, Leavy A, et al: Behavior therapy of anxiety disorders motivating the resisting patient. Am J Psychotherapy 38:533–540, 1984

Hare AP: Handbook of Small Group Research. New York, Free Press, 1962

Hargreaves W, Attkisson CC, Siegel LM, et al: Resource Materials for Community Mental Health Program Evaluation: Part 3—Evaluation Effectiveness of Services. Rockville, Md, National Institute of Mental Health, DHEW Pub. No. (ADM) 75–222, 1975

Hargrove EA, Bennett AE, Steele M: An investigational study using carbon dioxide as an adjunct to psychotherapy in neuroses. Paper presented at the 109th Annual Meeting of the American Psychiatric Association, Los Angeles, May 7, 1953

Haring NG, Phillips EL (eds): Educating Emotionally Disturbed Children. New York, McGraw-Hill, 1962

Harless WG, Dennon GG, Marxer JJ: CASE: A computer-assisted stimulation of the clinical encounter. J Med Educ 46:443–448, 1971

Harless WG, Templeton B: The potential for CASE for evaluating undergraduate psychiatric education. Paper presented at the NIMH Congress on Evaluation of Undergraduate Psychiatry. June 22–23, 1972

Harms E: The psychotherapeutical importance of the arts. Occup Ther 18:235–239, 1939

Harms E: Child art as an aid in the diagnosis of juvenile neuroses. Am J Orthopsychiatry 2:191–209, 1941

Harper RA: Psychoanalysis and Psychotherapy—36 Systems. Englewood Cliffs, NJ, Prentice-Hall, 1959 (repr—New York, Aronson, 1974)

Harper RA: Marriage counseling as rational process-oriented psychotherapy. J. Individ Psychol 16:197–207, 1960

Harper RA: Can homosexuals be changed? in Rubin I (ed): The Third Sex. New York, Basic Book Co, 1961

Harper RA: The New Psychotherapies. Englewood Cliffs, NJ, Prentice-Hall, 1975

Harrington JA, Mayer-Gross W: A day hospital for neurotics in an industrial community. J Ment Sci 1:224–234, 1959

Harris A: Day hospitals and night hospitals in psychiatry. Lancet 272:729, 1957

Harris FR, Wolf MM, Baer DM: Effects of adult social reinforcement on child behavior, in Guerney BG (ed): Psychotherapeutic Agents: New Roles of Nonprofessionals, Parents and Teachers. New York, Holt, 1969

Harris HI: Efficient psychotherapy for the large outpatient clinic. N. Engl J Med 221:1–5, 1939

Harris MR, Kalis BL, Freeman EH: Recipitating stress: An approach to brief therapy. Am J Psychother 3:465, 1963

Harris MR, Kalis BL, Freeman EH: An approach to short-term psychotherapy, in Barten HH (ed): Brief Therapies. New York, Behavioral Publications, 1971

Harris T: I'm OK—You're OK. New York, Harper & Row, 1967

Harrison SI (ed): Child psychiatric treatment: Status and prospects, in Noshpitz JD (ed): Basic Handbook of Child Psychiatry. New York Basic Books, 1979

Harrison SI, Robbins D, Esman AH: Psychotherapy with children and adolescents, in Karasu TB (ed): The Psychiatric Therapies. Washington, DC, American Psychiatric Association, 1984, pp 362–368

Harrower MR: The Evolution of a Clinical Psychologist. Transactions of the First Conference. New York, Josiah Macy, Jr, Foundation, 1947, p 12

Harrower MR: The measurement of psychological factors in Eisenstein VW (ed): Interaction in Marriage. New York, Basic Books, 9476(a), pp 169–191

Harrower MR: "Projective counseling." A psychotherapeutic technic. Am J Psychother 10:74–86, 1956(b)

Harrower MR: The therapy of poetry, in Masserman JH (ed): Current Psychiatric Therapies, vol. 14. Orlando FL, Grune & Stratton, 1974

Hart JT, Tomlinson TM: New Direction in Client-Centered Therapy. Boston, Houghton Mifflin, 1970

Hartert D, Browne-Mayers AN: The use of methylphenidate (Ritalin) hydrochloride in alcoholism. JAMA 106:1982–1984, 1958

Hartland J: Ego building suggestions. Am J Clin Hyp 3:89–93, 1965

Hartley D, Roback HB, Abramowitz SI: Deterioration effects in encounter groups. Am Psychol 31(3):247–255, 1976

Hartley RE, Frank LK, Goldenson RM: Understanding Children's Play. New York, Columbia University Press, 1952(a)

Hartley RE, Frank LK, Goldenson RM: New Play Experiences for Children. New York, Columbia University Press, 1952(b)

Hartley RE, Goldenson RM: The Complete Book of Children's Play. New York, Crowell, 1957, pp xiv, 462

Hartley RE, Gondor El: The use of art in therapy, in Brower D, Abt LE (eds): Progress in Clinical Psychology, vol. 2. New York, Grune & Stratton, 1956

Hartmann E: L-Trypotophan: A rational hypnotic with clinical potential. Am J Psychiatry 134:366–370, 1977

Hartmann H: Comment on the psychoanalytic theory of the ego, in Eissler RS, et al (eds): The Psychoanalytic Study of the Child, vol. 5. New York, International Universities Press, 1950, pp 74–96

Hartmann H: Technical implications of ego psychology. Psychoanal Q 20:31–43, 1951

Hartmann H: Ego Psychology and the Problem of Adaptation. New York, International Universities Press, 1958

Hartmann H: Essays on Ego Psychology. New York, International Universities Press, 1964

Hartmann H, Kris E: The genetic approach in psychoanalysis, in Hartmann H (ed): Papers on Psychoanalytic Psychology. Psychological Issues Mongr No. 14. New York, International Universities Press, 1964

Harvard Medical School and Psychiatric Service, Massachusetts General Hospital: Community Mental Health and Social Psychiatry: A Reference Guide. Cambridge, Harvard University Press, 1962

Hashagen JM: Supervision. J Psychiatr Soc Work 17:94–99, 1947–1948

Haskell D, Pugatch D, McNair DM: Time-limited psychotherapy. Arch Gen Psychiatry 21:546–552, 1969

Hastings DW: The psychiatrist and the clergyman. Northwest Med 47:644–647, 1948

Hastings DW: Psychologic impotence. Postgrad Med 27:429–432, 1960

Hastings PR, Runkle L, Jr: An experimental group of married couples with severe problems. Int J Group Psychother 13:84–92, 1963

Hatch WR, Bennet A: Effectiveness in Teaching New Dimensions in Higher Education, No. 2. Washington, DC, Office of Education, U.S. Department of Health, Education, & Welfare, 1960

Hathaway SR, Meehl PE: An Atlas for the Clinical Use of the MMPI. Minneapolis, University of Minnesota Press, 1952

Haun P: Psychiatry and the ancillary services. Am J Psychiatry 107:102–107, 1950

Haun P: Recreation: A Medical Viewpoint. New York, Teachers College Press, Columbia University, 1965

Haun P: Recreation in medical psychiatric therapy, in Masserman JH (ed): Current Psychiatric Therapies, vol. 7. Orlando FL, Grune & Stratton, 1967

Hauri P: Behavioral treatment of insomnia. Med Times 107:36–47, 1979

Havens LL: The development of existential psychiatry. J Nerv Ment Dis 154:309–331, 1972

Havens LL: The existential use of the self. Am J Psychiatry 131:1–10, 1974

Havens LL, Jaspers K: American psychiatry. Am J Psychiatry 124:66–70, 1967

Hawkins D, Pauling L (eds): Orthomolecular Psychiatry. San Francisco, Freeman, 1973

Hawkins RP, et al: Behavior therapy in the home: Amelioration of problem parent-child relations with the parent in a therapeutic role. J Exp Child Psychol 4:99–107, 1966

Hawkinshire FBW: Training procedures for offenders working in community treatment programs, in Guerney BG, Jr (ed): Psychotherapeutic Agents: New Roles for Nonprofessionals, Parents and Teachers. New York, Holt, 1969

Haylett CH, Rapaport L: Mental health consultation, in Bellak L (ed): A Concise Handbook of Community Psychiatry and Community Mental Health. Orlando FL, Grune & Stratton, 1964

Hayman M: A unique day therapy center for psychiatric patients. Ment Hyg 41:245–249, 1957

Haynes JM: Divorce Mediation: A Practical Guide for Therapists and Counselors. New York, Springer, 1931

Heath RG, et al: Brain activity during emotional states. Am J Psychiatry 131:858–862, 1974

Hecht MH: The development of a training program in pastoral counseling at a mental health center. Int Ment Health Res Newsletter 7:12–16, 1965

Heckel R, et al: Conditioning against silences in group therapy. J Clin Psychol 18:216, 1962

Heckel R, et al: The effect of musical tempor in varying operant speech levels in group therapy. J Clin Psychol 19:129, 1963

Hedlund JL, Vieweg MS, Wood JB, et al: Mental Health information systems: A state-of-the-art report. Health Care Technology Center. Columbia, Mo, University of Missouri Press, 1979

Heidegger M: Being and Time. New York. Harper & Row, 1962

Heilbrunn G: Results with psychoanalytic therapy. Am J Psychother 17:427–435, 1963

Heiman JR, LoPiccolo L, LoPiccolo J: Becoming Orgasmic: A Sexual Growth Program for Women. Englewood Cliffs, NJ, Prentice-Hall, 1976

Heiman P: On counter-transference. Int J Psychoanal 31:81–84, 1950

Heimann P: Discussion of O. Kernberg's paper: Instincts, Affects, and Object Relations at the meeting of the New York Psychoanalytic Society. New York, 1966

Heimlich EP: Paraverbal techniques in the therapy of childhood communication disorders. Int. J Psychother 1:65–83, 1972

Helfer R, Hess J: An experimental model for making objective measurements of interviewing skills. J Clin Psychol 26:327–331, 1970

Hellenbrand S: Client value orientation: Implications for diagnosis and treatment. Soc Casework 42:163–169, 1961

Henderson RB: In defense of clinical psychology. Can Men Health 14:17–19, 1966

Hendin H, Haas AP, Singer P. Gold R, et al: Evaluation of posttraumatic stress in Vietnam veterans. J Psychiatric Treatment and Evaluation 5(4):303–307, 1983

Hendrick I: Facts and Theories of Psychoanalysis (3rd ed). New York, Knopf, 1958

Hendry CE (ed): Decade of Group Work. New York, Association Press, 1948

Henry WE, Sims JH, Spray SL: The Fifth Profession: Becoming a Psychiatrist. San Francisco, Jossey-Bass, 1971

Herbert WL, Jarvis FV: The Art of Marriage Counseling. A Modern Approach. New York, Emerson Books, 1959

Herink R (ed): The Psychotherapy Handbook. New York, The New American Library, 1980

Herr VV: Mental health training in catholic seminaries. J Rel Health 1:127–152, 1962

Herr VV: Mental health training in catholic seminaries. J Rel Health 5:27–34, 1966

Herrigel E: Zen in the Art of Archery. New York, Pantheon, 1953

Herschelman P, Freundlich D: Large group therapy with multiple therapists, in Masserman JH (ed): Current Psychiatric Therapies, vol. 12. Orlando FL, Grune & Stratton, 1972

Hersen M, Bellack AS: Social skills training for chronic psychiatric patients: Rationale, research findings, and future directions. Comprehensive Psychiatry 17:559–580, 1976

Hersen M, Bellack AS: Staff training and consultation, in Hersen M, Bellack AS (eds): Behavior Therapy in the Psychiatric Setting. Baltimore, Williams & Wilkins, 1978

Hersen M, Eisler RM, Miller PM: Development of assertive responses: Clinical measurements and research considerations. Behav Res Ther 11:505–522, 1973(a)

Hersen M, Eisler RM, Miller PM, et al: Effects of practice instructions, and modeling on components of assertive behavior. Behav Res Ther 11:443–451, 1973(b)

Herz MI, Endicott J, Spitzer RL, Mesnikoff A: Day versus inpatient hospitalization: A controlled study. Am J Psychiatry 127:1371, 1971

Herz MI: The therapeutic community: A critique. Hosp Community Psychiatry 23:69–72, 1972

Herz MI, Szymanski HV, Simon JC: Intermittant medication for subtle schizophrenic outpatients: An alternative to maintenance medication. Am J Psychiatry 139:918–922, 1982

Herzberg A: Short treatment of neurosis by graduated tasks. Br J Med Psychol 19:36–51, 1941

Herzberg A: Active Psychotherapy. Orlando FL, Grune & Stratton, 1945, p 49

Herzog E: Some Guide Lines for Evaluative Research. Washington, DC, U.S. Department of Health, Education, & Welfare, 1959

Hess AK (ed): Psychotherapy Supervision. New York, Wiley, 1980

Heyder DW: LSD-25 on conversion reaction. J Am Psychol Assoc 120:396–397, 1963

Hilgard ER: Theories of Learning (2d ed). New York, Appleton-Century-Crofts, 1956 (4th ed, 1974)

Hill G, Armitage SG: An analysis of combined therapy—individual and group—in patients with schizoid, obsessive-compulsive, or aggressive defenses. J Nerv Ment Dis 119:113–134, 1954

Hill JA: Therapist goals, patient aims, and patient satisfaction in psychotherapy. J Clin Psychol 25:455–459, 1969

Hiltner S: Religion and Health. New York, Macmillan, 1943

Hiltner S: Religion and pastoral counseling. Am J Orthopsychiatry 17:21–26, 1947

Hiltner S: Pastoral Counseling. New York, Abington, 1949

Hiltner S: Hostility in counseling. Pastoral Psychol 1:35–42, 1950

Hiltner S: Pastoral Counseling. New York, Abington, 1952

Hiltner S: The American Association of Pastoral Counselors: A critique. Pastoral Psychol 15:8–16, 1964

Hiltner S, et al: Clinical Pastoral Training. New York, Federal Council of Churches of Christ in America, 1945

Hinckley RG: Group treatment in psychotherapy. Minneapolis, University of Minnesota Press, 1951

Hines PM, Hare-Mustin RT: Ethical concerns of family therapy. Professional Psychology 9:165–171, 1978

Hingtgen JN, Coulter SK, Churchill DW: Intensive reinforcement of imitative behavior in mute autistic children. Arch Gen Psychiatry 17:36–43, 1967

Hinsie LE, Campbell RJ: Psychiatric Dictionary. New York. Oxford University Press. 1960 (4th ed. 1970)

Hirschowitz J, Casper R, Garver DL, et al: Lithium response in good prognosis schizophrenia. Am J Psychiatry 137: 916–920, 1980

Hoagland H (ed): Hormones, Brain Function and Behavior. Orlando FL, Academic Press, 1957

Hobbs N: Helping disturbed children: Psychological and ecological strategies. Am Psychol 21:1105–1115, 1966

Hobbs N: Mental health's third revolution, in Guerney BG, Jr (ed): Psychotherapeutic Agents: New Roles for Nonprofessionals, Parents and Teachers. New York, Holt, 1969

Hobbs N, Rogers CR (eds): Client-centered Psychotherapy. Boston, Houghton Mifflin, 1951, pp 278–319

Hoch PH: Drugs and psychotherapy. Am J Psychiatry 116:305–308, 1959

Hoch PH, Kalinowsky L: Somatic Treatments in Psychiatry. Orlando FL, Grune & Stratton, 1961

Hoch PH, Polatin P: Narcodiagnosis and narcotherapy, in Bychowsky G, Despert JL (eds): Specialized Techniques in Psychotherapy. New York, Basic Books, 1952, pp 1–23

Hoch PH, Zubin J: Relation of Psychological Tests to Psychiatry. Orlando FL, Grune & Stratton, 1951

Hoch PH, Zubin J (eds): Comparative Epidemiology of Mental Disorders. Orlando FL, Grune & Stratton, 1961

Hoeper EW, Nyez GR, Cleary PD, et al: Estimated prevalence of RDC mental disorder in primary medical care. Int J Ment Health 8:6–15, 1979

Hoffer A: An alcoholism treatment program—LSD, Malvaria, and Nicotinic Acid. Preprint of the 2d Conference on the Use of LSD in Psychotherapy, May 1965

Hoffer A: How to Live with Schizophrenia. New York, University Books, 1966

Hoffer A: Megavitamin B-3 therapy for schizophrenia. Can Psychiatr Assoc J 16:499–504, 1971

Hofling CK, Leininger MM: Basic Psychiatric Concepts in Nursing, Philadelphia, Lippincott. 1960

Hofling CK, Meyers RW: Recent discoveries in psychoanalysis. A study of opinion. Arch Gen Psychiatry 26:518–523, 1972

Hofmann H: Religion and mental health. J Rel Health 1:319–336, 1962

Hogan RA, Kirchner JH: Preliminary report of the extinction of learned fears via short-term implosive therapy. J Abnorm Psychol 72:106–109, 1967

Hogarty GE, Anderson CM, Reiss DJ, Kornblith SJ, et al: Family psychoeducation, social skills training and maintenance chemotherapy in the after care treatment of schizophrenia. Archives of General Psychiatry 43:633–642, 1986

Hollander D, Harlan J: Antacids vs. placebos in peptic ulcer therapy. A controlled double-blind investigation. JAMA 226:1181–1185, 1973

Hollander FI: The specific nature of the clergy's role in mental health. Pastoral Psychol 10:14, 1959

Hollander FI: Mental health teaching materials for the clergy. J Rel Health 1:273–282, 1962

Hollander M: The Practice of Psychoanalytic Psychotherapy. Orlando FL, Grune & Stratton, 1965

Hollis F: The techniques of casework. Soc Casework 30:235–244, 1949

Hollis F: Casework: A Psychosocial Therapy. New York, Random House, 1964; 2d ed, 1974

Hollister LE: Optimum use of antipsychotic drugs, in Masserman JH (ed): Current Psychiatric Therapies, vol. 12. Orlando FL, Grune & Stratton, 1972

Hollister LE: Clinical Use of Psychotherapeutic Drugs. Springfield, Ill, Thomas, 1973

Hollister LE: Psychopharmacology. Audio-Digest Foundation Cassette 3(23), December 9, 1974

Hollister LE: Drugs for mental disorders of old age. JAMA 234:195–198, 1975

Hollister LE: Clinical Pharmacology of Psychotherapeutic Drugs. New York, Churchill Livingston, 1978

Hollister LE, Conley FK, Britt RH, Shuer L: Long-term use of diazepam. JAMA 246:1568–1575, 1981

Hollon SD, Kendall PC: Cognitive self-statements in depression: Development of an automatic thoughts questionnaire. Cognitive Res & Ther 4:383–395, 1980

Holman CT: The Care of Souls: A Socio-Psychological Approach. Chicago, University of Chicago Press, 1932

Holmes GH, Rahe RH: The social readjustment rating scale. J Psychosom Res 11:213, 1967

Holmes M: The Therapeutic Classroom. New York, Aronson, 1974

Holt H: Existential psychoanalysis: A new trend in the field of psychoanalysis. Trans. New York Institute of Existential Analysis 2(2), 1965

Holt H: The problems of interpretation from the point of view of existential psychoanalysis, in Hammer EE (ed): Use of Interpretation in Treatment. Orlando FL, Grune & Stratton, 1968

Holt H: Existential group therapy, in Kaplan HI, Sadock BJ (eds): New Models for Group Therapy, New York, Dutton, 1972(a)

Holt H: Existential psychoanalysis, in Freedman AM, Kaplan HI (eds): Treating Mental Illness, New York, Atheneum, 1972(b)

Holt H: Existential psychoanalysis, in Freedman AM, Kaplan HI, Saddock BJ (eds): Comprehensive Textbook of Psychiatry II (2d ed), vol. 1. Baltimore, Williams & Wilkins, 1975, pp 661–668

Holt RR (ed) New Horizon for Psychotherapy: Autonomy as a Profession. New York, International Universities Press, 1971

Holt RR, Luborsky L: Personality Patterns of Psychiatrists, vol. 1. New York. Basic Books, 1958

Homan WF: Child Sense. New York, Bantam, 1969

Homans GC: The Human Group. Orlando FL, Harcourt, 1950

Homme, LE: Control of covenants, the operants of the mind. Psychological Record 15:501–511, 1965

Hora T: Beyond countertransference. Am J Psychother 10:18–23, 1956

Hora T: Ontic perspectives in psychoanalysis. Am J Psychother 13:134–141, 1959(a)

Hora T: Existential group psychotherapy. Am J Psychother 13:83–92, 1959(b)

Horney K: The Neurotic Personality of Our Time. New York, Norton, 1937

Horney K: New Ways in Psychoanalysis. New York, Norton, 1939

Horney K: Self-Analysis. New York, Norton, 1942

Horney K: Our Inner Conflicts. New York, Norton, 1945

Horney K: Neurosis and Human Growth. New York, Norton, 1950

Horowitz FD: Social reinforcement effects on child behavior. J Nurs Ed 18:276–284, 1963

Horowitz L: Transference in training groups and therapy groups. Int J Group Psychother 14:202, 1964

Horowitz MJ: Image Formation and Cognition. New York, Appleton-Century-Crofts, 1970

Horowitz MJ: Stress Response Syndrome. New York, Aronson, 1976

Horowitz MJ: Stress Response Syndromes and Brief Psychotherapy. Strecher Monograph Series No. 14, Philadelphia: Institute of the Pennsylvania Hosp, 1977

Horsley JS: Narcoanalysis. J Ment Sci 82:416, 1936

Horsley JS: Narco-Analysis. London, Oxford University Press, 1943

Horsley JS: A critical discussion of the relationship between hypnosis and narcosis and of the value of these states in psychobiological medicine, in LeCron LM (ed): Experimental Hypnosis. New York, Macmillan, 1952

Hospital Focus: Enuresis-therapies, luck and devices. May 15, November 1, 1964

Howard KI, Orlinsky DE: Psychotherapeutic processes, in Mussen P, Rosenzweig M (eds): Annual Review of Psychology. Palo Alto, Calif, Annual Reviews, 1972, pp 615–668

Howe HS: Progress in neurology and psychiatry. NY State J Med 51:102, 1951

Hoyt MF: Therapist resistances to short-term dynamic psychotherapy. J Am Academy of Psychoanalysis 13:93–112, 1985

Hubbard JP, Templeton B: The future of medical education and its implications for psychiatry, in Usdin G (ed): Psychiatry: Education and Image. New York, Brunner/Mazel, 1973

Hubbard LR: Dianetics: The Modern Science of Mental Health. New York, Hermitage House, 1950

Hubbs R: The sheltered workshop. Ment Hosp 11:7–9, 1960

Huddleson JH: Psychotherapy in two hundred cases of psychoneurosis. Mil Surg 60:161–170, 1927

Hudson JT, Harrison GP, Jonas JM: Treatment of bulimia with antidepressants. Psychiatric Annals 13:965–969, 1983

Hudson JL, Pope HG, Jones JM et al: Hypothalamic-pituitary-adrenal axis hyperactivity in bulimia. Psychiatry Res 8:111–117, 1983

Hughes EC: Psychology: Science and/or profession. Am Psychol 7:441–443, 1952

Hulse WC: The therapeutic management of group tension. Am J Orthopsychiatry 20:834, 1950

Hulse WC: Transference catharsis, insight and reality testing during concommitant individual and group psychotherapy. Int J Group Psychother 5:45, 1955

Hulse WC (ed): Controversial issues, Part 2, in Stokvis B (ed): Topical Problems of Psychotherapy, vol. 2. Basel, Switz, Karger, 1960

Hulse WC, Lowinger L: Psychotherapy in general practice. Am Practitioner Digest Treatment 1:141–145; 588–598; 926–932; 1024–1030, 1950

Hulse WC, Lulow WV, Rinesberg B, Epstein NB: Transference reactions in a group of female patients to male and female coleaders. Int J Group Psychother 6:430, 1956

Hume PB: Community psychiatry, social psychiatry and community mental health work: Some interprofessional relationships in psychiatry and social work. Am J Psychiatry 121:340–343, 1964

Hume PB: Searchlight on community psychiatry. Commun Ment Health J 1:109–112, 1965

Hume PB: General principles of community psychiatry, in Arieti S (ed): American Handbook of Psychiatry, vol. 3. New York, Basic Books, 1966, pp 515–541

Hunt J McV, Kogan LS: Measuring Results in Social Casework: A Manual of Judging Movement. New York, Family Service Association of America, 1950

Hunt W: The use of the countertransference in psychotherapy supervision. J Am Academy of Psychoanalysis 9:361–373, 1981

Hurvitz N: Interaction hypotheses in marriage counseling. Fam Coordinator 19:64–75, 1970

Huseth B: Half-way houses—a new rehabilitation measure. Ment Hosp 9:5–8, 1958

Huseth B: What is a halfway house? Function and type. Ment Hyg 45:116–121, 1961

Hussain A: Behavior therapy using hypnosis, in Wolpe J, et al (eds): The Conditioning Therapies. New York, Holt, 1965, pp 54–61

Hussain MZ: Desensitization and flooding (implosion) in treatment of phobias. Am J Psychiatry 127:1509–1514, 1971

Husserl E: Ideas. New York, Macmillan, 1931, 1962

Huston P: Treatment of depression, in Masserman JH (ed): Current Psychiatric Therapies, vol. 11. Orlando FL, Grune & Stratton, 1971

Imber SD: Patient Direct self-report techniques, in Waskow IE, Parloff MS (eds): Psychotherapy Change Measures. Washington, DC: DHEW Publ No. (ADM) 74–120, 1975

Imber SD: Lewis PM, Loiselle RH: Uses and abuses of the brief intervention group. Int J Group Psychotherapy 29:39–49, 1979

Ingersoll TG, et al: A survey of patient and auxiliary problems as they relate to behavioral dentistry curricula. J Dent Ed 42(5):260–3, 1978

Ingersoll TG, Seime RJ, McCutcheon (eds): Behavioral dentistry: Proceedings of the first national conference. Morgantown, West Virginia University Press, 1977

Insel T et al: Obsessive-compulsive disorder. Arch Gen Psychiatry 40:605, 1983

Irvine LF, Deery SJ: An investigation of problem areas relating to the therapeutic community concept. Ment Hyg 45:367–373, 1961

Irving HH: Divorce Mediation: A Rational Alternative to the Adversary System. New York, Universe Books, 1980

Isaacs S: Social Development in Young Children. London, Routledge, 1930

Ishiyama T: Music as a therapeutic tool in the treatment of a catatonic. Psychiatr Q 37:437–461, 1963

Jackson DD: The question of family homeostasis. Psychiatr Q (Suppl) 31:79–90, 1957

Jackson DD: The family and sexuality, in Whitaker C (ed): The Psychotherapy of Chronic Schizophrenic Patients. Boston, Little, Brown, 1958

Jackson DD: Family interaction, family homeostasis, and some implications for conjoint family psychotherapy, in Masserman JH (ed): Individual and Familial Dynamics. Orlando FL, Grune & Stratton, 1959

Jackson DD: Action for mental illness—what kind? Stanford Med Bull 20:77–80, 1962

Jackson DD, Satir VM: Family diagnosis and family therapy, in Ackerman N, Beatman FL, Sherman SN (eds): Exploring the Base for Family Therapy. New York, Family Service Association, 1961

Jackson DD, Weakland JH: Conjoint family therapy, some considerations on theory, technique and results. Psychiatry 24 (2, Suppl):30–45, 1961

Jackson J: A family group therapy technique for a stalemate in individual treatment. Int J Group Psychother 12:164–170, 1962

Jackson J, Grotjahn M: The treatment of oral

defenses by combined individual and group patient interview. Int J Group Psychother 8:373, 1958(a)

Jackson J, Grotjahn M: The reenactment of the marriage neurosis in group psychotherapy. J Nerv Ment Dis 127:503–510, 1958(b)

Jackson J, Grotjahn M: The efficacy of group therapy in a case of marriage neurosis. Int J Group Psychother 9:420–428, 1959

Jacobsen C: Preclinical Training of the Clinical Psychologist. Transactions of the First Conference. New York, Josiah Macy, Jr, Foundation, 1947, pp 16–21

Jacobson E: Progressive Relaxation. Chicago University Press, Chicago, 1929

Jacobson E: Progressive Relaxation. Chicago, University of Chicago Press, 1938 (3rd rev ed, 1974)

Jacobson E: The Self and the Object World. New York, International Universities Press, 1964

Jacobson E: Psychotic Conflict and Reality. New York, International Universities Press, 1967

Jacobson E: Depression: Comparative Studies of Normal, Neurotic and Psychotic Conditions. New York, International Universities Press, 1971

Jacobson E, Kehlet H, Larsen V, et al: The autonomic reaction of psychoneurotics to a new sedative: Benactyzine, NFN, Suavitil (benzilic acid diethylaminoethylester hydrochloride). Acta Psychiatr Kbh 30:637, 1955

Jacobson GF, Wilner DM, Morley WE, et al: The scope and practice of an early-access brief treatment psychiatric center. Am J Psychiatry 121:1176–1183, 1965

Jacobson NS, Margolin G: Marital Therapy: Strategies Based on Social Learning and Behavior Exchange Principles. New York, Brunner/Mazel, 1979

Jacobziner H: Glue sniffing. NY State J Med 63:2415–2418, 1963

Jaffe J: Verbal behavior analysis in psychiatric interviews with the aid of digital computers. Disorders Commun, vol. 42. Research Publications Association for Research in Nervous and Ment Disorders, 1964

Jaffe JH: Cyclazocine in the treatment of narcotic addiction, in Masserman JH (ed): Current Psychiatric Therapies, vol. 7. Orlando FL, Grune & Stratton, 1967

Jaffe JH, Brill L: Cyclazocine—a long-acting narcotic antagonist: Its voluntary acceptance as a treatment modality by narcotic abusers. Int J Addict 1:86–99, 1966

JAMA: Editorial: An evaluation of psychoanalysis. 101:1643–1644, 1933

JAMA: Editorial: Music therapy. 162:1626, 1956

JAMA: Editorial. 183:879, 1963

JAMA: Editorial: 220:1231–1236, 1972

JAMA: The use of sucrose polyester in weight reduction therapy. 248(22):2963–2964, 1982

JAMA: Worksite anti-alcoholism saves jobs, money. 249:2427–2433, 1983

JAMA: A sharper focus for psychotherapy. 252(6):741, 745, 749, Aug 10, 1984

JAMA: The first amendment and cigarette advertising 256(4):502–9, July 25, 1986

Jameison GR, McNiel EE: Some unsuccessful results with psychoanalytic therapy. Am J Psychiatry 95:1421–1428, 1939

James W: The Varieties of Religious Experience. New York, Longmanns, Green, 1941

Janis IL: Psychological Stress: Psychoanalytic and Behavioral Studies of Surgical Patients. New York, Wiley & Sons, 1958

Janis IL: Adaptive personality changes, in Monat A, Lazarus, RS (eds): Stress and Coping: An Anthology. New York, Columbia University Press, 1977, pp 272–284

Janov A: The Primal Scream: Primal Therapy. The Cure for Neurosis. New York, Putnam, 1970

Jaques E: Measurement of Responsibility. London, Heinemann, 1956

Jaques E: Equitable Payment (rev ed). Carbondale, Southern Illinois University Press, 1961

Jaques E: Time-Span Handbook. Carbondale, Southern Illinois University Press, 1964

Jaques E: Progression Handbook. Carbondale, Southern Illinois University Press, 1968

Jaques E: Changing Culture of a Factory. London, Routledge & Kegan, 1970(a) (repr 1951 ed)

Jaques E: Work, Creativity and Social Justice. New York, International Universities Press, 1970(b)

Jaques E: Measurement of Responsibility. New York, Halsted, 1972

Jaretzki A: Death with dignity-passive euthenasia. NY State J Med 76:539–543, 1975

Jason L: Rapid improvement in insomnia following self-monitoring. J Beh Ther Exp Psychiatry 6:349–350, 1975

Jaspers K: Von der Wahrheit. Munich, Germany, Piper, 1947

Jaspers K: General Psychopathology. Chicago, University of Chicago Press, 1963

Jellinek EM: Clinical tests on comparative effectiveness of analgesic drugs. Biometrics Bull 2:87, 1946

Jencks SF: Recognition of mental distress and diagnosis of mental disorder in primary care. JAMA 253:1902–1907, 1985

Jenkins RL: Behavior Disorders of Childhood and Adolescents. Springfield, Ill, Thomas, 1973

Jenkins SR: The development and evaluation of a musical thematic apperception test. Proceedings of the National Association of Music Therapy, pp 101–113, 1955

Jennings S: Remedial Drama. New York, Theatre Arts Books, 1974

Jens R: Desoxycorticosterone in certain psychotic cases. Northwest Med 48:609, 1949

Jensen-Nelson K: Massage in Nursing Care (2d ed). New York, Macmillan, 1941

Jensen SE: A treatment program for alcoholics in a mental hospital. Q J Stud Alcohol 23:243–251, 1962

Jersild AT: When Teachers Face Themselves. New York, Columbia University Press, 1955

Jersild AT: What teachers say about psychotherapy. Phi Delta Kappan 44:313–317, 1963

Jersild AT: Personal communication, 1966

Jersild AT, Lazar EA, Brodkin AM: The Meaning of Psychotherapy in the Teacher's Life and Work. New York, Teachers College Press, Columbia University, 1962

Jewish Board of Guardians: Conditioned Environment in Case Work Treatment. New York, the Board, 1944

Jewish Board of Guardians: The Case Worker in Psychotherapy. New York, the Board, 1946

Johnson AM: Sanctions for superego lacunae, in Eissler KR (ed): Searchlights on Delinquency: New Psychoanalytic Studies. New York, International Universities Press, 1949, pp 225–245

Johnson AM: Juvenile delinquency, in Arieti S (ed): American Handbook of Psychiatry, vol. 1. New York, Basic Books, 1959, pp 840–856

Johnson AM, Szurek SA: The genesis of antisocial acting out in children and adults. Psychoanal Q 21:323, 1952

Johnson BS: Psychiatric-Mental Health Nursing: Adaptation and Growth. Philadelphia, Lippincott, 1986

Johnson D, Sandel S: Structural analysis of movement sessions: Preliminary research. Am J Dance Ther 1:32–36, 1977

Johnson D: Developmental approaches in drama therapy. Int J Arts in Psychother 9:183–190, 1982(a)

Johnson D: Principles and techniques in drama therapy. Int J Arts in Psychother 9:83–90, 1982(b)

Johnson D, Sandel S: Structural analysis of movement sessions: Preliminary research. Am J Dance Ther 1:32–36, 1977

Johnson JA: Group Therapy, a Practical Approach. New York, McGraw-Hill, 1963

Johnson JJ: Technology, in Williams TA, Johnson JH (ed): Mental Health in the 21st Century. Lexington, Mass, Heath & Co, 1979, p 160

Johnson PE: Personality and Religion. New York, Abingdon, 1957

Johnson PE: The church's mission to mental health. J Rel Health 12:30–40, 1973

Johnson W: People in Quandaries. New York, Harper & Row, 1946

Johnston R: Some casework aspects of using foster grandparents for emotionally disturbed children. Children 14:46–52, 1967

Joint Commission on Mental Illness and Health: Americans View Their Mental Health. Report 4. New York, Basic Books, 1960

Joint Commission on Mental Illness and Health: Digest of Action for Mental Health. New York, Basic Books, 1961

Jolesch M: Casework treatment of young married couples. Soc Casework 43:245–251, 1962

Jones CH: A day-care program for adolescents in a private hospital. Ment Hosp 12:4–6, 1961

Jones E: The relation of technique to theory. Int J Psychoanal 8:1–4, 1924

Jones E: Decannual Report of the London Clinic of Psychoanalysis, 1926–1936

Jones HG: The application of conditioning and learning techniques to the treatment of a psychiatric patient. J Abnorm Soc Psychol 52:414–419, 1956

Jones M: Social Psychiatry. London, Tavistock, 1952

Jones M: The concept of the therapeutic community. Am J Psychiatry 112:647–651, 1956

Jones M: The treatment of personality disorders in a therapeutic community. Psychiatry 20:211–220, 1957

Jones M: Toward a clarification of the therapeutic community concept. Br J Med Psychol 32:200–205, 1959

Jones M: Therapeutic millieu innovator assails institutional conservatism. Roch Report 3:1–2, 1973

Jones MC: The case of Peter. Pediatr Sem 31:308–318, 1924(a)

Jones MC: The elimination of children's fear. J Exp Psychol 7:382–390, 1924(b)

Jones WHS: Hippocrates, vol. 1. London, Heinemann, 1928, p 318

Joseph H, Heimlich EP: The therapeutic use of music with "treatment resistant" children. Am J Ment Defic 64:41–49, 1959

Josselyn I: The Adolescent and His World. New York, Family Association of America, 1952

Josselyn I: Psychotherapy of adolescents at the level of private practice, in Balser B (ed): Psychotherapy of the Adolescent. New York, International Universities Press, 1957

Jourard SM: I—Thou relationship versus manipulation in counseling and psychotherapy. J Individ Psychol 15:174–179, 1959(a)

Jourard SM: Seif disclosure and other-cathexis. J Abnorm Soc Psychol 59:428–431, 1959(b)

Journal of the American Medical Association, vol. 242, August 10, 1979, p 545

Journal of Pastoral Care: Pastoral Counseling at a Crossroad. 26, 1972 (entire issue)

Journal of School Health: Mental Health in the Classroom. Columbus, Ohio, American School Health Association, 1968

Judah JS: Hare Krishna and the Counterculture. New York, Wiley, 1974

Jung CG: Psychology of the Unconscious. New York, Moffat, Yard, 1916

Jung CG: Studies in Word Association. London, Heinemann, 1919

Jung CG: Psychological Types or the Psychology of Individuation. Orlando FL, Harcourt, 1923

Jung CG: Modern Man in Search of a Soul. New York, Orlando FL, 1933, 1934

Jung CG: The Structure and Dynamics of the Psyche. Hull RFC (trans). New York, Pantheon, 1960

Jung CG: Memories, Dreams, Reflections. Jaffe A (ed). New York, Pantheon, 1961

Kadis AL: The alternate meeting in group psychotherapy. Am J Psychother 10:275–291, 1956

Kadis AL: Early childhood recollections as aids in group psychotherapy. J Individ Psychol 13:182, 1957

Kadis AL: The role of co-ordinated group meetings in group psychotherapy, in Moreno J (ed): Progress in Psychotherapy. Orlando FL, Grune & Stratton, 1958

Kadis AL: Alternate meeting, in Hulse W (ed): Topical Problems of Psychotherapy, vol. 2. Basel, Switz, Karger, 1960

Kadis AL: The exploratory phase in the treatment of married couples: The phase of decision making. Int Ment Health Res Newsletter No. 3/4, p 7, 1963

Kadis AL, Krasner JD, Winick C, Foulkes SH: A Practicum of Group Psychotherapy. New York, Hoeber, 1963

Kadis AL, Markowitz M: The therapeutic impact of co-therapist interaction in a couples group. Paper presented at the 3rd International Congress of Group Psychotherapy, Milano-Stresa, July 16–22, 1963

Kagan J: Change and Continuity in Infancy. New York, Wiley, 1971

Kagan J: The form of early development. Arch Gen Psychiatry 36:1047–-1054, 1979(a)

Kagan K: Overview: Perspectives on human infancy, in Osofsky JD (ed): Handbook of Infant Development. New York, Wiley, 1979(b)

Kagan J, Kearsley RB, Zelazo PR: Infancy, Its Place in Human Development. Cambridge, Harvard University Press, 1978

Kahn RL, Perlin S: Hospital-community integration in psychiatric therapy, in Masserman JH (ed): Current Psychiatric Therapies, vol. 4. New York, Orlando FL, 1964, pp 246–252

Kales A, Caldwell AB, Soldatos CR, Bixler EO, et at: Biopsychobehavioral correlates of insomnia II. Pattern specificity and consistency with the Minnesota Multiphasic Personality Inventory. Psychosom Med 5:341–356, 1983

Kales A: Evaluation and Treatment of Insomnia. New York, Oxford University Press, 1984

Kales A, Caldwell AB, Soldatos CR, Bixler EO, et al: Biopsychobehavioral correlates of insomnia II. Pattern Specificity and Consistency with the Minnesota Multiphasic Personality Inventory. Psychosomatic Medicine 45:341–356, 1983

Kalinowsky LB: The use of somatic treatments in short-term therapy, in Wolberg LR (ed): Short-term Psychotherapy. Orlando FL, Grune & Stratton, 1965, pp 201–211

Kalinowsky LB: Convulsive Therapies, in Freedman AM, Kaplan HI, Sadock BJ (eds): Comprehensive Textbook of Psychiatry, vol. 3, (3d ed). Baltimore, Williams & Wilkins, 1980

Kalinowsky LB, Hippius H: Pharmacological, Convulsive and Other Somatic Treatments in Psychiatry. Orlando FL, Grune & Stratton, 1969

Kalinowsky LB, Hippius H, Klein EH: Biological Treatments in Psychiatry. Orlando FL, Grune & Stratton, 1982

Kalinowsky LB, Hoch PH: Shock Treatments, Psychosurgery and Other Somatic Treatments in Psychiatry (2d ed). Orlando FL, Grune & Stratton, 1952

Kalinowsky LB, Hoch PH: Somatic Treatments in Psychiatry. Orlando FL, Grune & Stratton, 1961

Kalis BL, Freeman EH, Harris MR: Influences of previous help-seeking experiences on application for psychotherapy. Ment Hyg 48:267–272, 1964

Kallmann FJ: Heredity in Health and Mental Disorder. New York, Norton, 1953

Kallmann FJ: Psychiatric aspects of genetic counseling. Am J Hum Genet 8:97–101, 1956

Kallman FJ: Some aspects of genetic counseling, in Neel JV, Shaw, MW, Schull WJ (eds): Genetics and the Epidemiology of Chronic diseases. Washington, DC, U.S. Department of Health, Education, & Welfare, 1965

Kallmann FJ, Rainer JD: Psychotherapeutically oriented counseling techniques in the setting of a medical genetics department, in Stokvis B (ed): Topical Problems of Psychotherapy. Basel, Switz, Karger, 1963

Kallmann FJ, Rainer JD: The genetic approach to schizophrenia: Clinical, demographic, and family guidance problems, in Kolb LC, Kallmann FJ, Polatin P (eds): Schizophrenia. Boston, Little, Brown, 1964

Kanfer FH: Self management methods, in Kanfer FH, Goldstein AP (eds): Helping People Change (2d ed). New York, Pergamon, 1980, pp 334–389

Kanfer FH, Phillips S: Behavior therapy. Arch Gen Psychiatry 15:114–127, 1966

Kanfer FH, Phillips S: Learning Foundations of Behavior Therapy. New York, Wiley, 1970

Kanfer FH, Saslow G: Behavioral analysis. Arch Gen Psychiatry 12:529–538, 1965

Kanner L: Early infantile autism. Am J Orthopsychiatry 19:416, 1959

Kant O: Deceptive psychoneurosis. Psychiatr Q 20:129, 1946

Kantorovich NV: An attempt at associative-reflex therapy in alcoholism. Nov Refleflsol Fiziol Nerv Syst 3:436–447, 1929 (Abstract appears in Psychol Abstr 4:493, 1930)

Kaplan HI, Sadock BJ: Comprehensive Group Psychotherapy. Baltimore, Williams & Wilkins, 1971

Kaplan HI, Sadock BJ (eds): Comprehensive Group Psychotherapy (2d ed). Baltimore, Williams & Wilkins, 1983

Kaplan HS: The New Sex Therapy. New York, Brunner/Mazel, 1974

Kaplan HS: The illustrated Manual of Sex Therapy. New York, Quadrangle, 1975

Kaplan HS: Disorders of Sexual Desire and Other New Concepts and Techniques in Sex Therapy. New York, Brunner/Mazel, 1979

Kaplan HS: The Evaluation of Sexual Disorders: Psychological and Medical Perspectives. New York, Brunner/Mazel, 1983

Kaplan HS, Moodie JL: Therapies for psychosexual dysfunction, in Karasu TB (ed): The Psychiatric Therapies. Washington DC, The American Psychiatric Association, 1984, pp 675–699

Kaplan L: Mental Health and Human Relations in Education. New York, Harper & Row, 1959

Kaplowitz D: Teaching empathic responsiveness. Am J Psychother 4:774–781, 1967

Karasu TB, Conte HR, Plutchik R: Psychotherapy outcome research, in Karasu TB (ed): The Psychiatric Therapies. Washington, DC, The American Psychiatric Association, 1984, p 850

Karasu TB, Plutchik R, Conte HR, et al: The therapeutic community in theory and practice. Hosp Community Psychiatry 28:436–440, 1977

Kardiner A: The individual and His Society. New York, Columbia University Press, 1939 (rev ed—Westport, Conn, Greenwood, 1974)

Kardiner A, Linton R, DuBois C, West J: The Psychological Frontiers of Society. New York, Columbia University Press, 1945

Karle W, Corriere R, Hart J: Psychophysiological changes in abreactive therapy. Psychother: Theory Res Prac 10:117–122, 1973

Karliner W: Indokolon therapy, in Masserman JH (ed): Current Psychiatric Therapies, vol. 6. Orlando FL, Grune & Stratton, 1966, pp 252–259

Karliner W, Wehrheim HK: Maintenance convulsive treatments. Am J Psychiatry 121:113, 1965

Karnosh LJ, Mereness D: Psychiatry for Nurses: Essentials of Psychiatric Nursing. St Louis, Mosby, 1962

Karoly P: Operant methods, in Kanfer FH, Goldstein AP (eds): Helping People Change (2d ed). New York, Pergamon, 1980, pp 210–247

Karpf FB: The Psychology and Psychotherapy of Otto Rank. New York, Philosophical Library, 1953

Karpf FB: Rankian will or dynamic relationship therapy, in Masserman JH, Moreno JL (eds): Progress in Psychotherapy, vol. 2. Orlando FL, Grune & Stratton, 1957, pp 132–139

Karpman B: Objective psychotherapy. J Clin Psychol 5:189–342, 1949

Karpman SB: Developments in transactional analysis, in Masserman JH (ed): Current Psychiatric Therapies, vol. 12. Orlando FL, Grune & Stratton, 1972

Karush A: Adaptational psychodynamics, in Stein MI (ed): Contemporary Psycho-therapies. New York, Free Press, 1961, pp 305–318

Kasius C (ed): A Comparison of Diagnostic and Functional Casework Concepts. New York, Family Service Association of America, 1950, pp 78–169

Katz AH: Self-help and mutual aid: An emerging social movement? Annual Review of Sociology 7:129–155, 1981

Katz AH, Bender EI (eds): The Strength in Us: Self-Help in the Modern World. New York, Franklin-Watts, 1976

Katz JL, Weiner H, Gallagher TF, Hellman L: Stress, distress and ego defenses. Arch Gen Psychiatry 23:131–142, 1970

Katz M: Agreement on connotative meaning in marriage. Fam Process 4:64–74, 1965

Katz MM, Lyerly SB: Methods for measuring adjustment and social behavior in the community. Rationale description, discriminative validity and scale development. Psychol Res 13:1503–55, 1963

Katz NW: Hypnosis and the addictions: A critical review. Addictive Behaviors 5:41–47, 1980

Katz RC, Johnson CA, Gelfand S: Modifying the dispensing of reinforcers: Some implications for behavior modification with hospitalized patients. Behav Ther 3:579–588, 1972

Katz S: Office management of borderline personality disorders. Psychiatric Annals 12:610–617, 1982

Kaufman I: The role of the psychiatric consultant. Am J Orthopsychiatry 26:223–224, 1956

Kaufman MR: Psychiatry: Why "medical" or "social" model? Arch Gen Psychiatry 17:347–358, 1967

Kayton L: Clinical features of improved schizophrenics, in Gunderson JG, Mosher LR (eds): Psychotherapy of Schizophrenia. New York, Aronson, 1975, pp 361–395

Kazanjian V, Stein S, Weinberg WL: An Introduction to Mental Health Consultation. Pub Health Monogr No. 69. Washington, DC, U.S. Government Printing Office, 1962

Kazdin AE: History of Behavior Modification. Baltimore, University Park Press, 1978

Kazdin AE: Therapy outcome questions requiring control of credibility and treatment–generated expectancies. Beh Ther 10:81, 1979

Kazdin AE, Wilson GT: Evaluation of Behavior Therapy: Issues, Evidence and Research Strategies. Cambridge, Ballinger, 1978

Kellam SG, et al: Mental Health and Going to School. Chicago, University of Chicago Press, 1974

Kelly G: The Psychology of Personal Constructs. New York, Norton, 1955

Kelly JA: Social Skills Training. New York, Springer, 1982

Kelman H: Techniques in dream interpretation. Am J Psychoanal 25:3–26, 1965

Kelman H: Helping People: Karen Horney's Psychoanalytic Approach. New York, Science House, 1971

Kempler W: Family therapy of the future. Int Psychiatry Clin 6:135–158, 1969

Kennedy N: Section Three (untitled) on the social worker's role, in Helping the Dying Patient and His Family. New York, National Association for Social Workers, 1960

Kern HM, Jr: Community psychiatric training—a public health approach, in Goldston SE (ed): Concepts of Community Psychiatry: A Framework of Training. Pub Health Service Publ No. 1319. Bethesda, Md, National Institute of Mental Health, 1965, pp 79–87

Kernberg O: The treatment of patients with borderline personality organization. Int J Psychonal 49:600–619, 1968

Kernberg O: Borderline personalities. Bull NY State Distr Branches, Am Psychiatr Assoc Nos. 1 & 6, 1974

Kernberg O: Borderline Conditions and Pathological Narcissism. New York, Aronson, 1975

Kernberg O, et al: Psychotherapy and psychoanalysis: Final report of the Menninger Foundation's Psychotherapy Research Project. Bull Menninger Clin 36 (1, 2), 1972

Kernberg O: Object Relations Theory and Clinical Psychoanalysis. New York, Aronson, 1976(b)

Kernberg O: Internal World and External Reality. New York Aronson, 1980(a)

Kernberg O: Melanie Klein, in Kaplan HI, Freedman AM, Sadock BJ (eds): Comprehensive Textbook of Psychiatry. Baltimore, Williams & Wilkins, 1980(b)

Kernberg O: Self, ego, affects, and drives. J Am Psychoanal Assoc 30:893–917, 1982

Kessel K, Hyman HT: The value of the psychoanalysis as a therapeutic procedure. JAMA 101:1612–1615, 1933

Ketal RM: Psychotropic drugs in emergency

care. Audiodigest Psychiatry. Psychiatric Emergencies, vol. 4, no. 9, May 12, 1975

Kettle J: The EST Experience. New York, Kensington, 1976

Kierkegaard S: A Kierkegaard Anthology. Bretall R (ed). Princeton, NJ, Princeton University Press, 1951

Kiev A: Magic, Faith and Healing. New York, Free Press, 1964

Killen JD, Taylor CB, Telch MJ, Saylor KE, et al: Self–induced vomiting and laxative and diuretic use among teenagers. JAMA 255:1447–1449, 1986

Killins CG, Wells CL: Group therapy of alcoholics, in Masserman JH (ed): Current Psychiatric Therapies, vol. 7. Orlando FL, Grune & Stratton, 1967

Kimble GA: Hilgard and Marquis' Conditioning and Learning (2d ed). New York, Appleton-Century-Crofts, 1961

Kimble GA, Kendall JW, Jr: A comparison of two methods of producing experimental extinction. J Exp Psychol 45:87–90, 1953

King GF, Armitage SG, Tilton JR: A therapeutic approach to schizophrenics of extreme pathology. J Abnorm Soc Psychol 61:276–286, 1960

King NJ: The behavioral management of asthma and asthma-related problems in children: A critical review of the literature. J Behav Med 3:169–189, 1980

King O: Sleep deprivation therapy in depressive syndromes. Psychosomatics 21:404–407, 1980

Kinross-Wright J: The current status of phenothiazines. JAMA 200:461–464, 1967

Kirchner JH, Hogan RA: The therapist variable in the implosion of phobias. Psychotherapy 3:102–104, 1966

Kirsch MA, Glass LL: Psychiatric disturbances associated with Herard Seminars Training, II: Additional cases and theoretical considerations. Am J Psychiatry 134:1254–1258, 1977

Klaesi J: Uber die therapeutische Anwendung der "Dauernarkose" Mittels Somnifen bei Schizophrenen, Ztschr f d ges Psychiat u Neurol 74:557, 1922

Klapman JW: Group Psychotherapy: Theory and Practice. Orlando FL, Grune & Stratton, 1946 (2d rev ed, 1959)

Klapman JW, Lundin JW: Objective appraisal of textbook-mediated group psychotherapy with psychotics. Int J Group Psychother 2:116–126, 1952

Kleegman SJ: Frigidity in women. Q Rev Surg Obstet Gynecol 16:243–248, 1959

Klein DF: Psychopharmacological treatment

and delineation of borderline disorders, in Hartocollis P (ed): Borderline Personality Disorders. New York, International Universities Press, 1977, p 365

Klein DF, Davis JM: Diagnosis and Drug Treatment of Psychiatric Disorders. Baltimore, Williams & Wilkins, 1969

Klein DF, Gittelman R, Quitkin F, et al: Diagnosis and Drug Treatment of Psychiatric Disorders: Adults and Children, (2d ed). Baltimore, Williams & Wilkins, 1980

Klein DF, Rabkin JG: Anxiety: New Research and Changing Concepts. New York, Raven Press, 1980

Klein G: Two theories or one? Bull Menninger Clinic 37:102–131, 1973

Klein GS: Psychoanalytic Theory: An Explanation of Essentials. New York, International Universities Press, 1976

Klein M: Personification in the play of children. Int J of Psychoanaly, 10:193–204, 1929

Klein M: The Psychoanalysis of Children. London, Hogarth Press, 1932

Klein M: The Psychoanalysis of Children. London, Hogarth, 1932; New York, Norton, 1935 (repr, 1975)

Klein M: Notes on some schizoid mechanism. Int J Psychoanal 27:89–110, 1946

Klein M: Contributions to Psychoanalysis, 1921–1948. London, Hogarth, 1948

Klein M: In Richman J (ed): On the Bringing up of Children by Five Psychoanalysts (2d ed). New York, Brunner/Mazel, 1952

Klein M: The psychoanalytic play technique. Am J Orthopsychiatry 112:418–422, 1955(a)

Klein M: The psychoanalytic play technique, its history and significance, in Klein M, Heiman P, Money-Kyrle R (eds): New Directions in Psychoanalysis. The Significance of Infant Conflict in the Pattern of Adult Behavior. New York, Basic Books, 1955(b)

Klein M: New Directions in Psychoanalysis. New York, Basic Books, 1957(a)

Klein M: Envy and Gratitude: A Study of Unconscious Sources. London, Tavistock, 1957(b)

Klein M: On the development of mental functioning. Int J Psychiatry 39:84–90, 1958

Klein M: Uber das Seelenleben des Kleinkindes. Psyche (Stuttg) 14:284–314, 1960

Klein M: Narrative of a Child Analysis. New York, Basic Books, 1961 (rev ed—Delacorte, 1975)

Klein M: Our Adult World and Other Essays. New York, Basic Books, 1963

Klein M: Mourning and its relation to manic depressive states, in Klein, Melanie (ed): Love, Guilt and Reparation and other Works, 1921–1945. New York, Delacorte Press, 1975, pp 344–369

Klein WH, et al: The Training of Youth Counselors. Washington, DC, Institute for Youth Studies, 1966

Klein WH, LeShan ES, Furman SS: Promoting Mental Health of Older People Through Group Methods: A Practical Guide. New York, Mental Health Materials Center, 1966

Klein-Lipshutz E: Comparisons of dreams in individual and group psychotherapy. Int J Group Psychother 3:143–149, 1953

Kleitman N: Patterns of dreaming. Scientific Am 203:82–88, 1960

Klemperer E: Changes of the body image in hypnoanalysis. Paper presented at the Annual Meeting of the Society for Clinical and Experimental Hypnosis, New York Academy of Science, New York, 1953

Klepac RK: Micro–computers in behavior therapy: A sampler of applications. The Behavior Therapist 7:79–83, 1984

Klerman GL: Psychoneurosis: Integrating pharmacology and psychotherapy, in Claghorn JL (ed): Successful Psychotherapy. New York, Brunner/Mazel, 1975(a)

Klerman GL: Combining drugs and psychotherapy in the treatment of depression, in Greenblatt M (ed): Drugs in Combination with other Therapies. Orlando FL, Grune & Stratton, 1975(b)

Klerman GL: Long-term treatment of affective disorders, in Lipton MA, DiMascio A, Killam KF (eds): Psychopharmacology: A Generation of Progress. New York, Raven Press, 1978

Klerman GL, Rounsaville BJ, Chevron ES, et al: Manual for Short-Term Interpersonal Psychotherapy (IPT) of Depression, Unpublished manuscript, fourth draft. June 1979

Klerman GL, Rounsaville BJ, Chevron ES, et al: Manual for Short-term Interpersonal Psychotherapy (IPT) of Depression. New Haven, Boston Collaborative Depression Project, June 1982, 5th Draft

Klerman GL, Weissman MM, Chevron ES, Rounsaville BJ: Interpersonal therapy, in Karasu TB (ed): The Psychiatric Therapies. Washington DC, The American Psychiatric Association, 1984, pp 387–396

Klerman GL, Weissman MM, Rounsaville BJ, et al: Interpersonal Psychotherapy of Depression, New York, Basic Books, 1984

Kline F: Personal Group Therapy and Psychiat-ric Training. New York, Stratton Intercontinental, 1975

Kline NS: The practical management of depression. JAMA 190:732–740, 1964

Kline NS: Drugs in the treatment of depression: Clinical studies, in Solomon P (ed): Psychiatric Drugs. Orlando FL, Grune & Stratton, 1966

Klopfer B, Kelly DM: The Rorschach Technique, Yonkers, World Book, 1942

Knee RI: Psychiatric social work, in Hurtz RH (ed): Social Work Yearbook. New York, National Association of Social Workers, 1957, p 431

Knight RP: Evaluation of the results of psychoanalytic therapy. Am J Psychiatry 98:434–446, 1941

Knight RP: A critique of the present status of the psychotherapies (1949), in Knight RP, Friedman CR (eds): Psychoanalytic Psychiatry and Psychology. New York, International Universities Press, 1954, pp 52–64

Kniskern DP, Gurman AS: Clinical implications of recent research in family therapy, in Wolberg LR, Aronson ML (eds): Group and Family Therapy. New York, Brunner/Mazel, 1980

Knobloch F: On the theory of a therapeutic community for neurotics. Int J Group Psychother 10:419–429, 1960

Knobloch F: Czech-type therapeutic unit successfully used in Canada. Psychiatr News 8:32–33, 1973

Koegler R, Brill Q: Treatment of Psychiatric Outpatients. New York, Appleton-Century-Crofts, 1967

Kohl RN: Pathologic reaction of marital partners to improvement of patients. Am J Psychiatry 118:1036–1041, 1962

Kohut H: The Analysis of the Self. New York, International Universities Press, 1971

Kohut H: The Restoration of the Self. New York, International Universities Press, 1977

Kohut H, Wolff ES: The disorders of self and their treatment: An outline. Int J Psychoanal 59:413, 1978

Kolansky H, Moore WT: Marijuana. Can it hurt you? JAMA 232:923–924, 1975

Kolb LC: Consultation and psychotherapy, in Masserman JH (ed): Current Psychiatric Therapies, vol. 8. Orlando FL, Grune & Stratton, 1968

Kolb LC: Return of the repressed: Delayed stress reaction to war. J Am Acad Psychoanal 11(4):531–545, 1982

Kolb LC, Montgomery J: An explanation for transference cure: Its occurrence in psychoanalysis and psychotherapy. Am J Psychiatry 115:414–421, 1963

Kolb LC, Mutalipassi LR: The conditioned emotional response: A sub–class of chronic and delayed posttraumatic stress disorder. Psychiatric Annals 12:979–987, 1982

Koltes JA, Jones M: A type of therapeutic community. Ment Hosp 8:16–19, 1957

Konia C: Orgone therapy: A case presentation. Psychother: Theory Res Prac 12:192–197, 1975

Konopka G: Group therapy in overcoming racial and cultural tension. Am J Orthopsychiatry 17:593–699, 1947

Konopka G: Group work and therapy, in Hendry CE (ed): A Decade of Group Work. New York, Association Press, 1948

Konopka G: Eduard C. Lindeman and Social Work Philosophy. Minnesota, University of Minnesota Press, 1958

Konopka G: Group Work: A Heritage and a Challenge. Social Work with Groups. New York, National Association for Social Workers, 1960, pp 7–21

Konopka G: Social Group Work: A Helping Process. Englewood Cliffs, NJ, Prentice-Hall, 1963

Koppitz EM: The Bender Gestalt Test for Young Children. Orlando FL, Grune & Stratton, 1963, pp 73–83

Koranyi ER: Morbidity and rate of undiagnoses physical illnesses in a psychiatric clinic population. Arch Gen Psychiatry 36:414–419, 1979

Korzybski A: Science and Society. An Introduction to Non-Artistotelian Systems and General Semantics (2d ed). Lancaster, Pa, Science Press, 1941

Kosbab FP: Imagery techniques in psychotherapy. Arch Gen Psychiatry 31:283–290, 1974

Kosten TR, Rounsaville BJ, Kleber HD, et al: A 2.5 year-follow-up of depression, life crises, and treatment effects on abstinence among opioid addicts. Arch Gen Psychiatry 43:733–738, 1986

Kotkov B: Common forms of resistance in group psychotherapy. Psychoanal Rev 44:88, 1957

Kotkov B: Favorable clinical indications for group attendance. Int J Group Psychother 8:419–427, 1958

Kotler SL: Role theory in marriage counseling. Sociol Soc Res 52:50–62, 1967

Kraft AM: The therapeutic community, in Arieti S (ed): American Handbook of Psychiatry, vol. 3. New York, Basic Books, 1966, pp 542–551

Kraft IA, Vick J: Flexibility and variability of group psychotherapy with adolescence girls, in Wolberg LR, Schwartz EK (eds): Group Therapy 1973: An Overview, New York, Stratton Intercontinental, 1973, pp 71–91

Kraines SH: The Therapy of the Neuroses and Psychoses. Philadelphia, Lea & Febiger, 1943

Krakowski AJ: Protriptyline in treatment of severe depressions. A long-range pilot study. Am J Psychiatry 121:807–808, 1965

Kramer BM: The day hospital: A case study. J Soc Issues 16:14–19, 1960

Kramer CH, Kramer JR: Basic Principles of Long-term Patient Care: Developing a Therapeutic Community. Springfield, Ill, Charles C Thomas, 1976

Kramer E: Art Therapy in a Children's Community. Springfield, Ill, Thomas, 1958

Kramer E: Art as Therapy with Children. New York, Schocken, 1972

Kramer M: On the continuation of the analytic process after psychoanalysis (a self-observation). Int J Psychoanal 40:17–25, 1959

Krantz C, Jr, Truitt EB, Jr, Speer L, Ling ASC: New pharamaco-convulsive agent. Science 126:353, 1957

Krasner J: The psychoanalytic treatment of the elder people via group psychotherapy. Acta Psychother (Suppl 7), 205, 1959

Krasner L: Studies of the conditioning of verbal behavior. Psychol Bull 55:148–170, 1958

Krasner L: The psychotherapist as a social reinforcement machine, in Strupp HH, Luborsky L (eds): Research in Psychotherapy, vol. 2. Washington, DC, American Psychological Association, 1962, pp 61–94

Krasner L: The operant approach in behavior therapy, in Bergin A, Garfield S (eds): Handbook of Psychotherapy and Behavior Change. New York, Wiley, 1971

Krause MS: Defensive and non-defensive resistance. Psychoanal Q 30:221–231, 1961

Krause MS: A cognitive theory of motivation for treatment. J Gen Psychol 75:9–19, 1966

Krause MS: Behavioral indices of motivation for treatment. J Couns Psychol 14:426–435, 1967

Kremer MW: A reconsideration of change and insight in therapy. Paper presented at the 122d Annual Meeting of the American Psychiatric Association, Atlantic City, NJ, May 9, 1966

Kressel K: Resolving marital disagreements over money: A comparison of role-reversal and self-presentation. New York, Dabor Science Publications, 1977

Krich A: A reluctant counselee: A specimen

case, in Mudd EH, Krich A (eds): Man and Wife. New York, Norton, 1957, pp 258–275

Kriegsfeld M: How now: A Gestalt approach, in Grayson H (ed): Short-term Approaches to Psychotherapy. New York, Human Sciences Press, 1979

Kringlen E: Obsessional neurosis: A long-term follow-up. Br J Psychiatry 11:709, 1965(a)

Kringlen E: Schizophrenia in male monozygotic twins. Acta Psychiatr Scand (Suppl 178), Munksgaard, 1965(b)

Krippner S, Line MV: Passages: A Guide for Pilgrims of the Mind. New York, Harper & Row, 1972

Krippner S, Rubin D (eds): Galaxies of Life: The Human Aura in Acupuncture and Kirlian Photography. New York, Gordon & Beach, 1973

Kris E: On preconscious mental processes, in Rapaport D (ed): Organization and Pathology of Thought. New York, Columbia University Press, 1951, pp 474–493

Kris E: Psychoanalytic Explorations in Art. New York, International Universities Press, 1952

Kris E: On the vicissitudes of insight. Int J Psychoanal 37:445, 1956

Kris EB: Simplifying chlorpromazine maintenance therapy. Am J Psychiatry 114:836, 1958

Kris EB: Intensive short-term therapy in a day care facility for control of recurrent psychotic symptoms. Am J Psychitry 115:1027, 1959

Kris EB: The role of the day hospital in the rehabilitation of mental patients. Proceedings of the Institute for the Rehabilitation of the Mentally Ill. New York, Altro Health and Rehabilitation Service, April 1962, pp 33–36

Kroger WS: Systems approach for understanding obesity: Management by behavioral modification through hypnosis. Psychiatric Opinion 7:7–19, 1970

Kroger WS, Fezler WD: Hypnosis and Behavior Modification: Imagery Conditioning. Philadelphia, Lippincott, 1976

Krug O: The dynamic use of the ego functions in casework practice. Soc Casework 36:443–450, 1955

Krumboltz JD (ed): Revolution in Counseling: Implications of Behavioral Science. Boston, Houghton Mifflin, 1966

Krupp GR, Kligfeld B: The bereavement reaction, a cross-cultural evaluation. Paper presented at the 38th Annual Meeting of the American Orthopsychiatric Association, New York, March 23–25, 1961

Kubie LS: The use of hypnagogic reveries in the recovery of repressed amnesic data. Bull Menninger Clin 7:172–182, 1943

Kubie LS: Elements in the Medical Curriculum Which Are Essential in the Training for Psychotherapy—Training in Clinical Psychology. Transactions of the First Conference. New York, Josiah Macy, Jr, Foundation, 1947, pp 46–51

Kubie LS: Psychoanalysis and healing by faith. Pastoral Psychol 1:13–18, 1950(a)

Kubie LS: Practical and Theoretical Aspects of Psychoanalysis. New York, International Universities Press, 1950(b)

Kubie LS: Research into the process of supervision in psychoanalysis. Psychoanal Q 27:226–236, 1958(a)

Kubie LS: Some theoretical concepts underlying the relationship between individual and group psychotherapies. Int J Group Psychother 8:3, 1958(b)

Kubie LS: Psychoanalysis and scientific method. J Nerv Ment Dis 131:512, 1960

Kubie LS: Neurotic Distortion of the Creative Process. New York, Farrar, Straus, 1961

Kubie LS: The process of evaluation of therapy in psyciatry. Arch Gen Psychiatry 26:880–884, 1973

Kubie LS, Landau G: Group Work with the Aged. New York, International Universities Press, 1953 (rev ed, 1975)

Kubie LS, Margolin S: The therapeutic role of drugs in the process of regression, dissociation and synthesis. Psychosom Med 17:147, 1945

Kubler-Ross E: On Death and Dying. New York, Macmillan, 1969

Kuehn JL, Crinella FM: Sensitivity training: Interpersonal "overkill" and other problems. Am J Psychiatry 126:840–844, 1969

Kuhn R: Problems der praktischen Durchführung der Tofranil-Behandlung. Wien Med Wochenschr 110:245, 1960

Kunnes R: Radicalism and community mental health, in Gottesfeld H (ed): The Critical Issues in Community Mental Health. New York, Behavioral Publications, 1972

Kunstler P: Social Group work in Great Britain. London, Faber & Faber, 1955

Kupers TA: Public Therapy. New York, Free Press, 1981

Kurland AA, Savage C, Pahnke WN, et al: LSD in the treatment of alcoholics. Pharmakopsychiatr Neuropsychopharmakolog (Stuttg) 4(2), 1971

Kurland AA, Savage C, Unger S, Shaffer JW: Psychedelic psychotherapy (LSD) in the treatment of alcoholic patients. Paper presented at the 122d Annual Meeting of the American Psychiatric Association, Atlantic City, NJ, May 1966

Kurlychek RT, Glang AE: The Use of Microcomputers in the Cognitive Rehabilitation of Brain-Injured Persons. New York, The Haworth Press, 1984, pp 245–256

Kutash IL, Wolf A: Psychotherapist's Case Book. San Francisco, Jossey-Bass, 1986

Kwentus J, Major LF: Disulfiram in the treatment of alcoholism: A review. J Stud Alcohol 40:428–446, 1979

Kwiatowska HY: The use of families' art productions for psychiatric evaluation. Bull Art Ther 6(2):52–72, 1967

Labeck LF, Johnson JH, Harris WG: Validity of a computerized on–line MMPI interpretive system. J Clin Psychol 39:412–416, 1983

Lacan J: Some reflections on the ego. Int J Psychoanal 34:11–17, 1953

Lacan J: The Mirror Phase as Function of the I. Translated by J. Roussell. New Left Review 51:71–77, 1968

Lacan J: The Four Fundamentals of Psychoanalysis, in Miller JA (ed): Translated by A. Sheridan. London, The Hogarth Press, 1977(a)

Lacan J: Ecrits: A Selection. Translated by A. Sheridan. New York, Norton, 1977(b)

Lacan J: The Four Fundamental Concepts of Psychoanalysis. Translated by A. Sheridan. New York, Norton & Co, 1978

LaForgue R: Exceptions to the fundamental rule of psychoanalysis. Int J Psychoanal 18:35–41, 1937

Lager E, Zwerling I (eds): Psychotherapy in the Community. St. Louis, MO, Warren H. Green, Inc, 1983

Laidlaw RW: The psychiatrist as marriage counselor. Am J Psychiatry 106:732–736, 1960

Laing RD: The Divided Self. London, Tavistock, 1960

Laing RD: The Politics of Experience. New York, Pantheon, 1967

Laing RD, Esterson A: Sanity, Madness and the Family: Families of Schizophrenics (2d ed). New York, Basic Books, 1971

Laing RD, Phillipson H, Lee AR: Interpersonal Perception: A Theory and a Method of Research. New York, Springer, 1966

Lamb HR (ed): The Homeless Mentally Ill. Washington, DC, American Psychiatric Association, 1984

Lamb HR, Peterson CL: The new community consultation. Hosp Community Psychiatry 34:59, 1983

Lambert MJ: The effects of Psychotherapy. Montreal, Eden Press, 1979, pp 109–122

Lambert MJ, Utec JM: Therapist characteristics and psychotherapy outcome, in Lambert MJ (ed): The Effects of Psychotherapy, vol. 2. New York, Human Sciences Press, 1982

Lancet: Editorial: Treatment of enuresis. 1:1425, 1964

Lander J, Schulman R: The impact of the therapeutic milieu on the disturbed personality. Soc Casework 4:227–234, 1960

Landis C: A statistical evaluation of psychotherapeutic methods, in Hinsie LE (ed): Concepts and Problems of Psychotherapy. New York, Columbia University Press, 1937; London, Heinemann, 1938

Landy D: Rutland corner house: Case study of a halfway house. J Soc Issues 16:27–32, 1960

Landy D, Greenblatt M: Halfway House, Washington, DC, U.S. Department of Health, Education, & Welfare, 1965

Lang PJ: Experimental studies of desensitization therapy, in Wolpe J (ed): The Conditioning Therapies. New York, Holt, 1964

Lang PJ, Lazovik AD: Experimental desensitization of a phobia. J Abnorm Soc Psychol 66:519–525, 1963

Lang PJ, Lazovik AD, Reynolds DJ: Desensitization, suggestibility, and pseudotherapy. J Abnorm Soc Psychol 70:395–402, 1965

Lang PJ, Melamed BG, Hart JA: A psychophysiological analysis of fear modification using an automated desensitization procedure. J Abnorm Psycho 76:220–234, 1979

Lang PJ, Melamed BG, Hart JA: A Psychophysiological analysis of fear modification using an automated desensitization procedure. J Abnorm Psychol 76(2):220–34, 1970

Langdell JI: A unique English therapeutic community for adolescents: Finchen Manor, in Masserman JH (ed): Current Psychiatric Therapies, vol. 7. Orlando FL, Grune & Stratton, 1967, pp 36–42

Langen D, Volhard R: Zschr Psychotherapie 5:215, 1955

Langer M: Learning to Live as a Widow. New York, Messner, 1957

Langer M, Puget J, Teper E: A methodological approach to the teaching of psychoanalysis. Int J Psychoanal 45:567–574, 1964

Langs R: The Supervisory Experience. New York, Aronson, 1979

Laqueur HP: General systems theory and multiple family therapy, in Masserman JH (ed): Current Psychiatric Therapies, vol. 8. Orlando FL, Grune & Stratton, 1968

Laqueur HP: Mechanisms of change in multiple family therapy, in Sager CJ, Kaplan HS (eds): Progress in Group and Family Therapy. New York, Brunner/Mazel, 1972, pp 400–415

Laqueur HP, LaBurt HA: Conjoint family group

therapy—a new approach. Paper presented at the 122d Annual Meeting of the American Psychiatric Association, Atlantic City, NJ, May 1966

Lasagna L, Mosteller F, Felsinger JM, Beecher HK: A study of the placebo response. Am J Med 16:770–779, 1954

LaVietes R, Cohen R, Reens R, Ronall B: Day treatment center and school: Seven Years' experience. Am J Orthopsychiatry 35:160, 1965

Law SG: Therapy Through Interview. New York, McGraw-Hill, 1948

Lawrence MM: The Mental Health Team in the Schools. New York, Behavioral Publications, 1971

Lazarus AA: Group therapy of phobic disorders by systematic desensitization. J Abnorm Soc Psychol 63:504–510, 1961

Lazarus AA: Behavior rehearsal vs. nondirective therapy vs. advice in effecting behavior change. Beh Res Ther 4:209–212, 1966

Lazarus AA: In support of technical eclecticism. Psychol Rep 21:415–416, 1967

Lazarus AA: Behavior therapy in groups, in Gazda G (ed): Basic Approaches to Group Psychotherapy and Group Counseling. Springfield, Ill, Thomas, 1968

Lazarus AA: Behavior Therapy and Beyond. New York, McGraw-Hill, 1971

Lazarus AA (ed): Clinical Behavior Therapy. New York, Brunner/Mazel, 1972

Lazarus AA (ed): Multimodel Behavior Therapy. New York, Springer, 1976

Lazarus AA: The Practice of Multimodel Therapy. New York, McGraw-Hill, 1981

Lazarus AA, Abramovitz A: The use of "emotive imagery" in the treatment of children's phobias. J Ment Sci 108:191–195, 1962

Lazarus AA, Fay A: Behavior Therapy, in Karasu TB (ed): The Psychiatric Therapies. Washington, DC, The American Psychiatric Association, 1984

Lazarus RS: On the primacy of cognition. Am Psychologist 39(2):124–129, 1984

Lazarus RS, Alfert E: The short-circuiting of threat by experimentally altering cognitive appraisal. J Abnormal Social Psychology 69:195–205, 1964

Lazarus RS, Deese J, Osler S: Review of research on psychological stress upon performance. Res Bull 51-29, 1951

Lazarus RS, Folkman S: Coping and adaptation, in Gentry WD (ed): The Handbook of Behavioral Medicine. New York, Guilford, 1984, pp 282–325

Lazell EW: The group treatment or dementia praecox. Psychoanal Rev 8:168–179, 1921

Lazovik AD, Lang PJ: A laboratory demonstration of systematic desensitization in psychotherapy. J Psychol Stud 11:238–247, 1960

Leader AL: Social work consultation in psychiatry. Soc Casework 38:22–28, 1957

Leake CD: The Amphetamines, Their Actions and Uses. Springfield, Ill, Thomas, 1958

Leavy SA: The significance of Jacques Lacan. Psychoanal Q 46:201–219, 1977

Lebensohn ZM: American psychiatry and the general hospital. Med Ann DC 33:47–52, 1964

Lee RS: Religion psychotherapy and Freud. Paper presented at the Postgraduate Center for Mental Health, Carnegie Endowment Center, New York, April 9, 1957

Leedy J: Poetry therapy. Psychiatr Op 3:20–25, 1966

Leff JP, Vaugh CE: The interaction of life events and relatives' expressed emotion in schizophrenia and depressive neurosis. Br J Psychiatry 136:146–153, 1980

Lego S: Nurse psychotherapists: How are we different? Perspectives in Psychiatric Care 11:144–147, 1973

Lego S: The one-to-one nurse-patient relationship. Psychiatric nursing 1946-1974: A report on the state of the art. Perspect Psychiatr Care 18:1–14, 1980

Lego S: The American Handbook of Psychiatric Nursing. Philadelphia, Lippincott, 1984

Lehman HE, Ban TA: Pharmacotherapy of tension and anxiety, in Masserman JH (ed): Current Psychiatric Therapies, vol. 12. Orlando FL, Grune & Stratton, 1972

Lehner GFJ: Negative practice as a psychotherapeutic technique. J Gen Psychol 51:69–82, 1954

Lehrer P, Schiff L, Kris A: Operant conditioning in a comprehensive treatment program for adolescents. Arch Gen Psychiatry 25:515–521, 1971

Leiblum SR, Pervin LA (eds): Principles and Practice of Sex Therapy. New York, Guilford Press, 1980

Leichter E: Group psychotherapy of married couples' groups: Some characteristic treatment dynamics. Int J Group Psychother 12:154–163, 1962

Leighton AH: An Introduction to Social Psychiatry. Springfield, Ill, Thomas, 1960

Leighton AH, Clausen JA, Wilson RN (eds): Explorations in Social Psychiatry. New York, Basic Books, 1957

Leighton AH, et al: The Stirling County Study. Vol. 1: My Name is Legion. Vol. 2: People of Cover and Woodlot. Vol. 3: The Character of Danger. New York, Basic Books, 1959, 1960, 1963

Leitenberg H (ed): Handbook of Behavior Modification and Behavior Therapy. Englewood Cliffs, NJ, Prentice–Hall, 1976

Lemere F: Treatment of mild depressions in general office practice. JAMA 164:516–518, 1957

Lemere F: The danger of amphetamine dependency. Paper presented at the 122d Annual Meeting of the American Psychiatric Association, Atlantic City, NJ, May 1966

Lemere F, Voegtlin WL: An evaluation of the aversion treatment of alcoholism. Q J Stud Alcohol 11:199–204, 1950

Lemere F, Voegtlin WL, Broz WR, et al: Conditioned reflex treatment of chronic alcoholsim: VII. Tech Dis Nerv Syst 3:243–247, 1942

Lemkau PV: Mental hygiene in public health. Pub Health Rep 62:1151–1162, 1947

Lemkau PV: What can the public health nurse do in mental hygiene. Paper presented at the Mental Hygiene Conference for U.S. Public Health Service Nursing Consultants, Washington, DC, February 1948

Lemkau PV: Mental Hygiene in Public Health. New York, McGraw-Hill, 1955

Lemkau PV: Operation of the New York State Community Mental Health Services Act in New York, 1956. Paper presented at the Annual Meeting of the American Psychiatric Association. (Abstract in Goldston SE (ed): Concepts of Community Psychiatry: A Framework for Training). Pub Health Service Publ No. 1319. Bethesda, Md, National Institute of Mental Health, 1965, p 197

Leopold HS: Selection of patients for group psychotherapy. Am J Psychother 11:634, 1957

Leopold HS: The problem of working through in group psychotherapy. Int J Group Psychother 9:287, 1959

Lerner RC: The therapeutic social club: Social rehabilitation for mental patients. Int J Soc Psychiatry 6:101,1960

Lesse S: Management of apparent remissions in suicidal patients, in Masserman JH (ed): Current Psychiatric Therapies, vol. 7. Orlando FL, Grune & Stratton, 1967

Lesse S: The range of therapies in the treatment of severely depressed suicidal patients. Am J Psychother 29:308–326, 1975

Lesser IM, Rubin RT: Diagnostic considerations in panic disorders. J Clin Psychiatry 47, 6 (Suppl) 4–10, 1986

Lester D: The unique qualities of telephone therapy. Psychother: Theory Res Prac 11:219–221, 1974

Lester D, Brockopp GM (eds): Crisis Intervention Counseling by Telephone. Springfield, Ill, Thomas, 1973

Lester MW: Counterpoint in psychoanalytic thinking, in Abt LE, Riess BF (eds): Progress in Clinical Psychology, vol. 5. Orlando FL, Grune & Stratton, 1964

Leszca M, Yalom ID, Norden M: The value of inpatient group psychotherapy: Patients' perceptions. Int J Group Psychother 35(3):411–33, 1985

Leuner H: Guided affective imagery (GAI): A method of intensive psychotherapy. Am J Psychother 23:4–22, 1969

Levay A, Kagle A: Ego deficiencies in the areas of pleasure, intimacy and cooperation: Guidelines in the diagnosis and treatment of sexual dysfunctions. J Sex Marital Ther 3:10–18, 1977(b)

Levene H, Breger L, Patterson V: A training and research program in brief psychotherapy. Am J Psychother 26:90, 1972

Levenson AJ: Non-functional psychopathology in late life. J Psychiatric Treatment and Evaluation 4:63–72, 1982

Levi L: Society, Stress, and Disease. Vol. 1. The Psychosocial Environment and Psychosomatic Diseases. New York, Oxford University Press, 1971

Levi L (ed): Stress and distress in response to psychosocial stimuli. Acta Med Scand Suppl No. 528, 1972

Levick M: Adjunctive Techniques in Psychotherapy: Art Therapy in Psychiatric Patients. Nutley, NJ, Roche Laboratories, 1973

Levick MF, Dulicai D, Briggs C, et al: The creative arts therapies, in Adamson W, Adamson K (eds): A Handbook for Specific Learning Disabilities. New York, Gardner Press, 1979

Levin TM, Zegans LS: Adolescent identity crisis and religious conversion: Implications for psychotherapy. Br J Med Psychology 47:73–82, March, 1974

Levine A: The time has come. Bull NY State Distr Branches Am Psychiatr Assoc 8:1, 1965

Levine A: The present status of relations between psychiatry and psychology. Psychiatric Op 8(3):6–9, 1971

Levine M: Psychotherapy in Medical Practice. New York, Macmillan, 1942

Levine SV, Salter N: Youth and contemporary religious movements: Psychosocial findings. J Can Psychiatr Assoc 21(6):411–420, 1976

Levinson H: Executive Stress. New York, Harper & Row, 1970

Levitan S, Kornfeld D: Clinical and cost benefits of liaison psychiatry. Am J Psychiatry 138:790–793, 1981

Levitt EE: The results of psychotherapy with children: An evaluation. J Consult Psychol 21:189–196, 1957

Levitt EE: Psychotherapy with children: A further evaluation. Behav Res Ther 1:45–51, 1963

Levitz LS, Stunkard AJ: Therapeutic coalition for obesity: Behavior modification and patient self-help. Am J Psychiatry 131:423–427, 1974

Levy D: Attitude therapy. Am J Orthopsychiatry 7:103–113, 1937(a)

Levy D: Studies in sibling rivalry. Res Monogr 2. New York, American Orthopsychiatric Association, 1937(b)

Levy D: Trends in therapy: III. Release therapy. Am J Orthopsychiatry 9:713–737, 1939

Levy D: Development of psychodynamic aspects of oppositional behavior, in Changing Concepts of Psychoanalytic Medicine. Orlando FL, Grune & Stratton, 1956

Levy J: The use of art technique in treatment of children's behavior problems. J Psycho-Asthenics 39:258, 1934

Levy J: Relationship therapy. Am J Orthopsychiatry 8:64–69, 1938

Levy RA: A practical approach to community psychiatry in a remote city—What is sex-session psychotherapy? Paper presented at the 122d Annual Meeting of the American Psychiatric Association, Atlantic City, NJ, May 1966

Levy S: The hyperkinetic child—a forgotten entity: Its diagnosis and treatment. Int J Neuropsychiatr 2:330–336, 1966

Lewin K: The research center for group dynamics at Massachusetts Institute of Technology. Sociometry 8:126–138, 1945

Lewin K: Frontiers in group dynamics: Concept, method and reality in social science: Social equilibrium and social change. Hum Relations 1:5–41, 1947

Lewin K: Resolving Social Conflicts: Selected Paper on Group Dynamics. New York, Harper & Row, 1948

Lewin K: Field Theory in Social Science: Selected Theoretical Papers. New York, Harper & Row, 1951

Lewin KK: Brief Encounters. St. Louis, Green, 1970

Lewin K, Lippit R, White RK: Patterns of aggressive behavior in experimentally created "social climates." J Soc Psychol 10:271–299, 1939

Lewin R (ed): Child Alive: New Insights into the Development of Young Children. London, Temple Smith, 1975

Lewin W: Observations on selective leucotomy. J Neurol Neurosurg Psychiatry 24:37–44. 1961

Lewinsohn P, Biglan A, Zeiss A: Behavioral treatment of depression, in Davidson P (ed): The Behavioral Management of Anxiety, Depression and Pain. New York, Brunner/Mazel, 1976

Lewinsohn PM, Hoberman MH: Behavioral and cognitive approaches, in Paykel ES (ed): Handbook of Affective Disorders. New York, Guilford Press, 1982

Lewinson TS, Zubin J: Handwriting Analysis. New York, King's Crown, 1942

Lewis CB: Rehabilitation of the older person: A psychosocial focus. Phys Ther 64(4):517–522, Apr. 1984

Lewis DJ, Sloane RB: Therapy with LSD. J Clin Exp Psychopathol 19:19, 1958

Lewis JM: Marital therapy and individual change: Implications for a theory of change, in Myers JM (ed): Cures by Psychotherapy. New York, Praeger, 1984

Lewis JM, Usdin G: Treatment Planning in Psychiatry. Washington, DC, American Psychiatric Press, 1982

Lewis M, Solnot AJ: Residential treatment, in Freedman AM, Kaplan HI, Sadock BJ (eds): Comprehensive Textbook of Psychiatry II (2d ed) Baltimore, Williams & Wikins, 1975, pp 2246–2249

Lewis NDC: The practical value of graphic art in personality studies. I. An introductory presentation of the possibilities. Psychoanal Rev 12:316–322, 1925

Lewis NDC: Graphic art productions in schizophrenia. A Res Nerv Ment Dis Proc 5:344–368, 1928

Liberman RA: Behavioral approach to group dynamics. I. Reinforcing and prompting of cohesiveness in group therapy. Behav Ther 1:141–175, 1970

Licht S: Music in Medicine. Boston, New England Conservatory of Music, 1946

Lichtenberg B: On the selection and preparation of the big brother volunteer, in Guerney BG (ed): Psychotherapeutic Agents: New Roles for Nonprofessionals, Parents and Teachers, New York, Holt, 1969

Lidz T: Schizophrenia and the family. Psychiatry 21:21–27, 1958

Lidz T: The Person. New York, Basic Books, 1968

Lidz T: The Origin and Treatment of Schizophrenic Disorders. New York, Basic Books, 1973

Lidz T, Edelson M (eds): Training Tomorrow's Psychiatrist. New Haven, Conn, Yale University Press, 1970

Lidz T, Fleck S: Schizophrenia, human integration and the role of the family, in Jackson DD (ed): Etiology of Schizophrenia. New York, Basic Books, 1960

Lidz T, Lidz RW: Therapeutic consideration arising from the intense symbiotic needs of schizophrenics, in Symposium, Psychotherapy of Schizophrenia. New York, International Universities Press, 1952

Lieberman D: Follow-up studies on previously hospitalized narcotic addicts. Am J Orthopsychiatry 35:601–604, 1965

Lieberman RP, Wheeler EG, de Visser LAJM, et al: A positive approach to helping troubled relationships. Handbook of Marital Therapy. New York, Plenum, 1980

Liebman JS (ed): Psychiatry and Religion. Boston, Beacon, 1948

Liebman R, Minuchin S, Baker L: An integrated program for anorexia nervosa. Am J Psychiatry 131:432–436, 1974

Liederman PC, Liederman VR: Group therapy: An approach to problems of geriatric outpatients, in Masserman JH (ed): Current Psychiatric Therapies, vol 7. Orlando FL, Grune & Stratton, 1967

Lief HI: Subprofessional training in mental health. Arch Gen Psychiatry 5:660–664, 1966

Lief HI: Sexual problems in medical practice. Monroe, Wis, Am Med Assoc, 1981

Liegner LM: St. Christopher's Hospice, 1974. JAMA 234:1047–1048, 1975

Life Magazine: Synanon. March 9, 1962, p 56

Lifschutz JE, et al: Psychiatric consultation in the public assistance agency. Soc Casework 39:3–9, 1958

Lifton W: Working with Groups: Group Process and Individual Growth. Palo Alto, Calif, Science Research Associates, 1961

Lillie FR: General biological introduction, in Allen E (ed): Sex and Internal Secretions. Baltimore, Williams & Wilkins, 1931

Lin T-Y, Standley CC: The Scope of Epidemiology in Psychiatry. Geneva, Switz, World Health Organization, 1962

Lindemann E: Symptomatology and management of acute grief. Am J Psychiatry 101:141–148, 1944

Lindeman EC: Group Work and Education for Democracy. Proceedings of the National Conference of Social Work. New York, Columbia University Press, 1939, pp. 342–347

Lindner RM: Rebel Without a Cause: The Hypnoanalysis of a Criminal Psychopath. Orlando FL, Grune & Stratton, 1944

Lindner RM: Who shall practice psychotherapy? Am J Psychother 4:432–442, 1950

Lindner RM: Hypnoanalysis as a psychotherapeutic technique, in Bychowski G, Despert JL (eds): Specialized Techniques in Psychotherapy. New York, Basic Books, 1952, pp 25–39

Lindsley OR: Characteristics of the behavior of chronic psychotics as revealed by free-operant conditioning methods. Dis Nerv Syst 22:66–78, 1960

Lindsley OR: Characteristics of the behavior of chronic psychotics as revealed by free-operant conditioning methods, in Franks CM (ed): Conditioning Techniques in Clinical Practice and Research. New York, Springer, 1964, pp 231–254

Linn L: The use of drugs in psychotherapy. Psychiatr Q 38:138–148, 1964

Linn L: Occupational therapy and other therapeutic activities, in Freedman AM, Kaplan JH, Sadock BJ (eds): Comprehensive Textbook of Psychiatry II (2d ed). Baltimore, Williams & Wilkins, 1975, pp 2003–2009

Linn L, Schwartz LW: Psychiatry and Religious Experiences. New York, Random House, 1958

Linn L, Spitzer RL: DSM-III. Implications for liaison psychiatry and medicine. JAMA, 247(23): 3207–3209, 1982

Linn L, Spitzer RL: DSM-III: Implications for liaison psychiatry and psychosomatic medicine. JAMA 247:3207–3209, 1986

Linn L, Weinroth LA, Shamah R: Occupational Therapy in Dynamic Psychiatry. Washington, DC, American Psychiatric Association, 1962

Linton TE: Services for "problem" children: Contrasts and solutions. Int J Ment Health 2:3–14, 1973

Lipkin S: Round robin time-limited therapy. Amer Acad Psychotherapists Newsletter 2:37–42, 1966

Lippitt GL: Consulting with a national organization: A case study. J Soc Issues 15:20–27, 1959

Lippitt R, Polansky N, Redl F, Rosen S: The dynamics of power. Hum Relations 5:37–64, 1952

Lippitt R, Watson J, Westley B: The Dynamics of Planned Change. Orlando FL, Harcourt, 1958

Lippitt R, White RK: The "social climate" of

children's groups, in Barker RG, Kounin JS, Wright HF (eds): Child Behavior and Development. New York, McGraw-Hill, 1943, pp 485–508

Lipschutz DM: Combined group and individual psychotherapy. Am J Psychother 11:336–344, 1957

Lipton MA, Ban TA, Kane FJ, et al: Megavitamin and orthomolecular therapy in psychiatry. American Psychiatric Association Task Force Report No. 7. Washington, DC, the Association, July 1973

Liss E: The graphic arts. Am J Orthopsychiatry 8:95–99, 1938

Liston MF: Educational issues confronting mental health nursing, in Leninger MM (ed): Contemporary Issues in Mental Health Nursing. Boston, Little, Brown, 1973

Litchenstein E, Brown RA: Current trends in the modification of cigarette dependence, in Bellack AS, Herson M, Kazdin AE (eds): International Handbook of Behavior Modification and Therapy. New York, Plenum, 1982, pp 575–604

Little KB, Shneidman ES: Congruencies among interpretations of psychological test and anamnesic data. Psychol Monogr. Gen Appl 73:1–42, 1959

Little M: Counter-transference and the patient's response to it. Int J Psychoanal 32:32–40, 1951

Littner N: The impact of the client's unconscious on the caseworker's reactions, in Parad HJ (ed): Ego Psychology and Dynamic Casework. New York, Family Service Association of America, 1958, pp 73–87

Litton EM: Psychiatric aspects of symptom removal by hypnosis. Paper presented at the Conference on Hypnosis, Center for Continuation Study, University of Minnesota, Minneapolis, June 16, 1966

Liversedge LA, Sylvester JD: Conditioning techniques in the treatment of writer's cramp. Lancet 2:1147–1149, 1955

Livingston MS: On barriers, contempt, and the "vulnerable moment" in group psychotherapy, in Wolberg LR, Aronson ML (eds): Group Therapy 1975: An Overview. New York, Stratton Intercontinental, 1975, pp 242–254

Locke N: The use of dreams in group psychoanalysis. Am J Psychother 11:98, 1957

Locke N: Group Psychoanalysis: Theory and Practice, New York, New York University Press, 1961

Loeser L, Bry T: The position of the group therapist in transference and countertransference. An experimental study. Int J Group Psychother 3:389–406, 1953

Loewenstein RM: Drives, Affects and Behavior. New York, International Universities Press, 1953

Logsdon A: Why primary nursing? Nurs Clin N Am 8:283–291, 1973

Lomax DE: A review of British research in teacher education. Rev Educ Res 42:289–326, 1972

London P: The Modes and Morals of Psychotherapy. New York, Holt, 1964

Long EL, Jr: Religious Beliefs of American Scientists. Philadelphia, Westminster, 1951

Loomis EA: The Self in Pilgrimage. New York, Harper & Row, 1960

Loomis EA: Religion and psychiatry, in Deutsch A. Fishman H (eds): The Encyclopedia of Mental Health. New York, Encyclopedia of Mental Health, 1963, pp 1748–1759

Lorand S: Technique of Psychoanalytic Therapy. New York, International Universities Press, 1946 (repr. 1961)

Lorand S: Persuasions, Psychodynamics and Theory. New York, Gramercy, 1956

Lorand S: Modifications in classical psychoanalysis. Psychiatr Q 32:192–204, 1963(a)

Lorand S: Present trends in psychoanalytic therapy, in Masserman JH (ed): Current Psychiatric Therapies, vol. 3. Orlando FL, Grune & Stratton, 1963(b)

Lorr M, McNair DM: Expansion of the interpersonal behaviorial circle. J Personality Soc Psychol 2:823–830, 1965

Lovibond SH: The mechanism of conditioning treatment of enuresis. Behav Res Ther 1:17–21, 1963

Lovibond SH: Aversive control of behavior. Behav Ther 1:80–91, 1970

Lovibond, SH: Current status of the field: Contrasting perspectives. The future of behavioral interventions. Recent Developments in Alcoholism 1:241–7, 1983

Low AA: Recovery, Inc, a project for rehabilitating postpsychotic and long-term psychoneurotic patients, in Soden WH (ed): Rehabilitation of the Handicapped. New York, Ronald, 1950, pp 213–226

Low AA: Mental Health Through Will-Training. Boston, Christopher, 1952

Low NL, Myers GG: Suvren in brain-injured children. J Pediatr 3:259–263, 1958

Lowen A: Physical Dynamics of Character Structure. Orlando FL, Grune & Stratton, 1958

Lowen A: The Betrayal of the Body New York, Macmillan, 1967

Lowenfeld M: The world pictures of children: A method of recording and studying them. Br J Med Psychol 18:65–101, 1939

Lowinger P, Dobie S, Reid S: What happens to the psychiatric office patient treated with drugs? A follow-up study. Paper presented at the 120th Annual Meeting of the American Psychiatric Association, Los Angeles, May 1964

Lowrey LG: Psychiatry for Social Workers. New York, Columbia University Press, 1946, pp 342–366

Lowry F: A Philosophy of Supervision in Social Case Work. New York, National Council of Social Workers, 1936, pp 108–113

Lowy S, Gutheil EA: Active analytic psychotherapy (Stekel), in Fromm-Reichmann F, Moreno J (eds): Progress in Psychotherapy. Orlando FL, Grune & Stratton, 1956, pp 136–143

Luborsky L: A note of Eysenck's article, the effects of psychotherapy: An evaluation. Br J Psychol 45:129–131, 1954

Luborsky L: Principles of Psychoanalytic Psychotherapy. A Manual for Supportive-Expressive Treatment. Philadelphia, Lippencott, 1984

Luborsky L, Mintz J, Auerbach A, et al: Predicting the outcome of psychotherapy: Findings of the Penn Psychotherapy Project. Arch Gen Psychiatry 37(4): 471–481, 1980

Luborsky L, Singer B, Luborsky L: Comparative studies of psychotherapies. Arch Gen Psychiatry 32:995–1008, 1975

Luborsky L, Woody GE, McLellan AT, et al: Can independent judges recognize different psychotherapies? An experience with manual guided therapies. J Consult Clin Psychol 50:49–62, 1982

Lucas D, et al: Group psychotherapy with depressed patients incorporating mood music. Am J Psychother 18:126–136, 1964

Luchins AS: Group structures in group psychotherapy. J Clin Psychol 3:269–273, 1947

Ludwig AM: Altered stated of consciousness. Arch Gen Psychiatry 15:225–234, 1966

Ludwig AM, Levine J: Hypnodelic therapy, in Masserman JH (ed): Current Psychiatric Therapies, vol. 7. Orlando FL, Grune & Stratton, 1967

Luff MC. Garrod M: The after-results of psychotherapy in five hundred adult cases. Br Med J 2:54–59, 1935

Lundin LH, Aranov BM: Use of co-therapists in group psychotherapy. J Consult Psychol 16:76–80, 1952

Lundin RW: Personality—An Experimental Approach. New York, Macmillan, 1961

Luthe W: Autogenic training: Method, research and application in medicine. Am J Psychother 17:174–195, 1963

Luthe W (ed): Autogenic Training. Orlando FL, Grune & Stratton, 1965

Luthe W (ed): Autogenic Therapy, vol. 1–6, Orlando FL, Grune & Stratton, 1969–1973

Luthe W, Jus A, Geissman P: Autogenic state and autogenic shift: Psychophysiologic and neurophysiologic aspects. Acta Psychother 11:1–13, 1963

Lyle J, Holly SB: The therapeutic value of puppets. Bull Menninger Clin 5:223–266, 1941

Maas H: Social casework, in Friedlander WA (ed): Concepts and Methods of Social Work. Englewood Cliffs, NJ, Prentice-Hall, 1958, pp 48–65

MacDonald JM, Daniels M: The psychiatric ward as a therapeutic community. J Nerv Ment Dis 124:148–155, 1956

MacDonald MC: (1978, March 17). A new breed: Doctor of mental health. Psychiatric News, pp. 1, 35–37

MacDonald MC: (1978, April 7). A new breed: Doctor of mental health. Psychiatric News, pp. 3, 20, 22–23

MacDonald MC: (1978, April 21). A new breed: Doctor of mental health. Psychiatric News, pp. 1, 14, 18

MacGregor R, Ritchie AM, Serrano AC, Schuster FP, Jr: Multiple Impact Therapy with Families. New York, McGraw-Hill, 1964

Machover K: Personality Projection in the Drawing of the Human Figure. Springfield, Ill, Thomas, 1948

Machover K: In Anderson HH, Anderson GL (eds): An Introduction to Projective Techniques. Englewood Cliffs, NJ, Prentice-Hall, 1951, pp 341–360

MacKay HA, Laverty SG: G.S.R. changes during therapy of phobic behavior. Unpublished manuscript. Queens University, Ontario, Canada, 1963

Mack-Brunswick R: The preoedipal phase of the libido development. Psychoanal Q 9:293–319, 1940

MacKenzie KR: An eclectic approach to phobias. Am J Psychiatry 130:1103–1106, 1973

Mackie R, Wood J: Observations on two sides of a one-way screen. Int J Group Psychother 18:177–185, 1968

MacLean JR, MacDonald DC, Bryne UP, Hubbard AM: Use of LSD-25 in the treatment of alcoholism and other psychiatric problems. Q J Stud Alcohol 22:34–45, 1961

MacLenna BW, et al: Training for new careers. Commun Ment Health J June 1966

Madanes C: Strategic Family Therapy. San Francisco, Jossey–Bass, 1981

Maddun JF, Bowden CL: Critique of success with methadone maintenance. Am J Psychiatry 129:440–446, 1972

Maddux JF: Psychiatric consultation in a public welfare agency. Am J Orthopsychiatry 20:754–764, 1950

Maddux JF: Psychiatric consultation in a rural setting. Am J Orthopsychiatry 23:775–784, 1953

Maguire GP, Goldberg DP, Hobson RF, Margison F, Moss S: Evaluating the teaching of a method of psychotherapy. Br J Psychiatry 144:575–580, 1984

Mahler MS: Mother types encountered in child guidance clinics. Am J Orthopsychiatry 11:484, 1941

Mahler MS: On child psychosis and schizophrenia. Autistic and symbiotic infantile psychoses, in Eissler R, et al (eds): The Psychoanalytic Study of the Child, vol. 7. New York, International Universities Press, 1952, pp 286–305

Mahler MS: Autism and symbiosis: Two extremes of identity. Int J Psychoanal 39:77, 1958(a)

Mahler MS: On two crucial phases of integration of the sense of identity: Separation-individuation and bisexual identity. Abstracted in Panel on problems of identity, rep Rubinfine DI. J Am Psychoanal Assoc 6:136–139, 1958(b)

Mahler MS: On human symbiosis and the vicissitudes of individuation. J Am Psychoanal Assoc 15:740–763, 1967

Mahler MS: A study of the separation-individuation process and its possible application to borderline phenomena in the psychoanalytic situation, in Eissler R, et al (eds): Psychoanalytic Study of the Child, vol. 26. New Haven, Yale University Press, 1971, pp 403–424

Mahler MS: The Selected Papers of Margaret S. Mahler. New York, Aronson, 1975

Mahler MS, Furer M: On Human Symbiosis and the Vicissitudes of Individuation. New York, International Universities Press, 1968

Mahler MS, Furer M, Settlage CF: Severe emotional disturbanced in childhood, in Arieti S (ed): American Handbook of Psychiatry, vol. 1. New York, Basic Books, 1959, pp 816–839

Mahler MS, McDevitt JB: Thoughts on the emergence of the sense of self, with particular emphasis on the body self. J Am Psychonal Assoc 30:827–848, 1982

Mahler MS, Pine F, Bergman A: The psychological birth of the human infant: Symbiosis and individuation. New York, Basic Books, 1975

Mahoney MJ: Cognition and Behavior Therapy. Cambridge, Mass, Ballinger, 1974

Main TF: The hospital as a therapeutic institution. Bull Menninger Clin 10:66–76, 1946

Majumdar SK: Introduction to Yoga—Principles and Practices. New Hyde Park, NY, University Books, 1964

Makadon HS, Gerson S, Ryback R: Managing the Care of the Difficult Patient in the Emergency Unit. JAMA 252:2535–2588, 1984

Malamud DL: Objective measurement of clinical status in psychopathological research. Psychol Bull 43:240–258, 1946

Malamud IT: Volunteers in community mental health work, Ment Hyg 39:399–309, 1959

Malan DH: A Study of Brief Psychotherapy. London, Tavistock, 1963. (rev-ed—Springfield, Ill, Thomas, 1964)

Malan DH: The outcome problem in psychotherapy research. Arch Gen Psychiatry 29:719–729, 1973

Malan DH: The Frontier of Brief Psychotherapy. New York, Plenum Press, 1976(a)

Malan DH: Toward the Validation of Dynamic Psychotherapy: A Replication. New York, Plenum Press, 1976(b)

Malan DH, Heath ES, Bacal HA, Balfour FHG: Psychodynamic changes in untreated neurotic patients. Arch Gen Psychiatry 32:110–126, 1975

Malcolm, J: In the Freud Archives. New York, Knopf, 1984

Malhotra JC: Yoga and psychiatry: A review. J Neuropsychiatry 4:375–385, 1963

Maltz M: Psycho-cybernetics. Englewood Cliffs, NJ, Prentice-Hall, 1960 (paperback—New York, Pocket Books, 1973)

Manaser JC, Werner AM: Instruments for Study of Nurse–Patient Interaction. New York, Macmillan, 1964

Mangus AR: Role theory in marriage counseling. Soc Forces 35:200–209, 1957

Mann EC: Frigidity. Clin Obstet Gynecol 3:739–759, 1960

Mann J: Encounter: A Weekend with Intimate Strangers. New York, Grossman, 1970

Mann J: Time-Limited Psychotherapy. Cambridge, Harvard University Press, 1973

Mann NM, Conway EJ, Gottesfeld BH, Lasser LM: Coordinated approach to antabuse therapy. JAMA 149:40–46, 1952

Mannino FV, MacLennan BW, Shore MF: The Practice of Mental Health Consultation. New York, Gardner, 1975

Marcovitz RJ, Smith JE: Patients' perceptions of curative factors in short-term group psychotherapy. Int J of Group Psychotherapy 33:21–39, 1983

Marcus EH: Gestalt therapy, in Masserman JH (ed): Current Psychiatric Therapies, vol. 11. Orlando FL, Grune & Stratton, 1971

Marder SR, May PRA: Benefits and limitations of neuroleptics and other forms of treatment in schizophrenia. Am J Psychother 40:357, 1986

Mark SG, Pottash AC, Sweeney DR, Kleber HD: Opiate withdrawal using clonidine. A safe, effective, and rapid nonopiate treatment. JAMA 243(4):343–346, 1980

Markowitz M: Analytic group psychotherapy of married couples by a therapist couple, in Rosenbaum S, Alger I (eds): Psychoanalysis and Marriage. New York, Basic Books, 1967

Markowitz M, Kadis A: Parental interaction as a determining factor in social growth of the individual in the family. Int J Soc Psychiatry Congress Issue, 1964

Marks I: Cure and Care of Neuroses: Theory and Practice of Behavioral Psychotherapy. New York, Wiley, 1981

Marks I, Hodgson R, Rachman S: Treatment of chornic obsessive-compulsive neurosis by in-vivo exposure. Br J Psychiatry 127:349–364, 1975

Marks IM: Management of sexual disorders, in Leitenberg H (ed): Handbook of Behavior Modification and Behavior Therapy. Englewood Cliffs, NJ, Prentice-Hall, 1976

Marks IM: Review of behavioral psychotherapy: Obsessive-compulsive disorders. Am J Psychiatry 138:584, 1981

Marks JM, Stern RS, Mawson D: Clomipramine and exposure for obsessive-compulsive rituals, 1, 11. Br J Psychiatry 136:1–25, 161–166, 1980

Marlatt GA, Gordon JR (eds): Relapse Prevention: Maintenance Strategies in the Treatment of Addictive Behaviors. New York, Guilford Press, 1985

Marmor J: Some considerations concerning orgasm in the female. Psychosom Med 16:240–245, 1954

Marmor J: Psychoanalytic therapy as an educational process: Common denominators in the therapeutic approaches of different psychoanalytic "schools," in Maserman JH (ed): Science and Psychoanalysis, vol. 5. Orlando FL, Grune & Stratton, 1962, pp 286–299

Marmor J: Sexual Inversion: The Multiple Roots of Homosexuality. New York, Basic Books, 1965

Marmor J: Theories of learning and the psychotherapeutic process. Br J Psychiatry 112:363–366, 1966

Marmor J (ed): Modern Psychoanalysis: New Directions and Perspectives. New York, Basic Books. 1968

Marmor J: Dynamic psychotherapy and behavior therapy. Arch Gen Psychiatry 24:22, 1971

Marmor J: The future of psychoanalytic therapy. Am J Psychol 130: 1197–1202, 1973(a)

Marmor J: Limitations of free association, in Psychiatry in Transition. New York, Brunner/Mazel, 1973(b) pp 265–275

Marmor J: Psychiatry in Transition: Selected Papers. New York, Brunner/Mazel, 1974

Marmor J: Recent trends in psychotherapy. Am J Psychiatry 137:409–416, 1980

Marmor J: Experiental, inspirational, cognitive/emotive and other therapies, in Karasu TB (ed): The Psychiatric Therapies. American Psychiatric Association, 1984, pp 564–579

Marohn RC: (1977) The Delinquent Adolescent (Cassette recording). Glendale, Calif: Audio-digest Foundation, vol. 6.

Marohn RC, Dalle-Molle D, McCarter E, et al: Juvenile Delinquents: Psychodynamic Assessment and Hospital Treatment. New York, Brunner/Mazel, 1980

Marsh LC: Group treatment of the psychoses by the psychological equivalent of the revival. Ment Hyg 15:328–349, 1931

Marsh LC: Group therapy and the psychiatric clinic. J Nerv Ment Dis 82:381–393, 1935

Martin AJ: LSD treatment of chronic psychoneurotic patients under day hospital conditions. Int J Soc Psychiatry 3:188, 1957

Martin AJ: LSD analysis. Int J Soc Psychiatry 10:165–169, 1964

Martin AR: A psychoanalytic contribution to the study of effort. Am J Psychoanal 4:108, 1944

Martin AR: Reassurance in therapy. Am J Psychoanal 9:17, 1949

Martin AR: The fear of relaxation and leisure. Am J Psychoanal 11:52, 1951

Martin HH: American minister. Saturday Evening Post, April 24, 1965, p 21

Martin PA, Bird HW: An approach to the psychotherapy of marriage partners: The stereoscopic technique. Psychiatry 16:123–127, 1963

Martin PA, Lief HI: Resistance to innovation in psychiatric training as exemplified by marital therapy, in Usdin G (ed): Psychiatry: Education and Image. New York, Brunner/Mazel, 1973

Martin WR, Fraser HF, Gorodetzky CW, Rosenberg DE: Studies of the dependence producing potential of the narcotic antagonist 2-cyclopropylmethyl-2'-hydroxy-5, 9-dimethyl-6, 7-benzomorphan (cyclazocine, Win 20, 740, ARCII-C3). J Pharmacol 150:426–436, 1965

Martin WR, Jasinski DR, Haertzen Ca, et al: Methadone: A reevaluation. Arch of Gen Psychiatry 28:286–295, 1973

Mason AA: Psychotherapeutic treatment of asthma. Trans World Asthma Conference, 1965, pp 89–91

Mason AA: Personal communication. 1966

Mason AS, Granacher RP: Clinical Handbook of Antipsychotic Drug Therapy. New York, Brunner/Mazel, 1930

Mason AS, Tarpy EK: Foster home preparation cottage: A transitional program for the chronic mental patient, in Masserman JH (ed): Current Psychiatric Therapies, vol. 4. Orlando FL, Grune & Stratton, 1964, pp 218–221

Mason JW: A review of psychoendocrine research on the pituitary–adrenal cortical system. Psychosom Med 30:576–607, 1968

Masserman JH: Behavior and Neurosis. Chicago, University of Chicago Press, 1943

Masserman JH: Music and the child in society. Am J Psychother 8:63–68, 1954

Masserman JH: Practice of Dynamic Psychiatry. Philadelphia, Saunders, 1955

Masserman JH (ed): Individual and Family Dynamics. Orlando FL, Grune & Stratton, 1959

Masserman JH: Principles of Dynamic Psychiatry. Philadelphia, Saunders, 1961

Masserman JH (ed): Current Psychiatric Therapies, vol. 3. Orlando FL, Grune & Stratton, 1963

Masserman JH, Carmichael HT: Diagnosis and prognosis in psychiatry. J Ment Sci 84:893–946, 1938

Masters WH, Johnson VE: A team approach to the rapid diagnosis and treatment of sexual incompatibility. Pacif Med Surg 72:371–375, 1964

Masters WH, Johnson VE: Human Sexual Response. Boston, Little, Brown, 1966

Masters WH, Johnson VE: Human Sexual Inadequacy. Boston, Little, Brown, 1970

Masterson JF: Treatment of the Borderline Adolescent: A Developmental Approach. New York, Wiley, 1972

Masterson JF: Psychotherapy of the Broderline Adult. New York, Brunner/Mazel, 1976

Matarazzo JD, Conner WE, Fey SG, et al: Behavioral cardiology with emphasis on the family heart study: Fertile ground for psychological and biomedical research, in Millon T, Green C, Meagher R (eds): Handbook of Clinical Health Psychology. New York, Plenum, 1982

Matarazzo RG: Research on the teaching and learning of psychotherapeutic skills, in Bergin A, Garfield S (eds): Handbook of Psychotherapy and Behavior Change. New York, Wiley, 1971

Matheney R, Topalis M: Psychiatric Nursing. St Louis, MO, Mosby, 1965

Mathews S: On the Effects of Music in Curing and Palliating Diseases. Philadelphia, Wagner, 1906

Mathewson RH: The role of the counselor. Harvard Educ Rev 17:10–27, 1947

Mathewson RH: Guidance, Policy and Practice. New York, Harper & Row, 1949

Matte-Blanco I: The effects of psychotherapy. Int J Psychiatry 1:163–165, 1965

Matz PB: Outcome of hospital treatment of ex-service patients with nervous and mental disease in the U.S. Veteran's Bureau. U.S. Vet Bur Med Bull 5:829–842, 1929

Maultsby M: Against technical eclecticism. Psychol Rep 22:926–928, 1968

Maultsby M: Routine tape recorder use in REI. J Rational Living 5:823, 1970

Maves PB, Cedarleaf JL: Older People and the Church. Nashville, Tenn, Abingdon, 1949

Mavissakalian M, Turner SM, Michelson L, et al: Tricyclic antidepressants in obsessive–compulsive disorder: Anti–obsessional or antidepressant agents? 11. Am J Psychiatry 142:572–567, 1985

Max LM: Conditioned reaction technique, a case study. Psychol Bull 32:734, 1935

Maxmen JS: The Post-Physician Era: Medicine in the 21st Century. New York, Wiley, 1976

Maxmen, JS, Silberfarb PM, Ferrell RB: Anorexia nervosa. JAMA 229:801–803, 1974

May PRA: Treatment of Schizophrenia. New York, Science House, 1968

May PRA: For better or worse? Psychotherapy and variance change: A critical review of the literature. J Nerv Ment Dis 152:184–192, 1971

May R: The Meaning of Anxiety. New York, Ronald, 1950

May R: The nature of creativity, in Anderson HH (ed): Creativity and Its Cultivation. New York, Harper & Row 1959

May R: Existential bases of psychotherapy. Am J Orthopsychiatry 30, October 1960

May R, et al (eds): Existence. New York, Basic Books, 1958

May R, Van Kaam A: Existential theory and therapy, in Masserman JH (ed): Current Psychiatric Therapies, vol. 3. New York, Grune & Stratton, 1963

Mayeroff M: On Caring. New York, Harper & Row, 1971

McCabe OL: Psychodelic (LSD) psychotherapy: A case report. Psychother: Theory Res Prac 11:2–10, 1974

McCabe OL, Savage C, Kurland AA, Unger S: Psychedelic (LSD) therapy of neurotic disorders: Short-term effects. J Psychedelic Drugs 5:18–28, 1972

McCann RV: The Churches and Mental Health. New York, Basic Books, 1962

McCarthy BW: A modification of Masters and Johnson sex therapy model in a clinical setting. Psychother: Theory Res Prac 10:290–293, 1973

McCawley A: A double-bind evaluation of nomifensine and imipramine in depressed patients. Am J Psychiatry 136:841–843, 1979

McConaghy N: Aversion therapy of homosexuality, in Masserman JH (ed): Current Psychiatric Therapies, vol. 12. Orlando FL, Grune & Stratton, 1972

McCrady BS: Conjoint behavioral treatment of an alcoholic and his spouse, in Hay WH, Nathan PE (eds): Clinical Case Studies in the Behavioral Treatment of Alcoholism. New York, Plenum, 1982

McCrady BS: Alcoholism, in Barlow D (ed): Clinical Handbook of Psychological Disorders. New York, Guilford Press, 1985, pp 462–501

McDonald E: The masking function of self-revelation in group therapy. Int J Group Psychother 1:59–63, 1951

McGlashan TH: Intensive individual psychotherapy of schizophrenia. Arch Gen Psychiatry 40:909–920, 1983

McGovern WM: An Introduction to Mahayana Buddhism, with Especial References to Chinese and Japanese Phases. London, Routledge & Kegan, 1922

McGovern WM: A Manual of Buddhist Philosophy. London, Routledge & Kegan, 1923

McGrath JE (ed): Social and Psychological Factors in Stress. New York: Holt, Rinehart and Winston, 1970

McGrath JE: Settings, measures and Themes: An integrative review of some research on social-psychological factors in stress. In Monat A, Lazarus RS (eds): Stress and Coping. New York: Columbia University Press, 1977, pp 67–76

McGraw RB, Oliven JF: Miscellaneous therapies, in Arieti S (ed): American Handbook of Psychiatry. New York, Basic Books, 1959

McGregor HG: Enuresis in children. Br Med J 1:1061–1066, 1937

McGuire C: Teaching of psychotherapy. Paper presented at the Postgraduate Center for Mental Health, New York, November 1964

McGuire MT: The instruction nature of short-term insight psychotherapy. Am J Psychother 22:218–232, 1968

McGuire RJ, Vallance M: Aversion therapy by electric shock: A simple technique. Br Med J 1:151–153, 1964

McIntosh JR, Pickford RW: Some clinical and artistic aspects of a child's drawings. Br J Med Psychol 19:342–362, 1943

McKinley DA, Jr. et al: Architecture for the Community Mental Health Center. NIMH School of Architecture, Rice University, 1966. Available from the Mental Health Materials Center, New York, NY

McKinney F: Explorations in bibliotherapy. Psychother: Theory, Res Prac 12:110–117, 1975

McLean A: Occupational Stress. Springfield, Charles C. Thomas, 1974

McLean P: Psychiatry and philosophy, in Arieti S (ed): American Handbook of Psychiatry. New York, Basic Books, 1959

McLean PD, Hakstian AR: Clinical depression: comparative efficacy of outpatient treatments. J Consult Clin Psychol 47:818–836, 1979

McLellan AT, Luborsky L, O'Brien CP, Woody GE, Druley KA: Is treatment for substance abuse effective? JAMA 143: 1423–1428, 1982

McLellan AT, Luborsky L, Woody GE et al: Predicting response to alcohol and drug abuse treatments. Role of psychiatric severity. Arch Gen Psychiatry 40:620–625, 1983

McNeill J: History of the Cure of Souls. New York, Harper & Row, 1951

McNemar A: Psychological Statistics. New York, Wiley, 1949

McReynolds P, DeVoge S: Use of Improvisational Techniques in Assessment, vol. 4. San Francisco, Jossey–Bass, 1977

Meacham ML, Wiesen AE: Changing Classroom Behavior: A Manual for Precision Teaching (2d ed). New York, IEP, 1974

Mead GH: Mind, Self and Society. Chicago, University of Chicago Press, 1934

Mead M: From the South Seas. New York, Morrow, 1939

Mead M: Sex and Temperament. New York, Mentor, 1952

Meador BD: Client-centered group therapy, in Gazda GM (ed): Counseling and Group Psychotherapy (rev ed). Springfield, Ill, Thomas, 1975

Mebane JC: Use of Deanol with disturbed juvenile offenders. Dis Nerv Syst 21:642, 1960

Medical news: Value of antidepressant drugs over other therapy questioned, 190:37, 1964

Medical News: JAMA 252:1385–1392, 1984

Medical Society of County of NY: The dangerous drug problem. NY State J Med 66:241–246, 1966

Medical Tribune: 130 cases of spontaneous cancer regression surveyed. 4(92), November 18, 1963

Medical Tribune: Ralph Nader organization attacks mental health centers. 13:1, 1972

Medical World News: Shocking device for bed-wetters, May 12, 1972

Medical World News: Sex counseling and the primary physician. March 2, 1973

Meduna LJ: Carbon Dioxide Therapy. A Neurophysiological Treatment of Nervous Disorders. Springfield, Ill, Thomas, 1950

Meduna LJ: Physiological background of carbon dioxide treatment of the neuroses. Paper presented at the 109th Annual Meeting of the American Psychiatric Association, Los Angeles, May 7, 1953

Meehl PE: Psychopathology and purpose, in Hoch PH, Zubin J (eds): The Future of Psychiatry. Orlando FL, Grune & Stratton, 1962

Meehl PE: The effects of psychotherapy. Int J Psychiatry 1:156–157, 1965

Meerloo AM: Transference and resistance in geriatric psychotherapy. Psychoanal Rev 42:72–82, 1955

Meichenbaum D, Turk D, Burstein S: Nature of coping with stress, in Sarason IG, Spielberger CD (eds); Stress and Anxiety, vol. 2. New York, Wiley, 1975, pp 337–360

Meichenbaum DH: Examination of model characteristics in reducing avoidance behavior.

J Personality Soc Psychol 17:298–307, 1971

Meichenbaum DH: Cognitive Behavior Modification. New York, Plenum, 1977

Meichenbaum DH, Cameron R: The clinical potential of modifying what clients pay to themselves. Psychother Theory Res Prac 11:103–117, 1974

Meichenbaum DH, Goodman J: Training impulsive children to talk to themselves: A means of developing self-control. J Abnorm Psychol 77(2), pp 115–126, 1971

Meier EG: Social and cultural factors in casework diagnosis. Soc Casework 41:15–26

Meijering WL: The interrelation of individual, group, and hospital community psychotherapy. Int J Group Psychother 10:46–62, 1960

Meissner JH: The relationship between voluntary nonfluency and stuttering. J Speech Dis 11:13–33, 1946

Meissner WW: Annotated Bibliography in Religion and Psychology. New York, Academy of Religion and Mental Health, 1961

Meissner WW: The conceptualization of marriage and family dynamics from a psychoanalytic perspective, in Paolino TJ, McGrady BS (eds): Marriage and Family Therapy. New York, Brunner/Mazel, 1978

Melamed BG, Siegel LJ: Reduction of anxiety in children facing hospitalization and surgery by use of filmed modeling. J Consult Psychol 43:511–521, 1975

Melamed BG, Siegel LJ: Behavioral Medicine: Practical Applications in Health Care. New York, Springer, 1980

Meldman MH, Harris D, Pellicore RJ, Johnson EL: A computer assisted, goal oriented psychiatric progress note system. Am J Psychiatry 134:38–41, 1977

Meletsky BM: Self–referred versus court–referred sexually deviant patients: Success with assisted covert sensitization. Behavior Therapy 11:306–314, 1980

Melnick J, Tims AR: Application of videotape equipment to group therapy. Int J Group Psychother 24:199–205, 1974

Meltzer D: The Psychoanalytic Process. Perth, Scot, Clunie, 1973(a)

Meltzer D: Sexual States of Mind. Perth, Scot, Clunie, 1973(b)

Meltzer D: Explorations in Autism. Perth, Scot, Clunie, 1975

Mendell D: Discussion, in Death and Dying: Attitudes of Patient and Doctor. GAP Symposium No. 11, 1965, p 649

Mendelson D: Patient's prior expectation and discrepancies between expectation and actual perception of psychotherapy as factors in session absences. Unpublished doctural dissertation, Postgraduate Center for Mental Health, New York, 1973

Mennell JB: Physical Treatment by Movement, Manipulation and Massage (5th ed). Philadelphia, Blakiston, 1945

Menninger KA: Religious applications of psychiatry. Pastoral Couns 1:13–22, 1950

Menninger KA: What are the goals of psychiatric education? Bull Menninger Clin 16:156, 1952(a)

Menninger KA: A Manual for Psychiatric Case Study. Orlando FL, Grune & Stratton, 1952(b)

Menninger KA: Theory of Psychoanalytic Technique. New York, Basic Books, 1958; 1961

Menninger KA, Holzman PS: Theory of Psychoanalytic Technique (2d ed). New York, Basic Books, 1973

Menninger RW: Observations on absences of member patients in group psychotherapy. Int J Group Psychother 9:195–203, 1949

Menninger WC: Psychiatric social work in the army and its implications for civilian social work. Proceedings of the National Conference of Social Work, 1945

Menninger WC: Psychiatry and religion. Pastoral Psychol 1:14–16, 1950

Mental Hygiene Committee, National Organization of Public Health Nursing: Nurse as a mental health consultant: Functions and qualifications. Pub Health Nurs 42:507–509, 1950

Mereness D: The psychiatric nursing specialist and her professional identity. Perspect Psychiatr Care 1:18–19, 1963(a) 18–19

Mereness D: The potential significant role of the nurse in community mental health services. Perspect Psychiatr Care 1:34–40, 1963(b)

Mereness D: Problems and issues in contemporary psychiatric nursing. Perspect Psychiatr Care 2:14–21, 1964

Mergenthaler E: Textbook Systems: Computer Science Applied in the Field of Psychoanalysis. New York, Springer-Verlag, 1985

Merlis S, Beyel V, Fiorentino D, et al: Polypharmacy in psychiatry: Empiricism, efficacy, and rationale, in Masserman JH (ed): Current Psychiatric Therapies, vol. 12. Orlando FL, Grune & Stratton, 1972

Merrill S, Cary GL: Dream analysis in brief psychotherapy. Am J Psychother 29:185–193, 1975

Merry J, Reynolds CM, Bailey J, et al: Prophylactic treatment of alcoholism by lithium carbonate: A controlled study. Lancet 2:486–488, 1976

Mesnikoff AM: Ward group projects as a focus

for dynamic milieu therapy. NY State J Med 60:2395–2399, 1960

Meyer A: Objective psychology and psychobiology. JAMA 65:860–863, 1915

Meyer A: The philosophy of occupational therapy. Archives Occup Ther 1:1–10, 1922

Meyer A: The Commonsense Psychiatry of Dr. Adolf Meyer. New York, McGraw-Hill, 1948

Meyer E, Spiro HR, Slaughter R, et al: Contractually time-limited psychotherapy in an outpatient psychotherapy clinic. Am J Psychiatry 124 (Suppl):57–68, 1967

Meyer HJ, Borgatta EF: An Experiment in Mental Patient Rehabilitation. New York, Russel Sage Foundation, 1959

Meyerson A: Effect of benzedrine sulphate on mood and fatigue in normal and neurotic persons. Arch Neurol Psychiatry 36:816, 1936

Michaels J: Character structure and character disorders, in Arieti S (ed): American Handbook of Psychiatry, vol. 1. New York, Basic Books, 1959, pp 365–366

Michels R: Summation, in Meyers JM (ed): Cures by psychotherapy: What effects change? New York, Praeger, 1984

Midelfort CF: The Family in Psychotherapy. New York, McGraw-Hill, 1957

Miel J: "Jacques Lacan and the structure of the unconscious." Yale French Studies, 1966, pp 104–111

Miel J: Jacques Lacan and the structure of the unconscious, in Ehrmann J (ed): Structuralism. Garden City, Mich, Anchor Books, 1970, pp 94–100

Migler B, Wolpe J: Automated desensitization: A case report. Behav Res Ther 5:133–135, 1967

Milbank Memorial Fund: The Elements of a Community Mental Health Program. New York, the Fund, 1956

Milbank Memorial Fund: Programs for Community Mental Health. New York, the Fund, 1957

Milbank Memorial Fund: Progress and Problems of Community Mental Health Services. New York, the Fund, 1959

Miles H, Barrabee EL, Finesinger JE: Evaluation of psychotherapy. Psychosom Med 113:83–105, 1951

Miller D: Adolescence: Psychology, Psychopathology and Psychotherapy. New York, Aronson, 1974

Miller EC, Dvorak A, Turner DW: A method of creating aversion to alcohol by reflex conditioning in a group setting. Q J Stud Alcohol

21:424–431, 1960. Also in Franks CM (ed): Conditioning Techniques in Clinical Practice and Research. New York, Springer, 1964, pp 157–164

Miller JG: Elements in the Medical Curriculum Which Should be Incorporated in the Training of the Clinical Psychologist. Transactions of the First Conference. New York, Josiah Macy, Jr, Foundation, 1947, pp 41–46

Miller JG: Criteria and measurement of changes during psychiatric treatment. Bull Menninger Clin 18:130–137, 1954

Miller NE: Biofeedback and visceral learning. Annual Rev Psychology 29:373–404, 1978

Miller NE: Behavioral medicine: Symbiosis between laboratory and clinic. Annual Review of Psychology 34:1–31, 1983

Miller PM: Behavioral Treatment of Alcoholism. New York, Pergamon Press, 1976

Miller PM: Behavioral treatment of binge drinking, in Hay WM, Nathan PE (eds): Clinical Case Studies in the Behavioral Treatment of Alcoholism. New York, Plenum, 1982

Miller PM, Eisler RM: Assertive behavior of alcoholics: A descriptive analysis. Beh Ther 8:146–149, 1977

Miller PM, Mastria MA: Alternatives to Alcohol Abuse: A social Learning Model. Champaign, Ill. Research Press, 1977

Miller WB: The telephone in outpatient psychotherapy. Am J Psychother 27:15–26, 1972

Miller WR: Behavioral training in the treatment of problem drinkers, in Stuart RB (ed): Behavioral Self–Management: Strategies, Techniques, and Outcome. New York, Brunner/Mazel, 1977

Miller WR, Rosellini RA, Seligman MEP: Learned helplessness and depression, in Maser JD, Seligman MEP (eds): Psychopathology: Experimental Models. San Francisco, Freeman, 1977

Miller WR, Taylor CA, West JC: Focus versus broad spectrum behavior therapy for problem drinkers. J Consult Clin Psychology 48:590–601, 1980

Miller EC, Dvorak H, Turner DW: A method of creating aversion to alcohol by reflex conditioning in a group setting. Q J Stud Alcohol 21:424–431, 1960

Mills Report: Bull Assoc Am Med Coll 6:62, 1971

Minkowski E: Lived Time: Phenomenological and Psychopathological Studies. Nancy Metzel (trans). Evanston, Ill, Northwestern University Press, 1970

Mintz EE: Time-extended marathon groups. Psychother: Theory Res Prac 4:65–70, 1967

Mintz EE: Marathon Groups, Reality and Symbol. New York, Appleton-Century-Crofts, 1971

Mintz EE: On the rationale of touch in psychotherapy, in Sager CJ, Kaplan HS (eds): Progress in Group and Family Therapy. New York, Brunner/Mazel, 1972, pp 151–155

Mintz EE: On the dramatization of psychoanalytic interpretations, in Wolberg LR, Aronson ML (eds): Group Therapy 1974: An Overview. Orlando FL, Stratton Intercontinental, 1974, pp 175–185

Mintz J, Luborsky L, Christoph P: Measuring the outcome of psychotherapy: Findings of the Penn Psychotherapy Project. J Consult Clin Psychol 47:319, 1979

Mintz NL, Schwartz DT: urban ecology and psychosis. Int J Soc Psychiatry 10:101–119, 1964

Minuchin S: Conflict-resolution family therapy. Psychiatry 28:278–286, 1965

Minuchin S: Families and Family Therapy. Cambridge, Harvard University Press, 1974(a)

Minuchin S: Structural family therapy, in Arieti S (ed): American Handbook of Psychiatry, vol. 2 (2d ed). New York, Basic Books, 1974(b), pp 178–192

Minuchin S: Families and Family Therapy Techniques. Cambridge, Harvard University Press, 1981

Minuchin S, Fishman HC: Family Therapy Techniques. Cambridge, Harvard University Press, 1981

Minuchin S, Montalvo B: Techniques for working with disorganized low socioeconomic families. Am J Orthopsychiatry 37:880–887, 1967

Mira E: Myokinetic psychodiagnosis: A new technique for exploring the conative trends of personality. Proc Roy Soc Med 33:9–30, 1940

Mischel W: On the future of personality research. Am Psychol 32:246–254, 1977

Misiak H, Sexton VS: History of Psychology: An Overview. Orlando FL, Grune & Stratton, 1966

Misselt A: Implementation and Operation of Computer Based Education, MTC Report No 25, Final Report. Urbana, University of Illinois Computer Based Research Lab, 1980

Missildine WH: Your Inner Child of the Past. New York, Simon & Schuster, 1963

Mitchell C: Family interviewing in family diagnosis. Soc Casework 40:381–384, 1959

Mitchell HE: Application of the Kaiser method to parital pairs. Fam Process 2:265–279, 1963

Mitchell KB: Do pastoral counselors bring a new consciousness to the health professions? J Pastoral Care 26:245, 1972

Mitchell TW: Problems in Psychopathology. Orlando FL, Harcourt, 1927

Mittelman B: Complementary neurotic reactions in intimate relationships. Psychoanal Q 13:491–497, 1944

Mittelman B: The concurrent analysis of married couples. Psychoanal Q 17:182–197, 1948(a)

Mittelman B: Failures in psychosomatic case treatments, in Hoch P (ed): Failures in Psychiatric Treatment. Orlando FL, Grune & Stratton, 1948(b) pp 106–117

Mittelman B: Analysis of reciprocal neurotic patterns, in Family Relationships. New York, Basic Books, 1956

Modell W: The Relief of Symptoms. Philadelphia, Saunders, 1955

Moench LG: Office Psychiatry. Chicago, Year Book Publishing, 1952

Monahan J: The Clinical Prediction of Violent Behavior. Rockville, Md, NIMH, 1981

Money-Kyrle RE: Man's Picture of His World. New York, International Universities Press, 1961

Montgomery GT, Crowder JE: The symptom substitution hypothesis and the evidence. Psychother: Theory Res Prac 9:98–102, 1972

Moore FJ, Chernell E, West MJ: Television as a therapeutic tool. Gen Psychiatry 12:217–220, 1965

Moore GE: Some Main Problems of Philosophy. New York, Macmillan, 1953

Moos RH, Kopell BS, Melges FT, Yalom ID, et al: Fluctuations in symptoms and moods during the menstrual cycle. J Psychosom Res 13(1):37–44, 1969

Moos RH, Yalom ID: Medical students' attitudes toward psychiatry and psychiatrists. Men Hy 50(2):246–56, 1966

Moreno JL: Who Shall Survive? Washington, DC, Nervous & Mental Disease Publishing Co, 1934

Moreno JL: Psychodrama, vol. 1. Beacon, NY, Beacon House, 1946

Moreno JL: The First Book on Group Psychotherapy (3d ed). Beacon, NY, Beacon House, 1957

Moreno JL: Introduction. Psychodrama, vol. 1 (3d ed). Beacon, NY, Beacon House, 1964

Moreno JL: Psychotherapie de Group. Paris, Presse Universitaire de France, 1965, pp 169–180

Moreno JL: Therapeutic aspects of psychodrama. Psychiatr Op 3:36–42, 1966(a)

Moreno JL (ed): The International Handbook of Group Psychotherapy. New York, Philosophical Library, 1966(b)

Moreno ZT: Psychodramatic rules, techniques and adjunctive methods. Group Psychother 18:73–86, 1965

Morgan DW: Enhancing supervision of psychotherapy. Southern Med J 77:1406–1409, 1984

Morgenthau HJ: Death in the nuclear age. Commentary 32:231–234, 1961

Morris RD: The essential meaning of clinical pastoral training, in Hiltner S (ed): Clinical Pastoral Training. New York, Federal Council of Churches of Christ in America, 1945

Morrison GC (ed): Emergencies in Child Psychiatry. Springfield, Ill, Charles C. Thomas, 1975

Morrison JK, Layton D, Newman J: Ethical conflict in decision making, in Hansen JC, L'Abate L (eds): Values, Ethics, Legalities and the Family Therapist. Rockville, Md, Aspen Systems, 1982

Morse PW. Gessay LH, Karpe R: The effect of group psychotherapy in reducing resistance to individual psychotherapy. A case study. Int J Group Psychother 5:261–269, 1955

Mosher LR, Feinsilver RD: Current studies on schizophrenia. Int J Psychiatry 11:7–52, 1973

Moss CS: The Hypnotic Investigation of Dreams. New York, Wiley, 1967

Moss CS, Bremer B: Exposure of a "medical modeler" to behavior modification. Int J Clin Exp Hypn 21:1–12, 1973

Mosse EP: Painting-analysis in the treatment of neuroses. Psychoanal Rev 27:65–82, 1940

Moulton R: Multiple dimensions in supervision. Contemp Psychol 5:151–158, 1969

Mowrer OH: Learning Theory and Personality Dynamics. New York, Ronald, 1950

Mowrer OH: Anxiety theory as a basis for distinguishing between counseling and psychotherapy, in Berdie RF (ed): Concepts and Progress of Counseling. Minneapolis, University of Minnesota Press, 1953

Mowrer OH, Mowrer WM: A new method for the study and treatment of enuresis. Psychol Bull 33:611–612, 1936

Mowrer OH, Mowrer WM: Enuresis—a method

for its study and treatment. Am J Orthopsychiatry 8:436–457, 1938

Mueller EE: Rebels with a cause. Am J Psychother 18:272–284, 1964

Muench GA: An investigation of the efficiency of time-limited psychotherapy. J Counsel Psychol 12:294–299, 1965

Muench GA, Schumacher R: A clinical experiment with rotational time-limited psychotherapy. Psychother: Theory Res Prac 5:81–84, 1968

Mulac MD: Educational Games for Fun. New York, Harper & Row, 1971

Mullahy P: Harry Stack Sullivan's theory of schizophrenia. Int J Psychiatry 4:492–521, 1967

Mullahy P: Psychoanalysis and Interpersonal Psychiatry. New York, Science House, 1968

Mullahy PF: Harry Stack Sullivan, in Kaplan HI, Freedman AM, Sadock BJ (eds): Comprehensive Textbook of Psychiatry (3d ed). Baltimore, Williams & Wilkins, 1980

Mullan H: Conflict avoidance in group psychotherapy. Int J Group Psychother 3:243, 1953(a)

Mullan H: Countertransference in groups. Am J Psychother 7:680, 1953(b)

Mullan H: Transference and countertransference. New Horizon. Int J Group Psychother 5:169–180, 1955

Mullan H: Group Psychotherapy, Theory and Practice. With Rosenbaum M. New York, Free Press, 1962

Mullan H, Sangiuliano IA: Interpretation as existence in analysis. Psychoanal Rev 45:52–64, 1958

Muller JD: Cognitive psychology and the ego: Lacanian theory and empirical research. Psychoanal & Contemp Thought 5:257–291, 1982

Muller JP: Lacan's mirror stage. Psychoanal Inquiry 5(2):233–252, 1985

Muller TG: The Nature and Direction of Psychiatric Nursing. Philadelphia, Lippincott, 1950

Muller-Hegemann D: The effects of psychotherapy. Int J Psychiatry 1:157–158, 1965

Mumford E, Schlesinger HJ, Glass GV: The effects of psychological intervention on recovery from surgery and heart attacks: An analysis of the data. Am J Public Health 72:141–151, 1982

Mumford E, Schlesinger HJ, Glass GV, Patrick C, Cuerdon T: A new look at evidence about reduced cost of medical utilization following mental health treatment. Am J Psychiatry 141(10):1145–1158, 1984

Muncie W: Psychobiology and Psychiatry (2d ed). St Louis, MO, Mosby, 1948

Muncie W: The psychobiologic approach, in Arieti S (ed): American Handbook of Psychiatry, vol. 2. New York, Basic Books, 1959, p 1326

Muncie W: Personal communication, 1976

Munetz MR, Roth LH: Informing patients about tardive dyskinesia. Archives of Gen Psychiatry 42:866–969, 1985

Munster AJ, Stanley AM, Saunders JC: Imipramine (tofranil) in the treatment of enuresis. Am J Psychiatry 118:76, 1961

Munzer J: The effect on analytic therapy groups of the experimental introduction of special "warm-up" procedures during the first five sessions. Int J Group Psychother 14:60, 1964

Muro JJ: Play media in counseling: A brief report on experience and some opinions. Elem School Guide Counsel 3:104–110, 1968

Murphy G: Personality: A Biosocial Approach to Origins and Structure. New York, Harper, 1947

Murphy G: Human Potentialities. Baltimore, Penguin Books, 1975

Murphy LB: Personality in Young Children. Vol. 1, Methods for the Study of Personality in Young Children. New York, Basic Books, 1956

Murphy LB: Adaptional tasks in childhood in our culture. Bull Menninger Clin 28:309–322, 1964

Murphy M: The Social Group Work Method in Social Work Education. Vol. 2, A Project Report of the Curriculum Study, Werner W Boehm, Director and Coordinator. New York, Council on Social Work Education, 1959

Murray DC: The suicide threat: Base rates and appropriate therapeutic strategy. Psychother: Theory Res Prac 9:176–179, 1972

Murray EJ: A content-analysis method for studying psychotherapy. Psychol Monogr 70, No. 14 (Whole No. 420), 1956

Murray EJ, Cohen M: Mental Illness, milieu therapy and social organization in ward groups. J Abnorm Soc Psychol 58:48–55, 1959

Murray HA: Explorations in Personality. London, Oxford University Press, 1938, pp 530–545

Murray RA: Automated educational and vocational guidance system, in Schwartz MD (ed): Using Computers in Clinical Practice. New York, The Haworth Press, 1984, pp 387–392

Murray VF, Burns MM: The use of sodium amytal in the treatment of psychosis. Psychiatr Q 6:273, 1932

Muscatenc LC: Principles of group psychotherapy and psychodrama as applied to music therapy. Int J Group Psychother 14:176–185, 1961

Mussen PH, Conger JJ: Child Development and Personality. New York, Harper & Row, 1956

Muth LT: Aftercare for the Mentally Ill: A World Picture. Philadelphia, Smith, Kline & French labs, 1957

Muthard JE, et al: Guide to Information Centers in the Social Services. Gainesville, Regional Rehabilitation Research Institute, University of Florida, 1971

Myers ES: National health insurance: Prospects and problems. Psychiatr Ann 4:17, 1974

Myerson A: Effect of benzedrine sulphate on mood and fatigue in normal and neurotic persons. Arch Neurol Psychiatry 36:816, 1936

Myrick RD, Moni LS: The counselor's workshop. Elem School Guid Counsel 6:202–295, 1972

Nacht S: Technical remarks on the handling of the transference neuroses. Int J Psychoanal 38:196–203, 1957

Nacht S: Variations in techniques. Int J Psychoanal 39:2352–237, 1958

Napier A, Whitaker CA: The Family Crucible. New York, Harper & Row, 1978

Napoli PJ: Finger-painting and personality diagnosis. Genet Psychol Monogr 34, No. 2, 1946

Napoli PJ: Interpretive aspects of fingerpainting. J Psychol 23:93–132, 1947

Naranjo C: Contributions of gestalt therapy, in Otto H, Mann J (eds): Ways of Growth. New York, Pocket Books, 1971

Nash EM, Jessner L, Abse DW (eds): Marriage Counseling in Medical Practice. Chapel Hill, University of North Carolina Press, 1964

Nathan PE, Goldman MS: Problem drinking and alcoholism, in Pomerleau OF, Brady JP (eds): Behavioral Medicine: Theory and Practice. Baltimore, Williams & Wilkins, 1979

Nathan PE, Marlatt GA (eds): Experimental and Behavioral Approaches to Alcoholism. New York, Plenum, 1978

National Commission on the Protection of Human Subjects of Biomedical and Behavioral Research. Appendix DHEW Publication No (OS) 77–0002. Washington, DC, U.S. Government Printing Office, 1977

National Association for Mental Health (NAMH): The Mental Health Association in Planning for Comprehensive Community Mental Health Services, Sixth Annual Mental Health Association Staff Council Institute. New York, the Association, 1963(a)

National Association for Mental Health: The Mental Health Services, Seventh Annual Mental Health Association Summer Staff Training Institute. New York, the Association, 1963(b)

National Institute of Mental Health (NIMH): Planning of Facilities for Mental Health Services. Washington, DC, U.S. Government Printing Office, 1961

National Institute of Mental Health, Surgeon General's Ad Hoc Committee on Mental Health Activities: Mental Health Activities and the Development of Comprehensive Health Programs in the Community. Department Pub Health Service Publ No. 995. Bethesda, Md, the Institute, 1962

National Institute of Mental Health: Mental Health and Social Change: An Annotated Bibliography. DHEW Publ No. (HSM) 72–9149, 1967–1970. Washington, DC, U.S. Government Printing Office, 1970

National Institute of Mental Health: Community Mental Health Center Program: Operating Manual. Washington, DC, U.S. Government Printing Office, 1971

National Institute of Mental Health: Mental Health Consultation to Programs for Children. DHEW Publ No. (HSM) 72–9088. Washington, DC, U.S. Government Printing Office, 1972

National Institute of Mental Health: NIMH: Promoting Mental Health in the Classroom. DHEW Publ No. (HSMO) 73–9033. Washington, DC, U.S. Government Printing Office, 1973

National Institute of Mental Health (NIMH) Clinical Research Branch and Temple University: Proceedings of Conference on ECT. Efficacy and Impact. New Orleans, 1978

Naumburg M: The drawings of an adolescent girl suffering from conversion hysteria with amnesia. Psychiatr Q 18:197–224, 1944

Naumburg M: Studies of the "Free" Art Expression of Behavior Problem Children and Adolescents as a Means of Diagnosis and

Therapy. Monogr No. 71. Washington, DC, Nervous & Mental Disease Publishing Co, 1947

Naumburg M: Schizophrenic Art: Its Meaning in Psychotherapy. Orlando FL, Grune & Stratton, 1950

Naumburg M: Psychoneurotic Art: Its Use in Psychotherapy. Orlando FL, Grune & Stratton, 1953

Naumburg M: Dynamically Oriented Art Therapy: Its Principles and Practice. Orlando FL, Grune & Stratton, 1966

Naumburg M: Dynamically oriented art therapy, in Masserman JH (ed): Current Psychiatric Therapies, vol. 7. Orlando FL, Grune & Stratton, 1967

Naumburg M, Caldwell J: The use of spontaneous art in dynamically oriented group therapy of obese women. Acta Psychother 7:254–287, 1959

Nelson RC: Pros and cons of using play media in counseling. Elem School Guid Counsel 2:143–147, 1967

Nemiah JC: The psychological management and treatment of patients with peptic ulcer, in Weiner H (ed): Advances in Psychosomatic Medicine, vol. 6. Basel, Switz, Karger, 1971, pp 169–185

Nemiah JC: Psychoanalysis and individual psychotherapy, in Karasu TB (ed): The Psychiatric Therapies, Washington, DC, American Psychiatric Association, 1984, p 324

Nemiah JC: Obsessive-compulsive disorder, in Kaplan HI, Sadock BJ (eds): Comprehensive Textbook of Psychiatry IV, (4th ed). Baltimore, Williams & Wilkins, 1985, pp 904–917

Neufeld W: Relaxation methods in United States Navy air schools. Am J Psychiatry 108: 132–137, 1951

Newman FL, Rinkus AJ: Level of functioning, clinical judgment and mental health services. Evaluation and the Health Professions 1:175, 1978

Newman RG: Methadone maintenance treatment. NY State J Med 76(9):1536–1537, 1976

New York State Counselors Association: Practical Handbook for Counselors. Palo Alto, Calif, Science Research Associates, 1945

New York Times: Growth of community mental health in reducing the number of patients in hospitals. July 30, 1972

Nicholls G: Treatment of a disturbed mother-child relationship: A case presentation, in Parad HJ (ed): Ego Psychology and Dynamic Casework. New York, Family Service Association of America, 1958, pp 117–125

Nichols LA: The presentation and diagnosis of impotence in general practice. Coll Gen Practit 4:72–87, 1961

Nickerson ET: Recent trends and innovations in play therapy. Int J Child Psychother 2:53–70, 1973

Nickerson ET: Bibliotherapy: A therapeutic medium for helping children. Psychother: Theory Res Prac 12:258–261, 1975

Nictern S, Donahue GT, O'Shea J, et al: A community educational program for the emotionally disturbed child. Am J Orthopsychiatry 34:705–713, 1964

Niebuhr HR, William DD, Gustafson AM: The Advancement of Theological Education, New York, Harper & Row, 1957

Niebuhr R: The Self and the Dramas of History. New York, Scribber, 1955

Nordoff P, Robbins C: Creative Music Therapy. New York, John Day Co, 1977

Norris CM: The trend toward community mental health centers. Perspect Psychiatr Care, January–February: 36–40, 1963

North Central Association of Colleges and Secondary Schools: General Education in the American High School. Chicago, Ill, Scott Foresman, 1942, p 12

North EF: Day care treatment of psychotic children, in Masserman JH (ed): Current Psychiatric Therapies, vol. 7. Orlando FL, Grune & Stratton, 1967

Noshpitz J: Opening phase in the psychotherapy of adolescents with character disorders. Bull Menninger Clin 21:53, 1957

Noshpitz J: Youth pervades half-way house, at NIMH. Ment Hosp 10:25–30, 1959

Noshpitz J: Residential treatment of emotionally disturbed children, in Arieti S (ed): American Handbook of Psychiatry, vol. New York, Basic Books, 1975, pp 634–651

Noshpitz, JD: The psychotherapist in residential treatment, in Mayer MF, Blum A (eds): Healing Through Living. Springfield, Ill, Charles C. Thomas, 1971

Noshpitz JD, Shapiro T, Sherman M, Oldham JM, Lazarus LW, Newton NA: Milieu Therapy, in Karasu TB (ed): The Psychiatric Therapies. Washington, DC, American Psychiatric Association, 1984

Noyes AP, Haydon EM, van Sickel M: Textbook of Psychiatric Nursing. New York, Macmillan, 1964

Noyes AP, Kolb LS: Modern Clinical Psychiatry. Philadelphia, Saunders, 1963

Nunberg H: Practice and theory of psychoanalysis. Nerv Ment Dis Monogr No. 74, 1948

Nunberg H: Principles of Psychoanalysis. New York, International Universities Press, 1955

Nunberg H: Practice and Theory of Psychoanalysis. New York, International Universities Press, 1961

Nunnally J: The communication of mental health information. Behav Sci 2:222–230, 1957

Nyswander M: The Drug Addict as a Patient. Orlando FL, Grune & Stratton, 1956

Oates WE: Religious Factors in Mental Illness. New York, Association Press, 1955

Oates WE: Protestant Pastoral Counseling. Philadelphia, Westminster, 1962

Oates WE: Association of pastoral counselors; its values and its dangers. Pastoral Psychol 15:5–7, 1964

Oates WE: Do pastoral counselors bring a new consciousness to the health professions? J Pastoral Care 26:255–257, 1972

Oates WE, Neely K: Where to Go For Help. Revised enlarged edition. Philadelphia, Westminster, 1972

Oberndorf CP: Psychoanalysis of married couples. Psychoanal Rev 25:453–475, 1938

Oberndorf CP: Consideration of results with psychoanalytic therapy. Am J Psychiatry 99:374–381, 1942

Oberndorf CP, Greenacre P, Kubie LS: Symposium on the evaluation of therapeutic results. Int J Psychoanal 29:7–33, 1948

O'Connor JF, Daniels G, Karush A, et al: The effects of psychotherapy on the course of ulcerative colitis: A preliminary report. Am J Psychiatry 120:738–742, 1964

O'Connor JF, Stern LO: Results of treatment in functional sexual disorders. NY State J Med 72:1927–1934, 1972

Odenheimer JF: Day hospital as an alternative to the psychiatric ward. Arch Gen Psychiatry 13:46–53, 1965

O'Donnell JA: A follow-up of narcotic addicts. Am J Orthopsychiatry 34:948–954, 1964

Oettinger KB: Why a nurse mental health consultant in public health? J Psychiatr Soc Work 19:162–168, 1950

Oettinger L: Meratran. Preliminary report of a new drug for the treatment of behavior disorders in children. Dis Nerv Syst 16:299, 1955

Oettinger L: Use of Deanol in treatment of disorders of behavior in children. J Pediatr 53:671–675, 1958

Offenkrantz WCE, Elliot R: Psychiatric man-agement of suicide problems in military science. Am J Psychiatry 114:33, 1957

Ofman WV: Existential Psychotherapy, in Kaplan HI, Sadock BJ (eds): Comprehensive Textbook of Psychiatry IV. Baltimore, Williams & Wilkins, 1985, pp 1438–1443

Ogden TH: On projective identification. Int J Psychoanal 60:357–373, 1979

Ogden TH: Projective identification in psychiatric hospital treatment. Bull Menn Clin 45:317–333, 1981

Oldham JM, Russakoff LM: The medical-therapeutic community. J Psychiatr Treat Eval 4:347–353, 1982

Olds V: Role theory and casework: A review of the literature. Soc Casework 43:3–8, 1962

O'Leary KD, Becker WC: Behavior modification of an adjustment class: A token reinforcement program. Except Child 33:637–642, 1967

O'Leary KD, Drabman R: Token reinforcement programs in the classroom: A review. Psychol Bull 75:379–398, 1971

O'Leary KD, et al: Modification of a deviant sibling interaction pattern in the home. Behav Res Ther 5:113–120, 1967

O'Leary KD, Wilson GT: Behavior Therapy: Application and Outcome. Englewood Cliffs, NJ, Prentice-Hall, 1975

Olshansky S: The transitional sheltered workshop: A survey. J Soc Issues 16:33–39, 1960

Olsson PA: Psychodrama and group therapy with young heroin addicts returning from duty in Vietnam. Group Psychother and Psychodrama 25:141–147, 1972

O'Malley M: Transference and some of its problems in psychoses. Psychoanalytic Review 18:465–466, 1931

Opler M: Schizophrenia and culture. Sci Am 197:103–112, 1957

Opler M: Discussion: Scientific social psychiatry encounter existentialism. Phil Phenom Res 24:240–243, 1963(a)

Opler M: Need for new diagnostic categories in psychiatry. J Natl Med Assoc 55:133–137, 1963(b)

Orgel SZ: Effect of psychoanalysis on the course of peptic ulcer. Psychosom Med 20:117–125, 1958

Orgler H: Alfred Adler, the Man and His Work. New York, Liveright, 1963

Orlando IJ: The Dynamic Nurse-Patient Relationship. New York, Putnam, 1961, (paperback)

Orlinsky DE, Howard KI: Gender and Psychotherapeutic outcome, in Brodsky A, Hare-Mustin RT (eds): Women and Psychotherapy. New York, Guilford Press, 1979

Ormont L: Establishing the analytic contrast in a newly formed therapeutic group. Br J Med Psychol 35:333, 1962

Ormont L: The resolution of resistances by conjoint psychoanalysis. Psychoanal Rev 51:425, 1964

Orne MT, Wender PH: Anticipating Socialization for psychotherapy. Am J Psychiatry 124:1202–1212, 1968

Ornstein P: Selected problems in learning how to analyze. Int J Psa 48:448–461, 1967

Ornstein P: What is and what is not psychotherapy. Dis Nerv Sys 29:118–123, 1968

Ornstein P, Goldberg A: Psychoanalysis and medicine: I. Contributions to psychiatry, psychosomatic medicine and medical psychology. Dis Nerv Sys 34:143–147, 1973

Ornstein PH: Some surative factors and processes in the psychoanalytic psychotherapies, in Myers JM (ed): Cures by Psychotherapy. New York, Praeger, 1984

Orr DW: Transference and countertransference: A historical survey. J Am Psychoanal Assoc 2:621, 670, 1954

Osipow SH, Walsh WD: Strategies in Counseling for Behavior Change. New York, Appleton-Century-Crofts, 1970

Ost LG, Johansson J, Jerrelmalm A: Individual response patterns and the effects of different behavioral methods in the treatment of claustrophobia. Behav Res Ther 20:445–460, 1982

Ostow M: Religion, in Arieti S (ed): American Handbook of Psychiatry, vol. 2. New York, Basic Books, 1959, pp 1789–1801

Ostow M: The Use of Drugs in Psychoanalysis and Psychotherapy. New York, Basic Books, 1962

Outler A: Psychotherapy and the Christian Message. New York, Harper & Row, 1954

Overall JE, Hollister LE: Computer procedures for psychiatric classification. JAMA 187:583–588, 1964

Overall JE, Hollister LE, Johnson M, Pennington V: Nosology of depression and differential response to drugs JAMA 195:162, 1966

Overholser W: Physical medicine and psychiatry, some interrelationships. JAMA 138:1221, 1948

Ovesey L: The homosexual conflict: An adaptational analysis. Psychiatry 17(3) 1954

Ovesey L: The homosexual anxiety. Psychiatry 18(1), 1955(a)

Ovesey L: Pseudohomosexuality, the paranoid mechanism and paranoia. Psychiatry 18(2). 1955(b)

Ovesey L: Pseudohomosexuality and homosexuality in men: Psychodynamics as a guide to treatment, in Marmor J (ed): Sexual Inversion. New York, Basic Books, 1965

Ovesey L, Gaylin W, Hendin H: Psychotherapy of male homosexuality. Arch Gen Psychiatry 9(1), 1963

Oxford Universal Dictionary: Oxford, Eng, Clarendon, 1955, p 584

Pacella BL: A critical appraisal of pastoral counseling. Paper presented at the 122d Annual Meeting of the American Psychiatric Association, Atlantic City, N.J., May 1966

Pack GT: Counseling the cancer patient. Surgeon's counsel. The physician and the total care of the cancer patient. Scientific Session of the American Cancer Society, 1961

Pahnke, WN, Kurland AA, Unger S, et al: The experimental use of psychedelic (LSD) psychotherapy. JAMA 212:1856–1863, 1970

Palmer HD, Braceland FJ: Six years with narcosis therapy in psychiatry. Am J Psychiatry 94:35–37, 1937

Palmer MB: Social rehabilitation for mental patients. Ment Hyg 42:24–28, 1958

Palmer RD: Desensitization of the fear of expressing one's own inhibited aggression: Bioenergetic assertive techniques for behavior therapists. Paper presented at the Association for the Advancement of Behavior Therapy, Washington, DC, September 1971

Paneth HG: Some observations on the relation of psychotic states to psychosomatic disorders. Psychosom Med 21:106–109, 1959

Panzetta AF: Toward a scientific psychiatric nosology. Arch Gen Psychiatry 30:154–161, 1974

Paolino TJ, McCrady BC(eds): Marriage and Marital Therapy: Psychoanalytic, Behavioral, and Systems Theory Perspectives. New York, Brunner/Mazel, 1978

Papanek E: Das Kinderheim Seine Theorie und Praxis im Lichte der Individual Psychologie. Acta Psychother 4:53, 1956

Papanek E: In-service training of educators for maladjusted youth. Proceedings of the 4th Congress of the International Association of Workers for Maladjusted Children, Laussanne-Paris, 1958

Papanek E: A new approach to institutional care for children, in Adler K, Deutsch, D (eds): Essays in Individual Psychology. New York, Grove, 1959, pp 139–152

Papanek E, Papanek H: Individual psychology today. Am J Psychother 15:4–26, 1961

Papanek H: Combined group and individual therapy in the light of Adlerian psychology. Int J Group Psychother 6:136–146, 1956

Papanek H: Recent developments and implications of the Adlerian theory for clinical psychology, in Abt LE, Riess BF (eds): Progress in Clinical Psychology, vol. 5. Orlando FL, Grune & Stratton, 1963

Papanek H: Adler's concepts in community psychiatry. J Individ Psychol 21:117–126, 1965

Papanek H: Personal communication. 1966

Papp P (ed): Family Therapy: Full Length Case Studies, New York, Gardner Press, 1977

Pardes H: Why students are not entering psychiatry. Resident and Staff Physicians April, 1979

Paredes A, Gogerty JH, West LJ: Psychopharmacology, in Masserman JH (ed): Current Psychiatric Therapies, vol. 1. Orlando FL, Grune & Stratton, 1961

Paredes A, Ludwig KD, Hassenfeld IN, et al: A clinical study of alcoholics using audiovisual self-image feedback. J Nerv Ment Dis 148:449–456, 1969

Park LC, Covi L: Nonblind placebo trial. Arch Gen Psychiatry 12:336–345, 1965

Parker B: Psychiatric Consultation for Non-psychiatric Professional Workers. Pub Health Monogr No. 53, Washington, DC, U.S. Government Printing Office, 1958

Parker B: Some observations on psychiatric consultation with nursery school teachers. Ment Hyg 46:559–562, 1962

Parloff MB: The family in psychotherapy. Arch Gen Psychiatry 4:445–451, 1961

Parloff MB: Discussion of group therapy with schizophrenics. Int J Group Psychother 36:353–360, 1986

Parloff MB, Waskow LE, WOlfe BE: Research on therapist variables in relation to process and outcome, in Garfield SL, Bergin AE (eds): Handbook of Psychotherapy and Behavior Change: An Empirical Analysis, (2d ed). New York, Wiley, 1978

Parloff MB, Wolfe B, Haldey S, Waskow LE: Assessment of Psychosocial Treatment of Mental Disorders: Current Status and Prospects. Report by NIMH Working Group, Advisory Committee on Mental Health, Institute of Medicine, National Academy of Sciences, 1978

Parsons T, Shils EA: Toward a General Theory of Action. Cambridge, Harvard University Press, 1951

Paschalis AP, Kimmel HD, Kimmel E: Further study of diurnal instrumental conditioning in the treatment of enuresis nocturna. J Behav Ther Exp Psychiatry 3:253–256, 1972

Paterson AS: Electrical and Drug Treatments in Psychiatry. London, Elsevier, 1963

Patrick T, Dulack T: Let Our Children Go. New York, E.P. Dutton & Co, 1976

Patterson CH: Theories of Counseling and Psychotherapy. New York, Harper & Row, 1966

Patterson GR: A learning theory approach to the treatment of the school phobic child, in Ullmann LP, Krasner L (eds): Case Studies in Behavior Modification. New York, Holt, 1965

Patterson GR: Behavioral intervention procedures in the classroom and the home, in Bergin AE, Garfield SL (eds): Handbook of Psychotherapy and Behavior Change. New York, Wiley, 1970

Patterson GR: Families: Applications of Social Learning to Family Life. Champaign, Ill, Research Press, 1971

Patterson GR: Some procedures for assessing changes for marital interaction patterns. Oregon Research Institute Bull 16 (7), 1976

Patterson GR, Gullion ME: Living with Children: New Methods for Parents and Teachers. Champaign, Ill, Research Press, 1968

Patterson GR, Reid JB, Jones, RR, et al: A social learning approach to family intervention, in Families of Aggressive Children, vol. I. Eugene, Ore, Castelia, 1975

Patterson RL: Overcoming Deficits of Aging. New York, Plenum, 1982

Patterson RL, Jackson GM: Behavior modification with the elderly, in Hersen J, Eisler R, Miller P (eds): Progress in Behavior Modification, vol 9. Orlando FL, Academic Press, 1980

Patterson V, Levene HI, Breger L: Treatment and training outcomes with two time-limited therapies. Arch Gen Psychiatry 25:161, 1971

Patton GO: Foster homes and rehabilitation of long-term mental patients. Can Psychiatr Assoc J 6:20–25, 1961

Paul GL: Effects of insight, desensitization, and attention-placebo treatment of anxiety: An approach to outcome research in psychotherapy. Unpublished doctoral dissertation, University of Illinois, 1964

Paul GL: Insight Versus Desensitization in Psychotherapy: An Experiment in Anxiety Reduction. Stanford, Calif, Stanford University Press, 1966

Paul GL: Insight versus desensitization in psychotherapy two years after termination. J Consult Psychol 31:333–348, 1967

Paul GL: Inhibition of physiological response to stressful imagery by relaxation training and hypnotically suggested relaxation. Behav Res Ther 7:249–256, 1969(a)

Paul GL: Physiological effects of relaxation training and hypnotic suggestions. J Abnorm Psychol 74:425–437, 1969(b)

Paul GL, Shannon DT: Treatment of anxiety through systematic desensitization in therapy groups. J Abnorm Psychol 71:124–135, 1966

Paul GL, Tobias LL, Holly BL: Maintenance psychotropic drugs in the presence of active treatment programs. Arch Gen Psychiatry 27:106–115, 1972

Paul GL: Psychological Treatment of Chronic Mental Patients. Cambridge, Harvard University Press, 1977

Paul GL, Lentz RJ: Psychosocial Treatment of Chronic Mental Patients: Milieu vs. Social Learning Programs. Cambridge, Harvard University Press, 1977

Paul NL: Cross-confrontation procedure via tape recordings in conjoint family therapy. Paper presented at the 122d Annual Meeting of the American Psychiatric Association, Atlantic City, NJ, May 1966

Pauling L: Pauling blasts APA report on orthomolecular psychiatry. Psychiatr News 9:4, 1974

Payne FD, Wiggins JS: MMPI profile types and the self-report of psychiatric patients. J Abnorm Psychology 79:1, 1972

Payne J: Ombudsman roles for social worker. Soc Work January 17, 1972

Payot I: The Education of the Will. New York, Funk & Wagnalls, 1909

Pearce JK, Friedman LJ: Family Therapy: Combining Psychodynamic and Family Systems Approaches. Orlando FL, Grune & Stratton, 1980

Pellegrino V: A new voice: A new life. Todays Health 52:44–49, 1974

Pelletier KR: Theory and applications of clinical biofeedback. J Contemp Psychother 7:29–34, 1975

Pepper M, Redlich FC, Pepper A: Social psychiatry. Am J Psychiatry 121:662–666, 1965

Perelman JS: Problems encountered in group psychotherapy of married couples. Int J Group Psychother 10:136–142, 1960

Perlman H: Social Casework: A Problem-Solving Process. Chicago University of Chicago Press, 1957

Perlman H: Intake and some role consideration. J Soc Casework 41:171–177, 1960(a)

Perlman H: Social casework, in Kurtz RH (ed): Social Work Year Book—1960. New York, National Association Social Workers, 1960(b), p 535

Perlman H: The role concept and social casework: Some explorations. I. The "social" in social casework. Soc Serv Rev 35:370–381, 1961 II. What is social diagnosis. Soc Serv Rev 36:17–31, 1962

Perlmutter F, Durham D: Using teen-agers to supplement casework service. Soc Work 10:41–46, 1965

Perls FS: Gestalt therapy and human potentialities, in Otto HA (ed): Explorations in Human Potentialities. Springfield, Ill, Thomas, 1966

Perls FS: Gestalt Therapy Verbatim. Moab, Utah, Real People Press, 1969

Perls FS, Hefferline RF, Goodman P: Gestalt Therapy. New York, Julian, 1951

Perls FS: The Gestalt approach and eyewitness to therapy. Palo Alto, Calif, Science and Behavior Books, 1973

Perry MA: Modeling and instructions in training for counselor empathy. J Counseling Psychology 22:173–179, 1975

Perry MA, Cerreto MC: Structured learning training of social skills for the retarded. Mental Retardation 15:31–34, 1977

Perry MA, Furukawa MJ: Modeling methods, in Kanfer FH, Goldstein AP (eds): Helping People Change (2d ed). New York, Pergamon, 1980, pp 131–171

Peters GA, Phelan JG: Practical group psychotherapy reduces supervisor's anxiety. Personnel J 35:376–378, 1957(a)

Peters GA, Phelan JG: Relieving personality conflicts by a kind of group therapy. Personnel J 36:61–64, 1957(b)

Peterson S: The psychiatric nurse specialist in a general hospital. Nurs Outlook 17:56–58, 1969

Pfister HP: Farbe und Bewengung in der Zeichnung Geisterskranken. Schweiz. Arch Neurol Psychiatry 34:325–365, 1934

Pflug B: The effect of sleep deprivation on depressed patients. Acta Psychiatr Scand 53:148–158, 1976

Philander DA, Yorkston NJ, Eckert E, et al: Bronchial asthma: Improved lung functions after behavior modification. Psychosomatics 20:325–327, 330–331, 1979

Phillips EL: Psychotherapy: A Modern Theory and Practice. London, Staples, 1957

Phillips HU: Essentials of Social Group Work Skill. New York, Association Press, 1957

Phillips JS, Kanfer FH: The viability and vicissitudes of behavior therapy, in Frederick CJ (ed): The Future of Psychotherapy. Boston, Little, Brown, 1969, pp 75–131

Piaget S: The stages of the intellectual development in the child, in Harrison SI, McDermott, JF: Childhood Psychopathology. New York, International Universities Press, 1972

Pickford RW: Some interpretations of a painting called "abstraction." Br J Med Psychol 18:219–249, 1938

Pierce CM: Enuresis and encopreses, in Freedman AM, Kaplan HI, Sadock BJ (eds): Comprehensive Textbook of Psychiatry, vol. II (2d ed). Baltimore, Williams & Wilkins, 1975, pp 2116–2125

Pierce CM, et al: Music therapy in a day care center. Dis Nerv Syst 25:29–32, 1964

Piers MA: Play and mastery, in Ekstein R, Motto RL (eds): From Learning for Love to Love of Learning. New York, Brunner/Mazel, 1969

Pietropinto A: Poetry therapy in groups, in Masserman JH (ed): Current Psychiatric Therapies, vol. 15. Orlando FL, Grune & Stratton, 1975, pp 221–232

Pinckney ER, Pinckney C: The Fallacy of Freud and Psychoanalysis. Englewood Cliffs, NJ, Prentice-Hall, 1965

Pincus HA, Straia JJ, Houpt JL, et al: Models of mental health training in primary care. JAMA, June 249(22):3065–8, 1983

Pines M: Group therapy with "difficult" patients, in Wolberg LR, Aronson ML (eds): Group Therapy 1975: An Overview. New York, Stratton Intercontinental, 1975, pp 102–119

Pins A: Changes in social work education and their implications for practice. Soc Work 16:5–15, 1971

Piotrowski Z, Schreiber M: Rorschach, perceptanalytic measurement of personality changes during and after intensive psychoanalytically oriented psychotherapy, in Bychowski G, Despert JL (eds): Specialized Techniques in Psychotherapy. New York, Basic Books, 1952, pp 337–361

Pittman FS, DeYoung MS, Flomenhaft K, et al: Crisis family therapy, in Masserman JH (ed): Current Psychiatric Therapies, vol. 6. Orlando FL, Grune & Stratton, 1966, pp 185–196

Plunkett RJ, Gordon JE: Epidemiology and Mental Illness. New York, Basic Books, 1960

Plutchik R, Kellerman H: Emotions Profile Index. Los Angeles, Western Psychological Services, 1974

Pohl R, Berchou R, Rainey JM: Tricyclic antidepressants and monoamine oxidase inhibitors in the treatment of agoraphobia. J Clin Psychopharm 2:399–407, 1983

Polak P, Laycob L: Rapid tranquilization. Am J Psychiatry 128:640–643, 1971

Pollak VE: The computer in medicine. JAMA 253:62–68, 1985

Polster E, Polster M: Gestalt Therapy Integrated: Contours of Theory and Practice. New York, Brunner/Mazel, 1973

Poole N, Blanton S: The Art of Real Happiness. Englewood Cliffs, NJ, Prentice-Hall, 1950

Pomerleau OF, Brady JP (eds): Behavioral Medicine: Theory and Practice. Baltimore, Williams & Wilkins, 1979

Pope H, Judson JI, Jones JM et al: Bulimia treatment with imipramine: A placebo–controlled, double–blind study. Am J Psychiatry 140:554–558, 1983

Poussaint AF, Ditman KS: A controlled study of imipramine (tofranil) in the treatment of childhood enuresis. Paper presented at the 120th Annual Meeting of the American Psychiatric Association. Los Angeles, May 1964

Powdermaker FB: Psychoanalytic concepts in group psychotherapy. Int J Group Psychother 1:16, 1951

Powdermaker FB, Frank JD, Abrahams J: Group Psychotherapy: Studies in Methodology of Research and Therapy. Cambridge, Harvard University Press, 1953

Powell DR, Arnold CB: Antismoking program for coronary–prone men: An evaluation study NY State J Med: 1435–1438, 1982

Powell LH, Friedman M, Thoresen CE, Gill JJ, Ulmer DK: Can the type A behavior pattern be altered after myocardial infarction? A second year report from the recurrent coronary prevention project. Psychosom Med 46:293–313, 1984

Powers E: An experiment in prevention of delinquency. Ann Am Acad Pol Soc Sci 77–88, 1949

Powers E, Witmer H: An Experiment in the Prevention of Delinquency. New York, Columbia University Press, 1951

Practitioners Conference, NY Hospital, Cornell Medical Center. Sterility and impotence. NY State Med J 57:120–144, 1957

Pratt JH: The class method of treating consumption in the homes of the poor. JAMA 49:755–759, 1907

Pratt JH: The influence of emotions in the causation and cure of psychoneuroses. Int Clinics 4:1, 1934

Pratt JH: The use of Dejerine's methods in the treatment of the common neuroses by group psychotherapy. Bull N Engl Med Ctr 15:1–9, 1953

Pratt JH, et al: Extrasensory Perception After Sixty Years. New York, Holt, 1940

Pray KLM: The place of social casework in the treatment of delinquency. Soc Serv Rev 19:235–248, 1945

Pray KLM: A restatement of the generic principles of social casework practice. J Soc Casework 28:283–390, 1947

Prescott D, et al: Helping teachers understand children. Understanding the Child 14:67–70, 1945

Proceedings of the Brief Psychotherapy Council, under the auspices of the Chicago Institute for Psychoanalysis, October 1942

Proceedings of the Second Brief Psychotherapy Council (1. Psychosomatic medicine. 2. Psychotherapy for children. Group psychotherapy. 3. War psychiatry), under the auspices of the Chicago Institute for Psychoanalysis, January 1944

Proceedings of the Third Brief Psychotherapy Council, under the auspices of the Chicago Institute for Psychoanalysis, October 1946

Proskauer, S: Focussed time–limited–psychotherapy with children. J Am Child Psychiatry 10:619–639, 1971

Prowse M: A night care program. Nurs Outlook 5:518–519, 1957

Pruyser PW: Towards a doctrine of man in psychiatry and theology. Pastoral Psychol 9:9–13, 1958

Pruyser PW: Religion and psychiatry. A polygon of relationships. JAMA 195:197–202, 1966

Psychiatric Bulletin: Houston, Tex, Medical Arts Publishing Foundation, 1950–1951, and issues thereafter

Psychiatric Manpower Bulletin: (American Psychiatric Association) No. 2, May 1963

Psychiatric News 7:22, 1972

Psychiatric News 9:1, 1974

Psychiatric News 20:12, 1985

Psychiatry and Medical Education. Report of the 1951 Conference on Psychiatric Education. Washington, DC, American Psychiatric Association, 1952

Psychotherapy and Casework. Symposium of the Boston Psychoanalytic Society and Institute. J Soc Casework, 1949

Psychotherapy Curriculum Consultation Committee, American Psychological Association: Recommended standards for psychotherapy education in psychology doctoral programs. Professional Psychol Spring, 1971

Pumpian-Mindlin E (ed): On Psychoanalysis as Science. New York, Basic Books, 1956

Pumpian-Mindlin E: Considerations in the selection of patients for short-term therapy. Am J Psychother 7:641–652, 1957

Quarti C, Renaud J: A new treatment of constipation by conditioning: A preliminary report, in Franks CM (ed): Conditioning Techniques in Clinical Practice and Research. New York, Springer, 1964, pp 219–227

Quaytman W: Impressions of the Esalen (Schutz) phenomenon. J Contemp Psychother 2:57–64, 1969

Rabin HM: Any answers to the compelling arguments against encounters and marathons? Psychother Bull 4:16–19, 1971

Rabiner EL, Gomez E, Gralnick A: The therapeutic community as an inside catalyst, expanding the transferential field. Am J Psychother 18:244–258, 1964

Rabinovitch RD: Reading and learning disabilities, in Arieti S (ed): American Handbook of Psychiatry, vol. 1. New York, Basic Books, 1959, pp 856–869

Rachman AW: Marathon group psychotherapy: Its origins, significance and direction. J Group Psychoanal Proc 2:57–74, 1969

Rachman AW: Group psychotherapy in treating the adolescent identity crisis. Int J Child Psychother 1:97–117, 1972(a)

Rachman AW: Identity Group Psychotherapy with Adolescents. Springfield, Ill, Thomas, 1972(b)

Rachman AW: The issue of countertransference in encounter and marathon group psychotherapy, in Wolberg LR, Aronson ML (eds): Group Therapy 1975: An Overview, New York, Stratton Intercontinental, 1975, pp 146–163

Rachman S: The Effects of Psychotherapy. International Series of Monographs in Experimental Psychology, vol. 15. Elmsford, NY, Pergamon, 1972

Rachman S: The modification of obsessions: A new formulation. Behav Res Ther 14:437–444, 1976

Rachman S: Obsessional–compulsive checking. Behav Res Ther 14(4):269–277, 1976

Rachman SJ, Hodgson R: Obsessions and Compulsions. Englewood Cliffs, NJ, Prentice-Hall, 1980

Rachman S, Hodgson R, Marks IM: The treatment of chronic obsessive-compulsive neuroses. Behav Res Ther 9:237–247, 1971

Rachman S, Marks IM, Hodgson R: The treatment of obsessive–compulsive neurotics by modeling and flooding in vivo. Behav Res Ther 11:463–471, 1973

Rachman S, Teasdale J: Aversion Therapy and Behavior Disorders. Coral Gables, Fla, University of Miami Press, 1969

Rachman S, Wilson GT: The Effects of Psychological Therapy (2d ed). New York, Pergamon Press, 1980

Rado S: Developments in the psychoanalytic conception and treatment of the neuroses. Psychoanal Qt 8:427, 1939

Rado S: Mind, unconscious mind, and brain. Psycosom Med 11:165, 1949

Rado S: Emergency behavior: With an introduction to the dynamics of conscience, in Hoch PH, Zubin J (eds): Anxiety. New York, Grune & Stratton, 1950, pp 150–175

Rado S: Psychoanalysis of behavior: Collected Papers, vol. 1. Orlando FL, Grune & Stratton, 1956

Rado S: Obsessive behavior, in Arieti S (ed): American Handbook of Psychiatry, vol. 1. New York, Basic Books, 1959, p 342

Rado S: Psychoanalysis of Behavior: Collected Papers, vol. 2. Orlando FL, Grune & Stratton, 1962

Rado S: Relationship of short-term psychotherapy to development stages of maturation and stages of treatment behavior, in Wolberg LR (ed): Short-term Psychotherapy. Orlando FL, Grune & Stratton, 1965, pp 67–83

Rado S, Daniels G: Changing Concepts of Psychoanalytic Medicine. Orlando FL, Grune & Stratton, 1956

Rafferty FT: Day treatment of adolescents, in Masserman JH (ed): Current Psychiatric Therapies, vol. 1. Orlando FL, Grune & Stratton, 1961, pp 43–47

Raginsky BB: Sensory hypnoplasty with case illustration. Int J Clin Exp Hypn 10:205–219, 1962

Rahe RH, Arthur RJ: Life–change patterns surrounding illness experience, in Monat A, lazarus RS (eds): Stress and Coping. New York, Columbia University Press, 1977

Rainer JD: Genetic counseling in a psychiatric setting, in Masserman JH (ed): Current Psychiatric Therapies, vol. 7. Orlando FL, Grune & Stratton, 1967

Rancurello ML: Antidepressants in children: Indications, benefits, and limitations. Am J Psychother 40:377–391, 1986

Rangell L: Similarities and differences between psychoanalysis and dynamic psychotherapy. J Am Psychoanal Assoc 2:734–744, 1954

Rank O: The Trauma of Birth. New York, Harcourt, 1929

Rank O: Will Therapy and Truth and Reality. New York, Knopft, 1947

Rapaport D: Emotions and Memory (2d ed). New York, International Universities Press, 1950

Rapaport D: The autonomy of the ego. Bull Menninger Clin 15:113–123, 1951

Rapaport D: The theory of ego autonomy: A generalization. Bull Menninger Clin 22:13–35, 1958

Rapaport D: On the Psychoanalytic Theory of Motivation. Lincoln, University of Nebraska Press, 1960

Rapaport D, Gill M, Schafer R: Diagnostic Psychological Testing, vol. 1. Chicago, Year Book Publishers, 1946 (rev ed—New York, International Universities Press, 1968)

Rapaport HG: Psychosomatic aspects of allergy in childhood. JAMA 165:812–815, 1957

Rapaport L: The state of crisis: Some theoretical consideration. Social Service Review 36:211–217, 1962

Rapaport L (ed): Consultation in Social Work Practice, New York, National Association of Social Workers, 1963

Rapaport RN: A social scientist looks at the therapeutic community: Suggestions for developing action research, in Proceedings of the World Congress of Psychiatry, Montreal, Canada, 1961

Rapaport RN: Principles for developing a therapeutic community, in Masserman JH (ed): Current Psychiatric Therapies, vol. 3. Orlando FL, Grune & Stratton, 1963, pp 244–256

Rapaport RN, et al: Community as Doctor: New Perspectives on a Therapeutic Community. Springfield, Ill, Thomas, 1960

Raskin DE: Problems in the therapeutic community. Am J psychiatry 128:492, 1971

Raskin HA: Rehabilitation of the narcotic addict. JAMA 189:956–958, 1964

Raush HL, Bordin ES: Warmth in personality development and in psychotherapy. Psychiatry 20:351–364, 1957

Ravenette AT: Maladjustment: Clinical concept or administrative convenience: Psychologists, teachers and children: How many ways to understand? Assoc Educ Psychol J Newsletter 3:41–47, 1972

Ray MB: The cycle of abstinence and relapse among heroin addicts. Soc Prob 9:132–140, 1961

Redkey H: Rehabilitation Centers Today. DHEW Rehab Service Ser No. 490. Washington, DC, U.S. Government Printing Office, 1959

Redl F: Resistance in therapy groups. Hum Relations 1:307, 1948

Redl F: The concept of a therapeutic milieu. Am J Orthopsychiatry 29:721–737, 1959

Redl F: When We Deal with Children. New York, Free Press, 1966

Redl F, Wattenberg WW: Mental Hygiene in Teaching. Orlando FL, Harcourt, 1959

Redlich FC, Freedman DX: The Theory and Practice of Psychiatry. New York, Basic Books, 1966

Redlich FC, Pepper MP: Social psychiatry. Am J Psychiatry 119:637–642, 1963

Redlich FC, Pepper MP: Social psychiatry. Am J Psychiatry 120:657–660, 1964

Reeder CW, Kunce JT: Modeling techniques, drug abstinence behavior, and heroin addicts: A pilot study. J Counsel Psychology 23:560–562, 1976

Rees TP: Back to moral treatment and community care. J Ment Sci 103:303–313, 1957

Reese HH: In Podolsky E (ed): Music Therapy. New York, Philosphical Library, 1954

Reeve M: The role of the supervisor in helping the student to a professional orientation, in FSSA pamphlet: Some Emotional Elements in Supervision. (Report of a group discussion.) 1937

Reeves RB: When is it time to die? Prologomenon to voluntary euthanasia. N Engl Law Rev 8:183, 1973

Regier DA, Goldberg ID, Taube CA: The de facto US mental health services system. Arch Gen Psychiatry 35:685–693, 1978

Reich A: Symposium on the termination of psychoanalytic treatment and on the criteria for the termination of an analysis. Int J Psychoanal 31:78–80, 179–205, 1950

Reich W: Zur Technik der Deutung und der Widerstandsanalyse. Int Ztschr Psychoanal 13, 1927

Reich W: Über Charakteranalyse. Int Ztschr Psychoanal 14, 1928

Reich W: The Function of the Orgasm. New York, Orgone Institute Press, 1942

Reich W: Character Analysis (3d ed). New York, Orgone Institute Press, 1949

Reider N: Remarks on mechanisms of nonanalytic psychotherapy. Dis Nerv Syst 5(1), 1944

Reiff R: Mental health manpower and institutional change. Am Psychol 21:540–548, 1966

Reik T: Dogma and Compulsion: Psychoanalytic Studies of Religion and Myths. New York, International Universities Press, 1951

Rein M: Social work in search of a radical profession. Soc Work 15(2):13–28, 1970

Reinherz H: The therapeutic use of student volunteers. Children 2:137–142, 1964

Reinkes JH: The use of unfamiliar music as a stimulus for a projective test of personality, in Proceedings of the National Association of Music Therapy. Kansas City, Kans, the Association, 1952, pp 224–230

Reisman JM: Toward the Integration of Psychotherapy. New York, Wiley, 1971

Reitman F: Facial expression in schizophrenic drawings. J Ment Sci 85:264–272, 1939

Reitman R: The Use of Small Computers in Self–Help Sex Therapy, in Schwartz MD (ed): Using Computers in Clinical Practice. New York, The Haworth Press, 1984, pp 363–380

Rennie TAC: What can the practitioner do in treating the neuroses? Bull NY Acad Med, January 1946

Rennie TAC: Trends in medical education (discussion). Commonwealth Fund. New York, NY Acad Med Inst Med Educ, 1949

Rennie TAC, Woodward LE: Mental Health in Modern Society. New York, Commonwealth Fund, 1948

Resnick R, Volavka J, Freeman AM, Thomas M: Studies of En-1639A (Maltexone): A new narcotic antagonist. Am J Psychiatry 131:646, 1974

Revenson TA, Wollman CA, Felton BJ: Social supports as stress buffers for adult cancer patients. Psychosom Med 45:321–331, 1983

Review Panel on Coronary–Prone Behavior and Coronary Heart Disease, A Critical Review: Circulation 63:1199–1215, 1982

Reyna LJ: Conditioning therapies, learning theory, and research, in Wolpe J, et al (eds): The Conditioning Therapies: The Challenge of Psychotherapy. New York, Holt, 1964, pp 169–179

Reynolds DK: Morita Psychotherapy. Berkeley, University of California Press, 1976

Reynolds R, Siegle E: A study of casework with sado-masochistic marriage partners. J Soc Casework 40:545–551, 1959

Rhine SB: Experiments bearing on the precognition hypothesis. J Parapsychol 2:38, 1938

Rhoades W: Group training in thought control for relieving nervous disorders. Ment Hyg 19:373–386, 1935

Rhoads JM, Feather BW: Transference and resistence observed in behavior therapy. Br J Med Psychol 45:99–103, 1972

Rhoads PS: Management of the patient with terminal illness. JAMA 192:661–667, 1965

Rhys-Davids TW: Dialogues of the Buddha, Translated from the Pali of the Digha nikāya, 3 vols. London, Frowde, 1899–1938

Richardson C: The formal rites and ceremonies of the church, in Maves PB (ed): The Church and Mental Health. New York, Scribner, 1953

Richelson E: Are receptor studies useful for clinical practice? J Clin Psychiatr 44:4–9, 1983

Richmond ME: Social Diagnosis. New York, Russell Sage Foundation, 1917

Richter R, Dahme B: Bronchial asthma in adults: There is little evidence for the effectiveness of behavioral therapy and relaxation. J Psychosom Res 26:533–540, 1982

Rickels K: Anti-anxiety drugs in neurotic outpatients, in Masserman JH (ed): Current Psychiatric Therapies, vol. 7. Orlando FL, Grune & Stratton, 1967

Rickels K, Baumm C, Raab E, Taylor W, Moore E: A psychopharmacological evaluation of chlordiazepoxide, LA-1 and placebo, carried out with anxious medical clinic patients. Med Times 93:238–245, 1965

Rickels K, Clark TW, Ewing JH, Klingensmith WC: Evaluation of tranquilizing drugs in medical out-patients (meprobamate, prochlorperazine, amobarbital sodium and placebo). JAMA 171:1649–1656, 1959

Rickels K, Weise CC, Sandler K, Schless A, Zal M, Norstad N: Nomifensine impriamine and placebo in depressed outpatients. Int Pharmacopsychiatry 17 (Suppl): 73–88, 1982

Rickers-Ovsiankina MA: Rorschach Psychology. New York, Wiley, 1960, p 441 (repr—Huntington, NY, Krieger, 1976)

Rieff R, Riesman F: The Indigenous Nonprofessional: A Strategy of Change in Community Mental Health. New York, National Institute of Labor Education, 1964

Riess BF: Changes in patient income concomitant with psychotherapy. J Consult Psychology 31:130, 1967

Riess BF: Consensus techniques in diagnosis and group therapy of adolescents, in Wolberg LR, Schwartz EK (eds): Group Therapy 1973: An Overview. New York, Stratton Intercontinental, 1973, pp 92–100

Riessman F: New Approaches to Mental Health Treatment for Labor and Low Income Groups, New York, National Institute of Labor Education, 1964

Riessman F: The "helper" therapy principle. Soc Work 10(2):27–31, 1965

Rifkin A, Quitkin F, Carilla C, et al: Lithium carbonate in emotionally unstable character disorders. Arch Gen Psychiatry 27:519–523, 1972

Rimm DC, Masters JC: Behavior Therapy: Techniques and Empirical Findings. New York, Academic Press, 1974

Rimm DC, Masters JC: Behavior Therapy: Techniques and Empirical Findings, (2d ed). Orlando FL, Academic Press, 1979

Ringness TA: Mental Health in the Schools. New York, Random House, 1967

Rinsley DB: Diagnosis and treatment of borderline and narcissistic children and adolescents. Bull Menn Clin 44:147–170, 1980(a)

Rinsley DB: Treatment of the Severely Disturbed Adolescent. New York, Aronson, 1980(b)

Rinsley DB: Borderline and Other Self Disorders: A Developmental and Object–Relations Perspective. New York, Aronson, 1982(a)

Rinsley DB: Object relations theroy and psychotherapy with particular reference to the self–disordered patient, in Giovacchini PL, Boyer LB (eds): Technical Factors in the Treatment of the Severely Disturbed Patient. New York, Aronson, 1982(b) pp 187–213

Rinsley DB: Notes on the pathogenesis and nosology of borderline and narcissistic personality disorders, J Am Acad Psychoanal 13:317–328, 1985

Rioch MJ: The transference phenomenon in psychoanalytic therapy. Psychiatry 6:147–156, 1943

Rioch MJ: Changing concepts in the training of therapists. J Consult Psychol 30:290–292, 1966

Rioch MJ, Elkes C, Flint AA: Pilot Project in Training Mental Health Counselors. Pub Health Service Publ No. 1254. Washington, DC, U.S. Government Printing Office, 1965

Rioch MJ, Elkes C, Flint AA, et al: National Institute of Mental Health pilot study in training mental health counselors. Am J Orthopsychiatry 33:678–679, 1963

Rippon TS, Fletcher P: Reassurance and Relaxation. London, Routledge & Kegan, 1940

Roazen P: Freud, Political and Social Thought. New York, Knopf, 1968

Robbins BS: The theoretical rationale for the day hospital, in Proceedings of the 1958 Day Hospital Conference of the American Psychiatric Association, Washington, DC, 1958, p 5

Robertiello RC: Telephone sessions. Psychoanal Rev 59:633–634, 1972

Robertiello RC, Forbes SF: The treatment of masochistic character disorders. J Contemp Psychol 3:41–44, 1970

Roberts A, Rheinhardt L: The behavioral management of chronic pain: Long term follow up with comparison groups. Pain 8:151–162, 1980

Roberts DE: Psychotherapy and a Christian View of Man. New York, Scribner, 1950

Roberts JAF: An Introduction to Medical Genetics. London, Oxford University Press, 1963

Roberts R, Hee R (eds): Theories of Social Casework. Chicago, University of Chicago Press, 1970

Robertson WMF, Pitt B: The role of a day hospital in geriatric psychiatry. Br J Psychiatry 111:635–640, 1965

Robinson AM: The Psychiatric Aide, His Part in Patient Care. Philadelphia, Lippincott, 1964

Robinson DS, Nies A, Ravaria CL, et al: The monoamine oxidase inhibitor, phenelzine, in the treatment of depressive-anxiety states. Arch Gen Psychiatry 29:407–413, 1973

Robinson RL: Criticisms of psychiatry, in Usdin G (ed): Psychiatry: Education and Image. New York, Brunner/Mazel, 1973, pp 1–25

Roche Report: California dialogue: Defining psychotherapy, insight. 2:1–9, 1965

Roche Report: Civic treatment centers recommended for adolescents. 3(18):3, 6, 1966

Roche Report: Distorted video images quickly elicit repressed material. 3(5):1–11, 1973

Roche Report: Video psychiatry comes of age. 4(4):1–8, 1974(a)

Roche Report: Psychiatrists urged to abdicate therapeutic roles. 4(5):3, 1974(b)

Rochkind M, Conn JH: Guided fantasy encounter. Am J Psychotherapy 27:516–528, 1973

Roche Report: Frontiers of Psychiatry, Nov 15, 1981

Rockwell WJK, Pinkerton RS: Single-session psychotherapy. Am J Psychother 36:32–40, 1982

Rodin G, Voshart K: Depression in the medically ill: An overview. Am J Psychiatry 143:696–705, 1986

Rogawski AS (ed): Mental Health Consultations in Community Settings. New Directions for Mental Health Series, vol. 3. San Francisco, Jossey-Bass, 1979

Rogers CR: Counseling and Psychotherapy: Newer Concepts in Practice. Boston, Houghton Mifflin, 1942

Rogers CR: Therapy in guidance clinics. J Abnorm Soc Psychol 38:284–289, 1943

Rogers CR: The development of insight in a counseling relationship. J Consult Psychol 8:331–341, 1944

Rogers CR: Significant aspects of client-centered therapy. Am Psychologist 1:415–422, 1946

Rogers CR: Some implications of client-centered counseling for college personnel work. Personal Counselor 3:94–102, 1948

Rogers CR: Client-Centered Therapy. Boston, Houghton Mifflin, 1951

Rogers CR: Client-centered therapy: A current view, in Fromm-Reichmann F, Moreno JL (eds): Progress in Psychotherapy. Orlando FL, Grune & Stratton, 1956

Rogers CR: A theory of therapy, personality, and interpersonal relationships, as developed in the client-centered framework, in Koch S (ed): Psychology: A Study of Science. Vol. II, General Systematic Formulations, Learning and Special Processes. New York, McGraw-Hill, 1959

Rogers CR: On Becoming a Person: A Therapist's View of Psychotherapy. Boston, Houghton Mifflin, 1961(a)

Rogers CR: The characteristics of a helping relationship, in Stein MI (ed): Contemporary Psychotherapies. New York, Free Press, 1961(b)

Rogers CR (ed): The Therapeutic Relationship and Its Impact: A Study of Psychotherapy with Schizophrenics. Madison, University of Wisconsin Press, 1967

Rogers CR: Freedom to Learn: A View of What Education Might Become. Columbus, Ohio, Merrill, 1969

Rogers CR: Carl Rogers on Encounter Groups. New York, Harper & Row, 1970

Rogers CR: My philosophy of interpersonal relationships and how it grew. J Hum Psychol 13:3, 1973

Rogers CR: Client-centered psychotherapy, in Freedman AM, Kaplan HI, Sadock BJ (eds): Comprehensive Textbook of Psychiatry, vol. II (2d ed). Baltimore, Williams & Wilkins, 1975, pp 1831–1843

Rogers CR: A Way of Being. Boston, Houghton Mifflin, 1980

Rogers CR: Freedom to Learn for the 80's. Columbus, Charles E. Merrill, 1983

Rogers CR, Becker RJ: A basic orientation for counseling. Pastoral Psychol 1:26–28, 1950

Rogers CR, Gendlin ET, Kiesler DJ, Truax CB: The Therapeutic Relationship and Its Impact: A Study of Psychotherapy with Schizophrenics. Madison, University of Wisconsin Press, 1967

Rogers CR, Sanford RC: Client–centered psychotherapy, in Kaplan HI, Sadock BJ (eds): Comprehensive Textbook of Psychiatry (4th ed). Baltimore, Williams & Wilkins, 1985, pp 1374–1388

Rogers CR, Truax CB: The therapeutic conditions antecedent to change: A theoretical view, in Rogers CR (ed): The Therapeutic Relationship and Its Impact: A Study of Psychotherapy with Schizophrenics. Madison, University of Wisconsin Press, 1976

Rogers D: Mental Hygiene in Elementary Education. Boston, Houghton Mifflin, 1957

Rogers F: Patients respond to music program. Ment Hosp 14:642–643, 1963

Rokeach M: Long–term value change initiated by computer feedback. J Person Soc Psychol 32:467, 1975

Rolf I: Structural Integration. San Francisco, The Guild for Structural Integration, 1958

Rolf I: Rolfing; The Integration of Human Structures. New York, Harper & Row, 1973

Roman M: Creating the future, in Williams TA, Johnson JH (eds): Mental Health in the 21st Century. Lexington, Mass, D.C. Heath & Co, 1979, pp 11–20

Romano J: Has psychiatry resigned from medicine? Med Op 2:13–16, 1973

Rome HP: Group psychotherapy. Dis Nerv Syst 6:237–241, 1945

Rome HP: Psychiatry growing up. Editorial. Psychiatr News 1:4, 1966

Rome HP, et al: Symposium on automation. Technics in personality assessment. Proc Mayo Clin 37:61–82, 1962

Ropschitz DH: The role of extra-mural therapeutic social clubs in the mental health services of Derbyshire. Int J Soc Psychiatry 5:165–173, 1959

Rorschach H: Psychodiagnostics: A Diagnostic Test Based on Perception. Berne, Switz, Huber, 1942

Rose AE, Brown CE, Metcalfe EV: Music therapy at Westminister Hospital. Ment Hyg 43:93–104, 1959

Rosen E: Dance in Psychotherapy. New York, Bureau of Publications, Teachers College, Columbia University Press, 1957

Rosen JM: The treatment of schizophrenic psychosis by direct analytic therapy. Psychiatr Q 21:3–37, 117–119, 1947

Rosen JM: Direct Psychoanalytic Psychiatry. Orlando FL, Grune & Stratton, 1962

Rosen JM: Direct psychoanalysis, in Masserman JH (ed): Current Psychiatric Therapies, vol. 4. Orlando FL, Grune & Stratton, 1964, pp 101–107

Rosen JM, Chasen M: A study of resistance and its manifestations in therapeutic groups of chronic psychotic patients. Psychiatry 12:279, 1949

Rosen V: The initial psychiatric interview and the principles of psychotherapy: Some recent contributions. J Am Psychoanal Assoc 6:157, 1958

Rosenbaum CP: Events of early therapy and brief therapy. Arch Gen Psychiatry 10:506–512, 1964

Rosenbaum M: Group psychotherapy and psychodrama, in Wolman BB (ed): Handbook of Clinical Psychology. New York, McGraw-Hill, 1965

Rosenbaum M: The responsibility of the group psychotherapy practitioner for a therapeutic rationale. J Group Psychoanal Process 2:5–17, 1969

Rosenbaum M, Berger M (eds): Group Psychotherapy and Group Function: Selected Readings. New York, Basic Books, 1963

Rosenberg PP, Fuller M: Human relations seminar: A group work experiment in nursing education. Ment Hyg 39:406–432, 1955

Rosenfeld HA: Psychotic States. London, Hogarth, 1965

Rosenthal AJ, Levine SV: Brief psychotherapy with children: Process of therapy. Am J Psychiatry 128:141–146, 1971

Rosenthal D, Frank JD: Psychotherapy and the placebo effect. Psychol Bull 53:294–302, 1956

Rosenthal L: Countertransference in activity group therapy. Int J Group Psychother 3:431–440, 1953

Rosenthal L: A study of resistances in a member of a therapy group. Int J Group Psychother 13:315, 1963

Rosenthal L, Nagelberg L: Limitations of group therapy: A case presentation. Int J Group Psychother 6:166–179, 1956

Rosenthal MJ, Sullivan ME: Psychiatric Consultation in a Public Welfare Agency. Washington, DC, Children's Bureau, 1959

Rosenthal SH: A qualitative description of the electrosleep experience, in Wulfsohn NL, Sances A (eds): The Nervous System and Electric Currents, vol. 2. New York, Plenum, 1971, pp 153–155

Rosenthal SH: Electrosleep: A double-blind clinical study. Biol Psychiatry 4:179–185, 1972

Rosenzweig A: A transvaluation of psychotherapy: A reply to Hans Eysenck. J Abnorm Soc Psychol 49:298–304, 1954

Rosenzweig S: Some implicit common factors in diverse methods of Psychotherapy. Am J Orthopsychiatry 6:412–415, 1936

Roskin G: Drug addiction and its treatment: An analysis. Roche Report 3:1–8, 1966

Ross A: Behavior therapy, in Wolman BB (ed): Manual of Child Psychopathology. New York, McGraw-Hill, 1972

Ross H, Johnson AM: The growing science of case work. J Soc Casework 27:273–278, 1946

Ross MW: Clinical profile of Hare Krishna devotees. Am J Psychiatry 140:416–420, 1983

Ross TA: An enquiry into prognosis in the neuroses. London, Cambridge University Press, 1936

Rossi E (ed): Collected Papers of Milton H. Erickson. New York, Halsted Press, 1980

Rossi EL: Dreams and the Growth of Personality. Elmsford, NY, Pergamon, 1972

Rossi E, Ryan M (eds): Life Reframing in Hypnosis: The Seminars, Workshops and Lectures of Milton H. Erickson, vol. 2. New York, Irvington, 1985

Rossi E, Ryan M, Sharp F (eds): Healing in Hypnosis: The Seminars, Workshops and Lectures of Milton H. Erickson, vol. 1. New York, Irvington, 1983

Rossman I: Clinical Geriatrics. Philadelphia, Lippincott, 1971

Roth J: An intervention strategy for children with developmental problems. J School Psychol 8:311–314, 1970

Rothman T, Sward K: Studies in pharmacological psychotherapy. Arch Neurol Psychiatry 75:95–105, 1956

Rubenstein C: The treatment of morphine addiction in tuberculosis by Pavlov's conditioning method, in Franks CM (ed): Conditioning Techniques in Clinical Practice and Research. New York, Springer, 1964, pp 202–205

Rubins JL: Five year results of psychoanalytic therapy and day care for acute schizophrenic patients. Am J Psychoanal 36:3–26, 1976

Rubinstein D: Family therapy, in Hoffman FH (ed): Teaching of Psychotherapy. International Psychiatric Clinics. Boston, Little, Brown, 1964

Rubinstein MA, Chipman A, Nemiroff RA: Simultaneous family and individual therapy of a hospitalized mother and daughter. Paper presented at the 122d Annual Meeting of the American Psychiatric Association, Atlantic City, NJ, May 1966

Ruck F: Alkoholentziehungskur mit Hilfe eines bedingten Reflexes (Apormophinentpziehungskur). (Conditioned reflex treatment of alcoholism.) Psychiatr Neurol Med Psychol (Leipz) 8:88–92, 1958

Ruesch J: Social factors in therapy, in Psychiatric Treatment, vol. 31. Assoc Res Nerv Ment Dis. Baltimore, Williams & Wilkins, 1953

Ruesch J: Disturbed Communication. New York, Norton, 1957

Ruesch J: General theory of communication in psychiatry, in Arieti S (ed): American Handbook of Psychiatry, vol. 1. New York, Basic Books, 1959, pp 895–908

Ruesch J: Social psychiatry. Arch Gen Psychiatry 5:501–509, 1965

Ruesch J, et al: Psychiatric Care. New York, Grune & Stratton, 1964

Rund DA, Hutzler JC: Emergency Psychiatry. St. Louis, CV Masky Co, 1983

Rush AJ: Cognitive therapy. Weekly Psychiatry Update Series. Lesson 52. Princeton, NJ, Biomedia, Inc, 1978

Rush AJ, Beck AC: Cognitive therapy of depression and suicide. Am J Psychother 32:201–219, 1978

Rush AJ, Beck AT, Kovacs M, et al: Comparative efficacy of cognitive therapy in pharmaco therapy in the treatment of depressed outpatients. Cognitive Ther Res 1:17–37, 1977

Rush AJ (ed): Short–term Psychotherapies for Depression. New York, Guilford, 1982

Russell MAH, Raw M, Jarvis MJ: Clinical use of nicotine chewing gym. Br Med Journal 280:1599–1602, 1982

Rutherford BR: The use of negative practice in speech therapy with children handicapped by cerebral palsy, athetoid type. J Speech Dis 5:259–264, 1940

Rutledge KA: The professional nurse as primary therapist: Background, perspective, and opinion. J Operational Psychiatry 5:76–86, 1974

Rutter M: Maternal Deprivation Reassessed. Middlesex, England, Penguin Books, 1972

Ruud E: Music Therapy and its Relationship to Current Treatment Theories. St. Louis, Magnamusic–Baton, 1980

Ryan WC: Mental Health Through Education. New York, Commonwealth Fund, 1939

Ryle G: Philosophical Arguments. New York, Oxford University Press, 1945

Sabath G: The treatment of hard-core voluntary drug addict patients. Int J Group Psychother 14:307–317, 1964

Sabshin M: Theory and practice of community psychiatry in the medical school setting, in Goldston SE (ed): Concepts of Community Psychiatry: A Framework for Training. Pub Health Service Publ No. 131. Bethesda, Md, National Institute for Mental Health, 1965, pp 49–56

Sacks MH, Carpenter WT, Jr: The pseudotherapeutic community: An examination of anti–therapeutic forces on psychiatric units. Hosp Community Psychiatry 25:315–318, 1974

Safer DJ, Allen RP: Hyperactive Children, Diagnosis and Management. Baltimore, University Park Press, 1976

Sager CJ: The effects of group psychotherapy on individual psychoanalysis. Int J Group Psychother 9:403, 1959

Sager CJ: Insight and interaction in combined individual and group therapy. Int J Group Psychother 30:14, 1964

Sager CJ: The treatment of married couples, in Arieti S (ed): American Handbook of Psychiatry, vol. 3. New York, Basic Books, 1966(a), pp 213–224

Sager CJ: The development of marriage therapy: A historical review. Am J Orthopsychiatry 36:458–467, 1966(b)

Sager CJ: Transference in the conjoint treatment of married couples. Newsletter (Society of Medical Psychoanalysts) 7:9–10, 1966(c)

Sager CJ: Marital psychotherapy, in Masserman JH (ed): Current Psychiatric Therapies, vol. 7. Orlando FL, Grune & Stratton, 1967

Sager CJ: Marriage Contracts and Couple Therapy. New York, Brunner/Mazel, 1976

Sager CJ, Kremer M, Lenz R, et al: The married in treatment. Arch Gen Psychiatry 19:205–217, 1968

Sager CJ, Kaplan HS: Progress in Group and Family Therapy. New York, Brunner/Mazel, 1972

Sakel M: The Pharmacological Shock Treatment of Schizophrenia. Wortis J (trans). New York, Nerv & Ment Dis Monogr, 1938

Salk L: What Every Child Would Like His Parent to Know. New York, McKay, 1972

Salter A: Conditioned Reflex Therapy: The Direct Approach to the Reconstruction of Personality. New York, Putnam, 1961

Salter A: The theory and practice of conditioned reflex therapy, in Wolpe J, et al (eds): The Conditioning Therapies. New York, Holt, 1966

Salzinger K: Experimental manipulations of verbal behavior: A review. J Gen Psychol 61:65–94, 1959

Salzman L: Countertransference: A therapeutic tool, in Masserman JH (ed): Current Psychiatric Therapies, vol. 2. Orlando FL, Grune & Stratton, 1962

Salzman L: Therapy of obsessional states. Am J Psychiatry 122:1139–1146, 1966

Salzman L: The Obessive Personality. New York, Science House, 1968

Salzman L: Psychoanalytic therapy of the obsessional patient, in Masserman JH (ed): Current Psychiatric Therapies, vol. 22. Orlando FL, Grune & Stratton, 1983, pp 53–66

Salzman L: Psychotherapeutic management of obsessive–compulsive patients. Am J Psychother 39:323–330, 1985

Salzman L, Thaler FH: Obsessive–compulsive disorders: A review of the literature. Am J Psychiatry, 133(3):286–296, 1981

Sandell R: Influence of supervision, therapist's competence and patient's ego level on the effects of time–limited psychotherapy. Psychother Psychosom 44:103–9, 1985

Sanders SH: Behavioral assessment and treatment of clinical pain: Appraisal of current status, in Hersen M, Eisler RM, Miller PM (eds): Progress in Behavior Modification, vol. 8. Orlando FL, Academic Press, 1979

Sanderson RE, et al: An investigation of new aversive conditioning treatment for alcoholism, in Franks CM (ed): Conditioning Techniques in Clinical Practice and Research, New York, Springer, 1964, pp 165–177

Sandison RA, Whitelaw JDA: Further studies in the therapeutic value of lysergic acid diethylamide in mental illness. J Ment Sci 103:332–343, 1957

Sandison RA, Whitelaw JDA, Spencer AM: The therapeutic value of lysergic acid diethylamide in mental illness. J Ment Sci 100:491–507, 1954

Sandler J, Rosenblatt B: The concept of the representational world. Psychoanal Study of the Child 17:128–145, 1962

Sandler J, Sandler AM: On the development of object relationships and affects. Int J Psychoanal 59:285–296, 1978

San Mateo County Department of Public Health and Welfare: Spectrum of San Mateo County Mental Health Services. San Mateo, Calif, San Mateo Department of Public Health & Welfare, 1961

Santayana G: The Life of Reason (2d ed). New York, Scribner, 1948

Sarason IG, Ganzer VJ: Modeling and group discussion in the rehabilitation of juvenile deliquents. J Counsel Psychol 20:422–429, 1973

Sargant W, Shorvon HJ: Acute war neuroses. Arch Neurol Psychiatry 54:231, 1945

Sargant WW, Slater ETU: Introduction to Physical Methods of Treatment in Psychiatry (4th ed). Baltimore, Williams & Wilkins, 1963 (New York, Aronson, 1973)

Sarlin CN, Berezin MA: Group psychotherapy on a modified analytic basis. J Nerv Ment Dis 104:611–667, 1946

Sarwer-Foner GJ: Patterns of marital relationship. Am J Psychother 17:31–44, 1963

Sasaki RF: Rinzai Zen Study for Foreigners in Japan. Kyoto, The First Zen Institute of American in Japan, 1960

Saslow G, Matarazzo J: A setting for social learning. Ment Hosp 13:217–226, 1962

Saslow G, Peters AD: A follow-up study of "untreated" patients with various behavior disorders. Psychiatr Q 30;283–302, 1956

Satir VM: Schziophrenia and family therapy, in Social Work Practice, 1963. (Published for the National Conference on Social Welfare, Columbus, Ohio. New York, Columbia University Press, 1963

Satir VM: Conjoint Family Therapy. Palo Alto, Calif, Science & Behavior Books, 1964(a)

Satir VM: Symptomology: A Family Production. Palo Alto, Calif, Family Project Institute, 1964(b)

Satir VM: Conjoint marital therapy, in Green BL (ed): The Psychotherapies of Marital Disharmony. New York, Free Press, 1965

Saul LJ: On the value of one or two interviews. Psychoanal Q 20:613–615, 1951

Saul LJ: The Technic and Practice of Psychoanalysis. Philadelphia, Lippincott, 1958

Saul LJ: Reactions of a man to natural death. Psychoanal Q 28:383, 1959

Saul LJ, Beck AT: Psychodynamics of male homosexuality. Int J Psychoanal 42:43–48, 1961

Saul LJ, et al: Can one partner be successfully counseled without the other? Marr Fam Living 15:59–64, 1953

Saul LJ, Rome H, Leuser E: Desensitization of combat fatigue patients. Am J Psychiatry 102:476–478, 1946

Savage C: Countertransference in the therapy of schizophrenics. Psychiatry 24:53–60, 1961

Savage C, Harman W, Fadiman J, Savage E: LSD: Therapeutic effects of the psychedelic experience. Psychol Rep 14:111–120, 1964

Savage C, McCabe OL: Residential psychedelic (LSD) therapy for the narcotic addict: A controlled study. Arch Gen Psychiatry 28:808–814, 1973

Savage C, McCabe OL, Olsson JE, et al: Research with psychedelic drugs, in Hicks RE (ed): Psychedelic Drugs. Orlando FL, Grune & Stratton, 1969

Sawyer J: Measurement and prediction, clinical and actuarial. Psychol Bull 66:178–200, 1966

Scarborough HE, Denson BW: Treatment of therapeutic blockades with theopental (Pentothal) sodium and methamphetamine (Desoxyn), 1948–1957. Psychosom Med 20:108–116, 1958

Schaefer DL, Smith JJ: A dynamic therapy for schizophrenia. Am J Occup Ther 7:5, 1958

Schaefer R: The Clinical Application of Psychological Tests. New York, International Universities Press, 1948

Schafer R: New Language for Psychoanalysis. New Haven, Yale University Press, 1976

Schafer R: The Analytic Attitudes. New York, Basic Books, 1983

Schamess G: Group treatment modalities for latency age children. Int J Group Psychother 26:455–474, 1976

Scharfstein SS, Towery OB, Malowe ID: Accuracy of diagnostic information submitted to an insurance company. Am J Psychiatry 137:70–73, 1980

Schedlinger S: Psychoanalysis and Group Behavior. New York, Norton, 1952

Scheflen AE: Analysis of thought model which persists in psychiatry. Psychosom Med 20:235–241, 1958

Scheflen AE: A Psychotherapy of Schizophrenia. Springfield, Ill, Thomas, 1961

Scheflen AE: Communication and regulation in psychotherapy. Psychiatry 26:126–136, 1963

Scheflen AE: The significance of posture in communications systems. Psychiatry 27:316, 1964

Scheidlinger S: Group process in group psychotherapy. A critical analysis of some current trends in the integration of individual and group psychology. Am J Psychother 14(1,2—entire issues), 1960

Scheidlinger S: Concept of regression in group psychotherapy. Int J Group Psychother 18:20, 1968

Scheidlinger S: Group psychotherapy in the 1980's: Problems and prospects. Am J Psychother 38(4): 494–504, 1984(a)

Scheidlinger S: Psychoanalytic group psychotherapy today–an overview. J Am Psychoanal 12(2):269–84, 1984(b)

Scheidlinger S, Porter K: Group therapy combined with individual psychotherapy, in Karasu T, Bellak L (eds): Specialized Techniques in Psychotherapy. New York, Brunner/Mazel, 1980

Scherz FH: Multiple-client interviewing: Treatment implications. J Soc Casework 43:120–125, 1962

Schiavi RC: Male erectile disorders. Annu Rev Med 32:509–520, 1981

Schilder P: The analysis of ideologies as a psychotherapeutic method, especially in group treatment. Am J Psychiatry 93:601–617, 1936

Schilder P: Results and problems of group psychotherapy in severe neuroses. Ment Hyg 23:87–98, 1939

Schilder P: The cure of criminals and the prevention of crime. J Crim Psychopathol, 149–161, 1940

Schindler W: Countertransference in family-pattern group psychotherapy. Int J Group Psychother 3:424–440, 1953

Schlessinger N: Supervision in psychotherapy. Arch Gen Psychiatry 15:129–134, 1966

Schmideberg M: The mode of operation of psychoanalytic therapy. Int J Psychoanal 19, 1938

Schmideberg M: The borderline patient, in Arieti S (ed): American Handbook of Psychiatry, vol. 1. New York, Basic Books, 1959, p 415

Schmideberg M: A major task of therapy: Developing volition and purpose. Am J Psychother 15:251–259, 1961

Schmiege GR: The current status of LSD as a therapeutic tool: A summary of the clinical literature. J Med Soc NJ 60:203–207, 1963

Schneck JM: Hypnoanalysis. Personality 1:317–370, 1951

Schneck JM: Self-hypnotic dreams in hypnoanalysis. J Clin Exp Hypn 1:44–53, 1953

Schneck JM: Hypnosis in Modern Medicine (3rd ed). Springfield, Ill, Thomas, 1963

Schneck JM: The Principles and Practice of Hypnoanalysis. Springfield, Ill, Thomas, 1965

Schneider SJ: Quit by mail: The computer in a stop-smoking clinic, in Schwartz MD (ed): Using Computers in Clinical Practice. New York, The Haworth Press, 1984, pp 359–362

Schoech D: Computer use in human service. New York, Human Sci Press, 1982

Schofield W: In Welsh GS, Dahlstrom WG (eds): Basic Readings on the MMPI in Psychology and Medicine. Minneapolis, University of Minnesota Press, 1956

Schopbach RR: Art in psychotherapy. Henry Ford Hosp Med Bull 12:301–316, 1964

Schorer CE, Lowinger P, Sullivan T, Hartlaub GH: Improvement without treatment. Paper presented at the 122d Annual Meeting of the American Psychiatric Association, Atlantic City, NJ, May 1966

Schuckit MA: Drug and Alcohol Abuse: A Clinical Guide to Diagnosis and Treatment. New York, Plenum Press, 1980

Schullian D, Schoen M (eds): Music and Medicine, New York, Schuman, 1948

Schultz JA, Luthe W: Autogenic Training—A Psychophysiologic Approach in Psychotherapy. New York, Grune & Stratton, 1959

Schuster DB, Sandt JJ, Thaler OF: Clinic Supervision of the Psychiatric Resident. New York, Brunner/Mazel, 1972

Schut JW, Himwich HE: The effect of Meratran on twenty-five institutionalized mental patients. Am J Psychiatry 111:837–840, 1955

Schutz W: Interpersonal Underworld. (Original title: Firo: A Three-Dimensional Theory of Interpersonal Behavior.) Palo Alto, Calif, Science & Behavior Books, 1967(a)

Schutz W: Joy: Expanding Human Awareness. New York, Grove, 1967(b)

Schwab JJ, Schwab RB: The epidemiology of mental illness, in Usdin G (ed): Psychiatry: Education and Image. New York, Brunner/Mazel, 1973, p 67

Schwarcz, GA: A review of rapid neuroleptization. Rapid medical control of acutely psychotic patients. National Assoc of Private Hospitals 13:12–16, 1982

Schwartz A: Parameters in the psychoanalytic treatment of a dying patient. Assoc Psychoanal Med, December, 1961

Schwartz CG: Rehabilitation of Mental Hospital Patients. Pub Health Monogr No. 17. Washington, DC, U.S. Government Printing Office, 1953

Schwartz EK: The development of clinical psychology as an independent profession. Prag Clin Psychol 3:10–21, 1958

Schwartz EK: Non-Freudian analytic methods, in Wolman B (ed): Handbook of Clinical Psychology. New York, McGraw-Hill, 1965

Schwartz EK: The treatment of the obsessive patient in the group therapy setting. Am J Psychother 26:352–361, 1972

Schwartz EK, Abel TA: The professional education of the psychoanalytic psychotherapist. Am J Psychother 9:253–261, 1955

Schwartz EK, Wolf A: Psychoanalysis in groups: Three primary parameters. Am Imago 14:281–297, 1957

Schwartz EK, Wolf A: Psychoanalysis in groups: The role of values. Am J Psychoanal 19:37–52, 1959

Schwartz EK, Wolf A: Psychoanalysis in groups: The mystique of group dynamics, in Hulse W (ed): Topical Problems of Psychotherapy, vol. 2. Basel, Switz, Karger, 1960

Schwartz EK, Wolf A: Psychoanalysis in groups: Some comparisons with individual analysis. J Genet Psychol 64:153–191, 1961

Schwartz EK, Wolf A: Psychoanalysis in groups: A creative process. Am J Psychoanal 24:46–59, 1964(a)

Schwartz EK, Wolf A: On countertransference in group psychotherapy. J Psychol 57:131, 1964(b)

Schwartz JL: Smoking cures: Ways to kick an unhealthy habit, in Jarvik ME et al (eds): Research on Smoking Behavior. NIDA Res Mongr 17, Washington, DC, U.S. Government Printing Office, 1977

Schwartz MD (ed): Using Computers in Clinical Practice. New York, The Haworth Press, 1984

Schwartz MF: The core of the stuttering block. J Speech Hear Disord 39:169–177, 1974

Schwartz MS, Shockley EL: The Nurse and the

Mental Patient. New York, Russell Sage Foundation, 1956

Schwartz W: Group work and the social scene, in Kahn A (ed): Issues in American Social Work. New York, Columbia University Press, 1959, pp 110–137

Schwitzgebel R: Reduction of adolescent crime by a research method. J Soc Ther Correct Psychiatry 7:212–215, 1961

Schwitzgebel R, Kolb DA: Inducing behavior change in adolescent delinquents. Behav Res Ther 1:297–304, 1964

Science News, Vol. 122, November 13, 1982, p. 309

Science 228:1510–1511, 1985

Searl MN: Some queries on principles of technique. Int J Psychoanal 17:471–493, 1936

Searles HF: The informational value of the supervisor's emotional experiences. Psychiatry 18:135, 1955

Searles HF: The Nonhuman Environment in Normal Development and in Schizophrenia. New York, International Universities Press, 1960

Searles HF: Collected Papers on Schizophrenia and Related Subjects, New York, International Universities Press, 1966

Sechehaye MA: Symbolic Realization: A New Method of Psychotherapy Applied to a Case of Schizophrenia. Wursten B, Wursten H (trans). New York, International Universities Press, 1951

Sechehaye MA: A New Psychotherapy in Schizophrenia. Orlando FL, Grune & Stratton, 1956

Seeman J, Raskin NJ: Research perspectives in client-centered therapy, in Mowrer OH (ed): Psychotherapy: Theory and Research. New York, Ronald, 1953, p 205

Seevers MH: Psychopharmacological elements of drug dependence. JAMA 206:1263–1284, 1968

Segal H: Introduction to the Work of Melanie Klein. New York, Basic Books, 1964

Segal J: Biofeedback as a medical treatment. JAMA 232:179–180, 1975

Seitz PFD: Experiments in the substitution of symptoms by hypnosis, II. Psychosom Med 15:405–422, 1953

Seligman E: Behavior therapy, in Grayson, H (ed): Short–term Approaches to Psychotherapy. New York, Human Sciences Press, 1979, pp 11–55

Selmi PM, Klein MH, Greist JH, et al: An investigation of computer–assisted cognitive–behavior therapy in the treatment of depression. Beh Res Methods & Instrumentation 14:181, 1982

Selvini-Palazzoli M, Cecchin G, Prata G: Paradox and Counterparadox. New York, Aronson, 1978

Selye H: Stress, The Physiology and Pathology of Exposure to Stress. Montreal, Acta, 1950

Selye H: Stress and psychology. Am J Psychology 113:423, 1956

Selye H: The Stress of Life. New York, McGraw–Hill, 1976

Selzer ML: The Michigan Alcoholism Screening Test: The quest for a new diagnostic instrument. Am J Psychiatry 127:1653–1658, 1971

Senay EC: Substance Abuse Disorders in Clinical Practice, Littleton, MA, John Wright, 1983

Senay EC, Dorusw, Renault PF: Methadylacetale and methadone. JAMA 237:138–142, 1977

Serban G, Siegal S: Response of borderline and schizotypal patients to small doses of thioxipene and haloperedol. Am J Psychiatry 141:1455–1460, 1984

Sermat V, Smyth M: Content analysis of verbal communication in the development of a relationship: Condition influencing self–disclosure. J Personality and Soc Psychol 26:332–346, 1973

Servadio E: Transference and thought-transference. Int J Psychoanal 37:1, 1956

Shafii M: Childhood psychosis, in Noshpitz JD (ed): Basic Handbook of Childhood Psychiatry, vol. 3. New York, Basic Books, 1979, pp 555–567

Shapiro AK: Etiological factors in placebo effect. JAMA 187:712–714, 1964

Shapiro D: Neurotic Styles. New York, Basic Books, 1965

Shapiro DA, Shapiro D: Meta–analysis of comparative therapy outcome studies: A replication and refinement. Psychol Bull 92(2):581–604, 1982

Shapiro D, Schwartz GE: Biofeedback and visceral learning: Clinical applications. Semin Psychiatry 4:171–184, 1972

Sharfstein SS, Beigel A: Less is more? Today's economics and its challenge to psychiatry. Am J Psychiatry 141:1403–1408, 1984

Sharfstein SS, Towery OB, Milowe ID: Accuracy of diagnostic information submitted to an insurance company. Am J Psychiatry 137:70–73, 1980

Sharoff RL: Therapy of drug addiction. Curr Psychiatr Ther 6:247–251, 1966

Sharoff RL: Narcotherapy, in Freedman AM, Kaplan HI (eds): Comprehensive Textbook of Psychiatry. Baltimore, Williams & Wilkins, 1967

Sharpe EF: The technique of psychoanalysis.

Int J Psychoanal 11:251–277, 361–386, 1930: 12:24–60, 1931

Sheehan DV: Current Concepts in Psychiatry: Panic attacks and phobias. Engl J Med 307(3): 156–158, 1982

Shehi M, Patterson WM: Treatment of panic with alprazolam and propanolol. Am J Psychiatry 141:900–901, 1984

Sherwood S: Long–term Care: A Handbook for Researchers, Planners and Providers. New York, Spectrum Publishers, 1975

Shick JFE, Freedman DX: Research in nonnarcotic drug abuse, in Arieti S (ed): American Handbook of Psychiatry, vol. 4. New York, Basic Books, 1975, pp 592–593

Shlien JM: Cross-theoretical criteria in time-limited therapy. Paper presented at the 6th International Congress of Psychotherapy, London, 1964

Shlien JM, Mosak HM, Driekers R: Effects of time limits: A comparison of two psychotherapies. J Counsel Psychol 9:31–34, 1962

Shlien JM, Zinring FM: Research directives and methods in client-centered therapy, in Hart JT, Tomlinson TM (eds): New Directions in Client-Centered Therapy. Boston, Houghton-Mifflin, 1970, p 33

Shobe FO, Gildea MCL: Long-term follow-up of selected lobotomized private patients. JAMA 206:327–332, 1968

Shor RE: The fundamental problem viewed from historic perspective, in Fromm E, Shor RE (eds): Hypnosis: Research Developments and Persepctives. Chicago, Aldine, 1972

Shore MF, Massimo JL: Comprehensive vocationally oriented psychotherapy for adolescent delinquent boys: A follow-up study. Am J Orthopsychiatry 36:609–615, 1966

Shorr JE: Psycho-imagination Therapy. New York, Stratton Intercontinental, 1972

Showalter L: Mental health counselors—new professionals? The NIMH pilot group ten years later. Semin Psychiatry 3:288–291, 1971

Sider RC, Clements C: Family or individual therapy: The ethics of modality choice. Am J Psychiatry 139:1455–1459, 1982

Sider RC: The ethics of therapeutic modality choice. Am J Psychiatry 141: 390–394, 1984

Sidowski JB, Johnson JH, Williams TA: Technology in Mental Health Care Delivery Systems. Norwood, NJ, Ablex Publishing Corp., 1980

Siegel NH: What is a therapeutic community? Nurs Outlook, 12:49–51, 1964

Sifneos PE: Two different kinds of psychotherapy of short duration. Paper presented at the 122d Annual Meeting of the American Psychiatric Association, Atlantic City, NJ, May 1966 (Am J Psychiatry 123:1069, 1967)

Sifneos PE: Short-Term Psychotherapy and Emotional Crisis. Cambridge, Harvard University Press, 1972

Silber E: The analyst's perception in the treatment of an adolescent. Psychiatry 25:160–169, 1962

Sills GM: Historical developments and issues in psychiatric mental health nursing, in Leninger MM (ed): Contemporary Issues in Mental Health Nursing. Boston, Little, Brown, 1973

Silver LB: Acceptable and controversial approaches in treating the child with learning disabilities. Pediatrics 55:406, 415, 1975

Simmons JQ, Leiken SJ, Lovaas DI, et al: Modifications of autistic behavior with LSD-25. Am J Psychiatry 122:1201–1211, 1966

Simms LM: Use of hydroxyzine in neuropsychiatric states. Dis Nerv Syst 19:225, 1958

Simon A, Epstein LJ (eds): Aging in Modern Society. Washington, DC, American Psychological Association, 1968

Simon B, et al: The recognition and acceptance of mood in music by psychotic patients. J Nerv Ment Dis 114:66–78, 1951

Simon J: Observations on 67 patients who took Erhard Seminars Training. Am J Psychiatry 135:686–691, 1978

Simon RM: On eclecticism. Am J Psychiatry 131:135–139, 1974

Simpson GM: Antipsychotic drugs, in AMA Drug Evaluations. Chicago, Am Med Association, 1983

Singer E: Key Concepts in Psychotherapy. New York, Random House, 1965

Singh AN, Sexena B, Gent M: Clomipramine (Anafravil) in depressive patients with obsessive neurosis. J Int Med Res (Suppl 5) 25, 1977

Skinner BF: Science and Human Behavior. New York, Macmillan, 1953

Sklar AD, Yalom ID, Zim A, et al: Time-extended group therapy: A controlled study. Comp Group Studies 1:373–386, 1970

Slack CW: Experimenter-subject psychotherapy: A new method of introducing intensive office treatment for unreachable cases. Ment Hyg 44:238–256, 1960

Slack CW, Schwitzgebel R: A Handbook: Reducing Adolescent Crime in Your Community. Privately printed, 1960

Slavin S: Education, learning and group work. J Educ Sociology 24:143, 1950

Slavson SR: An Introduction to Group Therapy. New York, Commonwealth Fund, 1943 (paperback—New York, International Universities Press, 1970)

Slavson SR: Current practices in group therapy. Ment Hyg July 1944

Slavson SR: Differential methods of group psychotherapy in relation to age level. Nerv Child, pp 196–210, 1945

Slavson SR: The field and objectives of personality disorders, in Glueck B (ed): Current Therapies of Personality Disorders. Orlando FL, Grune & Stratton, 1946(a), pp 166–193

Slavson SR: Recreation and the Total Personality. New York, Association Press, 1946(b)

Slavson SR: The Practice of Group Therapy. New York, International Universities Press, 1947

Slavson SR: Child-Centered Group Guidance of Parents. New York, International Universities Press, 1949

Slavson SR: Analytic Group Psychotherapy with Adults, Adolescents and Children. New York, Columbia University Press, 1950(a)

Slavson SR: Transference phenomena in group psychotherapy. Psychoanal Rev 37:39, 1950(b)

Slavson SR: Child Psychotherapy. New York, Columbia University Press, 1952

Slavson SR: Sources of countertransference and group-induced anxiety. Int J Group Psychother 3:373–388, 1953

Slavson SR: Criteria for selection and rejection of patients for various types of group psychotherapy. Int J Group Psychother 5:3–22, 1955

Slavson SR: The Fields of Group Psychotherapy. New York, International Universities Press, 1956(a)

Slavson SR: The nature and treatment of acting out in group psychotherapy. Int J Group Psychother 6:3, 1956(b)

Slavson SR: Are there "group dynamics" in the therapy group? Int J Group Psychother 7:131, 1957

Slavson SR: When is a "therapy group" not a therapy group? Int J Group Psychother 10:3–21, 1960

Slavson SR: A Textbook in Analytic Group Psychotherapy. New York, International Universities Press, 1964

Slavson SR: Reclaiming the Delinquent by Para-Analytic Group Psychotherapy and the Inversion Technique. New York, Free Press, 1965, p 766

Sletten IW, Altman H, Ulett GA, et al: Routine diagnosis by computer. Am J Psychiatry 127:1147–1152, 1971

Sloane P: Report of the second panel on the technique of supervised analysis. J Am Psychoanal Assoc 5:539–545, 1957

Small IF, Matarazzo R, Small JG: Total ward therapy groups in psychiatric treatment. Am J Psychother 17:254–265, 1963

Smallwood JC: Dance-movement therapy, in Masserman JH (ed): Current Psychiatric Therapies, vol. 14. Orlando FL, Grune & Stratton, 1974

Smith AB, Berlin L, Brassin A: Problems in client-centered group therapy with adult offenders. Am J Orthopsychiatry 33:550–553, 1963

Smith BK: No Language But a Cry. Boston, Beacon, 1964

Smith BM, Hain JD, Stevenson I: Controlled interviews using drugs. Arch Gen Psychiatry 22:2–10, 1970

Smith CM: A new adjunct to the treatment of alcoholism: The hallucinogenic drugs. Q J Stud Alcohol 19:406–417, 1958

Smith EWL (ed): The Growing Edge of Gestalt Therapy. New York, Brunner/Mazel, 1976

Smith ER, Tyler R: Appraising and recording student Progress, in Adventures in American Education, vol. 3. New York, Harper & Row, 1942, p 18

Smith G: Psychotherapy in General Medicine. New York, Commonwealth Fund, 1946

Smith ME: Perphenazine and amitriptyline as adjuncts to psychotherapy. Am J Psychiatry 120:76–77, 1963

Smith MJ: When I Say No, I Feel Guilty. New York, Dial Press, 1975

Smith WL, Glass GV, Miller TI: The Benefits of Psychotherapy. Baltimore, Johns Hopkins University Press, 1980

Smith WG: A model for psychiatric diagnosis. Arch Gen Psychiatry 14:521–529, 1966

Snell JE: The use of music in group psychotherapy, in Masserman JH (ed): Current Psychiatric Therapies, vol. 5. Orlando FL, Grune & Stratton, 1965, pp 145–149

Snyder F: Progress in the new biology of dreaming. Am J Psychiatry 122:377–391, 1965

Snyder F: Toward an evolutionary theory of dreaming. Paper presented at the 122d Annual Meeting of the American Psychiatric Association, Atlantic City, NJ, May 1966

Snyder WU: A short-term nondirective treatment with an adult. J Abnorm Soc Psychol Clin Suppl 38:87–137, 1943

Snyder WU: Casebook of Non-Directive Counseling. Boston, Houghton Mifflin, 1947(a)

Snyder WU: The present status of psychotherapeutic counseling. Psychol Bull 44:297–386, 1947(b)

Soal SG, Bateman F: Modern Experiments in Telepathy. New Haven, Yale University Press, 1954

Sobel HJ (ed): Behavior Therapy in Terminal Care: A Humanistic Approach. Cambridge, Ballinger, 1981

Sobey F: The Nonprofessional Revolution in Mental Health. New York, Columbia University Press, 1970

Soibelman D: Therapeutic and Industrial Uses of Music. New York, Columbia University Press, 1948

Sollod RN, Kaplan HS: The new sex therapy: An integration of behavioral, psychodynamic, and interpersonal approaches, in Claghorn JL (ed): Successful Psychotherapy. New York, Brunner/Mazel, 1976

Solnit AJ: Learning from psychoanalytic supervision. Int J Psychoanal 51:359–362, 1970

Soloff PH, George A, Nathan RS, Schultz PM, Alrich RF, Perel JM: Progress in pharmacotherapy of borderline disorders: A double-blind study of amitryptyline, haloperodol, and placebo. Arch Gen Psychiatry 43:641–697, 1986

Soloff PH, Schulz PM, Nathan RS, et al: Progress in pharmacotherapy of borderline disorders. Arch Gen Psychiatry 43:691–697, 1986

Solomon A, Loeffler FJ, Frank GH: An analysis of co-therapists interaction in group psychotherapy. Int J Group Psychother 3:171–180, 1953

Solomon AP, Greene BL: marital disharmony: Concurrent therapy of husband and wife by the same psychiatrist. Dis Nerv Syst 24:21–28, 1963

Solomon JC: Active play therapy. Am J Orthopsychiatry 8:479, 1938

Solomon JC: Active play therapy: Further experience. Am J Orthopsychiatry 10:763–781, 1940

Solomon JC: Therapeutic use of play, in Anderson HH, Anderson GL (eds): Introduction to Projective Techniques. Englewood Cliffs, NJ, Prentice-Hall, 1951

Solomon JC, Axelrod PL: Group psychotherapy for withdrawn adolescents. Am J Dis Child 68:86–101, 1944

Solomon P (ed): Psychiatric Drugs. Orlando FL, Grune & Stratton, 1966

Soo ES: Applications of object relations concepts to children's group psychotherapy. Int J Group Psychother 35:37–47, 1985

Solow C, Silverfarb PM, Swift K: Psychosocial effects of intestinal bypass surgery for severe obesity. N Engl J Med 290:300–304, 1974

Sonneman U: Handwriting Analysis. Orlando FL, Grune & Stratton, 1951

Soskin RA, Grof S, Richards WA: Low doses of dispropyltryptamine in psychotherapy. Arch Gen Psychiatry 28:817–821, 1973

Spangaard J: Transference neurosis and psychoanalytic group psychotherapy. Int J Group Psychother 9:31–42, 1959

Spector S: Behavior therapy in anorexia nervosa. JAMA 233:317, 1975

Spence D: Narrative Truth and Historical Truth. New York, Norton, 1982

Spence DP: On some clinical implications of action language. J Am Psychoanal Assoc 30(1):137–168, 1982

Spencer AM: Modifications in the technique of LSD therapy. Compr Psychiatry 5:232–252, 1964

Sperber E, Feitas R, Davis D: Bulletins of Structural Integration, vol. I, II. 1969

Spero MH: Thoughts on computerized psychotherapy. Psychiatry 41:279–288, 1978

Spiegel D, Yalom ID: A support group for dying patients. Int J Group Psychother 28(2):233–45, 1978

Spiegel H: Is symptom removal dangerous? Paper presented at the 122d Annual Meeting of the American Psychiatric Association. Atlantic City, NJ, May 1966

Spiegel H: A single-treatment method to stop smoking using ancillary self-hypnosis. Int J Clin Exp Hypn 18:235–250, 1970

Spiegel H, Spiegel D: Trance and Treatment: Clinical Uses of Hypnosis. New York, Basic Books, 1978

Spiegel JP: Homeostatic mechanisms within the family, in Galdston I (ed): The Family in Contemporary Society. New York, International Universities Press, 1958

Spiegel JP: The resolution of role conflict within the family, in Bell NW, Vogel EF (eds): The Family. New York, Free Press, 1960

Spiegel JP: Our colleagues. Psychiatr News 9:2, 1974

Spiegel R: Specific problems of communication in psychiatric conditions, in Arieti S (ed): American Handbook of Psychiatry, vol. 1. New York, Basic Books, 1959, pp 909–949

Spiegelberg H: The Phenomenological Movement, A Historical Introduction. The Hague, Neth, Martinus, Nijhoff, 1960

Spitz HH, Kopp SB: Multiple Psychotherapy. Psychiatr Q Suppl 3:295–311, 1957

Spitz RA: Hospitalism, in Eissler RS, et al (eds): The Psychoanalytic Study of the Child, vol.

1. New York, International Universities Press, 1945

Spitz RA: Anaclitic depression, in Eissler RS, et al (eds): The Psychoanalytic Study of the Child, vol. 2. New York, International Universities Press, 1946, p 313

Spitz RA: Genese des premiéres relations objectales (Development of the first object relationships). Rev Fran Psyche, 1954

Spitzer RL: Clinical criteria for psychiatric diagnosis and DSM-III. Am J Psychiatry 132:1187–1192, 1975

Spitzer RL, Cohen J: Common errors in quantitative psychiatric research. Int J Psychiatry 6:109–131, 1968

Spitzer RL, Endicott J: A re–analysis of the reliability of psychiatric diagnosis. Br J Psychiatry, pp 341–347, 1974

Spitzer RL, Endicott J, Cohen J: The Psychiatric Status Schedule. Technique for Evaluating Social and Role Functioning and Mental Status, New York, N.Y. State Psychiatric Institute and Biometrics Research, 1967

Spitzer RL, Endicott J, Diagno II: Further developments in a computer program for psychiatric diagnosis. Am J Psychiatry 125:12, 1969

Spitzer RL, Endicott J, Fleiss, RL, Cohen J: The psychiatric status schedule: A technique for evaluating psychopathology and impairment in role functioning, Arch Gen Psychiatry 23:41–55, 1970

Spitzer RL, Williams JBW: Classification of Mental Disorders, in Kaplan HJ, Sadock BJ (eds): Comprehensive Textbook of Psychiatry. Baltimore, Williams & Wilkins, 1985, pp 591–613

Spivack G, Platt JJ, Shure MB: The Problem–Solving Approach to Adjustment. San Francisco, Jossey-Bass, 1976

Spotnitz H: Group therapy as a specialized psychotherapeutic technique, in Bychowski G, Despert JL (eds): Specialized Techniques in Psychotherapy. New York, Basic Books, 1952(a) pp 85–101

Spotnitz H: A psychoanalytic view of resistance in groups. Int J Group Psychother 2:3, 1952(b)

Spotnitz H: Resistance reinforcement in affect training of analytic group psychotherapists. Int J Group Psychother 8:395, 1958

Spotnitz H: The Couch and the Circle. A Story of Group Psychotherapy. New York, Knopf, 1961

Spotnitz H: Discussion of Stoller's accelerated interaction. Int J Group Psychother 18:236–239, 1968

Spotnitz H: Touch countertransference in group psychotherapy. Int J Group Psychother 22:455–466, 1972

Spotnitz H: Acting out in group psychotherapy, in Wolberg, LR, Schwartz EK (eds): Group Therapy 1973: An Overview. New York, Stratton Intercontinental, 1973, pp 28–42

Spotnitz H, Gabriel B: Resistance in analytic group therapy: A study of the group therapeutic process in children and mothers. O J Child Behav 2:71, 1950

Sprague RL, Sleator E: Effects of psychopharmacologic agents on learning disorders. Pediatr Clin North Am 20:719–735, 1973

Staats AW, Staats CK: Complex Human Behavior. New York, Holt, 1963

Stace WT: Religion and the Modern Mind. Philadelphia, Lippincott, 1952

Stainbrook E: The hospital as a therapeutic community. Neuropsychiatry 3:69–87, 1955

Stainbrook E: The hospital as a therapeutic community, in Freedman AM, Kaplan HI (eds): Comprehensive Textbook of Psychiatry. Baltimore, Williams & Wilkins, 1967, pp 1296–1300

Stampfl TG: Implosive therapy in behavior modification techniques in the treatment of emotional disorders, in Armitage S (ed). Battle Creek, Mich, Veterans Administration, 1967

Standard S, Nathan H: Should the Patient Know the Truth! New York, Springer, 1955

Stanton A: Milieu therapy and the development of insight. Psychiatry 24 (Suppl):19–30, 1961

Stanton AH, Schwartz MS: The Mental Hospital: A Study of Institutional Participation in Psychiatric Illness and Treatment. New York, Basic Books, 1954

Stanton HE: Weight loss through hypnosis. Am J Clin Hypn 18:94–97, 1975

Stanton HE: Short–term treatment of enuresis. Am J Clin Hypnosis 22:103–107, 1979

Starfield B: Enuresis: Its pathogenesis and management. Clin Pediatr 11:343–349, 1972

Stark P: A psychoanalytic view of male homosexuality. J L Is Consultation Center 3:3–13, 1963

Stegar J, Fordyce W: Behavioral health care in the management of chronic pain, in Handbook of Clinical Health Psychology. New York, Plenum, 1982

Stein A: Some aspects of resistance in group psychotherapy. J Hillside Hosp 1:79–88, 1952

Stein A: Indications for group psychotherapy and the selection of patients. J Hillside Hosp 12:145, 1963

Stein A: The nature of transference in combined

therapy. Int J Group Psychother 14:413, 1964

Stein A: Reconstructive family therapy. Newsletter (Bleuler Psychotherapy Center) February 1966

Stein C: Practical pastoral counseling, in Masserman JH (ed): Current Psychiatric Therapies, vol. 12. Orlando FL, Grune & Stratton, 1972

Stein EH, Murdaugh J, MacLeod JA: Brief psychotherapy of psychiatric reactions to physical illness. Am J Psychiatry 125:1040–1049, 1969

Stein J, Euper JA: Advances in music therapy, in Masserman JH (ed): Current Psychiatric Therapies, vol. 14. Orlando FL, Grune & Stratton, 1974

Steinglass P: Family systems theory and therapy: A clinical application of general systems theory. Psychiatric Annals 14:582–586, 1984

Steinhaus AH: Neuromuscular relaxation and mental health. Psychiatr Spectator 3:1, 1963

Steinhelber J: An investigation of some relationships between psychotherapy supervision and patient change. J Clin Psychology 40:1346–1353, 1984

Steinman LA, Hunt RC: A day care center in a state hospital. Am J Psychiatry 117:112, 1961

Stekel W: Der Vetischismus, Berlin, and Wein, Urban and Schwarzenberg, 1923

Stekel W: Peculiarities of Behavior. New York, Liveright, 1924

Stekel W: Frigidity in Women. New York, Liveright, 1926

Stekel W: Impotence in the Male. New York, Liveright, 1927

Stekel W: Sadism and Masochism. New York, Liveright, 1929

Stekel W: Sexual Aberrations: The Phenomenon of Fetishism in Relation to Sex, vol. 2. New York, Liveright, 1930

Stekel W: Sexual Aberrations. New York, Liveright, 1949

Stekel W: Technique of Analytical Psychotherapy. New York, Liveright, 1950

Stekel W: Patterns of Psychosexual Infantilism. New York, Liveright, 1952

Steketee G, Foa EB: Obsessive–compulsive disorder, in Barlow DH (ed): Clinical Handbook of Psychological Disorders. New York, Guilford, 1985, pp 69–144

Steketee G, Foa EB, Grayson JB: Recent advances in the behavioral treatment of obsessive–compulsives. Arch Gen Psychiatry 39:1365–1371, 1982

Sterba R: The dynamics of the dissolution of the transference resistance. Psychiatric Q 9, 1940

Sterba R, Lyndon BH, Katz A: Transference in Casework. New York, Family Service Association of America, 1948

Stern A: On the counter-transference in psychoanalysis. Psychoanal Rev 9:166–174, 1924

Stern K, et al: Observations on a ceramics workshop for psychiatric patients. Can Psychiatr Assoc J 2:114–125, 1957

Stern MM: Free painting as an auxiliary technique in psychoanalysis, in Bychowski G, Despert JL (eds): Specialized Techniques in Psychotherapy. New York, Basic Books, 1952(a) pp 65–83

Stern MM: Spontaneous art in therapy and diagnosis. Prog Clin Psychol 1:290–311, 1952(b)

Sterne S: The validity of music on effective group psychotherapeutic technique, in Proceedings of the National Association of Music Therapy. Kansas City, Kans, the Association, 1955, pp 130–140

Stevenson GS: Mental Health Planning for Social Action. New York, McGraw-Hill, 1956

Stevenson I: Processes of "spontaneous" recovery from the psychoneuroses. Am J Psychiatry 117:1057–1064, 1961

Stevenson I: The use of rewards and punishments in psychotherapy. Compr Psychiatry 3:20–28, 1962

Stevenson I: Discussion, in Wolpe J, et al (eds): The Conditioning Therapies. New York, Holt, 1966

Stevenson I, Buckman J, Smith BM, Hain JD: The use of drugs in psychiatric interviews: Some interpretations based on controlled experiments. Am J Psychiatry 131:707–710, 1974

Stewart MA: Hyperactive children. Sci Am 222:94–98, 1970

Stewart MA: Treatment of bedwetting. JAMA 232:281–283, 1975

Stewart RL: Psychoanalysis and Psychoanalytic Psychotherapy, in Kaplan HI, Sadock BJ (eds): A Comprehensive Textbook of Psychiatry IV. Baltimore, Williams & Wilkins, 1985, pp 1331–1365

Stewart WA: Psychoanalytic therapy, in Frosch J, Ross N (eds): The Annual Survey of Psychoanalysis. A Comprehensive Survey of Psychoanalytic Theory and Practice, vol. 7. New York, International Universities Press, 1963, pp 354–355

Stieper DR, Wiener DN: Dimensions of Psychotherapy. Chicago, Aldine, 1965

Stierlin H: Psychoanalysis and Family Therapy. New York, Aronson, 1977

Stimson GV, Oppenheimer E: Heroin Addiction. Treatment and Control in Britain. London, Tavistock, 1982

Stock D: Interpersonal concerns during the early sessions of therapy groups. Int J Group Psychother 12:14, 1962

Stock D, Thelen H: Emotional Dynamics and Group Culture. New York, New York University Press, 1958

Stollak GE: An integrated graduate-undergraduate program in the assessment, treatment, and prevention of child psychopathology. Professional Psychol 4:158–169, 1973

Stollak GE: Education for early childhood consultation. J Clin Child Psychol 3:20–24, 1974

Stoller FH: Marathon Group Therapy. Los Angeles, Youth Studies Center, University of Southern California, 1967

Stoller FH: Accelerated interaction: A time-limited approach based on the brief intensive group. Int J Group Psychother 18:220–235, 1968

Stoller FH: Videotape feedback in the group setting. J Nerv Ment Dis 148:457–466, 1969

Stolorow RD, Atwood GE: Faces in a Cloud. New York, Aronson, 1979

Stolorow RD, Lachmann FM: Psychoanalysis of Developmental Arrests: Theory and Treatment. New York, International Universities Press, 1980

Stone AA: The *Tarasoff* Decisions: Suing psychotherapists to Safeguard Society. Harvard Law Review 90:358–378, 1976

Stone L: Psychoanalysis and brief psychotherapy. Psychiatr Q 20:215–236, 1951

Stone LA: Residential Treatment, in Noshpitz JD (ed): Basic Handbook of Child Psychiatry, vol. 3. New York, Basic Books, 1979, pp 231–262

Stone WN, Tieger ME: Screening for T-groups: The myth of healthy candidates. Am J Psychiatry 127:1485–1490, 1971

Storrow HA: Money as a motivator. Pub Welfare 20:199–204, 1962

Storrow HA: Psychotherapy as interpersonal conditioning, in Masserman JH (ed): Current Psychiatric Therapies, vol. 5. Orlando FL, Grune & Stratton, 1965

Strachey J: The nature of the therapeutic action of psychoanalysis. Int J Psychoanal 15:127, 1934

Strachey J: Symposium on the theory of the therapeutic results of psychoanalysis. Int J Psychoanal 18:125–189, 1937

Strachstein H: Bibliography—Group Analysis. New York, Postgraduate Center for Mental Health, 1965

Strang R: Educational Guidance: Its Principles and Practice. New York, Macmillan, 1947

Straus E: The Primary World. New York, Free Press, 1963

Strauss AA, Kephart NC: Psychopathology and Education of the Brain-Injured Child, vol. 2. Orlando FL, Grune & Stratton, 1955

Strauss AA, Lehtinen LE: Psychopathology and Education of the Brain-Injured Child, vol. 1. Orlando FL, Grune & Stratton, 1947

Strauss BV: The role of the physician's personality in medical practice (psychotherapeutic medicine). NY State J Med 51:753, 1951

Strauss JB: Two face the group: A study of the relationship between co-therapists, in Wolberg LR, Aronson ML (eds): Group Therapy 1975: An Overview. New York, Stratton Intercontinental, 1975, pp 201–210

Strauss JS: A comprehensive approach to psychiatric diagnosis. Am J Psychiatry 132:1193–1197, 1975

Strean HS: Non-verbal intervention in psychotherapy. Psychother: Theory Res Prac 6:235–237, 1969

Strean HS: Social change and the proliferation of regressive therapies. Psychoanal Rev 58:581–594, 1971–1972

Streiker JD: The Cults are Coming: Nashville, Abingdon Press, 1978

Stringer LA: Children at risk: II. The teacher as change agent. Elem School J 73:424–434, 1973

Stroebel CF, Glueck BC: Biofeedback treatment in medicine and psychiatry: An ultimate placebo? Semin Psychiatry 5:379–393, 1973

Stroh G: A therapist's reactions as reflected in his reporting on a psychotherapeutic group. Int J Group Psychother 8:403–409, 1958

Strunk O, Jr: Empathy: A review of theory and research. Psychol Newsletter 9:47–57, 1958

Strupp HH: An objective comparison of Rogerian and psychoanalytic techniques. J Consult Psychol 19:1–7, 1955

Strupp HH: A multidimensional analysis of therapist activity in analytic and client-centered therapy. J Consult Psychol 21:301–308, 1957

Strupp HH: Psychotherapists in Action. Orlando FL, Grune & Stratton, 1960

Strupp HH: The effects of psychotherapy. Int J Psychiatry 1:165–169, 1965

Strupp HH: On the technology of psychotherapy. Arch Gen Psychiatry 26:270–278, 1972(a)

Strupp HH: Needed: A reformulation of the psychotherapeutic influence. Int J Psychiatry 10:119, 1972(b)

Strupp HH: Psychotherapy: Clinical, Research,

and Theoretical Issues. New York, Aronson, 1973, pp 377–418

Strupp HH: Psychotherapy research and practice: An overview, in Garfield SI, Bergin AE (eds): Handbook of Psychotherapy and Behavior Change: An Empirical Analysis (2d ed): New York, Wiley, 1978

Strupp HH, Binder JL: Psychotherapy in a New Key. New York, Basic Books, 1984

Strupp HH, Fox RE, Lessor K: Patients View Their Psychotherapy. Johns Hopkins University Press, 1969

Strupp HH, Hadley SW: A tripartite model of mental health and therapeutic outcomes with special reference to negative effects in psychotherapy. Am Psychol 32:187–196, 1977

Strupp HH, Hadley SW, Gomes B, Armstrong SH: Negative effects in psychotherapy: A review of clinical and theoretical issues together with recommendations for a program of research. Support provided by NIMH, Contract 278–75–0036(ER). To be published

Strupp HH, Hadley SW, Gomes-Schwartz B: Psychotherapy for Better or Worse: An Analysis of the Problem of Negative Effects. New York, Aronson, 1977

Stuart GW, Sundeen SJ: Principles and Practice of Psychiatric Nursing. St. Louis, C.V. Mosby, 1983

Stuart RB: Behavioral control of overeating. Behav Res Ther 5:357–365, 1967

Stuart RB: Operant–interpersonal treatment for marital discord. J Consult & Clin Psychology 33:675–682, 1969

Stuart RB: Helping Couples Change: A Social Learning Approach to Marital Therapy. New York, Guilford, 1980

Stueks AM: Working together collaboratively with other professionals. Community Ment Health J 1:316, 1965(a)

Stueks AM: The community mental health view of mentally ill and mentally restored patients. Perspect Psychiatr Care 3(1), 1965(b)

Stunkard A: New therapies for the eating disorders. Arch Gen Psychiatry 26:391–398, 1972

Stunkard AJ: From explanation to action in psychosomatic medicine. The case of obesity. Presidential address, 1974. Psychosom Med, 37:195–236, 1975

Stunkard AJ (ed): Obesity. Philadelphia, Saunders, 1980

Stunkard AJ: Obesity, in Bellack AS, Hersen M, Kazdin AE (eds): International Handbook of Behavior Modification and Therapy. New York, Plenum, 1982

Stunkard AJ: The current status of treatment of obesity in adults, in Stunkard AJ, Stellar E (eds): Eating and Its Disorders. New York, Raven, 1984

Stunkard AJ: Obesity, in Kaplan HI, Sadock BJ (eds): Comprehensive Textbook of Psychiatry, Baltimore, Williams & Wilkins, 1985, pp 1133–1142

Subcommittee on Occupational Therapy, American Psychiatric Association: An opinion survey concerning occupational therapy. On file with the Council of the American Psychiatric Association. Washington, DC, the Association

Suess JF: Milieu and activity therapy with chronically disturbed female patients. Psychiatric Q 32:1–12, 1958

Suess JF: Short-term psychotherapy with the compulsive personality and the obsessive-compulsive neurotic. Am J Psychiatry 129:270–275, 1972

Sullivan HS: The modified psychoanalytic treatment of schizophrenia. Am J Psychiatry 11(3), 1931

Sullivan HS: Conceptions in Modern Psychiatry. Washington, DC, William Alanson White Psychiatric Foundation, 1947

Sullivan HS: The Meaning of anxiety in Psychiatry and in Life. Washington, DC, William Alanson White Foundation, 1948

Sullivan HS: The theory of anxiety and the nature of psychotherapy. Am J Psychiatry 12:3–12, 1949

Sullivan HS: The Interpersonal Theory of Psychiatry. New York, Norton, 1953

Sullivan HS: The Psychiatric Interview. New York, Norton, 1954

Sullivan HS: Clinical Studies in Psychiatry. New York, Norton, 1956

Sullivan HS: Schizophrenia as a Human Process (1930). New York, Norton, 1962

Sundberg ND, Tyler LE: Clinical Psychology. New York, Appleton-Century-Crofts, 1962

Super DE: Guidance and counseling, in Social Work Year Book. New York, American Association for Social Workers, 1951, p 220

Sutherland JD: Notes on psychoanalytic group therapy. I. Therapy and training. Psychiatry 15:111–117, 1952

Suzuki DT: An Introduction to Zen Buddhism. London, Rider, 1947

Suzuki DT: Essays in Zen Buddhism (1st ser, 2d ed). New York, Harper & Row 1949

Suzuki DT: Essays in Zen Buddhism (2d ser, 2d ed). London, Rider, 1952

Suzuki DT: Essays in Zen Buddhism (3d ser, 2d ed). London, Rider 1953

Suzuki DT: An Introduction to Zen Buddhism (2d ed). London, Rider, 1957(a)

Suzuki DT: A Manual of Zen Buddhism (2d ed). London, Rider, 1957(b)

Suzuki DT: The Training of the Zen Buddhist Monk (1st Am ed). New York, University Books, 1959

Swanson MG, Woolson AM: Psychotherapy with the unmotivated patient. Psychother: Ther Res Prac 10:175–183, 1973

Swason DW, Maruta T, Swenson W: Results of behavior modification in the treatment of chronic pain. Psychosom Med 41:55–61, 1979

Swenson WM, Pearson JS, Rome HP: Automation technics in personality assessment: Fusion of three professions, in Proceedings of Conference on Data Acquisition and Processing in Biology and Medicine. Elmsford, NY, Pergamon, 1963, pp 149–156

Swenson WM, Pearson JS, Rome HP, Brannick TL: A totally automated psychological test: JAMA 191:925–927, 1965

Syz H: The concept of the organism-as-a-whole and its application to clinical situations. Hum Biol 8:489–507, 1936

Syz H: Trigant Burrow's thesis in relation to psychotherapy. Prog Psychother 2:147–155, 1957

Syz H: Reflection on group of phyloanalysis. Acta Psychother Suppl ad 2:37–88, 1963

Szasz TS: Psychiatric aspects of vagotomy II. A psychiatric study of vagotomized ulcer patients with comments on prognosis. Psychosom Med 11:187–199, 1949

Szasz TS: Psychoanalytic training: A sociopsychological analysis of its history and present status. Int J Psychoanal 39:1–16, 1958

Szasz TS: Myth of mental illness. Am Psychol 15:113–118, 1960

Szasz TS: The Myth of Mental Illness. New York, Hoeber, 1961

Szasz TS: Law, Liberty and Psychiatry. New York, Macmillan, 1963

Szasz TS: Ethics of Psychoanalysis. New York, Basic Books, 1965(a)

Szasz TS: Psychiatric Justice. New York, Macmillan, 1965(b)

Szurek SA: Notes on the genesis of psychopathic personality trends. Psychiatry 5:1, 1942

Szurek SA: Remarks on training for psychotherapy. Am J Orthopsychiatry 19:36–51, 1949(a)

Szurek SA: Some impressions from clinical experience with delinquents, in Eissler KR (ed): Searchlights on Delinquency. New Psychoanalytic Studies. New York, International Universities Press, 1949(b), pp 115–127

Szurek SA, Johnson A, Falstein EI: Collaborative psychiatric treatment of parent-child problems. Am J Orthopsychiatry 12:511, 1942

Taba H: With Perspective on Human Relations. Washington, DC, American Council on Education, 1955

Tabachnick N: Research Committee Report on Psychoanalytic Practice. The Academy 17:9–12, 1973

Taffel C: Anxiety and the conditioning of verbal behavior. J Abnorm Soc Psychol 5:496–501, 1955

Taft J: The Dynamics of Therapy in a Controlled Relationship. New York, Macmillan, 1933

Taft J (ed): Family Case Work and Counseling: A Functional Approach. Philadelphia, University of Pennsylvania Press, 1948

Tagge GF, Adler D, Bryan-Brown CW, Shoemaker WC: Relationship of therapy to prognosis in critically ill patients. Crit Care Med 2:61, 1974

Taggert M: The AAPC information project. J Pastoral Care 26:219–244, 1972

Takakusu J: The Essentials of Buddhist Philosophy. Honolulu, University of Hawaii Press, 1947

Talbot E, White RB, Miller SC: Some aspects of self-conceptions and role-demands in a therapeutic community. J Abnorm Soc Psychol 63:338–345, 1961

Talbott DR: Are tranquilizer combinations more effective than a single tranquilizer? Am J Psychiatry 121:597–600, 1964

Talbott JA, et al: The paraprofessional teaches the professional. Am J Psychiatry 130:805–808, 1973

Talbott JA, Ross AM, Skerrett AF: The Chronic Mental Patient in the Community. Washington, DC, American Psychiatric Association, 1978

Talbott JA: The Chronically Mentally Ill. Treatment Program, Systems. New York, Human Sciences Press, 1981

Talbott JA (ed): The Chronic Mental Patient in the Community. Orlando FL, Grune & Stratton, 1984

Tallent N: Clinical Psychological Consultation. Englewood Cliffs, NJ, Prentice-Hall, 1963

Tallman FF: Treatment of Emotional Problems in Office Practice. New York, McGraw-Hill, 1961

Tannenbaum F: Crime and the Community. Boston, Ginn, 1938

Tanner BA: Two case reports on the modification of the ejaculatory response with the squeeze technique. Psychother: Theory Res Prac 10:297–300, 1973

Tanner LN, Lindgren HC: Classroom Teaching

and Learning. A Mental Health Approach. New York, Holt, 1971

Tarachow S: An Introduction to Psychotherapy. New York, International Universities Press, 1963, p 41

Tart CT: A comparison of suggested dreams occurring in hypnosis and sleep. Int J Clin Exp Hypn 12:263–289, 1964

Tart CT: The hypnotic dream. Psychol Bull 63:87–99, 1965

Tart CT: Types of hypnotic dreams and their relation to hypnotic depth. J Abnorm Psychol 71:377–382, 1966

Tarumianz MD, Bullis HE: The human relations class: A preventive mental hygiene program for schools. Understanding the Child 13:3–10, 1944

Tauber ES: Exploring the therapeutic use of the countertransference data. Psychiatry 17:331–336, 1964

Taylor FK: A history of the group and administrative therapy in Great Britain. Br J Med Psychol 31:153–173, Parts 3, 4, 1958

Teicher A, de Freitas L, Osherson A: Group psychotherapy and the intense group experience: A preliminary rationale for encounter as a therapeutic agent in the mental health field. Int J Group Psychother 24:159–173, 1974

Terman LM, Merrill MA: Stanford-Binet Intelligence Scale; Manual for the Third Revision, Form L-M. Boston, Houghton-Mifflin, 1960

Teuber HL, Powers E: Evaluating therapy in delinquency preventive program, in Association for Research in Nervous and Mental Disease: Psychiatric Treatment. Res Publ 31. Baltimore, Williams & Wilkins, 1953, pp 138–147

Tharp RG: Psychological patterning with marital partners. Psycho Bull 60:97–117, 1963

Thelen HC: Dynamics of Groups at Work. Chicago, University of Chicago Press, 1954

Thelen HC, et al: Methods of Studying Group Operation. Chicago, Human Dynamics laboratory, 1954

Thigpen CH, Cleckley H: A case of multiple personality. J Abnorm Soc Psychol 49:135–151, 1954

Thomas A: Simultaneous psychotherapy with marital partners. Am J Psychother 10:716–728, 1956

Thomas A, Chess S: The Dynamics of Psychological Development. New York, Brunner/Mazel, 1980

Thomas DR, Becker WC, Armstrong M: Production and elimination of disruptive classroom behavior by systematically varying

teacher's behavior. J Appl Behav Anal 1:35–45, 1968

Thomas EJ: The Life of Buddha as Legend and History: London, Routledge & Kegan, 1931

Thomas EJ: The History of Buddhist Thought. London, Routledge & Kegan, 1933

Thomas EJ: Early Buddhist Scriptures. London, Routledge & Kegan, 1935

Thomas EJ: Selected socio-behavioral techniques and principles: An approach to interpersonal helping. Soc Work 13(1), 1968

Thomas EJ: Behavioral modification and casework, in Roberts R, Nee R (eds): Theories of Social Casework. Chicago, University of Chicago Press, 1970

Thompson C: Psychoanalysis: Evolution and Development. New York, Hermitage, 1950, pp 241–242

Thompson CE: The attitudes of various groups toward behavior problems of children. J Abnorm Soc Psychol 35:120–125, 1940

Thompson TL, Byny RL (eds): Primary and Team Health Care Education. New York, Praeger, 1983

Thorndike EL: The Psychology of Wants, Interests, and Attitudes. New York, Appleton-Century, 1935

Thorndike RL, Hagen E: Measurement and Evaluation in Psychology and Education (2d ed). New York, Wiley, 1961

Thorne FC: A critique of nondirective methods of psychotherapy. J Abnorm Soc Psychol 39:459–470, 1944

Thorne FC: Directive psychotherapy: IV. The therapeutic implications of the case history. J Clin Psychol 1:318–330, 1945

Thorne FC: Directive psychotherapy: VII. Imparting psychological information. J Clin Psychol 2:179–190, 1946

Thorne FC: Principles of directive counseling and psychotherapy. Am Psychol 3:160–165, 1948

Thorne FC: An eclectic evaluation of psychotherapeutic methods, in Jurjevich RM (ed): Direct Psychotherapy, vol. 2. Coral Gables, Fla, University of Miami Press, 1973, pp 847–883

Thorne RB: Bibliography—Group analysis. New York, Postgraduate Center for Mental Health, 1966

Thornton EE: Professional Education for the Ministry: A History of Clinical Pastoral Education. Nashville, Tenn, Abingdon, 1970

Tibbetts RW, Hawkings JR: The placebo response. J Ment Sci 102:60, 1956

Tiemann WH: The Right to Silence. Richmond, Va, Knox, 1964

Tien HC: From couch to coffee shop: A new

personality via psychosynthesis. Roche Report 2(18, 19), 1972

Tillich P: The Courage to Be. New Haven, Conn, Yale Union Press, 1952

Tippin J, Henn FA: Modified leukotomy in the treatment of intractable obsessional neurosis. Am J Psychiatry 139:1601–1603, 1982

Tischler GL: Evaluation of DSM-III, in Kaplan HI, Sadock BJ (eds): Comprehensive Textbook of Psychiatry (4th ed). Baltimore, Williams & Wilkins, 1985, pp 617–621

Titmuss RM: Community care of the mentally ill. Can Ment Health Suppl No. 49, November-December 1965

Tobias M: Disturbed child—a concept. Am Pract Dig Treat 10:1759–1766, 1959

Tompkins SS: Thematic Apperception Test. The Theory and Technique of Interpretation. Orlando FL, Grune & Stratton, 1947

Topping R: Treatment of the pseudo-social boy. Am J Orthopsychiatry 13:353, 1943

Torkelson LO, Ramano MT: Self-confrontation by video tape: A remedial measure in teaching diagnostic evaluation. JAMA 201:773–775, 1967

Torraine EP, Strom RD (eds): Mental Health and Achievement: Increasing Potential and Reducing School Dropout. New York, Wiley, 1965

Torrance EP: Guiding Creative Talent. Englewood Cliffs, NJ, Prentice-Hall, 1962

Toulmin S: The Philosophy of Science: An Introduction. New York, Longmans, Green, 1953

Tourney G: Therapeutic fashions in psychiatry, 1800–1965. Paper presented at the 122d Annual Meeting of the American Psychiatric Association, Atlantic City, NJ, May 1966

Towle C: Social case work in modern society. Soc Serv Rev 20:165–180, 1946

Towle C: The Training and Function of a Psychiatric Social Worker in a Clinical Setting. Transactions of the First Conference. New York, Josiah Macy, Jr, Foundation, 1947, pp 31–40

Towle C: The Learner in Education for the Professions. Chicago, University of Chicago Press, 1954

Trager H: The Primary Teacher, in Intercultural Attitudes in the Making. 9th Yearbook of the John Dewey Society, 1949

Trager H, Yarrow MR: They Learn What They Live: Prejudice in Young Children. New York, Harper & Row, 1952

Trail PM: An account of Lowenfeld technique in a child guidance clinic, with a survey of therapeutic play technique in Great Britain and the U.S.A. J Ment Sci 91:43–78, 1945

Trappi R: Computer psychotherapy: Is it acceptable, feasible, advisable? Cybernetics & Systems: Int'l J 12:385, 1981

Traxler AE: Techniques of Guidance. New York, Harper & Row, 1945 (3d ed, 1966)

Trecker HB: Social Group Work, Principles and Practices. New York, New York Women's Press, 1946, pp 16–18; Whiteside, 1955

Trimble MR: Epilepsy, antidepressants, and their role of nominfensine. J Clin Psychiatr 45:39–42, 1984

Trosman H: Dream research and the psychoanalytic theory of dreams. Arch Gen Psychiatry 9:27–36, 1963

Trower P, Bryant B, Argyle M: Social Skills and Mental Health. Pittsburgh, University of Pittsburgh Press, 1978

Truax CB, Carkhuff RR: For better or for worse: The process of psychotherapeutic personality change, in Recent Advances in the Study of Behavior Change. Montreal, McGill University Press, 1964, pp 118–163

Truax CB, Carkhuff RR: Toward Effective Counseling and Psychotherapy: Training and Practice. Chicago, Aldine, 1967

Truax CB, Mitchell KM: Research on certain therapist interpersonal skills in relation to process and outcome, in Bergin AE, Garfield SL (eds): Handbook of Psychotherapy and Behavioral Change. New York, Wiley, 1972, pp 299–244

Truax CB, Wargo DC: Psychotherapeutic encounters that change behavior: For better or for worse. Am J Psychol 20:499–520, 1966

Tullis F: Rational diet construction for mild and grand obesity. JAMA 226:70–71, 1973

Turner RM, Ascher LM: Therapist factors in the treatment of insomnia. Behav Res Ther 20:33–40, 1982

Tyhurst JS: The role of transition states—including disasters—in mental illness. Symposium on Preventive and Social Psychiatry sponsored by the U.S. Walter Reed Army Institute of Research, Walter Reed Army Medical Center, Bethesda, Md, April 1957

Tyler R: The influence of the curriculum and teaching on the development of creativity, in Ekstein R, Motto RL (eds): From Learning for Love to Love of Learning. New York, Brunner/Mazel, 1969

Ulett GA, Akpinar S, Itil TM: Quantitative EEG analysis during hypnosis. Electroencephalogr Clin Neurophysiol 33:361–368, 1972(a)

Ulett GA, Akpinar S, Itil TM: Hypnosis: Physiological, pharmacological, reality. Am J Psychiatry 128:799–805, 1972(b)

Ulett GA, Goodrich DW: A Synopsis of Contemporary Psychiatry. St. Louis, Mosby, 1956

Ullman M: On the occurrence of telepathic dreams. J Am Soc Psychical Res 53:50, 1959

Ullman M, Krippner S: Dream Studies and Telepathy. New York, Parapsychology Foundation, 1970

Ullmann LP, Berkman VC: Efficacy of placement of neuropsychiatric patients in family care. Arch Gen Psychiatry 1:273–274, 1959

Umbarger CC, et al: College Students in a Mental Hospital. Orlando FL, Grune & Stratton, 1962

Ungerleider JT, Wellisch DK: Coercile persuasion (brainwashing) religious cults, and deprogramming. Am J Psychiatry 136(3):279–282, 1979

Upham F: Ego Analysis in the Helping Professions. New York, Family Service Association of America, 1973

Upton D: Mental Health Care and National Health Insurance: A Philosophy of and an Approach to Mental Health Care for the Future. New York, Plenum Publishing, 1983

Urban HB, Ford DH: Some historical and conceptual perspectives on psychotherapy and behavior change, in Bergin AE, Garfield SL (eds): Handbook of Psychotherapy and Behavior Change: An Empirical Analysis. New York, Wiley, 1971

Ursano RM, Dressler DM: Brief vs. long-term psychotherapy: A treatment decision. J Nerv Ment Dis 159:164–171, 1974

U.S. Children's Bureau: Trends and Developments in Public Child Welfare Services. Child Welfare Reports No. 4. Washington, D.C, U.S. Government Printing Office, 1949

U.S. Department of Health, Education, & Welfare, Public Health Service: Narcotic Drug Addiction, Ment Health Mongr 2. Washington, DC, U.S. Government Printing Office

U.S. Department of Health, Education, & Welfare, Public Health Serivce: The Protection and Promotion of Mental Health in Schools. Ment Health Mongr 5. Washington, DC, U.S. Government Printing Office

U.S. Department of Health, Education, & Welfare. Secretary's Committee to Study Extended Roles for Nurses: In Extending the Scope of Nursing Practice. Washington, DC, U.S. Government Printing Office, 1971. (See also Am J Nurs 7:12:2346–2351, 1971)

U.S. Department of Health, Education, & Welfare: Report on Licensure and Related Heatlh Personnel Credentialing. Washing-

ton, DC, U.S. Government Printing Office, June 1971

U.S. Office of Education, National Institute of Mental Health: Mental Health and Learning. Washington, DC, U.S. Government Printing Office, 1972

U.S. Public Health Service: An Introduction to Mental Health Consultation. Washington, DC, U.S. Department of Health, Education & Welfare, 1962

U.S. Social Security Administration: Annual Report of the Federal Security Agency, 1949

Vahia NS: Hindu philosophy and psychology. Lecture presented at the Postgraduate Center for Mental Health, New York, 1962

Vaillant GE: A twelve-year follow-up of New York City addicts—characteristics and determinants of abstinence. Paper presented at the 122d Annual Meeting of the American Psychiatric Association. Atlantic City, NJ, May 1966

Vaillant GE: Theoretical hierarchy of adaptive ego mechanisms: A 30–year follow–up of 30 men selected for psychological health. Arch Gen Psychiatry 24:107, 1971

Vaillant GE, Semrad EV, Ewalt JR: Current therapeutic results in schizophrenia. N Engl J Med 271:280–283, 1964

Valenstein AF: Some principles of psychiatric consultation. Soc Casework 36:253–256, 1955

Vandenbos GR, Pino CD: Research on the outcome of psychotherapy, in Vandenbos GR: Psychotherapy: Practice, Research, Policy. Beverly Hills, Calif, Sage Publications, 1980

Van De Wall W: Music in Institutions. New York, Russell Sage Foundation, 1936, pp 48–73

Van Dyke PB: Hypnosis in surgery. J Abdominal Surg 7(1, 2), 1965

Van Egeren LF, Fabrega H, Jr, Thornton DW: Electrocardiographic effects of social stress on coronary–prone (Type A) individuals. Psychosom Med 45:195–203, 1983

Van Ophuijsen JHW: Therapeutic criteria in social agencies. Am J Orthopsychiatry 9:410–420, 1939

Van Putten T: Milieu therapy: Contraindications. Arch Gen Psychiatry 29:640–643, 1973

Van Riper C: The Nature of Suttering. Englewood Cliffs, NJ, Prentice-Hall, 1971

Vasconcellow J, Kurland AA: Use of sustained-release chlorpromazine in the management of hospitalized chronic psychotic patients. Dis Nerv Syst 19:4, 1958

Vass I: The acting-out patient in group therapy. Am J Psychother 19:302–308, 1965

Vassilou G, Vassilou V: Introducing operational goals in group psychotherapy, in Arieti S (ed): Second Biennial of Psychiatry and Psychotherapy. New York, Basic Books, 1973

Vassilou G, Vassilou V: On the synallactic aspects of the grouping process, in Wolberg LR, Aronson ML (eds): Group Therapy 1974: An Overview. New York, Stratton Intercontinental, 1974, pp 158–174

Vaughn CE, Leff JP: The influence of family and social factors on the course of psychiatric illness. Br J Psychiatry 129:125–137, 1976

Vaughn CE, Snyder KS, Freeman W, Jones S, Falloon IRH, Liberman RP: Family factors in schizophrenic relapse: A replication. Schizophr Bull 8:425–426, 1982

Verebey K (ed): Opioids in Mental Illness: Theories, Clinical Observations, and Treatment Possibilities. New York Acad of Science, 1982

Vernon MD: Backwardness in Reading: The Study of Its Nature and Origin. New York, Cambridge University Press, 1957

Vernonon PE: The significance of Rorschach Test. Br J Med Psychol 15:199–217, 1935

Verplanck WS: The control of the content of conversation: Reinforcement of statement of opinion. J Abnorm Soc Psychol 51:668–676, 1955

Vigilante J: The future: Dour or rosy. Soc Work 17(4), 1972

Visher JS, O'Sullivan M: Nurse and patient responses to a study of milieu therapy. Am J Psychiatry 127:451, 1971

Vitoz R: Treatment of Neurashenia by Means of Brain Control. Brooks HB (trans). London, Longmans, Green, 1913

Voegtlin W, et al: Conditioned relfex therapy of alcoholic addiction, III. An evaluation of present results in the light of previous experience with this method. Q J Stud Alcohol 1:501–516, 1940(a)

Voegtlin W, et al: The treatment of alcoholism by establishing a conditioned reflex. Am J Med Sci 199:802–809, 1940(b)

Vogel GW, Thurmond A, Gibbons P, et al: The effect of REM deprivation on depression. Psychosomatics 14:104–107, 1973

Volgyesi FA: "School for Patients," hypnosistherapy and psychoprophylaxia. Br J Med Hypn 5:8–17, 1954

von Dedenroth TEA: The use of hypnosis in 1000 cases of "tobaccomaniacs." Am J Clin Hypn 10:194–197, 1968

Wachpress M: Goals and functions of the community mental health center. Am J Psychiatry 129:187–190, 1972

Wachtel PL: Psychoanalysis and Behavior Therapy: Toward an Interaction. New York, Basic Books, 1977

Wachtel PL: The Politics of Narcissism. New York, The Nation, 1981, pp 13–15

Waelder R: The principle of multiple function. Psychoanal Q 5:45–62, 1936

Waelder R: Basic Theories of Psychoanalysis. New York, International Universities Press, 1960

Wagman M: PLATO DCS: An interactive computer system for personal counseling. J Counsel Psychol 27:16, 1980

Wagman M, Kerber KW: PLATO DCS, an interactive computer system for personal counseling. Further development and evaluation. J Counsel Psychol 27:31, 1980

Wagner G, Green R: Impotence. New York, Plenum, 1982

Wagner JA: Children's Literature Through Storytelling. Dubuque, Iowa, Brown, 1970

Wagner PS: Prospects for psychiatry and psychoanalysis. Int Psychiatry Clin 6(3):5–28, 1969

Wahl CW: Section Two (untitled) on the psychiatrist's role, in Helping the Dying Patient and His Family. New York, National Association for Social Workers, 1960

Walder E: Synanon and the learning process: A critique of attack therapy. Correct Psychiatry J Soc Ther 11:299–304, 1965

Walen SR, Hauserman NM, Lavin PJ: Clinical Guide to Behavior Therapy. Baltimore, Williams & Wilkins, 1977

Walker HM, Mattson RH, Buckley NK: Special class placement as a treatment alternative for deviant behavior in children, in Modifying Deviant Social Behaviors in Various Classroom Settings. Mongr No. 1. Eugene, Department of Special Education, University of Oregon, 1969

Walker RG, Kelley FE: Short-term psychotherapy with hospitalized schizophrenic patients. Act Psychiatr Neurol Scand 35:34–56, 1960

Wallace AFC: Human Behavior in Extreme Situations. National Academy of Sciences, National Research Council, Publ No. 390, Diaster Study No. 1. Washington, DC, the Council, 1956

Wallace CJ, Boone SE, Donahoe CP, Foy DW: The chronic mentally disabled: Independent living skills training, in Barlow D (ed): Clinical Handbook of Psychological Disorders. New York, Guilford Press, 1985, pp 462–501

Wallace CJ, Nelson CJ, Liberman RP, et al: A review and critique of social skills training with schizophrenic patients. Schizophrenic Bulletin 6:42–63, 1980

Wallace RK: Physiological effects of transcendental meditation. Science 167:1751–1754, 1970

Wallerstein JS, Kelly JB: Surviving the Breakup: How Children and Parents Cope with Divorce: New York, Basic Books, 1980(a)

Wallerstein JS, Kelly JB: Effects of divorce on the visiting father–child relationship. Am J Psychiatr 137(12): 1534–1539, 1980(b)

Wallerstein RS: The goals of psychoanalysis. A survey of analytic viewpoints. J Am Psychoanal Assoc 13:748–770, 1965

Wallerstein RS: The current state of psychotherapy: Theory, practice, research. J Am Psychoanal Assoc 14:183–225, 1966

Wallin JEW: Education of Mentally Handicapped Children. New York, Harper & Row, 1955

Welsh BT, Stewart JW, Wright L: Treatment of Bulimia with Monoaminc Oxidase Inhibitors. Am J Psychiatry 139:1629–1630, 1982

Walsh J: Continuous narcosis: The Advantages of oral somnifaine—a comparison. J Ment Sci 93:255, 1947

Walsh JJ: Health Through Will Power. Boston, Stratford, 1913(a)

Walsh JJ: Psychotherapy. New York, Appleton-Century, 1913(b)

Walsh WB: Validity of self–report. J Counsel Psychol 14:18–23, 1967

Walsh WB: Validity of self–report: Another look. J Counsel Psychol 15:180–186, 1968

Walters L: In Podolsky E (ed): Music Therapy. New York, Philosophical Library, 1954

Walters RH, Leat M, Mezei L: Inhibition and disinhibition of responses through empathetic learning. Can J Psychol 17:235–243, 1963

Walters RH, Llewellyn TE: Enhancement of punitive behavior by visual and audiovisual displays. Can J Psychol 17:244–255, 1963

Walton D, Mather MD: The application of learning principles to the treatment of obsessive-compulsive states in the acute and chronic phases of illness. Behav Res Ther 1:163–174, 1963(a)

Walton D, Mather MD: The relevance of generalization techniques to the treatment of stammering and phobic symptoms. Behav Res Ther 1:121–25, 1963(b)

Walton HJ: Outcome in treated alcoholism. Paper presented at the 122d Annual Meeting of the American Psychiatric Association, Atlantic City, NJ, May 1966

Walzer H: Casework treatment of the depressed patient. Soc Casework 42:205–512, 1961

Warner R: Recovery from Schizophrenia. New York, Methuen Inc, 1985

Washburn S, Vannicelli M, Longabaugh R, Scheff BJ: A controlled comparison of psychiatric day treatment and inpatient hospitalization. J Consult Clin Psychol 44:665–765, 1976

Waskow IE: NIMH Treatment of Depression Collaborative Research Program (Pilot Phase) Revised Research Plan. Rockville, Md, Psychosocial Treatments Research Branch, NIMH 1980

Waskow IE, Parloff MB (eds): Psychotherapy Change Measures. Washington, DC: DHEW Pub. No. (ADM) 74–120, 1975

Wasserman MD, Pollak CP, Spielman AJ, et al: The differential diagnosis of impotence: The measurement of nocturnal penile tumescence. JAMA 243:2038–2042, 1980

Wasson BG: Mushroom rites in Mexico. Harvard Rev 1:14, 1963

Watkins HR: Hypnosis and Smoking: A five-session approach. Int J Clin & Exp Hypn 24:381–390, 1976

Watkins JG: Hypnotherapy of War Neuroses: A Clinical Psychologist's Casebook. New York, Ronald, 1949

Watson AS: The conjoint psychotherapy of married partners. Am J Orthopsychiatry 33:912–922, 1963

Watson G: The role of the teacher, in Witty PA, Skinner CE (eds): Mental Hygiene in Modern Education. New York, Ferrar & Rinehart, 1939

Watson G: Areas of agreement in psychotherapy. Am J Orthopsychiatry 10:698–709, 1940

Watson N: The mental health practitioner of the future, in Williams TA, Johnson JH (eds): Mental Health in the 21st Century. Lexington, Mass, D.C. Heath & Co. 1979, pp 109–117

Watterson DJ: Problems in the evaluation of psychotherapy. Bull Menninger Clin 18:232–241, 1954

Watts AW: The Way of Zen. New York, Pantheon, 1957

Watts MSM, Wilbur DL: Clinical management of "functional" disorders. JAMA 148:704–708, 1952

Watzlawick P: A review of the double-bind theory. Fam Process 2:132–153, 1963

Watzlawick P, Beavin JH, Jackson DD: Pragmatics of Human Communication: A Study of Interactional Patterns, Pathologies, and Paradoxes. New York, Norton, 1967

Watzlawick P, Weakland JH, Fisch R: Change: Principals of Problem Formation and Problem Formation and Problem Resolution. New York, Horton, 1974

Watzlawick P, et al: How real is real? Confusion, disinformation, communication. New York, Random House, 1976

Waxenberg SE, Fleischl MF: Referring therapist's impressions of a therapeutic social club. Int J Soc Psychiatry 11:3, 173, 1965

Wayne GJ: The hospital-affiliated halfway house, in Masserman JH (ed): Current Psychiatric Therapies, vol. 4. Orlando FL, Grune & Stratton, 1964, pp 213–217

Weakland JH: Family therapy as research arena. Fam Process 1:63–68, 1962

Weathers L, Liberman RP: Modification of family behavior, in Marholin E (ed): Child Behavior Therapy. New York, Gardiner Press, 1978

Webster DR, Azrin NH: Required relaxation: A method of inhibiting agitative-disruptive behavior of retardates. Behav Res Ther 11:67–78, 1973

Wechsler D: WAIS: Manual: Wechsler Adult Intelligence Scale. New York, Psychological Corporation, 1955, p 20

Wechsler H: The ex-patient organization: A survey. J Soc Issues 16:47–53, 1960(a)

Wechsler H: Halfway houses for former mental patients: A survey. J Soc Issues 16:20–26, 1960(b)

Wechsler H: Transitional residences for former mental patients: A survey of halfway houses and related rehabilitation facilities. Ment Hyg 45:65–76, 1961

Wedding D: The Word Processor as a Patient Education Tool in Psychotherapy, in Schwartz MD (ed): Using Computers in Clinical Practice. New York, The Haworth Press, 1984, pp 281–386

Weinberg J: Geriatric psychiatry, in Freedman AM, Kaplan HI, Sadock BJ (eds): Comprehensive Textbook of Psychiatry, vol. II (2d ed). Baltimore, Williams & Wilkins, 1975, pp 2405–2420

Weinroth LA: Occupational therapy, in Freedman AM, Kaplan HI (eds): Comprehensive Textbook of Psychiatry. Baltimore, Williams & Wilkins, 1967

Weinstein EA, Kahn RL: Symbolic reorganization in brain injuries, in Arieti S (ed): American Handbook of Psychiatry, vol. 1. New York, Basic Books, 1959, pp 974–976

Weir-Mitchell S: Fat and Blood (4th ed). Philadelphia, Lippincott, 1885

Weisenbaum J: Computer Power and Human Reason. San Francisco, W.H. Freeman, 1976

Weisman AD: Thanatology, in Kaplan HI, Sadock BJ (eds): Comprehensive Textbook of Psychiatry, IV. Baltimore, Williams & Wilkins, 1985, pp 1277–1286

Weiss DM, Margolin RJ: The use of music as an adjunct to group therapy. Am Arch Rehab Ther 3:13–26, 1953

Weiss E, English OS: Psychosomatic Medicine. Philadelphia, Saunders, 1957

Weiss RL, Cerreto MC: The marital status inventory: Development of a measure of dissolution potential. Am J of Family Therapy 8(2):80–85, 1980

Weiss RJ, Payson HE: Gross stress reaction I, in Freedman AM, Kaplan HI (eds): Comprehensive Textbook of Psychiatry. Baltimore, Williams & Wilkins, 1967, pp 1027–1031

Weissman AW: The Dysfunctional Attitude Scale: A validation study. Dissertation Abstracts International 40:1389–1390B, 1979. (University Microfilm No. 79–19533)

Weissman MM: The psychological treatment of depression: Evidence for the efficacy of depression alone, in comparison with, and in combination with pharmacotherapy. Arch Gen Psychiatry 36:1261–1269, 1979

Weissman MM, Paykel ES: The Depressed Woman: A Study of Social Relationships. Chicago, University of Chicago Press, 1974

Weizenbaum J: A computer program for the study of natural language communication between man and machine. Comm ACM 9:36, 1966

Wender L: Dynamics of group psychotherapy and its applications. JNMD 84:54–60, 1936

Wender L: Group psychotherapy: A study of its application. Psychiatr Q 14:708–718, 1940

Wender L: The psychodynamics of group psychotherapy. J Hillside Hosp 12:134, 1963

Wender P: Minimal Brain Dysfunction in Children. New York, Wiley, 1971

Wender PH, Reimherr FW, Wood D, Ward M: A controlled study of mathylphenidate in the treatment of attention deficit disorder, residual type, in adults. Am J Psychiatry 142:552, 1985

Wenkart A: Existential Psychotherapy: Its Theory and Practice. Nutley, NJ, Roche Laboratories, 1972

Werner H, Kaplan E: The acquisition of word

meanings: A developmental study. Child Dev Mongr 15, Ser No. 1, 1950

Werry JS: The conditioning treatment of enuresis. Am J Psychiatry 123:226–229, 1966

Wershub LP: The plague of impotence. J NY Med Coll, Flower Fifth Ave Hosp 1:17–26, 1959

West LJ, Stein M (eds): Critical issues in Behavioral Medicine. Philadelphia, Lippincott, 1982

Westman JC: Psychiatric Day Treatment, in Noshpitz JD (ed): New York, Basic Books, 1979, pp 288–299

Weston WD: Development of community psychiatric concepts, in Freedman AM, Kaplan HI, Sadock BJ (eds): Comprehensive Textbook of Psychiatry, vol. II (2d ed). Baltimore, Williams & Wilkins, 1975, pp 2310–2326

Wheelwright J: Jung's psychological concepts, in Fromm-Reichmann F, Moreno JL (eds): Progress in Psychotherapy, vol. 1. Orlando FL, Grune & Stratton, 1956, pp 127–135

Whiffen R, Byng-Hall J (eds): Family Therapy Supervision. New York, Academic Press, 1982

Whiles WH: Treatment of emotional problems in children. J Ment Sci 87:359–369, 1941

Whitaker CA: Psychotherapy with couples. Am J Psychother 12:18–24, 1958

Whitaker CA, Malone TP: The Roots of Psychotherapy. New York, McGraw-Hill, 1963

Whitaker DS, Lieberman MA: Psychotherapy Through the Group Process. New York, Atherton, 1964

White A, Fichtenbaum L, Dollard J: Measures for predicting dropping out of psychotherapy. J Consult Psychol 28:326, 1964

White JG: The use of learning theory in the psychological treatment of children, in Franks CM (ed): Conditioning Techniques in Clinical Practice and Research. New York. Springer, 1964, pp 196–201

White RB, Talbot E, Stuart CM: A psychoanalytic therapeutic community, in Masserman JH (ed): Current Psychiatric Therapies, vol. 4. Orlando FL, Grune & Stratton, 1964, pp 199–212

White V: Studying the Individual Pupil. New York, Harper & Row, 1958

Whitehead AN: Science and the Modern World. New York, Macmillan, 1925

Whitehorn JC: Guide to interviewing and clinical personality study. Arch Neurol Psychiatry 52:197–216, 1944

Whitehorn JC, Betz BJ: Further studies of the doctor as a crucial variable in the outcome

of treatment with schizophrenic patients. Am J Psychiatry 117:215, 1960

Whitelaw JDA: A case of fetishism treated with LSD. J Nerv Ment Dis 129:573, 1959

Whiteley JM, Flowers JV: Approaches to Assertion Training. Monterey, CA, Brooks–Cole, 1977

Whitfield CL: Treatment of alcohol withdrawal without drugs, in Masserman (ed): Current Psychiatric Therapies. Orlando FL, Grune & Stratton, 1980

Whitfield CL: Outpatient management of the alcoholic patient. Psychiatric Annals 12:447–458, 1982

Whittington HG, Zahourek R, Grey L: Pharmacotherapy and community psychiatric practice. Am J Psychiatry 126:551–554, 1969

Whybrow PC, Akishkal HS, McKinney WT: Mood Disorders: Toward a New Psychobiology. New York, Plenum, 1984

Wickes IG: Letters to the editor: Treatment of enuresis. Lancet 2:413, 1964

Wickes TA: Examiners' influence in a testing situation. J Consult Psychol 20:23–26, 1956

Wickman EK: Difference in the attitudes of teachers and mental hygienists, in Children's Behavior and Teacher's Attitude. New York, Commonwealth Fund, 1928

Wickramasekera I: Aversive behavior rehearsal for sexual exhibitionism. Behav Res Ther 7:167–176, 1976

Wikler A: Opioid Dependence: Mechanisms and Treatment New York, Plenum, 1980

Wilcox PH: Psychopenetration. Dis Nerv Syst 12:1, 1951

Wilden A: On Lacan: Psychoanalysis, Language and Communication. Contemporary Psychoanalysis 9:445–470, 1973

Wilder J: Facts and figures on psychotherapy. J Clin Psychopathol 7:311–347, 1945

Wilder J: The law of initial values. Psychosom Med 12:392, 1950

Wilder J: Modern psychotherapy and the law of initial values. Am J Psychother 12:199, 1958

Wilder JF, Caulfield S: A "high-expectations" half-way house—a follow-up. Paper presented at the 122d Annual Meeting of the American Psychiatric Association, Atlantic City, NJ, May 1966

Wilker A: Opioid Dependence: Mechanisms and Treatment. New York, Plenum, 1980

Wilkins GD et al: A therapeutic community development in a state psychiatric hospital. Med J Aust 2:220–224, 1963

Wilkins LG, Stein SH: A dynamic approach to symptom amelioration: An integration of psychoanalysis, hypnotherapy and behavior modification. Paper presented at the meeting of the American Psychological Association. Honolulu, Hawaii, September 1972

Will OA: Schizophrenia: Psychological treatments, in Freedman AM, Kaplan H (eds): Comprehensive Textbook of Psychiatry. Baltimore, Williams & Wilkins, 1967

Will OA: The psychotherapeutic center and schizophrenia, in The Schizophrenic Reactions. New York, Brunner/Mazel, 1970

Willard H, Spackman CS (eds): Principles of Occupational Therapy. Philadelphia, Lippincott, 1947

Williams CD: The elimination of tantrum behavior by extinction procedures. J Abnorm Soc Psychol 59:269, 1959

Williams DB: California experiments with halfway house. Ment Hosp 7:24, 1956

Williams DD: Therapy and salvation. Union Seminary Q Rev 15:303–317, 1960

Williams DD: The Minister and the Care of Souls. New York, Harper & Row, 1961

Williams F: Family therapy: Its role in adolescent psychiatry. Adoles Psychiatry 2:324–339, 1973

Williams RB, Gentry WD: Behavioral Approaches to Medical Treatment. Cambridge, Mass, Ballinger, 1977

Williams RL, Webb WB: Sleep Therapy. Springfield, Ill, Thomas, 1966

Williams T: Telephone therapy: The faceless therapist. Crisis Intervention 3:39–42, 1971

Williams TA, Johnson JH (eds): Mental Health in the 21st Century. Lexington, Mass, D.C. Heath & Co, 1979

Williamson EG: How to Counsel Students. New York, McGraw-Hill, 1939

Williamson EG, Darley JG: Student Personnel Work, An Outline of Clinical Procedure. New York, McGraw-Hill, 1937

Williamson FE: Art therapy as creative activity. Ment Hosp 10:18–19, 1959

Willis RW, Edwards JA: A study of the comparative effectiveness of systematic desensitization and implosive therapy. Behav Res Ther 7:387–395, 1969

Wilmer HA: Social Psychiatry in Action: A Therapeutic Community Springfield, Ill, Thomas, 1958

Wilmer HA: Television as participant recorder. Am J Psychiatry 124:1157–1163, 1968

Wilson G: Group Work and Case Work—Their Relationship and Practice. New York, Family Welfare Association of America, 1941

Wilson G, Ryland G: Social Group Work Practice: The Creative Use of the Social Process. Boston, Houghton Mifflin, 1949

Wilson GT: Toward specifying the "nonspecific" factors in behavior therapy: A social learning analysis, in Mahoney MJ (ed): Psychotherapy Process. New York, Plenum, 1980

Wilson GT, Franks CM: Contemporary Behavior Therapy: Conceptual and Empirical Foundations. New York, Guilford, 1982

Wilson GT, O'Leary KD: Principles of Behavior Therapy. Englewood Cliffs, NJ, Prentice–Hall, 1980

Wilson TG: Behavioral treatment of obsessive-compulsive disorders. Cassette Tape T29. New York, Biomonitoring Applications, 1976

Wilson HS, Kneisl CR: Psychiatric Nursing. Menlo Park, Addison–Wesley, 1979

Windholz E: The theory of supervision in psychoanalytic education. Int J Psychoanal 51:393–406, 1970

Wing JK, Cooper JE, Sartorius N: Measurement and Classification of Psychiatric Symptoms. London, Cambridge University Press, 1974

Winick C: Psychiatric day hospitals: A survey. J Soc Issues 8, 1960(a)

Winick C, Holt H: Uses of music in group psychotherapy. Int J Group Psychother 13:76–86, 1960(b)

Winick C, Holt H: Seating position as non-verbal communication in group analysis. Psychiatry 24:171–182, 1961

Winkelman HW, Jr, Saul SD: The riddle of suggestion. Am J Psychiatry 129:477–481, 1972

Winnicott DW: Hate in the counter-transference. Int J Psychoanal 30:69–74, 1949

Winnicott DW: Symptom tolerance in paediatrics. Proc Roy Soc Med 46:675–684, 1953

Winnicott DW: Collected Papers—Through Pediatrics to Psycho-Analysis. New York, Basic Books, 1958

Winnicott DW: The Maturational Process and the Facilitating Environment. New York, International Universities Press, 1965

Winnicott DW: Playing and Reality. Roche Report 6(6), 1969

Winnicott DW: The squiggle technique, in McDermott JF, Harrison SI (eds): Psychiatric Treatment of the Child. New York, Aronson, 1977

Winokur M: A family systems model for supervision of psychotherapy. Bull Menn Clin 46:125–138, 1982

Winston S: Dance and movement therapy. Psychiatr Op 3:26–31, 1966

Winter G: The pastoral counselor within the community of faith. Pastoral Psychol 10:26–30, 1959

Wisdom JO: Foreword, in Lazerowitz M (ed): The Structure of Metaphysics. New York, Humanities, 1955

Wise CA: Pastoral Counseling: Its Theory and Practice. New York, Harper & Row, 1951

Wise CA: A meeting of American Association of Pastoral Counselors in St. Louis: A Report. Pastoral Psychol 15:47–52, 1964

Witmer H: The later social adjustment of problem children: A report of thirteen follow-up investigations. Smith College Studies in Social Work 5:1–98, 1935

Witmer HL (ed): Teaching Psychotherapeutic Medicine. New York, Commonwealth Fund, 1947

Wittkower ED, La Tendresse TD: Rehabilitation of chronic schizophrenics by a new method of occupational therapy. Br J Med Psychol 28:42, 1955

Wobraich ML: Stimulant drug therapy in hyperkinetic children: Research and clinical implications. Pediatrics 60:512–518, 1977

Wolberg A: The "borderline" patient. Am J Psychother 6:694–710, 1952

Wolberg A: Lectures given in class No. 218 at the Postgraduate Center for Mental Health, New York, 1959

Wolberg A: The psychoanaytic treatment of the borderline patient in the individual and group setting, in Hulse W (ed): Topical Problems of Psychotherapy, vol. 3. Basel, Switz, Karger, 1960, pp 174–197

Wolberg A: The contribution of social casework to short-term psychotherapy, in Wolberg LR (ed): Short-term Psychotherapy. Orlando FL, Grune & Stratton, 1965, pp 305–327

Wolberg A: The Borderline Patient. New York, Stratton Intercontinental, 1973

Wolberg A, Padilla-Lawson E: MPAG: A generic concept of mental health consultation. Paper presented at the Postgraduate Center for Mental Health, New York, October 1959

Wolberg A, Padilla-Lawson E: The training of mental health consultants at the Postgraduate Center for Mental Health. Int Ment Health Newsletter 4:3–8, 1962

Wolberg A, Padilla-Lawson E: The psychotherapist as a mental health consultant. Paper presented at the Annual Meeting of the American Orthopsychiatric Association, Chicago, March 1964

Wolberg A, Padilla-Lawson E: The goals of community mental health consultation, in Masserman JH (ed): Science and Psychoanalysis, vol. 8. Orlando FL, Grune & Stratton, 1965, pp 243–261

Wolberg LR: The psychology of Eating. New York, McBride, 1936

Wolberg LR: The spontaneous mental cure. Psychiatr Q 18–105–117, 1944

Wolberg LR: Hypnotic experiments in psychosomatic medicine. Psychosom Med 9:337–342, 1947

Wolberg LR: Medical Hypnosis, vol. 1, 2. Orlando FL, Grune & Stratton, 1948

Wolberg LR: Current practices in hypnotherapy, in Fromm-Reichmann F, Moreno JL (eds): Progress in Psychotherapy, vol. 1. Orlando FL, Grune & Stratton, 1956

Wolberg LR: Hypnosis in psychoanalytic psychotherapy, in Masserman JH, Moreno JL (eds): Progress in Psychotherapy, vol. 2. Orlando FL, Grune & Stratton, 1957

Wolberg LR: Child institutionalization as a psychotherapeutic procedure, in Glueck S (ed): The Problem of Delinquency, Boston, Houghton Mifflin, 1959(a) pp 755–762

Wolberg LR: Hypnotherapy, in Arieti S (ed): American Handbook of Psychiatry, vol. 2. New York, Basic Books, 1959(b) pp 1466–1481

Wolberg LR: The efficacy of suggestion in clinical situations, in Estabrooks GH (ed): Hypnosis: Current Problems. New York, Harper & Row, 1962, pp 127–136

Wilberg LR: Hypnoanalysis (2d ed). New York, Grune & Stratton, 1945, 1964(a)

Wolberg LR: The evaluation of psychotherapy, in The Evaluation of Psychiatric Treatment. Orlando FL, Grune & Stratton, 1964(b), pp 1–13

Wolberg LR: Short-term Psychotherapy. Orlando FL, Grune & Stratton, 1965

Wolberg LR: Psychotherapy and the Behavioral Sciences. Orlando FL, Grune & Stratton, 1966

Wolberg LR: The Technique of Psychotherapy (2d ed). Orlando FL, Grune & Stratton, 1967, pp 44–51, 293–312

Wolberg LR: Hypnosis; Is It For You? Orlando FL, Harcourt Brace Jovanovich, 1972

Wolberg LR: Amytal, in Wolman BB (ed): International Encyclopedia of Psychiatry, Psychology, Psychoanalysis and Neurology, vol. 2. New York, Aesculapius, 1977, pp 29–31

Wolberg LR: Handbook of Short-term Psychotherapy. New York, Thieme-Stratton, 1980

Wolberg LR: Hypnoanalysis, in Kutash IL, Wolf A (eds): Psychotherapist's Casebook. San Francisco, Jossey-Bass, 1986, p 311

Wolberg LR, Aronson M (eds): Group Therapy: An Overview. New York, International Medical Book Corp. (New Thieme–Stratton) 1974–1979

Wolberg LR, Aronson M (eds): Group and Family Therapy. New York, Brunner/Mazel, 1980–1983

Wolberg LR, Kildahl JP: The Dynamics of Personality. Orlando FL, Grune & Stratton, 1970

Wolberg LR, Schwartz ED (eds): Group Therapy: An Overview. New York, International Medical Book Corp,. (New Thieme–Stratton) 1973

Wolf A: The psychoanalysis of groups. Am J Psychother 3:525–558, 1949; 4:16–50, 1950

Wolf A: Psychiatry and Religion. M.D. International Symposium No. 3, New York, M.D. Publishers, 1955

Wolf A: The arcadian ingredient in group psychotherapy, in Wolberg LR, Schwartz EK (eds): Group Therapy 1973: An Overview. New York, Stratton Intercontinental, 1973, pp 1–11

Wolf A: Remembering Mannie: Emanuel K. Schwartz, PhD, DSSc, June 11, 1912–January 22, 1973, in Wolberg LR, Aronson ML (eds): Group Therapy 1975: An Overview. New York, Stratton Intercontinental, 1975

Wolf A, Bross R, Flowerman J, et al: Sexual acting out in the psychoanalysis of group. Int J Group Psychother 4:369–380, 1954

Wolf A, Schwartz EK: Psychoanalysis in groups: Clinical and theoretic implications of the alternate meeting. Acta Psychother Psychosom Orthopsychiatry 7 (Suppl): 404, 1959

Wolf A, Schwartz EK: Psychoanalysis in groups: The alternate session. Am Imago 17:101–106, 1960

Wolf A, Schwartz EK: Psychoanalysis in Groups. Orlando FL, Grune & Stratton, 1962

Wolf M, Risley T, Mees H: Application of operant conditioning procedures to the behaviour problems of an autistic child. Behav Res Ther 1:305–312, 1964

Wolf S: Effects of suggestion and conditioning on the action of chemical agents in human subjects—the pharmacology of placebos. J Clin Invest 29:100–109, 1950

Wolf S, Pinsky RH: Effects of placebo administration and occurrence of toxic reactions. JAMA 155:339–341, 1954

Wolfe J, et al: Emotional education in the classroom: The living school. Rational Living 4:22–25, 1970

Wolff IS: The psychiatric nurse in community mental health centers. Perspect Psychiatr Care 1:11–18, 1964

Wolman BB: Hostility experiences in group psychotherapy. Int J Soc Psychiatry 10:57, 1964

Wolman BB (ed): Psychoanalytic Techniques. New York, Basic Books, 1967, pp 147–559

Wolpe J: Objective psychotherapy of the neuroses. S Afr Med J 26:825–829, 1952

Wolpe J: Reciprocal inhibition as the main basis of psychotherapeutic effects. AMA Arch Neurol Psychiatry 72:205–226, 1954

Wolpe J: Psychotherapy by Reciprocal Inhibition. Stanford, Calif, Stanford University Press, 1958

Wolpe J: The systematic desensitization treatment of neurosis NNMD 132:180–203, 1961

Wolpe J: Behavior therapy in complex neurotic states. Br J Psychiatry 110:28–34, 1964(a)

Wolpe J: The comparative clinical status of conditioning therapies and psychoanalysis, in Wolpe J, Salter A, Reyna LJ (eds): The Conditioning Therapies. New York, Holt, 1964(b)

Wolpe J: The effects of psychotherapy. Int J Psychiatry 1:175–178, 1965

Wolpe J: The Practice of Behavior Therapy. Elmsford, NY, Pergamon, 1969

Wolpe J: Orientation to Behavior Therapy. Nutley, NJ, Hoffman-LaRoche, 1971

Wolpe J: Advances in behavior therapy, in Masserman JH (ed): Current Psychiatric Therapies, vol. 12. Orlando FL, Grune & Stratton, 1972

Wolpe J: The Practice of Behavior Therapy (2d ed). New York, Pergamon Press, 1973

Wolpe J, Flood J: The effect of relaxation on the galvanic skin response to repeated phobic stimuli in ascending order. J Behav Ther Exp Psychiatry 1:195–200, 1970

Wolpe J, Lang PJ: A fear survey schedule for use in behavior therapy. Beh Res Ther 2:27–30, 1964

Wolpe J, Lazarus AA: Behavior Therapy Techniques. New York, Pergamon, 1966

Wolpe JP, Brady M, Serbes WS, et al: The current status of systematic desensitization. Am J Psychiatry 130:961–965, 1973

Wolpe J, Salter A, Reyna LJ (eds): The Conditioning Therapies. New York, Holt, 1964

Wolpin M: Guided imagining to reduce avoidance behavior. Psychotherapy: Theory Res Prac 6:122, 1969

Wolstein B: Countertransference. Orlando FL, Grune & Stratton, 1959

Woltmann AG: The use of puppets in understanding children. Ment Hyg 24:445–458, 1940

Woltmann AG: Mud and Clay. Personality Symposium No. 2. Orlando FL, Grune & Stratton, 1950

Woltmann AG: The use of puppetry as a projective method in therapy, in Anderson HH, Anderson GL (eds): Introduction to Projective Techniques. Englewood Cliffs, NJ, Prentice-Hall, 1951

Woltmann AG: Play therapy and related techniques, in Brower d, Abt LE (eds): Progress in Clinical Psychology, vol. 1. Orlando FL, Grune & Stratton, 1952

Woltmann AG: Concepts of play therapy techniques. Am J Orthopsychiatry 25:771–783, 1955

Woltmann AG: Play therapy and related techniques, in Brower D, Abt LE (eds): Progress in Clinical Psychology, vol. 2. Orlando FL, Grune & Stratton, 1956

Woltmann AG: Play therapy and related techniques, in Brower D, Psychology, vol. 3. Orlando FL, Grune & Stratton, 1959

Wong N: Clinical considerations in group treatment of narcissistic disorders. Int J Group Psychother 29:317–345, 1979

Wood E: Yoga. New York, Penguin, 1959

Wood LF, Jacobson NS: Marital distress, in D.H. Barlow (ed): Clinical Handbook of Psychological Disorders. New York, Guilford, 1985

Woodward LE: Family life education, in Social Work Year Book. New York, American Association of Social Workers, 1951, pp 181–182

Woody GE, McLellan AT, Luborsky L, et al: Severity of psychiatric symptoms as a predicator of benefits from psychotherapy: the Veterans Administration Penn Study. Am J Psychiatry 141:1172–1177, 1984

Woody GE, O'Brien GP, McLellan AT, et al: Psychotherapy as an adjunct to methadone treatment, in Meyer RE (ed): Psychopathology and Addictive Disorders. New York, Guilford Press, 1986

Woody RH: Behavioral Problem Children in the Schools. Recognition, Diagnosis, and Behavioral Modification. New York, Appleton-Century-Crofts, 1969

Woody RH: Psychobehavioral Counseling and Therapy: Integrating Behavioral and Insight Techniques. New York, Appleton-Century-Crofts, 1971

Worcester A: Care of the Sick, the Dying and the Dead. Springfield, Ill, Thomas, 1935

Worcester A: Care of the Aged, the Dying, and the Dead. Springfield, Ill, Thomas, 1961

Worchel P, Byrne D: Personality Change. New York, Wiley, 1964

Worden JW: Grief Counseling and Grief Therapy. New York, Springer, 1982

World Health Organization (WHO): Occupational Health. WHO Tech Rep Ser No. 66, 1953, p 11

World Health Organization: The Mentally Subnormal Child. WHO Tech Rep Ser No. 75, 1954

World Health Organization Epidemiology of Mental Disorders. WHO Tech Rep Ser No. 185, 1960

World Health Organization: International Classification of Diseases, vol. 1. Geneva, Switz, WHO, 1965

Wortis RP: Music therapy for the mentally ill. J Gen Psychol 62:311–318, 1960

Wright MW: Clinical psychology—progression or regression. Can Ment Health 14:20–25, 1966

Wright R: Hydrotherapy in Psychiatric Hospitals. Boston, Tudor, 1940

Wynne LC, Ryckoff IM, Day J, Hirsch SI: Pseudo-mutuality in the family relations of schizophrenics. Psychiatry 21:205–220, 1958

Yalom ID: The Theory and Practice of Group Psychotherapy. New York, Basic Books, 1970, p 83: 2d ed, 1975

Yalom ID: Research in EST. Am J Psychiatry 134(2):213, 1977

Yalom ID: Existential Psychotherapy. New York Basic Books, 1980

Yalom ID: Inpatient Group Psychotherapy, New York, Basic Books, 1983

Yalom ID: Bloch S, Bond G, et al: Alcoholics in interactional group therapy: An outcome study. Arch Gen Psychiatry 35(4):419–425, 1978

Yalom ID, Bond G, Bloch S, et al: The impact of a weekend group experience on individual therapy. Arch Gen Psychiatry 34(4):399–415, 1977

Yalom ID, Greves C: Group therapy with the terminally ill. Am J Psychiatry 134:396–400, 1977

Yalom ID, Lieberman MA: A study of encounter group casualties. Arch Gen Psychiatry 25:16–30, 1971

Yamakami S: Systems of Buddhist Thought. Calcutta, University of Calcutta, 1912

Yaskin JC: The psychoneuroses and neuroses. A review of a hundred cases with special reference to treatment and results. Am J Psychiatry 93:107–125, 1936

Yates AJ: The application of learning theory to the treatment of tics. J Abnorm Soc Psychol 56:175–182, 1958

Yates AJ: Behavior Therapy. New York, Wiley, 1970

Yates AJ: Theory and Practice in Behavior Therapy. New York, Wiley, 1975

Yates BT: Improving Effectiveness and Reducing Costs in Mental Health. Springfield, Ill, Thomas, 1980

Yates DH: An association set method in psychotherapy. Psychol Bull 36:506, 1939

Yates DH: Relaxation in psychotherapy. J Genet Psychol 34:213–237, 1946

Yeats-Brown F: Yoga Explained. New York, Vista House, 1958

Yeomans NT: Notes on a therapeutic community. I. Preliminary report. Med J Aust 2:382, 1961

Yesavage JA, Karasu TB: Psychotherapy with Elderly Patients. Am J Psychother 36:41–55, 1982

Yesudian S, Haich E: Yoga Uniting East and West. New York, Harper & Row, 1956

Young H: A Rational Counseling Primer. New York, Institute for Advanced Study in Rational Psychotherapy, 1974

Young JE: Loneliness, depression, and cognitive therapy, in Peplau LA, Perlman DA (eds): Loneliness: A sourcebook of Current Theory. Research and Therapy. New York, Wiley, 1982, pp 388–389

Young RA: Treatment problems of the psychologist. Round table, 1949. I. The status of the clinical psychologist in therapy. Am J Orthopsychiatry 22:312, 1950

Ytrehus A: Environmental therapy of chronic schizophrenic patients. Acta Psychiatry 34:126–140, 1959

Zabarenko L, Pittenger RA, Zabarenko RN: Primary Medical Practice. A Psychiatric Evaluation. St Louis, Green, 1968

Zabarenko RN, et al: Teaching psychological medicine in the family practice office. JAMA 218:392–396, 1971

Zachry CB: The psychotherapist and the school. Nerv Child 3:249–257, 1944

Zaks A, Jones T, Fink M, Freedman AM: Naloxone treatment of opiate dependencies: A progress report. JAMA 215:408, 1971

Zander A, et al: Role Relations in the Mental Health Professions. Ann Arbor, University of Michigan Press, 1957

Zarr ML: Computer-mediated psychotherapy: toward patient-selection guidelines. Am J Psychother 38:47–62, 1984

Zaslow R: A theory and treatment of autism, in Berger L (ed): Clinical Cognitive Psychology: Models and Integrations. New York, Irving Pub Co, 1969

Zborowski M: Differences and similarities, in Monat A, Lazarus RS (eds): Stress and Coping. New York, Columbia University Press, 1977, p 106

Zeig JK (ed): A Teaching Seminar with Milton H. Erickson. New York, Brunner/Mazel, 1980

Zeig JK: Ericksonian Approaches to Hypnosis and Psychotherapy. New York, Brunner/Mazel, 1982

Zeig, JK: Ericksonian Psychotherapy, vol. 1. New York, Brunner/Mazel, 1985(a)

Zeig JK: Experiencing Milton H. Erickson. New York, Brunner/Mazel, 1985(b)

Zetzel EA: The effects of psychotherapy. Int J Psychiatry 1:144–150, 1965

Zetzel ER: A developmental approach to the borderline patient. Am J Psychiatry 127:867–871, 1971

Ziferstein I, Grotjahn M: Group dynamics of acting out in analytic group psychotherapy. Int J Group Psychother 7:77–85, 1957

Zigler E, Phillips L: Psychiatric diagnosis: Critique. J Abnorm Soc Psychol 63:607–618, 1961

Zilbergeld B: Male Sexuality: A Guide to Sexual Fulfillment. New York, Bantam, 1978

Zilboorg G: The fundamental conflict with psychoanalysis. Int J Psychoanal 20:480–492, 1939

Zilboorg G: Fear of death. Psychoanal Q 12:465–475, 1943

Zilboorg G: Scientific psychopathology and religious issues. Theolog Studies 14:283–297, 1953

Zilboorg G: Psychoanalytic borderlines. Am J Psychiatry 112:706–710, 1956

Zilboorg G: Psychoanalysis and Religion. New York, Farrar, Strauss, 1962

Zilboorg G: Psychiatry and Medical Practice in a General Hospital, New York, International Universities Press, 1964

Zimberg S, Wallace J, Blume SB: Practical Approaches to Alcoholism Psychotherapy. New York, Plenum, 1978

Zimmerman EH, Zimmerman J: The alteration of behavior in a special classroom situation. J Exp Anal Behav 5:59–60, 1962

Zimney GH, Weidenfeller EW: The effects of music upon GSR or children. J Music Ther 15:108–117, 1978

Ziskind E: Training in psychotherapy for all physicians. JAMA 14:1223–1225, 1951

Zitrin CM, Klein DF, Warner MG, Ross DC: Treatment of phobias: I. Comparison of imipramine and placebo. Arch Gen Psychiatry 40:125, 1983

Zrull JP, Patch D, Lehtinen P: Hyperkinetic children who respond to d-amphetamine. Paper presented at the 122d Annual Meeting of the American Psychiatric Association. Atlantic City, NJ, May 1966

Zubin J: Standard control groups for the evaluation of therapy. Proceedings of the 2d Conference of Mental Hospital Administrators and Statisticians. Pub Health Serv Publ No. 226. Bethesda, Md, National Institute of Mental Health, 1953, p 63

Zubin J: The effects of psychotherapy. Int J Psychiatry 1:153–155, 1965

Zucker H: Problems of Psychotherapy. New York, Free Press, 1967

Zucker KB: Teacher or teacher-therapist: Training for special educators? Contemp Educ 42:115–116, 1971

Zucker LJ: Psychoanalytic assessment of ego weakness. Am J Psychother 17:275–285, 1963

Zuk GH: Family therapy, in Haley J (ed): Changing Families. Orlando FL, Grune & Stratton, 1971(a)

Zuk GH: A Triadic-Based Approach. New York, Behavioral Publications, 1971(b)

Zuk GH: Engagement and termination in family therapy, in Wolberg LR, Aronson, ML (eds): Group Therapy 1974: An Overview. New York, Stratton Intercontinental, 1974, pp 34–44

Zuk GH, Boszormenyi-Nagy I (eds): Family Therapy and Disturbed Families. Palo Alto, Calif, Science & Behavior Books, 1967

Zulliger H: Psychoanalytic experiences in public schools practice. Am J Orthopsychiatry 10:37–85; 595–609, 1940: 11:151–171, 356–370, 1941

Zusman J: Primary prevention. Secondary prevention. Tertiary prevention, in Freedman AM, Kaplan HI, Sadock BJ (eds): Comprehensive Textbook of Psychiatry, vol. II (2d ed). Baltimore, Williams & Wilkins, 1975, pp 2326–2346

Zweben JE, Miller RL: The systems games: Teaching, training, psychotherapy. Psychother: Theory Res Prac 5:73–76, 1968

Zwerling I, Wilder JF: An evaluation of the applicability of the day hospital in treatment of acutely disturbed patients. Isr Ann Psychiatry 2:162–185, 1964

Author Index

Subject Index

Note: Page numbers followed by *t* refer to tables.
Page numbers followed by *f* refer to figures.
Boldface type refers to main discussions.